1 MONTH OF
FREE
READING

at

www.ForgottenBooks.com

By purchasing this book you are
eligible for one month membership to
ForgottenBooks.com, giving you
unlimited access to our entire
collection of over 1,000,000 titles via
our web site and mobile apps.

To claim your free month visit:

www.forgottenbooks.com/free778985

ISBN 978-0-428-96146-6
PIBN 10778985

THE

CATHOLIC WORLD.

A

MONTHLY MAGAZINE

OF

GENERAL LITERATURE AND SCIENCE.

VOL. LIII.

APRIL, 1891, TO SEPTEMBER, 1891.

NEW YORK:

THE OFFICE OF THE CATHOLIC WORLD,

120-122 WEST SIXTIETH STREET.

—

1891.

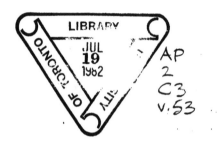
Copyright, 1891, by
VERY REV. A. F. HEWIT.

THE COLUMBUS PRESS, 120-122 WEST 60TH ST., NEW YORK.

CONTENTS.

POETRY.

NEW PUBLICATIONS.

THE

CATHOLIC WORLD.

VOL. LIII.　　　APRIL, 1891.　　　No. 313.

THE PASCHAL MOON.

THROUGH seas of light,
A vision bright,
Slow moves the Paschal moon.
Its sails are set, .
Its prows are wet
With the mist of night's still noon.

To barren lands,
To empty hands,
To hearts that ache and wait,
The buds of Spring,
The hopes that sing,
It bears, a shining freight.

ALICE WARD BAILEY.

THE CHECK TO THE HOME-RULE MOVEMENT.

> "Ah ! but our hopes were splendid,
>   Annie, dear ! "

wrote Thomas Davis, in one of those bursts of song, half addressed to his country and half to his betrothed. In a second
couplet he adds :

> " How sadly they have ended,
>   Annie, dear ! "

And so the song goes on. The first, indeed, literally describes
what our position had been ; but to the second, dark as our hopes
are, we refuse to subscribe.

Those who are now most despairing were the persons who
had formed a wrong estimate of the future when our sun was
in its zenith. Those were the persons who had reckoned that,
immediately that a general election took place and Gladstone returned to power, Home Rule was a thing of the next day. Let
us suppose for the moment that this untoward affair had not
taken place in Irish politics ; let us suppose that there was still
such a united party as there once had been, and that it was
still led by the unquestioned skill and diplomacy of an innocent
and stainless leader ; what would have taken place ? Gladstone
would be returned to power. In due course he would introduce
a Home-Rule bill, or he might possibly secure the passing of some
act in the direction of extension of the franchise, in order to render certain a Liberal return in the event of its being necessary
to appeal once more to the country. Necessary it would have
been, for the House of Lords would, without the shadow of a
doubt, cast out the Home-Rule bill on its first appearance at their
chamber after passing through the Commons. In any case,
therefore, it is only after a second election that Home Rule could
be carried. So far, then, we are not a whit worse off now than
then. It is only after a second election that, under the most
favorable circumstances, we could expect the passing of the measure ; and by the time of a second election the atmosphere here
in Ireland will be so cleared that undoubtedly a compact and
united party can and will be returned.

Later on in this paper it may become necessary to expand

this matter somewhat. At present I put forward this question: Suppose nothing more could, *by the present agitation*, be gained than has been gained; are we to look upon the work of the last ten or twelve years as so much waste of power? By no means. Victories have been won the fruits of which cannot be filched from us. Waterloo may be won and rewon, the Rhine crossed and recrossed, but victories in the moral order once accomplished can never be undone. Slavery can never again, while the stars and stripes float in the breeze, become a legalized institution of the American Republic. And Ireland, poor Ireland, by the sacrifice and bravery of her women as well as her men, nay, even of her little ones, has secured victories in the moral and legislative order. Behind the ramparts we have built not alone a future generation, but even our own can stand and fight for larger liberties and national self-government.

Take the peasant-farmers, say; you knew a man, bound neck and heels by the terms of a lease which he could not fulfil, and his landlord would not forego his pound of flesh. Let us say the man owned 100 acres of land, or thereabouts, at the yearly rent of £200. The farm did not yield a margin of £200, but Shylock was at liberty by law to demand the terms of his bond, and the executive government were prepared to enforce it. The result would be that out on the roadside the man would have to go with his family, two or three boys and one or two girls—children of nice manner and character, like the growing boys or girls you know. Instead, the agitation has broken through the unjust sacredness of Shylock's bond; the man is declared free to go into the courts, and they (one-sided even as they are) have declared that £150 is the full market value of the bond. That man is in his house; his family are around him; they have what little comforts they have among themselves, but they have the sweetest and most sacred pleasure of all, the blessing of one another's society and love. The father's hand is over the children; the children's love is around the father. No money could buy that domestic joy and peace.

But look at the money side of it. £50 is left that man yearly; two years £100, four years £200, and so on; and that £50, or £100, or £200, instead of being dragged away out of the country, and squandered in such a manner as to excite in Burns's *Twa Dogs* the astonishment of one of them—

> " Hech! sir—is that the gait
> They waste sae mony a braw estate?"

is spent at home, and remains in the country. The grocer, and draper, and shoemaker, and school-master all come in for their share. In money, since the League began, that man did not subscribe more, perhaps, than half one year's reduction. Now, there he stands, ready at the first moment an opportunity offers to improve his position, and to help his fellows to do so. Broadly speaking, the agitation of the past ten years has been worth to Ireland some four or five millions sterling annually; and has, moreover, by legislation as well as by organization, made them defiant of the arrogant feudalism that has ground them to the earth.

The laborer, too, has succeeded in emancipating himself. Now he holds a little plot of land and a cottage secure " while grass grows or water runs " (to use one of our Irish expressions). He cannot be disturbed while he pays a certain weekly rent. That rent is being reduced almost universally through Ireland this year by reason of the distress; and it is pretty safe to say that the thin end of the wedge is, all unconsciously, got in, and that year by year this weekly toll will grow " small by degrees and beautifully less." The laborer has, moreover, a vote. It is a loss to the poor man that the Nationalist vote so tremendously predominates, else he might better his position if only he could stifle his patriotic tendencies. In the north of Ireland, however, where the labor vote would be a matter of importance, it may be that the Nationalists in the Board of Guardians will try by some means of this kind to win their votes. But, unless otherwise advised, the poor Catholic laborer will vote Nationalist, and scarcely to save his children from starvation would vote otherwise; whereas the poor Protestant laborer will, on the other hand, almost to a certainty vote with his religion. But this is by the way. The main fact is that both classes, the tenant-farming and the laboring, have gained advantages solid and *pretio. estimabilia.* Just now it is a mercy that it has been so, for were it not for those four or five millions of an annual reduction for the past few years, the bulk of the country would at present be undergoing the same agonies of famine that, unhappily, are felt along the western seaboard. The depreciation in the price of the staple commodities of the country—*i. e.*, in grain, butter, beef, and mutton—has been such that were the *onus* of these few millions still hanging round the people's necks the effect could be none other than famine.

These advantages have, however, been bought at a very dear price. War, even when it emancipates, leaves human corpses on the field. Groups of tenantry here and there have acted as the vanguard in the tenant war. The Cloncurry tenantry, for instance, on the borders of Limerick and Tipperary, have been living in Land League huts ever since '81, when they were evicted from their holdings. Look for a moment at what that means. There were young children growing up in some of these homes. Their parents intended to give them a nice education, as well as their means would afford. The little girls were to be sent to convent boarding-schools—our Catholic girls are sent nowhere else; the boys prepared for trades or even professions. The fathers and mothers had, perhaps, some darling hopes. There the children remained. Should they be now reinstated they have grown too old to be sent to school or apprenticed to trades. Or, again, their girls and boys were grown, and the parents were looking to settle down their poor girls in life. The crow-bar and the battering ram came, and their hopes were as low as their homes. For a long, long decade these people have been enduring that deferring of hope that maketh the heart sick. Later came Clanricarde at Woodford, Smith Barry at Youghal, Massarene in Louth, Olphert in Donegal; oh, 'tis a long litany! Kenmare, Clongorey, Wicklow, Cashel, Tipperary! These are the prisoners of war on our side. Alone with ourselves, when we brood over the hardships and sufferings that these poor people have undergone, we are tempted to cry out that our victories have been dearly bought; but without spilling of blood there is no conquest, and these seem the only serious drawbacks. Were it not for these the country at large may exult, for advantages of a broad and useful kind have been obtained, and while it would reasonably regret the present check, it could at the same time feel that the past ten years have not been all lean kine. But the present check does not cast us into despair. The pending cloud, dark as it is, is not without its silver lining. This is the way we look at it.

Events never stand still, and their onward march must lead to greater privileges for our people. The river, flowing to the sea, might as well think of returning to its source as that we can be robbed of the liberties we have won. Slowly but surely we must go on from vantage ground to vantage ground. The ultimate goal we are fighting for—viz.: the triumph of Home-Rule—is to be won, not so much by ourselves single-handed as by an honorable alliance with one of the two great English parties. It cannot be won without both, much less despite of both. Either of the two must act as an ally; and our position of independence as a parliamentary party and their position of being evenly balanced, make the fact of alliance a matter of political necessity. But which? Will it be with the Tories? For two reasons—no! One reason is, they already made promises and deceived. The second reason is, that the Tories, if they had the will, have not the way. The Liberals could not well oppose; if they did oppose, the majority of Tories and Irish Home-Rulers would swamp them to zero. Our alliance is, therefore, almost necessarily with the Liberals. It has been prophesied, or attempted to be prophesied, by one who did not always prophesy so, that the Liberals cannot return to power at the next election. The very best proof of the falsity of that prophecy is shown in the hesitation of the Tories to appeal to the country. There is no man that would not willingly fling down two to gain seven if he saw the way of doing it. The Tories have two years yet of power to run, if they decide on holding to office; but if they appealed to the country, and were victorious, they would, instead of two, have seven. Their hesitancy, therefore, does not corroborate the prophecy, and, if ever there was a favorable time for them, it is now.

It is all but certain that the Liberals will return to power; the one vital fact we ask of the future is to put Gladstone in office; send us John Morley once again as Irish Secretary, and give the Irish electorate a fair field of squaring matters. Gladstone in office means that Ireland would be freed, or at least eased, from three things that gall us most bitterly at present: 1st, harsh or unjust evictions; 2d, the divisional magistrates' caricature of law courts; 3d, the cruelty and autocracy of the police force. Remove these galling burdens, find just means of reinstating the evicted tenants, give the country a moment to draw its breath, and with one united and supreme effort it will, with God's blessing, cleave its way to legislative freedom.   R. O. K.

THE TRUE STORY OF A CONVERSION.

THAT God in his overwhelming mercy is continually calling human souls from the depths ot ignorance and schism into the glorious light of the one true church is a fact too well known to us, both in England and America, to require any special explanation. But in the countries of the north ot Europe—such as Denmark, Norway, and Sweden—where the light of faith has been so long extinguished, such miracles of grace are more rare, and the account of the conversion of a lady of high rank in the first-named country, through the intervention of the present Cardinal Mermillod, may not be uninteresting to our readers across the. Atlantic. We will give it very nearly in her own words.

"Brought up by a good and pious mother in the beautiful old Castle of H——, my sisters and myself were trained in the straitest sect of Lutheranism. I learned all that our popular histories tell us of the horrors of the Catholic religion, and never failed to thank God for the purer light which had been revealed to us. I remember trembling with indignation when the old professor who taught us used to dilate on the terrors of the Inquisition, the intrigues of the Jesuits, the vices of the popes, the brutality of Gregory VII., and the like. Then, when he went on to speak of the immorality of the priests, the ignorance of the monks, and the gradual but certain decay of the Catholic faith throughout the world, I felt myself greatly relieved, and used to look forward confidently to the glorious day when the pure Gospel would be everywhere preached, when the Bible should be once more given back to souls groaning under the Catholic yoke, and when the hymns of Luther would be sung in the basilica of St. Peter's, while all the idols which now filled it would be trampled under foot. I had never seen a Catholic in my life, for the mission of Svendborg did not then exist; and if I had ever met one I should have been very careful to avoid so dangerous a contact. The very idea that such people existed filled me with a vague terror, mingled with a deep pity for their ignorance and superstitions. I had, in fact, such a fear of meeting one that I remember feeling quite faint when, in a railway carriage in Germany, I found myself for the first time face-to-face with a Catholic priest.

The author of the *Imitation* says that "those who travel much sanctify themselves with difficulty." But he had evidently not been in northern lands. To such people I should, on the contrary, strongly urge the need of travel to open their eyes; and advise them to leave countries where Catholicism does not exist and find out for themselves into what gross errors they had been led by those who speak only of the horrors and iniquities of the Church of Rome.

"God gave me this grace, for when I married my husband's delicate health obliged us to go south, and in 1880 we started for the Island of Corsica. I was then just twenty-one years of age, and, although I carried a great Bible in my trunk, I practised my religion very little. I used to like to go into the churches of Ajaccio, however, and felt a great sweetness in being able to pray at any time, kneeling on those marble pavements, where everything seemed to speak to me of God; whereas in my Protestant home all the churches were shut except on Sundays. I went there so often, in fact, that my husband became alarmed and forbade it. A Protestant pastor, strangely enough, interposed in my favor, telling my husband that it was, after all, an innocent pleasure; that there was no fear of my orthodoxy being affected, and that there was no reason why I should not enjoy the beauty of the Corsican churches; so that after that I was left alone.

"One day I went to a great convent in the Rue 'Cours Grandval' and, ringing at the cloister gate, asked to be allowed to visit it. It was the first time I had ever seen any Catholic nuns close at hand and my object was pure curiosity. They were very kind to me and showed me all over their beautiful gardens, which were full of roses and lilies. Then I was taken into the parlor, and there something that I said made them ask me if I were a Catholic. My answer filled them with surprise and pity, and when I went on to assure them that I came from a country where people had done without Catholicism very well for upwards of three hundred years, the disgust they evidently felt for me wounded my self-love and I hastened to take my leave, not, however, before the superior had gently said she 'would pray for me.' I was much too indignant at the moment to feel any gratitude for her prayers, and was only relieved when I got outside and heard the convent gates close behind me.

"When I came back to the hotel I mentioned my 'escapade' to my friends at the table d'hôte, who could not find words strong enough to blame my imprudence. 'Thank God that you have been kept safely,' exclaimed one Anglican minister ; while a Calvinist added: 'To go off like that—all alone—without giving us any warning ! What if you had disappeared altogether and never been allowed to come back ? '. A third said: 'You would not have been the first victim, I assure you. You do not know, perhaps, that there are vast subterranean chambers in Catholic convents where people are constantly immured. I, who speak to you, have known more than one person who, having ventured as you did to-day, have been entombed in cold, damp, dark dungeons, where an abjuration was extorted from them by dint of hunger and ill-usage.'   ·

"I was horrified at these apparently truthful revelations, and took very good care never to venture again near a convent. After that I became indifferent to the subject. My curiosity had been satisfied, and the little I had seen and heard gave me (however absurd this may seem) a certainty that I *knew all about it*, and that the superiority of my education made Catholicism of no earthly danger to me.

"Filled with this comfortable self-complacency I went to Switzerland, where we passed the summer of 1881. If others prepare themselves by prayer and solitude to listen to· the voice of God, my preparation was of a very different kind. We stayed at a beautiful hotel in Geneva, which was full of people of every nationality. English, Americans, Russians, Spanish, French, Poles, Austrians, even Turks, met day by day round that crowded table d'hôte and made more or less acquaintance. We happened to be placed at a table near a Polish family—the Comtesse M—— and her son, with whom we became very intimate till our acquaintance ripened into real friendship. Comtesse M—— was a fervent Catholic, but was very careful not to shock or wound my Protestant susceptibilities. When the men went to smoke we used to sit together and talk after dinner, and almost always the conversation turned on religious subjects. Comtesse M—— was not only very clever and intelligent, but a thorough woman of the world, so that with infinite tact she never uttered a word that I could take amiss, in spite of the ridiculous things which I said to her on Catholic subjects, which I had been told by my Lutheran advisers. When her son came in and joined us, he was less indulgent, and I used to see that he was convulsed with laughter now and then at my stories of popes and priests and nuns, though he tried to look grave and remained silent. He evidently thought me extraordinarily simple

and credulous (not to say stupid) for believing such things, and
I felt inclined to be angry with him, yet could not but admire
his own strong and honest convictions, so that we remained
good friends.

"It was about that time that Monseigneur Mermillod had re-
turned from Sweden and settled himself at Monthoux, near
Geneva, a beautiful villa belonging to the Comtesse Élise de
Montailleur, which she had placed at his disposal. Comtesse
M—— invited me to go with her and pay him a little visit,
saying it would interest me to hear about his journey to the
north, and that he would be sure to receive me with kindness.
I hesitated for a long time before I could make up my mind
to visit a bishop of so terrible a sect as I still thought the
Roman Catholics were, but at last yielded to her persuasions,
saying to myself 'that he could not be more terrible than the
brigands we had met in Corsica; that my husband knew where
I was going and would come and rescue me if necessary, and
that Comtesse M—— herself would protect me.' So, the next
morning, we started through the beautiful country round
Geneva, with glimpses of the lake at every turn, till we reached
the Swiss frontier and perceived on a height the church and
house of Monthoux, partly hidden by the trees. Driving
through a high gate, we came to a door covered with roses and
beautiful creeping plants, in the midst of a lovely garden, which
door opened into a pretty sitting-room on the ground-floor.
Whilst the servant went to announce us, I made a rapid inven-
tory of everything in the room so as to try and judge of the
tastes of the owner. The pictures on the walls and the books
and papers on the table all pleased my fastidious taste. Then
the bishop came in. Comtesse M—— presented me and he began to talk of his Swedish journey, which put me at my ease
at once. A little later he showed me some Danish newspapers
which had been sent to him, giving an account of several
episodes in his Scandinavian mission, and asked me to translate
them for him, which I gladly undertook to do. But when a
few words were said about religion I thought I ought to be on
my guard, and I asked him not to make any attempt to convert me, as I was firmly resolved never to become a Catholic.
He only smiled, and then he and Comtesse M—— began talking
of serious things and of those eternal truths which are common
to both Protestants and Catholics, while I listened with more
and more interest, thinking of my good and pious mother and
feeling that, after all, good people felt alike on all really im-

portant points. Before our visit ended the bishop had won not
only my respect but my confidence and affection.

"A few days later, his secretary, Canon Guillermin, came to
fetch the translations I had promised him. We were then staying at Veyrier-sous-Salére, the great heat of Geneva having
compelled us to leave that town for the summer. I happened
to be out when the canon called and he found my husband
alone. This was really a providential circumstance, for they
entered at once into a conversation on religious subjects, and my
husband did not hesitate to pour out freely all his prejudices
and erroneous ideas as to the Catholic Church; but only to find
them dispelled one by one. He never made any objection
after that to my seeing the bishop, which I often did, either at
his own house or in the great convent of Mère Émilie, which
was near our home. Monseigneur Mermillod gave me many
interesting Catholic books to read, and, as I had nothing else to
do and the weather was too hot to go out in the middle of the
day, my husband and I spent more than half our time in reading. I found out every day not only how absurd my ideas
were about the ignorance, superstition, and idolatry of Catholics,
but also that I really knew nothing whatever either of religion,
philosophy, or history. In the evening I used often to meet and
talk to the village children, and when I told one of them once
that he worshipped the Virgin Mary the boy laughed in my
face, and gave me so clear a theological answer that I was both
ashamed and confused at my ignorance. Strangely enough, all
this time I never dreamed of becoming a Catholic myself. I
studied the question as I should have done natural history or
any other science, without ever thinking of it as affecting my
own soul. The good canon came very often to see us both, and
we became very fond of him and used to enjoy the theological
disputes we had together, in which, I am bound to say, we
always came off second-best. But his patience and sweetness
were unalterable, even when I used to say to him: 'Yes! I see
you are right; but as for me, nothing would ever induce me to
become a Catholic!'

"At last I became secretly alarmed at the inclination I felt
growing in me towards Catholicism. I remembered all I had
been taught about guarding my pure Protestant faith against the
insidious wiles of the papists; so that I resolved to go and consult a noted Lutheran pastor at Geneva, to open my heart
to him, and get him to reawaken my Protestant zeal and
strengthen me against the ravening wolves who were striv-

ing to entrap and destroy my soul. I went accordingly and
knocked at the pastor's house. It was his wife who opened the
door, together with half a dozen little children, who were sent
in different directions to look for their papa. He was not, however, to be found; and his wife then suggested that I should
tell *her* what I wanted and she would explain it all to her husband. But I had imbibed too many Catholic notions about confession to find such a proposal acceptable, and therefore begged
her to ask the pastor to come and see me. He did so several
times; but when I propounded my difficulties to him he
answered me so vaguely and so unsatisfactorily that I was more
perplexed than ever. The canon had only asked me to pray to
God for light, and this I did with my whole heart. My husband
was in the same state of mind as myself; yet we neither of us
thought it would be possible for us to become Catholics, knowing the very strong Protestant feeling in both our families and
the horror which such a step would inspire in their minds. My
only consolation was in going to Monthoux and having long
talks with the bishop, who, in spite of his overwhelming occupations, always found time to give me an explanation of my difficulties and to say a few words of hope and encouragement,
which were as balm to my troubled spirit.

"At last I resolved on a desperate measure in order to test
our real position; and that was, to ask the Lutheran pastor to
admit us to holy Communion in his church. He, knowing our
state of mind, hesitated to give us the permission; and, in fact,
refused it. Then I said to him: 'Well, I feel I must have
Communion in some way or other; and if you will not give it
to us, we will go to Monseigneur Mermillod.'

"The poor man, alarmed at the bare thought of our leaving
the Protestant Church, at once fixed on the Sunday following;
and I went to the bishop to tell him what we had settled to do.
I implored him to forget, for a moment, that he was a Catholic
bishop and to advise me only as a kind and disinterested friend;
for, of course, as a bishop, he could only condemn our intended
action. He said only a few, wise words and did not attempt to
dissuade us.

"On the Sunday following, accordingly, after the table d'hôte
in the evening, when we had made a copious repast, I announced to our astonished friends that we were going to the Protestant temple to make our Communion.

"In Denmark the custom is as follows:

"After what is called 'confession,' which consists in an exhortation from the pastor, while the penitents say nothing, every one goes up to the communion table and kneels, while the minister pronounces the absolution and imposes his hands on the head of each person, after which he gives them the bread and wine.

"But in Geneva, as the pastor's wife told me, this antiquated but reverent mode of action is entirely '*out of fashion.*' Every one stays in his or her place while the minister sits on a little stool, and then the communicants rise and receive the bread and wine standing before him. This was the last time that we either of us set our foot in a Protestant church. If we had our doubts before, we then acquired a blessed certainty that the truth was only to be found in the Catholic faith.

"We walked home in silence towards the hotel. It was late and the moon had just risen behind Mont Blanc. When we came to the bridge, my husband stopped and, pointing in the direction of Monthoux, said to me: 'I have had enough of this. We cannot lose our souls to please our families, and cannot resist God's grace any longer under the pretext of wanting still further time for reflection. I see clearly which is the true church of our Lord Jesus Christ, and I am determined to belong to it. If you think as I do, let us go to-morrow to Monthoux and ask monseigneur to receive us?'

"My joy may be imagined. I had never dared hope that my dearest husband would so soon share my convictions; and now all difficulties had vanished, and *together* we were to take this, the most important step in our whole lives! The next morning my husband was not very well, but he would not hear of any further delay, so that I went over alone to Monthoux and informed Monseigneur Mermillod of our determination and the result of our Protestant Communion. I added our earnest entreaty that he would himself receive us into the church. He assented most kindly, congratulating me warmly, and fixed on the 26th of October for the day of our joint reception.

"The intervening time was spent in earnest preparation for the event. The good canon multiplied himself in giving us the needful instruction, while the Comtesse M——, who was to be my godmother, gave me a beautiful rosary and crucifix blessed by the pope.

"The day came, and the little church of Monthoux was gaily decked with flowers by our sympathizing friends.

"My husband made his confession first, I walking up and down in an agony outside the church meanwhile, not knowing how great is the sweetness and ease of that sacrament when once it is fully understood.

"Then on two *prie-dieux*, before the altar, we knelt and both made our abjuration; after which Holy Mass was said, and we received from the bishop's hand the Bread of Life. Then he deigned to give us the sacrament of Confirmation, addressing us in that paternal and beautiful language with which those who know him are so familiar.

"Of the intense happiness of that hour I cannot speak. We both seemed flooded with grace and blessings, and as if life would never be long enough to express our deep and heartfelt gratitude.

"Nine years have now elapsed since that day, and each year has only found us more thoroughly contented and more deeply grateful for the infinite grace vouchsafed to us, while so many of our countrymen are plunged in the darkness of heresy and schism."

It is almost impossible for English or Americans, who see and hear so much of Catholicity, and so many of whom have some friend or relation in that faith, to believe the amount of ignorance, prejudice, and actual violence which exist in the northern countries of Europe against the Catholic Church. All we can do is to pray, and that earnestly, that the light may once more be vouchsafed to all "who sit in darkness and the shadow of death," so that in God's good time all may be one in faith and hope and in that divine charity which "hopeth all things," "believeth all things," and which "never faileth."

MARY ELIZABETH HERBERT.

A QUESTION OF TEMPERAMENT.

I.

THE smile grew broader as Miss Garrison progressed through page after page of the voluminous letter, and by the time she read "Yours ever faithfully, Addie," it had developed to the extent of showing a set of very regular teeth of perfect whiteness. There was a merry twinkle in her eye also. In this good-natured merriment there was the faintest suggestion of cynicism.

"So you have gone the way of the flesh, have you?—that is, of young and pretty feminine flesh," she thought to herself, as she tossed the letter on her writing-table. "I told her she would be engaged before the close of her first season, and she is. So much for my prophetic instinct. She was just the kind of a girl to fall in love with something. I suppose you have got to be congratulated, and, judging from the description which you give of your 'young man,' I think I can offer my felicitations with a good conscience. Let me see: ' tall, broad-shouldered, massive without being bulky, gray eyes that shade into violet.' O Addie!" and the white teeth flashed into view again, "I am afraid they are a watery light blue."

Then she went on to herself with the phrases of the letter: "His features, not very sharply cut, are strong, and his mouth and chin are very handsome indeed; hair light brown, thick but fine and glossy, and with a waviness to it ; and his complexion bronzed but clear."

Miss Garrison went over these details with great relish, and really tried to build up an image of the man to whom her friend had entrusted her heart, although such a process is always unsatisfactory. "I wish she had sent a photograph with the description," she said to herself. "No doubt she meant to be accurate. That remark about his 'not very sharply cut features,' with the supplementary one that 'his mouth and chin are very handsome *indeed*,' and the painful silence about Mr. Paul Arkenburgh's nose inclines me to the belief that it may be a good, honest turned-up one. I am sure Addie would not have omitted some word about it if it had been a definite nose of any other kind. Well, it would have to be almost a broken nose not to be amply compensated for by 'eyes that shade into violet' and a stunning mouth and chin.   It is a dreary waste of countenance, indeed, which handsome eyes cannot redeem, and I have seen a fine mouth and smile make a perfectly ugly man fascinating.   So, if Addie has not hopelessly idealized her Launcelot, I should think he would do, as far as looks go."

"By the way," she continued, in analytical revery over her friend's letter, "she hasn't said a word about his intelligence or his moral character.   That he is a model of virtue is taken for granted, I suppose, and that he has been employed for some time as confidential clerk in the same office with Addie's father must be considered as a voucher for good business qualities at least.   Nowadays that counts more than a taste for literature or philosophy.   So I think on the whole I may congratulate you, Mrs. Paul Arkenburgh that is to be, with an approving conscience.   I should have had to do it anyhow, but it is nicer to do it without having to say to one's self: 'What in the world *could* she have found in that man?'"

Miss Garrison, having analyzed herself into this frame of mind, sat down and wrote straightway a sympathetic little note of felicitation to Miss Archer on having reached that delightful stage of young womanhood where an engagement ring on the finger notes a circumscription of horizon but a great access of delight within the contracted sphere.

The two girls had been at Vassar together, and were very good friends despite a radical difference in temperaments.   Miss Garrison felt to herself that there was much in Addie Archer which the girl could have lacked advantageously, but there was much there which appealed to her.   Miss Archer was a pretty blonde, quick and lively, and with a pronounced disposition to enjoy life as thoroughly as possible which made her forgivably frivolous.   But constant high spirits are such a grateful thing in a friend, outside of a lachrymose or serious juncture, that they are recognized as a virtue.

Miss Garrison was a young woman of character and ideas. She was quite capable of cutting her hair short and devoting herself to female suffrage if the admission of women to the polls should strike her as a desirable thing for her sex.   Fortunately, nothing like this had ever struck her.   She dominated her sprightly friend by the superior force of her will, and it had seemed the most natural thing in the world that Addie should have dutifully submitted to her a close description of the young man who had won her.

After they were graduated at Vassar, Miss Garrison had gone to Europe with her uncle, who was her guardian and greatest friend. Nearer relatives she had not. She enjoyed an income ample enough for her individual needs, though not large enough to give her the prestige of an heiress. It was at Cannes that she received this letter from Addie Archer. After a few weeks there they were to go to Florence, Naples, Rome, and Venice; then back to America.

The Archers were people who were almost in the inner circle of New York society. Miss Garrison was quite inside the invisible lines which hedge about that small, exclusive body from friction with the coarser outside people, who, poor things! are doomed, not to "outer darkness," but to that gray mist which lies round and about the fancied sphere of golden light in which the elect of the great world rejoice and have their being.

Mr. Archer was apparently a successful business man, and there was a well-founded hope in the hearts of his wife and daughter that some day, and that a not very distant one, they would reach the round of the social ladder which was the object of their ambitions.

Mr. Archer was the president of a line of surface cars and Paul Arkenburgh was a confidential clerk in the company's office. Young Arkenburgh owed his promotion to the influence of Mr. Archer, who had recognized his excellent business qualities, and by his recommendation and praise of the young man's clear head, fidelity to work, and integrity had secured his prompt advancement. Arkenburgh was more than grateful for this generous patronage. A disposition of great intensity and much warmth was somewhat masked in him by the reserve which so frequently accompanies great force of character. But gratitude with him was not an emotion to begin yesterday and end to-day. The sense of a kindness done to him abode in his soul with a fixity as tenacious as that of honor in the soul of a gentleman.

Mr. Archer's interest in his promising clerk was not exhibited merely in their business relations. He frequently took him to his place at Irvington, and the young man gradually acquired a familiar footing in the family. When Paul Arkenburgh realized that the pretty, frolicsome daughter of his employer was the one fair maid to make " this and that other world " for him, before speaking to Addie Archer he had frankly spoken to the girl's father to learn whether he would object to receiving him as a son-in-law.

To Mr. Archer's credit, although he had counted on a more distinguished alliance for his only child than one with his own clerk, he was too sensible a man to undertake to shape the destiny of the girl in contradiction to her wishes. Moreover, he not only had really a regard for Arkenburgh, but he detected in him those qualities which require only opportunity to lead to success. It was with a quiet conviction of his own foresight in regard to Paul's future that he bade him urge his suit with Miss Archer, and assured him that, if he found favor with the girl, he had nothing worse to anticipate than Mrs. Archer's disappointment.

That worthy creature, working to break down the barriers which barred her entrance to the land of promise held by the chosen few, had waited for an influential son-in-law as a useful and expected auxiliary. She was not likely, then, to see her daughter marry Mr. Archer's clerk with perfect acquiescence.

"But if Addie says 'Yes,' and you have me and her to back you, the mother will have to come down, that is all," said Mr. Archer, with a nice estimate of the situation.

What Addie said we already know from the warm letter to Miss Garrison announcing her engagement. It was written and sent off the day following a very charming interview with Mr. Paul Arkenburgh in the conservatory. That the strong, monumental young man should have won her airy fancy was one of those surprises which Cupid sometimes works for his own amusement and the wonder of the world. That a severe, earnest young fellow should lay his strongly beating heart at the feet of a gay, volatile girl was, on the other hand, a venture in love so much in the order of masculine selections for wifehood as to occasion no surprise in any one who has marked the course of love's currents in the human male.

It may be said here, however, that the thought which occurred to many minds when they received the news, to wit: that Arkenburgh had viewed the young girl in connection with her father's bank account, was entirely wrong. Paul had fallen as honestly in love as a healthy young man, heart-free, possibly could. Had Addie Archer been a shop-girl it would not have affected his suit in the least. He loved the bright, pretty creature, and men of his stamp, when they love, marry for it. He had too much confidence in his own ability to compass the goods of fortune to make their presence in the person of his beloved anything that could be called an inducement. Miss Archer had not enlarged upon his personal attractions to any extent in her letter to Miss Garrison. Paul Arkenburgh's grayish eyes did deepen into an exquisite violet, and though his nose was one of those resolute features which present more determination than form it was not ugly. The sturdy, broad-shouldered man, with the clear mastery in the expression of his gray eyes and the strong, square chin, with a mouth that resolved itself into an exceedingly winning smile, was to any woman's eyes a wonderfully attractive youth.

They loved each other so much that they were glad to rise earlier that they might the quicker renew the consciousness of how sweet it was. Thus the commencement of love's young dream was fair and smooth.

II.

Four months later, at the beginning of June, Kate Garrison and her uncle Hartwell returned to America as a large number of their compatriots were drifting across the ocean to Europe. Miss Garrison was not sorry to be back on her native shores once more. She had enjoyed her pleasant wanderings on the Continent in the genial companionship of an uncle who found in his niece such a reproduction of his cherished sister, the mother of the girl, that he could not be kind enough to her. But she wanted to see old friends and old scenes. She was to remain with her uncle for a fortnight, and then she had promised Miss Archer to put in a few weeks with her at Newport.

It was only the second day after her return that she found herself in the lower part of the town. A very late wedding at Trinity Church had drawn her thither, and after it was over she decided to go to her uncle's office on Broad Street and see if there were any prospect of his returning home with her, at least after luncheon.

She found him bundling together two or three papers with heads neatly written in red ink, his hat on, ready to go out. He greeted her warmly, and when he had heard why she came said dubiously and with regret:

"I have got to go to court, for there is every reason to think that a case of mine will be reached this morning. But it is not certain, and, if it does come up, there is a chance of old Wiggins getting another postponement. How would you like to go to court with me, and if the case is put off, or doesn't come up at all to-day, I'll go home with you. Were you ever in a court?"

"No, never," she replied, "and I had rather go than not."

So Mr. Hartwell stuck two or three of the documents into the inside band of his hat and then set that rather antiquated article with much precision on his head. They left the office together, walked up Broadway and along Park Row until they came to City Hall Park, which they crossed. Miss Garrison next found herself entering a square brown-stone building, to the second floor of which they were borne in a lift. The Court of Special Sessions was on this floor, at least that part of it in which Mr. Hartwell had, or expected to have, his case.

It was a large square room, with the sunlight streaming in from long windows, which were open to allow the soft air to circulate through the room. At the end, to the left of the door, was the judge's seat with some red stuff draped back of it against the wall. Miss Garrison felt that the dignity of the law would not have been impaired at all if the red drapery had not been so obviously dusty.

In front of the judge's desk, which stood on a platform two or three feet high, was an enclosure where the clerk, the district-attorney, and other court officials were. At the right of this space was the jury-box, in which twelve disconsolate-looking men were sitting in various stages of relaxation.

Outside this enclosure was a larger space with benches in it, which was barred off by another railing from the last section of the court-room. Back of this was what looked like a large wardrobe. It was the enclosure in which the prisoners were kept when brought from their cells until they had to appear before the court.

Miss Garrison looked about the place with its cheaply frescoed walls and long windows, and felt it was rather a mean-looking court-room. The people in it did not impress her much more favorably. They had a cheap look, too, and she began to think that those who attend the sessions of justice, even as spectators, are not drawn from the cream of humanity.

Her uncle had put her in the enclosure just below the judge's desk. He told her his case was to come on next, and that she would not have to wait very long. The judge was a rather fine-looking man. He was tall and portly, and though his hair was liberally sown with gray he did not seem more than forty-five or six. He wore moustaches, had large, bright eyes, and also had a fashion of gnawing the finger-nails of a white, shapely hand. He was clean-shaven with the exception of his moustaches.

Miss Garrison did not have to wait long.   She saw her uncle
rise and address some remarks to the court.   Then another
lawyer got up and addressed remarks to the court.   From what
was said by the judge, Miss Garrison gathered that the case
was put off till some other time.   She saw her uncle put his
papers promptly into his high-hat and pick up his cane.

At that moment a noise and slight commotion at the other
end of the court-room attracted her attention.   She glanced that
way and saw a tall, broad-shouldered young fellow walking
down the aisle.   He carried himself with notable dignity.   Straight
as an arrow, with a set expression on his face, and his resolute
eyes betraying a stanch unacceptance of his surroundings, he
approached the railing in front of the judge's desk like one who
had come to call him to stern account.

There was something in his carriage and looks which excited
Miss Garrison's curiosity.

"What is he going to do?" she whispered to her uncle, who
had approached her side.   She delayed, her gaze fastened on the
young fellow.

"He is going to be done, I believe," said her uncle with
grim humor.   "He stole a lot of money, and he is to be sentenced!"

A thief!   Her first thought was that he looked like a man
who would steal a great deal of money if he stole any.   He did
not suggest petty larceny in the least.   But her next thought,
as clear and strong as a logically deduced judgment, was that
the young man had stolen nothing.   His face, his clear, unflinch-
ing eye, the calm dignity of his fine mouth and square chin, the
character of the broad, smooth forehead, and, more than all, the
peculiar dignity with which he carried himself made it a matter
of no doubt to her mind that he was guiltless.   Her intuition
told her this.

His eyes were fixed calmly on the judge: not defiantly, not
resignedly—only unshrinkingly, and with a sense of contained endurance as of one who assists at a necessary but painful ceremony.   There was not a flicker of change in the strong face as
the learned judge declared that after an impartial trial he had
been convicted of a gross breach of trust and had been adjudged
guilty of having embezzled fifteen thousand dollars.

"If I am disposed to accord you the lightest sentence which
the statutes decree, it is because this is your first offence, and that
your character seems to have been irreproachable before this
lapse.   But the evidence in your case, though circumstantial, has

been of a kind to force conviction of your guilt on twelve impartial citizens. You have declined to enter any plea either of 'guilty' or 'not guilty.' I sentence you, therefore, to five years of hard labor in Sing Sing. I hope that, as you have youth and so much that seems praiseworthy in your character, this term of imprisonment will not blight your life but may be a safeguard to your future career when you are released."

During the slow, measured delivery of the judge's words Miss Garrison had not once removed her eyes from the face of the man. The longer she looked the more certain was she in her soul that he was innocent. At the close of the fatal speech he turned with the same calm repose and air of mastery and walked down the aisle erect and firm, the officer at his side. Not a shadow of emotion had crossed his face.

"Come! let us go," exclaimed Miss Garrison to her uncle.

They followed after the sheriff and his prisoner. Something chanced to delay them so that Miss Garrison found herself by the side of the sentenced man. Pushed by the crowd behind her she was even forced against him for a moment.

He moved a little, slowly turned toward her, and when he saw it was a lady made a slight bow as of apology.

Her eyes were fixed upon him with a look of interest which she did not care to disguise. As he apologized by this quiet show of courtesy for something not his fault, his clear eyes were turned full upon her own. The girl had a conviction of her ability to read character, and the intimate sense that the man before her was guiltless of all crime struck her with such force that, in an impulse of honest sympathy, she stretched forth her hand and, looking straight into his eyes, said in a low, earnest voice: 'I believe you are perfectly innocent."

He took her hand with a respectfully firm grasp, which was hardly a pressure of the fingers. "Thank you," he said, with intense feeling, while his eyes lit up with a light that would have confirmed her had she needed confirmation. The soft gray deepened with feeling. The firm lips relaxed into a softer expression, lending a sudden charm to his rather stern face. She felt the full stress of gratitude conveyed by his words and kindled look. Then he bent his head slightly again and passed on.

"My dear," said Mr. Hartwell, with some nervousness, "that was a very singular thing to do! I do not think you should have spoken to that fellow at all. Certainly not to tell him that. The court has found him guilty. He is a criminal."

"And I found him innocent," she cried warmly. "Uncle

Hartwell, I am sure that he has not done the thing he was charged with. I could not help letting him feel as he stood there, so alone and deserted, that there was one soul who believed in him. I should have felt like a coward not to have spoken to him as I did when I felt it so strongly. There is some mistake, I am sure. I would do the same thing again."

"I am afraid you have made the mistake, my dear. What do you know about crime or criminals?" Mr. Hartwell inquired with a proud disdain.

"Nothing—about criminals," she retorted quickly.

Miss Garrison could not get the thought of the young fellow out of her mind. She felt glad that she had happened into the court-room and was thus able to say one cheering word to a stricken man. How his eyes had lit up as he neither confirmed nor denied her conviction in regard to him! There had been no need of words.

The next day she eagerly read the morning papers to find out who he was and with what he was charged. When she found the account and read the prisoner's name she experienced a strange shock. It was none other than Paul Arkenburgh!

She got other papers of an earlier date to learn all she could of his alleged crime. In them she read the story, given at length on account of the criminal's engagement to the daughter of Mr. Archer, the president of the company from which the money had been stolen. It seemed that on a certain day of the week the company paid off the men. The money for this was deposited in the safe two or three days before, and was put in envelopes ready for distribution on pay-day, Monday.

Friday the money was in the safe. Saturday morning it was gone. By a singular coincidence, that same Saturday morning one of the men employed in the office, who lived some little distance up the Hudson, had noticed Arkenburgh at the window of a train going north, which passed the station where he was waiting to take the cars into town. Arkenburgh had not seen him.

When this man got to the office he learned that the money was taken. Arkenburgh had left the key for the cashier in an envelope. Mr. Archer had been ill enough for two days to remain at Irvington, and he had not come down that morning. He was telegraphed at once that the money had been taken and that Paul Arkenburgh, the only one of the clerks who knew the combination for the safe, had been there yesterday until the office was closed and had been seen by chance that morning on a train going north! Mr. Archer was asked if they had not better telegraph to Albany and the way-stations, ordering Arkenburgh's arrest.

Mr. Archer wrote back that he was too ill to do anything himself that day, but to take such measures as they thought best.

Thereupon the official did take such measures that Paul Arkenburgh was arrested when he was leaving the train at Albany. He had seemed disturbed and vexed. He declared that it was a mistake and an insult, and that he would explain matters to Mr. Archer when he got to New York.

Despite Mr. Archer's illness, he was at the station to meet him, and accompanied him to jail. There he had a long private talk with Arkenburgh.

When Arkenburgh was brought to trial he declined to plead "not guilty," refusing to make any answer to the charge. The evidence was strongly against him. No one but he knew the combination for the safe, except Mr. Archer, who had been confined to his home for two days before the robbery, and for the greater part of the day following it.

Testimony on all sides was in favor of the fine character Arkenburgh had always borne. The most the opposing counsel could get against him, as an offset in this respect, was his reserve. He seemed a quiet fellow, not accustomed to talk of his plans or views, and yet very thoughtful.

Everything seemed to tell against him as far as they told against any one. The safe had not been broken open. The result was his conviction. And Miss Garrison had witnessed the closing scene in the drama by being present in court the day he was sentenced.

"It is thought," said the paper which gave the best account of the robbery, "that Mr. Archer hoped for Arkenburgh's acquittal in view of the fine character he had always borne. It is known that he strove to induce the company to decline prosecuting the guilty clerk on the ground that he could probably be induced to refund the money. And here was a strange feature in the case. Arkenburgh had nothing with him when he was arrested but a small travelling bag, in which there was no money. His room had been searched by the detectives, but no money found. All he had with him was one hundred and some odd dollars in bills, none of which were identified as of those stolen from the bank.

"Arkenburgh must have had an accomplice to whom he entrusted the money. He was not known to have any woman friend who could have assisted him. There was no woman in the case, apparently."

"Paul Arkenburgh is innocent!" Miss Garrison exclaimed aloud upon finishing the paper. "But who could have taken the money, then? Why did he say he could explain it all to Mr. Archer, and then decline to make any answer to the charge."

She sat motionless, the paper in her lap, thinking very intently. For fully half an hour she remained quiet, her mind working at the problem with great activity. She tried to divest herself of the idea that Arkenburgh was innocent that she might feel the force of the circumstances which had convinced the jury of his guilt. But she could not get any hypothesis which would make it plausible in this way. Was human nature capable of a hypocrisy so deep that this man, convicted of a crime which he had committed, and laboring under the sense that he had played his game and lost, could have flashed into his violet eyes that look of intense, quiet gratitude at her testimony of a belief in his innocence? could have thrown into his voice that simple, earnest, manly dignity as he thanked her?—she, a stranger whom he had never seen before and could never expect to behold again.

No! She had not sounded the depths either of human depravity nor risen to the heights of human rectitude, but there could be no sufficient reason for such duplicity as this, she thought.

Then who had stolen the money, and why was this innocent man without a protest, without even the usual plea of "not guilty," passing to an ignominious punishment that would blast his career?

There could be no motive but policy or love. Which could it have been? There seemed no room for the first. There appeared no ground for the second.

The result of Kate Garrison's long deliberation was that she resolved to go to Newport and pay her visit to Miss Archer as soon as she had seen one or two legal persons in New York.

III.

"Oh! I am so glad to see you, Kate."

Miss Archer's tone was warm and eager, but there was the sound of tears in her voice as she greeted Miss Garrison. It was a week after that young woman's deep cogitation over the

case of Mr. Paul Arkenburgh. Before she left New York for
Newport she had had a long interview with the lawyers who
had conducted the case against that unfortunate young man.
At the end one of them had said to her: "It is a pity the
prisoner did not have you to conduct his defence."

Miss Garrison had smiled and remarked: "The defence may
be possible still." Then she had left him with her belief in the
young man's complete innocence quite unimpaired and with a
rather contemptuous opinion of the legal profession.

She had hardly arrived at the cottage in Newport which Mr.
Archer had rented for the season and taken off her things before Miss Archer dragged her into her bed-room and told her
with tears and lamentations, and a touch of indignation, the
story of the robbery. She was intensely vexed with Arkenburgh
for exposing her to the mortification of public gossip and a
scandal which threatened to impair her social interests.

"You have no doubt of his guilt?" asked Miss Garrison,
when Miss Archer had finished her story of the robbery.

"I wish I could have for my own sake," Miss Archer replied
bitterly. "It is mortifying to think that one has been engaged
to a thief. Unfortunately, there is no room for doubt. Poor
papa is quite broken up over the thing. He implores me to be
less severe in my feelings against Arkenburgh. He was really
fond of him, and cannot reconcile himself to the thought of such
perfidy. Oh! why should I have gotten into such a dreadful
complication?" she exclaimed irritably, a look of vexation in
her face. "It seemed sacrifice enough to marry only a clerk in
papa's office and then to have him show his appreciation of my
generous forgetfulness of the difference in our positions by dis-
gracing himself and me. Isn't it awful, Kate? O Kate! don't
you feel what this is to me?"

She looked at her friend imploringly, the flush of mortified
vanity reddening her cheeks. Miss Garrison hardly knew what
to say. If the girl believed her lover guilty of theft she could
not be blamed for feeling so keenly hurt about the matter. But
even so, Miss Garrison thought, with some severity, perhaps, that
a more dignified bearing would have seemed better than the ready
querulousness of outraged pride or vanity. Miss Archer had no
room for any consideration except her humbled self.

"Your father was ill at the time this thing happened?" Miss
Garrison asked after a moment, in which she had nodded her
head in a slow, doubtful way, capable of being construed into
sympathy for Miss Archer.

"Yes; that only made it worse. It seems as if Arkenburgh were taking advantage of papa's absence"

"What was the matter with your father?" inquired Miss Garrison with kindly interest.

"He had a severe attack of rheumatism in his leg so that he could not move. He was unable to leave his room, and it was only by the greatest effort that he could get to town to see Paul after he was brought back from Albany. But he would go to New York to see him. He did his best to prevent the company from pushing the case, he was so lenient toward Arkenburgh. Papa really made him. It was through him that Paul was so rapidly advanced. Don't you see how much worse that made it seem in him to act so shamefully?"

Miss Garrison did not make an immediate answer. She only took her friend's hand and held it in her own.

Then she said quietly: "Do you love him still, Addie?"

Miss Archer raised her head indignantly, with the tear-drops clinging to the lashes of her eyes, and said, rather viciously: "Love a thief? Love a man who has been as ungrateful and cruel as that? My shame and wonder is that I could have ever loved any one who could be capable of such things. At first I did not believe it, and wanted to go to him and ask him how he could have done such a thing," she went on with charming consistency: "But papa would not hear of it. He cannot bear to have the subject mentioned. Once when I spoke of Arkenburgh as a 'thief' papa reproached me quite strongly for it. He said that Paul had always been kind to me and that it was unwomanly to throw stones at him when he was down. As if making me a byword were not doing enough to offset any little good-natured kindness before," she exclaimed in another burst of indignation.

"Supposing it were all a mistake, and Mr. Arkenburgh were proved perfectly innocent," said Miss Garrison soothingly:

"How can it be proven when they have tried him and found him guilty?" the other cried impatiently. "It is foolish to pity him or make such suppositions about him. No; I do not care for him and I wish I had never seen him."

"I am sorry for you, Addie," said Miss Garrison, "but it would be much worse if you still loved him, or if you had any doubt about his guilt. You will soon forget him. Do not think about him any more. These things have only to be lived down, and they are lived down pretty quickly in America. Everybody will sympathize with you. We won't talk about it any more; but just have as jolly a time as we can this summer. You must go out just as much as possible, and act as if this had never occurred."

Then Miss Garrison began asking about friends and what kind of a season it was at Newport, etc., until she had brought Miss Archer to a more cheerful mind. After a little while, on the plea of fatigue, she bade her friend " good night," and retired to her room, glad to get by herself and think. Her fancy flew from the picture of the querulous girl full of wrathful feeling for her former lover to that lover as she had seen him, his eyes growing dark with the intensity of his gratitude for her declaration of belief in his innocence. He was in a prison now, coarse clothes, with stripes of ignominy on them, presenting him as an offender against society. She found herself more in sympathy with the man who was a stranger to her than with the petulant girl whom she called her friend.

" You are innocent!" she cried vehemently to herself, " and if I can help to prove you so I will." And Miss Garrison had the elements in her of almost quixotic devotion when her judgment and her feeling were alike touched. She had not been in Newport more than a day or two before she found an opportunity to converse with Mr. Archer alone. It was something she had desired ever since her arrival. Miss Archer had been invited at the last moment to take a place left vacant in a coaching party, and had accepted with much pleasure on her friend's insistence that she should go. Mrs. Archer was sick with a headache, but she told Miss Garrison not to forego the afternoon drive on that account. Whereupon that young lady had proposed to Mr. Archer to accompany her, and to her surprise he had consented.

The carriage bowled over the road along the cliffs, the velvety softness of the sea-air gently fanning their faces, while the blue water broke with a lisping contentedness upon the shore. Suddenly, after a slight pause, Miss Garrison said:

"I suppose you were awfully vexed by the conduct of your clerk, Mr. Archer, weren't you ?"

A look of pain shot for a moment over the ruddy face of Mr. Archer and his brow contracted. His lips also were pressed tightly together for a moment. Then he said slowly:

" Yes, more than can be imagined. It is an exceedingly painful subject. My daughter's relation to the young man made it doubly trying. Nobody would have suspected him of such a thing. But it is done, and there is nothing more to

be said about it. It is too painful to be talked about, Miss
Garrison. I rarely allude to the subject. There is no use in it
now."

"There is only one thing I wish you would tell me, Mr.
Archer, and then we will let the subject drop. Why did he say
when he was arrested that he would explain everything satisfactorily and then, after he had come back, refuse to say a
word?"

Mr. Archer glanced at the girl, but she wore an expression
of idle feminine interest only. Then he said:

"He may have had some thought of defence which no one
knew. He was quite excited when I saw him on his return to
New York. But he agreed with me that in view of what had
happened the simplest thing was to submit to whatever the trial
would lead to. I did my best to get the company not to prose-
cute the case, but could not prevail with the managers. He
was a fine young fellow, and no one had a word against him
before this trouble. But, as I said, it is too painful to dwell
upon, Miss Garrison, and I shall really feel obliged if you will
quietly banish the whole thing as far as possible. We never
speak of it now. It is done and cannot be recalled. He was
a fine fellow."

He sighed heavily as he finished speaking and passed his
hand over his forehead, which had contracted again. During the
rest of the drive he was rather silent. Miss Garrison felt that
she would gather very little from any conversation on the subject, even had it been possible to broach it again after her host
had so pointedly begged that all allusion to it should be
avoided.

Miss Archer returned from her expedition in better spirits
than her friend had yet experienced in her. In the course of
her talk with Miss Garrison she mentioned meeting a Mr. Caldwell from the West, who was visiting a friend in Newport.
According to her report, he was a young man of thirty, of
agreeable manners, and rich. He had evidently awakened a
pleasant feeling in Miss Archer.

The next day the two girls went to the Casino in the morning to attend the tennis championship games. It was a soft,
gray morning, the air cool with soft white clouds floating in the
sky. Miss Garrison was absorbed to a degree she would not
have cared to admit to everybody with the thought of discovering the truth about Paul Arkenburgh. She must find out. Believing him innocent, she felt the injustice of the punishment

he was undergoing, and he had no friends. She did not analyze very closely whether the personality of the stalwart young clerk had helped to arouse this desire to vindicate him or not.

On the other hand, if she were utterly mistaken—in which case Paul Arkenburgh was, to her mind, much worse than a thief—she wished to know it too, because then she could dispel the thought of assisting him. If he had stolen the money she could not feel any interest in him, for he was an awful hypocrite as well as a thief. He had conveyed to her a sense of innocence in a way that could only have been the deepest, craftiest dissimulation if he were guilty. Hypocrisy was a more odious crime to her than larceny.

But in the meantime she could not think of any measure to pursue for the moment. As the subject was barred in the Archer family, there was no hope of getting any clue by talking about the matter. So she resolved to enjoy her visit to her friend and to help Addie as much as she could.

The grounds of the Newport Casino are very lovely, and they never show to better advantage than on a soft gray summer day. A crowd of men and women were gathered about the tennis court and wandering about on the sward with a Watteau-like effect. The son of a New England millionaire was playing with a college champion from England, and the interest shown by the young women was not entirely due to the skill displayed by the players.

The two girls were standing a little outside of the crowd when Miss Archer greeted with some warmth a young fellow who strolled up. She presented him to Miss Garrison. It was Mr. Caldwell. He was a slender young man in a white flannel suit with white shoes. He was good-looking and talked animatedly. Miss Garrison was only moderately interested in him, but she saw that her friend considerably brightened under his advent.

He asked permission to introduce a friend of his, also from the West, a Mr. Derwent. It was the first time he had been in Newport, and Miss Garrison graciously showed him about the Casino. He was a business man who had been successful in some ventures, and even in his outings and moments of recreation he showed an inclination to touch on matters connected with profit and loss which amused the young woman.

After a slight break in their conversation, he said to Miss Garrison: "Is the young lady with you the daughter of George Archer?"

"Yes," said Miss Garrison.

"Was she very badly broken up by the way Arkenburgh acted?"

"Of course it was a great trial," she answered. "The young man never gave any indication of such a nature, and naturally it was a terrible shock to a girl just engaged to him."

"I was very much surprised when I heard of it," Mr. Derwent continued. "I knew Arkenburgh slightly. I thought at one time he might go into a scheme with me. He was a fine business fellow, and I felt he would get ahead. The man who introduced me to him tried to get him to join me. It had some chance of turning the wrong way; and I suppose Arkenburgh did not want to risk what money he had laid by and throw up a good position. But he was thinking about it a good deal, for this other fellow told me only a little while before this robbery Arkenburgh had spoken to him about it again and wanted to know when I was coming East. I was in Albany at the time, and my friend told Arkenburgh that I would treat with him if he chose to see me. Perhaps he thought stealing fifteen thousand dollars was a surer thing than running the risk of losing two or three thousand," Mr. Derwent added with a laugh.

Miss Garrison's interest had been aroused from the moment Paul Arkenburgh's name was mentioned, and she had listened most attentively.

"Do you think he stole the money?" she asked quietly.

"Why, I thought they proved it at the trial, didn't they?" he returned nonchalantly. "You can imagine I had no such opinion of him when I wanted him to go into a scheme with me."

"There was strong circumstantial evidence, I believe," said Miss Garrison carelessly. Then, after a moment's pause she asked: "Was there any reason he could have had for not wishing it known that he was thinking of going into this scheme of yours?"

"Oh! I don't know, unless he felt people might think he had a taste for speculation. The risk might have seemed too great for a man with not much money to go into it. But he would have made a good thing out of it. It is turning just as I expected, and I will get good returns for my investment."

"You were in Albany about the time he got into this trouble, then?" she said.

"Just at that time. I had been there a week when I read the newspaper account of the robbery."

"And your friend told you that Mr. Arkenburgh had talked with him about a wish to see you in regard to this matter?"

"He said he wanted to know when I would come East, and I suppose he was thinking about this. It was only about two months before that I had broached it to him."

"And you say your friend told him you were in Albany then?"

"Yes. Morris told him he had better not wait too long if he meant to go into it with me, and then Arkenburgh went into himself again and said no more about it one way or the other. He never talked much about anything."

The conversation turned to something else. Miss Garrison was a little absent-minded at moments. She was saying to herself: "This would account for his going to Albany just at the time of the robbery, which seemed so suspicious." Arkenburgh had declined to give any reason for this trip, and the prosecution had made quite a point of it. It had seemed strange to Miss Garrison, but now she felt that she had discovered a reason for this. He had gone there to confer with Derwent. With his usual secretiveness he had said nothing of his purpose. Then, when he was arrested for the robbery, the very fact that he kept silent on a point which seemed to tell against him fitted in with her idea that he was innocent, but for some reason cared to do nothing to clear himself of the charge. There could be no motive in this except to screen some one. Who could it be?

She recalled his indignation on being arrested. Then he had seen Mr. Archer and had said or done nothing to prove his innocence afterward. Could it be that Mr. Archer had made it clear to him that defence was useless?

She was very thoughtful while they were at the Casino. That night, when Miss Archer and herself were sitting together before going to bed, she strove to placate that young woman by a hearty sympathy with her hopes. At last she said carelessly:

"Addie, was Mr. Arkenburgh of a very generous disposition?"

"How strange you should take such an interest in that man!" her friend replied, with a touch of the pettish indignation which the name of her former lover seemed to always awaken. "I thought he was very generous, but he was a reserved man and, as a rule, never showed his feelings very much. But it looks

like generosity, doesn't it, to disgrace himself and thus put me
and papa and mamma in such a hateful position? If there was
anybody he ought to have felt gratitude toward it was certainly
papa. His advancement was due to papa's taking such an active
interest in him. No; I do not think he had any generosity,"
she concluded emphatically. "But why do you take such an
interest in a thief?" she asked vindictively.

"It certainly is not because he is a thief," Miss Garrison
returned with some coldness. "Did, it never strike you as somewhat surprising that so very exemplary a man should all at once
steal fifteen thousand dollars?"

It was on the tip of her tongue to explain that Mr. Derwent,
by what he had said to her that day, had confirmed her belief
in Arkenburgh's innocence. But on second thought she said
nothing about it. A rather startling suspicion had entered her
mind while her friend had been speaking. It was one she was
loath to entertain, but she could not dispel it.

The time of her visit was drawing to a close. She was not
sorry. Her interest in Miss Archer had somewhat faded when
she saw how she bore herself in the matter of Paul Arkenburgh.
She could not sympathize with the ease with which Miss Archer
had rallied from her regard for him. Given that he had stolen
the money, she need not have been so ready to vituperate one
who had never shown her personally anything but the warmest
devotion. A little pity would not have been misplaced, Miss
Garrison thought.

Another young friend of hers at this juncture afforded her a
surprise, half pleasant and half a doubtful pleasure. This friend,
who had rather fallen out of Miss Garrison's sight for some
months, wrote and asked her to visit her. She was at a country
residence her family had. Miss Garrison felt a curious sensation
when she learned that they lived in Sing Sing!

Somehow it took a very short time for her to decide on
accepting it, and. three days after leaving Newport she found
herself in the same village with Paul Arkenburgh; she the idle
summer guest in a handsome house and he the State's prisoner,
in a suit of brown and black, in the big prison down by the
river.

Something like a shudder passed over her as she was whirled
along in the train by a big gray building with hundreds of narrow windows from which the imprisoned light escaped in a sickly
glow on the mist of a drizzly evening. She let herself fall back
with a sigh, when she could no longer see it, into her com-

fortable chair in the Pullman car. *Was* Arkenburgh innocent? Or was he a cool, unsuccessful criminal, suffering just punishment, and she a foolish, quixotic creature of vain imaginings? She could not assent to the latter possibility very well because she knew herself too perfectly. "I have good reasons for thinking he may be innocent!" she said to her heart, in rebuttal of the idea of foolishness in such an opinion. She did not reflect that her first impression of Paul Arkenburgh's innocence was based entirely on feeling. Or would she have denied this, and have maintained that her firm, quick conviction on that point was an intuitional judgment based on premises existent if intangible, and deduced therefrom with unconscious logic? She undoubtedly did so feel it.

JOHN J. À BECKET.

(TO BE CONCLUDED.)

"HAST THOU SEEN HIM WHOM MY SOUL LOVETH?"
(*Cant. iii.* 3.)

Jesus as the Gardener.

WHOM seekest thou? Whom wouldst thou bear away
    Within thy close embrace?
Who, thinkest thou, would choose the night to stray
    Unto this lonely place?

Thine own sweet child, perchance, from thy fond arms
    Escaped in playful mood,
And wandered, fearing not the night's alarms,
    Unto this garden wood?

Mary Magdalen.

Oh yes! a wanderer He, indeed, who from Heaven's coast
    Down-gazing on this sin-shamed earth
Pitied, then fell in love: who knoweth not the cost
    And sharp, deep pang of true love's birth?

Methinks the greatness of His love did more exhaust
    Than life, with all its price, is worth.
Prithee, didst thou, perchance, this Lover e'er accost
    Somewhere on this wide, weary earth?

Jesus.

The world is full of lovers as of men;
   And every one, from serf to king,
Doth judge his own love past all others' ken
   Or e'en of their imagining.

Nay, more: what lover e'er found what he sought?
   Herein lies love's chief joy and pain:
That which is past all price to give for naught,
   And yearn for love as great in vain.

Yet would I know upon whose path thy eager feet
   Press forward in such amorous haste:
That He hath won such love as thine doth prove a feat
   Of love like God's, as His as chaste.

Mary.

Dost not know HIM? Thou speakest but in jest.
   'Tis He who deigned to look at me, and won
By that sweet glance more love than heart confessed
   Since time its tireless course began to run.

O hour of wondrous bliss and love untold!
   In Heaven I'll smell the od'rous spikenard still.
My contrite eyes may now naught else behold;
   His image dear doth all their vision fill.

No music, tho' of angels, to my list'ning ear
   May bring its charm. He sang a rapt'rous strain
Which lifted me from hell to Heaven to hear:
   "Of many sins much love doth pardon gain."

Hast thou not heard what all men surely know;
   Aye, every weeping angel in the skies;
Glad souls in Limbo, and those steeped in woe
   Beyond the limit where Hope's promise dies?

Alack! He lost what all true lovers lose,
   E'en I. What love, what seek I, more than Life?
And such I find not: but yet may not choose
   To die like Him and end the woeful strife.

What falleth to all lovers Him befell.
  His God-like love was scorned with rare despight,
E'en direful death. Crown, spear, and torturing nail
  Poured forth His life-blood till His soul took flight.

From Paschal moon the silver, shimmering light
  Fell full athwart His Body on the Rood.
His locks were wet with dews of coming night.
  Himself, the cross, the ground, all drenched with blood.

The arms that held Him until death did yield
  What never mine ! We bore the priceless load
Earth gave to Heaven here. This silent field
  Became the grave of earth's own Maker, God.

They rolled the heavy stone upon my heart;
  Ten thousand worlds as much would never weigh.
Yet was I joyful ; since no cunning art
  Could lift that stone and take my Love away.

Now is the day when these fond eyes should see,
  And mine own hands anoint His blessèd clay.
Alack ! some power hath robbed earth's richest treasury,
  And rapt the shrine that held my Life away!

Good sir ! if Him who is all mine hast found,
  And hidden safe till love could claim its own,
Show me where thou hast laid Him on the ground,
  And I will take Him—I who should, alone !

                    Jesus.
        " Mary ! "

                    Mary.
        " Rabboni ! "
                              ALFRED YOUNG.

THE FORERUNNER OF THE METRIC SYSTEM OF MEASURES.

As we make use of a fact, endorse a creed, or utilize an invention we frequently lose sight of the mental effort which the devising and elaboration cost. In order to rightly appreciate what our antecedents have done for us it is well to occasionally make a halt in our rapid march long enough to contemplate the rise and development of those institutions which are now a part of our life—which had only the beginnings in theirs. In doing this we frequently call up before us names of those long-forgotten, and realize anew who first placed the principal from which we are incessantly drawing the interest.

And now, while many wise men are glorifying the French nation for having given us such an elaborate, harmonious, and unique system of measures; while learned bodies throughout the land are urging its adoption; while governments are legalizing or enforcing its use, should not some mention be made of that modest priest who suggested the system long before its Academician propounders knew aught of ife? Judging from the life of Gabriel Mouton, he would care but little to have the memory of his notable labors revived, but it is due us to know who it is that deserves our gratitude, and in rescuing his name from oblivion others may be led to feel that if forgetfulness is to be their reward some one will find it his pleasure to throw aside the surrounding pall and give to their names a newness of life.

In order to fully appreciate what our hero proposed and accomplished it is necessary to go back to the beginning of the seventeenth century. At that time the sciences were only on the brink of being; for it would be inaccurate to give the name of science to that mass of hypothetical speculation of which all natural philosophy previously consisted. The purpose of the ancients was to divine natural causes, not to investigate them. The art of examining nature in order to constrain her to reveal her secrets was unknown; it remained for Galileo to make this discovery. He showed that the human mind is too feeble and too evanescent to progress by virtue of its own strength through the labyrinth of natural facts; that it is necessary at every step to classify those phenomena which approximate to one another.

To this Bacon added that, in the multiplied opportunities which nature offers for inquiry, experiments industriously prosecuted are necessary to conduct to a course of new phenomena which shall neither entangle nor mislead.

It was while the sciences were in this formative period that Ferrara, a city of Italy, gave to the world one who was to soon become famous. At the age of sixteen John Baptist Riccioli was admitted into the society of the Jesuits, and before he had completed his course of study many regarded with amazement the progress which he made. Rhetoric, poetry, philosophy, and scholastic divinity were his favorite subjects, and these he was soon called upon to teach in the Jesuits' colleges at Parma and Bologna. While engaged in teaching he became interested in geography and astronomy. These he found so fascinating and so promising of rich fruit that he obtained permission from his superiors to quit all other employment that he might devote himself exclusively to those sciences.

While studying everything on these subjects that fell in his way he met with *Eratosthenes Batavorum*, by Snellius, a geometer of Holland. In this book was described the means by which Snellius in 1615 determined the length of a degree of the earth's meridian, and hence the circumference of the earth. This important problem concerning the size and shape of the earth had received the earnest attention of Greek and Egyptian philosophers, and called forth methods puerile and ineffectual from Fernel, the court physician to Henry II. of France, and the Arabian Caliph Almamon.

In order to know the length of a degree, it is necessary to know the exact latitude of two points on the earth's surface. The difference in these latitudes will give the amplitude of the arc which connects the parallels of these points. Now, if the linear distance between these parallels be also known, the length of one degree will bear the same ratio to the length of this arc that one degree bears to the amplitude of this arc. Therefore this problem is made up of two parts: to determine the amplitude of an arc, and to know its length.

It is said that Ptolemy pointed out the fact that in order to determine the length of an arc it was not necessary to measure along a meridian. Still, no one was willing to accept this belief until Snellius demonstrated it to be a fact. He went still further, saying that, since it is not absolutely essential to measure on a meridian, it is not necessary that the terminal points should be connected by a straight line, but the line may be broken—that is, made up of a number of straight lines joined end to end. This, perhaps, suggested at once that at least some of the lines might have their lengths computed, thereby saving the trouble of measuring them. It was, of course, known at that time that in a triangle if one side and the angles be given the remaining sides can be found. The known side might be short, while the computed sides could be relatively longer. From this it was but a step to realize that a side which has been computed in one triangle may become the known side in an adjoining triangle, and aid in determining the remaining sides of the latter. Thus triangle could be joined to triangle, link by link, forming what is now called a chain or net; with only one side, called the *base*, determined by direct measurement.

Snellius measured a base on the frozen meadows of Sverterwoude, and laid out a chain of triangles stretching from Alkmaar to Bergen. He determined the angles by measurement and the sides by computation step by step from the base. Then, knowing the length of each side, the summation of a set of contiguous lines, gave the length of the *broken* line joining the terminal points. However, these lines, not having the same direction, it was necessary to calculate what the length of each line would be if it had the direction of the imaginary line which connected the two ends; that is, he found the *projection* of each line on this direction, then the sum of these projections gave the distance required. With this oblique line and the bearing, it was easy to find its projection on the meridian, or the length of the arc which united the parallels of the terminal stations. The determination of the latitudes gave the amplitude and the length of one degree, found as has been intimated. This method, then followed for the first time, contains the fundamental principles of all subsequent geodetic operations.

It was the description of these operations which fell into the hands of Riccioli, just when he was anxious to make some valuable contribution to the world's stock of knowledge. He had already projected a great work, the *Almagestum Novum*, following in the main the plan of Ptolemy's monumental work, but he wished to produce something more than a compilation—he would hand down some original observations, and thereby stimulate others to reap as well as to gather.

With his mind glowing with such noble aspirations, ready to enter upon any investigation which had the promise of results worthy of the effort, we find him upon Mount Serra-Paderno, where his order possessed a country place. While here he wrote his *Astronomia Reformata* and *Chronologia Reformata.* In the former he gave the diverse and divergent views of astronomers of all ages, and sought by diligent comparisons to bring order out of these chaotic beliefs and deduce principles broad enough to include all that was meritorious and accurate enough to accord with observed phenomena. As one of the divisions of his subject included a discussion of solar units, he found a variety of values for the distance from the sun to the earth and the latter's size. Then, as he looked away toward the Ghirlandina, that graceful tower of Modena's cathedral, he thought of what Snellius had accomplished in far-away Holland. Is it not natural that the thought should come to him that perhaps here was the desired opportunity to enrich the world's knowledge ? Perhaps his value of a degree might emphasize that found by his predecessor, and so one more authenticated result could take its place in his *Reformata.*

In 1645, in connection with Grimaldi, also a member of the society of Jesuits, he began the task of measuring the arc between Mount Serra-Paderno and Ghirlandina, following in many respects the method devised by Snellius, using a measured base and joining the terminal points by means of a net of triangles. The amplitude of the arc was only one-fourth of a degree, which would not establish great confidence in his results, but adverse criticism is forestalled by our ignorance as to the length of the unit which was employed.

But, as it frequently happens, the work of Riccioli in this direction cannot be estimated by the value of his immediate results. As the Chinese pay homage to the parents of a great man rather than to his children, so should we honor Riccioli, who laid the foundations for him who proposed a decimal metrology, and not to the French nation which adopted it.

In the mutual interchange of courtesies a copy of Riccioli's work found its way to the College of St. Paul at Lyons, where it met at the hands of Gabriel Mouton a cordial reception. Of Mouton, unfortunately, but little is known ; we hear of him as choir-master at the collegiate church, and only in a few other places. He had sent a copy of tables of some trigonometric functions to the Academy of Sciences at Paris, and the secretary in presenting it to the Academy referred to Mouton as a very skilful mathematician. All encyclopædias seem to be ignorant of his existence, and no bibliography gives more than the title of the one book which he wrote. This title has an unattractive beginning: " *Observationes Diametrorum solis et lunæ apparen-tium . . .* " ; nor is anything of importance referred to until after *fifty-one* words are given. One seldom reads a Latin title beyond this point, which explains why so few have noticed that " *Huic adjecta est . . . una cum nova mensurarum geometri-carum idea,*" and even if one should read all the way through it is not probable that any great expectations would be aroused by this " *nova idea.*" In recent times, at least, but few persons have had the opportunity of even seeing the book, judging from its apparent rarity, as evinced in a two years' search through the libraries of this country and Europe which revealed the existence of only one copy—and that one is in a Boston library. And a dealer has sought for a year in vain for a copy. This scarcity does not detract from the credit due the pro-pounder of this " *idea,*" but merely explains why he has been obliged to rest in oblivion so long.

Let us now see what this scheme is which occupies pages 427–448 of the above-named book. He begins very modestly, thinking perhaps others have hit upon a similar system, and does not show any desire to contend for priority. He says: " Although here matters of measurement are discussed, they are not perhaps new to all, from the fact that in the vast variety of measures that are in use to-day in all parts of the world it is possible that these which I propose may coincide with some of them. Nevertheless these measures are new both as to their nature and the method by which they are de-termined and protected against any danger of alteration." Then, appreciating the great advantages possessed by our deci-mal notation, he concluded that in his new system ten should be the number of times each unit should be contained in the next higher. This of itself was a grand proposition, devised without any reference to any system then in vogue and totally independent of all.

In addition to this proposal, which alone is worthy of our commendation, he went far beyond the expectations of his time, by taking the length of his unit from the *length of a terrestrial degree,* using one minute of this degree for his longest unit, the *milliar.* Going down the scale from milliar we come to *centuria,* by hundreds; *decuria,* by tens ; and *virga,* which was to be the primal or fundamental unit. To know exactly how far to carry the subdivision of this unit it was necessary to know the length of the degree of the great circle of the earth, for the earth was then regarded as the perfect sphere. Just here we see the influ-

ence of our Jesuit astronomer.   Mouton says :. " Of all the observations that I know, ancient as well as modern, those of John
Baptist Riccioli please me most, both on account of their wonderful harmony and the singular diligence which the above-mentioned author has exhibited in treating of them, and also the
industry manifested in the labor of twelve years, which he bore
with an unwearied mind for the sake of the truth that was to be
attained.   Indeed, I have such confidence in these observations
that I should regard my own, if I had any, as inferior to them.
But hitherto I have been unable to accomplish anything; in this
subject, although I am very fond of such things."

The twelve years here referred to were occupied by Riccioli in
collating and comparing ancient earth measurements to see how
they would harmonize with the work of Snellius or his own.   He
saw in these different results an endorsement of his value for a
degree, 64,363 Bologna steps.   Mouton accepted this value, and
taking one-sixtieth of 321,815 feet, to which the above is equivalent, he gavé 5363.58 feet as the value of his milliar, and one-
thousandth of this was 5.36+, which represented a virga.   With
wonderful acumen he perceived that this would be too long for the
small unit, which would be in frequent demand, and therefore proposed a second unit one-tenth as long as the virga, which he
called *virgula*, saying : " The virga is the smallest among the
larger measures, and the virgula is the largest among the smaller
measures."   Then realizing that still smaller units might be preferable to parts of a larger one, he subdivided the virgula by the
scale of ten, giving *decima*, a tenth part; *centesima*, a hundredth
part, and *millesima*, a thousandth part.

This system can be expressed in English equivalents if we
take the most recent value for the length of a mean degree as
follows :

Milliar...................................... 72908.	inches.
Centuria.................................... 7290.8	"
Decuria............................. .... 729.08	"
Virga....................................... 72.908	"
Virgula.................................... 7.2908	"
Decima....... .... .72908	"
Centesima.................................. .072908	
Millesima................................. .0072908	"

In order to aid in the introduction of his system Mouton ascertained the relation between the foot of Bologna and that of
Paris, perhaps hoping that the French government might see its
merits and authorize its adoption ; or he might have desired that

it receive the commendation of the Academy. To give the reader
an idea as to the length of the virgula, he had it, with its decimæ
and one decima, divided into centesimæ, printed on the margin
of a leaf, with the naïve acknowledgment that it is not given
with such accuracy that copies could be taken from it as if it were
a standard, a remark made useless by the careless trimming of
the binder.

Just when this scheme suggested itself to Mouton is not
known, but it was prior to 1665, as some observations in connection with the fixing of his standards were made in March
of that year.

In 1673 Huyghens published his famous treatise concerning
the movements of pendulums, wishing simply to establish his
claim to priority in the application of the pendulum to clocks,
but he had announced his invention to some friends as early
as 1658, and had made some clocks about this time. Galileo
had already shown that pendulums were isochronal, and others had
proven that the squares of the number of vibrations of two
pendulums are to each other in the reciprocal ratio of their
lengths; but it remained for the transcendent genius of Mouton
to combine these principles and establish the fact that the
length of a pendulum in terms of any given measure which
makes an oscillation in a fixed time can be made to preserve that measure and re-establish it should the standard become damaged or lost—a method which was afterwards adopted by the English Parliament without any reference to Mouton, its inventor. He, however, gives due credit to Huyghens
when he writes: "In making use of the following and similar
experiments a very exact knowledge is required of the time
that has elapsed in the meanwhile. In order to obtain this
knowledge we must have recourse to the clocks of Christian
Huyghens, which are constructed with hanging weights.

"This Huyghens was a man of remarkable learning, and one
to whom posterity will always be largely indebted for his
great assistance in mathematics. His clocks excel all others,
and correspond so nearly to the daily revolution of the sun
that nothing more accurate can be hoped for."

So with a clock, which he regulated so as to record exactly twenty-four hours while the star Sirius was making a
complete revolution, he made a number of experiments which
resulted in his knowing the length of the pendulum in terms
of the virgula, which made an oscillation in a second of time
as indicated by this clock. Nor did he stop here. He was so

convinced of the accuracy of his work and the correctness of his method that he suggested that all nations could determine the relation of their measures to his by simply determining the length of the seconds' pendulum in terms of their units—that is, to use the pendulum as a go-between. That one may not doubt his honesty, he gave in detail the observations themselves.

· If we should compare this system with the metric measures of length, we should find at least two important points of superiority: the unit is derived from the length of one minute, and is, therefore, an exact part of a degree, quadrant and circumference, while the metre has *nine* degrees as its smallest multiple; then the names are etymologically far superior—centuria, by hundreds, is better than hektometre; and, besides, all of the terms are from one language and not from two—Greek in addition to Latin. Then, again, those who use the metric system find that the metre is rather long for the class of measures which we express as fractional parts of a foot, while it is too much of a jump to go to the centimetre and very few use the decimetre. The virga, about six feet, would come in very well for expressing distances for which we now use yards. If these views be correct, Mouton's duplex units, virga and virgula, are preferable to the metre.

It is hoped that this establishes the claim of Mouton as the originator of the decimal system and the inventor of a method of preserving linear units by means of the pendulum. The effort has also been made to show that he acknowledged the assistance which he received from Riccioli; how Riccioli did not forget to mention Snellius, and the latter in the very name of his book erected a monument to Eratosthenes, the first to attempt to measure the length of a degree. But have Mouton's successors shown equal magnanimity? If so, would his name have been so long forgotten and his book preserved by accident only?

To answer the first question we quite naturally turn to the history of the metre. The day around which the lustre of this work clings is June 17, 1799. After nearly nine years' labor an arc of the meridian had been measured, the earth's quadrant had been computed, and now a bar whose length was one-ten-millionth of this quadrant was formally presented to the two *Conseils du Corps Législatif.* It is quite natural that the members of the *Commission des Poids et Mesures* should rejoice over the conclusion of their work, a work which readily sustained the severest criticism; nor is it surprising that their spokesman should say: "To employ as a fundamental unit

of all measures a type taken from Nature herself, a type as unalterable as the globe which we inhabit, to propose a metric
system all of whose parts are intimately interdependent,
and whose multiples and sub-divisions follow a natural progression, simple, easy to comprehend, and always uniform,
is certainly an idea beautiful, grand, sublime, worthy of the
brilliant century in which we live." In the detailed account of
the operations which were then given there is interspersed a
large amount of praise for the participants—from Talleyrand,
who laid the proposition before the Assembly on May 8, 1790,
down to the laborers who carried in the prototype on this
august occasion. But one looks in vain for even a mention
of the humble, conscientious, credit-giving priest who was the
first to propose "a type taken from Nature herself, as unalterable
as the globe which we inhabit."

Was Mouton entirely forgotten in the interval which elapsed
between the publication of his book and the adoption of the
metric system? To answer this question it has been necessary
to look through the entire literature of astronomy and geodesy
covering this period.

In volume ii. of the *Mémoirs of the Paris Academy* we find
an account of the observations made in 1672, 1673, and 1674
by Picard, that brilliant priest of Rillé. Picard was elated over
the success of his geodetic work—which in itself amounted to
but little, but which gave Newton a value for the earth's radius
which enabled him to establish the hypothesis of universal gravitation. As this fact just alluded to is the most notable instance
that ever occurred of theory pausing for practice, we may be
pardoned for introducing it here.

Newton had attempted to prove his theory of universal gravitation by comparing the force of gravity on a body at the
moon's distance with the power required to hold the moon in
her orbit. He used in his computations the diameter of the
earth as somewhat less than 7,000 miles. The result failed to
show the analogy he had conceived, but twenty years later,
when Picard's length of a degree was made known, increasing
the diameter of the earth by about one thousand miles, Newton was able to demonstrate that the deflection of the orbit of
the moon from a straight line was equal to a fall of sixteen
feet in one minute, the same distance through which a body
falls in one second at the surface of the earth. The distance
fallen being as the square of the time, it followed that the
force of gravity at the surface of the earth is 3,600 times as

great as the force which holds the moon in her orbit. This number is the square of sixty, which therefore expresses the number of times the moon is more distant than we are from the centre of the earth; this required a diameter of 8,000 miles for the earth.

Newton recognized the force drawing an apple to the ground from a tree-top, a stone from the top of the loftiest structure, a drop of water from the highest cloud, to be the same as that which draws the moon to the earth, both to the sun, with an equalizing centrifugal force to keep each in its place. But he did not regard an hypothesis as sufficient; it needed verification, so when at twenty-three from inaccurate data his demonstration failed, he laid aside his theory, so brilliant in conception, so insufficient in action. Had Picard announced his result fifty years later, the ripeness of the time would have passed by with only Newton's failure to check the search for that grand essential theory without which we could have no exact astronomy, no celestial mechanics. The French geometer "builded more wisely than he knew"; the English philosopher harmonized theory with fact, applied the finite to the infinite, and harnessed the worlds with invisible traces.

After making this great contribution, Picard sought new glory in making astronomic observations at some of the principal cities of France. One of these places was Lyons, and in discussing his observations made when there he says: "M. Mouton in his discussion of a universal measure, said that at Lyons a simple pendulum whose length was equal to a Paris foot— a length given him by Auzout—made 2,140.4 vibrations in half an hour, from which he concluded that the length of the seconds' pendulum would be 36 inches 6.3 lines." This application of the pendulum evidently pleased Picard, for he takes from Mouton this idea: "If one had the length of a seconds' pendulum expressed in the usual measures of each country, one could know the relations of these measures as if they had been directly compared with one another—besides this, one could detect at any time in the future a change in their lengths."

As late as 1776 De la Condamine said: "M. Mouton, priest at Lyons, was the first whom I know to propose a unit deducible from the pendulum; this was in 1570; proposed by him in 1668 (it should be 1665), adopted by Picard in 1672, and by Huyghens in the same year." This is quoted by Todhunter without comment, as he could not see the original work.

Cassini, in 1757, refers to Mouton as one whom "we know

only as a priest and master of the choir at the collegiate church of St. Paul." Perhaps this was to prevent people from supposing that his own scheme was not taken partly or wholly from Mouton. He proposed to take one-six-millionth part of a minute of a terrestrial arc, and call it a foot. He also suggested that the unit be a toise, 60,000 toises being contained in a degree. This was simply taking one-thousandth of a minute, which was Mouton's *identical* plan.

Thus it is seen that Mouton's idea was not lost sight of by those at least who wished to profit by it. He was quoted often enough and by such men as to make us believe that either conspiracy or cruel fate threw over his name the shadow of forgetfulness. And when we come to that monumental work—*Base du Système Métrique*, which recounts the incentives, beginnings, methods, and results of the commission which deduced a standard of length, following a scheme proposed a hundred and thirty years before, and using a nomenclature too much like the former to be original—we seek in vain for a proper recognition of obligation and find in a few lines a mutilated account of Mouton's scheme, while he barely escapes condemnation in some words of faint praise from those to whom he bequeathed the notion of a universal measure.

It is confidently believed that he who was known only as a priest and chorister was the originator of the decimal system of measures based upon geodetic data, and the "brilliant century" which deserves credit for the inception of a system which now promises to become universal was not the *eighteenth* but the SEVENTEENTH.

J. HOWARD GORE, PH.D.

Columbian University, Washington, D. C.

GALVESTON BEACH.

I.

WONDERFULLY beautiful is Galveston Beach.   It stretches
from where the tramway bounds it in front of the Beach Hotel
out beyond the old ramshackle building of the Catholic orphan-
age.   At least this is the Galveston beach that I knew in the
winter of 18—.   Broad and smooth as marble, hard as marble to
the foot, kissed all day by the spice-scented waters of the Mexican Gulf; and warm are those kisses and sweet, for all the world
like the kisses that come from the lips of a young and chaste
lover, shy and gentle, half-stolen, half-given, as the clear spreading of the surf washes up over the white sand, and murmurs and
whispers in low, melancholy chords, singing the love-songs to the
sands which only the sea can sing.

I first saw it in the latter part of the month of November, 18—.
It was early morning—early, that is, for the easy-going ways of a
delightfully easy-going clime.   Six o'clock, and all the island was
a flood of gold and silver light, from out a sky without a cloud,
and the gulf and land a wealth of sun-brightness, and in from the
sea came the breeze, gentle and sweet, and soft and cool, that
wishes you a thousand welcomes genuine and true, over and
over; a Southern welcome does the gulf breeze give you all the
day long.

I stood and looked down the long stretch of white sand.   How
broad it seemed and how straight away, as it lengthened out some
miles in the distance!   Not a mere ribbon of sand by the surf, as
many another beach, with turnings and twistings and pools
of water, and litter of sea-weed, with broken timber, along
which stand bizarre hotels, and railway tracks and merry-go-
rounds, and side-shows, and dime museums, and catchpennies
a thousand and one, with crowds of more bizarre people, gathered
from east and west and north and south.   No; not a Coney Island, nor a Long Beach, nor an Old Orchard; but a grand, broad
avenue, flanked on one side by the opal surf and on the other, one
hundred feet away, by the sand-hills and sand-pines which hold
the bank firm and guard the city in times of unusual tides.   I
stood and looked down this glorious beach of pure white sand,
unspotted by even a foot-print, all aglow with flashing light, now
silver, now golden.   What is in this maze of atmosphere?   For,

though the sunlight flashes it does not dazzle. You cannot call it a mist, for out beyond the white curling surf miles and miles away you catch a glimpse of the sails and topmasts of a ship as she sinks out of vision beyond in the horizon, and like a purple scarf thrown across the sky is the smoke of a Morgan steamer yonder in the south. The very air is amber-tinted. How else describe it?

On this stretch of beach, as I stood and looked down the cool, inviting isle, there was naught of life save light; neither bird nor beast nor man; not even the flitting of the sand-piper in and out the crest of the surf, taking her dainty meal of dainty fishes or things that swim in the sea. No flocks of gulls nor gathering of pelicans; no chattering chickadee nor call of mocking-bird; no sound nor sign of life save the murmur of the gulf waves and glinting of mellow sunbeams on the opal water and the silvery land. Coming down from the North, hastening away from the slush and the mud and the cold, gray, smoke-laden sky of Chicago; hastening away from the chill winds of that other sea, that cold, steel-blue inland sea, Lake Michigan; hastening away from the flurry of snow in bleak November in the bleak North winter, and coming to stand here on Galveston beach, in warmth and light, soothed by a breeze that had romped and played amidst the spice-groves of the southern islands before it scampered across the gulf to lose itself amidst these white sands, was like going from the hard realities of every-day life to the fairy-lands of child-hood's dreams. It is an unbroken sameness, is this beach of Galveston. Only the gulf waters are opal in color, though not always so. I have seen them emerald and ruby and topaz; I have seen them white with the clearness of the diamond, and I have seen them glow as though red of liquid fire. Only the great, broad, white beach is always white and smooth, and firm and clean. I have never seen the beach strewn with sea-weed nor littered over. After a fierce storm I have seen a great tree, likely out of the Orinoco or some other South American stream, half-buried in the sand over against the hills. But the next storm took it away. Only the gray sand-hills that fringe the beach and keep the tide-waters back from flooding the island, blown there by the wind, telling you that nature guards the life of the quaint and lovely city that lies beyond.

There is an unbroken sameness, but yet the sight of it never tires you. Whether it is the breeze so sweet to breathe and feel which never fails; whether it is the never-clouded sky, save when the great white army of the day-clouds begin their lazy march across the blue above you; whether it is the wondrous atmosphere, amber and golden at noon, purple and golden at morning and night, an atmosphere that one seems to both feel and see; or whether it is the great, mysterious gulf beyond you, so gentle, so calm, so resonant of mystic sounds, that shows you by day-time and by night a thousand changing hues, Galveston beach is never the same though always the same. You walk along it and it does not yield to your feet. Where your foot has pressed it there is a white mark which outlines the shape of your foot. You look again and the mark is gone.

As I stood there looking down this long vista of surf and sand there came an impulse to saunter onward which was stronger than resistance. And so I started onward, and strolled for two miles along this gulf shore. Sometimes· I would pause to look out at the gulf itself. There was nothing but the changing waters flashing back the softened sun-rays. Then on I would saunter and again pause to look back, half expecting to see a crowd following me, who like myself had discovered this wonderland and were coming out to enjoy. You reluctantly yielded to the influence of the silence about you and became silent yourself. I remember I began to hum to myself the music to which Jean Ingelow's "O Fair Dove! O Fond Dove!" is set, but gave it up, as I was frightfully out of tune with the minor chord that the surf made falling on the sand. Then, like a boy who wants to keep his courage up, I began to whistle "When the Flowing Tide comes in," and the breeze sighed disapprobation. And then I paused again and yielded me to the influence of the sea, of the sun, of the sweet zephyrs, of the silence, and from that day to this I have loved the beach of Galveston. My return to the city was prosaic enough. I had no eye for its quaintness, nor heart of sympathy for its warm, hospitable people. I sat about the dingy old hotel up-town somewhere; I dreamed all day of my new love and longed for the cool of evening to visit the beach again.

II.

One afternoon in December I happened to be on the beach, when I witnessed a scene I shall never forget. A "norther" had been blowing for three days previous. · Any one who has ever visited Galveston, or in fact any part of the gulf coast, and remained for any considerable time during the winter months knows what a very disagreeable thing a "norther" is. First· there comes a spell of sultry, clammy weather, when your clothes stick to you and everything is humid to the touch. · Then sud-

denly and without warning there comes hissing from the north
a wind so cold, so keen and cutting, that it penetrates your very
bones. You are wise to get into flannels and stay indoors. It
is sure to blow for three days, and it may blow for nine. But
a nine days' "norther" is an exception. In fact, I did not experience one during my winter on the gulf. The only one disagreeable remembrance I have of my stay in the island city is
of this particular "norther" to which I refer. It had kept me
indoors and had deprived me of my usual walk along the beach.
About noon this day the sky had cleared, and gently the south
breeze began to beat up against the north wind, till it gained
way and at last conquered. It was like an invitation to me to
hasten to the lovely beach. So forth I went, to gaze on the
lovely waters of the gulf, to ramble along the white sands, to
feel the fanning of the lazy, sweet south wind in my face, to
be warmed, too, by the wondrous sunlight, everywhere streaming
out from the west, as a glorious December sun slowly sank toward
the western horizon.

I had gone for a mile or so down the beach, and over
against the sand-hills, where a great cypress-tree lay embedded
in the sand, a waif of the three days' storm just passed. I sat
down to rest and enjoy the scene. Suddenly my ear caught the
sound of gleeful shouting and laughter, and turning I saw coming up the beach in the hurry-skurry of a mad gallop a troupe
of children on Texan ponies. It was a veritable game of chase
and tag. First a slender girl on a spotted pony led the van,
her broad hat dangling by its strings, her fair, curly locks
all awave in the breeze, her small riding-whip plied fore and
aft with vim, her left arm extended, full and loose rein given
to her pony, her shouts of laughter mingled with her shouts to
her horse: "On, Rocco; forward, Rocco; go 'long, go 'long!"
The sleek little brute seemed to enjoy the sport. For, with his
ears thrown back and neck and head extended, he strained
every nerve to keep the lead. She rode with the ease and grace
and skill of an Indian. Her body took every motion of the
pony. Pressing hard after came a boy on a slate-colored pony,
which, were it not for its ugly large head, so common among these
Texan ponies, might have been taken for a two-year old thor-
oughbred racer, so light of limb, so deep of chest, so sleek of
coat was he. The boy brought his pony up till his nose was
even with the rider of the spotted animal, and then with a
bound he passed, "tagging" as he went. He had sent his
spurs home to get that bound and spring out of the little ani-

mal he was riding. · Then I saw a feat of horsemanship by the girl that even a rider in a Wild West show might have envied. While at full speed she whirled her pony about and rode him directly across the track of the third rider. Surely there will be an accident, I exclaimed as I rose to my feet, for they cannot check the ponies in time to avert a collision. But just as I thought they would come together and go down there was a swift slant movement and they passed. The girl on the spotted pony threw out her arm as she passed, and laughingly cried, as she touched the other rider: "You are it, Fannie!" Nor was I through witnessing this wonderful equestrian performance by these children. Fannie and her opponent by their movements had fallen somewhat behind the other children. I saw Fannie, after she had been "tagged," deliberately raise herself in her saddle and select her victim from among the group of the three riders before her. It was the boy who had tagged the girl on the spotted pony. On she flew, bending forward and patting her little animal on the neck, and I could see that she was talking to him. Then she began to whip and to spur at the same time. There was a grand response from her pony. In a burst of speed he gained on the boy's pony. He seemed to know what was wanted of him; he strained every muscle and nerve. When the boy saw that he was to be overtaken, he too gave whip and spur. But there was no response. He had already ridden hard and fast, and had winded his horse in his first effort. The girl was now close on his right quarter. With shout and call and whip and spur he urged his pony on. Seeing that he was about taken he whirled and made straight for the surf. Quick as a flash she whirled, and as his pony plunged into the water she reached out her hand and, touching him, cried "tag," and quickly whirling again avoided the surf. From the other children there came a shout of natural compliment to a wonderfully fine bit of riding. And this brought the game to an end, for both children and ponies were tired indeed, for they had ridden over a mile in the game, and fast and hard riding it was.

They had dismounted and had thrown themselves on the sand and were hotly discussing the game just ended. My landlady had given me a magnificent Marshal Neil rose as I was leaving the house. I was wearing it in my coat. Rising, I walked over to where the children were gathered, and as I came up I overheard them saying: "You never would have 'tagged' me, Tom, had I known you were so near before I began to spurt." "Yes, I would," said Tom, the boy who had "tagged" the first

girl, " for my pony can outrun yours on a long stretch. And,
Fannie, if Topsy were not afraid of the surf you never would
have touched me." As I came up, I unpinned the rose from
my coat, and going up to the child they called Fannie, I said:
" Will you permit me to offer you this as a prize for your
beautiful riding," as I extended her the rose. " Why, did you
see me ? Papa says that I ride well, but that I am too bold."
And then she blushed, remembering she had not thanked me,
and rising she made me a very pretty bow, and with the grace
of a studied actress said : " I thank you very much, sir." I
got to know Tom, and Fannie and Bell, Will and Nora well
before I left Galveston. I often met them on the beach, and
have witnessed races between Rocco and Topsy, Bay and
Gilder and Star, their ponies. They were the children of two
families of circus riders, who, like myself, had come to Galveston for the winter, for Fannie's papa, like myself too,
could not stand the winter of the North. I will never forget
the look of intense pleasure, and also of intense surprise, on
Tom's face when one day he saw a pair of beads in my hand.

Somehow the melodies of the beach, the sweet anthems of
the gently falling surf, the quiet and the peace of the place lead
one to prayer. It was my custom to say my rosary here during
my afternoon walks. Tom had ridden out in search of me, and
had come on me while I was thus engaged. Before I could slip
my beads in my pocket he had discovered them. " Why, Mr.
Neville, we are all Catholics, too"—his face a very picture of surprised pleasure. And right good little Christians they were, too.
For I had often seen them in the old cathedral at High Mass
on Sunday. And very devout and attentive they were, those
little circus riders. Many a hard lesson have I watched them go
through away out there on the lonesome beach, with only Uncle
Tom and myself for an audience and papa for a master. As I
walked back along the water's edge that afternoon, with the surf
throwing golden-red kisses to the golden-red sun, as he sank
out of sight, I could not help but ask myself, Was there ever
given such a glorious play-ground for lovely children as this
glorious old beach of Galveston ? And yet the only children I
ever saw in winter were children from the North and strangers.

III.

If I desired to study either light or sound I surely would go
somewhere on the coast of the Gulf of Mexico. Nowhere can
you find such weird and strange effects of light—so weird and

strange at times as to thrill you with a feeling of mystery—as here by these gulf waters. Nowhere does sound, coming you know not whence, take on such rhythmic music in minor chords as along these sand-shores. I remember a day and an evening spent on Galveston beach—how can I ever forget the one or the other?—when it seemed to me that I was in the midst of the mystery of light and sound. The day had dawned in a haze and the sun had come from the east blood-red, nor did it fight its way through the mist and clouds in clear bright light till long after noon. And yet, though ill-defined and uncertain, the sunlight was blinding, coming as it did in reflection from great banks of fog that hung over the waters, reflected, too, back and forth from the waves of an angry gulf, then reflected back again from the glistening white sand of the beach, and again reflect- ed by the mist in the atmosphere, glaring red sunlight every- where, baffling and mystifying you and wearying your eyes till you shaded them again and again with your hat brim and hand. There was a whispering and a moaning, a sound of sigh- ing and calling, a ballad of heart-aches, a melancholy sounding in the fitful wind that came straight from the south, so unlike the gentle, steady breeze that usually welcomed my coming to the beach. I walked far that morning, nor had I a companion, nor did I meet one on my return an hour or more after noon. By the time I had come to the tramway that skirts the beach for a short space it had cleared entirely, nor mist, nor fog, nor cloud was there anywhere, and the breeze had resumed its gentle, steady blowing from the South. If the sunlight effects had as- tonished me during the day, the light which came from moon and stars, and the phosphorescent glow of the waters, delighted and soothed me as I strolled along the beach that same night in company with Col. ——.

Never were heavens more beautiful, never were stars more wonderfully aglow, nor was moonlight so creamy silver as on that night. The colonel and I had come down to the beach late in the evening to stroll and smoke a cigar. He was one of the few Galvestonians with whom I had become intimately ac- quainted, a Southern gentleman of the old school, a man much my senior, but with a gentle, genial nature, a manner so refined and winning, a joyousness of soul almost boyish, that made him companionable to any one fortunate enough to know him. Of course he had been through the war, a commander of a regi- ment of cavalry. Though he bore the marks of both sabre and ball, he had escaped death; he had never been captured, nor

had he ever surrendered. When they heard of Lee's surrender
to Grant, he had turned his war-horse south, and rode home
and turned the noble animal out to his old pasture; had hung
up his sword and pistols. The war was over, to be sure, but his
commission as colonel was in his desk at home, his sword was
on the wall above it, his pistols flanked it on either side. He
was unconquered and, if you will, unconquerable. He was a
gentleman and would respect your opinions; but you felt he
pitied you if you could not see that which was so entirely
true to him, namely, the States were the development of the
colonies. The colonies, as a fact of history, were each independently sovereign; so therefore the States. Each State being
independently sovereign could, as an exercise of that sovereign
right, withdraw from the Union, and that hence secession had
not been a crime, but merely an exercise of a just right.

We had gone farther down the beach than we had intended,
being fascinated by the beauty of the night. Sitting there on
the sand we watched the moon go down—a blood-red moon
like the sun of the dawn. We sat on and smoked and were
talking of the wonders of the night, and the sea before us gave
evidence of the existence of God. Suddenly in the south, low
against the horizon, there was a flash of pale blue light and
quickly another, by the flash of which we saw the arm of an
ugly-looking cloud. Then we noticed that the breeze had ceased,
and then we knew that a storm would soon be on us, and we
were three miles down the beach. The colonel was a man who
did not know fear, and I did not fear because I was ignorant of
what was before us. But the way he said, "Neville, we must
hurry," made me apprehensive.

We had not made half a mile before the lightning flashing
showed us the nature and extent of the storm fast driving in
toward the shore. The surf began to beat on the sand and it
was evident that a high tide would run. On we hurried, with
the spreading waters from the surf coming higher and higher on
the beach. Never had I seen a storm so sudden in its coming.
Twenty minutes before and the moon had gently gone down and
all the heaven was ablaze with starlight. And now there was
inky darkness with only the lightning flashes to guide us.
"Colonel, we are in the water," I cried, as I felt the waves run
over my feet. "Go farther in toward the sand-hills." But then
a flash of light showed me the colonel just in advance and hard
against the hills. His only answer was "For God's sake, hurry,
Neville!" We pushed ahead, soon wading in the incoming tide,

which washed about our feet. The play of lightning was now'
incessant. I fancied I could hear the swish and swash of it as
it fell and flashed and darted among the waves and clouds.
The great mass of black clouds, rolling on towards the island
seemed to kiss the very waves. Now there came a blinding flash
and crash of thunder that seemed to take us from our feet, and
I threw out my arms vainly grasping at the darkness for support.
In that flash of lightning I saw a surf, white and direful, that
seemed scarce a yard away, and the next instant I was in water
to my waist. "Keep your feet, Neville, and come this way,"
shouted the colonel. Though I knew I was all but within reach
of him, I could not see him, and could scarce hear his voice
above the incessant peals of thunder. "This way, Neville, for
God's sake, quick!" he called. "Here! This way, over the
sand-hills!" And then I felt him sway against me as we both
went down, and a great wave went over us. Then I felt myself
thrown forward and I struck hard against something. Instinctively
I threw out my arms and grasped and held fast to what I struck
against. I was now above water again. "Colonel!" I cried.
"Here!" he answered, and again a great wave swept over us and
I saw just as we went under that we were in the second fall
of the surf, and not in the worst of it, and that gave me hope.
In an instant I knew where we were. We had come back as
far as the cypress-tree, my trysting-place, and were now clinging to it. When the next wave came I tried to notice if it
moved, and it did not, and I thought we were safe. And so we
were. Clinging to it we had passed through the worst, for the
storm had rolled on and swept across the island. It was one of
those sudden, awful storms of the gulf coast. One half hour later
we were on the beach, along the white line of which was beating
a surf so strong and heavy as to make the very island tremble.

Never can I forget the colonel's simple and touching piety
as he asked me to kneel with him there on the wet sand that
we might "thank the good God for the tender mercy he had
shown us this night." He prayed out loud, and there was a
tender pathos in his voice, and earnest manliness in his words,
that touched my heart to hear. He asked God to teach him to
know that he was ever in his hands. Then he asked "that the
same sweet mercy that we this night have tasted" might ever be
shown to the dear ones over there in his home in the island city.

The next morning, before I was up, his black man was
at my boarding-house with a great bunch of roses and a note
to inquire if I were all right. And very shortly after breakfast

the colonel himself came along, and we went and sat on the gallery and smoked and talked over the night's experience. As he left me he said: "Mr. Neville, you must excuse me for having kept you kneeling so long there in the wet and in your wet clothes last night, but I was very much affected by the thought of God's goodness." Excuse him! Dear old colonel! that prayer is a sweet memory for a lifetime.

IV.

One of the ways I had of amusing myself as I strolled along the Galveston beach was watching the fishermen, and there were many of them. Many weeks I had envied them as I watched them standing waist-deep in the water only half clad, intent on their lines. How stupid it seemed to me. Why do they not "set" their lines and take a jolly swim in that very jolly surf?

On coming to Galveston I had presented letters of introduction to Dr. W——, to whom I was duly accredited as a patient. This 'good man of science and medicine' had forbidden my going into the water. "We never bathe in the surf during the winter months, and I am constrained to deny you the pleasure," was what he said when I had asked to be recommended to a bathing-house. One morning I had gone down to the surf somewhat later than usual and was seated out in front of the Beach Hotel enjoying a cigar, when a number of ladies and gentlemen passed by me and entered the two pagoda-like buildings which used to stand well out over the water and were devoted to bathing purposes. Presently they emerged and entered the surf, and what a glorious time they had! They were members of a New York opera troupe that opened at the Galveston Opera House that night. The temptation was strong upon me, and going over to the hotel I ascertained that I could have a bathing suit and room, the which I forthwith procured, and from that day to the end of my sojourn by the gulf a daily swim was my custom, the doctor's advice to the contrary notwithstanding. He never found me out, and as I grew stronger and better day by day, I never felt that I was in duty bound to tell him, and never did.

But I was going to tell you of the fishermen. They were mostly Dagoes, swarthy fellows of the Austro-Italian type as far as I could make them out, fishing with nets and without skill, but with wonderful success. I have seen them load their carts with as fine a lot of fish as ever came out of the sea and in bewildering variety. To a mind more scientific and inquiring than my own here would have been a month's occupation

to name and classify these wonders of the gulf: fish of all shapes
and sizes, of all colors and hues; fish good to eat and fish
worthless for the table, from the beautiful ribbon fish, that the
white gulls would carry off squirming about their bodies as
they sailed away, to that royal fish of fishes, the red snapper.
The fishermen that amused me most were the blacks. There
was one strong fellow who lingers in my memory because of his
magnificent physique. Straight as an arrow and moulded like
an Apollo, with a well-formed head, well poised on a shapely
neck that was let into shoulders which were a perfect type of
manliness; as he stood there, clothed only in a cotton shirt,
which, wet by the spray, clung to his form and only served
to bring out the lines of his chest and trunk all the more perfectly, he made a picture against the white surf that I have
often recalled. Among my beach friends was an artist who
was spending the winter in Galveston. I chanced to meet him
one morning as he was starting down the beach, and so hailed
him and asked: "What is your work to-day?" "Nothing,"
he answered; "I am in search of something new." "Then
come, let me show you a subject worthy of your skill,—an
Apollo in ebony." We strolled down to where I knew my
black friend was accustomed to fish, and there he was outlined
in bold relief against the white surf. Down went the traps of
the artist. Up went his umbrella. Forth came all the para-
phernalia of his profession, and by noon was finished a splendid
sketch of the black Apollo.

This negro fished with a zeal and patience that Walton
would have lauded. He never was distracted by persons passing on the beach, whether on foot or in carriage or on horseback.
His long line well in hand, he kept his eye fixed on the point
beyond the surf where he knew the red snapper swam. I had
noticed him for some weeks before I got interested in his fishing, for he was as constant at his post as I was in my walk.
It seemed to me that he had dull fishing. I had never seen
him take a fish. I made up my mind to watch him. I carried
with me a field-glass, so without intruding on his privacy I
could observe him. But it was always the same stately pose as
he stood there with fixed eye that I observed whenever I
turned my glass upon him. However, one day as I was passing I observed an unusual tensity in his pose and his left hand
was slightly extended, and his head inclined slightly forward.
Suddenly there was a swish of the line in the surf as he drew
back his right hand to full length. Then hand-over-hand he

began quickly and deftly to haul in the line, at the same time walking backward from the water and out onto the sand· of the beach.   Far out I could see the darting of a splendid .fish as he flashed red and white beneath the water.   But sooner than it takes me to write this he had landed a fine specimen of the red snapper.   When he had unhooked it he threw it far back on the beach and began leisurely to do up his line.   In the interest and excitement of the catch I had come close up to him.   Here was my chance to make his acquaintance, and so I ventured to observe: " That is a fine. fish you have taken."   " Yes, sir."- Very laconic, I thought.   " Do you take many ? " again I ventured.   " I don't care to take more . than one, sir."   " It must be tiresome fishing, you seem to be obliged to wait so long for a strike."   " Yes, sir."   In the meantime he had gotten into his clothes, not a very extensive wardrobe, consisting merely of a much-battered hat and a pair of overalls in addition to the wet shirt he was wearing.   I turned and was about to try to engage him again in conversation when he bowed to me, saying as he did, and the bowing was with much grace and dignity, " I bid you good morning, sir."

I often saw him afterwards, and respected his reserve.   Somehow he was and is to me a type of the solution of the negro question of which you hear so much North and so little South. Let him alone and give him the opportunity.   In due time he will take the fish, let the task be ever so difficult.   Be that as it may, I will always recall the manly beauty of my black friend of Galveston beach, and have been much disappointed in never hearing of the picture my artist friend made of him in any of the exhibits of the New York societies devoted to American works of art.   He was dark of skin to utter blackness.   His nose and mouth were well formed and straight and delicate.   The only imperfect portion of his anatomy were his hands and feet, both unduly large.   I wonder what part of the Congo country his ancestors came from ?   To what line of royal African chieftains did he belong ?   Surely he was of no ordinary stock.   And his progeny ?   Where in this new civilization of America will be their place ? · Let the negro answer for himself.

Wonderfully beautiful is Galveston beach !   Delightful were the days spent there in the winter of 18—, when there came to me health and strength, from where there abides with me the memory of fair sunlight, soft breezes fraught with a thousand perfumes from off the waters of the wondrous Gulf of· Mexico. :

HENRY H. NEVILLE.

THE WITNESS OF SCIENCE TO RELIGION.

II.—HOW I PROVE A MIND IN NATURE.

THE most extreme sceptic in our day will not call in question the reality of physical science. He is well aware that the steam-engine, the telegraph, electric lighting, and the artificial pro-duction, let us suppose, of aniline dyes, are facts outside his own mind, of which he is the spectator, but in whose bringing about he has taken no share. He may pretend to argue, but he cannot and does not believe, that were his mind non-existent these things would cease to be. They are, in the strictest sense, objective to him. Science is not a dream in the mind shut up within itself. It is experimentally true and valid, proving its truth by the exquisite adaptation of its methods to results which are rapidly changing the face of the world. It has at once laws, or fixed and yet flexible procedures, and powers whereby its designs become facts, transferred into the region where Nature, the reality of things, must be obeyed if it is to be subdued. Testing hypothesis by observation, it moves from conquest to conquest. Day and night are spent in watching the ways of that world outside us by scientific men; and all their triumphs have been achieved in consequence of the fidelity with which they have noted the processes of Nature as disclosing something objective, and not merely tricking them into the fancy that they saw, or heard, or handled, when they had no such experience. Herbert Spencer has well said that "If Idealism be true, science is a dream." In other words, we cannot deny the objective validity of what we perceive without passing a sponge over the characteristic and undoubted achievements in subduing the material universe to our service, which have made the nineteenth cen-tury so different from the past. But who, I repeat, though he were the most stubborn disputant, could question these facts or imagine he was himself their author?

Here are truths which in a spirit of candid investigation I desire to employ in the solution of the gravest of all problems— the question of Theism. From my reader I ask no more than to put himself in the same frame of mind, without prejudice but not without a rational concern in the success of the undertaking, which he would deem suitable to an inquiry about the laws of

light, the conservation of energy, or the phenomena of animal
and vegetal existence. I shall make no appeal to sentiment, and
none to authority. I do not pretend to start with a definition of
what we shall find. With abstract vague terms, like the Infinite
and the Absolute, I trust to have as little to do as possible.
And I shall adduce no argument which does not convince myself.
Are these conditions accepted? Let us see, then, how the scien-·
tific inquirer must proceed when the question arises within him,
Is there another Mind besides my own in the universe?

· I cannot discover any starting point but this; and although I·
have looked at the matter in every light during a period of·
thirty years, I am always coming back to the same centre, as if
it were the law of investigation compelling me to obey it by its
very nature that I should begin by ascertaining that I know a
mind, an intelligence, which is not myself, to be in objective
existence, and then only advance to the farther problems of
Natural Theology. Or I may put it in the manner following:
Physical Science has been reduced to fundamental laws; as first,
that Matter is indestructible and is measured by weight, and
second, that Energy is indestructible and is measured by work.
But a third law suggests itself in the form of a question propounded, from the nature of the case, to all those who have
studied matter and energy in their relations, viz.: "Is not Mind
indestructible, and measured by adaptation?" The answer to this
third and final inquiry, if affirmative, will furnish the grounds
of Rational Theism. Should it be in the negative, or turn out
to be unattainable with our present powers of reasoning, we
shall be driven to conclude that a science of Rational Theology cannot exist.

The argument, however, which affirms a Mind in Nature
distinct from my own, is so clear and strong that I do not
hesitate to call it mathematical or self-evident in its cogency.
For the alternative to admitting its full force is scepticism
with regard to any marks of design whatever outside my own
mind. By mind in this series of papers I mean, not sense
or instinct, but conscious intelligence, or the faculty which
adapts means to ends, being aware that it does so. Which
premised, I argue as follows: If certain phenomena did not
manifest the action of an adapting mind outside me, in the
case where I am only a spectator, they would not do so
even in the case where I am, and know that I am, the
agent. But they do manifest intelligence where I am the
conscious agent. Therefore they manifest intelligence where I

am only a spectator.   In other words, a Mind objective to
me and distinct from mine exists in the universe.

Will the reader keep a firm hold of this piece of reasoning ?   I am going to prove it step by step, and then to
draw out from the conclusion some of the marvellous truths
which are hidden within its depths.   But one thing at a
time.   The end must not anticipate the beginning. I do not
start like :Spinoza by defining Substance, or, like some theologians, with a disquisition on the properties of. "Being in itself."   For me the commencement is my own thinking energizing self at the moment when I am writing these words.

This written page, I say, exhibits to my certain knowledge
the conscious deliberate adaptation of means to ends.   I am
employing paper, ink, pen, and an arrangement of alphabetic
characters to manifest the thought which is in me.   Precisely
this is what I understand by " design."   To express my thought
outwardly is the end, or the purpose, or the " final cause," of
this particular combination of material instruments which are not
my mind, nor is my mind identified with them, and yet they
show it forth.   Hence this page exhibits conscious intelligence
(such as it is), and does so by means of a complex adaptation
of things which are distinct from mind, to me and to every
other intelligence which apprehends the English language.

By what mental process do I know for certain that mind
is here manifested?   Suppose I answer that I cannot tell ; that
it exceeds my powers of analysis to find out; that nobody has
ever explained the process to my satisfaction?   Will that invalidate the certitude I undoubtedly possess of the fact?   If it
did, then the ignorance under which all men, except skilled
anatomists or physiologists, labor regarding the action of the
muscles by which they talk or eat, would mean ignorance of the
fact that they do talk and eat—which is absurd.   Hence I
may pass over the question *how* I know, and simply affirm
that I *do* know the fact alleged, namely, that this written page
exhibits mind by means of the characters inscribed on it.   And
if any one objects that a fortuitous concurrence of the parts
would have produced the semblance of mind in like manner, I
reply that since fortuitous here must mean "unintelligent," or
else it would prove nothing—I deny that the unintelligent could
produce intelligence.   For what stands written here is not the
mere *semblance* of mind, but exhibits mind, and is intelligence.

This shall be my first answer.   But my second is that I *know*
it is not by fortuitous concurrence that these characters exhibit

mind, for I *meant* them to do so.   Therefore the possibility of chance is altogether excluded.

Whereupon I put this further question.   If intellect and intention have concurred in the production of certain phenomena, is it possible to know for certain that they have done so under any circumstances, or must I always remain ignorant of it, unless it was my own intellect that concurred?   To bring out my meaning: I know that I intended the above page to manifest thought.   And I know that it does manifest thought.   Now, suppose I open Shakespeare and begin to read "Othello.".   I am absolutely certain that, if thought is manifested in "Othello," it is not thought produced by me.   Have I, nevertheless, the power of affirming that it is thought, even though not mine?   Can any mind which is capable of understanding English doubt that "Othello" manifests thought?   But if it does, then "Othello" is the work of a thinker who intended by that combination of words to express his own ideas, and who has succeeded—rather magnificently, I fancy—in what he undertook.   *How* do I know?   That is quite another question.   But once more, I do know that here is intelligence manifested which is not mine.   I am not the agent, but the spectator, the recipient.   I read, I did not create, the meaning of "Othello."

If I am to doubt, if I cannot affirm with complete certitude, that I perceive the mind exhibited in Shakespeare's plays, I shall, with as good reason, be driven to doubt whether a meaning is conveyed in my own pages.   For, although I may be conscious that I remember writing them, and did intend to put a meaning into them, how can I tell, now, that I have succeeded according to my intention?   By whatever process of mental interpretation I discern the characters to manifest mind in the one instance, by the same I do so in the other.   I will not undertake to say, nor am I required to discover, what set of faculties I put in motion to attain this end; any more than I need be capable of describing before a medical board of examiners what the apparatus was by which I walked yesterday from my house to Oxford.   I know that I accomplished the journey, and my memory remains as a sufficient guarantee for the change of place involved.   Thus, too, I interpret "Othello" with perfect confidence that, to a certain extent, I have seized the author's meaning.   Yet I never saw Shakespeare, though I hope one day to see him and to learn more of his mighty mind and heart.   All I can grasp of him now is contained in these printed characters.   Are they only a fortuitous concurrence of atoms?   How senseless and ridiculous the inquiry sounds? But observe that, in repelling the suggestion with scorn, I am not going by the testimony of another. It is the direct perception of intelligence, looking at me, answering to my own thought, in the printed Shakespeare, which furnishes me with a prompt, irresistible argument, superior to any number of sceptical hypotheses adduced in opposition to it.

What, then, is the conclusion? Is it not this, that unless I deny the possibility of ascertaining, in any conceivable instance, the tokens of mind outside my own consciousness, I must affirm that they are ascertainable in all cases by a similar process? Where the arrangement of phenomena *would* betoken mind if I myself produced them, and where I know that I did not produce them, there mind is manifested other than my own. I call such Objective Mind, as implying that it is distinct from me, is not I, but Another. In philosophical language, this other would be termed a second Subject. Grant that one single other Ego exists, besides this which is now committing its thoughts to paper, and a world of spirit or intellect rises into view. As the Laureate sings:

"Speak to Him, thou, for He heareth, and spirit with spirit can meet;
Closer is He than breathing, and nearer than hands and feet."

Wonderful as it may seem, the soul of the vanished Shakespeare is more intimate, more familiar, to me than the breath of my nostrils or the physical changes in the brain which accompany my thought. Is there not a vivid side-light, as it were, cast upon death and the grave by these reflections? Neither are they guesses; they state the sober truth of which we have experience from hour to hour. "Being dead, he yet speaketh." What can death be, if it does not silence even the echo of the soul's voice —the Bath Kol, as Hebrew divines poetically name it—long after the living spirit has passed away? Can death possibly end all? Why, it does not *end* a particle of matter, nor can it kill one throb of energy. To science, arguing by induction, matter and energy last for ever. Shall mind, so enduring in its feeblest reverberations, be quenched when the senses fail it? The sun which sinks is yet the sun that rises on a new day, and at that very instant. So Goethe, in his famous line:

"Untergehend sogar, ist immer die selbige Sonne."

But let me not anticipate. I go now a step further in my demonstration of mind outside my own. Shakespeare I read without difficulty, and am persuaded that his words have their intended significance, even though it baffles me sometimes to follow the trains of subtle and wide-glancing thought in which he abounds. But how if I am an English boy of ten and a volume of Greek is put into my hands for the first time? It will be all Greek to me, I humbly confess. Left to myself, perhaps I should not at once perceive that it was intended to convey a direct intellectual meaning at all. I might take it for an odd sort of picture-book, or be simply puzzled by it. In a few years, however, the case may be quite altered, and now I feel as certain that the Greek volume has a definite sense, and was written to convey such a sense, as that "Othello" is not a heap of gibberish. What, I ask, has come to pass in the meantime? Æschylus now stirs my admiration and sympathy no less than Shakespeare does. I follow the drift, I grasp the significance of the "Prometheus Bound," with quite as high a certitude that I am not projecting my own mind into the tragedy, as I have when studying the Moor of Venice. The meaning was always there, though I did not apprehend it at first. But education under a good master has supplied me with a key; the mere pictorial signs, which had only color and shape for the child's eye, have now grown intelligible, thanks to the process of interpretation which we call grammar and syntax. By means of them, when applied in detail, I observe how letter is joined to letter, syllable to syllable, word to word, and sentence to sentence. It is a never-ceasing process of *Adaptation*, employed in obedience to the supposition or postulate that the strange letters were intended to signify something or other. And the reward as well as the sufficient proof of my investigation is that in due course I arrive at a high and tragic meaning, full of a grave beauty, which the mind I call Æschylus desired to manifest outside itself to other minds, capable of being moved and interested even as it was. The transference of his thought to me, its reproduction (doubtless in a fashion far from perfect, though real in its measure), is a fact which I cannot question when the thing is done. Were a man unacquainted with Greek to tell me, however, that I could not have grasped the sense of the poet because the letters, being capricious formations, could have no meaning, and that therefore Æschylus himself was a myth, or only a shadow cast from my own brain, what could I think except that the speaker was not serious, or that he was mad?

The evidence of a meaning in the "Prometheus Bound" is, then, that I find a meaning there, ample and consistent with itself, unfolded through many parts to a sublime catastrophe. The adaptation of my mind to the play, and of the play to my mind, is proof beyond cavil of my having attained to an Objective Design, which is manifested in the Greek characters I was once unable to interpret. I know for certain that Æschylus, the writer of this drama, lived and thought and had the ideas—apart from incidental misunderstandings into which I may have fallen—that I have collected from him. What else he was I may never learn; but so much is self-evident, and all I discover by and by concerning him will not make it false. Adaptation is here an undeniable fact, proving the existence of a mind distinct from me and very unlike mine, not only in the range but in the quality and character of its ideas. When I read the "Prometheus Bound" I enter upon a world so new and strange to a nineteenth century European as to be extremely startling. I could not be more amazed if I were thrown among Polynesians, than in certain respects I am by the contest of Zeus and the human-loving Titan which is depicted with such pathos and power in these thunder-rifted scenes. Nevertheless, I recognize everywhere in them grave thought, human passion, artistic design. I cannot be agnostic as regards Æschylus. Instantly, as soon as the words form a sentence in my brain, I perceive that they have a meaning. The mental equation resulting from the correspondence between the printed letters and my intelligence proves itself, without need of further witness. I not only "move about" in that world, but I "realize" it; I am at home with the personages, I feel that they do not put my intellectual being to confusion. The reality of which they are signs and tokens is of a piece with my very nature; and yet I created neither them nor it. Æschylus spreads out before my mind's eye like a prospect which I can appropriate when I choose; and though clouds and darkness rest upon great tracts of it, and there is a murmur of thought deep and indistinguishable like the sound of the sea on its furthermost edge, I do not for a moment imagine that the poet's soul was a mere chaos because my sight and hearing no longer make out the phenomena distinctly. From what I have already gleaned, I argue to the rest. A larger intellect than mine would see more and more deeply, but never would it find that excess of understanding implied lunacy, violation of the laws of thought, or a mind constituted on a plan which was no plan but a congeries, not to be comprehended, of warring atoms.

The reader will have gone along with my purpose, I trust. He will have been aware that I am not talking of Æschylus or

Shakespeare, neither do I wish him to concern himself about "Othello" or the "Prometheus Bound." I want him, as an intelligent observer of facts, using his own mind impartially, to weigh this question well, whether, namely, if the material universe and his own consciousness offer him phenomena for interpretation, precisely as the Greek or English tragedies offer him such, and if, on applying the key of science here called "adaptation," he finds it will turn in the lock and that he may move about in an objective spiritual world, even as he may in the poets' realm, understanding much of what he sees—whether he is not bound to conclude in the one case as in the other? If there is thought manifested in "Othello," and it is not mine, there was a thinker, Shakespeare. But again, since there is adaptation, or correspondence, between my mind and the words of "Othello," there is thought in "Othello," which is objective to me. On the same principle, without alteration of a syllable, it is clear that if, and in so far as, there is adaptation in the universe, part fitting to part, and the details combining to form series after series of ends, there must be a Thinker—whose name is unspeakable. For the grandeur of *this* correspondence is overwhelming. I say nothing yet of an Infinite Mind. Mark me, if the word infinite slips in at this stage, I mean only indefinite, that which goes on and on till sight can discern no more, while reason pronounces that the horizon is not the end of existence. But I do say that if adaptation can be made out, Mind is made out; and that the universe of matter and energy, as soon as it becomes legible, shows in the background the universe of spirit. Call the world a poem, a tragedy, a combination of wheels within wheels, and you imply an overruling, an indwelling mind. Do you deny that the action manifests the mind? Then tell me how you can affirm that the page you are now reading is the product of a mind, three thousand miles away, which you never knew but by these characters. The alternative is scepticism, first, as regards *my* mind who am addressing you at this moment across the Atlantic, and next as regards your own whenever you attempt to express its meaning outwardly. Thus, to this extent, Theism, or the affirmation of Objective Thought in the universe, rests on precisely the same foundation as the belief to which every man is irresistibly compelled, that he is not the only thinker in existence, but that there are others besides him. We read in the first Epistle of St. John, "If ye love not your brother whom ye see, how shall ye love God whom ye do not see?" With even greater cogency I affirm that when we refuse to acknowledge adaptive Thought in the phenomena of Nature, we are thereby hopelessly precluded from recognizing it in the works of man, whether they be the devices of our own hands and brain, or the manifold creations of the artist, the poet, and the mechanician.

And here let me warn the student not to be led astray by the innumerable fallacies which lurk in the abstract terms wherewith modern treatises of unbelief are so plentifully sprinkled. He will be told that the above argument is tainted with "anthropomorphism," and that it concludes by "analogy," which is never more than a probable ground of inference. The true and sufficient answer to this kind of sophistry, for such it is, lies ever at hand if we will have recourse to it. Instead of losing ourselves in a maze of idle and obscure terminology, let us keep a steady eye upon the facts. Is it or is it not true, that I know with absolute certitude of the existence of other thinking beings distinct from myself and in no sense the coinage of my own brain? Certainly it is true, beyond question and beyond cavil. If, then, my agnostic disputant maintains that I know of them by "analogy," it follows that analogy is in the highest degree a ground of certitude. For the man who should seriously believe that he alone existed, and that all seeming others were a delusion under which he suffered, would be far more insane than the majority of those now shut up in our asylums. So great and evident is the force of that reasoning which the objector would lightly brush aside as "analogical." And I challenge him to this encounter. Let him set down any argument, inductive or deductive, by which he proves what we all admit, viz., that there exist thinking beings apart from our own Ego ; and I will match his argument with one as undeniable, of the like texture as regards premises and process, of which the conclusion shall be that there is a Mind in Nature. If it be "anthropomorphic" to affirm the existence of God, it is no whit less anthropomorphic to affirm the existence of men. Either the reasoning is valid in both cases or it avails in none, is vitiated from the beginning, and moves in a circle. To accuse me, therefore, of pressing analogy beyond its legitimate functions, or of indulging in metaphysical day-dreams, (which is all that is meant by "anthropomorphism"), because I employ in regard to Nature the same process which my opponent finds necessary in regard to all other mental existences besides his own, is throwing dust to confuse a most momentous issue.

That suggestive German thinker, Fichte, perceived long ago

where the truth of the matter lay. Once break the charmed circle of the Ego, make the mind a transparent window and no mere painted glass, and you may gaze abroad upon the universe of God and Man. Fichte, however, deemed that the circle was for ever closed. With deadly logic he resolved God and Man, the world and all that belongs to it, into phantoms of a mind which was its own prison whence it could never escape. There, indeed, we behold "anthropomorphism," consistent and complete, but as frail in its wealth of dreamy color as any soap-bubble blown by a child. For one breath of clear thinking smites it to atoms. Did Fichte really hold what he affirmed, the existence of his sole and solitary Ego? Could he affirm it to his consciousness? Or was he simply arguing, as so many clever men have done before and since, in a vacuum? The supreme test always is, What does my consciousness affirm as certainly known to me? Fichte's "anthropomorphism" would not, and could not, abide that decisive question. He knew, and I know that he knew, of others distinct from himself, each of whom was just as much an Objective Ego as he was. Again I say, the process by which he knew may be inscrutable; the result is certain. We *can* break the charmed circle of our own personality. We do see and encounter others who are not ourselves in disguise. The world is not the masquerade of a lonely being passing through endless forms, which he looks upon in the glass of consciousness without recognizing his own features. Scepticism of this fantastic pattern is shivered in a moment when it dashes upon the rocks of experience. The only marvel is that any one should have been at the trouble of inventing it.

I have already implied that the so-called "argument from design," as explained some distance back, appears to me unanswerable, as it did to Agassiz, to Owen, to Paley, to Leibnitz, to St. Thomas Aquinas, to St. Augustine, and to the disciples of Socrates. It is the reasoning which always and everywhere convinces plain men that Nature exhibits a most high and glorious art, whereof human invention is but the dimmest shadow. In certain schools, nevertheless, we find it, though not altogether cast aside, yet disparaged. Carlyle, speaking in the name of many, somewhat confused and turbid minds as I must think them, sneers it away as "mechanical," adding that its proper outcome is the stark atheism of a Diderot. "Canst thou by mechanism find out God?" he seems to say. I would reply with great reverence but in nowise timidly, "Yes, by mechanism as by mysticism, each after its proper method." I do not deny that there is a kind of reasoning from mechanism which dishonors God. And I say not that mechanism is the last stage as well as the first of the reasoning upon which I proceed. But what is any mechanism, great or small, from the voltaic battery to the system of gravitation binding suns and planets together, except incarnate thought—thought made visible in matter, force, and motion? Mechanism by its very nature involves the conception of means and ends; in other words, of a purpose which all the parts subserve. It cannot proceed "nohow and nowhither," as long as it remains a mechanism. But "How" and "Whither" imply adaptation, direction, a "final cause." It is of the essence of mechanism to eliminate chance; for if the parts might all act at random, there would be nothing produced, and the machine itself would fall to pieces. On the other hand, where we see parts conspiring to a whole and the end resulting from their action, our mind is immediately carried to the thought of a maker who contrived, or designed and put together, the elements here combined in unison. Be it Paley's watch or Leibnitz's "pre-established harmony," the argument is as conclusive as it is clear and simple. I defy any one who reads with attention the instances, alleged by Paley in his *Natural Theology*, of design as exhibited in the anatomical structure of the human body to point out a flaw in the reasoning. And I mention Paley because it is often suggested or openly declared that the Archdeacon of Carlisle was a shallow mind which has had its day. Paley's defects are well known to me, but they take nothing from the cogency of these particular arguments. There is, I affirm, no way of meeting them except the gambler's way—the "dice-box theory," it has been aptly termed—in which it is alleged that "given infinite time and infinite atoms, we must expect an infinite number of combinations to take place, and these seemingly ordered ones among them." This doctrine, tricked out in a vesture of scientific terms, is now known as Darwinism. It is nothing less than a crusade against thought in the universe, and would avail equally, as I have shown, against any possible "not myself" which was alleged to exhibit marks of intelligence as against the Divine Mind. But to insist on the machinery in things is not Darwinism. Nor is evolution Darwinism. It is not only right but expedient to search out the relation between evolution and design. I know of few investigations more fertile in results, more conducive to a religious frame of mind, or more necessary for these times. In my next article I will endeavor to sketch the general subject as it appears to me. Meanwhile

the conclusion upon which I would invite theologians as well as ·
men of science to meditate is, that where we see mechanism, in
ourselves or in the world without, there we see mind or the
results of mind.   The mechanical system of the universe reveals
a Prime Mover, whose Thought fashioned it and appointed the
ends to which it is determined, as certainly as the words and
the rhythm of Shakespeare and Æschylus lay open to us the
spirit whereby they were dictated, and the persuasive genius that
for ever in them glows and burns as with heavenly fire.   That
old Hebrew psalm, the *Cæli enarrant*, has set to immortal
music a theology of Nature upon which science every day pours
a more entrancing light.   " The Heavens are telling the glory of
God, and the firmament showeth the work of His hands.   Day
unto day uttereth speech, and night unto night showeth knowledge.   There is no speech nor language where their voice is not
heard.   Their sound is gone out through all the earth, and their
words to the end of the world.".

Will any Darwin or Haeckel silence that Credo of the open-
eyed seeker after truth?   I can never think it.

WILLIAM BARRY.

ODE.

For the Silver Jubilee of Archbishop Williams.

I.

WHAT are the years of Time ?
Pale motes that flash and fade beneath the sun ;
Phantoms of griefs matured and joys begun ;
        Or giants striding on with steps sublime,
That echo and will echo till the last
Great trumpet tone of earthly pomp be past.
Weakest and strongest of all powers that press
The changeful souls of men to curse or bless,
            As with poor, puny skill,
They shape them to their ends for good or ill,
Making them serve as sceptre or as rod ;
Foreknowing them as branches of the tree
            Of dread Eternity
That stands for ever in the courts of God !

        What are the years of Time ?.
A little span of shade, and then the light

A little space of day, and then the night
A little spell of sorrow and delight:
 With dirges tolling or with joy bells' chime!
Swift as the winds, and aimless too as they,
Their heedless moments fleet and fly away:
Yet can their calm, slow-moving, noiseless feet
Drag the great world to triumph or defeat;
Lure forceful wrong behind the prison bars,
Or lead the feeble steps of right beyond the morning stars!

II.

And the short Life of Man,
 Measured by moments' span—
How shall we count its varied force, or mate
Its lordly might divine, its pitiful, poor state?
Frailer than all frail things: a flash; a breath;
A sigh expiring on the lips of death;
A reed wind-shaken; or a power supreme
Greater than height or depth; a kindling gleam
By that great light of Love Immortal thrown
 Athwart the clouds by doubt or darkness driven,.
To shine with ray eternal as Its own,
 And with Itself to share the bliss of Heaven.

III.

Time, and the Life of Man! What darkness cast
By their grim deeds doth cloud the shuddering past;
When moved alone by erring human will,
Each small ambition worked its petty ill;
Ruled its short hour with stern destroying might,
And left its pathway seared with awful blight.
Or if some kindlier impulse touched the mind
To gentler thought for welfare of mankind,
'Twas but as summer winds that come and go;
 Or like the waves in motion
 Above the restless ocean,
While silently the sombre depths sleep dark and cold below.

IV.

But when the Christian came, his soul aflame
With the great glory of his Master's name;
Burning with Faith, and Charity divine,
And fire of Hope that makes the world to shine

With steadfast splendor; bringing unto earth
The joy immortal of immortal birth—
Then for the first time Man, with heart elate,
Did know the worth and honor of his state.
Alone no more, nor selfishly allied
To narrow schemes of policy or pride,
To weak vainglory, to the greed of pelf,
To the poor worship of the poorer self,—
But to the Power serene that dwells above,
        Uplifted by humility of love;
Unawed by stern misfortune's fiercest blow,
Serene alike in triumph and in woe,
Made strong by sacrifice, made rich by grace,
The help, the hope, the saviour of his race.

What wondrous fire makes eloquent his speech
Whose voice inspired beyond the earth doth reach;
What strange, sweet force doth make his weakness strong,
        Whose heaven-directed hand
Is nerved by all the radiant, mighty throng
        That near the Father stand—
Fair messengers of love, who linger there
With listening hearts to hear and grace to answer prayer!

V.

Time and such Life! Ah! world that flings away
The Christian's glory from thy crown to-day,
Think, ere too late, what spendthrift fools they be
Who fling their choicest treasure in the sea;
Destroy the one sole grandeur that hath shown
To Death a greatness loftier than its own;
Kill the rich grain that future fields might bless,
And leave the world but empty nothingness.

VI.

Thou, on whose pathway to its native heaven
The silver star of Jubilee hath risen;
Thou, whose ripe years in such accord have sped
With seed of faith in virtue harvested;
Whose loving labor still hath been to raise
The spirit bowed, to joy of prayer and praise;
Whose hands upraised in benediction win
Sweet Mercy's stream to cleanse the stains of sin,—

How in thy nature's high, benignant plan,
Time and the hour have blessed the life of man.

Under thy fostering touch,
What new, fair armor hath been wove, for right
    To use against wrong's mastery, and such
Dark shapes as do with human progress fight:
    The Midas blight that turns to sordid gold
Our hopes and aspirations, Eden born;
The lesser lights, that greater light do scorn;
    Doubt's haggard face and cold,
That turns to seek the gloom and shuns the face of Morn.

VII.

Prince of the House of God! what lot more blest
Than thine, that, lifted on the topmost crest
Of Faith's high mountain, the rich growth doth trace
Of thy fair realm across the centuries' space?
No passing bauble hers of mortal power;
    But for her lofty dower
Humanity's large virtues made more great;
The poor man taught to honor his estate;
Wealth made to hold its regal fee in trust,
To help the weak or hold itself accurst;
Wisdom, refined by Truth's eternal grace,
Making the world a glad abiding place
For all her children; Science seeking cause
To show the Giver greater than His laws;
And Charity, the all-ennobling gift
Which nearest to the throne of Heaven its foster-child doth lift.

VIII.

Onward her March of Empire! onward, and onward for ever,
    While the spirit of life doth own its heritage proud and blest;
While misery stumbles and gropes, and joy of the earth can never
    Grant to the heart content, or give to the tortured rest.
For hers are the only gifts which man, the Immortal, prizeth;
    Hers is the light that liveth though stars and suns shall
        cease,
Till the stream whose fountain is God to its bountiful source
    upriseth
    And the strife of the finite world is merged in infinite Peace.
                    MARY ELIZABETH BLAKE.

THE STAGE FROM WHIPPLE'S CORNERS.

MRS. SLOCUM'S ample figure completely obscured the small north window of the little sitting-room. She was watching for the stage that was to bear away their only Thanksgiving guest.

"I'm sorry enough it an't so Ben can carry ye down, Mr. Willoughby; the mare's been lame afore, but not so bad, and the roads being so rutty I do feel she ought to stand in."

The gentleman thus addressed sat in the rear of the giant base-burner, his feet resting on the fender that, like the other numerous glittering nickel edges and knobs, divided attention with the uncanny isinglass windows peering from all sides into the flaming pit.

"I beg you will not give it a thought, Mrs. Slocum," he said in a voice that betrayed his refinement. " I should greatly hesitate to come again if I felt that I must add to your labors."

"Well, naow there he comes, and it makes me easy about your goin' off alone so, to know that Jonathan Sebell's a-drivin' himself, for of all the keerful, accommodatin' men he's the prince. Just look how he's got them back curtains strapped down. I reckon maybe ye can sit in there, and no gust of wind ever gits ahead of Jonathan. Ah! he'll make it comfortable most anywhere. Good-by. It has been a real downright satisfaction to have ye at our table once more. To be sure it's sad to think of them that's gone, but it's the doin's of the Lord, and we mustn't repine.

"Here's Ben with the hard-wood block het up hot. Ben," she called, tapping on the window, "shove up the curtain a mite, so as I can see who's in."

Mr. Willoughby grasped his satchel, drew on his last glove, and, with a parting word of kindness, passed into the wintry air. Here he went through the farewell to Ben, conscious of the watchful eye of the driver, who beat his arms and stamped his feet to keep time with the lively tune of "Yankee Doodle" that he was whistling. The adieux being over, the new passenger looked at the vehicle that was to carry him from Whipple's Corners to the railroad station, a distance of something more than three miles.

It was rather disappointing. Built after the fashion of a "democrat wagon" and fitted with a home-made "canopy top," it had also submitted to the further ignominy of glazed curtains that, not being of the required width, yawned between the straps and buttons and let in draughts of air far more dangerous than a full exposure.

There were two seats; that in the rear was occupied by three females, swathed in shawls, and that indescribable length of wrapping material called in the masculine sense "a comforter," and in the feminine "a cloud." The front seat had the disadvantage of tipping forward, and, as it was extremely narrow, nothing but positive pressure against the dashboard prevented the occupants from falling headlong upon the horses' heels. A sense of gallantry had induced the driver to bestow two of the three blankets upon the "ladies," and as he now proceeded to assist Mr. Willoughby into his place, he added what he could to the importance of the threadbare robe that he produced by a fierce injunction to "tuck up, tuck up; nothin' keeps the cold out like bein' snug; loose wrappin', like loose livin', don't warm a man's heart much."

Mrs. Slocum's departing guest took time to nod once more to his late hostess, as the shambling horses responded to their master's reiterated "Get up alang," and then the keen, frosty air reminded him that the hard-wood block, so kindly furnished by Ben, would be a most welcome addition to his outfit. In vain his feet sought it. At length, certain that he saw it deposited in the wagon, he lifted the blanket and peered about the floor.

"Be you lookin' for that het stick?" asked one of the enormous mummies on the back seat. "Because if you want it, I'll shove it for'ard; but Miss Peters here is a feeble woman, an I tho't to heat her up a leetle."

What man could be so ungallant as to require the return of his property after that? Certainly not Mr. Willoughby, whose heart was as tender as a girl's, and he tried to warm his own chilled members with the consciousness that the "feeble woman" was made comfortable. It did not work as well as those things sometimes do, for he was not used to country drives, and indeed for many years had been a stranger to the New England climate.

Jonathan Sebell, however, thoroughly accustomed to the requirements of his steeds, tucked the reins between his knees, folded his arms and entered into conversation.

. " Is your name Slocum ? "

" No ; it is Willoughby."

" Not livin' in these parts."

" No ; I am at present located in Boston."

The victim vainly hoped by a gentlemanly reserve, and a free-will offering of certain prominent features in his existence, to forestall impertinent inquiry; but alas!

" Preachin' ? "

" Not now."

A little silence, broken at the first turn in the road.

" Ever been up this way afore ? "

" Yes, in years gone by."   He hoped to turn the interrogator's mind toward the physical changes and thus avoid personalities.

" Seems as if I'd seen ye ; guess you must be a relation of Miss Slocum ? "

" Not any."

" Maybe connection, then."

" Yes."

" Through your wife ? "

" Yes."

" She a Slocum or a Garrett ? "

" She was a Garrett."

" Ah! dead then.   Thought it queer she wa'n't along for Thanksgiving, and her the relation, too."   He paused long enough to drive out of the road to accommodate a heavy load. After the terrific jolting had subsided the conversation opened again.

" Can't be Ann Gadsby's man ?—Miss Slocum's first cousin on her mother's side."

" That was my wife's name— "

" And I used to see Ann Gadsby gallopin' to school on her pony, just as if the house was afire," he chuckled.

" Ann Gadsby, leetle Ann Gadsby!   I wonder now what complaint took her off ? "

It was beginning to grow uncomfortable to Mr. Willoughby, notwithstanding his patience, and the approach to a wayside post-office was a positive relief.   Here they stopped, and, with much inconvenience to his passengers, the driver drew out a diminutive mail-pouch and went into the building.   The wind swept around the stage with a vindictiveness that humbled the minister.   He shrank within himself until the blanket almost concealed him. Five minutes went by. Ten had almost passed when a deep bass voice, from the interior of the vehicle, gave utterance to the sentiment that Jonathan must be "a-toasting himself clean through." Presently, he appeared, bearing evidence in his face of a thorough-going fire somewhere.

"Tired a-waitin'?" he asked cheerily. "Guess I was gone longer than usual; had to help Charity sort the mail—she's partly froze; fixed her fire up good, too. Cleaned out the clinkers and fetched a hod o' coal. Must do a neighborly turn now and then. Lord knows I try to," he added with self-satisfaction, while Mr. Willoughby hoped that his attacks of benevolence would hold off until they reached the station. He was absorbed with this idea when he became conscious that his tormentor had returned to the old charge.

"Ann Gadsby! she was a pretty cretur. I'll bet you thought so oncet. Seems as if I ree-call the weddin'. Naow it can't be you are married ag'in?"

The poor gentleman appealed to felt his heart sink. How could he present all his private life for the inspection of these strangers. Yet how could he avoid it? There was no escape but the railroad station that was far in the distance. "Hey?"

With great embarrassment and inward quaking the minister faltered out: "Well, yes."

"Don't say so! Who'd 'a' thought Ann Gadsby, chirk as she used to be, would 'a' laid in her grave and her man married ag'in years afore the old stage stopped runnin'." He sighed, and then, as if remembering his duty toward the living, he chirruped to the horses and turned smilingly toward his companion to say: "There's them that think it ag'in Scripture for a preacher to marry at all, and them that says it's a rebuke to the cloth for him to marry twicet, and there's them that think it's right an' accordin' to natur'. You seem to be of the latter-most opinion."

Before Mr. Willoughby could rally the bass voice announced: "Most of men air this way of thinkin', or leastwise of doin'."

Was ever a drive of three miles so long? Some thought of getting out to walk crossed the minister's mind, but the consciousness that the roads were rough and the way unknown turned the balance in favor of quietly bearing the torture.

It was a pleasure to see a red flag fluttering at the door of a farm-house, for Jonathan drew toward the gate remarking: "'Nother passenger; mostly good business after Thanks-- givin'."

The new arrival proved to be a small lad who, with a little squeezing, was comfortably and safely wedged between the two men. His answers to the questions put by the driver as to the family affairs had scarcely died out, and Mr. Willoughby's fears were beginning to present themselves again, when a new subject of interest appeared. It was nothing less than the figure of a huge man in the middle of the road, gesticulating violently. The stage stopped.

" Humph! not much room for me."

" Plenty, plenty! Always room for one more," cheerfully answered the driver, springing to the ground and offering his hand for the parcels the stranger held.

How he was to bestow himself was a question even after the huge man was in the wagon. Various methods were resorted to, and at last, after some reluctance on the part of the boy, the fleshy person granted him the privilege of sitting on the edge of despair, while Mr. Willoughby gazed in horror upon the selfish new-comer. Jonathan's voice recalled him.

" Which of you men will drive team and let me run alongside ?· I'm always willing to accommodate."

The minister did not think of offering, feeling but too certain of his inability ; but the positive refusal of the big man, and the certainty that the small lad's mittens were poor protection against the biting cold, made it a duty, and as he took the stiff reins in his benumbed ·fingers he had at least the satisfaction of seeing a look of content gather on the boy's face.

At any rate it was not far to the station now, and so they pegged on, with the happy consciousness that the horses could not go very fast, and the added bliss of knowing the driver to be within call in case of accident.

Mr. Willoughby began to feel it a clear case of gain when silence reigned, but an unusual bumping brought exclamations of fright from the back seat and caused him to look for the deserter. Not a sign of him was to be seen. The bumping continued, and a horrible fear crept into his mind that the springs were broken or the wheel about to tumble off. In vain he searched the road for the owner of the vehicle. Matters were becoming serious when suddenly a dashing steed, drawing a most comfortable low phaeton, halted beside them, and Jonathan Sebell put out his shaggy head to say, in a commanding tone,.

"Drive up sharp now; an't no time to lose. I'll meet you at the depot; drive up sharp," and on he went quite as well satisfied as if his shivering passengers also were behind a nimble pair of young horses.

To "drive up" was no easy matter, even if Mr. Willoughby had been accustomed to the business. There was no whip, the right horse was lame, and the left lamentably lazy. To add to his misfortunes the passengers began to grumble, and the small lad to whine out that if he did not get to this train his grandmother would never let him go again. In vain he chirruped and shouted "Git up alang," just as he had heard the original driver do ; there was something evidently lacking in the intonation, it would not work; when to his great relief a sudden bend in the road revealed the dingy railroad station and the figure of Jonathan Sebell beckoning them on.

The whistle of the incoming train greeted the ear of the exhausted minister just as the last mummy was released from the back seat, and he heard the bass voice roar, " I never see sich drivin' in my life "; while Mrs. Peters, who proved to be a ruddy-faced invalid, squeaked out: "I dunno' what I'd done without that hot block." His hands were too numb to take the change from his purse with which to pay for the stage ride, so he presented it open to the driver, who selected seventy-five cents, and remarked placidly as he put it in his pocket: "It an't a payin' business, this staging, but it's a mighty sight of convenience to strangers."

S. M. H. G.

THROUGH MEXICO BY RAIL.

THE traveller will have reached the city of the True Cross by steamer either from Europe or by the commodious Ward Line from New York. The port is an open roadstead, the ship will anchor some way out, south of the island of San Juan de Ulúa, and will then be boarded by the health officer and port captain. License being granted to land by these worthies, the passenger, possibly ignorant of the speech of the land, will have the felicity of bargaining with Mexican or negro boatmen (there is a considerable negro element here) for conveyance of himself and his effects to the shore, and his store of silver pesos will be materially lightened. This is supposing calm weather to prevail; during a "norther" all idea of landing must be dismissed. And now ensues the custom-house inspection at the land end of the mole. "What sort of an ordeal is this?" Why, that depends. Last year we noted with compassion the arrival of a Methodistical Cornish mining captain, bound with his numerous olive-branches for Pachuca. The first thing remarked in his huge chest was a pile of tracts, designed for the enlightenment of the benighted natives. These observed, the official duly rummaged the trunk with ungentle assiduity, and a quantity of really valuable china was reduced to potsherds. He then gave his attention to the chest of a lady, but, seeing that she was met by a clean-shaven, black-coated gentleman of apparently priestly appearance (actually her husband), and that within her box was a large crucifix, he passed her with a graceful bow and without further inquisition.

The Hôtel de Méxique should be patronized; it faces the custom-house, benefits by the sea-breeze, and commands from the upper stories a cheerful view of the shipping and of the bustling activity of porters and carters. The landlord is a genial and handsome Frenchman. However, the Hôtel de Diligencias in the lovely tropical plaza hard by is preferred by some, who from the balcony can of an evening enjoy the music of the military band and watch the long procession of muslin-robed, black-eyed señoritas. Here also is the principal church, in no way remarkable; some government buildings, and the inevitable portales or covered walls, with shops, restaurants, and cafés. The zopilotes, or vultures, are honored scavengers, tame

as pigeons, and untold pains and penalties are in store for him
who should harm one of them—possibly incarceration in the
darksome, dripping dungeons of the fort of San Juan de Ulúa
on the island of that name, already mentioned. Here it was
that Cortés landed in 1519, on Holy Thursday. Next day he
set foot on the site of the present city, which he named from
the day. The place has for centuries been a terror to seafar-
ing folk from the deadly vomito which used to reign here
during the summer months, but for some years past yellow
jack has been practically expelled by dint of improved sani-
tation. Yet the stoutest Mexican in the interior will shudder
at the bare notion of visiting the place; regard you with
horror if you contemplate the trip, bless himself devoutly, and
relate for your warning ghoulsome stories which he can personally vouch for. However, Vera Cruz is a bustling and thriving place, and cab-fares, washing-bills, and such like incidental
charges, demonstrate that the pay of working folk here is on
a totally different scale to that prevailing in the frugal interior.

There is, of course, a large foreign colony resident here, and
they ordinarily like the place, but there will be little to delay
the casual traveller, who must leave the Mexican Railway's
terminus for the higher country at the unconscionable hour of
a quarter before six in the morning. He will find the train
built on the American model, with first, second, and third
class cars (no Pullmans or Wagners), and a special car for the
military guard. The conductors and most of the officials are
Mexicans, and, as in Europe, are the servants of the public, an
arrangement which those accustomed to it will prefer to the
lordly airs of the railway man prevalent in a certain republic
which shall be nameless. Steaming through the fortifications
of Vera Cruz into the sandy region adjacent there is little to
interest us. We cross the Laguna de Cocos, near which, in
1847, the garrison surrendered to General Scott. Although it is
nearly half a century since the project of building a railway in
Mexico assumed definite shape, yet the English line was long
the only iron road to be found in the republic; and the work of
railway construction, which forms so important and essential a
feature in the period of progress on which the land of Humboldt's predilection has now entered, owes its origin to the war-
rior and statesman who has so long guided the destinies of the
nation. The writer some months ago had occasion to traverse
the greater portion of the Mexican railway system in his task of
preparing a series of fourteen papers on the subject for a Mexi-

can journal, and though it would be impossible within the compass of one article to enumerate all the points of interest noted on this journey, yet an endeavor will be made to give a brief sketch of a subject that may prove worthy the attention of the general reader.

The principal lines of rail are four, and all these run into the capital of the republic. They are: The Mexican and the Interoceanic roads from Vera Cruz to the City of Mexico, and the Central and National lines from the United States, with their branches. The International, though entering Mexico from Texas, may be practically considered a feeder to the Central. Besides these there are many other local lines to be treated of in their place.

First in point of time and in excellence of construction, beauty of scenery, and general interest, is the Mexican Railway, or the Vera Cruz line, as it is often called in Mexico. The first contract for this line was made in 1842, and during the ensuing nine years no more than eleven and one-half kilometres of road were completed from the port of Vera Cruz inland. At the close of 1850 this contract was annulled, as the conditions had not been complied with. The work effected was only worth half a million dollars, but the constructors had received four times that amount from a two per cent. duty on imports at Vera Cruz granted them towards building expenses. The government then took charge of the work, and in six years doubled the mileage at about a third of the previous cost. But serious work did not commence till 1857, when Comonfort's government granted a concession for construction to Señor Antonio Escandon, selling him the fifteen miles of road, which had taken as many years to build, for three-quarters of a million dollars. The government thus far had lost a cool two million dollars, and nothing practical had been accomplished.

Enough has been said to show the leisurely manner in which the work was done; revolution, French invasion, wars —all these were fruitful causes of delay, yet a little progress was fitfully made and a big debt accumulated. Escandon actually transferred his concession to the Mexican Railway Company in 1864, during the empire of Maximilian, and though, three years later, on the Constitutional government resuming its authority, the validity of these transactions was not acknowledged, Juarez abstained from inflicting the penalty of forfeiture on the company. The branch to Puebla was completed two years later, and on the last day of 1872 the road was solemnly blessed at the Buena Vista terminus in Mexico by the archbishop, and a thanksgiving service was held in the cathedral. Next day President Lerdo de Tejada, with the principal men of the country, started from Mexico for Vera Cruz, in two special trains, stopping at all the intervening towns to join in the rejoicings, and returning to the capital in eight days.

The main line is 263 miles in length, and the Puebla branch 30 miles. The cost of the work amounted to more than $36,-000,000, or over $123,000 a mile. It is certainly one of the most costly railroads ever built, which is attributable to extravagance, misfortunes, and extreme natural difficulties. For instance, as the government insisted on construction being carried on from each end of the line at the same time, an enormous amount of material had to be hauled from the coast to the capital at a prodigious outlay. However, it is a solidly-built road of standard (4 feet 8½ inches) gauge, with substantial stations and excellent rolling stock. The average net income of the line has been about a million and a half dollars a year. The palmy days for shareholders were those when the Central and National roads were under construction, when the Mexican Railway bled its future rivals on the transportation of their material employed on the southern extremities of those lines. The company's capital is over eight million pounds sterling, divided, roughly speaking, into two and one-quarter millions of ordinary stock, two and one-half millions eight per cent. preference, and one million of six per cent. second preference stock, two millions six per cent. debentures, and one-quarter of a million of second mortgage stock. The state granted a concession of over half a million dollars a year for twenty-five years from 1868, and though the condition of the public finances prevented the full payment to be made for some years, it has now been resumed, being raised by a charge of six per cent. on custom-house receipts. It is not easy to see whence ordinary stockholders are to derive a dividend, either now or in the future. Even should the second preference obtain a trifle, the capital of the company is too great, towns and new industries do not develop on the line as in the Western States of the American Union, and the opening of the Interoceanic to Vera Cruz and of the various railways to the port of Tampico will introduce formidable rivals.

At Tejeria is the junction with the tramway which the line runs to Jalapa, a charming place, eighty miles from Vera Cruz, and capital of the State. The journey takes a dozen hours and the road lies through wild tropical jungle. When the Interoceanic completes, the line connecting these two cities, it is reasonable to suppose that steam will triumph over mule-power and the present tramway be disused or modified. An hour or two from the coast and the lovely views of the mountains are observed, and the rich pastures give place to coffee and sugar estates, banana groves abound, the trees are seen to be loaded with orchids and other glorious parasites, and we cross the Atoyac River over a bridge three hundred and thirty feet long and thirty feet above the stream. Though solidly constructed, this was demolished two years ago by heavy floods, which swept along huge boulders and fallen trees with irresistible impetuosity. Traffic was interrupted for some weeks, but the bridge is now restored and stronger than before. The grade now attains the heroic proportion of four per cent. and powerful double-ender Fairlie engines are employed and several tunnels are passed through. In twenty miles we ascend twelve hundred feet.

Córdoba we shall not notice in detail, for should we attempt to describe this delightful little lotus-eater's island no space would remain for other subjects. It is embowered in a wilderness of tropical fruits and flower-gardens, and the voyager should devote a week to the study of its glories. This is the point of departure of the Ferro-carril Agricola de Córdoba, or General Pacheco's Railway. It is to traverse and develop a marvellous country, but progress made is proportional to the genius of the country where "it is always afternoon." We were indebted to the Scotch engineer in charge for a ride on his locomotive over the few miles of line completed. This genial official impresses on new-comers the necessity of abstaining from fruits and qualifying all water drank, if fever is to be fended off; but he is not a very successful illustration of the triumph of his recipe. Onward still, amid scenes of wild magnificence, through tunnels, over ravines, but ever upwards. The bridge over the Mettac Ravine is 350 feet long and nearly 100 above the stream; it is built on a curve of 325 feet radius and on a three per cent. grade. Then we come on Orizaba, where we fain would linger, and in the body, if so it might be; but we must press on. The Barranca del Infiernillo—the Ravine of Hell—where there is a sheer drop of six hundred feet from the ledge along which the line crawls, La Joya, with the red-tiled town of Maltrata, in the centre of this radiant valley rightly named the Jewel, the remarkable contortions, twistings, and circlings of the line in its endeavors to scale the opposing heights—all these and numerous other marvels of natural glory and engineering skill must be seen to be appreciated, for there is little to equal and nothing to surpass it that we are acquainted with.

At Esperanza the Fairlie locomotive is detached, for we have now ascended about eight thousand feet and the remainder of the journey is through an elevated and comparatively uninteresting country. We traverse wide valleys bounded by barren heights, vast herds graze on the pastures, and wide expanses are devoted to cultivation. From Apizaco the branch to Puebla commences, 29 miles in length. Apam is the centre of the pulque district. The country for miles around is planted with huge magueys (*agave Americana*), and special trains, laden with the queer-flavored fluid thence derived (apparently a mixture of sour cider and soda-water), stored in clumsy barrels, leave daily for Mexico. We run past the suburb of Guadalupe—where is the shrine of the national patroness—as it is growing dusk, and terminate our journey at the handsome stone station of Buena Vista, one of the most pleasing features of the capital.

As the Interoceanic line is a formidable rival to the one just treated of, a rapid sketch of it will be in order. The first concession to construct a railway from Acapulco, on the Pacific, to Vera Cruz by way of the capital was granted more than a dozen years ago, and this was followed by others, which were consolidated in one, to Francisco Arteaga, dated 1883. Five years later a most capable Spaniard, Don Delfin Sanchez, a son-in-law of Juarez, took this concession to London and sold it to an English company, together with the portions of the line already constructed, for £800,000, he remaining president of the construction company, and by far the most prominent person in the enterprise. A year ago the writer went, as a guest of Mr. Sanchez, with a party of railway officials and journalists on a trial trip over the eastern portion of the line as far as Perote, 211 miles from the capital. We occupied three days on this excursion, making Puebla, 130 miles from Mexico, the first day, visiting Perote the following day, and then returning to our starting point. The terminus is at San Lazaro, to the east of the palace, near the unsavory *cloaca maxima*, or open drain, containing all the accumulated filth of a place of 300,000 people. The death-rate of the city is six times that of the London suburb from which this is written. The drainage works now being actively carried out by the firm of Reed & Campbell, of London, may mitigate this evil.

The Interoceanic is a narrow-gauge (three feet) line and reached Jalapa last summer; before long it will be at Vera

Cruz; directly it reached Puebla, the Mexican Railway felt the
effects of competition and had to lower its rates, to the benefit
of the public. At one point we noticed a considerable and well-
constructed tunnel, but these as a rule are avoided. At another
place a deviation from the original line had been made, saving
nine kilometres in a short distance, by the prosaic but practical
expedient of proceeding in a straight line along the level plain
and abandoning the graceful curves and sinuosities amidst the
neighboring mountains in which the ambitious Mexican engineer
originally employed had indulged. At Irolo, the point of departure by the Mexican branch line for the great mining town
of Pachuca, we cross the Mexican and Hidalgo Railways and
encounter an abandoned portion of track formerly built by the
National, misled by some visions of dreamland. The utilitarian
spirit of the dominant powers in Mexico is aptly illustrated by
the fact that even in pious Puebla the Interoceanic station, that·
of San Marcos, is located in the ancient church of that name.
Some months ago, remarking to a Mexican gentleman that the
building of the new Catholic church in the Calle de San Francisco was clearly unnecessary when so many ancient churches
remained unredeemed from secular uses, he rejoined that these
were worn-out old temples, three hundred years old, and fit only
for warehouses, and that the people wanted something new and
up to date; it sounds grotesque to us antiquarian English, who
wistfully regard our mutilated Norman abbeys and who recently
restored the chapel at Dover Castle in which the Roman garrison once worshipped to (parliamentary) Christian uses.

The south-western branch of the Interoceanic does not as yet
extend much over one hundred miles. A daily train consisting
of ten freight and two passenger cars is run each way. We
skirt Lake Texcoco and see fishermen afloat in canoes or drying
their nets on the shore. At Ayotta the fruits of their toil are
proffered to us by their wives, and to a Japanese traveller a
basket of uncooked fish might prove attractive, but we decline
the finny array. After three hours Amecameca, a town of ten
thousand inhabitants, is reached. This is the starting point for
the ascent of Popocatepetl. There is no real mountaineering work
to be done; still for some twenty-five dollars and three days' toil
one may ascend nigh on eighteen thousand feet above the sea-
level, trudge painfully through deep snow, and be lowered into
the crater in a sulphur-gatherer's bucket. Here the Sacro Monte
jostles the railway track, where is the cave formerly the abode
of Fray Martin de Valencia, one of the " Twelve Apostles " of

Mexico. He was greatly beloved by the Indians, who are said to have secretly removed his body from Tlalmanalco and interred it here. In·the shrine of the holy sepulchre is an image of the dead Christ said to have been placed here in 1527 by the holy man himself, and greatly reverenced. The image is carried to the parish church on Ash Wednesday and kept there till Good Friday, when it is restored with great ceremony to the shrine. Of the Holy Week pilgrimage, the Passion play, and kindred subjects much might be said, but we must onwards. At Ozumba breakfast is served; but the traveller should be on the alert, for he is not advised of the name of the station, of the half-hour's halt, the meal, or of anything else.

We now run downwards, winding and ophidianizing it to a surprising extent, passing corn-fields, grazing lands, and pine-clad heights till, after seven hours' travel, we reach the town of Cuantla, running into the church and convent of San Diego— we beg pardon, the freight and passenger station. This town of eleven thousand inhabitants is rectilineal and dreary enough, but the scenery has changed as if by magic, the magic of abundant water. The rich, broad valley is occupied by league after league of bright, waving sugar-cane, and factory chimneys taper upwards at intervals. At the hacienda of Santa Iñez 13,000 acres are tilled, 1,800 men and as many animals are employed. We then reach the bright little town of Yantepec, nestling amid extensive orange-groves. Coffee and bananas, corn and sugar are raised, and, except where vast masses of limestone protrude, the very mountains are clothed to their summits with a rich growth of nutritious herbage. The bridge, the government buildings, the flowering plaza, everything is spick-and-span, and bears evidence of care and thrift; but the church, dating from 1567, is gradually lapsing into decay, having fallen on evil days.

The Mexican Southern was attempted by various governors of Oaxaca (the president's native State), and General Grant at one time held the concession. But the actual concession was granted in April, 1888, to Mr. Read, eight per cent. interest on the amount expended being guaranteed for fifteen years by the government. The line is to run from Puebla to Oaxaca, and to be thence continued to Salina ·Cruz, the Pacific terminus of the Tehuantepec line. The company is an English one, and a strong one too, and the work is being pushed with energy. The line has the drawback of having no connection with the capital or gulf, but it traverses a district unsurpassed in Mexico for population or natural resources, and the advent of the iron

horse will be the signal for establishing new industries, reopen-
ing abandoned mines, and breaking untilled acres. Puebla we
have already mentioned. It has a population of 90,000, with
twenty-six factories of cotton, cambric, glass, crockery, soap,
etc. It is the third city of the republic, but is easily first in
beauty, cleanliness, and the piety of its inhabitants. Tehuacan,
with 25,000 inhabitants, is another flourishing place on the line;
also Tecomavaca; and Oaxaca, with 28,000 inhabitants, possesses a mint and various factories; it is lighted by electricity,
has a telephone system, and is the centre of a district famous
for its sugar, cotton, cochineal, silk, cacao, indigo, rice, coffee,
tobacco, honey, dye-wood, timber, and fruits. We have mentioned the Tehuantepec Railway; it is to connect the Atlantic
and Pacific, crossing the isthmus from which it is named. The
line is some 200 miles long, and runs from 16° to 18° north
latitude. When completed it will become the property of the
government. The enterprise was attempted forty years ago, a
company for the purpose being formed at New Orleans, but it
was too soon after the treaty of Guadalupe-Hidalgo, and the
Mexican government, seeing in it another Yankee aggression
prevented the realization of the project. Colonel McMurdo, an
American resident in England, finally obtained the concession;
he died last year, but the work is being continued. Tehuantepec (population 8,000) is the only place of any importance in
the neighborhood of the line. The highest point to be traversed
is only seven hundred feet above the sea, and natural obstacles
are but slight. The soil is rich, and yields abundant crops of
tropical products in the few places where it is cultivated. The
advantage to be derived from the line is the material shortening
of the sea voyage between various great centres of commerce.
For instance, from Liverpool to San Francisco is 16,552 miles
by way of Cape Horn, 8,885 by the Panama Railway, and
8,276 by Tehuantepec. Whilst we are in Southern Mexico we
must mention the lines running out of Merida, the capital of
Yucatan, a place of 62,000 inhabitants. The lucrative henequen
industry has made its planters the wealthiest in the republic,
and the Yucatanese are indignant if called Mexicans. A line of
thirty miles in length connects Merida with the port of Progreso.
There is another standard-gauge line to Sotuta, whilst narrow-
gauge tracks of fifteen, twenty-five, and sixteen miles long connect the state capital with the towns of Valladolid, Peto, and
Calkini respectively. These lines are worked by steam-power,
and prosper like everything else in this favored but sweltering

district. The Hidalgo Railway is noteworthy as being an exclusively Mexican undertaking. It connects the capital by a narrow-gauge track seventy-seven miles long with the great mining
town of Pachuca. Here, and in the immediate neighborhood, is
a population of 25,000, with a strong contingent from Corn-
wall. It has upwards of two hundred mines, including the celebrated Real del Monte. It is contemplated to extend this line
to the port of Tuxpan on the gulf coast, much nearer to the
capital than Vera Cruz.

The Mexican National Railway may possess more interest
for Americans than any of the foregoing, as by it, by way
of St Louis, San Antonio, Texas, and Laredo, is the nearest
route from New York to the City of Mexico. In the spring of
1881 the writer journeyed from San Antonio to Laredo and
thence into Mexico, but it was on horseback; railway contrac-
tors' camps were encountered and railway gossip was in vogue.
Two years later we made the journey by rail, regarding contemptuously from the comfortable railway car the arid desert
over which we had twice ridden some few months previously
without a drop of water for thirty-six consecutive hours. Mr.
Ruskin pined for some romantic nook remote from telegraph
cable or shrieking locomotive. It is possible that with larger
experiences of travel he might not find the iron horse so objectionable an institution after all. We can personally vouch for
the marked benefit that the line under consideration has proved
to the country which it serves. It would not interest the general reader to treat of the difficulties and delays which beset
the construction of the line, and we have already supplied papers
to THE CATHOLIC WORLD on Monterey, Saltillo, and San Luis
Potosi, three state capitals on the main line. Suffice · it to say
that this road from Laredo to Mexico, which was opened for
traffic on the first of November, 1888, is of three-feet gauge and
838 miles long. Some lovely scenery is traversed, especially between Monterey and Saltillo, and from Mexico to Toluca, the
capital of the State of Mexico. The conductors as yet are
Americans; Pullman cars are run on all trains as well as first,
second, and third-class cars; there are well-served refreshment
stations at reasonable intervals, and every effort is made to
insure the comfort of travellers. The branch line, ninety-six
miles in length, from Acámbaro by Morelia to Lake Pátycuaro
should be visited without fail by every tourist in Mexico; but
if we once commenced the description of the city of palaces and
the noble Mexican Westmoreland our whole remaining space.

would be occupied, so we content ourselves by repeating: visit, if possible, the ancient Valladolid and we shall have your heartiest thanks for the suggestion. Other branches are from the capital to El Salto, 42 miles; from Matamoras, at the mouth of the Rio Grande, to San Miguel, 75 miles (where a mixed train makes the journey either way three times a week with little profit to the company), and various smaller tracks used and unused, making a total of 1,232 miles. The company also owns the Texas-Mexican line connecting Laredo and Corpus Christi, but as the rails only weigh thirty pounds to the yard and are in poor condition, no one for pleasure would embark in the mixed train which occupies some fifteen hours in doing 161 miles, through a lonely mesquit wilderness. But this portion of the National line's property is not in Mexico. The vice-president of the line and manager in Mexico is the Honorable Chandos Stanhope, a son of Lord Chesterfield. The original concession for this line was granted to Mr. James Sullivan, and the undertaking originated in America, but the major portion of the bonds are now held in England.

The Monterey and Gulf line is an American enterprise commenced in February, 1889, but when we visited it in the following October one hundred kilometres had been completed, and from the commencement the line had more than covered expenses. The project is to connect Monterey with the port of Tampico, opening up a new and marvellously fertile district, where cotton, corn, sugar, coffee, and other sub-tropical products thrive. We were shown some beautiful specimens of ebony, mahogany, mesquite, and other woods from the virgin forests along the line, which should prove a source of considerable profit. The lumber used at Monterey now is imported from Louisiana, and the price used to be sixty-two dollars a thousand. Speaking of new industries to be initiated in these parts, we have just seen a notice in a Mexican paper of a Virginian dairy-man, whom we remember commencing business in a small way in the neighborhood of Monterey four years ago. He now has a herd of 200 Jerseys, sends milk into the town, and supplies butter all along the National line at seventy-five cents per pound. He has already realized a little fortune, and we sighed for his appetizing butter in the capital last winter when a higher price was charged for some villainous oleomargarine or similar abomination. Mr. Wolssner, the American consul at Saltillo, with his wife's uncle, Mr. Martinez, has for some time operated timber yards at Saltillo and Montercy, and these gentlemen are now establishing soap-works at the latter town. The Monterey and Gulf Railway Company induced an American company to erect extensive sugar-works at Linares, saw-mills were contemplated, and no doubt plenty of flourishing industries will be set on foot. What a shame it seems that millions of stunted and starving wretches are dragging out an attenuated existence, or rather enduring a lifelong penance, in our smoke-roofed slums, when vast unpeopled tracts of fertile land lie fallow beneath these genial skies!

One great drawback the Gulf Railway experienced in construction was that its material had to be brought to Laredo by the standard-gauge lines of the United States, then transshipped onto the three-foot National, and at Monterey transferred once again, as the Gulf line has very wisely adopted standard gauge. To avoid this constant vexation and expense the line has built a branch of one hundred and five kilometres to Venadita, on the Mexican International, to connect with the standard-gauge system of the country. This last-named line is under the control of Mr. Huntingdon, and is really a branch of the Southern Pacific, having been commenced soon after its completion from San Francisco to New Orleans. From Spofford Junction, in Western Texas, a branch thirty-four miles in length runs to Eagle Pass. There the Rio Grande is crossed by an iron bridge 930 feet long to Piedras Negras, whence it is 384 miles to Torreon, on the Central, the present termination of the line. There is little of interest on this road, but it passes through the Sabinas coal-fields, alluded to by Humboldt, which are said to occupy two or three thousand square miles. A branch line twelve miles in length has been opened from Sabinas to the Hondo coal-mines, and hundreds of thousands of tons of this coal are shipped off, this being at present the only source of supply in the country, to the best of our knowledge. The coal sells in the capital at sixteen dollars a ton. There is a probability that the line will be extended to Durango. Then the celebrated Mercado iron mountain, the greatest mass of iron in the world, will be available for practical purposes. As it is, the International may be regarded as a portion of the Central Railway, and by adopting this route and changing at Torrean 439 miles is saved between Mexico and New York, in place of making the entire journey by the Central. The distance by the National is still less, but some prefer travelling by a standard-gauge line. One of the most luxurious trains in the world is the Montezuma special, running occasionally between Mexico and New Orleans by the International. It is provided with library and writing-room, dining, drawing, and

sleeping cars (there are, in fact, six private drawing-rooms decor-
ated with different-colored draperies, artistic painting, and satin-
wood), bath-rooms, barber's shop, and every convenience of a
well found Atlantic mail steamer.   How happy Dives could
be if Lazarus would only leave his gate! but obtrusive Michael
Davitts and other journalists, and General Booths, persist in thrusting blood-curdling pictures of East London squalor and despair
before our complacent spectacles; so that to eat, drink, and be
merry becomes a difficult feat.

The Mexican Central is the most important railway in the
republic.   The enterprise is a Boston one, dating from 1880. The
work of construction was pushed rapidly from Mexico and
Juarez (Paso del Norte), the company having to pay ruinous
freight rates for shipment of material needed at the southern
end of its line to the Mexican Railway, which took the opportunity of bleeding its future rival and reaping a golden harvest.
In March, 1884, the line was open for through traffic, being
about two thousand kilometres in length and having been built
at the rate of a mile a day.   But branches to both oceans
formed a part of the scheme; that to Tampico was commenced
in July, 1881, and in spite of serious natural obstacles this
branch was completed last summer, being 380 miles long, and
passing from Aguas Calientes, on the main line, through San
Luis Potosi to the gulf. Through the exertions of the late
General Corona, governor of Guadalajara, who was so cruelly
murdered before the eyes of his American wife last year (1889),
the branch from Irapuato, on the main line, to the second city
of the republic was commenced in May, 1887, and its whole
length of 155 miles was completed by the following April amidst
wild enthusiasm (at least so the accounts of the arrival of the
first train at Guadalajara have it; never having witnessed any
Mexican display of whole-hearted jubilation we remain sceptical).
Mr. Edward Jackson, formerly of the Mexican, is general
manager at the Buena Vista terminus in Mexico. He is an
Englishman and a Catholic, fairly good recommendations in
Mexico. The traffic of this line shows a steady increase, and
goods lie by the track awaiting shipment for weeks together at
times, the carrying resources of the line being strained to the
utmost. The following table speaks for itself:

Years.	Ores carried.
1884	1,356 tons.
1885	6,133 "
1886	20,791 "
1887	41,175

And if later statistics were near us they would exhibit a still more marked development of the country tributary to the line.

Space does not permit us to dwell on Zacatecas, Leon, Aguas Calientes, and a number of other thriving cities located on this line, nor for the same reason can we dilate on the Sonora Rail·way, 353 miles in length, from Benson, Arizona, on the Southern Pacific, to Guaymas, on the Pacific. South of this is a shaky old track, forty miles long, from the port of Altata to Culiacan, dignified by the name of the Sinaloa and Durango Railway. But we do not wish to strike a false or jarring note. As a whole the Mexican railway system is most efficient and creditable and the cry is still they come; the air is heavy with concessions, from that of a line three thousand miles in length, from the Rio Grande to South America, downwards. But there are enough trunk lines now, and what is needed is an extended tramway system to connect country places with main lines. Mexican highways are so bad that grain and other bulky produce cannot be carried at a profit. But the Mexican tram-car system, with its sleek, plucky little mules pelting along at full gallop (what would befall them should they stumble!), cannot be surpassed. Existing lines often pay handsomely, and we anticipate that by advancing on the lines here indicated the erstwhile drowsy old land of Montezuma will be still more thoroughly awakened from its quondam lethargy, and will at length take its befitting place as one of the most prosperous countries of the world.

CHARLES E. HODSON.

THE LIFE OF FATHER HECKER.*

CHAPTER XXIII.

A REDEMPTORIST MISSIONARY.

" I WOULD not have become a priest had I lived in Europe, for I never had or could have any strong attrait for sacerdotal functions. But I felt that the Church in America was in need of all the help that could be given by her children for the work of the priesthood." Father Hecker said this when near his end, and a full knowledge of his character bore him out in it. The sacerdotal, the ecclesiastical, were qualities which he had assumed with full consciousness of their sanctity, yet they united with his other characteristics in a way to leave traces of the point of contact. He was certainly an edifying priest, and to hear his Mass was to be spiritually elevated by his joyous fervor. But you would never say of him " he is a thorough ecclesiastic, he is a typical priest." The external aids of religion he imparted with a reverence which displayed his faith in his priestly character as a dispenser of the sacramental mysteries of God. But the other mysteries of God which are hidden in his providential guidance of men, he could expound with the instinctive familiarity of a native gift; the voice of God in nature, in reason, and in conscience, and its response in revelation he could elicit with a power and unction rarely met with. He has left the following words on record: " After my ordination the duties of the sacred ministry appeared to me most natural; the hearing of confessions and the direction of souls was as if it had been a thing practised from my childhood, and was a source of great consolation."

The year spent in England after ordination was occupied by Father Hecker mainly in parochial duties at Clapham and some neighboring stations attended by the Redemptorists of that house. Father Walworth enjoyed some missionary experience with Fathers Pecherine and Buggenoms, but Father Hecker had only been at one or two small retreats—one at Scott-Murray's estate in company with Father Ludwig and another at that of Weld-Blundells in Lancashire; but in neither of these had he preached or given any instructions, serving only in the confessional and in hunting up obstinate sinners. He certainly did preach once before leaving England, perhaps only once, and that was at Great Marlowe, near London, in the church built by the Hornihold family. It was on Easter Sunday, 1850, and was well remembered by Father Hecker and referred to in after years. He thought the sermon a good one as a beginning, but it seems to have given him no encouragement, and we venture to think that if it profited his hearers somewhat it also amused them a little. He needed a teacher, and he found one in Father Bernard, the newly appointed provincial of the American province.

In 1850 Father Bernard Joseph Hafkenscheid * was made Provincial of the Redemptorist houses in America. His patronymic was too formidable for ordinary use, and he was universally known as Father Bernard. He was in the prime of life on taking this office, and although he had spent twenty years on the missions in Holland, his native country, in Belgium and England, he yet showed no signs of these labors; he continued them for fourteen years longer, for the most of the time in the Netherlands, his death resulting from accident in 1865. By common consent he is ranked in the highest order of popular preachers. He had entered the community from the secular priesthood shortly after his ordination; he had made a brilliant course of studies at Rome, which was crowned by the doctorate of the Roman College. He was physically a tall, powerful man, and of majestic bearing. His features were full of intelligence, his glance penetrating, his voice clear, sympathetic, and vibrating, his gestures expressive. If half that is handed down of Father Bernard be true, he was a wonderful preacher of penance and of hope, his high gifts of natural eloquence served by a perfect education and inspired by a most enthusiastic love of the people.

He was a popular preacher in the best sense of the term, calm in demeanor and simple in language as he opened, but when at the point of fervor pouring forth his soul in a fiery torrent of oratory, whose only restraint was the inability of the human voice to express all that the heart contained. In style impassioned, he yet often chose language bordering on the familiar, but was not vulgar. He is an instance of the fallacy of the saying that the preacher must stoop to his auditory if he would be popular. Father Bernard was ever true to himself,

---

* The reader is referred to his life by Canon Claessens (Catholic Publication Society Co.) It is all too brief, yet is a good summary of the career of the great Redemptorist missionary, one of St. Alphonsus' noblest sons.

never appeared less than an educated priest and grave religious, and yet he was a most popular preacher. The great truths of eternal life are a universal heritage, and the use of plain words is not getting down from good style even in the literary sense, and a familiar manner is a trait of affection. We have stopped the reader for this moment with Father Bernard because he was Father Hecker's teacher of mission preaching and instructing, and was ever beloved by him as an appreciative friend and a wise and indulgent preceptor. He had made his first visit to America with Father de Held in 1845, but remained only a few months to acquire information and gain impressions for a report to the Rector Major. He made a second voyage in January, 1849, acting as superior of the American houses, as Vice-Provincial, and remained about eighteen months. The United States now forming a separate province and Father Bernard made Provincial, he demanded Fathers Hecker and Walworth as his subjects, and they were given to him.

A letter from Father Hecker announces his departure for New York as fixed for some time in October, 1850; but delays occurred, and the following is an extract from one to his mother, dated January 17, 1851; it says that the departure is fixed for some day the same month:

"Oh! may Almighty God prosper our voyage, and may His sweet and blessed Mother be our guide and protector on the stormy sea. And may my arrival in America be for the good of many souls who are still wandering out of the one flock and away from the one shepherd! I hope that to no one will it be of more consolation and benefit than to you, my dearest mother."

The ship was named the *Helvetia* and sailed from Havre the 27th of January, the captain being a genuine down-east Yankee, and the crew a mixed assortment of English and American sailors. Father Bernard's party consisted of Fathers Walworth, Hecker, Landtsheer, Kittell, Dold, and Giesen, and the students Hellemans, Müller, and Wirth, the American fathers having come to Havre from London by way of Dover, Calais, and Paris. The weather was unfavorable during nearly the entire voyage, the ship being driven back into the English Channel and forced to anchor in the Downs. They were beaten about for two weeks before they got fairly upon the Atlantic, and while crossing the Newfoundland banks were in danger from icebergs. Nearly all the party were more or less sea-sick, including Father Hecker.

This did not prevent his attempting the conversion of the boat-swain, who seemed the only hopeful subject in the ship's company. There were a hundred and thirty steerage passengers, emigrants for the most part from Protestant countries, though a party of Garibaldian refugees and a few equally wild Frenchmen enlivened the monotony of sea-life by some bloody fights. There were but two cabin passengers besides the Redemptorists,. and the former being confined to their staterooms by nearly continual sea-sickness, the cabin was turned into a "floating convent," to borrow Father Dold's expression in a long letter descriptive of the voyage, given by Canon Claessens in his *Life of Father Bernard.*

The wintry and stormy voyage had already tested the missionaries' patience for some weeks, when Father Bernard informed the captain that he and his companions were going to make a novena to St. Joseph to arrive at New York on or before his feast, March the 19th. "St. Joseph will have to do his very prettiest to get us in," was the answer. And when the ship was still far to the east, being off the banks, and the weather quite unfavorable, and only three days left before the feast, the captain called out: "St. Joseph can't do it—give it up, Father Bernard." But the latter would still persevere; and that night the wind changed. The Yankee ship now flew along at the rate of fourteen miles an hour. When the eve of St. Joseph's Day came they were wrapped in a dense fog, and the captain, dreading the nearness of the coast, hove to. When day dawned the fog lifted, and the ship was found to be off Long Branch, and a wrecked ship was seen on the shore; she had been driven there during the night. The pilot soon came aboard and they sailed through the Narrows and into the harbor of New York, having spent fifty-two days on the ocean. As they approached the city a little tug-boat was seen coming to meet them. It bore George and John Hecker and Mr. McMaster, whose cordial greetings were the first welcome the young Redemptorists heard on their return to the New World. They were soon at their home in the convent in Third Street, and on the sixth of April following the first mission was opened in St. Joseph's Church, Washington Place, New York.

Here is Dr. Brownson's greeting, from his home in Chelsea, Mass., received by Father Hecker soon after his arrival:

"My very dear friend, you cannot imagine what pleasure it gives me to learn of your arrival in New York. . . . I want to see you much, very much. You have much to tell me that it is needful that I should know, and I beg you to come to see me. Tell your superiors from me that your visit to me will be more than an act of charity to me personally, and that it is highly necessary—not merely as a matter of pleasure to us two—that we should meet; and tell them that I earnestly beg to have you come and spend a few days with me. I am sure that they will permit you to do so in furtherance of the work in which I as well as you are engaged, and I have a special reason for wishing to see you now. I would willingly visit you at New York or anywhere in the United States, but there is no place so appropriate as my own house. . . . I am more indebted to you for having become a Catholic than to any other man under heaven, and while you supposed I was leading you to the church, it was you who led me there. I owe you a debt of gratitude I can never repay. . . .. Come, if possible, and as soon as possible."

At the Third Street house the new-comers found Father Augustine F. Hewit, a convert from the Episcopal Church, in which he had tarried for a few years on his way from Calvinism to the true religion. He had been a secular priest for a short time previous to entering the order. He was directed to join the newly-formed missionary band, and was destined to be more to Father Hecker than any other man, and to succeed him as superior of the Paulist community.

After more than five years' absence Father Hecker thus finds himself in America, the land of his apostolate, a member of a missionary community whose external vocation is the preaching of penance, and the conversion of sinful Catholics to a good life. A mission is a season of renewal of the religious life among the people of a parish. It is a course of spiritual exercises in which the principles of religion are called forth and placed in more active control of men's conduct, and by means of which their emotional nature is stimulated to grief for sin, love of God, yearning for eternal happiness. The sermons and instructions are given twice, and sometimes oftener, each day, during the early mornings and in the evenings. These exercises are conducted in the parish church, but not by the parish clergy. The people see among them the members of a religious order, men set apart, by the interior touch of the Holy Spirit and the public approval of the church, for this particular work—powerful preachers, confessors as indefatigable as they are patient, priests full of masterful zeal, moving in disciplined accord together against vice. The call they address to the people is the peremptory one: "Do penance, for the kingdom of heaven is at hand." Their words are given forth not from the usual pulpit, but from a platform at the communion railing, and in the presence of a high black cross set up in the sanctuary. They wear no surplice or stole while preaching, the only insignia of their office being a crucifix on their breasts. The bishop usually extends to them greater powers than are commonly given for reconciling sinners who have incurred ecclesiastical censures. The Holy See empowers them to extend the most abundant spiritual favors in its gift in the form of indulgences, and the pastor informs the congregation several Sundays beforehand that he expects the entire Catholic population of his parish to attend the mission and receive the sacraments.

To be absorbed in such labors as above described, was not the primary object of Father Hecker's vocation, but he accepted his place joyfully as chosen by the evident will of God. The missionary life was never in his eyes what the reader might surmise it to be—a mere interlude in his career, a period of patient waiting. Such is far from having been the case. The missions are eminent works of Catholic zeal, and there is not any vocation known to the active ministry which may not commute with them on equal terms. Human nature has never felt influences more deeply religious than those set at work by missions, recalling the effects of the preaching of the Apostles themselves. Remorse of conscience, loathing for sin, terror at the divine wrath, confidence in God, sympathy for our crucified Saviour, the ecstatic joy of the new-found divine friendship, utter contempt for the maxims of the world, iron determination to love God to the end—these are the sentiments which, by the preaching of missions, are made to dominate entire parishes in a degree simply marvellous. Nor can it be said that these dispositions are fleeting. Allowing for exceptions, especially in large cities, their permanency is often an evidence of the solidity of the motives which inspired them, as well as of the supernatural graces which gave them life. Every missionary will bear witness, as Father Hecker often did, that he has never assisted at a mission in which he was not profoundly impressed by the tears of hardened sinners. Every parish priest, however much he may regret the backsliding of some, will testify to the valuable results of missions among his people: the quickening of faith and the revival of supernatural motives, drunkards reformed, restitutions made, lust cleansed away, families united,

the church thronged with worshippers, saloons deserted. Father
Hecker never thought that all this was too dearly bought by
the dreary toil of the confessional, the discomforts of for ever
changing residences and living in strange places, nor even by
the growing nerve-troubles which the fathers are often subject
to, from brains superheated over and over again in the burning fires of mission preaching. Father Hecker did not think
the privileges of such a life too dearly bought even by the
postponement of his proper apostolate, and was ever glad of his
labors as a missionary.

They schooled him in public speaking. In his antecedents
there was abundant reason for diffidence, and he knew full well
that what was good enough language for an harangue to the
Seventh Ward Democracy would be ridiculous in a Catholic
pulpit. Nor was he deceived into the notion of his ability to
preach because he could influence men in private. Conversation is not public speaking, and the defects of grammar, or any
other such defects, if pardoned in an earnest and honest man
in private interchange of views, if committed on the public
rostrum are unpardonable and are usually fatal. Father Hecker
found in the incessant practice of the missionary platform, and
in the assistance of his present superior, exactly what he needed by way of preparation. Besides the mission sermon at
night—the great sermon, as it was called—there is a short doctrinal instruction at the same service and a moral one on the
sacraments or commandments in the morning. These became
his share of the mission preaching, and the school in which
he acquired that direct, convincing, and popular manner of discourse for which he was afterwards renowned as a lecturer.

We find the following among the memoranda :

" When I came over to America with Fathers Bernard and
Walworth, Bernard wanted to know what I could do. Well, by
that time I had given up all hopes of any public career. I
couldn't preach. My memory and intellectual faculties generally
were so influenced by my interior state that theology was out
of the question. The lights that God had given me about the
future state of religion in this country were still clear as ever,
but I thought that I should have to confine myself to imparting them to particular and individual souls whom the providence of God should throw in my way; for I was persuaded
that the Redemptorist community was unfitted for the future
work I had caught a glimpse of, and I was entirely contented

to live and die a Redemptorist, and was quite certain that I should. So, when Bernard asked me what I could do, I told him to get me some place as chaplain of a prison or public institution of charity, as that was about all that I was capable of. But he thought differently.

"My first instructions on the missions were almost word for word given me by Bernard. I didn't seem to have a single thought of my own."

To preach, whether to Catholics or to non-Catholics, one must learn how, and Father Hecker with all his gifts knew that this gift seldom comes from above except by way of reward for steady labor. The opportunity of the missions, and of Father Bernard as a guide, was eagerly accepted in lieu of the prison chaplaincy.

The missions also enabled him to know the Catholic people. The non-Catholics he already knew from vivid recollection of his own former state and from that of his early surroundings; Brook Farm and Fruitlands had completed his knowledge of the outside world; but the Redemptorist novitiate and studentate and his sojourn in England did not give him a similar knowledge of the Catholic people, priesthood, and hierarchy. To the average looker-on Catholicity is what Catholics are, and Catholics in America viewed from a standpoint of morality were then and still are a very mixed population. Why the fruits are worse than the tree is a sore perplexity even to expert controversialists, and Father Hecker had need to equip himself well for meeting that difficulty, a patent one in the rushing tide of stricken immigrants then pouring into America. The missions are an unequalled school for learning men. All men and women in a parish are made known to the missionary, for they walk or stumble through his very soul.

Nor can one fail to see the use of missions as an evidence to the non-Catholic public itself of the supernatural power of Catholicity over men's lives. To practical people like Americans there is no oral or written evidence of the true religion so valid as the spectacle of its power to change bad men into good ones. Such a people will accept arguments from history and from Scripture, but those of a moral kind they demand; they must see the theories at work. A mission is a microcosm of the church as a moral force. It shows a powerful grasp of human nature and an easy supremacy over it. It is an energetic, calm, and clean-sweeping influence for good, bold in its choice of the most sublime truths of supernatural religion as the

.sole motives of repentance. And it uniformly achieves so complete a victory over the best-entrenched vices that non-Catholic prejudice is invariably shaken at the spectacle. And in America the pioneer work of the apostolate must be to remove prejudice. The character of the men who conduct these exercises, their courage, intelligence, devotedness, discipline, and ready command of the people; the indiscriminate humanity which rushes to hear them, to pray, to confess their sins, to listen with mute attention—long before day-break and in the hours of rest after work —all regardless of social differences or of moral ones, soon become well known to the public and. generally excite comment in the press. All this contributes to prepare non-Catholics to hear from the same teachers the invitation which our Lord intended in saying: "Other sheep I have which are not of this fold; them also must I bring, and they shall hear my voice, and there shall be one fold and one shepherd."

Furthermore, it was necessary that Father Hecker should be made personally known to the bishops and priests of the country. The time was coming when he would have a public cause to advance, and their approval is a necessary sign of divine favor. Now, the missionary is closely studied by them and soon is intimately known, for there are too many things in common between priests but that they can readily test each other. Before the Paulist community had been organized, Father Hecker had been the guest of the most prominent clergymen of the entire United States, and of many even in the British Provinces, and was a well-known man throughout the Catholic community. Meantime the humiliations of his study-time had been quickly recovered from, if they had ever been a real hindrance to public effort, and we find no sign of protest on his part or of request to be let off from giving instructions beyond his answer to Father Bernard as above recorded. As he loved his vows as a Redemptorist, so he loved the work of the missions, because they were God's will for him; because they are a work of the highest order of good for souls; because the reputation of Catholicity is always raised in a community by a mission, and a good name is necessary for a controversial standing; because in them he daily learned more of men and of the means to win them; and because the members of the divine order of the episcopate and secular priesthood must be well known by him and he well known to them before any extensive work could be done among non-Catholics; and the missionary becomes a familiar friend everywhere he goes. Hence controversial sermons were sometimes preached during the missions, lectures of the same sort given after them, and during their continuance many converts received into the church. Father Hecker, as we have tried to show the reader, was a very observant nature, always learning lessons from life, and ready to try his 'prentice hand on what material offered in the way of converting Protestants at every opportunity public and private.

Nevertheless, the missions could not be made the ordinary channel of direct influences for turning sceptics and Protestants to the true religion. The attempt to make them so, involving, as it does, a notable interspersion of controversial sermons, has never been tried by the Redemptorist or Paulist Fathers to our knowledge, and when done by others has resulted in not enough of controversy for making solid converts, and too little penitential preaching for the proper reformation of hard sinners among Catholics. Father Hecker fully appreciated this. He threw himself into the mission work just as it was with the utmost ardor, and learning from Father Bernard how to prepare the matter for the morning and evening instructions, his natural gifts, together with hints and suggestions from his brethren, supplied him with the best possible manner of giving them. The writer has often served on missions in parishes where Father Bernard's new-formed band had preached in former years, and the testimony is universal that as a doctrinal and moral instructor Father Hecker was unequalled among missionaries. He was so frank, so clear, so lively, so impressible, and, in a certain way, so humorous, that he carried the people away with him. And he carried them all, high and low, learned and simple. With persons of education his homely words did not break the charm, nor did his simple but extremely well chosen illustrations do so—all taken, as they were, from common life or the lives and writings of the saints. He never preached the great sermons and never aspired to do it. He never sought to arouse terror or to be pathetic. He always reasoned and *instructed*. In truth, he was not competent to deal adequately with such subjects as Death, Judgment, and Hell—that is to say, as they are preached at missions, for the emotions have honest rights on such occasions, and Father Hecker acknowledged his deficiency in emotional oratory. But, to tell you the qualities of true sorrow, or to show you how to make a true confession, to picture the manliness of virtue and the dignity of the Christian state, he was unsurpassed. And the general effect remaining after his instructions was always a bright understanding of just what to do for a good life, with many happy examples to aid the memory,

together with a, strong personal affection for the holy man
who showed religion to be a most happy as well as most
reasonable service of God. To his penitents in the confessional
he was ever most kind and patient. " No school of perfection,"
he once said, " can equal the self-denial necessary to hear
confessions well." God is now rewarding him, we trust, for
the cheerful, often even bantering, words of encouragement he
gave to the multitudes of poor sinners who knelt at his
feet during the toilsome years he spent on the missions;
and for the enlightenment and encouragement of his big-hearted
influence, and for his trumpet notes of hope in the early morning instructions. After the hard pounding of the night sermons
it is always sought to pick the sinner up out of the dust and
to hearten him by the early instructions, as well as to guide
him to the precise methods and means of reform and of a good
life for the future. As to the sacrament of penance, the saying of St. Alphonsus is a maxim with us all : " Be a lion in
the pulpit, but a lamb in the confessional."

The reader must indulge us in thus dwelling so long on the
Catholic missions, for we are inclined to say many words of
praise of so lovely a life, in which the same men sow and reap
a great harvest in the same week, expend their vitality in
preaching the word and administering the sacraments and com-
forting sinners who are wholly broken down with the truest con-
trition.

In 1851 the American Redemptorists had before them a missionary field almost untouched. Public retreats had been given
from time to time in the United States by Jesuits and others,
but the mission opened at St. Joseph's Church, New York City,
on Passion Sunday, 1851, was the first mission of a regular
series carried on systematically by a body of men especially devoted to the vocation. The merit of inaugurating them is chiefly
due to Father Bernard, who had no hesitation in getting to
work with his three American fathers; though Father Joseph
Müller, rector of the Third Street convent, and Rev. Joseph
McCarron, the rector of St. Joseph's Church, had something to
do in arranging the details and in facilitating the work. Several
Redemptorists from Third Street helped in the confessionals.*

We have space for only the following extracts from the brief
record of the missions, preserved by the fathers. They illustrate

---

* Observers of coincidences will be interested to notice the arrival of the missionaries in
America on St. Joseph's day, under the Provincial Bernard Joseph Hafkenscheid, to open
their first mission at St. Joseph's Church, the pastor being Joseph McCarron, the mission
having been negotiated by Joseph Müller, the rector of the Third Street convent. Father
Hecker had a special devotion for St. Joseph.

how earnestly Father Hecker worked. In the record of the second mission at Loretto, Pa., we find this :

The instructions and Rosary were generally given by Father Hecker, who received from the people the name of "Father Mary." . . . During the first few days the people did not attend well ; but after Father Hecker had gone through the village and among a clique of young men who were indifferent and dis-affected to the clergy, and the evil geniuses of the place, and after some fervent exhortations had been made to the people, they flocked to the mission and crowded the church.

At Johnstown, Pa. : After two or three days a man happened to die on the railroad, and all the men at that station, per-haps a hundred in number, accompanied the corpse to the church. Father Hecker seized the opportunity to address them and to give them a mission *ferveroso.* And the next day he went on horseback, accompanied by the pastor, Father Mullen (since Bishop of Erie), to several stations and addressed the men, inviting them to attend the mission. The result was suc-cessful. Procession after procession marched in, filling the church, and numbers of them stayed all day, lying on the grass about the church. . . . Father Hecker called out a noted politician, who had not been to the sacraments for many years until the mis-sion, to receive the scapular as an example, and the good man did not fail to receive a plentiful supply of holy water from the vigorous arm of the said father.

The following entry in the record under date of February, 1852, made after a mission given in St. Peter's Church, Troy, N. Y., will be of interest to missionaries, and to others who are observant of their methods : " At Youngstown, Pa., (the preceding December) the experiment of preaching from a plat-form had been successfully tried and was repeated here, as at other missions since (Youngstown). On the platform a large black cross, some ten feet or more in height, was erected, from the arms of which a white muslin cloth was suspended. This use of cross and platform has thus been regularly introduced into the missions.'" Previously it had been the custom to erect a large cross out of doors in front of the church as one of the closing ceremonies of the mission.

Fathers Hecker, Hewit, and Walworth, led by Father Bernard, made a unique band of missionaries, one, we think, hardly equalled since they yielded their place to others. Each was a

man of marked individuality, whose distinct personality was by
no means obscured by the strict conformity to rule evident in
their behavior.   Fathers Hewit and Walworth were orators, differing much from each other, both full of power.   Father Hecker
was a born persuader of men, and could teach as a gift of nature,
earnest in mind and manner.   His two companions saw him learn
by hard work how so to modulate his voice and to manage it
and his manner as to exactly suit himself to his duties as the
instructor of the band, while they delivered finished discourses
at the night services, many of them masterpieces of mission oratory.   Their very poise and glance on the platform stilled the
church, and their noble rhetoric clothed appeals to the intelligence and to the heart in most attractive garb.   In Father
Hecker you saw a man who wanted to persuade you because
he was right and knew it, and because he was deeply interested in your welfare.   He sought no display, and yet held you
fast to him by eye and ear.   He had no tricks to catch applause,
for he had no vanity.   He said what he liked, for he was totally
devoid of diffidence or awkwardness, and his best aid was his
invariable equipment of an earnest purpose.   "But I don't believe," said Father Walworth to the writer, "that Demosthenes
ever worked through greater difficulties than Father Hecker in
making himself a good public speaker."

Father Bernard managed the missions for the first year, and
dealt with the pastors as superior of the band, meanwhile
devouring more than his share of the work in the confessional.
The least experience shows that there can be little of the discipline of the barracks order on the missions, and all the fathers
must of necessity consult together, the superior leading in the
observance of such community devotional customs as are possible, and setting a good example in stooping to the burdens
which all must bear.   As to Father Bernard, the Americans
could only admire and love him.   In his own tongue a renowned orator, he yet never preached in English while with these
three men unless on rare occasions, such as when one of them
was prevented by sickness.   From him they received the manner of giving missions handed down from St. Alphonsus, and
they have transmitted the tradition to their spiritual children in
all its integrity.

Nearly two years passed of hard missionary campaigning under
Father Bernard, when he was recalled to Europe, and Father Alexander Cvitcovicz took his place.   His last name was seldom used,
for the same evident reason as in his predecessor's case.   Father

Alexander was a Magyar, past the meridian of life, long accustomed to missions in Europe, learned, devout, kindly, and of a zeal which seemed to aspire at utter self-annihilation in the service of sinners. "It was not unusual for Father Alexander," says Father Hewit in his memoir of Father Baker, "to sit in his confessional for ten days in succession for fifteen or sixteen hours each day. He instructed the little children who were preparing for the sacraments, but never preached any of the great sermons. In his government of the fathers who were under him he was gentleness, consideration, and indulgence itself. In his own life and example he presented a pattern of the most perfect religious virtue, in its most attractive form, without constraint, austerity, or moroseness, and yet without relaxation from the most ascetic principles. He was a most thoroughly accomplished and learned man in many branches of secular and sacred science and in the fine arts; and in the German language, which was as familiar to him as his native language, he was among the best preachers of his order. . . . We went through several long and hard missionary campaigns under his direction, until at last we left him, in the year 1854, in the convent at New Orleans, worn out with labor, to exchange his arduous missionary work for the lighter duties of the parish."

Father Walworth now became superior, and the missions went on in the same spirit and with the same success as before. In the record of the one given at the church of Our Lady, Star of the Sea, Brooklyn, we find the following entry: "Missionaries, Fathers Walworth, Hecker, Hewit, and George Deshon (late lieutenant Ordnance, U. S. A., a convert from the Episcopal Church. This was his first mission)." Father Deshon had been ordained not long before, and soon began to share the instructions with Father Hecker. This was in February, 1856, and in November of the same year, at St. Patrick's Mission, Washington, D. C., they were joined by Father Francis A. Baker, ordained in the preceding September, a distinguished convert from the Episcopal ministry of the city of Baltimore. Much we would say of him, his eloquence and his very amiable traits of character, but all this and more is well said by Father Hewit, in his memoir of Father Baker, published after the latter's death in 1865 (Catholic Publication Society Co.) This increase of members allowed a division of the band for smaller-sized missions.

In our judgment those men were a band of missionaries the like of whom have not served the great cause among the English-speaking races these recent generations. Fathers Walworth,

Hewit, and Deshon have survived their companions of those early days, and may they long remain with us, calm and beautiful and devout' old veterans of the divine warfare of 'peace!

Father Hecker gave several retreats to religious communities of men and of women during the six or seven years we are considering, devoting for the purpose portions of the summer months usually unoccupied by missions. Copies of notes of his conferences, taken down by some of his hearers, are in our possession and may aid us further on in' giving the reader a view of his spiritual doctrine.

The following extract from the Roman statement summarizes what we. have been telling in this chapter, and introduces the reader to Father Hecker's first missionary activity as a writer:

"My superiors sent me back to the United States, and on my return being asked by my immediate superior in what way he could best employ me, my reply was, in taking care of the sick, the poor, and the prisoners. The stupidity which still reigned over my intellectual faculties, and the helplessness of my will, and my sympathy with those classes led me to choose such a sphere of action as most suitable to my then condition. And although the conversion of the non-Catholics of my fellow-countrymen was ever before my mind, yet God left me in ignorance how this was to be accomplished. Such strong and deep impulses, and so vast in their reach, took possession of my soul on my return to the United States in regard to the conversion of the American people, that on manifesting my interior to one of the most spiritually enlightened and experienced fathers of the congregation on the subject to obtain his direction, he bade me not to resist these interior movements, they came from God; and that God would yet employ me in accordance with them. Such were his words. After a few weeks in the United States the work of the missions began. My principal duties on these were to give public instructions and hear confessions, and up to this time (1858) these missionary labors have occupied me almost exclusively.

"The blessings of God upon our missions were most evident and most abundant and my share in them most consoling, as usually the most abandoned sinners fell to my lot. But holy and important as the exercises of the missions among Catholics are, still this work did not correspond to my interior attrait, and though exhausted and frequently made ill from excessive fatigue in these duties, yet my ardent and constant desire to do something for my non-Catholic countrymen led me to take up my pen. That took place as follows: One day alone in my cell the thought suddenly struck me how great were my privileges and my joy since my becoming a Catholic, and how great were my troubles and agony of soul before this event! Alas! how many of my former friends and acquaintances, how many of the great body of the American people were in the same most painful position. Cannot something be done to lead them to the knowledge of the truth? Perhaps if the way that divine Providence had led me to the church was shown to them many of them might in this way be led also to see the truth. This thought, and with it the hope of inducing young men to enter into religious orders, produced in a few months from my pen a book entitled *Questions of the Soul.* The main features of this book are the proofs that the Sacraments of the Catholic Church satisfy fully all the wants of the heart. . . .

"But the head was left to be yet converted; this thought led me to write a second book, called *Aspirations of Nature;* and which has for its aim to show that the truths of the Catholic faith answer completely to the demands of reason. My purpose in these two books was to explain the Catholic religion in such a manner as to reach and attract the minds of the non-Catholics of the American people. These books were regarded in my own secret thoughts as the test whether God had really given to me the grace and vocation to labor in a special manner for the conversion of these people. The first book, with God's grace, has been the means of many and signal conversions in the United States and England, and in a short period passed through three editions. The second has been published since my arrival in Rome. . . .

"On an occasion of a public conference (discourse) given by me before an audience, a great part of which was not Catholic, the matter and manner of which was taken from my second book, my fellow-missionaries were present; and they as well as myself regarded this as a test whether my views and sentiments were adapted to reach and convince the understanding and hearts of this class of people, or were the mere illusions of fancy. Hitherto my fellow missionaries had shown but little sympathy with my thoughts on these points, but at the close of the conference they were of one mind that my vocation was evidently to work in the direction of the conversion of the non-Catholics, and they spoke of such a work with conviction and enthusiasm."

This last event occurred in St. Patrick's Church, Norfolk,

Va., in April, 1856, and is thus mentioned by Father Hewit in the record of the mission: "Father Hecker closed with an extremely eloquent and popular lecture on 'Popular Objections to Catholicity.'"

The *Questions of the Soul* was well named, for it undertakes to show how the cravings of man for divine union may be satisfied. It does this by discussing the problem of human destiny, affirming the need of God for the soul's light and for its virtue, proving this by arguments drawn from the instincts, faculties, and achievements of man. The sense of want in man is the universal argument for his need of more than human fruition, and in the moral order is the irrefragable proof of both his own dignity and his incapacity to make himself worthy of it. Father Hecker urged in this book that man is born to be more than equal to himself—an evident proof of the need of a superhuman or supernatural religion. Eleven chapters, making one-third of the volume, are devoted to showing this, and include the author's own itinerarium from his first consciousness of the supreme question of the soul until its final answer in the Catholic Church, embracing short accounts of the Brook Farm and Fruitlands communities, and mention of other such abortive attempts at solution. Three chapters then affirm and briefly develop the claim of Christ to be the entire fulfilment of the soul's need for God, with the Catholic Church as his chosen means and instrument. These are entitled respectively, "The Model Man," "The Model Life," and "The Idea of the Church." Three more chapters discuss Protestantism, stating its commonest doctrines and citing its most competent witnesses in proof of its total and often admitted inadequacy to lead man to his destiny. Bringing the reader back to the Church, the fourteen last chapters fully develop her claims, dealing mostly with known facts and public institutions, and citing largely the testimony of non-Catholic writers.

It is something like the inductive method to infer the existence of a food from that of an admitted appetite, as also to learn the kind of food from the nature of the organs provided by nature for its reception and digestion. So the longings of man's moral nature, Father Hecker felt, when fairly understood, must lead to the knowledge of what he wants for their satisfaction—the Infinite Good—and that by a process of reasoning something equivalent to the scientific. Such is the statement of his case, embracing with its argument the introductory chapters. The inquiry then extends to the claimants in the religious world, not simply as to which is biblically authentic or historically so, but rather as to which religion claims to satisfy the entire human want of God and makes the claim good as an actual fact. It is wonderful how this line of argument simplifies controversy, and no less wonderful to find how easily the victory is won by the Catholic claim. The reader will also notice how consistent all this is with Father Hecker's own experience from the beginning.

The literary faults of the book are not a few ; for if the argument is compact, its details seem to have been hastily snatched up and put together, or perhaps the occupations of the missions prevented revision and consultation. There is a large surplusage of quotations from poets, many of them obscure, and worthy of praise rather as didactic writers than as poets ; yet every word quoted bears on the point under discussion. To one who has labored in preparing sermons, each chapter looks like the cullings of the preacher's commonplace book set in order for memorizing ; and very many sentences are rhetorically faulty. But, in spite of all these defects, the book is a powerful one, and nothing is found to hurt clearness or strength of expression. What we have criticised are only bits of bark left clinging to the close-jointed but rough-hewn frame-work.

The *Questions of the Soul* was got out by the Appletons, and was at the time of its publication a great success, and still remains so. The reason is because the author takes nothing for granted, propounds difficulties common to all non-Catholics, sceptics as well as professing Protestants, and offers solutions verifiable by inspection of every-day Catholicity and by evidences right at hand. Catholicity is the true religion, because it alone unites men to God in the fulness of union, supernatural and integral in inner and outer life—a union demanded by the most resistless cravings of human nature : such is the thesis. There can be little doubt that prior to this book there was nothing like its argument current in English literature ; a short and extremely instructive account by Frederick Lucas of his conversion from Quakerism is the only exception known to us, and that but partially resembles it, is quite brief, and has long since gone out of print.

The *Aspirations of Nature* deals with intellectual difficulties in the same manner as the *Questions of the Soul* does with the moral ones. The greatest possible emphasis is laid upon the two-fold truth that man's intellectual nature is infallible in its rightful domain, and that that domain is too narrow for its own activity. The validity of human reason as far as it goes, and its failure to go far enough for man's intellectual needs, are the two theses of the book. They are well and thoroughly proved; and no one can deny the urgent need of discussing them: the dignity of human nature and the necessity of revelation. Like Father Hecker's first book, the *Aspirations of Nature* is good for all non-Catholics, because in proving the dignity of man's reason Protestants are brought face to face with their fundamental error of total depravity; enough for their case surely. If they take refuge in the mitigations of modern Protestant beliefs, they nearly always go to the extreme of asserting the entire sufficiency of the human intellect, and are here met by the argument for the necessity of revelation.

An extremely valuable collection of the confessions of heathen and infidel philosophers as to the insufficiency of reason is found in this book, as well as a full set of quotations from Protestant representative authorities on the subject of total depravity. Over against these the Catholic doctrine of reason and revelation is brought out clearly. The study of the book would be a valuable preparation for the exposition of the claims of the Catholic Church to be the religion of humanity, natural and regenerate— the intellectual religion.

As might be expected from one who had such an aversion for Calvinism, the view of human nature taken by the author is what some would call optimistic, and the tone with regard to the religious honesty of non-Catholic Americans extremely hopeful. Perhaps herein was Dr. Brownson's reason for an adverse, or almost adverse, criticism on the book in his *Review*. He had given the *Questions of the Soul* a thoroughly flattering reception, and now says many things in praise of the *Aspirations of Nature*, praising especially the chapter on individuality. But yet he dreads that the book will be misunderstood; he has no such lively hopes as the author; he trusts he is not running along with the eccentricities of theologians rather than with their common teaching; fears that he takes the possible powers of nature and such as are rarely seen in actual life as the common rule; dreads, again, that Transcendentalists will be encouraged by it; and more to the same effect. But Father Hecker, before leaving for Europe in 1857, had submitted the manuscript to Archbishop Kenrick and received his approval; nor did Brownson's unfavorable notice ruffle the ancient friendship between them.

The *Aspirations of Nature* was put through the press by George Ripley, at that time literary editor of the New York *Tribune*, Father Hecker having gone to Rome on the mission which ended in the establishment of his new community. Mr. McMaster had assisted him similarly with the *Questions of the Soul.* The second book sold well, as the first had done, and has had several editions. It is not so hot and eager in spirit as the *Questions of the Soul*, but it presses its arguments earnestly enough on the reader's attention. It is free from the literary faults named in connection with its predecessor, reads smoothly, and has very many powerful passages and some eloquent ones.

THE CATHOLIC TRUTH SOCIETY.

THE Catholic Truth Society of America celebrated its first anniversary with great enthusiasm, March 10, in Cretin* Hall, at St. Paul, Minnesota. The spacious edifice was filled to its utmost capacity by the members and friends of the new society, and the stage was occupied by the officers and directors, Archbishop Ireland, and a number of prominent clergymen and laymen. Hon. William J. Onaban, of Catholic Congress fame, and one of the first to join the society, was the speaker of the evening. He delivered an able and eloquent address on " Rights and Duties of Catholics as Citizens."

The work accomplished by the Catholic Truth Society during the first year of its existence may be summarized, from the corresponding secretary's first annual report, as follows :

Under Section 1, viz., "the publication of short, timely articles in the secular press (to be paid for if necessary) on the fundamental doctrines of Catholicity," eight articles have appeared.

Under Section 2, viz., "the prompt, systematic correction of misstatements, slanders, or libels against Catholicity," thirty-five articles have appeared.

Under Section 3, viz., "the promulgation of reliable and edifying Catholic news of the day, as church dedications, opening of asylums and hospitals, the workings of Catholic charitable institutions, abstracts of sermons, and anything calculated to spread the knowledge of the vast amount of good being accomplished by the Catholic Church," ninety-two articles have appeared. Adding to these the similar articles published by the sev-

* Named in honor of Rt. Rev. Joseph Cretin, first Bishop of St. Paul.

eral local conferences of the society, the total number for the year approximates one hundred and fifty, and if we remember that most of these articles have appeared in the daily papers with circulations ranging from fifteen thousand to forty thousand each, it will be evident that the number of publications has run up into the hundreds of thousands. Surely this is a novel and efficacious means of "disseminating Catholic truth"! Besides this, upwards of seventy contributed articles concerning the society and its work have appeared in the Catholic press of the country.

Under Section 4, viz., "the circulation of books, pamphlets, tracts, and Catholic newspapers," the following books have been disposed of at publishers' prices: *New Testament, Imitation of the Blessed Virgin, Catholic Belief, Vaughan on the Mass, Facts of Faith and Rational Religion,* amounting in all to 1,835 volumes. The following original pamphlets, tracts, and leaflets have been published: *Refutation of Calumnies,* 8,000; *Vail-Burgess Debate,* 10,000; *How Catholics Come to be Misunderstood,* 6,000; *Who Can Forgive Sins?* 8,500; *Church or Bible?* 10,000; *The Catholic Church and the American Republic,* 2,000; *Sacrificial Worship Essential to Religion,* 2,000; *Some Things Catholics Do Not Believe,* a leaflet, 15,000; *Astounding Admissions,* one-page leaflet, 300; *Prospectus,* 23,000. Total 84,800.

Under Section 5, viz., "occasional public lectures on topics of Catholic interest," eight lectures have been given.

Under Section 6, viz., "supplying jails and reformatories with good and wholesome reading matter," an average of twenty-five Catholic papers, pamphlets, tracts, and magazines have been distributed weekly at four different institutions of this kind, and also at the Soldiers' Home.

The demand for such an organization as the Catholic Truth Society and the universal interest felt in its work are eloquently attested by the following summary of membership: St. Paul, 144; Minneapolis, 58; Minnesota cities, 92; Illinois, 19; Kentucky, 7; Missouri, 8; Colorado, 10; Michigan, 3; New York, 19; District of Columbia, 2; New Jersey, 8; North Dakota, 4; South Dakota, 3; North Carolina, 2; Iowa, 8; California, 8; Pennsylvania, 9; Massachusetts, 47; Delaware, 1; Maryland, 1; Maine, 1; Arizona, 1; Connecticut, 2; Indiana, 2; Louisiana, 1; Texas, 2; West Virginia, 1; Alabama, 1; Nebraska, 1; Rhode Island, 3; Tennessee, 4; Kansas, 7; Montana, 1; Ohio, 8; Wisconsin, 4; Canada, 1. Total, 493.

Sixty-nine of these are women, and the number also includes the following affiliated conferences, established in the order named. One in Worcester, Mass., with thirty-seven members and Very Rev. Vicar-General Power as censor, and another in Newark, N. J., with fifteen members and Rt. Rev. Monsignor Doane as censor. Both these societies have done excellent work during the few months of their existence. Besides local work, the former has distributed upwards of two thousand of the society's original pamphlets, and the latter a similar number of its leaflets. We are also informed by the latest mails that local societies are in process of formation, though not yet affiliated, in St. Louis, Kansas City, New Orleans, New York, Brooklyn, and Jersey City.

With this brief summary of the results of the first year's work of the society before me, I shall venture a few observations suggested by them

There are certain aspects of the Catholic Truth Society that seem to be deserving of special notice. Perhaps the only really novel feature about it is the one by which it proposes to utilize the secular and non-Catholic press in spreading a knowledge of Catholic truth. It is a method of "carrying the war into Africa." Of course no intelligent Catholic will for a moment underestimate the power of the Catholic press, the importance of the field it fills, or the value of the results it has obtained. But not one, on the other hand, can deny that its field of usefulness is circumscribed by well-defined limits, beyond which it has little or no influence. What does the public at large know about the Catholic press? How many non-Catholics ever read a Catholic journal? The exceptions are only sufficient to prove the rule. With many, alas! the very name "Catholic" is enough to arouse suspicion and thwart the good that is intended. We are forced to admit, therefore, that when the mountain will not come to the prophet the prophet must go to the mountain.

Another feature of the work proposed by the Catholic Truth Society also makes it necessary to have recourse to the columns of the secular rather than the Catholic press. "Misstatements, slanders, and libels against Catholic truth" do not usually appear in Catholic papers, hence that is hardly the place to correct them. Moreover, the value of a correction often depends largely on the promptness with which truth is sent travelling on the heels of error. This promptness can never be secured in the columns of our Catholic weeklies. The damage is done in the secular dailies, and they are the ones that must repair it. Nor is this in reality an unreasonable demand to make of the secular press. Newspaper editors do not as a rule wilfully or knowingly slander or libel their readers. They aim to give the

news impartially ,and correctly.   Now, the statistics furnished
even by our adversaries show conclusively that Catholicity to-day
is numerically the representative religion of the principal cities
and towns in the land, as, indeed, it is of the United States at
large and the entire western hemisphere, including North and
South America.   Notwithstanding its heavy losses, Catholicism
has steadily forged ahead till it is to-day the banner religion
of America.   It is not surprising, therefore, that there should be
an increasing demand for reliable information concerning it.
Again, it is admitted that much of the best newspaper work in
the land is done by Catholics.   Surely, then, American Catholics
would be false to their country if, knowing the truths that must
be of such vital importance to it, they do not reveal the knowledge they possess.   When pagan Rome built her magnificent
highways she supposed it was for her legions to carry her eagles
to the ends of the earth ; but in reality it was to enable the
apostles to carry the cross beyond the eagles.   So to-day, when
the miracles of science are annihilating time and space, men
imagine it is only to increase their material progress, but in
reality it is to serve God's purpose in spreading the knowledge
of the true religion in which all were to be saved.   The means
are at hand, the opportunity offers, and the Catholic Truth
Society has surely a magnificent mission to accomplish.

   Another feature of the society worth noticing is the method
of its extension.   A supplement to its prospectus, issued at an
early date in its history, suggests that local "conferences"
should be formed in cathedral cities.   While this would certainly
appear to be the most proper and orderly manner of extending
it, there seems to be no good reason why it should not take
root wherever it is needed, wherever there is work of this sort
to be done, and laymen competent and willing to do it.   Thus
there might be parish conferences, college conferences, and university conferences.   The work could be modified so as to suit
the requirements of each particular case.   For instance, in a
college, where there would be no opportunity for jail work, that
feature might be omitted ; or, if the students were burdened
with a surplus of suitable literature, they might collect it and
forward it periodically to neighboring conferences in cities or
towns, where there was need of it, for distribution in workhouse or jail.   There is another quarter in which good Catholic literature might be still more welcome, as will appear
from the following extract from a letter addressed to the
writer by a soldier at Fort Lewis, Col. :

"It has occurred to me that no better use could be made of your tracts and leaflets than to circulate them among the soldiers and settlers on the distant frontiers, many of whom seldom or never see a priest or receive any religious instructions. We have often sent us here large packages of tracts from Protestant sources, and these are all the religious (if I may so use the word) books or publications we ever see. Now many, perhaps fully one-half, of the soldiers in the regular army are Catholics or the children of Catholic parents. Very often they have been but poorly instructed in their religion, do not know how to defend it when assailed, which is often the case, and in time grow careless, indifferent, or perhaps ashamed of it, and end by losing or denying the faith. If you could send me a few of your publications I would see that they are placed where they will do the most good. I am a soldier myself, with pressing necessity for my scanty pay, and, therefore, can do but little else to help on the good work of your society."

Again, other Catholic societies might join as a body and the special literature be sent to a single address, and then passed from one member to another. The American Catholic Historical Society of Philadelphia and the Columbian Reading Circle of Vincennes were the first to apply for this sort of membership.

And this brings me to a question which, I am sure, never occurred to my own mind or the minds of any of the founders of the society till it was propounded by an outsider; nor should I consider it worthy of notice had it not been repeated more than once. "Why," it has been asked, "if the Catholic Truth Society is so important in its character and mission, was it started in the distant north-western city of St. Paul, and not in some older and larger city?" "It was founded in St. Paul because it was not founded elsewhere," was the blunt reply of a Western editor. The very question reminds me of the words of the carping Jews: "Can anything of good come out of Nazareth?" As well ask why the devotion to the Sacred Heart originated in Paray-le-Monial rather than Paris, or why the English Catholic Truth Society has its headquarters in Birmingham rather than London, or why Christ was born in the little hamlet of Bethlehem rather than the magnificent city of Jerusalem. God's ways are not man's ways. The Holy Spirit breatheth where he will. If, however, it be true that the early settlers of a community impress their characteristics upon their descendants for generations, may not the same law hold good in the spiritual order? If there be any truth in the opinion of theologians that each city and town has its guardian angel who shapes and controls its destiny, it appears to me that a Catholic Truth Society is just the sort of an organization we might expect to emanate from a city which claims as its patron saint the great apostle who was the foremost preacher of Catholic truth to the Gentiles—St. Paul. If there be any who find fault with the Catholic Truth Society of America on account of the place of its nativity, I can only reply, in the words of Gamaliel : " If this counsel or this work be of men, it will come to naught ; but if it be of God, you cannot overthrow it." As if truth would not be suppressed, however, the originators of the society stated, in the very first line of their very first prospectus, that " the Catholic Truth Society is one of the results of the Catholic Congress of Baltimore." If it bids fair to become the chief and most permanent result, it is because so many recognize it as the legitimate offspring of that memorable gathering. Nor can I refrain from mentioning the significant fact that several of the Paulist fathers, who had been courageously carrying on this very work in New York for years before the Catholic Truth Society was thought of, were among the first to welcome it to the field and joyfully enter its ranks.

I trust, therefore, that I am justified by the importance of the subject in explaining more fully the necessity of united effort, the practical workings of the plan adopted for carrying on the project, and the advantages resulting from affiliation with the parent society. For this purpose I shall quote freely from the circular letter addressed by the society to all new conferences seeking affiliation.

The work of the Catholic Truth Society of America is twofold : local and national. The local work certainly presents sufficient variety to suit the tastes, talents, and inclinations of all its members. It offers a magnificent field for individual efforts, which should be limited only by individual ability and opportunities.

The national work consists chiefly in the publication of a series of Catholic Truth Society pamphlets, tracts, leaflets, etc., especially designed for this purpose. It is evident that it would lead to great confusion and unnecessary expense, if to nothing worse, if a dozen different branch societies should attempt to publish pamphlets under this title, each according to its own peculiar notions. This part of the work is modelled after the plan of the English Catholic Truth Society, which, though it extends throughout the entire kingdom, has only one central publishing bureau at Birmingham. In America, therefore, as in England, our motto must be: " For ten who can write, ten thousand can subscribe and one hundred thousand can scatter the seed."

Now, this national work involves almost the only item requiring any considerable pecuniary outlay. The local work being done through the press, by lectures, and the like, involves only nominal expense. It was thought that if the Catholic Truth Society of America could be organized throughout the entire country, as it gave early promise of being, the annual subscription of one dollar would be sufficient to meet the expense of the national work. This is the only fund it has, or calculated on having, to meet it; hence it is evident that if each new local Catholic Truth Society should retain all of these subscriptions, each new society, instead of strengthening, would only weaken the national organization, and, indeed, might frustrate the plan entirely. It is freely conceded, however, that each branch must necessarily incur some expense, and, while it has been thought that seventy-five per cent. of the annual dues would be the lowest amount with which the national work could be carried on, the experience of the parent society, whose expenses would naturally be the heaviest, has shown the other twenty-five per cent. to be sufficient for local expenses.

Now, how must the national work be done? How must the expense be met?

It is proposed to furnish this special literature to all affiliated branches of the Catholic Truth Society from the start on a basis, not of *first cost*, but of *cost of reproduction* from electros. The first cost of many of the pamphlets is nearly double the figure at which they are sold, and the reproduction cost is taken as a basis, leaving a loss to be covered by membership fees until, in each case, over ten thousand copies shall have been reproduced, when the cost will be but a trifle under the prices named. The slight margin there will then be will be expended in mailing pamphlets gratuitously to non-Catholics of reasonably good will.

For example: pamphlet number five, Father Damen's *Church or Bible ?* (32 pages) is furnished from the start to affiliated branches at one dollar and fifty cents per hundred copies (3,200 pages); though 10,000 copies must be produced to overcome the cost ($64) on the first two thousand. Unless enough members can be secured to make it reasonably certain that ten thousand copies can be disposed of through their agency it would be useless to print so many. But where, then, would the cheap literature be ? And unless the parent or central society receives the seventy-five per cent. of the annual subscriptions, for the present, at least, how could the first cost of production be met ?

In other words, while the branch societies were receiving this special literature at cost of reproduction the parent society would be paying the first cost, which is so much greater that it would be a physical impossibility for it to do so unless some philanthropic millionaire should endow the concern; or all its members were not only very generous but very wealthy also; which does not happen to be the case. It is the unanimous opinion of printers, publishers, and newspaper men who have been consulted that this plan is the most economical one that can possibly be devised.

Now let us see what its workings would be if adopted by a new conference. Suppose it to have forty members. Forty dollars are collected ; thirty dollars are sent to St. Paul. Each one of these forty members receives a sample copy of each number in the series of Catholic Truth Society publications for one year. Suppose the series includes eight numbers; forty members would therefore receive three hundred and twenty (320) copies for thirty ($30) dollars; but the other ten dollars ($10) if invested in the same manner at club rates would buy six hundred and sixty-six (666) copies. That is, the last ten dollars would have more than twice the purchasing power of the first thirty dollars ; but, if some one had not paid the first thirty, the ten would have had no purchasing value at all, since the series could not have been published. If each branch could dispose of the literature at cost, it would get the money invested back again ; and it might be used over and over in the purchase and distribution of literature. If, however, it should be distributed gratis, it is evident somebody would have to pay for it.

Of course, as the membership increases the number of publications would increase, and each member would get more in return for his first seventy-five cents; and, as it is also certain that there is a limit to the number of publications which it would not be wise to exceed in a single year, the seventy-five cents would even be found more than sufficient to meet the expense ; and the rate might be lowered to perhaps twenty-five per cent., leaving still greater purchasing power for the residue. With a membership of 10,000 and the united efforts of all local conferences as its chief distributing agencies throughout the country, the Catholic Truth Society of America might scatter a million tracts gratis, or nearly so! The society has no desire to confine itself in the selection of worthy and proper matter for this series of publications to home talent; though lack of funds might compel it to do so in the beginning. The second year's series is to consist of twelve pamphlets, issued monthly, and to be contributed by some of the most distinguished lay and ecclesiastical writers in the country.

Some of the advantages of a society thus constituted may be summed up as follows:

First. Each member thus contributes his share of the *expense* in the disseminating of Catholic Truth, and the encouragement of wholesome Catholic reading; which are the main objects for which the society was organized.

Second. By co-operation it becomes possible to do what no single conference, by its own unaided effort, could possibly accomplish.

Third. A new literature, not heretofore in existence, is thus created; specially designed for this purpose, and presumably the best, most useful, suitable, and appropriate for this work that can be produced.

Fourth. Each member and conference thus obtains access to a limitless supply of literature at prices that cannot be duplicated in the United States. One dollar invested in it has a purchasing power of five or even ten dollars invested elsewhere.

Fifth. By affiliation every one participates in the spiritual advantages of all the Masses and prayers offered for the work, and such other spiritual benefits as are sure soon to follow.

Sixth. The union and organization so necessary to a society of this kind will be firmly and permanently established.

The letter referred to concludes as follows: "Nor can we help thinking that a Catholic Truth Society ought to participate to a high degree in the unity which constitutes so conspicuous a feature of the truth it would disseminate and the church it would defend."

I cannot conclude this article better than by quoting the words of Rev. Thomas O'Gorman, D.D., of the Catholic University of America, one of the earliest friends of the new society: "If the movement spreads and every town and village gets up a Catholic Truth Society, then, indeed, will the Church in America stand forth as 'the light of the world,' as 'a city seated on a hill,' as 'a standard set up among nations,' inviting all beneath its folds."   WM. F. MARKOE,

Corresponding Secretary.

THE OLD WORLD SEEN FROM THE NEW.

THE world of politics has been the scene of a number of events not indeed of a very sensational character but of no little interest and importance. The first place must be given to the unlooked-for resignation of Signor Crispi. With him departs, for the present at all events, the last of the triad of strong men who, a year ago, seemed to hold an almost impregnable position. Bismarck and Tisza had held office for much longer periods than Crispi, but the latter seemed even more indispensable to the Italian kingdom than either of the former to Germany and Hungary. What adds to the surprise at his fall is the fact that, only a few weeks before, a general election had resulted in an overwhelming victory for him and his policy, and so Catholics were looking forward to the future of the church in Italy with fear and the worst forebodings. He, however, who exalts himself shall be humbled. The overbearing manners of the Italian premier exasperated his own supporters and led him to his ruin. The financial burdens involved in the maintenance of the Triple Alliance, no mitigation of which could be hoped for from Signor Crispi, formed the basis for the opposition to him; and the new ministry is seeking by a diminution of these burdens to preserve its power. That it will succeed is very doubtful, for it is said to be made up of men of but third and fourth rate capacity, and hopelessly at issue, besides, with each other on almost every important point of policy; nor can there be any doubt but that Signor Crispi will make use of every means to regain control. Catholics, however, cannot but be thankful for the change; certain measures proposed by Crispi against the church have, we believe, been abandoned, and one member of the new ministry is well known as an advocate of a conciliatory policy.

In Austria an unlooked-for dissolution of the Reichsrath has involved the empire in an electoral contest. Since his accession to office the policy of Count Taaffe, the Austrian premier, has been to foster the nationalist sentiments of the numerous races of which the empire consists. Unfortunately, in Bohemia, besides the Czechs, there are a large number of Germans, and a way of reconciliation had to be found for the two opposite aspirations resulting from this fact. A compromise was made ; but the Young Czechs, with the ardor, and, perhaps, inconsiderateness of youth, thought it to be disadvantageous to their race, and therefore they repudiated it. This threw everything into confusion, and Count Taaffe is going, it is said, to make of his opponents hitherto, the German Liberals, allies and supporters by adopting their policy. This he can do without inconsistency, for an Austrian minister is in the same position as a minister of the German Empire—a servant of the emperor and not of the Parliament, and retains office so long as the emperor wishes. He is not the most prominent and devoted defender of certain political ideas, in the fortunes, good or bad, of which he must share, but a more or less skilful manipulator of party combinations to accomplish what the emperor judges to be best for the country. And so Count Taaffe, having found the policy heretofore pursued impracticable, makes an appeal to those who have been his opponents, and should this appeal be successful the count will remain in power in opposition ·to his former friends and supported by his former enemies.

The movement in favor of the amelioration of social ills by legislation has reached Austria also, and it is expected that measures for this purpose will form one of the principal aims of the new government. So much is this the case that one of Count Taaffe's colleagues, being of less pliable material than was suitable, has resigned, and has been succeeded by a gentleman who has made himself somewhat conspicuous for his advocacy of the necessity of state help and for his warnings against the dangers of individualism.

One of the many parties which war against ·one another in Austria is the Anti-Semitic, which has for its object · legislative action against the Jews. Although some of the supporters of · this party are Catholics and what are called Clericals, the Austrian episcopate in a pastoral which they have issued stigmatize as un-Christian the hatred preached by agitators against members of other religious bodies, thereby condemning the proceedings of this party. This recalls the terms in which Cardinal Manning spoke of the Jews in reply to an address recently presented by them to him, and his action on behalf of the oppressed Jews in Russia shows that it is not in the Catholic Church that this ancient nationality finds its oppressors.

*　　　*　　　*

In Spain there has been a general election, the first, we believe, with universal suffrage. The Conservative ministry was in power, and the elections have resulted in an increase of its strength. The Republicans have been worsted at the polls, and have a smaller number of representatives in the newly-elected Cortes.

Portugal has been the scene of a military revolt which was suppressed in a few hours. Whether it was a political movement or merely the disorderly action of discontented soldiers is not quite clear. At all events, the Republican flag was hoisted, and Republicans rallied to the side of the revolters; but unless in process of time there should be a notable increase of courage within the breasts of the defenders of a republic, the kings of Portugal will hold their throne in peace for many years to come; for at the first appearance of the loyal regular troops the revolters, and a few civilians who had joined their ranks, fell upon their knees and prayed for mercy.

*

Two of those unexpected events which are proverbial of French politics have taken place within the last few weeks. The first of these was the suppression of Sardou's play "Thermidor." This play is a dramatic denunciation of the Reign of Terror under Robespierre, and the defenders of this Reign of Terror have proved themselves so numerous and so powerful in Paris that, after vainly resisting for a time, the government on their demand forbade the continuance of the play. The dark significance of the matter lies in the fact that the government of the Republic should be so weak and the sympathizers with the worst period of the Revolution so strong.

The second event was the treatment of the Empress Frederick on her visit to Paris, a visit which seemed at first, especially after the favorable impression produced in France by the emperor's letter on the death of Meissonier, to give promise that France and Germany were to enter upon more friendly relations to each other. It is too early yet to form an estimate of the consequences of conduct which to outsiders appears the extreme of childish folly; but, if we may believe the reports in the newspapers, a complete change in the German emperor's external and internal policy may be the result.

In Germany legislation is being pushed forward on behalf of the working classes and in practical execution of the measures proposed at the Labor Conference at Berlin. What is of greater interest to Catholics, however, is the fact that a bill has been introduced into the Prussian Diet for the restoration to the church of the moneys, amounting to about sixteen millions ot marks, which were withheld by reason of fidelity to conscience on the part of the bishops during the *Culturkampf.* It is expected, too, that in the matter of elementary education concessions will be made by the government.

Philosophical students of the vanity of human life and of the mutability of human fortune will find in Prince Bismarck's present position an impressive illustration of that trite old theme. The once mighty ruler of the German Empire is able now to make his voice heard only by means of the press on which in former days he laid so heavy a hand and for which he had so great a contempt. And on account of his utterances it is said, and that on good authority, that he has incurred the emperor's grave displeasure, and that it was even contemplated to bring him to trial. It is said, too, that in his family there has been the greatest alarm, and that the Princess Bismarck is filled with fears for the security, honor, and even the life of her husband. He has been entreated to take refuge in England from the impending danger. This was the state of things in the month of February, but before these lines are in print all may have changed, and the prince may possibly have been restored to honor and power.

*   *

The death of the heir to the Belgian throne formed the occasion for the manifestation of what seems to be a universally felt sentiment of loyalty to the reigning family. The extension of the suffrage is the subject of chief political interest at the present time. That there should be an extension seems to be admitted by all, for the electorate at present only numbers 130,-000 persons. The question in dispute is whether the suffrage should be made universal, or whether it should be based, as in England, on occupancy. The workingmen, who have declared for universal manhood suffrage, have addressed an appeal to the Belgian bishops, entreating them to intervene with their great authority in behalf of this reform of the constitution.

*

How much bigotry remains within the breasts of those who, in season and out of season, are wont to vaunt themselves as lovers of liberty, has been revealed to the world by the opposition to Mr. Gladstone's Religious Disabilities Bill. No one has more distinguished himself in this matter than the high-priest of the City Temple, Dr. Joseph Parker. Although he has been one of the most prominent supporters of Mr. Gladstone in his advocacy of Home Rule, in this matter he had to renounce his allegiance and to enter upon an active opposition to the measure. This he did by a letter to the *Times* and by calling a public meeting to be held in his place of worship. In the letter, after affirming that he heartily assents to the absolute removal of all disabilities for religious belief, he brings forth the old charge—a charge which sent the martyrs under Elizabeth to the gallows and to the quartering-block—that "Popery is a state policy first and a religious faith second." This he proves by a quotation from the bull *Unam Sanctam:* "The temporal authority should be subject to the spiritual power." What adds a certain piquancy to his argument is the citation of a passage from Mr. Gladstone's own pamphlet *Vatican Decrees*, in which he said that "Rome requires a convert who now joins her to forfeit his moral and mental freedom, and to place his loyalty and civil duty at the mercy of another," and Dr. Parker accordingly proceeds to describe the bill as one "to remove the disabilities of men who have forfeited their moral and mental freedom to hold the office of lord chancellor, etc." How Mr. Gladstone vindicates his consistency we shall see later.

It is only fair to state that Dr. Parker did not carry with him the whole of his co-religionists in his opposition to the bill, although we cannot give the names of any of his brother-ministers who took up the defence of the bill; and 30,084 Baptists throughout the country signed a petition against it. We are not here concerned to enter upon a discussion of Dr. Parker's reasons for his opposition. We cannot help, however, pointing out the inopportuneness of the time which he chose for advancing the assertion that Popery (to use his courteous phrase) was first a state policy—a time when the voice of the Nonconformist conscience, all honor to it, had hurled from power an all-powerful political leader. This occurrence shows that even so rude and imperfect an organization as that of the Nonconformists exerts an influence on state policy; and we are ready to admit that the church, when it is right and proper for it to do so, ought also to exert an influence, and its influence will naturally be greater in proportion to its own greater perfection as a religious body.

When the bill came before the House of Commons it was rejected. The government opposed it, but, as any one who will read the debate will see, without casting any slur upon the loy-

alty of Catholics.   A few Conservatives, however, voted against
the government, among them being the eldest son of Lord Salisbury.   Why Mr. Gladstone introduced the bill is a puzzle to
which no one has offered a satisfactory solution; and although
it may seem ungracious, after this effort to remove one of the few
remaining disabilities, to call attention to the fact, still we think
that the truth ought to be known that Mr. Gladstone has not
squarely retracted or pretended to retract a single accusation
made against the church in his celebrated pamphlet.   His consistency he vindicated in his speech by saying that the effect ·of
his first pamphlet, in which he had impeached certain declarations of the See of Rome as dangerous to the civil allegiance
of those who adopted and concurred in them, was to draw forth
from his Roman Catholic fellow-subjects assurances that they did
give a full, entire, and undivided allegiance.   These assurances
convinced him, and he therefore inserted in his second pamphlet
the words: "I cannot but say that the immediate purpose of my
reply has been attained in so far that the loyalty of my fellow-
Roman Catholic subjects in the mass remains evidently untainted
and secure."   The reader will notice that this is not so much a
withdrawal of the accusation as the conceding that British Catholics are to be excepted from it.   And so Mr. Gladstone holds
the same position now which he· held when he issued his second
pamphlet : he believes in the loyalty and trustworthiness of English Catholics, because they are either disloyal and unfaithful to
the authorized teaching of the church and its head, or too unintelligent to understand just what that teaching is.

Let us add that one of the lessons taught by the fall of Parnell is that the only entirely trustworthy security for a good
cause is in the intelligence, honesty, and courage of its supporters
at large, and that even so good a friend as Mr. Gladstone seems
to be should not absorb the entire allegiance of advocates of
Irish claims.

Although this attempt to remove these particular disabilities
has failed for the present, it is clear that whenever a serious effort
is made they will no longer be maintained.   Political reasons of
the moment led the government to act in opposition to their removal; there would have been a revolt of their Irish supporters.
The bigotry of some of these may be estimated by the fact that
one of the members for Belfast has called upon his constituents
and friends there to boycott the meetings which Sir Henry James
is going to address because he spoke and voted in favor of Mr.
Gladstone's proposal ; and this notwithstanding the fact that Sir

Henry is one of the chief and most influential supporters of the Unionist cause.

The friends of the temperance cause in Great Britain were two years ago rejoicing in what seemed clear proof of the remarkable progress of their principles. Deficit followed deficit in the revenue derived from spirituous beverages, until it had become the custom for the chancellor of the exchequer to estimate the income from this source at a smaller and smaller amount year by year. Unfortunately, a mistake was made in assigning the cause for this diminishing consumption. The years in question were years of no little depression in commercial activity; and when two or three years ago there was a revival of trade and prosperity, there followed what Mr. Goschen termed "a rush to alcohol," which brought him in, instead of a deficit, a very large surplus. This took place in 1889. During 1890 commercial prosperity has been fairly well maintained, and so, we are sorry to say, has also been the demand for intoxicating liquors. We take from the letter on the Drink Bill, published annually by Dr. Dawson Burns, a few interesting particulars. For 1890 the expenditure on drink in Great Britain was £139,495,370, as compared with £132,213,276 in 1889, being an increase of £7,282,194. This is at the rate of £3 13s. per head of the population, or £18 5s. per family of five persons. This expenditure amounts to one-twelfth of the estimated income of all persons in the United Kingdom and one-fifth of the national debt. It was £32,000,000 more than the whole capital in the Post-office Savings-banks, and 4½ times the amounts deposited in both kinds of savings-banks. It was 4½ times the gross receipts from passenger traffic on all the railways of the United Kingdom in 1889, and 3½ times the gross receipts from their goods traffic, or nearly as much again as the receipts from both traffics combined. Comparing the drink expenditure with the income of all denominations for maintenance and extension, which is estimated at about £18,000,000 yearly, it is found that the nation spends about eight times as much on drink as on religion, or that it gives to Bacchus £1 for every half-crown it gives to Christ. General Booth asked for £1,000,000 for the full application of his scheme, and is considered to be asking for an enormous sum; but it is not one-seventh of the *increased* expenditure on liquor in 1890, and only one hundred and fortieth part of the gross expenditure. These facts show how great is the work still to be done before England, however free she may be, can be said to be sober.

In spite of Conciliation Boards and the unsuccessful Scottish Railway strikes the conflict between capital and labor is still going on. The present battle is between the ship-owners and their men. Hull, Sunderland, Liverpool have been the scenes of skirmishes; in Cardiff and London there have been pitched battles. The former place was chosen by the men because the various unions of the employees were thought to be better organized than in any other part of the kingdom. The principal combatants were the Shipping Federation on the one side and the Firemen and Seamen's Union on the other, but the conflict as it proceeded involved others. The men seem to have taken the initiative, they having refused to work with non-unionists and having blocked a vessel manned by " free " men. It is true that they accuse the other side of trying to exclude all unionist men. The most that can be truly said, however, is that the Shipping Federation gives a preference to those who have the Federation ticket, but does not refuse this ticket to unionists. In fact the Cardiff fight was another of the battles of the " new unionism," which seeks to exclude all " free " men from work in a ship along with union men. The brunt of the fight fell, however, on the allies of the Seamen—the coal tippers—who struck partly out of sympathy and partly for grievances of their own. Being unskilled laborers their places were easily filled, and before a week was over the fight ended in the discomfiture of these allies. Violence, breach of contract, disunion among the unionists, mistake in the choice of time, led to their defeat. The most disappointing feature in this matter is that it shows that the efforts to form a Conciliation Board which were made last year have proved abortive. It must not be thought, however, that the movement in favor of such boards is at an end. The London Conciliation Board, of which we gave an account a few months ago, is said to have done a large amount of good work for the trades with which it is concerned, although no detailed account of this work has been published. Cardinal Manning and Mr. Sydney Buxton have been urging upon it to invite the representatives of both sides in the dispute at the London docks to a friendly conference, with a view to an amicable arrangement of this serious and complicated conflict. According to the rules of the board it cannot take action unless requested to do so by one of the parties; in this case, however, Mr. Buxton and the cardinal think a relaxation of the rules might be made.

Lord Randolph Churchill has recently publicly advocated

the formation of State Boards of Arbitration to which the parties in dispute may have recourse. He has not gone so far as to advocate the legal obligation of such recourse, and to other practical politicians the establishment of merely voluntary boards by the state seems inadvisable. Our own experience with them bears out this view. The subject is, however, taking a firm hold of the public mind in Great Britain. The president of the Board of Trade in the present government looks forward to a time in the near future when strikes' will have become as antiquated and barbarous a means of settling trade disputes. as duels are for the settling of private disputes.

Meanwhile. the owners of ships have been strengthening their organization, so that it seems very unlikely that the men will have strength to cope with it. Of the 8,000,000 tons of shipping which requires organization 7,000,000 are banded together in a firm union, under a single committee, to resist in all parts of the kingdom the claims of the unionists to exclusive employment. This is the main point in dispute, and it seems that if in any trade the employer has a right to the control of his employees it should be the shipping trade, where discipline is so important for safety and success; all the more reason for both sides to be willing to arrive at an understanding.

On the other side the work of organization is being extended. The great source of weakness for the unionists is, of course, the supply of men ready and anxious to work upon which employers can fall back; the agricultural laborers, either directly or indirectly, are the source of this supply. Their wages are very low, and they are consequently always ready to better themselves by coming into the cities. To cut off this resource a number of representatives of organized city labor have been sent into the country, and have met with considerable, although by no means startling, success.

In Parliament the labor question is attracting more attention than has ever been given to it before, and it appears probable that there may be a reversal of the long-established attitude of the state towards industrial questions. No fewer than five bills have been introduced into the two houses dealing with the single subject of the regulation of work-shops and factories. In the House of Lords, Lord Thring, a political economist of the old school, has been forced by the evidence brought before the sweating committee to admit the existence of evils which require legislative action for their remedy, and has brought in a measure.

for that purpose. Lord Dunraven, to whom the appointment of that committee was due, and who acted as its chairman, proposes a bill more far-reaching in its operation than Lord Thring's. In the House of Commons Sir Henry James has brought in a bill which has been approved by a large number of factory workmen; Mr. Sydney Buxton is in charge of a fourth measure, while the government has its own bill, which will be brought forward by the Catholic member of the cabinet, Mr. Henry Matthews. There is no doubt but that the latter bill will be passed, the proposals of the other bills being incorporated so far as they commend themselves to the wisdom of Parliament. And the wisdom of Parliament, being to a very large extent a matter of political expediency, will pay, it is clear, due attention to the just claims of workingmen; for a class which out of the six or seven millions of electors numbers between four and five millions is not to be despised.

Another question which will be brought before Parliament is the regulation by legislation of the hours of labor. This proposal involves many difficult questions, and meets with opposition from all sides, from workingmen, and from Radical and Gladstonian members of Parliament. In the case of miners, however, it seems highly probable that the Eight Hours' Bill, supported by a vast majority of the men, will pass into law.

The most important event, however, which we have to chronicle is the fact that the government have decided to appoint a royal commission for the purpose of making an exhaustive inquiry into the relations between employers and employed. This may result in postponing legislation for a time, but will insure the collecting of full and reliable information on the points at issue and will lead to the passing of well-considered measures, beneficial to the best interests of every class. A royal commission does not consist exclusively of members of Parliament, but of the best-informed men to be found in the kingdom on the particular question, and as the evidence is published, these commissions become, irrespective of the conclusions of the commissioners, of extreme value to students.

The movement among French Catholics inaugurated by Cardinal Lavigerie seems to be gaining in power and influence. It is not, however, without opponents. Bishop Freppel has made a visit to Rome to represent, it is said, to the Holy Father the objections entertained by many good Catholics, among whom we must reckon that distinguished servant of the church in France, the Comte de Mún. It is thought that but little success has attended the efforts of the bishop. All this, however, is very much a matter of conjecture. What is certain is that the Royalists have had a meeting at Nîmes, at which one of the leaders of this party, M. d'Haussonville, delivered an address in opposition to the policy of the cardinal. He said that. a few deputies who had formerly been among the staunchest champions of royalty were now inclined to support the new policy. These deputies, he said, were affected by what is called in literature the feeling of despair. While recognizing the fact that Catholics were at liberty to take any political side which recommended itself to their minds even in countries where the form of government or the dynasty was in dispute, he maintained that the Republicans in France òf every shade had found in the words *Le Cléricalisme, voilà l'ennemi*, the cry which never failed to rally their confused ranks. He therefore came to the conclusion that it was impossible for any degrading capitulation or demoralizing truce to be made with them, and that all Royalists should adopt the device of their exiled prince-historian, *J'attendrai*, and never lay down their arms before the day after victory of the royalist cause.

To this speech a reply has been made by a Conservative deputy, M. Piou, who has lately returned from a visit to the Pope. In this reply M. Piou endeavors to define precisely the position, objects, and aims of those practical politicians who have adopted Cardinal Lavigerie's ideas. It is their intention to form a Conservative party, which, apart from all dynastic preoccupation, shall take its stand on constitutional ground to defend the great interests of the country; and he proceeds to express his conviction that any party which should enter into conflict with the very form of government would be doomed to impotence. He then proceeds : " We all appeal to the national will. We all proclaim that the country has control over its destinies. Do we not mean to recognize its supreme power only if it employs it according to our desires ? . . . When the country has spoken, the right is with it." The last sentence is quoted from a speech of M. Thiers made in 1864. To the objection that the Republicans will not be conciliated, but will continue to act against the church, he answers that his appeal is not to them but to the universal suffrage possessed by the French people. " We have neither concessions to expect nor conditions to dictate. We have to fight and to merit victory by our courage and wisdom." And in opposition to the passive attitude advocated by the Comte d'Haussonville M. Piou calls upon his former allies among Royalists to fight for faith and country on a basis which now, after so many elec_ tions, may be looked upon as acceptable to all Frenchmen. This, then, is the new movement—a movement which, accept- ing as final the decision of the people of France in favor of a Republican form of government, proposes to work against the irreligious measures taken by the defenders of that form up to the present time and contemplated in the future. It will meet with opposition from many quarters, but there is reason to believe that it will finally succeed.

⁂   *   *

Notwithstanding the bitter and unfair opposition of Professor Huxley, the lofty contempt of the *Times*, the withdrawal of sup- port by those Evangelicals who are led by Mr. Webb-Peploe, and the abuse of all kinds with which he has been assailed, General Booth within three months of the publication of his book has received the sum of £100,000 for which he appealed. In fact, on the thirtieth of January last the subscriptions amounted to £102,000, and they have not ceased to pour in since that date. A practical beginning has accordingly been made of the "Way Out." On the 23d of January the "Ark" was opened. This is to be a poor man's Métropole, where for fourpence he can have a bed in a four-bedded room, and for sixpence a little room to himself, with the conveniences for washing his clothes and a hot bath for himself. On the 30th of January the "Prison Bridge" was opened. This is a place which will accommodate fifty men, and by means of it those who have been in prison can pass from vice and disgrace to a new life of honesty and virtue. The "Red Maria" waits at the prison gates for discharged prisoners and brings them to the Bridge. Here work will be given in one or other of the factories of the Army and the former prisoners will be on the same foot- ing as the other workers. On the 31st of January another Food and Shelter Depot was opened, and in Bradford and Leeds build- ings are being prepared for the same purpose. A secretary for emigration has been appointed to furnish information for intend- ing emigrants, secure information as to the reliability of situa- tions offered them, and to be of general service to them. Nego- tiations, too, are in progress for securing land for the farm colony. We rejoice that the work is thus fairly started.

The principle of the uncontrolled management of the plan the general has rigidly maintained, even at the cost of much support. A trust-deed has, however, been executed by means of which all moneys subscribed for the social part of the Army's work will be secured to it alone, and to prevent these funds from being used for the general purposes of the Salvation Army. This deed will enable any subscriber to initiate proceedings against the general for any breach of the provisions of the deed. The intervention of the attorney-general will, however, be necessary in such a case. Means of providing against a too rigid and inelastic set of rules are provided by the deed itself. For should the general at any time think that the scheme may be advantageously extended, altered, or modified in some manner not wholly inconsistent with the main object thereof, he shall be at liberty to do so under the written consent of two-thirds of a committee. This committee is to consist of eighteen persons, of whom the general has the right to nominate six, and the Archbishop of Canterbury, the president of the Wesleyan Conference, the chairman of the Congregational Union, the chairman of the Baptist Union, the Attorney-General, and the chairman of the London County Council would each have the right to nominate two persons. In this way it is hoped to secure at once faithful adherence to the plan as proposed and the power of adaptation to new needs and wants.

All this we commend to the serious consideration of Catholics whose zeal, wealth, or state of life calls them to be fishermen of the "submerged."

TALK ABOUT NEW BOOKS.

MR. ANDREW LANG'S new volume* is mainly made up of essays reprinted from various periodicals, American and English. Of the five written expressly for it, that on " Homer and the Study of Greek," and those which treat respectively of Mr. R. L. Stevenson and Mr. Rudyard Kippling, are among the best in a good collection ; probably that on Homer is the very best. At the same time, one would be glad to spare from it Mr. Lang's parodies on certain actual and certain possible translators. They impart an air of tomfoolery to what is in other respects a digni- fied and persuasive plea for the retention of Greek in schools, whence the modern spirit is striving to thrust it out. Begin with Homer, is Mr. Lang's contention ; make boys, like Ascham and Rabelais, " jump into Greek and splash about until they learn to swim," instead of wearying them with " grammars *in vacuo*," and there will be less complaint against it as a useless wearying of school-boy flesh. What pleasure will be lost to coming genera- tions of English if Homer is to appeal to them only through the disguises imposed upon him by Pope and Fenton, Broome, Chapman, or William Morris ! True ; and yet how much pleas- ure has been and will be given to lovers of poetry by a certain sonnet in which an English poet who had no Greek made mem- orable his first acquaintance with Chapman's version. Better than nothing, Mr. Lang would answer, and yet the translators, " from Chapman to Avia, or Mr. William Morris, are all eminently con- scientious, and erroneous, and futile. Chapman makes Homer a fanciful, euphuistic, obscure, and garrulous Elizabethan, but Chap- man has fire. . . . Homer is untranslatable. None of us can bend the bow of Eurytus, and make the bowstring ' ring sweetly at the touch like the swallow's song.' The adventure is never to be achieved ; and if Greek is to be dismissed from education, not the least of the sorrows that will ensue is English ignorance of Homer."

But if this is the best among these essays, the one which follows it, on " The Last Fashionable Novel," is by odds the worst, and, to our notion, fails to put in any valid claim to ex- istence. With this exception, and possibly another in the case of the paper on Thomas Haynes Bayly, who was a very minor

* *Essays in Little.* By Andrew Lang. New York : Charles Scribner's Sons.

poet indeed, though twenty-five years ago every maid who owned
a piano was thrumming and humming his "Gaily the Trouba-
dour" and "The Mistletoe hung in the Castle Hall." Mr. Lang's
volume is sure to afford · entertainment to readers whose taste
inclines them to literary and critical chit-chat. There are many
readers and lovers of good books to whom gossip of this sort
makes no appeal. They like to read of deeds, and things, and
of men who made no books but were, in a manner, the quarry
from which books are · dug out by other men. But perhaps these
readers are, after all, in a minority; at all events the critical
essayists get in all times a fair share of attention. And Mr. Lang
deserves it as well as any of them. Though he is neither a
phrase-maker and hunter after rare epithets like Mr. Henley, nor
an unerring artist in words like his other compatriot, Mr. Stevenson, his judgment is sounder, less personal, and more to be
relied on than that of either. His style, too, is flexible and expressive. Mr. Henley is too fond of extremes—he likes weights
better than balances. If he heaps a full measure of praise on
one scale—the Dickens scale, say — the Thackeray on the other
side flies up and kicks the beam; he has been robbed· of every
claim to love and admiration save that extorted from a determined stylist by the contemplation of a perfect style. Mr. Stevenson, too, although he exerts a gentle compulsion on his reader
and will be followed to the end of whatever journey they undertake in company, though it lead to the condemnation and execution of one of the reader's long-cherished friends, gets judged in
turn and placed among the artists rather than the critics. It is
a good place, and no doubt any of us would prefer it were the
choice granted. Only, if the artists would stick to their brushes
and let other and less kindly tools alone, it might be better. Mr.
Lang is more generous and more just, and his essays on Dumas,
on Thackeray and Dickens, on Stevenson himself, and on Kipling, that "young Lochinvar of fiction," as some one has happily called him, are both agreeable in manner and discriminating
and sound in matter.

The Cassells begin a new series of fiction which they call
the "Unknown Library" with a novelette* having a Russian
Nihilist for its heroine. It is a very clever piece of work. The
scene is laid in an English country house to which comes
Mademoiselle Ixe as governess to three or four young children,
one of them a peevish invalid, who have been the terror and
discomfiture of several predecessors in her line. There is no

Mademoiselle Ixe. By Lanoe Falconer. New York: Cassell Publishing Co.

serious study of character undertaken in the tale, but there is
hardly one of the personages who appear on its narrow stage
who is not at once definitely brushed in with a secure stroke
and plenty of verisimilitude to common English types. Mademoiselle Ixe is herself wrapped in a profound mystery which
hangs about her until the author voluntarily lifts it, and
which gives a possible clue to the lines likely to be followed by
the subsequent tales of this "Unknown" series. Mademoiselle
Ixe embodies well that passion of the Nihilist, comprehensible at
all events even though mistaken, which governmental Russia
seems bent on doing all in its power to foster. The self-devotion of a soul which has no religion save love of country and
humanity, and which sees both of these helpless and hideously
outraged in the name of law, is combined in her with thorough
womanliness, extreme tact, far-seeing persistence, and complete
intellectual acceptance of her *rôle* as the illegal avenger of legalized crime. And Russia as it stands, with its foul places laid
bare by the hands of its own subjects, is so great an offence
against civilization, religion, and even nature, that what under
more ordinary circumstances would be universally classed as
private vengeance, has a tendency to assume other proportions
and to put forth an almost unchallenged claim to be ranked
with that of Judith and of Jael. From the Christian standpoint
there is room for condemnation, but, human nature being what
it is, there is not much room even there for surprise when those
who sin without the law of equity and humanity are punished
without it.

The first story by Dorothea Gerard which fell under the
present writer's notice was such a vigorous piece of work that
her name upon the title-page of a new novel seemed for some
time thereafter the herald of solid entertainment within. But,
neither when writing alone, nor in collaboration with E. Gerard, has she succeeded in striking again the bold, sure note
which gave character to *Orthodox*, her study of Jewish customs
and prejudices in Poland. But her material in that case was
fresher than any likely to come in the way of English novelists
working in the oft-sown field of British life and manners.

The scene of the new novel,* of which she is "joint author,"
is laid partly in a Scotch country house and partly in Venice.
The young girl whose abnormal sensitiveness gives the book its
rather promising title, is the daughter of a widowed Scotch
laird with peculiarities which make him anything but a com-

A Sensitive Plant. By E. and D. Gerard. New York : D. Appleton & Co.

fortable parent to have in the house. Still, he is a man of honor and uprightness, and the little Janet might easily be worse off than she is under his care and that of Aunt Penny, his maiden sister. The plot is not of absorbing interest and the story is far too much drawn out and padded. Its interest, never more than mild even when Olympe and her scheming mother come on the stage at Venice, with their very old tricks of flirtation and match-making, turns wholly upon Janet's inability, imposed upon her by her shrinking temperament, to manifest the love she feels for Captain Chichester, the friend of her scapegrace brother Robert. The latter has committed a murder —or, better, has unintentionally killed a young man in sudden drunken rage—and circumstances combine to make Janet believe that the crime, whose particulars she does not know, was committed by the captain. This belief, however, by no means lessens her love for him; and as the murder has no structural use in the story, it seems to have been introduced chiefly to bring out this accentuation of Janet's character and passion. There is some amusing by-play in the scenes where the *gourmet* D'Obson, wrongly believing Janet to have been the concocter of a marvellous lobster *soufflé*, wooes her assiduously, bombarding the fortress of her maiden innocence with cookery books and essays on "The Position of the Oyster in General History," while carefully guarding her from any knowledge of truffles. "I would as soon put a novel of Ouida's or Paul de Kock's into your hands as a treatise upon truffles—God forbid!" he says to her with fervor.

The announcement of a new book * by Olive Schreiner was something like an event for those in whose memories her singular first venture, *The Story of an African Farm*, was still vivid. The present volume, so exactly like its predecessor in style that no one familiar with that could well have mistaken its authorship, even had it been anonymous, will not much enhance her reputation. It seems to have diminished it in the eyes of the critic of the *Anti-Jacobin*, who, however, curiously misunderstands her drift in the dream called "Across my Bed." He says it is a "temperance tract" and blasphemous into the bargain. But the "wine" in which the people of her dream dabble and drink their fill is plainly enough the blood of the poor and wretched, out of whom the materials of life and joy have been crushed in order to give their oppressors a double share. And as to blasphemy, there seems no intention of the sort, although the great

* *Dreams.* By Olive Schreiner. Boston: Roberts Brothers.

name of God is handled more colloquially and freely than necessity required or reverence and good taste would sanction. ·The longest of these "Dreams" is reprinted from the "African Farm," where, had it been left, one might 'have praised this book more freely. On the whole, Miss Schreiner remains for the present an unknown quantity; a power, certainly, but one whose value and precise direction are indeterminate. She feels her sex—or, better, the wrongs endured by her sex—very keenly; and that seems to us a good thing. As she puts it in the most suggestive of these sketches, the one called "Three Dreams in a Desert," man cannot help his long-prostrate sister to her feet. "*She must help herself.* Let her struggle till she is strong."

The volumes of the Saint-Amand series, which are nominally concerned with Josephine and Marie Louise, not only maintain but increase their interest as they go on. The latest * of them, continuing the story of the Napoleonic decadence, brings it down to the emperor's arrival at Elba, May 4, 1814, and the final departure of Marie Louise from France, which took place just two days earlier. The imperial pair, who ought never to have met at all and who were never to meet again, had met for the last time late in January of that year. There is, therefore, in this volume none of those bits of domestic life and fatherly joy which until now have cast a flickering and illusive glow over a picture whose tints began to fade at the very moment when they seemed to have been made imperishable by the Austrian marriage. When Napoleon returned to Fontainebleau on the last of March, 1814, a defeated man, but not acknowledging defeat; on the eve of abdication, but full of futile plans for recovering power; a would-be suicide to whom even poison was to refuse the refuge against humiliation, neither wife nor son were there to greet him. But it was his own fault that they were not; Marie Louise was still faithful to him and to her conception of her duty, and she would have been ready to welcome him in defeat and accompany him into exile. As for him, he had already begun to acknowledge that his marriage had been a fatal blunder. Saint-Amand, who writes as a novelist and a Christian as well as a lively and accurate historian, stops his narrative to conjecture the probable reflections of the emperor when he re-entered this abode of his former glory:

* *Marie Louise and the Invasion of* 1814. By Imbert de Saint-Amand. Translated by T. S. Perry. New York: Charles Scribner's Sons. 1891.

" He might have said to himself : ' Here I inflicted. pain on my tender and devoted Josephine·; here I dealt harshly with the pope, that venerable man, who came to Paris from Rome for my coronation. I am punished for my sins. I recognize the hand of God in my .chastisement. Had I not repudiated Josephine, she would now be by my side. I did wrong to imprison the pope. He, not I, is free ; and who knows if I may not soon be a prisoner ? ' "

. Saint-Amand says well that it would need a Shakspere to describe the mental agonies which attended this great downfall. Nothing is lacking to its horrors save the touch of meanness in the vanquished man, and the loss of self-respect involved in fretting uselessly at small ignominies. No such great ascent has been followed by an overthrow so imposing, so dignified, and so pathetic. Rising and falling, sinning, repenting, and expiating, he arrests attention and conquers sympathy and admiration less as a man than as the incarnation of some great natural force. One regards him with a feeling akin to that awakened by the majestic harmonies of a Beethoven sonata or the great Paul Veronese in the *Salon Carré* of the Louvre, the *Marriage at Cana*—with a sense, that is, of the immense reserves of force imprisoned at times in men to all seeming like ourselves. There is no escaping him, no belittling of him, possible on the pages of history. His sins were many, and each of them came back to whip him with a scourge knotted by his own hands. Such disgrace as the defection and unworthiness of Marie Louise could fasten on him he had inflicted on the Count Walewska ; the Duke of Reichstadt avenged the Duke of Enghien ; the captive pope at Fontainebleau, restored with honors to his own· place, was set over against the new Prometheus on the black rock of Saint Helena, gnawed by remorse and released· only by penance and a lonely death. As' Saint-Amand says :

" To have died before the expiation of Saint Helena would have been for Napoleon the renunciation "—the word is ill-chosen—" of the noblest crown, that of martyrdom. The great man needed the purification of long sufferings. For his soul, so long the slave of passions, to become free, his body had to· be captive. If we look at things from the Christian's standpoint, thinking of eternity, it was his jailers who were to be his liberators. At Fontainebleau he had not been defeated enough.· He had not drunk the bitter chalice to the dregs. He needed one more final defeat—that of Waterloo. He needed meditation and remorse on the wave-beaten rocks.

He needed the dialogue between his stormy thought and the murmur of the ocean. There it was that he at last was to attain real greatness, where he was to deserve a glance from the God of pity; there that, after enduring nobly one of the most pathetic and grand expiations known to history, he was to utter those ever-memorable words: 'Not every one who wishes can be an atheist.' "

The purposes of the reading circles and clubs which abound on all sides, and which we take to include the task of giving young readers some acquaintance with writers and books whose fame has survived through centuries, but which, unaided, make no imperative appeal to modern taste, should be furthered by the colorless but sufficiently copious and accurate sketch* of Petrarch's life just brought out by Roberts Brothers. No analysis of his work is made in it, and no specimens presented in translation. But a fair general idea of the circumstances of his life and the complexion of his times may be gathered from it. Laura's lover, however, though he attracted the admiration, esteem, and friendship of most of his contemporaries, will probably not strike the reader of Miss Ward's biography as a very sympathetic figure. Some close co-ordinate or subsequent study of the sonnets and the prose " Dialogues on Contempt of the World," in which St. Augustine is the poet's interlocutor, will be necessary for whoever desires to think of Petrarch as anything more than a persistent lay figure in literature. He was more than that, but the author of this sketch has not succeeded in vivifying him in her representation.

Âtman† is one of those seemingly spiritual but actually material novels dealing with the mysterious and the occult which are one of the prevalent fashions of the day. It is better written than some of them, and shows (if it shows anything more than a ready pen and a sense of mercantile values in fiction), how ineradicable is the tendency of men who have either lost, or outraged, or never possessed Christian faith to dabble in natural magic. As the witches of whom Görres has so many strange tales to tell rubbed themselves with powerful unguents and swallowed hideous compounds in order to escape from their flesh and attend the " Sabbath," so the modern inquirer into the mysterious ties which knit soul and body to-

* *Petrarch: A Sketch of his Life and Work.* By May Alden Ward. Boston : Roberts Brothers, 1891.

† *Âtman:* The Documents in a Strange Case. By Francis Howard Williams. New York: Cassell Publishing Company. 1891.

gether seeks for a drug, a process of some sort or other, which shall be efficacious to unbind them.   So Bulwer did, and so did Stevenson in that clever tale of Jekyll and Hyde, whose moral and whose manner lifted it out of the rut where by virtue of its conception it belonged.   Mr. Williams's device of a chemical combination capable of holding a soul in solution, and preserving it indefinitely in a "small crystal vial, wedge-shaped, and fitted with a ground-glass stopper," whence it can be transferred to a soulless body at the operator's will, is nonsensical rather than grotesque.   And the grotesque marks the limit to which adventurers in the occult may go unlaughed at.   As for the transfusion process, it labors under the difficulty foreseen by Mrs. Glasse when writing her recipe for jugged hare.   First catch your living but soulless human body.   That done, there is no saying what else might not happen.

Mr. Stevenson, as we said just now, and not with sufficient accuracy, lifted his story out of the materialistic rut by virtue of its moral.   But, in truth, he was dealing with a more real problem—it was the two selves, the man of sin and the man of God, the old man and the new of whom St. Paul writes, that he had in view; the problem which, as he says himself somewhere in the story, lies at the root of religion.   The materialistic vein showed itself in the notion of the chemical salt and the physical presentation of either of the two selves.   But that was an allegory, and not a would-be juggler's trick.   The idea is doubtless as old as Cain or Adam, and is found in the serious literature of all lands which have one.

In the readable translations from five of Plato's dialogues * just brought out by the Scribners, occurs one of the most notable expressions of this truth of natural religion.   This admirable little volume contains portions of the Charmides, Lysis, Laches, Euthydemus, and Theætetes.   Our quotation is from the last, which is also in all respects the most interesting of them all. Socrates has been saying that it is

"not possible to destroy evil, for the opposite of good must needs always exist; nor is its abiding-place to be imagined among the gods, for it hovers of necessity about mortal nature here below.   Therefore it behooves us to make good our escape hence to yonder place as fast as may be.   And the way of escape is this—to grow as like unto God as possible; and to grow like him is to become just and holy and wise withal."

* *Talks with Athenian Youths.*   Five selected Dialogues translated from Plato.   New York : Charles Scribner's Sons.

Then he goes on to say how difficult it is to persuade men that virtue is to be sought and vice shunned for this reason and not in order to make a good appearance in the eyes of other men. God is never unjust, he says, and nothing is more like Him than the man who has made himself most just. The knowledge of this truth is wisdom and true virtue; "all else that looks like cleverness or wisdom is in matters of politics mere coarseness, and in the arts vulgarity." Some men glory in this cleverness, because they know not the reward of unrighteousness, which is that they shall become that which they have voluntarily resembled. Not stripes and death is their penalty, for these are frequently incurred by the just, but rather something impossible to escape from. Then Theodorus asks what the sage means, and he replies:

"Two living types, my friend, are set before them—the one divine and of perfect blessedness, the other with naught of the divine, and of utter misery. But this they do not perceive, and their excessive folly and stupidity makes them unconscious that on account of their evil deeds they are growing like the one and unlike the other. And the penalty they pay is that the life led by them is in the likeness of that which they resemble. If we tell them that unless they get rid of their boasted cleverness, they will not, even when dead, be received into that place which is free from evil, but must ever continue here upon earth in that way of life which is like unto themselves—evil consorting with evil—they will listen to us, but only as clever knaves might listen to a set of fools."

"Indeed they will, Socrates."

"I am quite aware of it, my friend. There is, however, this about them, that if they are confronted with one person alone, and made to give their reasons for what they censure—that is, if they are willing to stand their ground and not run away like cowards—they end, my good sir, by being strangely dissatisfied with their own reasons."

The world moves but changes not, says the modern reader coming on these words of ancient wisdom.

I.—HISTORY OF THE CATHOLIC CHURCH IN THE UNITED STATES.*

One might think that after the death of Archbishop Carroll the history of the American Church would be a matter of routine,

* *History of the Catholic Church in the United States,* from the division of the Diocese of Baltimore, 1808, and death of Archbishop Carroll, 1815, to the Fifth Provincial Council of Baltimore, 1843. By John Gilmary Shea. New York : John G. Shea.

a chronicle of appointments and of the formation of new dioceses, the establishment of religious communities, seminaries, colleges, and asylums, and the collection of the statistics of the gradual increase of the Catholic people. But although the present volume gives all this, and does it well, it does very much more. We cannot say that Dr. Shea leads us through such interesting scenes as he has done in the two previous volumes of his great work, which treat of the pioneer age of our Church; yet he narrates the events of what was a critical period among us, and sketches the characters of the men who led the clergy and people safely through it. They were not great men in the ordinary meaning of the term, although Bishop England was a great orator and a useful writer, and Bishops Bruté and Flaget were saintly prelates. But these, with Archbishops Neale, Maréchal, Whitfield, and Eccleston, Bishops Cheverus, the two Fenwicks, Du Bois, Du Bourg, and Rosati, had some extremely difficult problems to solve with very inadequate means to do it. They labored with zeal and suffered with much fortitude to supply the people with clergy from—God knows where. They struggled against a rebellious element among the people, who were bent on Protestantizing the parish corporations by means of the State authority; these prelates hewed down the bulkiest portion of this obstacle to the union of priest and people, preparing for its final removal under Bishops Hughes and Kenrick. They introduced into the country many of the charitable and educational religious societies since grown so great, or they fostered their infancy into active life. They did something for Catholic literature when to succeed in doing anything was to work wonders. They managed after enormous trouble to expel from the papal ante-chambers the advisory lobby of a foreign episcopate, which sought with almost fatal results to rule the American Church as an annex of a church itself the gasping victim of cruel persecution. They secured a *modus' vivendi* among the bishops by means of the first four provincial councils, clearing up, after infinite difficulty, the way to Rome and back for official business. And they chose out and put into office the men under whose powerful influence Catholicity became a great religious force in America, Kenrick, Purcell, and Hughes, the first years of whose era is lapped by the record given in this volume.

All this the reader will find told by Dr. Shea in this volume with unquestionable honesty; and he will also find many curious bits of history of personal, local, and general interest, interspersed with the details of dates and places which are essential to the end sought for in such a work.

The author has one more volume to prepare and then his work is done. And may God grant him the time to do it, and freshen his heart with renewed courage, and reward his industry with adequate temporal compensation, as he is sure to do with the consoling reflection of a lifetime devoted to works of the highest usefulness to both church and state !

2.—THE ORIGIN OF THE ENGLISH PRAYER-BOOK.*

In the first meeting of Convocation held in the reign of Edward VI. a petition of the Lower House to the Upper speaks of certain books which had been prepared by the order of Henry VIII. by a committee of prelates and learned men, such books being the "uniform order" for divine service which the committee had been appointed to devise. To these books former historians of the Book of Common Prayer did not have access. It was unknown what had become of them; some have even questioned their existence. The identification of the lost work or works with a certain MS. in the Royal Library has enabled Mr. Gasquet and Mr. Bishop to re-write the history of the origin of the Anglican Prayer-Book from a new standpoint, with fuller and more exact knowledge, and less of inference and conjecture.

The aim of the authors has been to bring out facts, not to enter upon a polemic against the Reformers or their work. This is what men of all parties want and most prize: for if the facts can be ascertained, it is easy for each one to draw his own conclusions; and Catholics have of all parties least to dread and most to hope from a full disclosure.

As an illustration of this we may cite the following as showing the position occupied by bishops who had renounced the pope: Canon Dixon in his *History of the English Church* gives this account of the proceedings which took place after Henry's death: "Even before the prince [Edward VI.] was crowned it came into the mind of Cranmer, so great was his loyalty, that it was *desirable* for himself and the other bishops to renew the commissions as functionaries of the new king. He therefore issued or caused to be issued without delay those curious instruments, etc." This is bad enough, but not so bad as the reality. Canon Dixon's account leaves to Cranmer the initiative. The truth is that the new supreme 'head of the church to which the

---

* *Edward VI. and the Book of Common Prayer.* An Examination into its Origin and Early History, with an Appendix of unpublished Documents. By Francis Aidan Gasquet, O.S.B., and Edmund Bishop. London : John Hodges ; New York : The Catholic Publication Society Co.

bishops had submitted exacted it, and that it was not merely desired, as Canon Dixon says, but required of them. The Harleian MS., 2308 f. 25 d. (cited by Mr. Gasquet), gives the following resolution of the council: "Item, whereas all the bishops of the realm had authority of spiritual jurisdiction by force of instruments under the seal appointed *ad res ecclesiasticas* which was determined by the decease of our late Sovereign Lord King Henry VIII., . . . and forasmuch as for the better order of the affairs of the realm it is thought convenient the same authority be renewed unto them: it was therefore ordained that they should cause new instruments to be drawn in form of the others they had before, . . . and thereupon every of the said bishops to exercise their jurisdiction in such manner as they did before by virtue of their former grants" It was in compliance with this order of his superiors, therefore, that Cranmer took out his new commission, and this he did the very next day, thus himself recognizing the claim which the state so peremptorily and unmistakably made that he and the rest of the bishops should be the mere delegates of the king. And much as the Church of England has changed in other respects, in this it remains the same. A reader of the London *Gazette* for the 12th December last will find the following order in council: " *Whitehall*, Dec. 12.— The Queen has been pleased to order a *Congé d'Elire* to pass the great Seal, empowering the Dean and Chapter of the Cathedral Church of Worcester to elect a Bishop of that See, . . . declared vacant by Her Majesty's Order in Council; and Her Majesty has been pleased to recommend to the said Dean and Chapter [here follows the name of Lord Salisbury's nominee], to be by them elected Bishop of the said See of Worcester."

The language of this order is a little more courteous, perhaps, than that of the earlier order, but it may be thought by some that it only adds insult to injury to be recommended to elect a person already elected, and to be bound to elect under pains and penalties, for such, as every one knows, is the real state of things.

Father Gasquet has already by his former work on the English monasteries of the reign of Henry VIII. established his reputation as a student of the sources of history, as a reliable authority, and as an enlarger of the field of knowledge; and every reader of the former work will know the character of the present. No student of the English Prayer-Book, or, indeed, of the history of the period of the English reformation, can feel sure that he is master of this subject unless he has read this book.

We regret that the space at our disposal precludes a more detailed notice of it, but every one should read it for himself.

3.—COLUMBUS.*

In the charming *Dialogues on Art· in Literature* of Francisco Cardoso, Don Fabio the Dreamer says: "He whose biography shall be faithful, shall have his vices painted by his friends, his virtues delineated by his enemies; Indifference shall describe his works, and Veracity shall compound the whole." On this Don Arturo the Objector remarks: "This Veracity is a very dull fellow, and withal most uninteresting." And the Dreamer replies: "Objector, thou art vain and immoral! Veracity is more precious and beautiful than fine gold and diamonds—" "And rarer withal," interjects Don Arturo.

Nowhere rarer than in history and biography. So rare that were Tarducci's life of Columbus what it is not, a dull, dry work, the simplicity and brilliant truthfulness of his narrative would make it delightful reading, and the epithet brilliant is used advisedly, for of the many fine qualities this life of Columbus possesses, none is characterized more firmly, none shines so brightly, as its utter truthfulness. A hundred times whilst reading the work one finds himself saying, "How true this is, how like Columbus." And this last expression explains another and not small characteristic of the work. You are made thoroughly acquainted with the man Columbus. You think and talk with Columbus, not about him. You view things through his eyes, not the eyes of the author. You comprehend the motives of the hero and discoverer, because you are made to comprehend the man. You are made to perceive blemishes in him; they cause you keen sorrow, but you do not cease to love the man who has now become your friend and companion. You see his weaknesses, and that he is never ignoble. You are made to know in him a saintly hero of stupendous mind and mighty soul, and never for a moment do you forget that he is a man with strong passions, and with weaknesses like to yourself. We know of few biographies that so perfectly reveal the nature of the subject treated as this, by Tarducci.

The simplicity with which the tale tells itself is extraordinary. There is no striving for an effect that is always reached. For example: Columbus has proceeded to Barcelona after his first

* *The Life of Christopher Columbus.* By Francisco Tarducci, after the latest Documents. Translated from the Italian by Henry F. Brownson. Detroit: H. F. Brownson, Publisher.

voyage, to meet Ferdinand and Isabella ; he has related his passage across the seas, and his wondrous discovery, and has rejoiced at the thought of the spreading of the Gospel to the
natives of these newly-discovered lands. " The words of Columbus so moved the sovereigns that as soon as his fervent discourse was ended, they both fell on their knees and raised their
joined hands to Heaven, weeping with joy and gratitude to
God. And all the ministers, high officers of the court, and
grandees of the kingdom, that were present, followed their example ; a lively feeling of religious thankfulness drew every
thought to God, and in the general commotion, instead of profane applause and huzzas, the choir of the royal chapel intoned
the _Te Deum._ Las Casas, describing the solemn enthusiasm of
that thanksgiving, says : " _It seemed as though each one enjoyed
at that instant a foretaste of the delights of paradise._"

Space admits of but one other quotation. Columbus has taken possession of San Salvador : " When the ceremony of taking
possession was over Columbus caused two large pieces of wood to
be cut, and, making a rude cross, raised it on the same spot where
the royal banner had been placed, ' to leave a sign that possession
had been taken of that land in the name of Christ.' He did the
same ever after in every land he discovered, whether large or
small, leaving everywhere the sign of redemption, as in a place
that had come under the dominion of the Christian religion." . . .
" The Spaniards remained on shore all day, refreshing themselves
after the voyage among the delicious groves of the island, and
only returned to the vessels late in the evening, full of wonder at
what they had seen."

At any time would Tarducci's life of Columbus have found a
hearty welcome and been pronounced an event in the world of
letters. Verging as we are on the fourth centenary of the discovery that changed a world, the Englishing of this great work has
a singular appropriateness. It would, indeed, be pleasant to give
unqualified praise to the translator, as it has been given to the
author. The veracity Don Arturo likes not obliges us to admit
that, while there is no question but that the translation is accurate, the translator has not always avoided the ambiguities of
our language, neither are his sentences always smooth and
flowing.

That this work will attract wide-spread attention there can
be no doubt ; let us hope that it will attract all the attention
Catholic readers should give to it. Fortunately for the translator,
the work he has given the English-speaking public is of such a

character as not to depend on any one portion of the public for its circulation. It will be bought and read and reviewed by Protestant readers and publishers. When this has been done and the excellence of the work approved of by our dissenting brethren, then our Catholic laity, who will have failed to buy it at once, will bethink themselves that they have room on their book-shelves for a copy. It is the life of one of the noblest characters that ever lived, the greatest of all discoverers, Christopher Columbus, whose least glory is not his saintliness of heart and mind, his devotion to Holy Church.

It is a pleasure to note the excellence of the engravings contained in these volumes, and the extremely low price at which the work is sold.

THE COLUMBIAN READING UNION.

ALL COMMUNICATIONS RELATING TO READING CIRCLES, LISTS OF BOOKS, ETC., SHOULD BE ADDRESSED TO THE COLUMBIAN READING UNION, NO. 415 WEST FIFTY-NINTH STREET, NEW YORK CITY.

COPIES of our book-lists and leaflets have been sent gratis to all the institutions devoted to higher education which are mentioned in the Catholic Directory of the United States as select schools, colleges, and academies. We had hopes that our communications would get some recognition at least from the teachers of literature, whose zeal for the diffusion of good books by Catholic authors might reasonably be expected to become manifest by a kindly word in favor of the useful work undertaken by the Columbian Reading Union. In many places we have failed to elicit any response, which leads to the undesirable conclusion that there are institutions claiming to give a finished education without inculcating the necessity of an elementary knowledge of Catholic literature.

*

The religious communities have given us many assurances of their interest in our movement, and cheerfully volunteered to pray for its success. We are directly indebted to their exertions for many new members. While thanking them one and all for past favors, we especially request a continuance of their good prayers to assist in overcoming the culpable indifference among Catholics which is the greatest obstacle to the missionary work yet to be done through the agency of Catholic literature. It is a consolation to know that within the sacred enclosure of the cloister there are holy nuns praying to St. Teresa for blessings upon the Columbian Reading Union and its members. A reverend mother in the Sunny South writes that our " work cannot but procure glory for God and save souls." From another religious living in the frozen North we received this cheering message : " I wish I could tell you what a comfort it is to know you are engaged in the work most needed now. I am too full of your laudable enterprise, which is and was my own pet scheme, to trust myself to say my say in a sufficiently coherent way to stand the test of cold print. If I were within reach of your Reading Circle, I do believe I would carry my presumption so far as to claim the privilege of speaking to the members at every meeting. I can only pray that our beloved Father Hecker's ideas may continue to be realized by his loyal sons. He must look down on you all with more than paternal love."

*　　　*　　　*

We are always pleased to get letters from young men, knowing as we do that in many places they have little opportunity to get at the works of Catholic authors. They read what comes *easily* within their reach, especially, and sometimes exclusively, newspapers. In the United States there are thousands of young men like the one who writes this letter :

" I have been recommended by a Christian Brother to write to the Columbian Reading Union for a list of books, with any information you could conveniently give. Will say that I am a Kerry boy, twenty-one years old, and five years in this country; and while I passed second stage of sixth class in the National schools to home, yet I read but few books there. In this country, however, I have learned, to some extent, to appreciate the value of books ; but my time for study is limited, as, being a bookkeeper, I work the greater part of my evenings. I would feel grateful for any information you might give, though, I suppose, it is difficult to wisely recommend books to one whose tastes you are not familiar with. To assist you, if possible, I will state what reading I enjoy. I love to read Dickens, not so much for his stories as for his sarcasm and the portrayal of those odd characters of his. I have greatly enjoyed *Ben Hur, Fabiola, Vicar of Wakefield*, and a few of Bulwer's works. I have the complete works of Bulwer. Which, if any, of them would you recommend me to read ? While I do not exactly know what I want, my preference is for historical novels, something not too deep or heavy. D. H. S.

" *St. Paul, Minn.*"

If our young friend from Kerry has access to a public library he will find in the *Encyclopædia Britannica* an impartial criticism of Bulwer's numerous writings in prose and verse. Many of his novels are pervaded with a low tone of morality, though his avowed purpose was to show " the affliction of the good and the triumph of the unprincipled." We would highly recommend to the writer of the above letter and to all Catholic young men a studious perusal of the work entitled *Rational Religion*, by Rev. John Conway, editor of the *Northwestern Chronicle*. It is a modern book for the modern need, the book for a busy man who is obliged to mingle with freethinkers and other non-Catholics.

*   *   *

The secretary of the Catholic Young Men's National Union has kindly sent us the proceedings of the sixteenth convention, held at Washington, D. C., October 7 and 8, 1890. We know of no other publication which contains so much valuable information for young men striving for self-improvement. In a pamphlet of over a hundred pages there are many notable addresses by eminent representatives of the clergy and laity. Among the many excellent papers and speeches we read with intense pleasure the eloquent speech of Hon. T. C. O'Sullivan, of New York, which won for him the greatest oratorical triumph of the convention. The masterly essay on Catholic literature by Mr. Condé B. Pallen, of St. Louis, fills twenty pages. It should be taken up in sections at the literary meetings of the Catholic young men's societies and thoroughly discussed. It will bear the closest inspection of critical students qualified to appreciate extensive learning, felicity of diction, and philosophical accuracy.

Some of our ablest writers are still Catholic young men. What are we doing to encourage them in their efforts to produce literature? Are we anxious to find out their works? How do we welcome books written by them? How often have we shown our appreciation of Catholic authors by purchasing their books in preference to others?

M. C. M.

WITH THE PUBLISHER.

WITH this issue THE CATHOLIC WORLD opens its fifty-third volume, and celebrates its twenty-sixth birthday. And the testimony is almost universal that it is "getting on" in every good quality as well as it is in years. Certainly the past year has been, in every respect, a bright one. Not only has the magazine become better and stronger from both the editorial and the financial standpoint, but there are many signs which augur even greater success during the year that is to come. As the public which THE CATHOLIC WORLD addresses is steadily growing, so the management is determined that in all its features the magazine shall keep pace with this growth. This pledge has been given to our readers repeatedly, and the history of the magazine during the past year is abundant evidence of the fidelity with which it has been kept.

**

The high standard of THE CATHOLIC WORLD, so successfully maintained during a quarter of a century, will be maintained and, as far as possible, surpassed in 1891. Plans for its improvement are always under discussion, and are matured and realized as soon as practicable. Some of these plans point to fundamental improvements, and we trust it will not be long before we shall be able not only to announce but to realize the improvements contemplated. The features of special interest in the fifty-third volume will be those that have been so popular in the past : the " Life of Father Hecker," which the Boston *Herald* declares to be " one of the best written stories of religious growth and change which has recently been published"; the " Talk about New Books," which many of our contemporaries say " is alone worth the price of the magazine "; the discussion of subjects of present interest in a spirit which is said to be "always broad, vigorous, and in the best sense progressive "; the Columbian Reading Union, which has done so much good in behalf of a more earnest study and appreciation of our Catholic writers. " The Old World as seen from the New " will be a new feature in THE CATHOLIC WORLD for 1891, and will treat all subjects of interest to American readers, especially subjects kindred to the social questions of the day, in condensed and pithy style, and in a just, candid, and thoroughly

Catholic spirit. As already announced, a number of articles on subjects suggested by the coming Columbian centenary are in progress and will be published during the year. The department "With the Publisher" (unavoidably "crowded out" last month) has had from the beginning a strong hold on the interest of our readers, as the Publisher himself has reason to know. Many rely upon its lists of new books for the month, and special means have been and will be employed to make this feature as accurate and reliable as is possible. This number appears, as has been already announced, in a bright, new cover of heavy paper and with some changes in the type, to relieve it of some of the heavy appearance urged against the former cover. Altogether we hope to make the new volume a memorable one.

⁂

And to do this thoroughly we again must call for assistance from our readers. We would like each one to feel that he or she must do something towards such a result. THE CATHOLIC WORLD was founded in a missionary spirit; its readers should partake of the same spirit. There are few who cannot influence at least one person, there are many who can do more. Very probably, a new subscriber is not always secured, but your words will bear fruit some day or other, and you do much in making the magazine known. There are many Catholics, and intelligent Catholics too, who do not know of THE CATHOLIC WORLD, or who do not know why they should read it; a word or two from you will make them subscribers. Make it a point, dear reader, to inquire among your immediate acquaintances and see how many of them know of the existence of the magazine, or of what subjects it treats, or why they are not subscribers. The Publisher is certain that you will be surprised with the majority of the replies, and that ignorance rather than economy, ignorance of its existence or its aims and character, will be the most frequent reply.

⁂

Let the Publisher take the following extracts from letters received during the past month as an "object lesson" to show what THE CATHOLIC WORLD is worth to its readers. These extracts are often little more than a single sentence sent with a renewal of a subscription.

"I read it carefully and always with great satisfaction and profit."

"Times are hard and ready money is always scarce here, but THE CATHOLIC WORLD has long been a *necessity* in my household."

"I don't agree with it always, but then it is always a good stimulant for thought."

"I am a busy man and can't read much, but your 'Talk about New Books' keeps me better acquainted with current literature than many of my acquaintances who have much more leisure than I."

"I have taken the magazine for twenty-two years, and simply couldn't do without it."

"A great monthly and growing better with every volume. Why can't you illustrate it?"

"We have a complete set in our library, and have the numbers bound as each volume is completed. The well-thumbed pages testify to the value our students place upon it."

"I made my acquaintance with THE CATHOLIC WORLD for the first time when I was a seminarian and the friendship has lasted ever since."

"Your last number was unusually interesting and that certainly means much."

"I read it regularly when still a Protestant, and only God knows how much I owe to it as a means of receiving the grace of Faith, now crowned with the priesthood."

✱✱

The Publisher trusts that these remarks will stimulate others of his readers to add their testimony to the benefit they receive from the magazine, and that they will give their friends and acquaintances the benefit of such testimony. Do something for THE CATHOLIC WORLD for the coming year: if you have done something already, let the memory of it serve to stimulate you to do more; if you have done nothing thus far, let the thought be a rebuke to your inactivity. You are doing more than securing subscribers for THE CATHOLIC WORLD (though you can do that more readily and with less trouble than a regular subscription agent); you are serving the cause of Catholic literature, and it needs such service in this country and at the present time.

✱✱

The Publisher wishes that every earnest reader of the magazine would take these words to heart, and would act upon them, and act upon them at once, and as a part of his duty. Don't be afraid of the trouble or inconvenience; it is little compared with the results. Let every reader adopt for the coming year a good motto the Publisher saw recently: "All those who pass through the door of success will find it labeled 'Push.'"

The Publisher wishes to call attention to the following note from the Editor: "Articles sent to the Editor for consideration must be accompanied by a stamped and addressed envelope, as well as by postage sufficient to return the manuscript, if not found available. Otherwise the Editor will not feel bound to acknowledge receipt."

The Catholic Publication Society Co. has in preparation:

> *The Life and Writings of Sir Thomas More.* By Rev. T. E. Bridgett, C.SS.R.

> *The Life of the Blessed Angelina Marsciano,* Foundress of the Third Order Regular of St. Francis of Assisi. By Mrs. Montgomery.

> Also a new and uniform edition of Mrs. Hope's works.

Nature's Wonder Workers is the title of some "Short Life Histories in the Insect World," by Kate R. Lovell, which the Cassell Publishing Company have ready. In this book the author's aim is to interest the reader in what are called the "useless insects." The information has been carefully collected from the best and latest authorities on entomology, and may be relied upon as far as it goes. She has made an admirable book to put into the hands of the young, to teach them that the most despised creatures that cross their path have their use in the world and should not be wantonly destroyed.

Francis Turner Palgrave's well-known anthology, *The Golden Treasury of Songs and Lyrics,* probably the most popular collection of its kind in English, has just made its appearance in a new edition in larger type. More than fifty new pieces have been added to this edition, chiefly from collections of Elizabethan songs, and the notes have been carefully revised throughout. The book is published by the Clarendon Press, and Macmillan & Co. are the agents in this country.

Benziger Brothers have just issued:

> *Letters of St. Alphonsus Maria de Liguori.* Part I. General Correspondence. (This is vol. 18 of the Centenary Edition of St. Alphonsus' works.) 12mo, cloth, net, $1.25.

> *Manual of Indulgenced Prayers.* Arranged and Disposed for Daily Use by Rev. Bonaventure Hammer, O.S.F. 32mo. Prices from 40 cents to $1.40.

> *Percy Wynn; or, Making a Boy of Him.* By Francis J. Finn, S.J. (Neenah). A story of college life. 12mo, cloth, $1.

Readings and Recitations for Juniors. By Miss Eleanor O'Grady, author of "'Aids to Elocution," etc. 16mo, cloth, net, 50 cents.

They have in preparation:

A Martyr of Our Own Times. Life of Rev. Just de Bretenières, Missionary Apostolic, màrtyred in Corea in 1866. From the French of Right Rev. Mgr. D'Hulst. Edited by Very Rev. J. R. Slattery, Rector of St. Joseph's Seminary, Baltimore, Md. 12mo, cloth, net, 75 cents.

Saints of the Society of Jesus. By Rev. D. A. Merrick, S.J. 16mo, cloth, net, 25 cents; paper, net, 10 cents.

Harper Bros. have published:

Our Italy. By Charles Dudley Warner. A description of the climate, scenery, and resources of Southern California.

Campmates: A Story of the Plains. By Kirke Monroe.

Lamb's Tales from Shakespeare's Tragedies. Edited, with notes, by Dr. Wm. J. Rolfe, and intended both as a "supplementary reading-book for children and as an introduction to the study of Shakespeare."

Sir Robert Peel. By Justin McCarthy, M.P.

Reminiscences of President Lincoln. By L. E. Chittenden.

Mr. C. S. Parker has edited, and Mr. John Murray of London will issue this month, a volume of *Sir Robert Peel's Letters*, covering the period when he was the Chief Secretary for Ireland.

A new edition of Stewart Rose's *St. Ignatius and the Early Jesuits* is announced by Burns & Oates. It will contain about one hundred illustrations.

In their "English Men of Action" series Macmillan & Co. have just issued *Warwick, the Kingmaker*, by C. W. Oman, M.A.

Houghton, Mifflin & Co. have published the sixth volume of James Russell Lowell's collected writings, embracing his literary and political addresses during the period of his life abroad as minister to England.

A work of much interest is soon to be issued by the Putnams, *The Life and Writings of George Mason of Virginia.* By Miss Kate Mason Rowland, his great-granddaughter. He was a conspicuous figure in the "constitutional era" of this country. He opposed presidency as well as monarchy, advocated such ministerial government as now prevails in England, and was one of the three members of the Constitutional Convention of 1787 who refused to sign the Constitution.

BOOKS ˙RECEIVED.

LIFE OF JOHN BOYLE O'REILLY. By James Jeffrey Roche. His complete
Poems and Speeches. Introduction by Cardinal Gibbons. New York:
Cassell Publishing Co.

THE NEGRO PROBLEM. By W. Cabell Bruce. Baltimore: John Murphy &
Co.

FRANCISCAN TERTIARY ALMANAC for 1891. Containing Useful Historical
Notes. Compiled by the Franciscan (Capuchin) Fathers. Pantosoph,
Holywell, North Wales.

CHRISTIAN ART IN OUR OWN AGE. By Eliza Allen Starr. Notre Dame,
Ind. : Office of the *Ave Maria.*

SELECTED SERMONS. By the Rev. Christopher Hughes. Introduction by the
Rev. Walter Elliott, C.S.P. New York and Cincinnati: Fr. Pustet &
Co.

SEVEN SUNDAYS IN HONOR OF ST. JOSEPH. From the Spanish. New York,
Cincinnati, Chicago: Benziger Bros.

IN DARKEST LONDON. By John Law. London : William Reeves.

THE KEYS OF ST. PETER. By J. P. Val D'Ereamo, D.D. Dublin : Browne
& Nolan.

AT OBER–AMMERGAU. By P. J. O'Reilly. London : Catholic Truth Society.

HISTORY OF THE CHURCH. By the Rev. J. A. Birkhaeuser. Second edition.
Revised and enlarged New York and Cincinnati: Fr. Pustet & Co.

THE SOUL OF MAN. By Dr. Paul Carus. Chicago : Open Court Publishing
Co.

LADY MERTON. By J. C. Heywood. London : Burns & Oates ; New York:
Catholic Publication Society Co.

NOVENA IN HONOR OF ST. JOSEPH. New York: P. O'Shea.

COUNSELS OF ST. ANGELA. New York, Cincinnati, Chicago: Benziger
Brothers,

POEMS, SKETCHES OF MOSES TRADDLES. Cincinnati : Keating & Co.

NOS MAÎTRES. Par l'Abbé F. Brettes. Paris: Gaumé et Cie. New York :
Benziger Bros.

STARS IN ST. DOMINIC'S CROWN. By Thomas Austin Dyson, Priest of the
same order. New York: D. & J. Sadlier & Co.

THE NEW REFORMATION. By Prognostic. Published by the Author, New
York P. O.

VIEWS OF JESUS. By Joseph Henry Crookes. Boston : American Unitarian
Association.

PAMPHLETS RECEIVED.

OUR LADY OF MERCY. A Sermon by the Very Rev. Daniel I. McDermott,
Rector of St. Mary's Church, Philadelphia.

THE CATHOLIC CHURCH AND THE AMERICAN REPUBLIC. A lecture by Wm.
F. Markoe, Esq. St. Paul: The Catholic Truth Society of America.

MATERIA EXAMINIS PRO BACCALAUREATU IN S. THEOLOGIA. Apud Uni-
versitatem Catholicam Americæ.

KALENDARIUM FACULTATIS THEOLOGICÆ. Universitatis Catholicæ Americæ. Pro Anno Scholastico, 1890–91.

NINETEENTH ANNUAL REPORT OF THE LE COUTEULX ST. MARY'S INSTITU-
TION FOR THE IMPROVED INSTRUCTION OF DEAF MUTES. Albany:
James B. Lyon.

EIGHTH ANNUAL REPORT OF THE CATHOLIC BENEVOLENT UNION OF NEW
JERSEY. Newark: L. J. Hardham.

THE

CATHOLIC WORLD.

VOL. LIII.   MAY, 1891.   No. 314.

THE CATHOLIC CLERGY AND THE LIQUOR-TRAF-FIC BEFORE THE NEW YORK LEGISLATURE.

ON reliable authority the charge has been made frequently that the agents of the liquor-traffic are sapping the foundations of representative government by their incessant attempts to usurp the power of making and unmaking laws to advance their own selfish interests. They ask for nothing less than a vicious system of class. legislation. The ominous warnings of enlightened citizens and distinguished clergymen from all parts of the United States have failed in many sections of the country to arouse the public mind to a vivid sense of the impending dangers, held in check only by the legal safeguards of sobriety. While ministers of various denominations were preaching vigorously in their pulpits on the ideal splendor of Prohibition, and elucidating futile distinctions as to Bible wines, crafty liquor-dealers and avaricious brewers have multiplied saloons, secured the appointment of their own dupes on excise boards, and with threats and bribes have induced the police, together with judges on·the bench, to conspire with them against the enforcement of laws imposing reasonable restraints on the hateful vice of intemperance. Unblushingly they claim the exclusive right to name candidates for office, and glory in their shame when they collect and disburse large sums of money in every election for the defeat of able men pledged to the maintenance of law and order. Renegade lawyers, self-seeking aspirants for judicial honors, and especially ex-judges of profligate life, are now employed to degrade their noble profession in the service of the beer barons, who are by all odds the most dangerous monopolists now existing on American soil.

A rude awakening has taken place within the past few months in the minds of many observant citizens of New York. Evidence of a startling character was furnished, showing that the liquor-trade, wholesale and retail, had combined to purchase for certain bills of their own manufacture the right of way through both houses of the Legislature and a cordial welcome in the governor's mansion. Following quickly after this disclosure of an insolent and aggressive attempt to control the representatives of the people came the astounding news that the notorious all-night dance-hall bill, introduced by Mr. Stadler, had been read with approval twice by the senators of New York State, and by unanimous consent was ordered to a third reading. Two votes more would have made it a law in the Assembly. It was proposed that this license for dance-halls to sell liquors at all hours of the night be granted only to respectable parties. The excise committee of the Assembly refused to accept any amendments. Unseemly haste was shown to advance the bill, and to allow no opportunity for the discussion of objections. Law-abiding citizens were at a loss to discover the hidden power which impelled their representatives at Albany to vote for a bill that allowed dance-halls, dives, and other similar places full power to turn night into day by selling liquor without cessation. Among Catholics it is well known that some years ago the late John Kelly had to exert all the power at his command to banish from New York the disreputable concert-saloons, known as dives, which were kept open the whole night as haunts for the worst characters, to shelter vice and immorality.

According to the testimony of competent lawyers, the Stadler bill was well calculated to promote public disturbance of the peace, especially after midnight; and to foster intemperance and vice by giving legal sanction for all-night bars to the worst class of dance-halls. New incentives to excessive drinking during the hours devoted to rest would inevitably result from such a law. After discussing fully these dangers, several priests of New York City resolved to make a joint protest. Then it was suggested that many others would gladly take part in the movement, and accordingly a petition was prepared which met with general approval.

On Saturday, February 21, the circulation of the petition was begun, and when it was sent to the Speaker of the Assembly on Tuesday, February 24, a large number of signatures were appended. Many more names would have been added had there been time, but it was decided that prompt action was needed. Duplicate copies of the petition were forwarded to Mayor Grant and General Husted. Some of the clergymen sent a protest direct to their local representatives in the Legislature. In Brooklyn and other places the priests in various ways took action in this important matter to show that they are determined to do their duty as citizens and as pastors in defending the moral and material welfare of the community endangered by new measures introduced at Albany which would remove entirely the existing legal restraints justly imposed upon the liquor-traffic.

It will be noticed that the petition, which is here given, was framed to secure prompt and decided action, not to provoke discussion on open questions. As now existing the excise laws contain at least some salutary restrictions which can be enforced :

To the Honorable the Legislature of the State of New York :

We, the undersigned Catholic Clergymen of the City of New York, are entirely opposed to the Stadler bill or any other measure legalizing the sale of liquor after midnight.

We consider every such measure as highly detrimental to the moral and material welfare of the community.

We therefore petition your honorable body to reject any bill permitting the relaxation of existing laws.

(*Signed :*)

Very Rev. Mgr. J. M. Farley,
Rev. John Edwards,
" Daniel T. Cronin,
" Francis X. Kelly,
" W. J. Hogan,
" John J. Kean,
" Thomas F. Lynch,
" John J. Carr,
" Peter McNamee,
" Peter Spellman,
" William F. Dougherty,
" Michael C. O'Farrell,
" Francis P. Moore,
" Thomas F. Cusack,
" Matthew Bohn,
" Francis Delargy,
" John Hickey,
" Caspar G. Ritter,
" James J. Flood, .
" Patrick Kelly,
" Edward J. Holden,
" John F. Woods,
" James W. Power,
" John McQuirk, D.D.,
" P. F. McSweeny, D.D.,
" Daniel P. Ward,

Rev. P. J. Martin,
" J. H. Slinger, O.P.,
" J. P. Turner, O.P.,
" J. A. Leonard, O. P.,
" M. A. Sheehan, O.P.,
" P. V. Keogh, O.P.,
" T. S. McGovern, O.P.,
" George Deshon,
" Walter Elliott,
" Alfred Young,
" Edward B. Brady,
" Thomas V. Robinson,
" Clarence E. Woodman,
" John J. Hughes,
" Charles J. Powers,
" Martin J. Casserly,
Very Rev. Joseph F. Mooney,
Rev. Bernard J. Duffy,
" Edward H. Cronin,
" J. D. Roach,
" John J. O'Donnell,
" P. B. Frey,
" A. Duckgeischel,
" P. B. Grebbels,
" Francis May,
" Albert Locher,

Rev. M. Reid,
" Charles H. Colton,
" Benjamin J. O'Callaghan,
" John P. Chidwick,
" John J. McCabe,
" Edward P. Southwell, O.C.C.,
" Michael B. Daly, O.C.C.,
" J. E. Whitley, O.C.C.,
" Thomas I. Feehan, O.C.C.,
" W. J. Kelly, O.C.C.,
" Michael J. A. Welsh, O.C.C.,
" Albert J. Bader, O.C.C.,
" James A. Dooley, O.C.C.,
" Henry A. Brann, D.D.,
" Joseph F. Sheahan,
" Henry T. Newey,
" M. Callaghan,
" M. Cahill,
" J. Brosnan,
" F. M. Fagan,
" W. J. Guinon, D.D.,
" H. J. Kelly,
" N. J. Hughes,
" William Everett,
" Michael J. Phelan,
" Michael J. McEvoy,
" Christopher B. O'Reilly,
" Thomas W. Wallace,
" John Talbot Smith,
" Thomas W. Grennan,
" J. M. Galligan,
" E. V. Higgins,

Rev. L. Beck,
" P. J. Waldmann,
" M. A. Nolan,
" John J. Keogan,
" W. D. Hughes,
" Michael Otis,
" Gilbert Simmons,
" Alexander P. Doyle,
" Thomas McMillan,
" Arthur M. Clark,
" Walter E. Hopper,
" Thomas Burke,
" P. G. Tandy,
" James T. McEntyre,
" Peter J. Prendergast, D.D.,
" Matthew J. Dougherty,
" Wm. A. O'Neill,
" M. J. Mulhern,
" John J. Morris,
" John E. Burke,
" Thomas O'Keefe,
Very Rev. W. L. Penny,
"   " E. McKenna,
Rev. John T. Power,
" James Nilan,
" Joseph P. Egan,
" C. G. O'Keeffe,
" P. E. McCorry,
" James F. Mee,
" J. P. McClancy,
" P. J. O'Meara,
" Cornelius V. Mahony, D.D.

Necessarily there were many expressions of opinion given while the petition was in circulation. From the selections which follow it is obvious there is a general conviction that the time has come for a fearless utterance in church and in the market-place of Catholic teaching on intemperance and its sources.

The Rev. Father Phelan, in addition to sending a protest to Albany, published in a local paper this scorching letter:

"I have just signed a protest to the Stadler bill brought me by a clerical friend, and am not quite satisfied that I have done all my duty, but wish here to voice my protest publicly against any attempt on the part of our representative to vote in its favor. We have, as it is, an overflow of rum. Will the people of this city remain passive while the brewery syndicates are endeavoring to establish their pumps at every corner? Is there any want of it at present, or do we want more? There is a rider in this Stadler bill which will give to every hoodlum association with a concertina the right to sell beer all the night through.

"I asked a well-known gentleman in this city what he thought of Liverpool, and his reply was that there was an overflow of rum in it.

"Do we want such scenes enacted here as there—men, women,

and girls in all stages of inebriety, with pails and bottles in their hands, awaiting in hundreds the opening of the groggeries? Will the practical Catholic or the law-abiding citizen promote such a state of things? I am sure from my own experience that our Catholic congregations are in sympathy with their priests, and that if called together would voice their protest in no uncertain sound. I call, then, upon our representative to save us from this awful danger by at least not giving his vote to a bill that will be in the interest of brothels and dives of every sort.

" I call upon every father and mother living within the limits of this parish to see to it that his boy and girl be kept from such a danger, and to tell their representative that he cannot promote such evils with impunity. I am sure that I may call upon many a liquor-seller who loves decency and order to respond, and he will do so because of the burning shame that will mark us through the infamy that is sure to follow.

" Let us all strive to be on the side of law and order. We are not observing the excise laws as they stand; still, it is better to make a show of observance rather than have our city made by law one open dance-hall all the night long. I believe I express the feeling of fully six thousand people of my parish when I say that we do not want any such bill passed."

Rev. Father Power was asked his opinion of the Stadler bill, and shown a copy of Father Phelan's letter.

"I endorse," said he, "Father Phelan's letter. The passage of the bill means the sale of drink all night. It means that the power for evil of the dives is to be increased. The bill is disgraceful, and it has been my intention to write to our Assemblyman."

"The saloons are ruining the people," said Rev. Father Carmody, "and, unless something is done, I do not know what will become of us. The present generation is bad enough, but the next will be far worse. The State seems to care nothing for the well-being of the citizens. In one block near here there are seven saloons, all of the worst class, dealing out ruin to the poor people in whose midst they are situated. There would probably be one opposite the church were it not for my strenuous resistance. Clergymen may labor until they are gray-headed without being able to counteract the mischief which is done by the saloons. After remaining open all day and half the night the saloon-keepers should be satisfied. I am entirely opposed to any measure like the Stadler bill."

"The saloon is not a bedroom," said Rev. Father Kennedy, "and when midnight comes it is time for it to be closed. I am, therefore, wholly opposed to any measure that would extend the time when saloons might be open, or that would make night a period of noise and riot instead of sleep and quiet.

If it is desirable to allow the sale of wine at balls after one o'clock, there should be special licenses granted without resorting to a device that will allow every saloon in the city to remain open all night instead of those only whom it is proposed to affect. Allowing them to remain open after twelve o'clock, when every one should be home, is only multiplying the evil."

. At the Church 'of St. Paul the Apostle Rev. Father Elliott addressed the congregation, drawing their attention to the necessity of parents and guardians, as well as clergymen, doing everything in their power to lessen instead of increasing the facilities for the desecration of the Lord's Day. The saloons are now the means of doing untold harm among the families of the community, and every thoughtful Christian and patriotic citizen must feel it a matter of conscience to resist any attempt to relax the laws. He besought every one to use in his individual sphere all his influence for the protection of the community from still further havoc. The address was very impressive, and the feeling among the Paulist Fathers and their parishioners is strong and decided on this matter.

During his long residence at Albany the Rev. C. A. Walworth has had unusual opportunities to study the legal side of the temperance question. For many years he has rendered heroic service for law and order. In the pulpit and before numerous excise committees of the Legislature his voice has been heard defending the rights of virtue and morality. After the Speaker of the Assembly refused a hearing to the petition of the priests, Father Walworth delivered a powerful discourse to his people, in which he said :

"We know, brethren, what the liquor-league wants and demands. What do we want ? Shall we be quiet and say nothing ? Our Legislature opens its ears readily to the demands of the liquor-trade, and so confidentially that bills are almost passed before we hear of them. But when hundreds of Catholic clergymen speak to them in remonstrance they are spurned as unworthy of notice. Then wonderful rules develop from the blue book. It is good to be quiet and docile when our rulers are making laws for us; but is it disorderly to exercise the right of petition ? Is it wrong to feel hurt when the courtesy which is given to others is refused to us ? Are our interests less dear than those of the liquor-trade ? "

Under strong pressure of public opinion the Excise Committee of the Assembly reluctantly gave an hour for a hearing to the opponents of the Schaff bill, one of whom urged that the bill be sent to•the Sadducees, who say there is no resurrection. On this occasion Father Walworth forcibly insisted that God has a valid claim to be represented among law-makers. He said :

".I know of no place, whether it be in the church or the Assembly hall, where the voice of God has not a right to be heard. The people have spoken against this measure, and they have spoken against the unrestricted sale of liquors. They are not in the mist regarding these things. For many long years have their voices been heard against just such measures as this. I have heard a great deal about the doings of the Germans, who meet and drink their beer, and that it does not affect them. That is false. I have been among them at those times, and I declare that it is not so. When men stagger and talk foolishly they are drunk. Years ago, when the question came up as to whether or not ale and beer were intoxicating, it was referred to the Court of Errors, which declared that they were intoxicating.

"What is the voice that is now asking for this added authority? Is it the voice of the people of the State of New York, who are the true constituents of the members of the Senate and the Assembly? No; it is the fearful power of the 40,000 liquor-dealers, who now hold the whip over the political parties of the country, and tell them to do just as they ask. The Excise Association, which I represent, does not want this bill amended— does not want the bill at all. It is a vicious and mischief-making measure."

It has been said that there is nothing more sacred in the eyes of Americans than the right of petition. It is a right guaranteed by the United States Constitution, and by the Constitution of the State of New York. It is one of the inalienable rights, and cannot be nullified by sending a petition unread to a committee. A petition for the moral welfare of the community is an expression of public opinion, and should be read to the Legislature for its information. Blue books must be made subordinate to the Constitution, and so interpreted. The Continental Congress in 1774 declared that the foundation of all free governments is the right in the people to participate in their legislative council ; and that this right was ignored when the English king treated with contempt dutiful and reasonable petitions.

Thomas Jefferson was convinced that deliberative bodies have always permitted the reading of petitions. His own personal opinion is stated in these words: "I am for the freedom of the press, and against all violations of the Constitution to silence by force and not by reason the complaints or criticisms, just or unjust, of our citizens against the conduct of their agents." In his *Manual for Parliamentary Practice* Jefferson says: "Before any petition shall be received and read, whether introduced by the President or a member, a brief statement of the contents shall verbally be. made by the introducer."

It is very significant that the objections to the reading of the priests' petition in the New York Legislature seemed to emanate chiefly from members whose names are associated with the introduction of the worst excise bills ever prepared by the liquor-dealers in this country. The account of the attempt to cast aside contemptuously a deliberate judgment representing thousands of sober and intelligent citizens is well worth reproduction here from the privileged statement made to the Legislature by the Hon. Hamilton Fish, Jr., whose persistent action in this matter deserves honorable mention:

"Inasmuch as the Speaker of the House, in his remarks yesterday in justification of his course with reference to the petition of the Catholic clergy against the liquor-bills, saw fit to allude to my action in the matter, I ask the indulgence of the House in replying thereto. That the rules provide that petitions may be presented to the clerk cannot be controverted. The only way in which any petition, no matter from what source (other than State offices), can be read or brought to the attention of the House is by unanimous consent to its reading being granted by the House.

"Being familiar with the rules of the House, when the petition was handed down on Feb. 25 to the clerk by the Speaker I demanded the reading of the petition. The Speaker refused to even entertain the motion; and referred it to the Committee on Excise, where it has since lain buried, no opportunity being afforded for it to see the light of day or to permit the members of the House to become familiar with its contents. The following day, as the journal of the House containing the record of proceedings of the previous day, prepared by the clerk under the direction of the Speaker, made no mention of the motion made by me to have the petition read, I moved to correct the journal by inserting the fact that I had made such motion. The Speaker refused to entertain that motion. Upon several occasions since I have asked unanimous consent to present the petition from the same source and to have it read, and I have been refused permission by members of the majority party of this House, on one occasion by the Democratic leader.

"The Speaker in his remarks stated that he had no objection to the rules being so amended as to provide an order of business for the introduction of petitions. Allow me to call his attention to the fact that last week, when I gave notice of a motion to change the rules so as to permit the introduction and reading of petitions from religious bodies I was refused the opportunity by an objection made by a Democratic member. Every one familiar with the proceedings of this Assembly of the State of New York knows that the rules are waived almost daily and unanimous consent thereto is obtained. The rules of the House provide that bills may be deposited at any time during the session in a box to be known as the 'bill box,' and yet frequently bills are introduced by members arising in their seats. A conspicuous violation of the rules, and with the acquiescence of the Speaker, was the passage of the Rapid-Transit bill. It certainly would not have required as much exertion upon the part of the Speaker to have secured permission from his side of the House—for every objection to its reading came from that quarter—to the reading of the petition in question.

"The reference of the Speaker in his statement of yesterday to the communication of the grand jury of the county of New York, and his justification for holding it to be privileged under the rules, cannot turn the attention of this House and the people of the State from the fact that the right of people representing a large body of reputable citizens to present to the open Assembly a petition against what they considered a dangerous bill has been denied them. Neither is his ruling that grand juries are State officers tenable. No one would be so bold as to hold that a justice of the peace, although a part of the judicial system of the State, was a State officer, much less can it be held as to a grand jury.

"There has never been a moment from the time that the petition was presented to the present that there was any objection to its being read made by any member of the minority party, and that the House has not been made familiar with the contents of such petition can be charged only to the majority of this House.

"And, in closing, permit me to say that during the eight years, that I have been a member of the Legislature I do not recall another instance where a petition upon any moral question coming from a reputable source has been denied a reading when demanded."

From present indications it will be many years before Speaker Sheehan is allowed to forget his unfair discrimination against the reputable petition sent by priests well qualified to give advice concerning the moral welfare of the community. For a very short time his decision caused great rejoicing among the liquor-dealers and their legal (?) advisers. The Catholic people, however, do not allow such an insult to pass unrebuked. Without delay a number of prominent laymen took up the matter, and an effective plan was put into operation, which transferred the dis-. cussion of the clergymen's petition and the reasons for it from the Legislature to the domestic circle. It was decided to issue a circular embodying the suppressed petition, the teaching of the Catholic prelates of the United States on saloons, and a protest against the newly introduced Schaff Excise Bill, appropriately called "the liquor-dealer's dream." By the plan devised for the distribution of this circular it was read in one day by over half a million people. The signers of this second petition explained their attitude in these words:

"We have adopted this plan of publishing a circular to mani-' fest our hearty concurrence in the good work done by the clergy, and to secure for our fellow-Catholics a correct statement of the facts. As citizens, recognizing the right of appeal to the Legislature to prevent unjust laws, we also desire to enter our indignant protest against the members of the Assembly who voted to sustain the Speaker in refusing a hearing to the petition signed by so many of our distinguished priests. We now present it again to the Legislature, and at the same time enter a public protest against the Schaff Excise Bill."

A very important part of the work of the laity in giving practical effect to the circular was cheerfully undertaken by the Holy Name Society, which has several thousand members enrolled in New York City. The arrogance of the liquor-trade, and its bold defiance of the moral restraints necessary to check the growth of vice, received a severe rebuke in the resolutions passed by the members of this society, which has for its special object the prevention of vicious and profane language. As delegates in convention, and as individual members of the Holy Name Society, they decided that the sins of the tongue are directly traceable to intemperance and the saloons. They likewise declared their confidence in the Catholic clergy as the highest representatives of law and order, entitled to a hearing in the Legislature. St. John the Evangelist's Temperance Society, St. Paul's Guild, and many other similar organizations held special meetings, and devised practical measures to urge upon public officials their responsibility for the spread of intemperance. At these meetings the so-called Catholic saloon-keepers, conspicuous in nearly every parish for violating divine and human laws, were reprobated as unworthy members of the church, which has always and everywhere been opposed to the degrading sin of drunkenness.

Some may wish to inquire what practical results have followed from this movement begun by the Catholic clergy, and vigorously endorsed by the laity. The spontaneous action of the clergy has shown to all citizens, more particularly to non-Catholics, that the priests are in hearty accord with the decisions of the archbishops and bishops concerning the dangers to religion and country which flow from the liquor-traffic as it now exists. No theological opinion of former centuries, based on a limited knowledge of European society, can claim an authority equal to the positive judgment given by the prelates of the United States, at Baltimore, in the year 1884, contained in this passage:

"It is hardly possible for us to restrain our impatience when we see Catholic emigrants crowding in such numbers into towns. There they toil for their daily bread at the most laborious occupations; in those populous cities they remain, with scarcely any hope of securing more than the barest necessaries of life. There they live in filth and squalor, amidst liquor-sellers and saloon-keepers, and the most depraved of mankind. It is in such cities that the pitfalls of vice are most numerous; it is there that it is the most difficult to instruct children in Christian doctrine and train them up in sound morality.

"There can be no manner of doubt that the abuse of intoxicating drinks is to be reckoned among the most deplorable evils of this country. This excess is an unceasing stimulant to vice and a fruitful source of misery; vast numbers of men and entire families are plunged into hopeless ruin, and multitudes of souls are by it dragged headlong into eternal perdition. Now, because the ravages of this vice extend not a little among Catholics, non-Catholics are much scandalized and a great obstacle is set up against the spread of the true religion. Hence it behooves all Christians to be filled with zeal against this vice, and for the love of God and of country to endeavor to root out this pestilential evil.

"Finally, we warn Catholics engaged in the sale of intoxicating drinks to consider seriously by how many and how great dangers, by how many and how great occasions of sin, their business —though in itself not unlawful—is surrounded. Let them, if they can, choose a more becoming way of making a living. Let them, at any rate, strive with all their might to remove occasions of sin as well from themselves as from others. They must not sell drink to minors—that is to say, to those who have not come of age; nor to those who they foresee will abuse it. They must keep their saloons closed on Sunday, and never allow blasphemy, cursing, or obscene language. Saloon-keepers should know that, if through their culpable neglect or co-operation religion is brought into contempt, or men brought to ruin, there is an Avenger in heaven who will surely exact from them the severest penalties.

"There is one way of profaning the Lord's Day which is so prolific of evil results that we consider it our duty to utter against it a special condemnation. This is the practice of selling beer or other liquors on Sunday or of frequenting places where they are sold. This practice tends more than any other to turn the Day of the Lord into a day of dissipation—to use it as an occasion for breeding intemperance. While we hope that Sunday laws on this point will not be relaxed, but even more rigidly enforced, we implore all Catholics, for the love of God and of country, never to take part in such Sunday traffic, nor to patronize or countenance it. And we not only direct the attention of all pastors to the repression of this abuse, but we also call upon them to induce all of their flocks that may be engaged in the sale of liquors to abandon as soon as they can the dangerous traffic, and to embrace a more becoming way of making a living.

"And here it behooves us to remind our workingmen, the bone and sinew of the people, and the specially beloved children of the church, that if they wish to observe Sunday as they ought they must keep away from drinking places on Saturday night. Carry your wages home to your families, where they rightfully belong. Turn a deaf ear, therefore, to every temptation, and then Sunday will be a bright day for all the family. How much better this than to make it a day of sin for yourselves, and of gloom and wretchedness for your homes, by a Saturday night's folly or debauch. No wonder that the prelates of the Second Plenary Council declared that ' the most shocking scandals which we have to deplore spring from intemperance.' No wonder that they gave a special approval to the zeal of those who, the better to avoid excess, or in order to give bright example, pledge themselves to total abstinence. Like them, we invoke a blessing on the cause of temperance and on all who are laboring for its advancement in a true Christian spirit.

"A Christian should carefully avoid not only what is positively evil, but what has even the appearance of evil, and more especially whatever commonly leads to it. Therefore, Catholics should generously renounce all recreations and all kinds of business which may interfere with keeping holy the Lord's Day, or which are calculated to lead to the violation of the laws of God or of the state. The worst, without doubt, is the carrying on of business in bar-rooms and saloons on Sunday, a traffic by means of which so many and such grievous injuries are done to religion and society. Let pastors earnestly labor to root out this evil; let them admonish and entreat; let them even resort to threatenings and penalties when it becomes necessary. They should do all that belongs to their office to efface this stain, now nearly the only blot remaining among us, obscuring the splendor of the day of the Lord."

The supreme pastors of the Catholic Church, after mature consideration, gave a final decision on the question of saloons in their proximate relations to the vice of intemperance. Whatever concessions may be extorted from civil tribunals by the liquor-trade, it cannot claim to be a privileged business among Catholics. Let the responsibility of relaxing the laws which make for virtue and sobriety be placed where it belongs. Catholics worthy of the name will take no part in giving the sanction of law to the iniquitous demands for increasing the occasions of sin.

Church work in large cities is much impeded by the many temptations which surround the homes of the people. Among zealous members of the St. Vincent de Paul Conferences and other benevolent organizations the conviction is fast gaining strength that intemperance is not lessened by liberal gifts to those who squander their earnings in drink. Practical experience of life in tenement-houses has taught them, as it has taught many pastors, that obdurate evil-doers find refuge in the saloons and yield to no influence save the strong arm of the law. Hence the relaxation of legal restraints is an evil to be feared by the benefactors of the poor as well as by good citizens. From the ranks of the active workers in the cause of charity came many expressions of approval for the fearless denunciation of the Stadler and Schaff excise bills, both of which are now reported dead. Through the exertions of these enlightened laymen, prompted by love of the poor and by patriotism, a number of the Germans of New York earnestly lent their aid to this movement in defence of sobriety. Public opinion, as reflected in the columns of the press and in letters received from trustworthy sources, abundantly proves that Catholics have achieved a great moral victory at a time when the enemies of law and order were most sanguine of success.   THOMAS MCMILLAN.

Church of St. Paul the Apostle, New York City.

CHANGE.

TO-NIGHT the sea intones a sullen dirge,
    Wringing white hands of foam o'er wasted ships;
Another moon, in sportive mood, its surge
    Will laugh and sing like any lover's lips.

To-night, o'er wrecks of ruined hopes, thy voice
    Takes on a mourner's tone, O sobbing heart!
To-morrow thou 'lt forget it and rejoice.
    Through storm and calm most like the sea thou art,
      Of fickle mood!

Philadelphia.   PATRICK J. COLEMAN.

"EDUCATED ABOVE THEIR STATION?"

IT seems strangely incongruous in this day of almost phenomenal intellectual activity to hear the complaint raised every
now and then that our efforts to extend educational advantages
to their farthest limit is doing harm, not to single individuals
merely, but to a whole class—and that one of the largest. Yet
the fact is we do hear it charged, both in private discourse and
in public print, that our Catholic schools are educating the
daughters of poor parents above the station intended for them,
thereby leading them into discontent and unhappiness, and unfit-
ting them to become the wives of poor, uneducated Catholic
men. The inference is not boldly stated, but the one we are evidently expected to draw is that, therefore, we are not doing a
good thing for these girls. Such an idea is antiquated and un-
progressive enough to be startling. Its enunciation at once fills
the bolder advocates of unrestricted education with indignation,
while the more timid ones simply tremble as they foresee new
versions of old slanders against the church, bolstered up, for
proof, by quotations of such expressions from the mouths of
Catholic men and women. Yet those who suggest that less or
perhaps no education would be a better thing for the daughters
of the illiterate poor, deserve to be enlightened rather than condemned. In a blind way they have stumbled upon a really
great evil, for which they have assigned a wrong cause. For,
after all, facts in abundance can certainly be quoted by the pastor of every parish of any considerable size which might seem
at first glance to justify such a very discouraging conclusion as
the one given above. Indeed, not only pastors but almost every
Catholic who reads this paper will readily call to mind at least
one case in point: some young girl who has been given an education at the cost of much self-denial on the part of her poor
and illiterate but ambitious parents; and whose peevish discontent
in her home surroundings has seemed to grow in direct proportion to her advancement in science, literature, and art ; who despises the occupations and aims of her parents, yet strives in
vain to find better ones for herself, and who discovers at last
that her chances for usefulness and happiness are lessened, or
even destroyed, seemingly by the sole fact of her education.
The picture is pitiable enough, and unfortunately represents a

state of things so common as to fill every thoughtful mind with anxiety. No wonder, then, that even among the learned and wise some have been tempted to deprecate any educational movement which seems to threaten an increase of so serious a difficulty. Let us be glad that even in a blundering way our attention has been called to the matter, though happily certain that the conclusion we are asked to base upon the facts adduced is not a true one.

Both our objectors and the teachers whom they would call to account have failed to grasp the true meaning of the word education; for, in spite of much talking and writing to the contrary, the idea is still wide-spread that education consists merely in forcing into growing minds a greater or less conglomeration of facts, and, in the case of girls, in giving additionally an outward veneering of "elegant and useful accomplishments." This misconception of the thing for which the term education stands is the explanation of the very deplorable fact that many of our girl graduates seem, from their discontented and unfruitful lives, to have no reason for being, and is at the same time the excuse for those who ask, "Would it not have been as well for them if these girls had not been educated?" Certainly, if that which they have acquired is education, it would be better if they had not been educated. But they are not educated. Some attainments they have, such as undigested facts in science; second, third, or fourth-hand opinions concerning the masters of English literature; more or less skill in putting in points and commas, and in sewing embroidery silks into velvet, and, crowning all, a great many rules in etiquette. But this may not be education. It is often mental, and sometimes even moral, chaos, but it is not necessarily education; for education, as every work on pedagogy tells us, is a development of the enfolded powers, and has for its highest and final aim the production of a strong and noble character in its subject. Failing in this, it has failed in everything. And that school which sends out a girl graduate filled with a knowledge no matter how extensive, yet unimbued with a strong sense of the duty of cheerfulness and contentment; full of aroused activities, yet helpless to make or find for them a legitimate outlet, has not educated her, and deserves to bear the blame of her failure and of her unhappiness. If the number of such girls is notably large, our conclusion should be, not that *education* is bad for them, but that the methods pursued in the schools from which they come demand improvement. The thing such institutions offer as education is a counterfeit article, capable of doing active harm.

But those people who talk about educating a poor girl above her station have not only, along with many others, misapplied the term education. They labor under still another misapprehension when they speak of a poor girl's "station." What decides any girl's station in this democratic land and age of ours? Is there a nineteenth-century American who acknowledges any law that says the daughter of a hod-carrier must, for the sake of the eternal fitness of things, become the wife of a hod-carrier and the mother and grandmother of hod-carriers? Would the social edifice be in any danger if at this moment all the daughters of hod-carriers in America were resolved to become the wives of bricklayers and the mothers of architects? It is rapidly coming to pass under this supremely blessed American flag of ours that a girl's station is determined by the same laws as those which determine her brother's. Her station is upon that plane which she can reach and hold by her own abilities, and, consequently, it is hardly correct to say that a girl has any station at the age when she leaves school. Her father's station is not necessarily hers, and she has yet to attain the one which, by right of ability and force of circumstances, will properly belong to her. Now, if a girl's station depends upon her own abilities, native and acquired, and if true education means simply the full development of all her powers, how can there possibly be such a thing as educating a girl above her station? Her teachers will do well if they educate her up to her station. They can never hope to do more, and, unfortunately, as our schools go, they seldom do that much. But while our schools cannot, from the nature of things, commit the impossibility of educating a girl (be she poor or otherwise) above her station, some of them do unwittingly compass as full a measure of mischief as lies in their power. They do in perfect good faith decoy many a daughter of poor parents out of the station of her childhood without showing her the way to any other; or, if we permit ourselves the use of the word education in the false sense so often assigned it, we may say that these girls are educated below the station of their parents; for only too often a girl of this class seems after an extended school career incapable of even perceiving, much less of performing, the duties peculiar to her difficult situation. She gets an "education" which gives her taste enough to discern the defects of her home surroundings, but not knowledge sufficient to remedy them; which awakens desires for better things, but confers no skill to accomplish their fulfilment. No wonder that now and then some one feels impelled to question the wisdom of that "educating" process which is the undeniable cause of such results.

Those who undertake to train the daughters of poor and illiterate parents assume a task as great as it is delicate. For, if she be truly educated, such a girl must be to that rude, humble, and probably unwisely-administered household a bringer of light and a prophet of better things, both material and spiritual. Her scientific insight into the wonders of the economy of nature must show her ways of making the meagre income of the poor home compass more of the comforts of life ; her taste in literature must be the means of banishing pernicious reading from the domestic circle, and of introducing in its place that of a more wholesome character; her knowledge of artistic principles must help her to beautify the home, simply and humbly, yet truly ; and above all must her ethical and religious training, by teaching her gentleness, cheerfulness, and lovingness, and, above all, resignation to the Divine Will, do more than all else to mitigate the rudeness of the uncultured family life ; while, outside, a trained judgment and a power of alert observation must help her to find her own proper place, either in the ways already trodden by so many lagging, careless feet, or, better still, in some one of those numerous untrodden ways of which women are daily catching surer glimpses.

True, in spite of all this wise training, which is to make her a woman of cheerful action, of strong character, and firm religious convictions, our poor girl will still feel, as she feels now, an uncontrollable discontent, but it will be a fruitful, not a paralyzing discontent—that sort of discontent which is peculiarly an American virtue, and which has inspired noble souls since the beginning to strive cheerfully and hopefully for better things.

But before we can offer such education as this to those who need it we must have in our schools wide-awake women who hold a constant finger on the pulse of American life, who study daily, with scientific impartiality and accuracy, the needs of American women, and who are able to discover such matter for teaching and such methods of teaching it as will fit Catholic American girls to meet the requirements of their day.

Some of our schools are at present too closely bound to foreign and antiquated traditions. Methods and aims which were adequate to fit a daughter of the French nobility one or two hundred years ago to shine in a *salon* are still thought in some places sufficiently well suited to train an American girl of to-day to discharge her obligations as a wage-earning woman of the people.   The practice of such schools is in direct opposition to the custom of the church since the very beginning.   The church has in every age most truly and delicately gauged the needs of the time, and wisely and surely devised means for supplying them. For this reason the Catholic schools of the past were great and glorious successes.   They kept up with the march of progress, or rather they led the van.   They carried on the world's work. They accomplished the mission they set themselves to do.   But the needs of those bygone times are not our needs.   We have a different work to do.   Why, then, cling to the antiquated instruments which, though they wrought very well in the past, have since been superseded by lighter and better ones?

It is time that all of our educators were awake to these facts, as very many of them already are.   It is time that they were seeking a remedy.   Let not any Catholic stultify himself by such an absurd generalization as that education, in the true sense of the word, can be bad for any human being.   Heaven never gave us our God-like powers to die in the bud.   But let us frankly acknowledge the true state of the case, and let us all strive that the education our schools at present offer the daughters of our illiterate poor shall be suited to their needs, so that it may be truly called education, and not become a disturbing element in their lives rather than a promoter of either material or spiritual happiness.   Being thus squarely face-to-face with the difficulty, let us put our heads together in friendly counsel and try to discover ways and means for its vanquishment.   That discovery will not be made at once, nor will it be the achievement of any single mind.   It will come only after much thought, much experiment, much prayer; but it will undoubtedly come at last.   That it has not done so before in the case of some is to be regretted.   We must not stubbornly shut our eyes to the truth and refuse to believe the plain facts before us. · The blunderers who have talked about educating poor girls above their station have undoubtedly been a very great mortification to those of us who take so much pride in calling ourselves progressive; but, nevertheless, like many other blunt people, they have done us good if, in trying to answer them, we have been led to seek the truth of the matter.

Let us, then, study to give our poor girls, and all our other girls as well, not less education but infinitely more; but let us endeavor to give them the true thing and not a base and useless substitute.

B. N. TAYLOR.

ST. LANDRY'S DELINQUENCY.

DRENCHED in the carmine and gold of the after-dawn was the lake, the garden, the gallery, and Miriam dancing thereon. Her thin, rose-colored robe fluttered as she danced, her yellow hair shone, her dark eyes beamed innocently glad, and her lips sang the song of "White Lilies," the air of which her brother strummed on a banjo as he half-reclined in a hammock. Suddenly Miriam brought herself to a standstill and cried, clasping her hands: "Clyffe! I'm that happy I don't know what to do!"

He looked up at her and smiled, and his fingers, wandering among the banjo's strings, fell to picking the air of "Ben Bolt."

"Don't, Clyffe," Miriam implored.

"Don't what?"

"Don't play that! I won't listen to a thing to-day that is dreary or sad," she declared as she seated herself beside her brother and slipped her arm through his. "I never thought he'd care a bit for me," she continued dreamily.

"Neither did I; that is, I never thought about your marrying at all," said Clyffe, laying aside the banjo and taking her hand in his. "How did it come about, anyhow? I know it was not at the dinner-table, and it could not have been in the *salon;* you danced the entire evening. See here, Miriam! your being seventeen yesterday and getting an offer of marriage are not reasons for pinching my arm black-and-blue!"

"O Clyffe! I thought it was your coat-sleeve," Miriam exclaimed. "I'm nervous; I want to shout, or something; I was pinching to keep the inclination down." She paused, withdrew her arm from his, and said, looking thoughtfully out on the lake: "It was after dinner; he and I walked down to the lake and we sat under the palm. Clyffe! I never saw anything so beautiful as Lake Pontchartrain last evening!" *

"Unless it be Lake Pontchartrain this morning?"

"Unless it be this morning? Yes, it is very beautiful this morning," she agreed, heaving a little sigh of content.

"What did he say? I'd like to know; for my time will come some day," persisted Clyffe.

* Evening: in Louisiana any time between noon and midnight.

The quick glance she gave him was penetrating. He was not laughing. On the contrary he looked very earnest and serious. Then she said, and a flush that was not born of the sun but of her heart stole to her face: "You know, Clyffe, I cared for him from the first."

"But what did you all say?" urged Clyffe, seeing that she paused and showed no sign of pursuing her discourse.

"I did not say much, Clyffe," she returned earnestly. "I could but listen; he knows so much. He has read Homer in the original. Clyffe! I want to learn Greek; won't you help me?"

"What does a girl care for Greek?" ejaculated Clyffe with an air of superiority.

"Queen Mary did, and, and—lots of women! Madame Charleur knows Greek; and I want—" she insisted.

"Well, yes; but he did not propose to you in a Greek hexameter, did he?"

Again she looked up at him quickly. He was not laughing, but she was half in doubt of him. "You're not laughing at me, on your honor, Clyffe?" she asked.

"Well!" he evaded—"well, I won't—on my honor, I won't. Now, what did Captain St. Landry say?"

She again heaved a little sigh of content and answered: "As I told you, we were speaking of poetry, and he asked me what was my favorite poem. I said I liked 'The May Queen' better than anything else; but, I said, I was sure that the 'Iliad' was very pretty."

The corners of Clyffe's mouth twitched, but she did not perceive the twitching.

"And," she pursued, "he asked me if I did not think the May Queen had been very cruel to Robin; and I told him I did, and that I felt a great deal more for Robin than I did for her, for she died and went to heaven, but Robin had to live on and suffer." (Her voice had now sunk to a whisper.) "Then he took my hand in his, and he said: 'Little one, I am an old Robin'; and he did not say any more, for now I began to cry; for I knew he loved me. Then he put his one poor arm about me, Clyffe, and I was very happy." She had now hidden her face on her brother's shoulder.

"*We* were very happy before St. Landry came along," he said morosely. "See here, sister, if you are going to cry every time you think of him, I'm not going to believe much in your happiness."

Miriam sprang to her feet and cried, with a joyous laugh: "Clyffe, you're jealous! You'll see as much of me as ever."

"Shall I?" he inquired with sarcastic effusion. "But," he continued gravely, "this is going to be a nuisance; he'll want to come here every week or so—and, by the way, when is he coming for my permission?"

"He said he would ride over to see you this evening," she returned.

Clyffe groaned, and asked, "Have you told grandma yet?"

She nodded her head and said, "She is very glad. You are going out?" she asked, for he had moved as if to pass to the garden.

"I have to go down to the overseer's. Oh! I'll not miss the captain; I'll be back in time," he laughed.

"You know it is not that, Clyffe," she said shamefacedly. "Before you go won't you pick out a good book in Greek for me to begin with?"

Clyffe's wonderment showed strongly in his rounded eyes. "Miriam," he exclaimed, "is your head turned? Why, you don't know as much as the alphabet." Then he was going on to dissuade her from the pursuit of a knowledge of Greek, but, seeing her serious, eager look, he said instead: "I can't begin now, but I'll teach you the alphabet; I'll begin after breakfast."

Miriam smiled her thanks, and having said she was going to see if grandma was ready for her coffee, went into the house humming the air of "White Lilies," and Clyffe strode away in the direction of the white pavilion where dwelt the overseer.

PARENTHETICAL.

How it was that Palmetto Plantation had in so great part been preserved to Clyffe Tone, this story has nothing to do. Suffice it to say, that he had inherited it directly from his grandfather; that, barring the years spent at a university in Alabama, he had lived his life on it happily in the company of his sister. When he was a small child Death had been a frequent visitor at Palmetto, taking first his father, then his mother, and finally the grandfather. After this last event the children had been cared for solely by their grandmother. A love for English literature and a passion for hunting, together with a succession of visitors from the neighboring plantations and from New Orleans, kept the youth free of *ennui*. At the time Miriam and Clyffe held the conversation just related, the 26th of March, 1885, the house was full of visitors who had remained over-night after Miriam's name-day *fête*, and who would appear at breakfast. With them, however, this story does not concern itself.

Adjoining Palmetto, but five miles distant from the dwelling, was the plantation of Captain Theophile St. Landry, styled Idesia, a much smaller property than that of Clyffe Tone. The owner had in his very youthful days fought through a great war, in which he had not only lost his right arm but his entire estate. With genuine and heroic perseverance he set to work— a herculean task in those days—to regain a portion of his estate that he might have a home for his mother, the only one left to him of his family. His task was but accomplished when the mother died. St. Landry, after this, gave himself up to the study of the Greek and Latin authors for whom, like his great compatriot Viel, he had an abounding devotion. His love for Miriam Tone had been of sudden growth, and budding as it did when he was past middle-age, it had fastened its roots deep and strong.

" I never t'ought you goin' git married, Marse T'eophile," giggled old Tesis (Theseus), St. Landry's body-servant, as he helped to array his master for the expected visit to Palmetto. St. Landry making no remark, he went on : " Anyways, t'ought it might be Miss Colonel Sams ; she ain' quite so gaily like as Misse Miriam. Them Sams ain' no trash neither— "

" You rascal ! " shouted St. Landry, wheeling about. " Do you mean to imply that the family I am going to marry into are not worthy of the highest respect ? "

Tesis rested the hand that held a whisk on his hip, and with the other meditatively scratched his white wool. " Lawd give you sense, Marse T'eophile," he said slowly, peering at St. Landry. " I ain' replyin' ter no one. I ain' sayin' nothin' 'bout them Tones ! I knowed 'em way back afore you's born. They's 'sponserble people all erlong. I ain' got nothin' 'gin 'em. I was jes' a thinkin' how crickety things er turnin' out. They's you an' Miss Colonel Sams, ain' nothin' comin' out er that ; and they's Misse Miriam an' young Marse Rapides, mighty likely couple they is, and they ain' nothin' come out of that neither—"

" See here, Tesis," interrupted St. Landry grimly, " you are doing too much thinking and a great deal too much talking. Help me on with my coat, and then go see if my horse has been brought around."

Tesis did in silence all that he had been bid to do, and it was not till his master had ridden off to Palmetto that he uttered in an apostrophe to the surrounding landscape his protest against his ill-treatment. " I ain' ussen ter be talk ter that ar way," he said, with an outward wave of his hand. " He's own father dassen' do it. Seems no one ain' got no manners these days, an' fust thing you know old miss up en hebben she ha'nt you, axin' you: ' Tesis, what for you lettin' you Marse T'eophile forgit hisself for ? ' An' what Tesis tell her ? 'Fore the Lawd, I ain' teachin' him nothin' as ain' misbecomin' to er genterman. 'Pears this here gittin' married jes make him wufless—t'rowin' erway t'ree kervats, a cussin' he's own haar, raxelin' me. Ain' no use talkin', Tesis, you's gittin' too old for this worl' when you ain' no use for er fam'ly; an' you bes' haive the buryin' over afore the time er the weddin'."

Clyffe Tone made the interview between himself and the captain a short one. According to an honorable custom, it was necessary that St. Landry should inform him, the only male representative of the family, of his aspirations to the hand of Miriam. But Clyffe thought the information should be given and received in few words. He was very glad when the meeting was over, for, if the truth be told, he found the captain a difficult person to converse with. Their tastes were at variance ; the one was devoted to a Homeric, the other to an English literature, and the captain was precluded from the use of a fowling-piece. It was mysterious to Clyffe that any woman could be found to love this grizzled, one-armed Antinous, and that of all women Miriam, his sister, should be the one.

"And now I have but to make my excuses for my grandmother," was his way of ending the interview. " She has had to keep her room to-day ; you know an affair like that of yesterday is rather upsetting to a woman verging on to ninety years."

The captain hoped that Madame Tone would suffer no permanent ill from the little dissipation of the *fête ;* and Miriam, was she quite well ?

" She is never otherwise," laughed Clyffe. " She is down under the palm by the lake. Of course you'll take dinner with us, captain ; it's very near our dinner hour. Perhaps you'd like to bring her to dinner ? Miriam gets down there and forgets— "

He paused, overcome by the boldness of his proposition. The captain might be very much in love, but the captain was a

very magnificent person, and might not like being sent on er-
rands; even on such a one. He was straightway reassured, however, by a hearty grasp of the hand and a ringing " Thank
you, Clyffe; I should like to very much," as the captain turned
to seek Miriam, leaving Clyffe to wonder at this display of
heartiness on the part of one whom he had always considered a
remarkable specimen of frigidity.

Miriam had gone down to the shade of the palm, carrying
with her a little bundle of papers containing some simple directions for the pronunciation of the Greek alphabet written out for
her by Clyffe. She had persuaded her brother to keep with her
the secret of her pursuit of knowledge. " I shall surprise him
some day," she had said, the fires of love and ambition glowing
in her cheeks. She was busily conning the manuscript and
thinking, almost with tears, that she was very stupid, when the
captain's " Good evening," hesitatingly given, caused her to start
to her feet, and, with a guilty look, to conceal the troublesome
alphabet in her pocket. Mingled with her confusion was such a
delight at seeing him that she was speechless, and could but
extend her hand in welcome.

" I have just come from your brother," he said with some
stiffness. " I hope I have not disturbed you."

She cast on him a shy look of surprise. So overwhelmingly
glad was she to see him, so inferior did she feel herself to be to
him, that not for a moment did she doubt but that he must be
sure of her joy. Therefore she said nothing to remove the impression her confusion had made.

" Your brother says he is pleased he is to be my brother,"
St. Landry said, after a moment's pause.

" Of course he is," returned Miriam, so prettily and with so
much earnestness that it set his heart to throbbing. But the kiss
he gave her cheek was given reverently, not to flutter or alarm
her; for he knew that the perfume of the rose lasts long, even
when it is faded; but that this preservation be secured, the petals
must not be bruised or broken.

They seated themselves on the rude bench under the palm,
and hand in hand gazed out on the lake, stealing glances at
one another, but saying little. They were speaking of a trip he
proposed to take with her to a Northern lake, when suddenly he
asked: " Miriam, why do you always call me captain? Don't
you know my name?"

" Oh! yes," she replied; she knew it very well.

"Let me hear you say it," he insisted. "Slowly and distinctly."

"Theophile."

This was sweeter to his ears than the tune of "White Lilies," and yet he liked to hear that sung by her.

"And I know, at least I think I know, what it means," she said, somewhat abashed at her venturing to claim the possession of even so little knowledge.

"What does it mean, *cherie?*" he asked, pressing her hand to his cheek.

"A lover of God and man," she answered solemnly. "I found it from the roots in the dictionary."

"You went to so much trouble, *mignon!* Your fingers are too dainty to delve among dry roots," he said caressingly.

There was something almost wild in the imploring look she gave him. "Don't laugh at me," she cried. "I know so little, and it was all for you—"

"Clang! clang! clang!" the dinner-bell ringing from its turret by the house.

"We are late," said Miriam guiltily.

"And I was sent to fetch you," said St. Landry, not less so.

Early in April it was arranged that the wedding of Miriam and St. Landry was to take place in the latter part of July. St. Landry would have had it earlier, but Miriam objected. She objected that she might have time to fit herself to be the companion of the man who had asked her to be his wife; not, however, giving this as her reason.

St. Landry fretted under the postponement. Idesia was full of gloomy remembrance for him; his taste for books had palled on him, and he wanted Miriam's face in the house to drive away the gloom, and he would rather hearken to her airiest nothings than to the sublimest utterances of Homer. Unconscious of this, Miriam worked and tired her brain with unflagging zeal. Daily at Mass she stormed Heaven with petitions for her lover and implorings that she might become a learned woman. And by the end of May, considering what she had already accomplished, it might be believed that the last would be attained. Clyffe assisted her prodigiously, inwardly protesting, but always submissive to her femininity. In time the unaccustomed labor told on her. She grew pale and lost much of her plumpness. St. Landry believed himself to be the cause of her altering appearance, as indeed he was, but not in the way he supposed. The hour of his daily visit to her they·spent under the palm by the lake; and, not knowing that she passed her days in the house and that this, her one meal of fresh air, was what kept health in her, he took it into his head that the lake air was miasmatic. After this he insisted that they remain within in the *salon*, where the air was always heavy with the odor of flowers the grandmother loved. Miriam did not object; it was all the same to her wherever she was, if he were present.

. It was in May that, the overseer falling ill, Clyffe was obliged to give up his tutorship. "I don't know what I shall do," Miriam said to him after a week's despairing plodding alone; "I do not seem to get along without you, Clyffe."

"Well, what's the use of it, anyhow?" said Clyffe, somewhat sadly, as he looked into Miriam's pale, eager face. "St. Landry won't care for all this study of yours."

"Oh! don't say that, Clyffe," she implored.

"Of course he'll appreciate it when he comes to know," Clyffe hastened to explain, not heeding much what he said, only speaking to soothe her. "But, sister, you're too good for him as it is; why not give it all up? You're as white as a sheet; next thing you know, you'll be down in bed."

She shook her head in dissent, and asked: "Do you think Cousin Rapides would be hurt if you were to offer him money for teaching me? It would help him, for you know his academy brings him very little. Do you think you'll succeed in getting back any of his property for him?" she added.

"I'm sure I will. You know the present legislature has declared off such sales as those by which Rapides' plantation was appropriated. I'm working hard for him," answered Clyffe.

"And about the lessons? Do you think he'd mind taking money from you?"

"Put in the right way, I don't suppose he would. But you don't mean to go to the academy!" Clyffe exclaimed.

"No, no! He could come here in the evening, after school hours—"

"That's the time St. Landry always comes," interrupted Clyffe.

"I have thought of that," she continued, waving aside his objection. "I shall ask Captain St. Landry" (she never called him Theophile to Clyffe) "to come in the morning."

And so it was that Cyrille Rapides was engaged to teach his cousin afternoons, and St. Landry was asked to make his visits in the morning. "You will give me my way in this,

Theophile," begged Miriam.. " I'll tell you some day why I ask it."

"I would grant you your will in everything," he answered with a gallantry she thought superb.

But in his heart St. Landry did not like this change in hours. A morning visit must necessarily be shorter than one paid in the afternoon ; and, attributing the change to matters connected with Miriam's trousseau, he inwardly protested with vehemence against woman's passion for dress.

One June afternoon business about the fencing of a field took St. Landry to Palmetto. Now the approach to Palmetto is on rising ground, giving one a fine view of the lake, the palmetto grove from which the place gets its name, and in particular of the spot where stands the great palm. St. Landry reined up his horse to take in the scene, and his eye fell on the bench beneath the palm where were sitting Miriam and her cousin, their heads bent over a book which Miriam held. He suddenly remember-ed what Tesis had said of Miriam and her cousin, but, as quickly as it came, he threw the remembrance off, and hoped magnanimously that Rapides was going to get his dinner at Pal-metto, for the poor devil had not a too luxurious board of his own, he thought.

Had it not been for Tesis, St. Landry would have forgotten this incident. Tesis had become Miriam's enemy. Since his master's engagement to her Tesis had discovered a great change in his master. He no longer took an interest in that good ser-vant's tales of the past. He had even, on one occasion after a return from Palmetto, told Tesis he did not wish to be both-ered about things that were dead and gone; the present fully occupied his mind. Tesis was now convinced that his master was crazy. "All on ercount of a young misse as ain' no more sense 'n er hummin'-bu'd !" he grumbled to himself. " He better er married Miss Colonel Sams ; she jest he's age. She never lettin' 'im forget who he's father is. That young misse ain' keerin' for 'im, nohow. I jest knows that for a fac'."

This last-uttered opinion was confirmed in him when, in one of his frequent conversations with his chosen friend, Augustine, the butler at Palmetto, he learned that Miriam's afternoons were spent in the company of Rapides. "That's a fac', suh. Jest as sure as you name's Tesis St. Landry, suh," Augustine insisted when Tesis insinuated that he was stretching the truth.

It was not till Tesis had assured himself by personal obser-vation of the truth of this statement, and then only after much communing with himself, that he took it on himself to ask St. Landry: "How come, Marse T'eophile, you never go visit Misse Miriam no more evenin's?"

St. Landry was so accustomed to answering whatever questions Tesis put him that he replied before considering: "Because she is engaged at that time."

Blinking his eyes, Tesis drew nearer and questioned: "Does you know, Marse T'eophile, how she is engage'? Misse Miriam and Marse Rapides mons'ous gaily couple, they is."

St. Landry stared at him, then blazed out: "Confound your impudence! What business is it of yours?"

Tesis shook with indignation. Here he was, his master's interests alone at heart, and that master addressing him as if he were one of the boys in the field. Drawing himself up, he made a low bow, and said with overpowering politeness: "Marse T'eophile, I axes your pardon, but I'se jest 'bleeged t' tell you, you is gittin' mons'ous dismannerly."

The color rose to St. Landry's face, and, with a half-laugh, he held out his hand and said: "There, Tesis, that's all right; but for heaven's sake don't ask any more questions."

Tesis shook his master's hand gravely, and walked out of the room a man conscious of having done his duty. But he had left a thorn to rankle in his master's side.

The next day St. Landry did not pay his usual morning visit to Palmetto, thereby causing Miriam to feel uneasy and unhappy. Ashamed of himself for doing so, he did ride over in the afternoon, and from the rising ground before the house he saw under the palm· what he had seen before—Miriam and Rapides seated together.

The servant who came forward to take his horse told him that Clyffe, for whom he had asked, had gone to the village. "Misse Miriam," he added gratuitously, "she down yonder at the lake: she down there every evenin', she an' Marse Rapides."

"I'll not get down, then," said St. Landry, and turned his horse and cantered on the road home.

He felt depressed and anxious, and it must be granted that, from his point of view, he had much to alarm him. As low in degree as Miriam held herself in her own way, so in his way he held himself. He thought of himself as a man past forty who had lost an arm. That he was strikingly handsome did not occur to him. It is doubtful, even, if he knew it. Tesis on various occasions had let fall· much about Miriam in connection with Rapides, and St. Landry knew that the time she had given to him she now reserved for the man he had been led to believe had been her lover. What he could not reconcile to the thought that she regretted Rapides was her evident pleasure at being in his (St. Landry's) company. But of late had this pleasure been so evident? Had she not appeared to be wearied and listless? Had he but known the cause of her weariness and listlessness! And, last of all, he remembered that the very place he had wished her to abstain from was the place she chose to meet Rapides, whom she now believed to be her lover.

St. Landry went on the following morning to Palmetto an hour earlier than was his custom. The result of his meditations was that he had best come to an understanding with Miriam; that anything was better than the state of doubt he was in. Early as he was, he found Miriam waiting for him on the gallery. The smile of welcome she gave him served to bring out in greater relief the general wanness of her appearance, the feverish light in her eyes. A phenomenally bright brain, urged to it by a loving heart, and pushed on by a merciless teacher who rejoiced in the development of a prodigy, had accomplished much, but at the expense of Miriam's health. The night before she had broken down whilst attempting a difficult translation, and this morning her head ached and her body felt out of joint.

"What was the matter yesterday?" she exclaimed. "Why did you not wait? I was coming up to the house when you rode away?"

Instead of answering her he said gravely: "I asked you not to go to the lake in the evening— You are ill and feverish!" he broke off to exclaim.

"Only a little headache; it will pass," she said carelessly, going on to ask in deprecation, "You are not displeased with me, are you? I needed the fresh air."

"You know best; and understand, Miriam, although I might be displeased with something you did, I could never be displeased with you. Awkwardly put, this, *mignon;* but it is meant to be a pretty speech," he returned with a smile, as he moved to enter the hall.

"Don't go inside, Theophile," she entreated, laying her hand lightly on his arm to detain him; "it is so much pleasanter here on the gallery."

"As you please," he said, and, having placed a chair for her, seated himself at a little distance.

She had been endeavoring to read when he came, and still

held her book, the leaves of which she fluttered absently as she looked towards him, waiting for him to speak. She was a little afraid, for, in spite of his "pretty speech," she believed him to be displeased.

"What is that finely bound novel?" he asked with a smile; " *St. Elmo?* "

She reddened and wished she had put the book away before he came. "No," she answered hesitatingly, "it is a Greek tragedy."

"May I look at it?" he asked, charmed for the moment at the idea of Miriam reading a Greek tragedy.

She handed him the book, and he read the title aloud: "' *The Suppliants' of Æschylus: a translation.*" Oh!" he ejaculated coldly, "one of your cousin's books."

"No, it is Clyffe's, though it was Cyrille who recommended Æschylus to me," she replied truthfully, but wishing ardently that he would not question her further. She was not yet ready to surprise him.

He opened the parchment-covered volume where a book-mark had been placed. "So you are reading *The Suppliants?* "

She nodded her head in assent, and his eyes fell on the passage pointed out by the marker:

"Look on the woman's cause!"

he read aloud; then stopped, for a moment lost in thought. Drawing in his breath, he continued:

" Recall the ancient tale,
Of one whom thou didst love in time of old."

He closed the book hastily and returned it to her.

For a little while he sat thoughtful, patting the floor softly with his foot. Then he turned to her abruptly, and questioned: "You and your cousin have always been very intimate?"

"He has been the same to me as a brother," she answered warmly. "He was the first one to row me on the lake—" Miriam was now shivering. The fever had changed to a chill. "It *would* be better for me to be inside," she interrupted herself to say, and rising from her chair, preceded St. Landry to the great *salon,* where huge pots of plants were ranged against the marble pilasters, and smirking shepherds and shepherdesses held branches of scarlet and of white waxen candles.

She took up a shawl that lay across the back of a chair and, throwing it about her, seated herself and said: " Ah, that is more comfortable! And you would rather be in here, wouldn't you, Theophile?"

St. Landry was leaning against a console-table looking absently before him when she spoke. He now advanced to where she sat, and, resting his arm on the high back of her chair, he looked down on her, and asked slowly. "Your cousin visits you every evening at the hour you used to permit me to come, does he not?"

She turned half around in her chair the better to look up at him and, meeting much of coldness in his glance, could only falter, "Yes."

"God bless you, *mignon*, for telling me the truth!" he said simply, and bearing hard on the chair. "Now," he went on, "tell me another truth. You wished that I should not know of his visits?"

His seriousness, a seriousness that was akin to severity, frightened her. "No," she said, speaking rapidly; "I did not mind if you knew Cyrille came; I only wished to keep it a secret why he came."

"You are indeed truthful," he returned with bitterness.

"You are angry with me!" she exclaimed, starting up in her chair.

"Angry with you? No!" he replied. "Do you not know the creed we are taught: a woman cannot err? I have always found it easy of belief, and I do not know that you have made it less so; you will not lie, nor give evasive answers—you are honorable."

"Theophile, Theophile! what is it?" she cried. "Do you want to know why Cyrille has been coming here? I'll tell you—"

"Spare yourself," he interrupted. "I know, and I would rather not hear more from you about it. I am but flesh and blood, you see, and further candor might make me forget myself."

She felt like one who looks down from a great height. He knew of her efforts to make herself his equal, and they displeased him. "If I had known you would not like it I would have acted differently," she said sadly.

For a second of time he felt his love giving way. She was absurd — worse than childish. Did she suppose he would be pleased with what she had done? "Miriam," he said, "before bidding you good-by, let me say, you should have been frankly open with me before this. And, *cherie*, I do with all my heart

hope you will be happy.   Good-by!" And he took her hand
and kissed it, and turned and left the room.

She made no attempt to call him back; but, her head aching, her whole body ill, sat endeavoring to understand how
dreadfully she must have erred to be so wounded.

As he rode away from Palmetto to Idesia, St. Landry went
over the events of the last few months dating from the hour
when, under the palm, Miriam had promised to be his wife. A
confused mind begot a worse confusion, and he could only see that
without cause he had been recklessly and cruelly trifled with.
He was a man of deep religious feeling, and he combated the
red thoughts that assailed him.   But in the end the tumult of
wrath against Rapides that surged in his brain and wrought in
his heart warned him that he was dangerous.   He felt that the
man should not live ; and yet why should he blame Rapides ?
Was not Rapides' claim to Miriam a prior one to his ?

The shrill whistle of the *Allen*, the little steamer that plied
between the lake towns and New Orleans, resolved him.   Looking out through the vista of magnolias, he saw her gilt figure-
head glittering in the amber light of the afternoon sun as she
made for Rosaries, the village near by. , She would remain at
the village till sundown, long enough for Tesis to pack his valise
and for him to see his overseer.   Flight from the vicinity of Palmetto was his only safety.   How many defeats had he not suffered in his life, and would God mercifully grant him to preserve
his honor in this last defeat as he had in all the others ?

When St. Landry went aboard the *Allen* he was told that
there was no vacant state-room.   "A young man from hereabouts," informed the clerk, "has taken the last we had.   There
are two berths in it; you can have the other if you wish."   St.
Landry hesitated before deciding to take the empty berth.   "I
don't know that I'll need it," he said.   "But you'll be on the
safe side if you take it," advised the clerk.   He took the advice,
entered his name, and then went to sit at the far end of the
deck, away from the gay crowd of passengers, most of whom were
out on a pleasure-trip.

No case of insomnia, however obstinate, can withstand the
night air blown gently over Lake Pontchartrain, soft and heavily
freighted as it is with the odors of ten thousand, thousand flowers—the rose, the jessamine, the magnolia, the spicy myrtle, and
the oozing gum · of the incense-pine.   One by one, in pairs and

in little bands, the passengers went down to their berths; and then St. Landry, left alone and somnolent, went to the state-room he was now glad was partly his. He opened the door of the room softly, not to disturb the man within, and, having turned up the light, he let his eyes fall carelessly on the occupied berth, the curtains of which were undrawn.

He half fell onto a camp-stool standing by, jarring the cabin, and the sleeper sighed in his sleep and nestled his curly head more comfortably in the hollow of his arm.

Was the devil given power over him? Was there truth in that gloomy dying creed that from all eternity most men are foreordained to damnation, and was he one of the hell-created, and had he been brought here to work out his doom? How easy it would be!—and the fingers of his hand twitched nervously. The window open by the sleeping man's side—one blow on the head, and the body thrust into the purple water to be drawn under the steamer's wheel!

How low had he descended that so cowardly a thought could be born in him! No! let the man awake and defend himself. Let him have such advantage as two arms could give him over the one that was mighty with hate and frustrated love.

"Rapides! Cyrille Rapides, wake up!" he thundered, rising to his feet, his voice not loud but penetrating.

The sleeper yawned, stretched himself, and swung into a sitting posture on the side of the berth. "It is not day yet," he began; then, seeing who stood before him and not noting the scowl that sought to scorch him, he stretched out his hand and cried, "Why, St. Landry, man! what brings you here?"

St. Landry flung back the outstretched hand and said—and once as he spoke he unconsciously grit his teeth—"I did not come here to find you, but now that I have found you, you must kill me or I shall kill you."

Rapides, though the younger man, had the cooler head. He was now on his feet, and the tone he took in answering the man possessed was low and even. "I see you wish to quarrel," he said; "I shall not second you till I know the reason why I should either kill or be killed. What ails you, St. Landry?"

"You are a coward and you lie!" retorted St. Landry. "I was at Palmetto before taking the boat; she has told me everything— Not yet; let me finish! No woman's name is to be brought into this business; we have quarrel enough in that I have called you a liar and a coward. Men have died for less than that, and I, who have hated the duel, now tell you I think it a righteous institution."

Still cool and collected, Rapides returned: "I shall fight no duel with you, and least of all without a cause. As for your insult, your better self shall teach you to ask my pardon for it. Now, for God's sake, for the sake of Miriam Tone, be cool, St. Landry. What do you mean by no woman's name being brought into this?"

Rapides' coolness stunned him. "You," he stammered, "who have stolen her from me— "

"Stop!" interrupted Rapides under his breath; he was hot enough now. "You dolt! are you jealous of me?"

"She did not lie," cried St. Landry in scorn. "And," he continued, "since she has told me you are her lover, I do not see what *you* expect to gain by a lie."

"Were you to tell me on your oath that she said that, I would not believe you. That you are a disgrace to the uniform you wore, a scoundrel who, having tired of your engagement, are seeking an escape, no matter how, I can well believe— "

"That's enough!" broke in St. Landry. He was now at white heat, but it was with much courtesy he asked: "Before our little encounter, will you answer two questions?"

'I will—if I see fit."

"Is it not true," interrogated St. Landry, his tone suave, "that for weeks past your evenings have been spent at Palmetto?"

As it were in a flash, the state of the case was revealed to Rapides. "St. Landry," he exclaimed, "I see it all; let me make it as clear to you!" And, as concisely as it could be told, he related the story of Miriam's lessons and why they had been pursued. As this was told a thousand and one incidents, unheeded at the time they happened, were remembered by St. Landry, and confirmed to him the truth of Rapides' narration. "You are convinced, are you not?" asked Rapides when he had ended.

"I am," was all St. Landry could find to say, in his confusion.

The two men were now seated—St. Landry on the campstool, Rapides on the berth.

"What did you mean by saying that my cousin—I cannot repeat it, you remember your accusation?" questioned the latter.   •

"Rapides," returned St. Landry, "I have played the part of a second-rate Othello, and Tesis, my body-servant, has been my Iago." Then he told how he had misjudged and misconceived, and he did not spare himself.

"Miriam has been made very unhappy," said Rapides, when the other paused. "You had better return to Palmetto as quickly as you can and right the wrong you have done. If you take the train at New Orleans to-morrow morning, you can be with her by five to-morrow evening. Now you had better turn in and see if you cannot get some sleep. By the way," he added cheerfully, "congratulate me: through Clyffe Tone's exertions, more than mine, I am getting back a big slice of Rapides plantation. It is business connected with this that takes me to New Orleans."

"Congratulate you! With all my heart, and thank God I met you!" returned St. Landry reverently. "Before we turn in, however, let me fulfil your prophecy by begging your pardon—"

"That's all right," interrupted Rapides; adding, "I wish you a good night's rest."

Miriam had a bad night of it. She was feverish, and Clyffe feared that she was going to be very ill. The doctor when called in said otherwise. "She has been poring over her books too much and too long. Give her plenty of fresh air, and she will be all right in a week," was his dictum.

She told Clyffe nothing of what had taken place in the *salon.* She had no doubt but that St. Landry's farewell was final, and in justice to him she endeavored to feel that he had cause to be wroth with her. She would put him out of her heart after awhile; then she would tell Clyffe, not before. One thing was sure: she was not given to sentimentality, and she would not pine.

Late in the afternoon they wheeled the lounge on which she reclined, wrapped in a muslin robe, on to the gallery looking out on the lake. "Do you remember the morning I played on the banjo, and you danced and sang?" asked Clyffe, who was seated by her side. "You have given up all that. I wish, Miriam, you'd put aside your books. I'm sure St. Landry cares more for you than for anything you can gain from them. Come, what do you say?"

"I suppose," she answered dreamily: then rousing herself, "I'm so glad you succeeded about Cyrille's property! Do you know that there is a strophe in *The Suppliants* I learned by heart, because it reminded me of what you have done for him? Listen !"

"Friend to the stranger wholly faithful found;
Desert not thou the poor,
Driven from their homes by godless violence,"

she quoted, and then was silent, thinking of St. Landry's evident impatience yesterday with this very volume of Æschuylus. Her eyes were closed, and she was silent for so long that Clyffe thought she slept, and stole away about some concerns of the plantation.

The beat of a horse's hoofs on the ascending drive to the house caused her to open her eyes, and she saw through a rift in the cassias and myrtle that lined the road that it was St. Landry who was approaching. Her first impulse was to run to meet him. Feminine reticence told her to remain, and feminine propriety threw a silken shawl about her, and smoothed her yellow hair, and put her in a sitting posture on the lounge.

He flung the horse's reins to a servant who had been lounging in the shade of a myrtle, ran up the gallery steps, and walked rapidly to where she sat.

"Miriam," he exclaimed, "I have come to cry *peccavi*, to entreat your pardon, for I have sinned against you greatly."

She waved her hand to a chair which he did not take, and said, as if this were but a continuation of the scene of yesterday : "I do not understand. I have tried to make it out why you should be so angry. I learned that you might not find me altogether unlearned. It is true, though, I got to love study for itself, and Clyffe and Cyrille were very patient with me."

He hated himself for the jealous twinge this praise of her teachers gave him. He had not been patient. "Miriam," he said, "I knew nothing yesterday of the lessons given you by Rapides."

"Then what was it?" she asked, with a surprised look.

A strained look on his face, he told how he had wronged her. "May I hope for forgiveness?" he pleaded, his tale concluded, even to the telling of his meeting Rapides on the *Allen*.

As she listened without interruption to his confession her face had at first expressed wonder, but as he progressed it gradually assumed an expression that told of nothing but that she patiently waited for his narration to come to a close. And now, in response to his question, she said : "Of course I forgive you, though I cannot understand how you could think me so contemptible."

"And you will forget it all?" he entreated.

"It is very soon to ask me to forget it all," she replied, drawing her shawl about her.

"Miriam! *cherie!*" he implored; "there is no true forgiveness without a forgetting. Are not things to be with us as they were before?"

"If you mean" she returned coldly, "am I not to be your wife—" She stopped abruptly, continuing in a suppressed voice: "Yesterday, when you came to me, I was a girl? I have grown old since then. You shall never make me suffer so again. No; I cannot be your wife."

He caught his breath and leaned for support against the pilaster of a doorway.

"Miriam," he cried, his voice broken, "you do not mean to break my heart?"

"You must not think I do not spare you because, yesterday, you had no thought of sparing me—"

"I gave you up because I thought you would be happier without me. Yesterday I did not spare myself," he interrupted, driven to defend himself.

She thought for a moment over what he had said, and then went on: "You are right. You intended to spare me, and you were pitiless to yourself. But I cannot expose myself to a repetition of such mercy."

"Do you think that could happen again?" he exclaimed bitterly.

She felt a return of the swimming in her head, and she made haste to say: "You must leave me now. I have not been well. I cannot bear this any longer."

"Miriam," he asked, "before I go, can you give me no hope? I have no right to look for happiness, *cherie*—I who would now be a murderer but for the mercy of the good God; but, *cherie*, I long to be happy—have you no word for me?"

"If I should ever have, I shall send for you," she answered, not trusting herself to look up. "But go now."

He caught his one arm about her, and before she could resist he had kissed her cheek, and had left her. And having entered the house, she looked out through the venetian blinds to see him ride away.

The broad leaves of the palm had turned from a deep, cool green to a rich gold; the petals of the magnolia to a color that was russet in the shade and a fiery crimson in the sun; the summer roses were departing and the winter roses returning, and still Miriam had sent no manner of word to St. Landry. She had told Clyffe nothing but that she had concluded not to marry, although he pestered her with questions. Cyrille Rapides had interceded for St. Landry; the *curé* at Rosaries did not approve of the course she was pursuing; yet she persisted on her way, though she found it toilsome. If St. Landry came again, perhaps she would listen to him, she thought. But St. Landry did not come, and she began to feel that in reality all was over between them. Then she began to pray earnestly to Heaven that he would return to Palmetto.

One afternoon late in December Miriam went down to the seat under the palm, her first visit to it since the lessons Rapides had given her were broken off. She did not remain long, for the place brought up sad memories. As she turned to go home her eyes strayed to the palmetto grove, and she saw St. Landry standing under one of the trees. He took off his hat, but the only sign of recognition she gave was a little start of surprise. That evening Tesis brought her a note from his master. She opened it and read:

"I found that you never came to the palm, and for the sake of old times I have gone there very often. I shall not offend again.—ST. L."

"There is no answer," she said to Tesis, and then went in and cried over the note. That evening at dinner she complained to Clyffe of the palm. She found it unsightly and declared that it should be cut down. Clyffe replied that he thought otherwise.

For a week after this event she kept herself indoors, pretending to think it possible she might meet St. Landry anywhere within the bounds of Palmetto. At the end of the week she called to mind that, considering Palmetto was a property of some seven square miles, she was not exercising common sense in so rigidly housing herself. "Clyffe!" she announced one morning after breakfast, "I am going out for a stroll." Clyffe nodded his head, not knowing why this should be communicated to him. He would have wondered the more had he known that Miriam's stroll would but take her to the palmetto grove.

As she entered the grove she drew in with long breaths the scented air. Standing still she looked about, then advanced to one of the trees and touched it gently. "This is his tree," she thought; "for from here he could best see the palm—

Oh!" she cried in sudden alarm at seeing something black in the grass at her feet. Stooping cautiously, she picked - it up. It was a man's soft felt hat. Immediately upon this she heard a footstep advancing towards her from behind. Bending over, she crushed the hat to her bosom, her face white and red by turns.

"May I have my hat?" asked St. Landry's voice.

She turned about slowly, still bending over, and, with one hand pressing her bosom, handed him the hat. "I did not know that you were here," she denied eagerly in a voice that was almost a whisper.

"Are you displeased to find me here?" he asked.

She hesitated so long that he thought she would never answer, and was about to repeat his question, when she faltered; "No."

"I wrote you that I would never offend again," he said. "You see I have kept my word."

She looked up quickly, and before her face again fell he saw that she was smiling, though there were tears in her eyes.

She let him take her hand, and he whispered, "*Cherie*, am I forgiven? My penance has been long."

She bent her head persistently, and he pursued, "Everything is over and forgotten, *cherie?*"

Miriam withdrew her hand slowly, looked up as if about to speak, hesitated, then turned and walked away.

He stood staring after her, and the cool wind that had come up from over the lake stirred strongly among the palmettos.

FELIX GARNETT.

JOHN· BOYLE O'REILLY.*

A RARE quality in this book, and one which proves the author's fitness for the office of biographer, is his absolute subordination of himself to his theme. The biography becomes,
wherever possible, autobiography. Facts have the light of a
lucid style upon them. The story has the reader's undistracted
first thought. That it is well told is his pleasant after thought.·

In the circumstances under which he was compelled to write
it was hardly to be expected that Mr. Roche should have made
the most of his knowledge of the life and work of the lamented
dead. Succeeding to O'Reilly's editorship of *The Pilot*, these
pages were written, to quote from his modest preface, "in the
scant leisure of a busy life, made doubly so by the loss which
called them forth." He wrote in the bondage of contract, date,
and space, and with an embarrassing riches of material. Moreover, he was still too near his subject.

"The picture," he says again, "has not been over-colored by
the hand of friendship." Rather has Mr. Roche carried artistic
reserve too far. His conscientious effort to resist the fascination
of his theme makes him at times constrained.

Still, in all essentials, John Boyle O'Reilly is faithfully depicted ; and none can trace the story of his short and crowded
life to its pathetic close without re-echoing the words of Cardinal
Gibbons at the announcement of his death : "A loss to the
country, a loss to the church, a loss to humanity."

John Boyle O'Reilly was a man with a Providential mission,
whose scope is described by the words just quoted. He, was born,
as Thomas Wentworth Higginson well expressed it, to be interpreter and reconciler of race to race and of class to class. He came
to America to do a special work in the levelling of the mountains
of racial and religious prejudice ; in the filling up of the valleys
of abjection and abasement into which, at least in New England,
the people of his own faith and race were plunged ; and in hew-
ing straight ways whereon the erstwhile despised Irish Catholic
might advance even to worldly distinction without compromising

---

* *Life of John Boyle O'Reilly.* By James Jeffrey Roche. Together with his complete
Poems and Speeches, edited by Mrs. John Boyle O'Reilly. Introduction by his Eminence
James Cardinal . Gibbons, Archbishop of Baltimore. New York: Cassell Publishing Com-
pany.

the honor of his faith or ancestry. From this point of-view we will consider the story of his life; touching on the romantic vicissitudes of his youth only for their value as a preparation for his life-work.

John Boyle O'Reilly wrought out his mission unconsciously. This simple and self-distrustful man would have been the last to dream of himself as a man with a mission. His master-passion was Ireland. The man and his life-long conscious purpose are here, in this brief passage from his "Statues in the Block"—a passage, by the way, not excelled for strength and beauty by anything else he has written:

> " My Land! I see thee in the marble, bowed
> Before thy tyrant, bound at foot and wrist—
> Thy garments rent—thy wounded shoulder bare—
> Thy chained hand raised to ward the cruel blow—
> My poor love round thee scarf-like, weak to hide
> And powerless to shield thee—but a boy
> I wound it round thee, dearest, and a man
> I drew it close and kissed thee—mother, wife!
> For thee the past and future days; for thee
> The will to trample wrong and strike for slaves;
> For thee the hope that ere mine arm be weak
> And ere my heart be dry may close the strife
> In which thy colors shall be borne through fire,
> And all thy griefs washed out in manly blood—
> And I shall see thee crowned and bound with love,
> Thy strong sons round thee guarding thee. O star
> That lightens desolation, o'er her beam,
> Nor let the shadow of the pillar sink
> Too deep within her, till the dawn is red
> Of that white noon when men shall call her Queen ! "

Love of his own land must have a glorious growth in the soul of his ideal patriot.

> " Love of thee holds in it hate of wrong
> And shapes the hope that moulds humanity."

So it was with him. His broad humanity was the hospitable banyan-tree, developed from the plant of patriotism which grows in Irish soil indivisible from religion, " a plant of double root."

In sight of Dowth Castle, Drogheda, Ireland, where John Boyle O'Reilly was born on June 28, 1844, rises the Hill of Tara, scene of Ireland's ancient national and religious glories. Close beside it runs the river Boyne, name reminiscent of national and religious humiliation.

Dowth Castle, dating back to the days of' the English Pale, is not so well known by its nineteenth century name, the Net-terville Institution, so called for the nobleman who owned it in the beginning of the century, and, dying, devoted it and a por-tion of its lands to charitable and educational uses.   A National school was built on its grounds, of which William David O'Reilly, the poet's father, was head-master for thirty-five years.

On his father's side young O'Reilly traced his ancestry back for a thousand years, through the soldierly and chivalrous O'Reillys of Cavan. .This noble stock gave also to the New World Count Alexander O'Reilly, governor of Louisiana under the restored Spanish domination, the friend of prisoners and implacable foe of the slave-trade.   His mother, Eliza Boyle, a woman of strong character, cultivated mind, and much per-sonal beauty, was a near relative of Colonel John Allen, who distinguished himself in the French wars under Napoleon.

Amid this historic environment, and with these family tradi-tions, the boy lived until he had passed, not his eleventh year, as his biography states, but only his ninth, as the author was informed in a letter from O'Reilly's sister, received too late for use.

"He had to kneel on a chair to sign his indentures," she writes, . describing the day he left home to enter the printing-office of the Drogheda *Argus* as apprentice.   Writes his biogra-pher:

"The circumstances under which he was induced to begin the struggle of life at such a tender age were these: His brother William, two and a half years his senior, had been bound as an apprentice in the *Argus* establishment.   He was a delicate youth, and after six months' service was obliged by ill-health to give up his place.   John, then a fine, manly little fellow, hearing his mother lament the loss of the premium, which amounted to fifty pounds, offered to take his brother's place, and the offer was ultimately accepted."

There can be few reminiscences of a childhood so patheti-cally brief.   He tells himself of his dearest childish possession, "the little, brown, fat dog who wore the hair off his back with lying on it to play with the big dogs or with me."

"His smile was irresistible," writes his sister, "but I think his greatest charm was in his manner.   From earliest childhood he was a favorite with everybody, and yet the wildest boy in Dowth.   If any mischievous act was committed in the neighbor-

hood John was blamed, yet everybody loved him and would hide
him from my father when in disgrace."

He was, nevertheless, a steady and omnivorous reader, and a
constant verse-maker.   His first completed effort, written at the
age of eleven, was a grateful little elegy on Frederick Lucas, the
pioneer English Catholic Home-Ruler.

All through his life O'Reilly cherished the tenderest thought
of the pious mother from whose loving care he so early drifted.
She died while he was still in Australia, her life shortened by
her anxieties for her best-loved son.   We find his mother's memory often in his poems; never more sweetly than in one on
the name of " Mary " :

> " Sweet word of dual meaning ; one of grace,
>   And born of our kind advocate above ;
> And one by memory linked to that dear face
>   That blessed my childhood with its mother-love,
>
> " And taught me first the simple prayer, ' To thee,
>   Poor banished sons of Eve, we send our cries.'
> Through mist of years those words recall to me
>   A childish face upturned to loving eyes."

From his fifteenth to his nineteenth year young O'Reilly was
employed, first as type-setter, later as reporter, on the *Guardian,*
of Preston, England, making his home with an aunt, Mrs. Wat-
kinson, the beloved " Aunt Crissy " of his letters from America.
Here in this quiet old English Catholic town the soldier blood in
him began stirring.   The iron of his country's wrongs had entered his soul.   Like most of the young patriots of his time, he
would have no half-measures.   He dreamed of a great uprising
which would make Ireland a republic.

When recalled home in 1863 he became a Fenian, enlisted
in the Tenth Hussars, and bent all his energies to the spreading
of republican principles in the British army.

An indefensible act from the moral standpoint ? Yes ; but before passing capital sentence consider the state of Ireland in
1863. " She was a drugged, poisoned, stupefied body," said
O'Reilly to the writer of this review ; " and the Fenian movement was the beating of it to waken it out of the fast-settling
torpor of death." The English policy of endeavoring to combine religious freedom and national slavery had developed " the
Castle-priest " and his unconcealed hostility to Irish national aspirations. Often he was a model of piety and sincerity in his
own fashion ; with the martyr-spirit ready to leap in flame from

his death-wound. But Ireland's world-wide apostolate, even
though it had to be furthered by submission to English rule,
and not her petty national possibilities was his dream, There
was many a "Monsignor McGrudder" in Ireland in John Boyle
O'Reilly's young manhood; and if he was far outnumbered by
priests like "Father Phil," at least the hot-blooded young
patriots, conscious for the time being only of the bit and curb,
had not learned that such priests loved Ireland as truly, if more
wisely, than themselves. O'Reilly learned it, as he testifies in
his "Priests of Ireland" in 1873. But he learned it by bitter
experience.

"I never knew what it all meant till I found myself in prison," he said in later years. "They only said to us: 'Come,
boys; it may be prison or death, but it's for Ireland'—and· we
came "

As his biographer truly says:

"One does not weigh dangerous consequences against generous impulses at nineteen years of age. No more does he inquire with minute casuistry into the exact moral values of the
deed."

O'Reilly frankly admitted the errors and blunders of Fenian-
ism. Early in his American career, and strongly and steadfastly
through the whole course of it, he raised his voice against secret
societies. The most obstinate "Invincibles" of them all heard
his words with respect. He knew whereof he spoke; his patriotism had borne the supreme test; and, however little to their
faith or taste the policy of constitutional agitation which
O'Reilly heartily adopted at the inception of the Home-Rule
movement in 1873, they knew he urged it from a sincere heart.

But of the young Fenian in the British army:

"The magnetism of the boyish soldier," writes his biographer,
"won more converts to treason than his fervid eloquence. Even
the uncompromising loyalty and Protestantism of an Orangeman
from the 'black North' succumbed to his fascination, and did
not recover from the spell until the Fenian *malgré lui* found
himself a life convict and wondered how it had come about."

"You've ruined the finest regiment in the service," was
Colonel Valentine Baker's testimony to the thoroughness of
O'Reilly's work when finally, through the inevitable informer,
the latter was discovered and arrested.

After a rather farcical trial, on July 9, 1866, sentence of death was passed on all the military prisoners. The same day it was commuted in the case of O'Reilly and four others to life imprisonment. Subsequently, through the efforts of Lord Odo Russell, O'Reilly's sentence was further commuted to twenty years' penal servitude. We will not follow him through his various English prisons—Arbor Hill, where Robert Emmet had been before him ; Mountjoy ; Pentonville ; Millbank, where he had his six months' solitary confinement ; Dartmoor, where the midsummer task was the pounding of putrefying bones, the refuse of the prison, in a shed on the brink of the prison cesspool, and where the men were in such state of semi-starvation . that they would eat anything that a dog would eat.

Fac-simile pages of some of his letters to his family from prison are given in the life. While awaiting sentence in Arbor Hill he wrote :

"Not a word yet—not even a hint of what my doom is to be ;. but whatever it may be I'm perfectly content. God's will be done. It has done me good to be in prison ; there is more to be learned in a solitary cell than any other place in the world—a true knowledge of one's self."

.   .   .   .   .

"Never grieve for me, I beg of you. God knows I'd be only too happy to die for the cause of my country. Pray for us all ; we are all brothers who are suffering."

After the life-sentence :

"I wrote these slips before I knew my fate, and I have nothing more to say, only God's holy will be done ! If I only knew that you would not grieve for me I'd be perfectly happy and content. My own dear ones, you will not be ashamed of me at any rate ; you all love the cause I suffer for as well as I, and when you pray for me pray also for the brave, true-hearted Irishmen who are with me. Men who do not understand our motives may call us foolish or mad, but every true Irish heart knows our feelings and will not forget us. Don't come here to bid me good-by through the gate. I could never forget that. I'll bid you all good-by in a letter.
                    " God bless you !   JOHN."

O'Reilly had made up his mind to do his utmost to preserve the health of mind and body through the term of his imprisonment.

"Some people would call it strange "—we quote from a MS. of O'Reilly's printed for the first time in this volume—

"that I should still regard that cell—in which I spent nearly a
year of solitary confinement—with affection ; but it is true. Man
is a domestic animal, and to a prisoner with '20 years' on his
door the cell is Home. I look back with fond regard to a
great many cells and a great many prisons in England and
Australia, which are associated to my mind in a way not to be
wholly understood by any one but myself."

He bore the term of solitary confinement—a punishment
which has unhinged many strong minds—wonderfully well.

"He found solace," writes his biographer, "in his thoughts
and in the pages of *The Imitation of Christ*, which he was allowed to read ; but he endured many hours of the keenest anguish. At times his mind was abnormally active ; he felt an
exaltation of the soul such as an anchorite knows ; he had
ecstatic visions."

But sometimes the vigorous physical nature of the man—
and he was only twenty-three—asserted itself. He made three
successive attempts to escape, each ending in recapture and the
punishment cell.

O'Reilly was one of the sixty-three political prisoners on the
ship *Hougoumont*, which sailed for the penal settlement of West
Australia November 23, 1867. It carried also 320 criminal convicts. "A convict ship," wrote O'Reilly, describing the voyage, "is a floating hell." Its horrors were mitigated for him,
however, by the kindness of the ship's chaplain, Father De-
laney. Arrived at the penal settlement he found another friend
in the person of Father Lynch, Catholic chaplain of Freemantle prison, who had him detailed as assistant in the library, and finally it was a Catholic priest, Father Patrick
McCabe, who planned and helped his escape from the convict settlement of Bunbury, a little more than a year later.
Of his year in Bunbury his biographer writes :

"Among the criminals with whom he was forced to associate were some of the most degraded of human kind—murder-
ers, burglars, sinners of every grade and color of vice. They
were the poison flower of civilization's corruption, more depraved
than the savage, as they were able to misuse the advantages of
superior knowledge. They were the overflow of society's cesspool, the irreclaimable victims of sin—too often the wretched
fruits of heredity or environment. Happily for the young, generous, clean-minded rebel, who had been doomed to herd with
this prison scum, God had given him the instincts of pure humanity ; and ill-fortune, instead of blighting, had nourished their

growth. He looked upon his fellow-sufferers with eyes of mercy, seeing how many of them were the victims, directly or indirectly, of cruel, selfish social conditions. In the Australian-bush he saw humanity in two naked aspects: the savage, utterly ignorant of civilized virtues as of civilized vices; and the white convict, stripped of all social hypocrisies, revealing the worst traits of depraved humanity. Both were 'naked and not ashamed.' For the savages, so-called, he entertained a sincere and abiding admiration. 'Why,' he said, years afterwards, 'I found that those creatures were men and women, just like the rest of us; the difference between those poor black boys and the men of the Somerset Club was only external. I have good friends among those Australian savages to-day, that I would be as glad to meet as any man I know.'

The date of his escape from Bunbury is February 18, 1869. He was taken up by a Yankee whaler, the *Gazelle*, of New Bedford, Mass., Captain David R. Gifford commanding, Henry C. Hathaway third mate. Here it is well to advert to a slander which, writes Mr. Roche, "in keeping with its character, did not find voice until the subject of it was dead"—namely, that O'Reilly had broken his "parole" in escaping from the penal settlement. This slander may have had its root in the reference of Sir William Vernon Harcourt to O'Reilly's escape as the crime of prison-breach in the House of Commons in the winter of 1885, when amnesty was asked (without O'Reilly's knowledge, be it said) for O'Reilly and James Stephens. When O'Reilly learned of the inclusion of his name in the petition he promptly cabled: "Kindly withdraw my name."

After his death the London *Times* revived the cry of convict and prison-breach. Searching inquiry, continues his biographer, has failed to discover any one willing to stand sponsor to the lie of broken parole. Its prompt refutation came from Captain Henry C. Hathaway, now of New Bedford, Mass., and the Rev. Patrick McCabe, now of Waseca, Minn., both of whom were parties to his escape. Writes Father McCabe:

"ST. MARY, WASECA COUNTY, MINN.,

"November 19, 1890.

"MY DEAR MR. ROCHE:

"I have your letter of the 6th inst. Absence from home prevented an earlier reply. John Boyle O'Reilly never broke his parole, *never having one to break.* From the day that he landed from the convict ship *Hougoumont*, in Freemantle, up to the day of his escape from Bunbury, he had been under strict surveillance, and was looked upon as a very dangerous man and

treated as such. No man living knows this better than I do.
Silence the vile wretch that dares to slander the name of our
dear departed friend, and you will have my blessing.

"Yours sincerely,   P. McCABE."

O'Reilly landed in Philadelphia November 23, 1869, and on
the same day presented himself before the United States District Court and took out his first papers of naturalization. In
the summer of 1870 we find him settled in Boston, employed
by Mr. Patrick Donahoe, founder and proprietor of *The Pilot*,
as editor of that newspaper. Six years later, when through
blameless financial misfortunes *The Pilot* passed out of Mr.
Donahoe's hands, O'Reilly bought a one-fourth interest in it;
the Most Rev. John J. Williams, Archbishop of Boston, purchasing the rest. The new proprietors assumed the debt of $73,000
due to poor depositors in Mr. Donahoe's bank at the time of
his failure, and paid it out of the profits of *The Pilot* in ten annual instalments.

In entering into association with Archbishop Williams in the
management of *The Pilot* O'Reilly said to him: "I will conduct *The Pilot* as becomes an Irishman, a Catholic, and a gentleman. And," said the archbishop, after death had severed
their fourteen years' association, "he kept his word."

With his work as a journalist John Boyle O'Reilly began his
Providential mission. Twenty-one years ago the position of
Catholics in New England was far other than it is to-day.
They were strong in numbers. The splendid vitality of their
faith was manifest in its powers of endurance; but in wealth, influence, and independence of spirit they were woefully behind the
Catholics of other long-settled sections of the country. There
was reason for this. The immigration to Boston from Ireland,
whose beginnings antedate the present century, drew largely
from the most oppressed districts. The immigrants who fled from
landlord tyranny and Protestant intolerance at home found a
vigorous transplant of the arrogant Anglo-Saxon political feeling
to the "mere Irish" and a grim and dominant Puritanism awaiting them on the new shores.

Notwithstanding Matignon and Cheverus, and the Protestant
Governor Sullivan, Catholic and Irish were, from the outset,
simply interchangeable terms—and terms of odium both—in the
popular New England mind. In vain the bond of a common
language. In vain the Irishman's prompt and affectionate acceptance of the duties of American citizenship. To but slight

softening of prejudice even his sacrifice of blood and life on every battle-field in the Civil War, in proof of the sincerity of his political profession of faith. He and his were still hounded as a class inferior and apart. They were almost unknown in the social and literary life of New England. Their pathetic sacrifices for their kin beyond the sea, their interest in the political fortunes of the Old Land, were jests and by-words. Their religion was the superstition of the ignorant, vulgar, and pusillanimous; or, at best, motive for jealous suspicion of divided political allegiance and threatened "foreign" domination. Their children suffered petty persecutions in the public schools. The stage and the press faithfully reflected the ruling popular sentiment in their caricatures of the Catholic Irishman.

Naturally, in an atmosphere so closely resembling that of the land of bondage, the New England Catholics, as a community, developed marked characteristics of reserve, caution, and slight self-esteem.

It is true that while the church was poor and weak, and distinctively allied with the foreign element, it attracted many converts from old New England families of wealth, position, and intellectual prominence. These accessions, however, had no very perceptible influence on the fortunes of the body Catholic. The bond of unity of faith can co-exist with marvellous divergences on all other points; and the convert, who had neither racial nor social sympathies with the mass of his fellow-religionists, was hardly fitted to be interpreter and reconciler between them and the dominant class, with whom, in all but religion, his heart was.

What the despised "foreign" element needed was a lay leader, of one blood as well as of one faith with themselves. Catholic and Irish, he had also to embody in his own person, so brilliantly that the dullest or most unwilling eyes must see them, those qualities which the Protestant Anglo-American had heretofore most prized as the visible sign of his own superiority. He came in the person of John Boyle O'Reilly.

There was many a riper scholar, many a better lay theologian, among the Catholics of the United States, but lacking the natural gifts and the providential training which made O'Reilly the great educative influence which he became among Irish-Americans and all other Americans. It is ill to underrate the natural man. O'Reilly was gifted with rare beauty and personal magnetism. The rough experience of barracks, prison, and convict colony had not impaired the courtly manners which were his inheritance. He was naturally brave, modest, and tactful. Suffering had made him patient, sympathetic, and magnanimous. He was a pleasing speaker, a promising journalist. A true poet, he came in time to have part with Bret Harte and Joaquin Miller and John Hay in that literary movement which Mr. Roche happily calls "the renaissance of natural poetry."

He made this grand equipment effective, first by his loyal identification of himself with everything pertaining to his own race and faith. He preached to the first colored class-orator of Harvard in 1890 only what he practised in his own person in 1870, for in many ways the Irish Catholics in New England were at that time subjects of an ostracism hardly less galling than that which chafes the self-respecting negro to-day. "There are dignity and power in his hands," wrote John Boyle O'Reilly of Clement Garnett Morgan, "if he be true to himself, which consists in being true to his people. Let no weak nerve draw him for an instant from their loving association. Their virtues are his own; let him labor to reduce their faults. The Anglo-Saxon will accept him only when he has proved his strength in the mass." This was the spirit in which his presence appealed to Boston, and his words to the great constituency which he reached every week through *The Pilot*. The founder of *The Pilot* had built up for it a national circulation in the 40's, when it had the field of Catholic journalism almost to itself. This O'Reilly maintained in the face of a more critical generation, and with competitors springing up on every side to divide the field.

The unstinted infusion of his own individuality into its columns was the primal factor in this result; but he re-enforced his own work with contributions from able writers at home and abroad. He would have his paper an expression of the best thought, a mirror of the noblest achievements of the Irish blood and the Catholic faith the world over.

".Don't moan that the Catholic press is poorly patronized," he would say, "but give the people a good paper, and they must take it." By his dignified and wisely generous management he made a paper at whose quality not even the most bigoted anti-Catholic could sneer.

But John Boyle O'Reilly had not been many years in Boston before it became a very perilous pastime to sneer at anything pertaining to Irish Catholics. All un-American discrimination against them in politics or business met his instant and practical protest. He had a custom of publishing in *The Pilot* "free advertisements" for business houses which attempted, however adroitly, the "no-Irish" or "no-Catholic" policy. These advertisements would stand in a conspicuous place till the offending parties "came to Canossa," so to speak. They usually came after the second advertisement. In the same way he would track to their cover, and pillory to the public gaze, the dark-lantern anti-Catholic societies, no matter how plausible their proclaimed intent, or how close to him in social or literary interest their membership.

No man dared say twice to him: "We don't mean your kind of Irish or Catholic, O'Reilly." All that bore the name was his, bone of his bone and flesh of his flesh; and this man, who cherished no personal enmities, who forgave and succored even the wretch who betrayed him, was merciless in his resent-ment of an insult to the least of his people, until condign satis-faction had been made. Thus he inspired a wholesome fear in the bully, and won the respect of all honest and fair-minded non-Catholics, for there is nothing your New England Yankee honors above "grit."

"How gladly," writes his biographer, "he welcomed any praise of their virtues, how eagerly he jumped at the least ex-tenuation of their faults!" And for what fault or crime could he not plead, and generally with sound philosophical basis, some ex-tenuating circumstance? He had no patience with those exhort-ers, however well-meaning, who would reproach the Irish with a human vice or folly, as if it were their own exclusive national sin.

We have spoken of his enmity to secret societies. He pro-tested against them not only in the name of the religion which forbade them to his own people, but in the name of true Amer-icanism. They were a national danger, whatever the race or faith of their members.

Thus, when the whole country was shocked by the murder of Dr. P. A. Cronin in Chicago, in the May of 1889: "This is the worst crime ever committed through the agency of secret societies *since the murder of Morgan by the Free-Masons.*"

"One of the worst consequences of England's long misgov-ernment of Ireland," said O'Reilly to the writer of this sketch, "is the number of Irish people born, so to speak, with mal-formed consciences." It was in a pause on the eve of publica-tion, while awaiting the verdict in the Cronin murder case, and the conversation drifted to the origin of the evil seeds which bore this poison-fruit in America. He told us of strange characters in the penal settlements—men who had been mad-dened by the sins against justice which they saw daily committed in the name of law, growing to believe themselves heaven-commissioned to rid their country of tyrant or informer. "They were kindly, generous, scrupulous men on all other subjects," he added, "but here you struck flint. Enlightenment and remorse by-and-by? Never. They told their deeds with calm satisfaction. They ate and slept like little children. They bore their punishment with a martyr's equanimity." All of which reminds one of Faber's remarks somewhere about brutality in war and agrarian outrages, and the occasional theological difficulty of deciding how far these crimes may be also sins!

O'Reilly, in common with all true-hearted Irish Catholics, hated the too-numerous association of his people with the liquor-traffic. The green-bedecked saloon on St. Patrick's Day was unconcealed pain and shame to him. But here again he found the evil fruit of alien misgovernment. "Intemperance went into Ireland with foreign rule," he said at the banquet of the National Catholic Total Abstinence Union in Boston, in 1888. And he continued:

"You will find (and I say it as an outsider who has given the subject some consideration) that the saloon-keeper among the Irish people in this country is nearly always an emigrant. There are very few Irish-Americans born in this country who have gone into the liquor-trade. The people coming here from Ireland were unskilled. The thousands or tens of thousand industries which enter into the life of a prosperous nation were taken away from Ireland.

.   .   .   .   .   .

"They were left with no opportunities whatever of acquiring knowledge other than that which pertained to the servile work of tilling the land, while the land was held by strangers. In Ireland a man with seven sons had seven farm laborers in his house; in Boston, for instance, the same man would have seven sons at useful and perhaps different occupations. That is the reason why many of the men coming from Ireland, notwithstanding they were provident, thrifty, and ambitious, were tempted to go into the liquor business as a means of acquiring money more rapidly. That is one of the considerations which I think ought to be remembered by your organization as a reason for dealing leniently with men in that traffic. But I believe that of all the classes affected by it, the first to relieve itself from the influence of the saloon is going to be the Irish-American class, because of these two facts: that we are not drunkards—that we come from no degraded or immoral stock; and because we are learning all the manifold industries and means of an honorable living which are open to us in our American business centres."

O'Reilly valued his personal advantages, his early-won literary fame, and immense social popularity and influence chiefly. as they promoted the cause of his people. And how effectively they promoted it! As one of his thousand friends in the priesthood, the Rev. Arthur J. Teeling, truly said:

"Like Esther of old, he went among his country's enemies and made them her friends; he exalted the condition of the people of his race; he won for them, for his native land, respect and esteem."

"A convict self-emancipated, he set us free," said Thomas Wentworth Higginson of O'Reilly's work as a dispeller of old Puritan, anti-Catholic prejudice in Boston.

George Parsons Lathrop, the author, who has become a Catholic since O'Reilly's death, publicly owned that he had never been able to throw off the shackles of New England tradition and the narrowness of vision engendered by it, so as to see human life and thought in their entire relations, till he met O'Reilly in Boston literary club circles.

But if he was thus jealous for the rights of Irish-American Catholics, and intent on their intellectual and social advancement, he was never unmindful of their duties. He would have Irish-Americans the best of Americans, not only for their own sakes, but for the sake of America and Catholicity. Almost his first editorial utterance in *The Pilot* was a scathing rebuke to the Irish Catholics who had attacked the Orange parade in New York, on July 12, 1870. This while the Irish-American journals of New York and elsewhere (for the soothing of the wounded vanity of their constituencies) were denouncing Governor Hoffman for permitting the Orangemen to march, and denouncing the militia for the bloodshed and loss of life attendant on the subduing of the riots.

"Why," he indignantly demanded, "must we carry, wherever we go, those accursed and contemptible island feuds? Shall we never be shamed into the knowledge of the brazen impudence of allowing our national hatreds to disturb the peace and the safety of the respectable citizens of this country? Must the day come when the degrading truth cannot be muffled up: that the murderous animosity of Irish partyism has became a public nuisance in almost every corner of the world? We cannot dwell on this subject. We cannot, and we care not to, analyze this mountain of disgrace, to find out to which party the blame is attached. Both parties are to be blamed and condemned; for both have joined in making the name of Irishmen a scoff and a by-word this day in America."

He granted the bitterness of the Orange insults to the religion of the majority of Irishmen, and the Orange alliance with American Know-nothingism ; but added : " If our Know-nothing snake attack us, we must ever remember that we can cure its bite by the plant of toleration, and kill itself with the whip of ridicule."

This was a new Irish gospel from a layman, but singularly in line with the pastoral letter of Bishop Rosecrans, of Columbus, which appeared at the same time. Received with disappointment and displeasure at first—an Irish contemporary had naïvely voiced national sentiment by describing under the head of "Orange Outrage" the sound drubbing which several Orangemen, appearing in their regalia, had *received* at the hands of their Catholic neighbors !—O'Reilly's counsel commended itself to the approving second thought of his justice-loving countrymen.

Strangely enough, as his biographer notes, " the last words that he ever penned for *The Pilot*, after twenty years of untiring service as the guide and friend and counsellor of his people, were in condemnation of the foolish, futile, dangerous dissensions among men who, enlisted in the service of their country, would forget the enemy before them to turn their arms against one another."

O'Reilly had equally stern condemnation for Irishman or Englishman, Catholic or Protestant, who sought to introduce foreign issues into American politics. Of an attempt to form an " Irish-American Party" in 1872 he wrote : " The day is surely coming when the necessity of punishing the author of such criminal folly will be forced upon the Irish people of America." And a year later on the same theme :

" The Irishman who would proscribe a native American, and the native American who would proscribe an Irishman, are guilty of the same crime against the principles of the Constitution. But the Irishman is guilty of more than the other; when he joins a secret society he is recreant to his religion; when he joins a proscriptive society he is recreant to his citizenship."

He would as strongly have condemned the wild proposal of a "Catholic party" to-day. " Advance the Catholic cause on citizen lines," was his constant urging. Let Catholics by their character, education, patriotism, compel respect and the recognition of their right to that political or other preferment for which they are fitted. Let them advance themselves in journalism, letters, business, society, and everywhere remember that they have the honor of their faith in their hands.

O'Reilly attended the Catholic Congress held in connection with the American Catholic Centenary celebration November 11 and 12, 1889; and was appointed one of the committee on future Catholic congresses. This committee met in Boston, July 25, 1890. Ten days before the meeting he wrote of it to his friend, Thomas B. Fitz, president of the Catholic Union of Boston:

"I am a member of the committee, but I have almost decided to resign after giving my reasons to the committee. I am convinced that national conventions of citizens called as Catholics, or as Baptists, Methodists, etc., are uncalled for, and in the case of the Catholics particularly are apt to be injurious rather than beneficial.

.   .   .   .   .   .

"If we had reason, as the German Catholics have had, to protest against national legislation, we should be only doing our duty in holding national conventions. But we have no reason of this kind, nor of any kind, that I can see. I do not believe that the judgment of the Catholics of the country advises the project of formulating any distinct Catholic policy in America."

Similarly he spoke to Cardinal Gibbons—in Boston for a meeting of the American archbishops—on the day before the meeting. He added that if, however, such congresses should confine their papers and discussions to subjects coming legitimately under the jurisdiction of laymen, and should seek to remedy certain local disadvantages under which Catholics labor, he would certainly approve of them. He instanced as practical subjects the great question of colonization, whereby our people might be to a great extent diverted from cities and thickly-populated centres, to seek homes for themselves and their families in agricultural districts. "Aiding and directing emigrants," he continued, "especially emigrant girls—strangers in a strange land—is another matter which appealed to our race and humanity to consider and amend present conditions. The encouragement of temperance, a careful analysis of the labor problem, and such like practical questions, would offer abundant matter and range for profitable discussion."

The Cardinal showed great interest in O'Reilly's views, and said that they were well worthy of serious consideration, that there was much to be said in favor of them, that the Congress would be open to no objections, and could not involve any dangerous complications, and would be received with general favor by the American people if its programme comprised

benevolent and economic subjects, affecting the moral and social well-being of our people, and such subjects as would foster
and develop a healthy spirit of patriotism, a love for our political institutions, and if it at the same time exposed and denounced all political corruptions and innovations which endangered the perpetuity of our cherished civil heritage.

Archbishop Ireland, Archbishop Riordan, Bishop Spalding,
and other bishops, besides a majority of the laymen attending
the meeting, received Mr. O'Reilly's suggestions with equal
favor.

On the other hand, he entered heartily into the project of a
Catholic educational exhibit at the World's Exposition in Chicago in 1893, as a definite and immediate work to be furthered
by the committee on future congresses.

John Boyle O'Reilly was a steady and consistent advocate of
Catholic popular education. We are sorry to miss from his
quoted editorial utterances his article on the perfect Catholic
school.

"There is one way," he said, "to make Catholic parochial
schools the most popular in America, even with non-Catholics:
make them the best schools in the country by an all-round
training—intellectually, spiritually, physically, and manually.

"In intellectual and spiritual training the Catholic schools
are the best now; and in physical training, since the advent of
the parish gymnasiums, they are sure to excel; but to complete
their excellence they must train the pupils in the skilful use of
their hands, in the use of the few tools that underlie all mechanical work, in free-hand drawing, etc.

"The parochial and convent schools have an immense advantage as manual training-schools. They are independent, un-
hampered by cast-iron rules and ignorant committee inspection,
and free to take advantage of every form and opportunity of
instruction.

.   .   .   .

"Here are the elements of a Catholic school:

> "Spiritual Instruction;
> Intellectual Instruction;
> Physical Instruction;
> Manual Instruction.

"The Kindergarten system can best be utilized by our convent schools.

"The expense of this added instruction, which is immensely
beneficial, is not too heavy for the poorest parochial school. A
few small foot-lathes, with turning-tools, scroll-saws, hand-saws,
planes, chisels, hammers, drawing-paper, or blackboards, a few

hundred feet of cheap lumber, in a` shed, with a good mechanic to train the hands of the youngsters to draw the design and use the necessary tools, and you have a department of the school which will be more popular than the literary department, and certainly quite as useful. Such a school will turn out more youths likely to succeed in the varied walks of life than any school based on the present exclusively literary system of instruction."

"Here is one result of Mr. O'Reilly's editorial on the four-fold training," said the reverend director of the Cathedral schools in Springfield, Mass., to the writer a year ago, displaying at the same time their fine gymnasiums and industrial departments. O'Reilly nearly always took part in the opening exercises of the parochial school gymnasiums.

He educated his own children at the convents of the Visitation and the Sacred Heart. "I sent my children to the convent," he said, "and the convent sent me back angels." We have a pathetic memory of a little daughter fastening a medal of the Blessed Virgin on his canoe, and standing guard by him on Good Friday to see that he kept "the black fast" properly.

Notre Dame University conferred the degree of doctor of laws on him in 1881 ; Georgetown University the same degree at its centenary in February, 1889. His last public utterance was an address to the students of Boston College during the commencement week of 1890.

The project of an American Catholic University enlisted his warm sympathy and steadfast help. Invited to be the poet of its dedication day, he wrote for the occasion his "From the Heights."

To John Boyle O'Reilly the brotherhood of man was the most literal of truths. He worked for the Negro-American in the same spirit in which he worked for the Irish-American. The cry of the oppressed in Russia or Farther India or Central Africa smote his heart as sorely as if it came from his native Meath. A few months before his death he read with intense sympathy Cardinal Lavigerie's appeal for the suppression of the slave-trade in Africa. The cardinal declared that the infamous traffic could be suppressed by force of arms if only "one thousand men, prepared for suffering and sacrifice—men who desired no reward or recompense, except that which the consciousness of having given away time, health, and even life, brings with it—would undertake the task. If there are any such men in America," said the cardinal, " I will be glad to hear from them, and particularly glad to enroll the emancipated blacks in my little army."

" There !" exclaimed O'Reilly, " that is the work I would like to do."

" But for the hostages to fortune," adds his biographer, " I think he would have volunteered to raise the little army on the spot."

Of the four notable poems of his maturity, one was for Ireland, " The Exile of the Gael "; one for America, " The Pilgrim Fathers "; one commemorated Wendell Phillips; and one the negro proto-martyr of American liberty, Crispus Attucks. His only novel, *Moondyne*, written but a few years after his escape from Australia, was based, not, as one would naturally expect, on the Irish national struggle, in one phase of which he bore so notable a part, but on phases of English life. Its hero, Joseph Wyville, " Moondyne " to the Australian aborigines, was an Englishman. Its motive was the reform of the English penal system. This gives the measure of the man.

It may be remembered that *Moondyne* was severely criticised by some Catholic journalists on the ground that neither in its chief character nor its spirit was it Catholic. Answering a very intemperate attack on the book, O'Reilly said :

" To demand of a Catholic author that his chief character shall be a Catholic is absurd. A novelist must study types as they exist." . . . The author " put the man there who actually belonged to the place. The leading traits of ' Moondyne ' were mainly studied from the life. . . . There is not, could not be, an anti-Christian word in *Moondyne*. If there were it should not stand one moment. The words put up and knocked down by Mr. McMaster are not in *Moondyne*. They are his own."

It is relevant to repeat here the judgment of a wise priest, who was also a close friend of O'Reilly's :

" John Boyle O'Reilly's temptation, not always successfully resisted, was to make too much of the goodness of human nature, without due advertence to its need of supernatural help. This he was overcoming with maturing years, and the deeper knowledge and more regular practice of his faith. He thought so well of human nature because he judged other men by himself. He was a great natural man."

Here is the explanation of whatever may disappoint the Catholic reader in *Moondyne*.

A Catholic monarchist would condemn some of his poems as "revolutionary." But devotion to monarchical traditions forms no part of the religion which flourishes best in the atmosphere of freedom; and John Boyle O'Reilly was too firm in faith and reverence to be a revolutionist, in the evil, Old World sense of the word. His friend, the Rev. Thomas J. Conaty, D.D., read him aright: "Liberty was his life-idea—God its source and Humanity its application."

Absolutely free, as another priest, the Very Rev. Wm. Byrne, D.D , V.G., of Boston, noted, from "that intellectual pride and self-sufficiency which impel some men . . . to invent a way of salvation all their own," he was a practical Catholic. For many years previous to his death he had approached the sacraments every three months. He always kept the anniversary of his marriage with Holy Communion. He went to his religious duties with the readiness and simplicity of a child.

A Protestant friend, the Hon. E. A. Moseley, of Washington, sharer of many a vacation trip with O'Reilly, writes: "What most impressed me in Boyle's character . . . was his childlike faith in the teachings of his youth, his firm, unshaken conviction and his beautiful trust and repose in his religion."

He writes himself of the church to another Protestant friend: "A great, loving, generous heart will never find peace and comfort and field of labor except within her unstatistical, sunlike, benevolent motherhood. J., I am a Catholic just as I am a dweller on the planet."

If anything could have tried his faith it would have been an apparent conflict between the interest of the Irish national cause and the obligations of religion. But when the Papal rescript of 1888 against the "plan of campaign" and "boycotting" was proving a stumbling-block to many a patriotic Irishman in America and in the Old Land, O'Reilly simply said:

"If there be in our political machinery one or more separate practices that can be morally condemned, we shall not hesitate to change them for the better. We reiterate our deep respect for the word and person of the Holy Father; and we reassert our unquestionable right to continue our ancient and honorable struggle for national self-government."

In this spirit he wrote all through the troubled season which followed; and his wise, manly, and Christian course won warm commendation at Rome and from the Irish bishops.

Cardinal Gibbons, in his introduction to the Life of O'Reilly, praises "the conservative prudence, scarcely to be expected in one so vehement by nature," with which he usually handled burning questions.

"Kindness was the fruit, courtesy the flower, of John Boyle O'Reilly's character," writes his biographer. He was naturally kind, but let us remember that "kindness springs from that part of man's nature where God's image is engraven deepest." His charity included not only generous giving of money, time, and influence, but that which sometimes costs more—gentleness of judgment, kind interpretation of motive, prompt forgiveness of injuries. He was scrupulous in his regard not only for the rights but even for the vanity of others. "I hate sarcasm as a quality in life or in writing," he said. He found something to respect in every creature. If he impulsively wronged or hurt any one, he never rested till he had made generous reparation. He was slow to suspect and incapable of jealousy.

He put all these characteristics into his journalistic work. "Never do as a journalist what you would not do as a gentleman"; "Conquer by magnanimity," were his constant counsels to his associates. He could not have endured association with a suspicious or vindictive character. He would not admit the possibility of anything but generous rivalry and a community of interest among Catholic newspapers. He proclaimed with pleasure every addition to their numbers, every evidence of any one's prosperity. He would have no quarrel with another journalist of his own faith. "See only the good in those who are working for the common cause," was another watchword in his office.

So he lived and labored, growing steadily in helpfulness and reverence and mercy, tuning his life more and more harmoniously to the key-note himself had chosen: "Not love but sacrifice." He had made a great place for himself; he had wrought a great work for his fellow-men; and he was still young enough to justify the hope that nobler achievements were in store for him, when Humanity was called to write Irreparable against the calamity of his death. He had no peer; he left no heir-apparent to his own peculiar place and work; but his memory and example are vital forces still, and the sacrificial seed he sowed so lavishly must bear befitting harvest.

KATHERINE E. CONWAY.

"WAS CHRIST A BUDDHIST?"

THE QUESTION ANSWERED.

THE above question forms the title ot an article by Mr. Felix Oswald lately published in *The Arena*. This article is one proof of the general neglect into which sound logic has fallen at the present time, of the scarcity of solid science controlled by a justly rigorous adherence to principles in a certain section of the literary world, and of the extreme facility with which it admits fantastic theories under the guise of popularized science.

Every one who has the least knowledge of Christianity and Bouddhism, on reading the somewhat singular title of the aforementioned article, must say at once that the answer to the question it proposes is assuredly negative. How great, then, is the surprise of even the least intelligent reader when he finds Mr. Oswald asserting in the most naïve manner that Christ was a remote disciple of Sakyamouni! After such a statement, we look for at least some new and solid proof, and are extremely surprised to find the entire article filled up with mere assertions, supported only by the weakest reasoning, betraying an altogether insufficient knowledge of the subject, a lamentable ignorance, even, of those things which any writer who attempts to treat of topics of this kind is bound to know.

We will not stop to consider such sort of assertions as those which Mr. Oswald puts forth, when, *e. g.*, he tells us that the knowledge of Bouddhism must have been extended even as far as Palestine long before the birth of Christ. Statements of this kind cannot be hazarded without some evidence to back them ; and when history does not furnish even feeble and insignificant support to a thesis, one refrains from affirming it, or else incurs the just reproach of drawing on his imagination for his facts ; a procedure which science does not tolerate, and which renders the fanciful theorist unworthy of serious treatment.

We dismiss, therefore, these hypotheses of Mr. Oswald without discussion, and make him welcome to all the benefit he can get from them. The question how far Bouddhism was or was not propagated beyond India is one of secondary importance. What is essential is a comparison between religious doctrines,

legends, and narrations, and an examination of their mutual relations.

According to Mr. Oswald, Christ must have been an adept
of Bouddhism, the Gospel an echo of the Bouddhist books, because there are such resemblances between the founders of the
two great religions under consideration, between the histories
whether real or legendary of both, that the hypothesis of a derived origin of one from the other imposes itself upon every impartial mind.

This is the point we are going to examine, in order to discover how far the hypothesis of Mr. Oswald is tenable. We
will begin with doctrines. What were the doctrines preached by
Sakyamouni become a Bouddha? It is not easy to determine
this question, if one consult Western authors. Moreover, one
who adopts this course is easily exposed to the accusation of
having chosen the opinion most favorable to the view sustained
by himself and to his personal religious beliefs. In order to
avoid this accusation we will borrow from the Bouddhists themselves the statement of their profession of faith. This procedure is very much facilitated by the recent publication of a
Bouddhist Catechism, edited by a doctor of the religion of
Bouddha for the use of his coreligionists and of Bouddhist
missionaries in Christian and Mohammedan countries. Its author is the Bhikshu or mendicant monk Subhadra, who is a
high authority among the believers in Nirvâna. His work
being too long to be quoted entire in this article, we shall
give a very exact abstract of its contents, preserving the very
words of the author.

The catechism of Subhadra is composed of an introduction
explaining the fundamental principles of the Bouddhist doctrine,
and of three sections explaining in detail each of these fundamental principles.

The introduction describes at the outset the Bouddhist.

He is one who reveres Bouddha as the dispenser of spiritual
light, the supreme teacher and guide of all living beings; who
also, believing in his doctrine, observes its precepts and has
given a public testimony of his faith by repeating the formula of
Recourse, so-called.

This formula is thus composed:

I have recourse to Bouddha.

I have recourse to the doctrine (*Dharma,* the law).

I have recourse to the community of believers (*Sangha*).

By this formula one professes faith in Bouddha as his spiritual master, recognizes his doctrine as the basis and essence of truth and rectitude, and acknowledges the community of the elect as the faithful interpreter of the teachings of truth.

This formula is obligatory, and only after professing it in presence of a reunion of the faithful does one really become a member of the great Bouddhist community.

Its three members are like three stars guiding the sea-farer over the sea of the world; and one must add to it another formula expressing his respect for this sacred triad.

Section 1.   The Bouddha.

Bouddha is the founder of the kingdom of truth and righteousness, the Blessed One who is self-illumined, perfect in holiness, in wisdom, and in mercy.

He is neither a god nor the envoy of a god, come for the salvation of the world.   He is a mere man, but infinitely superior to ordinary men; one of the long series of sublime, self-illumined Bouddhas who appear in the world at long intervals and are so morally and spiritually superior to suffering and dying humanity that the childish imaginations of the multitude transform them into Gods or Messiahs.

Bouddha is only a term of quality denoting a man who has acquired the true knowledge and moral perfection by his own efforts.

After this preamble the author relates the life of Bouddha.

The young prince who was destined to receive this title was a son of King Suddhodana, and Queen Maya, who reigned over the Indian tribe of the Sakya.   He received at birth the name of Siddhartha, "the one who has perfectly attained his end." He was born in the year 623 B.C.   Certain Brahmins of the royal court foretold that he would become a powerful monarch; or otherwise, if he should renounce the world, a perfect Bouddha.   Afterwards a holy hermit came from the Himalaya to venerate him and proclaim him the master of perfection and salvation.

King Suddhodana, ardently desiring to see his son occupy the throne with glory, tried to hinder him from meditating on spiritual things, and to attach him to the world by luxury and enjoyments.   He kept him confined in palaces and gardens where everything breathed pleasure and indulgence.   He had a court composed of numerous young people, and the companions of his pleasures contributed to keep him attached to them.   At the age of sixteen he was married to the Princess Yasodhara (bearer of glory), and numerous young girls, trained in the arts of music and the dance, nourished continually in his heart the love of diversions.

In spite of these unceasing allurements, the Bouddha none the less became disgusted with the world and its vanities. This reaction was occasioned by the view of four objects successively presented before his eyes. The first of these was a decrepit old man, the second a diseased man covered with sores, the next was a corpse, and the last a venerable hermit. He was led by the sight of these objects to perceive the nothingness of life, and the miseries which belong to it and at last bring it to a termination in death. No longer regarding earthly existence as a good and a boon, but as an evil which one ought carefully to shun, and seeing in sensual pleasures a source of corruption and misfortunes, he resolved to pursue an end better than a wretched life terminating in death. From this time forth he sought for the means of escaping from suffering, death, from the re-births in which he believed like the disciples of the Brahmins, and resolved to imitate the holy hermit the sight of whom had so deeply moved him.

The trial which he underwent was made more violent by the efforts of his relatives and his wife, who left nothing untried to turn him aside from his new design. But nothing could shake his resolution. One night, while all were sound asleep, he arose noiselessly, cast a parting glance upon his wife and child, had his horse saddled, and departed hastily in the darkness, flying with the utmost speed of his horse. He was accompanied by his faithful squire Tcharna. After a long gallop he halted, gave his arms, jewels, and horse to his companion, and sent him back to recount what he had witnessed to his relatives and his wife.

Being left alone, Siddhartha remained seven whole days on the bank of a river engaged in meditation upon the great truths which had impressed his mind; after which, having exchanged clothes with a beggar whom he met in that neighborhood, he went to the capital of the kingdom of Magadha, called Ragagriha, or dwelling-place of kings.

In that place, seeking for the truth of which he had yet obtained only imperfect glimpses, and wishing to arrive at the solution of the great problem of pain and death, he attended the school of two learned and pious Brahmins whose reputation was high in Magadha.

They instructed him to seek for salvation in religious practices, whose effect should be to incline to mercy that principle which is the author of the world. But Siddhartha, who had on this occasion taken the name of Gotama, soon felt the emptiness and insufficiency of their doctrines, and betook himself to other Brahmins who taught mortification as the means of obtaining deliverance from earthly evils and from re-birth. Yielding at once to their persuasion, he gave himself up to the most violent austerities, and that for the space of six years. He went so far as to lose his bodily strength and to fall into a state of weakness which was nearly mortal. He then understood that these austerities served only to trouble his soul and arrest his progress in the path of virtue. He abandoned them without hesitation, and was himself abandoned by his companions in penance as an ascetic who was a traitor to his duty.

Caring little for their disapproval, Gotama went on his way, meditating and seeking always in his mind the solution which he had been so long pursuing.

A prophetic dream had apprised him that he was approaching the goal of his efforts. After a long meditation, he sat down under a fig-tree, his face turned toward the East, resolved not to get up till he had reached the end of his aspirations.

He was then and there attacked by a violent temptation. All the human desires of greatness, glory, and pleasure arose in him at once, and the goods of the earth presented themselves before him under the most seductive aspect.

He felt as if he were vanquished ; but he remained unconquerable, shook off these dreams, rejected these phantoms, and came forth victorious from the mortal combat.

Then the veil which hid from him the truth fell from before his eyes ; he was suddenly enlightened (bouddha), and the truth was disclosed to his view.

He understood the cause of birth, decay, pain, death, and rebirths, and at the same time the remedy for these evils—the way of deliverance of Nirvâna. From this time he was bouddha.

He had to undergo, nevertheless, a last trial, a final temptation on the part of Mara, the spirit of evil and pleasure. He issued from this, as from the first conflict, victorious, repulsed the advances and seductions of the tempter, and protested that he would not die until he had preached and solidly established his doctrine, and thus provided the true and only means of salvation for men and gods. For, according to the Bouddhists, the gods, if they exist, are finite and transitory beings, subject to rebirths, like men, although their life should extend to a period of many millions of years. The Bouddhist pays no regard to them, and looks upon the *Saint* of his doctrine as superior to all gods.

The new Bouddha immediately began his itinerant work of sowing the good seed of the word. The first persons whom he encountered were the five ascetics who had quitted his company when he abandoned the life of mortification which he had led at the outset. They still wished to shun him as an apostate from the true faith, but his majestic appearance, the sublime expression of his countenance, made such a profound impression upon them, that they felt themselves vanquished, and submitted to his direction after a first sermon, in which he explained to them the fundamental principles of his doctrine. Henceforth they recognized in him the man perfectly enlightened, the teacher of the truth, the guide to Nirvâna.

The Bouddha immediately received them as disciples and with them formed the first community (sangha), the primordial germ of the great Bouddhist church. The five converts were actually a productive germ, and in five months the number of his ascetic disciples had already reached sixty, besides a great many lay adherents.

Seeing himself at the head of such a numerous troop of disciples, the Bouddha resolved to disseminate the good doctrine in the world, and sent forth his disciples singly to preach the way of salvation, giving them their commission in these words:

" You are now free from all bonds, human or divine. Go, preach salvation to all living beings through compassion for men. There are many people in the world of a right heart and a pure intention who will perish unless they hear you preach the doctrine of redemption. Go, and they will become, through you, supporters and confessors of the truth."

After bidding farewell to his disciples, Bouddha continued his peregrinations, converting Brahmins, nobles, and kings. In the course of his journeys he came to his natal city. His father, shocked at first by the poverty of his mode of life as a mendicant ascetic, was eventually convinced by the words of the seer and introduced him with honor into his palace. There he made a similar impression on the heart of his wife Yasodhara, and received his son into the community of the elect. Soon afterwards he departed, to continue his mission far and wide in the world, and during forty-five years he incessantly preached the word of salvation. He went from city to city and from hamlet to hamlet, exhorting the people and teaching them by maxims and parables. During the rainy season only he retired to the abode of some one of his disciples, or to one of the

demesnes which had been given to the infant community by
opulent believers.

Meanwhile the reputation of the Bouddha and of his doctrine increased daily. Thousands of men and women of every
rank and condition pressed around him, desiring to enter the
monasteries of both sexes and to pronounce the higher vows,
while a countless crowd embraced the practices enjoined upon
persons living in the world.

Neither the Bouddha nor his disciples became the object of
any persecution. The only instance of attempted violence was a
conspiracy planned by one of the chiefs of the elect against
his life, for the sake of getting rid of him and usurping his
place. Bouddha triumphed over his hatred by his inexhaustible goodness, and the unhappy man abandoned his criminal
project.

When he was eighty years old, the Bouddha felt his strength
failing and his death drawing near. He informed his disciples
of his condition, and admonished them to hold firmly and exclusively to the rules he had traced, rejecting unwaveringly
everything which had even the appearance of a deviation.

A little after he sank into an extreme feebleness, and asked
for water to assuage his thirst. His disciple Amouda ran to a
neighboring spring, the water of which was always troubled and
dirty. O wonder! the water had become pure and limpid. At
the same time the face of the Bouddha became so shining that
a robe of cloth of gold in which he had been vested seemed
to lose all its lustre.

On the morrow he had himself laid upon a couch between
two withered trees, when suddenly the two trunks were covered
with blossoms which fell down upon the blessed man, while soft
music was heard in the air.

The Bouddha said: "You see, my brethren, how heaven and
earth honor me; but the true honor which ought to be given
to me is to follow my instructions." He reminded them anew
of the necessity of always conforming to his teaching, not believing themselves to be left without any guide after the death
of their chief, but looking to his doctrine for guidance. "Forget not," he added, "that whatever is born perishes. Put forth
all your efforts to arrive at the deliverance"; and saying this,
the blessed man departed from life.*

---

* It is worthy of remark that our Bhikshu [from whom the author of the article has taken
the above narration.—*Ed.*] has passed over certain features of the legend which are little
honorable to the hero. For instance, it relates that the Bouddha died from the consequences
of an indigestion brought on by his gluttony.

We have dwelt thus long on this part of our subject in order that our readers may know well what sort of person he was
whom some prefer to Christ. Let us now pass on to our next
section.

Section 2. The Law and Doctrine. The law is the true way
of salvation, comprehended by intuition, announced by the Bouddha and consigned to the holy books of the Bouddhists. These
books are divided into three parts, containing, respectively, the
words, discourses, maxims, and parables uttered by the Bouddha
himself during his earthly life ; the moral and disciplinary precepts
dictated by him for the direction of his communities ; the metaphysical doctrines upon which the moral principles of the Bouddhist are founded. In order to comprehend this last class of
books it is requisite to have reached a high perfection and the
state of intellectual superiority to which it gives rise.

These books contain the pure truth, which is not found
elsewhere, and which one ought to believe firmly ; yet he should
by no means think that these truths were communicated by
a divine or celestial revelation. That would be an essential
error. The Bouddha was illuminated by himself, and was indebted only to a light which arose spontaneously within his own
intelligence. The revelation is the doctrine and the lessons
which he taught to men involved in the darkness of ignorance
and human passions.

An essential feature of the doctrine of the Bouddha is, that
he delivered it to men only from his natural goodness and compassion, in order to aid them to escape from a condition in
which they drag themselves from one miserable existence to another, from a current which bears them along through a thousand pains and sufferings from birth to death, and from one life
to another.

Bouddha's principal task was to discover the cause of all
these miseries ; and he found it in the desire to live—in attachment to life.

The man who has gained insight into this truth must before
everything else eradicate this desire from his heart, and he will
succeed in doing this if he acknowledges and meditates upon
the four great fundamental truths, namely : that life is inseparable from human miseries, that these miseries have a source, that
this source must be cut off, and that to do this is possible. The
man who is persuaded of these four axioms has lost the desire
of life and is ripe for redemption.

The Bouddha insisted strongly on the sufferings of life, which was for him truly and only *a vale of tears.* Birth, sicknesses, old age, death, the loss of loved ones, the enforced contact with hated individuals, etc., made up the perpetual themes of his pessimistic homilies and his exhortations to renounce their cause, to wit, the love of personal existence, which one should eradicate to the ·last fibre from his heart.

But this does not suffice for salvation, since it is necessary besides to follow the sublime eight-fold way, viz.: rectitude of view, of aspiration, of speaking, of manner of living, of conduct, of efforts, of reflection, of recollection.

The believer should abandon the two extremes of sensual pleasures which. debase, and of asceticism which torments and saddens without contributing to salvation.

The middle way just indicated alone conducts to wisdom, to perfect understanding, .to deliverance, to Nirvâna. But what is this Nirvâna or final state of the liberated man to which he is bound to aspire with all his desires, and after which he must strive with all his efforts?

There are few conceptions which have given rise to more diverse expositions and have remained more uncertain. For some it is annihilation, for others it is absorption in the great All. For ·others still it is a sort of paradise.

According to our Bhikshu, it is a state of the heart in which every desire, every passion, every feeling of fear, pain, malevolence, have entirely disappeared ; a state of repose, of peace, and joy, through the assurance of complete and inamissible deliverance. But it is impossible to define Nirvâna by language; no one knows what it is unless he has experienced it in his heart.*

The Nirvâna is the deliverance which one can attain even in this life. Nevertheless, many men are at present incapable of it ; all they can do is to secure a series of re-births, each more fortunate than the foregoing one, until they reach the final term. In itself re-birth depends from our will ; it is produced only by the force of our attachment to life; this is the true creative power which other religions have personified in God ; it is the agent —creator, preserver, and destroyer, which is the true and only divine trinity. The conditions of re·birth depend from the man and his acts, or rather from *the act,* from that which is called the *Karma* (act). This Karma which works in us is not an individual virtuality, but a general potency diffused through the universe, and operating in every being ; it is the law of causes and effects in

---

* It is altogether improbable that this was the primitive notion of the Bouddha's teaching. For him it was, more than probably, the annihilation of individual personality.

the moral world, the law making causes produce their necessary consequences, individualizing itself in each one, and playing the part of what Christians call providence, destiny, or even God. But it is a blind and necessary force, operating fatally.

The world has not been created; it has not come out of nothing; it is not the work of a divine creator—a notion which sprang from human ignorance, since there is no personal God, and no such thing as creation. As for the origin of the universe, Bouddha has said nothing about it, regarding the knowledge of this subject as useless for salvation.

Moreover, human language cannot render an account of it, because finite forms cannot express the eternal. Hence, whenever men have attempted to explain it, they have been able to put forth only vain speculations, false and contradictory theories.

When one shall have arrived at perfect illumination, he will then comprehend the true idea. But, to this end, he must be firmly resolved to walk in the eight-fold way. Every one can do this, on condition that he strive sincerely and enter into a community of the elect, in order to live secluded from the world, and aiming unceasingly at perfect wisdom. Few, alas! are able to resolve to take this course.

Besides the ascetics there is also a class of laical adherents to Bouddhism whose obligations are entirely different, and who cannot attain to perfection and the Nirvâna because of their attachment to earthly goods and, in consequence, to life.

A Bouddha, no more than any other, can deliver us by his personal merits. God himself cannot preserve any one from the consequence of his acts, which follow them as a shadow follows a body, and spring from them necessarily. Wherefore, the whole Bouddhist doctrine may be résumed in the one word "justice"; and the notion of mercy is entirely shut out.

The chastisements which are the consequences of crimes, even the most grievous, are not in themselves eternal, although they may be indefinitely protracted by the persevering impenitence of the criminal. These chastisements are not merely unhappy re-births, for Bouddhism recognizes also the existence of places of darkness and torment in which the criminal must expiate all his offences to the very last. Before this expiation has been accomplished good works can have no effect to restore the condemned to a terrestrial re-birth, to a new knowledge of the way of salvation, and to the possibility of re-entering this path.

The doctrine recognizes also the existence of places of delight, in which the fruit of good works is enjoyed until it becomes exhausted, after which one who retains an attachment to life is subject to a re-birth in fortunate conditions.

According to the Bouddhist doctrine, our actual being is only a form which vanishes at death. Hence the question arises, What is that in us which survives and becomes embodied by a new birth?

This something is nothing else than our will, our desire to live, which constitutes the essence of our being, and which, by the operation of Karma, seizes on the elements necessary to reconstruct and adapt to itself a new phenomenal form.

This being so, what is the will which is able to produce this kind of phenomena? Is it of the same nature with what we call a soul? By no means. The belief in an individual, subsistent soul, having only a temporary existence in the body, is a gross, heretical error in the eyes of Bouddhists. The principle called soul is only an aggregate of diverse faculties, which is dissolved at the death of the subject. What is reincarnated after death is the *individuality*, which takes a new personality according to its Karma, and perpetuates itself from one existence to another until the arrival at Nirvâna. Then only individualism is lost, and with it suffering, death, and re-birth finally cease.*

Repentance for faults is good and can aid in obtaining perfection and salvation, not by effacing faults and their consequences, but by determining the believer not to commit the same again and to follow the good way. But it has no retroactive effect. Such is also the effect of prayers, pious reading, etc., but nothing beyond. A Bhikshu ought not to make use of such means, which are proper only for beginners.

The universality of absolutely fatal laws leads the Bouddhist to acknowledge that salvation can be wrought out in all religions, although that of the Bouddhist renders it easier.

Our author finishes his catechism by a concise *résumé* of the essential characteristics of Bouddhism:

1. The reign of perfect goodness and wisdom without a personal God.

2. The persistence of individuality without an immortal soul.

3. Eternal happiness without a localized heaven.

4. The way of salvation without an external Saviour, wrought out by each one without prayers, sacrifices, or penances, without the ministry of priests, without the intercession of any saint, without any divine mercy, but by a natural and necessary law.

5. Complete perfection attainable in this life upon the earth.

---

* This proves that *Nirvâna* is really the loss of personal existence.

The teachings of the Bouddha are entirely exempt from errors. But the sacred books of Bouddhism which are not his work contain many which have crept into them in the process of time.

The doctrine of Bouddha is in itself eternal, but new conditions of the universe may demand modifications suited to the times. New Bouddhas will come to teach and establish these.

In fine, the actual Bouddhism is only one stage in the grand way of the illumination of humanity. Before Siddhartha other Bouddhas have appeared and revealed the doctrine of salvation. Others will come who will renew his mission. By the laws of nature one arises every time that the doctrine has become so obscured that men can no longer find the way which conducts to the deliverance.

Our author does not hesitate to place Christ among those Arhats who have arrived at the Nirvâna, and his doctrines among the teachings of the Bouddhas of past times; therefore his name ought to be venerated by Bouddhists. " Nevertheless, his doctrine was not entirely pure; at this day the European nations are in a condition to receive the true light and are ripe for deliverance."

The foregoing sketch of Bouddhism and its principal features may suffice for our purpose.

And now I demand of every man of good sense if it is allowable even to propose the question: " Was Christ a Bouddhist ? " though it were only to answer it in the negative.

Was there ever a doctrine more opposed to Bouddhism than are those of the Gospel ? Bouddhism denies the existence of God, recognizes neither the creator, the redeemer, nor the judge of men. In its doctrine there is no acknowledgment of providence, of heaven, of grace or pardon, of the human soul, or even of human personality; of anything in the universe except an assemblage of forces operating naturally and necessarily, as the magnet acts on iron and oxygen on the matter which it burns. According to this doctrine, life is an evil to be annihilated, prayer a folly, repentance a vain sentiment. Bouddhism recognizes neither church, doctrinal or disciplinary authority, or priesthood. But what need is there of all these details ? The perusal of the foregoing pages will have sufficiently convinced all our readers that the doctrine of Sakyamouni is in its essential principles and all its details the complete negation of Christianity. He who taught men to pray without ceasing, and to say in this continual prayer, " Our Father, who art in heaven, hallowed be thy name: thy kingdom come; give us this day our daily bread, and forgive us our trespasses," not only rejected the Bouddhist faith, but pronounced against it the most severe and complete condemnation. We affirm without hesitation that only stupidity, ignorance, or bad faith can explain the attribution of Bouddhist ideas to the divine Founder of Christianity.

There are indeed some analogies between certain teachings, we will not say of the two religions, for Bouddhism is not a religion, but of the two doctrines. Both have in common the conception of certain virtues, esteem of the excellence of virginity, of penitential acts, of the ascetic life. Also certain usages, ceremonies, processions, exorcisms, the use of bells calling to spiritual exercises, incense, etc.

So far as the first mentioned points of analogy are concerned, namely, the moral virtues, Mr. Oswald has not perceived that the resemblance is altogether external. Renunciation, asceticism has, in Bouddhism, in nowise the object of liberating the soul from servitude to the body, in order to give it freedom to raise itself toward God. It is intended only to destroy life and the desire of existence. But if it were otherwise, what would that prove? Can there not be a resemblance between two doctrines, without one being authorized to suppose that one has been borrowed or plagiarized from the other? To this question every sensible man will answer, that not only there can be, but there must certainly be features of resemblance between the Biblico-Christian religion and the beliefs, even the practices, of every people in whom human reason is not entirely extinct. In fact, Christian morality is evidently nothing else than the natural law developed, perfected, placed in a clearer light. The Christian dogmas are, in part, truths which man can attain by reason. Everywhere, where there remains a glimmer of reason, a ray of truth, there must be found a belief, a principle of conduct, showing a likeness to one or another point of the evangelical doctrines. Thus, every man who has not stifled the voice of conscience must perceive in himself a perpetual conflict between the senses and the spirit, and the necessity of subjecting the former to the latter. The Brahmins understood this before Bouddha, and so did likewise the Chinese philosophers. Christ could not do otherwise than sanction this principle by giving it its true expression in a perfect manner. The merit of virginity and of the ascetic life, for instance, was not ignored by the Romans, or the ancient Peruvians, as I have elsewhere shown (*Rev. des Qu. Scientif.*, 1889, I.) Would any one perhaps wish that Christ should have rejected every truth known in some corner of the globe, in order to avoid the reproach of plagiarism ? Such questions deserve no answer.

It is the same case with worship. Exterior worship is composed of certain rites expressive of the sentiments which man ought to cherish toward the God in whom he believes ; adoration, submission, gratitude, desire and hope for grace and pardon, finding utterance in prayer. Certain exterior acts are especially expressive in this sense, as the burning of incense, the lighting of tapers, chanting, instrumental music, religious processions, and the like. The true religion ought to employ these wonderfully efficacious means, as well as the others ; so much the more because by doing so it brings back those observances to their true destination, and re-establishes the rights of God over man and all other creatures. Besides, most of these usages had been customary during a long period among the Jews, and it is unreasonable to suppose that Christ would seek in the remote regions of the world for that which he had before his eyes, among his own people, and in their temple. Moreover, several of the customs cited by Mr. Oswald are of later origin among the Bouddhists, and no one can tell where is the priority.

But Mr. Oswald has found some other traits of resemblance, which must, perforce, furnish more conclusive evidence of plagiarism from India. These are certain facts related in the Bouddhist legends, and—who would believe it ?—the popery which is manifested in the Thibetan Lama, worshiped as God's vice-regent upon earth.

The ignorance which he exhibits in this place would provoke a smile were it not that the assurance with which he makes his assertions is capable of deceiving persons who are even less well informed than himself, and cause them to believe in the reality of his fancies. Mr. Oswald does not know that the legends of the life of Bouddha are much later than Bouddhism, and that no serious man would dare to maintain that they existed before the preaching of the Gospel in India during the first century of our era. It is very amusing, for example, to see him quoting the Thibetan *Ryya*, more than eight centuries posterior to the publication of the Gospels. Nor is he aware that Bouddhism did not penetrate into Thibet until the eighth century after Christ, when *Popery* had been known to the whole world for more than five hundred years.

But Mr. Oswald does still better than this. He speaks of *Feasts of the Immaculate Conception*, of *Masses for the repose of souls.* This is indeed to make mockery of his readers, for Bouddhism knows nothing of all this. To pray for the repose of the departed souls is simply to deny the Bouddhist principles, as we have already seen.

Many of the practices opposed to the original ideas of Bouddhism originated in the North, as offspring of what is called Northern Bouddhism, which had degenerated greatly from the primitive doctrine, and at an epoch when Christianity was known beyond the Pamir and the Indus.

Every one knows that the legend of Krishna was composed of traits partly taken from the Gospel. This fact alone should render all readers very circumspect in regard to pretended plagiarisms of Christian from Oriental sacred books.

In fine, we regret to say that Mr. Oswald falsifies the Bouddhist doctrines and legends in order to make them approach to the teachings and narratives of the Gospels. It is entirely false, for instance, that the Bouddhist believes in the necessity of redemption by a supernatural mediator. On the contrary, Bouddhism denies both the possibility of a redemption, the existence of the supernatural, and the utility of a mediator. Before whom should Bouddha fulfil the office of a mediator, since, according to Bouddhism, there is no God ?

If questions of this kind are to be treated in future, we respectfully request that a little more science and serious argument may be brought to the task.

Our conclusion is: that all the evidence in the case proves that Christ is the living negation of Bouddhism.

C. DE HARLEZ.

University, Louvain, Belgium.

A QUESTION OF TEMPERAMENT.

IV.

"HAVE you ever been in the prison here?" Miss Garrison asked of her friend the morning after she arrived. They were sitting on the veranda, with the sweet charm of the country about them, and nothing in sight to suggest the grim abode down by the river's bank.

"Oh, dear, no!" said Miss Forsythe, with a shrug of the shoulders and a grimace. "I am happy to say I never had any friends or acquaintances there."

"Do people never go to see the place through curiosity?" inquired Miss Garrison calmly.

"I believe they do—some people. Tom went there once with a man who was up here from New York, and from what he says about it I have no wish to see the place. You didn't feel any desire to go, did you?" She turned her head toward Miss Garrison with a look of surprise as the thought suddenly occurred to her.

"I did not know but that Sing Sing people felt in duty bound to know something about such a distinguished attraction," the other answered evasively and with a faint smile.

"I know. Before we came here I always used to feel as if people living in the place must feel something like prisoners But I do not believe I have seen it but once since we were here. That is, in the town. You can't help seeing the hateful place if you go by on the river, as we sometimes do in a yacht. You'd have to keep your face turned to the Jersey side resolutely to avoid looking at it; and the choice of evils is pretty close, isn't it?"

Miss Garrison made some excuse for going out by herself the next day. By inquiry, she found her way to the square brick building with its slits of windows. The warden's house, though connected with the prison, was rather pretty, with a luxuriant Virginia creeper climbing up the stone walls. She went to his office. The warden was a hale old fellow with a full white beard, which, somehow, failed to make him venerable. Miss Garrison learned that visitors were admitted once in two months and that next week she could come and see Arkenburgh.

"I shall try to do so," she said with decision. "I am very much interested in his case."

So some days later Miss Garrison, on the plea of a call, again made her way without any companion to the prison. She felt rather nervous. Such conduct was unconventional and she would not have liked it to be known. She was taken down a flight of steps and a turnkey opened a barred door for her. Then she was shown into a dark room with seats arranged around the wall. Two or three men, in suits of dingy whitish-brown with black stripes running around them, sat on these seats talking to friends or relatives, while keepers remained in the immediate neighborhood. Arkenburgh was sent for, and Miss Garrison seated herself in a chair, seemingly much more composed than she was in reality.

She had not very long to wait. The tall figure of Arkenburgh appeared, his closely-cropped hair revealing a head of almost classic elegance. But those wretched prison-suits seemed to refuse to look anything but slouchy and ill-fitting!

His bright eye was rounded and inquiring, and when he saw who it was a shadow passed quickly over his face. But a look of mingled respect and gratitude at once succeeded it. How much thinner he was than when she had seen him in the court-room! though his eye was as bright and unshrinking as ever.

He bowed with great dignity, and Miss Garrison stretched forth her hand. He took it and bent slowly above it, without any words.

"I did not know whether you would remember me or not," she said, smiling slightly. "I hope you do not mind my coming. I am here for a few days, visiting friends, so we are neighbors."

"You do not know me very well if you think I could ever forget to the day of my death what you were so kind as to do and say in that court-room. Your coming to see me is only another act of kindness, for which I am grateful."

His voice was rich and full, and he spoke with a grave self-possession which impressed the young woman. They seated themselves, and after a slight pause she asked: "Do you find your health good? And is the place very dreadful?"

"My health is very good. In fact," and a smile transformed his expression into one of winning sweetness, "the greater part of the prisoners really seem to thrive well on the prison air and diet. But, naturally, few would elect to remain here as a matter of choice—not even for their health's sake."

"Well, in one sense it must be easier to bear when one has

the consciousness of innocence to sustain him. Mr. Arkenburgh," she went on a little hurriedly, "I do not wish to pain you by any allusions to the past, but I am an intimate friend of Miss Archer's."

The sadness settled on his face again, but there was some sternness in it.

"Do you know how she is?" he inquired briefly.

"I saw her a few days ago and she was perfectly well," Miss Garrison answered.

"Has this affair troubled her much?" he asked after a moment's pause.

"She felt terribly, of course," returned the young woman.

"Yet you, who had never seen me, and knew nothing of me, felt that I was innocent; and she, who was promised to me as a wife, believes me guilty and has abandoned me."

There was almost solemnity in his repressed tones, but the grave face did not betray any strong feeling.

"Do not blame her too severely," Miss Garrison said. "You do not know how she has suffered, poor thing!"

"Pardon me; I do know how she has suffered," said Arkenburgh. "She wrote me so that I could not fail to see just what was rankling in her mind. She was filled with outraged pride that she had been associated with a felon. One would have supposed that I had deliberately tried to bring disgrace upon her. But in one sense I am glad she wrote just as she did. It helped me more than anything else could have done. That is past and through with, however," he continued calmly.

"What do you have to do?" asked Miss Garrison. "I hope you will not think this is merely idle curiosity."

"Do not have any fear that I shall misapprehend your motives," he answered earnestly, bending his calm eyes upon her with the greatest respect. "You have done me the greatest benefit any one ever did. You believed me innocent when twelve honest men had with due deliberation declared me guilty. I tell you now, in the name of all that is sacred, that your true woman's instinct was right. I am as innocent of this crime as you. I do not know as a condemned criminal's word is of great force, but I do know that to you it will be strong corroboration of your belief."

"It is, if there were any needed," exclaimed Miss Garrison. "I have tried to look at the matter calmly and study the evidence, but I have never faltered in my conviction. Only I do

not know whom you are trying to screen, or why you so pas-
sively let yourself be punished for another's sin."

She looked at him wonderingly. He was silent a moment,
while he met her glance with that straightforward expression in
his eyes which spoke of simplicity and rectitude. Then he said
slowly:

"If you are really kind and generous you will not seek for
an answer to those questions; neither from me nor elsewhere.
What I have done I did knowingly, and I would do it again
under the same circumstances. It is a question of temperament
with me, as much as that pure, womanly touch of sympathy and
belief, which I shall treasure my life through and which has
lightened the burden of this"—he touched his prison suit—"was
one of temperament in you."

"You ought not to put too much value on an action so
simple and spontaneous," she said deprecatingly. "I think anybody would have done the same. It was a sense of justice," she
added, smiling.

"You must let me feel that it was a very sweet and womanly
thing," he returned. "Are you interested in prisons?" he said
after a moment.

Miss Garrison felt an inclination to laugh. It was the first
time she had ever stepped within a penal institution, and she
felt how very remote from her was the philanthropic spirit which
the question implied.

"No," she answered. "I do not believe I have much of an
inclination for going round doing good. I am here on a short
visit, and I thought I would come and see how you were getting along. You may put the visit down to feminine curiosity
in part, for I would really like to know what you do in this
place That is, if you do not mind speaking about it," she added quickly.

"I shall be only too happy to gratify you in any way," Arkenburgh said with great simplicity. "My occupation is marking
the places for buttons on trousers and to do up the pieces into
bundles. It is not very æsthetic work, but it is considered one
of the most desirable things to do. I must tell you one pleasant
thing. My place in the workshop is in the corner, which is
bright and sunny, and from the window I can see the Hudson.
It is very pleasant," he added cheerfully, "to see the boats passing up and down. I work here all day. The food is very simple but clean, and, whether it is the regular occupation or the
variety afforded by going to meals, my appetite is excellent.

The cell is the worst part of the whole thing. It certainly is small. I can touch the top with my hand and almost reach from side to side with my outstretched arms. I could hardly endure this cramped space at first, but now I do not mind it very much. I am getting to be an old prison-bird, you know." He smiled faintly.

"That is about all there is to it. You can imagine that the most cruel part is working at something which does not contribute in the least to my advancement, and feeling that a portion of my life is practically going to waste. Still, good behavior secures a commutation of part of the term, and I behave myself very well."

"How I wish something could be done!" said Miss Garrison vehemently. "Is there anything that you would like?"

"No; thanks. Except that I would like to have you tell me your name, if you will," he said.

"My name is Garrison—Miss Katherine Garrison," she replied. "And now I must go, Mr. Arkenburgh," she went on, rising. "I believe you are innocent and that you could have established your innocence if you had wished to. Why you do not wish to I cannot conjecture, though I am beginning to get an idea about that, too," she said, nodding her head. "Perhaps I may see you again some time, though the warden tells me that visits are allowed only once in two months. I hope your health will keep good. Good-by!"

She extended her hand and he clasped it again, and again bowed above it with dignity and respect.

"Good-by! You have done a good work in coming to see me. It has exalted my ideal of a woman. Thank you once more for your generous instinct in regard to me."

Miss Garrison bowed and the turnkey escorted her to the door. She stepped into the warden's office on her way out and asked him if the prisoners were allowed to receive anything from friends or relatives. Whereupon the good man gave her a small printed slip, telling her that it set forth all that was allowed.

Having folded it and put it in her pocket-book, Miss Garrison regained the free outer air with a great sense of satisfaction. How good it seemed to be once more where the wind of heaven could freely play around her!

When she was alone in her room that evening she took the printed slip from her pocket and read it. It was as follows:

•   "SING SING PRISON, Nov. —, 18—.

"RULES FOR THE GUIDANCE OF THE FRIENDS OF PRISONERS IN THIS
INSTITUTION.

"Each prisoner is allowed certain privileges, by the Prison Authorities, only on condition of his good behavior. Disobedience to the Prison rules forfeits for him *all* privileges for such a length of time as the Agent and Warden may direct.

"*First.* He may receive a visit from his friends (one or more at the same time) ONCE in two months. When an extra visit is desired an application must be made to the Warden, giving the reasons therefor, which should be important. On Sundays and Holidays visiting is not permitted, the Prison being closed.

"*Second.* He may receive a box of delicacies to eat ONCE in two months. Coffee, tea, chocolate, and other articles which require cooking *here* not allowed.

"*Third.* He may receive chewing tobacco, underclothes, socks, handkerchiefs, towels, bedding, carpet for cell, looking-glass, hairbrush and comb, tooth-brush, shoes, slippers, gloves, and mittens. These articles may be sent at any time.

"*Fourth.* He may write one letter each month, and receive all letters, of a proper character, that come for him. His friends may write as often as they please. Extra letters are allowed to be written by him only in special cases of sickness or important business.

"*Fifth.* He may receive all papers, magazines, and books, of a proper character, that come for him. Daily and weekly political papers, criminal and sensational papers, immoral and sensational novels, not allowed.

"*Sixth.* All boxes and packages by express (which must be prepaid), and all mail matter, should be plainly marked with the prisoner's name in full, and *the date of his sentence.* Compliance with this rule will prevent mistakes in the Prison delivery.

"ALBERT F. BURROUGHS,
"*Agent and Warden Sing Sing Prison.*
"Approved:
"WILLIAM SANDFORD, *Sup't N. Y. State Prisons.*"

Miss Garrison made a running commentary on some of the rules. "I could send him a box of things to eat. They don't say anything about the size of the box. I wonder if he smokes? 'Carpet for cell.' I do not believe he has one, and I should think it would be a comfort. That bare stone floor! He can receive all the letters that come if they be of a 'proper character.' If I write it will certainly be a letter of a 'proper character.' Papers and books! Why, that is nice. They ought to be a relief after making button-hole places in trousers all day long."

She sat thinking, with the printed slip on her lap. "I wonder if he thought it was Addie waiting for him when he came
in. He certainly did not expect to see me, and there was a
little look of disappointment on his face when he saw it was I.
Oh! why is that man there?" she exclaimed impatiently. Then,
as if she did not like to think of it any more, she made her
preparations for the night and went to bed.

Miss Garrison spent a fortnight with her friend, Miss Forsythe, at Sing Sing. Then she went back to town. A week
later a large box came to Sing Sing prison for Paul Arkenburgh containing delicacies. There was no note or card with
the box. A Turkish rug, narrow and long, also came for him.

"The poor man is suffering unjustly and it is only decency
to try and make his lot as endurable as possible," the young
woman had said to herself when getting these articles ready for
Sing Sing. But it must be confessed that she found satisfaction
in the thought that no one knew anything about the strong interest she had conceived for a State prisoner.

IV.

A fortnight after she had returned to the city she received
a note from Addie Archer: "Papa has had a severe accident.
He was coming down stairs a week ago when he was seized
with a dizzy attack and fell. At first it did not seem as if it
was anything serious; but he must have injured himself inter-
nally, for he suffers a great deal and cannot leave his bed now.
The doctor says it is a very serious thing, but hopes that papa
will come out all right. You know how fanciful sick people are,
my dear Kate. Well, papa has got the idea in his mind that
you must come down here. He thinks you would have stayed
longer when you were here if you had enjoyed yourself, and he
fancies that the trouble about that dreadful man in prison, which
was so fresh and trying, made me remiss in my duties as a
hostess. Nothing will satisfy him but that I shall write and ask
you to come down for a while now. Will you? Pray, don't
fancy that because I am doing this to satisfy an invalid's caprice that I should not be delighted to have you come myself. I
wish you would come, although I am afraid it may not be very
pleasant for you, with papa so sick and mamma dreadfully upset. But I can assure you it will be a great relief to papa, and
I shall be ever so grateful if you will come."

Miss Garrison brought her lips closely together on reading
this letter and her brows contracted with thought. It did not

take her five minutes to decide, and having sent a telegram to announce her arrival, she took the Newport boat that evening.

"There was a positive, visible relief in papa when he heard you were coming, dear," said Miss Archer to her the next morning. "He said: 'Now, try and make it pleasant for her, won't you?' and of course I said I would, and I will. Isn't it odd what funny ideas people get when they are sick?"

Miss Garrison allowed that the vagaries of invalids were very unaccountable. She had felt the moment she got Addie's letter that Mr. Archer's desire might have more method in it than could be admitted. He was not a man to be carried away by a gust of hospitable feeling.

Naturally she expressed a desire to see the sick man. But for a day or two after her arrival he did not feel equal to it. The third day she was ushered into his room. Mr. Archer was confined to his bed, and Miss Garrison saw at once from the ravages illness had made that his condition was rather a perilous one. She talked to him cheerfully, and he tried to assume some interest, but his mind would wander off in an abstracted way. Once, on turning to look at him, she found his eyes fixed on her with a strange expression in them of doubt and anxiety.

He withdrew them as soon as he saw her attention was attracted, and turned his head restlessly on one side, while an expression of pain shot over his features. When she rose to go he said to her: "I am not very good company, but I hope you will find time to drop in on me sometimes, Miss Garrison. It is a relief to me to have a visitor to talk to."

Three days later the doctor found his patient so much worse that he ventured to inquire of him whether he had arranged his affairs, or if there was anything he would like to attend to in case of a relapse. "Not that there is much immediate danger, you know," the doctor said comfortingly, "but you are not strong, and it is always the safe thing to look out for everything in time, my dear sir."

The next day Miss Garrison dropped in to see him. He was evidently worse. He shook hands with her feverishly. "Can you stay here with me a little while, Miss Garrison?" he asked her. She replied that she would with pleasure. "Then, I think I will send the nurse out for an hour to get a little rest and air," and he insisted on the man's taking this recreation.

After he had gone Mr. Archer asked Miss Garrison to take a chair and seat herself near him. She did so. For some mo-

ments he said nothing. Once or twice he turned his eyes in a
pained way upon her. At last, by a great effort, he brought
himself to speak.

"Miss Garrison, I wish you to promise me solemnly that you
will regard what I am about to say to you as a sacred confidence. Tell me that—whether you will do what I want you to or
not—you will keep the information I have to impart a secret."

Miss Garrison leaned toward the sick man and assured him
that she would not betray any confidence he might repose in her.

"I have done something wrong," he went on, his forehead
contracting and his lips trembling at the revelation they were
about to make. "And then I have done another thing that has
troubled me more than the first. I want you to help me, for I
need some help very badly. I cannot speak to my wife or
daughter about it."

"I will help you all I can, Mr. Archer," said the young woman earnestly. She had a clear conviction now of what was
coming and half shrank from it.

"You know my clerk, Paul Arkenburgh, was accused and convicted of stealing fifteen thousand dollars from the company of
which I was president. He didn't take the money. I took it!"

The effort of making the disclosure left him panting and pallid. Miss Garrison was alarmed a little, though there was time
for one proud thrill of satisfaction. She had been right!

"Do not try to tell the rest now, Mr. Archer, if you find it
too painful. I know now and you have gotten over the worst
part. If you feel the strain too much, defer the rest until later."

"No. I must say it all now. I could not rest in my grave if I
did not try to repair this injustice. You do not know what a
noble fellow that young Arkenburgh is. He is honesty itself
'and the soul of generosity.'"

Mr. Archer gave a sigh that was very like a groan.

"It is the old story, Miss Garrison," he went on, with his lips
twitching nervously, while his face flushed. "I needed the money
only for a little while just at that time. I thought I could replace it before its absence would be noted. But Arkenburgh's
sudden trip to Albany just at the time the money was taken
drew suspicion on him. There was no way out of it for him except convicting me, for I was the only other person who had
the key. I was supposed to be confined at my house in Tar-
rytown at the time, too ill to move with rheumatism.

"He knew this, and when I saw him he said: 'It is much
better for me than for you to suffer this imputation.' And I

was weak enough to let him do it, Miss Garrison. It seemed a worse crime to break my wife's heart and ruin my daughter's career than to let him suffer for me. But I have paid for this by my suffering. It was terrible to see Addie turning against him as she did. I do not think she could have loved him very much or she would have suffered more on his account.

"I have done this evil and I want to repair as much of it as I can," he went on. "I am going to get you to write out a statement of the whole thing at my dictation, and I will sign it and we will get other witnesses to sign it. With that paper you ought to be able to secure his release from prison. The governor would set him free on such evidence as this of his innocence.

"I am not going to recover from this attack. It is my punishment, and I deserve it. But, if it can be possibly done—not for my sake, because I won't be here to feel it, but for my daughter's and her mother's—I would like not to be known as the—the guilty man. When I am dead will you try and do this, Miss Garrison? If you promise me I know you will."

He bent his sunken eyes on her with mournful intensity. Miss Garrison was greatly overcome, but she roused herself to say earnestly:

"I will try and do both of them, if they can be done. But it would be hard if Mr. Arkenburgh should suffer this unjust suspicion all his life. I will screen your name as much as can be. What led Mr. Arkenburgh to do such a noble thing?" she asked Mr. Archer gently.

"He was indebted to me for his rise in the world, and gratitude entered into his motive for such generosity. And then," Mr. Archer said sadly, "he was very much in love with Addie and he wished to spare her if he could."

The poor man sighed deeply. Then he said in tones of the bitterest feeling: "And she has turned against him because he is a thief! Oh! how cruelly she has stabbed me by her hardness and the contempt with which she has spoken of that fine fellow by this name, which belonged to her father and not to him!"

"Do not dwell on the thought any more now, Mr. Archer," said Miss Garrison. "It is sad enough. I would not talk about it any more for the present. I will write the statement any time you wish, and then you will feel that you have made some restitution, for it must release Mr. Arkenburgh from his unmerited imprisonment."

" Then you will help me ? I can count on you, can't I ? " the
sick man said eagerly.

" You may, assuredly," she said, taking the hand which Mr.
Archer stretched toward her.

She was glad to get away to give herself time to think over
the situation. The satisfaction of being borne out in her instinctive belief about Arkenburgh was almost lost sight of in the
mixed feelings which held possession of her now. There was a
good deal of repulsion toward Mr. Archer. By his own admission he was a thief ! She was the guest, then, in the house of
a man who had stolen money. Miss Garrison felt a most disagreeable sense of disgrace from such association.

But the poor man was suffering, and he had asked her to
help him. She would not be like Addie Archer. He wished
to make such amends as he could. Miss Garrison appreciated
that if the true facts in the case were to come out when justice
could not be done to the criminal, and only innocent people
would suffer, the good of such disclosure was hardly apparent.
Arkenburgh must be released and his reputation restored, if possible, without bringing disgrace on Mrs. Archer and Addie.

But if Mr. Archer should not die ! What could be done
then ? She would have a comfortable feeling, surely, in knowing
that an innocent man was bearing the punishment of another's
sin to spare two other innocent persons misery and disgrace. " I
hope he does die ! " she exclaimed to herself as this thought
arose. " It is the only way of getting things cleared up at all."

Then she thought of Arkenburgh, quietly and resolutely accepting five years of ignominious imprisonment through generous
feeling for the man who had befriended and helped him, and,
doubtless, with loving thought of sparing the woman he loved a
dark and blasting grief. And then Miss Garrison experienced
another lively emotion as she recalled Addie Archer's treatment
of her lover. She got fiercely indignant at the thought. " It
was all right to feel repelled at his being a thief. I feel that
way myself towards the poor man upstairs there. It
was right enough to renounce him, too, if she could believe
this thing of him. But she need not have shown so much un-
pitying hardness and contempt toward him. She need not have
poured all her pity out upon herself. Oh ! what a hateful tangle it is."

The next morning she was the recipient of another confidence. Miss Archer told her, under pledge of the greatest
secrecy, that she had engaged herself to Mr. Caldwell. The en-

gagement was to be kept strictly private for some time. Miss
Garrison was not quite as effusive in her congratulations as she
might have been. It must be admitted that her judgment and
feeling about the Archer family were largely affected by the
thought of a tall, resolute man in a dingy prison-suit of striped
cloth and with an invisible aureola around his shapely head. At
least Miss Garrison felt that the aureola was there. Her friend
was too full of her own happiness, however, to note the slight lack
of ardor in her confidante. The lovers had agreed that papa
was not to be disturbed about love or marriage until his health
was better.

In the afternoon Mr. Archer's nurse came and asked Miss
Garrison if she could pay another visit to that gentleman's sick-
room. Miss Garrison had been impatiently awaiting the sum-
mons and obeyed it with alacrity. She was eager to have in black
and white Mr. Archer's statement about the robbery. The invalid's gaunt eyes met hers the moment she entered the room,
and after the nurse had again been sent out for an airing, Mr.
Archer hurriedly broached the subject.

"There is ink and paper in that writing-table. Will you not
take down what I say about Paul Arkenburgh now?"

The young woman was soon in readiness, and the old man
began: "I, George Archer, do declare that Paul Arkenburgh
is wholly innocent of the crime for which he is now undergoing punishment in Sing Sing. I stole the money, fifteen thousand dollars, and he deliberately allowed himself to be convicted
of it in order to screen me and spare my family the disgrace of
such criminality. He did this through a sense of gratitude to
me for having helped him in his career. I feel that I
shall not live long, and I cannot pass into the future life without some effort to rescue this generous man from the burden
he is so heroically bearing for my sake. This paper, written by
Miss Katherine Garrison, will be witnessed as mine by her and
the undersigned, my nurse. This should secure Arkenburgh's
release and acquittal from the charge.

"If this can be done without my guilt being published I
pray that it may. But, if needs be, and there is no other way
of securing this result, then let it be known, since it is more just
that my own should suffer for my evil-doing than a stranger,
who has shown such magnanimity. I make this declaration with
my sound mind and in the full use of my faculties. So help
me God!"

"Now," said Mr. Archer, breathing heavily, "give me the

pen." He grasped it and wrote his name to the declaration with a trembling hand. As soon as he had done this he fell back in his bed and a sigh of relief escaped from him. Miss Garrison said nothing for a few moments, until he had somewhat recovered from the excitement of the confession. Then she said quietly: "You would like this to be witnessed by some one, would you not? I will write my name to it now."

"Yes; and when the nurse comes in he will sign it," said Mr. Archer. "If you will, I would like you to remain here until his return."

Miss Garrison readily consented. The sick man lay perfectly motionless, but with his eyes half-open. After a short time the nurse returned, and Miss Garrison explained to him briefly that the paper contained directions, which Mr. Archer had committed to her in writing, about something which he wished to have accomplished after his death. The nurse then signed it, and the young woman left the room with the vindication of Paul Arkenburgh's honor folded away within the bosom of her gown.

She would have liked to bid farewell to the Archers at once. But Mr. Archer seemed to view her departure with shrinking, and she could not bring herself to pain a dying man. So she remained. He grew weaker daily. One morning, about ten days later, when Miss Garrison came down to breakfast, Addie Archer advanced to meet her with eyes swollen from weeping. "Papa is dead," she said chokingly. "He died last night." Miss Garrison let the girl cling to her and weep, while the thought arose in her mind that the angel of death had slipped the bolts from Paul Arkenburgh's prison-door. She could not feel any regret at this death.

She stayed with them until after the funeral. Then she returned to New York, on the plea that she had much to do. That week, without letting any one know where she was going, she took the train to Albany. Not very long after this a communication was sent to the warden of Sing Sing prison telling him that Paul Arkenburgh was to be released, as his innocence had been clearly established.

V.

Two days later Miss Garrison was sitting alone in her room, buried in thought, when the servant said that a gentleman, who declined to give his name, wished to see her.

"Tell him I will be down directly," she said, rising from her chair at once. She had not seen or heard from Paul

Arkenburgh since her visit to the prison, but she knew that two days before he had walked forth from Sing Sing free and innocent. She knew that it was he. She gave a few hasty touches to her hair, and then glided rapidly down the stairs and entered the drawing-room.

Paul Arkenburgh had heard her step, and was watching the door as he stood drawn up to his full height. There was an air of distinction about his fine figure and handsome face which were much more in keeping with his dark clothes and gloved hands than they were with the dingy stripes of the Sing Sing prison-suit.

She advanced toward him, her hand stretched out, a smile of warm welcome lighting up her face. He clasped her hand and bent his head above it, the hair still closely cropped.

"I am very glad to see you, Mr. Arkenburgh," she said.

"Thanks," he said simply. "I am free, and one of the first things I wished to do with my freedom was to come to you. I wish you to tell me if I do not owe this in some way to you. I received a communication from the governor telling me that my innocence was proven by the confession of the guilty person, and also saying that the same generosity which had made me suffer to screen him would probably lead me to conceal the culprit's name now that I was free and declared innocent of all stain. Do you know who the person was, Miss Garrison?"

"Yes," she replied softly. "He is dead, and although he has done only the least that could be expected in this effort to save you from your generous sacrifice, I am sure you will be careful to keep his guilt from becoming public."

"I am not surprised that you, who felt that I was innocent when everything pointed to my guilt, should feel that I could not have any other wish than this. So far my release has escaped noticed in the papers. Otherwise I should fear that there might be conjectures based on Mr. Archer's recent death and my release which would be dangerous for the peace of mind of the survivors. But will you not tell me what part you played in my release?" he continued earnestly.

"I did nothing except convey to the governor a written statement which I wrote at the dictation of the real culprit, and which he signed and I and his nurse witnessed. It was very little. Do not let us speak of that, please. But I am sincerely glad that you are free."

"And I have not thanked you for the box you sent to the prison for me," said Arkenburgh. "You must not think me conceited in believing it was you who did this, for I know there was no other who could have thought of me. Miss Garrison, I can never repay you for these kindnesses, but I feel them to the bottom of my soul."

"They were trifles. Put them down to my philanthropic spirit," she returned lightly. "I am afraid your sensibility leads you into undue appreciation of small things done in your behalf."

"I wish you would help me with your advice on one point," he said, "if you will not allow me to show you my gratitude as much as I would like. This same person has arranged through a friend of his that I am to receive twenty thousand dollars. I could have borne the full term of my imprisonment to shield him through gratitude for what he did for me, and through understanding how he came to fall and what the consequences of his guilt would be should it become known. But I feel the strongest aversion to taking this money. It seems as if I were accepting not only a reward for what no money could have induced me to do, but as if it were meant for a sort of seal upon my lips—a bribe to silence. It cuts me deeply to feel that he could have thought me capable of being affected by such considerations; and yet I cannot escape this conviction."

His large, grave eyes were fixed upon her face with pleading earnestness as he waited for her to speak.

"And to think that such a man as that could have ever fallen in love with Addie Archer!" was the thought that rose in Miss Garrison's mind. Then she said slowly:

"I think you are wrong. There is no fault in this person's wishing to show his gratitude by such a course. If you could have heard him speak of your conduct you would know that he appreciated it and positively revered you for your noble action. I will tell you this. He declared in that written statement that if it were impossible to free you without publishing the real author of the theft then to publish him, for the sufferings of his own were more just than that you should endure such a punishment. No! I am sure that he knew his honor, or at least the fiction of his honor, was safe in your hands. His daughter's treatment of you was anguish to him. I believe," Miss Garrison added impressively, "that if the truth were known his death was materially hastened by the remorse of conscience which he felt. I think you should take the money and regard this poor man the more kindly for having given it to you. And you know how good my intuitions of motives and innocence are," she said archly.

"I believe I would follow your advice if it were against

every conviction I, had," exclaimed Arkenburgh with his grave simplicity, which quite took from his words the slightest air of being a complimentary phrase meant to flatter. "You have the clearest, most womanly instinct I have ever seen. You have a fine temperament."

"Thanks; you are very kind. But, pray, spare me, for I have all a woman's weakness for praise. Tell me what you are going to do?"

. "I am going West within a week. A man there once suggested to me a scheme which I am sure is a profitable one. It may be too late to go into it. I have lost some months. But the idea is one that may be applied elsewhere and I will make it go. This money which Mr.—which I have received, will enable me to make a much more advantageous attempt. Miss Garrison, I feel that I am paying the heaviest debt to gratitude now. This sojourn in a prison, wearing a felon's suit, seems to me to have left a taint on my life. I could never ask a woman to become my wife without telling her that at one time I occupied a cell in Sing Sing. And there are many who would not care to accept a life with that dismal passage in it."

"You are foolish there, I think," said Miss Garrison promptly. "Believe me, even crime can be lived down. How much more the innocent, suffering for an offence which one did not commit, and suffering endured from the noblest of motives. If you ever should tell a woman this thing without letting her also know your motive in having accepted such a trial then you will be doing an unjust thing. You would be foolishly, stupidly angelic," she said, smiling, but with considerable emphasis to the words.

"And do you think a fine, sensitive woman could accept as a husband a man who was once an inmate of Sing Sing prison?" he asked seriously. "One reason I am going West is to start in a new field where I will not be known. If his relatives are to be spared, all talk about my innocence must be avoided. Hence there may remain a doubt whether I was not pardoned for some reason that does not clear my name perfectly. Can I ask a woman to be my wife who cannot bear her head as proudly because she bears my name?"

Miss Garrison tapped her foot upon the ground. She saw the difficulty too well. At last she said, as the thought occurred to her: "But if you had served your full term and then have been released, and Mr.—and the man had lived, you could have had nothing but your word to give to the woman that you were innocent. Now you have your release and this paper signed by him. I did not let the governor keep that. I have it for you, and any time you wish you can give proof of your innocence. I will go and get you the paper now. I have kept it in my strong-box."

She rose and left the room, returning in a few moments with the folded paper. Arkenburgh took it and read it. Then he put it in his pocket.

"I cannot thank you enough," he said with that slow earnestness of speech which seemed to be his strongest expression of emotion. I hope you feel how deeply I appreciate your kindness. I convey sense of gratitude very poorly."

"You convey it very well, by deeds more than by words. Have I not had good proof of how you regard a benefit? But you must look at my action more simply and lightly. I felt you were undergoing a grievous wrong, and all I really did was what any one might have done. Do not think any more about it, please."

"As if I could forget!" he said, rising. "Yet, with my freedom and the prospect of beginning a prosperous career, I have never felt sadder in my life than I do now."

He stood, tall and stalwart, but with a look of dejection on his fine face.

"Will you see Miss—the Archers before you go away?" said Miss Garrison.

"No. Is it not more consistent with the wish of the dead man that I should avoid any contact with them? I never wish to see again in my life the face of Miss Archer. That was all a mistake, and the one thing I have to be grateful for to this experience, outside of what it has taught me of a noble woman, is that it saved me from being the husband of that girl. I can never forgive her for the way in which she treated me as," and his voice softened, "I can never forget the way in which you treated me. Good-by, Miss Garrison." Arkenburgh's serious manner was almost solemn.

"Good-by," she returned, struggling to make this parting wear more the air of any ordinary farewell. "I hope you will be successful beyond every hope in all that you desire."

There seemed every reason for a warm pressure of their hands. He bowed gravely and left her. Was there every reason why Miss Garrison should have hastened to her room and have busied herself about several things, while impatiently wiping from her eyes tears that would gather?

She felt irritable and dejected for days. She fought against it fiercely, taking part in whatever came along in the way of amusement with great energy. Occasionally she met Addie Archer. She could not refrain from a slight coldness in her manner towards the girl. It seemed to her as if she were living on another's blood, like a vampire. It vexed Miss Garrison that she should care so keenly for Paul Arkenburgh's interests or happiness, and this vexation made her more cold to Miss Archer for recalling that worthy. "To think that he could have ever loved that girl!" Miss Garrison said to herself on two or three occasions, when she had been subjected to this flux and reflux of disagreeable feeling. "It was cheap to escape that for a few months in Sing Sing." Which goes to prove that Miss Garrison was not superior to her sex in formulating judgments about her sisters.

The following spring she received cards for Miss Archer's wedding. She did not go, but she felt a strange mixture of delight and disgust over the event. For two or three seasons Miss Garrison went very much into society. During this time she received two or three offers of marriage, which she serenely declined. To the last applicant for her hand she vouchsafed the extraordinary remark that she did not think she would ever marry; which, strange to say, came very near the truth. She would rather have been burned at the stake than tell the reason why, though her dislike for Mrs. Caldwell seemed to increase, until at last she cut her dead with hardly any compunction of soul.

As season after season passed with Miss Garrison still in the field of virgins some comments began to be made on her staunch adherence to spinsterhood. But they did not reach her ears, and if they had would not have affected her. She knew very well what she was doing, and she meant to do it. She lived with her uncle, who was a cheerful soul, always ready to escort her to ball, opera, theatre, or reception.

Eight winters went on in this uneventful way, or, rather, the eighth was just beginning. Her uncle had proposed their spending it in Washington. Miss Garrison was nothing loath; and so a house was taken on K Street, and they transferred themselves to the Capital.

One evening, early in the season, they were at a reception at the German minister's. It was rather late in the evening, and Miss Garrison was standing talking with animation to the secretary of the legation when she felt the light tap of a fan on her shoulder and the voice of the hostess saying: "My dear, I want to present a friend of mine to you," and as Miss Garrison turned she beheld a tall man of the most imposing presence before her, with a violet gleam in his speaking eyes. She did not wait for the " Miss Garrison, Senator Arkenburgh ! " which the lady tried to deliver herself of before she extended her hand with a quick smile.

" Why, do you know each other ? " cried the lady. " And here I have been promising myself the pleasure of making two charming persons acquainted."

" We have known each other for a long time," exclaimed Miss Garrison, " and I am delighted with you for bringing me an old friend. But, I must confess, I did not know Mr. Arkenburgh was a senator. Pray, allow me to congratulate you, and do not think I take no interest in the current history of my country."

Senator Arkenburgh bowed with the dignity of old. There was the same frank look in his eye and the measured gravity of speech. Miss Garrison asked after his health, and how had he liked the West. Was it not nice to get East again ? Or perhaps he had been East frequently. No ? this was the first time ? Well, it was rather a triumphant return, this coming back to mount the steps of the Capitol as a ruler of the land.

" Yes, it is a triumph, after your last recollection of me," said Senator Arkenburgh. " Then I had just finished serving the State."

" And are you settled in Washington now ? " asked Miss Garrison, disposing of the remark with a brief, faint smile.

" Yes. I intended to go to New York to-morrow morning," said the senator, " but if you will kindly take my arm and accompany me a little out of this crush you may give me the information I was going to seek. It seems to me a happy augury that I should meet you almost at once at the first entertainment I have attended in Washington. Will you sit here for a few moments ? "

He had brought her to a secluded nook in one of the rooms comparatively deserted. Miss Garrison seated herself and, when he had taken a low chair and placed himself at her side, began a volley of questions. Hardly would one be answered before she proposed another. The spot and occasion seemed to have inspired her with great volubility. The senator had hardly a chance to do aught but answer.

At last, taking advantage of a very small break in the conversation, Senator Arkenburgh, bending slightly toward her, said : " May I not speak a little of yourself and of myself ? Or shall I fatigue you with the latter prosy subject ? "

" Oh ! you may talk of yourself as much as you please, but,

pray, leave me out.   There is so little about me as a conversational topic."

"First, then, let me tell you," Senator Arkenburgh went on with his firm, measured tones, "that I have succeeded in all the objects for which I went West.   My business ventures there have been unusually successful, and it seems to me that a place in the Senate of our country is an offset for that striped suit in Sing Sing.   But in my heart there has been an object higher and dearer far to me than either wealth or glory; and my object in going to New York to-morrow was to see if I had any hope of winning that."

Miss Garrison fanned herself and waited patiently for him to continue.

"When I left New York I carried with me the image of a noble woman in my heart.   There she has ever been, and my waking and my falling to sleep have been with the thought of her as a comfort and an incentive.   I was going on to New York to-morrow to ask her, if I found her unwedded, to be my wife, now that I can offer her something more worthy than what I had then to bestow.   But I do not need to go now, for I have found you here, and you are still Miss Garrison.

"This may seem abrupt," he went on, "and you may think it very little like a lover to have remained so long without word or sign to tell of what was in his heart.   But I wished to bring you something better than a prison-suit, and until I could I wished to leave you perfectly free.   Had I found you married, the remembrance of you would have been mine for ever, and that would have been more to me than marriage with any other woman. No one would have had a right to take that from me.   And if you had married, it would have been because your heart had been given to another, worthier than I, whom you loved.   And God knows I only desire your perfect happiness.   Now, tell me, with the same womanly candor and truth with which you spoke to me the sweetest words I have ever heard in my life, just after I had been sentenced as a thief—tell me if I may hope to win this greatest prize that I have set before myself."

She had let her fan fall in her lap, and her eyes had been downcast as she listened, motionless except for her quickened breathing.   As he finished she drew a long, slow breath before she raised her face to his, with the frankest smile upon her lips. Her answer was in her eyes.   He drew her head toward him and pressed his lips upon her forehead, folding his arms tenderly about her.   JOHN J. À BECKET.

THE LIFE OF FATHER HECKER.*

CHAPTER XXIV.

SEPARATION FROM THE REDEMPTORISTS.

THE events which led to the separation ot the band ot American missionaries from the Redemptorist community took place in the spring and summer ot 1857. A misunderstanding arose about the founding of a new house in Newark, N. J., or in New York City, which should be the headquarters for the English-speaking Fathers and become the centre of attraction for American subjects, and in which English should be the lan. guage in common use. Application had been made by Bishop Bayley, and afterwards by Archbishop Hughes, for such a foundation, but superiors, both in the United States and in Rome —the latter dependent on letter-writing for understanding the difficulties which arose—became suspicious of the aims of the American Fathers and of the spirit which actuated them. To establish their loyalty and to explain the necessity for the new foundation, the missionary Fathers believed that one of their number should go to Rome and lay the matter in person be- fore the General or Rector Major of the order. The choice fell on Father Hecker, who sailed on August 5, 1857, arrived in Rome the 26th, and was expelled from the Congregation of the Most Holy Redeemer on Sunday, the 29th of the same month, the General deeming his coming to Rome to be a violation of · the vows of obedience and poverty.

The grounds of his expulsion were then examined by the Propaganda, from which the case passed to the Holy Father, who sought the decision of the Congregation of Bishops and Regulars. Pius IX. gave his judgment as a result of the examin- ation made by the last-named Congregation ; but he had made a personal study of all the evidence, and had given private audiences to both the General and Father Hecker. It was de- cided that all the American Fathers associated in the missionary band should be dispensed from their vows as Redemptorists, including Father Hecker, who was looked upon and treated by the decree as if he were still as much a member of the Congre- gation as the others, his expulsion being ignored. This conclusion was arrived at only after seven months of deliberation, and was dated the 6th of March, 1858. The decree, which will be given entire in this chapter, contemplates the continued activity of the Fathers as missionaries, subject to the authority of the American bishops; their formation into a separate society was taken for granted. Such is a brief statement of the entire case. If the reader will allow it to stand as a summary, what follows will serve to fill in the outline and complete a more detailed view.

And at the outset let it be fully understood that none of the Fathers desired separation from the order or had the faintest notion of its possibility as the outcome of the misunderstanding. One of the first letters of Father Hecker from Rome utters the passionate cry, "They have driven me out of the home of my heart and love." We have repeatedly heard him affirm that he never had so much as a temptation against his vows as a Redemptorist. But in saying this we do not mean to lay blame on the Redemptorist superiors. In all that we have to say on this subject we must be understood as recognizing their purity of intention. Their motives were love of discipline and obedience, which they considered seriously endangered. They were persuaded that their action, though severe, was necessary for the good of the entire order. And this shows that the difficulty was a misunderstanding, for there is conclusive evidence of the loyalty of the American Fathers—of Father Hecker no less than the others; as also of their fair fame as Redemptorists with both the superiors and brethren of the community up to the date of their disagreement. When Father Hecker left for Rome the Provincial gave him his written word that, although he disapproved of his journey, he bore witness to him as a good Redemptorist, full of zeal for souls; and he added that up to that time his superiors had been entirely satisfied with him; and to the paper containing this testimony the Provincial placed the official seal of the order. On the other side, a repeated and careful examination of Father Hecker's letters and memoranda reveals no accusation by him of moral fault against his Redemptorist superiors, but on the contrary many words of favorable explanation of their conduct. When the Rector Major, in the midst of his council, began, to Father Hecker's utter amazement, to read the sentence of expulsion, he fell on his knees and received the blow with bowed head as a visitation of God. And when, again, after prostrating himself before the Blessed Sacrament and resigning himself to the Divine Will, he returned to the council and begged the General on his knees for a further consideration of his case, and was refused, he reports that the General affirmed that his sense of duty would not allow him to act otherwise than he had done, and that he by no means meant to condemn Father Hecker in the court of conscience, but only to exercise jurisdiction over his external conduct.

In truth the trouble arose mainly from the very great difference between the character of the American Fathers and that of their superiors in the order. It is nothing new or strange, to borrow Father Hewit's thoughts as expressed in his memoir of Father Baker, that men whose characters are cast in a different mould should have different views, and should, with the most conscientious intentions, be unable to coincide in judgment or act in concert :   •

" There is room in the Catholic Church for every kind of religious organization, suiting all the varieties of mind and character and circumstance. If collisions and misunderstandings often come between those who have the same great end in view, this is the result of human infirmity, and only shows how imperfect and partial are human wisdom and human virtue."

What Father Hewit adds of Father Baker's dispositions applies as well to all the Fathers. In ceasing to be Redemptorists, they did not swerve from their original purpose in becoming religious. None of them had grown discontented with his state or with his superiors. They were all in the full fervor of the devotional spirit of the community, and as missionaries were generously wearing out their lives in the toil and hardship of its peculiar vocation. But both parties became the instruments of a special providence, which made use of the wide diversities of temperament existing among men, and set apart Father Hecker and his companions, after a season of severe trial, for a new apostolate. They did not choose it for themselves. Father Hecker had aspirations, as we know, but he did not dream of realizing them through any separation whatever. But Providence led the Holy See to change what had been a violent wrench into a peaceful division, exercising, in so doing, a divine authority accepted with equal obedience by all concerned.

What Father Hewit further says of Father Baker applies exactly to Father Hecker :

" For the Congregation in which he was trained to the religious and ecclesiastical state he always retained a sincere esteem and affection. He did not ask the Pope for a dispensation from his vows in order to be relieved from a burdensome obligation, but only on the condition that it seemed best to him to terminate the difficulty which had arisen that way. When the dispensation was granted he did not change his life for a more easy one. . . . Let no one, therefore, who is disposed to yield to temptations against his vocation, and to abandon the religious state from weariness, tepidity, or any unworthy motive, think to find any encouragement in his example; for his austere, self-denying, and arduous life will give him only rebuke, and not encouragement."

After the expulsion the General begged Father Hecker to make the convent his home till he was suited elsewhere, and Father Hecker, having thanked him for his kindness and stayed there that night, took lodgings the following day in a quiet street near the Propaganda. During the seven months of his stay in Rome he frequently visited the General and his consultors, sometimes on business but at other times from courtesy and good feeling.

He at once presented the testimonials intended for the General to Cardinal Barnabo, Prefect of the Propaganda, who examined them in company with Archbishop Bedini, the Secretary of that Congregation. As may be imagined, the attitude of these prelates was at first one of extreme reserve. But every case gets a hearing in Rome, and that of this expelled religious, and therefore suspended priest, could be no exception. A glance at the credentials, a short conversation with their bearer, a closer examination of the man and of his claim, produced a favorable impression and led to a determination to sift the matter thoroughly. The principal letters were from Archbishop Hughes and Bishop Bayley. The former spoke thus of Father Hecker: "I have great pleasure in recommending him as a laborious, edifying, zealous, and truly apostolic priest."

Some of the letters were from prominent laymen of the City of New York, including one from Mr. McMaster, another from Dr. Brownson, and another from Dr. Ives; in addition he had the words of praise of the Provincial in America already referred to. Finally he showed letters from each of the American Fathers, one of whom, Father Hewit, was a member of the Provincial Council, all joining themselves to Father Hecker as sharing the responsibility of his journey to Rome, and naming him as the representative of their cause.

It is not our purpose to trace the progress of the investigation through the Roman tribunals. We will but give such facts and such extracts from letters as throw light on Father Hecker's conduct during this great crisis. One might be curious to know something about the friends he made in Rome. The foremost of them was the Cardinal Prefect of the Propaganda.

"The impression that Cardinal Barnabo made upon me," he writes in one of his earliest letters, "was most unexpected; he was so quick in his perceptions and penetration, so candid and confiding in speaking to me. He was more like a father and friend; and both the cardinal and the archbishop (Bedini) expressed such warm sympathy in my behalf that it made me feel, . . . in a way I never felt before, the presence of God in those who are chosen as rulers in His Church."

In another letter he says:

"He (the cardinal) has been to me more than a friend; he is to me a father, a counsellor, a protector. No one enjoys so high a reputation in every regard in Rome as the cardinal. He gives me free access to him and confides in me."

There is much evidence, too, too much to quote it all, that the cardinal was drawn to Father Hecker on account of his simplicity and openness of character, his frank manner, but especially for his bold, original views of the opportunity of religion among free peoples. Cardinal Barnabo was noted for his sturdy temper and was what is known as a hard hitter, though a generous opponent as well as an earnest friend. He espoused Father Hecker's cause with much heartiness; official intercourse soon developed into a close personal attachment, which lasted with unabated warmth till the strong old Roman was called to his reward.

Father Hecker speaks in his letters of spending time with him, not only on business but in discussing questions of philosophy and religious controversy, and in talking over the whole American outlook.

The cardinal became the American priest's advocate before the Pope, and also with the Congregation of Bishops and Regulars after the case reached that tribunal. "When I heard him speak in my defence," he said in after times, "I thanked God that he was not against me, for he was a most imperious character when aroused, and there seemed no resisting him."

Archbishop Bedini, the Secretary of the Propaganda, was another hearty friend. Our older readers will remember that he had paid a visit to America a few years before the time we are considering, and that his presence here was made the occasion for some of the more violent outbreaks of the Know-nothing excitement. He knew our country personally, therefore, and was acquainted with very many of our clergy; his assistance to the Roman Court in this case was of special value. He became so demonstrative in his friendship for Father Hecker that the Pope was amused at it, and Father Hecker relates in his letters home how the Holy Father rallied him about the warmth of his advocacy of the American priest's cause, as did various members of the Pontifical court.

At that time and for many years afterwards Doctor Bernard Smith, an Irish Benedictine monk, was Professor of Dogmatic Theology in the College of the Propaganda; he is now the honored abbot of the great Basilica of St. Paul without-the-walls. How Father Hecker came to know the learned professor we have been unable to discover; but both he and Monsignor Kirby, of the Irish College, became his firm friends and powerful advocates. Without Doctor Smith's advice, indeed, scarcely a step was taken in the case.

An unexpected ally was found in Bishop Connolly, of St. John's, New Brunswick. He had been robbed on his way between Civita Vecchia and Rome, and that misfortune gave him a special claim to the regard of the Pope, with whom he soon became a favorite. The Holy Father admired in him that energy of character and zeal for religion which distinguished him in after years as Archbishop of Halifax. On hearing of Father Hecker's case he studied it on account of sympathetic interest in the aspects of Catholicity in the United States, part of his diocese being at that time, we believe, in the State of Maine. How ardent his friendship for Father Hecker soon became is shown by his exclamation: "I am ready to die for you, and I am going to tell the Pope so." He even offered to assist Father Hecker in paying his personal expenses while in Rome. In a letter to the American Fathers of December 18 Father Hecker writes:

"Another recent and providential event in our favor has been the friendship of Bishop Connolly, of St. John's, New Brunswick. By his extraordinary exertions and his warm friendship for us he has succeeded in giving us the vantage ground in all quarters where we were not in good favor. I told you in the last note that he had spoken to the Holy Father in favor of our cause, but I had no time to give you the substance of what was said. Bishop Connolly is a full-blooded Irishman, but, fortunately for us, not implicated in any party views in our country, and seeing that the Propaganda regarded our cause as its own and had identified itself with our success, . . . it being friendly to us as missionaries, he exerted all his influence in our favor. His influence was not slight, for the Pope had conceived a great friendship for him, and heaped all sorts of honors on him. Well, he had a regular tussle with his Holiness about us and our cause, and when the Holy Father repeated some things said of me—against me, of course—he replied: 'Your Holiness, I should not be at all surprised if some fine day you yourself would have to canonize one of these Yankee fellows.' In one word, he left nothing unsaid or undone with the Pope in our favor; and the Pope suggested to him obtaining dispensation of our vows and forming a new company. 'They cannot expect me,' he said, 'to take the initiatory step; this would be putting the cart before the horse. Let *them* do this, and present their plan to me, and if I find it good, it shall have my consent.' . . . The bishop has also seen and won over to our favor Monsignor Talbot, who said to him: 'The only way now of settling the difficulties is to give the American Fathers the liberty to form a new company for the American missions.' In addition, the bishop wrote a strong document in favor of our missions and of us, and presented it to Cardinal Barnabo, which will be handed in to the Congregation of Bishops and Regulars, who have our affairs in hand. . . . If this good bishop should come in your way, whether by writing or otherwise, you cannot be too grateful for what he has done for us. After Cardinal Barnabo and Archbishop Bedini we owe more to him than to any one else.

"Wind and tide are now in our favor, and my plan is to keep quiet and stick close to the rudder to see that the ship keeps right."

On his way home from Rome Bishop Connolly wrote the following letter to Father Hecker, dated at Marseilles, January 20, 1858:

"From the deep interest I feel in your concerns you will pardon my curiosity in wishing to have the earliest intelligence of your fate in the Congregation of Bishops and Regulars. I could wish I were near you all the time, and have nothing else to attend to; but you have got One more powerful than I at your right hand. Fix your hopes in Him and you will not be confounded. After having done everything on your part that unsleeping energy as well as prudence could suggest, you must take the issue, however unpalatable it may be, as the undoubted expression of God's will, and act (as I am sure you will act) accordingly. . . . You must keep steadily in view the glorious principle for which you came to Rome, and which I am convinced is for the greater glory of God and the greater good of religion in America. If you can start as a religious body with the approbation of Rome, this would be the holiest and most auspicious consummation. . . . Be guided at every step by the holy and enlightened men whose sympathies you have won and in whose hands you will be always safe : Cardinal Barnabò *in primis*, and after him Monsignor Bedini and Doctors Kirby and Smith. United with them at every step, failure is impossible—you must and you will succeed. . . . I am sure that you know and feel this as well as I do (for we have been marvellously of the same way of thinking on nearly all points), but as I feel I must write to you, as it may be, perchance, of some consolation to you in your troubles, I thought it better to say it over again. . . . If a letter or anything else from me could be of any service, I need not tell you that I am still on hand and only anxious to be employed. [Here follows his address in Paris and Liverpool.] With all good wishes for your success, and with the hope of hearing the happy tidings from your own hand before I leave Europe, I am, Reverend dear Sir,

"Very faithfully yours in Christ,

"† THOMAS L. CONNOLLY,

"*Bishop of St. John's, N. B.*"

From what has been so far communicated to the reader, it will be seen that Father Hecker's case had the strength of friendship to assist it. But he was himself his best advocate. His traits of character were lovable, and the very incongruity of such a man forced to plead against the direst penalty known to a religious, was a singularly strong argument. His cheerful demeanor while fighting for his life ; his puzzling questions on social and philosophical points ; his mingled mysticism and practical judgment ; his utterance of political sentiments which, as he truly said in one of his letters, if spoken by any one but an American would elicit instant reproof ; his total lack of obsequiousness united to entire submission to lawful authority, all helped to make for himself and his cause friends in every direction.

The unanimous adhesion of the American Redemptorist missionaries was a powerful element in his favor, and a priceless boon for his own consolation. He was continually in receipt of such words as these : "We all desire you to consider us fully identified with you and to act in our name." "We have the

utmost confidence in your discretion, and your conservative
views are quite to our mind." His whole heart went out in
response to these greetings. On October 24 he writes to the
Fathers :

"The contents of your note were what I had a right to expect from you : sympathy, confidence, and reliance on Divine
Providence. How much these trials will endear us to each
other! If we keep together as one man and regard only God,
defeat is impossible. Do not forget to offer up continually
prayers for me. How much I see the hand of Providence in
all our difficulties! And the end will, I trust, make it evident as the sun."

But where he placed his entire trust is shown by the following, a part of the same letter :

"Our affairs are in the hands of God. I hope no one will
feel discouraged, nor fear for me. All that is needed to bring
the interests of God to a successful issue is grace, grace, grace;
and this is obtained by prayer. And if the American Fathers
will only pray and get others to pray, and not let any one
have the slightest reason to bring a word against them in our
present crisis, God will be with us and help us, and Our Lady
will take good care of us. So far no step taken in our past
need be regretted. If it were to be done again it would have
my consent. The blow given to me I have endeavored to receive with humility and in view of God. It has not produced
any trouble in my soul, nor made me waver in the slightest degree in my confidence in God or my duty towards Him. Let
us not be impatient. God is with us and will lead us if we
confide in Him."

During his stay in Rome he corresponded regularly with
his brother George, whose ever-open purse paid all his expenses. We have also found a very long letter of loving friendship from Doctor Brownson, conveying the profoundest sympathy. This came during the most critical period of the case and
gave much consolation. It called forth an answer equally
affectionate.
 . He received exceedingly sympathetic letters from Fathers de
Held and de Buggenoms. The former was at the time rector
of the house in Liège, and wrote a letter to Cardinal Barnabo, a

copy of which has been preserved, which treats most favorably of Father Hecker's character and discusses his case at length, petitioning a decision which should reinstate him in the order.

Late in November he sought an interview with Cardinal Reisach, holding him closely interested for two hours, conversing upon American religious prospects and quite winning his friendship. By means of such interviews, which, at Cardinal Barnabo's suggestion, he sought with the chief prelates in Rome, he became widely known in the city, and the state of religion in America was made a common topic of conversation.

The following introduces a singular phase in the case. It is from a letter written before the end of September, less than a month after his arrival:

"My leisure moments are occupied in writing an article on the 'Present Condition and Future Prospects of the Catholic Faith in the United States,' for the *Civilta Cattolica*. They have promised to translate and publish it."

The *Civilta* is still a leading Catholic journal, the foremost exponent of the views of the Society of Jesus. At that time it was the official organ of Pius IX., who read all its articles in the proofs, and it went everywhere in Catholic circles. The editors became fast friends of Father Hecker, though we are not aware that they took sides in his case. His article was divided in the editing, and appeared in two successive numbers of the magazine. It attracted wide attention, being translated and printed in the chief Catholic periodicals of France, Belgium, and Germany, and published by Mr. McMaster in the *Freeman's Journal*. In Rome it served a good purpose. To some its views were startling, but its tone was fresh and enlivening. It undertook to show that the freest nation in the world was the most inviting field for the Catholic propagandist. We suppose that the author's main purpose in writing was but to invite attention to America, yet he so affected public opinion in Rome as to materially assist the adjustment of the difficulty pending before the high tribunals. Cardinal Barnabo was quite urgent with Father Hecker that he should write more of the same kind, but either his occupations or his expectation of an early return home hindered his doing so. As it was, he had caused himself and the American Fathers to be viewed by men generally through the medium of the great question of the relation of religion to the young Republic of the Western World. That topic was fortunate in having him for its exponent. He was an object-lesson of the aspirations of enlightened Catholic Americans as well as an exalted type of Catholic missionary zeal. Very few men of discernment ever really, knew Father Hecker but to admire him and to be ready to be persuaded by him of his life-thesis : that a free man tends to be a good Catholic, and a free nation is the most promising field for apostolic zeal.

Soon after his arrival in Rome he made the acquaintance of George L. Brown, an American artist of some note, and a non-Catholic. He was an earnest man, and Father Hecker attacked him at once on the score of religion, and before December had received him into the Church. This event made quite a stir in Rome. The city was always full of artists and their patrons, and Mr. Brown's conversion, together with the articles in the *Civilta*, influenced in Father Hecker's favor many persons whom he could not directly reach. This was especially the case with the Pope, to whose notice such matters were brought by Archbishop Bedini, his office enabling him to approach the Holy Father at short intervals. He exerted a similar influence on all the high officials of the Roman court.

In spite of all this favor the usual delays attendant upon serious judicial investigations oppressed 'Father Hecker with the heavy dread of "the law's delay," detaining him in Rome from the first week in September, 1857, when the case was opened in the Propaganda, till it was closed by the decision of the Congregation of Bishops and Regulars early in the following March. Nor was the "insolence of office" quite absent. He was once heard to tell of his having been snubbed in the Pope's antechamber by some one in attendance, and often put aside till he was vexed with many weary hours of waiting and by being compelled. to repeatedly return.

"I had to wait for three days," we read in the memoranda, "and then was reproached and scolded by the monsignor in attendance for coming late. I had not come late but had been kept waiting outside, and I told him so. 'You will see those hills of Albano move,' said I, 'before I move from my purpose to see the Holy Father.' When he saw my determination he changed and gave me my desired audience."

When events had taken the question out of the jurisdiction of the Redemptorist order and into the general court of the Catholic Church, its settlement was found to be difficult. The restoration of Father Hecker by a judicial decision would not, it is plain, have left him and his companions in that harmonious relation so essential to their personal happiness and to their success' as missionaries. It was then suggested that they should petition for a separate organization under the Rule of St. Alphonsus approved by Benedict XIV., acting directly subject to the Holy See, thus making two Redemptorist bodies in the United States, as is the case with various Franciscan communities. It was also suggested that the Cisalpine, or Neapolitan Redemptorists, at that time an independent congregation, would gladly take the American Fathers under their jurisdiction. The alternative was what afterwards took place—the dispensation of the Fathers from their vows, in view of their forming their own organization under direction of the Bishops and the Holy See. A petition praying the Holy Father to give them either the Rule of Benedict XIV. in the sense above suggested, or their dispensations from the vows, was drawn up and forwarded by the Fathers remaining in America, the dispensation being named as the last resort. Father Hecker's legal case not being decided, he was advised by Cardinal Barnabo to reserve his signature to this document for the present. It will be seen at a glance that the dispensation from the vows and an entirely new departure in community existence was more in accordance with his aspirations. But no aspiration was so strong in him as love of his brethren, and he was fully determined not to be separated from them if he could prevent it.

Much delay was caused by waiting for further testimonials from American bishops confirmatory of the good character of the Fathers and of the value of their labors as missionaries. Father Hecker, meantime, wrote many letters to his brethren discussing the alternatives in question.

In one of October 24 he tells of a pilgrimage he made to Nocera, to the tomb of St. Alphonsus, bearing his brethren in his heart with him. He also visited the Redemptorist house there and in Naples, and was quite charmed with the fathers, who were entirely willing to receive the Americans into their organization, which, as the reader knows, was separate from that of the General in Rome. Knowing the mind of his brethren, and determined to take no step alone, Father Hecker would have been content with this arrangement had it seemed good to the Holy See. Meantime he tells how greatly he enjoyed his visit to Nocera, how he said Mass over the holy body of the founder, and adds: "Ever since I feel more consoled and supported and confident."

The following is from a joint letter of the American Fathers dated November 17; they prefer, in case Father Hecker is not reinstated, being separated from the order and made "immediately dependent on the Holy See, or the Prefect of the Propaganda, rather than anything else; . . . called, for instance, 'Religious Missionaries of the Propaganda,' if the Holy Father would make us such. With the Rule of St. Alphonsus and the same missionary privileges we now enjoy, and our dear Father Hecker among us again, we should feel happy and safe. . . . But we wait for the words of the Holy See to indicate our course."

His words to them are to the same effect: "Our first effort should be directed to the securing our hopes through the Transalpine Congregation [this means the regular Redemptorist order to which they then belonged]. . . . If this is not successful, then to endeavor to accomplish our hopes through the Cisalpine [Neapolitan] Fathers, who will be heart and soul with us and grant all our best desires. Or, thirdly, to obtain permission to act as a band of missionaries in our country under the protection, for the present, of some bishop. . . . It is a consolation to me to see that our affairs are so far developed and known, and our views are so identical that you can act on your part, and write, without having to delay for information [from me]. You can easily imagine that it was no pleasant state for me to be in while in suspense about what would be the determination you would come to. Thank God and Our Lady, your recent letter set that all aside! The work now to be done is plain, and the greatest care and prudence is to be exercised not to commit any fault, or make any mistake which may be to us a source of regret afterwards."

In another letter he says that Cardinal Barnabo spoke of the unpleasant relations likely to exist after his restoration to the order, and then continues:

"The cardinal had a long conversation with me, and he suggested whether God might not desire of me a special work. I told him I would not think of this while the dismission was over my head. He said, 'Of course not; for if you are a *mauvais sujet*, as the General thinks, God will surely not use you for any special mission.'" The letter here details more of the exchange of views between the cardinal and Father Hecker, the latter astounded to hear from this direction suggestions so closely tallying with his own interior aspirations about the apostolic outlook in America. "But," continues the letter, "you must well understand that I should not accept such a proposition for myself before having asked the best counsel of men of God and received their unhesitating approval of its being God's will. There are holy men here, and I take counsel with them in every important step; and they are religious, so that they are good judges in such important matters. . . . If God wishes to make use of us in such a design, and I can be assured of this on *competent authority*, whatever it may cost, with His grace I will not 'shrink from it. I call competent authority the approbation of good and holy men, and one like the cardinal, who knows the country, knows *all* our affairs now, and has every quality of mind and heart to be a competent judge in this important matter. Though you have made me your plenipotentiary, yet this is an individual affair, one we did not contemplate, one of the highest import to our salvation and sanctification, and must depend on God and our individual conscience.

"Even before making this proposition to you I asked advice from my spiritual director, and he approved of it. You may be confident that in every step which I take I endeavor to be actuated by the spirit of God, and take every means to assure myself of it, so that hereafter no scruple may trouble my conscience, and God's blessing be with me and you also."

He writes thus towards the end of September: "The more I think of our difficulties the more I am inclined to believe that they may have been permitted by a good God for the very purpose of a work of this kind. If wise and holy men say so, and we have the approbation of the Holy See, is it not a mission offered to us by Divine Providence, and ought we not cheerfully to embrace it?"

And on October 5: "I hope God has inspired you with some means of coming to my help. Indeed, it is a difficult position, and the best I can do is to throw myself constantly on Divine Providence and be guided by Him. You will remember, and I hope, before this reaches you, will have answered my proposition in my last note, whether or not you would be willing to form an independent band of missionaries to be devoted to the great wants of the country. I have considered and reconsidered, and prayed and prayed, and in spite of my fears this seems to me the direction in which *Divine Providence calls us.* . . . With all the difficulties, dangers, and struggles that another [community] movement presents before me, I feel more and more convinced that it *is this that Divine Providence asks of us.* If we should act in concert its success cannot be doubted—success not only as regards our present kind of labors, but in a variety of other ways which are open to us in our new country. . . . If you are prepared to move in this direction it would be best, and indeed necessary, not only to write to me your assent, but also a memorial to the Propaganda—to Cardinal Barnabo—stating the interests and wants of religion and of the country, and then petition to be permitted to turn your labors in this direction. . . .

" Such a course involves the release of your obligations to the [Redemptorist] Congregation, and this would have to be expressed distinctly in your petition, and motived by good reasons there given."

Further on in the same letter he adds : " Since writing the above I have had time for more reflection, and consulted with my spiritual adviser, and this course appears to be the one Divine Providence points out."

This very important letter ends as follows: " I endeavor to keep close to God, to keep up my confidence in His protection, and in the aid of Our Blessed Lady. I pray for you all ; you cannot forget me in your prayers."

Then follow suggestions about obtaining testimonials from the American hierarchy for the information of the Holy See in a final settlement of the entire case. The prelates who wrote, all very favorably, were : Archbishops Hughes of New York, Kenrick of Baltimore, Purcell of Cincinnati, Bishops Bayley of Newark, Spalding of Louisville (both afterwards Archbishops of Baltimore), Lynch of Charleston, Barry of Savannah, and De Goesbriand of Burlington, Vermont.

On October 26, while wondering what would next happen, he writes : " As for my part, I do not see one step ahead, but at the same time I never felt so closely embraced in the arms of Divine Providence." But on the next day : " It seems to me a great and entire change awaits us. . . . We are all of us young, and if we keep close and true to God—and there is nothing but ourselves to prevent this—a great and hopeful future is at our waiting. I know you pray for me ; continue to do so, and believe me always your wholly devoted friend and brother in Jesus and Mary."

On November 12 : " My present impression is that neither

union with the Cisalpine Fathers nor separation as a band of [independent Redemptorist] missionaries in the United States will be approved of here. . . . What appears to me more and more probable is that we shall have to start entirely upon our own basis. This is perhaps the best of all, all things considered. . . . Such a movement has from the beginning seemed to me *the one to which Divine Providence calls us,* but I always felt timid as long as any door was left open for us to act in the Congregation. . . . I feel prepared to take this step with you without hesitation and with great confidence. . . . I should have been glad, as soon as my dismission was given, to have started on in such a movement. But then it was my first duty to see whether this work could not be accomplished by the Congregation [of the Most Holy Redeemer]; and, besides, I was not sure, as I now am, of your views being the same as mine. . . . All indicates the will of Divine Providence in our regard and gives me confidence. . . .

"Father Hewit's letter, confirming your readiness to share your ortunes with me, was most consoling and strengthening. God knows we seek only His interest and glory and are ready to suffer anything rather than offend Him. . . .

"We should take our present missions as the basis of our unity and activity; at the same time not be exclusively restricted to them, but leave ourselves at liberty to adapt ourselves to the [religious] wants which may present themselves in our country. Were the question presented to me to restrict myself exclusively to missions, in that case I should feel in conscience bound to obtain from holy men a decision on the question whether God had not pointed out another field for me. . . . Taking our missions and our present mode of life as the groundwork, the rest will have to be left to Divine Providence, the character of the country, and our own spirit of faith, and good common sense."

In the same letter, that of December 25, he hopes that if the Holy See separates them from old affiliations they will form a society "which would embody in its life what is good in the American people in the natural order and adapt itself to answer the great wants of our people in the spiritual order. I must confess to you frankly that thoughts of this kind do occupy my mind, and day by day they appear to me to come more clearly from heaven. I cannot refuse to entertain them without resisting what appear to me the inspirations of God. You know that these are not new opinions hastily adopted. From the beginning of my Catholic life there seemed always before me, but not distinctly, some such work, and it is indicated both in *Questions of the Soul* and *Aspirations of Nature*. And I cannot resist the thought that my present peculiar position is or may be providential to further some such undertaking. . . . It might be imagined that these views were but a ruse of the devil to thwart our common cause and future prospects. To this I have only to answer that the old rascal has been a long time at work to reach this point. If it be he, I shall head him off, because all that regards my personal vocation I shall submit to wise and holy men and obey what they tell me."

Father Hecker had his first audience with Pius IX., after much delay, on December 22. "I felt," he said, in giving an account of it in after years, "that my trouble in Rome was the great crisis in my life. I had one way of telling that I was not like Martin Luther: in my inmost soul I was ready, entirely ready, to submit to the judgment of the Church. They had made me out a rebel and a radical to the Holy Father, and when I saw him alone, after the usual salutations, and while on my knees, I said: 'Look at me, Holy Father; see, my shoulders are broad. Lay on the stripes. I will bear them. All I want is justice. I want you to judge my case. I will submit.' The Pope's eyes filled with tears at these words, and his manner was very kind." The rest of the interview is given in a letter: "The Pope bade me rise and told me he was informed all about my affairs. Then he asked what was my desire. I replied that he might have the goodness to examine the purpose of my coming to Rome, 'since it regarded the conversion of the American people, a work which the most intelligent and pious Catholics have at heart, among others Dr. Ives, whom you know.' 'Yes,' he said; 'has his wife become a Catholic?' I replied in the affirmative. 'But what can I do?' he said; 'the affair is being examined by Archbishop Bizarri (Secretary of the Congregation of Bishops and Regulars), and nothing can be done until he gives in his report; then I will give my opinion and my decision.' 'Your decision, most Holy Father, is God's decision, and whatever it may be willingly and humbly will I submit to it.' While I was making this remark his Holiness paid the greatest attention, and it seemed to satisfy and please him. 'The American people,' he continued, 'are much engrossed in worldly things and in the pursuit of wealth, and these are not favorable to religion; it is not I who say so, but our Lord in the Gospel.' 'The United States, your Holiness,' I replied, 'is in its youth, and, like a young father of a family occupied in furnishing his house, while this is going on he must be busy; but the American people do not make money to hoard it, nor are they miserly.' 'No, no,' he replied; 'they are willing to give when they possess riches. The bishops tell me they are generous in aiding the building of churches. You see,' he added, 'I know the bright side as well as the dark side of the Americans; but in the United States there exists a too unrestricted freedom, all the refugees and revolutionists gather there and are in full liberty.' 'True, most Holy Father; but this has a good side. Many of them, seeing in the United States that the Church is self-subsisting and not necessarily connected with what they call despotism, begin to regard it as a Divine institution and return to her fold.' 'Yes,' he said, 'the Church is as much at home in a republic as in a monarchy or aristocracy. But then, again, you have the abolitionists and their opponents, who get each other by the hair.' 'There is also the Catholic faith, Holy Father, which if once known would act on these parties like oil upon troubled waters, and our best-informed statesmen are becoming more and more convinced that Catholicity is necessary to sustain our institutions, and enable our young country to realize her great destiny. And allow me to add, most Holy Father, that it would be an enterprise worthy of your glorious pontificate to set on foot the measures necessary for the beginning of the conversion of America.'

"On retiring he gave me his blessing, and repeated in a loud voice as I kneeled, 'Bravo! Bravo!'"

"Pius IX.," said Father Hecker afterwards, "was a man of the largest head, of still larger heart, moved more by his impulses than by his judgment; but his impulses were great, noble, all-embracing."

It will not be out of place here to look more closely into Father Hecker's conscience and study his motives. One might ask why he did not simply submit to the infliction visited upon him by his superior in the order, and humbly withdraw from notice till God should find a way to vindicate him. But his case was not a personal one. He was in Rome representing a body of priests and a public cause, and every principle of duty and honor required an appeal to higher authority. Nor was vindication the chief end in view, but rather freedom to follow the dictates of the Holy Spirit in accordance with Catholic traditions and wholly subject to the laws and usages of the Church. Beyond securing exactly this he had no object whatever. On February 19, 1858, he thus wrote to his brother George:

"But there is no use of keeping back anything. My policy has all along been to have no policy, but to be frank, truthful, and have no fear. For my own part I will try my best to be true to the light and grace given me, even though it reduces me to perfect insignificance. I desire nothing upon earth except to labor for the good of our Religion and our Country, and whatever may be the decision of our affairs here, my aims cannot be defeated. I feel, indeed, quite indifferent about the decision which may be given, so that they allow us freedom."

As illustrating Father Hecker's supernatural motives and rectitude of conscience the following extracts from letters to the Fathers will be of interest. In September, when the arrow was yet in the wound, he wrote:

"I have no feelings of resentment against any one of the actors [in this matter]. On the contrary I could embrace them all with unfeigned sentiments of love. God has been exceedingly good not to let me be even tempted in this way."

Again, on December 5:

"Your repeated assurances of being united with me in our future fills me with consolation and courage. We may well repeat the American motto, 'United we stand, divided we fall.' Never did I find myself more sustained by the grace of God. How often I have heard repeated by acquaintances I have made here: 'Why, Father Hecker, you are the happiest man in Rome!' Little do they know how many sleepless nights I have passed, how deeply I have suffered within three months. But isn't Almighty God good? It seems I never knew or felt before what it is to be wholly devoted to Him."

On December 9, after a long exposition of the need of a new religious missionary institute for America:

"Considering our past training, and many other advantages which we possess, I cannot but believe that God will use us, provided that we remain faithful to Him, united together as one man, and ready to make any sacrifice for some such holy enterprise; and my daily prayer is that the Holy Father may receive a special grace and inspiration to welcome and bless such a proposition."

. With his Christmas greetings he wrote: "From the start I have not suffered myself to repose a moment when there was anything to be done which promised help. Whatever may be the result of our affairs, this consolation will be with me—I did my utmost, and everything just and honorable, to deserve success. No one would believe how much I have gone through at Rome, but I do it cheerfully, and sometimes gaily, because I know it is the will of God."

On February 19, 1858: "The experience I have made here is worth more than my weight in gold. If God intends to employ us in any important work in the future, such an experience was absolutely necessary for us. It is a novitiate on a large scale. I cannot thank God sufficiently for my having made it *thus far* without incurring by my conduct the displeasure or censure of any one."

And a week afterwards: "You should write often, for words of sympathy, hope, encouragement are much to me now in these trials, difficulties, and conflicts. In all my Catholic life I have not experienced oppression and anxiety of mind in such a degree as I have for these ten days past."

March 6: "So far from my devotion to religion being diminished by recent events, it has, thank God, greatly increased; but many other things have been changed in me. On many new points my intelligence has been awakened; experience has dispelled much ignorance, and on the whole I hope that my faith and heart have been more purified. If God spares my life to return, I hope to come back more a man, a better Catholic, and more entirely devoted to the work of God."

The following is from a copy of a letter to Father de Held dated November 2: "One thing my trials have taught me, and this is the one thing important—to love God more. It almost seems that I did not know before what it is to love Him."

When it became evident that the Holy See would decide the case so as to make it necessary for the Fathers to form a new society, Father Hecker did not accept even this as a final indication of Providence that external circumstances had made it possible for him to realize his long-cherished dreams of an American apostolate; for he was at liberty still to refuse. He redoubled his prayers. His pilgrimage to the shrine of St. Alphonsus is already known to the reader; he caused a novena of

Masses to be said at the altar of Our Lady of Perpetual Help in the Redemptorist Church in Rome; he said Mass himself at all the great shrines, especially the Confession of St. Peter, the altar of St. Ignatius and that of St. Philip Neri; he earnestly entreated all his friends, old ones at home and new-found ones in Rome, to join with him in his prayers for light. •

He furthermore took measures to obtain the counsel of wise and holy men. Every one whom he thought worthy of his confidence was asked for an opinion. Finally he drew up a formal document, known in this biography as the Roman Statement, and already familiar by reference and quotation, and placed it in the hands of the three religious whose names, in addition to those of Cardinal Barnabo and Archbishop Bedini, appear at the end of the extract we make from its original draft. It opens with a summary of his conversion, entrance into religion, and missionary life, and embraces a full enough statement of the trouble with the General of the order—a matter of notoriety at the time in the city of Rome. He then describes his own interior aspirations and vocation to the apostolate in America, backing up the authority of that inner voice with the external testimonials of prelates and priests and laymen, whose letters had been procured by the Propaganda as evidence in the case before the Congregation of Bishops and Regulars.

"If God has called me," he continues, "to such a work, His providence has in a singular way, since my arrival at Rome, opened the door for me to undertake it. The object of my coming to Rome was to induce the General to sustain and favor the extension of our missionary labors in the United States. It was undertaken altogether for the good of the order, in the general interests of religion, and in undoubted good faith. Under false impressions of my purpose, my expulsion from the Congregation was decreed three days after my arrival. This was about three months ago, and it was the source of the deepest affliction to me, and up to within a short time my greatest desire was to re-enter the Congregation. At present it seems to me that these things were permitted by Divine Providence in order to place me in the position to undertake that mission which has never ceased to occupy my thoughts."

After some description of the state of religion in America the statement concludes:

"These [American non-Catholics] require an institution which shall have their conversion to the Catholic faith as its principal aim, which is free to develop itself according to the fresh wants which may spring up, thus opening an attractive future to the religious vocations of the Catholic young men of that country.

"Regarding, therefore, my early and extensive acquaintance among my own people, politically, socially, religiously, with the knowledge of their peculiar wants, with their errors also; and the way in which God has led me and the graces given to me; and my interior convictions and the experience acquired confirming them since my Catholic life, and also my singular position at present—the question, in conclusion, is to know from holy, instructed, and experienced men in such matters whether or not there is sufficient evidence of a special vocation from God for me to undertake now such a work."

What follows is placed at the bottom of the last page of the statement:

"EPIPHANY, 1858, ROME.

"This document I had translated into Italian, and I gave it to Cardinal Barnabo, Archbishop Bedini, Father Francis, Passionist—my director while in Rome—Father Gregorio, definitor, Carmelite, and Father Druelle, of the Congregation of the Holy Cross, and each gave a favorable answer."

Father Hecker often said that he was fully determined to forego the entire matter, go back to the Redemptorists, or drift whithersoever Providence might will, if a single one of the men whom he thus consulted had failed to approve him, or had so much as expressed a doubt. He had inquired who were the most spiritually enlightened men in Rome, and had been guided to the three religious whom he had associated with Cardinal Barnabo and Archbishop Bedini to assist him in coming to a decision.

The end came at last, and is announced in a letter of March 9, 1858:

"The Pope has spoken, and the American Fathers, including myself, are dispensed from their vows. The decree is not in my hands, but Cardinal Barnabo read it to me last evening. The General is not mentioned in it, and no attention whatever is

paid to his action in my regard. The other Fathers are dispensed in view of the petition they made, as the demand for
separation as Redemptorists would destroy the unity of the Congregation, and in the dispensation I am associated with them.
The Cardinal [Barnabo] is wholly content; says that I must ask
immediately for an audience to thank the Pope. . . . Now let
us thank God for our success."

On March 11: "We are left in entire liberty to act in the
future as God and our intelligence shall point the way. Let us
be thankful to God, humble towards each other and every one
else, and more than ever in earnest to do the work God demands at our hands. . . . The Pope had before him all the
documents, yours and mine and the General's, and the letters
from the Archbishops and Bishops of the United States. Archbishop Bizarri (Secretary of the Congregation of Bishops and
Regulars) gave him a verbal report of their contents and read
some of the letters. Subsequently the Pope himself examined
them and came to the conclusion to grant us dispensation. But
there was *I* in the way, who had not petitioned for a dispensation. And why not? Simply because Cardinal Barnabo would
have been offended at me if I had done so. . . . I could not
go against the wishes of the cardinal. A few days after he had
given me his views, and with such warmth that I could not act
against them, he saw the Pope, who informed him of his intention to give us dispensation and to set aside the decree of
my expulsion. On seeing the cardinal after this audience he
told me that I might communicate this to Archbishop Bizarri.
I did so by note, telling him that if the Pope set aside my expulsion and was determined to give the other American Fathers
dispensation from their vows, in view of the circumstances which
had arisen I would be content to accept my dispensation also.
This note of mine was shown to the Pope, and hence he immediately associated me with you in the dispensation.

"The wording of the decree is such as to make it plain that
it was given in view of your memorial, and its terms are calculated to give a favorable impression of us. . . . Archbishop
Bizarri told me yesterday, when I went to thank him for his
part, that in it the Holy See had given us its praise, and he
trusted we would show ourselves worthy of it in the future. I
rejoined that since the commencement of our Catholic life we
had given ourselves soul and body entirely to the increase of
God's glory and the interests of His Church, and it was our
firm resolve to continue to do so to the end of our lives. He

was quite gratified with *our* contentment with the decision, for
I spoke, as I always have done, in your name as well as my
own.

"But whom do you think I met in his antechamber? The
General [of the Redemptorists]. When he came in and got seated
I immediately went across the room and reached out my hand to
him, and we shook hands and sat down beside each other.
. . . In the course of the conversation he inquired what we
intended to do in the future. My reply was that we had
been guided by God's providence in the past and we looked
to Him for guidance in our future. . . . As to my return [home], the cardinal says I must not think of departing
till after Easter. Indeed, I see that before I can obtain an audience to thank the Holy Father it will be hard on to Easter.
If there be a few days intervening I will go to Our Lady of
Loretto to invoke her aid in our behalf, and for her protection
over us as a body and over each one in particular. In May,
earlier or later in the month, with God's blessing and your prayers, I hope to be with you. . . .

"The decree, which places us, according to the Canons, under
the authority of the Bishops, you will, of course, understand does
not in any way make us parish priests. The Pope could not
tell us in it to commence another congregation, although this is
what he, and Cardinal Barnabo, and Archbishop Bedini, and
others, expect from us. He [the Pope] said that for him to tell
us so [officially] would be putting the cart before the horse.
These are his words."

On March 18 : "It is customary here, before giving dispensation of vows to religious, to require them to show their admission
into a diocese. As this was not required in our case, we are consequently at liberty now to choose any bishop we please who will
receive us. 'Choose your bishop, inform him of your intentions, and if he approves, arrange your conditions with him.'
These are the cardinal's words, and both he and Archbishop
Bedini suggested New York. . . . My trip to Loretto has
come to naught, as I can find no one to accompany me, and
then my health, I fear, will not bear so much fatigue. I shall
come back with some gray hairs ; I thought to pull them all out
before my return, but on looking this morning with that intention I found them *too many.* However, that is only on the outside ; within all is right—young, fresh, and full of courage, and
ready to fight the good fight.' "

The following is a memorandum of his second audience with Pius IX. :

"Yesterday, the 16th of March, the Pope accorded me an audience, and on my entering his room he repeated my name, gave me his blessing, and after I had kissed his ring he told me to rise, and said : 'At length your affairs are determined. We have many causes to decide, and each must have its turn ; yours came finally, and now you have our decision.' ' True,' I replied, ' and your decision gives me great satisfaction, and it appears to me that it should be satisfactory to all concerned.' ' I found you,' he rejoined, ' like Abraham and Lot, and (making a motion with his hand) I told one to take this, the other that direction.' ' For my part,' I said, ' I look upon the decision as providential, as I sought no personal triumph over the General, but entertain every sentiment of charity towards him, and every one of my former religious brethren.' This remark appeared to move the Pope, and I continued : ' I thought of your Holiness' decision in the holy Mass of this morning, when in the Gospel our Lord reminds us not to decide according to the appearances of things, but render a just judgment ; and such is the one you have given, and for our part we trust that you will receive in the future consolation and joy [from our conduct].' ' As you petitioned,' he said, ' with the other Fathers' as one of the Congregation, in giving you dispensation I considered you a member of the Congregation.' ' So I understood it,' was my reply ; ' and as a [private] person I felt no inclination to defend my character, but as a priest I felt it to be my duty ; and in this regard your Holiness has done all that I have desired.' ' But you intend to remain,' he inquired, ' together in community ? ' ' Most assuredly, your Holiness ; our intention is to live and work as we have hitherto done. But there are many [spiritual] privileges attached to the work of the missions very necessary to their success, and which we would gladly participate in.' ' Well, well,' he answered, ' organize, begin your work, and then demand them, and I will grant them to you. The Americans, however, are very much engrossed in material pursuits.' ' True, Holy Father,' I replied, ' but the faith is there. We five missionaries are Americans, and were like the others, but you see the grace of God has withdrawn us from these things and moved us to consecrate ourselves wholly to God and His Church, and we hope it will do the same for many of our countrymen. And once our countrymen are Catholics, we hope they will do great things for God's Church and His glory, for they have enthusiasm' 'Yes, yes,' he rejoined, 'it would be a great consolation to me.' I asked him if he would grant me a plenary indulgence for my brethren and my friends in the United States. 'Well,' he said, 'but I must have a rescript.' 'I have one with me which perhaps will do,' I answered. Looking over it, he made some alterations and signed it. I knelt down at his feet and begged him to give me a large blessing before my departure, in order that I might become a great missionary in the United States—which he gave me most cordially, and I retired.

"His manner was very affectionate, and in the course of the conversation he called me '*caro mio*' and '*figlio mio*' several times. We could not desire to leave a more favorable impression than exists here in regard to us and our part in the recent transaction, and we have the sympathy of the Pope and the Propaganda. Rome will withhold nothing from us if we prove worthy of its confidence, and will hail our success with true joy. I look upon this settlement of our difficulties as the work of Divine Providence, and my prayer is that it may make me humble, modest, and renew my desire to consecrate myself wholly to God's designs."

He writes to the Fathers, March 27: "The seven months passed here in Rome seem to me an age ; and have taxed me to that extent that I look forward to home as a place of rest and repose. When I think of the fears, anxieties, and labors undergone I say to myself—enough for this time. On the other hand, when I remember the warm and disinterested friends God has given us on account of these difficulties, and the happy issue to which His providence has conducted them, my heart is full of gratitude and joy. To me the future looks bright, hopeful, full of promise, and I feel confident in God's providence, and assured of His grace in our regard. I feel like raising up the cross as our standard and adopting one word as our motto —CONQUER !

"I have just received the documents for you to give the Papal benediction at the missions, and will send them. A letter reached here this week from the Bishop of Burlington, Vt., and it is strongly in our favor; it concludes by saying that all that we required to make us a religious Congregation was the special blessing of the Holy Father."

Again, on April 3: "Monsignor Bedini asked of the Pope the special benediction that Bishop De Goesbriand suggested, and he replied: 'Did I not give it to Père Hecker, and through him to his brethren, when he was here?' 'But,' answered Monsignor Bedini, 'give them this benediction this time on the request ot the bishop.' And he answered: 'It is well; I do.' So there is a special blessing from the Holy Father in view of our forming a religious body. Indeed, that is so well understood here that several have inquired what name we intend to adopt, etc. Ot course to all such questions my answer is: 'I can say nothing; the future is in God's hands, and we intend to follow his providence.' . . .

" Good Cardinal Barnabo looks upon us with a paternal regard, and when I expressed in your name how warmly we returned his affection, and what a deep gratitude we owed him, he was deeply moved, and replied that he did not deserve such sentiments, and that he had only done justice. Since the settlement of our affairs I have let no occasion pass to express our gratitude to those who have befriended us ; and as for Cardinal Barnabo, Monsignor Bedini, Bishop Connolly, and Doctor Bernard Smith, Benedictine monk, they should be put at the head of the list of our spiritual benefactors and remembered in all our prayers. Now that we are a body, I would advise this to be done at once. The Holy Father stands No. 1; that is understood.

" How much I have to relate to you on my return ! Many things I did not venture to write down on paper, and many I can communicate to no one else but you. How great is my desire to see you !—it seems that I have no other.

" I have taken passage for Marseilles on Tuesday after Easter, the 6th of April, and intend to take passage on the *Vanderbilt*, which leaves Havre on the 28th. . . . I saw the General on Tuesday of this week, to take leave of him. After some conversation we left in good feeling, promising to pray *pro invicem.* God bless him l "

Before leaving Paris Father Hecker received extremely affectionate letters of congratulation from his old friends, Fathers de Held and de Buggenoms.

The following is the decree of the Congregation ot Bishops and Regulars : *

+ Nuper nonnulli ex Presbyteris Congregationis SSmi Redemptoris in provinciis Americæ Septentrionalis fœderatis existentibus SSmum D. N. Pium PP. IX. supplici prece deprecabantur, ut eis ob speciales circumstantias concederet ab auctoritate et jurisdictione Rectoris Majoris subtrahi, ac a proprio Superiore Apostolicæ Sedi immediate subjecto juxta regulam a Benedicto XIV., sanctæ memoriæ, approbatam gubernari. Quod si id eis datum non esset, dispensationem a votis in dicta Congregatione emissis, humillime expostulabant. Re sedulo

"Certain priests of the Congregation of the Most Holy Redeemer in the United States of North America recently presented their most humble petition to our Most Holy Lord Pope Pius IX., that in view of certain special reasons he would grant that they might be withdrawn from the authority and jurisdiction of the Rector Major and be governed by a superior of their own, immediately subject to the Apostolic See, and according to the [Redemptorist] Rule approved by Benedict XIV., of holy memory. If, however, this should not be granted to them, they most humbly asked for dispensation from their vows in the said Congregation. After having carefully considered the matter, it appeared to his Holiness that a separation of this kind would be prejudicial to the unity of the Congregation and by no means accord with the Institute of St. Alphonsus, and therefore should not be permitted. Since, however, it was represented to his Holiness that the petitioners spare no labor in the prosecution of the holy missions, in the conversion of souls, and in the dissemination of Christian .doctrine, and are for this reason commended by many bishops, it seemed more expedient to his Holiness to withdraw them from the said Congregation, that they might apply themselves to the prosecution of the. works of the sacred ministry under the direction of the local bishops. Wherefore his Holiness by the tenor of this decree, and by his Apostolic authority, does dispense from their simple vows and from that of permanence in the Congregation the said priests, viz.: Clarence Walworth, Augustine Hewit, George Deshon, and Francis Baker, together with the priest Isaac Hecker, who has joined himself to their petition in respect to dispensation from the vows, and declares them to be dispensed and entirely released, so that they no longer belong to the said Congregation. And his Holiness confidently trusts that under the direction and jurisdiction of the local bishops, according to the prescription of the sacred Canons,

---

perpensa, Sanctitas Sua existimavit hujusmodi separationem unitati Congregationis officere, et S. Alphonsi instituto minime respondere ideoque haud permittendum esse. Cum autem relatum sit oratores nulli labori parcere in sacris expeditionibus peragendis, et in proximorum conversione, Christianaque institutione curanda, et idcirco a pluribus Antistibus commendentur, visum est SSmo Domino magis expedire eos a præfata Congregatione eximi, ut in sacri ministerii opera promovenda sub directione Antistitum locorum incumbere possint. Quapropter Sanctitas Sua presbyteros Clarentium Walworth, Augustinum Hewit, Georgium Deshon, et Franciscum Baker, una cum presbytero Isaac Hecker, qui eorumdem postulationibus quoad dispensationem a votis adhæsit, a votis simplicibus, etiam permanentiæ in Congregatione SSmi Redemptoris emissis, hujus Decreti tenore, Apostolica auctoritate dispensat, et dispensatos, ac prorsus solutos esse declarat, ita ut ad eamdem Congregationem amplius non pertineant. Confidit vero Sanctitas Sua memoratos Presbyteros, qua opere, qua exemplo, qua sermone, in vinea Domini sub directione et jurisdictione Antistitum locorum, ad præscriptum SS. Canonum adlaboraturos, ut æternam animarum salutem alacriter curent, atque proximorum sanctificationem pro viribus promoveant.

Datum Romæ, ex Secretaria Sacræ Congregationis Episcoporum et Regularium, Die 6 Martii, 1858.

[L. ✠ S.]   G. CARD. DELLA GENGA, *Præf.*

A., ARCHIEPISCOPUS PHILIPPEN, *Sec.*

the above-mentioned priests will labor by work, example, and word in the vineyard of the Lord, and give themselves with alacrity to the eternal salvation of souls, and promote with all their power the sanctification of their neighbor.

> " Given at Rome, in the office of the Sacred Congregation of Bishops and Regulars, the 6th day of March, 1858.

[L. S.]   G. CARDINAL DELLA GENGA, *Prefect.*

" A., ARCHBISHOP OF PHILIPPI, *Secretary.*"

NOTE.—I wish to add to this, that the relations between the Redemptorists and Paulists are, and I trust will continue to be, most amicable.

AUG. F. HEWIT, C.S.P., *Superior.*

ARRIÈRE PENSÉE.

MAY! I adore the air of you,
The tinting of your skies of blue;
    Your fields by daisy-buds empearled,
    Your cherry-blossoms wet, and hurled
By wandering winds; your clover new
That lies a green bespread with dew;
Your meadow larks—O merry crew !—
    Ah! is it wrong to love May's world?
    May I adore!

I know I love the changing view
Because it changes all day through.
    The leaves are closed and then uncurled;
    Their beauty, whether wide or furled,
Comes from our God—Him, changeless, true:
    May I adore!

MAURICE FRANCIS EGAN.

THE OLD WORLD SEEN FROM THE NEW.

THE temperance campaign has opened in Great Britain under cheering auspices. Three important points have been gained, the first of which is the second reading of the Liquor-Traffic Local Veto Bill for Wales. Of 364 members present 185 voted in favor and 179 against the bill, thus giving a majority of six for the second reading. The government as a government did not take sides, but left its supporters free. The Catholic Home Secretary, Mr. Matthews, however, both voted and spoke against the bill. Official Liberals, like Sir Charles Russell, have declared in favor of securing for the people complete control over the liquor-traffic, and Cardinal Manning, in a letter to a meeting held in support of the bill, declared that " the only adequate remedy for the drink-traffic is the local veto, by which the people may be able to protect themselves and their homes It is the only means of defence."

The bill deals with Wales only; it assigns "vetoing districts," and gives to one-tenth of the rate-payers of any district the right to secure a public meeting of the rate-payers. This meeting, when duly summoned, is empowered to decide any one of three questions: first, whether at the expiring of the existing licenses all the public-houses in such a district should be closed. If two-thirds of the rate-payers then present and voting say yes, the liquor-traffic ceases, all public-houses in that district are shut up, and this without any compensation, and for the period of five years, for which time the question is settled when the vote is in the affirmative. Should the vote be negative, the question may be raised again in two years' time. A second question, however, may be put to the meeting at once, in case the temperance advocates fail in securing the two-thirds majority for complete closing, and that is, Whether the public-houses in the district should be limited to a certain fixed number? If this question, being put to the vote, is answered in the affirmative by a bare majority of those voting, then all the licenses in the district are to be consecutively numbered by the licensing authority, according to his discretion, and no license is to be granted to any present holder bearing a number higher than that specified in the resolution. Should the second proposal be negatived, a third course may be adopted. A resolution may be

proposed in favor of issuing no new licenses, and of merely renewing year by year those already in existence.   This, if carried by a bare majority, becomes the law for that district.
Such are the main proposals of the bill, which has passed its
second reading.   How it will fare in committee and what will
be the reception accorded to it in the House of Commons remain to be seen.

*   *   *

The second point which the temperance cause has gained
is, the decision in the highest court—the House of Lords—that
the holder of a license has no legal right to its renewal, and
that, however well he may have conducted his house, it is at
the discretion of the licensing authorities to close it if they judge
fit to do so.   This is in opposition to the view which has hitherto prevailed and to common practice, which has been that, provided the liquor-seller has complied with the laws regulating his
trade, he has a right to a renewal.   On the other hand, although
it is decided that full discretion is possessed by the licensing authority, yet it is held that it is a *iudicial* discretion—a discretion,
that is, which is not arbitrary or contrary to what the laws permit—and it is very doubtful whether a magistrate or a board of
magistrates which should refuse to grant licenses on the ground
that the liquor-traffic ought to be entirely prohibited would be
sustained in such decision by the higher courts.   For as long as
the law of the land permits the traffic under certain conditions, a
magistrate entirely vetoing it would, in all probability, be held
to have exceeded his powers.

*   *   *

The third point gained by the temperance party is the in-
timation that the National Liberal Federation, of which Mr.
Schnadhorst is the animating spirit, and which is the controlling
" machine " of the Liberal party, is about to adopt its principles
and to incorporate them into the Liberal profession of faith.
This is at once an indication of strength already attained—for,
as Mr. Schnadhorst himself said, the National Liberal Federation, as such, cares more for votes than principles in themselves—and an important auxiliary for the future.   That the
victory is not yet attained, however good may be the ground
for anticipating it, is proved by the fact that the revenue from
the excise this year has exceeded the estimate by £1,000,000.

*   *   *

The active warfare between union labor and free or non-
union labor, of which we have several times made mention and

which has been carried on so long and on so large a scale, has, to all appearances, at last come to an end, and has resulted most disastrously for the New Unionists. The last conflict was between the Seamen and Firemen's Union as principals on the one side, and the gigantic organization of the ship-owners, the Shipping Federation, on the other. The conflict was carried on chiefly in London and at Cardiff, and at the outset the Union most interested had allies in the dockers, stevedores, and others. Efforts were made to bring the unions of the railway servants and of the miners into co-operation. These efforts, however, failed, and in the end the Seamen's and Firemen's Union was left alone, being abandoned by its allies. The secretary made an effort to have a general strike at every port, but met with so much opposition from local branches that he was compelled to declare the strike to be ended. This defeat, together with those at Southampton, in Scotland, and at Liverpool, seems to show that the New Unionism is still a long way off from the realization of its programme. It has also shown those in sympathy with this programme that the strength of the unionists is not to be measured by the success of the great London strike; a success which was due to various causes. In all likelihood the strike-policy will be abandoned for a time. The *Labour World*, which is edited by Mr. Michael Davitt, advises the unionists to devote themselves to the work of organization for two or three years, and to renew the war after having in this way attained sufficient strength.

*   *   *

A more powerful influence for peace will be found in the appointment, announced by the government, of a royal commission for inquiry into the relations between employers and employed. It is certain that no better plan for bringing about a peaceful settlement could have been adopted. These questions are the most important of our times, and they are also the most difficult. It is of supreme importance that those who are called upon to legislate or in any way to deal practically with these matters should be in possession of the fullest knowledge, and there is no way so well adapted to attain this knowledge as by means of a body of men, skilful and competent themselves, who shall have power to summon before them all who have any information worth giving. The Sweating Committee of the House of Lords shed a flood of light over many dark places in Great Britain, and has been the means already of promoting several measures for the removal of injustice. This new commission

will be wider in its scope and greater in its influence, and
we hope and believe that until it has reported there will be
a cessation of the conflict so far as the same involves principles,
and that the evidence it will call forth and the report on that
evidence will lead to some solution of the questions at issue.

*   *   *

It has taken the government nearly two months from the
time of its announcement of the appointment of the commission
to settle the terms of reference and to select the commissioners.
We hope that this is rather a token of the care and attention
which has been given to the matter than an augury of the future and of delay and hesitation in making the report. The
terms of the reference are as follows: "To inquire into questions affecting the relations between employers and employed,
the combinations of employers and of employed, and the conditions of labor, which have been raised during recent trade disputes in the United Kingdom, and to report whether legislation can with advantage be directed to the remedy of any of the
evils that may be disclosed; and if so, in what manner? The
number of commissioners is very large, no less than twenty-six,
and includes representatives of all the different interests. The
Marquis of Hartington, a large landholder, presides. He has already been the president of several very important commissions,
and by general consent he is as good a president as could
have been chosen. The government is represented by Sir
Michael Hicks-Beach and by Sir John Gorst, whose recent utterances on the labor question have attracted so much attention,
and who was present as one representative of Great Britain at
the Berlin Labor Conference, and who has, as he himself says,
long been a close student of these questions. We have no room
to go through the complete list; suffice it to say that employers
of labor and employed, the old political economists and the new, the
old unionists and the new, have all their representatives. Certain
prominent men in the recent agitations, like John Burns and
Michael Davitt, have not been chosen, but persons of similar
opinions are on the board, and will secure a full hearing, as witnesses for those who do not act as commissioners.

*   *   *

Meanwhile, besides the New Unionism, there has sprung up
recently a "New Conservatism." The appointment of this labor
commission is itself an evidence of this. A clearer proof,
however, is found in the words and actions of by no means a
small number of prominent Conservatives. Lord Randolph

Churchill has spoken in favor of the legal eight-hour day for miners. Sir John Gorst, who is Under-Secretary for India in the present ministry, advocates, among other things, the appointment of a Minister of Industry to deal with all questions which affect the working-classes. Mr. Howard Vincent and Sir R. Paget spoke in the House of Commons in support of a measure so socialistic in its character that it was opposed even by labor members. And it is worth pointing out that it is from workingmen that much of the proposed legislation meets with opposition. The legal eight-hour day, even for miners alone, is far from meeting with the unanimous approval of those affected. But whatever differences may exist all are agreed upon one point, and that is that of all questions the labor question, in its various-ramifications, is by far the most important of those with which politicians have to deal.

*   *   *

The bills introduced into Parliament are a further evidence of this. As we mentioned last month no less than five measures dealing with the regulation of factories and workshops were under discussion. Two of these have been referred to committees to be consolidated and amended. Further proposals affecting more or less directly the position of the working classes have been brought before the House. It may be remembered, perhaps, that during the political campaign of 1885 the demand that each agricultural laborer should be made the owner of "three acres and a cow" was warmly advocated by Radicals, barely tolerated by Liberals, and vehemently opposed by Conservatives. Mr. Gladstone, however, having formed his alliance with the Irish party at the opening of the session of 1886, by adopting a resolution in furtherance of this plan brought about the overthrow of the Conservative government. But Home Rule for Ireland took precedence. Many changes have taken place since that time, but Mr. Jesse Collings, its promoter from the beginning, has been true to his cause, and with the help of his former opponents, and, in fact, without a division, has obtained for his Small Holdings Bill a second reading. It is true that an important concession has been made in the omission of any compulsory power requiring the local authorities to purchase or private persons to sell. But it will undoubtedly, if passed, go far to attain the object sought—the fixing of the agricultural laborer on the soil. For it enables the local authorities to borrow money from the treasury at a low rate of interest for the sake of purchasing land to be let in small parts not larger than fifty acres. A remarkable proviso, and one which seems to be a step towards the nationalization of land—resembling in appearance but really very different from Mr. George's plan—is that three-fourths of the purchase money, with interest, is always to remain a charge upon the property, thus constituting the state a perpetual owner of the land dealt with in that manner. This proposal is in accordance with the recommendations of a committee which reported in 1888. We doubt very much whether such a proposal will not defeat the end and object of the measure, which is to attach to the soil the people who at present are but toilers for the advantage of others, and to do this by giving them the rights and privileges of proprietorship. For can any one who has to pay for ever so large an annual quit-rent feel himself to be really a proprietor?

*   *   *

Friends of State Socialism, as well as its opponents, have in the British Post-office and its action towards the messenger companies an instructive object-lesson—an exemplification in practice worth a ton of theory. The post-office in Great Britain has by law a monopoly of the carriage of letters and of telegraphic business; and through the parcel-post system it does a very large part of what is done in this country by the express companies, although it has no monopoly. The district messenger system, however, has only been started within the last few years, and this in a manner far from being as perfect as that which has existed for twenty years or more in this country. Within the last few months a second company has introduced the electric call. The British citizen was just beginning to enjoy privileges and conveniences to which Americans have become habituated when, the postmaster-general interfered, and declared that the monopoly of the post-office was being infringed, and that the companies must entirely abandon the carrying of letters. But to appease the indignant citizens a post-office messenger and express service has been started, far less efficient and useful than those which private enterprise was carrying on. The points in this matter which deserve the consideration of those who advocate the extension of the sphere of state action are these: The post-office, having a monopoly, goes on for years in its old routine, and makes no effort to introduce improvements which have long been accomplished by private enterprise in other countries. As soon as private enterprise undertakes to supply this deficiency, and just as it is in a fair way to do so, the post-office intervenes, requiring that the undertaking shall be given up as illegal. Shamed, however, by the indignant remonstrances of the public, the post-office offers to do the work itself; but its plan is found to bear no comparison in general usefulness to the suppressed service, and to be enmeshed in the bonds of red-tapeism. The postmaster-general has been severely censured for interfering, but, it seems to us, without warrant; for if the law really has given such a monopoly he is but a servant and minister of the law, and has no dispensing power. And even if it should appear, as is maintained by the companies, that their undertaking is not illegal, such a result would but strengthen the case of those who oppose the extension of state action in these matters; for it would be an instance of the way in which officials invariably magnify their office.

*　　　*　　　*

The most interesting event in the political world during the past month has been the election of the Austrian Lower House. As anticipated, Count Taaffe's allies, the Old Czechs, were defeated, and even almost annihilated. The Young Czechs, enemies of all compromise with the Germans, as well as being Radicals, have driven their opponents out of the field. Count Taaffe has therefore to seek for support elsewhere. Austrian politics are interesting to a student of the constitutional form of government as an example of the manner in which extremes may meet in this as in other things, for in Austria, as in Russia, the emperor's will is, to a very large extent, law, and not only is he himself, like the English monarch, above parties, but the minister of his choice enjoys to a certain extent the same privilege. This, however, is brought about in a way just the opposite to that by which it is accomplished in Russia. In Russia the people are politically slaves; in Austria they are perfectly independent and free. They are so perfectly free and independent, indeed, that in a house which has only 353 members there are no less than sixteen parties—German Liberals and German Conservatives; Old Czechs, Young Czechs, and Independent Czechs; Clericals pure and simple and Italian Clericals; Poles, Ruthenians, Roumanians, Slavonians. This is only a partial list of these parties. The most numerous is that of the German Liberals, consisting, as it does, of 110 members; but, standing alone, it is powerless. In this divided house a ready resource for a minister is to form a coalition, and this he does by persuading a sufficient number of parties to adopt his ideas, making of course some concessions in return. Thus he gets his majority. Count Taaffe, himself a

Conservative Clerical, has lost his former supporters in this election, and therefore has sought, by forming an alliance between the German Liberals, his former opponents, and the Poles and Ruthenians, to obtain the requisite majority.   The German Liberals, it seems, have proved themselves somewhat impracticable, but after long negotiation the ministry has been reorganized by the admission into it of one German Liberal, one Pole, and one representative of the Czech land-owning nobility.   The policy of the emperor and this ministry is to group all the moderates together against extremists of every school.

*   *   *

In Italy the most important event has been the misunderstanding between that country and our own about the lynching in New Orleans, but as in these notes we do not discuss home politics we will say nothing on this point.   The Rudini ministry still retains office, to the surprise of many.   It has inaugurated its financial economies, for effecting which it was created—diminishing the length of service for soldiers, curtailing the expenditure on the African colonies, and effecting various other savings. There can be no doubt that the effect of these proceedings has been to shake the Triple Alliance, rendering somewhat doubtful the renewal which should take place in 1892.   It would seem, too, that the protectorate over Abyssinia, which it was thought had been accepted by that state, is by no means an accomplished fact, Count Antonelli having returned from his mission without success.   As to the relations between the new government and the church, there is not much to say, except that it seems to be more courteous in tone and manner, and that, perhaps, is something for which to be grateful after the coarse brutality of Signor Crispi.

*   *   *

The death of Prince Napoleon is the chief thing to chronicle with reference to France, and so low have the Bonapartists fallen that, while interest was, of course, taken in the event, it was not looked upon as a matter of the least importance.   Even the division in the ranks of this ever-dwindling party between the prince's followers and those of his eldest son, Victor, has not been healed, for he died unreconciled and unforgiving, and in his last will he has directed his followers to look for counsel in political matters to his second son, Prince Louis.   As regards his submission to the church, we have the best reason to believe that it was really and sincerely made, for the Abbé Puyol, who gave him the last sacraments, has publicly declared that the prince was fully conscious. It is to be remembered also that, un-Catholic and •anti-Catholic as the actions and words of the greater part of his life had been, nevertheless almost the last public action of the prince in politics was a manifesto in defence of religion and against the persecution it was undergoing at the hands of the French Republic in 1883. How sincere he was in this we leave it for others to judge.

The hoped-for *rapprochement* between France and Germany has been definitely put an end to by the action of the German emperor in re-imposing the severe restrictions upon intercourse between Alsace-Lorraine and France. Indeed, the bonds of union between the enemies of Germany— France and Russia— seem to be growing closer, if we can take the decoration of President Carnot by the czar as anything more than an act of politeness ; and it certainly seems to imply something more. In other respects the course of events in France has been satisfactorily peaceful. Cardinal Lavigerie's policy (if we may so call it) seems to be daily gaining in strength; in recent elections the adherents of the republic have been returned with greater majorities. The government is—strange to say—acting with vigor in the repression of betting and gambling, and protectionism is waxing more and more powerful. These events, together with diplomatic contests with England as to Egypt and Newfoundland, are the only incidents worthy of mention in the current affairs of France.

*   *   *

As in France so in Germany, a death is the chief thing to chronicle. In Dr. Ludwig Windthorst the Catholics of the German Empire have lost their bravest and most successful champion, and the despoiled king of Hanover a devoted and self-sacrificing advocate. At the time Prince Bismarck was all-powerful there was but one man of whom he was afraid, and but one man who succeeded in thwarting schemes upon which the prince had resolved, and not only in thwarting but to a large extent in reversing them. This man was Windthorst. · And what he achieved was through power of intellect alone and skill in parliamentary tactics, and in spite of great personal disadvantages ; for he was far from pleasing in appearance, being hump-backed, near-sighted, and almost a dwarf. If the detailed account of his life could be written, it would be of immense value for showing what service a layman can render to the church in our times, and might perhaps stir up to emulation laymen in other lands to serve the church and the causes which she has at heart —temperance, purity of politics, the well-being of the poor. He lived to see the fall of his great opponent, and to receive him-self from the emperor marks of special esteem and regard.   May his great, honest soul rest in peace ! We hope that he may have a worthy successor.

The youthful sovereign of Germany seems to be finding out the truth of the saying that in politics nothing succeeds like suc-cess.   The failure of his endeavors to enter into more friendly relations with France, and his peevish, ill-tempered infliction of punishment on his own subjects for the bad behavior of the "howling dervishes" of Paris, are making even Germans some-what critical as to his claim of absolute control over every de-partment of government.   And what his subjects feel is more clearly brought home to the minds of his allies : want of confidence in a man so full of confidence in himself is being more and more keenly felt, and a general feeling of uneasiness and appre-hension exists.

*   *   *

The other countries of Europe present little to which intelli-gent interest is attached.   In Servia and Roumania, and also in Norway, there have been changes of ministry.   Servia presents the spectacle of an ex-king now wrangling with a queen divorc-ed from him by an invalid decree made by a state bishop ; then bringing accusations against a former prime minister of having connived at murder, to which accusation a *tu quoque* is the re-joinder.   In Bulgaria a state assassination has taken place, and it is thought that it found its inspiration in the same country as that to which was due the. kidnapping of Prince Alexander. Russia proceeds inexorably on her way of repression, grinding down her Jewish subjects, narrowing the sphere of individual action, depriving of religious freedom those even to whom it has been most solemnly promised.   So seldom is it that there is anything pleasing to record of this dismal prison-house that we may mention the following incident of a more agreeable character.   On the 13th of March the emperor and the empress, and his majesty's four brothers, with their imperial consorts, at-tended the funeral of their old English nurse, who had died at the age of eighty-two.   The czar and the grand dukes walked on foot through the melting snow and dirt behind the hearse along the Neva Quay from the Winter Palace to the church, while the empress and the grand duchesses followed in carriages.   They remained in church as chief mourners throughout the funeral service.   It is a pleasure to be able to record such an act of kindness.

TALK ABOUT NEW BOOKS.

THE title of Doña Emilia Pardo Bazan's novel * holds out a promise which her performance does not adequately keep. It is true that there always have been, and doubtless will continue to be, Christian women who, through a more or less mistaken notion of duty, assume of their own free will the galling yoke of a loveless marriage and bear it without flinching to their life's end. But there is not only nothing distinctively Christian in such conduct, but we must insist that only the patience and fortitude with which the burden continues to be carried condones the great initial fault of having stooped to take it up. There have been places and times and isolated cases which seem to admit of an alternative opinion ; but times change, and so do manners, and ways of considering vital social questions. And among such questions none is so vital as that of marriage, whether looked at from the natural or the Christian point of view. Generally it it is the hinge on which life makes its most important turn. Catholic theology recognizes its individual and fundamental character in affirming that the parties contracting it are themselves the ministers of the sacrament by which humanity renews itself and supplies the material for the supernatural order. Hence the invidiousness of applying so great a title as a " Christian Woman," a title which connotes so much and which is applied by excellence to the stainless Mother of Jesus Christ, to the story of Carmen Aldao and her repulsive marriage.

But to say this is not to deny the title of Christian to Doña Pardo Bazan's heroine. It is merely to question the motive for delineating her in such a way that the criticism passed upon her conduct by Luis Portal, the free-thinker of the tale, shall seem entirely just. It is more than that: it is Christian, although it is coupled with deserved slurs against excrescences which human weakness and wickedness have often succeeded in confounding with Christianity itself: .

" You say," Portal remarks to Salustio, " that Señorita Aldao realizes the ideal of a Christian woman. Nonsense, my boy ! Will you kindly tell me what attractiveness we can find in that ideal if we examine it carefully ? The ideal for us ought to be

* *A Christian Woman.* By Emilia Pardo Bazan. Translated by Mary Springer. New York : Cassell Publishing Co.

the woman of the present, or, better, of the future; a woman who could understand us and share our aspirations. You will say that she does not exist. Then let us try to manufacture her. She will never exist if we condemn her before she is born.

"What are the virtues which you attribute to your aunt, and which you admire so much? In what do they consist? They appear to me negative, irrational, brutal. Don't start up in that way—I said brutal. She has married a man who is repulsive to her, given herself up to him like an automaton: and all for what? In order not to sanction by her presence another person's sins. Who can be held responsible for anybody's actions but his own? That young lady is either demented or a stark fool; and the friar who countenances her and seconds her—well, I don't care to say what I think of him, because my tongue would run away with me. He understands better than she does what she is binding herself to, and he ought to have prevented such a barbarous affair."

That, indeed, is precisely what "the friar" had sought to do within the limits of judicious warning and advice. Portal goes on to say:

"*A woman such as our modern society needs would go out to service, would take in sewing, or scrub floors, if she was not happy in her father's house, if her self-respect was wounded, but she would never give up her liberty, her heart, and her person to such a husband.* You must have caught the infection of Christianity. You must get rid of it. A perfect Christian woman! And why is it that you are charmed with a perfect Christian woman? Are you, perchance, a perfect Christian man? Do you aspire to be one? Or do you believe that the destined progress of society depends upon the wife being a Christian and the husband a rationalist?"

The trouble with Carmen is precisely that, though undeniably a Christian, she is not by any means a perfect Christian woman. Not only must one say that her special reason for marrying Don Felipe was a poor one, but it must be added that there is not now, whatever there may seem to have been in days when civilization was one-sided, because it had failed to assimilate or comprehend that equality of the sexes which the Gospel initiated and is to perfect, any good reason why women should consider it praiseworthy to contract a loveless marriage. We strongly suspect, indeed, that it was precisely this lesson which the author of the novel had it in mind to teach. Her delineations of Carmen and the Franciscan friar, Father Moreno, might well have been the work of a high-minded

Christian woman, heartily attached to her traditional faith, and anxious to help clear away the obstacles which retard its triumph in our modern life. Were that unmistakably her motive, one could hardly quarrel much with the object-lesson she has so vigorously given. The as yet untranslated sequel to the present story perhaps shows her hand more completely. Taken by itself, this one does not afford quite grounds enough for passing judgment on the animus of its production.

A French novel* by M. Henry Rabusson takes up the marriage question from a somewhat unusual point of view. Madame d'Orgevaut, a young and charming widow whom death had soon released from the burdens of a *mariage de convenance*, has two suitors, to one of whom her heart seriously inclines. This is M. Gaetan Faurel d'Ambérieu, a distinguished savant whose name, whose manners, and whose person, all seem to indicate high-breeding and high principles. The other is the Prince de Dhun, a nephew of the late Count d'Orgevaut, whose admiration for his aunt not only antedated her widowhood but had once found insulting expression during her husband's lifetime. The rebuff then received, and the coldness with which he had been ever afterwards treated, ended in converting into a real passion what had begun as a criminal caprice. The Prince de Dhun has been an evil-liver, and his unreturned love, when rendered hopeless by Madame d'Orgevaut's second marriage, makes him a physical wreck. As M. Rabusson puts it:

"It is hard for love to take root in the heart of a libertine, but when by chance it does find a place there, it disorganizes and absorbs it; where all the energies are worn or weakened, nothing can resist the great resolvent. Paul de Dhun had, therefore, no desire for a reaction; the news of Luce's marriage, the failure of the last attempt to save her—the idea of which had come to him too late—had given the last blow to his moral courage. As for his vitality, long since compromised by lesions of his heart and lungs, which the recent prostration of his whole being had aggravated more, even, than the excesses of his youth, it was departing little by little, escaping from him drop by drop, leaving, day by day, his cheeks more wan, his eyes more sunken, and his back more bent. He had aged so in four or five months that there was little left for him to do but die, in order to cease filling everybody with pity."

We quote in order to give the reader a complete if offensive idea of Madame d'Orgevaut's rejected suitor. The man whom

---

* *Madame d'Orgevaut's Husband.* By Henry Rabusson. Translated by Frank Hunter Potter. New York: Dodd, Mead & Co.

she accepts has the misfortune to displease all her friends, whose votes are unanimous in favor of the prince. They are actuated by an instinctive distrust of M. Faurel d'Ambérieu, which nothing seems to justify until an accident reveals that he is not of noble birth but simply the son of one Faurel, a schoolmaster in the village of Ambérieu, so that he is, or appears to be, travelling under false pretences. This fact, however, when ascertained and speedily imparted by Luce d'Orgevaut's well-intentioned relatives, has no effect, since it had been told her in advance by her lover himself. He has confessed that he had applied for and obtained legal sanction to adopt his present name, thinking it would help him to advance in his chosen pursuits, and also— but this only in response to a close question from Luce—that it would aid him to a better marriage than he could otherwise aspire to. But his love for her, like hers for him, is unmistakably genuine, and his timely avowal of his little vanity enables her to triumph when others seek to damage him with her by revealing it.

Gaetan's confession, however, has not been complete. The vanity which induced him to assume the coveted "particle" is a constitutional weakness, and pardonable. There has been a bad action in his life—one which offends against the male code of honor, and makes its detected perpetrator a pariah in the eyes of his own sex as certainly as an offence against purity lowers a woman in the estimation of both men and women. Pressed, not exactly by poverty but by an ambition which needed for its realization greater resources than he could command, he once stole money entrusted to him, intending to risk it at cards, and replace it when he should succeed in winning. He did win, he would have restored it, and his honor would have seemed unstained, had he not been discovered by the benefactor from whom he had taken it, at the very moment of success. He was repentant, he was pardoned, and his secret kept. But for a letter written by him spontaneously in a burst of gratitude, confessing his sin explicitly and avowing his shame and sorrow, no trace of it would exist save in his memory and that of the man he had wronged. Forgiven by Daniel Bréchet, Gaetan has also forgiven himself, and so completely that he does not realize that pardon cannot obliterate a fact so damning, and that for him all question of contracting marriage with "an irreproachable woman" was settled negatively in advance. It is not until the night of his marriage with Luce, and it would never have been at all had not circumstances then forced the avowal from him, that he fully makes known his past. A breach opens instantly between the pair, and, although it is apparently patched over for the time, it continues to widen until the woman's love dies out, killed by the knowledge of the man's shame, and they separate. When Gaetan, who has slain the Prince de Dhun in a duel, tells her that she had never had any true tenderness for him ; that she lied when she pretended to pardon him and promised to forget, and that, being a woman, she is "not even capable of indulgence," she replies :

"Well, I will tell you why I have not been able to pardon, to forget. You think that it is chiefly because you deceived me in concealing your past. You recollect, no doubt, fine scenes in dramas or comedies, where one sees the guilty one purified by confession and raised up by love? Ah! no, that is not true. In life, nothing is raised up, nothing is purified. It belongs only to God to efface, to cause to disappear the traces of a fault, because it is in His power alone to forget or recollect at will. And do you know why no one will ever see, in reality, a happy or even a peaceful married life where there is not a stainless past on either side, unless there be on both sides equality in vileness? The guilty person who is really worthy of being rehabilitated comprehends that there is no rehabilitation possible, save in a solitude courageously and voluntarily borne ; he understands that there will always be in his conscience and in the memory of others, in that of the being whom he loves, something which would protest against this lustral pardon. Saint Mary Magdalene never married. What I tell you is the truth! The rest are paradoxes of writers, illusions of fools! . . . Those who knew your secret, who might have spoken, did not speak ; circumstances and your will prevented them. . . It is you who have been compelled to speak, and what accuses you is your unworthiness; it is against that you are struggling. And I will repeat to you, if it can spare you one regret, I could not have been happy, even though you had confessed everything to me before we were marred. Certainly I should have forgiven you before ; I was able to do it afterward! I should have forgiven you more willingly, I grant that. But who would have taken away my memory? Who would have reconstructed the pedestal which I had raised for you, and which you would yourself, of your own accord, have thrown down? Bah! paradoxes, illusions! Now let us separate. I can bear no more. The cup has overflowed; this duel, this murder, this new crime with which I find myself associated this time with a share of real responsibility, terrifies me, 'drives me to despair. Ah! unhappy—"
"Ah, what an accent! Perhaps you loved him, after all."
"*No! but I regret with my whole soul that I did not love him.*"

Condemning first of all this low view of the rehabilitating power of repentance, we go on to remark that the lion in the fable said of the pictures wherein men were continually represented as victors in the hunt, that if lions had been the artists the pictures might have been different. Probably a woman capable of writing a novel as serious, well-considered, and just in sentiment as this of M. Rabusson's would not have put into Luce's mouth the sentence we have italicized. What is it but an admission—a blunt avowal, rather, that in the novelist's eyes unpardonable sins are reducible to offences against the male — men commit them when they rob other men; women when they lose the one virtue which man prizes in his chosen mate. This blot aside, M. Rabusson's novel, which, by the way, has been put into admirable English by the translator, is interesting, powerful, and well worth reading.

There is room, as we all know, for people of good taste to differ in opinion concerning Mr. Kipling as a story-teller. There can hardly be much where Miss Mary E. Wilkins's merits in the same line are concerned. The present collection * has, perhaps, some failures to hit their author's highest mark in it; perhaps, we say, having heard a usually hypercritical judge remark that he "liked even her failures"—but not because we recall any of them to which we should care to apply the term. They seem to us, without exception, not merely faithful transcripts of New England life in some of its humbler forms—they could be that and yet remain uninteresting and unamusing — but full of point, wonderfully clever in diction, and as complete in direct and artistic reproduction as an instantaneous photograph taken by a competent judge of a sitter's best points. For the matter of that, these little sketches, in which there is hardly a line or a word too much, leave the same impression as pictorial representations do. They are cut out, as it were, with a single stroke of the die. Miss Wilkins, we believe, describes her method by saying that the conclusion of a story is always what first occurs to her, and that all else arranges itself to lead up to it. Certainly, like the wasp, these stories carry their sting in their tail. Only, it is seldom anything so venomous as to deserve such a remark. Where all are so good it is not easy to name favorites. There is "The Solitary," which compresses into a dozen pages an idea which George Eliot expanded into *Silas Marner*, and which François Coppée has handled, and handled not so well, in our judgment, in "The Captain's Vices." "Sister Liddy" is full of

* *A New England Nun and Other Stories.* By Mary E. Wilkins. New York: Harper & Brothers.

the material of pathetic laughter, while " A Village Lear " is pathos pure and simple. " A Gala Dress," " An Innocent Gamester," " A Village Singer," and " A Poetess " possess a predominantly melancholy charm, but laughter and tears lie side by side in this writer's storehouse of things new and old.

It must be owned that one avows with some hesitation a preference for such a story as " The Solitary " above those in which an artist like François Coppée * treats an almost identical motive—that of the regenerating power of unselfish pity or love. It is a matter of material and environment rather than of conception and handling which weighs down the balance with the present critic; something homely and familiar in accent, something purer too, if less intense, in sentiment, which wakens a readier sympathy with the surly Nicholas Gunn than with Captain Mercadier or the ex-criminal Jean François Leturc. But the Frenchman's tales are very excellent specimens of the short story, somewhat marred, it is true, in translation by awkward turns of speech which a little care might easily have remedied. " At Table " is hardly to be called a story; it is the reverie of a dreamer who, at a costly banquet, is haunted by the thought of the pain and labor and risk of life which have gone to the making of this hour of pleasure for a few rich people. An accent of Tolstoï breaks through it. " An Accident " is the most intense in a collection whose chief note is, perhaps, intensity. In form it is the confession of a murder, made to the Abbé Faber at the Church of St. Médard, in Paris. " The Sabots of Little Wolff " is a charming little Christmas tale for children, more German than French in sentiment and conception. " A Voluntary Death " is painfully morbid and un-Christian.

Mr. J. C. Heywood by no means fulfils as a novelist his promise as a poet. The two-volume tale† which is, we suppose, the first-fruits of his Catholic life, could hardly be his and not possess many merits. But its defects, considered purely on the literary side, are also many. It is ill-constructed, it abounds in slang, its characters, notably " Vivy " and her lover, " The Hon. Frank Glyder," are painfully caricatured, and the whole American business of " Bill Mundly," " Mumps," and " Parley " has an air of being dragged in by the ears, so as to relieve the monotony of catechism by broad farce. Somehow they do not mix well. One understands the pressure which tends to constrain al-

---

* *Ten Tales.* By François Coppée. Translated by Walter Learned. New York: Harper & Brothers.

† *Lady Merton: A Tale of the Eternal City.* By J. C. Heywood, author of *Herodias, Antonius, Salome,* etc. London and New York: Burns & Oates.

most every convert who has had a literary training, to open his mind and heart to the general public concerning that great change which has, for the first time, brought home to his intelligence the adequate and satisfying object on which mind and heart were meant to feed. If he be a poet, which Mr. Heywood has convincingly proved himself to be; or a novelist, which he quite as certainly has not yet shown; his first thought is like enough to cast his mental and moral processes into the form of a tale or poem. For the motives on which these are naturally built are love and beauty; and what he feels is that he has found the very source of love and the embodiment of beauty. Not only are there to him no dry pages in the catechism, but history is a mirror reflecting the face of God and His dealings with mankind. For that reason, too, the Catholic reader, as such, gets a pleasure from even tales like Mr. Heywood's, which present almost no attractive side to the general reader.

There are some very clever ones among Mr. Briggs's rhymed charades.* These, for example, whose answers we will not offend the reader's perspicacity by giving:

> "The queen, with beauty's fatal gift accurst,
> Calmly laid down my second on my first.
> Thus can the mind the body frail control,
> And every man be valiant but my whole."

> "My first, if frequently repeated,
> Implies a speaker self-conceited.
> Devotion to my third is reckoned
> A flagrant instance of my second.

> "Would you have the voice of Spurgeon?
> Use my whole to keep it mellow.
> You will find the Russian sturgeon
> An accommodating fellow.
> He will give you all the sound
> Where the substance may be found."

Mr. Egan's new book,† which we are glad to see accompanied by a third edition of his deservedly popular collection of shorter tales, is very pleasant reading. Mr. Egan, like another of our still younger writers, Mr. Harold Dijon, has caught the true idea of what fiction intended for youthful Catholic readers should aim at. Example, not precept, is the story-teller's trade. No one can escape a moral, more or less obvious, whatever view of art or morality he holds or supposes himself to hold; but it

---

* *Original Charades.* By L. B. R. Briggs. New York: Charles Scribner's Sons.

† *The Disappearance of John Longworthy.* By Maurice Francis Egan. Notre Dame, Ind.: office of the *Ave Maria.*

The Life Around Us. A collection of stories. By Maurice Francis Egan. New York and Cincinnati: Fr. Pustet & Co.

is wise not to insist on making it too prominent, to which-
ever extreme of the ethical line one's education or predispo-
sitions may incline him. Mr. Egan has a light hand and a
penetrating eye ; he is familiar with many varieties of society,
especially in the Eastern States ; his literary knowledge is ample and varied and his taste excellent. To all these advantages,
so desirable for one who would paint the " Life Around Us "
so as to accentuate its true bearing on the life that is to come,
he adds a thoroughly Catholic feeling and a graceful, unstudied
manner of delineation and expression. *The Disappearance of
John· Longworthy*, whose central motive is perhaps to show
the futility of attempts to reconstruct society on the model proposed some years ago by Mr. Walter Besant, is a clever study
of life in New York among two or three varieties of the class
sometimes known as " second-growth Irish." The girls, Mary
and Esther ·Galligan, are very well done, and so, in her very
different line, is Nellie Mulligan. It would be a very desirable
result of work like this of Mr. Egan's, if the too common and
most deplorable type embodied in Miles Galligan—the hard-
drinking, self-seeking, small politician—could be made an offence
in the eyes of all our young people. Until it can be eliminated
or frowned down, too many of our nicest girls will continue to
aver with Esther when she meets that very different specimen,
Arthur Fitzgerald, that "a nice young Catholic man," honest,
intelligent, self-respecting, sober, religious, yet bent on success
by all honorable means, is a companion who rarely comes in
their way.

Mr. Robert Buchanan's new novel * is sensational as a matter
of course, yet not so much so as some of his previous work.
There is an ill-assorted couple in it who are severed in the first
place by what the man mistakes for murder or very near it.
He knocks his wife down in order to rob her of money bestowed
by an Anglican curate for the purpose of saving their sick baby's
life, and leaves her bleeding and unconscious. We mistake, however, in employing the word " rob "—in England, it seems, if
Mr. Buchanan's version of the law is correct, a man cannot rob
his wife, since all that she has, no matter how obtained, is his,
not hers. The wife recovers after the husband has fled, and
presently falls heir to an independent fortune, in the enjoyment
of which she and her little girl are living when the story takes
them up again seven years later. The woman lives under an

---

* *The Wedding Ring: A Tale of To-day.* By Robert Buchanan. New York: Cassell
Publishing Co.

assumed name, so as to evade her husband should he be still living. Her nearest neighbor, Sir George Venebles, has been seeking her hand in marriage for some years, but has always been refused it. Presently Mr. Bream, the Anglican curate of the first act of the drama, turns up again as assistant to the very High Church and celibate rector of the village where Sir George is magnate. He and Mrs. Dartmouth recognize each other, but keep their secret until an accident reveals to the curate the death of the first husband. He makes known the fact to the widow and Sir George, who immediately affiance each other. They have barely done so when the husband reappears, as plausible a villain as ever, demanding not merely the property and the child, to which English law entitles him, but also the affection, respect, and obedience to which he has also a clear legal title. The story is an old one, and Mr. Buchanan has not greatly varied it in presentation, except in the use he makes of the rector and the curate. The former is on the husband's side in every particular, takes his repentance for genuine, and rates his once-esteemed parishioner, the wife, as a very poor specimen of what Christianity can do, because she even hesitates as to her duty. In his view she ought to reserve nothing; her plain obligation is "to receive with tenderness the gentleman to whom she owes a wife's duty, a wife's obedience." The curate, on the other hand, goes in energetically for divorce and her remarriage to Sir George, a programme not carried out in the end only because the returned prodigal is murdered on his wife's doorstep by a man whose domestic happiness he had ruined and whose wife he had abandoned as well as betrayed.

Mr. Aldrich's new volume * of poems is, of course, melodious, correct, and agreeable in versification. Perhaps it is not often much more than that, except for an occasional pleasant conceit, or a picture like that embodied in the subjoined lines, called "Memory":

> " My mind lets go a thousand things,
> Like dates of wars and deaths of kings,
> And yet recalls the very hour—
> 'Twas noon by yonder village tower,
> And on the last blue noon in May—
> The wind came briskly up this way,
> Crisping the brook beside the road ;
> Then, pausing here, set down its load
> Of pine-scents, and shook listlessly
> Two petals from that wild-rose tree."

* *The Sisters' Tragedy. With Other Poems, Lyrical and Dramatic.* By Thomas **Bailey** Aldrich. Boston and New York : Houghton, Mifflin & Co.

1.—AN EXPOSITION OF THE EPISTLES OF ST. PAUL.*

"The Catholic Standard Library," of which Piconio's commentary forms a part, is published in a very neat style. The present volume contains the commentary on the Epistles to the Thessalonians, to Timothy, to Titus, to Philemon, and to the Hebrews. The translation of Piconio's text is excellent, but we cannot admire the version of the Scriptural text, although it is verbally accurate. The great excellence of the commentary of Piconio has been long and universally recognized.

2.—THE PACIFIC COAST SCENIC TOUR.†

This is not a particularly brilliant book of travel, but it is a particularly honest one, which is far better. Much of the ground covered by the author is familiar to the writer of this notice; indeed, we have been over a portion of it within the last six weeks, and so we are in a position to judge the correctness of his statements, and the accuracy of his descriptions. And we are simply surprised to find how faithfully our most vivid impressions are reflected and our actual experiences are re-echoed in the pages of this book. Mr. Finck depicts things in their every-day garb, and as they appear to the ordinary traveller without exaggeration and without affectation. He is not without enthusiasm, however, and his descriptions, while always sober and accurate, are often full of spirit and animation. The tour that he takes us through embraces, beyond all question, some of the very finest scenery on the face of the globe, and he gives us in a few skilful touches the grand outlines and distinctive features of these wonderful and varied scenes. Could the great scenic attractions of this country be grouped close together, as they are in Switzerland and Italy, few Americans would visit Europe for the sake of the scenery, for we have here in vast profusion all that they have there, and very much more besides. Nor is it at all unlikely that in the near future the tide of tourist travel will abandon the beaten paths of the Alps and the Apennines, and turn westward to explore the fragrant forests and virgin lakes and towering peaks of the Sierra Nevadas, the Cascades, and the Rockies. Here are still new wonders to marvel at and new worlds to conquer; and here without doubt the poetry and romance of the future will find their most congenial home.

---

* *An Exposition of the Epistles of St. Paul.* By Bernardine à Piconio. Translated and edited from the original Latin by A. H. Prichard, B.A., Merton College, Oxford. London: John Hodges.

† *The Pacific Coast Scenic Tour.* By Henry T. Finck. New York: Charles Scribner's Sons. 1890. Illustrated.

3.—THE INTERIOR OF JESUS AND MARY.*

A truly exquisite edition of a great work that has passed through more than twenty editions in French, and has been translated into every European language.

The book treats of a subject which should attract more attention than all else, and this is nothing less than the life of our Lord and his Blessed Mother. Not that it portrays their exterior life as told in the Gospel, but the spirit of that life, "hidden to the wise and prudent, but revealed to little ones." It is, therefore, a book for interior souls, and such souls will be astonished at the riches disclosed to them by Father Grou, riches suitable for every feast and season.

The work may be used as a book of meditation or of spiritual reading. The author would have us go to God with the greatest simplicity, leaving aside all studied discourse, and not attaching too much importance to reasonings and methods. "Let the heart alone speak, and let it express what it feels. When it has no feeling, let it groan over its insensibility; let it complain lovingly to God of this, and let it tell him all by its silence." "The soul that is under the action of God is never for one movement idle, as those imagine who have no true idea of what rest in God really means."

We concur with the editor of this translation in recommending the treatise *Abandonment; or, Absolute Surrender to Divine Providence* (Benzigers, New York), as an excellent sequel to the *Interior of Jesus and Mary.*

4.—SUMMA APOLOGETICA DE ECCLESIA.†

This work is one more contribution to the great number of manuals of apologetic literature already in the field. The learned author gives his production the rather pretentious title of *Summa.* In his preface, however, he rather hesitatingly asserts the claim. The whole object of the work is not revealed in this initial declaration. In the same preface he tells us that he had, when writing, a twofold object in view, to wit: the demonstration of Catholic truth and to point out to theologians the sources of arguments apt for that purpose; and, furthermore, to develop the value and use of each of those sources.

Our author follows the method of the illustrious Cano in dis-

* *The Interior of Jesus and Mary.* From the French of the Rev. J. Grou, S.J. New York: The Catholic Publication Society Co.; London: Burns & Oates.

† *Summa Apologetica de Ecclesia Catholica.* Auctore de Groot, Ordinis Prædicatorum. Ad mentem Sti. Thomæ Aquinatis.

tinguishing ten theological sources, but on account of his special aim he departs from the order established by his predecessor. In the first volume we are brought immediately face to face with the church, which is a sufficient motive of credibility on account of the notes and marks with which she is clothed.

Lacordaire accounts for the fact that there is no complete defence of Christianity because the restless tide of time multiplies ever and always new proofs, and, on the other hand, the objections which are raised are infinitely variable, the difficulties of each generation becoming contemptible with the lapse of years. This is undoubtedly the motive which inspired our author to put into a new ·dress the arguments with which numberless compendiums have made us familiar—wretched compendiums, Dr. Ward used to call them. Father de Groot, however, by following closely the scholastic method, renders his matter more lucid than most writers of his class of whom we have any knowledge, since Hurter's excellent work can scarcely be called a compendium.

The whole work is divided into twenty-two questions, embodying a lucid exposition of the subjects treated of. In places the various opinions current in schools are enumerated, followed by the author's thesis and its proofs ; finally the objections drawn from the nature of the subject or contingent facts are ably refuted. The style is so simple and didactic that it cannot fail to materially assist the student.

The author pays his respects to the schismatic churches at more length than is usually done in works of this kind. He is evidently familiar with the best German, French, and Italian apologists. He is not, however, so happy in his English selections. We have, for instance, the hackneyed piece of verbose rhetoric written by Macaulay on the Papacy, and which has done so much service to Continental authors that it has richly earned its *nunc dimittis*.

The learned Dominican devotes the fifth article of the ninth Question to an explanation of the sense which the church attaches to condemned propositions, and beginners will find his elucidation of this rather intricate technology very useful. The eleventh Question treats of the relations between church and state, and seems to us to be the best in the book.

5.—THE GOSPEL OF ST. LUKE IN VERSE.*

This is a translation of the Gospel of St. Luke from the Vulgate version into Latin hexameters. It is an ingenious and elegant composition, the version faithful, and the poetical construction correct.

*Sanctum Evangelium .Secundum Lucam in Carmina Versum. (Auctore Reverendo Domino Stephano Mazzolini.) For sale by Benziger Brothers.

THE COLUMBIAN READING UNION.

ALL COMMUNICATIONS RELATING *TO READING CIRCLES, LISTS OF BOOKS, ETC., SHOULD BE ADDRESSED TO THE COLUMBIAN READING UNION, NO. 415 WEST FIFTY-NINTH STREET, NEW YORK CITY.

The Ozanam Reading Circle has been favored with a letter from one of the most earnest workers in the cause of Catholic literature. It contains many suggestive statements in the Socratic form of interrogations. We commend it to the studious members of all Catholic Reading Circles:

"Is it not a veritable bringing of coals to Newcastle to say anything to the members of the *Ozanam Reading Circle* by way of suggestion?

"Merely as a sign of acknowledgment of a keenly-felt honor does the undersigned respond to a request made by the Rev. Father McMillan, and on the assumed strength of what the reverend father unknowingly calls 'experience,' here are a few detached observations.

"The associates in this laudable enterprise, fathered by the energetic Paulists, must by this time feel more than sanguine of success—full success. Alas! who that has looked on or shared in any great enterprise has been perfectly satisfied? The ultimate realization of our ideals is for another world, but a relative success in this work, how can we doubt of it when the impulse given is so strong and the guiding hands so sure? Onward, then, with hearts uplifted, and though it has come to be a sort of an article of faith that all literary associations die within the fifth year of their existence, let this one, which is not a literary club of the usual style, show that permanency is possible. But what is your design? What is the highest object you have in view?

"It has occurred to me frequently, while reading of your doings in THE CATHOLIC WORLD, that perhaps it would be well to do in your case what St. Bernard deemed advisable to do in his, after he had gone to the monastery; to ask himself, often, what he was about—'Bernard, what brought you here?' It is the writer's experience that members of similar associations are apt to fall too easily into what might be called the community spirit (wrongly understood, of course) and rest quite content to go along with the rest, satisfied that as the body knows what it is about, individual members need not concern themselves with keeping bright and warm and strong the true community spirit—a fatal error. Has this movement in favor of a better acquaintance with Catholic literature for its sole object to make known to Catholics that they possess treasures worth their while to take note of?

"A noble object surely. Matthew Arnold, in one of his essays on the 'Strength of Catholicism,' says something to this effect: If he were a Catholic living in England he would suffer much, but he would find also much to comfort him. Among the consolations he would give himself would be a frequent visit to the reading room of the British Museum, and there he would linger in loving contemplation of the vast section, stretching on and up from the 'Hell of the yellow law-books to the Heaven of the *Acta Sanctorum*' devoted to the Abbé Migne's collection, which contains all that concerns the Catholic Church from every point of view, dogma, discipline, art, literature, science, etc. He says: 'In this same room you may also find all the theological works of the various forms of Protestantism; but what a poor show they make, beside this array of condensed Catholicism.' We surely do not need assurances from Matthew Arnold or from any other outsider of our superabundant wealth. And yet I do fear that too many even of our educated Catholics are not fully informed in this matter. Do we really need to be told how rich and varied is the store from which we can adorn and arm and feed ourselves? Whether we really need this information or not, we will not discuss, but let us feel sure we are engaged in a good work in proclaiming our treasures. But this cannot be the sole motive of our combined efforts. Is it not rather to awaken in our hearts an enthusiasm for carrying the light to those who, thanks to much of the popular literature, are growing to believe that enthusiasm is a folly, that there is nothing worth striving for?

"Do we not wish to counteract the pernicious effect of the flippant reading of the day by working ourselves up to a relish for *studious* reading? And is not the means we have been advised to take something like a beginning of that after-course of studies so many have been longing for? The students in colleges, convents, and common schools can only go so far. How far? Indeed, only to the borders of the great wonderland of study. And must education be deemed ended when the medals have been pinned on amidst the flourish of pianos, violins, harps, etc. Bishop Spalding said something boldly true last summer at one of the commencements; something to the effect that there was a tendency to rest satisfied with the medal and diploma —that we too easily believed all sufficient these outward signs of inward progress. It would be well to heed such warnings as went with Bishop Spalding's cheering words to the graduates. But how are we going to solve the problem of a continued and studious life with the demands of our social and domestic environments? A great many seem to think the problem unsolvable and give it up, and content (?) with the *carpe diem* philosophy, are heard of no more among the light-bearers; they drop out of the ranks, or rather, they drop into the great nameless, aimless multitude. Would that it were the multitude for which Christ said he 'had compassion'! Will these Reading Circles, then, not help us to reach a satisfactory indication of the ways and means of doing one's duty to home and to other claimants, yet leaving us time enough to strive for personal perfection in every sense of the word? Will not communion with the divinely lighted minds of our great Catholic writers help immensely towards this perfection of mind and heart and soul? I think so, and if I were a travelling agent of your association canvassing members, I think I would feel sure of being in the right lines in holding out to the recruits the assurance that membership would mean for them a means of living up to their education and vastly more.

"Is it not an imperative duty for each member of such a favored section of the Columbian Reading Union as the 'Ozanam' to be on fire for the more and more clearly defined object of these associations?

"We must not let ourselves be talked out of our purpose nor sneered out of it. Let us work with wakeful souls. How shall we keep our souls awake amidst all the inducements to comfortable somnolence? Hero worship! Will that help? Let us try and find only the true heroes and heroines as we shall find them, busy and ceaselessly busy in our very midst; busy even in what the world deems the idle haunts of prayer, busy in the seclusions sacred to the higher Christian life. The saints are of all times. Should we fail to discern the living, acting ones in our midst? Then let us 'sit down and take thought' from what the written records show; let us familiarize ourselves with our *Acta Sanctorum*, not merely look at the goodly volumes on the top shelves of our libraries.

"Memoirs, too; biographies and letters of our saintly 'kith and kin' whose names are neither in the library nor in the martyrology, but whose names are surely written in heaven. It is to be regretted that we have not more good English translations of the many treasures in that line the French possess; such translation is a work for those of the members whose education and leisure permit. We want ever so many books done in the style of Kathleen O'Meara's *Ozanam;* of Mrs. Craven's *Lady Fullerton;* of Chocarne's *Lacordaire*, and pre-eminently of Father Elliott's *Father Hecker*. Is not this life going to be a great argument in favor of the possibility of the 'Modern Spirit' being proved a good spirit when it is properly directed? Has not Father Hecker given the lie beautifully to those who hold that the practical, realistic American cannot be a saint? 'Ever old, ever new,' holds good of the saints of God as of the God of the saints. We must insist, then, on the reading of biographical literature—not, however, to the exclusion of every other or any other.

"The books not directly Catholic in tone concern us closely. We want to know, and often to show, why they fall short of their purpose in spite of their fascinating form, why their arguments are not convincing. We can the better see what ails Carlyle when we know Newman well; why Matthew Arnold's suggestions do not cheer us when we read Father Hecker's Analysis of the Age; and George Eliot's *Romola*, despite its artistic and other merits, signifies very little to those who have read Capecelatro's *St. Philip Neri*, and so on with all of them. Comparative studies would be far more satisfactory than a too prolonged investigation into one side only.

" Will it not be feasible, as your association grows, to institute a course of lectures on the Philosophy of History, following, let us say, our own Allies' splendid work, *The Formation of Christendom?* These lectures would help much toward the interpretation of literature. Novels have a great hold on all readers, and they touch on all questions of time, and even of eternity. The philosophy of life, as shown in history, would help us benefit by some of these novels, and save us from the false theories they advocate. To sum up as briefly as possible, let us then—

1. Endeavor to know what we want, and why we want it.

2. Let us cultivate a taste for *studious* reading.

3. Let us always have a good Catholic work on hand, whatever amount of attention we choose to bestow on the magazines, reviews, and other books.

4. Let us try to find out the means by which those whose station in life does not permit a full participation in our work can be benefited as much as possible (cheap editions, *à la* Franklin Square, *à la* Harper, or any other way known to the publishers).

5. Let every member assume the right to act as an *irrepressible* agent in favor of at least one good Catholic weekly. We have many which are very good. Why should we not try also to make THE CATHOLIC WORLD reach a few more thousands?

Ottawa, Ont.   M. L. M."

*   *   *

The co-operative plan, upon which we rely so much for the work of our Reading Union, has been selected by the Rev. S. B. Messmer, D.D., as the only feasible way under the circumstances now existing of establishing at the Catholic University a truly representative " Library of American Catholic Literature." Besides documents bearing on canon law and church history, Dr. Messmer hopes to get odd copies of magazines, local publications giving the history of missions, parishes, convents, educational and charitable institutions; also biographies of men who have had some part in the development of the Catholic Church in this country. The members of our Reading Circles are requested to assist in this praiseworthy undertaking.

*   *   *

Through the Columbian Reading Union a lady has been directed to a priest to receive instructions for admission to the church. In a letter received from her she says that she is delighted with her "first encounter with a real shepherd of the one true church." Though her family suspect that something strange has happened, she hopes to overcome the obstacles in her way. She has found Father B. "kindness itself," and relies implicitly on his judgment in her case. We commend her to the prayers of our zealous members.

     *   *   *

We shall welcome any further suggestions concerning Canadian authors. This letter has given much encouragement to those preparing the list of authors known as Catholics.

"I have read with much attention and benefit that portion of THE CATHOLIC WORLD devoted to the Columbian Reading Union. I was much interested in your list of Catholic authors. Before I read the fact in your list, there were many of the names among them I had no idea were Catholics.

"I did not notice many names of Canadian authors on your list. In fact we here have but few English speaking, or rather writing, Catholics who have published works. Our writers as yet confine themselves to a less lasting form of literature. However, I think you might justly add to your list the following:

"Very Rev. M. F. Howley, D.D., vicar-apostolic of the west coast of Newfoundland, quite a prominent man in that colony, and author of *An Ecclesiastical History of Newfoundland*, published in 1888 by Doyle & Whettle, of Boston.

"Rev. A. McD. Dawson, LL.D., at present of Ottawa, Ontario, whose latest work, *A History of the Scotch Catholics in Canada* was published last year, if I mistake not, in the office of the *Catholic Record* newspaper of London, Ontario. Dr. Dawson has also published a *Life of Pius IX.* and several other works in prose and verse.

"Joseph Pope, too, at present private secretary to Sir John A. McDonald, our Canadian premier, last year published a work on the early French voyages to Canada, which I have seen favorably reviewed. Mr. Pope is a brother of Miss A. M. Pope, who has contributed several articles to the WORLD.

"If I might make a suggestion, I think if you would publish a·list of such novels by Catholics as may be had at a price to compete with the prices usually paid for novels, with the publishing house, etc., you would assist such of us, away here in the East, as have no means of seeing the general catalogues of publishing houses. But you are now doing a great deal and we must not expect too much.   C. F. HAMILTON.

 " North Sydney, C. B."

A list of cheap editions of good novels was prepared by the Columbian Reading Union over two years ago. For lack of funds it could not be published. No generous millionaire has yet appeared for this important work of assisting the publication and dissemination of our leaflets and book-lists.   M. C. M.

WITH THE PUBLISHER.

THE Publisher regrets that the third paper of Dr. Barry's series of articles on Science and Religion did not reach THE CATHOLIC WORLD in time to appear in this issue. It is ready for the June number, however, and the series will go on to completion without any further interruption.

**

The Publisher has not space enough at command to reproduce all the flattering comment that came from all sources on the occasion of the celebration of THE CATHOLIC WORLD'S last birthday. And with congratulation there was invariably some just and good criticism—always worth more than a gross of compliments. In this respect the Publisher is glad to note that his correspondents are beginning to make use of his invitation to help him by their suggestions, and are replying to his request for some " good-natured growls." Of course he cannot attend to all at once, but he means to devote some of his space in each issue to all in turn whose criticism is just and good-natured. Here is a specimen taken from his mail of last month, and he may be pardoned for quoting at length :

" As an old subscriber to THE CATHOLIC WORLD I beg to offer my congratulations as it enters upon the twenty-seventh year of its existence, bearing evidence of renewed life and vigor. During the past twenty-six years it has indeed proved invaluable to many readers, but it has been especially helpful to those who, finding themselves under the bondage of a false creed, had many difficulties to fight against on their way to ' the promised land.' And many a one whose peaceful home is now within that land ' flowing with milk and honey ' can, doubtless, thank THE CATHOLIC WORLD for the helping hand it gave him in his struggles from darkness to light.

" The contents of the magazine being so admirable, its exterior would, perhaps, pass without comment had not the Publisher drawn the attention of his readers to the ' bright new cover ' in which the beginning of the fifty-third volume makes its appearance. The heavy paper and the slight typographical change are certainly improvements over former numbers. Fain would I say the same of the color. I pray, Mr. Publisher, is

it intended to illustrate a certain concoction advertised on the
back cover? Has each number been dipped in 'Scott's Emul-
sion of Pure Cod Liver Oil with Hypophosphites of Lime and
Soda'?

"Time, however, may cure its bilious complexion. But,
even though the ailment be permanent, the value of its inner
self will always make it a welcome visitor to

"Your obedient Servant.

In reply the Publisher begs to assure his correspondent that
while he feels the new cover is open to some criticism because
of its color (commercially known as "moss rose," but which he
is sure a jury of his countrymen would pronounce a yellow),
he is nevertheless convinced that it is far "brighter" than the
dress of its predecessors. Perhaps it goes too far in this respect, but a defect of this kind can readily be remedied in the
future. The change is, in any event, a step towards improvement, and is meant as a step only. We hope soon to be able
to decide upon an original design for the cover which will be at
once "bright" and pleasing.

* * *

Another writer laments the fact that the eclectic character of
the first volumes of THE CATHOLIC WORLD is no longer maintained. The Publisher is not sure that the majority of his readers would desire a return to that feature of the earlier volumes
of the magazine. We need all our present space, generous
as it surely is, for original matter. It was and is among the
purposes of THE CATHOLIC WORLD to give opportunity to
Catholic and American writers, and of these there are now a
number large enough to make it no longer necessary to fill up
the pages of the magazine with translations from the Catholic
Continental periodicals. This, of course, was not the sole reason
for the custom in the past, but it must be remembered that in
those days contributors to our pages were not as numerous as
at present. But the eclectic feature has in itself many good arguments in its favor—so good, indeed, that the present management is considering the advisability of issuing from this office at
as early a date as is possible, either a new Catholic eclectic magazine, or of adding to THE CATHOLIC WORLD a new department
devoted entirely to translations and summaries of the best articles
in the Continental magazines. The Publisher has so many plans
at present under consideration that he cannot undertake to say
which of these plans may be adopted.

One thing is certain. To add fifty or sixty more pages to
the present magazine at the same subscription price, or to realize
any of the many plans contemplated for its improvement, we
should have a larger number of readers. Between good materials and promising opportunities and their realization there is a
chasm as deep as that between good flour and good bread, deep
enough to be blue at the bottom. To stride that chasm something of a Colossus is needed. Between its plans and their realization THE CATHOLIC WORLD needs the Colossus of a big
subscription list. Again the Publisher reminds his readers that
on them rests the realization of these plans; they are the builders of that Colossus. And hence he repeats his old question to
the reader of these lines: What are *you* doing towards the
building ?

***

F. A. Brockhaus, of Leipzig, has just published a posthumous
work of the distinguished archæologist, Dr. Henry Schliemann.
The first portion was completed by the author just before his
death, and describes the excavations made at Troy last year. In
the concluding part, written by Dr. W. Doerpfeld, full particulars
are given of the various discoveries made, which in many
respects confirm and complete Schliemann's published accounts
of the results of his labors.

Longmans, Green & Co. have just issued *The System of the
Stars,* by Agnes M. Clerke. Miss Clerke is a Catholic and a frequent
contributor to the pages of the *Dublin Review,* as many of our
readers may remember. Her *History of Astronomy in the Nineteenth Century,* published five years ago, met with the warmest
commendation from writers best qualified to speak on the subject, and her authority to discuss the most profound questions
raised in the science of astronomy is unquestioned. Her present
volume forms the subject of a flattering and lengthy critical
review by Mr. A. W. Benn in a recent issue of the *Academy,* in
which the hope is expressed that she " may be encouraged to
follow up this admirable work with a companion volume on the
solar system." The work is said to be in no sense a popular
treatise, but is one which, in the opinion of her reviewer, may
be consulted with profit by many specialists. All of this is
profitable reading, and worth remembering in the present discussions concerning the possibilities and opportunities for the higher
education of Catholic women.

In the second series of his *Historical Oddities* (London: Me-
thuen & Co.) S. Baring-Gould betrays, in his second essay, a

surprising "oddity" in giving to the celibacy of the priesthood a genesis from the principles of the Gnostic heretics.

D. Appleton & Co. have published Thomas A. Janvier's new book, *Stories of Old New Spain*. These fascinating tales of life in Mexico and our Southwest form a new page in our literature, for the author has preserved the coloring, atmosphere, and strange character of the life as vividly as Kipling has delineated certain phases of life in India. For this volume Mr. Janvier has written a new story entitled " A Mexican Night," and the collection includes "San Antonio of the Gardens," which has been called the most beautiful American short story of recent years.

Robert Clarke & Co., Cincinnati, announce for publication early this month *The Spanish Conspiracy*, by Thomas Marshall Greene, author of the *Historic Families of Kentucky*. The book is a review of the early Spanish movements in the Southwest; contains proofs of the intrigues of Wilkinson and Brown, and gives a history of the early struggles of Kentucky for autonomy.

Roberts Brothers have just published a new novel by George Meredith entitled *One of Our Conquerors*.

A book of some value to all who are interested in the subject of copyright law in England and America will soon be issued from the press of G. P. Putnam's Sons. It will contain contributions from Brander Matthews, R. R. Bowker, and Haven Putnam.

The Catholic Publication Society Co. has just published:

> *The Hidden Life of Jesus:* A Lesson and Model to Christians. By Henri-Marie Boudon. Translated from the French by Edward Healy Thompson. Third edition.
> *Life and Writings of the Blessed Thomas More.* By Rev. T. E. Bridgett, C.SS.R.
> *Interior of Jesus and Mary.* By Père Grou. New edition. Revised and edited by Rev. S. H. Frisbee, S.J., of Woodstock College. 2 vols.
> *The Blessed Sacrament and the Church of Saint Martin at Liège.* By the Abbé Cruls. Translated by permission of Monseigneur Doutreloux, Bishop of Liège, by Wm. S. Preston. Illustrated.
> *Acts of the English Martyrs, hitherto unpublished.* By Rev. John Hungerford Pollen, S.J. With a Preface by Rev. John Morris, S.J. Quarterly Series.

The same company announces:

> *Life of the Blessed Angelina Marsciano, Foundress of the Third Order Regular of St. Francis of Assisi.* By Mrs. Montgomery.

Mrs. Hope's Works. A new and popular edition in uniform binding.

St. Ignatius Loyola and the Early Jesuits. By Stewart Rose. Third edition. With about one hundred illustrations.

Benziger Brothers' new publications are :

How to Get On. By Rev. Bernard Feeney.

The Holy Face of Jesus. By the Sisters of the Divine Compassion.

They have in preparation :

Life of St. Aloysius. Illustrated.

Hunolt's Sermons. Vols. VII., VIII.: The Good Christian.

The New Third Reader of the Catholic National Series. Illustrated.

Hand-book of the Christian Religion. Translated from the German of Rev. Father Wilmer, S.J., by Rev. James Conway, S.J.

Simplicity in Prayer.

Dodd, Mead & Co. announce for early publication :

Samuel Houston (1793–1862), by Henry Bruce, in their series "The Makers of America."

The Journal of Maurice de Guerin. With a biographical and literary memoir by Sainte-Beuve. From the twentieth French edition by Jessie P. Frothingham.

In their series the "World's Great Explorers," *Ferdinand Magellan.* By F. H. H. Guillemand.

Macmillan & Co. have published Mr. William Winter's new book, *Gray Days and Gold,* and a new edition of his *Shakespeare's England,* issued in uniform style.

They announce a new edition of Landor's *Imaginary Conversations,* in six volumes, the first of which was issued in April. It is hoped that the whole publication will be completed by December. The edition is by Mr. C. G. Crump, who edited the "Pericles and Aspasia" for the "Temple Library" series. The text will be a reprint from the complete edition of Landor's works published in 1876, compared with previous editions, and a bibliography is added to each conversation showing the various forms in which it was originally published. There will be short explanatory notes. A limited edition on large paper will also be published.

BOOKS RECEIVED.

THE BLESSED SACRAMENT, AND THE CHURCH OF ST. MARTIN AT LIÈGE. From the French of Dean Cruls. By William S. Preston. New York: The Catholic Publication Society Co. ; London : Burns & Oates.

MAY DEVOTION. By C. Deymann, O.S.F. New York and Cincinnati: Fr. Pustet & Co.

MEDITATIONS ON THE VENI SANCTE SPIRITUS. By a Sister of Mercy. New York and Cincinnati: Fr. Pustet & Co.

A CHRISTIAN APOLOGY. By Paul Schanz, D.D., D.Ph. New York and Cincinnati: Fr. Pustet & Co.

FIRST LESSONS IN ENGLISH GRAMMAR. PRINCIPLES OF ENGLISH GRAMMAR. Used by the Christian Brothers. New York: Wm. H. Sadlier.

LIFE OF FRANCIS HIGGINSON. New York: Dodd, Mead & Co.

BUSINESS BOOK-KEEPING. By George E. Gay. Boston : Ginn & Co.

PERCY WYNN. By Francis J. Finn, S.J. New York, Cincinnati, Chicago: Benziger Bros.

THE HOLY FACE. From the French of Abbé J. B. Fourault. New York, Cincinnati, Chicago : Benziger Bros.

THE DISEASES OF PERSONALITY. By Th. Ribot. Chicago: Open Court Publishing Co.

L'ŒUVRE DES APÔTRES. Par l'Abbé E. Le Camus. Paris : Letouzey et Ané.

HEALTH WITHOUT MEDICINE. By T. H. Mead. New York : Dodd, Mead & Co.

SONGS OF THE LIFE ETERNAL. By Edward R. Knowles. Boston.

ORDER IN THE PHYSICAL WORLD. From the French. By T. J. Slevin. London : John Hodges; New York, Cincinnati, Chicago : Benziger Bros.

EXPOSITION OF THE EPISTLES OF ST. PAUL. By Bernardine à Piconio. Translated by A. H. Prichard, B.A. London : John Hodges; New York, Cincinnati, Chicago: Benziger Bros.

MEDITATIONS ON THE GOSPELS. By Père Médaille, S.J. London : Burns & Oates; New York : Catholic Publication Society Co.

REPORT OF THE KANSAS STATE BOARD OF AGRICULTURE. Topeka : Kansas Publishing House.

GUIDE IN ECONOMIC, SOCIAL, AND POLITICAL SCIENCE. Edited by R. R. Bowker and George Iles. New York and London: G. P. Putnam's Sons.

HISTORICAL SKETCH OF THE PHILADELPHIA THEOLOGICAL SEMINARY. Philadelphia : Hardy & Mahony.

THE LIFE OF FERDINAND MAGELLAN, AND THE FIRST CIRCUMNAVIGATION OF THE GLOBE—1480-1521. By F. H. H. Guillemard, M.A., M.D., Cantab., late lecturer in geography at the University of Cambridge. New York : Dodd, Mead & Co.

PAMPHLETS RECEIVED.

ITEMS OF INTEREST TO THE MEMBERS OF THE CATHOLIC TRUTH SOCIETY OF AMERICA.

FIRST ANNUAL REPORT OF THE CATHOLIC TRUTH SOCIETY.

ADDRESS OF ARCHBISHOP IRELAND TO THE CATHOLIC TRUTH SOCIETY.

THE CATHOLIC CHURCH AND THE AMERICAN REPUBLIC. By Wm. F. Markoe. St. Paul: Catholic Truth Society.

SACRIFICIAL WORSHIP ESSENTIAL TO RELIGION. By the Rev. P. R. Heffron, D.D. St. Paul : Catholic Truth Society.

CATHOLIC YOUNG MEN'S NATIONAL UNION CONVENTION. Brooklyn, 66 Court St.: Chas. A. Webber.

THE STUDY OF THE IRISH LANGUAGE. By the Rev. Wm. Hayden, S.J. Dublin : M. H. Gill & Son; London: David Nutt.

ARGUMENT OF HANNIS TAYLOR UPON A PETITION FOR WRITS OF HABEAS CORPUS, AGAINST THE RECENT ACTS OF CONGRESS KNOWN AS THE ANTI-LOTTERY LAW.

CATHOLIC YEAR BOOK OF THE ARCHDIOCESE OF BOSTON. Boston: Catholic Publishing Co.

THE

CATHOLIC WORLD.

| VOL. LIII. | JUNE, 1891. | No. 315. |

THE LADY OF ERIN.

IT is hard to realize the lives of persons who inhabit countries remote from our own; it is harder still, perhaps, in the
case of our own people who are separated from ourselves by
long lapse of ages. For we think it no wonder that we do not
understand the ways of foreigners, but find it strange indeed
that those whose blood, language, and religion we inherit
should yet differ so widely from ourselves in manners and customs. Hence the difficulty of interesting readers, city readers
especially, in the life and times of the saint whose merits I
intend briefly to set forth in this paper. Country folk lead a
less artificial existence, and hence have a quicker appreciation of
plain, natural manners in whatsoever age or clime. It may assist
all to place the Celtic virgin and take in her surroundings if
they will bear in mind that the Irish people of thirteen hundred
years ago bore a great resemblance to the inhabitants of Palestine as we know them from Bible history. When we tell them
how St. Briyid entertained kings, they may picture to themselves such monarchs, more or less, as those four of whom
Abraham—himself, too, a chieftain—with his three hundred and
eighteen followers defeated in a night attack (Genesis xiv. 14);
when we set before them our heroine engaged in domestic duties,
let them assist their imaginations with the delightful account of
how the noble and beautiful Rebecca fetched water for the
camels of the stranger at the well (Genesis xx. 20); when they
read of leprosy in Erin, and are surprised at the novelty, they
may fancy how this was naturally to be expected in times when
the tribal system made every village the fortified capital of an
independent chief, who was almost constantly at war with his

neighbors, and maintained himself by robbing those who were weaker than he was. In such a state of things the proper culti- vation of the soil became impossible, commerce was at a stand- still, and therefore not only war stalked abroad, but slavery, misery, disorder, and disease existed in a degree not exceeded perhaps even in the modern history of that beautiful but most unhappy country.

With this preamble, I proceed to give my readers what I have very sparingly gleaned out of Father O'Hanlon's history of the great woman-saint of the Irish, he himself having sifted the store of at least a dozen biographies by writers of various times and nationalities, ancient and mediæval, Irish, English, Italian, and German.

Her name (Briyid in Irish, Brigid or Bride in English; Father O'Hanlon follows the general manner of the Irish clergy at the present day, and spells it always Brigid) signifies *fire* or *flame*, and fire is always associated with her memory, not only for this reason, but because she was the beacon-light of all the women of Erin, and a fire was kept burning at her shrine in Kildare for seven hundred years after her departure for heaven.

St. Briyid is, among the Irish, the flower and ideal of con- secrated virginity, just as St. Patrick of the clerical state, and St. Columba of the monastic profession.

She was illustrious, however, not in Erin alone, and in Caledonia and Britain, but throughout Western Europe, and especially in Belgium and Germany, whither Irish missionaries had carried her fame. Her office was recited in those countries, and she had great popular veneration. Hence we find that her life was written not only by many Irishmen, but also by St. Antoninus, Archbishop of Florence, in 1450, and by other Italians. A life of her was published in Germany in 1478, a few years after printing was invented. Even in our own day two English Protestants—Bishop Forbes and Rev. S. Baring- Gould—have written her life.

The more distinguished a person is the more people talk of him, and the more stories and anecdotes of every kind are related. Hence St. Briyid's life is full of legends, either true or based upon some fact in her career. That people spoke so of her shows how much they esteemed her holiness, to whom they thought God could refuse nothing. Hence Certani, an Italian priest, and one of her biographers, entitles his work: *The Life of S. Briyid of Erin; or, Wonder-working Holiness.*

The missionaries that went out from Erin in those days carried her fame, as I said, and so did the nuns of her order who. founded convents in other countries. As for Erin itself, not only was the name of Briyid common amongst women, but there are hundreds of places called after her, showing where there had been, or now is, a church, a school, or a convent founded by her, or dedicated to God in her honor.

The names Tempul Breeda, or Bride's Church, Kilbride, Rathbride, Tegbride, Bridewell, Bride's Glen, Bride River on the. Liffey, Breeda River on the Lee, Innisbride, etc., are found all over Erin. There are churches now used by Protestants in England, Scotland, Wales, and the Isle of Man called St. Bride's, Kirkbride, etc. These are old Catholic churches of St. Briyid. In Scotland she was the patroness of the Douglas family, as you know who have read Scott's *Marmion* (canto vi. 14). King Edward III. of England had a daughter named Brigid who became a nun.

In Erin there are many holy wells named Tubber Breeda, to which people go to pray, and hang a rag on a thorn-bush near by, by way of an offering or an ornament. The poor creatures cannot afford anything better. But they pray with more devotion at these waters, blessed by the saints of old, than in the new and beautiful temples erected in the nineteenth century, and prefer that their bones should be laid in the grass-grown graveyard nigh the ruins of Tempul Breeda, rather than under the showy monuments of Glasnevin.

There is another practice in some parts of Erin, in memory of the processions in ancient times on saints' days—that is, the girls carry a little image about which they call *Briyid Og*, in English Young Briyid. They also hang a ribbon or handkerchief from the window, as the people used to hang out tapestry and flags formerly, by way of decoration, and they make Celtic crosses in a circle and wear them gracefully on the right shoulder on St. Briyid's Day.

St. Briyid is represented in art as a nun sometimes, other times as an abbess; sometimes with a dog by her side, or a wolf; or with a vine trailing round her dress, or a flame of fire over her head, or the sun on her breast, or a dove in her hand; all these things referring to incidents in her life, or else symbolizing her kindness even toward animals, her innocence, the fruitfulness of her mission as foundress of convents, or the blaze of holiness whereby she illuminated Erin. There is a statue in the cathedral of St. Omer, in France, showing her as a dairy-maid, in allusion to the fact that she used to milk cows and make but-

ter and attend to all the other domestic duties, as was the custom in those days for women in every position in life.

Of the fame of St. Briyid at the present day it is not necessary to speak.   The children of the Gael, like those of Israel,
have been scattered all over the world.   Wherever they go they
build a church of St. Patrick and one of St. Briyid, and the sun
never sets on the spires that sustain the cross of Christ under
which her name is invoked.   Even now the stranger in Erin is
restoring the ancient cathedral of Kildare from the ruins that
have lain there for fourteen hundred years.   The old round
tower is still there, too, in excellent preservation.   But though they
may be credited with patriotism and taste in thus trying to preserve one of Erin's most glorious monuments, they have lost the
faith of Briyid, and are so few in number that they have been
obliged to build a partition in the church for the greater comfort
of their small congregation, who would shiver in the grand old
Catholic temple.

Briyid was born at Fogart, County Louth, in the year 456,
of Dubtach and Broca, converts of St. Patrick and persons in good
circumstances.   She received such education as was customary
then for persons of her condition, we cannot say precisely what,
but probably reading, music, writing, and embroidery.   Still, like
the illustrious women of the Bible, and according to the simple
manners of her time, even among the wealthy, she used to fetch
water, herd sheep, milk cows, and attend to all household cares.
Thus she grew up in usefulness, good health, and piety, and
when about sixteen years of age, declining to marry, was allowed
by her parents to build a little hut for herself under a great oak-
tree on the borders of the Currach.   Her cell was called *Kil-Darra*,
that is, the Cell of the Oak.   In the course of time seven other
girls were induced by her example to live a similar life.   Then
they all were blessed by the bishop, and the first convent in Ireland was thus established.

These women did not live in cloister—that is, restricted to
their own houses, like the Presentation nuns or those of the Visitation—but led a life somewhat similar to that of our Sisters of
Charity, only still more free.   They not only did their own house-
work but also herded their sheep and cattle on the magnificent
field called the Currach, or race-course of Kildare, six miles long
by two broad, the richness of which is so great that the pasture
each morning seems as fresh and luxuriant as ever, in spite of
the numberless flocks and herds that always graze upon it.   St.
Briyid used to spend much of her time out in the fresh air, mind-

ing the sheep, and was a very early riser, two things very conducive to health, as one of the old chroniclers of her life remarks.

The nuns used to copy out the Sacred Scriptures and other useful books, for there was, of course, no printing. They used to make vestments for the priests, altar-cloths, etc., and also sing the Divine Office, for we read how Briyid sent messengers to Rome to get advice about the proper prayers and chant which were to be used. She also wrote a rule for the many convents founded by herself, and some treatises, which have perished in the troublesome days gone by. In her days hotels were very rare or perhaps unknown in most parts of Ireland, and travellers had to seek hospitality in private houses. Hospitality was considered one of the first of virtues, and the nuns exercised it to a remarkable degree. They entertained bishops, priests, kings, and their followers—all classes of persons. As there were no regular hospitals in those early days of Christianity, the sick as well as the poor used to travel about, begging of all, and stopping overnight wherever they found a welcome. The state of things in Erin caused immense numbers of such wanderers to be seen all over the land, for, as the Annals of Innisfail say, Erin was in those days "*a trembling sod.*" There were incessant wars and quarrels, public and private, rebellion, murder, and treachery. The claims on the hospitality of our saint were, therefore, constant, and so serious as to take up a great part of the nun's time and labor. They were regular innkeepers, in fact, in all but the reckoning, and their monastery was known to all the country around as the "House of Fire." The reason of this was that they kept a great fire always burning in an enclosure adjoining their residence, so that travellers arriving night or day might have a fire to sit down by and warm and rest themselves. You have read the poet's allusion to this in the song:

"Like the bright fire that blazed in Kildare's holy fane,
And burned through long ages of darkness and rain, . . .
Erin, O Erin ! thus bright through the tears
Of a long night of bondage thy spirit appears."

This hospitable fire, whose brightness shining across the Currach invited the weary traveller to shelter and warmth, was kept up during St. Briyid's life and during the three hundred years that her convent flourished after her death.

In 835 the Danes plundered Kildare and destroyed the monastery, but the fire escaped extinction. The country people took care not to let it go out until the scattered nuns came again together, and thus it was tended not alone for its sacred purpose of hospitality, but also in memory of the *Mistress of Erin*, *Light of Leinster*, the *Pearl of Kildare*, as St. Briyid was variously styled.

It was only in the year 1220, after the conquest, that Henry of London, the English Catholic Bishop of Dublin, thinking, perhaps, that there was danger of superstition in the popular reverence for the holy fire, ordered it to be finally extinguished. This was seven hundred years after our saint's death, which took place February 1, 523.

It is no wonder that this fire was held in veneration, for the hospitality to the rich and the kindness to the poor which it witnessed were indeed akin to divine. It is related that St. Briyid was one day listening to a sermon on the Eight Beatitudes, and after it was over proposed to her seven companions that each should choose one virtue for special cultivation. She was very modest herself and would have the others begin, but they insisted that she should lead. Whereupon she chose the virtue of Mercy, and this is, perhaps, the most conspicuous trait in her character.

Her life is full of anecdotes of her liberality to the poor. She received generous gifts from the wealthy, but immediately bestowed them on the needy, and God frequently increased her store in a wonderful or even a miraculous way when provisions fell short. Once when a poor person asked an alms she handed him a gold chain which a rich woman had bestowed on her. Another time she gave a cow to a poor leper, bidding him go and choose the best in her herd. Once again she broke a silver cup in three pieces to divide amongst as many beggars. There was no money in Ireland then, as it appears, or else the saint kept none in hand.

People afflicted with leprosy were common in those days, because, as I said in the beginning, the constant wars prevented tillage, and fruit and vegetables were therefore very scarce. This class of people, having no asylums, roamed about the country begging, and of course often called at the convent-gate. St. Briyid, by her prayers, sometimes cleansed them of their dreadful disease, always relieved their necessities, and even put up with their impudence, and defended them against those who could stand less than herself. One day a woman brought her a present of apples. While they were talking some lepers came up asking alms. Briyid bade the woman divide the fruit among them.

"Indeed, then, I will not," said the woman. "I brought these apples not for lepers, but for yourself and your nuns." The saint rebuked her for her want of charity, and said: "Your trees shall never bear fruit again "—which prediction was verified.

Another time two lepers came along covered with their frightful sores. The holy virgin blessed water and bade one of them wash the other. He did so, and behold! the washed one became sound and whole. "Now you wash your comrade," she said to him that had been cured. He would not, and was going away, but the saint herself washed the second poor wretch, and rid him of his loathsome disease, God working by her hands, while the selfish and ungrateful man got his malady back again. As I have said, the lepers sometimes abused her kindness.

At one time the King of Leinster visited the convent and was entertained by the nuns. After his departure Briyid and her sisters sat down to their own dinner with whatever poor persons were present. One of these, a leper, refused to eat unless he got the spear which he had seen the king carry. Briyid actually sent a messenger after the king, who, out of respect for her, readily bestowed the weapon. Meanwhile the holy abbess kept the dinner waiting, and at last, on the return of her messenger, the troublesome leper received the spear and consented to eat, when they all sat down again together.

"The just man is kind even to his beasts," says the Holy Bible (Proverbs xii. 10). So Briyid, like so many other saints, could not bear to see even a brute suffer, and one day, getting ready some bacon for certain guests, gave half of it to a poor dog that came hungry and whining to her feet. The legend tells us that still there was meat in plenty for the table, God miraculously supplying the want, and approving her tenderness of heart. Says the poet:

> "He prayeth well who loveth well
> Both man and bird and beast;
> He prayeth best who loveth best
> All things, both great and small,
> For the great God our Father,
> He made and loves them all."

The legends tell other things that go to show how she loved animals, and they obeyed her, as they did our first parents in Paradise, and others of the saints we read of. A wild boar escaping from the hunters took refuge among her swine one day. She blessed him, and he stayed there ever after. So a flock of wild ducks came at her call, and quacked their salutations around her; and even a wolf once leaped into her chariot and allowed her to pat his shaggy head. Some of these stories may be but stories; at any rate they show what the people thought of the holiness of the Virgin of Kildare.

St. Briyid's life was mainly a public one, as I shall explain later on, and we have but scant account of the internal affairs of her convent. They say, however, that she was naturally modest in her manner, notwithstanding that great force of character which raised her to be head of all the nuns in Erin, and caused her counsel to be sought even by the bishops of the church. She preferred simple and lowly employment, and delighted in following the sheep over the wavy slopes of the Currach.

At one time, when she and her sisters found themselves in another convent on Holy Thursday, we read that St. Briyid herself took the task of washing the feet of those nuns who were sick, and therefore unable to assist at the solemn celebration of the *Mandatum*. So going one day to see a neighboring family, and finding the women all indisposed, Briyid and her nuns milked the cows for them, as well as set the house in order. On another occasion she was short of corn, and went to get some from the bishop. "I am sorry, dear sister," he answered, "but I fear I have hardly any for myself." " Oh! yes you have," was the reply; "there is plenty of it in your barn." They went out to see, and the bishop found abundance of grain where he knew there had been a very scant supply. He ascribed this to the power of Briyid with God, and invited her to help herself of what she had given him. So she and her nuns took each one a sack of grain and returned home.

We have a glimpse of the hidden life of the convent in the following exquisitely beautiful narrative: One of the nuns named Daria was blind, but perfectly submissive to this stroke of Providence, and very edifying to all by her patience and sweetness. The holy abbess was conversing with her one evening about the beauty of the Son of God and the happiness of heaven, and their hearts were so full that they knew not how time sped. At last the sun came up over the Wicklow hills, and Briyid seeing the lovely landscape, sighed for her poor sister whose eyes were closed to all this beauty. Then she bowed her head and prayed, and rising signed with the cross of Christ the dark orbs of her gentle sister. Daria opened her eyes and saw the golden ball in the east, and the dewdrops glistening on the flowers, the graceful trees and the emerald green so grateful to the sight. Looking a little while she said: "Close my eyes again, dearest mother, for when the world is visible to the eye, God is seen less clearly by the soul." And Briyid prayed, and Daria's eyes grew dark once more.

From what has been already said you will understand that Briyid and her companions were not at all recluses or hermits. Quite the contrary. Not only did they work on their own land, but they assisted their neighbors, visited the sick, attended church festivals in the country around, and travelled whenever their own affairs or their neighbors' good required it. Nay, more, they went about teaching the people their catechism, assisting the missionaries in this great work.

Tachet de Barneval, a French writer quoted by Father O'Hanlon in his life of our saint, says distinctly that in those days not only priests but nuns went throughout Erin preaching and teaching. I have no doubt that the priests did the preaching, but the nuns then taught the catechism and prepared the women especially and the children for the sacraments. We know from the holy Scripture how women accompanied the apostles themselves,[*] and the early history of the church shows us deaconesses consecrated to this work by the hands of the bishop. Even in our own days, when the tradition of those rude ages, long after Brigid's time, in which women had to be kept behind grates and bars, has not yet died out, the pastors of the church in pagan as well as Christian lands are fain to confess that it is on women's aid they must chiefly rely for the holy and most important work of religious instruction. It was St. Vincent de Paul, the Apostle of Charity and the founder of the sisters of that name, that, in 1630, first broke down the iron barriers and stone walls that separated the nuns from the people, who were famishing for want of their words and their presence, and allowed the God-given companion of man to take her proper place at the side of the priestly messenger of Christ.

Briyid therefore travelled a great deal, being invited by the bishops, successors to St. Patrick, to found convents in their respective dioceses. In spite, however, of the war-troubled character of the times, she nor her companions ever met with disre-

---

* I. Corinthians ix. 5, St. Paul writes: "Have we not power to lead about a woman, a sister, as well as the rest of the apostles, and the brethren of the Lord, and Cephas? Or I only and Barnabas, have not we power to do this?" Acts xviii. 18, 26: " But Paul, when he had stayed yet many days, taking his leave of the brethren, sailed thence into Syria, and with him Priscilla and Aquila. . . . Now a certain Jew, named Apollo, born at Alexandria, an eloquent man, came to Ephesus, one mighty in the Scriptures. . . . This man therefore began to speak boldly in the synagogues Whom when Priscilla and Aquila had heard, they took him to them, and expounded to him the way of the Lord more diligently."

spect. It is true that it could not be said of them, as it was of
that one who tested the virtue of Erin in the days of Brian :

> " Rich and rare were the gems she wore,
> And a bright gold ring on her wand she bore " ;

but they went without escort, clad only in the armor of innocence, and recognized by their dress as consecrated virgins of the
Lord ; and no Irishman, seeing them, thought of aught else but
the honor and blessing derived from their visit to his native place.

The saint thus visited every part of Ireland, and nothing is
more common in her life than stories of how she lodged in the
homes of the people where there was no convent to stay in, and
often requited their hospitality by miraculously increasing their
store. They tell of how once, when she was going along the
road with her companions, an insane man met them and alarmed the sisters a good deal. But Briyid, going forward, said to
him : " O man ! announce to us the word of God." The mad-
man at once made answer : " O holy Briyid, I obey thee. Love
God, and all will love thee ; honor God, and all will honor thee ;
fear God, and all will fear thee."

Briyid, like all the children of Erin, as the French chronicler
before quoted says, delighted in music. Now, the harp was
found in every comfortable house, and the stranger who could
play on it was sure of a double welcome. One day, going into
the house of a chief to obtain the release of a captive, while
waiting for him to come in, she asked that some one should
give them a little music. Those present all asserting their want
of ability, one of the nuns said to a boy : " Go and ask Mother
Briyid to bless your hands, and then you'll be able to play."
The child did so. The abbess took his hands in her own, prayed, and blessed him, and he began to play beautifully. When
his father entered he was astonished, and, recognizing God's
work in favor of St. Briyid, readily granted the favor she had
come to ask.

The respect for St. Briyid made her protection very desirable,
and the number of poor and sick that applied to her for help
was so great, as well as that of the pilgrims, lay and clerical,
who came to visit her, that a town grew up near her convent.
It was a place of refuge which, whosoever entered, no one dared to lay a violent hand upon him until the abbess heard his
case and decided upon it. In the course of time it was made
the see of a bishop, and Briyid was held in such esteem by
the hierarchy that she had the naming of the first incumbent.

Later on the see became an archbishopric, and shared dignity
with Armagh itself, St. Patrick's own see, for the names and
honors of Patrick and Briyid have always been associated in Irish
history.

Kildare flourished as a home of sanctity and learning from
the death of Briyid in 523 until the invasion of the Danes in
835, when it was plundered by those barbarians and its library
and records destroyed. The Danes themselves becoming Catholics, the convent was rebuilt, and with much changing fortune
continued to spread the light of faith and education, and to dispense the bread of mercy, till at last it withered and died under
the harsh, cold spell of the Sassenach conqueror in 1172, and
its holy fire was, as we have said, put out finally in 1220.

Nevertheless, although the nuns died out, the monks were naturally more able to make their way in those dark and evil days,
and the Franciscans and Carmelites built monasteries at Kildare within the same century that saw the last of St. Briyid's
daughters. The Carmelites, in fact, have clung to the spot with
such marvellous tenacity that they have a house there at the present day, although many a time during the past seven hundred
years have they been forced to fly with a price set on their
heads. After the Catholic emancipation in 1829 things improved
in Erin, and to-day there is an order of women there called
Brigidines, and another styled Sisters of the Holy Faith, both
founded under the patronage of the Virgin of Kildare.

The holy nun passed out of this life, as said before, on the
1st of February, 523, and her sacred remains were laid in the
same tomb at Downpatrick, in Ulster, with those of the national
apostle and of St. Columba, the great patron of cloistered men.
This, the most holy spot in Erin, was violated and destroyed, of
course, by the heretics in the days of Henry VIII., but it is said
that the head of St. Briyid was saved by a priest, and carried
to Neustadt in Austria, and afterwards given by the Emperor
Rudolf II. to the Jesuits' Church at Lisbon, in Portugal.

I had the happiness in 1880 of visiting that fair spot in
Down where the ancient Catholic church, now in the hands of
strangers, still tops the lovely hill on which St. Patrick laid its
corner-stone one thousand four hundred years ago. There is a
hole in the old graveyard alongside, which the people point out
as having been the grave of the three great Irish saints, and this
is constantly kept open on account of every visitor reverently
taking a handful of earth from the sacred spot. Attempts have
been frequently made to mark the place by a suitable monument ;

but the stranger is in the land, ever ready to tear down the monuments, whether of the saints of the old church from which he has gone out or of the nation to which he is a declared enemy. However, though her grave be desecrated, her memory is green as the sward that, fresh each morning, covers the hills of Down with a carpet more grateful to the eye than Persian looms could ever furnish; her example still shines out "through the long night of bondage," and round the world wherever her children have been scattered, as brightly as the hospitable fire which so long blazed in " Kildare's holy fane."

So we have passed in review the records of St. Briyid's career. I have omitted most of the wonders that are found in it, because I think they are its least wonderful part. When a person from childhood up always walks in the presence of God, and, so different from the great majority of us, tries to do his pleasure in every thought, word, and deed, what else should we expect than that God should favor such a one, shower his choicest gifts upon her, and make all nature obedient to her will, united, as it always was, with his own. Hence the miracles done by the saints are only what should be expected   The wonder would be indeed if there were none found in their lives. The real wonder is that our heroine was able, amid the seductions and temptations of the world, the devil, and the flesh, to keep so pure in God's sight, to lead a life so unselfish, to work heroically during three score and ten years for God, her neighbor, and her native land.

Again, what attracts one in St. Briyid is the plainness and simplicity of her way of living. Evidently there was nothing about her house that made any one feel unwelcome there. The rich admired its neatness, the poor saw at once that Briyid was as natural in her ways as themselves, but, withal, that exquisite politeness which sprang from genuine gladness to see her guests and which took care that they made themselves at home round her fireside. It was the same when she visited others, and accepted their hospitality for a night. Consecrated virgin and all as she was, she dropped in so easily into their household circle that they felt no uneasiness at her presence, or at the thought that they could not make her comfortable, but their hearts laughed with hers at the music of the harp, their souls burned within them at the holy fire of her conversation, and they preserved the memory of her visit as if Mary herself had come down to see them. Hence it was that they used to call her the Mary of Erin, that is to say, the one who best realized their idea of the Queen of Virgins. Indeed, I think of Joseph, the carpenter, and Mary, the artisan's wife, and Jesus, their hard-working son, in the little village of Nazareth, when I read of Briyid's simple ways. In that school at Rome, Trinità del Monte, where the daughters of the wealthiest and most influential families of Europe are educated, the Blessed Virgin is represented in a famous and beautiful painting as the *Mater Admirabilis*—"Mother most admirable." Do you know how they depict her? Sitting at home spinning flax with a wheel. So I think the Irish artist's ideal of Briyid as the dairy-maid, the *Colleen Dhas Cruitha Nambo*, is more charming and more useful than if he had made her a richly-dressed lady or a nun rapt in ecstatic devotion. It is more charming because the farmer's daughter carries us further away from the artificial nonsense of fashion and deceit, and brings us "nearer to nature's heart," and hence to the God of nature; it is more useful because it shows us the nobility and holiness of labor, and renews for us the pattern left us by Jesus, Mary, and Joseph in the workshop of Nazareth.

O blessed toil! O sacred hospitality! O holy simplicity of Divine-Human Nature! How sweet are thy attractions, how fascinating thy contemplation! In the light of thy beauty verily all artifice in manner, posture, speech, or dress revolts one's very stomach. O single, seamless robe of Christ, knit doubtless by the busy hands of thy Virgin Mother, how forcible a lesson of Christian poverty dost thou teach! O Son of God without a stone whereon to lay thy Head! O consecrated one-story cottage in little Nazareth, what eloquence there is in thy littleness, thy plainness, thy simple furniture!

I suggest these thoughts to you, dear readers, in order that when, as I hope, you take up the life of St. Briyid, or the history of Erin, you may not be shocked, or even, perhaps, disgusted on account of your nineteenth century materialistic notions of elegance, comfort, and propriety, at the plain, simple ways of people in patriarchal times. I acknowledge here and now the valuable lesson received from an illiterate Irishman, to whom I had expressed myself somewhat as you perhaps would if you had the surroundings of St. Briyid, or even of Nazareth, photographed for your inspection: "'Tis the manner of the country," he said. And on reflection I felt that his brief, unpretending answer contained a sufficient explanation. But, in addition, you must remember that "'tis the manner" of the wise to disregard fantastic and unnecessary lodging, dress, or food; "'tis the manner" of the saints to make all accidents of the body of no account in comparison with the care they take of the soul.

Little reck they the perishable casket if only they can preserve and beautify and cherish the living immortal jewel that lies within. "'Tis their manner," in short, to imitate the Son of God. This, too, is the constant injunction of the church upon those who are to follow Jesus Christ more closely. Of their dress and life generally she says what the Third Plenary Council of Baltimore (No. 78) decrees of the priest's house: "Let the priest's house be so gotten up that all luxury, as well as unholy and worldly decoration, be far from it, and everything about suggesting piety, order, and plain neatness, proclaim to all that a servant of our Crucified Saviour lives there."

This double consideration, therefore, the manner of those early days, and the practice of that religious poverty which she professed, as well as her own lofty and noble character, explains the simplicity of the life of her who gained so much influence that she was called *Hiberniæ Domina*, the Lady of Erin.

And this is the manner that produces heroes in civil as well as in religious society Search the annals of the United States, and see if our greatest rulers of men have not come nearly always from the village, the farm, or the prairie. Of the saints I will not speak, except to remind you that immediately upon receiving the seed of Christianity Erin began to bring forth holy men and women, scholars and missionaries, to whom Europe and ourselves owe the civilization we enjoy to-day. During three centuries the lamp of learning which had been extinguished in Gaul, Germany, Italy, and Spain was kept alive in Hibernia. All those countries, except perhaps the last, were evangelized by Irish priests, and many a continental city, such as Salzburg, Tarentum, Lucca, San Gallen, venerated an Irishman among its bishops in those ages; while not only did they establish many monasteries and convents throughout Europe, but the two first universities, Paris and Pavia, were founded by Irishmen. If you seek authority for these and similar assertions, I refer you to the Frenchman Montalembert, in *The Monks of the West*, and to the Englishman Butler, *Lives of the Saints*, March 10, 17, and elsewhere.

And yet Erin suffers and Erin weeps. She is a slave unto her enemies and the enemies of God's Church. Europe owes her a debt of gratitude beyond estimation; America is her debtor for many material and spiritual advantages. And yet "the age of chivalry is past"; the selfish nations neglect and ignore Erin, who preserved for them religion and learning, just as they do Poland, who saved them from barbarism and slavery. Even the holiness of her sons and daughters obtains no official recognition from the church, and since the fire "in Kildare's holy fane" was put out not a single confessor or martyr have the efforts of Irishmen succeeded in placing on the altar which they honored by their lives and in whose defence they died.

Yet she is Innisfail, the "Isle of Destiny." Her children are scattered like those of Israel, to be witnesses to God and His Christ the world over and the ages along. This is itself a sublime mission. Perhaps, in the secret designs of Providence, a still grander one is reserved for the land of Patrick, Briyid, and Columba.

Pray for us, O Holy Virgin Brigid! that we may always love God and our neighbor, always love what is simple, natural, and true, having a contempt for all that is artificial and false. Pray for thy native land, that God may grant her peace and glory amongst the nations.   EDWARD McSWEENY.

Mount St. Mary's, Emmittsburgh, Md.

DEUS LUX MEA!

Newman died saying "I see the Light!"; Goethe, "More light!"

I ENVY them whose sturdy hearts
　　Welcome the brunt
Of battle, dark with mortal darts;
　　Well to the front
They stand, though the long line hath broke,
Breathing alone the fiery smoke.
　　I envy them, yet only so
　　If the last breath that spends their life
　　Sees Wrong enleaguèd with the foe,
　　And Right triumphant in the strife.

And sturdy him, whose trembling bark
　　Now troughs the sea,
Now upward cleaves the Stygian dark
　　So awfully
Storm-brooding on the quickening brine;
And crests the billows for a sign
　　Of beacon-safety; if at last,
　　Long stranger to the cheering light,
　　Half-wrenchèd from the straining mast,
　　He sees a new day born of night.

And· him whose high ideal shone
    Dimly and far;
·Not as the pillar-cloud led on,
    But as a star
Hid in the mists of earth and sky,
Glimmers inconstant from on high.
    Yet so, if with unwearied art,
    Still fashioning stairways to the Height,
    At last his strong and patient heart
    Sees darkness swallowed up of Light!

I envy him who holds as nought
    His little years;
But gives the Master he hath sought
    Sweat and tears;
Dead to the pride of power and pelf,
Dead to the world and dead to self;
    Yet so, if he who daily dies,
    Seek nevermore surcease of strife;
    Give holocaust for sacrifice,
    · Till Death be swallowed up of Life.

I envy not the sturdy will,
    And stirring brain,
And heart content to drink its fill
    Of the world-pain,
And the poor stumbling feet that bleed
Incessant o'er some thorny mead,
    If but a glow-worm lead them on
    To visionary fields of light,
    And after all the toiling done
    The Daylight darkens into Night!

                    HUGH T. HENR

Philadelphia.

SCOPE AND HISTORY OF THE TALMUD.

THE good Capuchin father, Henricus Seynensis, on one occasion triumphantly clinched an argument by exclaiming, "*Ut narrat Rabbinus Talmud!*" taking for granted that the Talmud was not a book but a man.

The same mistake might not be impossible even now. Notwithstanding the many centuries of its existence—for it was begun six hundred years before the birth of Christ, and ended six hundred years after—and notwithstanding the numerous allusions to it in works upon every department of art, science, or literature, the notions abroad in regard to it are strangely various, vague, and contradictory. By some it is credited with divine inspiration; by others it is scorned as a mass of childish folly. In fact, no book except the Bible has perhaps been so frequently referred to, and yet, at the same time, so little known. Nor, in this fleet-footed age of ours, can we greatly wonder at this neglect, when we hear the verdict of one of the most ardent and most learned Talmudists of this century on this vast work. "In the whole realm of learning," says Emanuel Deutsch, "there is scarcely a single branch of study to be compared for its difficulty to the Talmud. Yet," he adds encouragingly, "if a man had time, and patience, and knowledge, there is no reason why he should not, up and down ancient and modern libraries, gather most excellent hints from treatises, monographs, and sketches, in books and periodicals without number, by dint of which, aided by the study of the work itself, he might arrive at some conclusion as to its essence and tendencies, its origin and development. That work, every step of which is beset with pitfalls, has not yet been done for the world at large."[*]

In the Middle Ages the Talmud was regarded with suspicion and dislike, partly as being the principal depository of those "traditions of men" denounced by our Lord as making "the Commandment of God of no effect," and partly as being in no inconsiderable measure the work of Jewish continuators subsequent to the birth of Christ, and therefore implicitly if not formally anti-Christian in its later tendency. Hence the repeated

---

[*] See *Literary Remains* of Emanuel Oscar Menahem Deutsch, who was for eighteen years attached to the Library Department in the British Museum. He died in 1873, at Alexandria.

edicts that were from time to time issued against it, beginning with that of the Emperor Justinian, A.D. 553.[*]

When Pope Clement V., in 1307, was asked to renew the condemnation pronounced against it by some of his predecessors, he wished, before acceding to this request, to know what were really its contents, but found no one who could tell him. Whereupon he proposed that chairs for the study of Hebrew, Arabic, and Chaldee, the three tongues nearest to the idiom of the Talmud, should be founded at the Universities of Bologna, Salamanca, Oxford, and Paris, expressing his hope that in due time one of these universities might produce a translation of this mysterious book. This hope was never realized.

About two centuries later, one Pfefferkorn obtained the permission of the Emperor Maximilian (then before Pavia) for a fresh confiscation and conflagration of all discoverable copies of the Talmud. Reuchlin, the most learned Hebraist and Oriental scholar of the time, was put on the junto which was to give weight and effect to the imperial decree. Reuchlin, however, declined to have any hand in the wholesale destruction of a book "written by Christ's nearest relations." If, he said, it were found to contain anything contrary to Christianity, the more effectual remedy would be to refute it rather than to burn it; since burning was but "a ruffianly argument." Upon this, Pfefferkorn and his party denounced Reuchlin as a renegade and a Jew; but he kept his ground, and, when the emperor asked him his opinion, reminded him of the wish of Pope Clement V. to found Talmudical chairs at four of the chief universities. Meanwhile the contest spread throughout Europe; every authority, whether ecclesiastical, imperial, or literary, eagerly enlisting on the one side or the other in the fray. The *Talmulphili*, as they were called, eventually carried the day. To them to stand up for Reuchlin was to stand up for the Church. "*Non te*," Egidio di Viterbo wrote to him—"*Non* TE, *sed Legem, Non Thalmud, sed Ecclesiam!*"

In 1520 appeared the First printed Edition of the Talmud. Being issued with more haste than care, it is not without many mistakes; still, it contains fewer than any subsequent edition. With the Third, that of Basle, in 1578, began the era of revision by a "Censor," whose irresponsible manipulations wrought marvels, his one anxiety being to trim and lop an utterly Oriental and Jewish production to fit in with the notions of the Europe of

---

[*] *Novella* 146, Περι Ἑβραων, addressed to the Præfectus Prætorio Areobindus (quoted by Deutsch).

the day. Even the names of persons and places were changed
for others "evolved" out of his own head, when such substitution fell in with his private ideas of edification to the reader.
The result of these achievements was to tangle and break the
clue to a labyrinth already most difficult to thread. Many scores
of Talmudical codices, more or less fragmentary, still exist, however, scattered in the great public libraries of Europe, from Oxford
to Odessa, from which to construct a reliable edition. One such
edition was begun several years ago, but, like the two "Translations of the Talmud," commenced at different periods, this also
has come to a stand-still.

What, then, is this strange and complex work? Briefly, the
Talmud * may be described as the Book of the Oral Law of the
Jews, forming an uninspired, but more or less authoritative, supplement to the Pentateuch. And yet this definition is about as
complete and satisfactory as that which describes the teeming
earth as an oblate spheroid, composed of land and water. The
Talmud is much more than a legal code: it is the storehouse of
the archives of Israel. Its origin is coeval with the return from
the Babylonian Captivity, when all the records of the people's
faith and history which had escaped destruction were collected
with the utmost care, and the interpretation and exposition of
these treasured documents formed into a·science. This science,
which gradually assumed enormous proportions, was called MID-
RASH, an expounding.† · The Talmud is the storehouse of "Midrash" in all its branches. Although not at first easily discernible amid the tangled thickets of this luxuriant wilderness, there
are two main currents flowing through the Talmud: the one,
Prose; the other, Poetry; the one, Law; the other, Legend. The
former is strictly didactic—investigating, comparing, arguing; the
other, pensive, imaginative, fanciful, rich in parable and proverb,
delighting in allegories, many of which, having lost their key,
babble unmeaningly their insoluble enigmas, while around and
within them the sublime strangely mingles with the grotesque.
These two currents in the "Midrash," which gradually embraced
the whole of the Sacred Text, were respectively called Halachah
and Haggadah. The Halachah—Rule, Norm—concerned itself
with all the legal, levitical, and ceremonial rules and observances;
the Haggadah (Legend, Saga, illustrative story), chiefly with the
prophetical, historical, and poetic portions of the Scriptures.

* The primary meaning of the word is "study," "learning," from *lamad*, to learn; next,
"arguing"; lastly, it came to be the name of the great *Corpus Juris* of Judaism.

† From *darash*, a word used for the verb and substantive alike; as our word "study" is
used both for the process and the result.

The Talmud, with its two main elements of Law and Legend, is divided into Mishna and Gemara — Text and Commentary. Both these terms originally meant "learning," but Mishna expresses rather a "repetition of the Law," a "second Law," while Gemara has come to mean a complement or filling-up or expansion of the Mishna, as the Mishna is of the Mosaic Law. The Pentateuch always remained the immutable and divinely-given constitution—the Written Law; whereas the Mishna and Gemara, together forming · the Talmud, was the compilation of the Oral or Unwritten Law. This oral or corollary code of enactments must have begun almost simultaneously with the Sinaïtic dispensation; receiving developments of detail from the primitive Council of Elders in the Desert, and, later on, incorporating the verdicts of the "Judges within the Gates."

Putting aside all consideration of the fabulous number of books spoken of by apocryphal writers as having been given to Moses, together with the Pentateuch, it is evident from Scripture itself, and also from the testimony of Josephus, that there were certain laws and customs, not expressly mentioned in the Pentateuch, in use long before the Talmud was in existence. Such, for instance, as the prohibition to carry burdens on the Sabbath;[*] the list of the four principal fasts of the year;[†] the abstaining from certain kinds of food prepared by heathens;[‡] and the three daily times of prayer.[§] The custom of saying grace before meals, alluded to in the First Book of Kings,[||] we meet with also in Josephus (*Antiq.*, b. xii.), where King Ptolemy Philadelphus invited the Jewish Priest to bless the food, and give thanks for it, before partaking thereof. Again, the prohibition to use oil prepared by the heathen existed at the time of the Macedonian conquest. Seleucus Nicanor, who wished to gain the favor of the Jews, commanded that those of their nation in Syria and Asia should receive money instead. These and many such by-laws can only be gathered from the Mishna, which also contains evidence that the pristine severity of the penal laws was considerably mitigated in course of time, either by the introduction of exceptional formalities or in other ways.

In the long space of time which intervened between the Mosaic period and that of the Mishna, the Urim and Thummim had been lost, and Malachi, the last of the Prophets, had died. The Law was now all in all, as the one authoritative guide, the basis of every regulation affecting the life of the Jewish people. The

* Jer. xvii. 21, 22, *et seqq.*   † Zech. viii. 19.   ‡ Dan. iv. 10.
§ Dan. i. 8. || I. Kings (I. Samuel) ix. 13.

scrolls, few and scanty, brought back to Judæa by the exiles returning from Babylon, alone embodied their history and poetry,
the sacred Law, and the utterances of the prophets — precious
remnants saved out of a vast mass of writings which had irre-
mediably perished.

The reorganization of these documents was taken in hand by
the *Sofarim,* or "Men of the Great Synagogue," that most important religious and political Assembly, founded by Ezra or Esdras,
and which arose with the commencement of the emphatically
Jewish period which is not ended yet—the period succeeding the
Israelitish, as that succeeded the Hebrew era.

From this epoch date the collection of the Canon, the institution of the Targoumim, or translations of the Scriptures into
Aramaic, and certain of the Midrashim—interpretations or para-
phrases. These being either moral lessons drawn from some
particular text, legendary stories bearing upon the subject, or
else exegetic explanations. Several Midrashim attained their
present form as late as the sixth or seventh century, their
authors having, out of several ancient and fragmentary remnants, compiled one complete " Midrash."

The most important Midrashim are, the Mechilta, the Siphra,
the Siphri, the Pesikta, the Midrash Rabbah, the Midrash Tanchouma, the Midrash Schocher Tob, and the Ialkout.* The
Mechilta, Siphra, and Siphri together constitute a commentary
on nearly the whole Pentateuch. They are the oldest of the
Midrashim, dating from the first to the beginning of the third
century. The Pesikta, by R. Kahana, is on some chapters of
the Pentateuch, and on the Prophets. The Midrash Rabbah, on
the Pentateuch, Ruth, Ecclesiastes, Lamentations, and the Book
of Esther. The Midrash Tanchouma, or Ielamdenou, on the
Pentateuch. The Midrash Schocher Tob, on the Psalms, Proverbs, and a part of Samuel. The Ialkout, the latest of the Midrashim, is also the most complete, and the only, one which
takes in all the Books of the Old Testament. In this Rabbi
Simeon collected together, in the order of the verses of the
Bible, the various commentaries upon them scattered throughout
the Talmud and the earlier Midrashim.

The compilation of the Talmudic Code was entirely in the
hands of the Scribes. They, as our Lord said, " sat in MOSES'

---

* Mechilta, custom, usage, rite. Sifra,Sifri, the book, (Levit.) books. Pesikta, decision,
statute. Midrash Rabbah, the " Great" Commentary. Tanchouma, consolation. Ielamdenou, " we will teach," our teaching, instruction. Schocher Tob, that which takes in much
lit., " good drinker "), receptacle of many things.

seat." The task of the earlier Scribes from the Return from Babylon to the year 220 B.C.* was above all to arrange, pre-serve, and guard the sacred canon of Scripture. They scrupu-lously counted not only its words, but its very letters, in order to secure it from all possibility of interpolation or corruption. Moreover, with a view to preserve the true pronunciation of the Hebrew, the popular idiom having become a curious mixture of Hebrew, Syriac, and Aramaic, it became necessary to point the text with its vowel sounds, these having been for the most part omitted, until then, in the writing of Hebrew. This punctuation is said to have been the work of Ezra. New rules, safeguards, and aids to the better keeping of the old precepts, were also made, as "fences about the Law."

The class of Scribes called "Repeaters," and also "Master-builders," or Banaïm, succeeded, from 220 B.C. to 220 A.D. This momentous period comprised the Macchabean struggle, the Birth of Christ, the Destruction of the Temple † and of Jerusa-lem, and the Dispersion of the Jews.

Palestine, during these 440 years, was ruled by Persians, Egyptians, Syrians, and Romans in turn. But whatever happen-ed, and in spite of proscription, ruin, and death, the work of the teachers and expounders of the Law went on; sometimes the dying Masters, amid their tortures, naming those who were to take up their work. The highest ecclesiastical tribunal of the Jews was the "Great Sanhedrim." There were also two "Lesser Sanhedrim." When, in the New Testament, the Priests and Elders and Scribes are all mentioned together, the Great Sanhe-drim is referred to. This consisted of seventy-one members, all, intellectually and physically, picked men, not only learned in the Law, but also in the wide range of subjects bearing upon it. Moreover, the polyglot state of Palestine in those days necessitated their being good linguists, no member of the Great Sanhedrim being allowed to trust to an interpreter in the ad-ministration of justice.

These Masters and Doctors of the Law were regarded by the people with the highest veneration and esteem, although not a few of the most eminent among them were humble tradesmen—weavers, carpenters, tanners, sandal-makers, bakers, and cooks.

---

* The time of the Græco-Syrian persecutions.

† One of the most cherished legends of the Talmud tells how, when the Roman legion-aries entered the Holy of Holies, the Priests and Levites, led by the venerable High-Priest Simeon, bearing aloft the golden key of the Sanctuary, ascended to the summit of the burn-ing pile, whence, with all the emblems of their sacred trust, they threw themselves into the flames, rather than suffer them to fall into the hands of the conqueror.

One newly-elected president of this great assembly was found busy and begrimed among his mounds of charcoal. Idleness, as is shown by many an aphorism in the Talmud, was regarded as a hateful and despicable vice. "Labor is honorable, and honors the laborer"; "Toil keeps the toiler warm"; "Work is better than piety that is idle"; "Idleness begets hypochondriacs"; "Add a trade to your studies, then will you be free from sin"; "The tradesman at his craft need not rise up before the greatest of the Doctors." These are a few out of many maxims in the same sense. One reason for enjoining the pursuance of a trade was to render payment unnecessary for the nobler calling of Teacher. "Even as God freely and without price taught the Law to Israel, so ought we without price to teach it to our brethren" (*The Ialkout* on Exodus, § 286). "Rabbi Tzadok was wont to say: 'Make not of sacred learning a crown for thy pride, nor a shovel to dig with; for, as saith Hillel, He who maketh a trade of the holy Law, he shall thereby perish.'"

The Talmud gives abundant testimony to the energy with which, after the return from the Captivity, and still more after the wars of the Macchabees, the Pharisees and many of the Priesthood planted colleges and schools, and in every possible way exerted themselves to facilitate education, alike in Judea and among the Jews scattered throughout the whole Roman Empire. The regulations, minute and stringent, with regard to public instruction, are carefully laid down, extending even to the supervision by the parents of their children's tasks to be prepared at home; good grounding being particularly insisted on. As we have said, almost all the teachers, even in these schools, taught gratuitously, looking upon their office as holy and honorable, and upon their pupils as their children and friends. The honor in which the office of teacher was held is shown by the drift of numberless similitudes and legends. In one of these it is related that, the land being parched with drought, the most pious men wept and prayed for rain, but without result. "Then an insignificant person, one who seemed to be of no account, prayed also; when, behold! the clouds gathered in the sky, and the rain came down. 'Who, then, are you?' exclaimed the pious men—'you, whose prayers alone have prevailed with God?' And he said: 'I am a teacher of little children.'" Again: "When God was about to give the Law, he asked the people what surety they had to offer that they would keep it. They answered: 'Abraham.' But God said: 'Abraham sinned; Isaac, Jacob, and even Moses sinned': these will not suffice.' 'Wilt thou then, O God, accept our children to be our sureties and our witnesses?' And God accepted the little children."

About the year 30 B.C., Hillel I., the great Master of the Law, who was called the 'second Ezra,' became President* of the Great Sanhedrim. The Talmudic records are full of his meekness, patience, and piety, and contrast his lofty yet lowly spirit with the petulance of his jealous rival, Shammai. Hillel seems to have been the first to see the necessity of bringing into some sort of order the enormous mass of Oral Tradition which had, by his time, accumulated. He began by endeavoring to reduce the six hundred sections then in existence to six. But he died; and another century elapsed before the task was taken up by Akiba.

Akiba, a poor shepherd lad, had become, through his great love for the beautiful daughter of "the richest and proudest man in Jerusalem," first, an indefatigable student, and, by degrees, "the second Moses," one of the most famous Doctors of his time. He too, rashly heroic in his patriotism, and deluded by belief in Bar Cochab as the Messiah, was cut off in his prime by the sword of the Roman executioner. The day of his death was also that of the birth of Jehudah "Ha Kadosh," or "the holy," the great Rabbi who was to accomplish the work.

Rabbi Jehudah, who lived during the reigns of Antoninus Pius and Marcus Aurelius, was the first to collect in a written form all the traditionary laws (c. A.D. 180) and embody them in the Mishna. It is said that he undertook the work with great reluctance,† for hitherto it had been held as an inviolable rule that, except for private use, or in the way of notes of remembrance, oral tradition, as the word itself implies, must only be transmitted by word of mouth, and that, by the Divine injunction in Deuteronomy (iv. 2), "Ye shall not add unto the word that I command you," it was forbidden to write it down. The Law itself was to be read by all, expounded and administered, and every doubtful point settled, by the Great Sanhedrim; but even the decisions of this, the nation's highest tribunal, were not written down, lest they might thus appear to be invested with authority as precedents. There was for Jehudah only a choice between two evils. His people were just breathing again after the fearful slaughter under Hadrian, consequent upon their having taken up arms to hinder the erection of a temple to Jupiter

* The President was also called Nasi, " Prince "; the Vice-President, Ab-Beth-Din—
" Father of the House of Judgment."
† Hyman Hurwitz, *Essay on the Existing Remains of the Hebrew Post-Macchabean Sages.*

on the sacred site of the Temple at Jerusalem,* and during which
persecution—a period of mutual massacres of Jews and Romans
—their schools were scattered or destroyed, and their most
learned men cut off. He knew that the lull in the storm might
be but momentary; and, since the knowledge of the "unwritten
Law" must either be entirely lost, or one of its precepts must be
broken, he chose the latter alternative, "the loss of a single limb
being preferable to the loss of the whole body." Another consideration which weighed with him was, the impossibility of even
an Oriental memory retaining the mass of commentary and exemplification ever accumulating around the Scriptural Text. Although the Jews, in regard to their powers of memory, were in
no respect behind the followers of Brahma or Zoroaster, who to
this day repeat entire Vedas without the slightest error or omission though understanding not a word, still there is a limit to
the most abnormal human capacity. Jehudah therefore applied
himself diligently to the work, and thus the Mishna † or Talmudic
Text, was compiled. Being written in Hebrew‡ (which even at
that time had become the language of the learned), and in a
style extremely concise, it required elucidation and development.
These explanations, continued by the friends and successors of
Rabbi Jehudah, and couched in the idiom of the period,§ formed
the Gemara, the complement or commentary. In this way were
produced the two 'Gemaras,' known as the Jerusalem Talmud,
redacted at Tiberias, about A.D. 390, by the Rabbi Jochonan, in
the East Aramæan idiom; and the much larger and more esteemed Babylonian Talmud. This latter, written in Western
Aramæan, at Syra in Babylonia, was compiled in great part by
Rab Aschi, 365-427 A.D., continued by his son Mar, and completed by Rab Abina, Rabbi Joshua, and the first Saboraïm ‖ at
the close of the fifth century. This forms the most trustworthy
Canon of Jewish tradition.

   The Babylonian Talmud is about four times as large as the
Jerusalem Talmud. It fills 2,947 folio leaves, in twelve volumes.
But neither of the two codes was written down at first, and
much that once existed has been lost. Besides the official Mishna, into which R. Jehudah admitted only the best authenticated
traditions, those of a more apocryphal character were collected

---

* The number of Jews who then perished is estimated at 580,000—slain in fighting, mas-
sacred, or executed.

† Plural, *Mish-na-yoth*—Repetition or secondary laws.

‡ Hebrew into which many Chaldæan and other Eastern words had become mingled.

§ An idiom largely composed of Chaldæan, Syrian, with some Greek and Latin elements.

‖ The latest class of the Scribes, which succeeded to the Gaonim ("Noble" ones?).

into a sort of external Mishna, called Boraïta, still further additions forming the Tasefta, or Supplement. The Mishna proper, the condensed abstract of about eight hundred years' legal exposition of the Mosaic text, is divided into 6 Sections, containing in all 72 Chapters, subdivided into 524 Paragraphs. The subjects of the Sections are as follows:

Section I. Seeds. This, which begins with a chapter on prayers, deals with agrarian laws, forbidden mixtures in plants, animals, and garments, and regulates Tithes and portions to the Priests, Levites, and the Poor.

Sec. II. Feasts. On Feasts, fasts, ceremonies, and sacrifices, with special chapters on the Feast of the Exodus, of the New Year, the great Day of Atonement (this being especially solemn and impressive), the Feast of Tabernacles, and that of Haman.

Sec. III. Women. On betrothal, marriage, divorce, and vows.

Sec. IV. Damages. Includes much of the civil and criminal law, commercial regulations, and the law of trover. This section ends with the highly esteemed "Sentences of the Fathers"* (*Aboth*).

Sec. V. Sacred Things. Sacrifices; the First-born; also on the measurements of the Temple (*Middoth*).

Sec. VI. On Purification; and the ceremonies and rules for different cases.

For all practical purposes the Mishna was appealed to in preference to the Mosaic Law; just as in England Blackstone is appealed to as the practical exponent of English jurisprudence founded on the laws of Edward 'the Confessor and Alfred the Great. The rules laid down in the Mishna for the administration of justice are singularly minute, careful, and humane, and its admonitions to the judges stringent and impressive—*e. g.*: "He who unjustly hands over one man's goods to another shall pay for it to God with his own soul." "In the hour when the judge sits in judgment on 'his fellow-men, let him feel, as it were, a sword pointed at his own heart."

In criminal cases, the cross-examination of the witnesses was exceedingly strict; and in no case, however trifling, was a man addicted to gambling, betting, a usurer, or a slave, allowed, either for or against, as a witness. The *Lex Talionis* does not exist in the Talmud. "Paying measure for measure is in God's hands only." Bodily injuries inflicted are to be compensated by money.

---

* The five chapters composed of these "Sentences," with a chapter from the Boraïtha, and under the title of "Traité d'Aboth," form the concluding portion of a work by Rabbi Moses Schul, *Sentences et Proverbes du Talmud et du Midrasch.* Paris, 1878 (Imprimerie du gouvernemente).

The Sadducees had insisted on the literal carrying-out of the rule, "an eye for an eye," etc., but had been overruled by the Pharisees. In the extreme punishments of flagellation and death, the thirty-nine strokes of the Mosaic code were the utmost permitted, this number being reduced if endangering the life of the culprit.

The four modes of capital punishment * were: stoning, slaying by the sword, strangling, and "burning." In the two last the criminal was. immersed up to the waist in soft mud, and two men, by tightening a cord, wrapped in a soft cloth, round his neck, produced instant suffocation. All that the "burning" consisted of was to throw a lighted wick into the mouth at this last gasp. The judges of capital offences had to fast all day; nor was the sentence executed until it had been again examined by the Sanhedrim on the morrow. The place of execution was at some distance from the court, to give time for any fresh testimony in favor of the culprit, who was also allowed to stop four or five times, and, if he still had any plea to urge, be taken back before the judges. A herald went before him, proclaiming his name and crime, adding the words: "Whoso knows aught in his behalf, let him declare it!" Ten yards from the place of execution it was said to him: "Confess thy sins, that thou mayest have part in the world to come." At least he must say: "May my death be a redemption for all my sins!"

The ladies of Jerusalem formed a society which provided a beverage of mingled myrrh and vinegar, that, like an opiate, benumbed the man carried to execution. It was this benumbing beverage, offered the Divine Victim, which, "when he had tasted thereof, he would not drink."

The Mishna, although it aims at being merely a civil code, at the same time has more regard to the intention in the fulfilment of a precept than to the fulfilment itself, and teaches that "He who does not stop short at the Gate of Justice, but proceeds within the line of Mercy, in him the spirit of the wise has pleasure."

Jurisprudence, however, is only one branch of the widely-spreading Talmudic tree. From the times of the institution of the Great Synagogue down to the completion of the Babylonian Gemara, the legal, philosophical, historic, and poetical development of the Jewish people was embodied, age after age, in this extraordinary work. In its pages fable and allegory are interwoven

---

* Capital punishment was practically abrogated before the Romans had taken it out of the hands of the Sanhedrim (Deutsch).

with graphic portrayals of the scenes, customs, and ways of thought of old-world empires and of peoples which have long ago dropped out of the life of nations. Not only does it mirror the larger features of its long contemporary history, but a thousand details which fill in the picture, give it life, and (if we may adapt a quotation) impart that "touch of nature" which "makes the *Ages* kin." Every topic it deals with is pointed and illustrated by the proverbs and similitudes which have always formed the favorite vehicle of popular Oriental teaching. Our Lord, whose ministry is full of them, did but adopt and perfect the immemorial method of his people. "Despise not the proverb and the parable," says the Midrash Rabbah,* for it is through them that men will listen to the precepts of morals and religion. If a king has lost a precious jewel or a piece of gold, does he not find it by lighting a small wick not worth a farthing?" Again: "The rules of religion are like a basket filled with good fruit, but lacking handles, and therefore cumbersome to lift about. A man of sense makes handles to the basket, and moves it wherever he may list. And what are these handles but proverbs and pithy sayings?"

Among these, in an Oriental setting, are not a few which we had thought peculiarly our own. Not only has La Fontaine drawn upon the Haggadahistic stores of the Talmud for some of his most telling Fables, but many a page of mediæval and more recent writers, from Dante to John Bunyan, owes its inspiration to the same source; the framework of their fiction being hewn out of this "forest primeval," even when not adorned with its flowers and foliage, or enwreathed with its arabesques of mythic monstrosities—phantasmagoria from the dreamland of the Past. For, mingled with the treasures of the Talmud, is a large amount of dross. Many a worthless shell from which the pearls are lost is embedded in its strange mosaic. Some writers account for the admission of objectionable matter by the exaggerated veneration in which the Jews held their "wise men," and every word, under whatever circumstances, that fell from their lips. Also, by the scruples of later Scribes to omit anything they found in the Oral Traditions, although it is probable that, in a long course of transmission, passages had come to be widely distorted from their original form.† Some indeed of the wild stories of Lilith,

---

* On Canticles i. 1.

† There can be no doubt that many an allegorical and symbolical expression has come to be mistaken by commentators as intended to narrate a fact, not merely to suggest a type— *e. g.*: "Adam," it is said, "reached from earth to heaven"; but this expression was intended to indicate that in the spiritual part of his nature he was like the angels, and like the animals

Asmodeus, and certain allegorical monsters, were transferred bodily from the Zend Avesta, others from the Vedas, not a few of
the Talmudic angels and demons having also been adopted
from Persian and Zoroastrian sources.

The great Masters of the Law, with all the wiser portion
of the Jewish nation, strongly condemned these wild extravagances.   Rabbi Joshua Ben Levi, for instance, in the Jerusalem Talmud, says, in reference to a portion of the Haggadah :
" He who writes it down will have no part in the world to
come ; he who expounds it will be scorched, and he who listens to it will remain empty-handed, reaping no reward "—a
verdict which in any case explains the attitude of the popes*
who condemned the book, or warned the faithful against it.
Also, in its exposition of Scripture it is not only sometimes far-
fetched and obscure, but also at variance with it—*e. g.*, in
denying the doctrine of original sin, and in - apparently inculcating two opposite beliefs as to the personality of Satan
and the eternity of future punishment.

The Talmud handles freely the creation of the Cosmos, not
interpreting the " Days " of Creation otherwise than as successive periods of unknown duration, and assuming "destruction
after destruction," before the Divine Creator was satisfied with
the earth as a habitation for man.   According to the Haggadahistic legend, the minds of the heavenly host were much divided on the subject of the creation of man, some pleading for
and some against it. "Suddenly God turned to the contending
hosts, and deep silence fell on all.   Then, kneeling before the
Throne of Glory, appeared the Angel of Mercy, and he
prayed and said : ' O Father ! create Man, thy noble image
upon earth ! I will fill his heart with compassion towards all
creatures. They will praise thee through him.' Then appeared
the Angel of Peace. He wept, saying : ' O God ! Man will disturb thy peace ! Man will invent war, bloodshed, confusion,
horror ! ' Then cried the Angel of Justice : ' Thou wilt judge
him, O God ! He shall be subject to my law, and Peace shall
dwell again on earth.' The Angel of Truth entreated, saying :
' Cease to create, O Father of Truth ! With Man thou createst
the lie ! ' Then from the deep silence came the Divine word :
' Thou shalt go with him—thou, Mine own Seal—Truth. Be-

in the lower. Again, "Adam had two faces, the one looking to the East, the other Westward."
But this was but a fanciful way of saying that man's spiritual nature tends towards the source
of light and knowledge, while his material nature inclines towards the regions of darkness or
debasement.

    * Julius III., 1553 ; Paul IV., 1559 ; St. Pius V., 1566 ; Clement VIII., 1592 and 1599.

tween heaven and earth shalt thou abide, an everlasting bond uniting both.' "

. The abode of Truth, midway between earth and heaven, may help to account for her various obscurations, whether by the clouds of heaven, mysteries which veil her, or the smoke of earth—the mistakes and misconceptions which mask and distort her face and form.

The Talmud is full of the ministry of angels. Besides the "Seven Angelic Princes," and the Guardian Angels of the Nations and of men, every word of God and every good deed of man "becomes an angel."

On Friday night (it is written in the Haggadah), when a Jew left the Synagogue a good angel and an evil one accompanied him. If, on entering his home, he found the table spread, the lamp lighted, and his wife and children in festal garments, ready to do honor to the holy day of rest, the good angel said : "May all thy future Sabbaths be like this ! Peace unto this dwelling— Peace!" And the evil angel, against his will, said, perforce, "Amen !" If, on the contrary, the house was in discomfort and disorder, the evil angel derided him, saying : "May all thy Sabbaths and week-days be like this!" And the good angel, weeping, had to say "Amen !" There is here no direct word to the housewife, and yet she could not well be more shrewdly admonished.

To us, as Christians, the special interest of the Talmud lies in its numerous and vital points of contact with the New Testament. The terms, "Salvation," "Redemption," "Baptism," "Grace," "Son of GOD," "Son of Man," "Kingdom of Heaven," were among the household words of the exponents of the Law to which Christianity gave their full and highest meaning. Even the formula, "Father, Son, and Holy Spirit" (Ab, Ben, ve Ruach ha Kadosh), was theirs before it was ours. They had a term corresponding to our word "Trinity," namely Shilosh, and, in Aramaic, Talilutho ; and in some of their earliest post-biblical literature the doctrine intimated by that term has a categorical expression as distinct as any that are found in the creeds of the Church.*

The souls of men are said to have been all created together and hidden away from the moment of creation. Each time that a child is to be born, a soul is ordered to go and inhabit the

---

* Etheridge, *Glossary to "the Targums of Onkelos, Lev., Deut.,"* p. 6, where he gives some remarkable passages from the Zohar and elsewhere, conclusively proving his statements.

body of this new human being. The soul, being a pure spirit, is cognizant of everything, and being grieved at this command, supplicates its Creator to spare it that painful trial, in which it sees only sorrow and affliction. Then an angel, at the moment of the soul's union with the infant frame, touches the mouth of the child, causing it to forget all that has been. Had Wordsworth this Talmudic teaching in his mind when he wrote his "Intimations of Immortality" from recollections of early childhood?

> "Our birth is but a sleep and a forgetting.
> The soul that rises with us, our life's star,
> Hath had elsewhere its setting, and cometh from afar.
> Not in entire forgetfulness
> And not in utter nakedness,
> But trailing clouds of glory do we come
> From God, who is our Home."

Very piteous are the manifold endeavors of later Jewish interpreters to explain, in accordance with their unbelief in Christ as the Messiah, the great Prophecies concerning him. To take but one of these as an example—the fifty-third chapter of Isaiah, their treatment of which did not satisfy even their own nation on account of its diversity. Of the commentators who wrote after Christ, one says of this "Section," that it relates to Job; others say, to Hezekiah; others, to Isaiah himself; others, to Jeremiah. Some, in the hopelessness of explaining how one and the same person could be a suffering and dying Messiah and yet their Deliverer and a King victorious over his enemies, divided Isaiah's description of his sufferings and his glory between the "Messiah Ben Joseph" and the "Messiah Ben David"; while the most part saw in it the portrayal of their own nation. And further, "this Parashah," says Ibn Crispin, "the commentators agree (?) in explaining of the Captivity, although the singular number is used in it throughout." The *Karaïtes** appropriated it to "the wise of their own sect," while their opponents, the *Rabbinic* Jews, applied it to some of their own "righteous." Rabbi Tanchum speaks of it as pointing to "one of the generation in exile; . . . the mystery connected with him not being revealed.' He protests against the notion of its being hyperbolical or allegorical, as some writers had taught, and seems to think that the intention of the Prophet

---

* The Karaïtes were a class of commentators who threw off the shackles, as they considered them, of Rabbinical rules and antecedents; and to the *Karaïtes* were opposed the *Rabbinists*, who held to the customary methods of interpretation.

was, not to be understood. Shelomo Levi, Moses Elsheikh, and many others complain that all their commentators are at variance as to the Prophet's meaning, and Ibn Ezra says of these expositors that "they shut the door of literal interpretation against themselves, and then wearied themselves to find an entrance." He himself goes back "to the teaching of our Rabbis —the King Messiah." The application of the subject to the Jewish nation was the one most widely adopted by the later exponents, yet, even in the controversy with Christians, the belief that the Messiah would die was not extinct in the second century. "The Holy One," it is written in the P'siqtha,[*] "brought forth the Soul of the Messiah, and said to Him, Art thou willing to be created and to redeem my sons after 6,000 years? He replied, I am. And God said, If it be so, thou must take upon thyself chastisements, in order to wipe away their iniquity; as it is written, 'Surely He hath borne our sicknesses.' And the Messiah answered, 'These will I gladly take upon myself.'" To this teaching of the older Traditions, Rashi,[†] in his earlier notes on the Talmud, returned. In the graphic story in which Joshua Ben Levi inquires of Elias and Simeon Ben Yochai as to the coming of the Messiah, he is told to seek him for himself, and that he will find him sitting at the gates of Rome, among the poor who bare sicknesses. Rashi explained the words by reference to this "parashah" of Isaiah: "And he, too, is stricken; as it is written, And he was wounded for our iniquities, and our sicknesses he bore."[‡] But if Rashi wrote his commentary after A.D. 1096, and the hideous massacres of Jews in Speier, Worms, Maintz, and Cologne, by the wild and profligate rabble which swarmed thither after the first crusaders were gone, the sufferings of his people might well have been in his mind when he wrote it. And "Sitting at the Gates of Rome" might very probably refer to the shelter repeatedly afforded to the persecuted Jews by the Vicar of the Christ whom their fathers had crucified.

The doctrines of the Resurrection and of Immortality are enunciated in the Talmud with no faltering voice, while this present life is spoken of as a wayside inn, where, on our pilgrimage to our true country, we tarry, as it were, but for a night; or, as a porch or outer court, in which we prepare ourselves for admittance into the Palace, our Father's House. And having reached

---

[*]According to Hulsius, *Theologia Judaica*, p. 328; quoted by Dr. Pusey in his introduction to *The Jewish Interpreters of Isaiah*. Oxford, London, and Leipzig, 1877.
[†] Born, 1040; died, 1115 A.D.   [‡]Sanhedrim. Chelek fol. 98 col. 1.

the heavenly home, the saved are represented as actively advancing in excellence, and in the development of all the highest faculties of their nature. This is the interpretation of the text: "They shall go from strength to strength: every one of them appearing before God in Sion."

In this brief notice we have but attempted to shed a glimmer of light from the lamp of the learned into one or two of the countless intersecting galleries composing that catacomb of buried ages called the Talmud, for the sake of those who have not yet begun to explore its perplexing precincts for themselves. From this catacomb's storied walls we will, in conclusion, transcribe yet another parable: "There was One who betrothed to himself a beautiful maiden, and then departed far away. The maiden waited long, but still he came not. Friends and rivals mocked, saying, 'He has forsaken her. He will return no more for ever!' She went alone to her chamber, and took out the letters in which he had promised to be true to her. Weeping, she read them, and was comforted. And after many days her Betrothed returned. He asked her how she had kept her faith so long, and she answered by showing him his letters. Israel, in misery and captivity, was mocked by the nations for her hope of redemption. . . . God would in due time redeem her and say, 'How couldst thou alone, among all the mocking nations, remain faithful?' And Israel would answer, pointing to the Law, 'Had I not here thy promise?'"

ELIZABETH RAYMOND-BARKER.

THE INDIANS OF CANADA.

IN an eloquent passage which lies buried in one of our prosaic blue books the late Hon. Joseph Howe, who was at the head of the Indian Department in 1872, expressed the hope that those who came after him would never forget "that the crowning glory of Canadian policy in all times past, and under all administrations, has been the treatment of the Indians." And, judging from the remarks made from time to time complimentary of the manner in which the Indian question has been dealt with on this side of the border, it would seem that Joseph Howe's hope has been so far fulfilled. But the lot of the Indian in this northern land was not always a happy one. Close upon the heels of the zealous French missionaries came the greedy French traders, plying the Indians with vilest liquor that they might the more readily and cheaply dispose of their furs. One would fancy on reading the history of this baneful traffic, against which the priests protested and Laval hurled his anathemas in vain, that the traders of France had exhausted the resources of alcohol in their dealings with the Indians; yet it is of record that the natives expressed their preference for the English because they did not, like the French, water their liquor! In 1759 an English official reported that he had ordered rum and flour to make a feast for certain Indians that they might forget the death of a relative; and, as late as 1829, an Indian superintendent closed an address to the Ottawas by a promise to give them a few gallons of rum.

Notwithstanding the unscrupulous traffickers in rum and peltries, and other adverse influences, the sons of Loyola and other missionaries did much during the French *régime* for the lifting up of the native races. The Executive Council of Lower Canada were constrained to state, in their valuable report of 1837 on Indian affairs, that "since the cession of the Province to Great Britain, when the crown succeeded to the position which the Jesuits had formerly occupied in respect to the Indians, no advance has been made, if indeed ground has not been lost, in Indian education." This tribute to the Jesuits is all the more valuable because it was made in the days before representative government obtained in Canada, when the minority ruled in Quebec, and the Executive Council was practically an English Protestant institution.

Early in the seventeenth century the Indians of Canada came in contact with the French; and the Marquis Duquesne de Mennonville, in addressing the Iroquois chiefs whom he had assembled in Montreal in 1755 for the purpose of securing their alliance, thus depicted the difference between the effect of French and English colonization on the natives: "Go and examine," said he, "the forts which our king has erected: you will see that the land beyond their walls is still a hunting-ground. Our forts have been set up, not as a curb on the tribes, but to be useful for your trade with us; while no sooner do the British enter upon possession of your lands than the game deserts them, the forest falls beneath their blows, the soil is bared, and hardly will you find a bush left on your own domains to shelter you." The Indian title was not recognized by the French. They came and possessed such of the land as they desired, and for the use and benefit of those of its former lords who gathered about the missions and fortified places. Allotments were made by the new seigniors. When the flag of Britain replaced the *fleur-de-lis*, King George by solemn proclamation guaranteed to the Indians their lands and hunting-grounds, and reserved to the crown the privilege of treating with them for the alienation of any portions thereof. For many years after the cession what is now Ontario was but an Indian hunting-ground, with here and there on the frontier a few military outposts. When settlement advanced treaties were made with the Indians for the surrender of their vast domain, compensation being made to them sometimes in kind—occasionally very trifling—but more frequently in the form of permanent annuities at the rate of ten dollars for each member of the tribe to the number comprised therein at the date of treaty. Large tracts of land were reserved for the Indians, and laws were passed to protect their lands from trespass and themselves from fraud and fire-water. But, unfortunately, enforcement does not always follow the enactment of statutes. The "great frauds and abuses," which the king's proclamation and subsequent legislation were intended to stay, still continued. "The protection," says the commissioners' report of 1845, "which the government intended to throw over the Indians was not and could not be sufficiently maintained."

In truth it may be said that, with few other exceptions than the missionaries, the dealings of European peoples with the Indians were marked rather by avarice than justice; while the policy of governments was mainly shaped with a view to making them useful allies in war, the difference in this regard between two proud nations of civilized Europe being, at one time, in the graphic words of Philippe de Gaspé, that "the King of France was paying his red allies only fifty francs for an English scalp," while "His Britannic Majesty, richer or more generous, was paying a hundred for the head of a Frenchman." Not until time had proved that the peace of 1815 was likely to be a lasting one was anything worth speaking of done in Canada by the governing power towards the civilizing of the Indians. Even as late as 1828 the deputy superintendent-general of Indian Affairs complained that "since the war . . . the officers have done little more than superintend the issue of the presents, while the more important object of keeping alive the affections of the Indians to the government . . . has been altogether overlooked"; and, in another place, he points out that "a continuance of kindness" to the Indians who came annually from the United States to the distribution of presents would dispose them "again to take up the tomahawk when required by King George." Happily the time never came, and the tomahawk has ceased to be regarded as one of the "resources of civilization." In his despatch of the 14th June, 1836, Lord Glenelg assured the then governor of Canada "that he looked upon the moral and religious improvement of the Indians and their instruction in the arts of civilized life as the principal object to be kept in view in our intercourse with them."

The old desire to make of the Indian merely an ally in war now gave way to the laudable one of making him a useful member of the commonwealth in times of peace; and several interesting reports on the condition of the native races and the best manner of leading them into the ways of civilization were written at the instance of the imperial authorities. Many a suggestion since given forth as new may be found in these old reports; and through them there runs a due appreciation of that most powerful of all civilizers, religion. Sir George Murray, in his despatch of the 15th of June, 1830, dwelt on the necessity of encouraging in every possible way the spread of religious knowledge and education among the tribes, and, wiser than certain theorists of this generation, he gave it as his "decided opinion that these inestimable advantages should be allowed to flow in through whatever channel they may find their way." In his exhaustive report of 1839 Mr. Justice Macaulay stated that much had been accomplished by missionary piety and zeal; that "every proper encouragement should be afforded to those who undertake the work of Indian conversion," and that "they should be frequently consulted and deference paid to their opinions and views."

In the voluminous report of the commissioners appointed to inquire into the affairs of the Indians in Canada, which was laid before the Legislative Assembly in 1845, are these, among other valuable recommendations: " That measures should be adopted to introduce and confirm Christianity among all the Indians, . . . and to establish them in settlements; that the efforts of the government should be directed to educating the young, and to weaning those advanced in life from their feelings and habits of dependence; and that, for this purpose, schools should be established and missionaries and teachers be supported at each settlement." Further on this report reads: " Your commissioners do not find that the greatest progress in civilization has been generally made in settlements under the charge of the local superintendents, nor that their services are to be compared in this respect to those of the missionaries."

The confederation of the Provinces in 1867, and the subsequent absorption of British Columbia and the intervening Hudson's Bay country, into the Dominion brought under one central management the affairs of a large Indian population in various stages of savagery and civilization. Many of the Indians of the older Provinces were rapidly reaching the point where the line dividing them from other citizens becomes indistinct and gradually vanishes ; while in the newly-acquired territory were tribes as ignorant of our ways as the natives whom Cartier found in the lodges of Hochelaga. In the older-settled parts of the country there had been considerable intermingling of the exotic and indigenous races, and heredity was helping environment in the work of assimilation. Indeed, the great difference between the Indians of the Provinces and the other dwellers therein may be said now to consist in that a greater proportion of the former act on the principle of letting the morrow always care for itself. The report of the Indian Department for 1890 describes them as "being, as a rule, self-supporting." The policy of the department, we are told, is based on the theory that " if a man will not work neither shall he eat." What a pity the rule could not be made absolute and general! These Indians have at their credit in the hands of the government funds derived from the sale of surplus land, timber, etc., and rent of land leased, amounting to very nearly three millions and a half. Tne millions belong to the Ontario bands. Few of those in Quebec had much land or valuables to dispose of, and in the Provinces further east

care was taken not to overburden the natives with estates. The
interest on the trust fund, which is at 4, 5, and 6 per cent.,
amounted last year to $162,257 70 and the collections ön the
same account to $115,710 44. No appropriations are made from
the capital sum except for works of a permanent character. The
interest is charged with the cost of local management, medical attendance, works of a temporary nature, and a share of the educational expenses ; but it is supplemented by an annual vote from the
public chest of upwards of fifty thousand dollars, about twenty-four
thousand dollars of which goes to education, sixteen thousand to
pay annuities under treaty in Ontario, and over four thousand to the
relief of Indians without funds in Quebec. Only three hundred
dollars of it is required for a similar purpose in Ontario. This
parliamentary appropriation, with their share of the cost of running the Indian Bureau at Ottawa, marks the extent to which
the same thirty thousand Indians in Ontario and Quebec are a
drain on the federal exchequer. The interest money remaining
after certain proportions have been set aside for the fixed charges
just specified is equally divided among the members of the different bands in the ratio in which the bands share in the capital.

The Indian population of Ontario is returned at 17,776. But
they are not all the descendants of native Indians, for Canada
had an influx of red as well as white loyalists. The famous Six
Nations of the Mohawk Valley, who fought on the side of King
George, thought it best to go north with the flag of Britain ;
and under the great seal they were given a tract of excellent
land, six miles in depth on each side of the Grand River, extending from the head of that stream to its entrance into Lake
Erie, and comprising 694,910 acres. They have increased and
multiplied and are now a prosperous community of 3,425 souls,
owning about one-third of the total trust-fund. But though they
have lived for generations in the centre of a Christian community that appears to be constantly moved by a great desire
to rend the veil of papal darkness which shrouds Quebec, 630
of these Indians are officially classed as pagans. They have
still their harvest festivals and their fantastic rites; and with
the schools and churches stands the "Long House," where
once a year is offered the sacrifice of a snow-white dog. The
Indian report for 1888 put the number of pagans at 862 ; and,
whether due to it or not, the falling off synchronizes with the
attacking of Ontario's heathen stronghold by a detachment of
General Booth's army.

The other principal tribes in this province are the Ojibbewas,

Ottawas, Oneidas, Algonquins, Mohawks, Mississagas, and Dela-wares. The Oneidas and Mohawks are akin to the Six Nations, and the Delawares are the descendants of a colony of Indian converts to Moravianism, who migrated from the United States near the close of the eighteenth century and took up their abode on lands set apart for them by the Canadian government. A few hundreds of the Ontario Indians are still nomadic. The some seventeen thousand who enjoy fixed habitations had about sixty-five thousand acres of land under cultivation in 1889. In that year, though the harvest was light, they raised 277,995 bushels of grain, 89,561 bushels of potatoes, and 7,628 tons of hay. Their other industries were valued at $182,521. Comfortable houses, substantial outbuildings, improved machinery, and well-conditioned stock are no longer unusual with the Indians of On-tario; and they have their quota of prudent husbandmen, the fruits of whose labors have won prizes at provincial fairs. The nomadic Indians are mainly Ojibbewas living north of Lakes Hu-ron and Superior, in a country which is still largely a primeval wild. Here they lead their old-time life, finding in forest and stream sufficient for the day. Over nine thousand of the Ontario Indians are Protestants, about six thousand five hundred are Catholics, eight hundred are classed as pagans, and the religion of upward of thirteen hundred is marked "unknown." There were seventy-four schools in operation last year, with 1,824 children on the rolls and an average attendance of 1,000. Twenty of these schools are Catholic, thirty-two Protestant, and twenty-two undenominational. Several of the teachers are Indians. There are four industrial schools—three Protestant and one Catholic—with an average attendance of three hundred.

In the Province of Quebec there are 13,600 Indians, nearly one-half of whom still live the life of nomads in the almost unencroached upon country to the north of the settled line along the Ottawa and St. Lawrence. The patrimony of the Quebec Indians is not nearly so extensive as is that of their Ontario kinsmen, and much of the land is far from being as fertile; but from the nine thou-sand acres which those who had permanent dwelling-places culti-vated in 1889 they garnered 50,655 bushels of grain, 21,357 bushels of potatoes, and 2,150 tons of hay. Their other indus-tries were valued at $183,105 — a sum proportionately much in excess of that derived from similar sources by the Indians of Ontario. Many of the Indians permanently located depend large-ly on hunting and trapping for a livelihood, and farm on a very small scale. That they are not, however, intrinsically unfitted for dull labor is proved by the fact that the Algonquins of the county of Ottawa, who still give a deal of time to the chase, did much work last year at road and bridge making on their reserve. Contracts were given to certain of the Indians who undertook to employ only Indian labor. The work was done quite satisfactorily and paid for from the funds of the band held in trust by the government. The Iroquois of Caughnawaga and St. Regis—somewhat Gallicized remnants of the old Six Nation Confederacy, dubbed Iroquois by the French—the Hurons of Lorette, and the Abenakis of Becancour and Saint François du Lac are the most advanced of the Indians of Quebec. Very faint indeed is the line dividing them from other citizens. Many of them evince a decided bent for handicrafts, and their earnings from the manufacture and sale of useful and fancy wares are considerable. It is absurd to expect every Indian to become a soil-tiller. They have their peculiar bents just like other peoples. The small band of Quebec Amalecites, who disposed of their land some years ago and live partly as hunters and partly as artificers, have probably no more aptitude for agriculture than those of our own race who prefer the factory to the farm. Nothing has been done towards the training of the Quebec Indians in manual arts, though the question of establishing industrial schools in their midst has been frequently broached. There are, according to the official returns, only nineteen Indian day-schools in Quebec, five Protestant and fourteen Catholic. They have 516 pupils enrolled and an average attendance of 291. Four hundred and thirty-seven is given as the number of Protestants, and over six thousand are placed under the heading "religion unknown"; but it may be safely said that, with the exception of very few more than the four hundred and thirty-seven, the Indians of Quebec cling to the faith delivered to their ancestors by the Catholic missionaries of France.

The native race is thinly scattered over the eastern maritime Provinces. There are 2,428 Micmacs in Nova Scotia and Prince Edward's Island, and 1,569 Micmacs and Amalecites in New Brunswick. These tribes are branches of the Algonquin family. The French brought them Christianity, and they have kept the faith. After the final cession of the country to England settlement went on without any attention being given to the straggling Indians; but in time small quantities of land were here and there set apart for them. They have about four thousand acres under cultivation, and in 1889 they raised 5,714 bushels of grain, 18,899 bushels of potatoes, and 2,091 tons of hay. Their other industries were valued at $52,250. Like other people down by the sea, some of the Indians prefer fishing to farming, while others roam about in gypsy fashion, earning their bread by the cunning of their hands. The Micmac seems to be by nature an expert cooper and basket-maker. They have twelve day-schools —all Catholic—at which 241 pupils were entered last year. The average attendance was 119 The establishment of an industrial school has been suggested, but no step has as yet been taken in that direction. These Indians are an unobtrusive people, and they are as industrious as can be expected in view of the circumstances to which they have been subjected. They cost the country in 1889-90 $15,225 34.

The entry of British Columbia into the Dominion added to Canada's population some thirty-five thousand five hundred Indians, ranging as to social advancement all the way from the "superior race" of Shuswhaps to the Ahts, whom Dr. Powell, in his report of 1873, described as "a nation of savages." Catholic, Methodist, and Church of England missionaries were working among them, and churches and missions and convents and schools had been established long before the civil authorities gave thought to the natives.   Dr. Powell spoke very highly of the character and general condition of the Indians of the interior, but those of the coast he described as having been corrupted and depraved by "the lower grades of the white race" with whom they came in contact.   None of them, however, seem to have been, even when left to themselves, very high-toned moralists.   They developed a more elastic system of changing spouses than is afforded by the Chicago courts; and they have as decided a penchant for gambling as the members of a select baccarat club.   But they appear to have been always very good workers, not afraid of labor in any form, and able to take a hand at whatever offered.   Twenty years ago they were spoken of as "large contributors to the general revenue," and the exports of furs and fish oils were credited "nearly, if not all," to the Indians.   The departmental report for 1890 tells us that their course is still marked by "manly independence, intelligent enterprise, and unflagging industry."   They engage in farming and fruit-culture, fishing and fish-canning, hunting and trapping, and general work.   They are producers and consumers on a large scale, and their personal property is valued at nearly a million dollars.   The houses of those of them who live on the northwest coast are described as "superior to the habitations of fairly well-to-do white people," and "flower-gardens, house-plants, and in some cases luxurious and ornamental articles of furniture,. make their homes very attractive." Good work has been done by the missionaries in elevating the moral tone of the natives, and the labors of the Catholic priests have been especially fruit- ful in beneficial results. Speaking of a most impressive religious celebration held by Bishop D'urieu, "at which over a thousand Indians of different tribes were assembled," the Indian superin- tendent for British Columbia, in his report for 1890, states that "it would have been impossible to find any such concourse of people more orderly and devotional than were these Indians, gathered together from distant places, who doubtless years ago came in contact but to war with one another, and who, not so long since, were imbued with the most cruel and heathenish superstitions." Of the nearly twenty-four thousand Indians who live within the nine agencies of British Columbia, 5,242 are Protestants, 6,264 are heathens, and the remainder are Catholic. The others inhabit regions which have not yet been trespassed upon by census enumerators. The government has established and maintains four industrial boarding-schools in this Province, three of which are under the auspices of the Catholic Church. There are twelve ordinary schools—eight of which are Protestant —supported by the Indian Department. The total cost to the federal exchequer of the British Columbia Indians was $102,- 074 44 last year, $34,943 21 of which was expended in the con- struction and maintenance of industrial schools. Previous to the purchase of its monopoly, and the accession of the country to Canada, the Hudson's Bay Company were the actual rulers of the territory stretching from Lake Superior to the Rocky Mountains. Whatever tricks of trade were indulged in by indi- viduals at the expense of the unsophisticated natives—and tradi- tion says they were many and very fraudulent—the company succeeded in securing the good-will of the Indians. But with the passing away of the dominion of the traders many events occurred to disturb the mind of the red man. Louis Riel made his first attempt at rebellion by leading an armed resistance to the establishment of a provisional government on the banks of the Red River; the small white population was suddenly augmented from the east; from the south came a flow of fire- water, which, in the words of old Crowfoot, was killing his people fast; and on the plains the buffalo was disappearing with a rapidity which pointed to speedy extinction. The government lost no time in grappling with the Indian problem thus thrust upon it. The labors of the missionaries did much to smooth the way for the coming in of the civil power. No difficulties worth speaking of were met with in negotiating with the Indians, and between 1870 and 1877 seven treaties were made with the Saulteaux (akin to the Ojibbewas of old Canada), the Piegans, the Crees, the Bloods, and the Blackfeet. A corps of mounted police was formed, Indian agents were appointed, and a branch Indian office established in the centre of the new country. By the treaties the Indians relinquished their right and title to the territory in consideration of the perpetual payment of $5 a head to every man, woman, and child; the payment of $25 a year to each chief and $15 a year to each deputy or councillor, together with official clothing, flags, medals, etc. ; the allotment of reservations of land in the proportion generally of one square mile to a family of five; and the supplying of the requisite implements, cattle, seed, etc., to enable the Indians to make a beginning at farming. The government, at the urgent request of the Indians, covenanted to prevent the sale of intoxicants on reservations, and to establish and maintain schools. The Indians selected their lands, and reservations were made for the different bands in the localities in which they had been in the habit of living. Most of them seemed to understand that the pressure of events made a change in their mode of life a necessity. Some of them, in what is now the Province of Manitoba, had made beginnings, lived in houses and planted garden-plots; but as you went west the attempts at agriculture grew ruder and rarer, though there was evidence everywhere that the red man was becoming gradually seized of the conviction that he would have to look more and more to Mother Earth for subsistence. In 1878 the Hon. David Laird, then at the head of the Territorial Indian office, reported that "if it were possible to employ a few good, practical men to aid and instruct the Indians at seed-time," he was " of the opinion that most of the bands on the Saskatchewan would soon be able to raise sufficient crops to meet their most pressing wants." In the following year agriculturists were sent into the country to conduct farms which would serve as models for the Indians; but this system was not productive of very beneficial results, and, instead of conducting model farms, the farming instructors now devote their time to superintending and directing the work of the Indians. The latter has proved to be the better system. A religious system of education was adopted and has been adhered to with good results.

The first break in the smooth flow of Indian affairs in the Canadian Northwest was occasioned by Riel's second, and to him fatal, rebellion. It was not, it must be borne in mind, strictly speaking an Indian uprising. The half-breeds and their leaders tried to rouse the whole Indian population of the territories to arms; but, though the two peoples are bound by many ties, they were only in part successful. Several of the bands preferred quiet to war, and others were kept in the paths of peace by the missionaries, two of whom—Fathers Lacombe and Scollen—were specially mentioned in this regard in the report of the Indian Department for 1885. Without passing in review the details of departmental management, it is clear that the participation of the Indians in the rebellion was caused by influences working from without rather than from within the bands. The trouble was but of short duration, and all traces of it were quickly wiped out. The leaders in the perpetration of savage murders were executed, and others of the Indians whose blood-guiltiness was less in degree were punished in different ways. Affairs took again their normal course.

In Manitoba and the Territories there are about fifty-two thousand Indians. Nearly half of these live in the far north; no treaties have yet been made with them, and they are outside the jurisdiction of the department. The official report deals only with the other half, and it divides them, as to religion, thus: 3,459 Catholics, 8,086 Protestants, 11,566 pagans, and 2,632 of unknown faith. A careful enumeration would probably somewhat change these figures; but they are sufficiently accurate to convey a general idea of the religious condition of the Indians. There were ninety-nine day-schools in operation last year, seventy-two of which were Protestant and twenty-seven Catholic. The government paid the salaries of the teachers, in whole or in part, and contributed *per capita* allowances to six Catholic and ten Protestant boarding-schools. Two industrial schools have been established and are wholly maintained by the government, under the direction of a Catholic and Protestant clergyman respectively. Two Catholic and one Protestant school outside treaty limits receive aid from the government. There were two thousand children enrolled at the different schools last year, and the average attendance was 1,162. The day-schools cost the government last year $56,031 75, and the industrial and boarding-schools $127,347 30. The total expenditure in connection with the Indians of Manitoba and the Territories in 1889–90 was $940,261 72. Of this amount $356,361 71 went for rations and clothing, $129,627 to pay annuities, $79,143 10 for agricultural implements, seed, cattle, and the running of farms; $6,716 23 for grist-mills, $3,059 08 to the Sioux—about a thousand who came across the border some years ago—and $187,975 55 to pay expenses of management, etc. These Indians had 11,950 acres of land under cultivation, and broke up 1,174 acres of new land in 1889. They raised, though the year was not a fat one, 43,051 bushels of grain, 68,628 bushels of potatoes and other vegetables, and 17,886 tons of hay. Their individual earnings from other sources aggregated nearly a quarter of a million dollars. The Indian Superintendent for Manitoba, in his report for last year, felt called upon "to congratulate the department upon the general prosperity and contentment prevailing among the different bands," and, in referring to Indian affairs in the Territories, the superintendent general tells us in his report for 1889-90 that the eventual transforming of the wanderers of the plains into self-supporting members of the commonwealth has been " removed from the pale of uncertainty." The peace of the Territories is effectually guarded by a corps of one thousand mounted police, and the commissioner of that force states in his report for 1887 that, with the exception of the Bloods, the Indians behave " remarkably well."

The Indians of Canada are not dying out. If statistics can be relied upon, they are increasing. Their number is now put at 122,585. In 1889–90 they cost this country $1,178,446 16, upwards of seventy thousand dollars of which was required to meet the expenses of the general management of their affairs at Ottawa. In addition to the Parliamentary appropriation, $281,174 31 of the trust fund was expended.

Space has permitted of merely a bird's-eye view of the position of the Indians of Canada. But enough, perhaps, has been written to show that, if an earnest, honest, common-sense policy obtains, our Indian problem will, within a measurable time, dwindle " down to naught."

J. A. J. McKenna.

Ottawa, Ont.

CHUNKY.

I SEE you're looking for my finger-ends; you'll look a good while to find 'em; they an't been there for twenty-five years; whole first joint gone—see! but I kep' my thumbs an' I got a nail on one of 'em, too. That nail's handy to pick up with, mighty handy.

I suppose you'd like to know how I come by these 'ere stumps. Well, I rubbed 'em off on coal an' slate an' rock—like you grate horseradish.

I was working then at the Night-hawk, an' me an' Chunky was together; we was always together; lived under one roof you may say; yonder's the house—second o' them black double ones —No 3 was his'n, No. 4 was mine.

Chunky he had a stepmother. She was real good to him, but he said she made him kind o' homesick for his own mammy. So he stayed with us a good bit o' the time. When we started picking slate—that was at the Chenowith—we worked alongside, an' my mammy she used to give Chunky his bath in our kitchen 'cause we had big tubs, an', besides, there was five on 'em over to Chunky's to get washed. Well, six days in a week, as soon as ever he was dried off an' dressed, he'd say: " Sure'n I'm obliged to ye, Mrs. Deane "—only he called it Dane, 'cause he was Irish, Chunky was.

We kep' a cow, an' after work me an' Chunky used to go after her. She had the run o' the whole mountain, an' some-times we'd catch her down to Soldier Creek, then ag'in 'way up by the Whippoorwill, or maybe she'd be off on the Back Track. Often it'd be after dark when we'd get home; then my mammy she'd give us both some supper. Onct I lamed my toe going barefoot, so I couldn't walk for a long time. Chunky he went after the cow himself, an' my mammy she didn't want him to do it without pay. But do you think he'd take pay? No, he wouldn't; he said he was making it up square for the suppers an' scrub-bings she'd given him. He hadn't no dark corners to him, Chunky hadn't.

I was a little older than him, an' bigger, so I left the break-er first an' went inside to tend door. Then we couldn't get out at the same time; but Chunky'd stay around an' wait for me.

When I come up on the lift, there he'd be a-sitting under the trestling, his eyes, most dancing out of his face, an' he'd say: " Here y'are, Frid! " He couldn't say Fred, you know, being Irish.

After I got to be door-boy he wasn't content to stay in the breaker, an' he sought for promotion; but just then we had a new mine-boss come. He was a Welshman an' he did nothing but try to get rid of all that wasn't o' the same name. At any rate, he'd put in none new but Welshmen. He hated the Irish; but he couldn't hate Chunky, 'cause nobody couldn't do that, you know, so he didn't turn him away, but he wouldn't advance him.

When Chunky was seventeen an' I was near nineteen—I'd got to be driver then—we made up our minds to quit the Chenowith. The Night-hawk was just built, an' the mine belonged to the Rainbow Company. We liked the superintendent an' the boss there, an' David Davis was getting too much for us. He went beyond what a boss is meant for.

So we applied at the new place, an' got laborers' positions together. This suited first-rate; we went down an' come up in company, ate our dinners together, an' went snacks, if the one of us had anything better than the other in his pail.

Then I got married. 'Taint' much good getting married on laborers' wages, but youngsters want their own way, an' I had mine. I scratched on awhile; then the first baby made me jump around a little more lively. I went to mining, an' the boss set me to work in a new vein.

This was hard on Chunky. You see, when you get married your mind's took up away from your old friends. My woman an' me we liked to have Chunky set with us an' talk, an' then we liked to have him go.

But Chunky he felt kind o' lonesome, an' when I was moved he couldn't stand it very good. One day he says: " Wouldn't ye like to have me working for you, Frid ? Maybe the boss'll let you exchange laborers wid Thornton." Thornton was him we'd worked for together. Then I see how he felt the separation, an' I says to him: " All right."

Thornton didn't like it much, 'cause Chunky'd been the best fellow at the Chenowith, an' he was the best at the Night-Hawk —anywhere you'd put him he'd be the best: but the boss was with us, an' so it got fixed that I was to have Chunky, an' Thornton was to have one o' my men.

Then Chunky was happy, an' I liked it, too, for by that time I was getting kind o' used to being married, an' looked round a bit. Besides, when there was two babies 'stead o' one—an' it wasn't long 'fore there was two—'twasn't so peaceful to home; so I got in the way o' going to Chunky's house, or walking with him like we did when we was lads.

Well, do you know we growed that thick ag'in that my woman she got jealous. She said Chunky an' me was too fond of each other, but Chunky said: "Is it me ye're beginning to be jealous of now, Mis Frid?"—that's what he always called her—"sure an' ye had a right to be so always, for I've never let him out o' me heart."

He'd stuck to me tight, that's the truth, an' he never let on that I'd dropped him for a while. He was true-hearted, Chunky was.

He had a soft spot in him for babies, too. He could get my little ones to sleep quicker'n their mother could. The biggest one an' him was great friends—he was always for having her along on a walk—she'd not cry a bit when she was on Chunky's shoulder.

Well, things went along pretty good, and then come the winter when my third baby was born. That was a boy, an' we was some proud to our house. But you'd think our pride was nothing by the side o' Chunky's; he just took that baby for his'n.

We wanted to call it Patrick Edward — that was Chunky's real name — but Chunky he said we must call it Fred or he'd go to law about it; an' one day, before we'd come to a conclusion, in walks Chunky with a silver mug marked *Frederick Deane; from his friend, Patrick Edward Mulroy*. So that settled it.

All this time Chunky was only doing laborer's work. I couldn't noways coax him to leave me for a better position, though the boss'd given him anything he'd asked for. It just seemed that by the side o' the pleasure o' working in my company wages was no account.

One day, when I'd been urging him, he says with a kind o' trembling in his throat: "I'm all right, Frid; let me stick to you till the end." An' he did, Chunky did.

Next spring, when little Fred was going on six months old, Chunky said to me: "I've transferred me money in the savings-bank to the name o' Friderick Dane, Jun."

"An' what made you do that?" says I. "Because it's me

pleasure to do it," says he, an' I knowed there was no turning Chunky when he'd made up his mind, so I dropped it.

On the twenty-ninth of April we went down to our work, me an' Chunky, like we'd always done. My other man was sick, an' we two worked alone. There wasn't many working near us—our chamber was the last in the vein.

Chunky had just sent up a car, an' the driver boy told us it was nigh onto twelve when he left the foot o' the shaft. So I said we'd quit an' eat our dinner. I went an' fetched our pails from the gangway where we'd hung 'em away from the rats, an' I was just handing Chunky his'n when he cried out sudden: "Look out!" an' I didn't look out none too soon, for the whole roof come down between us an' the gangway, an' there we was boxed up in the chamber like we'd been trapped.

Chunky blowed out my light quicker'n a wink, an' I blowed out his'n, an' for a minute we said nothing. Then we both begun to holler. But we didn't waste breath that way long; we knowed the cave-in 'd be discovered soon or late, an' then we'd be missed.

So we sat down an' waited.

Waiting in the dark an't ever pleasant, but when you're not certain you'll ever see light ag'in it's like being alive in your coffin. At length I says to Chunky: "We'd better eat something"—we'd never let go our pails. "All right" says he, "but let's only take a wee bite, for maybe we'll require more before we get out."

"Like enough," I says, but I didn't know what I was talking about then.

Well, they say we was in there ten days; if they'd call it ten months I'd believe 'em easier. We hadn't no way to tell the time, an' it seemed like we'd set there a week without moving, when Chunky says:

"If they're not coming to dig us out, it's ourselves as must dig."

Then he proposed we should find how much victuals we had in the pails an' set apart as little as we could get along on for one meal.

After we'd done this I hunted round for the pick an' the drill, but they was nowhere to be found. Then I remembered they was lying near the opening when the cave-in come, so that was the end of 'em.

But we couldn't set still no longer. We thought maybe

'twasn't much of a fall, an' we could dig through anyway; so at it we went.

, You've heard tell o' tooth an' nail—well, that's the way we worked, but after awhile we found it worse business than we'd bargained for. The chamber was a good large one, but we didn't dare fill it up; the best we hoped to do was to make a hole through to get more air. So we took turns boring. Sometimes we'd come ag'in a solid chunk o' rock that wouldn't be bored, then we'd have to turn aside an' take another course for a distance.

Whenever we struck coal we thought ourselves lucky; then we scratched like rats under a red-hot pan.

Do you wonder I an't got any finger ends?

All this time we heard no noise outside. I'd say: "Chunky, we can't live it out"; an' he'd say: "We must try to."

The only way we knowed we hadn't been there for months was the way the victuals lasted us. Chunky was getting awful weak though. I knowed it by his voice, an' by the sound of his digging. He wasn't ever so strong as me, and he couldn't keep up on such short fare.

I didn't know how 'twas, but the victuals held out wonderful. We only took a few mouthfuls at a time, but after I'd eat a good many times, my pail didn't get no lower. I mentioned this to Chunky, an' he says: "Maybe it's a miracle the saints is a-working for us"; he believed in the saints, Chunky did; he was better'n I was every way.

At length he got so weak he couldn't work no more; I had to scratch along by myself. Now an' then we thought we heard picks outside, an' that kep' us up some, but we wasn't sure.

After Chunky got so weak, I didn't like to take my sleep— 'twas kind o' like leaving him alone. Onct when I was resting a bit, an' trying not to shut my eyes, I spoke to him so he'd know I was awake; but he didn't answer me. That scared me, an' I touched him. He was breathing, but his body was like a bag o' bones.

Then a thought hit me on the side o' my head, an' I felt for the dinner-pails. Chunky's was empty an' mine was more'n half full. Then I knowed why he was so weak: he'd chawed loud an' made believe eat, but he hadn't took a mouthful.

This beat me all to pieces, an' I just set there an' cried, an' that woke up Chunky. He says—his voice was like a baby's:

"What's got ye, Frid?" An' I busted out: "What made

you do it, Chunky?" An' Chunky he didn't say nothing at all. Then he heard me, at the dinner-pail an' he knowed what I was after, so says he : "I'm past ateing now, Frid." An' I asked him agin what made him do it; an' first he was still like he'd died, but soon he says, choking a bit:

"I knowed there wasn't enough for the two of us."

That made me mad, an' I says, speaking kind o' strong: "You've as much right to live as me."

Then Chunky he put up his hand an' felt round for my face, an' he patted me like he used to pat little Frid, an' says he: "No, ye've the best right; ye're the one as 's got the babies, Frid." An' I couldn't say no more, 'cause Chunky'd take his own way anyhow.

This was about the last talking he did, only to say a little prayer now an' then. Well, you may know I didn't enjoy my bites much after that. I wouldn't a' touched another crumb but for hurting Chunky's feelings; he'd made me swear I'd do my best to keep alive. But I was growing weak myself by this time.

The day Chunky died I heard the picks outside for sure, but I went on digging to keep from going crazy. I was beginning to go out o' my head an' I didn't know when I was took out. They said I was nigh dead what with the foul air I'd breathed, an' the starving an' the grieving; and indeed I was sick a long time. But I got well ag'in—all but my finger-ends; they never growed back.

My boy Fred he went to a pay-school on the money what Chunky left him. He's a heap better eddicated than his daddy ever was, or Chunky either; but all the eddication in the world won't never put a soul in him like Chunky had.

EDITH BROWER.

SOME PLAIN WORDS WITH AGNOSTICS.

ACCORDING to Richard Holt Hutton the word Agnostic, as at present used, owes its origin to the suggestion of the well-known naturalist, Professor Thomas Henry Huxley. An Agnostic is one who denies that anything beyond this material universe is known or is even knowable. To a greater or lesser extent he is a sceptic, a doubter. Though he may admit the reality of phenomena, his knowledge, he tells us, goes no further.

Sceptics have existed from time immemorial, and were of old strongly represented in the Grecian schools of Pyrrho of Elis. In our own time the more advanced sceptics not only deny the possibility of knowing that which lies beyond the reach of our senses, but also maintain that we are not able to possess any certain knowledge of the reality of things, not even of material phenomena. Their life is like a dream; they live in the midst of beings of whose very existence they are in doubt; they find no connecting link between the inner world of thought and the outer world of the numerous realities that surround them—not even with their own bodies. That such a system must sap the basis of all religion is evident; for how is it possible to honor or adore that which we know not? how can we aspire to a higher end if we are in doubt whether such a higher end exists? or how will we be in a condition to perform duties the foundation of which is hidden to us?

Scepticism and agnosticism, then, are the enemies of religion, both natural and revealed. They are the despair of the human intelligence—the awful *give-up* in the search for truth, the natural outcome of the many errors into which the human mind has fallen.

It is next to impossible to argue with a sceptic, for when we proceed to discuss a question with an intellectual adversary it is necessary that we agree with our opponent at least in some points. We must have common premises whereupon to build our reasoning. But the only principle of the sceptic is that he doubts of everything. The sceptic assures me that the world is for him a vast enigma; that he can establish no relations between his inner self and the outer world; that the stars above his head, the waving trees around him, the rushing waters that his ear hears and his eye admires, the music of the birds and

the life with which the universe teems are, perhaps, only the creations of his own imagination. He advances even farther, and in
his most doubting mood tells me that perhaps his own individuality does not exist—that he may be only the thought of some
universal mind. I feel, in listening to him, the difficulty of my
position as party to a discussion ; the very ground seems to sink
from under my feet. What reply shall I make ? whence shall I
draw my arguments? where shall I find a premise that my sceptic
shall admit ? But, lo ! here is one. The sceptic is firm at least
in one point : his doubt. He knows that he doubts. Of all else
he has no knowledge ; but there is one certainty in his mind,
and that is his doubt, for, were he to doubt whether he doubts
or not, then he could not assure me that he does doubt. But
even in that case he must finally come to some certain affirmation if he does not want me to fall into an infinite series of doubts,
before which absurdity even a sceptic would hesitate. Upon this
frail platform we will endeavor to build up our argumentation,
and, if possible, convince our sceptic.

You tell me, sceptical friend, that you doubt, but in your
very doubt I behold your existence ; for if you did not exist it
would be impossible for you to doubt, as doubt is a state of an
existing mind. Your existence mirrors itself in your doubt. By
the very fact, therefore, of your admitting that you doubt you
must necessarily admit your existence.

There is, moreover, within you, and you cannot deny it,
that inner self-consciousness which admits of no doubt concerning your existence. But if you admit your existence, and are
forced to admit it, I am equally forced to admit mine. But my
consciousness assures me that I am a distinct person from you—
in other words, that you and I are not the same person. This
you also admit by the very fact of your disputing with me, for
if you and I were the same person a contradiction would be
the result, for you doubt and I do not doubt ; consequently if
you and I were identified we would be the *I* doubting and not
doubting about the same thing at the same time, which is an
absurdity.

If, then, you admit that you and I are distinct persons, we
have only the same reasoning process to follow to establish
the existence of all other persons with whom we come in contact. We may, then, conclude that we possess certainty at
least of the existence of ourselves and of persons distinct from
ourselves. And let me remark in passing that certainty is a

state of the mind that· excludes all reasonable doubt. I say reasonable doubt; for groundless doubts can always be experienced without hurt be they ever so devoid of common sense.

If we ˙admit the existence of the world of human personality, we must also accept the reality of the material world around us; for we see that it strikes all individuals in the same manner. Certainly the senses of some may be deceived; but it is impossible that the˙senses of all should be so perverted that they should be deceived in their primary objects. Such a deception would prove a universal confusion˙ and contradiction in the senses, which would be something unnatural and incredible—a state of things for belief in which we have not the slightest ground. Hence, when the human race beholds the moon above its head in its different phases, that moon really exists; for otherwise the entire human race would be laboring under a hallucination. Moreover, to admit the non-reality of the outer world we should be forced to admit that all the senses are illusory in their action; for in walking through. a flower-garden, for instance, our hands touch the flowers and our sense of smell perceives their perfume and our eyes behold their color; and thus it is with all else.

But why reason on this subject? Does ˙ not common sense, does not our inner conviction assure us that the outer world has a true, a real existence, that our senses do not deceive us; and do not sceptics themselves believe this, at least practically?

In all this many, perhaps most, agnostics will agree with us but when we endeavor to ascend higher, to that which is above the senses, they bid us halt; for of the spiritual world they say, we can know nothing. Will they admit that we have the power of reasoning? Certainly. But what is reasoning? It is the exercise of a faculty of the mind by which we draw conclusions from certain known principles or facts. Thus I take a walk upon the sea-shore, and as I look upon the sand I behold the impression of feet. I know without any proof that, as there can be no effect without a cause, these impressions must have been produced by some feet. I would be unreasonable were I not to admit this. Hence, I conclude that some one has been here. But I may proceed further. From the nature of the footprints I am enabled to conjecture. the time when they were formed. It is low tide now; at high tide the place where the footprints are would have been under water. Had they been made at a previous low tide the water at high tide would have. obliterated all trace of them, consequently they have been formed·

quite recently; and thus from their position I can estimate pretty nearly the time when they were formed. I am also able to know with certainty in what direction the persons went, and from the nature of the footprints I may even find out with certainty by what kind of beings they were made. From the footprints I conclude that they were left by a man, a woman, and a child. My conclusions are certain because they have been logically drawn from evident premises

And is not this same mode of reasoning followed even by Agnostics in their zoölogical, geological, and archæological studies? They tell us how the earth existed thousands and millions of years ago, what its climate was, what kinds of animals wandered around upon its surface, what birds lived in its atmosphere, and what fishes swam in its waters. But if it is in my power to reach causes, the effects of which I possess some knowledge of, why may I not by the same process of reasoning arrive at causes of which I have no knowledge? I know that the effect gives evidence of the nature of its cause. If, then, I study the universe, may I not reason as I do when I behold footprints upon the sand?

The world did not make itself; I did not make it, nor any being like me. It is a great effect, hence the world must have had a cause. This also Agnostics are willing to admit, but they deny that I can obtain any knowledge of the nature of that cause. But if the effect indicates the nature of the cause, I must logically conclude that all I admire in the universe must have *eminently* pre-existed in its cause, and that therefore the First Cause must be far more perfect than the world itself I could not suppose for an instant that it could be less perfect, for no one can give what he has not, and if the Cause of the world did not possess the perfections with which the effect is endowed, those perfections never would have existed, for nothing can produce itself. And it is plain that a perfection which is creative is supreme and infinite. But among the perfections found in the universe I remark intelligence; therefore, the world must have had a cause endowed with intelligence, otherwise it is impossible to understand whence intelligence could have originated.

I know what Agnostics will answer; they will tell me that intelligence is only a higher-development of material forces. Be it so, for argument's sake; but it is, at all events, an organized development, and every organization presupposes an intellectual agent. Moreover, that material force which produces intellect must have come from somewhere—it must have pre-existed in the

First Cause, and therefore the First Cause is intelligent. I am well aware that Agnostics will find replies even to this, but replies based only upon gratuitous assumptions and by no means upon experience. If they tell me that intelligence is only an accidental effect of many causes, it will be my turn to demand proofs.

Moreover the perfect harmony of the universe convinces me that the world was produced by intelligence. If, walking upon the sea-shore, I were to notice a name written in the sand, how ridiculous it would be were I to assert that the name had been written by the waves, or that it had been produced by accident. Will not every one conclude that some one had been there to trace the characters in the sand? Am I required to be less reasonable when I behold the beautiful universe and trace it to its cause? Whence came the stars, and the laws that rule them, the plants, the animals, the mind of man; were they all accidentally produced by some blind, unthinking agent? One must be a fool, Agnostic or not, to harbor such a thought for a single instant.

Whose mind arranged the laws that govern mathematics? In what intelligence did they take their being? In none? Are they the · outcome of chance? Only an insane man could seriously assert this. It is then evident that I am able to form some idea of the nature of the world's First Cause. It must be a mighty intelligence.

Moreover there have been men, great and learned men, who have believed that they know much about that First Cause. In the kingdom of thought these men have ruled the human race. Are they all to be now rated as fools? And has wisdom only been born in these latter times in the Agnostic school of Professor Huxley and Mr. Herbert Spencer?

Mr. Herbert Spencer says so; it is Professor Huxley's opinion. But what does Plato say, and Aristotle and Socrates and Seneca, and Augustine and Aquinas, and a host of others—what do they say? And must these men be eclipsed by these later lights, the Agnostics? The beauty and order of the universe served to convince Plato, Aristotle, and Cicero of the existence of an intelligent First Cause, and the minds of these illustrious men never fell into Agnosticism. And who is there among the Agnostics who can stand against the great teacher and king of the ages, Jesus Christ?

"Whence," says St. Augustine, " do I know that you live, as I see not your soul? Whence do I know it? You will answer, because I speak, I walk, I work. Fool, from the works of the body

I recognize a living man; can you not from the works of the creature recognize the creator?" Does it not seem as though, sending his piercing eye through the centuries to come, Augustine addressed himself in these words to our modern Agnostics?

We sometimes hear people say that they will take nothing on authority, but will reason for themselves. Whether such persons do reason for themselves or not, the fact is that the vast majority of mankind are led by others, to whom they leave most of the reasoning. A most important question, therefore, is, Who shall be the teachers of men? For instance, it is now universally believed that the earth revolves around its own axis and performs a yearly revolution around the sun. This is taught in all the schools, it is learned in early childhood, and unhesitatingly believed by all, although it is an apparent contradiction to what we perceive by the senses. But why is it admitted? Is it because all have reasoned the matter out and have proved it satisfactorily? No; for, perhaps, not one in a hundred knows the arguments by which the earth's rotation is proved? Nevertheless they admit it, because the learned teach it, because they read it in books and all believe it. As it is with this dogma of science, thus is it with a great many other things in the world. Why has Agnosticism become popular among a certain class of people? Because some men of reputation have taught it, and perhaps because it has a high-sounding name. But how many of those who call themselves Agnostics are able to give any reason, even a plausible one, for their opinions?

If we will be led by others, why not go to those whose knowledge has been the admiration of centuries—to a Plato, an Aristotle, a Cicero, an Augustine, or an Aquinas—above all, to Jesus Christ and his apostles. Have, perhaps, our wonderful modern inventions thrown new light upon such subjects—a future state, the authority of conscience, the existence of God? They have not even elucidated the first principles of science in the natural order, and they confess it; how, then, can they be expected to render a clear account of the world above the senses?

We do not depreciate the progress our modern world has made in certain branches of science, but we are not afraid to assert that our many discoveries have added little or nothing to first principles of morality and metaphysics, and are, as a rule, merely limited to facts, and the generalizations deduced from them.

Let, then, sceptics doubt; let them grope in the dark, and let Agnostics love their darkness; we thank God that we are children of the light, and that the eternal radiance of an uncreated Deity is reflected upon our intellects by the wondrous works of creation. We behold his loveliness in the flowers of the field; his light shines upon us through the starry realms above our heads. We hear his voice in the storm-wind, his whisper is in the gentle zephyr, and we love to gaze upon the reflection of his countenance mirrored on the bosom of the deep. We know there is a God, for the heavens proclaim his glory. We know him because our souls crave him and are unrestful till they possess him. We know him though we comprehend him not. We know him, we love him, and it is our highest ambition to serve him for ever.

CHARLES WARREN CURRIER, C.SS.R.

THE WITNESS OF SCIENCE TO RELIGION.

III.—EITHER SCIENCE IS A DREAM, OR RELIGION IS TRUE.

BY an argument as simple as it appears to me conclusive, I have endeavored to prove these two things. First, that I recognize outside of the facts, and collocations of facts, like the words I am at this moment writing, which exhibit thought, design, or purpose—which, in other terms, are the effects of what philosophers have named a Final Cause—I know, and cannot but know, that this page manifests, by means of written sentences, the intention I had in putting it together. But secondly, by a like process (whether of direct perception or by reasoning from the analogy of my own acts), I am certified of the existence of other minds, with which I can enter into communion. To deny that purpose as manifested in the products of my own hands and brain, would be scepticism, were it possible, as in fact it is not. Equally sceptical would it be to call in question the ten thousand phenomena which I did not originate, but which have no meaning unless they proceed from an intellect framed on the pattern to which mine corresponds. Intercourse with other men could never take place, did I not incessantly refer their expressions to the common standard within me, and apply, so to speak, the key of mental interpretation which I carry about, to their language, gesture, and visible motions.

Even as I understand them, so do they understand me. There is a Light of the Intellect as surely as there is a sun in Heaven. Deny it, or take it away, and darkness follows. The mind which cannot affirm what other minds perceive and in their turn acknowledge, is stricken with paralysis. Therefore I conclude that a world of intellect, or a mental universe, exists, of which we are all members and citizens. How do I arrive at the knowledge of it? I answer, by interpreting phenomena according to the laws, axioms, and ascertained inferences of my individual reason.

Now this, and none other, is the foundation upon which science, inductive as well as deductive, is built. Deduction starts from self-evident truths, for which no ground can be assigned except their self-evidence. In other words, the mind certifies that they are objectively valid; that they cannot be dreams or delusions. They are *per se nota.* Induction, again, yields either certain or probable results, by appealing to a principle of which the value must be determined by some other than the inductive process itself—in short, by the intellect affirming at its own risk. Every physical science photographs, as it were, a portion of the universe. But it does more. It introduces among phenomena a method, an intelligible order; it ranges details in their places, connects them as antecedents and consequents, and casts them in the moulds of our mental categories. True it is that the senses bind them up after a fashion, or, as I may say, sift and sort the momentary impressions, and reduce the boundless chaos to an ordered whole, writing its record on the brain tablets and in the nervous system. Nevertheless, sense is not science. The brain may register feelings, but it is not the brain which interprets them so as to furnish us with scientific induction, nor does it elicit answers to the questions no mere brain has ever put, of the How, and the What, and the Why. To set down a list of sensations in shorthand may be useful, or even indispensable, before I attempt to reason about things. Only I cannot end there, and call my list a chapter of science. Induction mounts up to laws; deduction confessedly begins with axioms. And what are laws and axioms but mental statements, tested, if you please, by the experience of the five senses, yet in nowise depending on them for their truth or validity?

Religion and science agree, therefore, in one grand postulate, which I will call the fact of a real correspondence between our minds and the Nature of Things. Evidently, if that postulate is unfounded, or not self-evident, I can never know anything outside my own consciousness, and the world of matter, no less than the kingdoms of the spirit, is an empty dream. For in what way do I lay hold of the physical phenomena round about me, except by bringing to bear upon them the ideas of Reality, Substance, Existence, of Quantity, Quality, and Relation, every one of which is a mental form? Or how could *they* affect me, the thinking subject, if they did not by an inscrutable process give rise in my mind to these very conceptions? All physics, from this point of view, are metaphysics. Only by piercing into things with thought can we be said to understand them. It is thought which affirms law and order, invariable succession, the uniformities of action and reaction, the fixed times, and conditions, and quantities, according to which elements unite to form compounds and are dissolved again. The whole range of physical science is subject to number, to mathematics. But the late Professor Jevons, with whom I agree, has shown that number is a logical idea, founded on the apprehension by the mind (not by the senses, be it observed) of diversity. Animals have experience of various objects, but they cannot count them; still less can they reflect upon the abstract notion implied in the fact of variety and not to be seized except by a purely mental process. Let us consider now what this involves.

Either the principle of number is valid for the things themselves, or science, which cannot go one step without it, is a sort of algebraic castle-building. Induction everywhere proceeds by number, weight, and measure, in the province of physical research. It is constantly employed about numerical proportions, and can hardly lay the balance aside for a moment. We dare not, then, imagine the idea of number to be wholly subjective, and not in the things outside us, without ruining physical science from foundation to summit. On the other hand, if it be allowed that number is rooted and established in the material universe, and not painted into them by the pencil of our metaphysic fancies, it follows that forces, elements, and energies of what kind soever are built up in the likeness of Objective Thought, and are stamped with intelligence. To quote the beautiful Platonic language, they are seals or impressions of an archetypal mind. For number, I have said, is a logical idea. The great system in which we find ourselves cannot, then, be simply alien from us, a blind and brutal something of which we shall never grasp the meaning because it has none. It must have a meaning. Every idea into the sphere of whose illumination it is brought, shows its meaning more and more, lights up its heights and depths, and is constantly revealing how profoundly the Greeks were in the right when they named it the Cosmos, or the system of things ordered by reason.

Inductive science, I repeat, is not an echo, but an answer—the response to questions carefully and cunningly devised by a mind which moves about in worlds akin to it. Modern teachers would scout the notion that in unlocking one after another the closed doors of the great universe, they are but travelling through the stages of hallucination, or playing with dice which they have loaded beforehand. Nothing will persuade them of the unreality ascribed, by German metaphysicians like Fichte, to the phenomena with which they deal. The laws of gravitation, electricity, magnetism, spectrum analysis, and the rest, are to them as real as their own existence. On what ground, do we ask? The reply must be at last that intellect, observing and experimenting in accordance with its proper nature, has affirmed their truth. Verification is simply the establishment of a perfect correspondence between facts outside us and reason within us. It gives back, in forms commensurate with our mind, the realities by which we have been impressed ; and that could never be, unless the world were a system of intelligible principles, co-ordinated into one by most subtle and far-reaching harmonies. Scientific inquiry sets out with an assured confidence in the possibility of the end to which it is directed, and that end is explanation. Not, of course, that we look with our present limited senses, imperfect instruments, and easily fatigued attention, to attain the knowledge which alone would deserve to be called adequate. But whether we compass the explanation or no we feel certain, when the problems of matter and life are put before us in the several instances, that an explanation there is. No one could so befool himself as to think, in the presence of any phenomena whatsoever, that they had neither a cause by which they came to be, nor a purpose to which they were subservient. The idea of a cause is involved in the very fact of their being at all ; and that of a purpose in their belonging, as they manifestly do, to the general system of things. For we never meet with isolated phenomena; while among the myriad facts which fall under observation, not one completely and adequately explains itself. Thus it is that Science makes progress. It moves backwards along the series of efficient causes, and onward along that of ends or purposes. At every step it inquires how and why? But the chain of connection, as

I cannot too frequently observe, is woven by the intellect out of its own ideas. The great hierarchy of laws and forces is at once real and notional—neither blind, unintelligible matter (which I hold to be a contradiction, if not in terms yet in fact), nor abstractions which have no footing in things visible. This I will show by a further argument derived from the nature of induction as we practise it.

When we predict the future from the past, or—what comes to the same thing—when from a given number of specimens we decide the characteristics of all others belonging to that particular class, it is evident that our inference derives its strength from a principle tacitly assumed, which enables us to dispense with complete observation. We cannot argue from particulars to particulars. How, then, do we proceed? Either we assume the "uniformity of nature," as writers tell us nowadays, or we trace out a necessary connection between a given cause and the events or the attributes which we inductively predicate. Again, it may be said, with Professor Jevons, that we "invent hypotheses, until we fall upon one which yields inductive results in accordance with experience," and then, on the supposition that the conditions do not change, we hazard our prophecy. In every case—and here is my first point—we are driven back to an abstract principle, or set of principles, which the mind formulates and then proceeds to test. If experience bears them out in only a single case, some degree of probability in their favor arises. But as the witness of experience grows, the evidence multiplies; chance is more and more eliminated; and a certain number of coincidences between the facts and the hypothesis will suffice to persuade the reason that our theory is not only probable but true. Sir Isaac Newton has in this way demonstrated the law of gravity; nor is scientific induction possible except on the like method. From which I go on to my second point. That hypothesis, I affirm, ought to be received as certain and indubitable which, if it be granted, the phenomena of the universe are shown to have a reasoned connection one with the other, and to be susceptible of explanation on a piece, or systematically; while, if it be rejected, no account whatever can be rendered of that which makes the universe to be a whole composed of so many agreeing parts, and conspiring to exist and to advance in the manner of which we are conscious. For such an hypothesis fulfils all the conditions of scientific induction. It explains the facts; and by the facts it is verified in its turn. Now I say that the only view which is allowable to a properly trained mind, on summing up the evidence of phenomena with the aid of the most precise investigation, is that the present system of things has been established and is carried forward by a self-conscious intellect before which the past and the future alike are spread out, to which the infinite details were known from the beginning, and by which the ends or purposes of things, and the great final purpose to realize which they all combine, were foreordained. Theologians call that Supreme Intellect by the name of Providence. Mankind have ever worshipped it as God.

I am not pretending to be wise above what is written. But I cannot help seeing the order of the world; and order means mind, or it becomes not merely an enigma but a contradiction. Resting on the corner-stone of knowledge, which is self-evidence; and appealing to the test of induction—that is, to experiment—I say that an Objective Intellect does account for το ἐυ και καλως, as Aristotle calls it, for the intricate yet harmonious, the endless yet simple, arrangements of things, by which all are means and ends in a system that has lasted unnumbered millions of ages. I am convinced that to deny the governing Intellect is to commit ourselves to Chance or Hazard.   Who can really hesitate between these alternatives when they are understood? Mind or no mind; that is the question. *What* a question for scientific men, who have won all their triumphs, wrought their daily stupendous miracles, conquered matter, and made space and time their servants, by carrying the hypothesis of Mind victoriously into every corner of the universe ! Do any of them seriously contend that intellect will explain the details, but that there is no intellect in the whole ? What was known of nature two thousand years ago fills, in mere outline, the volumes of that penetrating genius whom I have quoted above. In our day no single mind is capacious enough to hold the knowledge pouring in upon us, The intelligible bounds of the world have been put back and are hourly receding.   New sciences spring up, methods of greater subtlety and power are devised from year to year.   What other inference can we draw from all this, astounding as it seems, except that Nature reveals thought in larger and more wonderful measure the more we lay our minds to it ?   Not chance nor chaos; not the haphazard jostlings and crossings of Lucretian atoms, but wheels within wheels, purpose subservient to purpose, organisms uniting in systems which they carry on and which reciprocally lead them to perfection.   Such are the facts to which science bears witness.   The assumption of Mind as directing and ordaining these million-fold correspondences is altogether reasonable. It offers no internal contradiction in itself. It is founded on absolute fact, since, as I showed at the beginning of this article, I know with certainty of the correspondence between my own intention and the results which my hand and mind achieve together. The existence of one single organism or piece of complex contrivance in the world outside us would prove it to a demonstration, simply because the probabilities against definite orderly results accruing by mere accident amid indefinite variations are beyond measure great. But instead of a single organism, myriads past all human counting live and move in earth and sky and sea, and have done so during ages upon ages. There is no calculus by which we could represent the improbability of the supposition that all these things have come to pass without a Mind. The dicer's fancy that, if the letters composing Virgil's *Eneid* were thrown from a tower they would fall into the identical words, lines, and fable which the poet has written, is sense and reason compared with the Agnosticism which hints that perhaps the whole system of the fixed stars and nebulæ, of suns, and planets with their satellites, and of organic life from its commencement in the Laurentian rocks till to-day, may have leaped out of a storm of molecules, whirling in all directions, and bent towards no definite end. But this mad supposition is involved in the denial of a guiding intellect. For what guidance could there be in its absence ?

As I view the great orders of Being one above another, appearing by successive stages in the world's history, what strikes me more than anything else is the adaptation of matter to life, of life to mind, and of mind to the general system of things. So clear, so overwhelming is the presence of intellect in the combinations I perceive, from the laws of light and chemistry in the remotest nebula to the microscopic building up of organisms, that nowhere can I discern a break or a gap into which hazard might enter. I cannot deny the universal nexus of finality. I grant that life does not spring from dead matter, any more than spirit can be drawn out of sense by skilful handling of its constituents. All the more wonderful, then, is that increasing purpose which, as Tennyson declares, has run through the ages, binding them in a drama every incident of which must have been foreseen and provided against. It is obvious, nay, inevitable, to attribute these multitudinous, ever-renewed adaptations to a cause with which we are already acquainted, and which, if conceived on such a scale as the phenomena warrant, will account for them adequately. We know of one such cause, and one only—intelligent Design. There is simply no other hypothesis to which we can resort, if this be not accepted.   For Chance is but a word to denote our ignorance; and Necessity, which some have invoked, must be either blind or seeing.   Is it seeing?   Then that is what I mean by Intelligence. Or blind?   So far as it is blind, the guidance of things must be to it impossible, and Chance returns under a different name Whatever is false, this is true, that we cannot omit Intellect from the nature of things, and still hope to understand them.

Agnosticism, I do not doubt, is on the increase.   Many otherwise thoughtful minds take refuge in it as a sanctuary from the storms of speculation, the wrangling which too often passes under the title of metaphysics, and the mysteries which they seem unable to face.   I have not attempted to deny that we are surrounded on every side with mysteries   I feel, in the words of Goethe, that "man is a dark being," inscrutable in many ways to himself and mostly unexplored.   I am sure that the wisest among us would fail to explain the nature of any process, within him or without him, which goes beyond simple addition or subtraction.   But I am just as certain that there are no contradictions in the things themselves, else they would not exist; and, if this be so, it is our powers of understanding that fail, not the intelligibility of the facts.   None, perhaps, have grasped so firmly as mathematicians the suggestive truth, that, as our methods of investigation improve, so do fresh prospects open into Nature.   The problems we have solved may be considered elementary and few in comparison with those which remain.   But the facts are given, and our reason affirms with absolute certitude that some explanation of them must be as possible as they are real.   Agnosticism here interposes, not without effect, to declare that the hypothesis of blind and dead matter is evidently no explanation at all.   If we are to set up Matter as the First Cause, it goes on to say, we must define it after a new fashion, perchance as "the mysterious Something," by which all other things have come to be.   Now my argument is that we cannot stop short in this way, even if we would, at the category of mere and bare existence.   The same mental necessity which compels us to affirm that "Something is and has been from everlasting," drives us on to the assertion that without Mind nothing whatever could have existed at any time.   And when I say mental necessity, while, on the one hand, I recognize that it is due to the nature of my intellect, or is, in this sense, prior to experience, on the other I can point to the conquests of science as my warrant for declining to believe that the certitudes of reason are only subjective.

I do not claim for the human faculties immunity from error, except when they claim it themselves. I can imagine other and more richly endowed senses, and an experience of worlds to us unseen and consequently incomprehensible, by the side of which our sphere of intuitive knowledge would seem little more than a child's in comparison with an angel's. But the first truths, elementary though they be, are still the mainstay of the largest wisdom. It may sound trifling to enunciate the equal validity of religion and science, because they are both products of the same human intellect. Yet it is the ground on which we shall find our arguments resting in the last analysis. And if the world has gone after its scientific teachers, relying on their word, making use of the inventions they have hit upon, and persuaded thereby that they have been all along in touch with reality, what reason can it allege for doubting the evidence of inductive theology, which, I say, does but apply to the whole those very methods whereby physical science has mastered the parts and the details? Even a mechanical order of things is impossible unless mind has designed it. How much more the organic world, the instincts of animals, and man himself the microcosm? Shall we grant the validity of an idea so low in the scale as "invariable succession," and turn from purpose and design as anthropomorphic? Are not all our primary notions anthropomorphic?

But I think the reason is not far to seek. Power and succession, which are ideas on a level, as it were, with energy in space and movement in time, seem to have nothing of the personal in them. They may amaze and terrify, but they cannot properly be said to demand admiration or worship. They leave us lords of ourselves, owning no master, though liable to be shattered by a turn of the great wheels. It is otherwise with the admission of a true Final Cause. If we live and move in the presence, in the all-encompassing sphere, of a Conscious Mind, which called us into being and controls our steps, it is manifest that we owe Him positive duties. Although Mind, considered in the abstract, is not immediately equivalent to a Moral Order, yet the line of argument, once we have broken with agnostics and materialists, cannot but lead on to it. The first step is decisive. In affirming an Objective Intellect we lay down one parallel over against which, by equally valid methods, we may proceed to drawn a second, and affirm an Objective Conscience. The purpose of the Supreme, to which all other purposes converge, must be good, cannot conceivably be evil. And of this, too, induction furnishes proofs and tokens. The noblest achievement of a mind conversant with laws is to have established the Moral Law on adamantine foundations. Hence it is that men to whom life seems, ethically, mere disorder, without aim or purpose which they can discern, or even a struggle for existence in which good succumbs to ill, and the vilest sit in high places by reason of their wickedness, deny that First and Fairest to which idealists look up. A beautiful theory, they admit, were not experience against it. Facts are what they are; and the test of experience, to which I have myself appealed, they tell me contradicts my supposition of an overruling Providence. It is a real, not an idle speculative objection. It has been urged by serious thinkers, and deserves such answer as I can give with the aid of inductive knowledge. I will consider it, therefore, in my next article. Meanwhile, let us meditate on the grave and exquisite lines in which Wordsworth has sung of the essential harmony between Science and the Ideal of Righteousness by which, indeed, the world is governed :

> " Stern Lawgiver! yet thou dost wear
> The Godhead's most benignant grace;
> Nor know we anything so fair
> As is the smile upon thy face.
> Flowers laugh before thee on their beds,
> And fragrance in thy footing treads;
> Thou dost preserve the stars from wrong,
> And the most ancient Heavens, through thee, are fresh and strong."

WILLIAM BARRY.

A QUESTION OF GROWTH.

A WELL-BRED looking woman in a close-fitting dress of some soft black stuff, and with her hand outstretched toward him— this was what he saw standing before him ; what he heard, to his dismay, was a clear voice saying :

"You and I were introduced long ago, weren't we, Mr. Nicholson ? "

"Oh! yes indeed, long ago," he declared, taking the offered hand and striving to echo the cordiality of the greeting, while he inwardly cursed his luck that the meeting had taken place so far in the dim past that he could recall nothing of it.

The shade that fell over the lady's face when she perceived herself forgotten was but momentary, and gave place to a smile as she hastened to his relief by saying, in the same clear, cheerful tones: "How stupid of me to have lost sight of the years that have passed since then ! Perhaps you would know Margaret Somerville, though Margaret Tyler seems almost a new acquaintance."

"How could I have hesitated ?" he exclaimed, possessing himself of her hand once more in renewed greeting. "And I remember Margaret Somerville so tenderly, too."

"So do I," answered the lady laughingly. "She is, indeed, one of the tenderest memories of my life."

"Have you any kindly recollections of Fred Nicholson ? " he queried, regarding her closely and striving to trace in this self-poised woman, with the friendly, good-comrade glance that met his directly, the resemblance to the shy girl whose blue eyes always reminded him of dewy violets half-hidden.

"The way I greeted his *evolution* a moment ago answers that. I wonder if you represent the 'survival of the fittest' in Fred Nicholson," she added with a touch of what might have been coquetry in her tone.

"It is very warm. Shall we walk on the piazza awhile, and give you a chance to find out?" he suggested. "Margaret and Fred used to be partial to the piazza, do you remember? I can smell the honeysuckles now."

"And hear Lew Hamilton strumming on that old guitar while he and Flora Monroe quarreled about his discords !

Weren't they a happy set of young folks that summer ?—though Fred insisted on posing as a cynic."

"And Margaret preached to him," he continued. "She was a capital preacher and he was a good listener. Do you recollect that he always went to see her when the rest of the boys were at church ? "

Thus these two, met by chance in this Asheville boarding-house, where all sorts and conditions of men and women gathered, fell to discussing the days, more than ten years past, when Margaret Somerville had returned to the primitive village, with the shy convent ways and the elaborate convent politeness about her, and had met handsome Fred Nicholson, who seemed to her a *blasé* man of the world and a great sinner whom she must strive to save, albeit he was but twenty-five and ranted at woman's faith and the world's treachery and religion's insufficiency with the fluency of a provincial who had read Bulwer and Byron and had gotten himself jilted by a country girl. Curiously enough they spoke of their old selves in a sort of indefinite, impersonal way, so conscious were they both of the gulf which lay between that past and their present. But Mrs. Tyler laughed outright after awhile ; which made her companion exclaim : "That was Margaret Somerville's laugh, that was like your old self ; and now tell me about your new self."

He was sorry that he had asked the question when he saw her face grow grave on the instant.

"There. is little to tell," she said quietly. "You heard, of course, of my husband's death two years ago. Since then I have been living here because I am stronger in this climate, and so can work better ; for I must work ; I am too poor to live without it even if I would. And you—what brought you here ? "

"The restlessness of the times I suppose," he said. "I am tired staying on the farm and making just a thousand or two a year raising bright tobacco. I want to turn my money over and add to it faster, so I am looking for a booming town ; if I could find the boom here I should be glad, for my lungs are not strong."

She regarded him critically.

"You have the boom fever, and I am sorry ; but nothing will cure you as soon as losing some of those thousands you have made so safely. I will help you to-morrow by introducing some real-estate men. They will convince you that this is the town, beyond peradventure or mistake. I don't like that about the

weak lungs, though," she added.   "Have you still the cough
which used to trouble Fred and Margaret?"

It was very sweet to the lonely man to catch the cadence of
interest in the last words; he had heard nothing like it since his
mother's death.

"Did the cough trouble Margaret?" he asked, lingering a
little on the name; he remembered that he never called her by
it in those old days and he wondered now why he had not. "I ·
didn't know she thought much about it."

"It is a pity you did not," said Mrs. Tyler lightly; "it
might have resulted in your conversion.   Margaret used to pray
for that—those were ages of *faith*, you know."

Some inflection of bitterness, some emphasis on the word
faith made him ask:

" Are these ages of unfaith ? "

" No," she answered, noticing · the resentment in his tone,
"but they are days of knowledge."

" And faith is lovelier than knowledge."   If he meant to
pique her by that, he failed, for she replied calmly as ever:

"Yes, it is far lovelier ; and yet knowledge is faith lost in
certainty.   A girl believes all things and hopes all things ; a
woman recognizes her own and other people's limitations, and so
hopes but little."

" Margaret Somerville was not given to philosophizing," he
said.

" Margaret Tyler *does* philosophize," she replied ; " and perhaps that marks the difference between simple faith and half
knowledge.   But have you learned to play whist in all these
years?   I have, and my partner is beckoning to me now. Come
and let me find a partner for you, won't you ? "

" No, I think not.   I prefer sitting here to smoke and **dream**
about Margaret and Fred."

"I wouldn't, if I were you," she admonished him.   " **Fred**
and Margaret are dead; leave them in their graves."

" Are they past resurrecting ? " he asked, letting his voice fall
half-unconsciously into the tender tones which had once seemed
music to the convent girl's unworldly ears.   Perhaps it was the
memory of that which made the ring of sadness in Mrs. Tyler's
answer.

" Why should we wish to resurrect them ? They played their
parts."

"But did they play them to the end ? " he asked, **still**
tenderly.

She looked at him in that frank, good-comrade fashion again.

"It seems to me they did," she said simply; "and they enjoyed it very much—while it lasted"

Then she left him to his cigar and to the memories which seeing her had awakened. He saw again the old-fashioned, dilapidated North Carolina village, where Fred Nicholson had gone to make some extra money during the summer by writing for the clerk of the court. A very heart-sore and disappointed young fellow he was, for had not the cotton crop failed the year before, and had not Helen Hunter jilted him for a richer man? He recalled the day when, as he, along with other villagers, lounged around the red warehouse at the railroad station to see the one daily train come and pass, Margaret Somerville alighted from it and entered her father's carriage.

To night so vivid were those old days that he could hear again his own sneer as he remarked, when he saw her new and glittering gold medal :

"There goes another sweet girl graduate, ready to set the river on fire with her brilliancy."

And the loyal way that Edgar Hartley answered:

"She is mighty sweet, and a lot too smart for most of us fellows; but *you* can talk to her, Nicholson. Let me take you to see her Sunday."

And their Sunday call, when they sat out on the long veranda, festooned in climbing vines, and his verdict that she was not pretty, with his later decision that she was unusual.

It seemed but the evening before that he had gone to the hop expecting to find her, and was told by Flora Monroe that she would not be there, when suddenly the music and the girls and the dancing lost charms for him, and a few moments later he was standing before Margaret, as she sat in the moonlight on the honeysuckle-porch. He could see her surprise at his coming, and her swift blush when he told her *she* was not there, so he left; and then the holy sort of light which came into her face as she endeavored to explain to him some incomprehensible thing about Father G.'s having come unexpectedly that day, and her not liking to go to a dance the night before receiving Holy Communion. He felt again the influence of the subdued gentleness of her manner that night, which accorded with the moonlight and the flowers, and which made him say to her at parting:

"Pray for me to-morrow. I feel as if I had been in church."

After that he went oftener and oftener to the house, and fell to saying tender words when he got there, always uncertain of his own meaning, and even more uncertain of what she thought he meant.

Some one of the self-appointed curators of other people's affairs, of which every village has one or two, had told her about his flirtations, and she, being distrustful of him and ignorant of herself, elected to treat him as if he were flirting with her, and stood constantly upon the defensive, piquing him sometimes, puzzling him sometimes, pleasing him ever.

It was a wonderfully pleasant summer, and looking back upon it now he perceived that it was Margaret Somerville who made it so; but he was not particularly conscious of this at the time. Perhaps if she had accepted his love-making in good faith, as one might suppose a motherless, convent-bred girl would have done, it might have become serious ; but she had taken him lightly, or seemed to do so, and he had been content that she should.

When his work was done he had gone back to his home, had written to her once or twice, and had abused those nuns for making a prude of her when she refused to keep up a correspondence. Then he discovered that his farm would produce bright tobacco, and that Helen Hunter had a young sister far prettier than Margaret or than Helen herself. He heard of Margaret's marriage with a degree of resentment, but in the end he accepted it, and thought more and more vaguely and infrequently of her and the summer they spent together until her unexpected presence in this Asheville boarding-house called up the past with sudden vivid distinctness. His cigar burnt his fingers at this point and awoke him to realities. "Hang it all!" he exclaimed as he threw away the stump, "I must have been a fool. Why couldn't I see that girl liked me throughout? If I had—"

If he had—ah! well, who can tell what the outcome of an "if" would have been ?

Mrs. Tyler did not play whist to her partner's edification that evening. There was a far-away look in her eyes and a smile on her lips. Was she, too, seeing the honeysuckle-porch ?

Whatever she saw, she did an unusual thing when she got to her room for a woman as devoid as she was of personal vanity. She walked straight to the mirror and studied the reflection there closely. "Men forget," she said as she turned away. "To think of his failing to recognize me ! But somehow he disappoints me. I wonder if I have outgrown him, or he me ? "

Then she became absorbed in a book on her table, and to a degree forgot the incident of the evening. She was a very busy woman, having long ago decided that to live out of one's self is the only way worth living. And yet she dreamed that night that she was a girl again, and that as she stood on the river's bank she blew a thistle, saying the while the magic words: "He loves me, he loves me not"; and she awoke before the thistle was blown away.

II.

There comes in the month of February a week or two that seems a foretaste of the spring, when the sunlight shines with delicate suggestion of vernal warmth, and the gardens send their hints in the shape of hyacinths and crocuses, and the woods whisper of coming joys through the trailing arbutus, which graciously smiles from its bed of moss or its shelter of red colt's-foot.

Nicholson had chanced to reach Asheville just at this enchanted time, and it seemed to him as if he, too, were awakening. The world within doors and without appeared full of revelations to him. He had lived on his farm and read the newspapers and an occasional novel, varying the monotony by a yearly two weeks' trip to New York or some other city, where he usually took in whatever theatrical performances were on the boards during his stay, and was lunched and dined and shown "the sights of the town" by the crowd of good fellows from his section of North Carolina and Virginia (his farm was near the line) who had drifted to the great centres to better or to worsen their fortunes.

His county people respected him and looked up to him—the older ones remembered his father and grandfather; the working men of all classes admired a man whose farm was made to be so productive; the young men envied his clothes—was he not known to have them made by a Baltimore tailor, and did he not possess a full dress suit?—and the girls felt themselves honored when noticed by a man who usually treated young women with a most attractively polite indifference? Who is it that has declared a man to be the result of his surroundings? Fred Nicholson had, if the truth must be told, grown to accept this universal good opinion as his due, and enjoyed, though but half-consciously, the pleasing certainty that he was not as other men, inasmuch as birth and breeding had lifted him a degree above them. But here in Asheville he found himself in close daily contact with men and women from everywhere, with all degrees of culture, and he was startled to discover how little he knew of the world's thought on any of the thousand "isms" in which much of it had crystallized.

Yet the greatest revelation to him was Margaret Tyler. He saw her easily and quietly fall into whatever discussion arose around her, holding her positions with a firmness which seldom became insistence; ready to turn from these graver talks to lend a hand in whatever scheme might be devised for the amusement of the house; and displaying a many-sidedness of information and of sympathies which amazed him in her whom he remembered as being a self-conscious and scrupulous girl, whose womanhood he would have predicted to be strong but straight-laced.

There was a sort of self-ignoring about Mrs. Tyler which never became self-effacement; her individuality displayed itself in her every action—most of all, perhaps, in the way that she went to her daily work from among these people, who had no need to toil, and who regarded her pityingly because she was obliged to win her bread.

Although he did not put it into words, she affected him much as the weather of that Asheville February did, bright and genial, with a touch of cold in it, and with an occasional haze which obscured the landscape while it gave charms to it, and which might tell of past storms or future changes. There was in her, too, or he began to think there was, the same subtle suggestion of unexhausted warmth and promise of a spring.

The comparison took shape with him when one day, as they were walking together, a little child ran toward them with handfuls of white hyacinths and yellow jonquils, plucked from one of the good old-fashioned gardens in the town.

"Please, Mrs. Tyler, pin 'em on," pleaded the child; "they'se pretty, just like you."

"Do you think she is pretty?" asked Nicholson with a smile which emboldened the little one to answer:

"Yes; don't you."

Margaret glanced at him with a laughing challenge in her eye; he had often bemoaned Margaret Somerville's lack of beauty.

"No," he said, looking down at the child; "I don't think she is a bit pretty."

"That's all you know," was the small champion's contemptuous response. "I guess if she teached you Sundays and told you 'bout the child Jesus, and the way he used to work like us children have to do, you'd think she was. An't you pretty, Mrs. Tyler?" And the questioner's upturned face was full of simple confidence. Mrs Tyler knew everything, of course.

Margaret stooped and kissed the child.

"I am pretty to you, little one, because you love me."

"Now pin on the flowers; then he'll be bound to call you pretty, too," suggested the young diplomat.

"Let me pin 'em on, won't you?" Saying which she climbed up on the fence and covered the bosom of the black dress with the delicate blossoms, leaning back against the arm which Margaret had thrown around her to admire her work and to glance up at the eyes which regarded her tenderly.

"She was right," said Nicholson as they walked away. "You are pretty when you look like that. Your face was a study when you were holding that child."

"I think most childless women have that sort of yearning love for children," she answered with a sigh. "The hours I spend with them are my best. Their love fills my life's void."

"I don't like to hear you speak of your life's void," he remonstrated. "I never saw a fuller life than yours seems to be, and you are always so cheerful and bright."

Somehow the words were discordant to her; and yet she had no right to expect him to understand. Why should he?

"Did you ever, as a child, watch the negro weavers putting the cloth in the loom?" she asked irrelevantly. "I remember how careful they were to get the warp right, and then how easily they would shuttle the filling back and forth, as if it were nothing much. Well, that is just what I am in the world —only a part of the filling. If I can brighten the warp here and there my mission is accomplished."

"If you were any one but you," said Nicholson indignantly, "I should call that speech a barefaced 'fishing for a compliment.' But it is just like you to make it. You have always undervalued yourself; it has led you to make mistakes in the past and will do so again. I live in dread of hearing you say that you have decided to take the veil—a woman like you going and shutting herself up in a convent to teach ragged children! But I should not be a bit surprised at it—it would be of a piece with that 'filling' speech."

Such a masculine tirade as this is calculated to please a woman; somehow it makes her conscious of her own superior reasonableness.

"It is a pity for me to disappoint you," said Mrs. Tyler, more brightly, "but I am afraid I shall have to—I have no vocation for a convent life, unfortunately; though why unfortunately?" she continued more to herself than to him. "God's work needs many hands; if my part of it lies in the world then I should be satisfied—and I am; I am generally well content."

They had stopped and were facing one of those vistas of mountains and forest that constantly break on the vision through the streets of this mountain town.

"Do you know," said Nicholson, "sometimes you make me have a sensation of standing on tip-toe to reach you—or better, perhaps, to say you seem to be away up on a mountain and I am trying to climb to you?"

"How very fatiguing my society must be!" exclaimed Mrs. Tyler with the unction of one who had experienced a mountain climb. "Let us turn back and talk about something else—Miss Cunningham, for instance. She has half a million in her own right."

"I would rather talk real estate just now," said Nicholson, "if you can tell me the probable price of such a lot as that one there."

She could and did; and discussed values and investments, and profits and losses with such practical comprehension of the subject that, as they reached home, he complimented her by saying:

"You would have made a fortune if you had been a man."

"Heaven forbid!" she ejaculated. "It would be the last thing I would think of."

"Yet you spoke appreciatively of Miss Cunningham's half-million," he reminded her.

"Did I say anything against *marrying* a fortune?" she queried.

"Who said anything of marrying at all?" he asked with significant obtuseness.

She made no reply and started up the stairs, when he stopped her.

"Won't you do something for me?" he asked. "Won't you wear those flowers this evening. I hate to see you always wrapped in black."

She hesitated and a bright blush suffused her face; it was as if Margaret Somerville had been resurrected, Nicholson thought.

"Please do," he pleaded; "they make you look young again."

"Which means that I usually look weighed down by age," she said laughing.

"Let it mean anything you choose," he replied with the daring frankness he had with women, "only wear the flowers."

That evening at tea some one remarked that Mrs. Tyler had lightened her mourning and pointed to the bouquet of white hyacinths on her breast; but Nicholson noticed that Miss Cunningham wore the jonquils.

Asheville, N. C.   F. C. FARINHOLT.

(TO BE CONCLUDED IN THE JULY NUMBER.)

THE WARFARE OF SCIENCE.*

I.

FOR some fifteen years, Dr. White, ex-President of Cornell University, has been engaged in describing what he calls "the great sacred struggle for the liberty of science," and combating for this liberty. What is the hostile power with which Dr. White, in the name of science, is engaged in warfare? It is "interference with science in the supposed interest of religion."

I do not propose to contend against science, the liberty of science, or against the entire plea of Dr. White as the advocate of this liberty. All I wish to do is to offer a little aid to those who are interested in the subject, in clearing away misapprehensions and perplexities concerning the attitude of the Catholic religion and Catholic authority toward science in its present common acceptation, and toward scientific investigation.

At the outset, some general considerations having a wider scope than .our immediate topic may be allowed.

What is science in the most general sense? Subjectively, it is the reflective, intellectual, and certain knowledge which the mind has of the objects of knowledge. Objectively, it is all the knowable; being and truth in all their latitude as the adequate object of the intellect; in so far as.this object has been actually brought within the domain of subjective cognition.

Philosophy and History are included in this general defini-· tion, as well as Physics. No matter what the source of know-· ledge, whether sense or intellect, intuition, deductive or inductive ˎreasoning, experience or testimony, whatever is really known is an object of science. There may be controversy respecting objects or modes of thought, as to whether mental apprehensions and judgments are valid.and true; but when once the adequation between the intellect and some real object is admitted, there can be no reasonable dispute of the right of admission into the circle of science.

In the case of a divine revelation of truths and facts, all that is certainly known in this way must also be included within the circle of science. If the fact of revelation is certainly known, it

* *The Warfare of Science.* By Andrew Dickson White, LL.D., President of Cornell University. New York: D. Appleton & Co., 1890. Articles in *The Popular Science Monthly,* by the same author.

is *ipso facto* an object of science. If the contents of the revelation are known with certitude, they are, so far forth, objects of
science. The testimony of God is the surest and most rational
ground for an intellectual judgment that whatever is disclosed by
a divine revelation, or attested as true, even although knowable
or known in a purely human way, is certainly true, and cannot
be doubted without doing violence to reason.

All science is from God, and is a rethinking of his thoughts.
"Alle Klarheit im Menschen ist ein Nachdenken der Gedanken
Gottes" (Leo). The intellect is from God, and understands and
reasons by principles which have their foundation in His essence.
All nature, corporeal and spiritual, is a manifestation of the
thoughts of God. The book of nature and the book of revelation are both alike from God, and are opened before men, that
they may read therein and understand, as far as they are able to
do so.

It is self-evident that there can be no contradictions between
any leaves of the divine book. There can be no opposition
between any one part of science and any other. All are really
and intrinsically in harmony. All are scintillations from the same
light. Science has no warfare except with ignorance. One kind
of truth cannot be in conflict with any other kind. Every
branch of science must recognize every other. Every investigation is bound to recognize every fact and every truth which can
justify its claim to be accepted, from whatever source the
knowledge of it is derived. Metaphysics and Mathematics,
Astronomy and Geology, Biology and Mechanics, Cosmology
and Chemistry, Psychology and Physiology, Theology and Cosmogony, Philosophy and all branches of Physics must admit of
mutual control in their just limits, must not ignore each other,
and must take due cognizance of historical facts, so far as these
have a bearing upon any theories which run upon historical ground.

Scientific civil war is not conflict of science with science, but
of science with unscientific theories pretending to be scientific, or
of theories which may or may not have some real or apparent
probability with each other. The struggle is caused by *nescience*
on one or both sides.

As to the attitude of Christian Theology toward rational philosophy and all the sciences subordinate to it, the same reason
runs for determining the question, as in the case of the relation
between the purely natural sciences. In so far as there is truth
in both, they must be in harmony and cannot be in opposition.
Neither can they ignore each other. Discord and struggle among

those who contend in the name of religion and in the name of science, arise from mistakes and misunderstandings on one side or on both sides, concerning that which pertains. to revealed truth, or that which pertains to natural science, or concerning both objects at once.

Concord and unity are promoted by progress and increase of knowledge in all directions, on all sides. Real progress is an advance from partial science toward more complete science, toward objective truth, by investigation which tends to eliminate the nescience from which imperfections and errors in theories and systems proceed. It is an approximation toward absolute, universal truth. Science, in the strict and proper sense, is a knowledge of entities in their causes, which is perfected in proportion to its approach to a comprehension of the deepest causes, both efficient and final. The lines of progress from all points of departure must therefore converge toward the same object. Retrograde and deviating movements are not progressive, although the mere change of place and the velocity of transition over distance may present an illusive appearance of progression. All interference from any cause whatever which hinders movement on the true lines is an evil, and all interference which hinders or counteracts retrogression or deviation, if it is legitimate, is a benefit to the cause of science, and a favorable influence upon investigation.

Interference is of two kinds: a moral interference, by an opposition which endeavors to bring some professedly scientific movement into discredit as essentially bad and dangerous, or at least futile and irrational; and an interference by the exercise of authority. It is legitimate, if it is the exercise of a just and rightful influence or authority, without infringement of other rights, employed in a reasonable manner.

The particular contention with which we are at present concerned relates to both kinds of interference, on the part of persons possessing influence or authority, which they are charged with using against "science" "in the supposed interest of religion." Of course, the term "science" is used in that restricted sense to which it is confined in common parlance, and therefore placed in logical opposition to "religion" and all that is regarded as included under that term. This will be well understood by all without any formal definition. The contention is chiefly directed against the exercise of authority and influence, ecclesiastical and theological, by rulers and doctors in the Catholic Church, and it is this alone of which I shall take any notice.

Let us first inquire what it is which makes the struggle of science for liberty especially "sacred," and what is the good to be attained by its untrammeled development. The desire for knowledge is innate in rational nature. Its object is truth ; and liberty to seek for truth, to imbibe it freely, to keep and profess it, is good, and a ·divinely-given right ; because it gives freedom to the rational part of man to develop itself and advance toward intellectual perfection. The chief reason and end of life is, however, ethical, and intellectual improvement is subordinate, in individual men and in the race, to the ultimate end for which man was created.

The warfare of science is "sacred" only in so far as it is elevated and ennobled by an ethical character, and is waged in view of ennobling the complete rational nature of man in all its relations ; and that not merely for certain proximate ends, but for an ultimate end. "Alle Entwicklung menschlicher Dinge hat die Aufgabe einer Verklärung zur Freiheit in Gott, zu welcher der Mensch ursprünglich erschaffen ward" (Leo). Intellectually, this freedom is liberation from ignorance and error by enlightenment from the true, the beautiful, and the good, which have their source in the divine essence ; by the adequation of the intellect to the reality of being, its connatural object. The warfare of science is against ignorance, error, falsehood, which are a privation of this equality and of the liberty which springs from it. In this warfare no particular species of science stands alone. In the purely natural domain, philosophy, literature, art, and all special sciences are allies. Morally, this freedom is liberation from all that which is degrading to man and mankind, in the ethical order. In this order rational ethics cannot be separated from religion, although it is to a certain degree distinct from formal and explicit theology. Religion takes precedence of all causes and factors in civilization taken in its entire comprehension, in the complete development of humanity into freedom in God. All the elements and instruments of intellectual and moral perfection must be measured by this criterion and judged by reference to this standard. Whence and wherefore is the world, what is the origin and the end of man, what is his highest good, and in what way can his interior and exterior relations be reduced to order in view of his perfectibility as a rational being? These are the great questions which the mind of man wants to have answered. The knowledge of the truth in regard to these objects of spontaneous and inevitable inquiry is the highest science, the only science of supreme and indispensable importance.

All that human intelligence and effort have been able to accomplish in this line by the cultivation of the purely rational and natural faculties of man, and by their exercise with the aid of all means and instruments at their command, has been proved by long and wide experience, not, indeed, to be a total failure, but to be a shortcoming. The evidence of the moral necessity of a divine revelation to supply the inadequacy of rational philosophy, ethics, and the regulating principles of civilization, is abundant and conclusive. And beyond this the perpetual, irrepressible haunting of the idea and aspiration, the reminiscence and the expectation of a supernatural end and destiny for mankind, bear witness to the absolute necessity of a revelation of truths and precepts above the scope of reason. This divine revelation, begun at the creation of man, completed in Jesus Christ, is accredited as a fact by overwhelming evidence. The being and veracity of God are evident by a metaphysical demonstration. The truth of the Christian revelation is evident by a demonstration which is directly moral, but reductively metaphysical. It is irrational to deny or even to doubt the truth of either Theism or Christianity. It is an imperative demand of reason and conscience to give assent to whatever has been revealed, without the need of any other motive than absolute trust in the veracity of God, who is the absolute truth in being, knowing, and revealing. This revelation must take precedence of all rational science, but it cannot contradict it, and does not dispense with it and set it aside. Science, literature, and art must be ancillary to religion ; but it is a greater dignity and splendor which are given to them when they are appointed maids of honor to their queen, than those which they possess by their native nobility.

Christianity inaugurated an intellectual, moral, and social regeneration of mankind, not yet more than partially consummated. Christ took the religious tradition entrusted to the Jews, the Greek philosophy, and the organizing genius of Rome, entwined these silver strands with the golden strand of his own doctrine into the fourfold cord of his New Law, to bind around all nations and peoples, and draw them to himself. This achievement, which he accomplished from the cross, suffices by itself to prove his claim to be the divine Creator, Redeemer, and Sovereign Lord of the world. "I came into the world to bear witness to the Truth." "What is Truth ?" asked anxious, bewildered, doubting Pilate, as the mouthpiece of perplexed humanity seeking for truth. Historical Christianity answers the question : "I am the Truth :—this is Life, to know Thee, the true God and Jesus Christ, whom Thou hast sent."

Christianity adopted and baptized the entire family of the sciences, arts, political and social institutions of heathen descent. They reflourished in the new civilization of the, new world of Christendom, as the earth entered into a new stage of development out of the foregoing conditions of the Tertiary period. The great work began during the early age of struggle with heathenism and persecution by pagan Roman emperors.

And here I will let Monsignor Audisio speak for me in his beautiful language :

" We find in Christianity two very remarkable prerogatives. The first is, that it began by the reformation of morals. No subtle and sonorous disputes at the beginning, but the grand and magnanimous virtues which denote souls reintegrated in the ways of righteousness. The second prerogative is, that while the doctrines of all the philosophical and religious sects descended from sages to the people, as a work or product of human intelligence, Christianity, on the contrary, arose from the bosom of the people, which was incapable of inventing it, and seized on the intelligence of sages, not to perfect itself, but to perfect them. *We believe in Jesus Christ, we believe in his apostles, we believe in his ministers.* Such was the cry of the first Christians, the cry of the martyrs, the cry not of academies but of faith ; a faith inspired from on high, supported by public, manifest, invincible monuments. It was not academies which defined and perpetuated this faith, but a moral tradition remounting to its source, propagated and guarded by all the churches, under the magistracy of the bishops and the general presidency of the successor of Peter. The learned as well as the ignorant bowed the head under the yoke of this faith, which was proportioned to all minds and independent of all. This was the first age ; faith preceded science.

" In the second, the faith had already profoundly shaken and triumphantly occupied the schools, the army, the senate, the court of the Cæsars. Then reason, the natural revelation of God, reflecting upon the supernatural, unchangeable truths of the faith, and making them the object of its meditations, began to trace the first lineaments of Christian science, and the erudite voice of the apologists was heard. To refute calumnies, to demonstrate with invincible logic the truth of prophecies, the certainty of miracles, and consequently the divinity of the new religion ; moreover, to attack and mortally wound the divinities of paganism and their adorers, with their iniquities and infamies ; such were the enterprises of reason become Christian, enterprises so grand that they show admirably what a vast and sublime career the Gospel opened to intelligent minds. The pagans were stupefied, and the emperors returned no answer except silence and the sword.

"At the end of the second century, and at the beginning of the third, we see able hands applied to gather up these separated threads, to co-ordinate and construct the science of the faith. This phenomenon appeared with special *éclat* in the Christian school of Alexandria. This city being, so to speak, the *entrepôt* of all the philosophies, Divine Providence wisely made it the seat of a flourishing and solid Christian philosophy. There, in the midst of the degradation of pagan sciences, arose the *Model of future Universities and Academies.* There the Catholic idea, with the noble *cortège* of profane sciences and letters, expanded itself and formed an admirable system firmly linked together. The Holy Scriptures, studied in their ancient, original languages, were explained, commented, vindicated in an orderly manner; the foundations of philosophy and theology were cleared up, discussed, and mutually bound together. Apologetics and controversy were elevated to such a point as to confute in a peremptory manner the plagiarizing philosophers of the eighteenth century.

"This marvellous transformation of pagan into Christian philosophy, and of the simple faith which adores into a scientific and doctrinal faith, which, while respecting the impenetrable sanctuary of revealed truths, exposes their foundations, develops their conclusions, applies their consequences—this magnificent work received its principal augmentation under the pontificate of St. Pontianus (A.D. 232-237) and through the genius of Origen."*

This was, indeed, a sacred warfare of faith, science, and heroic virtue, carried on at Rome in the catacombs and at Alexandria in the schools, against ignorance, error, vice, and all that degrades the rational nature of man, and which the Catholic Church wages unceasingly against all the evil powers which seek to bring mankind into intellectual and moral servitude.

The necessity of sending this paper to the press obliges me to cut it short, and await a future occasion for bringing my remarks closer to the point at issue.

AUGUSTINE F. HEWIT.

---

* *Histoire des Papes sous les Empereurs païens.* Par G. Audisio, Chanoine de S. Pierre et Professeur à la Sapience. Traduite de l'Italien, p. 303.

THE LIFE OF FATHER HECKER.*

CHAPTER XXV.

BEGINNINGS OF THE PAULIST COMMUNITY.

DURING the seven months of Father Hecker's stay in Rome the band of American missionaries were busily occupied. Missions were given in the following order: Newark, N. J.; Poughkeepsie, Cold Spring on the Hudson, and Utica, N. Y.; Brandywine, Del.; Trenton, N. J.; Burlington, Brandon, East and West Rutland, Vt., and Plattsburgh, Saratoga, and Little Falls, N. Y. All these labors were undertaken subject to the authority of the Redemptorist Provincial and in a spirit of entire obedience. The mission at Little Falls closed on Palm Sunday, March 28, and the missionaries, with the exception of Father Baker, who was sent to Annapolis, Md., returned to the Redemptorist house in Third Street, New York. On the Tuesday after Easter, April 6, 1858, the official copy of the Pope's decision reached them, and they bade farewell to their Redemptorist brethren and to the community in which they had spent so many happy years, and witnessed, as Father Hewit has written, "so many edifying examples of high virtue and devoted zeal, to enter upon a new and untried undertaking."

Archbishop Kenrick, as soon as he heard of this, made a determined effort to secure Father Baker for the diocese of Baltimore, but the latter never for a moment faltered in his purpose to cast his lot with his brethren, and the archbishop gave up his claim upon him at the request of Cardinal Barnabo.

Their engagements called for two more missions before the season ended—one at Watertown, N. Y., and the other at St. Bridget's Church, New York City. The first of these opened on the 18th of April, and while waiting for that date the Fathers lived with Mr. George Hecker in Rutger's Place, saying Mass in his private chapel and following their religious rule as far as circumstances allowed, continuing meantime to obey Father Walworth, their former superior of the missions. They journeyed to Watertown, fearful lest the faculties for giving the Papal blessing and the mission indulgences should not arrive there in time. But late on Saturday night, April 17, they were received, much to the joy of the Fathers.

Here occurred a noteworthy coincidence. Watertown was at that time in the diocese of Albany, of which Bishop McCloskey was then the ordinary. He had received Father Hecker into the Church and had been his first guide in the spiritual life, and now he was the first to publicly welcome his brethren at the beginning of their new career. The following is from a letter of his to Father Walworth in answer to one announcing the recent changes:

"I am happy to hear that your difficulties have at length received their solution, and in a manner, I presume, as satisfactory as you could well expect. The future must now in great measure depend upon yourselves. You will, of course, have difficulties to surmount and prejudices to encounter, but I trust that with God's blessing your new community when once organized will continue from day to day to gain increased stability and strength, and be enabled to carry out successfully all its laudable aims for the good of our holy religion. The faculties already given you in this diocese you will not consider as being withdrawn by the act of your separation from the Redemptorist order, and there is nothing that I know of to interfere with your proposed mission in Watertown."

During the mission at St. Bridget's—that is, in the first half of the month of May—Father Hecker arrived in New York and measures were at once taken for the practical organization of the new community. Nothing was done hurriedly; a fair and full consideration of all questions from every point of view, which lasted until early in the month of July, enabled each one clearly to understand his new relation in its every aspect. Father Walworth not being entirely in agreement with the other others, withdrew to the diocese of Albany and took charge of a parish; he returned again in 1861, remaining with the community till 1865, when his health becoming quite shattered, he reluctantly decided to withdraw altogether. It need hardly be said that the relations between him and the community have always been most cordial. Meantime the others, Fathers Hecker, Hewit, Deshon, and Baker, organized by electing the first-named the Superior, and drew up and signed what was termed a Programme of Rule. This was submitted to Archbishop Hughes and by him approved and signed on July 7, 1858. The Apostle of the Gentiles was chosen as patron, and the name selected was, The Missionary Priests of St. Paul the Apostle, which has been popularized into Paulists. The habit agreed upon was in form somewhat like that of the students of the Propaganda in Rome, black throughout, with a narrow linen

collar and buttoned across the breast, being held at the waist by
a cincture.

The Programme of Rule adopts an order of spiritual exercises similar to that observed by the Fathers while Redemptorists. A perpetual voluntary agreement takes the place of the vows
as the security of stability, the members affirming that they
are fully determined to promote their sanctification by leading
a life in all essential respects similar to that led in the religious
orders. Besides the chastity imposed upon them by the priesthood
the other evangelical counsels of obedience and poverty are adopted
and their observance enjoined upon the members, together with
the daily and periodical exercises of community life. As to the
external vocation, the missions are named as the basis of general apostolic labors, and parish work also, though in a subordinate degree. The entire document looks forward to a complete Rule to be drawn up and submitted to the Holy See
at a future day, for which it actually furnished the outlines
some twenty years afterwards. The approval of the Programme
of a Rule by the Archbishop of New York gave the Fathers the
canonical status anticipated by the decree *Nuper nonnulli*. This
was confirmed by an official permission of the Holy See to the
Archbishop of New York to establish the Paulist Institute in his
diocese, with the consent of his suffragans, which was asked for
and obtained.

A little more than a fortnight after these events Father
Hecker wrote as follows to a friend:

"Before leaving Rome our Holy Father Pius IX. gave us
his special blessing for the commencement of our new organization, promised us any privileges we might need to carry on our
missionary labors, and held out the hope of his sanction, in
proper time, of the rules which we might make. In my last
visit to his Eminence Cardinal Barnabo he gave me advice how
to organize, what steps were to be taken from time to time,
and expressed a most lively interest in our undertaking. The
same did Monsignor Bedini. On my return we organized as
advised, wrote out an outline of our new institution and submitted it to the ordinary of this diocese, the initiatory step of
all such undertakings. He gave it his cordial approbation, and
said that he found no word to alter, to add, or improve. Thus
we are so far regularly canonically instituted.

"Our aim is to lead a strict religious life in community,
starting with the voluntary principle; leaving the question of

vows to further experience, counsel, and indications of Divine Providence.   Our, principal work is the missions, such as we have hitherto given, but we are not excluded from other apostolic labors as the wants of the Church may demand or develop. . . . We begin early this fall our campaign of missions, and we never had before us so fine a list.   One thing I may say, and I trust without boasting, we are of one mind and heart, resolved to labor and die for Jesus Christ, for the good of His holy Church, for the advancement of the Catholic faith.   We have the encouragement of a number of bishops, and also, we trust, the prayers, sympathy, and assistance of the faithful.   We shall have to face obstacles, opposition from friends and foes; but if we are the right kind of men and have the virtues which such a position as ours demands, our trials will only strengthen us and make us the better Christians.   Every good work must expect opposition from pious men, and our minds are made up to that."

After St. Bridget's mission the little community found itself homeless, and it remained so till the spring of the year 1859. But during part of this period Mr. George Hecker, taking his family to the country, gave up his whole house to the Fathers, servants and all, making provision for the supply of every want in the most generous manner.   For the greater portion of the time, however, especially between missions in the winter and spring of 1858–9, the Fathers depended for temporary shelter upon the hospitality of friends among the clergy and laity, even lodging for a short while in a respectable boarding-house in Thirteenth street, at a convenient distance from several churches and chapels where Mass could be said daily.

But in the spring of 1858 arrangements had been made with Archbishop Hughes for establishing a house and parish in New York.   The present site of St. Paul's Church and convent, then in the midst of a suburban wilderness, was chosen, and, by dint of hasty collections from private friends and with the help of a very large gift from Mr. George Hecker, money enough was paid down to obtain the deeds.   Sixtieth Street was not quite opened at the time, and this part of Ninth Avenue existed only on paper; but by energetic efforts made by all the Fathers and their friends, and by personal appeals in every direction, especially in the down-town parishes in which they had given missions, sufficient funds were raised to clear the ground and lay the foundations of a building which was to include both con-

vent and church. Early in the summer of 1858 circulars asking
assistance had been sent out to the clergy of the United States,
and by this means also a considerable amount was secured, the
very first answer with a handsome donation coming from Father
Early, President of Georgetown College. In the spring of 1859
the Fathers rented a frame house on Sixtieth street, just west of
Broadway, fitted up a little chapel in it, and lived there in
community till the new house was finished.

The corner-stone of the new structure was laid by Archbishop
Hughes on Trinity Sunday, June 19, 1859, in the presence of
an immense concourse of people. During that summer and fall
every effort was made to keep the builders at work. The task
was no easy one. The times were hard, the country still suffering from the effects of the financial crisis of 1857, and financial
depression being aggravated by the ominous outlook in the political world. But the house was finally completed, and was blessed
by Father Hecker on the 24th of November, the feast of St.
John of the Cross, one of his very special patrons. This was
within a few weeks of his fortieth birthday. On the 27th of the
same month, the first Sunday of Advent, the chapel was blessed
and Solemn Mass was celebrated in it. Thereafter the Fathers
had to act as parish priests as well as missionaries. A few
weeks before this the first recruit joined the little band in the
person of Father Robert Beverly Tillotson, a convert, who,
though an American, had been for some time a member of Dr.
Newman's Oratory. He was a charming preacher and a noble
character, much beloved by all the fathers, and especially by
Father Hecker. He died, deeply mourned, in the summer of
1868, having given the community nine years of most valuable
service. He came just in time to set free three of the Fathers
for missionary duty, the other two remaining in care of the
parish. This was at first small enough in numbers, though in
territory it reached from Fifty-second Street to very near Man-
hattanville. The accession of Father Alfred Young, of the diocese
of Newark, and the return of Father Walworth considerably
relieved the pressure, though the rapid growth of the parish and
the widening scope of the community's labors kept every one
busy enough.

The newly-founded Paulist community was heartily welcomed
by both clergy and people. Missions were given in various parts
of the country, applications being often declined for want of time
and missionaries. Several prelates, among whom were the Archbishops of Baltimore and Cincinnati, wrote to Father Hecker offer-

ing to establish the community in their dioceses; Bishop. Bayley, of Newark, also wished to secure the Fathers, and he was especially urgent in his request. One has but to know the intensely conservative spirit of the Catholic hierarchy and clergy to appreciate how stainless must have been the record of the Fathers to elicit such testimonials of good-will just after they had fought a hard battle on the ground of authority and obedience. As to the Catholic laity, the following extract from a letter of the poet George H. Miles, whose early death some years after was so deeply lamented, shows how they regarded the new community. It was written from Baltimore under date of August 13, 1858:

" MY VERY DEAR FATHER HECKER: . . . Since we last parted you have been to me one of those grand, good memories we take to heart and cherish. I have loved you better than you could believe, for I felt that in the extremity of sorrow or temptation you were the man and the priest I would have recourse to, could my own wish be granted. You are not wrong in considering me a friend; that is, if much love may atone for little power to befriend. . . . *Providentially*, it now appears, you men have always had an individual force that detached you completely from your *confrères*. To me and to the multitudes you were never Redemptorists, never Liguorians, but Hecker, Walworth, Hewit, Deshon, Baker. I mean to utter nothing disrespectful to the society which has blessed this nation in training and developing you and your new body of preachers, but I maintain that you stood so completely apart from that society, so absolutely individualized, that, etc."

The three years following Father Hecker's return from Rome were exceedingly active ones. The missions were maintained, money collected for the purchase of the property and the building of the convent at the corner of Fifty-ninth Street and Ninth Avenue, and, after the opening of the new church in November, 1859, the regular duties of a city parish were added.

"I am hard at work," writes Father Hecker to a friend, in the very midst of these labors, "in soliciting subscriptions for our convent and temporary church. I have worked hard in my life, but this is about the hardest. However, it goes. I had, a couple of weeks ago, a donation of $200 from a Protestant. Yesterday a subscription of $50 from another. *Sursum Corda* and go ahead, is my cry!" And, indeed, he was full of courage and confidence in the future, all his letters breathing a cheerful spirit.

Before giving Father Hecker's principles for community life, which we will do in the next chapter, it may be well to say a few words more about the attitude in which he and his companions had been placed, by the action of the Holy See, toward the Catholic idea of authority.

Just as he was about to sail for America he wrote to his brother George; "I return from Rome with my enthusiasm unchilled and my resolution to labor for the conversion of our people intensified and strengthened. I feel that the knowledge and experience which I have acquired are most necessary for the American Fathers in their present delicate position." And in truth his stay in Rome had prepared him for the new responsibilities in store for him. His sufferings there had purified his motives, his humiliations and his anguish had taught him the need of reliance, total and loving, on Divine Providence. He had studied authority in its chief seat, and he had done so with the depth of impression which a man on trial for his life experiences of the power of the advocates and the dignity of the judges. The result of that trial was of infinite benefit. The test of genuine liberty is its consonance with lawful authority, and in Father Hecker's case the newest liberty had been roughly arraigned before the most venerable authority known among men, tried by fire, and sent forth with Rome's broad seal of approval.

Without doubt the chief endeavor of authority should be to win the allegiance of free and aspiring spirits; but, on the other hand, no one should be so firmly convinced of the rights of the external order of God as the man who is called to minister to the aspirations of human liberty.

No man ought to be so vividly conscious of the prerogatives of authority as he who lays claim to a vocation to extol the worth of liberty. It was, therefore, fitting that Father Hecker should learn his lesson of the prerogatives of the visible Church from that teacher who has no master among men. At the same time Rome sent forth in the person of Father Hecker a living and powerful argument addressed to this Republic, that the Catholic Church is worthy of the heartiest allegiance of our citizens.

This providential aspect of the case should not be forgotten. When Father Hecker had been expelled from the Redemptorists it might have been thought that he was done for, and that if he had ever had a mission it had suffered total shipwreck, whether deserved or not. But in reality the very reverse was the truth. The disgrace of expulsion, the sudden horror of being thus cast out, a calamity which set him forth to all Catholics as a ruined

priest, had but served to bring him into the notice of the supreme authority of the Church. And when in this God had
wrought all His work His servant was purified within and mightily
strengthened without. In his inmost soul he was conscious of
his divine mission with a deeper certitude than ever before; and
as he began his apostolate he bore on his arm the buckler of
Rome, against which all the darts of enemies, if any should arise,
would strike harmless and fall to the ground.

It was fitting that the Paulist community, appealing to the
men and women of to-day with the credentials as well of their own
individual independence as of the good will of the Pope and the
Bishops, should be launched into existence from the very deck
of Peter's bark, and furnished with all the testimonials of ecclesiastical authority short of canonical sanction. This was the more
proper because, in a few years after the beginning of the community, European revolutionists were to be scourged with the
Syllabus, whose every word agonized the souls of unworthy advocates of liberty. That Pontifical document has created a literature of its own in comment and explanation, some tying more
knots in every lash and others mitigating its severity or palliating
the errors it smote with such pitiless rigor. But the best interpretation of the Syllabus is the Paulist community. It is a
body of free men whose origin was the joint result of the personal workings of the Holy Spirit in the soul of a man who
loved civil and political freedom with a mighty love, and the
decision of the highest court of Catholicity declaring him worthy
of trust as an exponent of the Christian faith. If the Syllabus
shows what the Church thinks of those who in the guise of free-
men are conspirators against religion and public order, the
approval of the Paulist community shows the Church's attitude
towards men worthy to be free.

Nor was Rome's course chosen without weighing the consequences, without a full estimate of the public significance of
the act. Father Hecker's adversaries fixed upon him every
stigma of radicalism and rebellion possible in a good but deluded priest. For seven long months they poured into ears
which instinctively feared revolt in the name of liberty, every accusation his doings and sayings could be made to give color
to, in order to prove that he and the American Fathers were
tainted with false liberalism. And he seemed to lend himself to
their purpose. His guileless tongue spoke to the cardinals, prelates, and professors of Rome about nothing so much as freedom, and its kinship with Catholicity. He seemed to have no

refuge but the disclosure of the very secrets of his soul. Dur. ing those months of incessant accusation and defence. Father Hecker talked Rome's high dignitaries into full knowledge of himself, until they saw the cause mirrored in the man and gave approval to both. Some, like Barnabo, were actuated by the quick sympathy of free natures; others, like Pius IX., arrived at a decision by the slower processes of the removal of prejudice from an honest mind, and the careful comparing of Father Hecker's principles with the fundamental truths of religion.

CHAPTER XXVI.

FATHER HECKER'S IDEA OF A RELIGIOUS COMMUNITY.

The beginnings of the Paulist community having been sketched, it is now in order to state the principles with which Father Hecker, guided no less by supernatural intuition than by enlightened reason, intended it should be inspired; and this shall be done as nearly as possible in his own words. The following sentences, found in one of his diaries and quoted some chapters back, embody what may be deemed his ultimate principle:

"It is for this we are created: that we may give a new and individual expression of the absolute in our own peculiar character. As soon as the new is but the re-expression of the old, God ceases to live. Ever the mystery is revealed in each new birth; so must it be to eternity. The Eternal-Absolute is ever creating new forms of expressing itself."

What the new order of things was to be in the spiritual life could be learned, Father Hecker held, by observing men's strivings after natural good. The tendencies which shape men's efforts to secure happiness in this world, in so far as they are innocent, indicated to him what choice of means should be made to propagate the knowledge and love of God. According to this, the most successful worker for a people's sanctification will be kindred to them by conviction and by sympathy in all that concerns their political and social life. Men's aspirations in the natural order point out the highway of God's representatives. As these aspirations change from era to era, so do the main lines of religious effort change, the highways of one age becoming the byways of another. It is true that no method for the elevation of human nature to divine union, which the Church has sanctioned, ever becomes quite obsolete, but the merest glance at the differences between the spiritual characteristics of the martyrs, the hermits, the monks, the friars, shows that one form of the Christian virtues succeeds another in general possession of men's souls. The new spirit, without crowding the old one off its beaten track, follows men to the new ways whither the providence of God in the natural order has led them. " First the natural man," says St. Paul, " and then the spiritual." Different types of spirituality are brought forward by Almighty God to sanctify men in new conditions of life. Among the foremost of these are religious communities of men and women. Hence their duty to adjust themselves, as far as faith and discipline permit, to the circumstances of the times. The power of a religious community for good will be measured by its ability to elevate the natural to the supernatural without shocking it or thwarting it.

Now, every one knows that this age differs materially from past ones. It differs by a wider spread of education and an uncontrollable longing after liberty, civil, political, and personal.

Father Hecker was penetrated with the belief that the intelligence and liberty, whose well-ordered enjoyment he had witnessed in America, and which he loved so deeply himself, were divine invitations to the apostolate of the Holy Spirit. He was profoundly impressed with the certainty of the development, the extension, and the permanence of these political and social changes ; and he knew that they demanded of men a personal independence of character far in advance of previous generations. And he knew, also, that for the sanctification of such men the aids of religion, though not changed in themselves, must be applied in a different spirit. Discipline and uniformity, though never to be dispensed with, must yield the first places to more interior virtues. The dominant influence must be docility to the guidance of the Holy Spirit dwelling within every regenerate soul. Applying this, towards the end of his life, to religious communities, Father Hecker wrote: " The controlling thought of my mind for many years has been that a body of free men who love God with all their might, and yet know how to cling together, could conquer this modern world of ours." The sentence may be taken as a brief description of the Paulist community as he would have it. And it is easily seen why free men loving God with all their hearts are suited to conquer this modern world ; because men are determined to be free.

The following extracts from notes, letters, and diaries more fully develop this idea:

" A new religious order is an evidence and expression of an

uncommon or special grace given to a certain number of souls, so that they may' be sanctified by the practice of particular virtues to meet the special needs of their epoch, and in this way to renew the spiritual life of the members of the Church and to extend her fold. A new community is this, or, it has no reason for its existence. The means to accomplish its special work are both new and old. It should lay stress on the new, and not despise but also make use of the old. 'The wise householder bringeth forth from his treasury *new* things and old.'"

"The true Paulist is a religious man entirely dependent on God for his spiritual life; he lives in community for the greater security of his own salvation and perfection, and to meet more efficiently the pressing needs of the Church and of humanity in his day."

"The Church always finds in her wonderful fecundity wherewith to supply the new wants which arise in every distinct epoch of society."

"A new religious community, unless its activity is directed chiefly to supplying the special needs of its time, wears itself out at the expense of its true mission and will decline and fail."

"We must realize the necessity of more explicitly bringing out our ideal if we would give a sufficient motive for our students and members, keep them in the community, bring about unity of action, and accomplish the good which the Holy Spirit demands at our hands. A Paulist, as a distinct species of a religious man, is one who is alive to the pressing needs of the Church at the present time, and feels called to labor specially with the means fitted to supply them. And what a member of another religious community might do from that divine guidance which is external, the Paulist does from the promptings of the indwelling Holy Spirit."

"A Paulist is a Christian man who aims at a Christian perfection consistent with his natural characteristics and the type of civilization of his country."

"So far as it is compatible with faith and piety, I am for accepting the American civilization with its usages and customs; leaving aside other reasons, it is the only way by which Catholicity can become the religion of our people. The character and spirit of our people, and their institutions, must find themselves at home in our Church in the way those of other nations have done; and it is on this basis alone that the Catholic religion can make progress in our country."

"What we need to-day is men whose spirit is that of the early martyrs. We shall get them in proportion as Catholics cultivate a spirit of independence and personal conviction. The highest development of religion in the soul is when it is assisted by free contemplation of the ultimate causes of things. Intelligence and liberty are the human environments most favorable to the deepening of personal conviction of religious truth, and obedience to the interior movements of an enlightened conscience. To a well-ordered mind the question of the hour is how the soul which aspires to the supernatural life shall utilize the advantages of liberty and intelligence."

"The form of government of the United States is preferable to Catholics above other forms. It is more favorable than others to the practice of those virtues which are the necessary conditions of the development of the religious life of man. This government leaves men a larger margin for liberty of action, and hence for co-operation with the guidance of the Holy Spirit, than any other government under the sun. With these popular institutions men enjoy greater liberty in working out their true destiny. The Catholic Church will, therefore, flourish all the more in this republican country in proportion as her representatives keep, in their civil life, to the lines of their republicanism."

"The two poles of the Paulist character are: first, personal perfection. He must respond to the principles of perfection as laid down by spiritual writers. The backbone of a religious community is the desire for personal perfection actuating its members. The desire for personal perfection is the foundation stone of a religious community; when this fails, it crumbles to pieces; when this ceases to be the dominant desire, the community is tottering. Missionary works, parochial work, etc., are and must be made subordinate to personal perfection. These works must be done in view of personal perfection. The main purpose of each Paulist must be the attainment of personal perfection by the practice of those virtues without which it cannot be secured—mortification, self-denial, detachment, and the like. By the use of these means the grace of God makes the soul perfect. The perfect soul is one which is guided instinctively by the indwelling Holy Spirit. To attain to this is the end always to be aimed at in the practice of the virtues just named. Second, zeal for souls; to labor for the conversion of the country to the Catholic faith by apostolic work. Parish work is a part, an integral part, of Paulist work, but not its principal or chief work—and parish work should be done so as to form a part of the main aim, the conversion of the non-Catholic people of the country. In this manner we can labor to raise the standard of Catholic life here and throughout the world as a means of the general triumph of the Catholic faith."

"I do not think that the principal characteristic of our Fathers and of our life should be poverty or obedience or any other special and secondary virtue, or even a cardinal virtue, but zeal for apostolic works. Our vocation is apostolic—conversion of souls to the faith, of sinners to repentance, giving missions, defence of the Christian religion by conferences, lectures, sermons, the pen, the press, and the like works; and in the interior, to propagate among men a higher and more spiritual life. To supply the special element the age and each country demands, this is the peculiar work of religious communities: this heir field. It is a fatal mistake when religious attempt to do the ordinary work of the Church. Let religious practise prayer and study; there will always be enough of the work to which they are called."

"Are the Paulists Religious? Yes, and no. Yes, of their age. No, of the past; the words in neither case being taken in an exclusive meaning."

"As regards the growth of the Paulist, he must develop in an apostolic vocation—that is, in apostolic works, Catholic, universal; not in works which confine his life's energies to a locality. He must do the work of the Church. The work of the Church, as Church, is to render her note of universality more and more conspicuous—to render it sensible, palpable. This is the spirit of the Church in our country."

The following refers to the second trait of the character above given: "A Paulist is to emphasize individuality; that is, to make individual liberty an essential element in every judgment that touches the life and welfare of the community and that of its members. Those who emphasize the community element are inclined to look upon this as a dangerous and impracticable experiment."

"*Individuality is an integral and conspicuous element in the life of the Paulist.* This must be felt. One of the natural signs of the true Paulist is that he would prefer to suffer from the excesses of liberty rather than from the arbitrary actions of tyranny."

"The individuality of a man cannot be too strong or his liberty too great when he is guided by the Spirit of God. But when one is easily influenced from below rather than from above, it is an evidence of the spirit of pride and that of the flesh, and not 'the liberty of the glory of the children of God.'"

What follows touches the relation between the personal and common life:

"Many other communities lay the main stress on community life as the chief element, giving it control as far as is consistent with fundamental individual right; the Paulists, on the contrary, give the element of individuality the first place and put it in control as far as is consistent with the common life."

".The spirit of the age has a tendency to run into extreme individuality, into eccentricity, license, revolution. But the typical life shows how individuality is consistent with community life. This is the aim of the United States in the political order, an aim and tendency which we have to guide, and not to check or sacrifice."

"The element of individuality is taken into account in the Paulist *essentially*, integrally, practically. But when it comes into conflict with the common right, the individual must yield to the community: the common life outranks the individual life in case of conflict. But the individual life should be regarded as sacred and never be effaced. How this is to operate in particular cases belongs, where it is not a matter of rule, to the virtue of prudence to decide."

"When the personality of the individual comes into conflict with the life of the community, the personal side must not be sacrificed, but made to yield to the common. In case of conflict, as before said, common life and interests outrank personal life and interests. It may be asked how, in the ordinary regulation and government of a community of this kind, the individual and common elements are to be made to harmonize? The answer is, that the one at the head of affairs must be a true Paulist—that is to say, keenly sensitive of personal rights as well as appreciative of such as are common: where the question is not a point of rule, its decision is dependent on the practical sagacity and prudence of the superior more than on any minute regulations which can be given. He who interprets the acts of legitimate authority as an attack on his personal liberty, is as far out of the way as he who looks upon the exercise of reason as an attack on authority."

"How about persons of dull minds or of little spiritual ambition coming into the use of this freedom? First, no such person should be allowed to enter into the community: such persons should be excluded. Second, a full-fledged Paulist should have passed a long enough novitiate to have acquired the special vir-

.tues which are necessary for his vocation. Absence of supernatural light is the cause why a man is not fit to be a Paulist,
for he cannot understand rightly or appreciate the value of the
liberties he enjoys. He either is or he becomes a turbulent element
in the community."

"A Paulist, seeing that he has so much individuality, should
have a strong, nay, a very strong attrait for community life; he
should be fond of the Fathers' company, prefer them and their
society when seeking proper recreation, feel the house to be
his *home* and the community and its surroundings very dear to
him; in the routine of the day all the community exercises and
labors are, in his judgment, of paramount obligation and importance.

"The civil and political state of things of our age, particularly
in the United States, fosters the individual life. But it should
do so without weakening the community life: this is true individualism. The problem is to make the synthesis. The joint
product is the Paulist."

"A Paulist should cultivate personal freedom without detriment to the community spirit; and, *vice versa*, the community
spirit should not be allowed to be detrimental to personal freedom. But when the individual life runs into eccentricity, license,
and revolution, that is a violation and sacrifice of the community life."

"The duty of the Paulist Superior is to elicit the spontaneous
zeal of the Fathers and to further it with his authority. For lack
of one's own initiative that of another may be used, and herein
the Superior offers a constant help. But the centre of action is
individual, is in the soul moved by the Holy Ghost; not in the
Superior of the community or in the authorities of the Church.
And if he be moved by the Holy Spirit, he will be most obedient
to his superior; and he will not only be submissive to the authority
of the Church, but careful to follow out her spirit."

In explaining the routine of daily life Father Hecker said:
"The member of a community who does not make the common
exercises [of religion] his first care is derelict of his duty. A
common exercise should be preferred to all other devotional practices or occupations whatever; as far as possible all other exercises ought to be made subordinate to common ones, which
should never be omitted without permission of the superior."

Father Hecker was once asked: "Which would you prefer: to
have a rule and manner of life adapted to a large number of men,
embracing many of a uniform type, men good enough for average

work, intended to include and seeking to retain persons of medi-
ocre spirit, and having a dim understanding of our peculiar institute ? or would you prefer the rule to be made only for a select
body, composed of such men as —— and ——, and the like ? ' "
[Answer :] " I should prefer the rule to be made for the smaller
and more select body of men. Religious vocations are not common, but special. It is a fatal mistake for religious to take the
place of secular priests."

No one can be misled by what he has read in the foregoing
pages into the notion that Father Hecker had any other aim than
the entire consecration of liberty and intelligence to the influence
of the Holy Spirit. To know Father Hecker well was to be more
deeply impressed with his longing for the reign of the Spirit of God
in men's souls than even with his love of human liberty. In his
esteem the worth of the latter was altogether in proportion to its
aptitude for the former. His love of liberty was that of a means
to an end—the perfect oblation of the inner man to God. He
aimed at individuality because of his belief in the action of the
Holy Ghost in the individual soul. Such action, he was quick to
maintain, is given to every Christian, but it is to be looked for in
a high degree in those who are called by a special vocation to
assist independent characters to find the spirit of God within
them ; or, if already known, to obey His direction implicitly.
Paulists after Father Hecker's heart would be men whom experience and study had rendered fit instruments for disseminating the
knowledge of the ways of God the Holy Ghost in men's hearts ;
for instructing the faithful how to distinguish the voice of God
in the soul from the vagaries of the imagination or the emotions
of passion, and able to stimulate a ready and generous response
to every call of God from within.

It is because of this indwelling of the Holy Spirit in every
regenerate soul that Father Hecker so vigorously maintained that
the freedom of the individual is a golden opportunity for the
Catholic apostolate, according to the text " Where the Spirit of
the Lord is, there is liberty." Freedom, he affirmed, was in absolute consonance with Catholic doctrine. But he furthermore
insisted that it has become the world-wide aspiration of men by
interposition of Divine Providence and with a view to their higher
sanctification ; and however grossly abused, it is yet a direct
suggestion to an apostolate whose prospects are in the highest
degree promising. And this is the answer to the question
which reasonable persons may well ask, namely: Why should

the new institution differ so radically from the old ones, which were certainly works of God ? Because the change of men's lives in the entire secular and natural order is in the direction of personal liberty and independence, and this change is a radical one. "The Eternal-Absolute is ever creating new forms of expressing itself." If, indeed, men's aspirations for liberty and intelligence be all from the powers of darkness, then let every longing for freedom be repressed and condemned, crushed by authority in the state, anathematized by the Church. But if men are yearning to be free, however blindly, because God by their freedom would make them holier, then let us hail the new order as a blessing ; and let those who love freedom and are worthy of it use its privileges to advance themselves and their brethren nearer to immediate union with the Holy Spirit.

It has been seen that the important question whether the end of the new community would be better attained with the usual religious vows or without them was decided in the negative. They were not definitely rejected in the beginning ; but starting without them, the Fathers were willing to allow experience to show whether or not they should be resumed. The lapse of time but confirmed the view that the voluntary agreement and the bond of fraternal charity were, under the circumstances, preferab'e as securities for stability and incentives to holiness.

There can be little doubt that Father Hecker's ideas on this feature of the religious state had been greatly modified between the writing of the *Questions of the Soul* and the end of the struggle in Rome. Much is said in that book of community life in the Catholic Church, and generally as rendered stable and its spirit of sacrifice made complete by the vows; and in the statement given in Rome to his five chosen advisers, he says that one reason for writing the volume named was to induce young men to enter the religious orders as the only means of perfection—meaning orders under vows. But when he was released from his own obligations and was confronted with the choice of means for following his vocation, the horizon broadened away until he could see beyond the institutions and traditions in which he had lived since entering the novitiate at St. Trond. His ideas of perfection in its relation to states of life underwent a change. Therefore he said, Let us wait for the unmistakable will of God before we bind ourselves with vows amidst a free people. He never depreciated the evident value

of these obligations; indeed, he seldom was heard to speak of
them. · But he knew from close observation the truth of the
words of the Jesuit Avancinus:

"The net (St. Matthew xiii. 44) is the Catholic Church,
or, to take a narrower view, it means the station in which you
are placed As in a net all kinds of fish are to be found, so in
your position, as in all others, there are good and bad Christians . . . Should yours be a sacred calling, you are not, on
that account, either the better or the more secure; your sanctity
and your salvation depend on yourself, not on your calling."
(*Meditations*, Fourteenth Friday after Pentecost.)

It never entered into the minds of the Fathers to question
the doctrine and practice of the Church concerning vows. But
personal experience proves the lesson of history, that what religion needs is not so much holy states of life as holy men and
women.

Looking back into the past, Father Hecker saw St. Philip
Neri, to whom he had a great devotion and for whose spiritual
doctrine he had a high admiration. The following is from an
exponent of that doctrine, and is much in point:

"Although our Fathers and lay brothers [Oratorians] make
no vow of obedience, as do religious, they are, nevertheless, no
way inferior in the perfection of this virtue to those who profess
it in the cloister with solemn vows. They supply the want of
vows with love, with voluntary promptitude, and perfection in
obeying every wish of the superior. And it is a thing for
which we must indeed thank God, that without the obligation
of obeying under pain of sin, without fear of restraint or other
punishment (except that of expulsion in case of contumacy), all
the subjects are prompt in this obedience, even in things most
humiliating and severe, according to the terms of the rule. All
take pleasure in meeting the wishes of the superior, etc." (*The
Excellences of the Oratory of St. Philip Neri.* London: Burns
& Oates, p. 136.)

Father Hecker did not dream that by relinquishing the vows
he and his companions in the Paulist community had cast away
a single incentive to virtue capable of moving such men as they,
or had even failed to secure any of the insignia adorning the
great host of men and women in the Catholic Church whose
entire being has been given up to the divine service. "The true
Paulist," said he once, "should be fit and ready to take the

solemn vows at any moment." He felt strongly the truth of the following words of the Jesuit Lallemant:

"A desire and hunger after our perfection, a determined will to be constantly tending towards it with all our strength—let this be always our chief object and our greatest care. Let us bear in mind that this care is more of the essence of religion [*i.e.*, of a religious order] than vows themselves; for it is on this that our whole spiritual progress depends. Herein consists the difference between true religious and those who are so only in appearance and in the sight of men. Without this care to advance in perfection the religious state does not secure our salvation; but nothing is more common than to deceive ourselves on this point." (*The Spiritual Doctrine of Father Louis Lallemant, S.J.* New York: Sadlier & Co., p. 111.)

With regard to stability, men of stable character need no vow to guarantee adherence to a divine vocation, and men of feeble character may indeed vow themselves into an outward stability, but it is of little fruit to themselves personally, and their irremovability is often of infinite distress to their superiors and brethren. The episcopate is the one religious order founded by Our Lord, and its members are in the highest state of evangelical perfection; yet they are neither required nor advised to take the oaths or vows of religious orders.

Neither Father Hecker nor any of his associates had the least aversion to the vows. On the contrary, they had lived contentedly under them for many of their most active years, and it will be remembered of Father Hecker that he never found them irksome, had never known a temptation against them.

The question which arose was a choice between two kinds of community, the one fast bound by external obligations to the Church in the form of vows, placing the members in a relation of peculiar strictness to the Canon Law; or another kind, in which the members trusted wholly to the strength of Divine grace, and their own conscious purpose never to give up the fight for perfection; which of these states would better facilitate the action of the Holy Spirit in the present Providence of God; and which of them would tend to produce a type of character fitted to evangelize a nation of independent and self-reliant men and women? The free community was chosen.

No doubt this involved some risk of criticism, particularly in the beginning, for it was a wonder to many that men should organize for a life-long endeavor after perfection and not swear to it, especially as none of the free communities existing in Europe had houses in America, for the Sulpitians belong to the secular clergy. And there was also danger of unworthy subjects creeping in under favor of a freedom they were unfit to enjoy. For it may be reproached against us that we are apt to be victimized by men ruled by caprice, indulging in extravagant schemes or deluded by wandering fancies; and also by superiors who would let everybody do as he pleased. No doubt such dangers are to be guarded against. But vowed communities do not claim to be free from difficulties. No state of life and no organization claims to be so perfect as totally to prevent abuse of power on the part of superiors or caprice and sloth on the part of members.

Both kinds of organized religious life have their difficulties: the one, the martinet superior and the routine subject; the other, the capricious subject and the lax superior. In one kind the bond of union as well as the stimulus of endeavor is mainly obedience, fraternal charity assisting; in the other it is mainly fraternal charity, obedience assisting; each has to overcome obstacles peculiar to itself.

What has been said in this chapter, besides serving to exhibit Father Hecker's principles as a founder, will be, we trust, a sufficient answer to the silly delusion which the Paulists have encountered in some quarters, that their society tolerates a soft life and supposes in its members no high vocation to perfection; or that the voluntary principle allows them a personal choice in regard to the devotional exercises, permitting them to attend or not attend this or that meditation or devotion laid down in the rule, as "the spirit moves them." This is as plain an error as another one which had much currency for years and which is not yet everywhere corrected: that the Paulist community was open to converts alone and received none others.

A CONVERT FROM JUDAISM.

THE subject of this sketch was born over fifty years ago in London (West End), England. Her parents were Jews, who adhered strictly to the precepts of their religion, and possessed an abundance of the goods of this world. She received a good Scriptural name, and her surname was that of a near friend of our Lord of whom frequent mention is made in the New Testament. She was the seventeenth child in a family of eighteen, and was born blind. Under the care of an able surgeon, after nine operations, she could see imperfectly, with the aid of glasses of extraordinary power. She was taught to read and write and sew, but was never skilful in these accomplishments. During her childhood her father moved with his family to the Island of Jamaica, giving her at this time a house and land, that on account of her affliction she might be well provided for. This property was taken from her when, a few years later, her father settled in New York and met with financial reverses.

Books were her chief diversion, and she read all that she could find, even borrowing of the servants, who were often of Catholic faith. These books, being mostly devotional, aroused her interest to such a degree that she sought a Catholic church and attended the services day after day, hoping to learn more of this religion, to which she was so strangely attracted. She literally haunted the churches, stealing away from her home and returning at all hours. Finally, approaching a priest, the Rev. Dr. Cummings, pastor of St. Stephen's Church, and confiding her difficulties to him, she asked for instruction in the Catholic faith. Dr. Cummings very kindly placed her in charge of his sister, a saintly woman, who gave her all possible aid in her search after truth; ministering also to her temporal needs, of which she was quite unmindful.

With characteristic impatience she asked to be received into the church without delay, which Dr. Cummings promised on condition that she would first inform her parents of her intention—a most difficult task, as she well knew the bitter opposition that would follow. After earnest deliberation she decided upon the following plan. One morning, before starting for Mass, she told one of her sisters that she was about to become a Catholic, obtaining her promise that she would communicate the fact to her

father and mother. Having thus satisfied her conscience, she
returned with a light heart, informing Dr. C. that she had done
as he required. *He therefore at once baptized her, and she became a happy Christian, filled with faith and zeal for the church.
Making no effort to conceal her joy, when at home she sang hymns
to the Blessed Virgin and practised devotions most unacceptable
to a Jewish household. But she bore the sign of the cross, and
each day brought new trials. She cheerfully fasted all day in
order to receive Holy Communion, leaving her home before the
family were up and returning when she would be unobserved at
evening. One comfort after another was taken from her, until
at last she was forced to seek temporary refuge elsewhere.
Through Dr. Cummings's kindness she was sent to a convent
in Canada, where a home had been offered her, but after
a few months her father asked for her return to his home,
promising to care for her and allow her the privileges of her
religion. He was extremely urgent, and she journeyed home
again, only to find a renewal of the experience of the past.

She was again deprived of religious liberty, and again left her
father's house, this time never to return, excepting occasionally to
see her mother and at her father's death. She was evidently unwelcome, and became as a stranger to her brothers and sisters. She
was unwilling to receive the shelter of any institution, public or
private, and tried in various ways to earn a living, working hard
but seldom with success. A voice of rare power and sweetness
was her one gift, but, without the means of cultivating it, was of
no practical use to her. Among her business enterprises was a
newspaper stand, but being oblivious to all that did not appear
to her in the direct line of vision through her extraordinary
glasses, her box was often emptied of her earnings by mischievous
boys while she was receiving money from her customers. She
was for several years nursery governess in a Catholic family,
where the children were greatly attached to her. She had for a
while the care of infants from the foundling asylum. She was
one of Dr. Warner's first agents for corsets. She kept a small
store, selling books and various useful articles, but owed more
in the end than she ever received. Always working, always
poor, and always active in charities, she served our Lord in
those less fortunate than herself, and received from her religion the
great consolations usually accorded to so zealous a Christian.
When apparently without resources of any kind, I learned one
day that she was paying the rent for a woman in destitute circumstances who had several small children and a husband who

was numbered among the "unworthy poor," for whom she probably begged.

All her life she would give of the little she possessed, excepting fine wearing apparel; when this fell to her lot she accepted it as her natural inheritance. She never begged for herself, but sometimes borrowed small sums when she had fasted for several days and hunger compelled her. Those of other creeds asked: "Why does not the church take care of her?" But she would be cared for in her own way, and kind Catholic friends assisted her, one lady paying her rent for many years that she might enjoy her own little home, humble though it was Others helped her in various ways, most unexpected assistance arriving in times of her greatest need from people far away whom she had not seen for years. One day, wishing to visit a friend who lived at a distance, and having no money, she went to the station and sat among the waiting crowd. I do not know why she did this, as it is quite contrary to the usual custom of people under the circumstances. After a while, to her surprise, she saw beside her on the seat a small roll of bills, and, seeking an owner for it among those who sat near her, she was assured by all that it did not belong to them and that she had probably dropped it. The sum was just what she needed, and as no one claimed it she joyfully purchased a ticket and took the train for the desired destination. Her Jewish traits were always predominant, tempered and softened by her frequent reception of the sacraments of the church. During the latter years of her life she was afflicted with a painful and incurable disease. Her strength gradually failing, she was confined to her bed and dependent entirely upon the charity of friends; this occasionally disappointing, she informed me that she was sometimes deprived of the only article of food she could eat, even on one occasion being obliged to return it to the grocer because she could not pay for it. At this juncture her brothers and sisters came to her relief, and aided her to procure the comforts she needed. Her brother selected a room at the Astor Hospital, it being considered best to remove her to that place, she reluctantly consenting to the change under the impression that it was a Catholic institution. She was greatly distressed on discovering her mistake, and begged to be taken to her brother's house. But her stay was brief, as she died within a week.

Two days before her death one of her former pupils was impelled to go to her, a distance of many miles, without knowing of her extreme illness nor of her removal to a hospital.

She was overjoyed to see her young friend, who, finding her so near her end, informed her old confessor, Father Freeman, S.J., who hastened to her bedside, hearing her confession and sending the parish priest to give her the last sacraments. In order to reconcile her to her new surroundings, her sister had been advised not to visit her for a day or two, so she died as she had lived, away from kindred and friends, but strengthened and consoled by the church she had loved so well and for which she had forsaken father and mother and all who had been dear to her in early life. She had been cared for as the lilies of the field, though she had tried to "toil and spin," and I trust she is now enjoying an eternal home, "not made with hands," such as "eye hath not seen nor ear heard, nor hath it entered into the heart of man to conceive," and rest such as God gives to those who suffer patiently for him and serve him faithfully on earth. The funeral of this poor girl took place at the church in Ninety-seventh Street. Two men bore the coffin within the door, where it was met by the white-robed priest and an acolyte bearing a censer, who proceeded up the aisle, and following the coffin were the Jewish relatives of the deceased, also two Protestant and two Catholic friends—a most remarkable procession, and one never to be forgotten. It occurred to me that our Lord could not but be pleased to see so many children of Israel, his chosen people, assembled in his church to show respect and affection for one of their own who had left them to become his disciple. These relatives, with one exception, followed her to her grave in a Catholic cemetery, having everything done according to the ritual of the church, her brother paying the expenses of her funeral. May our dear Lord reward them with the greatest of all gifts—the gift of faith.   C. S. H.

THE OLD WORLD SEEN FROM THE NEW.

A VALUABLE article on "The Church and the Workman" has been written by the Archbishop of Capua, Cardinal Capecelatro, for *Merry England.* The importance which the distinguished author attaches to the subject may be seen from his concluding words: "God Almighty, I hold, has so constituted the Christian life that in every age, or rather every series of ages, it appears with a new *apologia*, due to the new conditions of the race. Now, in our day, if I am not deceived, this new *apologia* will be the product of the Social Question. That question, formidable in the eyes of all, will surely make a great stride, a giant's stride, possibly before the old century dies and the new century dawns. And that progress will most certainly be made in the name of Jesus Christ living in his church. To many an old *apologia* . . . will be added the fresh *apologia*, derived from a Social Question solved by Catholicism and by the science it inspires." This extract indicates the spirit of the cardinal's utterances, a spirit similar to that which animates our own cardinal and the Archbishop of Westminster, to both of whom he refers, as well as to a prelate less well known to our readers, Monsignor Kopp, who took a leading part, in his own name and that of the Pope, in the Berlin Labor Conference. For Cardinal Manning he has the warmest words of praise, because he has not hesitated to put himself at the head of Christian Socialism, and for "going in advance of contemporary philanthropists, economists, philosophers, in his study of the possible means for restoring the dignity and amending the condition of the poor."

*   *   *

The quotations which we have made show clearly the attitude of Cardinal Capecelatro towards the Social Question of our time. While recognizing the fact that men are unequal in natural capacity and ability, and that as a consequence their respective shares of worldly goods will also be unequal, he maintains that the tendency of the church and of the doctrine which she teaches is to lessen, and in the end to remove that inequality; to what degree, however, this inequality will be removed no human intellect, the cardinal thinks, can pronounce; the more fully, however, the doctrines of the church are embraced, acted upon, and realized the greater will be the union that will exist between different classes and the less the distance between them. The present evils are due to the imperfect recognition of the church's doctrines on human equality, all men being of the same nature, having the same destiny, and being given the same means to arrive at it. But a clearer understanding of these doctrines and a more practical realization of them are to be looked for, and signs of it already appear; so much, in fact, has already been done that the cardinal concludes with the hope expressed, in the words already quoted, that we may see the church working out a complete solution of the social problem. The cardinal, of course, condemns any doctrine which denies that man is with respect to other men the true owner of the things he possesses justly, but maintains in the clearest language that it is absolutely false and anti-Christian to assert that the rich man is free to spend according to his whim the things he calls his own. After providing for his own necessities in his own condition, he owes, by the express command of Jesus Christ, what remains to the poor. There are other points of interest in this article, but enough has been said to show that the cardinal is in full accord with his English and American colleagues in the Sacred College, and that although the social and industrial conditions of the countries are very different, yet there is an equal recognition of the importance of the labor question and of the proper attitude of the church towards it. Meantime, the Pope's long-expected encyclical on the social question will very soon be published, and we have no doubt that it will confirm and develop with the highest authority the general positions of Cardinal Capecelatro.

*   *   *

No event of importance in the conflict between capital and labor has taken place in Great Britain since our last. There have been strikes, not for principle, however, but for increase of wages. Riots have occurred at Bradford, but the strike was rather the occasion than the cause of them—the right of public meeting being the real point in dispute. For the present there is a lull of expectancy—a looking forward to the report of the Royal Commission and to the evidence to be laid before it. The new unionists have recognized their inability to cope with their antagonists, and are devoting their energies to the perfecting of the organization and the federation of skilled and unskilled labor. On the other side, their successful antagonists in the recent battle—the Shipping Federation—are seeking to secure the fruits of victory by the bestowal of benefits upon the men in their employment—bribing them with paltry bribes, the

Unionists say. Every seaman or fireman who takes a Federation ticket (for which he pays one shilling for registration) will by virtue of that ticket, without any further payment, effect an insurance to the amount of £25 should he be killed or lost at sea while serving on a Federation ship. To obtain a larger sum payment will be necessary. It is hoped, too, that by means of further arrangements, insurance against partial disablement may be effected.

*   *   *

Although greater quiet reigns, the interest in industrial questions has by no means abated. The Labor Commission is just beginning to examine witnesses, and several committees of Parliament are engaged upon particular branches of the question— such as the hours of railway servants, the age of juvenile employment. Politicians of both parties are busy in imparting to the public, and especially to the electors, their ideas of the remedies called for. We have already referred to the plan proposed by the Conservative Under-Secretary for India, Sir John Gorst. A former member of Mr. Gladstone's last ministry, Mr. Mundella, has come forward to speak for official Liberals. His proposals include not merely the free education, but the feeding of poor children. For it is one of the strange phenomena of the present social system that thousands of children who come to school under compulsion of law come without breakfast and dependent upon charity for their dinner. Charitable organizations have taken the matter in hand; but in defect of these Mr. Mundella would have the state supply the meals—a long step indeed on the socialistic road. With reference to the legal eight-hour day Mr. Mundella speaks with befitting caution, but a proposal which he makes with reference to strikes seems worthy of greater attention than it has received. As into railroad accidents and wrecks inquiries are held by commissioners appointed by the Board of Trade, so Mr. Mundella would have the powers of the board extended so that it should hold similar inquiries with reference to every great strike or lockout, in order to learn the exact facts and to make them public. Free land and temperance reform form parts of Mr. Mundella's programme; the most startling recommendation, however, is the last—that the progressive income-tax which has been adopted in Switzerland should be tried in England, so that the richer a man is the more should he pay in proportion to his wealth, not merely for the old and well-recognized objects of state care and solicitude, but for the educating, feeding, and housing of the poorer citizens and their children.

A Conservative and a Gladstonian having spoken, the Liberal-Unionists could not be silent. Mr. Chamberlain's proposals deal with another aspect of the question. He is struck with the hard and painful lot which awaits the poor laborer after a life of toil and poverty. Of the old people in the United Kingdom above the age of sixty, one in seven is in receipt of parish relief, either in the workhouse or as an out-door pauper. That this should be the only outcome of the toilsome days of so many poor creatures Mr. Chamberlain considers to be a public calamity, and therefore it becomes a part of the state's care that, if possible, means should be taken to prevent it. He therefore proposes a plan—the details of which we have not space to give—which, if carried out, would enable each individual to receive at the age of sixty-five a fixed annual annuity sufficient for decent support for the remainder of his days. The state's share in this would be that it should pay upon each individual's deposits a higher rate of interest than the state itself could earn ; for this course the justification is, in addition to that already mentioned, the saving which would be effected in the poor-rates. This proposal is similar in general outline to the German method of state insurance, but differs in the fact that it is not to be compulsory.

*　　　　*　　　　*

The most important event affecting the labor movement is— setting aside the May-day demonstration, of which it is difficult to appraise the correct value—the International Congress of Miners, which has been held at Paris. This is the second meeting of this body, the first having been held at Jolimont, in Belgium, last year. The object in view is to extend the sphere of organization so that it shall not merely comprise all the miners of a single nation, but those of all other competing nations. The importance of this it is, perhaps, somewhat difficult for Americans to realize, we being out of the reach, under existing circumstances, of external competition. But it seems to be clear that the legal eight-hour day depends for its success on an international agreement. For how can England, for example, compete with Belgium if the miners in the one country work twelve hours a day and in the other only eight ? The necessity of this being recognized, an earnest effort is being made to bring about so desirable an end.

*　　　　*　　　　*

Those efforts, however, were crowned with but moderate success. The first object was to form a permanent federation of all the miners of Europe.   But, to begin with, there were only five countries represented: France, Belgium, Germany, Austria, and England.   A more serious difficulty arose as to the system of voting.   The English delegates represented nearly one-half of the total numbers who had sent delegates to the congress, and consequently if the power of voting on any permanent commit- tee were to be regulated by the number of the miners the voting power of the English delegates would be very great.   To this the other nations were opposed, and wished that the voting should be by nationalities, each nation having one vote.   As no agree- ment could be reached on this point, the permanent federation remains unaccomplished.   A committee, however, has been ap- pointed to devise a settlement of this question.   That such a difficulty should have arisen in these preliminary stages shows that, however desirable international federation may be, the obsta- cles to its attainment are many, and that, if they are to be re- moved, no small degree of tact, wisdom, and self-sacrifice will be required.

*   *   *

But although unsuccessful in this, on other points good work was done, or, at all events, bad work was prevented.   The move- ment on foot for an international strike of miners, in order to attain an eight-hour day, was brought before the congress by the Belgian delegates.   The proposal was discussed at length: and in the end it was decided that while an eight-hour day was desirable, it would be unwise and inexpedient for its attain- ment to take such a violent measure as an international strike, for such a strike would involve the whole community ; would bring about in a short time the total cessation of all business: and in this way the sympathy of all classes would be alienated. It was recognized that no strike can be successful unless it enlists the active sympathy of the public at large.   Accordingly it was decided that the question should be pressed upon the govern- ments of each country by all legal and constitutional means; and that it should only be after the failure of these that so drastic a proposal as a universal strike should be entertained.

*   *   *

A more positive result of the Congress was the decision to af- ford pecuniary assistance to the Belgian miners in their endeav- ors to secure an amelioration of their lot.   And truly there is a most urgent call for such amelioration.   One fact alone will show this.   A miner in England for a shorter day's work gets six shillings ; a miner in Belgium gets two shillings.   The cost of living, indeed, is less, but by no means in the proportion of three to one; and as a consequence the means of support of a Belgian miner are barely sufficient to enable him to prolong a miserable existence. The congress recognized that the Belgians were entitled to the fullest assistance in the strike which they were contemplating, especially as the means of seeking redress are not open to them on account of the restricted franchise existing in Belgium. Whether this promise has been kept seems doubtful in the light of recent intelligence.

*.   *   *

The Berlin Labor Conference summoned by the German Emperor formed an epoch, it was thought, in the labor movement, and it may be interesting to put on record the results of that conference up to the present time, so far as it has had results. For it would appear that in Austria, Belgium, France, Germany, Italy, the Netherlands, Portugal, and Spain no special legislative action has yet been taken to carry out the recommendations of the conference. In Hungary the Sunday Rest Act and an act for the relief of workmen incapacitated by illness have been passed. In Denmark a law stopping unnecessary and regulating necessary Sunday labor has been recently passed. In Switzerland there has been legislation limiting the working hours of railway servants. In Belgium and Switzerland laws are already in force in harmony with the principal recommendations of the conference. In India an approximation has been made to some of the regulations suggested, while in England the question of the age of juvenile labor is under discussion. As is well known, the English Factory Act passed many years ago had embodied most of the results at which the conference arrived.

*   *   *

The second reading of the Intoxicating Liquors (Ireland) Bill, which reading has been carried by a majority of 248 to 94, forms the chief feature in the Temperance movement during the past month. This bill provides for permanent enforcement of the Irish Sunday Closing Act of 1878, an act which was originally passed for four years as an experiment, and which, on account of its good results, has been renewed year by year since that time. By the present bill, moreover, the five cities of Dublin, Belfast, Cork, Limerick, and Waterford, which were not included in the former bill, are now brought within the scope of its provisions, so that for the whole of Ireland the public-houses will be closed throughout Sunday. In addition to this the bill provides for their closing on Saturdays at 9 o'clock P.M., and also that a person shall not be considered to be a *bona-fide* traveller unless he has travelled a distance of at least six miles instead of three, which the law fixed as sufficient hitherto. Such are the main provisions of this bill, which will place Ireland as well as Scotland and Wales in advance of England in this respect. For nowhere in England are the public-houses closed during the whole of Sunday; in fact, it is said that the attempt to do so for London would bring the strongest ministry to utter ruin.

* * *

Not merely is the actual success of the measure in the House of Commons a matter of importance and interest, but also the course of events which has led up to that success. As we have said, the bill has now been in force in a mitigated form for thirteen years, and the experience thus gained has formed the ground for the strengthening and extending its operation and rendering its provisions permanent. The genuine character of this experience has been ascertained by evidence elicited by a Select Committee appointed for the purpose of inquiry into the matter. Before this committee priests and ministers of all denominations, coroners, police officers, magistrates (with the exception of one or two of the police magistrates in Dublin), unanimously testified that Sunday closing had succeeded in Ireland and that it ought to be continued. So evident has been this success that the government announced that, provided certain amendments were made in committee, they would give their assistance in order to carry it through the remaining stages; and this is a matter of moment, for a private member has to encounter so many difficulties that the assistance of the government becomes almost necessary.

* * *

We do not wish to trench upon politics, yet we think it well that the attitude of the present representatives of Ireland towards this question should be known. Last year when the question came before the House, of 42 Irish members who voted (and there are 105 in all) 28 voted for the bill and 14 against. Of the select committee to which we have referred, which took evidence and reported in favor of the bill, eight of the members were Irish. This year the rejection of the bill was moved by an anti-Parnellite and seconded by a Parnellite. Mr. Sexton made, to use Mr. Parnell's words, " an eloquent protest " against the bill, which protest Mr. Parnell himself emphasized and amplified. Three Irish members spoke in favor of the bill and ten against it, and it was due to Mr. Parnell's taking advantage of the forms of the House that it was not at once referred to the Standing Committee on Law, and its progress was thereby delayed. When it came to the vote the members were divided, but as the division list has not been published we cannot say on which side the larger number voted. The opposition is being continued, and a week later the bill would have been advanced a further step had it not been for the objections of two anti-Parnellite members. Mr. Sexton promises to further the progress of the measure on condition that it is so modified that in the five exempted cities the public-houses may be allowed to be open from 3 to 5 on Sunday afternoon and until 10 on Saturday night.

*   *

Although the friends of temperance will rejoice at the progress of their principles, as evidenced by the legislative acts, the testimony of statistics will be far from satisfactory to them. During the past year in Great Britain there has been much increase in the consumption of alcohol, and, worst of all, in the consumption of spirits. In England there was an increase of 9 per cent. over the high figures of last year. In Scotland and in Ireland the increase was only 7½ per cent. Never before in England has the consumption reached so high a level, whereas for Ireland, as well as Scotland, it has frequently been reached before and sometimes passed. In France also there has been a great increase, the tax on alcohol having produced nearly five million dollars more than it did last year. In some of the French towns this increase is quite startling. For example, at Nîmes it has been as much as 31 per cent., at Lille 24 per cent., at Rennes 14 per cent., at Caen 10 per cent. Looking at these figures the friends of sobriety must not allow apparent success to lead them to any relaxation of their efforts for the good of their fellow-man.

*

In announcing its intention to make education in the elementary schools completely free, the government has taken the step which was rendered necessary by the establishment in 1876 of compulsory education. Mr. Forster's Elementary Education Act of 1870 forms the basis of the present system. Under it voluntary schools and Board schools divide the ground between them, the Board schools representing the secular system of education, while the voluntary schools insist upon religious training and instruction, the "rights" of those who object to this being safeguarded by the Conscience Clause. By arranging their schools in accordance with the act of 1870, the Catholic bishops of England, Ireland, and Scotland agreed to accept state aid and state inspection for the secular branches of study. Cardinal Manning in his little work on National Education has expressed this attitude of the Bishops: "Where public money is received there must be public audit, inspection, and a share in management; this is already exercised by the Department of the Committee of Privy Council in virtue of government grants." He further says that "some such defined or proportionate scheme of management under similar conditions by local authority would in no way diminish the independence of voluntary schools in matters of religion and morals." The official examinations have given public testimony in favor of the Catholic schools. Each school, as the law now stands, whether a Board or a voluntary school, derived its support from three sources, the Board school from the local rates, the contribution of the imperial government, and the children's pence; the voluntary school, instead of the local rates, has to rely upon voluntary subscriptions, but has equally with the Board school a contribution from the imperial government and the children's pence. What the government proposes to do now is itself to pay the children's pence in Board and voluntary schools alike, and thus to relieve the parents of the entire burden, except in so far as they are tax or rate payers.

The Board schools have had a great advantage over the voluntary schools, and, it would appear, will retain that advantage, because they can make up any deficiency by the power of levying rates, whereas the voluntary school has to solicit the free-will offerings of the charitably disposed. As we have said, the Board schools are the result of the efforts of those who wish to have the education imparted by the state made entirely secular. They made, in 1870, a fierce onslaught upon religious education, but the friends of the latter were strong enough to secure a place for religious schools in the national system. The act of 1870 was consequently a compromise upon this point; but although to a certain extent successful the advocates of denominational schools looked forward to the future with a certain fear and dread. The experience of the last twenty years, how-

ever, has given them greater confidence.   They have, in fact,
gained over some of their greatest adversaries.   The Birmingham League*was the main agency in the contest in favor of
purely secular education, and of this League Mr. Joseph Chamberlain was the animating spirit.   But time, and perhaps his political alliance with his former foes, the Tories, on the Home-
Rule question, have changed him, if not into a friend, at least
into a non-combatant.   Since the announcement made by the government he has made a speech in which he declares that the
greatest boon they had known in their generation had been conferred by the government on the working classes.   He admits that
he had thought that denominational schools would die out with the
establishment of Board schools, but that he had been mistaken;
for during the twenty-one years which had elapsed they had
doubled their accommodation and more than doubled their subscription list.   At the present time they supplied accommodations for more than two-thirds of the children of England and
Wales.   To destroy voluntary schools, to supply their places
with Board schools, would be to involve a capital expenditure of
fifty millions sterling and five millions yearly extra in the rates.
And so Mr. Chamberlain is warmly in favor of the acceptance
of the government plan.

And we have no doubt but that it will be accepted, although
some opposition will be offered to it by the extremists of both
parties: extreme Tories, who object to free education as socialistic; extreme Liberals, who will insist on the grant of money
being accompanied by a share in the management.   But the
masses of the people care for none of these things and will
readily accept relief, however illogical may be the principles
upon which it is given.   The present government is friendly to
the cause of religious education, and should it succeed in settling
this matter it will be a subject of satisfaction to all who have
that cause at heart.

No event of real importance has occurred to affect the political situation in Europe.   The leading question is whether or
not the Triple Alliance will be renewed.   There seems to be no
doubt that its non-renewal is, to say the very least, possible.   Italy is groaning under the burden of taxation involved

in the maintenance of its place in the Alliance, and the present premier has openly declared that he is by no means enthusiastic for it;
and while he is showing towards France a more friendly attitude, he has publicly stated that Italy's chief interest "lies in a
constant and steadfast agreement with England." Strange to say,
it is thought that the approaching general election in England
will decide the question as to whether there will be peace or
war in Europe. It is well known that Lord Salisbury's sympathies are with the Triple Alliance, and it is shrewdly suspected
that, if war were to break out, and British interests be at all affected, England would afford assistance to the Three Allied Powers.
This assistance would not be of any great value from a military
point of view, the English army being so small; but the English
navy could protect the coast of Italy, and by doing so could
free the larger part of Italy's half-million of men for active service in the field. This consideration has not been without its
weight in making Russia loath to attack her opponents. Mr.
Gladstone, on the other hand, is known to have French sympathies and to favor an alliance with France, but his unwillingness
to act at ·all is counted upon, and those interested would take
their measures accordingly. Which party, and therefore which
tendency, is to be in power, a general election will decide, and
in this way upon it the peace of Europe may depend.

*   *

The election of Prince Bismarck to the Reichstag may lead to
important consequences in Germany. It seems to have alarmed
the youthful sovereign of the German Empire. The circumstances
of the election are perhaps of greater interest than the election
itself. Of the four · candidates he, indeed, received the largest
number of votes, but a second ballot was necessary. The strangest
thing was that so little interest was taken that 45 per cent. of
the electors did not vote at all, and that the candidate who ran
the prince closest was a humble cigar-maker of the Social Democratic party. The death of Count von Moltke will scarcely have
any effect on the future, for his work had been finished some
years ago. In France the most notable event has been the harsh
manner in which the May-day demonstrations were treated. It
seems as if either the Republic took less account of the working
class than the neighboring monarchies, or that that class were less
favorably affected to the Republic. In Austria Count Taaffe is said
to have secured a permanent coalition of a sufficient number of

the political parties in the Austrian Parliament to enable him to retain power. Servia has got rid of the unwelcome presence of the ex king Milan by paying a large sum of money down, with the promise of an annual pension. It is to be hoped that the ex-queen may be prevailed upon to depart. Spain, having organized her Cortes, is promised by the Conservative ministry measures to improve the position of the working classes. Strange to say the leader of the Republicans, Señor Castelar, condemns them as socialistic. Portugal, long trembling upon the brink of bankruptcy, seems to have arrived at a crisis in financial matters. Her troubles are complicated and enhanced by her disputes with England, and by a strong Republican party. We may in a short time see stirring events in this little kingdom.

In order to make as clear as possible the present position of the temperance movement in Great Britain we append the following notes. With respect to the question whether compensation is legally due to the owner of a public-house on account of the non-renewal of the license, when such non renewal is refused on public grounds, the decision of the highest court, as we have said before, has settled that no legal claim exists. But it is worth mentioning that this applies only to what are called fully licensed houses. There is, however, a very large number of licensed houses which have a statutory right of renewal conferred by act of Parliament. In 1870 this class formed forty-four per cent. of the whole number of licensed houses in the country and nearly sixty per cent. of the houses in London. This large proportion possess an absolute vested right to compensation in case of the non-renewal of the license, provided the owner of the premises has properly conducted the business, and consequently the existence of this class cannot but prove a difficulty in the way of the diminution of the trade.

And notwithstanding the decision of the courts, the defenders of the necessity of compensation have not abandoned their position. They maintain that a man who has invested a large amount of capital and who has conducted his house properly has an equitable claim to compensation if he is displaced. The equity of this claim was formerly recognized by Mr. John Morley and even by Sir Wilfrid Lawson. But the last-named gentleman now maintains that, since the decision of the courts and since the condemnation of the liquor-traffic has manifested itself so plainly as it has done of late, every one in the trade has had sufficient notice, and that if he enters or continues in it he does so at his own risk. And now it may be taken as certain that all official Liberals, as well as avowed temperance advocates, are agreed in refusing money compensation. In short, all parties are agreed that there are too many public-houses and that the number ought to be diminished. But this is the extent of agreement: differences spring up as to the manner of accomplishing the agreed-upon diminution. Even the temperance advocates are not agreed as to what should constitute the licensing authority. At present the magistrates form this authority, and that it should be taken from them is admitted; but whether the power of licensing should be conferred upon the municipal and county councils, or whether a body should be formed *ad hoc*, like school boards are elected for control of elementary education, is a point in dispute. Meanwhile the House of Commons, by a recent vote, has affirmed the desirability of diminishing the number of liquor-stores and of giving to local authorities the control, provided that equitable compensation be made to those who hold licenses. To the necessity of giving equitable compensation the present government still adheres. There is, however, but little reason to think that on this point their policy will commend itself to the country.

TALK ABOUT NEW BOOKS.

THE final volume* of the series in which M. Imbert Saint-Amand treats of the Empress Marie-Louise accents more sharply than ever, though not, as we suppose, by deliberate intention on the part of its author, the insignificance of their heroine. Perhaps no woman could have shone at the side of Napoleon as Marie-Antoinette, for instance, does at the side of ·Louis XVI. In fact, the cases are almost reversed if these two examples are chosen for the terms of comparison, since in one of them the woman eclipses and dwarfs the man almost as profoundly as her sisters are extinguished in the other Even Josephine, charming, amiable, and gracious figure as she is, was hardly more than an episode—intrinsically an episode, one hastens to add, not made so merely by the fact of the divorce—in the great career into which she entered. As for Marie-Louise, she was a nonentity from first to last. As a dairy-maid she would probably have done her duty in an inconspicuously faithful manner. But the strain of her actual circumstances was too great for the material she was made of. Her attitude toward Napoleon is neither difficult to understand nor hard to forgive. It might easily have been more heroic, but in that case it would not have been so true. Saint-Amand lays his hand on the secret of it in the final paragraph of this volume, when he is comparing her with Catherine of Würtemberg, a woman who occupied toward Jerome Bonaparte a position precisely analogous to that in which Marie-Louise stood toward Napoleon. Neither woman was, in any but a purely legal sense, the wife of the man whom she called husband, since each of these brothers had been already united in Christian marriage to a woman still living when the second union was contracted. But one of them is quoted as an example of fidelity, and the other of faithlessness. " The difference," says Saint-Amand,

" between the conduct of Catherine of Würtemberg and that of Marie-Louise is easily explained. It must be admitted, women never push devotion and charity to heroism except when they have love for a motive—love human or divine, the love of the lover for her well beloved, of the wife for her husband, of the mother for her child, of the Christian for her God. Then the

---

* *Marie-Louise, The Island of Elba, and The Hundred Days.* By Imbert Saint-Amand. New York: Charles Scribner's Sons.

feeble sex becomes strong. Then are realized those grand words of the *Imitation of Jesus Christ:* 'Love is capable of all; it accomplishes many things which exhaust those who do not love. Love watches always, and even in slumber does not sleep. No fatigue wearies it; no fear troubles it; but, like a living and ardent flame, it always ascends on high and opens a sure passage through every obstacle.' Why was one of these princesses sublime, and the other vulgar? For a very simple reason: Catherine of Würtemberg was in love with Jerome; Marie-Louise was not in love with Napoleon."

But to that summary something yet remains to be added. It was not so much that Marie-Louise was not in love with the man whom of her own free will she would never have married at all, so deeply were her race prejudices and her religious training enlisted against him. But she did not rise even to the dignity of motherhood, let alone that of the Christian woman. Her chief accuser is not the prisoner of St. Helena, but the unfortunate captive of Vienna, the Duke of Reichstadt. She deserved still less that her name should have been the last upon his lips than that Napoleon should have lauded her fidelity and attested his satisfaction with her conduct in his will. Perhaps his praise of her was also a bit of acting. Taken as a whole, this volume is one of the most interesting of a highly interesting series. Waterloo and St. Helena are. names to conjure with even when the magician is less cunning than Saint-Amand.

The Scribners also bring out a neat little volume* containing ten tales of New York life by that unusually clever story-teller, Mr. Richard Harding Davis. His talent is hereditary if, as we suppose, the "mother" to whom his book is dedicated is Mrs. Rebecca Harding Davis. But if so, it has lost, in process of transmission, that over-tense and somewhat hysterical insistence on large morals and small moralities which made "Life in the Iron Mills" and some other studies by that lady so unnecessarily trying to the sensibilities of the general reader. Mr. Davis is very free from any blunder of that sort. And yet the best and most suggestive of these stories, "The Other Woman," is of sound psychology, and hence of sound morality, "all compact." The "Van Bibber" sketches are particularly amusing—better than that, they present their hero's personality with an almost startling vividness and particularity, and apparently without an effort. Mr. Davis has made an extraordinarily good start on a road considered very hard to travel—that of the short story.

* *Gallegher, and other Stories.* By Richard Harding Davis. New York: Charles Scribner's Sons.

The same house publishes, in paper covers, a collection of Mr. H. C. Bunner's stories.* They are all very good—very clever, too, though with a cleverness that is somewhat domesticated and familiar when compared with Mr. Davis's work. They have the touch of middle age, as it were, upon them, and the expertness of the handicraftsman whose art is also his business. " Mrs. Tom's Spree" is perhaps the best and freshest of them, but they are without exception wholesome in sentiment and pleasant to read.

The most satisfactory, however, of recent American accessions to the ranks of the short-story tellers, is, without any doubt in the mind of the present writer, Father John Talbot Smith, whose abominably illustrated but extraordinarily well-conceived, well-managed, and well-written volume, *His Honor the Mayor*,† is capable of giving a genuine sensation to even a hackneyed reader. Some of its contents were not new to us—three of the eight stories having appeared in this magazine, though under different titles, within the last half-dozen years. They stand the test of a second reading better than well. Nevertheless, the least to our taste of the whole collection is one of these old acquaintances, now called "One of Many" in place of its first title, "A Boy from Garryowen." Father Smith is more obviously didactic here than elsewhere—less happy, too, in the scenes where the ladies of Algernon's family and acquaintance figure than is apt to be the case with him. As a rule, his moral is like the backbone of a well-made and perfectly well-dressed man,—the stay and support of all that meets the eye, but not a thing that one is apt to think of. What gives pleasure in these examples of his work, is the sense of his easy mastery of his material, his close observation and wonderfully vivid reproduction of what he has been observing, the candor and openness of mind evinced in such portraits as that of the " Baron of Cherubusco," Deacon Lounsberry, Silas and Lyddy Bump, and the M'Guinness family. The style, too, is excellent; strong, individual, without a trace of mannerism, flexible and lucid, and in the matter of dialect, whether Irish, Canadian-French, or down-east Yankee, giving abundant testimony to the sensitiveness of the author's ear. Some of the character studies are inimitable—the comprehension, for example, of the pathos of Cyriac Dupuy's mental and moral attitude between the " Baron," on the one hand, who has long bought

---

* *Zadoc Pine, and other Stories.* By H. C. Bunner. New York: Charles Scribner's Sons.

† *His Honor the Mayor, and other Tales.* By John Talbot Smith. New York: The Vatican Library Co.

and wants to continue buying a vote which Cyriac cannot understand it to be a crime to sell, and Father O'Shaughnessy on
the other, whose influence as the exponent of the faith which is
ingrained in the poor fellow's otherwise unenlightened soul, is
irresistible when he tells him that he must never sell it again, let
the forfeit be what it may. Cyriac Dupuy is a masterpiece of
portraiture. And we recall nothing more true to reality—we had
almost said to nature, but the matter is on a level beyond nature—
than the death-bed scene in "A Novel Experiment," where Mary
Jansen's faith unconsciously reveals itself as the living root and
substance of her soul. Good too, but in a totally different vein, is
the "Four Sons of Jael," a study which rends the heart and
leaves it bleeding. It is evidently in the short story that Father
Smith is most at home. His novels hardly gave promise of such
very good work as he has put together in this volume.

Mr. Henry Harland's new novel * may not be autobiographic,
but it has immensely that air. The fortunes and misfortunes of
his pair of married turtle-doves, shipwrecked by a faithless guardian,
and finding a safe harbor over on the East Side with a most charming family of "Chairman Chews" until Thomas Gardiner, alias
Grandison Mather, makes such an astounding success of his first
novel that he can quit his distasteful desk "down town," and go to
live in Europe, make very pleasant reading in any case.

A more pretentious but less successful novel,† from the same
publishers, is *At Love's Extremes*. Neither extreme, as portrayed
by Mr. Thompson, is captivating, though either seems to have been
more than the hero of the tale deserves. Have we not found Mr.
Thompson preaching some rather severe doctrine lately, with a direct and adverse bearing on Mr. Kipling's popularity, on the ground
that his "virile" heroes are apparently so-called only because they
are really brutal, base, and very "low-down"? Yet is it not true
that any one of them, even the ex-Corporal Mulvaney, "now re-
juced," and repenting the Annie Bragin episode, would show up
in shining contrast to Colonel Reynolds in his relations with Milly
White, as Mr. Thompson has portrayed them? There is a suggestion of Miss Murfree's way of looking at nature and the "poor
white trash" in Mr. Thompson's treatment of the White family and
their surroundings.

The three new volumes‡ of Cassell's "Unknown Library,"

---

* *Grandison Mather.* By Henry Harland. New York: Cassell Publishing Company.

† *At Love's Extremes.* By Maurice Thompson. New York: Cassell Publishing Company.

‡ *The Story of Eleanor Lambert.* By Magdalen Brooke. *A Mystery of the Campagna, and
A Shadow on a Wave.* By Von Degen. *The Friend of Death: A Fantastic Tale.* Adapted
from the Spanish by Mary J. Serrano. New York: Cassell Publishing Company.

which have been sent us, are all very entertaining after a somewhat unusual fashion. The English tale, *Eleanor Lambert*, describes
two very good women in a clever and unpretentious way. The
Von Degen stories are rather blood-curdling, but extremely well
told. As for the Spanish one, the title describes it exactly. It
is fantastic, but harmlessly so. After reading all the numbers of this
series, the mystery of the title selected for it grows increasingly
dense to our understanding. The books are none the less pleasant
on that account, and their peculiar form should recommend them
to those who have, like Mr. Wegg, a liking for "portable
property." Perhaps it would recommend them to nobody else.

Carmela* is a very charming Mexican story—or, rather, the
scene is laid in Mexico, and the characters are a half-Mexican
heroine and some of her American relatives. To tell the truth,
there is a good deal of the guide-book in its construction.
What Mrs. Blake and Mrs. Sullivan, Mr. Janvier, and even Mr.
Ballou, have had to say within the last few years in praise of that
wonderfully beautiful land, is recalled to their readers by many a
page of description or of history in this little story. It is none
the worse on that account.   But if Christian Reid has by no
means neglected description and instruction, she has still less
omitted to leaven them with entertainment and spiritual beauty.
Devotion is quickened by her little tale.   Carmela is a most
charming heroine, and the story of her self-conquest and its reward is one to be heartily commended. The volume is got up
in better taste than premium books are apt to be by most of
our Catholic publishers. With more careful proof-reading it would
have left little to desire. Remediable defects are not easily pardoned
in any case ; but when they detract from the agreeable effect of
such noticeably good work as Christian Reid produces when she
is writing simply as a Catholic for Catholics, they are more offensive than ever.

Several other nicely-bound little volumes accompany *Carmela*,
all of them intended to serve the purposes of the approaching
premium season. We could wish them better adapted to that
end. Most of them are translated from the French by nameless
and irresponsible translators, and brought out with little heed on
the part of the publishers to the more than common need of careful type and presswork in books made for the use of young
folks. It is a special pity that the author of *Edith*,† who has

---

* *Carmela.* By Christian Reid. Philadelphia : H. L. Kilner & Co.

† *Edith : A Tale of the Present Day.* By Lady Herbert. Philadelphia : H. L. Kilner &
Co.

done so much good work in her time, should ever have blun-
dered into the production of a tale like this. Can any reason
be sufficient to justify telling a story of actual adultery in one
generation and attempted adultery in a succeeding one, to girls
just coming out of schools in which the great aim has been to
guard them from the knowledge of evil? This story has nothing
to recommend it. Its manner is as unattractive as its matter is
objectionable.

Mr. Besant writes always like an artist; that is to say, like a man
who thoroughly enjoys his own work, and does it quite as much for
the pleasure the doing gives him as for the sake of the substantial addition it may make to his bank account. That is one reason, doubtless, why his stories are invariably such agreeable companions for one's leisure hours. He is quite up to his own level
in *Armorel of Lyonesse,** which, though several months old, is,
we believe, the latest of his novels. The famous Belt case, which
was one of the sensations of London some eight or nine years
ago, seems to have given him the hint on which he constructed
Alec Fielding, the jack-of-all-trades—of all arts, rather. The first
part of the novel is the most delightful, the description of Sam-
son, Armorel's ancestral possession in the Scilly Isles, and the
life she led there, having a charm of a sort quite new to us in
Mr. Besant's work. Here he invades, so to say, a domain which
Mr. William Black long since seemed to have pre-empted, and
if he does not altogether wrest it from him, at least maintains
his right to co-dominion.

Mr. Black, on the other hand, although he is still faithful
enough to his old traditions to give his young people an excursion together in a house-boat, has laid the scene of his
own latest novel† in London, Mr. Besant's most familiar ground.
It is a very good novel, too. Old George Bethune is a clever
but painful study of self-deception carried to a point which Mr.
Black seems to think not altogether beyond nature and reason.
Perhaps, if he had left out certain little touches, such as the
dropping of the Scotch accent and the removal of the Scotch
plaid after the visit to Lord Musselburgh which is described
in the first chapter, Mr. Black might have succeeded more fully
in persuading his readers to be of the same mind with him.
Another feature which he has in common with Mr. Besant, that of
choosing lofty, high-spirited, and pure-minded girls for his hero-

---

* *Armorel of Lyonesse: A Romance of To-day.* By Walter Besant. New York: Harper
& Brothers.

† *Stand Fast, Craig-Royston!* By William Black. New York: Harper & Brothers.

ines, and making them ennobling influences on the men who love them, was never more prominent than in the present story. It can hardly fail to please any one in search of a good novel for the summer vacation.

The scene of Mrs. Barr's new story* is laid in the New York of nearly sixty years since. Andrew Jackson is President, and making war upon the United States Bank. It is the period of the riots between the Whigs and the Jackson Democrats in 1834, when for the first time the city elected its own mayor, an office up till then in the gift of the governor and the council. It is the period also of the abolition movement under the leadership of Arthur Tappan. The story, when dealing with the causes, occasions, and circumstances of the Bank difficulty, inclines to drag. Even Mrs. Barr's most convinced admirers—and she must have a good many of them by this time—will be apt to find the discussions on the merits and demerits of Jackson between Major Mason and his friend John Paul Keteltas, as well as the lectures on politics given to his daughter by the major, to border too closely on padding for the purposes of a novel. Even the love stories of the two girls, Virginia Mason and Jane Keteltas, are not specially interesting, The book, nevertheless, is good as a whole, and increases one's respect for its author's talent. She has some unfounded prejudices which in her own interest one would be glad to see her free from—but it is hardly a question whether, without them, she would be as acceptable as she is at present to the public for which she ordinarily caters and by which she must be supposed to live. One of her books, as we happen to know, turned out, when finished, to be too favorable to Catholics to prove acceptable to the publishers of her present tale and of a good many others of her writing. It has since been brought out by a house less narrow in its views. In Mrs. Barr's own interest, as we said just now, and for the sake of the keen spiritual insight and high aspiration which her work betrays, we can but hope that she will not let her light be permanently darkened by a too canny way of considering the available qualities of her talent. The most interesting part of this novel deals with life on a Southern plantation, and the struggle in Jane Forfar's heart and conscience between her love for a bad husband and the plain duty laid upon her of preventing some of his basest and most cruel actions. In such a predicament it is easy to divine what will be done by any heroine whom Mrs. Barr thinks it worth her while to

* *She Loved a Sailor.* By Amelia E. Barr. New York: Dodd, Mead & Co.

delineate. Mrs. Barr, by the way, if she were as just as we should like to see her, would have used the invective of which she has such command more freely upon the "native-born Americans" who bought votes in the election she describes, and who have continued to buy them ever since, and less freely upon the "Irish peasants, who could neither read nor write, and who knew nothing whatever of civil liberty." No man was ever able to sell what some other man did not want to buy, and the parties then in power, and for the most part now in power, who practised bribery and corruption, were the real tempters and the real culprits. But they, poor innocents, the "Jackson party who condescended to use the votes of such men," are let off by Mrs. Barr with the naïve remark that the Irish "in their rags and bluster were so evidently in the market that the *temptation to buy them was irresistible*"! Nowadays, we believe, it is the native American of the rural districts, neither ragged nor blustering, but with a keen eye to the money value of his vote, who chiefly supplies the market where vote-buyers congregate at election time.

There is a good deal of clap-trap in the singular title of Jókai's romance,* but the story itself is interesting and almost powerful. It is put into excellent English moreover. There is a painfully vivid description of a railway accident in one of the early chapters, the memory of which is as hard as a nightmare to be shaken off. The point of the story, so far as it bears on the title, is that human selfishness and malice are quite 'sufficient to explain the injuries inflicted by men upon each other, without seeking for an extra-human principle of evil. "The so-called hellish passions in men," says the hero, once a Hungarian doctor, afterwards a so-called "American Silver-king," "are created by that which is beneath him, the animal, the material element, and it is superfluous to look to that which is above him, a spirit, for a motive. . . . Human I am and have been, and human have been the temptations and trials that beset me. The only devil to whom, for a time, I sold myself, was the demon in my own breast; a poor, feeble spirit, and long ago subdued by the more potent angel of love and peace." Jókai's story would have stood very plumply on its feet without leaning against any special thesis whatsoever. But since he elected to demonstrate one, it becomes imperative to say that while the narrowly personal conclusion quoted

---

* "*There is no Devil.*" A Romance by Maurus Jókai. Translated from the Hungarian by F. Steinitz. New York: Cassell Publishing Co.

above is justifiable from the premises supplied by his story, those premises are absurdly inadequate to cover the wider ground taken in the subsequent and concluding sentences of the story : *" All beings existing,* good or bad, *are human and material, and only such.* There is no Devil ! " " You don't tole me so ! " responds the reader, finding conventional English unequal to his gratified surprise at such an unexpected display of omniscience.

Ten of Sainte-Beuve's famous " Portraits of Men " have been very well translated by Forsyth Edeveain, and brought out in convenient form by the Chicago publishing house of A. C. M'Clurg. They are prefaced by an interesting and appreciative critical memoir of their author by Mr. William Sharp. Pending such an adequate translation, if not of the *Causeries* entire, at least of all that is best and most characteristic in them, as one would like to see undertaken and brought to completion, this volume is very welcome. The essays of which it is composed show Sainte-Beuve to excellent advantage. His sensitiveness to impressions, his austere delicacy of sentiment, his willingness to praise, his openness and flexibility of mind, his faculty of selection, everything, perhaps, except that charm of expression whose aroma inevitably loses something in the best translation and much in any that is appreciably less than the best, may be studied in it. One would have been glad, for the sake of that sharper-edged weapon which he sometimes employed, to have found the *Causerie* on Lamartine included, or if space did not allow, to have bartered for it one of those selected— that on Camille Desmoulins, say. The contents include papers on " Goethe and Bettina," " Alfred de Musset," " Letters of Lord Chesterfield to his Son," " De Balzac," " The Memoirs of Saint-Simon," " Camille Desmoulins," " Diderot," " La Bruyère," " L'Abbé de Choisy," and " Fontenelle." Every one of them is entertaining and suggestive as well as instructive. To read Sainte-Beuve with appreciation is to get a higher sense of the value of literature pure and simple, and of criticism as in itself a fine art, for the pursuit of which native predisposition and aptitude are as essential prerequisites to anything deserving the name of success as they are in poetry, or music, or the plastic arts. More than any critic whom we know, Sainte-Beuve is stimulating. He discourages sloth ; he excites to emulation ; he awakens sympathy with that chosen pursuit of his which he has felicitously characterized in saying of himself : " I analyze, I botanize, I am a naturalist of minds. What I would fain create is Literary Natural History." We commend this little

volume as an excellent primer of that ever-fertile, inexhaustible
department of study, which is rarely, indeed, a source of un-
mingled pleasure, but which is never devoid of interest and
charm.

A new translation—and a very excellent one, by Jessie P.
Frothingham—from the twentieth French edition of Maurice de
Guerin's *Journal* has just been issued by Dodd, Mead & Co.
It is prefaced by Sainte-Beuve's well-known biographical and
literary memoir of the young poet. It needs no comment.
Guerin's soul, passionless and calm, except when disturbed by
the melancholy which belonged to his physical weakness, was
like a clear lake in which external nature mirrored itself. His
expression of what he saw and felt is as naïve and involuntary
as the sounds evoked by sunrise from the great statue on the
Theban plain. When Sainte-Beuve writes of him it seems to us
that his pen slips—he fails to appreciate how great a truth Guerin
saw, if only by a fleeting glimpse, when he wrote the beautiful
lines we are about to quote. Concerning them, Sainte-Beuve remarks that Guerin was attempting the impossible when he sought
to reconcile Christianity with Nature : " For there is no middle
course," says the critic, who, like Guerin himself at a later period, had an inadequate and too natural a view of Christianity ;
" the Cross obstructs more or less the free view of Nature ; the
great Pan has nothing to do with the Divine Crucified " What
Guerin had written to call forth this only half-true criticism—if,
indeed, it be in any profound sense true at all—was this :

" *Oh! c'est un beau spectacle à ravir la pensée*—this immense
circulation of life within the broad bosom of Nature, this life
which springs from an invisible fountain and swells the veins of
the universe ; obeying its upward impulse, it rises from kingdom
to kingdom, ever becoming purer and nobler, to beat at last in
the heart of man, the centre into which flow from all sides its
thousand currents. There it meets the Divinity ; there, as on
the altar where incense is burned, it evaporates, through an inef-
fable sacrifice, into the bosom of God. *I feel as if deep and
marvellous things could be said on the sacrifice of Nature in the
heart of man and on the Eucharistic immolation in this same
heart. The simultaneousness of these two sacrifices and the absorption of the one into the other on the same altar, this meeting
of God and of all creation in humanity, would, it seems to me,
open up deep and lofty vistas: sublimitas et profundum.*"

No, Sainte-Beuve ! That was not a mistake of Guerin's. The
core of Christianity is there.

I.—PROFESSOR LADD'S PHILOSOPHY.*

This treatise is not the first part of a text-book of systematic instruction in philosophy. Its purpose is rather to make a plea for philosophy, and to call the attention of the more advanced students in colleges, and of thoughtful, studious persons at large, to its dignity and importance. The author has not attempted to popularize his manner of treatment and his style; his readers will therefore find that very considerable previous knowledge and mental discipline, together with close attention and careful study, are necessary in order to understand and enjoy what is the product of original thought and much learning, and deals with very abstruse subjects. We fancy that Professor Ladd will find comparatively few readers of this kind, but they will be those who are best worth having.

The plea for philosophy is chiefly against Agnosticism, and it very ably and successfully shows the nature of this " metaphysical boomerang," as a weapon which comes back and kills the thrower.

But besides the general plea for the reality and importance of philosophy as against sceptics and despisers, the author tells us plainly, and gives us credit for being able to see for ourselves, that a positive system of philosophy is suggested and sketched in his pages.

We have looked with much interest to find these indications of fundamental principles of philosophy, and we can express considerable satisfaction with some which we think we have found. The reality of the subject and the object of sensible and intellectual cognition, and of the relation between them, is presented very clearly and distinctly. So, also, the convergence of all lines of thought toward their final meeting-point and the apex of all knowledge in the ultimate reality, the ground of all being and knowing. The course of reasoning proceeds steadily forward toward his Monistic conclusion, which we understand as implying, not merely a rejection of all dualism, but also of every form of pantheistic identification of God and Nature, and as an expression in other terms of the primary dogma of Theism, that God is First and Final cause, intimately and essentially present in all derived and dependent beings, distinct in their essences and actual existence from their creator and from each other, severally, but having all one origin, one archetype, and one reason and continuous ground of being in God.

* *Introduction to Philosophy.* An Inquiry after a Rational System of Scientific Principles in their Relation to Ultimate Reality. By George Trumbull Ladd, Professor of Philosophy in Yale University. New York: Charles Scribner's Sons.

The author's treatment of Realism and Idealism is suggestive and interesting. We quote with pleasure a passage which oc_curs near the end of the book, expressive of a hopeful view of the prospects of philosophy, which we think is fully justified. "We find, then, a proof of the substantial truthfulness of the con_clusions reached by our examination in the continued recurrence and constant but *gradually softening antagonisms* of the main philosophical schools and tendencies. We have italicized the words which are to our mind the most significant, and which we fully adopt in a very wide extension as an expression of the confident hope we entertain of a movement toward har_mony and unity in the sciences, philosophy and religion, to which we look forward as the grand achievement of the twen_tieth century.

Professor Ladd mentions only to scout the notion that we want an "American Philosophy." It is, really, an unmeaning phrase. We might as well talk of an "American Bible" or an "American Algebra." George Eliot describes a certain Lentu_lus who possessed a "consciousness of corrective illumination on the philosophic thinking of our race ; and his tone in assuring me that *everything which had been done in that way was wrong* gave my superstitious nature a thrill of anxiety." Doubtless it is such persons among us who raise the cry for an "American Philosophy." It is, however, to be desired and hoped for that, as we have eminent biblical scholars, mathematicians, and geolo_gists in America, we should have an increasing number of able teachers and diligent students of philosophy in our republic.

The purpose of Professor Ladd in preparing his *Introduction to Philosophy* is a noble and useful one. His volume is fit to exert a salutary influence on those who undervalue or disregard philosophy, who have become bewildered by wandering among the mazes of German Transcendentalism, or who have absorbed more or less of the poison of Agnosticism.

We do not say that he will conduct them to the ultimate goal which pure thought and rational philosophy can reach, but he will put them on the right road, and lead them far on the way.

There remains the author's view of the relation of phil_osophy to theology. He rejects the scholastic doctrine that phil_osophy is the handmaid of theology, and yet affirms that it can be rendered ancillary to theology in another way. The exposi_tion of the topic is not clear and definite enough to furnish a sufficient ground for criticism. Moreover, this would have to be formulated on theological principles, and we have no desire to enter upon the field of polemics at present.

Philosophy, as a science, is assuredly not *subaltern* to theology. Its principles are data of pure reason, and its methods are rational. We have no fear that its prosecution to the utmost limits of the capacity of thought will be dangerous to Christianity, or that there is any analogous reason of apprehension from the prosecution of any of the sciences. On the contrary, it is the neglect of philosophy and nescience which are dangerous.

In conclusion, we venture to recommend to all teachers of philosophy a careful perusal of Professor Ladd's *Introduction*.

2.—DEAN CHURCH AND CARDINAL NEWMAN.*

"What the Church of England would have become without the Tractarian movement we can faintly guess, and of the Tractarian movement Newman was the living soul and the inspiring genius. Great as his services have been to the communion in which he died, they are as nothing by the side of those he rendered to the communion in which the most eventful years of his life were spent. All that was best in Tractarianism came from him—its reality, its depth, its low estimate of externals, its keen sense of the importance of religion to the individual soul. . . . Whatever solid success the High Church party has attained since Cardinal Newman's departure has been due to its fidelity to his method and spirit. He will be mourned by many in the Roman Church, but their sorrow will be less than ours, because they have not the same paramount reason to be grateful to him."

It was in these terms that the author of this book wrote in the *Guardian* immediately after Cardinal Newman's death. His own death followed closely upon that of his life-long friend and master. Of the movement of which he speaks, and in which he took not a prominent part indeed, but a by no means unimportant one, he had prepared this account several years ago, the greater part of it having been printed at the time for private circulation. His last days were employed in the revision of these papers. Those who are acquainted with Dean Church's writings will welcome any work which proceeds from so fine a scholar, from a thinker so refined and so religious as those writ-

*The Oxford Movement: Twelve Years, 1833-1845. By R. W. Church, M.A., D.C.L., some time Dean of St. Paul's. London and New York: Macmillan & Co.

ings have shown him to be ; while the larger number who are
interested in that great Oxford movement, which has already had
so powerful an influence, will be glad to read this memorial of.
it by the one man who, after Newman, was best fitted for the
work.   Unfortunately he did not follow the master he so much
revered into the Catholic Church, and the point of primary interest to Catholics is, What was the reason which kept him back ?
This he sums up in the words : " The English Church was, after
all its defects, as well worth living in and fighting for as any
other. . . .   We had our Sparta, a noble if a rough and incomplete one."   He would perhaps not have been unwilling to
use Cardinal Newman's description of the Anglican communion
as " a palace of ice, hard and cold."   But this view of the
church shows how far the dean was from having grasped the
idea of the church as not a human but a divine institution ; in
our Lord's own words, " *My* Church."

It was not the author's intention, he tells us, " to write
a history of the movement, or to account for it, or adequately
to judge it and put it in its due place in relation to the religious
and the philosophical history of the time, but simply to preserve
a contemporary memorial of what seems to me to have been a
true and noble effort which passed before my eyes."   The
accounts of this movement which have already been written are
now so numerous that for one who is acquainted with them there
may not be much which is strictly novel in this volume, but for
the reasons already given it is a work of deep and lasting interest.

3.—A HISTORY OF A GREAT FESTIVAL.*

An interesting history not only of the institution of the feast
of Corpus Christi, but of St. Julienne of Cornillon, and of the
city of Liège itself in the thirteenth century.   The translator is
but right, we fear, in thinking that comparatively few Catholics
in our country know the history of the origin and establishment of the Feast of Corpus Christi.   And still less is known
of that of St. Julienne, who was the instrument of Divine Prov.-
dence in the establishment of the great festival.   No literature
is more beautiful than the literature of the lives of the saints,
and Dean Cruls' life of St. Julienne in this worthy translation
is a welcome addition to the library of the world's true heroes
and heroines.

* *The Blessed Sacrament, and the Church of St. Martin at Liège.*   From the French of Dean
Cruls.   By William Preston.   New York : Catholic Publication Society Co. ; London : Burns
& Oates.

This and the before-mentioned work are as fine specimens of the bookbinder's and printer's art as any that we have seen from American firms.

4.—MARY IN THE EPISTLES.*

It would be a mistake to infer from the title given to this excellent volume that everything that has been applied in it to the Blessed Virgin is held to be actually contained in the apostolic epistles. But after making all necessary deductions enough remains fully to sustain the thesis of the author, viz.: that there is a considerable amount of teaching on our Lady implicitly contained in the Epistles. This view is borne out by abundant quotations from the Fathers and ecclesiastical writers.

The aim of the work is positive rather than controversial; its treatment devotional rather than scientific. It is an admirable book for all seasons, but more particularly for May, the month of our Blessed Mother herself.

5.—KINDNESS.†

A selection from the conferences of a great spiritual writer treating of kindness. It is divided into four parts: the first treating of kindness in general; the second, of kind thoughts; the third, of kind words, and the fourth, of kind actions. All is treated in the inimitable way of the saintly Oratorian. It is late in the day to speak of Father Faber's literary work. It is known not alone to Catholics but to those outside the church. Never had the church a more devoted child than this holy man, and we wish heartily that this little compendium may have a wide circulation, for his words always draw one closer and closer to the love of our Divine Lord.

6.—MEDIÆVAL AND MODERN COSMOLOGY.‡

This is a severe criticism of the mediæval cosmology, and of the doctrine of the text-books of philosophy which follow the

* *Mary in the Epistles.* By the Rev. Thomas Livius, C.SS.R. London: Burns & Oates; New York: Catholic Publication Society Co.

† *Spiritual Conferences.* By the Rev. Frederick W. Faber, D.D. New York: James Potts & Co.

‡ *Mediæval and Modern Cosmology.* By Rev. John Gmeiner, St. Paul, Minn. Milwaukee: Hoffman Brothers Co.

scholastic system.   An argument is derived from chemistry against the theory of substantial form and first matter, and the connected theory of substantial generations.   In the chapter on the vital force of plants the vegetative soul is denied, and the vital force explained as a resultant form which is merely a harmony of chemical and mechanical forces in the organic molecules.   In the chapter on the animal soul the principle of sensitive life is represented as not merely a substantial form, educed from the potentiality of matter, and dependent on the body both for action and existence, but as a substantial entity immediately created by God.   Consequently, it is denied that it ceases to exist, *ipso facto*, with the dissolution of the body, and two conjectures are proposed: one that it is annihilated when the animal dies; the other, that it continues to exist in some unknown state, for some unknown purpose.   In the chapter on the human soul, the opinion that the soul gives first being to the organism and all its parts as the substantial form of the first matter which underlies the whole complex structure, is combated.   Father Gmeiner quotes Secchi, Tongiorgi, and Palmieri, besides several eminent scientists, in support of his several theses.

Cosmology is the one branch of metaphysics which is the most beset with difficulties, and there are more controversies among those modern philosophers who profess to be substantially scholastics and Thomists, in regard to the questions raised by Father Gmeiner, than in respect to all the rest of the scholastic system.   Therefore, we wish to see a more thorough discussion and a more elaborate treatment of all these matters than we have yet found in our text-books.   We hope Father Gmeiner's brochure will help to stir up this discussion.

7.—SOME EXCELLENT SERMONS.*

Among English-speaking people preaching is probably more valued and consequently of greater utility than among the Latin races.   It is, therefore, the fulness of joy for one of our Catholic congregations to have a good preacher as its pastor.   The parochial relation is perfected by truth, zeal, patience, kindliness, sympathy, learning, the treasure of the priest's soul borne to his people's hearts by words of paternal love.

* *Selected Sermons.* By Rev. Christopher Hughes, Pastor of St. Mary's Church, Fall River, Mass. New York and Cincinnati: Fr. Pustet & Co.

The priest who publishes sermons stimulates preaching, and this is one, if not the chief reason why such a volume as this is so welcomed by the public; and it is to aid Catholic pastors in performing rightly their high function of the ministry of the word of God that Father Hughes has published this volume of sermons, and we, having carefully read every one of · the sermons, are of the opinion that he has done his work well. The test of excellence in a sermon, no less than in a preacher, is experiment. Himself a good preacher, the author publishes but a comparatively small number of sermons out of very many actually preached by him, some of them more than once. The clergy are here invited to examine these sermons chosen from a multitude of others, really preached to an average city congregation, and preached over again, and now offered after careful revision. The style, though not unrhetorical, is good, clear, forcible English, the sentences short, the matter cleared of all extraneous thought, and the manner of all verbiage.

The sermons are all of them brief, so that they may be readily committed to memory by beginners, or serve as outlines for the more practised; dealing each with one idea of strictly religious value, simply viewed, well illustrated, powerfully advocated and enforced. The tone is at once earnest and priestly, adapted to the altar and the pulpit. Holy Scripture is happily and abundantly quoted. The range of subjects does not expressly correspond with the routine of the ecclesiastical year, though the topics chosen are such as to serve practically the same purpose. Some of the sermons are on the critical points of controversy of our times, touching the relation of the religious and the civil states of men, and the bearings · of our civilization on the spiritual life. Others of them are such as are not to be found, as far as our knowledge goes, anywhere printed in Catholic publications of this sort—that is to say, those which give utterance to the voice of religion on patriotic occasions, such as Decoration Day; and others, again, arouse tender memories of the cradle-land of our Irish-American congregations.

Education viewed from a stand-point at once Catholic and American is fully represented in the choice of subjects made by the author. There is a fine sermon on Religious Indifferentism and an inspiring one on Intemperance, preached at the opening of the Convention of the Catholic Total Abstinence Union in 1876. Prayer, confession, the Eucharist, sanctifying grace and its effects, are treated of with much power, the supernatural gifts of the Christian state being fully displayed. A beautiful sermon for·

Advent entitled The King's Return, a very moving and yet very
practical charity sermon entitled Almsgiving, one on the Uncan-
onized Saints of Ireland, one preached at the funeral of a priest;
others on the Blessed Virgin, St. Joseph, and St. Patrick—these
have impressed us as of particular use for the great body of Catholic preachers. Finally, these sermons, so brief, and so plain
and yet so full of instruction and so earnest in tone, are well
adapted for the private use of persons who are hindered from
attending Sunday Mass or who desire devotional reading.

8.—MANUAL OF CHURCH HISTORY.*

In the book before us we have the first volume of an ecclesiastical history which, in our belief, will be found of no little
service to students. The author's object has been to give a class-
book to young men who have but a comparatively short time
to devote to this particular department of history. And while
he has of necessity been forced to omit details and to abbreviate
the treatment of some important questions in order to keep
within the scope of his work, he has nevertheless presented his
readers with an excellent narration of the events of church history down to the pontificate of Gregory VII.

In his treatment of his subjects he has adopted the synthetic
method. His style is clear, simple, and orderly, and he has bestowed especial attention upon those topics concerning which
controversy has aroused particular interest. In handling objections, based on history, against the church's teachings, he has
given the facts necessary for solution.

9.—PERCY WYNN.†

A book about boys and for boys, by one who knows and
believes in the innate goodness of boys. This last is a consequence of the first, for he who does not believe in the innate
goodness of boys has not yet begun to know them. Not that
all the boys who play their parts in this story are saints. By
no means; a number of them are bad, very bad, real villains.
But the author proves that even in such characters there is
downright good; and this he does without sermonizing. Know-

---

* *Manual of Church History.* By the Rev. T. Gilmartin, Professor of Ecclesiastical
History, St. Patrick's College, Maynooth. Vol. I. Dublin: M. H. Gill & Son; London:
Burns & Oates; New York: Catholic Publication Society Co.

† *Percy Wynn; or, Making a Boy of Him.* By Francis J. Finn, S.J. Second edition.
New York, Cincinnati, Chicago: Benziger Brothers.

ing boys, he is always conscious of the fact that, if there is one thing a spirited, generous, warm-hearted, and frank youth will not give ear to, it is "goody goodiness."

Percy Winn is a story of boy-life at a Catholic boarding-school, and, as far as we know, it is the only one of its kind in the English language. We heartily wish there were a hundred like it.

It is evident that Mr. Finn believes in the truth of what St. Ignatius wrote to St. Francis Borgia: "A sound mind in a sound body is the most useful instrument wherewith to serve God." Playfair, Quip, Donnel, and Keenan have healthy minds, stout hearts, and muscular bodies. And that they can box with great effect when necessary every true boy will be glad to know. The defence of Percy from the attack of the two roughs, Buck and Dick, is a fine piece of writing, and exhilarating, wholesome reading. Sceptical Frank Burdock is well done, and we can vouch for the truth of Mr. Middleton. We have known many Mr. Middletons.

Percy Winn is not a sensational story, although full of stirring scenes that in less skilful hands would have degenerated into melodrama. The scene which depicts the death, by a railway track, of the anarchist who has tried to rob Percy exhibits decided power and a strong, beautiful reticence. From this scene, or rather from what follows it, we quote what is almost the only comment the author makes in what is strictly a book of action: "Let men call him socialist, anarchist, a creature worthy of the halter. Yes, let us punish our anarchists when they violate our most sacred laws. But we shall save prison fare, and more, if we treat the poor and the oppressed as true children of the One Father, who is in heaven."

The author has given us what has been desired so long that we had despaired of it—a real book for boys about genuine boys, by a Catholic who thoroughly understands boys; and we are more than glad that he promises a sequel to *Percy Wynn.* Nor will we be satisfied with one more. There should be a series as unending as those of Optic. Thus much we have said of a second edition, contrary to our custom, on account of the exceptional merit of the story.

10.—SOME PREMIUM BOOKS.

Premium books are usually new editions of old stories, not seldom of small literary value. Here, however, are five new books all above the average of such publications as we are now considering.

Jacques-Cœur * and *The Moor of Granada* † are two historical novels from the French: the first from the pen of Delanoue, the second from that of Guenot. They are both interesting and instructive, and are fairly well translated. Laid as the scenes are in stirring times, both books are full of incident, and *The Moor of Granada* is not without pathos.

The stories contained in the series entitled *The Knight of Bloemendale* ‡ are of very unequal merit. One of these stories, "The Mirror of Mary," is from the Japanese, and is a beautiful little gem. While this volume cannot at all be classed with the two aforementioned, it affords much pleasant reading for the children's "tired hour," when the sun beats too fiercely for play, or when the long winter evenings have come.

A History of Robert Bruce § is more than a history of that hero. It is the story of the Scottish people down to the reign of James VI. Strictly speaking, it is not a history, but an historical novel. Historical accuracy is attempted, and we think has been attained. The author's name is not given. Whoever he be, he tells a sprightly story with a considerable degree of vigor, and the attention of the reader is not allowed to flag. The lesson that he who is truest to God is the truest patriot is to be read between the lines of this excellent little work.

The History of the Last Cæsars of Byzantium ‖ is a literary work of very considerable importance. At the time of its first appearance in French, during the Russian-Turkish war, it attracted wide and well-deserved attention. The author traces the rapid progress of the Turks, the decline of the Greeks whilst province after province was subjugated, until at last the fall of Constantinople dealt the fatal blow to that power which had ruled the East for so many centuries.

Todiere has been scrupulously careful in collecting reliable accounts of the events connected with the period of which he writes, and we trust that this Englished edition may be as favorably received and as widely read as were those in French.

---

* *Jacques-Cœur.* By M. Cordellier-Delanoue. Philadelphia: Kilner & Co.
† *The Moor of Granada.* By Henri Guenot. Philadelphia: Kilner & Co.
‡ *The Knight of Bloemendale* and other stories. Philadelphia: Kilner & Co.
§ *A History of Robert Bruce, King of Scotland.* Philadelphia: Kilner & Co.
‖ *The History of the Last Cæsars of Byzantium.* From the French of L. Todiere. Philadelphia: Kilner & Co.

11.—HOW THE UPPER HALF LIVES.*

Life in a tenement-house is not the most pleasant or the most desirable in the world, nor is it one which we would voluntarily choose; but if a choice had to be made between it and Society Life as Mr. Ward McAllister has found it, without any hesitancy should we give the preference to a fairly decent tenement and its society. Doubtless there would be a certain amount of dirt and plenty of bad smells, a good deal of coarse and vulgar language and noise, but the utter vacuity and selfishness, silliness and vanity of Mr. Ward McAllister's society, culminating, as it does, in elaborated and cultivated gluttony, could not be found among men and women who earn honest bread and butter by the sweat of their brow. If this book should reveal the real character of what is called society to any one who may be casting longing eyes on this most fatuous sphere of human life, it will have served a useful purpose. Of what other use it can be it is hard to see. In Mr. Riis's most valuable and important work, *How the Other Half Lives*, noticed in THE CATHOLIC WORLD for February, the reverse of the medal may be seen.

12.—THE SOUL OF MAN.†

This work, like all others from the press of the Open Court Publishing Co., represents the Monistic or Haeckelian Positivism. Although denying the existence not only of a personal God, but even of the "Infinite and Eternal Energy whence all things proceed," to which Herbert Spencer pays willing and frequent tribute, Dr. Paul Carus, the leading exponent of the system in the United States, and the author of the book before us, resents the appellation to his system of the word "atheistic." He retains the terms "God" and "soul," he even speaks of the all-importance of the soul's salvation; but he understands by "God" the principle of order in the material universe, and by "soul" the sum-total of the abstract ideas and lofty sentiments which man possesses. Animals are not capable of thought, he concedes, in the narrower sense of the word; man alone, therefore, has a soul, and this soul is immortal, enduring after the death of the body, and passing on from generation to generation.

There is but one substance in the universe, and every atom of it contains the elements of the consciousness which becomes

---

* *Society as I Have Found It.* By Ward McAllister. New York: Cassell Publishing Co.
† *The Soul of Man.* An Investigation of the Facts of Physiological and Experimental Psychology. By Dr. Paul Carus. Chicago, Ill.: The Open Court Publishing Co.

manifest in animals, and of the mind which is at last developed in man. Form is more important than substance; substance changes, but form endures. Everything which exists is knowable: Spencer's antinomies resulted from his own confusion of thought. But the materialist who repudiates religion, who despises the past, who looks upon life as merely the evanescent product of a fortuitous aggregation of atoms, is in the eyes of the Monistic Positivist a false and evil teacher, and it was the d'Holbachs and the Diderots who by their dangerous teaching and evil living brought about the catastrophe of the French Revolution, in which the innocent suffered with the guilty.

Dr. Carus no more spares the Comtian Positivism than he does Agnosticism and Encyclopedism.

The Christian reader will be pleased not only with his numerous admissions, which are available as weapons against other forms of rationalism, but with his unconditional adhesion to the ethics of Christianity, and the reverential attitude which all his work reveals towards religion in general, and even towards those who have formulated and defended the special religious and psychological doctrines to which he is opposed.

The book is also a valuable repository of the latest and most authenticated data which modern science has contributed towards the solution of the problems of life and mind, particularly in the domain of physiological psychology. It is well printed, and abounds in plates and references which make the work invaluable to the student of these subjects.

THE COLUMBIAN READING UNION.

ALL COMMUNICATIONS RELATING TO READING CIRCLES, LISTS OF BOOKS, ETC., SHOULD BE ADDRESSED TO THE COLUMBIAN READING UNION, NO. 415 WEST FIFTY-NINTH STREET, NEW YORK CITY.

AN English friend, deeply interested in our movement, has sent us the circulars of the National Home Reading Union, which was recently established in an office at the Surrey House, Victoria Embankment, London, W. C. It aims at helping all persons who are conscious of intellectual interests to obtain the maximum of educational benefit from their reading. Those who have but little time for self-improvement are to be assisted in getting the books most suitable for studying the particular subjects in which they are interested. It is hoped that by directing home-study to definite ends a taste for recreative and instructive reading may be developed among all classes of the community. Many prominent names appear on the list of vice-presidents, including the head-master of Rugby School, the master of Downing College, Cambridge, the Marquis of Ripon, Sir John Lubbock, Justin Mac-Carthy, Frederic Harrison, and Henry Drummond. The methods proposed are:

"(a.) Courses of reading are drawn up by competent authorities which are adapted to different tastes and requirements and include the best books available in each subject.

"(b.) A monthly magazine is published for each of the two classes of readers, viz., general readers and young people, containing articles—by writers of known ability in their subjects—upon the books included in the courses, and is forwarded to every member of the Union. The articles prescribe the portions of the books which it is advisable to study during the month, point out and elucidate difficulties, and give directions for reading and connecting links between the books.

"(c.) Memoranda sheets, on which difficulties may be noted, are issued with the magazines. These may be returned to the central office, and answers appear in the magazine or are forwarded to the members.

"(d.) Members may join the Union individually, but the council encourage the formation of Reading Circles, that is, groups of not less than five members, who meet at intervals for the discussion of reading done at home under the guidance of the magazine.

"(e.) The council also promote the establishment of local committees, in order that the Union may be brought to the notice of all local organizations, as, for instance, religious denominations, literary and scientific institutions, co-operative societies, clubs, school-boards, and other educational bodies.   Such local committees may organize lectures and excursions, secure the placing of the Union books in the various libraries, public and private."

The members of the National Home Reading Union are urged to render assistance by personal work among their friends and by the formation of Reading Circles.   They are requested to send to the office information as to possible helpers in various parts of the country, favorable localities for the establishment of local committees, and methods by which the Union may be made known to public and private bodies.   To make the project self-supporting it has been calculated that a membership of twelve thousand is needed.   In the young people's section individual members pay annually one shilling and sixpence, members of circles one shilling.   In the section for general readers, the individual members pay the annual sum of three shillings and sixpence, members of circles three shillings.   The Union magazine and publications are sent regularly to the members.   It is urgently desired by the managers " that large numbers of those who sympathize with the scheme will go further, and become *members* of *both* sections at a fee of five shillings, or *subscribers* for one or more years at ten shillings and sixpence, one guinea, or higher sums.   Donations will be welcomed for the purpose of paying off the deficit on the first year's working, and placing the Union finances on a completely satisfactory footing."

The formation of this English Reading Union is a hopeful sign that the movement which it represents is needed everywhere.   We shall watch its development with a view to any profitable suggestions for the members of the Columbian Reading Union.

An ex-member of the Chautauqua Literary and Scientific Circle has written an account of the work appointed to be done during the time that she followed the course of reading sanctioned by that organization.   She has also favored us with some copies of the *Chautauquan*, a monthly magazine devoted to the promotion of true culture.   We are pleased to notice that the Chancellor, J. H. Vincent, D.D., does not teach that true culture consists in the possession of a framed diploma to be displayed at home with seals that " flash out upon it as stars in the evening sky."   He says :

"Our only aim is to promote reading. If we enlist people in the reading of good books on a wide range of subjects we shall at some point strike their taste, and thus promote the culture that comes from the use of one's faculties in the line of his inclination and opportunity.

"This being the modest standard of the circle, we have a right to expect that every member will honorably discharge his duty, reporting the books he has read and none else, filling out his memoranda (when he undertakes to do it at all) by his own hand, or by dictation, not by proxy, winning the honors he seeks in our circle by the honesty which will render his recognition a pleasure to himself and a credit to the management. If any member feels that his conscience would be quieted by re-reading portions of the required books, let him do it. If any member expects to gain distinction or place among us by unfairness, let him remember that self-contempt is the severest penalty we care to predict. Let us live honestly."

*   *   *

The ex-member of Chautauqua, who is now doing very satisfactory work in a Catholic Reading Circle, had no desire for diplomas of doubtful value. Her only anxiety now is to ascertain whether the Chautauqua readings furnished reliable information on the various subjects required by the course. The members of our Reading Union who have requested information on this matter will find many of their questions answered in this statement:

"My interest in Chautauqua work dates from the early autumn of 1884, when a *Chautauquan* was handed me and I read as follows: 'The Chautauqua literary and scientific circle is a school at home—a school after school, a college for one's house. It is for high-school and college graduates, for people who never entered college, for merchants, busy housekeepers, and for people of leisure and wealth who do not know what to do with their time.'

"Having read the announcement I glanced at the prescribed course of reading and decided that here was an answer to a question that had puzzled me. I was but recently graduated, had sipped *a little* at the Pierian spring, and longed for a deeper draught. To procure this at one of the higher colleges for ladies was my ambition and hope; but for the realization of this hope I was obliged to wait a few years, and in the meantime I was anxious to keep up my studies by a systematic course of reading. A local Chautauqua circle had just been organized in our village, and within a week after reading the announcement my name was added to its roll. Of the thirty members of the circle—teachers, professional and business men, housekeepers and students—I shall say but little, except that, notwithstanding the fact that we represented many and widely different religious denominations, we worked together in harmony, with enthusiasm. I think that in the history of this little circle there is no record of any one who ever failed to perform an allotted task. Much of the benefit we derived from the work was due to this spirit of earnest endeavor that animated each one for the improvement of self and others. Every member felt that part of the success of the meetings depended on personal efforts.

"We did not have an elaborate constitution; just a few rules to regulate the election of members and officers, the place and frequency of our meetings. We had a president, vice-president, secretary, and programme committee; each elected for six months. While we realized the necessity of having a capable leader, we also appreciated the fact that the work of the programme committee was of vital importance, and selected its members from our wisest and best. The full Chautauquan course of reading requires four years. We took the work two years, and then, as a circle, disbanded; not that we had lost interest in what we were doing, but in order that we might devote our time to other pursuits.

"The course of study for 1884–85 was as follows:

History and Literature.

" Barnes's History of Greece; Preparatory Greek Course in English, Wilkinson; College Greek Course in English, Wilkinson; Cyrus and Alexander, Jacob Abbott; The Art of Speech, Townsend; Talks about Good English, Richard Grant White; Glimpses of Ancient Greek Life, Mahaffy; Greek Mythology.

Science.

" Chemistry, Appleton; Huxley on Science; Animal Biology, *Chautauquan ;* The Circle of the Sciences, *Chautauquan.*

Religion.

" The Character of Jesus, Bushnell; How to Help the Poor, Mrs. James T. Fields; History of the Reformation, Bishop Hurst.

The studies for 1885–86 were:

History and Literature.

" Barnes's History of Rome, Steele; Preparatory Latin Course in English, Wilkinson; College Latin Course in English, Wilkinson; A Day in Ancient Rome, translated by Shumway; Relations of Rome to Modern History, Wilkinson; Modern Italy, Wheeler; Italian Biography, *Chautauquan ;* Roman and Italian Art, *Chautauquan.*

Philosophy and Science.

" Moral Philosophy, *Chautauquan ;* Human Nature, *Chautauquan ;* Political Economy, Steele; International Law, *Chautauquan ;* Physical Geography, *Chautauquan.*

General and Religious.

" Pomegranates from an English Garden, R. Browning; The Bible in the Nineteenth Century, Townsend; In His Name, E. E. Hale.

" Each member purchased a set of text-books and devoted about forty minutes a day to reading, in the order prescribed in the *Chautauquan* magazine, in which we found programmes for the weekly meetings. Sometimes we used them, sometimes took suggestions from them, but generally depended on our committee for an original programme.   The following is a specimen of the programme we used the fourth week of November, 1885, when we were reading principally Roman history and literature :

"1. Roll-call, with responses from Shakspere ; 2. Character Sketch : Julius *Cæsar* ; 3. Paper: Cæsar's Foreign Wars and His Object in prosecuting Them ; 4. Table-Talk : The First Triumvirate ; 5. Music ; 6. Essay : Comparison of the Roman and American Republics ; 7. Recitation : The Present, Adelaide Procter ; 8. Book Review : Ben Hur ; 9. Ten Questions on the Week's Reading ; 10. Critic's Report.

"In taking up this course of reading we were not restricted to the use of the 'Chautauqua' books.   On the contrary there were as many different authors read on one subject as there were members in the circle, and at our weekly meetings we heard the best thoughts of many of the best writers on the subjects discussed.   Every one in the circle found time to do the prescribed amount of reading, and some of us did a great deal more.   When I read the Preparatory Greek Course in English, which treats first of the land, the people and their writings in general, and then briefly of Xenophon's *Anabasis*, and Homer's *Iliad* and *Odyssey*, I read also complete translations of the works just named.   When I read the College Greek Course in English, which treats of the writings of Herodotus, Thucydides, Plato, Æschylus, Sophocles, Euripides, Aristophanes, Pindar, Theocritus, and Demosthenes, I read also good translations of their best-known works.   This was my introduction to Plato's *Dialogues*, the *Apology* of Socrates, *Crito* and *Phædo*, and to the dramatic poems of Æschylus and Sophocles.   Analytical and critical essays on such subjects then became intensely interesting to me, and I began to take from the library shelves with pleasure books that previous to this time would not have engaged my attention.

"When we studied Roman and Italian Art we studied that of Greece, Egypt, and Assyria, and read a translation of Winckelmann's *History of Sacred Art*, and then gathered some information about mediæval and modern art.   I think it was at this time that I began to read the works of Ruskin, which have never since failed to instruct and delight me.

" This collateral reading we did in connection with the course prescribed by Chautauqua, which was merely suggestive or used as a guide, so that we would all read on the same subject at the same time.

" What did the Chautauqua course do for me ?   It taught me to read thoughtfully and critically, and to see and appreciate new beauties in literature and art.   It prepared me to continue earnestly my search for knowledge, for it gave me a taste for studious reading.   S. E. D."

Sir John Herschel said that a taste for reading, and the means of gratifying it, can hardly fail to make a " happy man, unless, indeed, you put into his hands a most perverse selection of books." In many departments of thought the books selected for the Chautauqua course are very defective, and from a Catholic point of view decidedly objectionable. We have yet to see any book endorsed by Chautauqua which contains a reliable account of the glorious work for "Roman Art" and "Modern Italy" accomplished by the Sovereign Pontiffs of the Catholic Church.

*   *   *

We would like to see at least one Catholic author represented in the Chautauqua course of reading on Christian art. Americans of all denominations will gladly unite with Catholics in paying a fitting tribute to Miss Eliza Allen Starr, for her life-long labors in promoting the study of art as exemplified in the works of the great masters. By her lectures and writings she has introduced the art students of the United States to the studios of the renowned Catholic artists. In recognition of her claim on the attention of the Catholic reading public as one of the best of our own writers, the Columbian Reading Union has just published a list of her books, with an admirable introduction written by Miss A. M. Mitchell, of the Fénelon Reading Circle, Brooklyn, N. Y. The list has been sent to all the members of our Read ing Union, and we urge them to make it known among art students. We will cheerfully furnish it to any one following the · Chautauqua course of reading on art, on receipt of postage.

*   *   *

Miss Mitchell quotes Nathaniel Hawthorne's statement that "Christian faith is a grand cathedral with divinely-pictured windows. Standing without, you see no glory nor can possibly imagine any," standing within, every ray of light reveals a harmony of unspeakable splendors." She then continues :

"One cannot but feel that, in the present state of enlightment, there is an overwhelming percentage of those within the 'grand cathedral' on whom the unspeakable splendors are entirely lost because they are not sufficently familiar with the sacred legends of the church. Miss Starr, in *Pilgrims and Shrines*, has endeavored to give us these legends, weaving them in with her artistic descriptions of the monuments reared abroad to honor the church's elect. In *Patron Saints* she leads us on to a still more intimate acquaintance with those who bear the palm-branch of triumphant struggle, while in her most recent publication, *Christian Art in Our Own Age*, she encourages the belief that the artistic torch, so long flickering, is about to glow anew."

" Fifty years ago, when an interest in mediæval art began to manifest itself in England, those who were interested in the subject found themselves at a loss to interpret intelligently the motives that stimulated the conceptions of the artists of the Middle Ages; for Christian Art is so inseparably connected with the history of the Catholic Church that it is impossible to study the former without a knowledge of the spiritual triumphs of the latter. It was to meet this want that Mrs. Jameson published, some years later, her works on Sacred and Legendary Art; but lacking the sympathetic insight of one who stands within the temple of faith, it was impossible for her to view her subject other than obscurely. As we contrast Mrs. Jameson's work on religious art with that of Miss Starr, the position of the two women in regard to their subject is most apparent. One sees poetical conceptions which she analyzes with purely intellectual discrimination, the other through her spiritual relation with the artist sees as he saw, feels the devotional thrill that he felt, and works as he worked, hoping that those who read may receive the divine message."

In reply to an inquirer we may here add that some of Mrs. Jameson's relatives became converts, but we can get no positive proof that she herself joined the Catholic Church before her death. The notice of her life which appears in the latest edition of the *Encyclopædia Britannica* contains no allusion to her final religious convictions.   *   *   *

Not long ago we heard a statement to the effect that educational institutions in America should not be surrounded by a cloister if their light is to shine in places where it can do great good. Evidently this remark will suit the writer of the following letter :

" I agree with Professor Egan, in his article on the school question in the *North American Review*, that Catholic lay members take little trouble to answer questions, and often shirk responsibilities. They do not perform their share of the public work imposed on Catholics. Our most zealous members enter the religious life, and the world loses sight of them. But our Protestant friends, so inclined, join a crusade, a guild, sewing societies, clubs, etc., and every little act is published, put before the public, for influence, emulation, admiration. We know among our religious there are a thousand times more sacrifices made, almost daily, and noble work done. The world knows scarcely anything about it. We suspect it at times ; sometimes have personal cognizance of it. Why could not our own magazine and weekly papers bring into more prominence the lives of these workers ? Nearly every secular paper mentions some work done by the King's Daughters or others. Why should we let pass the heroic deeds done under Catholic auspices ? Do you think it would change the motive of the doers to bring them into prominence ? I am annoyed at the way our ideas are usurped. I remember one of the Jesuits gave an interesting account of some of the hardships and difficulties he had to encounter in a new part of the country, and I said : ' What a pity, father, to let that all pass unknown, unnoticed.' ' Yes,' he said, ' the French have a very good way of keeping a journal, jotting

down thoughts and experiences, which sometimes serve those who come after.'
J. E. P."

The writer of the above letter is a most active worker for Catholic Reading Circles, and has touched on a subject that may be profitably considered as bearing on the public manifestation of the heroic deeds performed without hope of earthly recognition or reward.

* * *

"Thanks to THE CATHOLIC WORLD, the 'Life of Father Hecker' has been to me not only a present pleasure, but a reminder of a time when his name was a household word, spoken in a home presided over by one who thirty-three years ago passed over the silent river. Perhaps he was her confessor. When a child I was often taken to the Redemptorists' Church, although it was not in our parish.

"If Reading Circles could only be started in the various parishes I have no doubt that they would soon prove as great a success as congregational singing. If somebody would only come forward and start them, and those who have means would send books, what a great work it would be. One way to counteract the pernicious effect of flippant reading would be to give occasional readings to outsiders, who might be glad of something that promised an evening's entertainment, yet who would not read good literature for themselves. Again, there are people who, from want of opportunity to know better, or who, from too stubborn clinging to their own opinions and prejudices, cry down all literature except the daily papers, and so make things unpleasant for those who wish to read. Some believe, or pretend to believe, that novel-reading is synonymous with vile reading, and yet will read the papers, some of which are schools for crime. If such as these could attend those readings perhaps their stubbornness would yield a little, some of the cobwebs be swept out of their brains, and their families get a chance to improve.

"There are no Reading Circles in this neighborhood that I am aware of; if there were I would become a member. I belong to —— parish. If there is a Reading Circle it has never been spoken of in the church, so I conclude there is none. I confess I am surprised at it, as I do not think we are behind the age in anything else except congregational singing. Nobody has come to start that yet; when they do they will find us ready. I wish success to the Columbian Reading Union, and hope we shall soon have plenty of Reading Circles. A. E. K."
" Brooklyn, N. Y.

We recommend the writer of this letter to express these ideas vigorously among her acquaintances, and get a few of her friends to join with her in a request for the formation of a Reading Circle. No doubt she will find the priest quite willing to assist.
M. C. M.

WITH THE PUBLISHER.

THERE is no place like the Publisher's desk to learn that there are "many men of many minds." The letter of an old subscriber, published in this department of the magazine last month, in which the "brightness" of the color of the new cover was questioned, opened the flood-gates of an epistolary torrent on the Publisher. With all sorts of suggestions of every one (almost) of the primary colors, there have been many who claim that the present is the best color that could be used from every point of view. We quote the following letter for the reason that it exactly hits the idea the Publisher had in adopting a change in the dress of the magazine:

.*.

"BUFFALO.

"REV. DEAR SIR: It is with some interest I look over 'With the Publisher' in THE WORLD, and in the current number I was rather amused at the objection raised by 'An old Subscriber' to the color of the new cover. I should say, Do not change; it is all right. With so many magazines on the book-stands it is well to have, and really quite important, something striking to appeal to the eye of the general public. The old color was negative; the new one is positive. Keep it.

"In connection with suggestions, etc., you solicit, allow me to ask if you have ever considered that the sale, and, possibly through it, the subscription, of THE WORLD might be increased by a little judicious advertising, and more particularly by generous dealing with the book and magazine sellers throughout the country. It cannot cost much to print a few hundred of each issue beyond the regular number, and these I would suggest be placed with the dealers to have upon their stands together with *Harper's, Scribner's,* etc. Arrange to have them returnable within a stated time, in this way protecting the dealer and enabling him to handle them without loss, as undoubtedly the sale and demand would not be brisk in the beginning.

"In this way THE WORLD would appeal to and reach many Catholics who at present never see and seldom hear of it. For instance, as a matter of information, I have inquired at all the book-stores and stands in this city for THE WORLD and found not one for sale. The same is true of other cities where I have been. In Chicago I found it at one stand; it may have been at others, but certainly was not at *all* where it should have had a place beside the standard magazines.

" The American is an inquisitive person, and is most likely
to feed upon whatever ·looks new; wishes to taste, as it were,
of new things. Why not give him the opportunity of feeding
upon Catholic· reading and the Catholic side of things. It will
do him no harm, ·and may be productive of much good. Is it
not worth trying ?

" Pardon the length of this letter, but there is much to say
when the start has been made.

" Very truly yours,

—— ——.''

· The Publisher admits the truth of all that is said in the
foregoing letter ; and, so far as it rests with himself, he has
done all he can to secure greater patronage from the news-
dealers. The magazine can be obtained by them from the
American News Company, through whom the dealers throughout the country are supplied with this as with every other
magazine and on the same terms ; for THE CATHOLIC WORLD
is " returnable." That some dealers find sale for the magazine
·is shown by the regular orders of the American News Company, but that these orders should be larger and that the
magazine should become better known at the news-stands is
frankly admitted. In the ordinary course of things the Publisher
cannot reach the dealers directly, nor can he add to the inducements already offered. The dealer studies the question of
demand ; he will supply what is ordinarily called for. The
inducements necessary to make it worth the experiment of offering a comparatively unknown publication, ·even when it is
returnable, are, unless the Publisher is in error, very much in
advance of the present resources of THE CATHOLIC WORLD.

Hence the Publisher would ask his readers to do the next best
thing to secure a better acquaintance with the news-dealers—to
make a demand for the magazine. If our readers generally would
inquire for it now and then, the dealer would soon be led by
mere business instinct to venture on the experiment outlined by
our correspondent. The demand at the various public libraries
of the country for Catholic books and the works of Catholic ·au-
thors, suggested and urged by the director of the Columbian
Reading Union, met with a ready response, as a general rule, in
the purchase of books that otherwise might never have found a
place on the shelves of these *public* libraries, as if the Catholic
body formed no part of the public. So in like manner a regular
demand might lead the news-dealers to understand that there *was*

such a thing as a Catholic reading public and that it was worth catering to.

*

And we have a Catholic reading public—a public that finds interest in Catholic reading. It is small, but it is giving many signs of healthy growth. And the Publisher is glad to find in the proceedings of the recent Second Convention of the Associated Catholic Editors of the United States abundant evidence of that growth, abundant grounds for the hope of better things to come. The Association has doubled its membership within the past year, and surely where the spirit of unity gains strength such as this that hope is a reasonable one.

*

There was but one thing that in the Publisher's idea marred this second convention, and he is surprised that in the published accounts no stricture, no mention even, was made of it. It was the sentiment which one of the principal speakers at the reception gave utterance to. He "never read," said he, "a Catholic paper," and "his confessor had never yet imposed it upon him as a penance." On such an occasion and before such an audience this remark surely deserved a decided rebuke. If the rebuke was not administered it was because the numbers of such alleged "educated" Catholics is decreasing. It's easy enough to find fault with anything under the sun; merely to find fault is shabby criticism. As a mere matter of comparison it would be well for those Catholics who manifest such scorn for the Catholic Press and who do nothing with their purse or their pen to make it better, to compare the intellectual pabulum served in the ordinary Protestant journal with its magnificent support with that furnished by Catholic periodicals generally. It would, we feel sure, be a revelation to many.

*

Attention is called to an article of much interest in the last issue of the *Dublin Review* (April, 1891), entitled "The Scholastic Movement and Catholic Philosophy," by Mr. Wilfrid Ward. It is the writer's purpose to direct attention to the lines of thought outside the church which may assist Catholic philosophers in solving the problems of life. Mr. Ward, himself a philosopher in the full sense of the term, would have Catholic thinkers divested of superstitious antipathy to the contributions of non-Catholics, especially contemporary writers, to the philosophical discussions of our time. In urging this he says:

" A recent and saintly Catholic thinker has maintained that

the narrowing of Catholic thought since the Reformation has been owing to a duty of this kind. Private judgment had run wild, and the idea of authority was thrown to the winds by Luther and his followers. A stern enforcement of authority became necessary to neutralize the danger ; no matter if the intellectual life in the church did suffer for the time. A more important interest was at stake—Catholic faith itself. Authority became more absolute, more stringent. A liberty at other times allowable, and even essential for vigor and life, became danger-ous. As martial law supersedes in time of rebellion the freer process of trial by jury, and other institutions essential to the rightful liberties of a people in a state of peace, so the neces-sary vindication of authority after the Reformation contracted and repressed the freedom of Catholic thought and speculation which characterized the middle ages. Authoritative suppression of opinion became more necessary, lest liberty, at other times desirable, should under the peculiar circumstances degenerate into license. But this interference with speculation, however necessary, naturally checks the ardor of a philosophical move-ment, and may even render philosophical thought impossible. And in the palmy days of mediæval philosophy, though the danger of scandalizing the weak was not forgotten, and the great masters of the second period of scholasticism were not accused, as Abelard had been, of unsettling young men by startling and dangerous disputations, it was recognized that, in the sphere of philosophy, careful, dispassionate, and, in a great measure, sympathetic study of all great thinkers was called for."

* * *

He would have this reign of " martial law," as he calls it, and which was necessitated by the assaults of the enemies of authority on our defences, brought to an end, since the hostile forces which gave it existence have themselves weakened and withdrawn. What he says in the following quotation in favor of more liberty for English Catholics applies with equal force to Catholics of all tongues :

" And at the present time, now that comparative peace is supervening after the struggle of the Reformation and spiritual rebellion has resolved its elements into renewed obedience in some and hereditary separation in others ; now that the sus-pended commerce of intellect is being resumed and the institu-tions essential for a flourishing community in time of peace are again coming into play ; now that English Catholics have their civil and political rights in a measure restored, have their hierarchy re-established, are making themselves felt in the great social movements of the day, are recognizing who are their friends outside the visible fold in these movements, are sur-mounting the indiscriminate sense that every man's hand is against them in the world of politics and society, we naturally have to look more exactly in the intellectual sphere as well as in other spheres at non-Catholic writers and their principles. Intellectual life becomes possible for us as political life and social life. In the absence of philosophical organization at such times as I have referred to our rulers may warn us against false prophets, against Kant, against Locke, against the Scottish school, as well as against thinkers whose principles are anti-religious, as out of accord in much or in little with the principles of the church. A wholesale flight is the only course when the weapons and resources of philosophy have been removed. But when the ruler's martial law is revoked and arms are once more allowed, and Catholic philosophy is called upon to deal with the matter, it must separate the wheat from the chaff."

It condemns Kant's theoretical scepticism, but it recognizes in his pages probably some of the deepest thoughts which the intellect of man has wrought out on the great principles of ethics. It treats him as St. Thomas treated Aristotle—interprets him for the best, claims his support where it can, examines him closely, parts company with him where he is clearly at variance with Catholic truth, but reverences him intellectually, and recognizes that his great thoughts—as all great thoughts—come from God. And so with our great English and Scotch thinkers; Catholic philosophy does not treat them as enemies, but it considers closely what they say, and welcomes the good, and examines and corrects what is inaccurate. The great fact that in the exercise of purely philosophical thought a non-Christian intellect may be supreme, and far superior to his Christian commentators, was emphasized once and for ever by the schoolmen, and to forget it is to forget a cardinal point in their teaching.

* * *

Who is meant by "a recent and saintly Catholic thinker" is shown by Mr. Ward at the conclusion of the following extract:

"To express briefly the practical conclusion towards which these remarks tend, there appear to be two conceptions of the direction which the Catholic philosophical movement should take. One tends rather to fall back on the scholastic phraseology, to devote its principal attention to the identical questions which St. Thomas had to deal with in contemporary Aristotelianism, to view modern thinkers, so to speak, at a distance, as enemies on the whole, to be read hastily, for the purpose of refutation; nervously, half in fear lest to read them carefully and fully will be to shake Christian faith, wholly in fear of adopting in any considerable degree opinions first advocated by thinkers outside the church. The same view is inclined to regard contemporary philosophical movements as something quite external to us and radically vicious, to be compared (more in their conclusions than in their trains of thought, which are not entered into) with individual scholastic conclusions, and where they differ to be considered simply false, while the scholastic conclusions are held to be simply true. Such, I say, is a not uncommon view observable among Catholic writers. But there is another view more or less prevalent in the writings of such thinkers as Father Maher, and which falls in with the general account of the history of Catholic thought given by Father Hecker."

To the older readers of THE CATHOLIC WORLD the line of thought pursued by Mr. Ward must be familiar; it formed the theme of Father Hecker's most vigorous writing, and was emphasized in his last published work, *The Church and the Age.*

***

Mr. William · Swan Sonnenschein, of the well-known firm of London publishers, has just issued a "guide for readers" of eleven hundred pages quarto under the title *The Best Books.* It is a monument to his patience and love of books. Its object is nothing less than the provision for both the special student and the general reader of a guide to the best available books (which, according to the compiler's estimate, number about fifty thousand) in every department of science, art, and literature down to 1890. It was a great task for a single man to attempt, but in the general opinion of those who are qualified to judge, he has been successful. Whether one wishes to investigate the English marriage laws, or to learn all about the Colorado beetle, or to discover what has been said of the state of departed souls, the authorship of the letters of Junius, or the intention of Shakspere in writing *Hamlet,* all that has to be done is to turn to Mr. Sonnenschein's index of authors, tables, and subjects, and in another moment the key of the special treasury of knowledge is in one's hands. The New York · agents are G. P. Putnam's Sons.

***

Mr. C. Kegan Paul, of the London publishing firm of Kegan Paul & Co., has written a volume of essays entitled *Faith and Unfaith, and other Essays.* Four of these essays treat of religious subjects, the three concluding papers deal with literary matters. In the words of a recent critic: " The book has this special interest: that it is the work of one who has handled the great records of spiritual life and history in the spirit of inquiring Liberalism, and who has found an answer in the august doctrines of Catholic Christianity."

> " Plurima quæsivi: per singula quæque cucurri :
> Nec quidquam inveni melius quam credere
> Christo."

Houghton, Mifflin & Co. have published the first volume of a *Journal of American Ethnology and Archæology*, by Professor J. Walter Fewkes. It deals principally with the results of the Hemenway Archæological Expedition among the Zunis.

The Catholic Publication Society Co. announces:

Life and Times of Dr. Richard Robert Madden. Edited by his son, Thomas More Madden, M.D.

Ireland and St. Patrick : A Study of the Saint's Character, and of the Results of his Apostolate. By Rev. W. B. Morris.

Cardinal Newman. Reminiscences of Fifty Years Since. By one of his oldest living Disciples, William Lockhart.

Life of the Curé of Ars. From the French of Abbé Monnin. Edited by Cardinal Manning. New and cheap edition.

Peter Paul & Brother, Buffalo, N. Y., announce for early publication *The Life and Times of Keteri Tekakwitha, the Lily of the Mohawks*, 1656–1680, by Ellen H. Walworth, author of *An Old World as Seen through Young Eyes.*

Harper & Brothers have published:

Criticism and Fiction. By W. D Howells.

The Poems of Wordsworth. Selected and arranged by Matthew Arnold.

A Memoir of the Life of Laurence Oliphant. By Margaret O. W. Oliphant.

A new novel from the pen of Marion Crawford is called *Khaled, a Tale of Arabia;* and is published by Macmillan & Co. The same firm has issued in its "Temple Library" series the *Essays and Poems of Leigh Hunt*, edited and selected by Reginald B. Johnson.

Longmans, Green & Co. announce for immediate publication the second volume of their new edition of James Martineau's works, which have been carefully revised by the author. It is devoted to *Ecclesiastical and Historical Essays and Reviews.* They also announce an *Introduction to the Study of the History of Language*, by Herbert A. Strong.

BOOKS RECEIVED.

CONSIDERATIONES PRO REFORMATIONE VITÆ. Conscripsit G. Roder, S.J. St. Louis: B. Herder.

SACRED ELOQUENCE. By the Rev. Thomas J. Potter. New York and Cincinnati: Fr. Pustet & Co.

THE HOLY MASS EXPLAINED. By the Rev. F. X. Schouppe, S.J. New York and Cincinnati: Fr. Pustet & Co.

THOUGHT ECHOES. By the author of *Wreaths of Song*. Dublin: Gill & Son.

INFORMATION READER. By E. A. Beal, M.D. Boston: School Supply Company.

THE PARNELL MOVEMENT. By T. P. O'Connor, M.P. New York: Cassell Publishing Co.

HOW TO GET ON. By the Rev. Bernard Feeny. New York, Cincinnati, Chicago: Benziger Bros.

READINGS AND RECITATIONS. Compiled by Eleanor O'Grady. New York, Cincinnati, Chicago: Benziger Bros.

LIFE OF ST. ALOYSIUS GONZAGA. By the Students of Rhetoric of '92 of St. Francis Xavier's College. New York: Sold by all booksellers.

A SIMPLE PRAYER-BOOK FOR CHILDREN. Philadelphia: H. L. Kilner & Co.

A FIRST PRAYER-BOOK FOR LITTLE ONES. Philadelphia: H. L. Kilner & Co.

MORES CATHOLICI; OR, AGES OF FAITH. By Kenelm Digby. Vol. III., containing Books VII., VIII., and IX. New York: P. O'Shea.

ORIGIN, PURPOSE, AND DESTINY OF MAN; OR, PHILOSOPHY OF THE THREE ETHERS. By William Thornton. Boston: Published by the Author.

OUR COMMON BIRDS, AND HOW TO KNOW THEM. By John B. Grant. With sixty-four plates. New York: Charles Scribner's Sons.

PAMPHLETS RECEIVED.

ADDRESS OF THE FRIENDS IN BEHALF OF THE INDIANS. Philadelphia: Friends' Bookstore.

FIFTEENTH ANNUAL REPORT OF THE TABERNACLE SOCIETY; OR, WORK FOR POOR CHURCHES. Washington: Wm. H. Lepley.

THE

CATHOLIC WORLD.

| Vol. LIII. | JULY, 1891. | No. 316. |

JUVENILE LITERATURE AND THE FORMATION OF CHARACTER.

JUST twenty years ago the house of Lothrop & Co., of Boston, published for the first time one of those collections of miscellaneous reading for children, illustrated and in brightly lithographed covers, which have since become so familiar. A small edition was slowly gotten rid of in the two years following. To-day the same firm sells of this style of book alone, distributed among some twenty different forms, 1,250,000 volumes annually. They publish besides from 75,000 to 100,000 copies of bound annuals; and from original manuscripts, an average of 75 new books yearly, with a sale of 150,000. With the subscription list of *Wide Awake* and its attendant magazines, which runs up now to over 100,000, this reaches a sum total of 1,580,000 books of purely juvenile literature, graded to meet the requirements of all ages between infancy and manhood. Remember this is the record of but a single firm in a single city, and that there is scarcely a publishing house of any size in any large American town which does not make additions to the vast number. While it is but fair to state that Lothrop leads in the stupendous amount of his sales, many other houses press closely upon his figures. Harpers, the Century Company, Lippincott, the Appletons, and others show almost as large provision for the wants of youth, in their several departments. The four leading magazines, *St. Nicholas*, *The Youth's Companion*, *Harper's Young People*, and *Wide Awake*, count three-quarters of a million of subscribers; and among their contributors are some of the choicest names in politics, in science, in art, and in literary work of the known world. In addition there comes from across the water a host of novel and beautiful things to swell the final amount. The admirable and infinitely varied treatises which French ingenuity has put into the form of narrative or fiction to beguile the imagination into acting as interpreter to the intellect; the equally diversified but not always so carefully finished work of English book-makers; and the folk-lore and fairy-tales of Germany and Denmark weigh down the shelves of our booksellers. This would alone give an enormous amount in numbers if one could reach the figures. On one of the pages in a late issue of Scribner there is a list of 71 new fine-art juveniles, all reprints from earlier English editions. The *American Publishers' Weekly*, giving in February, 1889, the *résumé* of work in this department during the preceding year in the United States alone, gives the number of individual new works—without counting new editions of older publications—at 487; remarking, meantime, that the list is rendered incomplete by the failure of so many houses, especially in the West, to send in their statements. There are to be added to this importations of British authors of other new juveniles to the number of 112. The same paper states that "nowadays books addressed to young people are so admirably written and illustrated that adult readers are glad to use them, which renders it difficult for one who desires to classify to know under which heading they should be placed." The figures here referred to show 470 juveniles as against 1,314 novels in England, and 487 juveniles against 1,022 novels in this country. In neither case does this estimate include magazines. Unfortunately there is no account which would give the number of copies sold from this bewildering array; but taking Mr. Lothrop's average as a basis of estimate, there would be not less than 1,200,000 individual volumes, with reprints in the shape of miscellaneous collections which would count at least 5,000,000 more.

If these statements could but be taken to represent a similar plethora of intellectual development what happiness for all concerned. But I have not even been able to reach any approximately correct estimate of the number of comparatively useful books sold, as against those comparatively useless or worse. The "penny dreadfuls" of England, the five-cent pamphlets of Beadle's wretched detective stories, the degraded style and doubtful influence of such papers as the *Fireside Companion* will count their millions in the list as well as Stevenson's *Kidnapped* or *St. Nicholas*. In spite of the reformatory and educational work of our public libraries and schools, our Chautauquas and

Reading Unions, the readers of this worse than worthless literature mount every year into hundreds of thousands, and publishers
are found reckless and vile enough to sow those seeds of death
for sake of the filthy profits they receive. It is only a few
seasons since *Peck's Bad Boy*, a work as subversive of manliness,
of reverence, of uprightness, and of refinement as if it had been
framed by some infernal ingenuity solely for purposes of perversion, sold its 250,000 copies; and made the fortunes of author
and publisher when it should have been the disgrace of both. It
is safe to say that each one of those 250,000 books passed
sooner or later through the hands of at least two or three young
people before it found its way to oblivion; and every one counts
for as much in the sales-list of those years as a copy of Bible.
stories or a volume of *Robinson Crusoe.*

This is but one of the dangers to which the tremendous
change of the last fifty years has left us open. At first sight
an unmixed good, this superabundance of material disguises the
germ of a subtle but most positive evil. Even supposing the
whole range of absolutely vicious contributions to be stricken
out and only the good and true left, there would still be reason
for a pause of apprehension at the threshold of this full granary,
which has taken the place of the old emptiness. It is hard for
loving hands to understand that beyond a certain point support
and guidance are snares instead of blessings. Some struggle the
child must have, some elements of danger and difficulty must be
left for his own overcoming, or the strength of his nature will
never be fully developed. There is, congenitally, sufficient leaning toward the curves of least resistance in humanity, without
eliminating altogether by disuse from the virtues of mankind the
elements of antagonism, of perseverance, and of stubborn self-reliance. There is danger of drifting toward the maelstrom of
indifference and ease, which has already swallowed up so much
promise, and which appears year by year to threaten more directly the integrity of character among us. The best minds of
the age are at work now upon the problem of simplifying life's
realities and meanings, so that the dawning intelligence shall
comprehend almost unconsciously, as it learns to walk or to talk.
The perceptions are no longer allowed to be strained beyond
their normal power in the effort to grasp the full meaning of
some great truth; but piece by piece, with infinite patience and
many twists and turns, the subject is brought within the child's
focus of vision. The texts for the school, the moral lesson at
the mother's knee and the church altar, the principles and re-

finements into which the plastic nature is to be taught to mould
itself, must be illuminated with light beyond that which comes
from their own merits, and be imbibed rather than inculcated.
There *is* now a royal road to learning, which little feet may
tread. It has been graded after the best plans of modern en.
gineering, every stumbling-block has been removed from its
course, it has been widened and paved, it has been smoothed
and swept and garnished, and poor as well as rich have been
made welcome to tread the highway. It remains now to be
seen whether this gracious and easy passage will induce such
sturdy muscle and brave pedestrianism as of old, when there
were ups and downs, miry spots, and stony places to be gotten
over. We have rid ourselves of the Slough of Despond and the
Hill Difficulty—pray Heaven that we may not also have ridden
ourselves of the energy formerly required to overcome them!

Another risk of which the plethora of juvenile writing is—
shall I say effect, or cause?—is that which at present attaches
itself to all our dealings with childhood, in allowing too much
scope to its preferences and impulses, under the illusion that we
are thus interfering less with the personality of the individual.
To be of use either to itself or to others, must not all individuality be trained into the service of loyalty, of reverence, and of
principle? The highest liberty can be known only where law
and order exist; outside that, all is license. To make the child's
will or the child's whim of the first importance in choosing the
books he shall amuse or enlighten himself with, is to jeopardize
not only intellectual training, but moral force. We do not yield
to the nursery rebellion against the daily bath, the early hour
for bed-time, the plainness of simple and wholesome diet. Why
should we risk for the spiritual constitution what we would consider hazardous or actually unsafe for the physical? We know
that the youthful mind, naturally eager and curious, passes with
delight from one field of emotion to another, but refuses, without
wise constraint, to remain long at any one quest. Allowed in
the beginning to roam unchecked in a desultory way, the demand for the excitement of change becomes first customary and
then habitual. Reading which requires any effort of thought or
strain upon the attention grows irksome, and is quietly dropped
for more congenial pages. Since the supply always answers the
demand, there results a flood of light and flimsy story-telling,
over-sweet with vapid sentimentalism, over-spiced with weak sensations, which sweeps the idle fancy away with it, and leaves
behind stagnant pool and treacherous marsh, where proper irriga-

tibn would have developed fertile and fair fields. A false standard of emotion is made to take the place of true feeling; and
where the old writers failed only through turgid expressions or
bombastic language, the new often go astray in conception and
sentiment. Our best writers to-day have admirably solved the
problem of simplifying expression while retaining purity of
thought. But the literature which stocks our Christian counters
and overflows our library shelves has shifted its shortcomings
from the form to the idea. It is the spirit instead of the letter
which now halts. The proportions of this Barmecide feast are
so great, and its debilitating influence on the mental growth of
the child so evident, that it sensibly diminishes whatever vainglory we might be apt to feel at the magnitude of the provision
made. It would be quite safe to assume that one-half the entire
number of books written for young people belong to this skim-
milk and adulterated candy grade—it would be nearer truth to
say it reached three-quarters of the total. If there could be a
Congressional decree creating a board of censors with full power
to destroy all this questionable travesty on the name of literature,
it would do more for the security of American progress and
prosperity than even the solution of the proper distribution of
the surplus. It is not wholly the vicious or the absolutely
worthless which is to be feared; but that other type which is
almost as unhealthy in its subtle undermining of pure taste and
sterling worth. Made simply to amuse, written as hack-work
by scribblers in whom the intellect is as arid as the imagination,
they are so managed as not to shock conventional morality, and
thus escape the censure they deserve. They make advances
upon sensitiveness by such slow but sure degrees that they act
as anæsthetics, lulling the conscience and deadening the will.
Their use is the more to be regretted in that the child's imagination, vivid, inexhaustible, glorious, is as ready to assimilate the
finished as the imperfect work; it is as easy to train his understanding of literary style upon Lamb's *Tales from Shakspere*
and Kingsley's *Stories from Homer*, upon Longfellow, and Scott,
and Tennyson, as upon Oliver Optic, and Miss Alcott, and the
host of lesser writers who fall infinitely below even these in
merit.

Before passing to the suggestions which prudence and thoughtfulness would naturally arrive at as means of remedy for these
dangers, there is a third which deserves a moment's notice. The
old proverb, "Beware of the man of one book," reflected not
only the ignorance and intolerance of a little learning, but also

the absolute knowledge of his subject which the student developed upon this principle possessed. To the boy or girl of that time his hero was an intimate personal friend. His interest was that of long acquaintance; adventure and incident were his own possessions, conned over, reflected upon, revelled in, until they were familiar as the faces and exploits of his brothers. What book of to-day is such portion of the life of its child-reader beyond the passing moment during which it claims his attention. What image is so fixed in memory as to hold its own amid the vaporous crowd of hurrying phantoms, silhouettes rather than substantial figures, which tread upon each other's heels through the excited imagination, and fade like shades thrown upon the disc of a magic lantern? Here is really the greatest evil which threatens the helpfulness and benefit of the rich material provided for youth by the helpfulness and generosity of the modern spirit. The curse of superficiality, the risk of losing that after-growth of the mind which is the harvest of cultivation, clings about our own times with a pertinacity which endangers future progress at least as much as the harshness of mental discipline which preceded it. The habit of skimming a book instead of reading it, of demanding amusement instead of study, of allowing curiosity to take the place of reflection, is becoming so common among young people that it leaves much to be desired in the dispositions they bring to the acquirement of information and refinement afterward.

It is precisely in this matter of careful reading, as food for digestion rather than delectation of the palate, that the basis of true culture lies as opposed to commonplace acquirement. The child whose taste has been formed upon good models, and who has been taught to extract not sweetness alone but nourishment from the delectable pages spread before him, is sure to develop into the man of cultivated understanding and elevated imagination. His perceptions will be more delicate in all the finer and nobler issues of life. As for the girl, to whom the habit of interest in study and earnestness of thought is to mean so much more; whose life, as a woman, is to depend so largely for its vitality, health, and usefulness upon the power to turn readily into communion with great and noble minds, the training is not only beneficial, it is indispensable. In spite of all the widening paths which the new apprehension of women's rights and privileges have laid open to her feet, she is still to be the housekeeper, the housewife, the house-mother by nature, by grace, and by inclination. From the close environment of these dear but wearing cares, from the

narrowing influence of this happy but monotonous routine, she
will find freshness, vigor, recreation of sense, soul and body, in
her wise love of books. It is this which will lead her from over-
critical self-concentration into wholesome interest in ampler and
more varied fields. The overpowering strain upon nerve strength
which the demands of modern society place upon those who
form it, and which has resulted in an epidemic of prostration as
alarming as it is prevalent, will find its best corrective in some
earnest mental exercise which shall invigorate instead of wearying.
The attention turned wholly into other channels for even very
short spaces of time will create for itself counter issues of abundant interest to offset the frivolous and useless preoccupations
which wear out so many sensitive temperaments. I remember
some twenty years ago, when arguments of this kind were much
less general than at present, being very much struck by a series
of "Lenten Talks" given by the celebrated Bishop Dupanloup
to the ladies of his congregation. The subject was the means of
enlarging ordinary life into healthier and happier channels, and
nobler uses and ideals. He claimed that for rich and poor, the
woman of fashion as well as the household drudge, the most
complete rest and relaxation would be found in fifteen minutes,
if no more could be spared, of thoughtful daily reading. This
was to be carried on regularly; not by those fits and starts which
are to solid improvement what jerks are to a steady pull; and it
was for study, not amusement. And he was quite right. Even
physically, as a distribution of the blood and nervous forces, it is
the surest tonic for fatigue and weakness. But the power to avail
one's self of this vivifying influence can only come to those
whose earlier life has been an apprenticeship in careful and
thoughtful habits. It must be the result of growth and
training.

It is among the juvenile literature of the day, rich, varied, and
plentiful as it is, that these tastes are to be formed upon which so
much of the fortune of the future is to depend. In it we have a
strong and brilliant blade ready for our youthful warriors. But
whether it is to cut its way upward to divine heights, or
downward to realms of stagnation and iniquity, depends upon
how the hand has been trained to use it. If there could be
introduced into the homes of America the habit of reading
aloud, it would be in itself a great safeguard. There would
be at least assured sobriety and carefulness in the matter of
approaching a book; there would be security in the choice
made when it was to be shared by an audience; there would

be the benefit of association of ideas as a help toward understanding and reflection. No other method could better help to weed the good from the bad. Even where the natural order is reversed and the child instead of the parent has the better education in books, the riper moral sense of the elders would still be able to. discern good from evil; while the great watchfulness exercised by the public libraries, and the suggestions of the school, would make the chances of improper choice infinitely less than they otherwise might be.

To the objection so frequently made that the child has often no taste for the class of reading with which the more mature judgment would provide him there is but one answer. Taste is as much a matter of education and habit as cleanliness or morality. There may be an exceptional boy or girl who naturally and without urging keeps face and hands washed, or intuitively chooses the proper solution of a problem which involves some subtle discrimination between right and wrong. But for one such example there will be a hundred to whom the intrinsic merit of soap and water is only revealed after forced application three times a day for at least six or eight years; or in whom conscience is not the slow growth of ceaseless precept and example, planted in a thousand tiny seeds by the loving Christian watchfulness of the parents and teachers. So about taste in reading. Here and there a child will be found with such strong congenital bias as sways him toward certain pursuits or recreations as surely as the flower bends before the blasts. Meantime the other ninety-and-nine of his comrades are purely creatures of the measures employed in their rearing. Brought up on elevated and true models; made early acquainted with pure, beautiful, and strong thought as well as good English, they will take to it readily and kindly as their native element when the time comes that bids them choose for themselves. Accustomed, on the other hand, to poverty of imagination and the glare of crude coloring, they will turn from the better things which they have never been taught to appreciate, to the poorer glitter which has caught their eager fancy. The trouble, as a rule, is that we do not recognize early enough the dawning intelligence which is biasing the little child and receiving an impulse upward or downward as the case may be. I believe most heartily, that long before the infant has been born into the changing fortunes of this life the mother has power to mould somewhat the soul which has been entrusted to her. Certainly as soon as its bodily eyes have been opened to the light it is

time to · guide it toward the goal of promise.   The bed-time
prayer and song, the nursery stories, are stronger agents than we
dream of in the formation of mental as well as moral habit.

So that, after all, it is to restriction of choice by the elder
mind that we must look for purifying the mass, until those leanings toward right ideals are established which we call inclinations.
It is this little leaven which must leaven the whole lump.   Of
all races on the face of the earth .the American most requires
the help of high inspiration and the guardianship of self-control
because of the chaos of conditions and temperaments from which
it emerges.

Obliged to look to itself for repression and direction, making its own laws and abiding by its own decisions from the
moment it reaches manhood, what is to train its undeveloped
powers—to teach it prudence, obedience to lawful authority, perseverance and integrity?   Are these qualifications to be gathered
from the crudeness of uncultivated taste, the license of unawak-
ened principle, the absence of wholesome restraint while young,
until the plastic mind and strong perversity of unbridled passions
have learned to mistake self-will for conscience, and absence of
belief for liberality of spirit ?   What is to get for the beginning
of life that understanding which is beyond all other getting ?
You might as well expect the youthful intellect to absorb without suggestion or assistance the alphabet, arithmetic, or chemistry,
as that those deeper problems of life and character should be
solved by one who has never been taught to regard them.   If
he does not receive his training from books, at least his elders
must or his teachers.   You may shift the responsibility of careful choice to some earlier period, but it is still there and must
rest somewhere.

It is an ungracious task to emulate Cassandra, predicting destruction in the smiling halls of peace and famine in the midst
of plenty.   Yet unless we change many of the conditions which
at the present time govern the distribution of juvenile literature
among our children this is the only *rôle* left the impartial observer.   There must be, not occasionally but always, that wise
and kindly parental oversight which directs without forcing the
preference toward high ideals.   There must be an understanding
that weakness of sentiment and poverty of style are nearly, if
not quite, as injurious to the character formed upon them as absolute taints to morality and undermining of principle.   There
must be, above all, the firm conviction that a cup of strong broth
or a slice of good bread, taken at regular intervals, is better for

the mental constitution than this constant nibbling at never-so-carefully chosen food, which is sure to induce mental dyspepsia. It is only by such beliefs crystallized into absolute rules of conduct on the part of elder minds that we can winnow the wheat from the chaff, the cockle, and the tares, and know that good seed is being sown in the rich fields of thoughtfulness and advancement, instead of in the stubborn soil of a barren curiosity.

MARY ELIZABETH BLAKE.

INSPIRATION.

AN organ thrilling in cathedral glooms,
  A song chance-heard, a robin's roundelay,
  A kiss, a clasp of hands, a sprig of spray,
A sudden waft of meadow-land perfumes,
An old name graven in a place of tombs,
  In winter-land a flower of spring astray,
  A face remembered after many a day,
A bridal bell, a funeral with plumes:

Trifles, you say? But in the poet's heart
  They set strange rhymes a-ringing, till, behold!
    Well-hewn beneath the master's cunning hand,
Touch unto touch and perfect part to part,
  Finer than Phidian stone or statued gold,
    His gradual-shapen dreams of beauty stand!

P. J. COLEMAN.

THE SCHOOL QUESTION IN THE PENNSYL-
· VANIA LEGISLATURE.

THE School Question will not down. A solution of the educational problem must be found. And this is demanded not only from a consideration of the justice of the case, but much more so in the interest of a sound public policy. It is as unwise from the standpoint of the statesman as it is plainly unjust in itself to impose weighty burdens on any one class of our population, and worse still to persist in ignoring the fair and reasonable claims of this same class for a redress of their grievances.

The Legislature of Pennsylvania is in our day the first public body to approach the school problem in the proper spirit. At the recent session and for the first time, probably, in the history of the commonwealth, a prelate of the Catholic Church and another prominent Catholic clergyman appeared in the capitol before a legislative committee in opposition to the present administration of the common-school system. On the invitation of the Senate Committee on Education, Bishop McGovern, of Harrisburg, and Father McTighe, of Pittsburgh, threw a flood of light on the dark side of the school question. The scene, it is said, was one which might make Thaddeus Stevens, the founder of the present State system of schools, feel a little uncomfortable in his grave; and yet the claims of the bishop and the priest were moderate and their argument dispassionate, their manner that of men earnest and conscientious in their belief, sincere as Christians and patriotic as citizens. Such was the impression they made on the committee, as reported by the press.

The occasion that brought these advocates of the Catholic cause before the Educational Committee of the Senate of Pennsylvania was briefly this: Senator Henry A. Hall, of Elk County, had introduced into the Senate a resolution calling for the appointment of a committee to devise some plan by which the parochial schools may be adjusted to the public-school system and thus receive a share of the school-tax. Here are the words of the resolution:

"*Resolved* (if the House concur), that a joint committee of six be appointed, whose duty it shall be to confer with the managers of such denominational schools throughout the State in order to learn of some feasible plan to be adopted whereby the control of such schools may be given over to the various school boards to become a part of the public-school system, and to be made practically non-sectarian, so as to come within the meaning of the Constitution, and if so, to draft and report a bill to secure that end."

The resolution was referred to the Committee on Education without any opposition, and, as before said, Bishop McGovern and Father McTighe were heard on the subject in committee.

There were eight members present, the majority of whom were Republicans; the chairman, Senator Flinn, is a Republican; one member of the committee is a Catholic, while Senator Hall, the author of the resolution, is a prominent Democrat and a Protestant. It was too late in the session to do more than begin hearing evidence, which will be continued, it is hoped, next winter, and may lead to decisive action in the constitutional convention likely to assemble within a couple of years.

The arguments and evidence in support of the resolution were clearly and forcibly presented. The committee was much impressed by the facts and proofs of injustice brought forward. The line of argument pursued was this: It was bad public policy to so limit and conduct the public-school system in the name of the whole commonwealth as to cut off from its benefits a large and patriotic body of citizens. A public-school system supported by the taxes of the whole people should be for the benefit of the whole people. The bill of rights recognizes the rights of conscience and protects every citizen in the exercise of them. But to so conduct the public-school system as to practically debar from its benefits something like a million of those who are taxed for its support, but whose conscience will not permit them to use it, is to deny them the use of it as conclusively and unjustly as if they were excluded by name.

Again, it was held to be bad policy to train children from childhood into two opposing classes, one class feeling itself excluded from part of the rights of citizenship; for it was maintained that there is no higher right than that of education. This condition of things, it was urged, was bound to provoke continued disturbance and vex the peace of the State. Therefore, in the interest of peace and kindly relations between all citizens, a just and satisfactory solution of the problem should be sought.

Attention was directed to the fact that there are about seventy thousand children in the Catholic schools of Pennsylvania,

and fully half that number·in those of the Lutheran and Episcopalian churches. If these were suddenly closed, the public
schools would have neither room nor teachers to. take care of
this vast body of children. In the eyes of a Catholic the public
school, as conducted up to date, appears as a state church. It
has been a proselytizing institution. Facts prove this. A Metho·
dist minister in Massachusetts had publicly stated that the
influence of the public schools was so great that in twelve years
1,800,000 Catholic children had been lost to the church. And
this arose solely from the fact that religion was not taught in
these schools. Catholic parents want their children to become
neither apostates nor infidels. Hence they are forced by the
State's action to pay a double tax to save the faith of their
children. The committee was reminded that this question could
only be settled by extermination or compromise. It would be
the duty of the commission, if appointed, to find a compromise
that will work justice all round.

At this writing the committee agreed to report the resolution
for printing, after which it will be recommitted for further consideration. It will interest the readers of THE CATHOLIC WORLD to
learn that, with one or two exceptions, the action of the Legislature on this subject has been favorably received by the leading
newspapers of the State. For instance, a writer in the *Pittsburgh
Press* closes a remarkable article with this suggestion :

"If the parochial and other denominational schools are to
receive State aid, let the superintendent of the city, borough, or
county be empowered to visit such schools at least once every
year, and report to the State the efficiency or inefficiency of the
secular instruction given in said schools, as well as in the public
schools."

But this grave problem concerns not alone the citizens of
Pennsylvania, but those of the whole United States. The action
of the Legislature of Pennsylvania directs attention to the
common schools and the future of our country. It opens up a
timely discussion of the very fundamental principles of education,
in which all alike are interested.

We are all agreed that there can be no question of more
vital importance to the American people than this : How are the
children who, in a few years, are to be entrusted with the
responsibilities of citizenship and the destinies of the nation to be
educated ? Every one, in a measure, realizes that the growth,
development, and prosperity of the State depend on the intelli-

gence of the people. Happily for the Republic of the United States, with its citizens principles on this subject have passed into proverbs. We are all alive to the necessity and force of popular education. Not one of us who does not believe that knowledge is power. There are many, however, who fail to understand that the power may be for good or evil. And hence arises much of the confusion of thought, and of the conflict of opinion that prevails among us.

If we aimed only at the material greatness and happiness of the nation, the extension of trade and commerce, the adding to the country's wealth, the enlargement of its territory, the facility and comfort of travel, and various other benefits that might be mentioned, then we could consistently be satisfied with a purely secular system of education. But if our purpose is, as assuredly it must be, to preserve our form of government, to keep the moral bonds of society strong and secure, to maintain peace and good-will among all classes, to create and develop a sense of duty and justice in the individual so that honest and harmonious relations may exist between man and man, then surely we need something more than mere intelligence. We want virtue in the people. Without it there is no hope for the safety and perpetuity of our institutions. The history of the nations enforces this truth. The fall of the Roman Empire was due to its moral ruin? Yet all will admit that Rome and the other civilizations of antiquity were richer and more learned in the time of their decay than during the period of their infancy and growth; but the moral correlative being wanting, they tottered to their fall.

And is it not significant that our enterprising press invites thoughtful and patriotic men to discuss the dangers that threaten American civilization; that such questions as the following are proposed : 1st, Will our present republican form of government last one hundred years longer ? 2d, And if not, why not? 3d, What is its greatest peril ? The answers collected from men holding very different views on other subjects are substantially the same. All are agreed that there is danger ahead. One or two express the opinion that our present republican form of government cannot last one hundred years longer. It is well to note that it is the true and best friends of our common country, not her enemies, who to-day are asking and answering these questions. It is agreed that the greatest peril arises from a decadence of virtue among the people. The Protestant Bishop Potter does not differ from Cardinal

Gibbons in saying that the impending danger lies in the "departure from those Christian principles upon which our very laws and institutions are based. As long as these Christian principles are maintained our institutions will, under God, survive and flourish. Our laws, which are only expressions of eternal law, will command our respect and therefore our loyal obedience. On the other hand, every departure from these Christian principles upon which our social fabric rests tends to the loosening of the foundation-stones of the Republic."

Let us view the situation in a slightly different light. Is it not clearly evident to all that false standards of morality are set up for the guidance of the people? that dangerous principles at variance not alone with conscience but reason are enunciated and daily acted upon by men prominent in business and political life? It is not necessary to multiply instances. Take the case of a foremost public man who, quite recently, stated boldly and without rebuke from his hearers that, to his mind, "the decalogue and the golden rule have no place in a political campaign." Or the case of one of the great plutocrats of the land, who gave forcible expression to his belief that the public had no rights which he was bound to respect.

The idea is essentially pagan that in any sphere of thought or action a man can escape from his conscience; that for any purpose or under any circumstances he can cease to know right from wrong, and to be bound by his knowledge. There is no moral teacher, heathen or Christian, of any age or school, who questions that the happiness of a republic depends on the virtue —I use the word in its widest sense—of its citizens. No American can be at once a good man and a bad citizen.

Regarding only, for the present, the preservation of our liberties and the perpetuity of our institutions we see from what has been said that virtue as well as intelligence is an essential condition. How is this virtue to be attained? That is the problem which to-day confronts the American people. In comparison with it all other issues shrink into insignificance. If we clear our minds of misconceptions and prejudices, getting a firm grasp of first principles, and following the lines of reason and justice, there is every hope of a safe and practical solution.

In the first place, let us try and understand the situation. There are many popular errors on the subject of education. The idea is quite prevalent that intelligence is the necessary foe of vice and crime; that when the future citizen is made intellectually smart, he is at the same time made morally good. All that

is needed to insure a decrease of mental or moral delinquency
is to remove illiteracy. How utterly false this notion is our daily
experience and statistics prove. The Socialists, Anarchists, and
Nihilists of to-day are by no means illiterate; the corrupt official,
the absconding cashier, the "boodle" alderman, the scheming
politician, and the merciless monopolist, all have had the benefits
of a more or less extended secular education; the men and
women who burst the bonds of domestic peace and happiness,
and those who crowd our divorce courts seeking relief from a
galling yoke, are they not reckoned among the intelligent classes
chiefly?

. If we turn to the records of our mentally and morally
deranged, as exhibited in our statistics of insanity and crime and
vice, it is the same disheartening truth is told. The number of
our criminals and insane increases while illiteracy decreases. The
tenth census shows that for the decade ending with 1880, population having increased thirty per cent. and illiteracy only ten
per cent. (a relative decrease), the number of criminals during the same period presents the alarming increase of
eighty-two per cent., while of insane persons the ratio
of increase is out of all proportion to that of population.
When confronted with such alarming facts, is it to be wondered
at that thoughtful and patriotic men are beginning to fear for
the welfare of the country and the stability of its institutions?
What shall the ending be if with greater educational facilities
there is to be increased crime, and every enlargement in the
seating capacity of our schools means a larger demand for insane accommodations and additional felons' cells? If the instruction of our common schools subdues the tendency to crime,
why is it that the ratio of prisoners, being one in 3,442 inhabitants in 1850, rose to one in every 1,647 in 1860, one in 1,021
in 1870, and one in 837 in 1880? Will the census of 1890
show more encouraging results? We fear that it will not.
Some persons regard the large and constant influx of foreign
immigrants as a partial explanation of this startling growth of
crime; but the facts deny the hope, for the great increase is to
be found among the native-born. The *Tenth Census Report*
says that, while in 1850 the ratio of foreign criminals to population was five times that of the native-born, in 1880 the ratio of
foreign criminals is but little in excess of that for native whites.
Father Young, of the Paulist Congregation, New York, in a late
number of the *Independent*, refuting the alleged statistics of
Mr. Dexter A. Hawkins, establishes beyond all doubt the same

unwelcome facts. Taking Massachusetts, where up to the last few years the public-school system was " the supreme and only system," he proves that something more than education, purely secular, is needed to account for the large relative excess of native-born paupers and criminals over those of the foreign-born.

At a session of the National Prison Congress, held in Boston during 1888, Mr. Brooker, chairman of the board of directors of the South Carolina penitentiary, declared that " it is a fearful fact that a large proportion of our prison population is of the educated class." No thoughtful American can view these facts and statements without alarm. They prove conclusively that secular education, however perfect or extended it may be, does not diminish vice, pauperism, and crime; and since these are everywhere justly regarded as the worst and most deadly foes of the state, a system of education that, judged by results, shows a tendency to increase rather than diminish such, must be set down as not alone imperfect, but radically defective. It fails in its results. It does not furnish the Republic with the expected quota of self-supporting, law-abiding, virtuous citizens. Perhaps there is no country in the world where the purely intellectual side of education has been so wonderfully developed within the present generation as in our own. The moral side, however, has been sadly neglected. And yet this is more important, because it is of more vital interest to the state and society. Here, in our Republic, where each individual voter helps to shape the destinies of the nation, makes and unmakes parties and policies, character is everything. If, then, our state is to exist, our citizenship must be not only intelligent but as virtuous as possible. The very life and welfare of our institutions depend on this.

It is because we have lost sight of this essential idea, or have not given it its proper place in our educational system, that results which all deplore, the startling increase of vice, pauperism, and crime, are brought about.

Let us illustrate the situation by an example. Suppose a verified report was made to the board of directors of any of our great railroad lines by the chief constructing engineer that bridges of accepted form were showing visible signs of weakness, the report would be listened to with the greatest consternation and dismay. The board of directors would, doubtless, institute the closest inquiry and most searching examinations; it would, undoubtedly, stop the construction of such bridges until the cause of failure had been determined and the remedy ascertained; and failing in this, the construction of such bridges would be permanently abandoned and more perfect structures substituted. Now, our theory of state education, as at present constructed, is evidently faulty and imperfect; facts which no sensible person can impugn prove it to be so. And of what utility are facts and experiences unless their lessons are heeded and their meaning properly interpreted? When the facts disclosed by our social statistics make it appear that, in the education of our youth, we have gone too far in our aim for material advancement and development of wealth, and that we are rapidly losing in the direction of moral growth and culture; that we are face to face with a condition of society which reveals illiteracy decreasing and crime increasing, a marvellous addition to the nation's wealth with more widespread destitution.

The problem is: How are we to remedy this state of things? How are we to adjust the moral balance of education so that in civic virtue and strength of character we may keep pace with our material, social, and political progress?

In the first place, since education rightly understood means the training of the whole man and of all the faculties, of the conscience and of the affections, as well as of the intellect, we must make due and necessary provision for the moral instruction of the future citizen. And since it cannot be questioned that morals rest on a religious basis, provisions should be made for the moral and religious training of children in our common schools. Over the door-way of every school in the land should be written, and on the tender hearts of our youth should be impressed, the sublime words of the poet: " Let all the ends thou aim'st at be thy God's, thy country's, and truth's."

This is a Christian country, in the sense that Christianity is " an original and essential element of the law of the land." To maintain and practically act on the truth of this proposition does not tend, in the least, to weaken or invalidate our cherished American principle of the entire separation of church and state. The Christianity affirmed to be an essential element of the law of the land is not the Christianity of any one class of the population, but the Christianity which is inherited and held in common by all classes of our Christian people.

This principle is expressed in many decisions of our courts. In a decision of the Supreme Court of Pennsylvania, in the year 1824, it is declared that " Christianity, general Christianity, is and always has been a part of the common law of Pennsylvania; not Christianity founded on particular tenets; not Christianity with an established church, and tithes, and spiritual courts; but Christianity with liberty of conscience to all men." Chief-Justice Kent, in a decision of the Supreme Court of New York, in 1811, laid down the same doctrine.

Cardinal Gibbons, in his admirable book, *Our Christian Heritage*, traces the influence and predominance of the religious element in our American civilization. The discoverers of the Continent, the first settlers, the founders of the Republic, the men who framed the Constitution, the illustrious signers of the Declaration of Independence, all our Presidents, from Washington to Harrison, were Christian believers. At the era of the Revolution all the colonies adopted Christian constitutions in assuming their new character as sovereign States. The daily proceedings of Congress and of State legislatures are opened with prayer by a Christian minister. Our laws are largely founded on the principles of Christian ethics; and so "intimately interwoven are they with the Christian religion that they cannot be adequately expounded without the light of revelation." The vast majority of the population are professing Christians.

Why, then, have we banished from the common schools of the land our Christian heritage? Why deprive the youth of the country of that Christian education to which, by every title that is just and sacred, it has the strongest claims? Why run counter to all history and experience in striving to preserve and perpetuate our institutions, which are established on Christian principles, whilst we ignore all positive moral and religious instruction in the schools? Is it possible, a student of our institutions might ask with astonishment, that the school-room is the only place into which our common Christianity cannot enter? Why, on the ground of making the public school unsectarian, introduce the worst and most objectionable form of sectarianism—the sectarianism of infidelity?

The general reply to these questions is: "The state has no right to teach religion; therefore, religion should not be taught in our public schools." That is false reasoning. The state, of course, has no right to teach any particular form of religion to the exclusion of others. No one asks that. That would be essentially a union of church and state, and it would involve injustice to all who differed from the system of religion taught by the state. What is asked of the state is that its citizens shall have the right of teaching their own religion to their own children wherever they go to school.

Others say: "It has been settled by the American people

that religion is to be left entirely to the home, the Sunday-school, and the church." The answer is, there is no settlement of this or of any question until it is settled right. Catholics and Protestants agree that these agencies are not adequate to teach religion; the latter as well as the former found and establish denominational schools. It is, a fact not widely known that in Wisconsin, where an objectionable school-law was the prominent issue in the late election, a single Protestant denomination, the Lutheran body, has 287 parochial schools to the Catholics' 193. Evangelicals of all denominations hold that their children should receive a religious education and training. To that end they are urged in conferences, synods, and general assemblies "to do their full duty to all children by gathering them into schools and colleges thoroughly Christian"; they are reminded by their leaders that "morality cannot be inculcated in the most effective manner without religious enforcements." It is true non-Catholics are not as logical and consistent as one could wish. They make provision for the children of the wealthier members only, whilst the education of the children of their poorer co-religionists is sadly neglected.

From what has been written it is quite evident that there is satisfactory unanimity of sentiment on the fundamental principle, namely, the necessity of the moral and religious element in popular education. All accept the practical wisdom of the statement of Guizot, a Protestant writer, who said: "In order to make popular education truly good and socially useful, it must be fundamentally religious. It is necessary that national education should be given and received in the midst of a religious atmosphere, and that religious impressions and religious observances should penetrate into all its parts. Religion is not a study or an exercise, to be restricted to a certain place or a certain hour; it is a faith and a law, which ought to be felt everywhere, and which after this manner alone can exercise all its beneficial influence upon our mind and our life."

And in our own country thoughtful men are fast coming to the same conclusion. President Eliot, of Harvard, recently wrote: "I am persuaded that it is a grave error to 'secular-ize' the public schools; first, because education would be thereby degraded and sterilized; secondly, because the attempt is too unnatural to succeed; and thirdly, because this policy never can make the public school the school of the whole population."

But some one will say: "If the public schools are secularized, who is to blame ? Are they not 'degraded and sterilized' because no feasible and satisfactory alternative, just and accepta- ble to all concerned, has been brought forward ? Let," it may be urged, " the different Christian bodies of the country come together and agree on some working plan that is fair and rea- sonable ; then the solution of the school problem will be soon reached." Prejudice and politics have too deeply impressed themselves on this subject to look for any immediate relief in any other way.

Happily, there are not wanting indications of a very marked change for the better in the tone and temper of public senti- ment on the school question. The urgency for reform comes from many quarters. Non-Catholics are beginning to see, what American Catholics have always fully understood, the important truth that Washington laid down in his Farewell Address to his countrymen. "Reason and experience," he wrote, " both forbid us to expect that national morality can prevail in exclusion of re- ligious principles." Hence do we find a growing popular desire on the part of our non-Catholic fellow-citizens to hear and read the views of representative Catholics on this subject. The resolution of the Pennsylvania Legislature indicates the growth and strength of this popular desire. It augurs well, too, for a satisfactory adjustment of the problem when the most eminent Catholic ecclesiastics are cordially invited to the national as- semblies of public-school teachers to discuss the question. This was done two years ago at the Nashville convention, and dur- ing the past year at the convention held in St. Paul, where Archbishop Ireland indicated a possible way out.

What " the way out" will eventually be it would be hazardous to conjecture. That there is such a way is clear to all minds that are free from prejudice, that have a thorough grasp of fundamental principles, that have given sufficient thought to the whole school question, and that are, above and beyond all other considerations, ready to do full justice to the entire population without infringing on the rights of any class. The Rev. Thomas Jefferson Jenkins, in the February number of THE CATHOLIC WORLD, shows how it is possible to have "American Christian state schools" by citing several instances where a local *modus vivendi* has been established.

God grant that the American people will see, before it is too late, the dangers that threaten our civilization and republican form of government from our false system of education ! As the scales fall from men's eyes they recognize what a noble and truly patriotic work the Catholic Church has done in keeping before the mind of the nation the true idea of education. Many will give thanks to God that he has preserved, to quote the words of the late Rev. Doctor Hodge, of Princeton, " the Roman Catholic Church in America to-day true to that theory of education upon which our fathers founded the public schools of the nation, and from which they have been so madly perverted."

MORGAN M. SHEEDY.

Pittsburgh, Pa.

A QUESTION OF GROWTH.

III.

THERE are still in the world some people, generally among those who congratulate themselves on having had ancestors rather than on the prospect of themselves being such to a coming generation, who believe they are uttering a truism when they assert that " it takes three generations to make a gentleman."

They forget that this dictum was formulated before it had ever entered the mind of man to conceive of the lightning-like rapidity with which progressive Americans achieve results which hitherto the plodding old world took centuries to evolve. In those days, too, when woman was but a secondary satellite of man, no one thought it necessary to calculate how many generations were needed to produce a lady ; and now it would be a useless speculation, since the American girl, with her marvellous adaptability and her infinite capabilities, has attracted the attention and aroused the admiration of two continents. Suppose some genteel apostle of antiquated aristocratic faith should have seen Mary Cunningham, for instance, with her delicately-curved lips, slightly aquiline nose, and near-sighted, gold-eye-glassed brown eyes ; suppose he or—your pardon ! it would have been she—could have heard Miss Cunningham's irreproachable English spoken in a voice that drawled almost imperceptibly, could one possibly have blamed madame if she had accepted the young lady at once upon such unmistakable evidence as of long and honorable descent ?

What was there about her, from her shining, silky hair to her faultlessly-gaitered foot, to warn aristocrats that she was the daughter of a man who worked his way up from the fireman on the engine to be owner of half a million of stock in the road? What suggestions were there in the Redfern gown of blue cloth to remind one that the wearer's mother was clad in emulation of the rainbow on the day that she wedded the fireman above mentioned?

There would be but one way for madame to meet this living and breathing and quietly elegant refutation of her fine theories, and she would take that eagerly. She would gravely discourse on the influence of education and association, and would draw from you the fact that Miss Cunningham was not born until her parents had already moved into a handsome stone house of their own, and that most of her life which was not spent at the best select schools had been lived in Europe, surrounded by all that made for culture and refinement.

Miss Cunningham herself would have yielded assent to every article of madame's creed of lineage and its advantages. In her secret soul she bowed in reverence before "the daughter of a hundred earls" It seemed to her, with her romantic tendencies and warm imagination, something to make one's pulses thrill and one's heart beat high to know that the blood which coursed through one's veins was the same that had once moved knightly arms to deeds of chivalry and lady's hands to acts of tenderness. Margaret Tyler, who had lived her life amid a class by whom gentle birth was accepted as a rightful inheritance, was not slow to perceive this bit of sentiment in Miss Cunningham's character, and was a little inclined to laugh at it.

One evening, when she and Miss Cunningham had been sitting alone in the bay-window, in deep conversation, which Nicholson soon discovered was about him from the glances both women cast toward him, Mrs. Tyler beckoned to him to come and take the seat which the young lady had just vacated. She surveyed him critically, her eyes twinkling with amusement. Somehow Nicholson objected to this kind of regard, and said petulantly :

"Is there anything wrong about me this evening? I could see that you and Miss Cunningham have been discussing me for the last half-hour, and now you are laughing at me."

"You are quite mistaken," Mrs. Tyler hastened to say. "I was at that moment metaphorically 'taking your measure' to decide what sort of figure you would cut as the hero of a romance."

"With you as the heroine?" asked Nicholson audaciously.

A quick flash of Mrs. Tyler's blue eyes told him he was even with her, and so soothed his ruffled feelings; but her voice was as calm and amused as ever as she replied:

"I thought you understood that *I* was merely to be the teller of the story, or shall I say the *prompter?* I have commenced my part already. Guess what Miss Cunningham and I were saying about you just now."

"As if a man could ever guess what two women were saying about him or anything else!" exclaimed Nicholson with lofty superiority. If there were in Mrs. Tyler's face any lines which told that she knew how to bide her time, the gentleman had no opportunity to observe them, for she turned at that moment and became to all appearances absorbed in the antics of a little boy who was dancing around the parlor in the unconscious freedom of a joyous child. Nicholson waited for her to resume the conversation, but she had suddenly become oblivious of his presence; and he really wished to know what they had said about him. Silence was a feminine weapon to which he was unaccustomed, and he at length confessed that it vanquished him by saying, somewhat shamefacedly:

"Were you and Miss Cunningham abusing me?"

Only the gleam of Mrs. Tyler's eye and the faint curve of the lip showed that she knew herself victor.

"No," she said, "not to any serious extent, as I might have done. The truth is you were shining with a sort of reflected glory. I was telling her about that silver service of yours with the Nicholson crest on it; and then I described your grand old house, with its octagon room opening out on the lilac-scented garden that was guarded by arbor-vitæ dragons, and the solid mahogany stair-rail, and the frescoed drawing-room ceiling. I told her, too, how your great-grandfather built it after his return from France, where he had been with Mr. Jefferson, and how tradition said he named the place Montmorenci in memory of the French lady he loved and lost. I dwelt on the grove of ancestral oaks about it, and the family portraits within it. Miss Cunningham's weak point is her love of blue-blood; and I assure you she is interested in you. I also told her just enough about Helen Hunter and you to awaken her sympathies. Now, isn't there material enough for a girl to make a hero out of?"

"What I want to know," said Nicholson with a quizzical smile, "is how you knew all that; you've never been to Montmorenci."

"It is but two miles from Shockoe Springs," explained Mrs.

Tyler a trifle hurriedly, " where grandma and Aunt Maria used to go; and they told me all about it, when—oh! ages ago—"

So she had asked minutely about him and his home that summer. He felt suddenly a keen sense of elation.

" How many ages ago?" he asked, leaning toward her while his voice dropped into lower and tenderer tones. When Mrs. Tyler seemed not to hear him he was still better pleased; it was a tacit confession that she was conscious of having betrayed herself.

" I was doing my best for you," she continued with somewhat strained lightness. " Foreign noblemen, I should say, must be getting scarce by this time. Why shouldn't an heiress be content with a well-to-do Southerner who has a family crest, and a genealogical tree with its roots in the time of Elizabeth?"

" When shall I propose?" asked Nicholson. " Is to-night an auspicious time? Of course I am more than willing, being quite as buyable as a foreign noble; but I suppose one still has to go through the form of being in love with the lady, hasn't he?"

Then that small woman chose to turn upon him and say indignantly: " Why should it be a form? Surely if ever a woman was made to be loved Mary Cunningham is that woman. And you and she would suit each other so well. I can picture her now brightening Montmorenci with her sweet presence and making a new man of you. All her money aside, I do wish you and she would fall in love and get married."

The speech instantly deadened the elation he had felt but a moment before. In the sudden chill and falling of his spirits he realized vividly that in these days he had been picturing another than Miss Cunningham in the halls of the old homestead.

" I wish you would not trouble yourself to marry me off," he said brusquely. " I can attend to such affairs for myself"

He had never before known that Margaret Tyler's voice had in it a ring like steel against steel.

" Can you pardon my presumption," she said icily, " when I tell you I thought we were friends? I shall not make the mistake again."

" Oh! forgive me, forgive me," he exclaimed, penitently, holding her skirts and detaining her as she rose to go. " How could you know that you were hurting me? How could you understand that there is but one woman in all this world whom I could see the mistress of Montmorenci?"

The look of quick sympathy which she turned upon him showed him how far she was from comprehending him.

"Why, you should have told me of your engagement before," she said, all resentment gone from her manner. "It seems to me I might have expected that much."

"But I haven't told you I was engaged," corrected Nicholson. "I only said that—that—"

"Oh!" she exclaimed, smiling at his floundering, "you mean that you would like to be. Will you tell me her name?"

Nicholson knew women too well to imperil his chances by telling her then. She would never have forgiven him for taking advantage of the avenue so directly opened by herself, even though she had done it in this obviously unintentional way. He saw clearly that this woman was to be wooed, and he had not lost hope that she could be won   "I will tell you all about it some day," he said; "it is a long story."

After that neither of them again referred to Miss Cunningham, and Nicholson fancied that there crept into Mrs. Tyler's manner a sort of reserve which gave to it a different quality from the friendliness that had hitherto characterized it. He began to find it difficult now to draw her into talking about that summer of *lang syne* which grew daily more interesting to him.

Sunday afternoon in an Asheville boarding-house is apt to be tedious. There really seems no place made for it in the week's programme. Cards are frowned down upon, driving is considered questionable, and the dull hours have to be gotten through somehow, generally in wishing it were Monday and occasionally by organizing impromptu chorus clubs, which begin by singing a hymn and can end with a negro shouting jubilee if there be two or three in the company who are able to delude themselves and the others into the belief that they have caught the fervor and the rhythm so natural to the colored enthusiast.

On one of these days when music was the refuge the group about the piano began singing those ballads which were street favorites yesterday and to-day supplanted by newer songs, which to-morrow will in their turn be relegated to backwoods villages and country lanes, if, indeed, they be fortunate enough to reach these pleasant by-ways.

As Nicholson turned over the pile of old music his eye suddenly fell upon a familiar title.

"Sing this," he said, placing the sheet on the rack as the lights were brought in, and taking a position where he could watch Mrs. Tyler, who sat apart delighting an old scholar's soul by her close listening to his discourse on the prehistoric races of America. Scarcely had the first notes of the air been played before Mrs. Tyler looked up quickly to find Nicholson's gaze fastened upon her. Their glances met, a common memory in both, and a blush as vivid as any girl's suffused her usually pale face.

"I had no idea you could sing like that," exclaimed a young lady to Nicholson when it was over. Nor had he—but his heart was singing.

When Lew Hamilton and Flora Monroe had sung that serenade in their end of the honeysuckle-porch had not Fred Nicholson and Margaret Somerville, in their end, entered into a solemn compact to think of one another whenever they heard that air, wherever they should be and whatever should betide? And Margaret Tyler blushed at the first chords of it, after all these years! She scarcely waited for it to be finished before she arose and left the room, and Nicholson followed her as she went through the darkened hall and stood before the western window, looking out upon the last expiring glories of the sunset"

"You remember?" he asked softly, as he stood behind her.

"Yes," she answered without turning to look at him, "I remember."

"If we had but known ourselves better in those old days," he said sadly, "how different it all could have been for you and me!"

She made no attempt to reply and he continued (restraining by a strong effort the desire to tell her the rest with his arm holding her close to his heart):

"Margaret Somerville was sweet and lovely; Fred Nicholson the boy had sense to see that; but you as you are in your noble womanhood make me bless God that it is given me to behold my highest ideal of woman.

"Sweetheart, Fred Nicholson the man loves you with the love of his life. Will you not turn around and tell him it has not come too late."

She put aside the hand which would have clasped hers and looked at him with eyes full of unshed tears. The conflict of emotions made speech an impossibility to her, and he guessed rather than heard the murmured words that told him she could not talk to him then—words she spoke as she moved away from him. Had she been a younger woman, or one accustomed to being swayed by impulse in the crises of life, she would have yielded then. It is inexpressibly sweet to a woman to know herself beloved, and in the agitation caused

by Nicholson's avowal, and the stirring of the old tender memories that clustered around him and her younger self, she believed at that moment that the quick beating of her own heart
meant that love for him was awakening there.

Even when she became calmer the visions she saw were
very fair. She pictured to herself the life they would lead at
Montmorenci—the placid, pleasant plantation life she knew so
well, and to which her family had been used for generations.
She saw herself falling easily and naturally into the *rôle* of lady
of the manor, which her mother and her grandmother, and their
grandmothers before them, had played so graciously. She contrasted this uneventful, quiet home-life, with its domestic duties,
which most women enjoy and which had their attractions for
herself, brightened by the warm social neighborliness of the old
county families, and crowned and sweetened by a strong man's
love and protection, with the loneliness of her present and the
future that lay before her, full of effort of some sort or another
as it would be to the end. Why should she presume to mark
out for herself, as she had done, lines so different from those
where other women were content to dwell? That this question
arose before her showed that the other part of her nature was
making itself heard.

No one knew so well as she her need of sympathy in the
intangibles. Could Nicholson give her that? Could she give
him support and sympathy always in the thoughts and aspirations that filled his mind? That home vision was wonderfully
fair, but would it in reality satisfy her? Would there be no
void in it?

Her religion was a sealed book to him; nay, more, the Lord
Jesus Christ, whom she adored as her God and loved as her
Friend, he who made for her the centre and sum of all that was
best on earth or in heaven, what was he to Nicholson?—"an
enthusiastic Jewish peasant"; or at most but the wisest and
purest of men. Rightly or wrongly, she measured the real by
standards that exalted it into the ideal; he thought these standards beautiful for her, but impossible for him, and smiled conde-
scendingly at her quixotic notions of honor and honesty. She
herself often doubted their practicability and wisdom, but she
knew she could never relinquish them.

Perhaps if she had married him in her girlhood, while her
character was in its formative state and she had as yet arrived at no convictions, they might have adapted themselves to
each other. Would it be possible now? In the question of

growth had she not left him behind her, and would she not be likely to make him as well as herself wretched by continual efforts to quicken his pace should they now start on the journey together?

Yet his companionship was very, very pleasant. She wondered how she should pass the days when he no longer made a part of them. Why should not one take the good things life offers and rest satisfied? "But what are the good things?" asked that other self which would not be silenced.

IV.

The next day it rained as it can rain in these mountains—a steady, uncompromising down-pour—the sort of day when nature so veils her face and wears so forbidding an aspect as to awaken in the veriest misanthrope the instincts which tell him that man is a gregarious animal and drives him to seek human companionship.

Not that Mrs. Tyler and Miss Cunningham phrased it this way when the latter sought the former's room in the afternoon and was welcomed with unfeigned warmth and eagerness. They said something or other about the influence of mind upon mind, which had evidently brought the visitor, since Mrs. Tyler had been thinking at that moment of going to seek her. The day was conducive to confidences, when aided by the influence of a bright fire and rocking-chairs, and it soon happened that the two women were talking with a sense of fellowship and comprehension which was new in their acquaintance with each other. When the mail was brought Miss Cunningham received a photograph which, after pondering over for a while, she handed to Mrs. Tyler, saying somewhat nervously:

"What do you think of him?"

Luckily the face was that of such a frank and kindly young fellow that Mrs. Tyler was not obliged to sacrifice truth to politeness and could admire it sincerely. "But somehow I had an idea there was as yet no *him* in your case," she ended by saying.

"There really isn't," Miss Cunningham replied, moved to frankness by the surroundings, "but he would like very much to be; and I—am ever so fond of him, you know. But you said that as if you had *hoped* there was no *him*, and I had fancied you were an advocate of marriage."

The older woman looked into the fire and said nothing. One

of the comforts of Mary Cunningham's society was that she permitted you to enjoy it in silence.

"So I am," she answered at last, "for most people; but marriage is a great risk for a girl like you."

"Why for a girl like me?" asked she, drawing near. Margaret felt that the talk, coming after last night, was as if she were
arguing her own case over again as well as advising the girl beside her.

"Because," she said, "you are a woman with ideals and a capacity for *idols*. Marriage shatters ideals and shows an idol's
clay feet."

Miss Cunningham looked disappointed.

"I dislike to hear a woman like you say cynical things,"
she remonstrated. "They are not in accord with your character."

The two earnest faces looked into each other; there was certainly no trace of the cynic in either.

"Yes, that speech has a flippant sound," said Margaret, accepting the rebuke, "and I did not mean to generalize. I meant
to say that a woman with your high ideals would find it difficult
to meet the man who would come up to them. Most women
have about them a quality which makes them easily take shape
from the conditions that bound them, and, to use the old simile,
they can be moulded to their husbands' characters. But you are
too sensitive and reserved to do that, and would pine your life
away, fret it out against prison-bars as it were, if you found
your marriage a disappointment. But, ah! if *he* is the right
kind," she continued, smiling down on the picture she held in her
hand, "and can answer the needs of your earnest and exacting
nature, then it will be very, very good, will it not? You could
make a glorious wife and mother, but it all depends on the man
you marry."

Another silence fell, and the firelight played over faces
sweet with womanly seriousness. It was perhaps a subtle bond
of sympathy between them that each as she seemed to gaze into
the glowing coals was asking her own heart if the man she was
seeing could meet the requirements of the best part of her.

"You do not think so highly of me as I do of you," Miss
Cunningham said after the pause had lengthened into a long half
hour. "I believe you would make a glorious wife and mother,
no matter who you married, and I wish you would marry. Yours
seems to me such a lonely life as it is."

Was one side of her own perplexity finding voice in these

sympathetic, womanly tones? If so, the other side must have answered when Mrs. Tyler spoke with a new inflection of firmness.

"The loneliness of an unmarried woman," she said, " is but isolation, and it need not be that if she will but still the cravings of her own heart until she can hear the beatings of the mighty world's heart that throbs around her and shows itself wherever there is a human being in need of sympathy or help; especially must this be true if she be a Catholic, for does she not then recognize in every act of kindness she extends a deed of love to those over whom the Heart of Jesus yearns with infinite and fraternal charity?

"But the loneliness of the married woman is desolation, the very existence of the feeling is a tacit wrong to the man whom she has sworn shall fill her life.

"It is good sometimes to call things by their right names, and that woman is, I believe, guilty of a crime who for the sake of being loved and cared for, the safety of being shielded, allows herself to be tempted into marriage. There is but one thing in all this world that should prompt a marriage—that is pure love; love so deep and true that it makes two generous people ready and glad to suffer all things, and renounce all others if need be, for the sake of each other's dear companionship. If there are some so constituted that none with whom they are thrown can awaken this exalted love, then they may be unfortunate, but they have no right to profane an ordinance of God by entering it from any but the highest motive."

She had spoken rapidly, as a woman does under strong excitement, and there was on her face a look of consecration which transfigured it. Her deep emotion communicated itself to Mary Cunningham, who presently slipped from her chair and knelt beside her.

"Dear Mrs. Tyler," she whispered as she put her arms about her, " cannot you and I love each other? We need one another, do we not?"

For answer Margaret drew the kneeling figure closer to her, and there was born one of God's rarest and most precious gifts —a deep and lifelong friendship between two women. Their talk was low and fragmentary after that, but when the twilight shadows filled the room and the firelight flickered in only occasional brightness, Mary Cunningham said tentatively:

"It seems to me a woman might love Mr. Nicholson that way; don't you think she might?"

If both women blushed who was there to see ? The kindly darkness had fallen over them.

"I remember that I came very near loving him myself once upon a time," Margaret replied, with a lightness which had been a stranger to her manner heretofore during their talk.

Perhaps both of them remembered the speech when, a day or two later, they found themselves thrown with Nicholson in the party which had been made up to go from their house to the mountains to search for arbutus, but the slight constraint wore off from all of them in the woods. The sudden sense of freedom and naturalness which comes when the pines whisper above one and the dried leaves and pine-needles rustle under one's feet, possessed them ; they were children or savages once more, and the party of conventionalized beings welcomed the sensation as only conventionalized beings can.

But the climb was steep, and Margaret Tyler had during the past few weeks been so played upon by varying emotions that her strength, at no time great, failed utterly as she reached the summit, and she sat down exhausted on the steps of the untenanted house which crowned it. Nicholson saw the sudden paling of her face and made no comment, but seated himself just at her feet, while the others, noting the position, left them to themselves.

It was a silvery day. The sky was covered with floating clouds that here were fleecy white and there shone in radiant grayness. The hidden sun revealed its position by the long streams of brightness which it sent downward athwart the shifting grays to bring out in clear perspective some dainty bit of landscape. Snow had fallen on the far western range during the night, and glistened against the cloud-masses, and shone in gleaming whiteness amid the blue of the lower hills, a blue which had in it the coldness of steel and the softness of soft veiling, with an airiness foreign to either of these, an airiness too light and exquisite to be adequately told of in words, and which affected one like the gentlest strains of music. The river shone by mirror-like snatches from its hidden course among the nearer and deeper blue hills. In the valley Asheville lay, what of it that was homely changed into picturesqueness, and whatever it had of fairness made infinitely more fair ; an occasional clump of trees just feathering into foliage told of the spring, and the only sound which reached them was the sighing of the wind as it waved the dark and slender pines to and fro.

On the other side of the ridge far below them Chunn's Cove smiled in its inexpressible quiet and peace, the subdued tints of the newly-ploughed ground, mingled with the fresh green of the growing oats or young grass; and a party of horsemen, the only signs of life, passed, moving atoms, on the red road which wound its devious way through the valley. The near mountains, which shut in the cove, stood solemn and silent with their tree-covered summits silhoueted against the dark eastern sky, and Craggy kept watch from the south clothed in misty purple shadows and crowned by lowering clouds, while through the gap, away and away into infinitude, stretched the blue, blue mountains, so losing shape and outline toward the horizon as to remind one involuntarily of the ocean.

For awhile neither Nicholson nor Margaret spoke; it was a scene and a time when God's glorious outer world says to the human soul, however tempest-tossed, "Peace, be still!" and the winds and the waves of sorrow and passion obey. Nicholson at last looked up at Margaret with tenderness and love shining in his eyes. She oddly remembered at that moment that her partiality for amethysts began because in her foolish girlish fancy their purple gleam reminded her of these same eyes.

"Sweetheart!" he said, referring to her evident weariness, "you are overtaxing yourself greatly. When are you going home with me to Montmorenci?"

He spoke with the air of one who has no doubt of his position, and his security and certainty of her sent a flash of resentment through Mrs. Tyler, and served to divest him of the glamour which her memories of their youth were continually throwing around him; but she did not reply at once, and he continued, still smiling up at her:

"Now you can understand, my Margaret, why you hurt me so when you suggested another mistress for Montmorenci. Margaret Somerville alone could reign there, ever."

He had an instinctive dislike to using her married name of late; there was in him a vague jealousy of her husband, though he was dead. She looked down at him regretfully.

"Margaret Somerville is no more," she said.

He caught the tone of her voice, and a quick fear rose in his face as he did so.

"But all that was best and sweetest in her lives in the developed woman," he replied gently.

"Ah! Margaret!" he exclaimed, as he caught the hand that rested on her lap, "you will not, you cannot tell me that your love for Fred Nicholson is one of the things that are dead ! "

" Then you think she loved you in those old days ? " she asked, a bitterness creeping into her voice.

" I think we loved each other, though we scarcely knew it," he answered, "and now it is given us to see—now when our lives may go on together to the end."

" How is it possible that you can ignore the years that have passed between that summer and this winter ? " she asked, after a pause. " Are you conscious of no change in yourself since then that you can speak as if it were but yesterday ? "

"It seems to me since I met you the other day that my love for you has filled all the years," he said tenderly. " I have but been waiting for you."

Nothing could have so conclusively proved how far she had outgrown her own fancy for him as the fact that she smiled at the extravagance of this speech. She had the faculty of occasionally seeing the humor of a situation at the wrong time.

" Shall we call that remark poetic license ? " she queried, lightly.

" Call it what you will," he replied, vexed at her tone, " it was but the simple truth. You would not have laughed at it on the honeysuckle-porch."

" No," she answered, " because I would have been so glad then to have heard you speak in earnest as you spoke just now."

The whole import of her words flashed over Nicholson.

" In Heaven's name," he said, vehemently, " why weren't you honest with me that summer, Margaret ? Why did you let us both throw our lives away ? "

She rose and stood looking down on him, even though he rose also. He thought he had never seen her so stately.

"Was *I* the dishonest one ? " she asked, proudly. " Did *I* say meaningless words of love which perchance might win a young heart's devotion simply to serve my own amusement ? Suppose *you* had been honest, Mr. Nicholson."

Ah ! suppose he had. At that moment Nicholson felt what many another one of us have felt before him, that he stood beside a grave for ever closed—and the name of the grave is a lost opportunity, and in it lies buried the might-have-been. But he was not thus easily going to give up the struggle for his life's hopes and happiness. There was anguish in his face and voice which melted all the woman's resentment into pity when he spoke again.

"Margaret, Gód knows I have repented the insincerity of those days, if it *was* insincerity—I believe I loved you even then—but now surely, when I see the light, you will not let a woman's pique stand between us; you are too noble and true for that! Dearest, come to me and hallow my life and sweeten your own."

He made a step toward her and held out his hands—but even as he did so that sense of her exaltation above him came over him; he knew not the meaning of the look on her face.

"Dear friend," she said—she knew he would wince at the words, but she could find no other—and her tones became but the tenderer and lower for the added evidence of his pain, "so far am I from pique or anger that the memories of that past have at times blinded me to the truth of the present, so tender and sweet were they. But October is not May, however bright the sun shines. Whatever I might once have been to you, I cannot now be other than I am. I belong to my work and must live my life untrammeled; I know what you would say," she continued, as he attempted to speak, "that as your wife I should do that, but I could not. Your strong, deep love, precious and sacred as it is and would be, would prove the greatest of trammels—for it calls for strong, deep love in return; and that I could never give."

Her voice died into a whisper and there was unutterable sadness in her eyes, which yet did not for an instant mar the gentle firmness of her glance and words.

The arbutus party returned the next moment and the homeward tramp began.

As they reached the town, Margaret Tyler was stopped by a, lady to advise about the nursing and care of some suffering street-waif—and Mary Cunningham and Fred Nicholson walked on together.

F. C. FARINHOLT.

THE WITNESS OF SCIENCE TO RELIGION.

IV.—THE INDUCTIONS OF *CONSCIENCE.*

THERE is one objection, fatal, as I hear it said, to arguments in Natural or Inductive Theology ; and it is, that they leave out the facts.   Fatal indeed, were it true.   Yes, I am told, they may serve as apologies, but they will not convince any one who has tasted the cup of bitter and real experience ; they sound plausible, but they are no less shallow than the writers who make use of them are unfeeling.   To the wounded heart what can they offer ?   Syllogisms—abstract reasoning which does not, nor ever will, take away the winter of its discontent ; for how shall we assuage grief or lighten sorrow with words, and dia-grams, and idle talk of the adaptation of life to circumstances ? " Read your Pascal," the brooding Pessimist will say, not with-out a touch of contempt, " your Leopardi and your Schopenhauer, nay, or your Dante and your Newman ; and then, if your daring so much exceeds your intellect, begin to prove, from the facts of life and the order of the universe, the existence of that Righteous Deity whom alone reason could admit, were any Deity admis-sible.   But remember that the deepest minds in the world's history have put aside your excuses for the existence of evil, the ever-springing pain of life, for the reign and triumph of death, for the disorders of the physical and the moral being of which we men are made, as at once futile and irreverent. Silence alone is great ; why do you trouble the stillness with reasonings that end in bewilderment and amaze ? "

Why ?   Surely because I must attempt to satisfy my reason, and Pessimism is no answer, but despair of an answer.   I have read my Pascal and the rest of that illustrious company more than once.   I feel that their eloquence is overpowering, but, if I must record the instinctive judgment of my nature when all is said and done, it is that Pascal trusts himself rather to feeling than to calm intellect, and is narrow and partisan, though on the side of goodness.   Much more do I suspect Schopenhauer and the tribe of cynical Pessimists, to whom the miseries of human kind afford a gloomy sport, as though disdain and not fellow-feeling were the clue to man's essence.   Ill-temper and congenital or acquired sadness do not, to my thinking, furnish reason with its best methods of research. I am well-assured that the confusion of the inward being which follows upon the silence here applauded, and the impotence in action so characteristic of its adepts, are a proof that the beginning is as great a mistake as the end is disastrous. What I feel constrained to seek until I find it, is the rational purpose of my existing as I am, a standard by which to live, and a final cause of the activities wherewith I have been endowed, so that when the end comes I shall have fulfilled, however inadequately, my part in the universe, as I see things inanimate fulfil theirs. I cannot live at random, or upon the impulse of the moment, without forfeiting my claim to be regarded as a reasonable being. For it is beyond cavil that my faculties are always urging me to act; and that, if I do not bring them to some harmonious issue, I am after a sort committing suicide, and running counter to the whole stress and strain of the tendencies which make me human I can simply not deny that every fibre of my being is instinct with purpose. The senses look for their gratification; the intellect desires knowledge, that is to say, truth; the will seeks after good; and the conscience bids it choose what is right and turn away from evil. My entire organism, as I know it, is founded and set up on the idea of purpose; and not only of purpose, but of moral purpose. And as it is with me, so is it with all men Whether they reflect or no upon the astounding mystery of their nature, with its faculties, laws, and innate aspirations, they too, like myself, exist in the kingdom of moral ends and means; they are a part of it; and never while they are conscious and free have they an escape through any door into the supposed but imaginary chaos where purpose does not rule. How, then, can I help asking whether the world without me, in which I have beheld such magnificent systems upon systems of the most exquisite order and adaptation, is not likewise a moral universe, of one pattern with the ideal held up to me by conscience? Did I cease to ask that question, I should cease to be man.

But I will not allow that my interrogation of nature ends in bewilderment and amaze. In deep wonder it does, in an *O altitudo*, to speak with St. Paul and St. Augustine. I do not pretend that our light shines except in a dark place; it is almost put out when the flood of noonday beats upon it, and I pass from the sanctuary of my own bosom, where conscience keeps the lamp burning, to that great and high prospect, the manifold existence of men, so little known to me, so full of trouble, so entangled in circumstance, so secret because it is so vast, so

much beyond my searching into by reason of its rich and puis-
sant variety. Let every one, then, speak for himself; and perhaps
it will be found that the most forbidding, the least encouraging,
of the phenomena which perplex the moral historian, may be
explained by a frank *Mea culpa*. There is something, no doubt,
besides the guilt of man; he submits to conditions and must
fashion and mould his character in time, amid surroundings he
would not have chosen. But still, he is himself, not another, still
less a mere mechanism of wheels and pulleys driven by a force
outside him. I do not require to make any assumptions but
these—which are self-evident, or conclusions from self-evident
premises—viz., that man in a normal state has some power of
shaping his character by acts of choice; and that, as I have
shown, the physical universe presents indubitable tokens of adaptation to ends foreseen, and in their realization co-ordinated to
issues of use and beauty.

The test of valid science is prediction. From its knowledge
of the past it foretells the future; which could not be, unless past
and future were fitted each to each by the intrinsic reasonables
of causes and effects, or of substances and their many modes and
accidents.

This is what we mean by order, purpose, and at last by
design, if we carefully examine our words. Blind forces, it must
be said again and again, would be incapable of producing
uniform results. The line upon which things move to definite
issues cannot but be a line of guidance or direction. And I
believe the most determined agnostic would allow that the order
of the world seems due, in its lower circles, to adaptation of part
to part;—as certainly the late Mr. Stuart Mill, no follower of
Paley, allowed that the whole cosmic order was due, though he
demurred to the notion of Omnipotence. However, I am not
discussing Omnipotence now; and all I say is, that were the
inanimate universe solely in question, the marks of design would
be overwhelming. But immediately this reply is made to me,
" On the supposition of an Objective Reason, you may perhaps
account for the orderliness of matter; how will you account
by the same for the disorder of life ? "

That is the problem. Matter, by which I understand the
entire system of energies acting in space and time exclusive of
living things, appears, strangely enough, to fall within the
domain of reason; while life is refractory, and the more so the
higher we ascend in the scale. Not that we have grasped the
essence, whatever it is, of physical energy; but we know its

laws in a certain measure, and are not put to confusion on looking out upon its activities. How different is the scene when we
turn to contemplate man, the race or the individual! He witnesses, by the mouth of all his prophets and teachers, that
he is an enigma to himself. "Unhappy that we are!" exclaims
Pascal, with his accustomed severity of tone, "more unhappy
than if there were nothing great in our condition. We have an
ideal of happiness, and we cannot reach it; we have an image
of the truth, and we possess nothing but a lie; we are incapable of absolute ignorance as of certain knowledge!" Who
shall disentangle so intricate a skein?

Well, let us begin at the beginning, and not, as so many do,
at the end. What are the facts of the case? That I find myself
simultaneously in two worlds; I am a denizen of the physical
universe, allied to it, imprisoned in it, if you will, by the texture
of nerves and brain, as I am of the spiritual by virtue of the
mind and conscience I possess. Now mark: if there is any
force in the difficulty put forward, it would follow that as a
physical being I exist in the realm of perfect law, where reason,
the deeper it inquires the more it is satisfied; while, as a spiritual being, I live and move amid confusion worse confounded.
The Supreme Power whose wisdom in adapting means to ends
where matter alone is concerned, has, so far as we can judge,
simply no limits, and who chooses from infinite contingencies an
order of being so stable and constant that for a myriad million
of years it goes through its courses untroubled, does, it would
seem, fall back in disorder as soon as a living organism, subject
to pain, emerges from the dark of its own nothingness. There
is harmony admitted in the clash of world-systems, in the rush
of constellations together; but none, not one single bar of music,
in the so-called struggle of that organism to maintain itself within
or to overcome the attack of its enemies from without. Divine
Wisdom made the outside of things; folly and unwisdom the
inside, which yet is their life! The mind which alone has the
idea of Truth is, we know not why or how, condemned on this
showing to eternal falsehood; and Conscience is lighted up by
the sun of Righteousness, only to discern that righteousness never
has existed, but is the dream of man the self-tormentor! Tor-
mented, surely, beyond all speech are we, if the ideal in whose
radiance we perceive our moral imperfection, and vex ourselves
daily because we come short of it, turns out finally to be the mirage of our own hunger and thirst, with the desert sands stretching
endlessly before us as we march, and the night bereft of its stars

descending upon our utter disappointment! There was, again it should seem, enough intellect in the nature of things to realize in visible forms the laws of mathematics and of chemical affinities; enough to make the brain of man responsive to echoes and pulsations from the remotest nebula; but not enough to appease the desire for justice and holiness which has been awakened in his heart;—enough, therefore, to design his misery, but not enough to make it the instrument of good. Will reason permit us to halt in this fashion between Wisdom and Unwisdom as the root of things? Must we not either fall headlong down the abyss with scepticism; or make sure that the foothold we have attained by means of physical science is the first round of a ladder leading upward to the light?

These considerations appear to me by no means fanciful, but of a most solid scientific worth, as showing that we cannot allow more to the axioms and postulates of physical inquiries than we allow to the primary dictates of the moral sense, as it is called. In both cases, the foundation is in the nature of the mind itself—here as conscience affirming the objective moral order, there as pure intellect declaring that an Objective Reason exists. To make the co-ordinations of science real, and to maintain at the same moment that moral truth and ethical justice have no substance, nay, not the shadow of a meaning, outside the thoughts of man—himself a figure passing swiftly over the stage and disappearing into the gulf where all phenomena vanish—I call a crime against logic, good sense, and experience. If the visible frame of things is held and knit together by the law of gravitation, no less certainly must I believe—or rather, I see and therefore I believe—that human society, and the very nature of the individual man, are coherent entities only because of that unchanging moral law to which we know that we are subject. The parallel is complete. I take the physical universe as it lies before me, and examining its ten thousand details with the aid of Newton's genius, I find that one formula explains and exhausts the action in space (I do not say, lays bare the essence), of its contending elements. However complex may seem their motions, and although I can make satisfactory trial of the law in but a few instances, I do not feel that I can refuse my assent when the physical philosopher announces that all bodies in the universe, so far as it is known to us, attract inversely as the square of their distance. Were they to act otherwise, the sciences of dynamics and of statics would have to be expunged from our text-books, and experience make a fresh start, as though nothing were ascertained concerning the motion of bodies. Apply this to the elementary ideas of moral good, of righteousness, and the reward of just and unjust actions, which are at least as connatural to our minds as the notions of weight, attraction, and repulsion. Could we imagine a human society which was not under the influence of them? Would not all the reasons we have for calling a polity, however civilized, human, in the strict and proper sense of the word, dissolve and pass away when the distinction between moral right and moral wrong had ceased to win acknowledgment from the men and women composing it? And in like manner must we judge of the individual. Righteousness, I say with Edmund Burke, is the law under which we are all born. Repeal or disown it, and man sinks to a beast of the field; his volitions become mere appetites, his desires the cravings of self-interest, his affections the instruments of his brutal passions. It is not true, therefore, that we can philosophize accurately about man, while disregarding his moral nature; and when we attribute mind to him we mean of necessity that he is a conscience also.

See, then, what is the force of my argument. When I would establish science, physical or metaphysical, on a sure foundation, I am compelled to recur to the very make and constitution of my intellect, affirming, in opposition to the scepticism of Kant or of Hume, that the laws of thought which I discover in myself are the laws of things; and that in this equation truth stands and must stand for ever. But the horrid doubt which appears as Scepticism where truth in general is questioned, takes the form of Pessimism so soon as the idea of goodness—of course I mean moral good—is refused its objective value. In the one case, though man affirms that truth, being the very form of his intellect, cannot be a phantom or delusion springing up in his own brain, the sceptic tells him that he knows nothing except such delusions. In the other, conscience itself declaring that it binds man as a subject, and is therefore the voice of a sovereign, the Pessimist replies by pointing to the chance-medley, as he deems it, of human existence, and asking where is the Judge and Master who rules the fray. With equal cogency might the objection be raised to a common man unversed in mathematics, that he ought to state the formula of three or more moving bodies before he was permitted to believe or to act upon the law of gravitation. But he knows that bodies have weight; and the man who attends to his conscience is perfectly well aware that the right and the wrong of the moral dictates have not

been put into things by his mere fancy, nor by that of any one
else   He possesses the certain knowledge (called, not unfairly,
intuition or mental insight) of his own present power of choosing
and the standard according to which he ought to choose—nay,
and ethically speaking, must choose under penalties. The vision
of the moral order is as steadfast and as permanent before his
mind's eye, as the vision of physical order is before the gaze of
science. To deny either is to shake the foundations of both.

If we term the first principle of inductive science the "uniformity
of nature," we may with as good reason define the first principle
of morals to be the supremacy of conscience. But the "Categorical Imperative" thus admitted, would lose all its binding force
and superhuman majesty, were it nothing more than a law imposed upon man by himself, the coinage of a frightened or
intoxicated brain. Nor is it an empty ideal which he is free to
follow or forget, an artist's dream (suppose), lovely indeed, but
melting into the cloud-forms of imagination ; else where would be
its authority ? The so-called "laws" of physical science are wanting in the element which truly constitutes law, for they have not,
in themselves, any power to coerce and bring about the effects
they describe. But the Moral Law is the first and greatest of
sovereign powers, from which, as our being testifies in its innermost depths, there is neither appeal nor escape. The dread
anticipations which are the immediate fruits of wrong-doing bear
witness that the Power we offend is beyond us to overthrow. If
the first stage of transgression be lawless liberty, rioting in its
own delight, the second, which comes quickly until blindness has
seared our vision, is, it cannot be doubted, a certain fearful looking for judgment to be executed upon us. Are not these things
disclosures of a new and terrible kingdom of means and ends,
wide as the world, commensurate with human existence, and
extending round it on every side, into eternity ?

Such are the facts, be the inferences from them what they
may. In conscience, as we know it, apart from all theoretic
determinations, there is discernible a threefold experience ; of
free-will able to choose ; of a command to choose right according
to the standard shown us ; and of guilt anticipating punishment
whenever we disobey the inward voice. I do not see what is
wanting here to the strictest induction. As for experiment and
verification, is not our life from hour to hour one perpetual
series of trials made and results accruing, as in a moral laboratory of the spirit ? Have we not knowledge from the past
whereby to foretell the future ? " Who hath resisted Him, and hath

had peace ? " If we understand these words as they were intended, we shall acknowledge that they are a summing up of the experience of the perverse and froward in every age. To break the moral law, to rebel against its commandment, is that very instant to lapse and be degraded into a lower creature. As he who thinks falsehood cannot hold the truth which he denies, so the man to whom sin is pleasing slips away from justice, and in being unjust, without further penalty, he is punished; the seed of death is already sown within him, and needs only time for its ripening. Is not this a demonstration plain that the nature of things is holy, and just, and righteous? For it not only does not, but I will dare to say that it cannot, save the unjust from the greatest and worst consequences of his injustice, which are not that he should endure pain of body or limb, neither that he should be mulcted of this world's goods, but that he should fall below the level of the just man, being degraded and spoiled of that spiritual essence which he flung from him in the very act of sinning. He never can be again what he was before he sinned.

I have implied throughout this argument two things, which in the nineteenth century are often denied and still oftener forgotten. One is that pain is not the greatest of evils; and the other, that moral guilt, as I am now considering it, cannot exist apart from the exercise of free-will. In addressing Christians, I take for granted that the doctrine of original sin, as held by them, is declared to be perfectly compatible with Divine Justice, and will not be urged against the objective existence of the moral order which I am defending. To the philosopher who abstracts from original sin, or does not believe in it, I point out with Aristotle that moral evil is the consequence of a free choice wrongly exercised. And furthermore that pain, in itself, has no moral quality, but is good or evil according to the end which determines its application. I must not be understood as saying that to inflict pain for the sake of pain is ever good. On the contrary, I hold it to be intrinsically bad and forbidden by that moral law which to me is the nature of things itself. But that pain, either inflicted or endured, may be a relative good, as the instrument of justice and sanctity, I think self-evident. And that not pain but deflection from the moral standard is the highest evil, must be granted by all who are not Utilitarians. Now I do not profess to argue from science in favor of a Utilitarian religion. The stand I take is that of all those to whom virtue or righteousness comes first, as the absolute end of man, and happiness, in whatever sense, comes in the second place, not at all as a thing indifferent to the Supreme Providence which governs the world, but still as subordinate to that Holiness without which no man shall see God. If I prove that our experimental and inductive knowledge bears witness to justice in the objective order, I shall have made out my contention. And I say that it does, and that I have proved it by appealing to the experience of our spiritual life which alone can throw light upon these problems, since to it alone they belong and apart from it have no intelligible meaning.

It is a hard saying in the ears of our luxury-stricken time that pain is not the supreme of evils. Yet men's softness, self-indulgence, and sensual cowardice cannot make a vain thing of the Cross of Christ, looked at, I do not say with the eyes of faith, but as confessedly the centre of human history, and the ethical force which has raised civilization to its noblest heights. There is a scale of perfection in the moral as in the material world; one thing is better than another, one ideal overtops the rest. To behold the triumph of justice, Plato has written in a passage of inspiring eloquence, we must consider the just man, who is truly such but does not seem so to his fellow-citizens, when they have scourged, racked, and bound him, nay when, after suffering every kind of evil, he is crucified. And to suffer injustice, Plato argues, is not the first of evils, for it cannot hurt the soul; but they are miserable who inflict that suffering on the blameless, and are themselves most to be pitied. But if before the Divine experience of the Gospel, even a Greek philosopher could, by the light of reason, discover that in apparent defeat and humiliation, in pain and wrong-suffering, there might be the very conditions of a perfectly just life, an ideal fulfilled to the uttermost, "all glorious within," though its outward seeming were mean and despicable, what will the impartial judge affirm, to whom the life of Jesus of Nazareth and its ever-enlarging consequences from age to age have been made manifest? I repeat that my argument is not addressed to believers; it borrows its strength neither from faith nor from authority. The patent facts of the New Testament which abide the coldest critic's scrutiny are my warrant when I would conclude, as the heart does even against the shrinking senses, that self-sacrifice opens to the moral intuition a range of most heroic, most pathetic and subduing, virtues, to which we cannot but assign the crown of goodness. While, on the other hand, since free-will, the voluntary surrender of ourselves to lower influences, yielding where we might and ought to resist, is a necessary condition of wrong-doing, it follows that, in the order of righteousness, every man remains his own master, nor can be injured unless he is willing. The spirit is superior to violation. Personal dignity and true honor stand in our own choice; and he only is conquered who suffers himself to be overcome.

Yet this is not the conclusion of the whole matter, though, as I would most earnestly contend, it ought to be " the master-light of all our seeing." Free moral choice, under conditions ranging from the easy to the heroic, and always involving some degree of martyrdom in witness to the ethical standard, is our one sure guide through the mazes of existence. But who will grant that the tragic defeat, though it be a moral victory, is the last scene of all, and that the curtain shall never rise again upon injustice caught in its own snare? When I refuse to barter virtue for happiness, and deny that it looks beyond itself to some future reward, I am not forgetting the scandal of every day,—goodness trampled underfoot, cunning and malice making sport of the innocent, injustice sowing with an assurance that it shall reap its golden harvest. These eclipses and disasters of the moral world, painted in too dark a color by the ready pencil of discontent, have still a terrible truth in them; the anguish of good men cries out that evil, if not in the nature of things, has a wide domain and a present power which extends over those to whom it is hateful and repellent. Shall the just perish for ever? Shall the mouth of unrighteousness never be stopped? Where is that balance of the moral order in which none shall eat the fruits of another man's devices, but every one, as the Categorical Imperative commands, shall be rewarded according to his works? We may allow that suffering is a means, provided that it be not the end. But if the ethical character, made perfect by endurance, lifted upon Calvary for all the world to contemplate its winning loveliness, shall straightway fall to dust and ashes, what can be the purpose, or how shall we talk of the reason which science would fain discover in that marvellous spec·tacle, the pattern and instance of virtues known to commoner experience? It is not enough to say with modern enthusiasts that self-sacrifice hands on the lamp of moral splendor from one century to another. That does not answer my question. I speak of justice, not of consequences. It is not just that wrong should go unpunished, or that goodness should be wantonly afflicted—and though, as I have said, there is a penalty inseparable from the very act of evil choice, and virtue is and must be its own reward, yet reason demands that, in the end, it shall be well with him that means well, and ill with him to whom injustice was pleasant.   By the law of gravitation, all things are kept in stable equilibrium and the visible world endures. Can I point to indications of a law in the spiritual order which fulfils the same office and renders to every free choice its due ?   I say yes, there is one great law which presents itself to us under a double aspect; the law that character tends to be permanent, and that spiritual energy is indestructible.   We may define it, indeed, as the highest form of the conservation of energy, or as Ethical Optimism; by which I mean that the supreme expression of intellectual and moral being is justice, and that the spirit of the just is immortal.   In my next paper I will touch upon the grounds for this momentous conclusion offered to us by inductive science.

WILLIAM BARRY.

THE REWARD FOR A CUP OF COLD WATER.

" Whosoever shall give to drink to one of these little ones a cup of cold water only . . . shall not lose his reward."—ST. MATT. x. 42.

DIVES IN HELL.

'Tis plain that He meant Heav'n as the reward for boon so
    small,
Since I would gladly give all Heav'n twice o'er to him
Who from his plenteous cup's cool, overflowing brim
Upon my burning tongue would let one drop in mercy fall.

ALFRED YOUNG.

THE AMERICAN STATE AND THE PRIVATE SCHOOL.

IN two of the Northwestern States, Wisconsin and Illinois, the question of the relation between the State and the school has been, within the last two years, very generally and very thoroughly discussed on the rostrum and in the press, and it was submitted last autumn to the arbitrament of the popular voice at the polls. The issue involved the claim of the State, as embodied in certain school laws passed by the General Assembly, to control the management and the studies even of the private and denominational schools that derive no aid whatever from the public funds. This claim of State control was pushed still further. Compulsory education laws were passed and for a short time enforced, which, whatever may have been the purpose of their authors, were held by many to invade the domain of parental rights. When these laws came to be applied by school directors they were found in many cases to be meddlesome, annoying, and oppressive, and excited determined opposition. The interference complained of extended chiefly to the following points :

1. Parents were obliged to send their children to *a school approved by the school board* or school directors.

2. To an approved school *in the district wherein the parents resided.*

3. For a *certain number of weeks* (say sixteen) *continuously, and at a time of the school year to be determined by the school board.*

4. *No school to be considered as a school,* within the meaning of this law, unless there should be taught therein, *in the English language, reading, writing, United States history, geography, and arithmetic.*

5. Truant children, when arrested, were to be sent to the nearest public school.

6. Any failure to comply with the several provisions of this law *subjected the offending parent to a fine, determined by the statute,* and to be paid into the court, *on the mere charge and testimony of the school director as the accusing witness.*

7. The failure to teach in the English language any one of the several branches named in the statute might, at the pleasure of a school director, have the effect of outlawing the school, and subjecting the parents of all the children frequenting such school to the penalties provided for in the law.

From the foregoing clauses of the Bennett law of Wisconsin and the Edwards law of Illinois, it is clear that this is not simply compulsory school legislation in the sense of securing to the children of criminally negligent or indifferent parents a certain amount of instruction, or of arresting the very real evil of truancy as it exists in certain of our large cities. Here is something very different. Here is State interference and State control in matters which had hitherto been considered as within the exclusive right and jurisdiction of the parents. This legislation formed a new departure. It attempted to extend over the child, the parent, and the private school an authority hitherto unknown, and to dictate to the family *how much* and *what sort* of schooling it must give the child, and *where* and *at what time.* It is not to be wondered at that such laws excited opposition. They were denounced as uncalled-for, unnecessary, unjust, oppressive, and tyrannical. They were said to be the work of fanatics, of enemies of religious schools, of doctrinaires devoted to State paternalism, of Know-nothings hostile to the German parochial schools. They were defended with equal warmth. Religious prejudice was invoked against the German Lutherans and the German Catholics, who fought for their parochial schools and who were virulently denounced as enemies of the public schools, assailants of American institutions, aliens in tongue and in spirit, and so on. The war was waged with a good deal of rancor towards the patrons of private and denominational schools. The issue was carried into the political arena and was fought out, first in Wisconsin, with a result which was almost as much of a surprise to the victorious Democrats as to the defeated Republicans. The party identified with the obnoxious Bennett law was overwhelmed at the polls and lost everything. In Illinois both political parties entered the contest by pledging themselves, in their State conventions, either to repeal the compulsory law or to amend its most objectionable clauses. But even this did not save the Republicans from defeat. They had been unwise enough to renominate for the office of State Superintendent of Schools Mr. Richard Edwards, the reputed author of the compulsory education law. To emphasize their condemnation of that law, the voters of the State of Illinois elected Mr. Edwards's opponent by thirty-five thousand majority.

The election in these States is over long ago, and the smoke of the battle has rolled away; it may be well to review the situation and note some of the lessons taught by the contest and its results. Such an analysis has its value for others than politicians. From the educational standpoint and as a question

of civics involving the relation of State and school, it will be
instructive to notice what principles were rejected or admitted
by either side in the contest.

In the first place, it is pleasant to observe that none of the
dire consequences predicted by the party that defended the compulsory law have followed the defeat of that party at the polls.
The "little red school-house" has not been closed. The English
language has not been abolished; nor does either of these valued
institutions seem to be threatened with any immediate disaster.

In the second place, the election has settled, so far as a decided majority can settle anything, that the time has not yet
come, if it ever will come, when the State, under the dictation
of a political party, can interfere with the right of parents to
educate their children in the schools of their choice, or can control and virtually suppress schools that derive no aid from the
public funds.

When it became evident that the issue between the advocates and the opponents of State control as embodied in the
compulsory school law, or of "State paternalism," as its enemies
called it, would be made a political issue, both parties addressed
themselves to the task of formulating the principles they were
prepared to maintain. Party lines were rigidly drawn; the two
great political parties were arrayed against one another chiefly
on the question of the compulsory law; and in their respective
State conventions they adopted certain principles on which they
appealed to the people for support. A comparison of these
principles will now engage our attention.

Let us first compare the principles of the two parties in the
State of Wisconsin. The Republicans, through their State officials,
chiefly the Governor and the Superintendent of Public Instruction, were committed to the compulsory school law, called the
"Bennett Law"; but certain provisions of that law, in fact its
chief and fundamental provisions, had been so vigorously assailed
and were so unpopular that the party felt the necessity of
making concessions. Accordingly we find them, as their opponents termed it, "hedging" in the following clauses of their
platform:

"We believe that the compulsory education law is wise and
humane in all its essential purposes, and we are opposed to its
repeal; but at the same time we assert that the parent or guardian has the right to select the *time of year* and *the place*,
whether *public* or *private*, and *wherever located*, in which his
child or ward shall receive instruction, and we pledge ourselves

to modify the existing law so that it shall conform to the foregoing declarations. . . . The Republican party recognizes as valuable auxiliaries in the work of popular education the private and parochial schools, supported without aid from public funds, and *disclaims absolutely any purpose whatever to interfere in any manner with such schools, either as to their terms, government, or branches to be taught therein.* . . . We repudiate as a gross misrepresentation of our purposes the suggestion, come whence it may, that we will in any manner invade the domain of conscience, or trample upon parental rights or religious liberty."

These disclaimers did not save the Republicans from defeat. The party was popularly identified with the Bennett law and was swept out of place by the tidal wave of reaction against State interference. This formal recognition of certain inalienable rights of parents in the matter of education, though it failed of its immediate purpose, is valuable on other accounts, as we shall presently see.

Let us turn now to the platform of the Democratic party. The authorship of this platform is credited to Colonel Vilas, since elected to succeed Mr. Spooner as United States Senator from Wisconsin. It is clear, bold, aggressive, and direct. This is what it says on the subject of the odious compulsory school law :

" The Bennett law is a local manifestation of the settled Republican policy of paternalism. . . Favoring laws providing for the compulsory attendance at school of all children, we believe that the school law in force prior to the passage of the Bennett law *guaranteed to all children of the State opportunity for education*, and in this essential feature was stronger than the Bennett law. The '*underlying principle*' of the *Bennett law is needless interference* with *parental rights* and *liberty of conscience.* The provisions for its enforcement place the accused at the mercy of the school directors, and deny his right to trial by jury and according to the law of the land. To mask this tyrannical invasion of individual and constitutional rights, the shallow plea of defence of the English language is advanced. The history of the State, peopled largely with foreign-born citizens, demonstrates the fact that natural causes and the necessities of the situation are advancing the spread of the English language to the greatest possible extent. We therefore denounce that law as unnecessary, unwise, unconstitutional, un American, and un-Democratic, and demand its repeal."

There was no mistaking this pronouncement. It went to the very root of the whole question. It attacked the " underlying principle " of State control over private schools, denounced the law in this sense and demanded its repeal. The people of Wisconsin, hitherto counted as a safe Republican State, by a very sweeping majority supported the party pledged to repeal the law.

Looking back over these two platforms, we find that their differences concern the scope and meaning of the compulsory law actually on the statute book, rather than the abstract question of State control over education. The Republicans profess to regard the Bennett law as " wise and humane in its essential purposes, and are opposed to its repeal." At the same time they "disclaim absolutely any purpose whatever to interfere in any manner with such (private or parochial) schools, either as to their terms, government, or branches to be taught therein." They also agree with the Democrats when they repudiate as a gross misrepresentation of their purposes the suggestion "that we will in any manner invade the domain of conscience or trample upon parental rights or religious liberty." They pledge themselves to modify the Bennett law so as to eliminate from it every clause that seems to interfere with parental rights or to control private schools.

The Democrats, on the other hand, see in the Bennett law not the benign purpose of securing to all children an elementary education, but a meddling and encroaching tendency which they call paternalism, and a fixed resolve to "interfere with parental rights and liberty of conscience."

However far asunder the two parties stood in their interpretation of the existing compulsory law, their differences as to principle were more apparent than real. To the thoughtful reader, who studies the public expression of party creeds put forth in these platforms, it is in the highest degree interesting and gratifying to note that both parties are sound on this vital question of State interference with private schools. If the principles enunciated in these party manifestoes are sincerely held by the rank and file of the two parties, there is not much reason to fear the encroachment of the State upon the rights of parents.

Let us now turn to the neighboring State of Illinois, where, though the contest was not so bitter, the same issue was involved. There the Democrats were first in the field with their declaration of principles. On this compulsory law question they hold "that the parental right to direct and control the education of the child should for ever remain inviolate, and that the provision of the law of 1889, commonly known as the Compulsory Education Statute, impugning that inalienable right, should be at once repealed."

To this the Republicans reply: "We are opposed to *any*

arbitrary interference with the right of parents or guardians to educate their children at private schools, no matter where located ; and we favor the amendment of the existing compulsory education law so as to conform to the declarations herein set forth, and also the repeal of so much of said law as *provides for public supervision of private schools."* So far the two political parties are at one in the rejection of all unnecessary or arbitrary interference with the parent's right to educate his child. Both parties then proceed to define their position on the question of compulsory education. The Republicans say: "We declare in favor of a compulsory education law, which will guarantee to all the children of the State ample opportunity of acquiring such an elementary education as will fit them for the intelligent performance of civil and political duties." The Democrats state their principles still more explicitly: "Compulsory education in the sense that parents who violate or neglect their parental duty may be compelled to its performance or punished for non-performance, is licit. Compulsory education in the sense of controlling or seeking to control, or to dislodge from their rightful place, those parents who are discharging their parental duties commensurately with the state of life of parent and child, is not allowable even to the State."

The principles thus admitted or rejected by the two great parties in Illinois as well as in Wisconsin, in so far as we can judge of principles from the platforms adopted under the pressure of political exigency, in the heat of a political campaign, appear to be substantially identical. What the one party rejects the other also rejects with a little more emphasis; what the one repudiates as foreign to its spirit and purpose, the other condemns as unjust, unnecessary, and unconstitutional. What the one admits, namely, the natural right of the parent to control and direct the education of his child, the other defends as an inalienable right with which the State cannot interfere. Where one disclaims all intention of arbitrary interference with the right of parents to educate their children in any school, no matter where located, the other declares that this parental right must for ever remain inviolable. So far, therefore, as the theory or abstract principle of State interference is concerned, there is not much room for choice between the two sets of resolutions. If the popular vote went so largely to the Democratic side, it was because popular opinion had come to identify the Republicans, despite their political platform, with the odious compulsory law which in practice contradicted their theory. The movement that carried two strongly Republican States over to the camp of Democracy is now generally admitted to have been a reaction against State paternalism, or that tendency towards what is called a "strong government" which characterizes a small and restless clique of doctrinaires. On this subject, as on all the fundamental questions which the popular mind can easily grasp, the people are undoubtedly sound, and may be trusted to approve no laws that unnecessarily and seriously interfere with parental rights or the rights of conscience. The people of these two prosperous States, and notably the patrons of private and parochial schools, are as progressive and as willing to make sacrifices for popular education as those of any State in the Union. They prove it by the burdens they voluntarily assume, to give their children the best possible education, according to their convictions and the dictates of their conscience. The line of State interference was sharply drawn in the contest through which those States passed last autumn, · and the result of the election set the limit· so emphatically that no one, for the present, can pretend to ignore or mistake it.

The State may assist parents to control habitual truants; it may compel negligent parents to provide their children with an elementary education; but it may not invade the domain of parental rights. It may not dictate the sort of school, public or private, religious or secular, domestic or foreign, to which the parent shall send his child; it may not prescribe the place, the time, the amount or the quality of schooling, or otherwise interfere with the management or control of schools supported without aid from the public funds. · Private and parochial schools enjoy the fullest right to exist and to flourish as "valuable auxiliaries in the work of popular education." In selecting a school, public or private, or in providing instruction for his children at home, the parent "exercises a right protected by the law of the land as well as by the law of nature and in exercising this right he need offer neither excuse nor apology."

These points, as we have already observed, may be considered settled, so far as a great and decisive political contest can be said to settle anything. It is worth a great deal to have had these principles so distinctly formulated and so generally admitted. They have cleared the atmosphere of much haziness and have helped to define the true relation between the State and the school.

E. A. HIGGINS, S.J.

St. Ignatius College, Chicago, Il..

THE OLD LANDLADY'S ALBUM.

THE old landlady came to our little village about the first of
October, just after the summer visitors had left for their homes
in the valleys. Being the only new member of a very small
community, she and all her belongings received a full measure
of attention, all other subjects having been so thoroughly discussed they had lost their relish. She lived just across the
street from us, and I learned to know her before I ever spoke
to her. When I threw open my shutters in the early morning
madame would be at her window, busy with her birds and
flowers, or walking up and down her wide galleries softly, as
though she felt all the glories of earth and sky which surrounded
her and yet her thoughts were far away.

Her white hair was put back smoothly from her brow, and,
after being plaited in two heavy·bands, was confined low on the
back of a head whose noble outlines would delight a sculptor.
She was always dressed in black, and though one would never
call her fashionable or stylish, there was about her a certain
elegance in costume and bearing which impressed the least
sensitive of those who saw her.

It was not long before I sought her acquaintance. Her
cordial smile and sincere voice put me thoroughly at ease,
almost as soon as I entered her cosy sitting-room. Her
manner, though so gentle and dignified, was alert and business-
like; her eyes, behind their gold-rimmed glasses, met yours frankly.
She seemed to comprehend you at once, to know you thoroughly;
and yet so kind was her judgment that she knew you at your
best—rather what you wished yourself to be than what you
really were.

She began the conversation, as many people do, about the
weather, but she spoke so enthusiastically of the ever-changing
moods of nature that I found myself valuing less cheaply the
charms of my mountain home; but when she began to extol
the delights of monotony, declaring it to be a "poultice to her
aching nerves," I avowed my detestation of all poultices, real or
figurative. She laughed as merrily as I did, but suggested that
the difference in our feelings could be readily explained by
considering the differences of age and occupation. "You are
young, ignorant of the big and busy world; you imagine it full
of pleasant adventures, but I have tested its promises and I am

quite willing to leave its crowded ways to those who love them."
Seeing a protest on my face, she continued: "I do not wish to
discourage you; the present generation of Southern girls will
probably not be called upon to endure the hardships and horrors
of a civil war. That great tragedy left me a widow with
children to educate, almost penniless and totally untrained to any
sort of business, but we naturally proceed along the line of least
resistance. The whole training of the average Southern girl
before the war consisted in learning to make herself agreeable
in society, as well as capable to direct her household affairs so
that the limitless hospitality which was practised in those days
by all people in good circumstances should cause no inconvenience to herself, her family, her guests, or her servants. Being
thoroughly trained in that school, having kept house on a large
scale in brighter days, my first thought was to do for pay, now
that necessity demanded it, what I had formerly done for habit
and inclination. So gathering together what I could I opened a
boarding-house in the capital of my native Tennessee, where I
had friends and kindred. As I have continued in that business
uninterruptedly for twenty years, my dear child, perhaps you
can understand why my nerves need soothing, for I assure you
the woman who fights steadily the ever-rising billows of detail,
which threaten daily to engulf the city boarding-house keeper,
is as busy as the shipwrecked mariner in mid-ocean with only
a plank between him and death."

"Oh! but madame," I cried, "you have fought the fight, you
have won the victory. I would be glad to know I could do
anything successfully."

"Victory is a fine word," she said soberly. "If success is
to be counted by dollars and cents, many a woman earns more
in one season by dancing or singing than I have done in twenty
years of steady application to duties teasingly small and merciless-
ly exacting; but I do not count success alone by dollars and
cents. Through all those long years I am sure I never lost
that instinct of hospitality which decided my choice of a business;
the fact that my boarders paid me money only emphasized my
duty as a hostess. Wits of the newspaper variety have always
made themselves merry over the comical situations which arise
from the different points of view occupied by Mrs. Tuffstake and
Mr. Haffed; but in our latitude, at least, these jokes rarely have
any foundation. Twenty years ago the boarding-houses of the
South were, as a rule, presided over by ladies whose instincts
and traditions prompted them to make a home, as far as was

possible, for all' who received the shelter of their roof. Yes,"
she continued musingly, "the life of a landlady is a laborious
one, but it is not without its pleasures. Do you see that large
album—every face in it is the face of a boarder, and many a
one the face of a friend."

I took the large and handsome volume in my hand and
began carelessly to turn the leaves, being more interested in
madame's conversation than in her boarders, when the pictured
face of a young woman arrested my attention. A wealth of
black hair above a low, broad brow; heavy eye-brows, almost
meeting, shaded large, mournful eyes—sorrowful they were, and
yet so eager! Only the bust, shoulders, and part of the arms
were visible, but I felt sure the hands must be tightly clasped—
so intent were those wonderful eyes.

"Ah! madame," I cried, interrupting her, "who is this?"
pointing to the picture.

"That is the picture of one whom I knew as Mrs. Johnson,
of St. Paul, Minnesota."

"Do tell me about her; she has such a singular expression."

"Her expression is no more singular than her life," madame
replied.

"Do tell me about her," I begged, and madame readily consented, adding that old soldiers love to recount the histories of
their battles.

"Really," she began, "Mr. Howells was not far wrong
when he divided mankind into three classes—men, women, and
boarding-house keepers. In the management of her business
affairs a boarding-house keeper needs the faculties of a man,
and those of a woman in the discharge of her domestic duties;
in addition to all that, she needs to be free from prejudices; the
progress of her busy life will do much to destroy them, however
ancient or deep-seated. But to the story."

Early in the seventies a young man came to the house with
a note of introduction, signed by the chief train-despatcher
at the L. and N. office. "Mr. Hugh Johnson," the note ran, "is on
duty in my office. I send him to you for comfortable room and
board." As I knew Mr. King very well, of course Mr. Johnson was made welcome. He was apparently about thirty years
old, quick and lively in conversation, and showed at once a
disposition to be very friendly and communicative. He came in
September, and spent all his leisure hours about the house, seeming to enjoy the wide halls and galleries of the stately old

mansion, which had once been the home of one of the most aristocratic families of Tennessee. It was not long before he gave me his history—how he had gained his not very perfect education by his own exertions, cared for his widowed mother, won the good-will of his neighbors in Pennsylvania, etc., etc.; and finally after establishing himself in business he had married about the close of the war, in which he earnestly assured me "he took no stock." (All my boarders knew I was a totally unreconstructed rebel.) He was passionately in love with his wife, but she, he learned too late, had married him to spite another lover, and of course things went rapidly from bad to worse; the only child, a little girl, died—the wife returned to her mother. By agreement he left the State, and, as quickly as the matter could be arranged before the courts, a copy of the divorce was forwarded to him in Texas. Telegraphers are a migratory race. He finally found himself in Nashville, and declared himself fortunate to be in a house whose mistress was so thoroughly a mother to her boarders, etc., etc.

The next day after this first outburst of confidence, Judy, my faithful black cook, came into my room and, with the familiarity born of life-long association, dropped into a chair near the open door and proceeded to unburden her mind.

"Now, Miss Nett," she said (my baptismal name is Jeannette), "I know times is changed an' you is 'bleeged to make yore livin'. Ise glad to git a boarder, an' I does my best to please 'em. I know de wah's done ceased an' we oughten to hate nobody, but I jes nacherally 'spises to see a Yankee 'bout dis house, an' dat ar las' white-eyed un's not fitten to be in no real lady's house."

"Why, Judy, what is the matter with Mr. Johnson? Didn't he give you the handkerchief you have on your head this very moment? And does he not declare that you make the best biscuits in the world?"

"Yes, an' he gin me dis too," she said, showing a round silver dollar; "but I doan like no white man—'ceptin 'tis some dese boys what we all knows—comin' flingin' little rocks at my winder an' callin' right easy 'Aunt Judy! Aunt Judy!' 'Who's dat?' I say. 'Me, Hugh Johnson,' he say. 'I an't none o' yore A'nt,' I tell him; but he keep on: 'Aunt Judy, jes lissen a minute—come to de winder; here is something for you.' Wid dat I jes kinder hist the winder a little bit, an' he gin me dis dollar, an' he say: 'Now, Aunt Judy, just open de hall door and don't tell madame. I have been out with a friend and had a

little too much wine.' Now, I knowed 'twas whiskey, an' he was
mos' too drunk to walk; but I let him in; 'twas mighty nigh
day. When de time come I fetched him up his brekfus', an' I
seed you didn't 'spect nuffin'. But now I done tole you, don't
you let dat white man beat you outen his bord. I done tole
you now"; and with a warning shake of her turbaned head she
disappeared to look after the affairs of her own peculiar domain.

Despite Judy's warning, Mr. Johnson won my sympathy, and
I spent some little time encouraging and admonishing him, in
which missionary efforts I was warmly seconded by one of my
boarders, a rich young widow, who had come from a country
town to enjoy the pleasures of a season in the gay capital.

In February he went away, having paid all that he owed, so
far as I knew, and avowing the most extravagant admiration for
Southern women in general, and for myself in particular the most
respectful affection and the warmest gratitude.

In a short time a postal card came to tell me that he had secured a good situation in St. Paul; after that nothing was heard
and but little thought about Mr. Johnson. The widow showed
some interest in his fate, but apparently that died out, and Mr.
Johnson was only a memory among many others. One day in
August I received a bulky envelope containing a long and enthusiastic letter, signed Hugh Johnson, filled with his courtship
and marriage to the "sweetest woman that ever lived upon the
face of the earth." "I know your kind heart," he continued;
"you will rejoice with me in my happiness, but that happiness
will never be complete until you know my wife. Next month
we will go to see my brother in Texas, and we will stop two
days with you, the kindest, the best," etc. I thought the letter
extravagant in its praise of me, if not of his wife, and I sighed
over the state of public sentiment which allowed divorced people
to re-marry without exciting disapprobation or even comment.
Before the war, in the South such occurrences were almost unheard of. However, I wrote a short note of congratulation, and
asked to be notified of the date of their arrival. Time, in accordance with a fixed habit, steadily dropped the days into the gulf
of the past, which flows just behind the marching column of humanity. September came and went, so did October—but not the
Johnsons. One dreary afternoon in November I was summoned
to the parlor to see a lady who wanted a room. She sent no
card. When I entered I saw a young lady most stylishly dressed
and exceedingly handsome, accompanied by a conductor on the
L. and N. road, as I knew by his uniform. I bowed, saying,

"I am madame."   As the lady made no reply the conductor spoke: "Madame, this lady asked me to bring her to your house, to which she had been directed by a friend of yours." With that he made a hasty retreat.

I looked at the lady for further explanation, but without speaking she gazed at me so wistfully, so strangely, that I was uncertain what to do or say. To break the awkward silence I reminded her that I had not the pleasure of knowing her name.

"My name is Johnson," she answered slowly, "and I live in St. Paul, Minnesota."

"Indeed! It seems odd that the one acquaintance I have in that city should bear the same name—Johnson—though it is not an uncommon one."

She gave me a startled glance. "Is your acquaintance a gentleman?" "Yes." "What is his given name?"

At the moment I had forgotten it, but I described him minutely.

"Was his name Hugh?" she asked.

"Yes," I answered, "and"—but the sentence was never completed, for without a sob or a groan my new acquaintance fell to the floor limp and insensible. I summoned assistance as hastily as possible; she soon revived sufficiently for Judy and the house-maid to get her up-stairs and in bed. Of course all debate about receiving an unknown person into the house had to be adjourned for later consideration.

After seeing to everything necessary for her comfort I told Miss Johnson I would leave her in Sallie's care until she had entirely recovered, as she protested she would in a few moments. She caught my hand and cried out, as one in mortal agony, "Madame, do not leave me; I have something to tell you."

I sent Sallie away and sat by the bed . "I have come all this way to see you, and to see you alone," she said. "I am Hugh Johnson's wife!"

"Why did you not write? Where is Mr. Johnson?"

"I don't know where he is—he is gone. I have come to ask you where he is."

"My dear lady, I know nothing of him. I have only one letter, which you shall read, telling of your marriage and promising to bring you to see me."

"Well," she continued, speaking rapidly, "you will hear from him very soon. Six weeks after we were married, when I was happier than anybody that ever lived on earth, Hugh left

me one evening to be gone half an hour to deliver the packages
in the express office to the 7.30 train. He delivered them all
right, the receipt was found next day, but he has never been
seen again. There was money gone. I know he did not take
it; my people call him a thief—he is not!" with rising excitement.
"While I stay at home I cannot hear from him—they keep my
letters—I know they do. He has told me a thousand times
about you—that you were a Christian and really afraid to do
wrong—that he would trust you with his life. You are Madame
——, this is No. —, and — street; I am safe—you will befriend
me!"

"What can I do, my dear child?"

"You will get a letter; he will try to communicate with
me through you; you will be my friend as you were his; only
promise me this, dear madame—let me stay here until I hear
from him. Don't deny me; I have money to pay my board
and I can earn more.".

The tears were streaming down her pallid cheeks, her lovely
hair fell loosely around her face, her distress was pitiable. Of
course I consented that she should stay; begged her to quiet
herself, and in every way I tried to comfort the poor creature.
After awhile she seemed to be asleep, and I went down to
look after the supper-table. Of course I told Judy all about
the affair and how sorry I felt for the unhappy, deserted girl.
Judy was but little touched by the recital. "She knowed that
Johnson was pore white trash the fust time she sot eyes on him."
However, she prepared a dainty meal, and, more from curiosity
than sympathy, carried it to Mrs. Johnson's room. One glance
at Judy's face when she returned from her errand was sufficient
index of her opinion of the new boarder; but that high-spirited
individual left no room for doubt by asserting unequivocally that
"dat gal was gwine to gib trubble if she didn't go straight
back to dem Yankees, whar she b'longed." Next morning Mrs.
Johnson came in to breakfast, quiet and dignified. One could
not call her a lady, though her movements were graceful, and
her voice exceedingly rich and full. At a glance it could be seen
that her blood, if not her birth, was foreign. Her whole appearance was anomalous and puzzling; evidently uneducated, she
occasionally quoted a line or two which bespoke acquaintance
with books; unused to the ways of polite society, there was
something far from commonplace in her free and harmonious
movements. After my morning duties were finished she sat by
my side while I wrote several letters of inquiry for her. The

most important were to Mr. King, who had gone West from Nashville, and to Mr. Johnson's brother in Texas, though there were several other friends of her husband and herself to whom I wrote, signing always my name with no mention of her. She seemed very much relieved, and confident that in a short time she would hear from her husband. She reiterated her conviction that he had tried to communicate with her in St. Paul, but that her friends, believing him guilty, had intercepted the letters. She told me that her mother died soon after the family came from Norway to America; her father was a sailor; he left her with a German family, sailed away and never returned. These people had treated her very well, probably as well as if she had been their own child. They had sent her to the public school, but had given her no other advantages; of her own accord she had cultivated her one small talent—she could draw and paint, after a fashion, without effort, and she had applied her skill to the production of all sorts of trifles which seem to have become articles of necessity to a very large class of American women. Her foster parents had allowed her to earn what she could in that way, and so she had bought the handsome clothes for her wedding, and also paid her expenses to Nashville. The old people were very indignant at her coming, and, indeed, it was a singular thing to do. " Suppose I had left the city ? " I asked her. " I knew you had not," she replied. " I felt *sure* you had not."

Among other things, she told me she had travelled for one season with a theatrical company, a place in which had been secured for her by a niece of Mrs. Hertwig her foster-mother, who held a good position in the troupe, but the life did not suit her. That episode in her history explained the elegance of her movements and the distinct tones of her voice. For a few days she was very quiet, and rarely spoke to anybody but me. If she noticed the attention she attracted among the boarders she gave no sign of it, though, of course, she had been introduced to every one of them.

Almost a week passed before replies to the letters began to come in. First, the brother knew nothing of him—in fact, he and Hugh were not on the best of terms. Then Mr. King knew nothing of him, but would send letters and telegrams to men in the business and would notify me promptly.

Apparently she felt but little discouraged. " She felt certain that Mr. Johnson would write to me as soon as it was safe to do so. In a few days we would hear."

The next morning she came down dressed for the street in a

picturesque walking-dress of dark green cloth and a dainty little hat to match. She carried in her hand a satchel of open straw-work, lined with green satin, filled with a number of sketches of all sorts of subjects on all sorts of materials for all sorts of orna-mental purposes. My enthusiasm for her art treasures was not very high, but I could easily believe she would find little diffi-culty in disposing of them to ladies who possessed, at least, as much money as taste. Fortunately for ber the æsthetic wave had just reached Nashville, and she came back at dinner–time flushed with triumph, having sold mats, tidies, throws, lambrequins, quantities of things, and having taken orders enough to keep her busy for some time. I had directed her carefully in what part of town to look for patronage. She declared herself almost happy. Hugh would write soon and all would be well.

After dinner she begged me to go up to her room. Of course she went over the whole story again and again—how he had no friends to clear up his good name, he could not have stolen the money, somebody else took it, he became aware of the theft and fled because he knew it would go hard with him among strangers. In my heart I thought the poor man was dead, but I did not say so of course.

" Madame, let me read some of his beautiful letters to you," she said after a pause.

To please her I consented, so she sat by the window and read aloud many letters he had written to her before they were married. They were of the usual order, full of praises for her beauty and protestations of his deathless love. He was older than she, but experience had taught him to value truly the happiness which he would find in their little cottage, etc. ; all commonplace enough, but to her it was the music of the spheres. Her face, as she care-fully replaced the letters in her trunk, was bright with emotion—the radiance from her loyal heart lit up every feature. In anticipation of finding him, she had brought his trunk, containing all his wardrobe. She opened it and showed me a little package of letters, which she had written to him, neatly labelled and put away in a box I recog-nized at once. At last she picked up a dainty envelope addressed to Mr. Hugh Johnson, which she said came after he left. " She was sure there was some mistake about the letter, as Hugh had never spoken to her about F——," a little town near Nashville from which the letter was mailed. She brought me the letter. It was very short.

" The $100 you borrowed for two weeks from me has not been received.—C. D."

The post-mark and the initials told that the widow's missionary zeal had cost her something.   Handing it back I merely said: "Evidently a mistake."   After Elise, as she entreated me to call her, had put away the letters, she came to the fire and talked hopefully of his coming at Christmas, which was now close at hand. My heart sank, for I began to fear he was a worthless scoundrel. As gently as possible I tried to insinuate my fears that he might never return.   The blood left her face, her short and irregular breathing alarmed me, but she rallied and said after a painful pause: "I feel, I know he will return, but I promise to say nothing more about him if he does not come by the first of January.   But, dear madame, do not send me away.   I will paint, I will work hard, I will do anything for you—only let me stay here; do not send me back where they hate him and constantly reproach me for loving him—him, so noble, so true, and so unhappy!"   "Hugh!" she cried, walking rapidly about the room, "should all the courts in the world pronounce you guilty I know you are innocent.   Call me, dear darling; I will fly to you at the ends of the earth."   Her eyes were blazing, her hands deadly cold.   I spoke to her reassuringly, reminding her that there were yet ten days till the New Year, and much might happen in that time.   She rewarded me with a bright smile, but sank into a chair faint and pallid.   After that interview my cogitations, when the Viking's Daughter—as the boarders called her—occupied my thoughts, were far from pleasant.   I did not want such a member of my family on such terms.   A landlady's responsibilities are serious enough without complications.   I had no means of verifying her statements.   I knew nothing about her.   I could only hope and pray for something to relieve the poor young creature of her sorrow and me of my burden.

The joyous hubbub of Christmas came and went.   After some persuasion Elise consented to go to church, though she protested it did no good, declaring she knew everybody would go to heaven when they died, and as for *this* world the good people always came in for their full share of trouble.   However, after she went once, she rarely missed a Mass; the novelty of the service, the lights, the music, the priest in his robes, and the little altar boys, diverted her mind.   Christmas day she showed me a small silver image of the Virgin, not more than an inch tall, which had been her mother's.   I advised her to invoke the aid of that Sweet Comfortress of the Afflicted, but she turned away with an incredulous smile.

As New Year's drew near I watched almost as eagerly for the postman as Elise did.   Nothing came until the morning of

December 31. The letter was from Mr. King, saying that he could hear nothing of Mr. Johnson, but reliable information from St. Paul left no room for doubt—it was a plain, prosaic case of making off with funds committed to his care, without extenuating circumstances.

Now, what was I to do?

The best room in the house had long been occupied by a lawyer and his wife, my very good friends as well as boarders. To Mr. Trewhilt I always went for advice in an emergency. Of course we had often discussed the Viking's Daughter, and he had laughed at the sentimentalism which had allowed her to stay in the house for a single day; but truly, after all these years have passed, I cannot see what else was possible under the circumstances. "Why, madame, show her the letter; she must go back to her own people, there is no other course."

I did not feel so confident, and my heart fell at the thought of her despair when informed of even a part of the contents of Mr. King's letter.

I waited until after dinner, thinking that the most comfortable and prosaic time to talk over exciting subjects.

She was in the sitting-room alone, running her fingers over the keys of the piano, drumming out an accompaniment for some simple ballad. I entered as cheerfully as possible.

"Mrs. Johnson," I began, "I received this morning another letter from Mr. King." She turned her large eyes eagerly towards me. I went on rapidly: "He can hear nothing from your husband, and thinks"—but the poor girl had fainted.

She was taken to her room and after a little while she seemed to be asleep. At supper-time Judy sent Sallie with a cup of tea, which came back untasted. After supper I went to see her. She seemed entirely prostrated—she wanted nothing; she would be well in the morning. I returned to my room with no light heart. In vain I tried to prepare my monthly bills and examine the accounts which awaited my attention. I sat sorrowfully looking into the fire, utterly bereft of the power to come to any conclusion concerning my unfortunate boarder. The clock struck ten, and I still sat gazing helplessly at the glowing coals when the door-bell rang sharply; thoroughly upset, dreading I knew not what, I hastened to answer it myself. The gentleman who rang it apologized for interrupting me, but "there was a very handsome young lady, with flashing eyes and black hair, inside the Capitol grounds. She refuses to stir unless madame will come for her. The night watchman locked the gates, as usual, at nine o'clock, not knowing any one was inside. Soon after that Policeman Bolton saw her in the bright moonlight flitting about over the terraces and steps, apparently talking to some one whom he could not see. When he approached her she looked at him with wide-open eyes and told him 'not to disturb her, she was expecting her husband, who had promised to meet· her there.' After some time she told Bolton she would go home if madame would come after her." Just then Mr. Trewhitt, who had heard the whole conversation through his open door, came into the hall. " Ah! madame," he cried, " that's your boarder— no doubt about it ; but come on, let's see what can be done."

A few steps brought us to Capitol Hill, that fine elevation upon which rests the noble State-house of Tennessee. Built of native marble, its massive Corinthian pillars and grand propor· tions are the pride of the whole State. The radiance of a full moon in a cloudless sky gave it a singular beauty that cold night, the last of the old year.

The heavy iron gate was still locked, though a messenger had been despatched for the key. Outside stood a motley crowd, principally men and boys, with a few of the gentler sex, colored cooks hurrying home with their buckets of cold victuals, and others who chanced to be on the street at that hour. Inside were the policeman and Elise, with her beautiful, pale face pressed close to the cold bars of the gate; her long hair, falling over her shoulders, contrasted with the white wrapper of soft merino which she wore. The heterogeneous crowd seemed awe-stricken by her appearance ; they made way for us at once. Some one said, " Here is madame." Elise raised her eyes, and, seeing me, began to shake the gate. But there was a delay until the key came. When the gate was opened she put her hand in mine, saying: " My man told me he would meet me at the Capitol, but there was such a crowd he did not come ; but he will come to-morrow night, will he not, dear madame ? "

The truth dawned on me. She was crazy; her sorrows had dethroned her reason. I spoke cheerfully to her, assuring her that Mr. Johnson would never come in that crowd, and that the best thing would be to go home. She went with us, but her excitement was alarming. After reaching her room she began anew the recital of her woes. Mr. Trewhitt, who declared he could not leave me alone with a mad woman, sat patiently while she read the letters and took all of Mr. Johnson's clothes out of his trunk. At the bottom she found a razor, which she said she had sharpened to cut her throat the day she knew he was dead or false to her. Mr. Trewhitt examined the razor, declared it very dull, and put it in his pocket, promising to have it put in good order for her.

That performance *was* a trifle exciting, but the day's fatigue, the cold walk, and the warm air of the room conspired with my comfortable position on the sofa to put me to sleep. As I dozed off I heard kind Mr. Trewhitt saying, "Yes, madame; no madame," as occasion required to the rapid speeches of Elise. When I awoke the cold gray of New Year's morning was struggling with the light from the flaring gas-jet. Elise was asleep, with her arms clasped over the trunk, and Mr. Trewhitt was asleep in the rocking-chair. I threw a blanket over Elise, turned down the gas, replenished the fire, and aroused Mr. Trewhitt. Outside the door we held a whispered consultation. I felt sure she would be all right when she awoke. He declared he could not help it if she was not; he must have a nap before breakfast. There was no nap for me. My time was absorbed between the necessary morning duties of a landlady and intense watchfulness of Mrs. Johnson's room.

When the breakfast-bell rang she came down looking worn, pale, and listless. She remembered nothing of the night's adventures, as she asked me how her room came to be in such disorder; but her interest in the matter was so slight that she was easily diverted from the subject.

After breakfast Mr. Trewhitt again advised me to send her home at once. "But," I replied, "she tells me she will never go home; but I can write to her foster-father "; which I did that day.

Of course the strange events of the night had come to the ears of the boarders, and their glances of curiosity or pity could not entirely escape Elise's attention, but she was too languid to take interest in anything; even her paint-box and brushes remained untouched.

The family physician was summoned, but, after a lengthy interview with the patient, he could give but little information. Diseases of the mind were difficult to diagnose; he was no expert, but he would advise her to be sent to an asylum for the insane. Sure enough! why had we not thought of that?

Mr. Trewhitt readily agreed to see Dr. Callender, of the State Asylum.

All that day I felt like a traitor to the poor girl, who followed me timidly from room to room, or sat pathetically gazing into the fire unconscious of the plans which had been formed for her.

Dr. Callender could not receive a patient who was not a citizen of Tennessee, Mr. Trewhitt reported that night. "But great heavens! madame," he cried, "there is *some* place for her besides your house, where she is not only dependent on your bounty but where she will seriously injure your business. Mrs. Trewhitt, I am sure, will prolong her holiday visit indefinitely if she hears there is a lunatic in the house. I will see the county and city authorities."

Upon investigation he found there was no place for her except the county jail! I had one hope yet—Mr. Hertwig would certainly come or send for her. Days passed and no answer to my letter. Elise would be quiet enough through the day, but as night came on she would get restless and be sometimes entirely unconscious of her surroundings. I moved her into a small room opening into my own, with the key on my side of the door. One night after I had seen her in bed I thought I heard the sound of opening a window. I hoped I was mistaken, but the thought came back again. My heart quaked a little, and I called Judy. That respectable personage had suffered greatly; "to see her mistis keep a bodin-house" was bad enough, but "a lunacy 'sylum wid jes one in it, and dat one a Yankee!" —words failed her.

She opened Mrs. Johnson's door cautiously and peeped in; the fire was low in the grate, but she soon discovered that the room was unoccupied! After a short search we found Elise on the banisters of the second floor gallery, clad in her night-clothes, her hair flying and her eyes blazing, as we could see by the light from the street lamp. The composure of a veteran landlady, who had served her novitiate as a refugee during four years of terror and bloodshed, almost forsook me at the sight. She sat easily, her bare feet hanging over the banisters; one false motion and she would be hurled to the pavement, crippled or dead!

Judy was not nervous. "Mis Johnson, what you doin' dar in de coie?" Elise turned her head slowly, and sighed rather than spoke: "I am waiting for my man."

We took her down-stairs and put her to bed, fastened the windows and the shutters, and tried to sleep; but there was little sleep for me with such a neighbor.

About the middle of January Mr. Hertwig's letter came.

He said "they were poor people; had no money to send for

Elise. This was her second serious offence, the first being the theatrical engagement, but considering her forlorn condition they would receive her once more if she would promise to have nothing to do with Hugh Johnson. As for the fainting spells, years ago she had been afflicted with them, but not lately." All this badly spelled and in mingled German and English.

I read the letter to Elise, and, God forgive me! interpolated expressions of affection. Mr. Trewhitt offered to get her a ticket from the county, if possible; if not, he and the other boarders would furnish it. "No," Elise said; "they could put her on the train, but she would jump off and kill herself rather than go home."

I was truly at my wits' end when help appeared from a most unexpected quarter.

If there is one thing besides the demonstrations of mathematics which Southern people believe, it is that the men of Dixie's Land are by nature, when the weaker sex is concerned, the most courteous, the most gentle, the most loyal, in a word the most chivalrous, men on earth. Between them and other men they admit no comparison. We hold, with scarcely less unanimity, that the men north of us are selfish towards women, that they are not only indifferent to the sweet courtesies of life, but in stern reality sacrifice a woman's interest as unhesitatingly as a man's.

After Mrs. Johnson came to the house there was another arrival from the North, a rosy-cheeked, sturdy young fellow, not more than nineteen years old, named Andrews. He had shown great sympathy for Elise, not only because she was a young and handsome woman, but because she was penniless, helpless, and among strangers. When nobody knew what to do and everybody felt the burden intolerable, Mr. Andrews proposed that he should write to his mother about the whole affair; his mother was half a doctor and entirely a Christian philanthropist, with a large house and ample means and leisure. Of course I was glad for him to write, but I agreed with Mr. Trewhitt, that nothing would come of it.

In the meanwhile Elise was sometimes better and sometimes worse, but always a source of exceeding anxiety. Mr. Andrews assured me that the end was near; and, indeed, as quickly as the mail could go and come the answer reached us. "Certainly," Mrs. Andrews wrote, "send the young lady along at once." Mr. Andrews was delighted, and Elise shared faintly in his joy. He could not leave his business, but a bachelor of means and leisure, such as nearly every boarding-house can supply, volunteered to escort Elise to her new home. Mr. Trewhitt obtained from the county and city authorities transportation for "Elise Johnson, a pauper and lunatic, and her guard." Armed with that, Mr. Lavalle and Elise, with her two handsome trunks, were driven from my door one bright morning in February. Truly we cannot always judge by appearances. Mrs. Andrews wrote of her patient's gradual recovery and final restoration. Young Andrews went further South and only the photograph remained to remind me of Elise. A few months ago a gentleman sent up his card, "C. Andrews, N. Orleans." The name did not recall to my mind the Knight of the Rosy Countenance—the hero who had so unselfishly, so quixotically rescued poor Elise—until he spoke; then, despite his heavy beard and the assured manner of a successful man, I joyfully recognized him.

He had married a Southern girl and was living in New Orleans. Of course I asked about Elise. He had never seen her since she left Nashville, but she had lived until about six years ago with his mother, who was much attached to her *protégée;* then she had gone off to become a member of some Roman Catholic community—he thought, the Little Sisters of the Poor. There was a convent near his mother's house. Elise soon learned to love the sisters. "We suppose that was the cause of her last freak"; and he looked at me with a merry smile.

"Johnson? He died seven or eight years ago in an Australian prison."   M. M.

THE LIFE OF FATHER HECKER.*

CHAPTER XXVII.

FATHER HECKER'S SPIRITUAL DOCTRINE.

HAVING given in the preceding chapter Father Hecker's principles of the religious life in community, a more general view of
his spiritual doctrine, as well as of his method of the direction
of souls naturally follows. And here we are embarrassed by the
amount of matter to choose from ; for as he was always talking
about spiritual doctrine to whomsoever he could get to listen, so in
his published writings, in his letters to intimate friends, and in
his notes and memoranda, we have found enough falling under
the heading of this chapter to fill a volume. Let us hope for
its publication some day.

It need hardly be said that Father Hecker did not claim to
have any new doctrine; there can be none, and he knew it well.
Every generation since Christ has had His entire revelation.
Development is the word which touches the outer margin of all
possible adaptation of Christian principles to the changing conditions of humanity. But in the transmission of these principles from
master to disciple, in practically assisting in their use by public
instruction, or by private advice, or by choice of devotional and
ascetical exercises, there is as great a variety of method as of
temperament among races, and even among individuals; and
there are broadly marked differences which are conterminous
with providential eras of history. This was a truth which Father
Hecker, in common with all discerning minds, took carefully
into account.

His fundamental principle of Christian perfection may be
termed a view of the Catholic doctrine of divine grace suited
to the aspirations of our times. By divine grace the love of
God is diffused in our hearts; the Holy Spirit takes up his abode
there and makes us children of the Heavenly Father, and brethren
of Jesus Christ the Divine Son. The state of grace is thus an
immediate union of the soul with the Holy Trinity, its Creator,
Mediator, and Sanctifier. To secure this union and render it
more and more conscious was Father Hecker's ceaseless endeavor
through life, both for himself and for those who fell under his
influence, whether in cleansing the soul of all hindrances of sin

and imperfection, or advancing it deeper and deeper into the
divine life by prayer and the sacraments.

His doctrine of Christian perfection might be formulated as a
profession of faith : I believe in God the *Father* Almighty ; I
believe in Jesus Christ the Only Begotten *Son* of the Father ; I
believe in the Holy Ghost the *Life Giver*, the spirit of adoption by whom I am enabled to say to the Father, *My Father*,
and to the Son, *My Brother*.

He wished that men generally should be made aware of the
immediate nature of this union of the soul with God, and that
they should become more and more personally conscious of it.
He would bring this about without the intervention of other
persons or other methods than the divinely constituted ones
accessible to all in the priesthood and sacraments. It was the
development of the supernatural, heavenly, divine life of the regenerate man, born again of the Holy Ghost, that Father Hecker
made the end of all he said and all he did in leading souls ;
and he maintained that to partake of this life which is " the light
of men," many souls needed little interference on the part of
others, and that in every case the utmost care should be taken
lest the soul should mingle human influences, even the holiest,
in undue proportion with those which were strictly divine.

" Go to God," he wrote to one asking advice, "go entirely to
God, go integrally to God ; behold, that is sincerity, complete,
perfect sincerity. Do that, and make it a complete, continuous act,
and you need no help from me or any creature. I wish to
provoke you to do it. That is my whole aim and desire. Just
in proportion as we harbor pride, vanity, self-love—in a word,
self-hood—just so far we fail in integrally resigning ourselves to
God. Were we wholly resigned to God He would change all in
us that is in discord with Him, and prepare our souls for union
with Him, making us one with Himself. God longs for our
souls greatly more than our souls can long for Him. Such is
God's thirst for love that He made all creatures to love Him,
and to have no rest until they love Him supremely. If my
words are not to your soul God's words and voice, pay no heed
to them. If they are, hesitate not a moment to obey. If they
humble you to the dust, what a blessing ! He that is humbled
shall be exalted."

" Peace is gained by a wise inaction, and strength by integral
resignation to God, who will do all, and more than we, with
the boldest imagination, can fancy or desire."

"May you see God in all, through all, and above all. May the Divine transcendence and the Divine immanence be the two poles of your life."

The natural faculties of the understanding and will, whose integrity Father Hecker so much valued, were to be established in a new life infinitely above their native reach, glorified with divine life, their activity directed to the knowledge of things not even dreamed of before, and endowed with a divine gift of loving. In this state the Holy Spirit communicates to the human faculties force to accomplish intellectual and moral feats which naturally can be accomplished by God alone. This is called by theologians supernatural infused virtue, and is rooted in Faith, Hope, and Love, is made efficacious by spiritual gifts of wisdom and understanding, and knowledge and counsel, and other gifts and forces, the conscious and daily possession of which the Christian is entitled to hope for and strive after, and finally to obtain and enjoy in this life.

That this union is a personal relation, and that it should be a distinctly conscious one on the soul's part, all will admit who think but a moment of the infinite, loving activity of the Spirit of God, and the natural and supernatural receptivity of the spirit of man. Although not even the smallest germ of the supernatural life is found in nature, yet the soul of man ceaselessly, if blindly, yearns after its possession. Once possessed, the life of God blends into our own, mingles with it and is one with it, impregnating it as magnetism does the iron of the lodestone, till the divine qualities, without suppressing nature, entirely possess it, and assert for it and over it the Divine individuality. "Now I live, yet not I, but Christ liveth in me." An author much admired by Father Hecker thus describes the effects produced in the soul by supernatural faith, and hope, and love:

"These virtues are called and in reality are *Divine* virtues. They are called thus not because they are related to God in general, but because *they unite us in a divine manner with God*, have Him for their immediate motive, and can be produced in us only by a communication of the Divine nature. . . . For the life that the children of God lead here upon earth must be of the same kind as the life that awaits them in heaven." (Scheeben's *Glories of Divine Grace*, p. 222; Benziger Bros.)

To partake thus of the inner life of God was Father Hecker's

one spiritual ambition, and to help others to it his one motive
for dealing with men. He was ever insisting upon the closeness
of the divine union, and that it is our life brought into actual
touch with God, whose supreme and essential activity must, by
a law of its own existence, make itself felt, dominate as far as
permitted the entire activity of the soul, and win more and
more upon its life till all is won. Then are fulfilled the
Apostle's words: " But we all beholding the glory of the Lord
with open face are transformed into the same image from glory
to glory, as by the Spirit of the Lord " (II. Cor. iii. 18).

Here are some of Father Hecker's words, printed but a year
or two before his death, which treat not only of the interior
life in general, but in particular of its relation to the outer
action of God on the soul through the divine organism of the
Church :

"St. Thomas Aquinas attributes the absence of spiritual joy
mainly to neglect of consciousness of the inner life. ' During
this life,' he says (*Opuscula de Beatitudine*, cap. iii.), 'we should
continually rejoice in God, as something perfectly fitting, in all
our actions and for all our actions, in all our gifts and for all
our gifts. It is, as Isaias declares, that we may particularly
enjoy him that the Son of God has been given to us. What
blindness and what gross stupidity for many who are always
seeking God, always sighing for Him, frequently desiring Him,
daily knocking and clamoring at the door for God by prayer,
while they themselves are all the time, as the apostle says,
temples of the living God, and God truly dwelling within them ;
while all the time their souls are the abiding-place of 'God,
wherein He continually reposes! Who but a fool would look
for something out of doors which he knows he has within ?
What is the good of anything which is always to be sought and
never found, and who can be strengthened with food ever
craved but never tasted ? Thus passes away the life of many a
good man, always searching and never finding God, and it is
for this reason that his actions are imperfect.'

"A man with such a doctrine must cultivate mainly the interior life. His answer to the question, What is the relation
between the inner and the outer action of God upon my soul ?
is that God uses the outer for the sake of the inner life.

"There seems to be little danger nowadays of our losing
sight of the Divine authority and the Divine action in the government of the church, and in the aids of religion conveyed

through the external order of the sacraments. Yet it is only after fully appreciating the life of God within us that we learn to prize fittingly the action of God in His external Providence. Such is the plain teaching of St. Thomas in the extract above given.

"By fully assimilating this doctrine one comes to aim steadily at securing a more and more direct communion with God. Thus he does not seek merely for an external life in an external society, or become totally absorbed in external observances; but he seeks the invisible God *through* the visible Church, for she is the body of Christ the Son of God.

"Once a man's hand is safe on the altar his eye and voice are lifted to God.

"It is not to keep up a strained outlook for times and moments of the interior visitations, but to wait calmly for the actual movements of the Divine Spirit; to rely mainly upon it and not solely upon what leads to it, or communicates it, or guarantees its genuine presence by necessary external tests and symbols.

"Not an anxious search, least of all a craving for extraordinary lights; but a constant readiness to perceive the Divine guidance in the secret ways of the soul, and then to act with decision and a noble and generous courage—this is true wisdom.

"The Holy Spirit is thus the inspiration of the inner life of the regenerate man, and in that life is his Superior and Director. That His guidance may become more and more immediate in an interior life, and the soul's obedience more and more instinctive, is the object of the whole external order of the Church, including the sacramental system.

"Says Father Lallemant (*Spiritual Doctrine*, 3d principle, chap. i. art. 1): 'All creatures that are in the world, the whole order of nature as well as that of grace, and all the leadings of Providence, have been so disposed as to remove from our souls whatever is contrary to God.'"

What follows has been culled from notes and memoranda:

"When authority and liberty are intelligently understood, when both aim at the same end, then the universal reign of God's authority in the Church will be near and the kingdom of God be established universally."

"The whole future of the human race depends on bringing the individual soul more completely and perfectly under the sway of the Holy Spirit."

"What society most needs to-day is the baptism of the Holy Spirit."

"That soul is perfect which is guided habitually by the instinct of the Holy Spirit."

"The aim of Christian perfection is the guidance of the soul by the indwelling Holy Spirit. This is attained, ordinarily, first by bringing whatever is inordinate in our animal propensities under the control of the dictates of reason by the practice of mortification and self-denial; for it is a self-evident principle that a rational being ought to be master of his animal appetites. And second by bringing the dictates of reason under the control and inspiration of the Holy Spirit by recollection, and by fidelity and docility to its movements."

"To attain to the spiritual estate of the conscious guidance of the indwelling Holy Spirit, the practice of asceticism and of the natural and Christian moral virtues are the preparatory means."

"To rise before the light appears, is vain;. to hinder the soul from rising when it does appear, is oppression. In the first place, the soul is exposed to delusions; in the second, it is subjected to arbitrary human authority. The former opens the door to all sorts of extravagances and heresies; the latter breeds a spirit of servility and bondage."

"To reach that stage of the spiritual life which is the consciousness of the indwelling and guidance of the Holy Spirit some souls need the practice of asceticism more than others, these latter being more advanced by the practice of the Christian virtues. Others, again, need the strenuous practice of both of these means of advancement until the close of their lives. And there is another class which reaches this degree of spiritual growth sooner and with less difficulty than the generality of souls."

"Whenever the guidance of the Holy Spirit is sufficiently recognized, then the practice of the virtues immediately related to this action and proper to increase it in the soul are to be recommended, such as recollection, purity of heart, docility and fidelity to the inner voice, and the like."

"It should ever be kept in view that the practice of the virtues is not only for their own sake and to obtain merit, but mainly in order to remove all obstacles in the way of the guidance of the Holy Spirit, and to assist the soul in following his operations with docility."

"Obedience in its spiritual aspect divests one of self-will and makes him prompt to submit to the will of God alone. Viewed as an act of justice, obedience is the payment of due service to one's superior, who holds his office by appointment of God."

"The essential mistake of the transcendentalists is the taking for their guide the instincts of the soul instead of the inspirations of the Holy Spirit. They are moved by the natural instincts of human beings instead of the instinct of the Holy Ghost. But true spiritual direction consists in discovering the obstacles in the way of the Divine guidance, in aiding and encouraging the penitent to remove them, and in teaching how the interior movements of the Holy Spirit may be recognized, as well as in stimulating the soul to fidelity and docility to His movements."

"The director is not to take the place of the Holy Ghost in the soul, but to assist His growth in the soul as its primary and supreme guide."

"The primary worker of the soul's sanctification is the Holy Spirit acting interiorly ; the work of the director is secondary and subordinate. To overlook this fundamental truth in the spiritual life is a great mistake, whether it be on the part of the director or the one under direction."

The great obstacle to the prevalent use of this privilege of divine interior direction is lack of practical realization of its existence by good Christians. And this want of faith is met with almost as much among teachers as among learners, resulting in too great a mingling of the human element in the guidance of souls. What is known as over-direction is to be attributed, as Father Hecker was persuaded, to confessors leading souls by self-chosen ways, or laboriously working them along the road to perfection by artificial processes, souls whom the Holy Spirit has not made ready for more than the beginning of the spiritual life. This is like pressing wine out of unripe grapes. Another practice which Father Hecker often deprecated was the binding of free and generous souls with all sorts of obligations in the way of devotional exercises. This is forcing athletes to go on crutches. The excuse for it all is that it really does stagger human belief to accept as a literal matter of fact that God the Holy Ghost personally comes to us with divine grace and gives Himself to us; that He actually and essentially dwells in our souls by grace, and in an unspeakably intimate manner takes charge of our entire being, soul and body, and all our faculties and senses.

"By sanctifying grace," says St. Thomas (p. I, q. xxxiii. art. 2), "the rational creature is thus perfected, that it may not only use with liberty the created good, but that it may also enjoy the uncreated good; and therefore the invisible sending of the Holy Ghost takes place in the gift of sanctifying grace and the Divine Person Himself is given to us."

It is the soul's higher self, thus in entire union with the Spirit of God, that Father Hecker spent his life in cultivating, both in his own interior and in that of others. He insisted that in the normal condition of things the mainspring of virtue, both natural and supernatural, should be for the regenerate man the instinctive obedience of the individual soul to the voice of the indwelling Holy Spirit.

To what an extent this inner divine guidance has been obscured by more external methods is witnessed by Monsignor Gaume, who places upon the title-page of his learned work on the Holy Spirit the motto "Ignoto Deo"—to the Unknown God! Objections to this doctrine are made from the point of view of caution. There is danger of exaggeration, it is said; for if in its terms it is plainly Catholic it may sound Protestant to some ears. And in fact to those whose glances have been ever turned outward for guidance it seems like the delusions of certain classes of Protestants about "change of heart" and "inner light."

"But," says Lallemant (and the reader will thank us for a detailed reply to this difficulty from so venerable an authority), "it is of faith that without the grace of an interior inspiration, in which the guidance of the Holy Spirit consists, we cannot do any good work. The Calvinists would determine everything by their inward spirit, subjecting thereto the Church herself and her decisions. . . . But the guidance which we receive from the Holy Ghost by means of His gifts, presupposes the faith and authority of the Church, acknowledges them as its rule, admits nothing which is contrary to them, and aims only at perfecting the exercise of faith and the other virtues. The second objection is, that it seems as if this interior guidance of the Holy Spirit were destructive of the obedience due to superiors. We reply: 1. That as the interior inspiration of grace does not set aside the assent which we give to the articles of faith as they are externally proposed to us, but on the contrary gently disposes the mind to believe; in like manner the guidance which we receive from the gifts of the Holy Spirit, far from interfering with obedience, aids and facilitates the practice of it. 2. That all this interior guidance, and even [private] divine revelations, must always be subordinate to obedience; and in speaking of them this tacit condition is ever implied, that obedience enjoins nothing contrary thereto.   .   .   .

"The third objection is that this interior direction of the Holy Spirit seems to render all deliberation and all counsel useless. For why ask advice of men when the Holy Spirit is Himself our director? We reply that the Holy Spirit teaches us to consult enlightened persons and to follow the advice of others, as He referred St. Paul to Ananias. The fourth objection is made by some who complain that they are not themselves thus led by the Holy Spirit, and that they know nothing of it. To them we reply: 1. That the lights and inspirations of the Holy Spirit, which are necessary in order to do good and avoid evil, are never wanting to them, particularly if they are in a state of grace. 2. That being altogether exterior as they are, and scarcely ever entering into themselves, examining their consciences only very superficially, and looking only to the outward man and the faults which are manifest in the eyes of the world, .   .   .   it is ·no wonder that they have nothing of the guidance of the Holy Spirit, which is wholly interior. But, first, let them be faithful in following the light which is given them; it will go on always increasing. Secondly, let them clear away the sins and imperfections which, like so many clouds, hide the light from their eyes: they will see more distinctly every day. Thirdly, let them not suffer their exterior senses to rove at will, and be soiled by indulgence; God will then open to them their interior senses. Fourthly, let them never quit their own interior, if it be possible, or let them return as soon as may be; let them give attention to what passes therein, and they will observe the workings of the different spirits by which we are actuated. Fifthly, let them lay bare the whole ground of their heart to their superior or to their spiritual father. A soul which acts with this openness and simplicity can hardly fail of being favored with the direction of the Holy Spirit" (*Spiritual Doctrine*, 4th principle, ch. i. art. 3).

Father Hecker had himself suffered, and that in the earliest days of his religious life, from want of explicit instruction about this doctrine. Father Othmann, whom our readers remember as the novice-master at St. Trond, was too spiritual a man to have been ignorant of its principles. Yet he seemed to think that either no one would choose it in preference to the method in more common use, or that he would not find his novices ready for it. But to Father Hecker it was all-essential. "When I was not far from being through with my noviceship," he was heard to say, "I was one day looking over the books in the library and I came across Lallemant's *Spiritual Doctrine*. Getting leave to read it, I was overjoyed to find it a full statement of the principles by which I had been interiorly guided. I said to

Père Othmann: 'Why did you not give me this book when I first came? It settles all my difficulties.' But he answered that it had never once occurred to his mind to do so." Besides the Scriptures, Lallemant, Surin, Scaramelli's *Directorium Mysticum*, the ascetical and mystical writings of the contemplatives, such as Rusbruck, Henry Suso (whose life he carried for years in his pocket, reading it daily), Tauler, Father Augustine Baker's *Holy Wisdom* (Sancta Sophia), Blosius, the works of St. Teresa, and those of St. John of the Cross—these and other such works formed the literature which aided Father Hecker in the understanding and enjoyment of the guidance of the Holy Spirit. Lallemant he returned to ever and again, and St. John of the Cross he never let go at all. It was always with him, always read with renewed joy, and its wonderful lessons of divine wisdom, expressed as they are with the scientific accuracy of a trained theologian and the unction of a saint, were to Father Hecker a pledge of security for his own state of soul and a source of inspiration in dealing with others.

To the ordinary observer a knowledge of the men and women of to-day does not give rise to much hope of the widespread use of this spirituality. But Father Hecker thought otherwise. He ever insisted that it must come into general preference among the leading minds of Christendom; for independence of character calls for such a spirituality, and that independence is by God's providence the characteristic trait of the best men and women of our times. God must mean to sanctify us in the way He has placed us in the natural order. He believed that the Holy Spirit would soon be poured out in an abundant dispensation of His heavenly gifts, and that such a renewal of men's souls was the only salvation of society. Some may think that he was over-sanguine; many will not interest themselves in such "high" matters at all. But some of the wisest men in the Church are of his mind, notably Cardinal Manning. And the signs of the times, if interrogated with regard to the problem of man's eternal destiny, give no other answer than the promise of a new era in which the Holy Ghost shall reign in men's souls and in their lives with a supremacy peculiar to this age.

The following extract from *The Church and the Age*, a compilation of Father Hecker's later essays, shows his estimate of the form of spirituality we have been discussing, as bearing upon the regeneration of society in general:

"The whole aim of the science of Christian perfection is to

instruct men how to remove the hindrances in the way of the action of the Holy Spirit, and how to cultivate those virtues which are most favorable to His solicitations and inspirations. Thus the sum of spiritual life consists in observing and yielding to the movements of the Spirit of God in our soul, employing for this purpose all the exercises of prayer, spiritual reading, the practice of virtues, and good works.

"That divine action which is the immediate and principal cause of the salvation and perfection of the soul, claims by right the soul's direct and main attention. From this source within the soul there will gradually come to birth the consciousness of the indwelling presence of the Holy Spirit, out of which will spring a force surpassing all · human strength, a courage higher than all human heroism, a sense of dignity excelling all human greatness. The light the age requires for its renewal can come only from the same source. The renewal of the age depends on the renewal of religion. The renewal of religion depends on a greater effusion of the creative and renewing power of the Holy Spirit. The greater effusion of the Holy Spirit depends on the giving of increased attention to His movements and inspirations in the soul. The radical and adequate remedy for all the evils of our age, and the source of all true progress, consist in increased attention and fidelity to the action of the Holy Spirit in the soul. 'Thou shalt send forth Thy spirit and they shall be created: and Thou shalt renew the face of the earth.'"

Lallemant's answer to the difficulty of excess of personal liberty in this method has been already given. Father Hecker's own is as follows:

"The enlargement of the [interior] field of action for the soul, without a true knowledge of the end and scope of the external authority of the Church, would only open the door to delusions, errors, and heresies of every description, and would be in effect only another form of Protestantism. But, on the other hand, the exclusive view of the external authority of the Church, without a proper understanding of the nature and work of the Holy Spirit in the soul, would render the practice of religion formal, obedience servile, and the Church sterile.

"The solution of the difficulty is as follows: The action of the Holy Spirit embodied visibly in the authority of the Church, and the action of the Holy Spirit dwelling invisibly in the soul form one inseparable synthesis; and he who has not a clear con-

•ception of this two-fold action of the Holy Spirit is in danger
of running into one or the other, and sometimes into both, of
these extremes, either of which is destructive of the end of the
Church. The Holy Spirit, in the external authority of the Church,
acts as the infallible interpreter and criterion of divine revelation. The Holy Spirit in the soul acts as the divine Life-
giver and Sanctifier. It is of the highest importance that these
two distinct offices of the Holy Spirit should not be confounded.

" The increased action of the Holy Spirit, with a more vigorous
co-operation on the part of the faithful, which is in process of
realization, will elevate the human personality to an intensity
of force and grandeur productive of a new era to the Church
and to society—an era difficult for the imagination to grasp,
and still more difficult to describe in words, unless we have
recourse to the prophetic language of the inspired Scriptures."

" The way out of our present difficulties," said Father Hecker,
speaking of the conflicts of religion in Europe, " is to revert
to a spirituality which is freer than that which Providence
assigned as the counteraction of Protestantism in the sixteenth
century—to a spirituality which is, and ever has been, the normal
one of the Christian inner life. That era accentuated obedience,
this accentuates no particular moral virtue, but rather presses the
soul back upon Faith and Hope and Love as the springs of life,
and makes the distinctive virtue fidelity to the guidance of the
Holy Spirit, imp.lling the Christian to that one of the moral
virtues which is most suitable to his nature and to the requirements of his state of life, and other environments."

But from what has been said it must not be inferred that
Father Hecker thought it safe to be without spiritual counsel,
above all when the soul seemed led in extraordinary ways. He
firmly believed in the necessity of direction, and that in the
sense intended by spiritual writers generally. In practice he
himself always consulted men of experience and piety. We have
seen how he sought advice, and was aided by it at every crisis
of his life. But he did not accept all that is said by some writers
about the surrender of the soul to one's father confessor. He
thought that confession was often too closely allied with direction,
and he was convinced that many souls' could profit by less introspection in search of sin, and more in search of natural and
supernatural movements to virtue. He condemned over-direction,
and thought that there was a good deal of it. He thought that there

were cases in which spontaneity of effort was too high a price to pay for even the merit of obedience. His sentiment is well expressed by St. John of the Cross in the ninth chapter of *The Ascent of Mount Carmel:*

"Spiritual directors are not the chief workers, but rather the Holy Ghost; they are mere instruments, only to guide souls by the rule of faith and the law of God according to the spirit which God gives to each. Their object, therefore, should be not to guide souls by a way of their own, suitable to themselves; but to ascertain, if they can, the way which God Himself is guiding them."

Leave much to God's secret ways, was one of Father Hecker's principles. "When hearing some confessions on the missions," he once said, "and when about to give absolution, I used to say, in my heart, to the penitent, Well, no doubt God means to save you, you poor fellow, or He wouldn't give you the grace to make this mission. But just how He will do it, considering your bad habits, I can't see; but that's none of my business."

Leave much to natural or acquired inclinations, was one of his maxims. He was not deeply interested in souls who by temperament or training needed very minute guidance in the spiritual life; to him they seemed so overloaded with harness as to have no great strength left for pulling the chariot. But he would not interfere with them; he knew that it was of little avail to try to change such methods once they had become habitual; and he recognized that there were many who could never get along without them. At any rate he was tolerant by nature, and slow to condemn in general or particular anything useful to well-meaning souls.

"It is vain to rise before the light," was another motto. "Make no haste in the time of clouds." These two texts of Scripture he was fond of repeating. "When God shows the way," he once said, "you will see; no amount of peering in the dark will bring the sun over the hills. Pray for light, but don't move an inch before you get it. When it comes, go ahead with all your might." Self-imposed penances, self-assumed devotional practices he mistrusted. He was convinced that the only way sure to succeed, and to succeed perfectly, was either that shown by an interior attraction too powerful and too peaceful to be other than divine, or one pointed out by the lawful external authority in the Church.

When asked for advice on matters of conscience his decisions were generally quick and always simple. Yet he often refused to decide without time for prayer and thought, saying, " I have no lights on this matter; you must give me time." And not seldom he refused to decide altogether for the same reason. One thing annoyed him much, and that was the blank silence and stupid wonder with which some instructed Catholics listened to him as he spoke of the guidance of the Holy Spirit as the way of Christian perfection, treating it as beyond the reach of ordinary mortals, intricate in its rules, " mystical," and visionary; whereas Father Hecker knew it to be the one only simple method, with a minimum of rules, useful for all, readily understood. What follows is a brief outline of the entire doctrine in its practical use in the progress of the soul from a sinful life onwards; we have found it among his memoranda:

"What must one do in order to favor the reception of the Holy Spirit, and secure fidelity to His guidance when received? First receive the Sacraments, the divinely instituted channels of grace: one will scarcely persevere in living in the state of grace, to say nothing of securing a close union with God, who receives Holy Communion only once or twice a year. Second, practise prayer, above all that highest form of prayer, assisting at Holy Mass; then mental and vocal prayer, the public offices of the Church, and particular devotions according to one's attrait. Third, read spiritual books daily—the Bible, Lives of the Saints, *Following of Christ*, *Spiritual Combat*, etc. But in all this bear ever in mind, that the steady impelling force by which one does each of these outward things is *the inner and secret prompting of the Holy Ghost, and that perseverance in them is secured by no other aid except the same hidden inspiration.* Cherish that above all, therefore, and in every stage of the spiritual life; be most obedient to it, seeking meantime for good counsel wherever it is likely to be had."

Father Hecker was of opinion that a larger number of persons can be led to perfection than is generally supposed, and he would sound the call in the ears of Christians generally far more than is commonly done. He was also persuaded that there are many souls whose whole lives have been entirely, or almost entirely, free from the taint of mortal sin, and these he considered should be the most active spirits among Christians. He thought that more room should be made for them in our discourses, and that everybody should not be lumped together in one mass as hardened sinners or as penitents.

To these innocent men and women the mediatorship of Christ should be made as distinct as possible, the elevation of the soul to divine union through the Incarnation brought out fully, and the redemption of man from sin and hell be included in it, and be absorbed by it. Too many souls who have never sinned mortally fail to struggle for· perfection, Father Hecker often said, because they never have heard any invitation but the call to repentance. The positive side of Christianity is the Incarnation, which lifts all men of good- will, repentant and innocent alike, into participation with the Deity. Father Hecker would talk by the hour of the need of bringing that view of our Lord's mission most prominently forward, the idea of redemption applying to innocent souls only on account of original sin, and by sympathy with their brethren infected by actual sin. And he would show that even hard sinners could often be brought to a good life more surely, and be enabled more certainly to persevere, by forcibly emphasizing the Incarnation and its benefits than by any other method. Their blindness and selfishness hinder hard sinners from easily appreciating our Lord's sufferings as borne on their account. Father Hecker regretted that the idea of redemption was so often presented in a way to give the impression that atonement was the whole office of Christ. There are many souls for whom access to Christ as Mediator was more in consonance with the truth than access to Him as Redeemer, Mediator in that case including Redeemer, rather than the Redeemer absorbing the idea of Mediator. Redemption from original sin is, of course, necessary to the mediatorship of a fallen race. But our Lord became Redeemer that he might be Mediator; he cleansed us from sin that he might lift us up to the Godhead; and in many souls Father Hecker knew that the process of cleansing began and ended with original sin and venial sins. Such souls often go their lives long with no compelling stimulus to perfection, because they cannot apply to themselves the accusations of sin commonly put into the directions for beginners.

Much has been already said of the aids to perfection which Father Hecker perceived in a right use of the liberty and intelligence of our times. He also insisted that the commercial and industrial features of our civilization were no obstacles to a high state of Christian perfection.

In a remarkable sermon, entitled "The Saint of Our Day," published in the third volume of the Paulist series, Father Hecker, after making a powerful exposition of the advantages of liberty and intelligence as helps to the interior life, insists that the opportunities and responsibilities peculiar to our civilization are capable of being sanctified to the highest degree. The model he proposes in this sermon is St. Joseph. He was no martyr, yet showed a martyr's fidelity by his trust in God.

"Called by the voice of God to leave his friends, home, and country, he obeys instantly and without a murmur. To find God and to be one with God, a solitary life in the desert was not necessary to St. Joseph. He was in the world and found God where he was. He sanctified his work by carrying God with him into the workshop. St. Joseph was no flower of the desert or plant of the cloister; he found the means of peifection in the world, and consecrated it to God by making its cares and duties subservient to divine purposes.

"The house of St. Joseph was his cloister, and in the bosom of his family he practised the sublimest virtues. While occupied with the common daily duties of life his mind was fixed on the contemplation of divine truths, thus breathing into all his actions a heavenly influence. He attained in society and in human relationships a degree of perfection not surpassed, if equalled, by the martyr's death, the contemplative of the solitude, the cloistered monk, or the missionary hero.

"Our age is not an age of martyrdom, nor an age of hermits, nor a monastic age. Although it has its martyrs, its recluses, and its monastic communities, these are not, and are not likely to be, its prevailing types of Christian perfection. Our age lives in its busy marts, in counting-rooms, in workshops, in homes, and in the varied relations that form human society, and it is into these that sanctity is to be introduced. St. Joseph stands forth as an excellent and unsurpassed model of this type of perfection. These duties and these opportunities must be made instrumental in sanctifying the soul. For it is the difficulties and the hindrances that men find in their age which give the form to their character and habits, and when mastered become the means of divine grace and their titles to glory. Indicate these, and you portray that type of sanctity in which the life of the Church will find its actual and living expression.

"This, then, is the field of conquest for the heroic Christian of our day. Out of the cares, toils, duties, afflictions, and responsibilities of daily life are to be built the pillars of sanctity of the Stylites of our age. This is the coming form of the triumph of Christian virtue."

With all, moreover, Father Hecker insisted on the practice of the natural virtues, honesty, temperance, truthfulness, kindliness, courage, and manliness generally, as preceding any practical move towards the higher life. He first explored the character and life of his penitent in search of what natural power he had, and then demanded its full exertion. He began with the natural man, and made every supernatural force in the sacraments and prayer aid in establishing and increasing natural virtue as a necessary preliminary and ever-present accompaniment of supernatural progress. Perhaps Father Hecker's antipathy to Calvinism sharpened his zeal for the natural virtues, and strengthened his advocacy of human innocence. The craving for the supernatural, he was convinced, would be strong in proportion to the enlightenment of the natural reason; the need of the grace of God is, of course, most urgent in a sinful state, but it would be more quickly perceived in proportion to the possession of natural virtue. As the exercise of reason is necessary to faith and precedes its acts, so the integrity of natural virtue is the best preparation for the grace of God. Many pages of *The Aspirations of Nature*, from which the following brief quotations are made, are devoted to the dignity of humanity and the need of placing the excellence of human nature in the foreground when con-sidering how man may attain to a high supernatural state:

"Every faculty of the soul, rightly exercised, leads to truth; every instinct of our nature has an eternal destiny attached to it. Catholicity finds its support in these and employs them in all her developments."

"The Catholic religion is wonderfully calculated and adapted to call forth, sustain, and perfect the tastes, propensities, and peculiarities of human nature. And let no one venture to say that these characteristics which are everywhere found among men are to be repressed rather than encouraged. This is to despise human nature, this is to mar the work of God. For are not these peculiarities inborn? Are they not implanted in us by the hand of our Creator? Are they not what go to constitute our very individuality?"

Humanity is a word of vague meaning to most ears, but to Father Hecker its meaning was a living thing of value second only to Christianity. Here is his summary of the relation of Catholicity to human nature, taken from the same source as the foregoing:

"Catholicity is that religion which links itself to all the faculties of the mind, appropriates all the instincts of human nature, and by thus concurring with the work of the Creator affirms its own Divine origin."

We give the following extracts from letters of spiritual advice, to show Father Hecker's views of mortification :

"Exterior mortifications are aids to interior life. What we take from the body we give to the spirit. If we will look at it closely, two-thirds of our time is taken up with what we shall eat, and how we shall sleep, and wherewithal we shall be clothed. Two-thirds of our life and more is animal—including sleep. I do not despise the animal in man, but I go in for fair play for the soul. The better part should have the greater share. The right order of things has been reversed : *con*-version is necessary. Read the lives of the old Fathers of the Desert. They determined on leading a rational and divine life. How little are they known or appreciated in our day! Their lives are more interesting than a novel and stranger than a romance."

"Self-love, self-activity, self-hood, is something not easily destroyed. It is like a cancer which has its roots extending to the most delicate fibres of our mental and moral nature. Divine grace can draw them all out. But how slowly! And how exquisitely painful is the process—the more subtle the self-love the more painful the cure."

"Never practise any mortification of a considerable character without counsel. The devil, when he can no longer keep us back, aims at driving us too far and too fast."

"How can the intellect be brought under direction of divine grace except by reducing it to its nothingness ?—and how can this be done except by placing it in utter darkness ? How can the heart be filled with the spirit of divine love while it contains any other ? How can it be purified of all other inordinate love except by dryness and bitterness ? God wishes to fill our intelligence and our hearts with divine light and love, and thus to deify our whole nature—to make us one with what we represent—God. And how can He do this otherwise than by removing from our soul and its faculties all that is contrary to the divine order ? "

"All your difficulties are favors from God ; you see them on the wrong side, and speak as the block of marble would while being chiselled by the sculptor. When God purifies the soul, it cries out just like little children do when their faces are washed.

The soul's attention must be withdrawn from external, created things and turned inward towards God exclusively before its union with Him; and this transformation is a great, painful, and wonderful work, and so much the more difficult and painful as the soul's attention has been attracted and attached to transitory things—to creatures."

He was often heard repeating the following verse from *The Imitation* (book iii. chap. xxxi.), as summarizing the necessary conditions of the active life: "Unless a man be elevated in spirit, and set at liberty from all creatures, and wholly united to God, whatever he knows and whatever he has is of no great weight." He wrote to a friend that he had studied that verse for thirty years and still found that he did not know all it meant.

We give what follows as characteristic of Father Hecker's manner as a director:

"At first, in all your deliberate actions, calm your mind, place yourself in the attitude of a receiver or listener, and then decide. Imperceptibly and insensibly grace will guide you."

"Don't care what people say; keep your own counsel. Use your own sense and abound in it; as the apostle says: 'Let every one abound in his own sense.' Don't try to get anybody to agree with you. No two noses are alike, much less souls. God never repeats."

"Nobody nowadays wants God. Every one has the whole world on his shoulders, and unless his own petty ideas and schemes are adopted and succeed, he prophesies the end of the world. You are on the right road—push on! Our maxim is: Be sure you are right and then go ahead!"

"How much that is good and noble in the soul is smothered by unwise restraint! The whole object of restraint is to reject that which is false and to correct the preference given to a lower good instead of to a higher one. As for the rest—*freedom!*"

"I know a man who thinks he don't know anything—who every day knows that he knows less; and who hopes to know nothing before he dies. O blessed emptiness which fills us with all! O happy poverty which possesses all! O beatified nothingness which can exclaim, *Deus meus et omnia!*"

It will have been seen by this time that Father Hecker's first and fundamental rule of direction was to have as little of it as possible. His method started out with the purpose to do away with method at the earliest moment it could safely be done. To be Father Hecker's penitent meant the privilege of sooner or later being nobody's penitent but the Holy Ghost's. The following rules of direction he printed in 1887:

"The work of the priesthood is to help to guide the Christian people, understanding that God is always guiding them interiorly.

"An innocent soul we must guide, fully understanding that God is dwelling within him; not as a substitute for God.

"A repentant sinner we must guide, understanding that we are but restoring him to God's guidance.

"The best that we can do for any Christian is to quicken his sense of fidelity to God speaking to him in an enlightened conscience.

"Now, God's guidance is of two kinds: one is that of His external providence in the circumstances of life; the other is interior, and is the direct action of the Holy Spirit on the human soul. There is great danger in separating these two.

"The key to many spiritual problems is found in this truth: The direct action of God upon the soul, which is interior, is in harmony with his external providence. Sanctity consists in making them identical as motives for every thought, word, and deed of our lives. The external and the internal (and the same must be said of the natural and supernatural) are one in God, and the consciousness of them both is to be made one divine whole in man. To do this requires an heroic life-sanctity.

"All the sacraments of the Church, her authority, prayer both mental and vocal, spiritual reading, exercises of mortification and of devotion, have for their end and purpose to lead the soul to the guidance of the Holy Spirit. St. Alphonsus says in his letters that the first director of the soul is the Holy Ghost Himself.

"It is never to be forgotten that one man can never be a guide to another except as leading him to his only Divine Guide.

"The guide of the soul is the Holy Spirit Himself, and the criterion or test of possessing that guide is the Divine authority of the Church."

What follows was published by Father Hecker in THE CATHOLIC WORLD in 1887. It throws new light on the questions we have been considering, abounding in practical rules of direction, and

therefore, though somewhat long, we venture to close the chapter
with it:

" ' If any one shall say that without the previous inspiration of
the Holy Spirit and His aid, a man can believe, hope, love, or
repent as he should, so that the grace of justification may be conferred upon him, let him be anathema.'

"These are the words of the holy Council of Trent, in which
the Catholic Church infallibly teaches that without an interior
movement of the indwelling Holy Spirit no act of the soul can
be meritorious of heaven. This doctrine, embodying the plain
sense of Holy Scripture and the unbroken teaching of the Church
in all ages, bases human justification on an interior impulse of the
Third Person of the Divine Trinity. This impulse precedes the
soul's acts of faith, hope, and love, and of sorrow for sin: the
first stage in the supernatural career, then, is the entering of the
Holy Spirit into the inner life of the soul. The process of justification begins by the divine life of the indwelling Spirit taking up
into itself the human life of the soul.

"Nor is this to the detriment of man's liberty, but rather to
its increase. The infinite independence of God and his divine
liberty are shared by man exactly in proportion as he partakes
of God's life in the communication of the Holy Spirit.

"If it be asked how the Holy Spirit is received, the answer
is, Sacramentally. ' Unless a man be born again of water and the
Holy Ghost, he cannot enter into the kingdom of God.' As man
by nature is a being of both outer and inner life, so, when made
a new man by the Spirit of God and elevated into a supernatural
state, God deals with him by both outer and inner methods.
The Holy Spirit is received by the sacramental grace of baptism and renewed by the other sacraments; also in prayer, vocal
or mental, hearing sermons, reading the Scriptures or devout
books, and on occasions, extraordinary or ordinary, in the course
of daily life ; and when once received every act of the soul that
merits heaven is done by the inspiration of that Divine Guide
dwelling within us. Even though unperceived, though indistinguishable from impulses of natural virtue, though imperceptibly
multiplied as often as the instants are, yet each movement of
heaven-winning virtue, and especially love, hope, faith, and repentance, is made because the Holy Spirit has acted upon the
soul in an efficacious manner.

"It is not to induce a strained outlook for the particular
cases of the action of the Spirit of God on us, or the signs of

it, that these words are written. The sacraments, prayer and holy reading, and hearing sermons and instructions, are the plain, external instruments and accompaniments of the visitations of God, and are sufficient landmarks for the journey of the soul, unless it be led in a way altogether extraordinary. And apart from these external marks, no matter how you watch for God, his visitations are best known by their effects; it is after the cause has been placed, perhaps some considerable time after, that the faith, hope, love, or sorrow becomes perceptibly increased—always excepting extraordinary cases. Not to 'resist the Spirit' is the first duty. Fidelity to the divine guidance, yielding one's self up lovingly to the impulses of virtue as they gently claim control of our thoughts —this is the simple duty.

"Having laid down in broad terms the fundamental doctrine of the supernatural life, it is proper to say a word of the natural virtues and of their relation to the supernatural. It has been already intimated that the goodness of nature is often indistinguishable from the holiness of the supernatural life; and, indeed, as a rule, impulses of the Holy Spirit first pour their floods into the channels of natural virtue, thus rendering them supernatural. These are mainly the cardinal virtues: Prudence, Justice, Fortitude, and Temperance. Practised in a state of nature, these place us in our true relations with our nature and with God's providence in all created nature around us; these are the virtues which choice souls among the heathen practised. They are not enough. When they have done their utmost they leave a void in the heart that still yearns for more. It is the purpose of the Spirit of God to raise our virtue to a grade far above nature. The practice of the virtues of faith, hope, and love, which bring the soul into direct communication with God, and which, when practised under the guidance of the Holy Spirit, are supernatural, following upon the practice of the cardinal virtues under the same guidance, place the soul in its true and perfect relation with God—a state which is more than natural.

"Let us, if we would see things clearly, keep in sight the difference between the natural and supernatural. In the natural order a certain union with God was possessed by man in all ages in common with every creature. The union of the creature with the divine creative power is something which man can neither escape from nor be robbed of. But in the case of rational creatures this union is, even in a state of nature, made far closer and its enjoyment increased by a virtuous life—one in which reason is superior to appetite; a life only to be led by one assisted, if not by the indwelling Holy Spirit peculiar to the grace of Christ, yet by the helps necessary to natural virtue and called medicinal graces. The practice of the four cardinal virtues—Prudence, Justice, Fortitude, and Temperance—in the ordinary natural state gave to guileless men and women in every age a natural union with their Creator. Although we maintain that such natural union with God is not enough for man, yet we insist that the part the natural virtues play in man's sanctification be recognized. In considering a holy life natural virtues are too often passed over, either because the men who practised them in heathen times were perhaps few in number, or because of the Calvinistic error that nature and man are totally corrupt.

"And we further insist on the natural virtues because they tend to place man in true relations with himself and with nature, thus bringing him into more perfect relation or union with God than he was by means of the creative act—a proper preliminary to his supernatural relation. Who will deny that there were men not a few among the heathen in whom Prudence, Justice, Fortitude, and Temperance were highly exemplified? They knew well enough what right reason demanded. Such men as Socrates, Plato, Epictetus, and Marcus Aurelius had by the natural light of reason a knowledge of what their nature required of them. They had faults, great ones if you please; at the same time they knew them to be faults, and they had the natural virtues in greater or less degrees. Thus the union between God and the soul, due to the creative act, though not sufficient, never was interrupted. The Creator and the Mediator are one."

THE WARFARE OF SCIENCE.

II.

WHOEVER admits revelation as a certain fact, and a certain interpretation of its genuine, authentic sense, must maintain its precedence over every kind of human knowledge. The data which it furnishes in theology, ethics, history, or any kind of science, as certainly attested by divine authority, must be true and beyond denial or question. Any theory which contradicts a revealed truth must be false, as surely as if it denied the reality of self-consciousness, the axiom that the whole is greater than a part, or the principle of contradiction.

If the fact of revelation is questioned, it only remains to fall back upon rational philosophy, pure and simple. Likewise, if revelation, being admitted, its certain, infallible interpretation is questioned, there must be the same recourse to rational philosophy as the tribunal of final appeal, although in the higher part of its domain as religious philosophy it will admit Christian elements. Professor Ladd's *Introduction to Philosophy* shows that this is the case.

A merely sentimental religion, which is not rational and philosophical, has no field and no forces or weapons for a warfare with science, and no claim to supremacy. All sciences in the natural and rational order are co-ordinated and regulated under the supremacy of their queen, philosophy. This is briefly but clearly shown by Dr. Barry in his article in our last number.

In order that Religion may be put in logical opposition to Science, it must have a supernatural entity, as a divine revelation proposed and proclaimed by an infallible witness, custodian, and judge. The Catholic religion and church is on one side, the whole complex system of human rational knowledge, summed up under the general title Philosophy, or Science, is on the other.

Some readers unfamiliar with the technical language of logic may fancy that the opposition connoted above between Catholic authority and rational science implies hostility. This is not so, but the term designates distinction between two objects of thought, as, for instance, the two opposite poles of the earth's axis.

The truths of revelation and the propositions presented to the mind as rational truths stand over against each other. The in-

fallible authority of the church is on one side, the authority of
reason on the other. What is the relation between the two? I
am writing only for Catholics, who may have perplexities in regard
to this relation, caused by the accusations made against the
church, as if she were an enemy to the just liberty and progress
of science. Therefore I merely make an exposition of the Catholic
idea. I assume the infallible authority of the Catholic Church as
the organ of divine revelation within its proper sphere, and the
infallible authority of reason within the limits of a certain domain.
They are concentric circles, and the circle of revelation is the
outermost, including the circle of reason.

The authority of the church is the divine right to keep and
teach the revealed truths of the deposit of faith, to define dogmas
and condemn errors, with a certitude which is rendered infallible
by the assistance of the Holy Spirit, not by the way of revelation
or inspiration, but by a divine providence and direction in the use
of all the means for understanding and proclaiming the contents
of the sources of faith, Scripture and Tradition. This infallible
authority is limited to the sphere of that which is explicitly,
implicitly, or virtually revealed—*i. e.*, to objects of divine faith
credible on the divine testimony, and those which are so related
to these that the revealed truth is a criterion of their certitude.

The direct, immediate, and principal object of the infallible
judgments of the church is the Faith, the Truth disclosed by
divine revelation. Every other matter, whether it be a fact or
a proposition, is accessory.

Now, the divine revelation was given in view of the highest
ethical, spiritual, and eternal good of the human race. It was
not given for the satisfaction of the *ingenium curiosum* of man.
It is not even a systematic theology. Much less, a formal, scientific philosophy, and least of all, a disclosure of the system of
the universe, a revelation of astronomy, cosmology, zoölogy,
chemistry, and natural science in general. The history contained
in the inspired books is recorded, for a sacred and religious, not
for a secular purpose. Its whole scope is to teach men what to
believe, what to hope for, what to do, in order to attain to the
love of God in Jesus Christ, and the possession of the inheritance of the sons of God in everlasting life.

Whatever is contained in the inspired books which is not
doctrinal, ethical, or of the nature of dogmatic fact, is accidental.
All of science and history, which is transmitted with the divine
tradition of religious and moral doctrine, but only accidentally
connected with them, has more or less of obscurity and ambigu-

ity, and admits of more than one interpretation. It is that which is certainly revealed, certainly understood in its true, authentic sense, attested and proposed by the church in her ordinary magistracy or by solemn definitions, which is the matter of Catholic faith. All that is revealed is *de fide in se,* all that is sufficiently proposed to us as revealed truth is *de fide quoad nos.* The church is infallible in making this proposition, but cannot transcend the divine limits of that which is *de fide divinâ in se,* in proposing dogmas as *de fide Catholicâ.* There can be no growth and increase in the deposit of faith itself since the age of the apostles, who transmitted the completed revelation, the word of God in Scripture and Tradition, to their successors. But there has been a continuous, gradual progress and development in the understanding and proclamation of the truth revealed by the divine word, in the reduction of implicit to explicit faith, as is shown in the History of Dogma, and of which the definition of the Immaculate Conception is a signal, recent example.

Theology is a science founded upon the dogmas of faith, and upon all the contents of Scripture and Tradition, which have not been explicated in the dogmatic teaching of the church. It is the product of *Fides quaerens intellectum.* In so far as it reproduces the testimony and judgments of the infallible church, it is only an instrument by which the church proclaims her doctrine and law, a mouth-piece of ecclesiastical tradition. It is in this sense that the unanimous consent of the Fathers makes a binding rule in doctrine, as a witness to that which has been believed and taught in the church always, everywhere, and by all.

When theology passes beyond this boundary it becomes a human science. Private doctors are not infallible. Their systems and text-books have the authority of the evidence and the reasons upon which their theories are based, and of the approbation which they receive from competent judges and common consent. They contain some amount of certain science, a great deal that is probable, and more or less, according to the genius of different authors, of hypothesis and conjecture. Of course, there is a wide field open to controversy, and the human liability to error. From the nature of the case, theology is progressive and subject to development, and sacred science in its comprehensive sense must borrow from many special secular sciences, and depend for its advancement upon their discoveries and improvement.

The luminous orb of revelation has its penumbra, which gradually fades away into the space of opinion and conjecture. The authority of the *Ecclesia Docens,* infallible in its central sphere, is modified and lessened as it changes from dogmatic to disciplinary, passing through all the gradations from the highest to the lowest, from the Roman Congregations to the mother teaching her little child the catechism.

The authority of reason is infallible in a certain sense, and under certain conditions. That is to say, the human faculties of cognition acting normally upon their proper objects do not deceive us. The senses, the intellect, the reasoning faculty, give us knowledge of which we are infallibly certain. The same is true of human faith in testimony. Metaphysical, physical, and moral certitude are attainable by the use of the natural faculties. True, we do make false and erroneous judgments. But this error to which we are liable is an accident. The infallibility of the church is secured against this accidental error in a supernatural way. The infallibility of reason has only natural safeguards against accidental errors, and therefore the authority of reason can only be called infallible with a restriction, in the concrete, and in respect to the judgments of individual minds. Making all due allowance for the fallibility of individual men, and the liability to error in the domain of rational thought and history, there are truths and facts which are certain, verdicts of the authority of reason which are infallible, and which we can apprehend as such, and employ as an unerring criterion of the adequation between our intellect and objective reality. These truths and facts are the principles and data of rational science in all its ramifications, of all the known and all the knowable within the boundary of natural human intelligence.

What now, we inquire, is the relation between revelation and natural science, the authority of the church and the authority of reason? The discussion of this topic in all its extension and comprehension is beyond the scope of our present intention. It is limited to the one, particular point, of the existence of a just *casus belli* in behalf of the liberty of science against oppression and interference from Catholic authority claiming a right of control and direction by which the progress of science is hindered.

The gist of the accusation so often made against the church by anti-Catholic writers, especially by those who attack her authority in the supposed interest of the physical sciences, is this: That the church has wished to impede the progress of the sciences in order to keep the human mind in a darkness favorable to her omnipotence. Or, if it is made in a milder form, that Catholic theology, seeing that science was emancipating itself and beginning to live its own independent life, wished to cut short these efforts to gain a liberty which would put an end to the dominion which it claimed to exercise over science. This suppos- ed antipathy of the church for the scientific development of hu- manity has never had an existence, but is purely imaginary. There is nothing in principle which places Catholic authority in a hostile attitude to the authority of reason, to any science what- ever, or to free scientific investigation. Due subordination of particular to more general sciences, of philosophy to theology, and of theology to the infallible authority of the church, does not imply vassalage and servitude. Theology, beyond the domain of the revealed dogmas proposed to faith by the infallible authority of the church, and the conclusions virtually contained in them which have been defined, has freedom to expand and pro- gressively develop itself, from the principles which it finds in Scripture, Tradition, and Reason. Philosophy proceeds, not from data of revelation, but from rational principles and by its own purely rational methods. Each particular science goes its own way, following its own proper line and methods of investigation. They are subject, however, to the laws which govern all thought, and which they receive from mathematics, if they follow mathe- matical methods, from logic and from metaphysics. Philosophy is bound to recognize all the certain truths of theology, and, as it necessarily comes into more extensive and intimate contact with the teachings of revelation, by treating of the same topics, than any other rational science, there has been more occasion for the exercise of control and direction by ecclesiastical authority in the case of philosophy than in any other department.

We are more immediately concerned, however, with the rela- tion between scientific discoveries and the interpretation of the Sacred Scriptures. On this head I will quote a few sentences from an article by Professor Gilbert, of the University of Lou- vain :

"Undoubtedly the Holy Scripture has an object very different from that of the human sciences, and *the labors of astronomers, physicists, and naturalists have in general no relation with the revealed dogmas.* No one, however, will go so far as to assert absolutely that every scientific doctrine or assertion is indifferent or inoffensive in respect to the point of view of faith and the in- terpretation of the Scriptures. Who could maintain this total separation between the object of the sacred writings and that of the natural sciences ? May there not exist, in the domain of physiology, of linguistics, of anthropology, points of very close contact with the instructions which the Bible gives us concerning the origin and destination of man ? One would need to be sin-

gularly rash to trace thus in advance an impassable line of de-
marcation between theology and the study of nature."*

Evidently, since the instruction from God through revelation,
and the instruction from God through nature, must both be true
and in harmony, theology and. natural science cannot ignore each
other.   There must be some general principles of conciliation.
Professor Gilbert remarks that these present no great difficulties
in the abstract, although serious difficulties may arise in their application to determinate cases.

The chief contention is about these general principles.   The
controversy about particular cases is of minor importance.   The
right of judging upon those mixed questions in which theology
and natural science are both involved is not a usurpation upon the
liberty of science, and does not trammel its legitimate exercise.
The judgments of the supreme authority in the church which are
dogmatic and irreformable scarcely come into the controversy at all.
They are in a region above the domain of science, taken in a sense
which prescinds from philosophy.   Even in the domain of philosophy there are but few definitions outside of natural theology and
ethics.   In the domain of natural science taken in the restricted
sense, what warfare its votaries have had to wage with theology has
been a struggle with disciplinary authority, and with private doctors,
singly or collectively.   This authority of discipline, existing in the
Holy See as its highest tribunal, in inferior tribunals, and after a
certain manner in the consentient teaching of recognized doctors of
sacred science, is a necessary adjunct of the supreme, infallible authority of the *Ecclesia Docens*.   Without this adjunct that authority
would be nugatory, and inapplicable to practical purposes.

A strange and bizarre notion of what is the Catholic idea of
the divine and infallible church under a supreme and infallible
head, has been widely prevalent, and, if less so at present, is still
obscuring the view of many intelligent persons.   They seem to
think that infallibility implies a continuous revelation and inspiration, extending to all kinds of matters, even to judgments on particular facts, and to acts of jurisdiction and government.   They
imagine, also, that infallibility implies impeccability, as if, supposing
the Catholic idea to be true, all members of the church, especially
priests, must be saints through a magical influence of the sacraments.   All ecclesiastical administration in spiritual and temporal
matters must be the wisest and best.   Theology, philosophy, polity,
and ritual must have come suddenly, like Adam from the Creator's

* *Revue des Questions Scientifiques*, tome deuxiène, p. 175.

hand, into full maturity admitting of no further development. Consequently, since history proves abundantly that the church has not shown itself to have this purely supernatural being, has been subject to human vicissitudes, and in many respects to have been similar to other human societies, bearing on her rolls names of men of all varieties of character, from the best to the worst, the conclusion is drawn that the church is not in any sense a divine, but a purely human institution.

This is a chimera. It is not the Catholic idea.

The church is supernatural and divine, but not in this exaggerated and exclusive sense. It is also natural and human, as man is both spiritual and corporeal. The treasures of faith, grace, sacraments, and spiritual power have been committed to earthly and fragile vessels. The citation of the misdeeds and mistakes of churchmen, supposing it to be perfectly correct, is none the less perfectly irrelevant. We are not bound in any way by loyalty to the Catholic cause to defend any of them, and we are bound by loyalty to truth, justice, and the law of God and conscience, to assent to the verdict of authentic and impartial history, in respect to all facts established by conclusive evidence.

Controversy, to be genuine and truly logical, must be a discussion of general principles, of fundamental facts, according to a comprehensive philosophy, and a philosophical view of the history of all human development, religious, moral, and scientific. On this ground the Catholic cause has always been victorious, and is invincible. We may justly and proudly adopt the language of Cardinal Wiseman, at the conclusion of his famous work on Science and Revealed Religion, " *Religio, vicisti.*"

Our modern opponents, who make war under the ægis of science, are not fond of this mode of controversy. Whether they attack natural religion, revealed religion, or specific Catholicity, they like to creep among particular facts, real or supposed, and single phenomena, and lead a long chase across dry deserts among interminable bushes, into caves and recesses among mountains, like the ancient Scythians. It is tedious work, though it may be useful or even necessary, to follow them into all their hiding places. At present, I am only intent, in respect to the particular topic in hand, on showing that the general principles of Catholic disciplinary authority and theology are not in opposition to scientific liberty and progress. As to particular applications of these principles in determinate cases, and interference in the interests of religion with science in a detrimental manner, there will be occasion to consider these matters later on.

The Council of the Vatican has made the following declara. tion :

" The church, so far from opposing the cultivation of human arts and sciences, aids and promotes them in many ways. . . . Nor surely does she forbid that these sciences, each in its own proper circuit, use their own proper principles and proper method; but recognizing this just liberty, carefully watches that they do not adopt errors repugnant to the Divine Doctrine, or, stepping over their boundaries, invade and disturb the domain of faith." *

St. Augustine had already traced out with a firm hand, in a manner which leaves little to be desired after more than a thousand years have passed, the rules to be followed in order to avoid a vain conflict between the Bible and sciences :

" In obscure matters, remote from our penetration, if we find in the Divine Scriptures certain things which are susceptible of various interpretations without damage to the faith in which we have been instructed, let us not hastily commit ourselves to any one of them in such a way that if perhaps a more thorough discussion of the truth show its nullity we become compromised with it ; and are drawn into a contest for our own opinion with which we strive to make the Scriptures agree, whereas we ought to endeavor to make our own opinion conform to the doctrine of the Scriptures."

Again, and still nearer to the point, St. Augustine expresses himself in a passage, which Prof. Gilbert remarks seems to have been well adapted to " open the eyes of the adversaries of Galileo " :

" It frequently happens that a man who is not a Christian knows something, by means of most certain reasoning or experience, about the earth, the celestial region, about the different elements of the world, the movements and revolutions of the stars, certain phases of the sun and moon, the periodical return of phenomena which mark the measurement of time, the natural characters and properties of animals, plants and minerals, and other similar objects. Now, it is most shameful and pernicious, and therefore most carefully to be avoided, that any infidel should hear a Christian speaking of these things, under the pretence of having derived his opinions from the Christian Scriptures, in such an idiotic manner that he cannot help seeing, as the saying is, how heaven-wide of the mark his notions are, and can scarcely keep from laughing. It is not much matter that the mistaken man should be laughed at, but it is lamentable that our sacred authors should be supposed by outsiders to have held such opinions, and should be re-

* Const. de Fide Cathol., c. iv.

proached and despised as ignorant men, to the great spiritual detriment of those for whose salvation we are solicitous. For, when they have found a man who belongs to the Christians in error about things which they know perfectly well, and referring his absurd notions to our sacred books, how can they believe what these same books teach on the resurrection of the dead, the hope of eternal life and the kingdom of heaven, so long as they suppose that they contain falsehoods in respect to questions wherein their own experience and irrefragable reasons have enabled them to perceive the truth." *

St. Jerome rebuked those who were accustomed to force the Scripture into a sense according to their private caprice, "ad voluntatem suam Scripturam trahere repugnantem"; forgetting that " many things in the Holy Scriptures are said according to the opinion of that time in which the events related took place, and not with a rigorous exactness."† St. Thomas of Aquin also says that in a certain passage the Sacred Scripture "speaks, *according to its customary method,* in accordance with the way of viewing things common among men."

In another place he lays down the following prudent rule :

" It seems to me that it is safer, in regard to opinions generally admitted by philosophers and reconcilable with our faith, not to affirm them as we do dogmas of faith, . . . nor to deny them as though they were contrary to faith, lest occasion be given to the wise men of this world of contemning the doctrine of faith."

The same great doctor expresses a doubt of the truth of the Ptolemaic astronomy, writing that "the presumptions which astronomers think to be discoveries cannot be necessarily true, since that which is perceived by our vision in respect to the stars can perhaps be explained *in some other way not yet known to men.*"‡

The Spanish Jesuit theologian Pereira, a little before the time of Galileo († 1610), wrote as follows :

" We should carefully guard against and absolutely abstain from adopting and maintaining in a positive and obstinate manner, in explaining the writings of Moses, any opinion in contradiction to certain conclusions derived from experience and reason in philosophy and the other sciences. For, since truth always agrees with truth, it is impossible that the truth of the Sacred Scriptures should be in opposition to the exact proofs and observations of the human sciences."§

---

* De Genesi ad litt., lib. l. c. 18, 19. † In Jerem. Proph., c. xxviii.
‡ In Job, c. xxvii. opusc. x lec¹. 17, l. ii., De Cœlo. § In Genesim ad princip.

Finally, even Cardinal Bellarmine, who probably had a principal part in the decisions of the Roman Congregation respecting the case of Galileo in 1616, affirms a principle of interpretation which fully justifies the universal assent which has been given to the heliocentric theory since the truth of it has been scientifically demonstrated. In a letter to the Carmelite Foscarini, who was a Copernican, he writes:

" If a true demonstration were given of the central position of the sun in the world, and of the position of the earth in the third heaven, the earth revolving around the sun and not the sun around the earth, it would then be necessary to proceed with great prudence in the explication of the Scriptures which seem to teach the contrary, and *rather to say that we have not understood them, than to declare false what has been demonstrated.*"*

As I have not space enough left to go into the case of Galileo in this article, I will conclude it with a sentence borrowed from an excellent article on " Leibnitz and the Sciences in a Monastery," by M. Charles Lamey :

" Although the philosophical age of Voltaire has passed, its consequences still remain and are everywhere felt. At the present time it is in the name of science that the church is constantly attacked with the expectation of accomplishing its overthrow. This design is more accentuated than ever before, and may we not recognize a precise indication of the. needs of our epoch in the words lately uttered by the Vatican Council (Const. de Fide, c. iv.) on the supreme importance of the sciences, their divine origin, and their natural alliance with the faith.
" It is these instructions which it behooves us to set in a clear light before the eyes of unbelievers in our days, and in a manner so unanswerable that they will ere long be constrained to admit that the church is the faithful promoter and natural ally of the sciences."†

AUGUSTINE F. HEWIT.

* Published from inedited MSS. by Signor Berti. *Copernico*, pp. 121-123.
† *Rev. des Qu. Scientif.*, vol. ii. p. 86.

A SPIDER-WEB, ALL GLITTERING.

NEAR my door is a spider's web of extraordinary size, and —you will hardly believe it, but I assure you—it is hung with sparkling brilliants, many of which are real jewels, pearls and diamonds! I am greatly tempted to approach and pick off some of the gems. Thousands of people are doing so, at least trying to. Few succeed, however, while a vast number get so entangled in the meshes that they cannot get away ; and so they die there.

It is the Louisiana State Lottery! Listen to what Father J. T. Tuohy says in this connection—and may God reward him for his bold, brave words! Truly is his sermon called "one of the most remarkable utterances on the social question ever heard from a Catholic pulpit."

He says : " The social question is a most important one ; and for a clergy consecrated to the service of God and of humanity, it is *the question of questions.* . . . Too long has the church let the discussion remain chiefly in the hands of her enemies. Catholics do not do their full duty by attending Mass and church services, or with half-shut eyes, in highly artificial albeit pious meditations, dreaming dreams of heavenly bliss, or by turning to the controversies of mediæval times, to indulge in their hair-splitting abstractions. . . . No thinking man of any experience can be blind to the fact that there is to-day a rapidly growing discrimination in the minds of the masses between Christ and the church. Christ and the church must be placed before them as one and inseparable."

Aye, aye! And responding to the inspiration of these magnetic words, I will try to do my little share, as a Catholic writer, towards "placing Christ and the church as one and inseparable," the friend of the poor, the hope of the masses.

I come, therefore, to arouse your interest, dear fathers and kind readers of this Catholic periodical, and to beg for your prayers, your sympathy, and your active assistance in behalf of my sorely-tempted State, unhappy Louisiana !

You, who do not live here, have as yet but slight idea of our lamentable condition. An almost inevitable net-work of webs is woven among us. Everywhere the insatiable spider says, "Won't you walk into my parlor ?"

And the masses walk right in; for where is there any one to warn them? The spider is fattening enormously, for who raises a hand to stay him? This now huge lottery began scarcely twenty-five years ago. Already it owns, virtually owns, the State. The press is in its power. Politics sways according to its control, and it plays upon human nature with absolute mastery. Nothing could be more alluring than its promises; more specious than its arguments; more fascinating than its methods. It throws dust in our eyes—gold dust so glittering that the best of us can hardly help being dazzled and blinded.

Its advocates, and many of them are honest, sincere people (aye, some of our very own too, alas!), say in its defence: " I don't see any harm in it. It isn't a sin. It does a great deal of good. Gives a great deal in charity. If it obtains a new twenty-five years' charter, it promises to the State one and a quarter millions yearly for twenty-five years! Magnificent! It would be folly to lose such an offer. The Lottery party is not a bit worse than any of our political parties. Then why all this outcry? We might just as well be governed by the Lottery party as by any other. As for its immense and dangerous power it's no greater than the railroads, for instance. So why oppose lottery and sustain railroads?"

Need I answer these fallacies? Only briefly, because the readers of this monthly are men of pure hearts and prayer-enlightened minds. They can readily see through even such pleasing sophistries.

If this lottery is not gambling, what is it? And if gambling is not to be condemned, what is?

We all know that the devil is always willing to give away fifty cents' worth of good if, under cover of that generosity, he can get back fifty dollars' worth of evil.

But so captivating are the Lottery's promises that they beguile us, and then our integrity is devoured by it, like flies by the spider.

Other corporations, monopolies, combines, and political parties may be as corrupt, but none of them are as powerful. None have ever begged to build our levees, and pay our public-school expenses, and support our insane, and clean, pave, and beautify our city, and endow our Charity Hospital—all for the small privilege of a twenty-five years' charter!

No wonder its opponents diminish steadily, while its advocates multiply and grow eloquent. No wonder they taunt us as being " fanatics, puritans, saints, fools, hypocrites." ·

No wonder they sneeringly say: "You can't legislate people moral. It's ridiculous to try. Gambling is an inherited instinct, and ineradicable. • No use forbidding it. You can't stop it. It should therefore be licensed, not prohibited."

They go further, and say: "The lottery is an admirable system of taxation; oppressive to no one; free to all, but compelling none. As for draining the poor—the poor would spend their money in worse ways if we had not the lottery; they *will* throw away their earnings. The poor are always wasteful; the wasteful always poor. And it's the best thing for them that the State benefit by their gambling habits."

What a pity that these wise and far-seeing counsellors were not around Moses when he was receiving the decalogue! They would have prevented him from losing his time that way. Because, of course, it was nothing but a loss of time—this transmitting laws which would inevitably be broken. How ridiculous to forbid impiety, and cursing, and profanity! They shouldn't be forbidden, because it's no use; they should be licensed. In fact, we ought not forbid nor oppose anything in the nature of sin or temptation. What does it matter whether other people fall or not, just so *we* keep out of the pitfalls? It's no affair of ours. "Am I my brother's keeper?"

And, indeed, many a well-meaning lottery friend declares, in all seriousness too: "We Catholics must not meddle with it. It's not a moral question. It's purely a business matter. It is to be judged from a commercial standpoint. The opposition is merely political. Religion has nothing whatever to do with it."

Certainly not! Politics and finances being the devil's own chosen domain, we mustn't interfere. "Hands off!" We must give him full sway. He is entitled to it. It doesn't matter at all that the people and the poor are thereby down-trodden, both body and soul. It's none of our business.

Ah! terribly true are Father Tuohy's words. The disaffection from us of the masses *is* rapid. We cannot deny it. And it is easily accounted for, too. In Father Faber's incisive words: "The scandal of the fact is so much greater than the scandal of merely acknowledging it, that we brave this latter for the sake of a greater good."

Cardinal Gibbons says the same thing, and attributes it to the same cause—the neglect, the seeming indifference of the church to the social question, the miseries of the poor, and the machinations of the rich. Cardinal Gibbons says: "The tolerance of.this is, unfortunately, in the pulpit. The close-fisted, affluent communicant who is sometimes not particular how he turns a penny, even to the point of downright dishonesty, is, as a rule, treated with marked deference by his pastor." And he further says that therefore "worldly men are confirmed in their worldliness, and the masses are repelled from the church that harbors and honors the mean sinner.",•

Equally pertinent to this subject are the welcome advices of our Holy Father's recent encyclical. Leo XIII. says that the social and labor questions of the day have assumed undeniable prominence, and therefore "the *necessity* of the church's dealing with them." We have a grand Pope, thank God!

Now, a composite view of the labor and social questions resolves them into one, namely, the MONEY QUESTION! That is *the* question of the day. It is at the root of every labor, social, and political problem of the times. And I contend that of all the iniquitous schemes whereby the shrewd get money from the masses, not one of them surpasses in iniquity this soft, glittering, and irresistible lottery. And that, therefore, there is no other evil against which Catholic people, press, and pulpit should be more determined, active, outspoken, and fearless.

With intense satisfaction I quote our Pontiff's attitude on these matters. The report says:

"The Pope desires to deprive his adversaries of the slightest pretext for pretending that the church has only charity as her programme, and nothing definite or precise to offer society. His object, above all things, has been the teaching of social justice."

Blessed words, and timely. For it were like gall and wormwood to the poor man, to be offered charity by a religion which would seem to say to him: "In your present troubles I take no interest. You must look out for yourself. I cannot lift a finger against your moneyed oppressors. I give good general advice, but as to any *definite, precise* action on such matters, that is out of my province. But when at length by fraud, compulsion, or" (worst of all) "cajolery, your earnings and your honor have been taken from you, and you are a wretched pauper, then I stretch out my hand—Come to me! I will give you alms; I will give you charity."

Aye, gall and wormwood! The workman turns away. Shall we blame him?

I heard a young lad talking about the lottery lately. He said: "Don't I wish I could strike Howard for $250! Phew! wouldn't I"—and he went on to build his air-castles. He had bought a lottery ticket. Need I point out how already one film of the spider's web has fastened upon that boy's mind? Already there is formed in him the ignoble desire of possessing what he has not earned. Thousands of boys are similarly ensnared. And is it not easy to see how that unmanly wish is excited, fostered, encouraged, played upon, by this corrupting lottery? Is it not obvious that the lottery's chief aim is to fan this desire until it become a passion?

Some months ago the *Catholic Review* referred editorially to our State Lottery. The article was on its front page, among those "Topics of the Hour" which every week tingle with vivid ideas on the live issues of the moment. I regret exceedingly not having it at hand in order to quote verbatim. Nevertheless, I am able to recall quite distinctly its spirit and purport. It commented with surprise upon the silence of many of our Louisiana clergy, their inertia in so momentous a crisis, when their influence could be of such avail and so beneficial. Yes, and there is no class of sufferers more sorely in need of that influence than we are, right now.

Humanly speaking our case is hopeless. The lottery is bound to win, because it has a measureless purse; and a measureless purse means measureless power. And then we are *so* poor. Many of our purest patriots say, "Louisiana is too poor; we *cannot* refuse the lottery." They never seem to be impressed by the *peculiar* fact, that while our State is "very, very poor," our lottery is very, very, enormously rich!

And so this "noble and beneficent institution" is having victories right straight along. But is the arm of God shortened? Ah! no, no. Pray then that he deliver us. The courageous stand taken by the priests of New York against the liquor-traffic; the strong and pregnant words of Father Tuohy; the timely sympathy of the *Catholic Review*, and the unmistakable utterances of our grand Cardinal and our glorious Pontiff—all combine to fill me with hope. I joy to think that very soon active steps will be taken, and I shall no longer writhe beneath the lash of taunts like the following from Protestant sources:

"Your church is a sphinx. Aha! I knew it long ago. She is dumb on this subject. She hasn't a word to say. She sanctions gambling. The Catholic Church has always approved of lotteries," etc., etc.

God grant that such accusers be silenced soon! And may God grant that the lottery be silenced too, and that no longer our people exemplify the song:

> "Will you walk into my parlor,"
>   Said the spider to the fly;
> "It's the prettiest little parlor
>   That ever you did spy,"

no matter how siren-like the coaxing, nor how dazzlingly fair the
glittering of that spider's web!

M. T. ELDER.

New Orleans, La.

AN OLD IRISH TOWN.

THERE are three towns in Ireland of pre-eminent interest to
the student and the antiquarian—Kilkenny, Galway, and Youghal,
and the last exceeds the other two in keen and vivid interest.
It is on the Atlantic seaboard; and down by the railway station,
where the summer visitors congregate in smart villas, there is a
steady roar and shock of Atlantic rollers inexpressibly fine and
splendid, even on a mild autumn day. What it is in a storm I
can only conjecture. The great sea-wall notwithstanding, the
ocean saps the land every day. It has sucked in the strand
steadily. What is now long stretches of undulating yellow sand
when the tide is out used to be bog-land and salt marshes. In
the last century they still dug turf there, and embedded in it
were quantities of fir and hazel trees. They took from it once the
skeleton of a great animal, or portions of it, and the horns of
moose deer were also dug out. The whole points to a primeval
forest; and an old history tells us that once, when a violent storm
had wasted the strand, there was laid bare a great expanse of
roots and limbs of trees. It is a treacherous tide hereabouts, and
if you stand below Clay Castle, the great promontory of cliffs to
the south-west of the town, the loose clay of which becomes
rose and blue and violet petrifactions, you may chance to find
yourself dry-shod some distance out, while the tide is bubbling
up and forming wide pools to isolate you. Fortunately for their
safety many of the villa-houses climb up the hill, towards where
the old town walls throw out a ruined bastion or buttress. Those
on the strand itself are doomed. It is worth a good many hours
of city life to stand by the sea-wall at Youghal and see the
rollers forming far out; first a dimple, then a long steady line,
then the great plunge at the land, and the dull roar and thud,
and high over you goes a cataract of fine silvery spray. This in

the goldenest autumn evening; in winter the sea is across the
road and stealing like a great gray serpent into the houses.

The town of Youghal is in a sheltered inlet. The river Blackwater—"The First Rhine" they call it; though why not the
Rhine "The German Blackwater"?—discharges itself into the sea
at Youghal. The town lies at its mouth, and over yonder are
the green Waterford hills, whither you may be ferried for a
penny. Once there was a strange traveller over the ferry. Of the
Desmonds, who made the fortunes of Youghal, there was at one
time an Earl Gerald, who died and was buried at holy Ardmore
of St. Declan, which, with its round tower and holy well and
other interesting ruins, lies still and quiet over there on the
sea-shore. But no saint's grave, or aught else, could satisfy
the dead earl, who desired to sleep at his own holy place of
Temple Michael on the Blackwater. So it came that all night,
in tempest or moonlight, when the waves were crooning their
summer song, or roaring like loosed lions, a strange voice,
like the voice of the dead earl, but hollow and terrible, went
crying across the waters: "Garault, arountha! arountha!"
(which is, Gerald, hurry! hurry!). "Give Garault a ferry."
So at last some young men of his clan went over by night
and lifted up the coffin and ferried him back, and at Temple
Michael he slept in peace.

Youghal is full of signs of its old consequence. The
houses are strangely important for those of an Irish country
town, and though many of them are degraded from their
first uses, they are not the less stately even in misfortune.
You enter Youghal through a street of those old houses, with
a boulevard of twisted elms blown away by the sea-wind.
Round and pointed chiselled doorways, trefoiled windows,
corbels and mullions, heraldic badges and friezes—all these
tell of vanished glories, and are everywhere. But if you pass
down by the College from the Raleigh house along the straight
roadway, perched on the hillside, and from which narrow alleys
wind down to the main street, you might easily believe yourself
in an English university town. On one side there are great old
houses well kept and prosperous-looking, on the other are the
college walls overhung with myrtle and valerian, and in their
season crested with yellow wallflowers and campanulas. Sir
Walter Raleigh brought the wallflower here as well as the
potato and the cherry. The descendants of his cherries still
flourish in the orchards at Affane on the Blackwater, where he
planted them. It is perhaps due to Affane that one sees lovely

fruit in Youghal. In a little room off the main street, converted to a shop, I have seen the most lovely apples and pears, making with baskets of red and yellow tomatoes a perfect feast of colors.

Sir Walter Raleigh and Spenser make many a one in love with Youghal. It is a place full of ghosts; the Desmonds jostle in the haunted air the gallant adventurer who had their estates when they were attainted, and further back are the Knights Templars, who had a preceptory at Rhincrew, at the mouth of the Blackwater, where perched high they could see the ships sailing in to bear them to the Holy Land. Some of them in stone, with crossed legs and sword in hand, are in St. Mary's Church, over against the bewildering monument of Robert Boyle, the "great Earl of Cork"; another shade, for he followed Sir Walter in the Desmond inheritance when one of the handsomest heads of all time fell under the executioner's axe in London Tower. Then Old Noll himself was here in the winter of 1649. The house where he lodged is a ruins in the main street. That Christmas-time one of his officers, Lieutenant-General Jones, died of a pestilential fever; he was buried in the Earl of Cork's chantry in St. Mary's church, and Oliver himself read the funeral service. One can picture that curious night-scene—my Lord Broghill, Sir William Fenton, and the other officers grouped about the open grave; on a bier the body of the dead soldier; by the flaming of torches the grim face of the Protector reading over the open grave his godly exhortation. In those streets it is not difficult to place him in his cloak and slouched hat. There he wintered in the mild climate—the south of Ireland is semi-tropical—and from this port he sailed away in May the year following, in the frigate *The President.*

The main street is spanned by a great clock-tower and gateway, the like of which I have never seen in any town in Ireland. Half-way down it is the "Red House," a fine example of Queen Anne architecture. It looks like the scene of one of Hawthorne's stories, standing back from the street in a grave stateliness, all stained to beautiful harmonious colors by the sun and the sea-wind; its gardens climbing up the hill at the back. You can have the Red House for the moderate rental of thirty pounds a year, but you will need to roof it, for it has been left long to the ghosts. In Youghal you could live in a very stately way on a very small income if you were inclined to be out of the world.

The Red House belonged to Mr. Drury, who owned the potteries. Youghal has made pitchers and vases of its red clay from time immemorial.. The pitchers can be obtained everywhere through the country for domestic purposes. They are as simple and beautiful in shape as that Rebecca carried to the well. Vases, pots, and pans there are of all sizes, and many pretentious, but I lost my heart to the big pitchers which one sees in the hand of every second urchin going to the fountain. As for the prices, we interviewed a dame who sat by the clock-tower. The pottery was closed for the time being owing to ·a coal strike, so I could not go to the fountain-head, so to speak, for my pitcher. This dame had a noble one among her wares. "What price?" we asked. She eyed us doubtfully, as if to measure the extent of our purses. "Well," tentatively, "you see it's very big. I'll have to charge yez fippence for that." "*Fivepence!*" we cried with one accord, and were misunderstood. "Well, yez needn't take it if yez don't like, but fippence it is." She was cautious in other matters. We asked her about the coal strike from which the town was suffering. She was bitter enough against it and its promoters, but would not satisfy our curiosity as to the strike leaders.

"A shut mouth ketches no flies," she said oracularly, nodding her shrewd old head.

Youghal has a stained-glass factory as well as a pottery. Few people know that Cox, Buckley & Co., the famous stained-glass house of London, have a branch factory in a little Irish town. It is there because Mr. Buckley, the junior partner, is a Youghal man, and in his prosperity remembered his native town. The factory employs nearly a score of hands. They are making windows for many big churches, Protestant and Catholic, and clients are just beginning to find out that they can place their orders at home and see the work in process. If you call you will be shown round by a most courteous and intelligent young Englishman. The offices are full of cartoons for the stained glass, beautiful large, simple designs, which remind one of Mr. Walter Crane's work, with perhaps a touch of Burne Jones thrown in.

If you are *fin de siècle* in politics, and interested in the Ponsonby tenants, eight miles outside of Youghal, you will be fortunate if you find so competent a witness to instruct you as a certain bright and handsome girl whose acquaintance we made in a shop in the main street. Her cleverness was simply a marvel. I should like to set her face-to-face with an exponent of the landlord view. She was an interesting example of the Irish inborn aptitude for politics. She was a farmer's daughter, one of eleven, I think, all of whom worked on the farm. She was the only one who had ever had the courage "to go foreign," as she put it, Youghal being about nine miles from home. I wish I could give her views of the land question, but they would take an article in themselves. Her views on marriage were pessimistic and more prosaic than I looked to find even among the Munster peasants, whose marriages are the merest contracts, though afterwards the bond is held inviolably. She never seemed to think that there could be a question of anything but money in marriage. "An' if I was saving ten years what could I buy with my money?" she demanded with some fierceness—"an ould show of a widower; though it's more likely *he'd* be looking for a girl with three or four hundred pounds. Marry for love!" in reply to our astonishment. "I've heard of people marryin' for love, foreign, in Dublin or Cork, but never in Youghal. I never heard of but one marriage for love in Youghal, *an' that was before my time,* an' it ended bad." She had evidently scant sympathy for that far-away love-affair which budded so out of place in the uncongenial air of Youghal.

In the main street, besides Cromwell's house and the clock-tower, are one or two other antiquities. There is the arched doorway of the convent of the Hospitallers of St. John, and their orchard, still walled away, is across the street. Then there is Sir Robert Tynte's castle, a square old keep, now a corn and coal store. After James II. came to the throne the story goes that some of the Youghal folk went near having a small Eve of St. Bartholomew on their own account in this tower. They seized and imprisoned there a little knot of Protestants, and one knows not what might have happened if the news had not been brought to a Catholic gentleman of the county, named Ronayne, a name still preserved and honored in Youghal. He rode in at hot speed, and exhorted the crowd to such good purpose that they yielded up their prisoners, whom he released nothing worse than frightened. For this service, when a Ronayne dies the town bell is tolled, a curious privilege.

Of course the antiquities of Youghal are St. Mary's Church, the College, and the warden's, or Raleigh's, House. In the latter, which now belongs to Sir John Pope Hennessy, Raleigh dwelt in 1588–89, when he was mayor of the town. He had received a grant of 12,000 acres or more of the Desmond's estates on their attainder, and this included Youghal. The house is like an old English manor-house, gabled, and with twisted chimneys; from its dense ivy the beautiful, irregular oriel windows look out. Here in the garden are the four yew-trees beneath which Raleigh sat smoking his pipe on that occasion when his servant

deluged him with water to put out the fire. The place is
smothered in myrtle-trees. Within the house is brown and
rich and ancient, full of carved wood and oak panelling. In
the oriel window of the drawing-room, once Sir Walter's study,
tradition says Spenser sat and read to his host the MS. of
"The Faëry Queene." The room is most beautiful, all of dark
oak, ceiling, walls, and floor, with a carved mantel of great
beauty and value. It has the figures of Faith, Hope, and Charity set in niches between elaborate garlands of one knows not
what. Everywhere about the room are portraits of Raleigh,
brown-eyed, olive-tinted, with his keen and delicate oval face,
his pointed beard, his ruff, his doublet of silk and mantle of
velvet. The furniture of the room is all old: an oak chest,
some carved chairs, a tall oaken dresser, which has turned
amid its carvings the device of Robert Boyle, Earl of Cork:
"God's Providence is Our Inheritance." Wax candles lit in the
tall sconces only make the place eerier. If Raleigh, courtly and
beautiful, came through the doorway one would scarcely feel
surprise.

This oriel looks toward St. Mary's, one of the most beautiful churches in Ireland. Around it the graveyard lies on a hill,
and is all very fair and peaceful. Not so long ago the chancel
was uncovered and partly ruined, but a generous and right-
minded rector restored it with fine judgment. The east window
has not its equal in this country for size and beauty. There is
a great square tower outside, more like a keep than a church-
tower. This is supposed to have subterranean connection with
the Raleigh house, and, indeed, in a corner of the dining-room
of the latter the boards of the floor lift up and reveal a passage.
But some former inhabitants threw earth down into the passage
and it has not been explored. Youghal, if one may believe the
stories, is tunnelled by subterranean ways. The Templars had
their secret ways down from Rhincrew to the sea-shore, and the
Desmonds also had their burrows. In old Strancally Castle, a
fortress of the latter, there is a ghastlier piece of ingenuity.
It is a chamber in the rock overhanging the water, where a
captive walked in unwarily and dropped sheer into the dark
water. "Drowning-holes" they call such *oubliettes.*

The great Earl Thomas of Desmond re-edified the church,
and built and endowed the college for a warden and eight fellows, with eight singing-men, who were to have a common table
and live after the collegiate manner. They were munificent
founders, those Desmonds. The North and South Abbeys, which

were Dominican . and Franciscan respectively, were founded by two Desmonds, father and son. There is no ruin of the South Abbey left. The North Abbey, now called "The Old Mass Yard," shows a beautiful bare window standing up amid stones and rubbish, and, far enough away to show the size of the church a portion of the western gable. The burying place of saints is miserably dirty, overgrown, and neglected, in pitiful contrast to its neighbor, St. Mary's.

The college of Thomas Fitzgerald, which he had endowed with £600 yearly, equal to more than £3,000 of our money, fell on evil days when Sir Walter Raleigh had yielded in his turn the spoil of the Desmonds to the Earl of Cork. This latter was the very prince of adventurers, so far as rapacity . goes. Sir Walter lost his handsome head, and what *quid pro quo* my Lord Cork gave him for his Irish estates remains unsubstantiated. To a surviving son of Raleigh's he gave a list, indeed, of various sums paid at times to his father, and on account of which the latter recommended his son Wat, since dead in the West Indies, to let Lord Cork have his Irish estates. "*For if you do not some Scot will get them,*" is put into the dead man's mouth, with saturnine humor. Lord Cork had need of all the revenues, and so much for a warden and fellows and singing men was not to be thought of, so he took up his residence himself in the college, and bade the scholars begone to a little school-house he prepared for them, and which is still the endowed school of Youghal. If you go there and pass through its pointed doorways you will see a beautiful Elizabethan ceiling of twisted and turned oak.

The south transept of St. Mary's Church, which was once called the Chantry of Our Saviour, Lord Cork took for the burying place of himself and his family. Over against the stone slabs of the Crusaders and the ancient monuments of the founders this maker of a family reared a monument which is the most grotesque witness to human vanity. In the midst lies the earl himself, first of his name, in a suit of armor, with the Elizabethan ruff above it, and the cap of the time on his grizzled head. His fierce painted eyes stare at you out of the marble in a way to haunt your sleep of nights. On a pedestal by his head kneels the figure of his second wife, who bore him nine children. Below you see all the tiny effigies going down in steps and stairs, with one pathetic little figure fallen forward, Geoffrey Boyle, who was drowned in the college well. At the earl's feet is his first wife, who died in childbirth, her one little son not surviving her.

Here he lies in the most elementary little cradle was ever seen off a christening cake. This first wife is robed gravely by contrast with the purple velvet and ermine of the second wife, the triumphant mother of children. As if all this pomp were not enough, there is over all the effigy of Joan Naylor, the earl's mother, in a great hat tied with ribbons and a ruff, solemnly contemplating from her cushion the skull she holds in her hands. The whole surprising edifice is of Italian marble, painted over in the taste of the time.

The great Earl of Desmond and his wife were buried here; probably the recumbent figures on slabs which are not named in a recess of the church wall may be their monument. Here also was buried that Countess Eleanor who survived seven English kings, and seems by the histories to have actually lived 140 years, though the rhyme says

> " . . . a hundred and ten,
> And died of a fall from a cherry-tree then."

It was not she, but the countess of the last unhappy Earl Gerald, who walked on foot to London to beg of Queen Elizabeth a sustenance out of the magnificent estates which once had been the possessions of the proud Desmonds.

The Earl Gerald, after the failure of the great Munster rebellion, was beheaded in a hut in the mountains by one Daniel Kelly, who received for that thirty pounds yearly from Queen Elizabeth, and who, it is satisfactory to learn, was afterwards himself hanged at Tyburn. The condition of Munster after the Desmonds fell must have been indeed appalling. Spenser's terrible description wrings the heart:

"Notwithstanding that the same was a most rich and beautiful country, full of corn and cattle, . . . they are brought to such wretchedness as that any stony heart would rue the same; out of every corner of the woods and glens they came, creeping forth upon their hands, for their legs could not bear them: they looked anatomies of death; they spake like ghosts crying out of their graves. They did eat the dead carrion (happy were they who could find them); yea, and one another soon after; inasmuch as the carcases they spared not to scrape out of the graves; and if they found a plot of watercress or shamrock they flocked there as to a feast."

Years after Queen Elizabeth sent back Gerald's young son,

whom she had taken to England and reared after the English manner. She wanted to set up a Queen's Desmond in Munster. His people, as she had counted, received him with passionate joy and welcome, flocking in from all parts of the country, and crowding about him so that his passage-way was long barred. Many of them remained all night around the place where he lodged, but great and bitter was the grief and disappointment when next day, being Sunday, he went to the Protestant church. From that hour he had no more following than any private gentleman, and after a while he returned to hide his diminished head in England. He died soon after, being a puny stripling at best.

I have told nothing of the glories of the Desmonds which were also connected with Youghal. But the old town would take half-a-dozen magazine articles if one were to tell leisurely all the things one desired about it and its associations. I had gathered so many bits for quotation; I have delicious extracts from my Lord Cork's diary and letters about that family he founded. But they must go. And one would need to abide a little in Youghal to appreciate the interest and claims of the old place, and the glamour of the past which lies upon it like a veil of silver mist wrought large with letters of gold.

KATHARINE TYNAN.

THE OLD WORLD SEEN FROM THE NEW.

As in these notes we have referred repeatedly to the labor and social question, we cannot pass by the recent Encyclical of Pope Leo XIII., ·of which the chief and the almost exclusive object is the discussion of the condition of the working classes with a view to its amelioration. Many articles would be required to bring out the true bearing and scope of this most important pronouncement, and we' must be content with calling attention to a very few points. After speaking of the extreme difficulty of the matter, the Holy Father, notwithstanding this difficulty, affirms that " all agree, and there can be no question whatever, that some remedy must be found, and quickly found, for the misery and wretchedness which press so heavily at this moment on the large majority of the very poor." No recognition is, therefore, to be given to those who are inclined to dismiss the wrongs of the poor and of the laborer from their thoughts and efforts under the plea that the world is under condemnation—those who maintain that the church's work is only a spiritual work, and who relegate entirely to a future life the redressal of the wrongs of this: " A remedy must be found and quickly found." Already we have a decision on a most important point.

For many apologists and defenders of the church, and even for many moral theologians, the attitude of popes and councils in former times toward usury and the strict condemnation and even rigorous repression of it have afforded no little difficulty. Owing to the long-continued domination of what is now the old school of political economy, such maxims as that supply alone regulates price seem to have been looked upon as laws of nature. To the modern order of things based upon this teaching it has been the effort of many to make the church's doctrine agree, or at least to show that it does not disagree. The Pope seems to take a different view of the matter. After attributing to the repudiation which has taken place of the ancient religion the fact that "the working-men have been given over, isolated and defenceless, to the callousness of employers and the greed of unrestrained competition," he proceeds : "The evil has been increased by rapacious usury, which, although more than once condemned by the church, is nevertheless, under a different form but with the same guilt, still practised by avaricious and grasping men." At all events the Holy Father attributes to usury a greater influence in causing present evils than is usually done. Usury in his eyes is by no means a sin of former ages exclusively; it lives and flourishes·now.

*   *   *

While the main object of the Encyclical is to show the solution of the labor question which is to be drawn from Catholic teaching, to which object far the greater portion of the document is devoted, the solution of the Socialists is rejected and condemned, and the right of private ownership in land and other property affirmed to be rooted in the law of nature. This is not the place to give an accurate and precise estimate as to how far this condemnation goes. But, so far as we can see, it would not affect any practical proposal yet made, or ever likely to be made in any English-speaking country, by responsible statesmen. For we can scarcely look upon the advocates of the nationalization of land as responsible statesmen. Socialism, as Cardinal Manning has pointed out, is a term hard to define, there being no agreement as to its meaning among its various advocates and opponents. According to the *Anti-Jacobin* the Irish Land Purchase Bill and the free education proposals of the Tory government in England are manifestly socialistic. We must, therefore, carefully learn from the Encyclical itself precisely what it is that is condemned, and we must also bear in mind the wide scope allowed ·by theologians for the exercise of *altum dominium* by the state, *servatis servandis*. The Socialism which is condemned is that held by those "who endeavor to destroy private property, and maintain that individual possessions should become the common property of all, to be administered by the state or by municipal bodies." What, therefore, is condemned seems to be the theory of those who are commonly called Collectivists.

*   *   *

· Although we have not touched the main body of the Encyclical, the space at our disposal precludes further comment. Suffice it to say that the Pope directs the course of thought and action between the extremes of undue state interference and regulation on the one hand, and of the *laissez faire*, as well of the theologian as of the political economist, on the other. Whatever leaning there may be is to the side of the working-man : because, as the Pope says, "to the material well-being the labor of the poor is most efficacious and altogether indispensable. Justice, therefore, demands that the interests of the poorer population be carefully watched over by the administration, so that they who contribute so largely to the advantage of the community may themselves share in the benefits they create. . . . Both philosophy and the Gospel agree in laying down that the object of the administration of the state should be, not the advantage of the ruler, but the benefit of those over whom he rules. When it is a question of protecting the rights of individuals, the poor and helpless have a claim to special consideration." We cannot conclude without a reference to the stress the Pope lays upon the obligation of rest, religious rest, on Sundays. He seems to go much farther in this matter than text-book theology, for he speaks of it as a rest not merely "sanctioned by God's great law of the ancient covenant," but "taught to the world by his own mysterious rest after the creation of man. *He rested on the seventh day from all his work which he had done.* This approximates to what the late Father Formby used so zealously to defend. The Holy Father treats of the questions of child labor and that of women, rates of wages, equalization of land-ownership, and the homes of workmen, short and long hours, and workmen's societies, inclining in every case to the side of the poor man and his family.

*   *   *

The chief events of interest in the Labor World are the May Day demonstrations in favor of the eight-hour day and the subsequent and consequent events. As we have already noted, systematic striking, as a definite settled policy, has been abandoned for the time being in Great Britain. A large number of strikes, it is true, have taken place—some of them, such as those of the tailors and the omnibus and cab-drivers, involving a great many men. The cause of these strikes is found, however, in matters of detail, and, as such, no special interest attaches to them. The May Day demonstrations belong to a different category. This year they assumed colossal proportions and caused grave anxiety to the authorities of many countries. It is instructive to note that while in monarchical England the demonstrators themselves bore public testimony to the courtesy and considerateness of the police, in republican France blood was shed and the most careful precautions were taken. No less than 42,000 soldiers were brought into Paris, in view of the celebration; and on the day itself these troops were engaged in the constant work of securing the "circulation" of the people. In Fourmies as many as nine lives were lost. The first warlike service to which the Lebel rifle, the new weapon of the French army, was put was against French citizens. That the carnage stopped when it did was due to the bravery and zeal of the *curé*, who rushed between the soldiers and his people. The loss of life was the greatest at Fourmies; but there was bloodshed also in Rome, and disturbances in many other places. The outcome of the demonstrations as a whole has been to make the statesmen of Europe apprehensive for the future, and to show them that an international organization of the work-ing-men (in whose hands the power is placed in most countries) is a thing which must be counted upon and reckoned with.

*   *   *

Belgium, however, is one of the countries in which the fran-chise is so restricted as not to admit of the working-men exer-cising their rightful influence upon legislation. And, as we stated last month, their lot in this country is all but unendurable, espe-cially that of the miners; nor should we in all likelihood greatly err if, between these two facts, we should trace the relation of cause and effect. For this reason the disturbances in Belgium did not end with the May Day processions. In despite of the advice of their councils, the miners determined to leave off work, and in the different parts of the country nearly seventy thousand men struck. Many disturbances ensued; business was brought to a standstill; bombs were thrown, and the anxiety throughout the kingdom was so great that rumors went abroad that it was the intention of the king to ask for the assistance of the German army, and French newspaper writers began to indulge in threats about what France would do in such an event. These rumors were, however, without foundation. For a long time the revision of the constitution has been a subject of discussion and agitation. In November last the question was referred to a committee. It was apprehended by the miners that such a reference might lead to the permanent shelving of the matter, and the main and imme-diate object of the strike was to prevent this. Success has so far attended their efforts that the committee has reported and the men have consequently returned to their work. When revision has been secured, they hope to secure legislation for the much-needed improvement of their position.

*   *   *

The proposals of Mr. Joseph Chamberlain for a system of national insurance have been widely discussed, and seem in a fair way to enter into the region of practical politics. A committee

of members of the House of Commons has been formed, or rather
has formed itself (for it has no official character), for the purpose
of working out the details of the scheme and embodying them in
a bill for presentation to Parliament.   The Rev. Canon Blackley,
an Irishman by birth, has for many years been an ardent advocate
of national insurance.   The defect of his scheme was its ambitious
character.   He aimed at securing for the working-men, through
state agency, provision for sickness and accident as well as a pension in old age.   This brought him into conflict with the friendly
societies which abound in England—*le pays de self-help*, as the
Count de Mun' styles it.   It seems a pity that one good thing
should so often place itself just in opposition to another.   But this
has always been the case and doubtless always will be.   These
societies provide for sickness and for accidents.   The magnitude
of the work thus voluntarily done may be estimated by a few statistics with reference to one of them—the Odd Fellows.   The adult
membership of this society is 673,000, the net increase during the
past year having been 21,000.   The juvenile membership was
greater, 738,000.   The income for the year 1889 was £1,300,-
000, the capital of the society being £7,358,000.   There is another society larger even than this, and many smaller ones.

*   *   *

It is clear, therefore, that to enter into a conflict with such
powerful organizations, and with the spirit which they represent,
the spirit of self-help and voluntary co-operation in contradistinc-
tion to that of reliance upon the state, was unadvisable.   Canon
Blackley, therefore, made no headway, notwithstanding his zeal.
But these societies have been unable to grapple with the question
of the superannuation even of their own members.   Mr. Chamberlain's scheme, therefore, aims at doing what the friendly societies either have not attempted or have failed in accomplishing ;
and as he does not aim at providing for sickness or for accident
no reason for conflict exists.   This renders it probable that a
measure will be passed—how soon it would be rash even to
form a conjecture, so uncertain nowadays are the ways of
Parliament.

*   *   *

Another gigantic organization for the mutual assistance of people
whose means are small has been holding its annual meeting.   We
refer to the Congress of the co-operative societies of Great Britain
and Ireland, which met at Lincoln in May.   This is another working-men's movement, managed and controlled by themselves, although not without the friendly assistance and advice of many

educated and experienced men, of whom the author of *Tom Brown's School Days* is the most widely known.   Its object is two-fold : co-operation in the supply. of goods so that the profits of sale accrue to the purchasers, all of whom must be members of the society, and co-operation in the production and manufacture of goods, so that the workman shall share in the profits of his work. In the first of these objects the success has been startling.   We must again give a few figures.   The first store was opened not very many years ago in a provincial town in England, in a miserable room lit by a tallow candle.   During the past twenty-five years the annual business of the retail stores has increased from about £4,000,000 to £28,000,000, and the members from 175,000 to over 1,000,000. The business of the wholesale societies in England and Scotland has grown from almost nothing to £10,000,000 a year in the same period.   The flour-mills do a business of about £2,000,000 a year.   £114,000 was paid last year for tea duty to the government.   These figures show what working-men are capable of doing for a cause which enlists their sympathies and from which they reap substantial and tangible advantages.   Why do they not succeed in such undertakings in America ?

This success in the co-operative distribution of goods has not been shared by the co-operative production of goods.   The society aimed no less at enabling the working-men to share in the profits of their toil than in lessening the expense of living by purchasing at their own stores ; but little or no success has so far attended their efforts in this direction.   The society has become an employer of labor like any other capitalist.   It has even failed in some instances to give satisfaction to its employees, and has been made to undergo the salutary correction of a strike.   It is not that the attempt has not been honestly made, but that ill-success has attended nearly every such attempt.   It would be very interesting and instructive to have an account of the precise reasons for this failure. If the working-man can himself be his own capitalist as well, the conflict between capital and labor must necessarily cease, and it is to this that many look for the solution of the problem.   But the fact cannot be overlooked that attempts have been made to secure this end, and that these attempts have met with very small success.   The failure, however, has not been so complete as to be disheartening.   Want of success will lead to a closer study of the problem ; and the future may remove the difficulties hitherto found so great.

The session, which opened with so much promise for social reformers, seems destined to frustrate their hopes. Little progress has been made with the various measures which have been brought before Parliament, and for some of them but little hope is entertained of their becoming law. It will be impossible to proceed with the Welsh Local-Option Bill—although it has received a second reading—as it is a private member's bill. Whether the Sunday-closing bill for Ireland will share the same fate it is hard to say. Mr. Sexton is relentless in his opposition to it in its present form, and may succeed in defeating a measure ardently desired by all friends of the temperance movement. The legal eight-hour day for miners has no chance of being carried. It is doubtful whether it will be so much as debated. In fact, there is by no means a unanimous agreement among those most nearly affected by it. The free—or rather the assisted—education proposals of the government are now before Parliament; but such is the state of public business that it may not be even in the government's power to pass them into law. We must console ourselves with the thought that progress when slow is on that very account the more likely to be sure and well considered.

*

A new labor movement has been started of which, whether it succeeds or fails, it will be interesting to note the result. Mr. Frank Smith, the commissioner of General Booth, who abandoned his post at the head of the social wing of the Salvation Army just as it was getting into working order, has devoted himself since that time to the support of working-men's claims. Not content with this, he has formed the plan of organizing a labor army. No doubt the training received under the general has suggested the idea, although the distinguishing mark of the Salvation Army, the supreme power wielded by its head, is not to form a feature of this new army. The hope is that it will embrace every working-man—as well those who belong to trade-unions as those who do not. It is to be a combination of all for political action. This is another evidence of the growing dislike to strikes which is felt by the capitalist and the working-man alike. The latter is turning to parliamentary action as the means most suitable for the relief of his wrongs; and strong efforts will be made to send to the House of Commons a large number of reliable labor members. This is a matter independent of the success or failure of the new labor army. The chief interest attaching to this is whether it will be possible for purely material and temporal advantages to organize a body at all analogous to the Salvation Army.

"A little knowledge is a dangerous thing." Of the truth of the old saying Mr. P. H. Calderon, the keeper of the Royal Academy, must by this time have a somewhat keen and unpleasant apprehension. Having read in an old life of St. Elizabeth of Hungary that on a certain Good Friday, before the altar and in the presence of the clergy, the saint "*omnino se exuit et nudavit*," he leaped to the conclusion that she stripped herself then and there of every shred of clothing, and accordingly has so represented her in a picture which is on view in this year's exhibition. The worst of it is, that it is no longer in the power of the artist to destroy this humiliating and disgusting manifestation of his ignorance, for the picture has been bought for the National Gallery, and as a consequence the folly of the painter will be handed down from generation to generation. The controversy has given yet another opportunity to Professor Huxley for airing his hatred of everything religious—a hatred which, from his eagerness to manifest it, is becoming almost ridiculous. Dr. Abbott also, who has had the prudence to assail Dr. Newman's truthfulness after the cardinal's death and not before, as did Kingsley, has by coming forward on this occasion given an indication of his animus. When the case is so bad that even the London *Times* had to decide in favor of "the member of the Jesuit order writing in Farm Street" against the Royal Academician, we have some hopes that on another occasion these eminent writers will be less precipitate.

*   *

During the past month it is in the little kingdom of Portugal that the most important events have taken place on the Continent, and although the *status quo* has been preserved for the time, and the future looks more promising, it would be imprudent to conclude that all danger is over. For many years Portuguese expenditure has been in excess of income, and loan after loan has been made to meet the interest on the debt. The revived interest in its colonies and the conflict with Great Britain in South Africa have also been sources of expense; for the colonies of Portugal, like those of the Continental powers, are governmental matters and not the outcome of the voluntary action of private citizens. A new loan was therefore necessary; but investors held back and the loan failed. This led to a crisis. The

Portuguese government issued a decree in virtue of which the payment of obligations was suspended for sixty days. This extreme measure, instead of completing the disaster, as many outside Portugal expected, inaugurated an improvement, and at the present moment there is a better outlook and something like a restoration of confidence.

What has materially contributed to this better state of affairs is the conclusion of an arrangement with England in settlement of the South African difficulty. Under this new agreement better terms have been secured by Portugal than under the treaty rejected last year by the Cortes. Lord Salisbury is said to have been influenced by two considerations in making these concessions. If Portugal were pressed too hard there was danger of bankruptcy, and much British capital is invested in Portugal. The other belongs to a higher category. As is well known, there is a strong republican party in Portugal, the spirit of which is such that it was thought there might be an uprising against the crown in the event of its being unable to conclude a satisfactory arrangement with England. Not to further such a blow to monarchical institutions, Lord Salisbury yielded.

Just after the conclusion of this satisfactory arrangement with England, and before waiting to present it to the Cortes to obtain its consent, the ministry resigned. For a fortnight it was found impossible to form a new cabinet. In the end, however, Portugal rejoiced in having a new government, the third within the period of eighteen months. It is thought that the republicans would have taken advantage of this opportunity ; but it was well understood that had they done so the Spanish forces would have occupied Portugal, with the probability that they would never leave it, and that the kingdom would be incorporated with Spain. This was more than the republicans cared to risk, and so they kept quiet. Meanwhile the outlook is brighter. The new ministry inspires confidence, especially the minister of finance, who is a man of ability, public spirit, and enlightened views.

Servia, as we noted last month, has got rid of the disturbing presence of her ex-King Milan. It was looked upon as equally necessary for the peace of the kingdom that the ex-Queen Natalie should depart. To effect this persuasion and entreaty were employed, but with characteristic obstinacy the queen would not yield until the government, unlawfully and arbitrarily and by the most injudicious of means, forcibly expelled her from the country. The unfortunate mode of procedure adopted by the ministry has excited sympathy for the queen, and wrought division among its supporters, and so, bad as was the effect of her presence, that of her enforced absence may be worse.

*　　　　*　　　　*

It is instructive to note, *apropos* of Queen Natalie, the practical workings of divorce in a schismatic church. This power is arrogated to itself by the synod. King Milan, bent on obtaining a complete separation from his queen, and not finding the synod compliant enough, prevailed upon the metropolitan, who was his tool, to supersede the synod and to pronounce the decree in his own name. And so the king and queen were divorced. But on account of a political change the metropolitan also is changed, and the new head of the Servian Church reverses the decision of his predecessor and declares the decree null and void. Here we have metropolitan against metropolitan; but to add to the confusion the decree of the second metropolitan has itself been declared to be *ultra vires* and in its turn null and void. To such a state are those reduced who have not the divine authority of the See of Peter to guide and rule them.

*　　　　　　*

The Marquis de Rudini still holds the reins of power in Italy, but his tenure is very precarious. His cabinet rests for support on the two extreme parties in the Chamber—the Conservatives and the Radicals—and closer acquaintance with each other does not make them better friends. A mere accident may displace the ministry at any moment, and no one can tell at what moment such an accident may occur. A warm sympathizer with the movement for the unification of Italy, and a personal friend and admirer of many of the men who brought it about, writes to the London *Times* to bewail the moral deterioration of the men who have taken their places. He finds the modern Italian politician destitute of public spirit and unwilling to sacrifice himself for the common good, a mere seeker of emoluments and personal advantages, untrustworthy and contentious. Party spirit we find a bad enough evil in England and America, but it would seem Italy is afflicted with a worse, for its politicians have not enough public spirit to be faithful even to a party, but each one

is seeking simply and solely his own advantage and nothing else.
This is the picture drawn of Italy by a warm admirer of the new
order of things. Meanwhile the people groan under the heavy
burden of taxation; how heavy it is may be judged by a representative case. An artisan's family in the city of Florence out
of the total income of £86 14s. are calculated to have spent
£8 17s. 10½d. in direct taxation and £13 14s. 11½d. in the
enhanced price of commodities due to indirect taxation, and this
although none of them smoked, and consequently did not pay
any share of the duty on tobacco. No wonder Italians are not
enthusiastic about the Triple Alliance.

*   *   *

The sufferings and persecutions which the Jews have been
forced to undergo form one of the most striking events of the
recent month. In Crete the populace made a violent onslaught
upon them, and many lives were lost. This, however, was the
unreasoning attack of the mob, and as such was ultimately
repressed by the authorities; but in Russia the measures taken
against them are a part of a deliberate plan of the government
itself. It would take many pages to describe in detail the character of these measures. Suffice it to say that they are of the
most inhuman and barbarous character. It seems evident that
the set policy and plan of the government is to drive into exile
some 5,000,000 of its own native-born subjects, and the only hope
that the friends of the victims have is that the czar will not
carry out the measures all at once, but that he will vouchsafe
time sufficient to enable friends to provide a home for the exiled.
It seems clear that Baron Hirsch has made arrangements to buy
and prepare in the Argentine Republic a large tract of land
for this purpose. Some are emigrating to Turkey, others are
finding their way to England, and doubtless also to this country.

*   *   *

As an illustration of the manner in which what takes place
in one country has unforeseen and apparently unconnected consequences in other and far-distant countries, this Russian persecution of the Jews may be instanced. The vast export of gold
from this country and whatever consequences it may have upon
our trade are due to the demand for gold in western Europe.
This demand arises from the fact that Russia has recalled the deposits she had made in England, France, and Germany These
deposits were withdrawn because the Rothschilds, out of sympathy
for the oppressed members of their race, would not finance a

new Russian loan. Although this may not be quite certain, it rests at all events upon excellent authority and is generally believed.

*

Bare mention of a few other European events will suffice. The youthful sovereign of Germany has given his high approval to the elevating and ennobling customs of duelling and drinking-bouts, both so much in vogue among German students. France is busy in raising her tariffs. We are glad to say that the French government has taken measures to afford the railway servants some degree of rest on Sundays. Austria remains under the skilful control of Count Taaffe. We cannot close without mentioning the inauguration of perhaps the most gigantic railway undertaking of modern times. The Russian government has definitely taken in hand the construction of a railway right across Siberia to the Pacific Ocean. It will cost, according to present estimates, $125,000,000, as well as a permanent subvention. Its object is strategic, but it may result in larger commercial advantages. Death has removed M. Jean Bratiano, the statesman who, under King Charles, formed Wallachia and Moldavia into the flourishing little kingdom of Roumania.

TALK ABOUT NEW BOOKS.

THE evil rumors that somehow or other have got into circulation concerning the state of Mr. Rudyard Kipling's health give a certain ominous character to the sentences with which Mr. Henry James lately closed the admirable sketch that introduces the only American collection* of his tales for which their author is responsible. Mr. James is ample, unstinted, and yet discriminating in his praise. Discrimination one counts on from him as a matter of course, but the generosity, not to say the lavishness, of commendation with which in this instance it is accompanied, and even the sense in the reader's mind that this also is but an additional testimony to the reality of the critic's accustomed virtue, comes as an agreeable surprise. Though Mulvaney carries his own credentials, and one needs no justification for having accepted them out of hand, yet it is pleasant to delight in him and in the circle of which he is, after all, only the central figure, in such good company. Concerning the future presumably wrapped up in such a present, Mr. James, while denying himself the luxury of prophecy, and declaring that he finds the young athlete "stepping out quite as briskly and still more firmly than ever," ended by saying :

"A whimsical, wanton reader, haunted by a recollection of all the good things he has seen spoiled; by a sense of the miserable, or, at any rate, the inferior in so many continuations and endings, is almost capable of perverting poetic justice to the idea that it would even be well for so surprising a producer to remain simply the fortunate, suggestive, unconfirmed and unqualified representative of what he has actually done. We can always refer to that."

Speaking for one, and with a memory recently refreshed by a renewed reading of a good deal more of Mr. Kipling's prose than is included in this volume, we find this " always " a well-chosen adverb. Even though the ill news should happily turn out unfounded, and Mr. Kipling as a producer may in the end survive himself, it can never be gainsaid that he made his own place in literature as positively and as precociously, the difference in their arts considered, as Mozart did in music. There are but two of the stories in the present collection which are new, and as the hero of one

---

* *Mine Own People.* By Rudyard Kipling. With a Critical Introduction by Henry James. New York: United States Book Company.

of these is an ourang-outang and of the other an elephant, it might under certain aspects seem invidious to say that Bimi and Moti Guj are not only "people," but as strictly Mr. Kipling's very own people as Mrs. Hauksbee, or Terence Mulvaney, or the ghastly "Man who would be King." But in reality there is something very far from offensive implied in the remark. These two stories intensify in a singular and unexpected way one's sense of that keen and abounding vitality, as receptive as a sponge to impressions and as ready to give them forth again, which to our own mind is singling itself out as Mr. Kipling's most unique and endearing characteristic. Even when he casts the plummet of his imagination into the depths that seem to lie below rationality, he brings up what one is fain to accept as deep-sea soundings, throbbing with articulate life. Bimi, "mit der half of a human soul in his belly," and Moti Guj, "a bachelor by instinct" like the drunken mahout, his master, recall what some one not long since reported Edison as saying—that to him everything in nature seems to possess a living soul, and that it is in the attempt to "put himself in the place" of things usually considered inanimate that he has oftenest obtained the secret of his marvellous inventions.

Mr. F. H. Smith, who speaks, we believe, as one "to the manner born," gives in Colonel Carter * an unusually pleasant description of one of the accepted types of the "high-toned Southern gentleman." It is very easy to comprehend the colonel's charm, to laugh good-naturedly at him, since circumstances of a congenital kind forbid laughing with him, and to rejoice in the good fortune which, through the unselfish generosity such men usually stand in need of, at last places him on his feet and permits him to settle up his grocer's account with something more to the latter's purpose than delightful manners and a flow of r-less eloquence.

Glencoonoge † is a story of Irish life into which neither politics nor religion enter as important factors. It is too long, and its interest is not at any point engrossing; still it permits itself to be read with a certain pleasure. Its author bears a name very ponderous with literary suggestiveness, and if his novel cannot be said to increase, neither does it greatly diminish the force of this antecedent attraction.

Those who not only read French with ease but are sensitive to the poetic and philosophic aspects of religion, will be sure to

---

* *Colonel Carter of Cartersville.* By F. Hopkinson Smith. New York and Boston: Houghton, Mifflin & Co.

† *Glencoonoge.* By Richard Brinsley Sheridan Knowles. Baltimore: John Murphy & Co.

find both pleasure and profit in a recent work * by M. Claude-Charles Charaux, professor of philosophy at the University of Grenoble. Following, but not too closely, in the path trodden by Châteaubriand in his *Génie du Christianisme*, he has brought fancy and imagination to the aid of a serene intelligence and an ardent faith, in order to devote all to the task of adorning and edifying the City of his love, the Church Catholic and Roman. To our mind he has made a very beautiful success. Among the dialogues of the first part, that entitled *Notre Dame du Hêtre* has given us especial pleasure. But the second part of the work, which is more exclusively devoted to philosophy, is also by far the most suggestive and noteworthy. The pair of dialogues on "Time and the Unity of Time," and "Space and Matter," in which the chief interlocutors are the youths who were afterwards General Duroc and Count Hercules de Serre, to whom their instructor, Laillet, a learned Augustinian monk, plays the part of Socrates in drawing fine distinctions from their lips, are especially valuable.

Some remarkably clever work may be found in a volume † called *Noughts and Crosses*, just brought out by Cassell's. There is a strongly individual touch in these sketches, and a refreshing novelty of tone and treatment. And in the quaint and delicate conceits of "Old Æson," "The Magic Shadow," and one or two others, there is vivid poetic insight as well. "Q" is plainly a man of imaginative substance, whose stores seem in no immediate danger of exhaustion. He has a style, too, which is not merely eminently his own, but a possession to be congratulated on.

In fact, those who have of late been dinning into the ears of whosoever could be got to listen, that the "short story" is a rare and almost impossible form of art, practicable only by the exceptionally gifted few, seem to be getting the lie direct from a more or less successful crowd of aspirants, new and old. Elizabeth Stuart Phelps, for one—in the title-page to this latest volume ‡ she discards the recently assumed addition to her name—has never appeared to better advantage than in the fourteen tales of which it is made up. She profits more than most writers by compression, her most evident weakness having always been a tendency to slop over and waste her motive power. These stories are of unequal excellence. The best of them are the clerical sketches like

<hr>

* *La Cité Chrétienne. Dialogues et Récits.* Par Claude-Charles Charaux, Professeur de Philosophie à la Faculté des Lettres de Grenoble. Paris : Firmin-Didot & Cie.

† *Noughts and Crosses.* By Q. New York : Cassell Publishing Co.

‡ *Fourteen to One.* By Elizabeth Stuart Phelps. New York and Boston : Houghton, Mifflin & Co.

" His Relict," " The Reverend Malachi Matthew," and that which gives its title to the collection. The painful story " Too Late " is full of the kind of sentiment and material which afford this writer her amplest scope and opportunity.

Mr. Stockton, too, is out with a collection* of his stories, old and new. The humor in them is as Stocktonian as ever, but somehow it fails to produce its old effect. Perhaps that is because one has become so accustomed to laugh in the right places with Mr. Stockton that both mirth and interest have acquired an invincible tendency to merge into something which retains but a shadowy likeness to either. " Euphemia among the Pelicans " is the pleasantest of these sketches.

An author who deliberately excludes love between the sexes from the means and motives of a proposed fiction, and yet produces a powerful novel whose interest does not flag at any point, deserves to be congratulated. And that is what has been done in *Jerry*† by Miss Sarah Barnwell Elliott. It is true that as a man Jerry takes less firm hold on the reader's sympathies than he did as an abused and frightened but indomitably plucky child. But there is so much in the book besides its hero; the study of old Joe Gilliam is so masterly, and all that relates to the mine is delineated with so firm a hand, that attention is enchained from the first page to the last. If the construction is thin in parts; if the Doctor seems to clamor for more explication than is furnished by his life of expiation and the scrap of conversation between him and Paul Henley's mother, overheard by Jerry at the ball, these are defects which, in their way, testify to the general solidity of the novel as a whole. To our notion it is among the best stories produced by Southern writers. For one thing, it is not overloaded with description; the interest is before all things human, and the dialect, though marked enough, is not pressed to that verge of weariness which makes one reflect on the possible advantages of phonetic spelling in reducing all story-tellers to a level where sense and not sound would be their only hope. As things stand, there must be many readers who, addressing the novelists of the period, would echo Joe Gilliam's sentiment with regard to Jerry's efforts to pronounce his first reading lessons after the Doctor's fashion :

" Joe's English was very demoralizing, and Jerry puzzled sorely over his words, speaking slowly and correcting himself when he

---

* *The Rudder Grangers Abroad, and Other Stories.* By Frank R. Stockton. New York: Charles Scribner's Sons.
† *Jerry.* A Novel. By Sarah Barnwell Elliott. New York: Henry Holt & Co.

remembered. And Joe was very lenient, treating these efforts as signs of the weakness of Jerry's intellect. ' Jest please yerself 'bout words, Jerry,' he said kindly ; ' *I don't rayly hev no feelin' agin one word or enother ; it's orl one to me, jest so I kin on'erstan youuns;* now jest pole erlong, but thet boy an' hisn's fly.' "

Iermola * is a charmingly told, and in parts almost painfully interesting, tale of Polish low life. The theme, almost identical with that of *Silas Marner*, is worked out with an abundance of local detail which seems very well managed, and is, at all events, very effective. The old Iermola, wakened to skill, energy, foresight, and invention by pure love for a helpless child, after a long life of apathetic resignation to hopeless poverty, is a very pathetic figure.

Mr. Crawford's new novel † dresses an old motive—the very oldest, perhaps, in all the world—in a characteristic and taking fashion. His hero is " one of the genii converted to the faith on hearing Mohammed read the Koran by night in the valley Al Nakhlah." For reasons for which we refer those in search of certain entertainment to the tale itself, Khaled has been allowed to assume mortal shape and to become the husband of the most virtuous and beautiful woman in the world, Zehowah, daughter of the Sultan of Nejed, for whose hand, left at her own disposal by her father, hundreds of princes have sued in vain. But, though granted mortal life, he can gain an immortal soul only after probation. " Zehowah will accept thee in marriage though she love thee not," says the angel who conveys to Khaled the decision,

" ' for Allah commands that it should be so. But if in the course of time this virtuous woman be moved to love, and say to thee, ' Khaled, I love thee,' then at that moment thou shalt receive an immortal soul, and if thy deeds be good thy soul shall enter paradise with the believers ; but if not, thou shalt burn. Thus saith Allah. Thus thou art rewarded, indeed, but wisely and temperately, since thou hast not obtained life directly, but only the hope of life."

The novel, managed in Mr. Crawford's best vein as to accessories and incident, continues to be a skilful variation on the theme of mutual wedded love, what it is and what it is not, and how impossible it is to attain it save by the pure grace of God. " You must love me as I love you, if you would save me from destruction," says Khaled, almost in despair, to the uncomprehending Zehowah:

---

* *Iermola.* By Joseph Ignatius Kraszewski. New York: Dodd & Co.

† *Khaled: A Tale of Arabia.* By F. Marion Crawford. New York and London : Macmillan & Co.

"Death is stronger than man or woman, but love is stronger than death, and all else is but a vision seen in the desert, having no reality."

"I will try to understand it, for I see that you are very unhappy," said Zehowah. She was silent after this, for Khaled's words were earnest and sank into her soul. Yet the more she tried to understand what the passion in him could be like, the less she was able to understand it, for some of Khaled's actions had been foolish, but she supposed that there must have been some wisdom in them, having its foundation in the nature of love.

"What he says is true," she thought; "I married him in order to give my people a just and brave king, and he is both brave and just. And I am certainly a good wife, for I should be dissolved in shame if another man were to see my face; and, moreover, I am careful of his wants, and I take his kefiyeh from his head with my own hands, and smooth the cushions for him, and bring him food and drink when he desires it. Or have I withheld from him any of the treasures of the palace, or stood in the way of his taking another wife? Until to day I thought, indeed, that this talk of love meant but little, and that he spoke of it as an excuse for marrying Almasta, who loves him. But when I said at a venture that he wished to make me jealous, he confessed the truth. Now all the tales of love told by the old women are of young persons who have seen each other from a distance but are hindered from marrying. And we are already married. Surely, it is very hard to understand."

*A Window in Thrums** is not less remarkable for its unlabored pathos and delicate humor than for the masterly selection of salient points and characteristic traits which attest its author's sense of fitness and proportion. It is hardly to be called a story, even though the connecting thread which binds the separate sketches to the personality of Jess is as strong as it is slender. The chapters are thrown together so loosely that their unity, though real, resembles that of the outdoor studies made by a consummate artist in a single locality and a single summer; each of them begun and finished at a sitting, in which the strokes are few, and each stroke tells. The figures stand out with astonishing vividness. Jess, in her kitchen window, studying life through the scanty specimens of humanity which pass up and down the brae, or come to visit her in the cottage she has not left in twenty years; Tammas Haggart, at the pigsty, sitting on an upturned pail, planning a home for impecunious geniuses, or dilating on his calling as a humorist to his admiring neighbors; Gavin Birse, the postman, trying to be off

---

* *A Window in Thrums.* By J. M. Barrie. New York: Cassell Publishing Co.

with the old love before being on with the new ; Jamie, with
the masculine shyness of a small boy, seeking to restrain the
sisterly adoration which makes him the butt of all the other
laddies, and yet unable, through pure softness of heart, totally
to conceal that he is not as indifferent to Leeby as he wishes to
appear ; Hendry, the weaver, upright, dull even where love for
Jess might quicken his comprehension, God-fearing, tender-
hearted—all of them are creations to be remembered.   Gavin's
errand to Mag Lownie, who has been engaged to him a year
or more, is thus narrated to Jess and Hendry by Tammas,
whom the reluctant wooer takes along with him as a witness.
He wanted one, because "if she winna let me aff, weel and
guid ; and if she will, it's better to ha'e a witness in case she
should go back on her word."

"Weel," said Tammas, "aff we goes to Mag's hoose, an
sure enough Mag was in. She was alane, too ; so Gavin, no to
waste time, juist sat doon for politeness' sake, an' syne rises up
again ; an' says he, 'Marget Lownie, I ha'e a solemn question
to speir at ye, namely this, Will you, Marget Lownie, let me,
Gavin Birse, aff ?' "
"Mag would start at that ?"
"Sal, she was braw an' cool. I thocht she maun ha'e got
wind o' his intentions aforehand, for she juist replies, quiet-like,
'Hoo do ye want aff, Gavin ?'
"'Because,' says he, like a book, 'my affections has under-
gone a change.'
"'Ye mean Jean Luke,' says Mag.
"'That is wha I mean,' says Gavin, very straightforrard.
"But she didna let him aff, did she ?"
"Na, she wasna the kind. Says she, 'I wonder to hear
ye, Gavin, but 'am no goin' to agree to naething o' that
sort.'
"'Think it ower,' says Gavin.
"'Na, my mind's made up,' says she.
"'Ye would sune get anither man,' he says earnestly.
"'Hoo do I ken that ?' she speirs, rale sensibly, I thocht, for
men's no sae easy to get.
"''Am sure o't,' Gavin says, with michty conviction in his
voice, 'for ye're bonny to look at, an' weel-kent for bein' a
guid body.'
"'Ay,' says Mag, 'I'm glad ye like me, Gavin, for ye have
to tak' me.' "
"That put a clincher on him," interrupted Hendry.
"He was loth to gi'e in," replied Tammas, "so he says,
'Ye think 'am a fine character, Marget Lownie, but ye're very
far mista'en. I wouldna wonder but what I was lossin' my place

some o' thae days, an' syne whaur would ye be? Marget
Lownie,' he goes on, '' 'am nat'rally lazy an' fond o' the drink.
As sure as ye stand there, 'am a reg'lar deevil!'

"That was strong language," said Hendry, "but he would
be wantin' to fleg [frighten] her."

"Juist so, but he didna manage 't, for Mag says, 'We a' ha'e
oor faults, Gavin, an' deevil or no deevil, ye're the man for me!'

"Gavin thocht a bit," continued Tammas, "an' syne he tries
her on a new tack. 'Marget Lownie,' he says, 'ye're father's an
auld man noo, an' he has naebody but yersel' to look after him.
I'm thinkin' it would be kind o' cruel o' me to tak ye awa' frae
him.'"

"Mag wouldna be ta'en in wi' that; she wasna born on a
Sawbath," said Jess, using one of her favorite sayings.

"She wasna," answered Tammas. "Says she, 'Hae nae fear
on that score, Gavin; my father's fine willin' to spare me.'"

"An' that ended it?"

"Ay, that ended it."

"Did ye tak' it doon in writin'?" asked Hendry.

"There was nae need," said Tammas, handing round his
snuff-mull. "No, I never touched paper. When I saw the
thing was settled, I left them to their coortin'. They're to tak'
a look at Snecky Hobart's auld hoose the nicht. It's to let."

Mr. Keenan's new novel * is a long and not uninteresting tale
of the civil war. Lincoln, Sherman, Stanton, President Davis
and his wife flit in and out of its pages, though none of them
can be said to contribute greatly to its action. It deals with
various battles in much detail, but intersperses war with love-
making which crosses Mason and Dixon's line without a with
your leave or by your leave. The conversations between the
various pairs of lovers take usually a sprightly, not to say epigrammatic turn, which suggests the footlights and the soubrette's
cap and jaunty apron.

Mr. Grant Allen has just been repeating, in _The Fortnightly_,
his old complaint against the restrictions imposed on British
authors by the dense stupidity and commonplace morality of the
British public. An Englishman, according to Mr. Allen, though
desiring in his heart of hearts such a world-wide fame as the
Kreutzer Sonata procured for Tolstoï, finds himself cabined, cribbed,
confined by the demands of the home public, and the fact that
his bread and butter depend on them alone. No hope of translation into foreign tongues awaits him, for none but English-
speaking people read English books—they are quite too tame for
the Continental palate. So says Mr. Allen, forgetting, per-

* _The Iron Game._ By Henry F. Keenan. New York: D. Appleton & Co.

haps, that Mr. George Moore's venture into the unmentionable lands whither the patrons of Mudie decline to be taken, gained no more extensive foreign repute than his own.   Mr. Allen feels that he would like to be free to say " all that is in him," and to see his brother novelists likewise set free.   An expert in novels or in popularized science—the two branches of literature which Mr. Allen most affects—would, we fear, be apt to conclude from the specimens given that enough is even better than a feast where his work is concerned.   He is nothing if not sensational in his tale *What's Bred in the Bone*,* where he harps on the note of heredity, although something—the influence of his British environment, one must suppose—makes him keep carefully within the limits against whose pressure he protests in *The Fortnightly*.   The heroine, though an English girl, is descended in a direct line from a " mesmeric sorceress who belonged to some tribe of far-Eastern serpent-charmers."   This ancestress married an Englishman in George the Second's time, after having been duly baptized, and became the mother of a large family, the women of which have continued to transmit to their daughters a marvellous intuition and a propensity to the Eastern snake-dance which, soon or late, breaks out unexpectedly in every one of them.   It generally defers its appearance until the first time they fall in love or see a live snake.   How Elma careered around her bed-room with a feather boa in her hand, in lieu of a snake, when her time came, and how shocked and alarmed she was, not knowing what had befallen her, and how her will finally conquered her propensity and allowed her to marry with a good conscience, those readers who desire to know must learn from the book itself.

The recent death of Madame Craven has called forth a beautiful tribute to her memory, from the pen of her friend the Vicomte de Meaux.†   It is not in the nature of a biographical sketch, which, indeed, had long ago been made in a manner unnecessary by such matters of personal history as were included by Madame Craven in her first and most famous work, *Le Récit d'une Sœur*.   All the world, one might say, became her intimate friends on the publication of that volume.   She wrote it when she was nearly sixty, and it is now in its forty-second French edition, besides having achieved a wide reputation in the admirable English translation of Miss Emily Bowles.   Beginning a

---

* *What's Bred in the Bone.*   By Grant Allen.   Boston: B. R. Tucker.
† *Madame Craven, née La Ferronnays.*   Par le Vicomte de Meaux.   Paris: Librairie Académique Didier.   Perrin et Cie.

literary career so late in life, she afterwards produced some fourteen or fifteen other works, some of them biographical, others
fictitious, but all having the same great motive, of inciting souls
to the love of God, which had first induced her to make what
must have been the painful effort of unveiling to the world the
inner lives of those she had held most dear. The Vicomte de
Meaux says that on his return from the Catholic Congress held
at Baltimore in 1889, he was able to tell Madame Craven that
she was the European author whom he had heard most frequently spoken of on this side of the water, and concerning
whom he had been questioned with the most interested and
affectionate regard. One can easily believe that who, like the
present writer, owes to her inimitable first volume the most
powerful external impetus determining the end of an old life and
the beginning of a new one. None of her succeeding volumes
have reached so wide a circle of readers, although *Fleurange*, the
best of her novels, has passed already into a twenty-eighth
edition, and, like the *Récit d'une Sœur*, has been crowned by
the French Academy.

Madame Craven reached the very advanced age of eighty-
two, and even then, says the Vicomte de Meaux, her death
seemed premature. At eighty-odd she was still youthful. But
her last illness, which lasted nearly a year, was at first marked
by a sort of aphasia, which soon passed into an absolute impossibility either to speak or write, while still leaving her hearing
and her intelligence untouched. It was plain that her affections
outlived all else, but the exchange of ideas, and the distinct
manifestation of her will and her desires, was thenceforward forbidden to her. Only at the very end, when she was apprised
that the last sacraments were about to be administered, the soft
groan which had become habitual on her lips, changed into a
sort of joyful cry. "When the Sacred Host was brought to her,"
says the Vicomte de Meaux, "her poor body, already almost
entirely inert, was seen to make an effort to rise, and her eyes
burned with a final glow. All was ended for her. A few hours
later, peacefully and without a struggle, she rejoined in the
bosom of God those good and charming beings whose history
she had written and whose memory she had made immortal."
She had survived all of her own generation, and had never borne
a child. But her nephew, Count Albert de Mun, son of that
dear sister Eugénie who had been most near of all to Madame
Craven's heart, still carries on most nobly the traditions of a
noble and God-fearing race.

Mr. Hamilton W. Mabie's essays* on various aspects of nature, reprinted from the *Christian Union*, in which they have been appearing during the last four years, are very pleasant reading. They are not particularly suggestive, it is true; but though they do not quicken thought, they present some agreeable pictures of out-door life as it affects one in a dreamy, semi-reflective mood. Mr. Mabie's prose is almost musical at times.   Accompanying this volume comes, from the same publishers, another † which Mr. Mabie prefaces in a manner to persuade one that he would be a more trustworthy guide out-of-doors than in the library for people whose tastes have not been conventionalized.   To us, at least, it seems as if no one who really knew and heartily loved his Shakspeare could be otherwise than bored, not to say disgusted, with Landor's *Citation*.   So that when we are told, as in this introduction, that "there is nothing in English which surpasses it in the quality of pure literature," and that it is a "transcription of life . . . so perfect of its kind . . . that we are reminded of the lavish and richly colored life of Egypt in ' Antony and Cleopatra,' and of the large simplicity and massive form of Roman life in 'Julius Cæsar,'" our interest in Mr. Mabie as an appraiser of literary values is extinguished once for all.

There is some excellent work in Miss Jewett's new volume,‡ and none that is not very good.   "In Dark New England Days" there is a certain weird, half-tragic force very simply attained, as most fine touches doubtless are. ."The Luck of the Bogans" is also very sympathetically told.   As a painter of New England life Miss Jewett is more subjective, more obviously reflective than her great rival in that field, Miss Wilkins.   But though her stories have not the crisp alertness and unavoidably contagious sense of humor which distinguishes the work of the author of *Sister Liddy*, they are, and possibly for that very reason, not less veracious as transcripts of ordinary New England life.   Miss Jewett's style is very charming.

* *Under the Trees.* By Hamilton W. Mabie. New York: Dodd, Mead & Co.
    † *Citation and Examination of William Shakspeare.* By Walter Savage Landor. New York: Dodd, Mead & Co.
    ‡ *Strangers and Wayfarers.* By Sarah Orne Jewett. New York and Boston: Houghton, Mifflin & Co.

I.—A CHRISTIAN APOLOGY.*

The translators of this admirable work are entitled to our warmest praise and thanks for the most opportune and useful task which they have undertaken and partly fulfilled. We are sadly lacking in original works in the very necessary branch of Apologetics in the English language. Those who might be capable of producing them are deterred by the great cost of publication, which publishers are unwilling to assume, having so little prospect of a sufficient sale even to defray their expenses, let alone making a reasonable profit. In Germany, on the contrary, the most solid and learned works, in this and other branches of sacred science, are continually appearing. Some of these—for instance, the works of Hettinger and Scheeben—have been translated and published in England, and there are others which it would be most desirable to have translated. This is being done for Dr. Schanz's Apology by English ecclesiastics, although it is issued by an American publisher. It is a work of extensive and thorough learning, especially in scientific and historical branches. It is not so strong in the metaphysical portion as in its other parts. The first volume embraces topics of religious history, biology, psychology, anthropology, natural theology, cosmology, the unity and antiquity of the human race, etc., under the general heading of " God and Nature." The second volume, the translation of which is now due, embraces under the general head of " God and Revelation " topics in the comparative history of religion, the origin and credibility of Christianity, Prophecy, Miracles, the Bible, and Christology. The third volume embraces the principal topics which fall under the general heading of " Christ and the Church," concluding with the Papacy and the relation between Christianity and general culture.

The author's style is very condensed, sometimes obscure, and evidently has presented great difficulties to the translators. The translation is very literal, too much so, in fact, usually correct, and sufficiently clear to make the sense intelligible. Nevertheless, it is sometimes more obscure than the original, often awkward, and showing marks of haste and oversight, which have led even to singular mistranslations, unless these are merely errors of the press. On page 437 we read that " Rambouillet has lately been vigorously belaboring the now defunct Motais, and he bids

* *A Christian Apology.* By Paul Schanz, D.D., D.Ph., Professor of Theology at the University of Tübingen. Translated by Rev. Michael F. Glancey and Rev. Victor J. Schobel, D.D. In three volumes. Vol. I., " God and Nature." New York and Cincinnati : Pustet & Co.

fair to continue the fight. He strenuously maintains that, according to Moses, the Cainites had long since gone forth from the land of Nod, etc." Now, this is the very thing that Motais maintained, and in the original we find that the word translated "maintains" is "bestreitet," which signifies "combats"; " er sucht vor allem zu *bestreiten,* dass Moses das Geschlecht Kains schon frühzeitig aus dem Lande Nod aufbrechen lasse" (p. 353).

The author has been criticised as falling short of the common doctrine of theologians on the guarantee of inspiration against all error in matters not pertaining to faith or morals. The translators have appended a cautionary note to a passage on page 367. Those who have not read the whole work in the original German will be better able to understand the views of Dr. Schanz when the translation of the second volume appears. It contains an entire chapter on Inspiration, from which we quote one passage: "Was aber den *Umfang* der Inspiration betrifft, so ist daran fest zu halten, dass die ganze Heilige Schrift das Wort Gottes enthält, aber doch nicht alle Theile in gleich unmittelbarer Weise. Jedenfalls ist für alle Theile als Minimum die *Irrthumslosigkeit* zu fordern, welche nur aus göttlichem Beistand und göttlicher Einwirkung zu erklären ist" (p. 343). In respect to the *extent* of inspiration, it must be firmly held that the entire Holy Scripture contains the Word of God, yet not, however, all parts in an equally immediate manner. In every instance, for all parts, the very least which must be exacted is *inerrancy,* which is only to be explained by divine assistance and divine influence.

The mechanical execution of the volume might pass muster were it not for the faintness of the impression.

2.—OUR COMMON BIRDS AND HOW TO KNOW THEM.*

On the farther side of the Harlem River, within easy reach by drive or walk, are some of the most charming woodlands imaginable. Along the Bronx, within a stone's throw of Fordham College, are dells and woods so exceedingly beautiful as to enchant one into long rambles and day-dreams and wild-flower gatherings and pencil sketching. During a recent ramble there we came across a great strapping, manly fellow wearing the uniform of St. John's cadets, sketching with an enthusiasm worthy of a true lover of nature. Not only may one find "woodlands wild" and the

* *Our Common Birds and How to Know Them.* By John B. Grant. With sixty-four plates. New York: Charles Scribner's Sons.

sweet perfumes that come from those humble little flowers, but also the wondrous variety of sound ; and, sweetest far, the songs of a thousand birds as they flit and glint midst the dank bowers of the spring woods.   And all this not more than one hour's ride from where we write here in the very heart of this great dusty, harsh-sounding, albeit attractive city of New York.   Those of us who are country bred and born, but who are now shut up amidst walls of stone and brick, with only a peep at nature now and then in the park, have a keener relish, I fancy, for things of na-ture than others.   Therefore we welcome Mr. Grant's book most heartily.   It is no uncommon book, though the author is very modest in his claim, as is shown by the very first line of his introduction.   However, Mr. Grant is an ornithologist of no mean ability.   His introduction tells you something about the book, his authorities, and a hint of method of bird study, and the region of his observation : " The birds which have come under the author's own observation, and whose habits are here recorded, were seen on Long Island, near Flushing, and at various points upon the Hudson between New York City and Peekskill."   Then follows the essay, " Our Common Birds and How to Know Them," well written, full of information, a practical lesson on how, where, and when to study the subject, very valuable to a lover of birds who desires to know some-thing more of them than mere unenlightened observation will give him.   The plates are beautiful illustrations, each accompanied by a descriptive text.   The plate of the blue jay—that winter dandy, a veritable Beau Brummell among birds—is wonderfully life-like. We do not agree with what the author says of the cat-bird.   Our own observation of this nightingale of the North leads us to think that it is not true to say that it has " skulking habits."   It may be, however, that our poetical friends of the honeysuckle bush—they nested there in our youthful days—were better bred than most cat-birds.   Has Mr. Grant ever seen the work of Dr. Howard Jones, of Circleville, Ohio—*Birds of Ohio and Their Nests ?*   When a book is limited to one hundred copies, and each copy costing $150—it can-not now be obtained for less than $300 a copy, we believe—every one does not get to see it.   Mr. Grant should see it, however.   *Our Common Birds and How to Know Them* is more accessible, and hence really more valuable.   Its index is copious, the price modest, its English excellent.

3.—MEDITATIONS ON THE GOSPELS.*

The general plan of these excellent meditations is that the Gospel of each Sunday furnishes the matter for the whole week. There is an appendix with meditations on special feasts of the saints. We have any number of books of meditations, from all of which some profit may doubtless be gained, but there are few that can be highly commended. Extravagant, high flown language, strained interpretations of Scripture; sentences which sound well but mean little practically; repetition of ideas in different words, are common faults, all of which are absent in the book before us. It combines brevity with great suggestiveness. Each sentence is in its right place and furnishes abundant material for thought, and there is a logical connection between each part of the meditation. We are happy, therefore, to recommend this practical, common-sense book of meditations.

4.—THE CENTENARY LIFE OF ST. ALOYSIUS.†

We trust we are not too late in congratulating the professor and students of the Rhetoric Class of '92 of St. Francis Xavier's College on their production of the *Life of St. Aloysius Gonzaga*. In a work of this kind, written by boys under nineteen, one would naturally expect to find bombast of language and crudity of thought. But such is not the case here. There is a gentle modesty and simplicity pervading the whole book which gives it a peculiar charm. We are told that almost ten thousand copies have been sold—surely a success unparalleled in devotional literature. It is not often that an ascetic book reaches its eighth edition within a few weeks—nor is it often that an ascetic book can have appreciative and laudatory criticism from secular papers such as the New York *Sun, Herald,* and *Recorder.* The modern young man, whose chief ambition is a life of luxury, can draw much profit from reading this little book.

5.—THE AGES OF FAITH.‡

Two years ago we praised the former volumes of this beautiful publication of Kenelm Digby's great work. What we said

---

* *Meditations on the Gospels for Every Day in the Year.* By Père Médaille, S.J. Translated into English under the direction of the Rev. W. H. Eyre, S.J. London: Burns & Oates, Limited; New York: The Catholic Publication Society Co.

† *Life of St. Aloysius Gonzaga.* Edited by Rev. J. F. X. O'Conor, S.J. New York: St. Francis Xavier's College.

‡ *Mores Catholici; or, Ages of Faith.* By Kenelm H. Digby. Vol. III. New York: P. O'Shea.

then we now reiterate concerning the third volume. Certainly
Mr. O'Shea's enterprise should receive ready support from the
public, so that the forthcoming volumes may soon be at hand.
We will quote the closing paragraph of the third volume: "The
monks and friars have conducted us to the threshold of those
true asylums of peace, of which, in the beginning, I said that
we should speak, where souls through powers that faith bestowed
won rest and ease and peace, with bliss that angels shared.
Our course tends unto the summit. 'On to the abbey!' as the
poet says. Already we have met the men who come from it,
whose strains still sound to us like the sweet south wind that
breathes upon a bank of violets: but no more yet of this; for
'tis a chronicle of day by day, not a relation for a visit, nor befitting this late meeting. Here will we repose and wait till the
morn, in golden mantle clad, shall walk o'er the dew of yon
bright eastern hill. So that, gentle reader, with respect to the
peace enjoyed and imparted during faithful ages, half yet remains unsaid."

6.—BELLS OF THE SANCTUARY.*

Catholic literature sustained a real loss in the sudden death
of Kathleen O'Meara in 1888, in the full maturity of the noble
career she had chosen, and to which she gave the full bent of a
pious and highly cultivated intelligence.

The life of the holy priest De Segur, and that of the saintly
Madame Legros, foundress and first novice mistress of the Sisters
of Charity, compose the third of the series of publications entitled *Bells of the Sanctuary*, and are the last bequest to us of
the gifted author. These lives are given in a clear, concise style,
are of intense interest, and have received the warm commendation of Cardinal Manning, who thus sums up the life of De Segur: "The life of Monseigneur Gaston De Segur is one of heroic patience, zeal, and piety, under an affliction which would
have crushed any soul which was not sustained, hour after hour,
by continual union with God. For six-and-twenty years he persevered in preaching and hearing confessions of students, soldiers,
working-men, and of the poor, daily and without intermission, in
total blindness."

His youth was innocent in the world; endowed with all social
gifts and great artistic powers, beloved by kindred and friends.

* *The Blind Apostle* and *A Heroine of Charity*. Third series of "Bells of the Sanctuary."
By Kathleen O'Meara. London: Burns & Oates; New York: The Catholic Publication
Society Co.

He began life in diplomacy; gave up all to become a priest; was sent to Rome by the imperial government in France, in an office of great distinction, with an open and certain ecclesiastical career, almost promised, before him; but in one day and in a moment one eye became absolutely sightless. The other soon began to fail. He returned to France, and shortly after, while walking with his brother, he suddenly said "I am blind." The other eye was also dark. Then begn a life truly heroic. To console his mother he went to Tours, to Lourdes, to Ars, if haply he might miraculously regain his sight. But he had made an absolute submission of his will to the will of God, and asked nothing but patience. For in his first Mass as a priest he had begged of our Blessed Mother whatsoever grace he needed most, and he believed that this affliction was the answer to his prayer.

Patience he had, and much need of it, not alone because he was blind, but in regard to the sufferings he endured from the spiritual blindness of those with whom he came in contact. To De Segur was granted what Gabriel Malagrida and other saints have beautifully called "the supreme happiness of the supreme ignominy." Which, being explained, is not only to be persecuted by the enemies of God, but by God's own servants; to be misinterpreted, misunderstood, and reviled, even by "the ministers of the Temple." In the midst of the untold good De Segur was doing for God's poor, at the very time when his life was threatened by the Freemasons of France, the holy priest, misinterpreted, misunderstood, and reviled, was suspended by the Archbishop of Paris. How gloriously God righted this holy man Miss O'Meara has well told.

The life of Madame Legros was truly heroic in devotion and celestial in wisdom. It was her wisdom that St. Vincent de Paul spoke of when he described her work. "Your convent," he said, "will be the house of the sick; your cell, a hired room; your chapel, the parish church; your cloister, the streets of the city or the wards of the hospital; your enclosure, obedience; your grating, the fear of God; your veil, holy modesty." The Sisters of Charity, who fill the world and are revered by all, are the reflection of her mind and example.

The book is well printed on tinted paper and is tastefully bound.

7.—THE VENERABLE MADELEINE BARAT.*

The object of this volume is to present to Catholics a cheaper and more popular history of the servant of God, the venerable Mother Barat, than the voluminous one translated from the French of the Abbé Baunard some years ago, and, while thus bringing it within the reach of a greater number of readers, to spread more widely the knowledge of her virtues and the lesson of her life. Mother Barat's virtues were many, no one of them more conspicuous than her deep humility. It was her profound humility which led to her great achievements; and if God gives us grace to build in the least measure on the same foundation we may hope to accomplish something towards the same end. Lady Fullerton asks, "Who was ever more simply humble, than Mother Barat?" and answers in the record of a life that not alone preserved its humility but as well the perfect simplicity which is the delicate bloom of that heavenly virtue.

Mother Barat felt deeply that we want saints in what is called society as well as amongst the poor. "Be apostles, my children," she said, as much to the young brides of the Faubourg St. Germain as to the nuns she sent to the shores of the Mississippi; and, indeed, it is true that were there more saints among the rich there would soon be but few poor. We regret to say that the publisher's part of this book is anything but well done.

* *The Life of the Venerable Madeleine Barat, Foundress of the Society of the Sacred Heart o Jesus.* From the French, by Lady Georgiana Fullerton. New York: P. O'Shea.

THE COLUMBIAN READING UNION.

ALL COMMUNICATIONS RELATING TO READING CIRCLES, LISTS OF BOOKS, ETC., SHOULD BE ADDRESSED TO THE COLUMBIAN READING UNION, NO. 415 WEST FIFTY-NINTH STREET, NEW YORK CITY.

Catholic authors are watching with interest the progress of the movement initiated by the Columbian Reading. Union. The letters from them printed in THE CATHOLIC WORLD have been eagerly read and discussed in various Reading Circles. We again renew our request that authors will kindly send to us any suggestion which may assist in the diffusion of Catholic literature. In the catalogue of Messrs. Houghton, Mifflin & Co., of Boston, we find eighteen books by Catholic authors. Six of, the number are from the pen of the well-known writer whose. name is signed to this letter :

"It is cheering to know that we are to have a complete list. of Catholic authors of our vernacular. There never was a time. when a solidarity of our literature was more needed than the present. A vast and ever increasing mass of printed matter is before the people, and infiltrates through all the homes of this nation. Much of it is pernicious, and of a nature to confuse the understanding as to what is true. It rises before us like some tower of Babel, seemingly pointing skyward, but in reality a fabric of error. How good and useful, then, to have a safe guide to point the way : how valuable for those who read, and how inspiriting for those who write.

"The literature of a country should be two-fold in its scope : it should not only be the exponent of the best thought of the age, but it should *lead* this thought to highest aims. Authors are the chosen intellectual standard-bearers. The public should follow those whose motto is 'Excelsior,' and turn away from low pessimistic realism. Yet how to know where to turn has been a perplexing question. Your careful labors will assist to dispel uncertainty. They will give light where light is needed, and future generations will profit thereby.

"MADELEINE VINTON DAHLGREN.

" Washington, D. C "

*　　　　　*　　　　　*

We gladly accept the offer of assistance contained in the following letter from Cork :

"For well-nigh forty years I have been an ardent reader, especially of Catholic literature ; have chiefly formed the library of the Catholic Young Men's Society here, and have collected a considerable number of volumes for my own use, perhaps a. thousand..

"While engaged in the pleasing duty of collecting donations of books for the reconstruction of our library about this time last year, I sent for a copy of a publication which, no doubt, would be of great use to your Reading Union: *A Catalogue of Books presented to His Holiness Pope Leo XIII. by the Catholics of Great Britain on the occasion of his Jubilee*, 1887; and inside a further title is: 'Papal Jubilee Library: A collection of books written or published by Catholics born or living in England during the years 1837–87. Presented to the Sovereign Pontiff Leo the Thirteenth on the occasion of his Golden Jubilee, December 31, 1887.' Should you desire to get a copy of this book and find that it is out of print, my copy would be most cheerfully placed at your service.

"My writing now is not entirely from a disinterested motive. Reading your articles in THE CATHOLIC WORLD entices me to ask for membership, provided that one so far removed as I am could benefit by membership. I would earnestly ask to be sent a copy of *Books and Reading*, by Brother Azarias, also a copy of the list of his works which you have published. For our young men's reading-room I should also ask to be furnished with any reports you publish, rules for your reading classes or other study movements.

"I think, from the books which I have collected for my own use, I may be able to somewhat assist your Union in its noble objects of encouraging the reading of Catholic works and enlarg· ing the scope of Catholic literature generally.

"THOMAS H. ATTRIDGE.

" *Cork, Ireland.*"

Under the guidance of the Very Rev. Canon Sheehan, Mr. Thomas H. Attridge, and others a library has been formed for the use of the Cork Young Men's Society. Its objects are well stated in this appeal:

"Much has been said of the want in Cork of the first requisite of intellectual progress—a good popular library. That want is now, at least partially, supplied. There is not an institution in the kingdom that we know of which offers as good ·a library on such terms and with such facility as the Cork Young Men's Society now presents to its members. There are not, perhaps, a dozen men in Cork who possess, except as subscribers to the comparatively expensive public libraries, such a collection of books as that of which every member of the Young Men's Society may now be master.

"Come then, brothers; whoso feels the noble ambition to know truly and think rightly throbbing at his heart, making his young blood bound, or preserving in age the vivacity of youth, let him avail of advantages such as he never had before. Whoso is resolved not to be a mere clod of the valley, or a mere imple- ment of commerce, let him come. Whoso would glance back through the world of the past, or look abroad upon the world of the present, or peer out into the world of the future, let him come. Let those come who would train their own minds for the rough practical contest with the world; who would not lose some of the greatest pleasures and advantages of life; who would not expose themselves unprotected to some of its greatest dangers. Let those come who would learn the great sciences, know the great deeds, grasp the thoughts, or listen to the sweet songs of our own time and of other days.

" Let us not leave refinement and cultivation of mind to those who call themselves our ' betters.' We have as good a right to enjoy and use the advantages of literature as any man in this land. Let us be convinced that any station is rendered noble and beautiful when its duties are performed and its opportunities are availed of; but self-indulgence, recklessness, and ignorance, these are in every station vulgar, disgusting, and deplorable. A scholar is a scholar, in purple or in rags; a clown is a clown, whether he wears a tradesman's cap or a duke's coronet."

"The character of the library is as good and as varied as the limited means of the society permit. Some of the departments, however, are almost empty, most of them are imperfect. It is for the members themselves, and those who think with them and those who would help the cause of religion and education amongst us, to say whether it shall so continue. Valuable books are mouldering in half the houses of Cork which would be of rich utility in the Young Men's Society. Persons die every week letting their libraries be sold or scattered, who by bequeathing them to the society would really promote God's glory and man's salvation. This should not be. But it is on the efforts of members themselves that most reliance should be placed.   .   .   .

" The circulation of good books is an obvious benefit. It is enforced not only by experience but by the most influential authority of the present time. In fact, every one who observes with attention the condition of the people and the signs of the times becomes alarmingly conscious that the spread of irreligious and immoral publications is just the one danger that society has now most to fear, and that we cannot hope practically to meet that danger unless we are prepared to supplant these publications by good ones. The licentious novel, the Protestant or infidel newspaper, the brilliant, self-assured, but false and foolish essay—these are the devil's weapons now; and as there is a change in the policy of evil, so there must be a change in the policy of good. Let us look to it while it is yet time. Man is no machine— never believe it. His hand is obedient to his head and heart: but these are ruled by ideas; and if you have allowed the insidious voice of error to beguile the one, and the fatal fascination of sin to seize upon the other, then you have allowed a man to be transformed into a demon; and if you let this go on, nothing is safe; law, property, life, honor, religion—all will sooner or later perish."

A representative of the Pacific Coast Women's Press Association informs us that its scope is broader than that of any other press association in the United States. Its very commendable purpose is to educate the younger members of the association, and to give to all the members practical assistance in their work. Books written by members are well advertised; readers and lecturers are secured a hearing before the best-known newspaper representatives; a circulating library and other means of self-improvement are to be supplied with earnest good-will and a deep spirit of helpfulness. As many of the members are Catholics, we may look to this Press Association for some of our future Catholic authors. The Pacific Coast has a climate very favorable for literary work.

* * *

Some of the members of our Reading Circles, gifted with a talent for writing, will be interested to know that the Pacific Coast Literary Bureau, 1419 Taylor Street, San Francisco, Cal., is prepared to take charge of the reading and criticism of all kinds of manuscript; and to revise for publication short stories, novels, poems, etc. The manager is Mrs. Emelie Tracy Y. Parkhurst.

We have received the following list of Pacific Coast Catholic writers: Charles Anthony Doyle, Sister Anna Rafael, Marcella Fitzgerald, Elizabeth Hogan, Elodie Hogan, W. S. Green, Emilie Tracy Y. Parkhurst, Mary Lambert, Teresa I. Talbot Condon, Agnes Manning, Carrie Stevens Walter, Harriet Skidmore, Kate Nesfield, Rose O'Halloran, Charles Warren Stoddard, Daniel O'Connell, R. E. White, and Rev. Father Crowley.

* * *

Since the publication of the list of Catholic authors in the January (1891) CATHOLIC WORLD a number of additional names have been sent to us from various places. Names only will not give us the desired information. Concerning such Catholic authors we wish to know: (1) the titles of books, (2) the names of publishers, (3) an indication of which books are now for sale. We would like to have our complete list of authors thoroughly reliable as a guide to book-buyers and for reference use in libraries. Though the task of arranging the data at our disposal is very tedious, we hope to get it completed during the summer months.

* * *

The missionary work to be done by Catholic literature is too often forgotten. In a Western State eight Catholic books of standard merit, though some of them are repulsively printed, have been read by a "would-be convert." He has made a good selection to start with, and if he will write again stating his difficulties, we shall cheerfully suggest a further course of reading. His letter is as follows :

"I have read *Faith of Our Fathers*, by Cardinal Gibbons ; and *Plain Talk*, by Segur; have managed to borrow a catechism; *Think Well On't* and *Catholic Christian Instructed*, by Challoner; *Papist Misrepresented*, by Gother ; Cobbett's *Protestant Reformation*, and the *Mission Book*. If these books are not quite suitable I am willing to purchase anything you specially recommend to be read. I am a would-be convert, a school teacher, and have just received an eye-opener and am anxious for more knowledge. There is no Catholic church nearer than seventy-five miles. I have never seen the priest, and no members in this vicinity have yet entered on their Easter duties. I am anxious to gain the greatest possible knowledge without reading the same over and over in different books, and to save time and expense; and then turn colporteur. Was about to sell Alden's *Manifold Cyclopedia*, but found it endorsed only by Protestants, and wanted to secure the full set of volumes before I became interested in Roman Catholicity. Can you please recommend a cyclopædia from Catholic origin which is more truthful and superior to Alden's *Manifold*?"

*   *   *

On Catholic subjects especially there is no cyclopædia more trustworthy than Appletons'. Two prominent Catholic writers, Rev. Bernard O'Reilly, D.D., and John Gilmary Shea, LL.D., were employed on the staff of revisers, while the list of contributors contains the names of several eminent Catholic scholars. Cardinal Gibbons gave his opinion of the work in these words :

"For the American reader and student I regard *Appletons' American Encyclopædia* as by far the best work of the kind that we have, and I cordially commend it to all as being just and fairly accurate in the vast amount of information it furnishes.

"J. CARDINAL GIBBONS.

"Baltimore, January 31, 1889."

*   *   *

A writer in the Michigan *Catholic* has given this favorable opinion of the Columbian Reading Union :

"For the last three years New York has been the head centre of the crusade in favor of Catholic literature. THE CATHOLIC WORLD has been there doing the laborious preparatory work. It has searched catalogues of publishers, consulted bibliographies, prepared courses of reading, and by its enthusiastic devotion it has succeeded in arousing the interest of every thinking reader in a cause so pregnant with the happiest effects. Ever since it came into existence this magazine has played a conspicuous part in defending and advancing the cause of Catholic education. We think the patient industry expended on its Columbian Reading Union will not be the least fruitful of its labors. Moreover, there is nothing selfish or narrow about the men who make this magazine. They are the first to hail the coming of the Catholic Reading Circle Review and to recommend it to American readers. This spirit of co-operation among the leaders will be a valuable example for all the promoters of the work. We must all work with zealous and united effort. The spread of Catholic thought, the knowledge of a long maligned, long misunderstood church and people is the great missionary work of the day. And every Catholic from the Pope to the peasant can do his part. In union there is strength. If we work with earnest and united effort success is sure to follow.—CLERUS."

* * *

The editor of the *Northwestern Chronicle*, Rev. John Conway, kindly endorses our work in very complimentary terms:

" Our readers in the cities of St. Paul and Minneapolis know of many excellent local literary societies. The societies in these two cities are doing very good work, but there is room for more of them. The Columbian Reading Union, whose headquarters is in New York, is setting a good example to the whole country. Its object is to promote the study of Catholic literature. How well it is succeeding may be gathered from the various reports of the different reading clubs which it has influenced. If the Union did no more than to prepare the long list of Catholic authors published in THE CATHOLIC WORLD, even this work entitles it to great praise. The list is restricted to those authors whose writings have appeared in English. Though by no means complete, it is a long and an honorable one, covering almost every field of literature. There are names in it which many people took for granted belonged to others than Catholics, although there was no reason why they should. The Catholic reader has a grand list from which to choose, and he is a mere snob and nothing more in literature who will not see merit in many of these writers. Those who note the trend of readers remark that some Catholics take a certain pride in stating that they never read a Catholic book. If these people were catalogued their place in the world of literature would be similar to the social position of those Catholics who boast that they never associate with their fellow-Catholics The former are intellectual nonentities ; the latter are the objects of secret contempt, concealed only through politeness. The Columbian Reading Union is doing a great deal to establish a healthy state of literature among Catholics. We wish it every success."

We hope that these words of encouragement will urge the members and friends of the Columbian Reading Union to renewed activity in assisting us to complete speedily our list of Catholic authors. M. C. M.

WITH THE PUBLISHER.

———

AMONG the many letters of good cheer which greeted the Publisher during the past month, and which are unhappily too numerous and often too lengthy to quote, there was one from which an extract will be opportune for the Publisher's text this month :

"Returning to ———— after an absence of seven months in Europe, I am glad to see the admirable change in THE CATH-OLIC WORLD, which has been welcomed in our house for many years—since April, 1865. Accept our congratulations, not only for the fine appearance of the magazine but for the excellent standard it has so long maintained."

* * *

This, my dear reader, is not a good month in which to call upon your enthusiasm for any kind of literature. You care for little else than to keep cool. Business is dull, vacation is at hand, you are fagged out with hard work perhaps, and you feel that your mind is unequal to anything heavier than a light diet of fiction. But the Publisher thinks it is just the time to tell you of his plans for the future; and he hopes, indeed he feels sure, that he has your attention and your interest.

* * *

For of course you have said "Amen" to the congratulations of his correspondent. You not only agree with what has been said of the magazine, but it is not unlikely that you think you would put it stronger. Of course you would, and of course you will when you send the next renewal of your subscription. Don't forget it, please, and in the meantime rehearse it frequently for the benefit of your immediate acquaintance. You know it is a fine magazine, that no effort is spared to make it such, that it has qualities which make it compare favorably with the best of its contemporaries. Don't be afraid to give these good qualities an equally good airing. You can't give the magazine and its aims too much publicity. It is in just such soil that it will thrive.

* * *

You may learn something of enthusiasm in this respect from

a few sentences taken at random from two letters received by the Publisher from readers of the magazine who are not Catholics. The first is from a gentleman who holds a prominent position in public life, and whose name is known and honored throughout the land : "I enclose my check for $4 for the coming year's subscription to THE CATHOLIC WORLD. Some one has been kind enough to send it to me. Although I am not a Catholic, I find it such manly, Christian reading that I am glad to pay for it." Another writes : "I always welcome it *first* among all the regular periodicals I receive, and though I am a Protestant I always recommend it to my friends."

If every reader of the magazine had something of this enthusiasm and put it into such practical shape it would speedily be felt in the right way at the Publisher's desk. I know the Publisher has said all this before, but he cannot say it too often. He has undertaken a number of plans which look to the improvement of the magazine, to the enlargement of the sphere of its usefulness. And he expects your support; he has counted on it in all that he has undertaken, and he feels that he will have no use for the word disappointment.

And what has the Publisher been doing? Well, he has been planning on a large scale—on so large a scale, indeed, that there are some folks who call him an optimist, a word which can be interpreted according to the taste and fancy of the interpreter. And he made the first step towards the realization of these plans when he plunged into debt and began the erection of a large building which will be used for the publication of THE CATHOLIC WORLD, and for spreading the Gospel generally through the medium of printer's ink. This building is now almost completed ; machinery, presses, and type have been purchased ; and he hopes it will not be long before the magazine will be printed, bound, and mailed from its new home and under his own supervision. The added control he thus obtains over every department of the magazine will enable him the more readily to adopt every new plan to make it better and stronger and more widely read.

All this is the result of months of thought and labor, and involves the expenditure of many thousands of dollars. It has been done with confidence in its ultimate success. It is done for the cause of God; His blessing is invoked upon it, and in His name we appeal to our readers for the help, the encouragement, and the generosity to further the cause which gives THE CATHOLIC WORLD a reason for its existence and continuance.

.*.

It must be of interest to our readers to learn of a very warm discussion in the London *Spectator* (April 18–May 30 inclusive) provoked by Dr. Abbott's attack on Cardinal Newman. The doctor, whose tendencies in religious thought are those of the Broad Church type, has recently published through Macmillan & Co. a work entitled *Philomythus*, in which he discusses Newman's *Essay on Ecclesiastical Miracles.* He characterizes the late Cardinal as "a lover of fables," and while disavowing any intention of accusing him of insincerity, harshly criticises him on personal grounds, condemns his style for looseness and slovenliness, and charges him in some instances with "self-deception and a monstrous manipulation of conscientious conviction." These views gave rise to the lengthy controversy noted above, in which both Mr. R. H. Hutton and Mr. Wilfrid Ward were enlisted in behalf of Cardinal Newman. The points raised are too numerous for summary in this department; the whole discussion is worthy of a regular article. We venture, however, to call the attention of our readers to the matter because of the interest which anything touching Cardinal Newman is sure to receive from Catholics generally.

.*.

In the wake of Mr. Sonnenschein's *The Best Books*, Henry Frowde, London, will issue at once *A Guide Book to Books*, by Mr. Sargent and Mr. Bernard Whishaw. The total number of books on all subjects recommended in this "Guide" is about six thousand. While its plan is similar to that laid down in *The Best Books*, arranging the titles by subjects, giving prices, publishers, etc., it differs from it in giving to each title brief descriptive notes. *A Guide to the Choice of Books* is the title of another work somewhat similar in character to those mentioned above. It is edited by Arthur H. Acland, and "has been prepared for those who have not competent advisers to tell them what to read, as well as to assist those who are responsible for libraries of books intended for popular or general use."

The International Academy of Volapük is now completing the normal grammar of the "universal language." It will be at once translated and published simultaneously in fourteen languages: French, English, Russian, German, Danish, Spanish, Portuguese, Italian, Hungarian, Roumanian, Dutch, Flemish, Swedish, and Japanese. The Academy of Volapük, founded in 1887 by the Munich Congress, and definitely established at the Paris Congress of 1889, is composed at present of thirty-five members, representing eighteen nationalities. The American members are Colonel Charles E. Sprague, of New York City; F. W. Mitchell, of Cambridge, Mass., and Lieutenant M. W. Wood, U.S.A., of Fort Randall, Dakota. · The publication of this normal grammar is designed to put an end to certain dissensions, "apparent," it is said, "rather than real," which now exist among the adherents of Volapük.

The famous Greek manuscript of the New Testament, which dates from the fifth century and constitutes one of the chief treasures of the Vatican Library, where it is well known to scholars by its catalogue number, 1209, is now being phototypically fac-similied by order of Pope Leo XIII., who intends to present a copy of the work to each of the principal libraries of Christendom.

Harper & Brothers have ready for immediate publication *Jinrikisha Days in Japan*, by Eliza R. Scidmore; *A Group of Noble Dames*, by Thomas Hardy, and *Unhappy Loves of Men of Genius*, by Thomas Hitchcock. They will also issue a new popular edition of W. C. Prime's *I Go a-Fishing*, and a library edition of H. Rider Haggard's *Eric Brighteyes*.

Literary Industries, a volume by Hubert Howe Bancroft, is announced as nearly ready for publication by Harper & Brothers. The work is largely autobiographical, and contains the story of the conception of Mr. Bancroft's great history, the manner of its composition, and the methods by which the materials for its completion were collected. There are many interesting reminiscences, also, of the famous men with whom Mr. Bancroft was from time to time thrown in contact, and numerous literary digressions, which give additional zest to an already entertaining narrative.

Teaching in Both Continents is the title of a volume by E. C. Grasby, which is introduced to American readers by Prof. W. T. Harris, which will be published by the Cassell Publishing Co. It is a comparative study of our school system in connection with those of other nations.

Robert Clarke & Co., Cincinnati, O., have just ready a work entitled *Beginnings of Literary Culture in the Ohio Valley*—historical and biographical essays on the early travellers and annalists, the pioneer press, early periodicals, the first libraries, pioneer schools, and numerous sketches of literary men and women, by Dr. W. H. Venable; *Pronao :* of Holy Writ—establishing, on documentary evidence, the authorship, date, form, and contents of each of its books, and the authenticity of the Pentateuch, by Rabbi Isaac M. Wise.

The Catholic Publication Society Co. has just published :

History of St. John's College, Fordham. By H. Gaffney Taaffe, A.B. Profusely illustrated.

The official translation of the Holy Father's Encyclical on the Labor Question.

The same Company announces :

The Science of the Saints in Practice. By John Baptist Pagani, second General of the Institute of Charity. Vol. III., September–December. (Vols. I. and II. have already been issued.)

Life of St. Francis di Girolamo, S.J. By E. M. Clerke. (New volume Quarterly Series.)

St. Ignatius Loyola and the Early Jesuits. By Stewart Rose. A new edition, with about 100 illustrations.

BOOKS RECEIVED. .

THE LIFE OF THE VENERABLE MADELEINE BARAT. From the French, by
Lady Georgiana Fullerton. New York: P. O'Shea.

TRANSLATIONS FROM HORACE. By Sir Stephen E. De Vere, Bart. London:
Walter Scott; New York: Thomas Whittaker; Toronto: W. J. Gage
& Co.

PROTECTION OR FREE TRADE. By Henry George. New York: Henry
George & Co.

MARY OF NAZARETH, a Legendary Poem (complete in Three Parts). By Sir
John Croker Barrow, Bart. London: Burns & Oates; New York: Catholic Publication Society Co.

CATHOLIC BELIEF; OR, A SHORT AND SIMPLE EXPOSITION OF CATHOLIC
DOCTRINE. By the Very Rev. Joseph Faà Bruno, D.D. Author's Ameri-
can Edition, edited by Rev. Louis A. Lambert. One hundredth thousand.
New York, Cincinnati, and Chicago: Benziger Bros.

THE AUTHORITY OF THE CHURCH, AS SET FORTH IN THE BOOK OF COMMON
PRAYER, ARTICLES, AND CANONS. Sermons preached in Trinity Chapel,
New York, during Lent, 1891. By Morgan Dix, S.T.D., Rector of Trinity
Church. New York: E. & J. B. Young & Co.

THE BIRTHDAY BOOK OF THE SACRED HEART. Being a collection of the
Maxims of the Saints in honor of the Sacred Heart. Compiled by Vincent
O'Brien. Dublin: M. H. Gill & Son.

THE LIFE OF THE BLESSED ANGELINA OF MARSCIANO, VIRGIN, PROMOTRESS
OF THE THIRD ORDER REGULAR OF ST. FRANCIS OF ASSISI. By the
Hon. Mrs. A. Montgomery. London: Burns & Oates: New York: Catho-
lic Publication Society Co.

THE PRECIOUS BLOOD. By Richard F. Clark, S.J. New York, Cincinnati,
Chicago: Benziger Bros.

INCA ROCCA, and Other Poems. By Chauncey Thomas. Boston: Damrell &
Upham.

DE INSIGNIBUS EPISCOPORUM COMMENTARIA. Auctore Petro Josepho Ri-
naldi-Bucci. Ratisbon, New York, Cincinnati: Fr. Pustet & Co.

PAMPHLETS RECEIVED.

TWENTY-THIRD ANNUAL REPORT OF THE HAMPTON NORMAL AGRICULTURAL
INSTITUTE.

AN APPEAL IN BEHALF OF THE UNITED STATES CATHOLIC HISTORICAL SO-
CIETY. By John Gilmary Shea. Elizabeth, N. J.

SAYINGS OF CARDINAL NEWMAN. Reprinted from *Merry England.* Boston:
The Pilot Publishing Co.

THE CATHOLIC PAGES OF AMERICAN HISTORY. A Lecture by Hon. J. L.
MacDonald. St. Paul, Minn.: The Catholic Truth Society of America.

OUR RIGHTS AND DUTIES AS CATHOLICS AND AS CITIZENS. A Lecture by Hon.
W. J. Onahan. St. Paul, Minn.: The Catholic Truth Society of America.

TWENTY-FIFTH ANNUAL REPORT OF THE TABERNACLE SOCIETY OF PHILA-
DELPHIA.

ON THE CONDITION OF LABOR. Encyclical of our Holy Father Pope Leo the
Thirteenth. New York, Cincinnati, Chicago: Benziger Bros.

THE

CATHOLIC WORLD.

VOL. LIII.   AUGUST, 1891.   NO. 317.

THE POPE AND THE PROLETARIAT.

IT is no exaggeration to say that not since St. Peter wrote his inspired epistles, eighteen hundred and fifty years ago, has a document of more world-wide interest and acceptance emanated from his chair than the recent encyclical of his illustrious successor, Leo XIII., on the Condition of Labor. The man, the subject, the treatment, the time all combine to place this encyclical among the noted documents of history. It is a new declaration of human rights, coming from the highest source on earth and bestowing the sanction of Heaven on every just and reasonable movement inaugurated for the relief of the toiling, struggling masses. And while it champions the cause of the poor and pleads for the rights of the wage-earners, it is a noble vindication of the rights of all classes; and society at large must henceforth recognize a benefactor in Leo XIII. The reception given this encyclical on every hand is a sufficient test of its importance and the broad and liberal spirit that animates it. Catholic and non-Catholic, conservative and radical, are alike loud in its praise. Only a very few grotesque bigots here and there, who still stultify themselves and maintain that nothing of good can come out of Galilee, have questioned its value.

This encyclical is remarkable not because it lays down any new principles or unfolds any new methods to be applied to the solution of the labor problem, but because it is the most complete and perfect summary of social economy from a Christian standpoint that has yet appeared, and shows how profoundly the Holy Father has studied the great economic questions of our day, and how keenly he realizes the condition and sympathizes with the lawful aspirations of the proletariat all over the globe.

In reading it we are continually surprised at the accurate knowledge displayed of the actual state of the working classes by one so far removed from contact with the work-a-day world; the ordinary limitations of place, position, surroundings are not noticeable, and Cardinal Manning could not address himself more intelligently to the labor problems of England or Cardinal Gibbons to those of America than does Pope Leo to the labor questions of the whole civilized world. His utterances on the subject are not simply those of a profound thinker, a great spiritual leader, but the utterances of a man in full sympathy with his kind and earnestly seeking to promote their temporal as well as their eternal interests. The great heart is visible throughout as well as the great head, and the undertone of sweet sympathy that is exhaled in every sentence, quite as much as the power of thought and grace of diction, will secure a hearing for this encyclical where papal document never before found entrance, and the name of Leo XIII. will become known and revered in the mine and the foundry, the factory and the workshop, among the toilers of all races and of all religions.

This, of course, is not the first time that a pope has come forward to defend and to define the relative rights and obligations of capital and labor, for the questions now involved have come before the Holy See many times already under somewhat different aspects. Nor can the bitterest enemy of the Papacy deny that the judgments of Rome on these and kindred subjects have ever been on the side of right and justice, and the sympathies of Rome have ever been with the weak and oppressed of every land. For centuries the voice of the Vicar of Christ was the only voice in the world raised to rebuke tyranny and oppression, and the victim of oppression, whether an injured queen or an outraged serf, found in the popes their most powerful protector. Pope Leo then, in descending into the area of social affairs to discuss questions that affect the well-being of the masses, is in full harmony with the best traditions of the Holy See and fulfils an important function of his office. Justice between man and man lies at the root of all morality, and if injustice is prevalent in any direction it is the part of the supreme arbiter of faith and morals to take cognizance of it and try to find a remedy for it. False theories, moreover, on the private ownership of property have been newly broached, and they must needs be judged and condemned by that tribunal from whose decisions there is no earthly appeal, and whose anathema blights with perpetual sterility all noxious growths.

The right of possession, the right to hold private property of whatever kind, is the foundation of all social order and civilization, and until this' primordial right is absolutely established and universally recognized no other right can be either sacred or secure.   Hence, as the Holy Father well remarks, "our first and most fundamental principle, therefore, when we undertake to alleviate the condition of the masses, must be the inviolability of private property."   And so the first part of the famous. encyclical is devoted not merely to a statement of the right of private property, but to a profound demonstration of it.   Pope Leo goes to the root of the question and shows that man, by the very nature of his being, has the *right* and the *necessity* of absolute ownership over that which his industry has created ;   and the right, moreover, of transmitting that absolute ownership to others, and this altogether independent of the law of society or of the state; for, as he says, "man is older than the state, and he holds the right of providing for the life of his body prior to the formation of any state."   Only in the exercise of its right of *eminent domain* can the state interfere with private possessions, and then justice requires that full compensation whenever possible be made.   The limits of state interference with the individual and with the family are also referred to and Cæsarism is shown to be at variance with the law of nature and the law of God. For man was not made for the state, but the state was organized for the benefit of man.   "If," says the Sovereign Pontiff, "the citizens of a state, on entering into association and fellowship, experienced at the hands of the state hindrance instead of help, and found their rights attacked instead of being protected, such association were rather to be repudiated than sought after."   The rights of the family, too, are inviolable, and the state can have no sort of claim to interfere with its privileges or its possessions. Marriage is a primitive right, and human law can neither abolish it nor legislate against its essential purpose or relationship, for "the family, a man's own household, is a society anterior to any kind of state or nation, with rights and duties of its own, totally independent of the commonwealth," says the Holy Father, and so it must be left perfectly free to pursue its own ends and to possess its own inheritance, as the same right of possession that belongs naturally to a man individually must also belong to him in his capacity as head of a family.   Domestic concerns, therefore, must be left entirely in the hands and under the complete control of the parents.   The state has no business to interpose its authority except in rare emergencies, where parental authority is powerless or inadequate. The vindication of the sanctity of the Christian home is not the least admirable and striking feature of this encyclical, and is in full harmony with the idea that a man's house is his castle and its independence must be respected to the last degree. The relationship between parent and child is also touched upon, and that universal stepmother, the state, is given to understand that she must keep her hands off and not obtrude her advice or assistance when they are not wanted. One short and pithy sentence sums up the subject: "Paternal authority can neither be abolished nor *absorbed* by the state, for it has the same source as human life itself." This is pretty strong doctrine for the paternal governments and military systems of Europe to swallow. The truth is, no sincere and consistent advocate of personal liberty could demand more freedom of action for the individual and for the family than Pope Leo postulates in this encyclical; and the man who, after a careful perusal of it, would still inveigh against the pope and the church as opposed to human rights must be an irreconcilable indeed. The broad spirit of humanity, the sincere benevolence, the noble poise and balance of justice that are everywhere manifest in this document, ought to convince the most sceptical that Leo XIII. is a true lover of mankind and in favor of the fullest liberty consistent with justice and good order.

Having thus established the fundamental principles on which civil society must ever rest, the Holy Father enters "with confidence," as he says, on the burning question of the Condition of Labor. In the opening page of his encyclical he speaks of the difficulties that beset the subject, for it is not easy, as he says, to define the relative rights and the mutual duties of the wealthy and the poor, of capital and labor; but something, he insists, must needs be done to ameliorate the condition of the working classes. To quote his exact words: "All agree, and there can be no question whatever, that some remedy must be found, and quickly found, for the misery and wretchedness that press so heavily at this moment on the large majority of the very poor." Now, in the solution of this pressing problem religion must be recognized as the chief factor, and all revolutionary dreams and socialistic Utopias must be abandoned. "Let it be laid down in the first place," he writes, "that humanity must remain as it is: it is impossible to reduce human society to a level." The Socialist's scheme of perfect equality is absurd on the face of it, for it is contrary to the course of nature itself. There are differences in the mental and physical constitution of men, and hence different degrees of success in life, and, as a consequence, difference in social position. Degrees in the social scale are not only the result of natural causes over which legislation can have no permanent control, but they are, moreover, necessary for the fulness of human life and the proper development of human society. Without these differences the world would be in a perpetual state of stagnation, and anything in the way of an advanced and complex civilization would be an impossibility.

All this is so evident that it seems quite unaccountable how men of intelligence and sincerity could entertain for a moment the naked hypothesis of Socialism, which so far from promoting the greatest good of the greatest number would drag mankind down to a state of savagery. The grades in social position are in reality productive of good to all classes and conditions and establish a mutual dependence that is the strongest bond of civil society. The rich cannot do without the poor, any more than the poor can do without the rich. "Each requires the other," says the Holy Father. "Capital cannot do without labor, nor labor without capital." And although abuses may and often do occur from the inequality between wealth and poverty, they are not to be compared to the prostration and dull monotony that would inevitably settle down on society were things reduced to a dead level. So that no remedy for the hard lot of the poor can be found in the wild dreams and crude theories of the socialistic school of reformers. Not philosophy, not political economy, not social science, but religion holds the key of the position ; for it is religion, exclaims the Sovereign Pontiff, that "teaches the rich man and the employer that their *work-people* are not their *slaves*, that they must *respect* in every man his *dignity*, and that it is *shameful* and *inhuman* to treat men like *chattels* to *make money* by, or to look upon them merely as so *much muscle* and *physical power*." This single sentence covers the whole situation and exposes the root of the evil. The grasping spirit of the age runs counter to the spirit of the Gospel, and the poor are oppressed in consequence. A recognition of Christian principles is the first great step in advance. Religion alone can hold up the balance of justice before the rich and the poor alike and enforce their mutual rights and obligations in the name of the great God. "It teaches," continues the Holy Father, "the laboring man and the workman to carry out *honestly* and well all *equitable* agreements freely made, and never to employ violence in representing his cause or to engage in riot or disorder, and it reminds the rich that to *exercise pressure* for the *sake* of *gain* upon

the *indigent* and the *destitute*, and to make one's *profit* out of the
need of *another*, is condemned by all laws, human and divine."

Where else, indeed, but to religion are we to look for the final
sanction of right and the final condemnation of wrong? Without
religion we cannot approach any of the great problems of life.
For if there is not something to look forward to beyond the
present then selfishness pure and simple is the only law of life,
and the world, as has been said, is only a vast pig-pen where the
biggist swine are sure to get the most swill; but we know that
life under any and all circumstances is full of sorrow and care,
that the brightest lives have a dark background, and when the
shadow falls where is there any refuge except in religion and the
immortal hopes it inspires? When the poor' man loses the
wife whom he loved or the children whom he reared and his
home is desolate, can he find any comfort in cold philosophy, in
political economy, in the theory of social equality? The whole
world is a blank to him, and life is a dark riddle unless there' is
a rift in the clouds through which the light of heaven shines in'
upon his soul, and bathes it in the bright beams of eternal
hope. No! without the aid of religion the labor problem, and
every other great problem the world presents, are simply insoluble. If there be only mechanical forces to rest upon they
are inexorable, and the miseries of mankind must go on and on
increasing as the world grows old and decrepit, until universal
law ceases to operate and chaos and darkness resume their sway
over earth and air and sea and sky.

. Not only must religious influence make itself felt, but the
church must bear a practical part in the work of relieving the
material miseries and improving the social condition of the
wage-earners. "Nor must it be supposed," writes the head of
the church, "that the solicitude of the church is so occupied
with the spiritual concerns of its children as to neglect their interests temporal and earthly. Its desire is that the poor, for example, should rise above poverty and wretchedness and should'
better their condition in life; and for this it strives." Leo XIII.
is evidently no advocate of the theory that religion has nothing'
to do with the material interests of this life and should confine'
itself to its purely spiritual domain. Religion is the highest good'
of humanity informed by the revelation of God, and no human'
good can be a matter of indifference to it or outside the just'
sphere of its influence. The church must concern herself with'
social problems whenever they come up and lend her potent aid'
in their solution. She has done so all along. The guilds and'

working-men's associations of the middle ages were her creation. She blessed them and directed them, and under her 'fostering care they fulfilled the objects for which they were founded. They perished at the period of the Reformation, or very soon thereafter, because the church could no longer guide and inspire them. They who would apply the *laissez faire* principle to religion in our times are not its friends. Religion is not an abstraction; it is a concrete reality, and should make itself felt in every pore of human society, and particularly in all that concerns the poor and suffering members of Christ. The same lips that pronounce the first Beatitude—"Blessed are the poor in spirit, for theirs is the kingdom of heaven"—must also be ready to utter the invitation, "Come to me all ye who labor and are heavy laden, and I will refresh you." There has been a little too much of the passive, some might be disposed to call it the contemplative, spirit of religion in certain schools of Catholic thought, and this earnest, energetic, advanced encyclical of the supreme head of the church is a rebuke to it. Religion must not be held in leash. It must be altogether free to fulfil its mission in the world, and to go about the Great Father's business in whatsoever direction that business may lead it. And next to the evangelization of the nations, and as a necessary step towards it, religion has no higher work in the world to-day than to labor for the relief and elevation of the masses.

Take the awful blight of intemperance, which is the cause of the greatest misery to the working-people of many lands, is religion not called upon to grapple fiercely with that? The last stronghold of slavery in Africa is now besieged, serfdom has altogether disappeared, and it only remains to lift off the heavy burdens from the shoulders of the sons of toil which a ruthless greed of wealth has imposed upon them, and mankind will be in a condition to listen to the Divine Master whose "yoke is sweet and burden light." Men cannot turn their gaze heavenward when they are bowed down to the earth with incessant labor and care; the aspirations of the soul are stifled in the sordid atmosphere that surrounds them. Even the day set apart by the Almighty himself for their rest and refreshment is frequently denied them, and the animal life and its wants absorb all their thoughts and efforts; there is neither time nor energy left for the functions of the soul. Thank Heaven! this condition of things does not yet exist to any very great extent in our country, but it certainly does elsewhere, and the Holy Father pours out his condemnations upon it all. He pleads for the ob-

servance of Sunday as the poor man's day of spiritual refreshment and bodily rest, and denounces the desecration of it
so common on the Continent of Europe. "No man," he says,
"may outrage with impunity that human dignity which God
himself treats with reverence, nor stand in the way of that
higher life which is the preparation for the eternal life of heaven."
In fine, the Vicar of Christ holds that religion, the Christian religion, the Catholic Church, which renovated society in the past,
must be the prime source of its renovation in the present; and
a return to Christian principles and institutions is a *sine quâ non*
for the adjustment of the difficulties and disorders that now
threaten the whole fabric of civil society.

But the Holy Father does not content himself with proclaiming these general principles and establishing their application by
cogent arguments; he recommends the adoption of positive
and practical measures for the relief of the working classes and
the permanent amelioration of their condition. And he appeals
to the state to do its part in the needful work of reform by en-
acting laws in favor of the rights of the poor and to guard them
against the rapacity of the rich. "We have said," he writes,
"that the state must not absorb the individual or the family;
both should be allowed free and untrammeled action as far as is
consistent with the common good and the interests of others.
Nevertheless rulers should anxiously safeguard the community in
all its parts, . . . and the public administration must duly
and solicitously *provide for the welfare and comfort of the
working people.*" The state is bound, of course, to enforce the
rights of each and all its citizens; this is the object of its existence. But Pope Leo insists that it is bound in an especial
manner to enforce the rights of the poor and to protect their
interests. "The richer population," he says, "have many ways
of protecting themselves and stand less in need of the help of
the state; those who are badly off have no resource of their
own to fall back upon and must chiefly rely upon the assistance
of the state; and it is for this reason that wage-earners, who are
undoubtedly among the weak and necessitous, should be especially cared for and protected by the commonwealth." The Holy
Father mentions, moreover, some of the contingencies in which
state interference between employers and their employees can
and ought to be invoked, as when there is danger to the public
peace, when family ties and obligations are relaxed or neglected,
when the spiritual interests of the wage-earners are at stake or
their morals are endangered through the unseemly mixing up

of the sexes, or other occasions of evil; and if the burdens imposed by employers are unjust, degrading, or repugnant to the
dignity of their employees as human beings, and if the labor
demanded be excessive, injurious to the health, or unsuited to the
age and sex of the operatives. "In all these cases there can be
no question," says the Pope, "that, within certain limits, it would
be right to call in the help and authority of the law." And,
again, when referring to strikes and other serious disagreements between capital and labor, he does not hesitate to say that
"the *laws* should be *beforehand* and *prevent* these troubles from
arising; they should lend their influence and authority to the
removal in *good time* of the *causes* which lead to conflicts between masters and those whom they employ." And, on the
other hand, repressive measures are to be resorted to only in
extreme cases and when no other remedy can be found. Nor
must the state enact laws that tell against the interests of the
working classes or impose excessive taxation upon them. The
policy of the state should be to encourage the industry of the
poor, to make them happy and contented in their own land, and
not to drive them into exile from their homes and their country
to secure a decent subsistence. While exceedingly jealous of
state interference in private affairs, as he has good reason to be,
Pope Leo demands the protection of the state for the weak
against the strong, and insists upon it that the law ought to
find redress for the grievances of the poor. Trusts and monopolies, child-labor, the sweating system, forced contracts, etc., are
all fit and proper subjects for legislative interference, and should
be taken in hand and dealt with by the strong arm of the
law.

The truth is, the most pronounced advocate of the rights of
the people under the constitution could not, in reason, demand
from the laws of the state more complete protection for their
every-day interests than Pope Leo concedes. To many it will,
no doubt, be a new revelation to find the oldest and the most
independent sovereign authority in the world pleading the popular
cause, and demanding for the masses, in the truest and best
sense, the "right to life, liberty, and the pursuit of happiness."
And that Leo XIII. does all this few who read his encyclical honestly and intelligently will be disposed to deny. Extreme radicals may, and doubtless will, scoff at it; but, on the other hand,
extreme conservatives, whether in church or state, will not find
much comfort in it.

The hours of labor and the important question of compensation receive due attention in this comprehensive document; and the attitude of the Holy Father on these subjects is in keeping with the humane and benevolent spirit that runs all through his encyclical: his plea is for the poor toilers' rights in everything. "It is neither justice nor humanity," he writes, "to so grind men down with excessive labor as to stupefy their minds and wear out their bodies." The length of the day's labor, he says, should be determined by the character of the work, the season of the year, and the physical capacity of the worker; and he proclaims that "every man should have *leisure* and *rest* in proportion to the wear and tear on his strength. Women should not be required to do work that is in any way unsuitable for them to engage in; and children should not be placed in workshops and factories until their bodies and minds are sufficiently mature."

These are wise and beneficent rules, and they should commend themselves to the intelligence and sense of humanity of the world at large. Life is intended to be, and for the great mass of mankind must be, a season of labor, but it is not therefore to be an unbroken drudgery. And we think the time will come when eight hours for work, eight hours for sleep, and eight hours for recreation will be very generally regarded as the proper standard for man's daily occupation in life. But, as Pope Leo intimates, it will be always a difficult thing to fix an absolute limit, for the hours of labor cannot well be otherwise than relative to the character of the work and the condition of the worker.

The matter of wages is also relative and a very difficult subject to deal with in the abstract. The Holy Father feels this, and approaches the vexed question with great caution. Nevertheless, his declaration on this head is among the boldest in his encyclical, and will bear a message of hope and encouragement to the ranks of the great labor army scattered all over the globe. He is thoroughly opposed to *starvation wages*, and while he upholds freedom of contract, he shows that in agreements between employers and their employees this principle is not always present, inasmuch as the laborer is often forced to barter his labor in order to sustain himself and his family; he must get employment or starve, there is no other alternative—he is then the victim of necessity. And in view of this Pope Leo makes his noble declaration on the subject of due compensation—a declaration that shall be quoted as long as employers are base enough to take advantage of the necessities of the poor and buy their sweat and blood at the lowest possible price. We give the

Pontiff's statement on this subject in full: "Let it be granted, then," he says, "that as a rule workmen and employers should make free agreements, and, in particular, should freely agree as to wages. Nevertheless, there is a dictate of nature more imperious and more ancient than any bargain between man and man—that the *remuneration must be enough to support the wage-earner in reasonable and frugal comfort.* If through *necessity* or *fear* of a worse evil the workman accepts *harder conditions*, because an employer or contractor will give him no better, *he is the victim of force and injustice.*" This declaration most assuredly leaves nothing more to be said on the question of fair compensation for labor. The wages received should insure the workman and his family a comfortable living in a modest way, and even admit of his saving something when due economy is practised. This is the test of fair wages, and there can be no better.

The Holy Father favors the establishment of private boards of arbitration rather than state boards to adjust the disputes and differences that may arise between employers and their employees about wages and other matters. He also recommends very earnestly and at considerable length the formation of working-men's societies for their mutual aid and support, but he takes very great care, of course, to insist that all such societies shall keep within their own proper bounds and honestly carry out the objects for which they are founded, and he is at great pains to warn workmen against joining any labor organization that is in the least un-Christian or revolutionary in its tendencies. He would have modern tradesmen's associations modelled on the ancient guilds. And when they are properly organized and peacefully pursue their own ends, the state must in no way interfere with them; they have a perfect right to exist, and it is nothing short of tyranny and oppression for the state to meddle in their affairs. This, of course, apropos of the utterly unjust and vicious attitudes of some of the European governments towards organizations that are perfectly legitimate and serve a good purpose.

Leo XIII. praises all who have taken an active part in founding sound associations to promote the welfare of the working classes, and he expresses the fervent hope that such societies will everywhere increase and continually prosper in their beneficent purpose. Finally, he implores the co-operation of all earnest men in the great work of alleviating the condition of the masses. "Every one should put his hand to the work which falls to his share, and that at once and immediately," he exclaims, for "at this moment the condition of the working population is the question of the hour, and nothing can be of higher interest to all classes in the state than that it should be rightly and reasonably decided." He particularly urges upon the ministers and representatives of religion the duty of "throwing themselves into the conflict with all the energy of their minds and all their strength of endurance." Indeed Pope Leo XIII. would seem to imply by his encyclical that the church should take the lead in a world-wide movement for the relief and elevation of the toiling, struggling masses; and surely the nineteenth century offers no ampler field for the exercise of her divine energy and the world no nobler cause than the cause of suffering humanity.

E. B. Brady.

FIESTA ON A MEXICAN HACIENDA.

"You would like," said our good friend, the *cura* of the parish where our lot in Mexico has been for some time cast, "to see a great hacienda and something of the life upon it? It gives me pleasure to be able to afford you the opportunity. Across the mountains from here, over in the valley of Ameca, lies a hacienda on which I spent five years as chaplain. The patronal feast of this estate is the Purification of the Blessed Virgin, and every year it is celebrated with great honor. The other day the *haciendado*, Señor C——, came, according to his custom, to invite me to participate in the *fiesta*, and I have his permission to bring with me some foreign friends. You will, therefore, prepare to spend Candlemas on a hacienda which is typical of our great estates, and to see a *fiesta* thoroughly Mexican in its character."

It is almost needless to say that this kind invitation was eagerly accepted. It was, indeed, an opportunity not to be neglected; for, although Mexican hospitality is equal to any demands made upon it, the stranger in the country can seldom obtain an inside view of the life of these vast estates, whose proprietors live among their tenants and dependents like feudal lords, and where there is a touching, patriarchal character in the relation of master and servants maintained through generations— a beautiful relation drawing forth some of the best feelings of human nature on both sides, one which the modern world is losing fast and replacing with the caste hatred and antagonism that exists between employer and employed when Christianity has been forgotten and the hard law of material gain alone rules the contract between them. On the hacienda to which we were invited the relation spoken of—formed by kindliness and consideration on one side, by loyalty and attachment on the other—exists in its perfection, because it has always rested upon a Christian basis, the family who have owned this great estate for an unbroken period of a hundred and thirty-five years having been for all that length of time distinguished for their devotion to the church and its precepts.

In this year of grace the feast of Candlemas fell upon Monday, therefore it was in the afternoon of Sunday that we made the drive of twenty-four miles to the hacienda, passing from one lovely valley into another, around the base of a great serrated mountain which lies between. Of our own valley we had often said, in the words of Cortés about the valley of Mexico: " *Es la cosa mas hermosa en el mundo*" *;* but we had now to acknowledge that its companion across the purple mountains was even more beautiful. How can one paint the picture which it presented in the still, golden light of that afternoon ? At least twenty miles wide by more than thirty long, it spread far as the eye could reach, vast levels of cultivated land alternating with stretches of woodland, a crystal river flowing through its midst, azure mountains encircling it, and over all the luminous Mexican sky, a vault of dazzling sapphire. Almost immediately on entering the valley we left the *Camino Real*—the " Royal Highway " from Guadalajara to the town of Ameca—and entered by a gateway upon the lands of the hacienda. Here we drove for twelve miles through an Arcadia of fertility, loveliness, and peace. The full extent of the estate is eleven leagues (thirty-three miles), and this for a great Mexican domain is not remarkable. Even in Mexico, however, there are lands and lands, and those of this hacienda are of peculiar richness and value, covering, as it does, the greater part of the fertile Ameca valley.

We had been driving nearly three hours when the *cura* suddenly pointed. " Yonder," he said, " is the church." A glance showed it standing on a hill above the river, its picturesque front and open Carmelite belfries outlined with beautiful effect against the sky. A few minutes later we lost the view, as our road turned and ascended in the rear the eminence on which the church and *casa grande* stand, passing through a village of the people employed on the estate, its houses of adobe covered with tiles and surrounded by enclosures of luxuriant tropical shrubs, of a better and more comfortable order than are often seen on the haciendas and ranches. " The people on this hacienda," said the *cura*, " are generally of a very high character, noted for their honesty and intelligence. They are treated with liberality and justice, make all they need for living, and I am sure that there is not a single person among them who does not know how to read and write, the proprietor supporting the schools in which the children are taught." It may be added that, observing the throngs which filled the church during the next day, we were struck with the corroboration of these words in the appearance of the people, their neatness and cleanliness of attire, their well-bred, self-respecting manner, and the intelligence of their countenances.

Driving rapidly up a gentle slope, we passed from the village through an immense gateway into a large, open square, capable of containing several thousand people, enclosed on one side by the long wall of the great house (*casa grande*) of the proprietor, and on the others by the schools, the shops of the various industries of the hacienda (as the carpenters, saddle-makers, etc.), the house of the *administrador* or agent of the estate, and also a pretty residence in which one of the brothers of the proprietor lives. Crossing this plaza, which had the true air of a Mexican *fiesta* from the numbers of people already moving to and fro, and the dealers in fruits, peanuts, *dulces*, etc., who had established themselves along the borders, with their wares displayed on squares of matting, we drove up to a flight of handsome steps, which descended to the plaza from the end of the corridor of the great house. Here a group of gentlemen stood to welcome us, and conspicuous among them was a truly splendid figure, that of the *haciendado* himself. A man in the prime of life, of superb stature and proportions, with a handsome head set on massive, well-carried shoulders, he would have been a striking personality anywhere; but here, on the threshold of his own stately home, dressed in the rich and beautiful Mexican costume which Mexican gentlemen seldom wear now except on their estates—a costume consisting of close-fitting trousers of black cloth, with double rows of silver buttons down each side, connected by delicate silver chains, and short jacket, also of black cloth, elaborately braided with silver—he was so entirely in accord with his position and his surroundings as to charm both the eye and the fancy.

Ascending the massive flight of steps, with their curving balustrades of stone, we found ourselves on the corridor which extends along the front of the house, and the unsurpassed beauty of the situation burst fully upon the gaze. We are told that admiration of nature is the special attribute of our days; but surely the man who nearly a century and a half ago planted his residence on this spot had the love of nature in his soul and must have enjoyed the superb panorama of valley and mountains which lay before him. It is impossible to conceive anything more beautiful than the view. The hill, which slopes so gently behind that one is scarcely aware of ascending it, descends abruptly in front to the level of the river flowing below, and from the front of the house, which faces on this side, the eye passes over miles of cultivated and wooded valley to the glorious mountains that with their noble lines sweep around the horizon, forming a vast amphitheatre of encircling heights, the nearest of which are at least ten miles distant, and which are robed in such divine colors, changing with the changing light of every hour, as can be seen only in the lucid atmosphere of this true " land of the sky."

From the broad corridor which extends into the platform before the church, twelve steps, running the whole length of the house and church, descend to what is termed an *atria* (*atrium*), which is that part of the terrace before the building enclosed by an Italian-like balustrade of stone into a paved court, containing in the centre a large, handsome fountain, and at the corners of which tall and beautiful carved stone columns stand. From this a path leads down the steep hill to a garden at the foot—a garden that as one stands looking through its barred gate, while waiting for the key of admittance, again recalls Italy, for, down a vista of shining foliage, one sees a fountain of gray old stone and gray stone benches like those one remembers in the gardens of Roman villas. But when we enter Italy is forgotten in the luxuriant beauty of this tropical paradise. Its broad alleys lead between thick groves of every variety of fruit-trees known to this fortunate land. Orange-trees, lemons, limes, the graceful tree which bears the guava, the mango, the cherimoya, the palm-like melon-zapote, the shining leaves and clustering berries of the coffee-tree ; these and a multitude beside, together with roses, magnolias, and oleanders, and long walks overarched by grape-bearing vines, supported from double rows of classic columns, make a spot where one might readily forget time in lingering, and where all the romance of the south seems to find a home.

But although we have thus turned from the threshold of the house for a glimpse of the garden that lies under its broad terrace, it was not in reality the first or most interesting of the sights which awaited us. The interior of the *casa* naturally commanded attention before its exterior. Like all Mexican houses it is built around an open court—a court so large that a regiment might be reviewed within it. It is paved, but devoid of plants, as befits the stately, almost severe character of the whole edifice. Between each, of the great arches that form the outer side of the corridors surrounding it there has, however, been planted an orange-tree; and these trees, inclining outward, form a circle of luxuriant green around the *patio* and fill the air with the fragrance of their blooms. Standing on the farther side of this court, and looking up beyond arches and the glistening boughs of foliage, amid which shines golden fruit, one sees a sight for a painter—the picturesque old wall and lovely belfry of the church standing out against the deep-blue sky, and looking down with solemn quiet into the inner heart of the home that has always yielded to God its first homage.

The apartments which open upon the corridors surrounding the four sides of the *patio* are many and spacious. Everything is on a grand scale, without ornament; but in its solidity, its extent, and its stateliness impressing one as having no need of it. A dining-room of immense dimensions extends back from the court, and on one side opens upon a lovely garden, where luxuriant creepers cover the sides of the walls with which it is enclosed, where flowers bloom and birds sing, and where a great green summer-house in the centre has been the scene of many a feast—notably the breakfast always given to the children of the estate when they make their First Communion. Then there are other courts enclosed by many domestic offices, by granaries and stables; and one, most charming and monastic in its air, in the rear of the church, where a small stone staircase against the wall leads up to a secluded apartment, a library, which must have been built by one who possessed the true soul of a scholar and understood the love of all scholars for silence and solitude. No sound from the house reaches this quiet spot; its walls are lined with book-cases, filled with Spanish and Latin volumes, and windows opening from the floor upon a stone balcony command a view of the valley toward the mountains that lie against the western sky, a wide picture full of enchanting beauty and infinite serenity. It is an ideal retreat for a student, a poet, or a saint—for any soul that loves communion with the great dead of past ages through their written words, and that, seeing God mirrored in the wonderful loveliness of his visible creation, would be led by it to lofty and touching thoughts of him.

And now, in the order of ecclesiastical processions—the greatest last—we come to the *cor cordium* of this Christian home, the sanctuary of God. As the exterior of the church towers in height and beauty above the house beside it, so does the richness of its interior far surpass anything to be seen in the residence.

Here man has offered his best to God, and, unlike some Catholics of whom we know elsewhere, does not leave a luxurious home to go and worship in a poor and humble chapel. The church, which will hold five or six hundred people, is built in the usual style of Mexican churches—that, more or less, of the Spanish renaissance—a style most picturesque and effective for decoration both within and without. Upon this church wealth has been lavished with a princely hand by the owners of the hacienda. The steps of the high altar are of silver; and behind extends from floor to ceiling, covering the entire sanctuary end of the edifice, a beautiful example of the highly ornate chirrigueresque work,* the best examples of which are seen in the chapel of Los Reyes (The Kings) in the cathedral of Seville, and in the chapel of the same name in the cathedral of Mexico. This richest of all possible modes of church decoration is a mass of elaborate carving executed in cedar and covered entirely with gold. Amid its multitude of intricate details are introduced statues of angels and saints, carved with exquisite skill and richly gilded; while its expensive character may be judged from the fact that the example of which we speak cost twenty thousand dollars. All the vestments and vessels of the altar are in accord with the magnificence that rules elsewhere; and even the tablet which is placed before the tabernacle, covering it entirely, is made of virgin silver beautifully wrought. A very large and handsome organ fills the gallery at the farther end of the church. "There is no better in Guadalajara, except those in the cathedral," said the *cura*.

No people understand better than Mexicans how to decorate a church effectively, either in an enduring or temporary manner; and very beautiful were the special decorations of this church for its great feast. Above and behind the high altar and two smaller altars in the sanctuary magnificent draperies of cloth-of-silver were arranged, while such immense wax tapers as one sees only in Mexico covered the altars, in the midst of masses of golden leaves and silver lilies. In the body of the church crimson draperies hung in graceful festoons, and hundreds of wax candles were attached by invisible wires, so that they seemed suspended in the air, to cords carried from the chandeliers in the middle of the church to the side walls, thus forming a succession of inverted arches of brilliant light, extending from the altar to the door, and filling the edifice with that soft radiance which multitudes of wax candles alone produce.

* So called from the Spanish architect and sculptor, Chirriguera, who practised it about the end of the seventeenth century.

As evening fell the *fiesta* appearance of everything deepened. In all directions men were at work preparing for the decorations of the night, hanging festoons of Chinese lanterns over the *atria* and between the arches of the corridor, and placing on the roof of church and house the oil-cups which, when lighted, make the most beautiful illumination possible. The plaza was fast filling with a distinctively Mexican throng, composed not only of the people of the estate but of many drawn from neighboring haciendas and towns—a lithe, sinewy people, with dark, gentle faces, quiet manners, full of courtesy and even of grace, and picturesque costumes, in which the bright red blankets of the men mingled with the soft tones of the blue and purple *rebozas* of the women. " I am always anxious on this occasion," said Señor C——, "fearing disturbance—chiefly from the outsiders who come to our feast; and in the permission to sell given to venders of refreshment, anything in the form of spirituous drink is always positively prohibited." Certainly all the merry-making on this occasion was of a most orderly character, and it was very striking to see now and then in the midst of the animated crowd a man or woman making his or her way to the church on bended knees, candle in hand and absorbed in prayer. Occasionally some person or persons would cast their blankets on the ground before these pilgrims, to soften a little the hard journey; but often no notice whatever was taken of the sight so wonderful to a stranger, so little wonderful here. Truly in these remote districts of Mexico, removed from foreign and (it must be said) contaminating influences, one seems to have stepped back into the Ages of Faith, when men had neither learned to deny their Creator nor to withhold from him the outward homage which is his due; when those touching practices of devotion prevailed which we have grown too cold, too mindful of the opinion of Protestants and infidels, to practise; when the rich man saw in the beggar at his gate the living representative of Christ, to be succored and honored accordingly, and when the Church of God sat enthroned in the splendor which is her right as Mother and Mistress of all men.

After nightfall the bells rang out their clashing peal, and as many of the people as could do so gathered within the church, where the Solemn Matins of the feast were sung. In accordance with established custom, an orchestra and singers had been brought from Guadalajara (the musical capital of Mexico) for the occasion. There were eighteen of these musicians, who arrived just before us in two large carriages sent to the city (seventy-five miles distant) for their conveyance. The music consequently was such as is seldom heard out of great capitals. Its perfect cadences filled both ear and soul, while the church itself was like a vision of the New Jerusalem. The altars a blaze of radiant splendor, the arches of dazzling light, the festoons of color, the officiating priests in their vestments of cloth-of-gold, the Most Blessed Sacrament throned high over all, amid clouds of curling incense, the throngs of devout kneeling people extending far into the outer court beneath the starry sky—all made such a picture as is only to be witnessed in a land where faith has not been weakened nor devotion grown cold.

The services in the church over, our attention and admiration were claimed by the brilliant illumination without. The façade of the church, its graceful open belfries, the long lines of its roof and those of the *casa grande*, were traced in fire against the sky, while on the side of the house overlooking the plaza, in immense letters of flame, were the words *Ave Maria Purissima.* The plaza itself was at this time a wonderful sight, thronged with the people who had been for hours constantly arriving, until now there must have been upon the ground at least ten thousand persons. In the vast throng there was a constant movement, but not the least sign of tumult or disorder. All was as quiet and well-ordered as if squads of police had been present. The orchestra from Guadalajara, stationed at the head of the steps of the corridor, were playing inspiring airs. In the middle of the crowded square stood a tall, light tower on which fireworks, that are a part of every Mexican *fiesta*, were arranged for display; now and then, over the heads of the people, in the interval of waiting, rockets went up, or small lighted balloons sailed away into the dark-blue depths of the sky, as if charged to carry to heaven the tidings of the joy in Mary's honor on earth. The lines of living fire around the roofs flickered in the night-breeze, and the bells of the church told their jubilation to all the valley in such tones as make one realize here how large a part bells are intended to play in the worship of God, and how in a Catholic land they do indeed

> "—— make Catholic the trembling air."

It was about ten o'clock when the signal for the commencement of the fireworks was given. A volley of squibs opened the entertainment; and then, as the fire thus started leaped from point to point along the wires which conducted it, there were a succession of brilliant pyrotechnic effects that threw wonderful reflections over the thousands of upturned faces, and culminated in displaying the figure of Our Lady of Guadalupe amid a shower of revolving lights on the summit of the tower.

With three priests in the house, there were next morning two Masses 'before the High Mass, which began at nine o'clock. Each of these Masses was attended by many more people than the church could hold. Far out beyond the doors they knelt in throngs, praying with a simplicity, a fervor, and an utter absence of distraction that would be remarkable enough anywhere else, but is not at all remarkable in Mexico. When the swinging clash of all the bells summoned us to the great Mass of the day, we looked from the tribunes where the family and their guests had their places upon a representative scene of this most Christian country. The church—which is, of course, without benches—was again closely packed with a reverent mass of worshippers, and beyond the great open arch of the door, that framed a noble picture of valley and distant mountains and bending sky, the kneeling forms of the people could be seen even to the end of the *atria*, their faces directed toward the altar with its shining lights and glistening draperies, their lips moving in prayer; the heads of the women draped in their graceful scarfs; the men, many of them, praying with extended arms and small, brown, toil-worn hands lifted in touching appeal to the Son of God, who on earth was himself a son of poverty and toil. And it was not the least edifying sight of the many around to see the stately *hacienda*, with lighted taper in hand, kneel reverently in the sanctuary during the whole of the long and elaborate ceremonial of the Solemn High Mass, offering in person his homage to God, and setting an example to his people of striking devotion. The Mass was beautiful throughout; beautiful in the splendor that surrounded it, in the full ritual that honored it, in the lovely music that accompanied it. The sermon (preached by the *cura* of Ameca) was eloquent and forcible, and it may be safely asserted that nowhere in the world was the feast of Our Lady's Purification more worthily celebrated, with more to delight the eye and satisfy the heart, than in the church of this Mexican hacienda.

The necessarily limited space of an article will not permit description of the popular festivities of the day, nor of the many beautiful and interesting scenes around the noble old house that has enshrined in the past and still enshrines in the present lives and characters formed in a mould so truly Catholic, and where the tradition of antique virtues lingers like a fragrance of the past.

There were many things to make one almost fancy one's self in a feudal castle. The hosts of retainers, the number of guests and members of branches of the family, and the hospitality apparently without limit. At least sixty persons sat down to a dinner that, with its many elaborate courses, lasted three hours. To speak of the charming hostess and lovely children of the house would seem a violation of the hospitality which, in grace and cordiality, left nothing to be desired; but certainly the strangers who met so kind a welcome within its gates are not likely soon to forget the pleasure given and the courtesy shown them there.

· The closing picture of that memorable day was too charming not to be sketched, in however light outline. · It was drawing toward sunset when the bells of the church again summoned the people, first for Rosary and Benediction, and then for a ceremony which always closes the *fiesta*. There is in the church a small but very ancient and highly venerated image of our Blessed Lady. This is taken in solemn procession around the plaza, pausing at three or four temporary altars to receive the homage of the people, and then carried back to the sanctuary. It is perhaps worth while to remind the reader that under the present oppressive laws of Mexico religious processions outside of the churches are prohibited, and can only take place on private estates, so that some idea may be formed of the good which Christian proprietors like Señor C—— are doing in helping to keep the faith of the people alive by feeding it with the devotional practices to which they are accustomed; for it should never be forgotten that faith and devotion are inseparable, and that where the second is neglected the first will soon be lost. The last golden rays of the sun were shining across the valley just as the tall processional cross emerged from the church door, and they caught and burnished it as well as the richly dressed statue following, borne on its flower-wreathed pedestal upon the shoulders of men. After the priests, and pressing close around them, came a throng of men and women, bearing for the most part lighted candles and saying the Rosary aloud. A parlor-organ was carried along, as well as the instruments of the orchestra, and when a halt was made at the temporary altars some of the sweetest of Mary's hymns rose on the air, while the people knelt in prayer and homage. With these pauses the procession was long in making its way around the large plaza, and before its return to the church dusk had fallen. In the twilight the multitude of flickering tapers borne aloft were like so many stars fallen from heaven to earth to light the pilgrims' way and honor her who is the Morning

Star. The plaintive music rose and fell with softest cadence, purple shadows had fallen over the valley ; but beyond the distant, dark-blue mountain-tops a golden glow showed where the fires of sunset had lately paled.. It was an exquisite and most touching scene. Ladies in silken gowns knelt in the dust of the plaza side by side with cotton-clad peasants, and from every lip rose but one refrain—familiar words clothed in sweet and stately Spanish—" Santa Maria, Madre de Dios, ruega por nosotros peca-dores, ahora y en la hora de nuestra muerte. Amen."

And so ended the Feast of the Purification on a Mexican hacienda, where nothing was done for effect, but everything with a noble simplicity and generosity for the glory of God alone. It was an occasion of edification, even in a land where such occasions abound, and made us feel again, as often before, that Catholics at home—both priests and people—may well come to Mexico to learn how God is served with a depth of inward devotion and a splendor ot outward service which shames our best efforts.

CHRISTIAN REID.

THE UNKNOWN BOUND.

I WATCHED a sail until it dropt from sight
Over the rounding sea. A gleam of white,
A last far-flashed farewell, and, like a thought
Slipt out of mind, it vanished and was not.

Yet, to the helmsman standing at the wheel,
Broad seas still stretched before the gliding keel.
Disaster ? Change ?—he felt no slightest sign ;
Nor dreamed he of that dim horizon line.

So may it be, perchance, when down the tide
Our dear ones vanish. Peacefully they glide
On level seas, nor mark the unknown bound.
We call it death—to them 'tis life beyond !

JAMES BUCKHAM.

'TONIA.

IN the women's work-room of the Warham Penitentiary there were two or three dozen women languidly at work. There is not, as a rule, much zest of industry among the state's compulsory servers, men or women, but always there is more purposeless performance of duty among the latter. The reasons are evident enough; among them being, perhaps, the greater variety and pleasantness of the work allotted to the men. The women in this particular institution had no occupation but various kinds of mending. They were of all ages and of varying degrees of degradation in appearance. The coarse, loose-fitting, blue-checked gowns they wore were far more slovenly looking than the gray stripes of the men. They worked in silence except for an occasional whispered word or two, an occasional cough or giggle. Without much nagging from the matron their apathy would have accomplished nothing. Only one of them seemed industrious—a young mulatto at the end of the row, who sewed with a feverish rapidity that betokened an anxiety to compel into inactivity thoughts that were vigorous and unwelcome. For half an hour her fingers flew, her eyes never left her work. At the end of that time there came a sound of noisy little feet along the corridor outside. The door opened and a child, about three years of age, came dancing in. The mulatto woman looked up and the sudden gleam of fierce affection that lit up her handsome eyes proved, more than the likeness between them, that this was her child. Most of the women smiled, looking for the moment as if the chubby hand of a little child had taken from their faces the mask of sin and weakness and placed there again the radiancy of innocence and purity. The matron took the little girl in her lap and started to talk with her. The mother sprang up from her work and stood gazing hungrily upon the child. "'Tonia!" she called. The matron turned to rebuke this breach of discipline. The little one sprang from her arms and rushed to her mother. Just then the bell sounded for the end of work. The women began filing away to their cells. The matron, a sharp-faced, kind-hearted woman, came up to the mulatto and said to her, "Send away 'Tonia now. I will come and talk to you in a moment."

When the other prisoners were disposed of, and the spring had been drawn that locked the tier of cells, the matron returned and said, kindly enough, to the mulatto, "You may get ready to go, Rosa. In an hour your time is up."

There was no reply, and the matron continued, somewhat sharply: "I hope you mean to behave and not get here again. You're a bright, smart young woman and this is not the place for you. Besides you've got your child to consider. It's your duty to make a respectable woman of her."

Rosa eagerly caught the matron's hand and said in a soft, sweet voice, singularly free from the negro accent and peculiarities of pronunciation: "Mrs. Last, what am I to do with 'Tonia? I can't take her with me, and I can't stay here with her, and I won't let her go into an asylum where strangers will be unkind to her and teach her to despise her convict mother. Do you think the superintendent would allow me to leave her here a few months till I have found work and made a little home for her? You will be good to her, I know, and the superintendent seems very fond of her."

Mrs. Last's sharp eyes measured Rosa up and down while she meditatively plaited and unplaited the hem of her apron. After a few minutes she said: "I will see Mr. Sefton. You may get ready to go. I will give you your things, and when you are dressed you may come to the office and Mr. Sefton will tell you his decision."

In half an hour the mulatto, dressed neatly in a plain dark gown, brown ulster much the worse for wear, and close-fitting bonnet, tapped at the door of the superintendent's private office. In response to his " Come in" she entered timidly and stood, with downcast eyes, just inside the door. The superintendent, a tall, loosely-built, shrewd-faced man of forty, looked keenly at her. She was clean, neat, intelligent-looking, and, with the exception of her color, possessed scarcely any negro traits.

"Well, Rosa," said he kindly, "Mrs. Last has been telling me your request concerning your little girl. It is quite contrary to all the rules, I am afraid, but I will see what can be done. I have a suggestion to make to you. I am very fond of children and I am a childless widower. Your little girl is a bright, lovable child and I am willing to adopt her as my own. But you will have to sign a paper agreeing to forego all claims on her hereafter. You must promise never to seek any communication whatever with her. In that case, I am willing to take her for my own, to educate her, and care for her in all respects as if she were my own daughter."

He paused. The mulatto trembled violently, her eyes dilated, but still she said nothing. "There is another thing," he continued; "a negro called John Hunter, a short-term man, who will be out in a few days, wants to take your little girl with him. He wants to turn over a new leaf, and he says she would keep him straight. It is a risk for the child, but in some respects it would be better for her to be with her own kind."

"No, Mr. Sefton, sir, I should never allow that. A nigger is not her own kind. My father was a French half-breed Indian, my husband an educated Italian."

Mr. Sefton smiled incredulously. "You are sure that is true, Rosa?"

"Yes, it is true. I am a thief but not a liar."

"Yes, it was thieving, I believe, that brought you here. How did you come to it?"

"My husband died when 'Tonia was a year old. My parents had died long before. I was alone in the world. All my life I had been poor. Carlo was an educated man, but always in ill-health, always discouraged, always unlucky. He left me penniless. For a year I managed to earn a living for my child. I could not do much. There were no influential friends to help me on and procure me congenial work. I did whatever I could get to do, but finally constant anxiety and lack of proper food and rest wore me out. I could not work any more. One day there was nothing in the house to eat. I was sick and faint. 'Tonia was crying for bread. At last I could stand it no longer. I rushed from the house in despair. I came back a thief, but 'Tonia went to bed that night satisfied and happy. I was too miserable to sleep at all. The next day I was caught, and—and then we came here, and you were very good, sir, to let 'Tonia stay here with me. But I can't let her go to the nigger, and I can't take her out with me."

She ended abruptly, a sob in her voice. Her black eyes filled with tears. Mr. Sefton cleared his throat.

"I can quite understand your feeling, my good woman, but I still think it might be a wise plan for the negro to take her. For your sake I wish you would decide to keep her yourself. I am still, however, quite willing to adopt her myself. I think I shall leave the decision to the child. A child's intuitions are sometimes clearer than any man's judgments. Will that satisfy you, Rosa?"

"Yes, sir."

It did, indeed, satisfy her. Her passionate mother-love fought against the idea of giving her "'Tonia" even to Mr. Sefton, which was the course that common-sense seemed to approve. Now her common-sense and her mother-love would at once be satisfied, for 'Tonia would come with her. Mr. Sefton sent for the convict, then for the child.

When 'Tonia came running into the room three anxious people looked at her. The mother, by a great effort, controlled her face and held back the tears that were gathering in her eyes. The effort was so great that her face became positively gray in the struggle. The passionate love in her heart was so completely held down that her expression became cold and repellent. The negro's broad face grinned cheerfully when he saw the child. He was a burly, good-natured fellow, whose convict stripes had not taken all manliness from him. Mr. Sefton's shrewd face re-laxed when he, too, looked at the little girl. A kindly smile lit up his blue eyes. 'Tonia glanced from one to the other. It was only her mother who looked coldly at her, although she half-invol-untarily put out her hand to the child, then resolutely drew back. 'Tonia came towards her, then stood still, afraid of this new, strange expression on " mammy's " face. She looked up at the negro and smiled in answer to his grin. Then she sprang toward Mr. Sefton.

" 'Oo want me, Missa Seffon ? "

" Yes, my child," he said gravely, and held out his arms to her. She clambered up to his shoulder and put up her little mouth to be kissed. The mother clinched her hands.

" 'Tonia," said Mr. Sefton, " I want to know what you wish to do. Your mother is going away. Will you go with her, or with John Hunter, who wants you too, or will you stay with me ? "

The negro came forward. " Missy 'Tony come wif John an' she hab good times. Marse Sefton, lemme hab her an' I'se a good man. I'se keep straight 'nuff ef she come 'long wif me. Tony gwine ter come ? " And the negro displayed his ivories in another good-natured smile.

'Tonia smiled, glanced from the negro to Mr. Sefton, and then slowly shook her head. The mulatto heaved a sigh of intense relief. The " nigger," at least, should not have her child. Her face still wore its intense, strained look, and her voice was nerv-ously husky as she stepped forward and said, " 'Tonia, come to mammy ! "

The child buried her face on Mr. Sefton's shoulder and made no answer. Rosa came nearer. There was pitiful entreaty in her broken voice : " 'Tonia, won't you come to mammy ? "

The little girl raised her head and looked gravely at her mother, then her baby voice said, very gravely and decidedly: "'Tonia 'fraid of mammy; 'Tonia stay wif Missa Seffon."

There was silence for a moment. Mr. Sefton put the child down and solemnly kissed her. He laid his hand for a moment caressingly on her head. "You shall stay with me always, 'Tonia," he said, "but now run away for a while."

John Hunter, grumbling loudly at the child's decision, was ordered back to his work. Rosa still stood, silent and motionless. Mr. Sefton looked at her very sadly and pitifully for a moment. When he spoke his voice was very gentle.

"Rosa, I am sorry for your grief; but the child has decided, and I trust it will be for the best. I solemnly promise you to love and cherish her as if she were my own. Now, will you sign this paper?"

She took the paper mechanically and read: "I solemnly promise never henceforth, in any way, to attempt to hold communication of any kind with my daughter Antonia, who is hereafter to be known as the daughter of Charles Sefton, superintendent Warham Penitentiary." Mechanically she took the pen and wrote in a firm, legible hand, "Rosa Corsini." She reread the paper, seeming for the first time to realize its meaning. A strange light came into her eyes. She drew a long, deep breath, regained her composure, and, rising from her chair, handed the paper to the superintendent.

"Now I am ready to go," she said slowly.

"You must first go and say good-by to 'Tonia," said he gently.

"No, I do not want to see her again. Now I can go. I could not consent to leave her if I were to look at her again."

"As you think best," he replied. "But tell me what you are going to do now that you are free again?"

He spoke very kindly, but her face hardened at his words. She gave a short, scornful laugh as she answered: "Do? What do you think an ex-convict can do? Is there any honest livelihood open for a woman who has served a year in the penitentiary? Do you think there is one home in this city ready to employ me as servant? Oh! there are plenty of charitable people, Mr. Sefton, in this big city, but their charity draws the line at the inmates of the penitentiary."

"You are too bitter," said Mr. Sefton. "You do not consider how few inmates the penitentiary has who are at all desirous to do well when they are free. I am sure you will do your best for the sake of your child, and I am sure you will succeed in earning an honest living. Come, I am going to give you a 'character' that may help to get you a place in some respectable family."

He went to the desk and wrote, with a slightly humorous smile on his thin lips:

"This is to certify that Rosa Corsini is a neat, competent, and conscientious servant.   CHARLES SEFTON."

Rosa took the paper, read it with a faint smile, and put it carefully in her pocket. Mr. Sefton took out his purse, counted out two ten-dollar bills, and put them in her hand as he cordially shook it. "This may help you a little," said he. "Remember that you have always my best wishes for your success. Good-by."

She turned to thank him, but he had quietly slipped out of the room. She put the money in her pocket, picked up her small bundle, and noiselessly left the office. In a few moments the heavy door of the penitentiary had opened and closed upon her. Rosa stood upon the stone flagging leading to the high gate in the great wall that surrounded the penitentiary and gave a last look at the white walls and grated windows of the dreary building that for a year had been her home. As she stood there the doors of the workshop in the rear of the enclosure swung open and a long line of convicts, marching with the prison lock-step, each man's hands upon his leader's shoulders, filed slowly from work. The dingy stripes of their ill-fitting garments, the tread so suggestive of shuffling chains, gave a spectator the impression of a serpent writhing past. Rosa shuddered as she looked at them, and hurried from the place. In her face the gray and hopeless look had deepened and intensified.

II.

We hear often of children's "laughing eyes," but I think we very seldom see them. There is generally a sweet seriousness in a child's innocent eyes. It seems almost as if seriousness were part of innocence. It is only when the first wandering consciousness of the glory and delight of the wide heaven and earth above and about has passed away that the carelessness of laughter and amusement takes its place and twinkles even from the soul's fair windows. So perhaps it was not so strange a thing as Mr. Sefton fancied that 'Tonia's great black eyes—bright, gay, active child though she was—should have been very serious and earnest. She was a remarkably beautiful child, in whose face it would have been difficult to trace either Indian or negro trait, excepting that her soft black hair fell in straight masses around her head and that her lips were too full for the delicacy of her other features. Her complexion was a clear olive, her hands and feet were finely formed.

Fortunately a child's remembrances fade quickly. At the end of a few weeks 'Tonia had grown used to "mammy's" absence, and soon had ceased to talk of her. She grew accustomed to Mr. Sefton's caresses and constant attention, and she learned to lisp "father" very prettily. She was a gleam of constant sunshine for the lonely man who had made her his daughter. He felt that since the death of his wife his heart had been frozen, but had suddenly been thawed back into life. All his plans now had reference to 'Tonia; his last thought at night was of her. Throughout the penitentiary the child had always been a favorite. The fact of her adoption by the superintendent seemed to make her even better liked. She loved to spend hours in the workshops, fascinated by the whirr of the machinery, watching with deep interest the long lines of busy, silent men. None were too abstracted, however, for a kindly glance, a smile, a half-whispered word for the child. Her influence was great even with these lawless characters; for in spite of the fact that a face of the Nero type, or of that of the utter sensualist, is not infrequent among them, there are more countenances that display weakness of will or good-natured irresoluteness in the penitentiary inmates than faces which show complete and hardened depravity. No man possessing a spark of goodness is insensible to the influence of a sweet and innocent child. Besides her mere unconscious childhood 'Tonia possessed the beautiful gift of song, most Godward-drawing of all God's gifts, and as she ran along the corridor outside the tiers of cells both men and women alike felt their hearts strangely moved by the unconscious trills and lilts of melody that fell in bird-like warblings from her lips.

One day, about six months after his adoption of 'Tonia, the superintendent found an official-looking envelope among his mail. It proved to be the announcement that a distant cousin, whose only surviving relative Mr. Sefton was, had recently died in England, making him sole heir to a very large fortune. A little while before this news would have left Charles Sefton quite unmoved, for he was an unambitious man, fond of work, and quite contented with the very moderate means that provided for his few personal wants. Now the case was different. It gave him keen pleasure to realize that his power of doing for 'Tonia had suddenly become almost unlimited. The final settlement of the affairs of his deceased relative demanded his immediate presence in England. Consequently he at once resigned his position, began his preparations for departure, and engaged a good mother-ly woman as nurse for 'Tonia. In a few weeks they were set-tled in London. His business did not detain him long, but he decided to remain in England till 'Tonia's education was far enough advanced to enable her to derive due benefit from the long course of travel he determined to give her. He took a charming little house in a fashionable quarter of London, en-gaged a small staff of servants, and began to live in every respect as became an American of taste and means. He was a man of a good deal of native tact and cleverness, and he had a quick power of observation, an insatiable desire to know whatever was best worth knowing, that, joined to his very evident wealth and his easy natural manner, soon made him a favorite in several circles of desirable and cultured society.

Somehow—possibly because little 'Tonia bore no resemblance to her American father—the legend originated with Sefton's new friends, and was by them transferred to newer acquaintances, that he had married a beautiful Italian girl who, dying when their child was but an infant, had left him ever afterwards mourning her memory and absorbed in its only living reminder. Sefton never openly contradicted this story, and when, with various em-bellishments, it reached the ears of his adopted child, she impli-citly accepted it, for she had quite lost all recollections of the real facts of her infancy. To her grief, however, she discovered that she was never to learn anything more definite of her beau-tiful Italian mother than her nurse's romantic conjecturings and imaginings could supply. When she asked her father some ques-tions on the subject he gave her a short and sharp answer, and bade her never repeat the queries. They grieved him, he said, and it was his earnest desire that her mother should never be mentioned between them again. 'Tonia obeyed him, but her thoughts dwelt often on the dead mother; whose face must have been like her own, "only much more beautiful"; whose voice, too, must have been like hers, "only much sweeter and lovelier." So this ideal mother, always sweet and gentle and beautiful, dwelt in the little maiden's heart, bringing with it, as does every generous ideal, the spirit of peace and content.

From the first Mr. Sefton resolved that Antonia's education should be broad and unconventional. All the instruction she re-ceived had for its object to develop her every latent power to

its fullest capacity.   Strength he wished for her characteristic.
'Tonia should be a strong woman ; that was his summary of all
that he wished for her in brain and heart and body.   As for
her soul, that he left pretty well to her own management.   He
professed no religion himself; she was to follow her own preference in the matter.   A chain of circumstances, the first being
the belief that it must have been her Italian mother's faith, led
her to Catholicity just as she was growing into womanhood.
Her father applauded her choice.   "You have chosen the strongest of all religions, my dear," said he.

Antonia's exquisite voice received the best training her father
could procure for her.   More than one enthusiastic master wished
to train her for concert or opera, where her success, they prophesied, was certain.   Mr. Sefton invariably refused to entertain the
idea.   "If Providence has put a nightingale in her throat," said
he, "it shall have every chance to fully develop its divine melody;
but not for the benefit of a mere money-paying, pleasure-seeking
public."

So there was no thought of a public career in the young girl's
enthusiastic and painstaking devotion to her music.   Perhaps the
thought that was most active in spurring her on to increased exertions in every line of culture was the wish to please the good
man who so freely placed unrivalled opportunities in her reach.
Each year that sped on left father and·daughter more closely and
entirely devoted to each other.

III.

In the little alcove of a crowded drawing-room a tall young
man, of about six or seven-and-twenty, stood chatting pleasantly
with a bright young English girl.   He was rather a good-looking
young fellow, though there was nothing remarkable about his appearance, unless it were the harmonious brown of his hair, eyes,
and moustache, or the quiet air of thorough breeding that seemed
to envelop him.   He was a wealthy American, of an honorable
New England family, who spent a good deal of his time abroad
and had a circle of friends in most of the European capitals.   He
was clever and intellectual, and amiable enough to be excellent
company when it pleased him to exert himself.   His greatest fault
was an intense dislike of the commonplace.   Only people and
things out of the common excited his interest, and, as is the case
with most mortals, it was seldom his fate to meet with them.   He
privately pronounced existence to be "agreeable enough, but some-

thing of a bore.' His name was Seymour Blaire. The young lady
with whom he was conversing was Miss Travers. They had been
friends for a long while and, as they had not met for several
months previously, their talk had been particularly animated. The
occasion was the first reception for the season of one of London's
most famous society leaders. The rooms were crowded and very
warm. Mr. Blaire plied Miss Travers's fan vigorously for a few
moments and then announced his intention of departing.

"Oh! you are not going yet," she said. "I particularly want
you to meet a very dear friend of mine who is to be here this
evening, though I haven't caught sight of her yet. She has been
on the Continent with her father for the past three years and only
returned to London a few weeks ago. This is her first season and
she's bound to be the rage before long."

"You have a delightfully flattering opinion of your friends.
What are the most shining qualities of this one, and what's her
name, by the way?"

"You are just ready to laugh at me, I know. I've a great
mind to tell you nothing about her."

"You know you are dying to talk of her."

Miss Travers closed her lips defiantly.

"Come; I admit myself curious. Tell me all about her. After all, it's a great point in her favor to be *your* friend."

Miss Travers smiled and relented.

"Well, I'll tell you her name, at any rate. Oh! there she is.
Don't you see that tall, gray-haired man standing at the door of
the music-room? That's her father. She is just beside him. I
declare, they have induced her to sing! She is going to the piano.
I am so glad you are going to hear Antonia sing."

"So her name is Antonia. It has a classical sound that seems
in keeping with the young lady herself. I don't think I'll wait to
hear her sing, though. I'll just slip away before she begins. I've
heard so many young ladies sing, you know. They're all very
much alike—not half bad, of course, for amateurs, but rather tiresome. Good-by, Miss Travers. I'm so glad I met you this
evening! Tell your mother that I mean to persecute her on her
Thursdays this season as much as ever."

A gloved hand was laid on his arm. "My dear Mr. Blaire, I
shall never forgive you if you don't wait, and I promise you you
will never forgive yourself."

"The thought of the first penalty," said he, "is more than
sufficient to make me listen to a dozen young ladies singing. As
for the second—," he shrugged his shoulders, and cast a second

look at the young lady, who stood turning over a pile of music at the piano. There was a distinction about her appearance that pleased him. The simplicity of her soft, trailing white gown and her low-coiled black hair suited his critical taste. She turned with a smile to the young man who was to play her accompaniment. With the smile a wave of animation swept over her face. After a word or two, she handed him the sheet of music she had selected and stood, tall and lithe as a young pine, waiting to sing. Seymour Blaire noted her attitude with involuntary admiration. "Her face is like a beautiful cameo," he thought. Then his moment of enthusiasm subsided. As the first chords of the piano sounded Miss Travers exclaimed in a rapturous whisper: "She is going to sing that exquisite little thing of Rubinstein's, '*Du bist wie eine Blume*'!"

The young man frowned slightly. The song was a favorite of his, but he had a theory concerning it. In his opinion it could only be well rendered by a singer who was at once a perfect artist and a pure-souled woman. He wished this beautiful girl had chosen something else.

After her first full, pure notes the low buzz of whispered voices ceased. The rooms were filled with eager listeners, who broke into enthusiastic applause when the last notes of the exquisite voice died away. On every side admiring comments, stupid or appreciative, were heard. But I think it was only a young man with abstracted brown eyes who said to himself: "It is as if a field of lilies had suddenly found voice!"

A little ripple of laughter recalled his thoughts. "Why, Mr. Blaire," said Miss Travers, "you look as if you had become a dweller among the stars. Did Antonia's singing bore you very much?"

"My dear friend, be merciful to me a Philistine!" he answered, with an attempt to shake off the gravity that had fallen upon him. "I owe you a thousand thanks for a few moments of intense enjoyment."

"That is very pretty. I think I must reward you for the nice things you can say, when it pleases you to try, by presenting you to Miss Sefton and her father."

"I should like it of all things," answered he meekly.

So in a few moments Seymour Blaire was talking to Antonia and her father as if they were old friends whom he had fortunately encountered after a long absence. He unconsciously exerted all the charm and fascination of manner he possessed as he chatted with these two who were, he realized immediately, so clever and so unaffected, so broad in view and experience. For the first time he had met a woman whose conversation afforded him at once complete intellectual satisfaction and a feeling of grateful repose. On the other hand, Mr. Sefton and his daughter were most favorably impressed with him. When they parted, the father gave him a cordial invitation to call on them. "My daughter is always at home on Tuesdays," said he, with a laugh, "and I am there whenever she is."

The invitation was acted upon as promptly as a due regard for appearances would permit, and the acquaintance thus established developed speedily into a comfortable intimacy. When Seymour Blaire did not meet Antonia and her father at a dinner or reception or ball—and as they were in the same circle of the social "swim" it generally happened that their engagements were identical—he spent a quiet and delightful evening with them at home. Miss Travers proved a true prophet. Antonia was indeed before long "the rage." Nature and education had made her that rare but not impossible combination, a woman of beauty, of rare gifts, of sound sense. Whether her face or her wonderful voice won her most popularity, or whether the last quality above mentioned was a help or detriment, I do not know. I know only that she was much in demand, that everybody was aware of the fact that she would one day be a very rich woman, and that this consideration may have had something to do with the shower of bleeding hearts that seriously afflicted her during the early part of the season. She confided to her father her opinion that mere friends were very desirable, but that would-be lovers were extremely tiresome. That was the nicest thing about Mr. Blaire; he was so friendly, so entirely free from any nonsense. She felt the greatest friendliness for him and wished to display it. Somehow she was never quite content with the result of her endeavors. She did not know why the mantle of reserve seemed to be always gathered around her when he was near. As for him, he loved her. He was happy when he was with her, happy when he thought of her, miserable when he meditated telling her his love. She was pure and cold as a snow maiden. How could any man have the impertinence to dream of being loved by her? He was very grateful for the gracious friendliness—though there was a bit of reserve about it—with which she always treated him. What right had he to ask any more?

One day he received a cablegram from his younger brother. It read: "Mother ill—nothing serious—but wants you. Come at once. Doctors think your presence necessary."

Young Blaire was very fond·ot his mother, so he lost no time in setting about his preparations for departure. After securing a state-room on a Cunarder that sailed in two days, he completed all arrangements for a probably long absence. One or two intimate friends had to be seen for a moment or two. Then he would go to the Seftons' and make his adieux. "After all," he reasoned, trying to drown an unreasonable pang that would make itself felt, "it is better to have an end of it. She will never be more than my friend. She is too cold to ever care for me. I can never even tell her that I love her."

He had argued himself into much propriety of thought and feeling when he made his farewell call. Mr. Sefton was out driv_ing, he was told, but Miss Sefton was at home. In a few minutes she joined him in the drawing-room. After a few indifferent remarks, he said, in a carefully casual manner: " I have come to say good-by, Miss Sefton. I am going home in a day or two, for a visit of indefinite length."

A shade of surprise crossed her face. Involuntarily she raised her eyes and gave him a glance in which he read amazement— and something more. It is one of the many responsibilities of Mother Eve & Co., this glance in which a woman unconsciously proclaims to the man her heart has chosen for its liege lord her willingness to swear vassalage and fealty unto him. There are divers ways of reading and misreading such a glance. In this case the man acted with more composure and common-sense than most men when such a revelation—unhoped-for as it is delightful— comes upon them. He tried to collect his thoughts for a moment with small success. He picked up a dainty bit of carving and seemed lost in its critical examination, while he said, very slowly: " I fear, Miss Sefton, my absence will be of no consequence to you."

No answer. He steadied his nerves, replaced the bit of carv_ing on the table, and tried again. "I mean, Miss Sefton, I wish that it were of some consequence to you. May—may I hope that it is ? "

He felt that he was unwarrantably bold, whatever her look had seemed to say. Antonia rose and half-extended her hand. Now was the time to display her friendliness, she thought; to give him a hearty handshake and a cheerful, sincere God-speed for his journey. Somehow she did neither. She only said two faint little words, "You may."

They were sufficient for the hearer. They were encouraging enough to open the floodgates of his eloquence. There was a good deal said on both sides after that, and with so satisfactory a result that, half an hour later, when Mr. Sefton came in from his drive, Seymour Blaire announced himself a candidate for the honor of being his son-in-law elect.

Mr. Sefton had a cordial liking for the young man. He knew that his character was irreproachable, his family connections and worldly prospects excellent. The union was in every sense desirable. Therefore his manner was very genial as he heartily pressed the young man's hand. "My dear fellow," said he, "if 'Tonia loves you I have nothing to say. I have no wish but her happiness, and if she thinks you are the man to secure it, why, I think so too."

After making a few remarks about his intended journey and assuring them that he would do his utmost, if his mother's illness were not much more serious than he fancied, not to protract his absence beyond a month, Mr. Blaire took his departure, promising to dine with them on the morrow, which was to be his last day in London.

At dinner the next day the conversation turned on the last novel of a brilliant young writer whose stories were the topic of the hour. The book is the history of a lie which makes the happiness of several lives that would have been made desolate by the true facts of the case. They were all agreed upon the cleverness of the writer, and, from general comments on the book and its characters, they passed to a discussion of the main fact contained in it.

"It is wrong to teach such a lesson," said Antonia decidedly.

"But whatever makes for happiness makes for final good," remarked Seymour Blaire.

"I'm afraid, my dear Blaire, that your own individual feelings at present are sufficient excuse for any obliquity of view you may express. I think 'Tonia is right. The author teaches a harmful lesson—in its general application, that is. Of course there are always individual instances where it would be wiser that the whole truth should not be known. Truth is sometimes very ugly, my dear," said Mr. Sefton, smiling across the round table at his daughter.

"That is so, father, and yet I think in every case it is better known. The facts of a man's life belong to him. No human being has a right to deceive another in what is so vital a concern to that other. 'The fool's paradise' cannot be cried out on too often. Every honest man or woman ought to prefer, a thousand times, a truth that brings unhappiness to an illusion or deceit that gives happiness."

• The young man's brown eyes kindled as he looked at the girl's earnest face. When she paused he bent towards her and raised her hand to his lips. •

"Antonia," said he gravely, "I promise you that in our life together I will give you always truth—and happiness, too, I hope."

She smiled her thanks. Then her earnest mood passed away. Both tried to forget the impending farewell, and each tried to outdo the other in gayety. With an effort Mr. Sefton shook off the shade of trouble that had settled over his face and tried to join in their liveliness. He felt that his sparkle was ineffectual, and wondered if they noticed it. He might have made his mind easy. For the first time in her life Antonia failed to observe every change in her father's face or voice. Another face and voice demanded all her attention.

When they adjourned to the drawing-room after dinner, Mr. Sefton remarked: "I am going out for a bit of a stroll while you young people make the most of your last evening. I suppose it will be a whole month, at least, before you have another evening together. Well, 'Tonia, do you think your old father will be able to comfort you?"

A kiss was the response. Mr. Sefton, looking quite content, went out. His stroll seemed to bring him very little comfort. The troubled look came back to his face as he paced slowly up and down. A hard decision lay before him. Was it or was it not his duty to tell 'Tonia the true facts of her infancy? Her chance remark had awakened thoughts that had not been in his mind for years. It quickened into intense life the one treasure he prized higher than even 'Tonia's happiness—his honor. His heart swelled with pride in the girl that she, too, should cherish truth and honorable dealing above all else. He decided to tell her everything. As he re-entered the house there was no longer any trouble in his face or in his thoughts. To-morrow he would tell her. After all, what difference could it make?

IV.

Three hours had elapsed while Antonia Sefton sat quietly by the open window of her pretty little sitting-room. She had scarcely moved from her position in the soft lounging-chair, and yet over her face had passed the shadows of many conflicting emotions. In her soul a battle had been fought and gained. A great desire to forget and ignore the facts of her childhood that

Charles Sefton's honorable nature had compelled him to make her acquainted with, a terrible temptation to leave Seymour Blaire ignorant of what must for ever change their position to each other, had raged passionately in her heart. Her keen sense of honor, her love of truth, gained the victory at last. With victory came the steady current of strength that a conquered temptation generally brings. The afternoon sunshine had gathered into the blaze of sunset and faded gradually into dusk when she rose from her chair. In the fading light the soft hangings, cushions, and rugs of her luxurious little apartment lost their rich colors, the outlines of chairs and couches were blurred and indistinct, but over her desk, at the opposite side of her room, the last faint ray of light still showed with some clearness a beautiful little painting of some Italian-faced Madonna which Mr. Sefton had given to Antonia on her last birth-day. There was in the sweet face a faint suggestion of Antonia herself, and she had hung the picture where it might be always in her view because it was to her the portrait of what her dead mother must have been.

The loss of an illusion is always a painful wrench. To Antonia, as she faced the picture, there came a moment of intense physical agony. Then she was overpowered by that torrent of grief that can only overwhelm a cold and self-contained nature, by way of establishing a balance, once or twice in a lifetime, with the habitual self-control. She flung herself passionately on the floor. Her whole frame was convulsed with sobs. In a moment every hold she had upon life had slipped from her hands. Her father, whom she loved with the most intense devotion, was not her father. The dead mother, whose beautiful image she had cherished for years, was a myth—the reality a mulatto, an ex-convict; Heaven knows what she had become, if she still lived! Her lover, who alone of all the men she had known was worthy to rank with her father, must be nothing to her hereafter. She clinched and unclinched her hands fiercely; she bit her lip till the blood came, and the same question rose in her breast that sooner or later rises in every heart when the inevitable anguish comes upon it: "Why must I, who am strong and vigorous, deserving of and anxious for happiness, endure this misery." It is the question that was asked and answered one night, long ago, under the olive-trees of a garden in Judea. Every soul, when suffering—particularly unmerited suffering—comes upon it, is compelled to accept this answer or be left desolate.

At last Antonia roused herself and rose slowly to her feet. She still trembled from the violence of her grief. She lit the

lamp that stood upon her desk, and stood for a long while gazing earnestly at the pictured Madonna which, a few hours before, had represented her mother.   Out of her mind the vision
and remembrance of her ideal mother seemed to fade as she
stood there.   In its place there rose the image of the loveless,
lonely, hunted life of the poor mulatto.   A great wave of pity
surged over her heart.   She went to the mirror and looked
steadily at the pale, sorrowful face, the heavy, tear-laden eyes
before her.   The grotesque thought came to her that she had
become, even in appearance, a veritable negro.   She looked at
her long, slim fingers, and fancied she saw a dusky tinge under
the nails.   A thousand invisible cords seemed drawing her to the
despised mulatto woman.

Finally she drew a long sigh; a firm look came over her full,
red lips and into her deep eyes.   Her conclusion was reached,
and, as she seated herself at her desk and drew towards her pen
and paper, it seemed impossible that she could ever have dreamed
of resolving otherwise—so true it is that only by taking hold of
the unendurable do we learn endurance.

She wrote rapidly for a few minutes, then threw down her
pen and read the brief lines she had penned.   They did not satisfy her.   It seemed cruel to say to the man who had hoped to
make her his wife: "Circumstances have arisen since we parted
that render our marriage utterly impossible.   It is equally impossible for me ever to see or hear from you again."

There was truth but too much austere pride in so cold a dismissal.   Now, truth and humility are very near neighbors, and
perhaps they were not altogether separated in the letter she
finally completed with more comfort to her aching heart.   In
this she said:

"MY DEAR SEYMOUR: When you asked me to marry you
you thought me the daughter of a man with whom any one
might be proud to ally himself.   To-day I have learned many
things, and my life's horizon has become very different.   I am
not the daughter of Charles Sefton, but was adopted by him at
the expiration of my mother's term of imprisonment in an American penitentiary, of which he was then keeper or superintendent.
I was then three years old.   I have absolutely no recollection
of my poor mother, of whom nothing has ever since been heard.
She was a mulatto, married to an Italian of good class who died
when I was a year old.   Her father was a French half-breed.
You perceive, my friend, what an impossibility your marriage
with a woman of such parentage is.   Family pride, even in you
who are so free from every mean prejudice, must absolutely for-

bid it. Even if you wished otherwise, after what I have told you, I know I could now never be happy as your wife. God knows what it costs me to lose you! But I realize, and you, too, will realize it for me, that there is but one thing for me to do—to spend my life, if need be, searching for my unhappy mother, and if I succeed in finding her still alive, no matter where or how, to devote myself entirely to her. That much, at least, I owe to her. I have only one request to make you, that you will permit me to drop out of your life and not allow my memory to sadden you. I do not ask you to forget me entirely, but I wish you to remember me as one gone for ever from your sight, whom you honored by your affection, and who gave to you her whole heart.   ANTONIA."

The letter folded and addressed, Antonia felt that the first and most painful step had been taken. It was with a sense of relief and of returning energy that she made her way to her father's study. He sat at his table, his white head buried in his hands. He looked up as she entered, the light in his eyes that her presence never failed to bring; but a great sadness came over his face when he saw the traces of the long afternoon of suffering upon her countenance.

He rose from his chair and went to her. He took both her cold little hands in his and, stooping, kissed her brow. "My 'Tonia!" said he.

She smiled—a wan, dreary little smile it was—and returned his caress. "Yes, father, always *your* 'Tonia. I have just been writing to Sey—Mr. Blaire. Will you read the letter, please?"

His quizzical glance met no responsive twinkle, so he sat down, turned up his reading-lamp, put on his eye-glasses, and gravely read the letter. As he replaced it in the envelope he said deprecatingly: "My dear, why should it make a difference? You cannot help but be always my daughter."

The girl put her arm about him and bent her head till her lips touched his silvery hair. "My father, I am always your daughter. But I am also the daughter of the poor mulatto, who needs the love and care of the girl whose father has given her such a bright and happy life."

"You feel it right, my child, to go to her?"

"I can do nothing else."

"Very well, my dear; I shall not thwart your wishes. Eighteen years ago, when I adopted you as my own, it was of your own free choice you came to me. I have often wondered what your life would have been had you chosen otherwise. If you had chosen the negro you might have been his salvation—

he was not a bad fellow at heart—but what a life you would have led! If you had gone with your mother you might have been an angel guiding her to good, or she might have been weak enough to drag you into the wretched ways of sin with herself. I hope all is best as it has been. You have made a lonely old fellow very happy, 'Tonia. And he ends by making you miserable."

"He ends by showing me my duty, by teaching me truth and honor as he has always taught me. Now, tell me, what is the first thing to be done to find my mother?"

"I think, if she is still living, she is probably in Warham. I will write to the superintendents of the various charitable institutions in the city and try to obtain news of her."

"But that is so slow. Can we not go to Warham ourselves?"

"If you wish it, child," he answered gently, "we will close the house and go immediately. It's high time we had an American tour, anyway."

She put her slim, brown hand softly on his gray head. "You are so good, dear," she whispered.

V.

On a bright September morning a cab drove rapidly through the streets of Warham. Mr. and Miss Sefton had arrived that morning in the city, and immediately after breakfasting at the hotel had begun their quest. Institution after institution was visited without result. The books of neither hospital nor almshouse showed the name of Rosa Corsini. The poormaster knew nothing of her. If she were still in the city there seemed but one other place to seek her. The same thought was in both minds as Mr. Sefton gave the order, "To the penitentiary!"

A few pencilled words on his card at once admitted Mr. Sefton and his daughter to the superintendent's private office. As one in a dream Antonia listened to the apologies, brief explanations, casual remarks that followed. She gathered only that a search was being made among the records for the name of the woman they were seeking. The compression of her lips alone told how intense was her emotion as she watched the superintendent rapidly turning over page after page.

"Ah!" said he finally, fixing his broad thumb upon the last page of the big book before him, "here we are. 'Rosa Corsini, mulatto, ten days for vagrancy.' I rather think that's the woman who was brought here a few days ago, and who seemed

to be in the last stage of consumption.   Her place is in a hospital, not here.   It often ·happens that people are brought here
who are much fitter subjects for the almshouse or hospital or
insane asylum.   It's doubtful, however, if that woman has many
days to live anywhere.   Two nuns who come here regularly to
see the prisoners, and who accomplish much good by their efforts
among them, were with her this morning.   I think they mentioned that the Catholic chaplain had prepared her for death.
Would you like to see her?"   And he looked curiously at his
visitors.

"Yes," replied Mr. Sefton.   "A family matter gives me a deep
interest in the affairs of this unfortunate woman.   My daughter
and I are most anxious to give her any assistance in our
power."

"Then, sir, we will go to her at once, if you and the young
lady will come this way."

As they were mounting the iron stairway they met the two
nuns descending.   The superintendent greeted them courteously,
and said : " This lady and gentleman are anxious to get some
information concerning the mulatto woman, Rosa Corsini.   I
know that you ladies have a way of obtaining the confidence
and affection of our prisoners that we, their official guardians,
never even dream of.   Therefore I think, if you will have the
goodness to come to the library with us, you will be able to
satisfy them far better than I.   First permit me, Sister Hildebrand, Sister Alphonse,—Miss Sefton, Mr. Sefton."

The two religious bowed, smiled, murmured an assent, and
the party entered a square, bare-looking room at the top of the
first flight of stairs.   It contained a couple of half-filled book-
cases and half-a-dozen wooden chairs.

As they entered the room Antonia impulsively grasped the
hand of the younger of the nuns, Sister Alphonse, a cheerful,
sweet-faced little woman, and, drawing her away from the others,
exclaimed : " Sister, come over here and tell me all you know of
this poor woman.   I must know everything.   I am deeply interested in her."

"My dear Miss Sefton," answered the nun gently, a ·slight
look of surprise crossing her serene face, " I shall be very glad to
tell you all that I know.   I am delighted to see so benevolent an
interest taken in one of the poor souls here, many of whom
never would be here were there a helping hand stretched out to
them in the need and privation that lead them into the wretchedness of sin.   This Rosa Corsini has been a very unhappy wo-

man. Even yet one can see in her traces of great natural refinement and some education. Although she has served several
terms here for theft or vagrancy, she seems always to have preserved a certain amount of self-respect that, joined to the grace
of God, kept her from greater evils. She had a child—her
'singing-bird,' she called her—who was adopted by a wealthy
gentleman of this city. After serving her first term of imprisonment she resolved to lead an honest life. Through a written
'character' given her by the superintendent she obtained an
excellent situation as housemaid in a wealthy family, where
she was treated with the greatest kindness till they discovered,
from the chance remark of a caller who had once visited this institution during Rosa's term of imprisonment and who remembered her face, that their invaluable housemaid was an ex-convict. One hour after the discovery Rosa was again a homeless
and hopeless woman. After that she lost all ambition. She
worked when she had the chance, but she did not attempt to
obtain another permanent, respectable situation. Once or twice
charity saved her from starvation, oftener theft. She led a dreary,
lonely life. She had neither friends nor relatives, and, as she
said to me when she told me her story, ' when a woman is once
spotted by the police there's no chance for her.' Unable to
work any longer, she was found on the street the other day in
an apparently dying condition and brought here as a vagrant.
Oh! my dear young lady, I hope there is room in heaven for
these poor vagrants, since it is only a prison-cell we can give
them on earth!"

The nun's bright eyes filled with tears and her voice was tremulous. After a pause, she continued: " Poor Rosa has been prepared for death and seems glad to have done with life, though
she is constantly talking of her child. The doctor says she cannot last through the day. I think she would die happy if she
could only have some news of her child."

Antonia had listened eagerly to the sister's narrative, her face
pale, her eyes full of tears. When it was ended she started from
her chair and, earnestly pressing the nurse's hand, said : " Thank
you, sister, for all you have told me. In return let me tell you
that Rosa shall die happy, for I am bringing her news of her
child."

Sister Hildebrand had been giving the same details to Mr.
Sefton. He, too, was strangely affected by the story. Antonia
said, as he came forward, " Father, let us go to her at once."

They bade the two religious good-by, the superintendent

again led the way, and in a few moments Antonia stood out-side the grating—serving as door and window for the cell—that separated her from her mother. One glance showed her the bare floor, the one wooden stool, the tiny shelf on the wall con-taining a few bottles of medicine, the comfortless cot on which rested a woman's motionless form. One thin hand lay on the coarse coverlid; the face was prematurely aged, but suffering had sharpened and spiritualized the features; the closed eyelids were suggestive of peace.

Mr. Sefton winced as he noticed, or thought he noticed, a startling resemblance even yet between mother and daughter. For an instant Antonia's thoughts reverted to the dream-mother she had so long believed in; then her whole heart was submerged in passionate tenderness for the dying woman before her. The superintendent turned the key and opened the grating. Mr. Sefton turned to his daughter and said in a low voice: "There isn't room for more than one visitor in that cupboard, so I'll stroll up and down the corridor, 'Tonia."

Mother and daughter were alone. The noise of the opening door had disturbed the mulatto's slumber. She moved uneasily; then her eyes opened, and she murmured in a husky whisper, "Who said ''Tonia?' Was I dreaming again?"

She caught sight of the beautiful, tall young lady bending over her bed. Her own dim eyes grew wistful as she looked into the eyes so full of love and pity. Antonia's warm hands clasped the thin, cold hands that were nervously playing with the coverlid. She forgot the discretion she had meant to exercise. She bent and kissed her mother's lips. "Mother," she whispered in a tremulous, low voice, "don't you see I am your 'Tonia?"

A look of glad surprise crossed the mulatto's face. "It is such a beautiful dream," she gasped.

Antonia's strong arm encircled her mother's wasted frame, her fingers smoothed the gray hair with a soft, caressing touch as she answered, "It is not a dream."

"Then this is heaven," murmured the feeble voice. "I have dreamed so often, so often, that I had her again—my little singing-bird whom I gave away. Sometimes she comes and pulls my dress and calls 'mammy,' just as when she was a little toddling child, and sometimes she takes my hand and we walk away off along a great, dusty road; but I never get tired, for she smiles into my face with her sweet eyes and sings all the time like a little canary bird."

"Shall she sing to you now, mother?"

There is only a faint, incredulous smile for answer. Antonia

holds her mother's hand in a closer clasp, and, standing erect,
begins to sing a quaint old hymn to the Virgin of Sorrows, each
stanza of which ends with the refrain, " Virgin, full sorrowful, pray
thou for us ! "

At first the tones are very sweet and low, then the exquisite voice
rings out in more powerful melody.   The mother listens as one in a
trance.   Never in a fashionable drawing-room, before the most cultured and appreciative audience, did Antonia sing so well.   The
pathos, the sweetness of her notes, surprise even her father, who is
pacing the corridor outside.   All along the tier of cells the calico curtains are drawn back from the gratings and eager faces peer into the
corridor.   Antonia does not know into how many wretched hearts
her tones are sinking as her wonderful voice breathes the last invo-
cation, " Pray thou for us ! "   She feels only that she is voicing the
plaintive heart-cry of the dying woman, whose eyes are streaming
with tears while she listens.

Suddenly she raises herself in bed and looks intently at Antonia.   " 'Tonia," she whispers, " you are not a little girl any
longer.   How beautiful you have grown !   Your voice is like an
angel's ! "

" No, mother, only like your little singing-bird."

Rosa smiles faintly.   Her breathing grows more difficult.   Finally
she gasps, " 'Tonia, if this isn't a dream, may I "—the voice is very
humble—" may I kiss you ? "

Antonia kneels at the side of the cot and raises her face as
she puts her arms about her mother.   The dying woman, gathering all her remaining strength together, bends her head and kisses
her daughter on brow and cheek and lips.   Then she sinks back
exhausted.   Once or twice she struggles to speak, but no word
leaves her lips, only a gasp ever fainter and feebler.   A convul-
sive movement goes through her frame.   In a moment Antonia
realizes that the end has come.   But on the dead face there is
a smile of infinite peace and content.

MARIE LOUISE SANDROCK.

THE WARFARE OF SCIENCE.

·'III.

THE different sciences justly claim for themselves their distinct autonomies, and the liberty of investigation on their own proper principles by their own methods. Catholic authority does not interfere with this liberty, or assume to overrule strictly scientific teaching by a higher scientific doctrine derived from revelation. Such a doctrine does not exist in the Sacred Scriptures, the only source from which it could have been derived, if the sacred writers had been inspired to disclose truths in this order. There is no royal road to knowledge in astronomy, geology, and similar things, for ecclesiastics, to be obtained by the study of the Scriptures. Ecclesiastics, doctors of the church, theologians, are on the same level with other men in this respect. The same is the case in regard to all the branches of human learning and art, politics, civil and social culture.

The history of Christian civilization is consequently a history of development and progress, like the history of all humanity. And, in this development, the two factors of conservatism and innovation are always at work, conditioning each other and modifying the rate and direction of progression in all lines of movement. Theology and philosophy, like other human sciences, develop in the same way, and under the same counterbalancing influences of conservatism and innovation. In so far as they are connected with other sciences, and obliged to follow methods of inductive reasoning from data furnished by the investigations of these sciences, their advancement is dependent on the course and the results of these investigations.

The resistance which discoverers in science, which innovating theories finally turning out to be true or at all events so probable as to merit general acceptance, have had to encounter from churchmen, is not to be exclusively referred to theological prejudice. To a great extent this resistance of Catholic authority was the effect of a conservative reaction of the dominant philosophy and science of the time against innovation. It was a struggle between old and long established scientific theories, and new, as yet merely hypothetical views, not entitled to be received as truth, but only as guesses at truth. Moreover, there was a great deal of pseudo-science, of charlatanism, in the form of alchemy, fortune-telling, astrology, necromancy, demonology, etc., prevalent in the middle ages. Suspicion was cast on men who deviated from the routine of the dominant schools for this reason, although in the case of genuine investigators it was unjust. The adepts in occult science and soothsaying were like the faith-curers, Christian-scientists, spiritists, and theosophists of our own day. Even religious and truly scientific men might sometimes try experiments in the borderland which had the appearance of dabbling in magic. Perhaps this was one reason of the quarrel between Roger Bacon and his superior which caused his imprisonment. The superior may have been in great part or entirely in the wrong; but this is no proof that the Franciscan Order was in principle opposed to science. The prohibition of medical studies and practice by Franciscans and Dominicans was because they were foreign to the religious vocation.

It would have been a miracle, considering the existing conditions during the period before the modern scientific revolution, if there had been no collision between Catholic authority and novel scientific theories. It was necessary that both theology and science should make great strides in their development before their real harmony could become evident. The Vatican Council has declared that: "The imaginary appearance of contradiction between them arises chiefly from this source, that the dogmas of faith have not been correctly understood and exposed, or that futile opinions have been mistaken for dictates of reason" (Const. de Fide, c. iv.) Imperfect theology and imperfect science coming together on common ground are liable to collision. It is the right and duty of Catholic authority to watch against the introduction of errors contrary to faith and the invasion of the proper territory of theology, under the disguise of scientific theories. But when there are not sufficient theological and scientific data at hand to determine, in a manner which is final and will never need to be reformed, some particular question of error and invasion, an undeserved censure may be pronounced. There is no recourse possible to divine revelation and inspiration. There is no supernatural insight into scientific truth. The prerogative of infallibility cannot be brought into play at will to meet every emergency. Ordinary discipline in respect to doctrinal matters depends on the judgments of theologians, on inferior tribunals, on the Roman congregations, which are a perpetual congress of theologians and, under the presidency of the Pope, form a papal tribunal which is not the *Cathedra Petri* and whose decisions are therefore not *ex-cathedra*.

There is no case of contradiction between any irreformable, infallible decision of Pope or Œcumenical Council and any certain conclusion of inductive science, or even any probable theory. Indeed, there are very few instances of collision between science and the disciplinary authority of the Holy See.*

One case which is often cited turns out on examination to be only imaginary. It is that of Pope Zachary, the Bishop Virgil, and the Antipodes.

Virgil was an Irish monk who went to Germany and labored as a missionary under St. Boniface. He was educated in an excellent school, and was acquainted with the fact that navigators had gone as far as Greenland, and even to our North American coast. He taught his scholars the rotundity of the earth and the existence of the antipodes which were inhabited by men. Some persons complained to St. Boniface that he was ventilating strange, unheard-of opinions, which as reported to the archbishop seemed to him contrary to the faith. St. Boniface wrote to the Pope on the subject, at the same time informing him that Virgil was making claim to a bishopric on the faith of a promise received from the Pope during a visit which he had made to Rome. The Pope replied that he was not aware of any such promise, and that he would exact from Virgil an account of his doctrines, and then determine what was to be done in the matter. Here the history of the case ends. There is no account of the communications which passed between the Pope, Virgil, and St. Boniface respectively. From the fact that Virgil was afterwards made Bishop of Salzburg we may infer that he convinced the Pope of his orthodoxy, and he was after his death canonized and highly venerated among the people of the country where he had labored.

On the strength of Pope Zachary's letter to St. Boniface he is accused of having censured the opinion of the existence of antipodes, implying, of course, the rotundity of the earth, as a heresy. The words of the Pontifi are as follows:

"Concerning his perverse and bad doctrine, by which he has spoken against God and his own soul, if it is made clear that he has professed that there is another world under the earth, *with other men having another sun and moon*, let him be expelled

---

* On the distinction between the infallible and disciplinary authority of the Holy See, see two articles: "The Divine Authority of the Church" and "Human Authority in the Church," in THE CATHOLIC WORLD, vol. xlii., November and December, 1885.

from the church by a council and deprived of the honor of the priesthood."

There is no question here of the rotundity of the earth or the antipodes in our sense of the word. The censure falls upon the opinion that there is another race of men in the opposite hemisphere. The inhabitants of this opposite hemisphere are called antipodes in the ancient authors, and not the hemisphere itself. Why was the assertion that such a race existed denounced as contrary to the doctrine of the Scriptures? Because it was supposed to be contrary to the doctrine of the unity of the human race, which pertains to the Christian faith, inasmuch as it is an essential dogma that all men fell in Adam and are redeemed in Christ. Now, the ancient Greeks, who had discovered the sphericity of the earth, supposed that the habitable regions opposite to their own were separated from them by an impassable burning zone, or by one of ice, or of water. This notion was transmitted to the Christian generations. So long as it prevailed there was no room for regarding the antipodes as descendants from Adam, who had colonized the opposite hemisphere from Asia. Hence, to assert their existence was equivalent to a denial of the unity of the human race. But, as soon as it was discovered that all parts of the globe are accessible and can have been peopled by descendants of Adam, the apparent contradiction between the assertion of the existence of antipodes and the doctrines of the faith disappeared. Virgil may have convinced Pope Zachary that he was right, a very probable conjecture which accounts fully for the fact that the impeachment of his orthodoxy was quashed, and that he was promoted to the episcopate and canonized.

The fathers of the church, whose language about antipodes is explained by what has gone before, did not generally reject the sphericity of the earth, much less condemn it as contrary to the Scriptures. Lactantius and Cosmas Indicopleustes do not represent the patristic doctrine, and even they do not censure the doctrine of the sphericity of the earth on the score of dogma. Origen, Ambrose, Augustine, Hilary, Gregory Nyssen, Gregory Nazianzen, James of Edessa, Isidore of Seville, and Ven. Bede either treat the question as one which is open to free discussion, or speak, respectively, with more or less of a leaning to the cosmographic system of Ptolemy.*

---

*See the article of Professor Gilbert, "Le Pape Zacharie et les Antipodes," *Rev. des Qu. Scientif.*, vol. xii., p. 478; Aug., De Genesi ad litt., lib. ii. c. g.; Orig., Periarchon, lib. ii. c. 3; Ambr., In cxviii. Psalm.; Serm. xii. Hexæmeron, c. vi.; Isid., Etymol. libri tres., cap. xxxii., xxxiii., lix.; Bede, De natura rerum; Patrol. Latin. Migne, t. xc. col. 193, 437–8, 453.

· As for Pietro d'Abano and Ceccho d'Ascoli, there is a great obscurity and uncertainty in regard to the alleged reasons for the persecution which overtook them. It may be that it sprang from passion and malice and was wholly unjust. But it had nothing to do with the antipodes,* or any matter of genuine science.

Giordano Bruno was a disreputable character, who no more deserves the name of a martyr of science than the anarchists hanged at Chicago deserve the name of martyrs of liberty.

The case of Galileo is the one signal instance of the condemnation of a true scientific theory by ecclesiastical authority. It is not at all requisite for my purpose that I should make a plea in justification of the Roman tribunal which censured the doctrine of this illustrious astronomer and obliged him to profess a retractation. The only point I aim at, is to show that in the Catholic Church, and in the exercise of her authority by defending the faith against errors under the garb of science, there is no hostility in principle to science or the scientific liberty recognized by the Council of the Vatican.

At the time of the censure on Galileo and his theory the heliocentric doctrine was not science, but hypothesis. There was no evidence of its truth except its fitness for explaining all the astronomical phenomena. There were objections to it which were insoluble in the then state of science. The geocentric theory was held by the whole scientific world, with few exceptions. In accordance with this common consent, the ecclesiastical judges of Galileo's case regarded his theory as scientifically false and absurd. The motive for pronouncing a theological censure upon it was, that it contradicted the literal sense of many passages of Holy Writ, and the interpretation of these passages by the common consent of the Fathers. By degrees the entire status of the heliocentric theory, and the prevalent view of its relation to theological doctrine, were changed through the progressive advance of science. Scientific discoveries removed the difficulties out of its way. Gradually an indirect demonstration of its truth was gained, which after the lapse of one hundred and fifty years was completed by Sir Isaac Newton. Since then direct proofs have been accumulating, as, for instance, by the discovery of the parallax of some fixed stars since the year 1838, and they are increased almost every day by astronomical observations.

According to Cardinal Bellarmine's principle of interpretation, as soon as the theory of Galileo became a scientific truth it became

Tiraboschi, *Storia della Lit. Ital.*, vol. v., book xi. cviii.-xviii.; Bernini, *Istoria di Tutte l. Eresie*, vol. iii., sec. xiv., Eivvana xxii.

necessary to abandon the literal interpretation of those texts of Scripture in which the inspired writers had been supposed to affirm the geocentric system as absolutely true, and to depart from the patristic comments in the same sense. It became manifest that the inspired writers spoke in accordance with the appearances which are presented to the senses, as is, even now, our customary method. As the philosophical and scientific prejudice of the old Aristotelian and Ptolemaic school waned before the rising sun of the Copernican system, theological prejudice gradually disappeared. The prohibition of the Roman congregations passed into desuetude.

"In 1664 the prohibition still remained officially in force. But the higher and higher position which the system of Copernicus gained among the learned necessarily induced a certain practical tolerance, and many Catholics had little scruple of professing it. . . . In the Congregation of the Holy Office of the 10th of May, 1757, under the pontificate of Benedict XIV., an important step was taken: they resolved to erase from the Index the article which prohibited works treating of the immobility of the sun and the mobility of the earth. . . .

"In France, Germany, and Italy the Copernican astronomy was taught, and works openly advocating this system were published with the approbation of the ecclesiastical censors, these works containing also the theories of Kepler and Newton. Cardinal Polignac and Muratori declared themselves distinctly in favor of these doctrines. F. Troili, S.J., published in 1772 a treatise on astronomy in which he refuted the 'system of Ptolemy and showed decisive reasons for adopting that of Copernicus. In 1755 Boscowich, in his memoir on the measurement of the arc of the meridian and in his other writings speaks absolutely as admitting the rotation of the earth. The astronomer Manfredi did the same. In 1790 the Abbate Guglielmini, assisted by a prelate of the household of Pope Pius VI., made a remarkable series of experiments at Bologna in order to demonstrate the rotation of the earth, by the deviation of bodies freely falling to the earth. I have before my eyes a MSS. course of astronomy given at the University of Louvain in 1786 by Van Lempoel, in which the superiority of the system of Copernicus over those of Ptolemy and Tycho, the proofs which sustain it, the nullity of the objections against it derived from the Holy Scriptures, are presented with a freedom and clearness which show that for many years these doctrines had been professed at Louvain. It is evident, then, that the prohibitions of 1616 and 1634 gave no one any uneasiness, and it is an exaggeration to say that the condemnation of Galileo had paralyzed the progress of astronomical science among Catholics." *

In 1820 a circumstance occurred which brought this famous and much discussed affair to its termination. Canon Settelé, a professor in a Roman college, applied for an *imprimatur* for his *Elements of Optics and Astronomy*, which was refused by the Master of the Sacred Palace, notwithstanding an order from the Pope to give it. The *imprimatur* was given by another prelate authorized by the Pope, and a decree was passed by the Congregation of the Holy Office formally permitting to the author the teaching of the Copernican system. Finally, September 11, 1822, a similar decree was published, and the works of Galileo, etc., which had remained on the Index were ordered to be erased from its pages.

The wonderful development of astronomical science has been accompanied and followed by a similar development of other sciences. Some of these sciences, and the theories and hypotheses connected with them, are, by their nature, in a vicinity to theology and interpretations of Scripture which have been in vogue. There have arisen controversies, in which theories and opinions on the two sides have come into conflict, and also various efforts of both scientists and theologians to bring about that conciliation which is so desirable. The Roman congregations have not interfered in these discussions by decisions having a disciplinary authority, but have left the adjustment of the relations between theology and the sciences to theologians.

In the question of cosmogony there is the same opposition between the conclusions of geology and the literal interpretation of the hexæmeron of Genesis, that exists between the Copernican astronomy and the literal interpretation of the respective texts of Scripture. Some theologians have steadfastly adhered, and a few still adhere, to this literal interpretation. The dominant sense of the majority is, however, that a sufficient latitude must be given to the interpretation of Scripture, to give full liberty to all those theories of geologists which are based on the data of genuine science. Even our opponents do not venture to censure this position as unorthodox, and Catholics enjoy, in this regard, a perfect scientific liberty. One word will suffice for a very famous and favorite theory, the nebular hypothesis of Kant and Laplace. This theory makes no claim to be more than a probable hypothesis. Yet, as there is no difficulty on

* Prof. Gilbert in the *Rev. des Qu. Scientif.*, April, 1891

the score of faith in admitting the long series of geological ages, embracing millions of years, neither is there any in respect to the preceding period of the development of the solar and stellar systems. This theory, in fact, is as generally favored by our eminent Catholic authors as by any other class of learned men.

The theory of evolution, in its application to the origin and development of the flora and fauna of the earth, is far too wide and deep a question to be treated in a cursory manner. There is no universal consent of scientific authorities on this head, and among evolutionists themselves there are serious divergencies of opinion. In my judgment, there is sufficient Catholic authority for the position, that it is a matter of purely scientific and philosophical investigation and discussion, in which theology is not directly implicated.

Anthropology, and the numerous questions connected with it, open up a field for inquiries into the human period of the earth's history and its earliest events, full of interest and replete with serious difficulties. The antiquity of man, the chronology of the period between Adam and Abraham, the peopling of the earth, the extent of the Noachian Deluge in respect both to the surface of the globe and to the race of mankind, the rise and progress of civilization, these are some of the numerous questions alluded to above. I must content myself, at present, with a reference to a series of articles in the fortieth and forty-fourth volumes of THE CATHOLIC WORLD, entitled " Scriptural Questions." Those who are at home in the German language will find it much to their advantage to consult the able and thoroughly scientific *Apologie des Christenthums* by Professor Schanz of Tübingen, and also the *Weltgeschichte* of Professor Weiss of the University of Gratz. The first volume of Dr. Schanz's work, in which the antiquity of man, the deluge, and kindred topics are treated, has already been published in an English translation.

There is no warfare of Catholic authority on any of these parts of the domain of science against liberty of investigation, or any of those certain conclusions which deserve the name of science. Conjectural and extravagant hypotheses do not deserve this name. These may be in opposition to faith, and also to sound philosophy, to genuine science, to history and common sense. Scientists, even some who are eminent in their particular branches, may invade the domain of philosophy and theology, and broach the most erroneous and destructive errors. When they avow themselves to be unbelievers in Christianity or Theism, we have a right to designate them by the names which denote their particular phase of unbelief or scepticism. Catholic authority has the right to condemn their errors and does a service to the cause of truth by waging war against them.

Moreover, we must be allowed, with all due respect for the physical sciences, to give religion, ethics, philosophy, history and letters, a place of higher importance in general education, making the proper exceptions in respect to some of these for professional specialists. Above all, we must insist on the paramount importance of religion in education, which for us Catholics means simply and exclusively the Catholic religion. If there are shortcomings in the courses of our educational institutions in respect to the sciences, we will endeavor to remedy the deficiency. So far as ecclesiastics have been behindhand in this regard the entire influence of Catholic authority, even the highest, is actively exerted to stimulate them to improvement and progress.

Authority and rational liberty are not in principle opposed to each other. Nor is the principle of authority a specific difference of theology. It is an universal principle, existing and necessary in every department of human development in the rational and moral order. This is eminently the case in the domain of natural science. A signal instance is presented in the defiant assertion of Judge Stallo that no answer has been given to the arguments of his famous book on the contradictions and unproved assumptions of prevalent scientific hypotheses, except an appeal to the consent and authority of scientists. The remarks of F. Kent in an excellent article on "The Office of Reason in Theology" are so much to the point, that I will conclude this paper by quoting them at length:

"The tone of superiority assumed by so many writers of the day is hardly in keeping with facts. We are told, however, that earlier ages were distinguished by a credulous and blind trust to authority, whereas the present lives by reason and proof. But is this the case? Do men nowadays make better use of their reason than in the ages of faith? Take, for instance, the general acceptance of the teaching of science. Does this rest on severe and formal reasoning or actual experience of the facts which are admitted? Undoubtedly a large number of facts in natural science have been ascertained with certainty, and many of its conclusions are proved to demonstration. Yes, but for whom is this proof? For all who accept the teaching? Surely not. Very few of the thousands who receive it without qualms, who take the word of Huxley and Darwin as gospel truth to measure heaven and earth withal, could give any proof of their teaching. Nay, there are many quite incapable of appreciating the force of the arguments when these are placed before them. Science, like religion, has its *ecclesia discens* and its *ecclesia docens*. Authority, after all, has more influence in our lives than we are aware of—more, maybe, than we care to acknowledge. Even in matters which are susceptible of strict proof most of us are content to go by faith. We accept the teaching of those who are masters of their several subjects, and go by reason only in so far as practical reason tells us that we do well to take their authority.

"Now, there is no reason to complain of the acceptance of scientific teaching on the authority of competent men. It would be the height of folly to reject and disbelieve all science which we have not proved for ourselves. Reason itself condemns such a course. For it is not only in strict proof and formal investigation that the voice of reason is heard. It is in the office of reason to weigh the credentials of an authority, and form a practical judgment as to its trustworthiness; and this reasonable belief is and must always be one of the most effective means of arriving at the truth. There is thus what may be called an element of faith in the wide-spread acceptance of modern physical science. Unhappily, credulity and superstition follow in its track.

"Because a man has made important discoveries, or has done other excellent work in the field of physics, he is practically taken as a guide and teacher, not merely on those matters on which he can claim to speak with authority, but on the higher subjects of philosophy and religion. No doubt there are some men who have been carried into the trackless desert of scepticism and unbelief by doubts and difficulties of their own. But it is likely that the number of those who have thus gone astray through the disordered workings of their own minds is not by any means considerable. The hosts of fashionable Free-thinkers and Agnostics, and Positivists and Atheists, are really led by the influence of others. They may talk of reason and smile at the simple credulity of darker ages, yet they are themselves the victims of a singular delusion, and afford one of the most striking examples of credulity and unreasoning faith that the world has seen. What, after all, is the ultimate basis of their assent to the form of unbelief which they affect? It is the word of some eminent man who has no claim to authority but his achievements in physical science, or the charm of his literary style. Popular Agnosticism is really a creed, or rather a system of credulity.

"In all this we see the natural result of the perversion of reason from its true office. The revolt against the just sway of lawful authority has ended in the tyranny of usurpers."[*] .

The miracles of St. Francis Xavier will form the topic of the next article.   AUGUSTINE F. HEWIT.

[*] *Irish Eccl. Record*, May, 1891.

THE HOUSE OF THE ROSE AND SWORD.

THERE is an old house on the Rue Royal about five minutes' walk from the garden of Monseigneur the Archbishop—a house that once seen would never be forgotten. That there are a hundred other houses in New Orleans as likely to impress themselves on one's memory does not detract from the special uniqueness of the "Rose and Sword." Once its bricks were yellow; they are now a creamy white, and the suns that bleached them have peeled the paint from the heavy oaken portal and the great venetian blinds. Each pair of windows—and each of the two upper floors has two pairs—has its own balcony; and the balustrade of each balcony has for balusters swords about which twine rose-branches all wrought in iron. Again, above the lintel of the portal is a great oaken shield on which is repeated the device of the Rose and the Sword; and from the base of the shield is thrust out another rose-twined sword, the lantern-bearer from which has hung no lantern since the year the then government ordered that, to show our happiness, we celebrate Mardi Gras as of old. Whether it was that there was so little of happiness to show, or what, there was no celebration of Mardi Gras, but much inspection of houses to know why we were sorrowful when the State of Affairs would have us glad. They came to Aunt Marie's room on the top floor, from the balcony of which one can see the broad banana leaves waving in monseigneur's garden. They wished to know why no candle had been lit. Aunt Marie did not tell that we had no candle, but paid the tiny fine that, tiny as it was, left us without a picayune.

That was our first year in the house of the Rose and Sword. After the great war mother and Aunt Marie had tried to hold on to the few acres of plantation still 'theirs. They held on for nearly five years. Then mother died. I was fifteen at that time. What can a girl of fifteen do? Aunt Marie was brave enough, as the good God knows; nevertheless she said to me: "I cannot keep the land for you, and I would but kill myself as your mother did if I tried. We will go to New Orleans; bread cannot be less scarce there than here, and we may find—we must find—a market for our embroideries and artificial flowers." It was well Aunt Marie decided on this, for presently the State of Affairs appropriated our house and little field. I think this was the time her heart broke. But before the representatives of the State of Affairs she was cheerful, even gay.

So we came to the house of the Rose and Sword. Aunt Marie knew the house. She had in the old time often visited the St. Juliens. Not that they still owned it. Oh! no; if any of them lived they were like ourselves. It was now a lodging-house, and Aunt Marie rented a room on the top floor from Madame Doussaint—she who leased the house. This was in 1870.

How did we live? Well, in truth it was hard. Aunt Marie could make from bits of paper, or silk, or velvet, and out of feathers, the most exquisite flowers, that, in all save the perfume, came near to rival those of the good God. She could embroider too. As for me, my sewing it was excellent. But there was so little sale for these things The good fathers at the cathedral and at the college bought from us. They could buy but little, for the city was full of women poor as Aunt Marie, and there was little with which to help us all. Aunt Marie always prophesied better times, always laughed and chatted cheerfully with me, and we often sang together. I know now that she did all this to give me heart. And she succeeded, for, though I was often hungry, I was not unhappy. No, not even when I thought of my father and mother and my brothers! Why should I be? They are in Paradise.

Once Aunt Marie did break down. That was in '72' when the tax was laid on the white artificial-flower makers and embroiderers. Aunt Marie laughed when she told me of it; but I cried. I was so young, and I was frightened, not knowing what would become of us, for we had no money to pay the license or the tax. But when Aunt Marie chided me and said, "Little one, suppose the State of Affairs knew of your tears?" I cried no more. She went on, however, to remind me of how poor our dear Lord was, and of the wounds of his sweet Heart, and I wept again, softened tears that made me hope.

What made the tax particularly hard on us at the moment was that Monseigneur the Archbishop had given Aunt Marie an order for flowers that would bring us a clear profit of at least ten dollars. I went with Aunt Marie to explain how it was that we could not make the flowers. Monseigneur listened quietly until she had finished telling him of our new trouble; then he opened a desk and, having taken a twenty-dollar gold piece from it, he said: "Madame, you must not refuse the church. You can," he continued after a pause, "*present* your flowers to her; the State of Affairs still permits us to give and to accept gifts." At this Aunt Marie wept as I have never seen one weep. She wept the pent-up tears of years, and the tears, too, rolled down the old cheeks of Monseigneur the Archbishop.

We stayed long that evening in the ancient cathedral; we were in thankfulness so drawn to the good God. As we went away I was glad to see the sunlight so bright on the tomb of my great-great grandfather, the Chevalier de l'Isle, who is buried there. I said to Aunt Marie that it was a good omen, and she was too content to reprove me for my superstition.

That evening, as we sat partly in the room, partly on the balcony, Aunt Marie said: "Rose, I have thought of something, now that we can no longer make flowers—except, of course, those for monseigneur; they are sacred. We are to make our fortunes!"

I smiled in doubt.

"Ah! infidel, you laugh," she cried, herself smiling. "Listen: we will make rice-cakes."

At this I laughed out so loud that Aunt Marie clapped her hand to my mouth. "You will attract the passers-by," she reproved. I blushed, and when I said it was so droll in her to say we would become rich by making rice-cakes I spoke in a whisper almost.

"Not by making them, but by selling them," she returned. I objected that I did not know how they were to be sold. "I shall tell you," she replied. "I shall carry them to the offices of the men in business. The clerks will buy my delightful cakes, Rose."

I was too amazed to speak. As noble as is her heart is the appearance of Aunt Marie. She to be a merchant of the banquette, to peddle cakes in the offices on Canal Street! She joked? No, no! it was in all sincerity that she spoke. We had to live; and we made cakes of rice early the next morning, and when they were ready, her thick white hair drawn back under her close black bonnet, Aunt Marie went out to sell them.

She would not return, she had told me, before some hours, and I was feeling very lonely over my sewing, when Madame Doussaint came in with some oranges for me and a great piece of news. She had rented her first floor that had been vacant so long. She was in high good humor, and insisted on my guessing the name of her lodger before she would tell me that he was a young lawyer named Eraste St. Julien, the last of the family that had once owned the Rose and the Sword, and the great Bellechasse plantation ·in Tangipahoa parish. We both thought it very sad, and madame talked long of the elegance of M. St. Julien's manner and of his handsome appearance.

Aunt Marie came home late, her cakes sold; but she looked badly and much fatigued. The cup of coffee I had ready enlivened her and set her to talking; but she told me nothing of her day's experience save that the city was swarming with women and children from the parishes in as hopeless a plight as ourselves. Tired as she was, Aunt Marie got to work at the flowers for monseigneur, and whilst she fashioned branches of lilies, I sewed and told her of Madame Doussaint's new lodger. The only remark Aunt Marie made to my news was, "I don't know but what I ought to claim his acquaintance, I knew his mother so well."

The next morning was Sunday, and as we returned from Mass a young man passed us whom I had noticed praying before the altar of the Holy Virgin. "It is Eraste St. Julien," whispered Aunt Marie. "He has changed very little from when I saw him as a boy." I was about to remark that Aunt Marie must have a good memory for faces to so well remember one she had not seen for nigh twenty years, when the clank of arms and the heavy tramp on the banquette of a body of the militia of the State of Affairs advancing behind us made me forget everything in my desire to reach home, which was in sight. I clung to Aunt Marie's arm, and we started at a trot for the Rose and Sword, followed by the laugh of the militia. In my eagerness to reach home I did not perceive that we had gained on M. St. Julien, who, seeing two unprotected women and the advancing militia, bowed and asked permission of Aunt Marie to accompany us home.

"We are there in a moment," said Aunt Marie, making a little motion with her hand to point out the house of the Rose and Sword.

"How fortunate!" he exclaimed. "I too live there."

We had now reached the house, and with a grave courtesy Aunt Marie thanked M. St. Julien and we passed on to our room, leaving him standing in the hallway. I was a little disappointed. I found that I had built on Aunt Marie's old friendship for M. St. Julien's family. She was very silent all that day, and I was abashed to speak of him to her.

Every day Aunt Marie went out with her basket of cakes, and in time she had so increased her custom as to be able to employ one Carl, who possessed a hand-cart, to deliver our cakes at a number of private houses and to the families of the troops that garrisoned the city.   One of the officers had showed to Aunt Marie much kindness.   "It was Captain Fletcher who gained me the custom of the garrison," she said to me.   "Do not forget him in your prayers, little one."   Things went well with us till August; so well that Aunt Marie spoke to Madame Doussaint of the possibility of her renting the second floor of the Rose and Sword.   And to me she said, half-laughing, half-crying, her arms about my neck, "What say you, little one, to one horse and wagon, so little, and Carl to drive?"

How we laughed and chatted and sang that evening!   We had had much of happiness in the house of the Rose and Sword, but that evening we could scarce contain ourselves.   And to make us merrier, if possible, Madame Doussaint came to join us at supper, bringing with her a little kettle of freshest red-fish court-bouillon.   "Eat, eat!" she cried to me at table; "he bring the color to your cheek so blanche, and the sparkle to your eye."

"She was my little angel, yes," murmured Aunt Marie, feigning to frown, and then crying out in a burst of laughter, "Gourmet! gourmet!"

About a week after this Aunt Marie met with the accident that came near to ending her good life.   She was on St. Claude Street, passing a dwelling that was being torn down, and a falling beam struck her leg, so that, as you know, she limps to this day. For more than a month she was unable to leave her bed, and it rested on me to keep up our trade in the rice-cakes.   With the help Madame Doussaint gave me I could have done this, had not Carl deserted me to go to a man who would pay him more than I could afford to give.   This desertion would have taken the life out of me had I had the time to spend in idle thought.   Mercifully there was much for me to do, and while I worked I formed my plan, and then communicated it to Madame Doussaint.

"You will go out with one basket as did the woman, your aunt, of the grand soul?" she said, knitting her brows in thought. "You will wear the close bonnet and the veil?" she continued, and I said I would, though I had not thought of them.   Then she implored me to give up my idea.   She was in no need of money for the room, and if we needed anything she could let us have it. I knew, however, that she was as poor as myself.   She had rented none of her rooms save the one Aunt Marie and I lodged in and the two occupied by M. St. Julien.   And, though madame never told me so, I felt that he was very poor and that he could

not pay her regularly.   Perhaps I had been led to believe this
last by my having learned that he cooked his meals himself, and
I very seldom perceived the odor of meat proceeding from his
apartment.

" Aunt Marie must not know I have gone out," I said to
madame when, my basket on my arm, I was preparing to leave
in the morning.   " Let her suppose I am resting in your room " ;
and madame said yes, yes, she would, and kissed me on either
check.

As I went through the hallway I met M. St. Julien, who
stared at me, astonished, then bowed and looked confused.

From hearing Aunt Marie speak of them, I had a tolerably
correct idea of what places to take my cakes, and everywhere I
went I found that our cakes were known, and from feeling
afraid to offer the contents of my basket I passed to the possession of a strong sensation of pride in our cooking.   I was
helped to this by the courtesy shown me, and the occasional
inquiry after my aunt, quietly put, and the expressions of
sympathy uttered concerning her misfortune.   My basket was
emptied early in the day, and I was crossing the plaza opposite the city hall on my way home when I saw M. St.
Julien advancing towards me.   I had been stopped before
by purchasers, and I began to dread that he wished to buy
of me.   He passed me without a bow or recognition of any
kind, and I felt that he knew I did not wish to be noticed by
him.

I was so overcome by this little encounter and so tired, for
the day was very hot, that I paused to rest myself on one of
the benches under the shade-trees.   I had not been seated long
when a man came up to me and said something in the negro
French of the plantation which I could not understand.   He was
rough-looking and I rose hastily to escape him, when he caught
me by the arm.   Not in a loud voice, for I was weak from terror,
I called out the name of the only man I at all knew, M. St.
Julien.   Helpless as I was from fright, I saw that the grove
of trees prevented me from being seen by the passengers in
the street, and I saw by the man's eyes that he had perceived
as much.

He had loosened his grasp of my arm and was again
speaking his jargon, when I uttered a shrill cry and sprang
from him to run against an officer in the uniform of a captain in the Federal service.   At sight of the uniform the fellow was about to take to his heels when the loudly-shouted

"Halt!" of the officer caused him to turn about and mutter, "I wasn't doin' no harm, boss."

"Lady," said the officer, uncovering, "this fellow has annoyed you?" I nodded my head, and he continued: "You wish to make a complaint against him?"

"No, no!" I denied eagerly, alarmed at the thought of appearing in a court-room.

Then, in no measured terms, the officer bade the fellow begone. He gazed irately in the direction the man had taken, then turned to me and said: "I regret that this has happened, and I beg you to believe me when I tell you that we soldiers have no part whatsoever in the present miserable state of the city." ·

I stammered something in French to the effect that I was not at all discomposed, and stooped to pick up my basket, which had fallen to the ground. He, too, stooped, begging my pardon, and in the confusion my veil fell back, and I saw that my defender was not only a stalwart but a very handsome man of about forty. And I saw that his face flushed and that he looked much surprised.

"Mademoiselle," he said, uttering the French title of compliment with difficulty, "you will pardon me—in the present state of the city you should not be abroad alone. My name is Fletcher. I am old enough to be your father. Permit me to see you safe home. Your family should not have permitted you to come out. Don't they know the state of the city?"

Though he spoke with much indignation, there was no mistaking the respect he showed me. In spite of this respect I, too, felt indignant that Aunt Marie should be so condemned, even though the condemnation was indirect. I broke out in a white heat to defend her, telling him of her accident, and how it came about that I was abroad, and that I was not afraid the men of my people would molest me.

It did not cool me to see him smile, and I winced a little when he said: "So the bakeress of the Rose and Sword is unwell! We have missed her cakes, I can assure you. And you are her niece, mademoiselle?"

Only then I remembered what Aunt Marie had told me of a Captain Fletcher's kindness to her, and now I felt a little shy of him. Instead of answering his last question, I reverted to his first. "I thank you," I said, "but there can be no danger for me on the banquette, and the Rose and Sword is not far off."

"As you will, mademoiselle," he said. "But may I beg another favor of you? I have a sister staying here on a visit; may she call on you?"

The expression "call on you" was new to me, and he must have perceived that I did not understand, for he explained: "May she visit you?"

I drew my veil closer about my face as I said, "We do not receive visitors—now—we have no place—"

I stopped short, and he said gravely: "Mademoiselle, this foolish pride of your people— I *may* tell my sister to call on you?"

I think I shook my head in affirmation, though, as I walked rapidly away, I repeated in French that we could not receive visitors.

I hurried, almost ran home, and as I ascended the steps of the Rose and Sword I saw M. St. Julien a few yards off, watching me as if on guard.

Fortunately I had not been missed by Aunt Marie, who had rested quietly all morning under the impression that I was in the little garden of the Rose and Sword; and this impression was confirmed by my taking to her a bouquet of roses that had been gathered by Madame Doussaint. On the same evening I was sitting by the half-closed blinds when Madame Doussaint came on tiptoe to the open door. In order not to disturb Aunt Marie, who slept, she put her finger to her lips and beckoned me out into the corridor. "Mademoiselle Rose," she said, " I have a message for you from M. St. Julien"; and she offered me a folded piece of note-paper.

"Should I receive a message from him?" I asked, hesitating and feeling that the piece of paper I now held burned my fingers.

"Surely," asserted madame; "he writes for your good."

"You know what he has written?" I faltered.

Madame signified by a nod of her head that she did, and then I opened the billet of M. St. Julien; and this is what I read: "Addressed to Mademoiselle Rose de l'Isle, September the eleventh, 1872: Daily a revolt of our people against the State of Affairs is looked for. M. St. Julien most humbly and with great respect does entreat mademoiselle not to leave the house of the Rose and Sword for the week to come. He petitions with reverence that mademoiselle consult with the respectable Madame Doussaint of these concerns."

Yes, I remembered it all, every word. I have it still in my escritoire.

. Even in the seclusion in which we lived rumor of a rising had reached us, and we longed for it to take place and we dreaded it. "He will take a part in the revolt, madame?" I asked.

"Is he a man, that you ask me that?" she flashed. Then she drew me to her and petted me. "You weep, my angel," she said; and when I had become quieted, questioned, "What shall I tell monsieur?"

"Tell him I thank him, and tell him I remain within," I said.

"And no more?" chirped madame.

I looked at her, and I saw that her eyes had guessed my secret. My face hid in my hands, I said as I turned to go to Aunt Marie, "Tell him, if you wish, I pray for him."

"Good!" called madame after me in a whisper, "that will make him most strong."

On the morning of the thirteenth of September Aunt Marie was able to sit up for the first time in many weeks. Madame Doussaint helped me to arrange a couch for her by the balcony, where she could refresh her eyes with a view of the garden of monseigneur and have a glimpse of the great river rushing to the far-off Gulf. The street had an unusually deserted look. Opposite, the shops of the dealers in old books and antiques, the shop of Madame Sylvanie with its faded bonnets in its window, were desolate, and the old man Simon, who owned the Café Reine at the corner, was the only human being in sight.

"You should have seen Rue Royal when I was young," sighed Aunt Marie, partly to me, partly to the cardinal bird gazing into the ivory cup of a magnolia blooming on the tree, the branches of which stretched out to the balcony.

I pressed her thin hand and sat thinking of the warning given me in M. St. Julien's note, and wondering when the revolt would come. Ignorant of my thoughts, for I had concealed from her all knowledge of M. St. Julien's admonition, fearing to alarm her and so retard her recovery, Aunt Marie began to tell me of the gay parties that she had accompanied to the French Opera, when suddenly she was interrupted by the clatter of a pair of horses and a carriage that drove up to the house of the Rose and Sword.

"Ah! our equipage for the promenade on the beach road to the lake!" exclaimed Aunt Marie, smothering a laugh in the folds of her handkerchief.

I was too intent on watching a woman, all in black silk from head to foot, who descended the carriage steps and then disappeared under the heavy shadow of the portal, to answer. Conscience put me a question that was answered in the affirmative by Madame Doussaint, who brought me a card on which was printed,

" *Miss Letitia Fletcher.*" My . heart beat hard as I handed the
card to Aunt Marie, for had I not kept it a secret to myself, my
meeting with Captain Fletcher ?   What a relief it was when she
said, after having read the name : " Will my Rose go down to this
lady ?   She has come to see why I have not served her for so long.
Let her know, and, my Rose, remember that she and hers have
been very kind to me."

I said that I would, and, directed by Madame Doussaint, I
went to the *salon* on the second floor, where I found the Miss
Letitia gazing out of the window.   She turned about abruptly, and
the cold look she gave me was penetrating.

" You are Miss de l'Isle's niece, I presume ? " she questioned.

I answered that I was, and in the mode taught me by Aunt
Marie I offered her a chair.   She stared at me, then burst into
a laugh that made her fair white face something beautiful, and
reminded me of her brother.

" You will be seated, mademoiselle, I entreat," I said.

For answer she dragged the chair I offered to the middle of
the *salon*, seated herself, and asked, " What is your given name ? "

I did not understand her question, and answered feebly that
I did not know ; then a sudden perception came to me that she
wished to know my Christian name, and I said, " My name is Rose
Marie de l'Isle."

" Well, Rosemary," she questioned, " how is your aunt ?
Captain Fletcher has told me all about her accident.   Does she
still send you out to peddle cakes ? "

I protested in a torrent of words, French and English, that I
had gone out without the knowledge of Aunt Marie, and that she
was unaware of my mishap in the plaza.

When I paused from fatigue, Miss Letitia asked:

" Well, are you through ? "

Under the circumstances it must have appeared droll, for again
Miss Letitia laughed when I bowed in assent as I had once seen
Aunt Marie bow to a representative of the State of Affairs.
Suddenly, however, her face straightened, and she reproved
me, saying, " Do you know that you have done very wrong ?
You have been acting a lie."

I stood up, and my eyes were big.   " A De l'Isle does not
lie, mademoiselle,' I said, my voice low and strong.

She stared at me and commanded, " Rosemary, sit down ! "

I was like a little child.   I obeyed her ; I sat down.

For quite five minutes she scolded me for my sinfulness.   " Now,
Rosemary," she finished, " I hope you are repentant."

With the sensation of having been scored by whips, I thanked Miss Letitia, and I believe I gave her the impression that I thought her charming.

"Well," she went on, "now that we have come to an understanding, I'll see your aunt. I want to speak to her about settling you. How would you like to have charge of a little girl, Rosemary, to teach her to read and write?"

"Mademoiselle," I entreated, "you will pardon me, but mademoiselle, my aunt, does not receive to-day; and, mademoiselle, you do me much honor, but I am one incapable."

"Don't you know how to read and write?" she demanded.

"Yes, yes, but— I will speak to my aunt," I stammered.

"You will do nothing of the kind; you are a pair of impracticable persons," declared Miss Letitia. "I shall speak to her myself."

What I would have said to this I do not know, for at that moment Madame Doussaint entered the *salon* with a message from Aunt Marie to ask Miss Letitia to her room.

She looked as if she had caught me in another prevarication. "Will you lead the way to your aunt?" she demanded, and I went quickly on the way upstairs, followed by her.

"Well, Marie," she began, and then stopped short; for my aunt, in her old-fashioned robe and her thick white hair visible, was very different from the withered woman in the close bonnet and veil. "I was grieved to hear of your accident, madame," she continued, stiffly, but with a grace that was peculiarly her own.

It was not long before Miss Letitia entered into the subject that brought her to the house of the Rose and Sword. I cast my eyes upon her to move her to pity, but she was implacable. She told of my deceit, the story of which made Aunt Marie to weep and caress me. And she called me her angel guardian, and made a grand heroine of me; persisting to do so even when reproved by Miss Letitia, who accused her of being my ruin. I think that Aunt Marie, as well as myself, was angry with Miss Letitia; but how changed we were when she went on to tell us that her brother had lost his wife some years before, and that he had a little girl of five years whom, if I would be a governess to, we would have money sufficient to make it not necessary to sell our cakes on the banquette.

"Now, my dear friends," said Miss Letitia, "let me be your friend. I know what it is to be poor, and I know what it is to be in trouble. When I was a young girl out West I worked hard with my mother, cooking and doing chores for a score or so of farm hands, and I say it in no spirit of boastfulness, but to let you know that I can understand what you have gone through. I earned enough to school me, and then I fell in love with a young farmer, who must needs go in the army, and one of your people killed him. Now, I an't bearing malice for that, neither am I heaping on coals of fire. I just want you to know, and that there is a deal to forgive on both sides. And may He forgive us our trespasses as we forgive those who trespass against us."

I was no longer afraid of her. I kissed her, and she called me a good little soul and stroked my hair. I think her heart was hungry. These people of the cold exterior often have warm hearts. I think it is like good wine that is set in ice; the ice does not kill its fire.

The little girl she spoke of lived in the North, and I would have to go to her. This made it very serious, and we said we would do as Miss Letitia advised. We would think it over.

After Miss Letitia left us neither Aunt Marie nor I spoke of her or of the proposition she had made for me. Rather, we strove not to think of it, although we felt that I must go, and I could not help but wonder what M. St. Julien would say if he were to know that I was going away from the house of the Rose and the Sword.

Before another twenty-four hours would pass enough was to happen to make us forget that my going away had ever been spoken of. About two of the evening Madame Doussaint, Aunt Marie, and myself were taking our bouillon, when we heard the tramp of many feet in the Rue Royal. We looked at one another instinctively, and madame, thinking it best, told Aunt Marie of the threatened revolt. She crossed herself in silence, and took up her beads.

Madame and I hurried to the blinds, and saw going up the banquette on the other side, taking the direction of the *Place d'Armes*, a long line of men. They marched two by two, shoulder to shoulder, with even tramp; these youths and old men so grave, with intent looks upon their faces.

"He is not there, madame," I said.

"He *will* be there," said madame resolutely.

No other body of men passed in the Rue Royal that evening, but occasionally two and three together, all with the intent look upon their faces. Early, before five, Madame Sylvanie and her little girl came out to put up the shutters of their shop to hide the faded millinery that no one wished to buy. A little later the old bookseller and the dealer in antiques gathered together their wares and fastened their doors.   And M. Simon, having drank a cup of coffee on the banquette, looked up and down the desolate street, shrugged his shoulders, and, having passed within, he closed the Café Reine for the night.   So still was it, I could hear the clank of the chain with which he fastened its door; so heavily still at sunset, that I could hear the boom of the evening gun out by Chalamette.

You who only know New Orleans with its laughter and bustle, and jingle of bells and perpetual blare of brass instruments, as if its world were but a circle .of *fête* days, can scarcely realize the oppressive silence of that night of the thirteenth and fourteenth of September, in 1872.   Neither Aunt Marie nor myself feigned to sleep.   I sat in a low chair by her couch, the couch we had prepared for her in the morning, my hand held in hers. We did not speak, only when the cathedral gong let us know the hours of the night her hand held mine more tensely. Twelve o'clock; one, and two, and three, and so on till the hot sun made yellow the edges of the slats of the blinds, and then the silence broke.

Tramp—tramp, tramp, tramp, tramp; TRAMP—TRAMP, TRAMP, TRAMP, TRAMP; *tramp—tramp, tramp, tramp, tramp*—the footsteps died away in the distance to where is the *Place d'Armes.*

I looked up at Aunt Marie; her cheeks glowed, her eyes burned.

Some one was knocking at the door, and I opened it to let in Madame Doussaint, carrying a tray.   "I have come to breakfast with you, my dears," she said, and sat down the tray. "There is coffee, and biscuit, and endive that is heavenly—Ah!" she cried, interrupting herself as she caught a view of Aunt Marie's face, "she is adorable"; and she threw her arms about Aunt Marie, who called her friend.

"Now, my angels," said madame, returning to herself, "we will make to ourselves strength of the coffee, and cool our tongues with the endive of paradise."

We had breakfasted and I was assisting madame to put away the cups and plates, when we heard afar off an angry roar and the report of rifles, that approached nearer and nearer till the air was torn to rags with the yells and shrieks of a mob, and the explosion of powder.

Madame and I ran to the blinds, and from our coigne of vantage we could see a multitude of men run into the Rue Royal from out the Rue Canal.   Some few bore flags, all carried pistols or rifles; some were wounded and bleeding; anon one fell to the

ground, to be trampled under by the rushing feet. Some would
turn to fire at their pursuers, and to shriek and yell their im-
precations; and some cried for mercy. And behind the multitude
came, shoulder to shoulder, the men of the intent look, silent and
merciless, to avenge great wrongs through the cruel muzzles of
the rifles that were cold and glittering in the flaming sun. I
heard, as it were in my sleep, the woman at my side, the woman who you know has so loving a heart, count coldly the
death of seventeen.

"Rose! madame! what is it?" cried Aunt Marie; and it was
madame who said, solemnly, "Mademoiselle, give thanks to
heaven!—the State of Affairs is dead."

I did not answer, for among the men of the intent look I
saw M. St. Julien, and every bit of my body was one prayer
alone for his safety. And whilst I prayed I saw him fall a little
beyond the house of the Rose and Sword, and the mob and
their pursuers turn into the Rue Toulouse.

Madame, too, saw this, and when I had looked in her face
our thoughts were as one. She took my hand and said, "Little
one, come with me." But first I went to Aunt Marie to tell
her that M. St. Julien lay in the street wounded or dead, and
that madame and I would go to bring him in. She said it was
good, and kissed my cheek with her hot lips.

We found other women in the streets caring for the wounded,
but we did not pause till I knelt by his side. He was not
dead, but blood poured from a wound in his side like wine from
a down-turned bottle. Madame tore off the muslin 'kerchief that
she wore crossed on her bosom and tied behind, and bound up
the wound, and, helped by the bookseller and Madame Sylvanie,
we got him into the house and laid him on his bed, the only
piece of furniture in his inner room.

Madame went to search for a surgeon, and while she was gone
I held my hand tight to the wound, which somewhat stopped the
flow of blood. But I make confession that I was a little sad that
I could not as well bathe his face with the fresh water, but had
to leave that to be done by Madame Sylvanie. And I make confession, too, that I did not think to ask any one to go to Aunt
Marie, not calling to mind that she was, no doubt, troubled as to
the condition of M. St. Julien.

Madame had to go far before she found a surgeon, and when
at last he came and made to me a compliment because of what
my hand had done, I thought of Aunt Marie and hurried to our
room. It was time. I found her feverish, her mind wandering.

. The surgeon prescribed various remedies, but all that day and
night her mind was gone. She would repeat that the State of
Affairs was dead, and then she would moan out a hope that the
tax would be removed from the flower-makers. "For," she would
say, "it is hard, messieurs, for an old woman, most gentle, to sell
on the banquette"; and then the tears would roll down her
cheeks.

Mon Dieu, those days, those days! Monsieur Time kissed me
on the forehead then, for, as you see, though I am but thirty-two,
I have the wrinkle on my brow.

The State of Affairs was not dead. An unwilling army was
called in to sustain it, and it rose again to see three more revolts
against its iniquity, and then, by its own weight of wrong-doing,
it fell, and we returned to our own. Before this was to be five
more long years were to pass.

Yes, I repeat, those were hard, hard days, the remainder of
September and the whole of October. There was ruin and beggary
for all in the house of the Rose and Sword, and for two of us, M.
St. Julien and Aunt Marie, it was a coquetting with death. The
time came when—by turns we took it—Madame Doussaint and I
stood in line with those who went to the gates of the good monseigneur to receive the dole of bread for the well, the little flask
of wine for the sick. We hid all this from Miss Letitia, who visited
Aunt Marie every day, and from the captain, her brother, who I
came to know as a friend through the attention he showed M. St.
Julien.

The day came, however, when I was obliged to tell Miss Letitia our secret. Through the love of the good God for us, Aunt
Marie recovered fast, but M. St. Julien did not mend. I could see
him failing before my eyes, and it pained me that I could not
procure for him the little things that the doctor said were so
necessary. When she was able to descend the stairs, Aunt Marie
accompanied me on my visits to him, and she, too, saw that he
failed, although he was always gay and cheerful in our presence.
Madame Doussaint told us that he mourned in secret at being a
burden. "You tell him that he is not a burden?" I asked.

"I tell him, my angel, that we rejoice to serve him," returned
madame, pressing my hand. "But," she added, "that does not
console him."

Poor madame! she also had a secret that she never revealed
till the danger had passed. Her lease of the house of the Rose
and Sword was almost run out.

One day when the doctor had been in to see M. St. Julien he called me aside to speak to me. " I see that my prescriptions for M. St. Julien are not followed out," he said, his voice hard and severe. " If I perceive any more of this carelessness I shall abandon his case unless he procure a capable nurse. I will not have him die on my hands ! "

I was a worm abased to the earth. I crawled upstairs to madame's *salon*, and there fell on my knees and covered my face with my hands.

" Well, child ! what is the matter ? " called Miss Letitia. I had altogether forgotten that I had left her in the *salon* when I went down to see the doctor. " Is St. Julien worse—what is it, Rosemary ? " she cried, holding me at arm's length and gazing into my face.

" I have killed M. St. Julien," I said, and my voice sounded to me as if it were some one else who spoke.

She drew me down into a chair by her side and asked me what I meant. I did not spare my words ; if I could have done so, I would have exaggerated our wretchedness. I told her how we had done all that we could, and I implored her, for the sake of the good God, to save M. St. Julien.

From that day Miss Letitia and Aunt Marie took charge of the house of the Rose and Sword, and of all who were in it. It was Miss Letitia who told us what to do, and no one questioned her bidding. Whatever she chose to do for us, and she chose to do much, we acquiesced in, for she never made us feel her kindness. What she did that was best for us, for it made us independent, was to get us the making of the dresses of the officers' wives and daughters. Our prosperity overflowed to the house of Madame Sylvanie in this way : one of our lady customers discovered madame's tact in the manufacture of bonnets, and told her discovery to others, who came and were pleased to be bonneted in the French mode. Even the old bookseller and the dealer in antiques had their trade increased by these same ladies, who could not fail to see their treasures as they passed in and out of the house of the Rose and Sword.

Now that M. St. Julien had recovered I saw but little of him. He was shy of me, and I was very shy of him. Ingrate that I am, I believe truly that, in spite of the prosperity in which he no longer shared, I was happier when he had to be cared for. Madame Doussaint would look from one to other of us when we

met him on the stairs, and he and I had so little to say; and
she would sigh when he left us and fall to talking of Captain
Fletcher, as if she wished to distract my thoughts from M. St.
Julien.

Captain Fletcher came frequently with Miss Letitia to visit
Aunt Marie, and it was he who told me that M. St. Julien was
going away from the house of the Rose and Sword to a little
property in the parish of Tangipahoa which had been left him by
a cousin who had died lately.

"It is well," I said with nonchalance ; "he is too impracticable
to be a lawyer ; he will be better in the field."

"He is a solidly good fellow," laughed the captain; "but,
as you say, mademoiselle, he is not practical."

"Yes, but he is—a little," I demurred. "Think to yourself how
all of himself he studied the law. I think you do not comprehend
the Creole, monsieur."

"I do not, no ! " he returned; and eyed me so curiously that
I blushed an angry red.

The next morning I heard M. St. Julien talking with Madame
Doussaint in the corridor, and I wished that I were a man that
I might go out and talk with him, and, perhaps, help him to
pack the trunk I now heard him drag from out the storeroom.
Presently I heard madame begin to sing, and I caught the refrain
of the ballad :

> "Tu fais, sous ton empire,
> Le doux martyre —"

which she cut short to call down the stairs to M. St. Julien, that
she would take his message to the Mademoiselle de l'Isle.

"Caught! " she cried, clapping her hands as she burst into
the *salon*, and I drew back, red in the face. "Ah! my angel,"
she went on, now wringing her hands, "I am disconsolate ! I
lose my friend, the best of men : M. St. Julien, he leaves my
house."

"I know," I replied.

"He has told you ? "

"No, the captain, he told me."

"The captain, the captain, always the captain; always, always,
mademoiselle ! " cried madame. "You love the captain, eh ? "

"Madame ! " I exclaimed, and called her most cruel, most
wicked.

"I am one demon ! " agreed madame; "one demon most

vile. I deliver my message, which is : M. St. Julien will do himself the honor to make his adieux to the Demoiselles de l'Isle, and I disappear."

I motioned for her to remain, but she said she had to call down my aunt. So, he was coming now.

After a short time aunt came to the *salon*, and, almost immediately following, I heard M. St. Julien's footsteps in the corridor. My aunt caught my arm so hard that she hurt me. " Courage, little one, courage !" she whispered.

We three had little to say, and that little was almost all said by my aunt. He told us that he was going to a little place in the country that had become his, and Aunt Marie asked if it were near Bellechasse ; and when he said it adjoined it, she said what a delight it was for him to be near the home of his father, and how adorable is the country. I think he would have remained longer had he not heard Miss Letitia talking to Madame Doussaint in the corridor. Then it was that he rose from his chair and said to me : " Mademoiselle, I shall ever hold in my heart the devotion of yourself, and you, mademoiselle "—he bowed to Aunt Marie—" when I was ill in the room that was desolate till you visited it." He bent over my hand and kissed it, and left the room.

" Aunt Marie," I said, my back turned to her, " Miss Letitia is coming; I would escape her." We could still hear her voice, now speaking to M. St. Julien.

" You will meet her if you go into the corridor ; it is best that you remain." She was cold, but she was doing what was best to keep me from breaking down.

We sat apart, waiting for Miss Letitia, the fresh wind blowing in sweet smells from the pots of jessamine in the balcony ; the time going slowly.

At last she came in, her fair face flushed, her whole body animated as I had never before seen her. " I am simply and totally disgusted !" she exclaimed. " I don't know what to make of you people ! You let things go wrong, you let yourselves be wronged, you let all manner of troubles come along, and you say nothing, do nothing, and I suppose you call it sublime patience. You do *explode* sometimes, I don't deny it. But your explosions do no one any good, not even yourselves. Here is St. Julien going off without a word to Rosemary; and I saying nothing further of Captain Fletcher's child, because I have been expecting every day to hear of their marriage."

"You have been our savior, but—" began Aunt Marie.

"Be quiet!" interrupted Miss Letitia. "I will listen to your pretty speeches when I get through, not before. I ask St. Julien if he has spoken, and he says no; and I find out that he thinks my brother is in love with Rosemary, and because he has befriended him, St. Julien says, he was bound in honor to stand aside; and I have not the least doubt, though his tongue is as smooth as a pat of butter, for a word he'd blow my brother's brains out, and he'd call that honor, too. Well, I tell you both, for fear you may have notions in your heads, my brother does not care a button for Rosemary—at least not in that way. Now, listen to me. I am going to send St. Julien to you. I don't want to know, Marie, what you think about it; you're a child for all your fifty years—" She paused, and then went on quietly, "I suppose I am abrupt, but, my dear friends, it is because I love you, and I can't bear to see people unhappy."

It seemed but a moment after Miss Letitia ceased speaking till Eraste held my hand and asked, "Is it true, Rose?"

"My friend," I whispered, and again he kissed my hand.

You ask if we have prospered; and you see the five angels the good God hath sent us; you see Aunt Marie, so rosy, so content; and then, besides, is not Bellechasse again our own? You are so droll, monsieur!

HAROLD DIJON.

LIFE OF FATHER HECKER.*

CHAPTER XXVIII.

THE PAULIST PARISH AND MISSIONS.

IN serving the parish, the Paulists, led by Father Hecker, endeavored to utilize the individual qualities of each member, as well as the advantages of a community, so as to bring them to bear as distinct forces upon the people. What George Miles had said of them as missionaries, as quoted in a previous chapter, applied to them as parish priests, and told accordingly in results. Their personal excellences found free room for activity, without any lack of oneness of spirit and without interfering with harmony of action.

The missionary makes an efficient parish priest. Accustomed to severe labor as well as to very moderate recreation, he pours the energy of apostolic zeal into parochial channels. A high order of preaching is often the result, combined with tireless application to visiting the sick, hunting up sinners, and hearing confessions. On the other hand, the experience of regular parish duty is of assistance to the missionary when he returns to his " apostolic expeditions," as Pius IX. called them ; he is all the better fitted to plan and execute his proper enterprises from having obtained a fuller knowledge of the ordinary state of things in a parish.

It will not be expected that a detailed account of the parish work of St. Paul's will here be given, or more than a brief summary of that of the missions. These latter were kept up with vigorous energy from 1858 till the close of the war in the spring of 1865. On April 4 of that year Father Baker died, and the missions, which had been a grievous burden to the little band, now became an impossibility. They were suspended till 1872, excepting an occasional one, given not so much as part of the current labor of the community, as to retain their sweet savor in the memory and as an earnest of their future resumption. But up to Father Baker's death this small body of men had preached almost everywhere throughout the .country, getting away from the South just before the war blocked the road. Eighty-one missions had been given, hundreds of converts had been received into the Church and many scores of thousands of confessions heard. Numerous applications for missions were refused for want of men to preach . them. Scarcely a city of any size in the United States and Canada but knew the Paulists and thanked God for their missions.

The Fathers conducted them in the same spirit as when they were Redemptorists, and followed, as the community still continues to do, substantially the same method. It is not easy to improve on St. Alphonsus. But they did not fail to bring out the qualities and call for the peculiar virtues demanded by Divine Providence in these times. Their preaching was distinguished by appeals to manliness and intelligence, as well as to the virtues distinctly supernatural. The people were not only edified by their zeal and religious discipline, but the more observant were attracted by the Paulists' freedom of spirit, and by their constant insistence on the use of the reasoning faculties to guide the emotions aroused by the sermons. The missionaries were men of native independence, and their religious influence was productive of the same quality. Great attention was paid to the doctrinal instructions. As to special devotions, the Paulists have never had any to propagate, though competent and willing to assist the pastor in his own choice of such subsidiary religious aids. Non-Catholics of all classes were drawn to hear the convert missionaries, and the exercises usually received flattering notices from the secular press. An unrelenting warfare was carried on against the dangerous occasions of sin peculiar to our country and people, and the Fathers were from the beginning, and their community is yet well known for particular hostility to drunkenness, and to the most fruitful source of that detestable and widespread vice, the saloon. Their antagonism to drunkenness showed their appreciation of its evil supremacy among the masses, and the condemnation of the saloon was a necessary result.

This attitude of the missionaries was often a bitter-sweet morsel to the pastors, nearly all of whom at that time had been trained in the Old World. They were glad of the good done; yet sorry to see their liquor-dealers put to public shame. One pastor is recorded as saying: " The only people that have looked sad at this mission are the first men in my parish, the rum-sellers." The following is a piece of evidence worth publishing, though it is but one of very many which could be produced. It is found in the Mission Record in Father Baker's handwriting :

" A Catholic one evening, on his way to the mission, stopped in a grog-shop and took a glass with the proprietor. ' Won't you go with me to hear the Fathers?' said the guest. ' No,' said the other, ' these men are too hard on us. They want all of us liquor-dealers to shut up our shops. If we were rich we could do it; but we an't—we are poor. These men are too high and independent; Father —— wouldn't dare to speak as they do. But after all,' continued he, 'they are good fellows; see the effect of their labors.' Then, taking out of his pocket a crumpled letter which he had received through the post-office, and which was badly spelled and badly written, he read as follows: ' SIR : I send you three dollars which I received by mistake three years ago from your clerk. And now.I hope that you will stop *selling damnation*, and that God may give you grace to stop it. Yours : A Sinner.' "

Whatever may have been the misgivings of some, the opposition of the Paulists to the liquor-traffic was approved by the most enlightened and influential prelates and priests of the country, as is shown by the number of cathedrals and other prominent churches in which the missions were preached. It should be added that this antagonism to drunkenness, to convivial drinking, and to saloon-keeping, not only received the unanimous applause of the Catholic laity, but edified the non-Catholic public, and brought out many commendations from the secular press as well as from the police authorities of our crowded cities. A mission is a terror to obstinate evil-doers of all kinds, but to habitual drunkards and saloon-keepers it is especially so. The attitude of the Church in America on this entire subject, as officially expressed by the decrees of the Third Plenary Council and by its pastoral letter, fully justifies the action of Father Hecker and his companions.

As soon as the church in Fifty-ninth Street was opened the community exerted itself to make the surroundings attractive. The building occupied but a small part of the property, the rest of which was laid out in grass-plats and gravel walks; many shade-trees and some fruit-trees were set out, and a flower and vegetable garden planted. It was Father Hecker's delight to superintend this work, and to participate actively in it when his duties allowed. The grounds soon became an attractive spot, to which in a few years church-goers from all parts of the city began to make Sunday pilgrimages. They came in considerable numbers every Sunday to assist at Mass or Vespers in St. Paul's quiet, country-like church. Meantime the residents of the parish, not very numerous and nearly all of the laboring class, formed deep attachments for their pastors, and an almost ideal state of unity and affection bound priests and people together.

Nearly the entire region was covered with market gardens, varied with huge masses of rock, and groups of shanties. Very many of the parishioners of that early period lived in these nondescript dwellings, of which they were themselves both the architects and builders, a fact which added not a little to their quaint and picturesque appearance. The sites upon which these "squatters'" homes were placed, and over which roamed and sported their mingled goats, dogs, and children, are now occupied in great part by blocks of stately residences and apartment houses; but we know not whether the grace of God abounds more plentifully now than it did then   At any rate, whoever heard Father Hecker in those primitive days call his parish "Shantyopolis,' could see no sign of regret on his part that he had a poor and simple people as the bulk of his parishioners.

Much attention was given to the preparation and preaching of sermons, with the result of a full attendance at High Mass on Sundays. Beginning with 1861, a volume of these discourses was published under Father Hecker's direction each year, till a series of seven volumes had been completed. These were very well received by the Catholic public, and were bought in considerable numbers by non-Catholic clergymen. They had an extensive sale, though when their publication was first proposed it was feared that they would not succeed. They are almost wholly of a strictly parochial character, brief, direct in style, abounding in examples from every-day life, and plentifully illustrated with Scripture quotations. Although Father Hecker preached regularly in his turn, only a few of his sermons were contributed to these volumes, but his suggestions and encouragement greatly assisted the other Fathers in preparing theirs, as indeed in all their duties, parochial and missionary. Some years after the series was ended two volumes of Five-Minute Sermons were published, providing short instructions for Low Masses on Sundays.

The Paulist Church also became well known for the attention paid to the public offices of religion, as well as for rubrical exactness in ceremonies, the greater feasts of the year being celebrated with all the splendor which a simple church-building and limited pecuniary means allowed.

Father Hecker was from first to last strongly in favor of congregational singing, and assisted to the best of his power in introducing it. It began in our church in modest fashion back in those early days, and was fostered zealously at the Lenten de-

votions and society meetings. It never failed of some good results, and has finally attained a flourishing state of success in
this parish. His attention to the children was constant. No
matter who had charge of the Sunday-school, as long as his
health permitted Father Hecker was there every Sunday that he
was at home, asking questions, talking to the teachers and children, enlivening all by his encouragement and cheerfulness.

He was a martinet on one question, and that was cleanliness,
and its kindred virtue, orderliness. He was never above working
with mop, broom and duster indoors, and shovel and rake in the
garden; and this trait added much to the appearance of things
as well as to the comfort of all concerned in the use of the convent and the church.

Though assiduous in every parish duty, his favorite task was
the relief of the poor. They multiplied in number in undue
proportion to the increase of the parish, drifting out this way
from the overcrowded quarters down town. Father Hecker enlisted the best men and women in the congregation in the work
of caring for them, organizing a conference of the St. Vincent
de Paul Society, in whose labors he joyfully and energetically
participated.

The death of Father Baker was, humanly speaking, a loss to
the community beyond all calculation, and was the great event
of the first period of the Paulist community. Father Hecker had
the very highest estimate of his holiness, and mourned him with
the mingled sorrow and joy with which saints are mourned.
The reader should get Father Hewit's Memoir of Father Baker
if he would know his virtues. Father Hecker was often heard to
say that few men understood his ideas so clearly as did Father
Baker and had so much sympathy with them. And his death
was the signal for an impulse whose power plainly indicated its
supernatural origin. Up to that time there had been but two
priests added to the community, and those who had offered
themselves as novices and been rejected, were, as a rule, little calculated to inspire hope. But from 1865 onwards good subjects,
mostly converts, applied in sufficient numbers, and in a few years
the missions were resumed. But what was of even more importance, the apostolate of the press, started in the publication of THE
CATHOLIC WORLD the month in which Father Baker's death
occurred, assumed a national prominence, and together with the
Catholic Tracts and the Catholic Publication Society set the Paulists
at work in their primary vocation, the conversion of non-Catholics
to the true religion. To this, and to Father Hecker's lectures, we

now turn. Of course we might dwell longer on the parish and the missions, about which there are many things of interest left untold, but only the lapse of time can sufficiently dissociate them from living persons to allow of their being made public.

'———

CHAPTER XXIX.

FATHER HECKER'S LECTURES.

THE suspension of the missions, if it was the result of necessity, was yet an aid to Father Hecker in devoting himself to public speaking in the interests of the Catholic faith. Between missions, it is true, he seized every favorable opportunity to address audiences on controversial topics, often doing so in public halls, as well as in churches. Meantime he could still further mature his plans, and, testing his methods by experiment, secure for future occasions a course of lectures fully suited to the end he had in view. More than ever did he study to fit himself for his apostolate. How, he asked himself, shall the living word be framed anew for our new people? How shall religious teaching be suited to the special needs of this age without detracting from the integrity and the venerable antiquity of the truth? He sought to answer these questions by recalling his own early difficulties, and by opening his soul to the voices of struggling humanity uttered everywhere around him. What men outside the Church were yearning for in matters social and religious was his incessant study. He read every book, he read every periodical which promised to guide him ever so little to know by what road Divine Providence was moving men's minds towards the truth. His eyes were ever strained to read the signs of God's providence in men's lives. And his conclusion was always the same: proclaim it on the house-tops that no man can be consistent with his natural aspirations till he has become a Catholic; preach it on the street-corners that the Catholic religion elevates man far above his highest natural force into union with the Deity—intimate, conscious, and perpetual.

As to systematic preparation for discourses to non-Catholics, Father Hecker had his own peculiar equipment. As the reader will remember, God had led him in no way more singularly than in his studies, and had led him straight. The doctrines of the Church were familiar to him, for they had quenched his soul's thirst. And he had preached them on the missions, the instructions on the Creed and the Sacraments falling to his share. He had given these waters of life to other souls, and knew their value. He was a close student of the dogmatic side of religion. He had, it is true, little taste for the refinements of theologians, unless they touched the questions of human dignity and the scope of the grace of Christ, which were vital ones to himself. He viewed religion with wide-sweeping glances, trying to discover every hill of vision or stream of sanctity. He had plain truths to teach, and he needed none other. He knew the organism of the Church in clergy and in people, for he had seen it both from without and within. He had felt the grip of authority fixed in his soul. He had agonized under the brand of punishment as it burnt into his flesh, and he had seen it changed into the badge of approval. Within and without he knew Catholicity, loved it daily more and more, and was daily more and more anxious to proclaim it to the world.

It was not from labored preparation of his lectures that success came to Father Hecker. Even those which seemed the most elaborately prepared he did not write out word for word. His verbal memory was not trustworthy, and he had to confide in his extemporizing faculty, which was very good, and which became in course of time quite reliable, giving out sentences clear, grammatical, and fit to print. " I have to *produce* a sermon for next Sunday," he once wrote to a friend. " For me a sermon is always a spontaneous production ; I cannot *get one up*. The idea must arise and grow up in my own mind. It is usually hard labor for me to produce it outwardly and give it suitable expression." But the effort did not appear in the delivery, for his style, although emphatic, was easy and familiar; his delivery, if not altogether according to the rules of elocution, nevertheless gained his point completely. No word of his was dead-born. His voice was not always clear, as he often suffered from bronchial troubles, but it was not unpleasant, and had a penetrating quality, being of that middle pitch which carries to the ends of a large auditorium without provoking the echoes. His appearance was very dignified, his tall frame, his broad face and large features showing with striking effect. His action was simple and not ungraceful, though frequently exceedingly energetic. As he never sought emotional effects his power may be known by his unfailing success in holding his audience perfectly attentive throughout long argumentative discourses. Energy of conviction was one of the strongest forces he possessed, and it took the shape of a gentle constraint with which his positive utterances of Catholic principles compelled assent. Sincerity of belief and liberty of soul were admirably blended in his manner. He never appeared in public without attracting many representatives of the mottled sectarianism of our population; and this pleased him much, for he loved them, felt at home with them, and was full of joy at the opportunity of addressing them.

He was chagrined at the apathy he sometimes met with among Catholics concerning the American apostolate. He found priests who would devote much labor to collecting money for the propagation of the faith among distant heathen races, but very few who would make a serious effort for the conversion · of their American fellow-citizens. Are Americans of less worth in God's eyes than pagans and Buddhists? he would ask. He thought no differently of the people of the United States than St. Paul did of the Corinthians and Macedonians, groaning and travailing with them to bring them forth members of Christ; or than St. Francis Xavier did of the Japanese.

If asked how he was going to convert people, he would answer: "I am a Catholic, and I know that I am right. I can prove that I am right. What more do I want than this, and honest men and women who will listen to me?" The confidence he had in the strength of the Catholic argument was absolute, and this he showed by his zeal. His sole study was how to transmute this force into missionary form. Of all the wonders of the intellectual world he felt that the greatest is the faith of Catholics, and he knew by the lesson of his early life that it is but slightly appreciated by the non-Catholic mind. That Catholics permit this ignorance to continue was a puzzle to him. And it was all the more annoying because any single one of them can multiply his influence indefinitely by his union with the most perfect organism ever known—the Catholic Church. The quiescence of a body of men, sincere and intelligent, infallibly certain of the means of obtaining eternal happiness, living in daily contact with other men ignorant and *inquiring* about this unspeakable privilege, and yet not taking instant measures to impart their knowledge, was to Father Hecker almost as great a wonder as the divine gift of faith itself, especially as Catholics are well furnished with leaders and are organized to spread the truth as one of their most sacred duties.

Mr. Wilfrid Ward, a Catholic philosophical writer of distinction, has explained in a brilliant little volume the influence upon controversy of what he styles *The Clothes of Religion*—race, political traditions, education, physical temperament. He puts into his instructive pages the sense of the great scholastic maxim, *Quidquid recipitur secundum modum recipientis recipitur*—Whatever is received, is received according to the mode (or character) of the recipient. The national character, the tendencies, the antecedents of the people addressed, the relative power of thought and of emotion in their mental activity; all these are not, indeed, the souls of men but the clothing of them, their armor and their weapons; and Father Hecker felt that such things must be taken into account in dealing with people, and that with the utmost discretion. His view about controversy with non-Catholics was indeed aggressive—that we had reached the point in the battle at which the legion, having cast its javelins, rushes on with drawn swords to closer conflict. But the combatants should be well trained, the captains should know the ground to be traversed, should understand thoroughly the weakness and strength of the enemy. It was not a new thing to bring Protestantism into court at the suit of human liberty. But it was a novelty to attack Protestantism as the very torture-chamber of free and innocent souls, and to do it in such a way as to draw thousands of the best Protestants in the land to listen. Such sentences in the morning papers as " An overflowing house greeted Father Hecker," " The immense hall has seldom been so completely filled," " Representative men of all creeds and of none were scattered through the large audience," had a tremendous meaning when the lecturer was known to be the most fearless assailant of Protestantism who had appeared for many a day.

Father Hecker well knew that the non-Catholic American aspires to deal with God through the aid of as few exterior appliances as possible. To come near God by his own spiritual activity without halting at forms of human contrivance is his spiritual ambition. His religious joy is in a spiritual life which deals with God directly, His inspired Word, His Holy Spirit. Father Hecker longed to tell his fellow-countrymen that the Catholic Church gives them a flight to God a thousand times more direct than they ever dreamed of. They think that the authority of the Church will cramp their limbs; he was eager to explain to them that it sets them free, clears the mind of doubt, intensifies conviction into instinctive certitude, quickens the intellectual faculties into an activity whose force is unknown outside the Church.

It was not with the truths of revelation alone that Father Hecker dealt in his lectures. The first principles of natural religion were the background of all his pictures of true Christianity: that God is good, that men will be punished only for their personal misdeeds, that men are born for union with God and.

in their best moments long for Him, that they are equal, being all made in the Divine image, endowed with free will and called to the one eternal happiness—such were the great truths with which he would impress his audience first of all, using them afterwards as terms of comparison with Protestant doctrine. This plan he followed rather than institute a comparison of historical claims or of Biblical credentials, the well-trodden but weary road of ordinary controversy. To him Protestantism was more an offence against the integrity of human nature than even against the truths of Christian revelation. And he would place Catholicity in a new light, that of reason and liberty.

The revolt of Protestantism was not more against God's external authority among men than it was against the equal brotherhood of the human race. Well done, Luther, Father Hecker would say, well and consistently done ; when you have proclaimed man totally depraved you have properly made his religion a Cain-like flight from the face of his Maker and his kindred by your doctrine of predestination. Father Hecker deemed it plainly unwise to forego the advantages of attacking such vulnerable points as the Protestant errors of total depravity and predestination for the sake of dwelling on the Biblical and historical credentials of Church authority. He knew, indeed, that extravagant individualism is to this day a fundamental Protestant error, but the waning power of its doctrinal assertion has deprived it of aggressive vigor. There is less danger of its assault upon the Church, Father Hecker thought, than of its sceptical tendency upon its own adherents. To emphasize the obligation of organic unity, in such a condition of things, was not good tactics ; it was to revive the spirit of resistance without arresting the evils of doubt. Authority in religion has high and undoubted claims ; but it is nevertheless true that the normal development of man is in freedom. Man is fitted for his destiny in proportion to his ability to use his liberty with wisdom, and Father Hecker endeavored to set non-Catholics themselves to work removing the obstacles to true spiritual liberty which Protestantism had planted in the way.

An appeal from Luther and Calvin to the standards of rational nature, to human virtue, to human equality, rather than to exclusively Catholic standards, was certain of success in a large class of minds. And this but led to the consideration of the Church's claims to elevate rational nature and natural virtue to that divine order which is above nature, and which is organic in the Catholic Church. Moral rectitude is a simpler test of truth than texts from a dead book, whose original tongues and whose perplexed exegesis are quite unknown to the vast mass of mankind. And Father Hecker recognized that the elementary truths of reason and the aspirations of humanity for better things are not unknown to any man or woman; these are everybody's personal means of testing truth. To pass them by in order to apply the remoter test of revelation is either to admit that Protestantism is not against the dictates of reason and man's aspirations, or to commence the argument against it at the wrong end.

In a letter to Cardinal Barnabo written in July, 1863, Father Hecker gives an account of how he went to work to secure and interest a non-Catholic audience:

"For several years past it has seemed to me that some more effectual means should be taken to reach the Protestant community. This last winter I ventured with this view upon an experiment. In three different cities I gave, in a large public hall, a course of conferences on religion, one every evening from Sunday to Sunday inclusive. The expense of the hall was paid by the priest of the place, the lectures were all free, and addressed exclusively to Protestants. The halls were crowded at each place, and that my audiences might be such as I desired to address, I begged Catholics to stay away. At the close of one of my lectures there were present twenty-five hundred persons, chiefly Protestants.

"My method was as follows: In treating any doctrine of our holy faith with a view to convincing my audience, I considered first what want in our nature it was related to, and to which it addressed itself. This want being discovered, I developed and illustrated it until my hearers were fully convinced of its existence and importance. Then the question came up, Which religion recognizes this element or want of our nature, and meets all its legitimate demands? Does Protestantism? Its answers were given, and found either hostile or incomplete. Then the Catholic Church was interrogated, and she was found to recognize this want, and her answers adequate and satisfactory. These answers were then shown to be supported by the authority of Holy Scriptures.

"The interest shown by my audience was remarkable, and the effect of this method was equal to my hopes. My experience convinces me that, if this work were continued, it would prepare the way for a great change of religion in this country, more particularly at the present time, when the public mind is favorably disposed to consider the claims of the Catholic Church."

The "want in our nature" appealed to was often in the political order, such as the love of liberty or man's capacity for self-government. This he dwelt upon at considerable length in the opening part of his lecture, viewing it as a philosopher would, and extending its application, as far as possible, to men generally. He thus chose his criterion for comparison of the two claimants in the religious world. His triumph was, therefore, often in an arena only semi-religious, or rather in that of natural religion. The effect was wonderfully good, though doubtless due in great measure to the manner in which his plan, so simply sketched in the letter above quoted, was developed before the audience. The entire doubting body of intelligent men was enlisted in varying degrees in favor of the Catholic teaching of man's relation to God and to his fellow-men, and against Protestantism. Americans could not help feeling disgust for doctrines which were condemned by the maxims of the Declaration of Independence.

Although there was nothing positively new in the method—something like it had been used by Archbishop Hughes against the Presbyterian champion, Breckenridge—yet the public was taken by surprise. The style of controversy universally in vogue was that of setting up texts of Scripture and bowling them down with other texts. But here comes an American Catholic and arraigns Protestant doctrine at the tribunal of American liberty. The thick-and-thin Protestant was thrown into a rage, and became abusive and often incoherent in his reply. The easy-going Protestant claimed that the doctrines assailed were obsolete, as his church had, at least implicitly, changed them. "Then change your church," said Father Hecker; "if you have come back to the right doctrine, why not come back to the true Church?" As to the average intelligent inquirer, he was uniformly influenced by these lectures against the Reformation and its entire teaching, with its dreadful effects of doubt and division among Christians.

Father Hecker had an intuitive perception of the peculiar difficulties of the American people, and ever showed the utmost readiness and skill in meeting them. He had a matchless power of laying bare the wants of the human heart, and an equal facility of pointing out the light and strength of Catholicity for their supply. His immense sympathy for an aspiring and guileless soul deprived of the truth, was most evident; he always looked it and spoke it and acted it before his audience. To do so was no effort on his part. He told of the promised land not as a native of it, but as a messenger sent into it, and now returned with such tidings as should hasten the steps of his brethren still wandering in the desert; and this sympathetic interest embraced the civil as well as the religious side of human nature. He claimed everything really American for the Catholic faith, and this was joy and gladness to many a weary heart drawn to the Church by her charities, or her beautiful symbolism, yet hindered by the phantom of absolute authority and the dread of losing the integrity of free citizenship. Incivism—will Catholic apologists never learn it?—is the heaviest stone flung at the Church in all free lands to-day. Father Hecker's blood fairly boiled that the Church of Christ, the very home of Christian freedom, and the nursing-mother of all civil well-being, should be thus assailed, while Calvin's and Luther's degrading doctrines should be paraded as alone worthy of a free people.

To say that Father Hecker "Americanized" in the narrow sense would be to do him injustice. The American ideas to which he appealed he knew to be God's will for all civilized peoples of our time. If fundamentally American they were not for that reason exclusively American. His Americanism is so broad that by a change of place it can be made Spanish, or German; and a slight change of terms makes it religious and Catholic. Nor had form of government essentially to do with it; human equality cannot be monopolized by republics; it can be rightly understood in a monarchy, though in such a case it does not assume the conspicuous place which it does in a republic. It was this broadness of Father Hecker's Americanism that made him acceptable to the extremely conservative circles of Rome, in his struggle there in the winter of 1858–9. Many men in the monarchies of the Old World may doubt the advent of republicanism there, but what sensible man anywhere doubts the aspiration of all races towards liberty and intelligence?

Father Hecker's repertory covered the entire ground between scepticism and Catholicism. In refutation of Protestantism the principal lectures were: *The Church and the Republic; Luther and the Reformation; How and Why I became a Catholic, or A Search after Rational Christianity;* and *The State of Religion in the United States.* On the positive side his chief topics were: *The Church as a Society, Why we Invoke the Saints,* and the Sacraments of Penance and Holy Communion. Others he had against materialism, spiritualism, etc.

As may naturally be supposed, some of his lectures succeeded better than others. One of those he personally preferred was *The Church and the Republic.* He opened by affirming, as the fundamental principle of the American nation, that man is naturally virtuous enough to be capable of self-government. He developed this in various ways till his audience felt that it was to be the touchstone of the question between the churches. He then exhibited the Protestant teaching on human virtue and human depravity, quoting extensively from Luther and from Calvin, as well as from the creeds of the principal Protestant sects, until the contrast between their teaching and the fundamental American principle was painfully vivid. There was no escape ; doctrinal Protestantism is un-American. He then gave the Catholic doctrine of free will, of merit, of human dignity, and of the equality of men and human brotherhood. The impression was profound. Great mountains of prejudice were lifted up and cast into the sea. The elevating influences of the Church's faith fixed men's eyes and won their hearts. To have it demonstrated that Catholicity was not a gigantic effort to combine all available human forces to maintain a central religious despotism in the hands of a hierarchy, was a surprise to multitudes of Protestants. To not a few intelligent Catholics the style of argument was a great novelty. Father Hecker's success proved that the claim of authority on the part of the Church could be established without much difficulty in men's minds, if it were not associated with the enslavement of reason and conscience, and if shown to be consistent with rational liberty. He insisted upon the positive view of the subject. He proclaimed the purpose of Catholic discipline to be essentially conservative of human rights, a divinely-appointed safeguard to the liberty and enlightenment of the soul of man. He further proclaimed that the infliction of penalties by Church authority was an accidental exercise of power provoked by disobedience to lawful authority.

Luther and the Reformation excited widespread remark, and yet to one accustomed to old-time controversy it seemed but a fragment of an argument. The lecture proved that Luther was not an honest reformer, because, having started to reform inside the Church and as a Catholic, he finished by leaving the Church and therefore the real work of reform. At the outset Father Hecker proved that Luther was but one, and by no means the most important one, of the great body of Catholic reformers of his time. These set to work to remedy abuses which had grown to such an extent as to have become intolerable. The genuine reformers, led by the Popes, went right on and did reform the Church most thoroughly, ending by the decrees of the Council of Trent. All this the lecturer proved by citations from numerous high authorities, all of them Protestants. Why did Luther leave the company of the true reformers ? or, as Father Hecker puts it, "Why did Luther change his base ? " Whatever reason he had for leaving Catholicity, it was not, as a matter of fact, on account of zeal for reform. The lecture concluded by emphatically and, in different terms, repeatedly denying to Luther the name of Reformer and to his work the name of Reformation. Such was the line of argument in a lecture which entertained the general public and enraged bigoted Protestants more, perhaps, than any of the others. The secret of its success was that it overturned the great Protestant idol.

With humanitarians, rationalists, indifferentists, and sceptics Father Hecker's lectures were popular, and such were his favorite audience. If he so much as aroused their curiosity about the Church, he deemed that he had gained a victory; this and more than this he always succeeded in doing. Regular "church members" he did not hope much from, though they came to hear him and he sometimes made converts even among them. The lecture system, then far more in vogue than at present, gave him hearers from all classes of minds, and especially those most intellectually restless and inquiring. He took his turn in the list which contained the names of Wendell Phillips, Beecher, Emerson, and Sumner, and found his golden opportunity before such audiences as had been gathered to listen to them. Thus into the drifts of thought and into the intellectual movements around him, into the daily and periodical press, into the social and political and scientific groupings of men and women, his lectures enabled him to breathe the peremptory call of the true religion, sure to provoke inquiry in all active minds, and in some to find good soil and bear the harvest of conversion. He searched for earnest souls; and his confidence that they were everywhere to be found was rewarded not only in many particular instances, but also by the removal of much prejudice throughout the entire country.

The writer of these pages saw Father Hecker for the first time on the lecture platform. He was then in the full tide of success, conscious of his opportunity and of his power to profit by it. We never can forget how distinctly American was the impression of his personality. We had heard the nation's greatest men then living, and their type was too familiar to be successfully counterfeited. Father Hecker was so plainly a great man of that type, so evidently an out-growth of our institutions, that he stamped American on every Catholic argument he proposed. Nor was the force of this peculiar impression lessened by the whispered grumblings of a few petty minds among Catholics themselves, to whom this apostolic trait was cause for suspicion. Never was a man more Catholic than Father Hecker, simply, calmly, joyfully, entirely Catholic. What better proof of this than the rage into which his lectures and writings threw the outright enemies of the Church? Grave ministers lost their balance and foamed at him as a trickster and a hypocrite, all the worse because double-dyed with pretence of love of country.

For the Protestant pulpits felt the shock and stormed in uni-son against this new exposition of Catholicity and against its representative. In some cases, not content with one onslaught, they returned to the charge Sunday after Sunday. All this was not unexpected. The secular press, however, were very generally favorable in their notices, excepting some of the Boston dailies. As a rule, the lectures were very fully re-ported and sometimes appeared word for word.

To reply to one's assailants after one has left the field of battle is no easy matter, and for the most part Father Hecker trusted for this to local champions of Catholicity; and not in vain. But it happened on one occasion that after he had lectured in a large town in Michigan, and had journeyed on to fulfil engagements farther West, he was at-tacked in a public hall by a minister of the place. On his return East Father Hecker stopped over and gave another lecture in the town, and not only refuted the minister but covered him with ridicule. In fact there was no great need of defence of Father Hecker's arguments, they were so simply true and so readily understood. Not one of his antagonists compared well with him for frankness, good humor, courtesy ; and they almost invariably shirked the issue and confined themselves to stale calumnies against the Church.

At Ann Arbor, Michigan, Father Hecker lectured in the Meth-odist meeting-house, then the largest hall in the town. The Michigan State University, at this town, had at the time about seven hundred students, nearly all of whom came to the lecture. The subject chosen was *Luther and the Reformation.* As it was announced, the audience loudly applauded Luther's name, and some one called for three cheers for him, which were given vociferously, especially by the students. Father Hecker smiled, waited till the noise was over, then bade them give him a fair hearing; which, of course, they did. Before he had concluded, his audience seemed won to his view of the question in hand, and showed it by the names and the sentiments applauded. At the end some one called out "Three cheers for Father Hecker!" and they were given most heartily. .

There seems nothing like a new discovery, as we have already said, in Father Hecker's controversial matter, or even in the method of its treatment. But joined with its exponent, blended into his personality, as it was, by the sincerity of his conviction, it was a discovery; flavored and tinctured by him, this wayside fountain had a new life-giving power to both Catholics and non-Catholics. Bishops, priests, and Catholic men and women in the world heard him with mute attention. Some Catholics, it is true, were stunned by his bold handling of those traditional touch-me-nots of conservatism—reason and liberty; and such drew off suspicious. But multitudes of Catholics felt that he opened up to full view the dim vistas of truth towards which they had long been groping; these could agree with him without an effort. A few had reached his stand-point before they knew him, and hailed with rapture the leader who, unlike themselves, was not kept back by either dread of novel-sounding terms or by the impotency of private station. But here and there he met Catholics as dead-set against him as the Judaizing converts had been against his patron, St. Paul. Their only love was for antiquity, and that they loved passionately and in all its forms, even the neo-antiquity of the controversy of the Reformation era. On the other hand many, when they heard him, said, "That is the kind of Catholic I am, and the only kind it is easy for me to be." Non-Catholics, earnest men and women, were often heard to say, "*If I were quite sure that Hecker is a genuine Roman Catholic* I think that I could be one myself"; and this some of them did not hesitate to publish in the newspapers, so that Father Hecker might have said with Job: "The ear that heard me blessed me, and the eye that saw me gave witness to me."

Father Hecker felt that he was a pioneer in thus dealing with rationalized Protestants. His eye was quick to see the signs of the breaking up of dogmatic Protestantism, and he was early out among the vast intellectual wreckage, endeavoring to catch and tow into port what fragments he could of a system founded on doubt and on the denial of human virtue and human intelligence.

"I want," he said on one occasion in private, "to open the way to the Church to rationalists. It seems to me to be now closed up. I feel that I am a pioneer in opening and leading the way. *I smuggled myself into the Church*, and so did Brownson." And now he wanted to abolish the custom-house, and open the harbor wide and clear for the entrance into the Church of all men who had been forced back on reason alone for guidance. The words above italicised were uttered with powerful emphasis and with much feeling. He quoted the following saying of Ozanam with emphatic approval: "What the age needs is an intellectual crusade"; and he affirmed that Leo XIII. had done very much to aid us in preaching it, and that Pius IX, rightly understood, had led the way to it. "The Catholics I would help with my left hand, the Protestants with my right hand," he once said. And non-Catholics, all but the bigots, liked him, for he was frank and true by every test. He was neither an exotic nor a hybrid, and they felt at home with him. He much resembled the best type of public men in America who have achieved fame at the bar or in politics; indeed, as we have already intimated, he really belonged to that type, for all his studies and all his training in the Catholic schools and convents, which had given him more and more of truth, more and more of the grace of God, had not changed the kind or type of man to which he belonged. He was the same character as when he harangued the Seventh Ward voters, or discussed the Divine Transcendence at Brook Farm. Scholastic truth sank deep into his soul, but scholastic methods stuck on the surface and then dropped away. "And David having girded his sword upon his armor began to try if he could walk in armor, for he was not accustomed to it. And David said to Saul, I cannot go thus, for I am not used to it. And he laid them off. And he took his staff which he had always in his hands, and chose him five smooth stones out of the brook."

If his duties in the Paulist Community and parish had allowed, Father Hecker could have lectured to large audiences during the greater part of the year, and been well paid for his labor. He soon became the foremost exponent of Catholicity on the public platform in the United States. From the close of the war till his health gave way in 1872 he was much sought after for lectures, and spoke in the different cities and very many of the large towns, besides being obliged to refuse numerous applications, constantly coming in from all parts of the Union and from all sorts of societies, secular, Catholic, and even distinctly Protestant. Meantime he was frequently called on to preach on such occasions as the laying of corner-stones of churches and their dedications. He also gave one of the sermons preached before the Second Plenary Council of Baltimore.

The following is the introductory paragraph of a long character sketch of Father Hecker from the pen of James Parton, the historian. It is taken from an article entitled " Our Roman Catholic Brethren," published in the *Atlantic Monthly* for April and May, 1868. The entire article is full of admiration for the Catholic Church and of yearning towards her, though written by a typical sceptic of this era:

" As usual with them [Catholics] it is one man who is working this new and most effective idea [the Catholic Publication Society] ; but, as usual with them also, this one man is working by and through an *organization* which multiplies his force one hundred times and constitutes him a person of national importance. Readers who take note of the really important things transpiring around them will know at once that the individual referred to is Father Hecker, Superior of the Community of the Paulists, in New York. . . . It is he [Father Hecker] who is putting American machinery into the ancient ark and getting ready to run her by steam. Here, for once, is a happy man—happy in his faith and in his work—*sure* that in spreading abroad the knowledge of the true Catholic doctrine he is doing the best thing possible for his native land. A tall, healthy-looking, robust, handsome, cheerful gentleman of forty-five, endowed with a particular talent for winning confidence and regard, which talent has been improved by many years of active exercise. It is a particular pleasure to meet with any one, at such a time as this, whose work perfectly satisfies his conscience, his benevolence, and his pride, and who is doing that work in the most favorable circumstances, and with the best co-operation. Imagine a benevolent physician in a populous hospital, who has in his office the medicine which he is *perfectly certain* will cure or mitigate every case, provided only he can get it taken, and who is surrounded with a corps of able and zealous assistants to aid him in persuading the patients to take it ! "

Mr. Parton having given us a picture of Father Hecker as he appeared to Protestants, the following exhibits him as Catholics saw him. It is an extract from Father Lockhart's clever book, *The Old Religion ;* the original of Father Dilke is Father Hecker :

" The day after our last conversation, having an introduction to the Superior of the —— Fathers in New York, my friends agreed to accompany me. I was particularly glad of this because

at er ke was one o t e most remar b e men o u   u c
in the States. Himself a convert, and a man of large views and
great sympathies, no one was better able to enter into the scruples and difficulties of religious Protestants on their first contact
with Catholic doctrines and Catholic worship.

" On sending in our names we had not long to wait in the
guest-room before the good father made his appearance. There
was a stamp of originality about him; tall in stature, not exactly
what we are used to call clerical in appearance, with a thoroughly
American type of face, and with the national peaked beard instead of being closely shaven as is the custom with our clergy
generally. I had met him before, without his clerical [religious]
garb, on a journey on board a steamboat. At first, I remember, I
had set him down as a Yankee skipper or trader of some sort; but
when by chance we got into conversation, I found him a hard-headed
man, shrewd, original, and earnest in his remarks; but when
our conversation turned to religious topics, and got animated, I
shall never forget how all that was common and national in his
physique disappeared. And when he spoke of the mystery of
God's love for man, his countenance seemed as it were transfigured, so that I felt that an artist would not wish for a better
living model from which to paint a St. Francis Xavier, making
himself all things to all men amidst his shipmates on his voyage
to the Indies."

From what has been said of Father Hecker's aptitude to win
non-Catholics to hear and believe him, it should not be thought
that in order to do so he was obliged to leave off any sign of
his priestly character. He was distinctly priestly in his demeanor,
though, as already observed, not exactly what one would call a
thorough " ecclesiastic." He ever dressed soberly. When he
arrived at a town on a lecture tour he always put up at the house
of the resident priest, if there was one, and, if he stayed over Sunday, preached for him at High Mass. He invariably corresponded
beforehand with the pastor of the town t o which he was invited by
a secular lecture society, requesting him to send complimentary
tickets to the leading men of the place—lawyers, doctors, ministers, merchants, and politicians. And when he appeared on the
platform it was always in company with the priest. He loved
priests with all his might and was ever at home in their company. It is not very singular, therefore, that some of his most devoted friends and most ardent admirers were priests, secular and
religious, born and bred in the Old World—among them some of
the most prominent clergymen in the country.

Father Hecker often met non-Catholics in private, being sought
out by prominent radicals, sceptics, unbelievers, and humanita-

rians. What they had heard from him in public lectures, or read of him in the press, drew them to him, or they were brought to see him by mutual friends. And here he was indeed powerful, overbearing resistance by the strength of conviction and the simple exhibition of Catholic truth. The sight of a man anywhere, whom he could but suspect of aptitude for his views, was the signal for his emphatic affirmation of them, sometimes leading him to controversy bordering on the vociferous on cars and steamboats. In such circumstances, and in all his other dealings with men, you saw his prompt intelligence, his fine sensibility, his lofty spirit, his forceful and occasionally imperious will to hold you to the point; but the quality which, both in public and private discourse, outshone all, or rather gave all light and direction, was an immense love of truth joined to an equal admiration for virtue.

THE WITNESS OF SCIENCE TO RELIGION.

V.—THE PHYSICAL BASIS OF IMMORTALITY.

WHAT are the most formidable questions which human thought can put to itself? They are these, I imagine: "Is there knowledge with the Most High?" and, "If a man die, shall he live again?" The first is that on which all controversy about Theism hinges. The second is the problem of immortality. Unless both receive an answer in the clear affirmative, I see no place whereon religion may plant the sole of its foot, no ark into which, from the wide ocean of despair, the heavenly wandering dove may be taken. What a courage and confidence in itself must not the reason possess that dares to solve these problems of eternity? And yet, solve them it will and ought, unless the daily life, its aspirations, longings, prophetic dreams, and duties from hour to hour, shall be counted more vain and delusive than the idlest fancies a poet ever nourished. The experience, not of one age or nation, but of all men, has surely proved that when we cease to look beyond the grave our existence is at once stripped of its meaning because it is denied a reasonable aim. It can henceforth devise no task equal to its powers, nor imagine a purpose worthy of them. When the agnostic reflects, he becomes a pessimist. "Once youth is over," said James Mill, "there is little to make existence desirable." And his son tells us in the most thoughtful pages of that sad volume, his *Autobiography*, how, when he himself mused on the time to come, and pictured the fulfilment of his great hopes for the world—they were earthly and utilitarian, bounded by the tomb—a voice asked him, "Should you be happy when your desire was given you?" and he could not but answer, with an accession of the deepest melancholy, "No, I should not."

It is the "witness of a soul naturally Christian," naturally immortal. Providence has not abandoned these vital truths to the exclusive keeping of the syllogism, or to such metaphysical insight and subtlety as not one in a thousand has ever possessed. The short way into the reality of things is by instinct. Man *feels* that he is destined to live hereafter. Upon that feeling he acts, with the carelessness and confidence of a child who takes it for granted that to-morrow will come when to-day is past. We shrink from the pain of dissolution ; we shudder even at the fancy while we reject it that the time can ever arrive when we shall be no more ; but so little do we think to be annihilated, that, as Bacon observed, "there is no passion in the mind of man so weak but it mates and masters the fear of death." If, like the brute creation, we did not apprehend its coming, our want of fear would be no argument. But to look forward, and then to look beyond, taking death as if a mere stage in our journey, is, I cannot help believing, a sign that we have in ourselves the answer of life; and that our very innermost essence, the spirit from which we could not be divorced without wholly ceasing to be, has uttered its infallible and unshaken judgment, *Non omnis moriar.*

Yet I am far from scorning the metaphysical proofs of an Hereafter. They appeal to me ; they convince me. I do not say that clouds and darkness are wanting round about the soul's pavilion, any more than about the footsteps of the Eternal Wisdom, whose pathways in the mighty deeps of existence are seldom known to us, and often only to be guessed at. Let us cherish, in the presence of the primal mysteries, which are at the same time pillars of smoke as of fire, that shame and reverence we owe them. It is not by glib and ready reasoning that we enter into truths so vast ; nor is speech equal to silence, provided only our silence be an affirmation and not a denial or an excuse to doubt. The stern and pensive teachers of mankind, Dante, Pascal, Carlyle, have bidden us hope for immortality and labor as in eternity ; but they believed with trembling, they were not high-minded. Their· faith, vexed by the storms of·life, shone like a beacon in the wild and windy night, with flickerings to and fro, ·as blown violently yet as never to be quenched. The immortal creature is weighed down by its burden of flesh ; and, musing upon many things, looks round the walls of its prison, bewildered sometimes, knowing that it shall escape, yet downcast with the long confinement. If a man die, shall he live again ? We answer that he shall ; but these tender-hearted Stoics, fretting themselves in the absence of the eternal prospect which ·they desire, are wistful and abound in difficulties, writing their deep mournful thoughts as with a pen of iron, singing as in the subdued minor key, their *Divine Pilgrimage* through the worlds invisible, and hoping, but, as one of them often said,· " with desperate hope," for the vindication of the ways of God to men. They behold the truth, according to the word of Augustine, in *ictu trepidantis oculi*, as in the lightning flash of tempests.

Surely we must respect their griefs and perplexities, which I know are shared by many who have neither the wit nor the occasion to publish what they think in their hearts. For myself, however, I cannot refuse to acknowledge how greatly I am borne up by the· multitude of facts, and the majestic ascending order of laws, which the modern sciences, not only physics but biology even more than physics, have brought to light, or in manifold new aspects have made to bear upon the question of man's future. Call the arrangements of uniformity, law ; and let the ever-expanding scheme of things be, as I have indicated in my previous articles, neither possible nor conceivable unless it is controlled by purpose. Look at man as a part of the universe, by all means ; but lay to heart the revelation which· comes when we perceive that the universe is a system of Thought, and that Matter is the garment, the symbol, and the effect of Mind. Understand by the very harmony and subordination of means to ends which makes the chronicle of our solar system, of our planet, of our geological succession, and of the present stage whereunto the orders and species of living things have arrived, how true it is that the visible has come forth from the invisible, and but serves as an instrument of that design which is perpetually unfolding to larger issues. Whether we reason backwards or forwards, it needs only to admit the idea of purpose, and from the past we can deduce the present, as from the present we explain the past. What I affirm in these words is not rhetoric, not sentiment, but proved and certain science. New orders of being rise out of the bosom of the old; and still the laws which govern them do not suffer repeal. In this sense the uniformity of law is no less demonstrable than the conservation of energy, or the indestructibility of matter. And since effects do not create the purpose which they subserve, but only obey and manifest it, the conclusion is forced upon our minds—I ask the reader who doubts me to make the trial for himself—that directing Thought must have preceded each and every system of reality, infinite or infinitesimal, throughout the universe. Nature without purpose would be simply unreason, and a contradiction in terms. But grant an intellect which has designed the whole and the parts according to a pattern, to express and incarnate its own Ideal, and we shall behold the same Nature wrapped in a blaze of light.

Now go a step further. All that we see is but appearance. The reality lies beneath, and we comprehend it with eyes not of flesh but of spirit. To the sense, our earth is solid and immovable, and the sun turns round it. To science, nothing whatever is solid; the earth is a projectile whirled through space; and the sun moves, not round the terrestrial globe, but in a descending flight towards the constellation Hercules. Conceive matter how we may, it is ruled by invisible, intangible, and imponderable forces. Every solid mass consists of millions upon millions of atoms which our microscopes cannot detect, which do not touch, and which are in perpetual motion. Our body is a rush of particles changing from instant to instant, never the same absolutely for two minutes together, and renewed in all its tissues every few months, if not even more rapidly. What is it that abides, then? The form of the organism? Not so. There was a time when the organism had no form; when the most searching scrutiny could not have told, from the mere inspection or analysis of the visible, what form would emerge in due course; when the matter was not organized at all. We must look elsewhere than to matter, formed or unformed, if we would account for the process which has resulted in the living, thinking, self-determining man. "That which makes the essence of the human being," says M. Flammarion, "that which organizes it, is neither protoplasm, nor the cell, nor those wonderful and fertile combinations of carbon and hydrogen, of oxygen and azote; it is the invisible and immaterial Force of the soul. That Force it is which groups, directs, and keeps in their fitting order the molecules beyond reckoning, out of which is built up the admirable harmony of the living frame." As there was Thought before the making of the worlds, or never a world could have been made; so there was

Life before organization, or the organism would for ever have been impossible. The body did not make the soul, but the soul the body.   •

If Life existed when the organism had not begun, it may continue to exist when the organism has perished, or has dissolved away into its particles. Science declares that the formative principle is fixed, the matter fleeting. Atoms are indestructible ; force persists under an endless variety of combinations. Why should not that life which fashioned the body out of the lowliest elements, and continues so to fashion it day by day, persist when the rush of particles has gone by? Because, you object, we have no ground for thinking that it can energize without some form of matter to act upon ? Well, I answer, suppose, for argument sake, that it cannot ? And let us prescind, as I am doing throughout these papers, entirely from Revelation. Is there anything to hinder the monad from drawing to itself out of the boundless realms of force, and according to law, those materials of which it may stand in need ? I have not affirmed that Life exists apart from atomic combinations. My statement, founded on the evidence of the microscope, is that Life creates organism, and therefore is its cause, not its effect. And again, that since the body is ever changing, the base and centre of stability is not that falling Niagara which sweeps over the brink and is whirled onward to the Ocean, but is the real and active force, the monad, or self-determined energy, by virtue of which alone the visible endures. If it follows hence that the monad requires a vehicle or instrument for its activities, I shall simply conclude that, as it was equal to the production of a first, so neither will it be at a loss to find a second.

We know already, in fact, that the soul has persisted through all the astounding changes of embryonic life, and has traversed childhood, youth, manhood, and old age. Did none of these destroy that primordial force ? Then what can or will ? Each transformation involved a crisis and the emergence or disappearance of marked and peculiar faculties. Yet the same being which was at first now is; and its physical and even mental present sums up, includes, and, as great authorities declare, may be said literally to photograph the multitudinous changes through which it has passed. I see here an argument for the continual upward course of a life which was once unconscious and little by little came to the knowledge and government of itself. But I see none to suggest a degradation of the vital essence. It has during a long journey discarded many visible wrappings, thrown aside instruments, and outlived experience. The body is ever dying, and at last it dies altogether. What shall be my inference, reasoning from analogy? What except that it has now discarded the visible in all its earthly forms, and is become, to men in the flesh, a denizen of the unearthly and the invisible? But not that it has undergone annihilation. Science refuses to believe in annihilation. That which was, is; that which is, shall be. There is not a single instance in which we can affirm the absolute destruction of atoms, forces, powers, or realities of which science has ever taken note. The atom is a centre of indestructible force. The monad we call soul or spirit, is a sanctuary of life without end.

That miraculous instrument, the spectroscope, has told us more about the substance and make of the universe than a hundred years ago the wisest of scientific students would have dreamt it possible to know. Every light from the abysses immeasurable of space reveals its own constituents; it comes to us with a message which is read off in the laboratory as though on a prearranged alphabet. Astronomy, taking a long step forward, is now become sidereal chemistry. But, as yet, it is only inorganic, and concerned with metals and non-metals, with vapors and flames and gases, in which no life subject to earthly conditions may be imagined to exist. Can we doubt, however, that amid the endless systems of star-clusters, with their attendant planets, the "chemistry of the carbon compounds" is not sufficiently advanced to match or to exceed the phenomena we are acquainted with on our own globe? In other words, does not the analogy of science forbid so improbable a supposition as that the organized life we know is the only life? And, as we have transformed our conception of matter by lifting it up into a dynamic system, must we not, arguing from the spectroscope, acknowledge that wherever the physical basis of life is given, there life will appear and will move along the cycle of evolution until man—yes, and more than man—comes upon the scene? Then there is a universe of conscious no less than of unconscious existence, and life is, at all events, as enduring as matter and force.

What follows? you ask. This, I reply: that we are not the crew, shipwrecked upon a lonely island, surrounded with the illimitable main, of which Littré has spoken; but that in our Father's house there are many mansions, and we, being even now tenants of the sky and dwellers in Heaven, may look upon ourselves as holding due rank in that great hierarchy. Our life is not an exception or

an accident, but is under law. The old geocentric notion whereby earth was unlike all things else has long since been discarded.
Earth is a planet, and the sun a star.   But astronomy warns us
that we must put away the equally absurd notion that life is
geocentric, or is a solitary miracle going forward on our globe in
the midst of a dead mechanical universe. It signifies nothing to an
ever-springing succession of worlds and ages whether intervals
occur during which organized life is not yet, or has ceased to
manifest itself, in this or that nook amid the constellations.   Let
us grant there may be seasons in the very star-clusterings, and a
winter of rest in the endless world-formations, which does but
lead in a more abundant harvest.   But the sidereal visions are
bringing home to the heart of science what was once the unimag-
inable truth that life is the purpose of matter and spirit its crown
and scope.   What Carlyle in *Sartor Resartus* lamented over as
" the gloomy Golgotha and Mill of Death," is now shown to be
the blossoming world-tree Igdrasil, whose roots go down into
the eternal deeps, and whose leaves are planetary systems teeming
with life.   Only thus, said the metaphysician from of old, as he
looked into the laws of thought, can matter and motion, sound
and light and color, have a meaning or perhaps even a reality.
Now comes the man of science with his tubes and glasses, to demonstrate the conditions upon which organisms arise out of the
hydrogen cloud, and to assure us that if the human faculties
depend for their exercise upon sulphur, carbon, and phosphorus,
there is no lack of them in the mighty systems of Orion, and
Cassiopeia, and the Seven Stars.

But even while the prerequisites of vital chemistry are discovered millions of leagues away from earth, and life is seen to be possible in the galaxies of the everlasting abyss, science here at hand
takes up strange and old-world superstitions to melt gold out of
them in its crucible.   What I must describe as the allotropism of
the soul is becoming daily manifest, not simply to Christians, who
have at all times believed in abnormal powers (both for good and
evil, be it observed), but to physicians concerned only with health
and disease, with the brains or the nerves of their patients.   No
philosopher would deny that our five senses might be supplemented, much to our advantage, by others, some of which even—like
the instinctive perception of magnetic or electric currents, and the
conscious performance of functions now carried out blindly in our
organism—might be sketched beforehand.   The power of the
will, again, to influence other minds and feelings, is real though

excessively obscure. Prevision of the future by instinct and not by reasoning is an undoubted faculty of some, perhaps of all, the lower animals. Why should it not find a heightened analogy in man himself? The particles of matter which affect one another incessantly do not touch; therefore it is plain that they act at a distance, or that we must give a peculiar meaning to the word presence when applied to them. May not the spiritual energy of man overleap intervening space, even as these do? Lastly—but I could much extend my catalogue of possible powers—since a variety of substances exist, without changing their nature, in forms which manifest quite different attributes, as for instance oxygen in the common form which was first discovered, and likewise in the form of ozone, or carbon as graphite and diamond, what is to hinder the human personality from existing in the like allotropic conditions? Of course we know that it does. Every man passes from waking to sleeping by a normal revolution which corresponds on the whole to that of the earth round its axis. We spend one-third of our existence in sleep; and the laws of that state, both physical and psychic, are of a kind which we could never, without experience, have so much as conjectured.

But science now admits a third state, partaking of the characters which mark these, and very aptly denominated sleep-waking. It does not appear to be diseased, like madness or lunacy; it discloses extraordinary powers of knowing, feeling, and acting. Whether as energizing or as merely receptive, it is *sui generis*. And the universal condition which it seems to exhibit in all those subject to it, is freedom from the trammels of the outward senses, resulting often, when it is carried to a certain height, in striking developments of the moral Ego, accompanied with intuitive knowledge which is denied to the waking state.

It will be seen that I accept, as proved, the leading and characteristic phenomena of hypnotism. I put forward no theory; and I am mindful, even while I omit to dwell upon them, of the difficulties which surround the whole subject. But the evidence of fact is such as no scientific man would now refuse to entertain; and for me it is sufficient as bearing out my contention, viz., that the dependence of the spirit on the organism is neither so close nor so confined as materialists have been wont to take for granted. We behold, if I may say so, in these phenomena, the butterfly—*l'angelica farfalla*, to quote Dante's phrase—unfolding its wings from the chrysalis in which it has been imprisoned; fluttering, though as yet unequal to flight. Significant, also, I think, is it that in the state of sleep-waking all fear of death vanishes. It will return when the senses unclose again ; but, like the fever which has been suspended in trance, it seems to be a disease of the less exalted condition, and mere weakness. Death, I conclude, holds of the phenomenal ; it is an instrumental cause, not a fixed state ; and belief in its reality is "the great delusion" which Amiel understood in a less reasonable sense. Death is the name, not of cessation, but of change ; and we die from moment to moment only that we may live. The individual persists by constant change of his material environment. What staggers man in the hour which he calls death is the total disappearance of vitality into the invisible. But he should remember that the principle of vitality never was or could be visible itself. It bound the molecules of gas and carbon together in a tangible form ; now, it binds them no longer and they are dispersed to all the winds. Why should that event destroy the spiritual monad, any more than the demagnetizing of an iron bar destroys the magnetic force which dwelt in it ? You cannot destroy force. Neither can you destroy the soul. It existed before the organism ; what is to hinder it from surviving when that has ceased ?

I have thrown out these few suggestions on the most momentous of all subjects, and I would invite the reader to weigh them candidly. In my opinion, they point to the beginnings which science has now made of a true and verifiable induction, founded upon facts, concerning the soul's natural and physical destiny. So far I have not dealt with moral considerations; my theme has been chemistry or biology, not ethics. But surely it is of the first importance to lay down a firm standing ground in nature, in the reality of the objective world, from which to argue for a life after the present. If immortality can be proved by reason— and I believe it can—we must secure a physical basis, a principle in the universe which now is, whereby to mount up along the ladder of existence and show how the future is rooted in to-day, in this very hour and moment in which I write. Astronomy comes, then, to our aid, and exhibits the universal possibility of life. The conservation of energy forbids us to think of atoms or forces as ever being annihilated. Organic chemistry reveals the need of a stable power, a self-determining monad, to govern and control the flux of the material particles which make up the body. Medical science allows or affirms a triple state of existence, each differing widely from the other in faculties and attributes, while the spirit itself persists, unaffected in substance by these wonder-working transformations. Biology records a series, still more disparate and astonishing, of changes through which the individual man climbs upwards from embryonic life to old age, where all the conditions of existence have varied, the conscious succeeding the unconscious, and the intellectual rising above the sensitive, yet by means of it as an instrument and a vehicle. What a long and romantic story, what enlargements of hope, what possibilities for the future! It is the ascent from life to life. Experience collects, registers, engraves upon the soul and the brain; but science is bold enough to declare that it can never lose one atom or one particle of those effects of energy which, dating back through millions upon millions of years, are yet photographed in every flying mote that shines in the sunbeam. Nothing is lost; nothing wasted. Even though we speak of degradation of energy, it is not meant that the present stage of any world merely sinks back into its past. Questions of transcendent difficulty confront us here; for the universe to which we belong flies onward through the pathways of space, bearing with it the whole visible scheme in which we are entangled. To what goal? And when shall it arrive? These are problems concerning which we must lay our hand upon our mouth. They are too high for us. But science, seeing and measuring, has given us the noblest, the most cheering of assurances. It affirms that no spark of energy can ever be put out; that all realities are immortal, and the soul of man along with them.

WILLIAM BARRY.

PROFESSOR BRIGGS ON AUTHORITY IN RELIGION.*

"THERE are," says Dr. Briggs, "historically three great fountains of divine authority—the Bible, the Church, and the Reason." Such a statement as this coming from a great leader in the Presbyterian Church is worthy of attention from Catholics. We cannot help sympathizing with one who enunciates such a truth as this (for rightly understood it is a truth), no matter by what means he has reached it. And although it is not possible for us to sympathize with his methods, which are largely those of the so-called "impartial and critical school," who attempt to explain divine facts in a purely human way, we may recognize some of the results for truth which his investigations have produced. In the present article I propose to consider his development of this remarkable proposition.

In his treatment of the question of Church Authority, which he discusses merely as an introduction to that of the authority of Holy Scripture, Dr. Briggs arrives at the following conclusions: The majority of Christians from the apostolic age have found God through the church. Their experience was not pious illusion and delusion. We have in Newman, says Dr. Briggs, the example of a sincere Protestant who, striving never so hard, could not reach certainty through the Bible or the reason, but who did find divine authority in the church. "The church is a seat of divine authority, and multitudes of pious souls in the present and the past have not been mistaken in their experience when they have found God in the church" (p. 26). "Protestant Christianity builds its faith and life on the divine authority contained in the Scriptures, and too often depreciates the church and the reason" (p. 28). "Those who question the fact that the church and reason are sources of divine authority go in the face of history and the creeds of the church" (p. 86). I am, says Dr. Briggs, a Protestant, and "I believe the Scriptures of the Old and New Testaments to be the Word of God, and the only infallible rule of faith and practice," but I think "the neglect of the church as a means of grace retards the use of the Bible itself as a means of grace, and dulls our sensitiveness to the presence of God" (p. 65). "It is one of the greatest faults

* *The Authority of Holy Scripture.* An Inaugural Address by Charles Augustus Briggs, D.D., Professor of Biblical Theology in Union Theological Seminary. New York: Charles Scribner's Sons.

of modern American Presbyterianism that it has become so un-churchly and takes such a low view of church and sacraments. Why do we use the sacraments if God does not make them by his divine presence and authority real means of grace to our souls? Why do we engage in the worship of the church unless we hope to meet God and his Christ, and feel in our souls the influence of the Holy Spirit?" (pp. 86, 87).

All of the above conclusions in regard to the authority of the church he deduces from the Presbyterian standard, the West-minster Confession, and in support of them quotes the follow-ing passages from it:

"The visible church, which is also catholic or universal under the Gospel (not confined to one nation, as before, under the law), consists of all those throughout the world that profess the true religion, together with their children; and is the king-dom of the Lord Jesus Christ, the house and family of God, out of which there is no ordinary possibility of salvation. Unto the catholic, visible church Christ hath given the ministry, oracles, and ordinances of God, for the gathering and perfecting of the saints in this life, to the end of the world; and doth by his own presence and Spirit, according to his promise, make them effec-tual thereunto."

"The grace which is exhibited in or by the sacraments, rightly used, is not conferred by any power in them; neither doth the efficacy of a sacrament depend upon the piety or intention of him that doth administer it, but upon the work of the Spirit, and the word of institution, which contains, together with a pre-cept authorizing the use thereof, a promise of benefit to worthy receivers."

"Worthy receivers, outwardly partaking of the visible ele-ments in this sacrament, do then also inwardly by faith, really and indeed, yet not carnally and corporally, but spiritually, re-ceive and feed upon Christ crucified, and all the benefits of his death: the body and blood of Christ being then not corporally or carnally in, with, or under the bread and wine; yet as really, but spiritually, present to the faith of believers in that ordinance, as the elements themselves are, to their outward senses."

"The Lord Jesus, as king and head of his church, hath therein appointed a government in the hand of church officers, distinct from the civil magistrate. To these officers the keys of the kingdom of heaven are committed, by virtue whereof they have power respectively to retain and remit sins, to shut that kingdom against the impenitent, both by the word and censures, and to open it unto penitent sinners, by the ministry of the gospel, and by absolution from censures, as occasion shall re-quire."

The modern Evangelical, and in many instances the modern Presbyterian, doctrine on the church, is widely different from that set forth by the Confession, as Professor Briggs plainly shows. The common teaching of most Evangelical divines now is, that the church is invisible, that it exists independently of all organization, and that neither Christ nor the Apostles did more than teach general principles of organization and establish a few rudimentary forms of association. Professor Briggs laments over this departure in doctrine, and is earnestly seeking to recall his brethren to the church idea of early Presbyterianism, because he sees the impossibility of establishing the doctrine of church authority in any sense without restoring the belief in a visible church. An invisible church cannot speak.

Now the question arises, What does Dr. Briggs mean by the divine authority of the church? This question, if it can be answered at all, must be considered with reference to his conception of the visible church, which I will endeavor to describe in his own words. In the first place, he emphatically denies that in the church there is any central ecclesiastical authority having divine right of government. The Church of Rome, he says, is "a true church," but only "one of the many branches of Christendom." The doctrine of papal supremacy has been "the mother of discord in Christendom. Until this barrier has been broken down the union of Christendom is impossible. The destruction of popery is indispensable to the unity of the church. The papacy is not the only form of ecclesiastical authority that has produced discord. . . . Protestant princes have been set up as little popes; kings and queens have usurped ecclesiastical authority. Any ecclesiastical government that usurps divine authority is tyrannical and schismatic from the very nature of the case" (*Whither?* p. 229).

With such views as these of governmental authority in the church, it may be asked, On what grounds does he hold that there is divine authority in the church? His answer to this question is [I] "believe that God inhabits his church and guides it in its official decisions, not inerrantly in every utterance, but in the essential doctrines in which the universal church is in concord" (p. 63). "In some doctrines the church has reached definite conclusions that will abide for ever" (*Whither?* p. 226). "It is noteworthy that there is agreement with reference to a single officer [in the church]—the pastor of the congregation. All Christian churches have pastors, and they cannot do their work without them. Here is a basis for union. It is agreed that he should be a man called of God to his work, and endowed with the gifts and graces that are needed for the exercise of his min- istry. It is also agreed that he should be ordained either by the impósition of hands or some suitable ceremony. This presbyter- bishop of the New Testament is found in all ages of the church and in all lands. Herein is the true historical succession of the ministry, in the unbroken chain of these ordained presbyters. Herein is the world-wide government which is carried on through them. This is one form of church government that bears the marks of catholicity, that is *semper ubique et ab omnibus*" (*Whith- er?* p. 230). "Christendom might unite with an ascending series of superintending bishops that would culminate in a universal bishop, provided the pyramid would be willing to rest firmly on its base, the solid order of the presbyter-bishop of the New Testament and of all history and all churches " (*Whither?* p. 238).

From the foregoing statements it would seem that divine au- thority in the church, as Dr. Briggs understands it, is not a living voice, but a scientific abstraction which he calls "the consensus of Christendom." Now, it will be seen at a glance that such an idea of church authority is radically different from the traditional one. The visible church, according to his conception of it, is an imaginary aggregation of all religious organizations called Chris- tian, without regard to their differences in doctrine, discipline, or worship. Unity is desirable, and might be reached, he would say, if all would make the concessions necessary, and he never questions the right of all to amend their constitutions for this end. We can only say that he, by this theory, reduces the church to the level of all human societies, and, according to it, the consensus of which he speaks, if it were attainable, could be only a human result. Divine authority in the church is, there- fore, manifestly an impossibility according to his theory of the church.

Protestantism, as every one knows, has from the very start practically repudiated the idea of church authority. Theoretically in the region of cloud and mist some have pretended to find it. Private judgment, under the name of historical criticism, has sometimes formed an ideal church in the early centuries, with an authority in the abstract; but nowhere outside of the Catholic Church has church authority ever been found in actual con- crete form.

Second in the order of the sources of divine authority Dr. Briggs places Reason, not because he exalts it above Holy Scripture, but because he considers it, next to the authority of the church, necessary to be known for the better understanding of the subject of his address; which, it must be remembered, is the Authority of the Bible. Reason, he says, he uses in the broad sense embracing the metaphysical categories, the conscience and the religious feeling. "Here," he affirms, "in the Holy of Holies of human nature God presents himself to those who seek him." Unless, he says, God speaks in the forms of reason the whole heathen world is lost for ever; unless God's authority is to be found in the modes of reason only external revelation would be possible, the inspiration of Holy Scripture could never have been, the church could not be. Without this divine authority in the modes of reason the inward work of the Holy Ghost cannot be explained. "It is impossible," he declares, "that the Bible and the church should ever exert their full power until the human reason, trained and strained to the uttermost, rise to the heights of its energies and reach forth after God and His Christ with absolute devotion and relf-renouncing love" (p. 66). In the above statements concerning reason, if it is viewed in its proper relation to external authority, he is correct. Such doctrine is in accordance with the principles of true philosophy and theology, and is favorable to the development and progress of Christian knowledge. And he is the more to be admired for recognizing in this way the authority of reason, because other theologians of his church have so generally ignored it. But unfortunately he does not stop here, but attempts to make of reason a wholly independent and adequate source of authority. "The Christian Church," he say, "is divided into three great parties —Evangelicals, Churchmen, and Rationalists." * This view of the one visible church consisting of different conflicting parties carries with it the idea of three sources of divine authority, contradicting each other, which is manifestly absurd. According to it Rationalism is just as true as Catholicism or Orthodox Protestantism. I think that Professor Briggs has been led to this broad church doctrine through his conviction that there must be a way of salvation for all who are in good faith, and his desire to reconcile this opinion with the Westminster doctrine that out of the visible church there is no ordinary possibility of salvation. Catholic theologians have solved this difficulty in a rational way by the well-known distinctions of soul and body of the church. But Dr. Briggs's solution of it destroys the belief in any external authority in religion, either church or Bible.

* Art. "Theological Crisis," *North American Review* for July, 1891.

The Holy Scripture, that source of divine authority which our author professes to hold as his "only infallible rule of faith and practice," now claims attention.

The Holy Bible, he maintains, has suffered from the obstructions heaped about it by the Christian Church ; popes, councils, fathers, schoolmen, and theologians, both Catholic and Protestant, have, he affirms, by their ecclesiastical decisions and dogmatic systems substituted for the authority of God the authority of their particular rules of faith. These he calls "the barriers of divine authority in Holy Scripture," of which he specifies six, viz., superstition or the use of the book as a sacred object, the theory of verbal inspiration, the maintenance of the traditional authenticity of its books, the claim of its inerrancy, the belief that the miracles recorded in it were departures from the law of nature, and the belief in the minute fulfilment of its predictions. Biblical criticism has, he declares, removed these barriers and opened the treasures of Holy Scripture to all mankind. If this be true then the higher criticism is the greatest boon that has ever come to mankind. But has Dr. Briggs shown this ? Let us examine and see, and with this object we will turn to his controversy with the conservatives of the Presbyterian Church.

In his book, *Whither ?* he heads one of his chapters "Shifting," and a very appropriate title it is. The conservatives of the Presbyterian Church, as they are called, whose chief representatives are Dr. Alexander, Dr. Hodge, Dr. Green, and President Patton, of Princeton, and Dr. Shedd, late of Union Theological Seminary, are very severe on Dr. Briggs for his Neo-Roman and Rationalistic tendencies; and he vigorously retorts by censuring them for abandoning the old Westminster line of defence of inspiration, viz. : internal evidence solely ; and he, falling back upon this and uniting with it modern higher criticism, carefully elaborates the proofs of Scripture inspiration and right interpretation which he so confidently expects will bring the nineteenth century to its knees before the Bible. Shifting, however, is something of which he cannot, as the assault which he has made upon the six barriers shows, proclaim himself guiltless ; and if by it he has brought men to their knees, there is, I fear, no assurance that they will continue in that attitude. It is a difficult position to keep, and my experience of human nature leads me to think that a book relating supernatural facts, which only proposes itself and offers therewith the conclusions which the higher criticism passes upon it, will not hold men in its subjection very long. I think that a divine messenger with credentials as valid as those of the authors of the Sacred Books themselves is the only power which can do it. I do not believe in the competency of human science to explain divine facts, but can believe that a divinely-established authority with perpetual divine assistance can do it.

Moreover, the Catholic Church, with the laurels of nineteen centuries upon her brow, is seen to-day advancing with giant strides into regions where a few years ago she was unknown, seeking men out, sending her ministers often to the most unattractive places, building her temples in the slums and filling them with people, erecting her cathedrals in the centres of fashion, pushing her fearless priests before the muzzles which soldiery are aiming at the starving and frenzied poor, alluring the proud and rich to serve the lowly and needy, carrying peace and comfort to the miserable, and with the Bible in her hand, proclaiming it to be her written constitution, her Book of which God is the Author ; and her claim to this Book accredits itself, because we know her sincere love for men's souls, her hatred of deception, and her supernatural wisdom too well to doubt her word. She manifests herself as the ideal church as far as she can be with men and women, such as we are, for her representatives. Her decrees, therefore, concerning inspiration, canonicity, and interpretation, we conclude, ought not to be questioned, because she is a standing miracle herself. We find, however, that mere human authorities, though their intentions have often been the best, have sometimes obscured the Bible and erected barriers that have hidden its treasures ; but if the question arises whether the divinely-commissioned church by her decrees has done so we must answer—*never*. The higher criticism which Dr. Briggs so extols is, I know, at best only human, and will never make the Scriptures more potent than the church has made them. A certain philosopher once met in the desert an old hermit, who before his conversion had enjoyed wealth and luxury among men. "What brought you here ?" he asked. The old hermit held up a much-worn copy of one of the Holy Gospels and said : "*That Book.*" "Man is fallible," says Dr. Briggs. True, and the sooner man finds out that he is not wiser than God's Church the better for him. Such a book as the Bible may well present difficulties which no one can explain, but our inability to solve them is not proof that they are insoluble. I can imagine and accept many solutions except one, viz. : that the Bible is not inspired. On this point the Catholic Church has solemnly defined that the entire books of the canon in all their parts were divinely inspired and have God for their Author.

Having stated the general principles by which Catholics are

guided in their investigations of the Bible, I will now consider in detail the author's views of what the higher criticism has done with the Bible. He maintains that it has proved the falsity of the theory of verbal inspiration. Certainly we cannot object to this conclusion. Very few, if any, modern Catholic theologians maintain it. "The doctrine* of inspiration approved by the church and Catholic theologians extends the divine authorship to all the sacred books, and to each part of the Scriptures, but does not affect the material form of the words, which are the writer's own expression, depending upon his individual style, genius, or culture. The assistance of the Holy Ghost is, however, such that the words chosen by the writer shall sufficiently and faithfully express the divine mind."*

In regard to the authenticity of the books, Professor Briggs maintains the higher criticism has proved that "the great mass of the Old Testament was written by authors whose names or connection with their writings is lost in oblivion" (p. 33). I am not aware that such a statement as the above is either directly or indirectly against Catholic faith, but it is certainly very bold, and is, I think, calculated to undermine belief in the Scripture in many minds. The demands of the higher criticism are surely not small. It would have Christian scholars surrender the Bible to it unreservedly and let it make a new interpretation of its contents, such as it can approve.

Professor Briggs has much to say about the teaching of theologians on the inerrancy of Scripture. He thinks that the higher criticism has proved that there are errors in the Scripture, but that these errors are in the circumstantials, and not in the essentials. What he means by this is difficult to understand. He is certainly walking boldly on dangerous ground. The extent of inspiration from the Catholic standpoint has, I think, been well described by Father Hewit in his article on *The Warfare of Science* in the last number of this magazine : "Whatever is contained in the inspired books which is not doctrinal, ethical, or of the nature of dogmatic fact is accidental. All of science and history which is transmitted with the divine tradition of religious and moral doctrine, but only accidentally connected with them, has more or less of obscurity and ambiguity, and admits of more than one interpretation. It is that which is certainly revealed, certainly understood in its true authentic sense, attested and proposed by the church in her ordinary magistracy, or by solemn definitions, which is the matter of Catholic faith."

* Lecture, *The Bible in the Catholic Church*, Mgr. T. S. Preston.

The traditional explanation of miracles, or. the claim that miracles disturb the laws of nature, is, according to Professor Briggs, an obstacle to faith in the Bible. " The miracles of the Bible," he says, "were the work of God, either by direct divine energy or mediately through holy men, energized to perform them; but there is no reason why we should claim that they in any way violate the laws of nature or disturb its harmonies. We ought not to be disturbed by the efforts of scholars to explain them under the forms of divine law, in accordance with the order of nature. If it were possible to resolve all the miracles of the Old Testament into extraordinary acts of Divine Providence, using the forces and forms of nature in accordance with the laws of nature; and if we could explain all the miracles of Jesus, his unique authority over man and over nature, from his use of mind cure, or hypnotism, or any other occult power—still I claim that nothing essential would be lost from the miracles of the Bible. . . . Christian men may construct their theories about the miracles of the Bible with entire freedom, so long as they do not deny the reality of the events themselves as recorded in Holy Scripture. The study of the miracles of the Bible has convinced me that they may be explained from the presence of God in nature in various forms of Theophany and Christophany, for where God is present we may expect manifestations of divine authority and power " (pp. 37, 38). This attempt to naturalize miracles, I think, rather increases than lessens the difficulty of believing in the reality of the events recorded. For to suppose that such unknown laws by which they can be accounted for exist, would imply that the laws of nature, as we ordinarily understand them, are not constant. Moreover, such a theory would destroy the character of miracles as divine evidences of revelation ; we ought, as our Lord declares their purport, to be led by them to believe in the supernatural doctrines which they substantiate, because we recognize them as events which the forces of nature of themselves could not have produced. But the notion, says Professor Fisher, that miracles are repugnant to nature, that the supernatural is antinatural, should be banished from our minds.[*] It is a misrepresentation of the teachings of orthodox theologians to say that they hold that miracles are "violations of the laws of nature."

On the whole, I conclude that Professor Briggs's treatment of the question of authority in religion is very unsatisfactory, and shows that he recognizes very little actual authority either in

* *The Beginnings of Christianity*, p. 465.

Bible or church, but very much in the higher criticism.   Would
that he had the light of the Holy Spirit to understand the three
sources of divine authority as *realities*, each having its own sphere
of action, and all of them united able to satisfy every soul in
quest of an eternal and immutable certainty, instead of regarding
them as forms which are so mixed with the human and imperfect
that he must try to get behind them to understand their meaning !   When the sun is over the hills why, we ask ourselves,
should one grope as if in the dark ?   However, it is encouraging
to know that Professor Briggs has caught glimpses of the divine
operations in ways which seem to be unknown to most of his
brethren.   Let us hope that he and others whose glances have
turned outward in the right direction may yet behold the full
light of God's revelation in all its splendor.

H. H. WYMAN.

SIR C. GAVAN DUFFY'S LIFE OF THOMAS DAVIS.

ANY book from the pen of Sir Charles Gavan Duffy must of
necessity be interesting and command a large share of public attention.   He always writes well and gracefully, and brings to his
subject the fullest possible knowledge.   This is especially the case
with his *Memoir of Thomas Davis*,* a book which we have long
been promised and which fully realizes the expectations formed
of it—expectations which were necessarily high because of the
reputation of the writer and because no man living was more
fitted to undertake the task.   He was one of Davis's most intimate friends and co-workers, and had in his possession many
valuable private papers and letters without which such a biography would be incomplete.   These letters (some of which have, it
is true, seen the light before) contribute in no small degree to the
interest of the book, showing as they do the unaffected modesty
and earnestness of Davis's character and the lovableness of his
nature, qualities which endeared him to all with whom he came
in contact, and which drew around him that brilliant circle who
afterwards came to be known as " Young Ireland," whose headquarters was the *Nation* office, and whose bond of union was

*Thomas Davis. The Memoirs of an Irish Patriot—1840-1846. By Sir Charles Gavan
Duffy, K.C.M.G. London: Kegan Paul, Trench, Trübner & Co. 1890.

their proud attachment to their friend. "It is very safe to say," wrote one of them, "that to the personal influence of Davis, to the grandeur of his aims, to his noble tolerance, to his impassioned zeal, and the loving trust which all generous natures were constrained to place in him, the Repeal Association was indebted not for Smith O'Brien only, but for Dillon, MacNevin, Meagher, O'Gorman, Martin, and Devin Reilly; and to the same influence they were indebted for their fate. . . . Yes, to them and hundreds more, he was indeed a Fate; and there is not one amongst them still alive but blesses the memory of the friend who first filled their souls with the passion of a great ambition and a lofty purpose."

These words were a noble tribute to a noble character, and if proof were needed of their truth we have it here in this memoir, which makes its appearance nearly half a century after its subject had been laid in his grave. "He was," says Sir Charles, "the most modest and unselfish of men, as well as the greatest and best of his generation."

To inspire noble ambition and heroic devotion was Davis's great power. That he should have exercised such an immense influence for good in Ireland was remarkable considering his ancestry. The posthumous son of an English Tory gentleman who married an Irish lady of Cromwellian descent, Thomas Osborne Davis was born at Mallow, in the County Cork, the 14th October, 1814. His youth was passed amidst the strictest Tory surroundings, and having received a good education he passed to Trinity College, Dublin, where he graduated in 1836. Two years later he was called to the bar, but he never practised at his chosen profession. He had not been long at college until he showed that he had emancipated himself from the traditional politics of his race, and began to develop signs of independence of thought not quite characteristic of the old school of conservatism. His address to the Historical Society, Trinity College, Dublin, delivered in his capacity of president when he was only in his twenty-sixth year, was marvellous in the depth of thought and wide range of reading which it manifested; and was a fitting prelude to the brilliant (though alas! short) career which followed. "He did," says Sir Charles, "much greater and more striking things than can ever be realized"; but, in truth, it was not so much what he did as the self-respect, self-reliance, manliness, kindliness, and tolerance which he practised and inculcated that have left his name as a precious legacy to his countrymen, and which brought "a soul into Ireland."

"It is the sure fate of a feeble fire," says Sir Charles, "to go out and be forgotten, but Davis's reputation has gone on gathering increased light and heat for nearly half a century."

The unhappy condition of Ireland at the time when Davis entered on public life might well have daunted the stoutest heart, but Davis was not one to be easily dismayed or to let obstacles stand in his way. He deplored the state of the country and the debasement of the people, and determined upon instituting a new order of things. Accordingly he, in conjunction with Charles Gavan Duffy and John Blake Dillon, established on the 15th of October, 1842, the *Nation* newspaper, "to direct the popular mind and the sympathies of educated men of all parties to the great end of nationality."

The Young Ireland party regarded English rule as the primary cause of the political degradation and social misery·of their country ; but they had no fanatical hatred of Englishmen, and most of them earnestly admired English political institutions, and entertained high respect for the great qualities, moral and intellectual, of the English race. Of the want of some of these qualities amongst their own countrymen they were fully conscious, but they also believed them to possess in rich abundance the germs of great national qualities, to develop and cultivate which was the ardent wish and hope of those who gathered round the *Nation :* to help "to create and foster public opinion in Ireland, and make it racy of the soil." They used these words as the motto of the paper, for, in their view of things, public opinion had to be "created." That which was called public opinion seemed to them a sorry sham. With the Protestants it meant the tenacious clinging to every shred of the old ascendency ; with the Catholics an entire submission to O'Connell. Davis wanted both Catholics and Protestants to unite in the struggle for nationality. The Young Irelanders fully recognized O'Connell's great abilities and noble services ; but Freedom's temple is a goal to reach which men must be united, and Davis and the others felt that an ignorant, distracted people, torn by factions and arrayed in two hostile camps, embittered against each other by both political and sectarian hate, could neither win nor retain independent existence.

The two primary duties, then, of an Irishman who loved his country were to educate and to conciliate ; and, under the guidance of Davis, the *Nation* essayed to do this. The new paper had been announced under auspices calculated to insure its success ; but its unexpected ability, the ground it broke in the national policy, and the vast intellectual resources it developed, eclipsed the prestige under which it had been deemed necessary to usher it into existence. Every variety of literary talent was to be found represented on its staff, "from grave to gay, from lively to severe." It was particularly strong in the light artillery of wit and banter, but nothing coarse or vulgar was ever admitted into its pages. The effect it produced upon Irish society was electric. It penetrated even the most exclusive Protestant and Tory circles, and everywhere found responsive echoes. It was at once a proof of greater powers than the country had yet witnessed, and a prophecy of a different fate from what she had hoped for.

The work done by Davis in connection with the *Nation* represents but a small portion of his literary labors, and yet it is not possible to refer the reader to any masterpiece of literary effort. "Literature," for its own sake, he almost despised. Whatever he wrote was written for some immediate or remote effect which he sought to produce ; it was, in fact, the writing of a journalist. "But there is enough of it," said his friend Wallis, "to make men love him, and guess at him—and what more can the best of readers do with the supremest writer, though he lived to the age of Sophocles or Goethe."

His prose writings are characterized by a nervous vigor which was peculiarly his own, combined with perfect simplicity and directness of expression. Of no writer could it be said with greater truth that the style was the man. What graces of style his writings possess are the products of genius and truth. Davis the poet will ever be dear to the Irish heart. For poetry, previous to the *Nation*, he had shown no capacity whatever. As a matter of fact he had never written even a line of poetry until about three years before his death ; although the warmth of his affections, and his intense enjoyment of the beauties of nature and art, ought early to have marked him out as one destined to sing as well as to think and to act. He attempted versification without any consciousness that he possessed the gift of song, and solely because he was full of the idea of its importance and power as a means of awakening popular emotion. The result was a collection of songs and ballads which number amongst them some of the most stirring vigor, and others of the utmost grace, tenderness, and beauty. The chief characteristic of his poetry may be briefly described as passion—no false or sickly sentiment, but the genuine outpourings of a nature which could feel intensely and love deeply. The verses which Sir Charles has included at the end of the volume are excellent examples of his pure and tender melody; linked with the name of the lady with whom he had hoped to link his life, they are alike worthy of the poet and their subject.

To determine Davis's exact position in the poetical firmament is no part of our present purpose, nor are we aware that any-thing would be gained by our attempting to do so. His poetry is unequal, and must be judged by a reference to his aims, and his mode of life. The greater, and by far the *best*, portion of it was written and published within a single year (1844), and that the most active of his short life. Had he lived, and been enabled to give the world the perfected fruits of an unincumbered leisure, we feel that he was capable of great things; as it is, none of his works, prose or verse, can be taken as an adequate expression of his creative power. The creation of an Irish literature, of which the justly celebrated "Library of Ireland" formed the nucleus, was the work of Davis. He was the soul which gave life to the thoughts and desires of every true Irishman; teaching them to rely upon themselves, and by their own labor to produce that of which they stood in need. To this end he himself spared no labor, working with an industry that was simply marvellous, and taking no credit to himself for anything he did. As an in-stance of his modesty in this respect, Sir Charles tells us how, when he had finished the collecting and editing of *Curran's Speeches*, he asked Maddyn to write a biographical sketch for it, and to have the volume published with his (Maddyn's) name on the title-page.

It was not in the nature of the man to lead a life of literary leisure. "Patriotism," as he himself said, "once *felt* to be a duty *becomes* so." And into the cause of Irish nationality he flung him-self with all the ardor of his intensely ardent nature. That the movement which has left such an indelible mark on the page of Ireland's history owed its inception, organization, and achieve-ments to Davis is undeniable, and had the lines he laid down been followed it is not too much to say that his ideas and aspira-tions were in a fair way to be realized. To quote the words of his biographer: "He had set himself the task of building up a nation—a task not beyond his strength had fortune been kind." But fortune did not prove kind; on the contrary, he saw the powerful organization in which he had trusted gradually weaken-ing and lowering its tone until it ceased to be respected. The disappointment was too much for Davis; he who had been the most hopeful of them all grew despondent.; the struggle against adverse influences wore out his delicate frame; and, in the very bloom of his manhood, death cut short his labors. The chapters which Sir Charles has devoted to the conflict with O'Connell and the new departure which followed, are, notwithstanding his previous contributions to this portion of Irish history, extremely interesting. "Without knowing the history of a time we cannot accurately comprehend its philosophy." What the destinies of Ireland might have been had Davis lived we can only conjecture. Speculations upon what might have been are idle, and not infrequently tinged with regret; let us, therefore, rather hope that the future of Ireland may be all that Davis himself would have wished for her.

For the rest but little remains to be said. In the course of the ten chapters into which the book is divided Sir Charles Gavan Duffy has traced Davis's career with a loving and sympathetic faithfulness. Never had a biographer a better subject, for there was nothing to conceal, nothing to be condoned. He never betrayed a friend or maligned an enemy. His private life was as blameless as his public life was praiseworthy—and of how few can that be said! There were no intrigues, social or political, to lay bare. Himself the very soul of truth and honor, Davis had an intense scorn of everything base or mean, and an earnest admiration of all that was elevated and pure. A stranger alike to the schemings of ambition and the rancor of faction, he was truly entitled to the name of patriot.

P. A. S.

Dublin.

THE OLD WORLD SEEN FROM THE NEW.

THE strike of the London omnibusmen and its success afford a few lessons not unworthy of notice. The first of these is, that the chief condition of success is that the cause should be such as to enlist the sympathy of the public. Such was the case with the omnibusmen, for their hours of labor were from fourteen to eighteen each day. This was felt by all to be intolerable. The next lesson is about a condition almost equally important, but circumstances do not make it always feasible. It is that the public must not be put to great inconvenience by the strike. Some inconvenience it is necessary to inflict, otherwise attention would not be excited. But great inconvenience the public is too selfish to tolerate. Of this the Scottish railway strike was proof. Now, the London public felt the want of the omnibuses, but not to a very unpleasant degree, for cabs and railways were at hand for long distances and short distances could be walked. It was due to these favorable conditions that the principal claims of the men were conceded.

Not, however, without a fight, nor without the intervention of distinguished outsiders. The Lord Mayor acted as intermediary and negotiated the terms of settlement. Cardinal Manning wrote, and the Marquis of Ripon spoke in support of the laborers' claims. Mr. G. F. Watts, the artist, has given the best expression of the views of thoughtful onlookers. In a letter sent by him to the organizers of the strike he says: "While I cannot pretend to understand how the business arrangements of firms and companies should be carried out, I feel that it is a monstrous thing to exact even as many as twelve hours' labor from any man. I fear in taking shares in companies the idea is always to secure as large a return for investments as possible, irrespective of every other condition; a principle, I believe, to be unworthy, unwise, and unsafe. The worship of Mammon, so universal in this age, has gone far to destroy our character as a noble people, and will, I believe, undermine the very existence of the nation. It must be understood that I am professing no socialistic principles, or any principles except those of justice and consideration for others."

In fact, the root of the present evils is to be found in the universal desire. which pervades every rank and class of society, high and low, rich and poor, to give as little as possible, whether in wages or in payment for goods—to buy always in the cheapest market. It is the public that is the sweater—the public which runs to the cheapest stores and gives the lowest wages. Fine sentiments are very pretty, and indignant exclamations at the wrong-doings of employers sound very grand, but this kind of philanthropy is very cheap and, we fear, worth very little. It would be more satisfactory to all concerned if people in general would bear in mind an elementary principle of Moral Theology, that it is as much a sin against justice to pay too little for an article as to ask too much for it ; that the face of the poor may be ground down as much by economical housewives as by tyrannical capitalists.

*   *

Nor is it the rich alone who are guilty of injustice: of this the strike above referred to affords an example. The drivers and conductors formed the majority of the strikers, but they were assisted by the horse-keepers, who form a large body of men. In the settlement, however, the latter's claims were entirely disregarded. The drivers and conductors having secured what they demanded, declared the strike at an end and left their humbler coadjutors to shift for themselves. This is not the only instance during the past month in which the claims of fellow-workmen have been set at naught by their comrades. At Newcastle the engineers in the shipping trade, because in their opinion the plumbers were encroaching upon their sphere of work, went out on strike, and on account of this action some 25,000 men stood in danger of loss of employment. .And so while in general we extend to the working-man our sympathy in their struggles, it must not be a blind sympathy ; for the fact cannot be overlooked that acts of injustice are not seldom committed by working-men in their dealings with each other. Is it not within the limits of possibility, too, that the employers may sometimes be right?

The great grievance of the omnibusmen was the long hours during which they were required to work. Yet they were themselves not without responsibility for this state of things. For the strike synchronized with the adoption of a ticket system which effectually prevented a long standing habit of peculation. Some time before it took place the managers of the companies had proposed to adopt this ticket system, but in deference to the wishes of the men the old method was allowed to continue, the men being willing to work more hours in order to have a longer time to carry on their depredations, and the employers conniving for the sake of securing their services at lower wages. It is hard to conceive a more demoralizing system for all concerned, both masters and men.

*　　*

The international character of the labor movement of our times has been strikingly exemplified in these omnibus strikes. It was in Paris that the first took place. Its success seems to have moved the London men to emulation. Hungary next became the scene of conflict; here, however, it was not the men but the masters who struck, moved thereto by certain onerous police regulations. Success attended their efforts. Then the movement returned to France, and first Lyons and then Bordeaux and Marseilles witnessed similar conflicts. Lyons and Bordeaux were the only places in which anything like rioting took place. In Bordeaux, however, there was somewhat serious trouble.

*　　*　　*

A more satisfactory exemplification of internationalism is found, however, in the action of many European legislatures. The Berlin Conference, far from proving fruitless, as many anticipated, is moving several countries to take measures for the improvement of the working classes. Its influence has been decisively felt in Great Britain with reference to child labor. In other respects, as is well known, the laws for the protection of operatives were, at the time of the conference, more satisfactory there than elsewhere. In the matter of child labor, however, the rest of Europe was in advance of England. The conference fixed the age at which a child was to be allowed to begin to work at twelve; in England it was lawful to begin at ten. The government bill for the Regulation of Factories and Workshops, as introduced by them, made no alteration in this respect, although the recommendation of the conference had received the express approval of Lord Salisbury. More than that, to an amendment

for raising the age to twelve the government offered strenuous
opposition. Strange to say, in doing this they acted—as they say
and as seems really to be the case—according to the wishes of
the parents most nearly affected. These parents, it appears, find
it hard to relinquish the earnings of the children under twelve.
The government would not even give its assent to a compromise
proposed by a conservative member by which the age was raised
to eleven. The feeling, however, in favor of this was so strong
that on a division the government were beaten. And so England, although she has not fully realized the recommendation of
the conference, has been induced to take this step toward it.

*   *

In other countries there is more zeal. France has gone beyond the recommendation of the conference; for a law has been
made by which the age for the legal employment of children in
some thirteen specified industries has been raised to thirteen.
One exception is made, rendering it lawful for children who are
above twelve to work on condition that they have passed the
required school examination. In other respects, too, legislation is
probable. The Minister of the Interior has introduced a bill for
the relief of destitute and deserving workmen. According to the
provisions of this bill a workman may voluntarily agree to have
certain deductions made from his wages with the view to the
ultimate enjoyment of a pension. To the fund for paying this
pension both the state and the employer will contribute, it being
made obligatory upon the employer to pay the share required of
him. In this way from three hundred to six hundred francs
yearly will be secured for the workman after the lapse of thirty
years. The cost to the state, should the five and one-half millions of working-men insure, is estimated at one hundred millions
of francs a year.

*

France has given yet another proof of her regard for the
laborer's welfare. A law was passed in 1848 by which the hours
of labor for all persons employed in state and municipal establish-
ments were fixed at twelve. This law has now been extended
to all engine-drivers, stokers, switchmen, omnibus-drivers, and
conductors, and other persons employed in transport companies
having concessions from the state or from local bodies. If the
Boulangists could have had their way this extension would have
included all day-laborers, miners, factory hands, and assistants in

large stores.   But this was further than the Assembly was prepared to go.
*   *

Nor is our chronicle of labor legislation yet complete.   In the
Austrian Reichsrath the Minister of Commerce has introduced a
bill "for the creation of institutions tending to facilitate conciliation
between employers of labor and their workmen."   The bill provides
for the appointment of workmen syndicates and for the establishment of boards of conciliation.   Trade corporations among the
mining operatives are also proposed.   These are so far only
projects.   The German emperor, however, in his speech on the
prorogation of the Prussian Parliament, expressed his satisfaction
that a law had been passed by which the taxation which bore
hardly on the poorer classes had been more equitably adjusted. .

*   *   *

The only conflict between labor and capital in which the distinctive principles of the "new" unionism formed the only direct
issue has taken place, not in the Old World but in one of Great
Britain's dependencies—Queensland.   This contest brings into view
several interesting points.   First of all, it shows, although not for
the first time, in one of the most recently settled and organized
of modern countries, the elements of strife exist as fully developed
as in the over-populated countries of Europe.   Another thing to
be noted is the attitude of the purely democratic government of
the colony toward the working-men.   The conduct of the strikers
called for active intervention.   They formed themselves into camps,
from which parties, mounted and armed, rode about the country
intimidating those who were willing to work.   Trains were
wrecked, many deeds of personal violence committed, property
was destroyed.   The strikers were some 10,000 in number, and as
the movement progressed talk of "social war" and the "Australian revolution" began to be heard.   The government, however,
did not flinch.   Some of the more outspoken and imprudent of
the leaders were arrested, and have since been convicted and
sentenced to various terms of imprisonment.

The ordinary police force proving too weak to cope with the
strikers, it became necessary to call out the military.   In the colony
there are no regular troops.   The only military organization possessed
by the state consists of what is called the Defence Force, formed
of men who, as a rule, are engaged in civil occupations, and only

liable to service in an emergency and for a limited time. Half of this force was called out. The men had to serve at long distances from their homes, to make long marches in a district where there are no railways, and to undergo many hardships and much fatigue; and this was done to protect "blacklegs" or "scabs." The government and people of the colony were led to make these sacrifices by the determination to maintain the right of men to work on their own terms, even though those terms were not union terms. There was no question of wages—by the admission of the men these were amply sufficient. Union of masters was pitted against union of men—and the union of masters has won. For, according to the last news the strike has been declared at an end. It seems clear that the determination that men shall be at liberty either to join or not a union is as strong in Australia as recent events have proved it to be in England.

*

The Labor Commission appointed by the English government has at last got to work. It has taken a long time to organize itself and to prepare its plan of operations. Perhaps it might not be wrong to speak of it as three commissions, for it has been divided into three committees, and among these the subjects of inquiry have been distributed. The first committee deals with the mining, iron, engineering, hardware, ship-building, and cognate trades; the second with shipping, canals, docks, railways, tramways, and agriculture; the third with the textile, clothing, chemical, building, and miscellaneous trades. In this way the vast field under investigation will stand a chance of being covered in time for a report before the general election. But, irrespective of this report, which will give the judgment of the commissioners, the facts given in evidence from day to day will form a mine of information accessible to all and simply invaluable. We hope to be able to lay before our readers the most important and interesting of the facts elicited.

*

Mr. Chamberlain's plan for providing pensions for the aged poor is making headway every day and taking more definite shape. Lord Hartington, the leader of the Liberal-Unionists, by no means a Radical, in a speech recently made includes it among the measures which his party have in contemplation. The committee for elaborating the plan and working out its details numbers sixty-six peers, and members of Parliament of all parties.

Many points have yet to be decided, but that there is to be no compulsion placed on working-men to effect the proposed insurance seems to be generally agreed. It has also been resolved that in case the insurer die before the attainment of the pension age the amount of money actually deposited by him may be with-drawn. How much the state will pay, at what age the pension will commence, and many other points remain to be settled. But from the attention the plan has excited, the amount of support it is receiving, and the state of political parties, we shall not be rash in concluding that a measure of this kind will pass through Parlia-ment next session.

*

For the first time since the passing of Mr. Forster's Act in 1870 the system of elementary education established by it is being subjected to fundamental revision. As our readers are doubtless aware, there are in Great Britain two parties diametri-cally opposed to each other on the school question. One party warmly defends and supports the giving of religious education in the elementary schools. This party is made up of the de-fenders of the Establishment, of the Catholics, and until quite re-cently of Wesleyan Methodists. The latter, however, have lately abandoned the cause. The other party wishes to have all the schools secularized, and finds its leaders and guides in infidels like Mr. John Morley, and, strange to say, derives its strength from the Nonconformists, Baptists, Congregationalists, and now the Methodists. The first party supports and maintains the voluntary schools, and seeks in Parliament all the help which national funds and laws afford them. The other party act, of course, in the opposite sense, and especially seek to extend the school boards, or, failing that, to bring the voluntary schools under public control.

When education was made compulsory in England, that it should become free became only a matter of time. The advo-cates of purely secular education were looking forward to this as the fitting opportunity for bringing all the schools into the power of the state, on the principle that he who pays should control. The present government, which is friendly to religious education and the voluntary schools, has brought in its Free Education Bill in order to frustrate this plan. The measure leaves the management of each school unchanged. Ten shillings yearly is given for each child in average attendance. It is perhaps inaccurate to call the bill a Free Education Bill, for it does not secure, and is not meant to secure, one dead-level of absolute freedom. The ten-shilling grant is calculated upon the basis of a three-penny fee for each child per week. As a matter of fact, the fees charged range from one penny to nine-pence per week. Consequently some schools will receive more than they have hitherto received in the way of children's pence, others will receive less. The schools which have hitherto received more will be allowed under this bill to charge the difference between the former fee and the three-pence given by the government, provided that a sufficient number of free places are found for those parents who wish for them. It is also left to the option of each school to accept or to reject the government grant.

*   *   *

Such are the main provisions of the new measure, which it is hoped by the government will settle the question permanently and settle it in favor of religious education. Whether this hope will be realized no one can tell. All we can say is, that the authors of the bill are sincere friends of the voluntary schools, and seem to have acted for no other purpose then to strengthen and preserve them. Only ten out of the six hundred and seventy-two members of Parliament voted against the second reading of the bill. In the course of the debate Lord George Hamilton, a member of the cabinet, paid a tribute of praise to supporters of Catholic schools in England, which will interest our readers as showing what English Catholics have done out of their poverty. "In the case of the Roman Catholic schools," he said "that subscriptions amounted to seventy-eight per cent. of the fees payable. That showed the subscriptions were high and the fees low, and that the subscribers were prepared to make sacrifices for their schools. In the case of the Wesleyan schools the statistics were reversed, the subscriptions amounting to only seventeen per cent." And speaking of the schools themselves, he said "the Roman Catholic schools were extraordinary in their efficiency, considering the small resources at their disposal." This is the spontaneous testimony of an impartial non-Catholic.

The fair treatment meted out to religious schools in Scotland is illustrated by the following case. The school board at Crieff, wishing, it would seem, to supplant neighboring Catholic and Episcopal voluntary schools, asked the Scotch Education Department what arrangements they required in regard to the religious teaching in public schools in order that the grants to the Episcopal and Roman Catholic schools in Crieff might be withdrawn and refused. To this the department replied, that where parents believed that religious instruction ought to be imparted to their children at school, it could not be said that sufficient provision, according to the terms of the Education Act, existed for the children in schools where no religious instruction is given, or where it is of a kind of which parents disapprove. From this reply it would appear that the Scotch Education Act—as interpreted, at all events, by its present administrators—gives a statutory right to parents to have their children taught their own religion at the expense of the state, even in places where the school board supplies sufficient secular education. If this is the case, religious education is more favored in Scotland than in England.

*   ..   *

One or two further proofs of the fair treatment accorded to the church in Great Britain may not be out of place. Some little time ago the ministers of the Establishment, assembled in convocation, made loud complaints that in many workhouses, while Catholic chaplains were appointed and received salaries, no provision was made for Episcopalian chaplains. And a few days ago the London *Times*, commenting on the opposition in Canada to Sir John Thompson being made premier, said: "Sir John Thompson is a Roman Catholic, and on that ground is denounced by some of the Protestant members of the Conservative party. . . . It is much to be regretted that Dr. Douglass, whose eighty years give him great authority among the Wesleyan Methodists, should have set the evil example of religious bigotry. Happily, more liberal views are entertained by other men of light and leading in that body."

*   *

We are unable, unhappily, to chronicle any marked advance of the temperance movement; in fact, hoped-for steps onward will be delayed for another year. The Welsh Local-Option Bill has been withdrawn, owing to the state of parliamentary business. Possibly the Irish measure may even yet be put through; but owing to the opposition of certain Irish members, of which we have already spoken, the likelihood of this is very small. But that the position of the publicans is beginning to be looked

upon as very insecure, on account of the legal decision of which
we have already spoken, is shown by the fact that a company
has been started to insure against loss of license, in the same
way as against loss by fire. Those who insure in this company
will receive the compensation which the law refuses. Doubtless
one good effect of this will be to remove the scruples of magistrates and make them more willing to take away licenses.
That public-house property, notwithstanding the temperance
movement and the legal decision, is still of enormous value is
proved by the fact that a public-house with only eighteen years
of lease to run sold a short time ago for sixty years' purchase—
twenty-five years' purchase being the average price paid for land
in England; seventeen years in Ireland.

*

A most important event for the future of Europe took place
quietly at the end of June. This was the formal renewal for six
years of that alliance between Germany, Austria-Hungary, and
Italy which is known as the Triple Alliance. Unless the un
foreseen should happen, this renewal will secure the peace—perhaps we should rather call it the armed truce—of Europe for
six years to come. Every one must feel gratified at this prospect of the postponement of war, and even hope against hope
that in the breathing-space given some man will arise great and
powerful enough to bring about a disarmament.

*

That Germany and Austria would renew the alliance was
never a matter of doubt. Strong opposition, however, arose in
Italy. As is well known, the country is groaning under taxation far heavier than it had to bear in the old days; the
strongest desire of every Italian is to get rid of some portion of
his burden; the Alliance requires the keeping its army up to a
very high standard of efficiency. The fall of Crispi, it was thought,
would lead to a change of policy. The Marquis di Rudini,
however, has followed in the steps of his predecessors and has
again pledged Italy to the Alliance. How he will at the same
time carry out the economies which are the *raison d'être* of his
ministry remains to be seen. The deficit for the financial year
1891-92, just announced, is no less than 5,424,096 lire. The
way of trangressors is hard.

*

But should not the Triple Alliance be called the Quadruple

Alliance? Is not Great Britain a secret party? This is the question which has been warmly discussed in France during the past month, and French newspaper writers profess themselves convinced of the affirmative. There can be no doubt that the present English government is friendly to the three allied powers and to their policy. It may even be the case that Italy would not have entered into the alliance unless it had received an assurance of that friendship. That it has received such an assurance is all that can be said. That there is no formal treaty binding England to take action is clear to any one who is at all familiar with the English methods. As to France and Russia, the powers against whom the Triple Alliance is made, it seems clear that no formal treaty has been made between them. Despotism and the principles of '89 find it hard to blend. What is certain, however, is that the unity of interests is sufficient to produce unity of action when the time comes.

*   *   *

Meanwhile the French Republic seems to be taking firm root. M. de Freycinet's cabinet has remained in power for the long period of sixteen months. The president was received with enthusiasm during his recent tour through the south. Cardinal Lavigerie's policy seems to be gaining ground. One of the bishops most opposed hitherto to the established form of government, Monseigneur Fava, of Grenoble, has publicly declared: "We accept the form of government which exists to-day in France— namely, the republic." The Orleanists, the Bonapartists, and even Legitimists—supporters, that is, of Don Carlos, " King Charles VII., of Spain, and XI., of France "—have held meetings and made speeches; but very little attention · is accorded to them. It seems probable that France is now secure in the possession of the first requisite for civilization—a stable form of government.

*   *   *

On the fifth of June Cardinal Richard consecrated the Church of the Sacred Heart, which has been in course of erection for many years on Montmartre. It has been built as an act of expiation on the part of the nation for the sins which brought about the disasters of 1870 and 1871. Five millions of dollars have been subscribed since 1873, when the movement was inaugurated by the late Cardinal Guibert. Another sign of the activity of French Catholics is the formation of the " Union of Christian France." It is understood to be a further result of Cardinal Lavigerie's appeal, although there is no open renunciation of the monarchy or adoption of the republic. Its object is to take political action for the obtaining of religious liberty of teaching, of charity, and of association, and for the revision of all that in educational, military, or fiscal legislation constitutes a violation of this liberty. Its programme embraces also the passing of laws to secure the observance of Sunday as a day of rest, and legislation for the establishment of institutions for the amelioration of the workmen's lot. We hope that the upshot of all will be more than the issue of a programme, and that French Catholics may be really moved to act in defence of their own interests.

*   *   ˷

Long months of hard work on the part of the representatives of all the European powers, and the sanguine expectation that the way had at last been secured for effectually putting an end to the slave-trade, have all been defeated and rendered useless by the action of the French Assembly. The Brussels Convention, of which we have given an account in former numbers, has been rejected by 439 votes to 104. The ostensible reason was the alleged revival of the right of search; but as no right of search was given, only a simple verification of the identity of vessels, the real reason must be found in something else. Possibly the utter failure of the convention may be averted. If it is forbidden to the Congo Free State to impose import duties, it is still in its power to impose export duties; and the other powers may carry out the provisions, leaving France in isolation, until from very shame she may fall into line with the rest of the civilized world.

˷   ˷   ˷

In Prussia the bill for restoring to the church the revenues withheld during the Kulturkampf, together with interest, has passed through both houses and has become law. By the retirement of the minister of public works, the emperor finds himself surrounded by entirely new men, only one of the old emperor's counsellors being left to emphasize the situation. Honors are being bestowed on those who have defended the youthful sovereign against one whom he describes as "an ungrateful vassal." The emperor has resumed his round of visits, Holland, England, and Norway being included in the first trip.

˸   ˷

In Austria most of the exceptional provisions against Socialists and anarchists have been abrogated, the authorities, in view of the more reasonable and pacific dispositions manifested by the working classes, being of opinion that they are no longer necessary. A closer alliance between Count Taaffe and the German Liberals is looked upon as probable. This would involve the abandonment of the Nationalist policy of the last twelve years, and a return to the work of liberal and constitutional development which went before the adoption of that policy. The peace secured by the Triple Alliance requires an increase of the war credits in the Austrian budget, and the arming of her soldiers with a cuirass impenetrable by bullets will, we hope, be a further safeguard against war.

*

The Balkan States, where the rivalry between Austria and Russia finds its sphere of action, present but little worthy of notice. That little consists in the rumor that a confederacy is being formed of the States which are under Russia's influence—Servia, Montenegro, and Greece—against Bulgaria, which enjoys the support of Austria. But little importance is, in our opinion, to be attached to these rumors. The uncertain *status quo* of these quarrelsome nationalities will, we think, remain in its uncertainty for a long time to come.

*

The long-standing dispute between Great Britain and Portugal has at last been settled, to all appearances permanently; and this little kingdom will now be able to devote itself to the readjustment of its finances and to the development of its long-neglected colonies. There are, indeed, among Portuguese statesmen some who by the sale of these colonies would find the means for effecting a financial equilibrium. If glory and prestige could make way for what would really be beneficial to the country this proposal would without doubt be carried out; but as things are it is scarcely to be expected. The new finance minister is a man of energy, skill, and experience, and is full of confidence that means can be found for effecting the necessary readjustment. In Spain, also, financial legislation is that which is of most pressing importance. Its character is of too technical a nature to be of general interest. A thing worthy of notice, however, is that in this, as in so many other countries, the legislature is interesting itself in behalf of the working-man. The securing to all in the employment of the state the rest of Sunday is the limit, however, of the present proposals.

TALK ABOUT NEW BOOKS.

As it was inevitable that a life * of Laurence Oliphant would be written, there seemed at first glance an obvious propriety in the fact that the work was to be undertaken by a kinswoman who was in so many ways qualified for the task. It is possible that this propriety was less real than it appeared, and that his biographer's defective sympathy with what was, after all, the essential thing in Oliphant and the true reason why a life of him finds buyers and readers, may prevent hers from being accepted as a fully satisfactory account of his career. But though this were certainly the case, and we feel persuaded that it is so in some measure, it would remain true that the first volume of this biography, which carries its hero through his first thirty-six years, could not well be improved. Mrs. Oliphant is very sensitive to the strong and peculiarly close affection which bound Laurence to his parents, and to the deep religious feeling he inherited directly from them, as well as to that side of his many-sided nature which kept him always a man of the world in a strict sense, even when he was most startlingly unworldly. Hence nothing could be better in its way than her presentation of him in these aspects.

Oliphant was born of Scottish parents in Cape Town, South Africa, in 1829, and though sent to England for his schooling, returned to his family without entering either of the universities —a fact to which his biographer is inclined to attribute many of his later eccentricities of thought. Be that as it may, there is something very charming in her account of the "education by contact" of this gay, impetuous, and brilliant youth, who at nineteen had entered into quasi-public life at Ceylon as secretary to his father, then chief-justice there. He became a barrister soon after, and had been engaged in twenty-three murder cases before he was as many years old. He never had much love for the law, however, and doubtless was glad of the very unlooked-for opportunity given him in 1851 to vary the routine of the courts by a tiger-shooting and elephant-catching expedition through Nepaul, in company with Jung Bahadour, on the return of the latter from his embassy to England. Oliphant was

* *Memoir of the Life of Laurence Oliphant and of Alice Oliphant, his Wife.* By M. O. W. Oliphant. New York: Harper & Bros.

twenty-one at the time, and from the notes he made of his observations and adventures he prepared his first book the following year. It was brought out in London, by Murray, in May,
1852, and ten days after its publication Laurence wrote to his
father that two thousand of the three thousand copies forming
the first edition had been sold, and that he had received "long
and favorable notices from the *Athenæum, Economist, Examiner,*
and *Literary Gazette.*" His reception from the reading world
was from that time assured, but it was not until thirteen years
later that he used his pen except to record his experiences of
travel. When, in 1865, he brought out his first novel, *Picca-
dilly*—written at the suggestion of Mr. John Blackwood and
issued as a serial in his famous magazine—he had already set
foot in the singular and little-frequented road he was thenceforward to travel until death. The novel is a curious production,
full of sharp and brilliant satire on society, " the wholly worldly "
and " the worldly holy," and yet interpenetrated by a certain
longing and vague mystic assurance of better things in store
for the world, sure to perplex as to their drift any reader who
should take it up in complete unacquaintance with its author's
career—as happened to the present writer some half-dozen years
since.

The interval between the production of these two books had
been packed with a succession of varied and unusual experiences.
Now one finds Oliphant doing missionary work in London
slums in company with parsons and society ladies; now on a
sporting expedition in Russia, or a diplomatic mission to Washington and Canada in the train of Lord Elgin in 1854; and,
again, in the following year, declining " a small governorship in
the West Indies," in order to go to the Crimea and try to engineer a diplomatic mission of his own concocting with Schamyl
in Circassia. There was plainly no lack of excitement and action in this life. It was also varied by the usual distractions of
an English gentleman to whom society is invariably cordial, and
by the less common introspection and study of his interior attitude towards God, begun early in life as a matter of filial duty,
and persevered in later through filial affection. His letters
to his mother were constant from all quarters of the world
whither he was led by a mercurial disposition, curiously harnessed
to and held in check by a thoroughly Scotch and canny resolve to carve out a desirable place for himself in life. He made
money readily, but he was no spendthrift; he loved pleasure
and society, but he was always coming to book with his con-

science and confessing himself in an artless, if not very contrite, way to his mother, who must have found a good deal to please as well as plenty to trouble her in the epistles which Mrs. Oliphant quotes so freely. Thus he writes her from Washington concerning a diplomatic dinner he had attended with Lord Elgin :

"We then adjourned with a lot of senators to brandy-and-water, champagne, and cigars till twelve, when some of us were quite ready to tumble into bed. Now I have no doubt you are perfectly horrified, and picture to yourself your inebriated son going to bed in a condition you never thought possible ; but, on the contrary, yesterday was a most profitable day to me. In the first place, though I did not restrain myself, I did not in the slightest degree exceed. I did .not touch anything else *but* champagne, and stopped exactly at the right moment. I felt all through that I was in a position not of my own seeking, and that if it was agreeable to me it was because I myself was at fault"

And, again, when his innocent attentions to the French girls in Quebec distress him with a fear lest he is not keeping up to his standard, he writes :

"Lord E. says he never knows what I am at ; at one moment going to the extreme of gaiety, at another to that of disgust and despondency. All he wishes is in a good-natured way to amuse people ; and he therefore can hardly sympathize with my reactions every now and then, which arise from my being too well amused myself."

It was always the latter reflection that bothered him.

"I am called upon to join in everything," he says, "and my conscience would not in the slightest degree twit me for doing so, *provided I was all the time bored instead of pleased.* The test of the thing is whether I like it ; and though I cannot say I do, I very soon would."

Later on, his religious introspection, which had hitherto been of the scrupulous and emotional character, began to be varied with doubts and speculations which afflicted the mother, from whom he made no effort to conceal them, more than his previous peccadilloes had done. He took to reading Theodore Parker, and then to philosophizing on his own account, but always with a certain practical turn which was characteristic of him. His difficulties concerned practice more than doctrines, and that not his own practice so much as that of "professing Christians," among whom he did not class himself as yet. If he once accepted the yoke, he thought he would feel bound to carry it more decorously than, for instance, a bishop whom he met in Shanghai when he was there in Lord Elgin's train in 1858:

"The bishop and his wife are becoming dabs at billiards," he tells his mother, "but the other night when the missionaries were dining he would not allow the billiard-room to be lighted, though he is generally the last to leave it. Woe unto you Evangelists and Puseyites, hypocrites!"

"But Laurence," says Mrs. Oliphant, "was little favorable to missionaries in general, and felt with many others that the good incomes, good houses, and worldly comfort of men who are supposed to be sacrificing everything for Christ's work, were jarring circumstances, to say the least." It was not alone in the spirit of self-sacrifice that he found them deficient, but in that of humanity.

"Like Lord Shaftesbury," he says, "they are truly English, and grumble at our not having murdered Yeh and given Canton over to pillage and slaughter. As a general rule, one thinks that justice ought to be tempered with mercy; but they would have vengeance tempered with justice!"

He speaks also of the contempt he feels (with a parenthetical acknowledgment that the feeling is wrong)

"for professors of a creed which has no power over them, but all the dogmas of which I am blamed for not subscribing to. When men who keep harems go to church regularly, and blame me for not going with them, I am apt to confound the faith with the individual, and swear at the whole concern. And so, because I do not confess to a good deal that seems to be hollow in the practice of a popular theology, I am put down as being without religion, and so lose any influence which, did I refrain from this, I might have, besides giving a totally wrong impression of my real convictions."

Here was plainly the stuff for a "comeouter" and practical enthusiast, if only the ground for thorough-going action should once seem solidly established beneath his feet. At the same time it was at least equally plain that this basis, were it found, would prove unusual, if not bizarre:

"I certainly do not understand God's dealings with men," he writes to his mother, "nor am I so presumptuous as to suppose

I ever shall; but if I did not exercise my reason there would be nothing to prevent my accepting the Koran or any other system of theology my fellow-creatures might assure me was right, and deny me the privilege of judging for myself. You say you would be glad if I could give up my career for God's service. I would willingly go into a dungeon for the rest of my days if I was vouchsafed a supernatural revelation of a faith; but I should consider myself positively wicked if upon so momentous a subject I was content with any assumptions of my erring and imperfect fellow-creatures, when against the light of my own conscience. . . . I would sooner go to the stake than do violence to what I believe to be the yearnings and whisperings—weak and imperfect, no doubt—of my divine nature."

It was not long after this—two or three years, at most, perhaps—that Oliphant became convinced he had come upon the traces of the revelation he was seeking. More than that, he had persuaded his mother to be of the same mind, and they had begun, though not openly as yet, to follow it together. He who had criticised the action of certain of his friends who became Catholics, on the ground that such a step implied weakness of will and judgment, and a desire to be dictated to on points of faith, was about to submit his whole life and conduct, in its most intimate and sacred relations, to a relentless scrutiny and arbitrary rule almost without a parallel, and to do so in the full persuasion that the man to whom he thus submitted exercised his sway by divine inspiration. Grant that persuasion—and it must be granted to a man of Oliphant's transparent candor—and what followed was only what might be expected from his power of self-devotion. One may wonder at the end, but the means to it are logical enough. It is difficult to give in a sufficiently condensed form an adequate idea of what it was that engrossed Oliphant's mind, so keen and practical, in the ordinary sense of those epithets, on one of its sides, and so mystical on another that, as has been said already, even his most extraordinary actions become practical and inevitable when judged from his own point of view. To him, at least, it was clearly a question of "What shall a man give in exchange for his soul?" and the answer he made is one of those which must be left to Him who is the only judge of consciences so delicate and lives so self-denying as his.

It was in 1860 that Oliphant first met the man to whose influence he so long allowed absolute sway over his external life, and whose teachings he never rejected, even after he had resumed his personal freedom of action. This person, whom Mrs. Oliphant describes at one time as "the obscure Swedenborgian preacher, the uncultured American who assumed over him the authority of God Himself," and again as "the prophet—or wizard, magician, as it seems fit to call him in the light of that tremendous indictment" (she alludes here to Oliphant's novel *Masollam*, written after he had shaken off his physical but not his spiritual bonds)—was Thomas Lake Harris. Whatever view he may have taken of Harris's conduct in after years, Oliphant continued to his latest day to believe that his original message had come direct from God— as is sufficiently evident not only from *Sympneumata*, the singular and almost incomprehensible joint production of Oliphant and his wife shortly before the latter's death, but from *Scientific Religion*, the equally curious but more comprehensible volume whose publication was almost coincident with Oliphant's own death. Harris was, briefly—*is*, perhaps, would be the better word, as he is still living—a Swedenborgian seer who claimed to have received a completion and correction of the revelations of the Swedish mystic. His initiation was into the "celestial sense" of Holy Scripture, Swedenborg having been "intromitted" into the spiritual one only. His doctrine, based upon the literal text, is both in terms and meaning more orthodox than that of Swedenborg, especially in his teachings on the Trinity and on heaven and hell. He abandoned, for example, that notion of "equilibrium" by which Swedenborg sought to demonstrate not only the eternity of both, but their absolutely inevitable sequence from the possession of free will. According to him, heaven *must* be based on hell, not merely here, but in any conceivable world occupied by rational creatures capable of choice—which is substantially the conclusion reached by Von Hartmann when he reluctantly abandons the suggestion of universal suicide as a refuge from the ills of conscious existence, on the ground that "the Unconscious," by the very law of its being, would be compelled to begin anew the same miserable round man knows too well already.

Like Swedenborg, Harris claimed to have visited in spirit not only the "third heaven" to which St. Paul was caught up, but various earths and suns of the universe, where he indeed found a state of things externally like that described by the Swedish seer in identical localities, but capable of another interpretation, which Swedenborg, on account of inherited and acquired prejudices, was incapable of receiving or transmitting. He received "according to his mode," is Harris's explanation. He thought he saw sin and disorder and punishment everywhere, chiefly because he had excogitated that very doctrine of "equilibrium," and carried it with him as a medium of vision. This explanation, as the reader of Father Hecker's " Life " may remember, is not un- like one suggested by him, before his conversion, in the case of Swedenborg and other mystics. Harris taught, on the contrary, that our earth is the only one in which sin has established an in- version of celestial order, and hence the only one in which pain and unhappiness are known. In every world, however, he found God worshipped in the divine humanity of Jesus Christ, and in many of them the knowledge that He had descended in it to our earth, suffered, died, and risen again for the redemption of those who would receive Him. Harris had a great natural flow of picturesque language and a poetic imagination, and his visions took a far more readable shape than those of Swedenborg; which, to be sure, is not giving them excessive praise. He included in them, however, a practical doctrine concerning a new descent of the Spirit of God, and certain consequences flowing from the belief that the sexes, separated by the fall, would be reunited in the re- generation. So far as one can make out, it was the latter teach- ing, with the practical conclusion from it, that each soul has its own counterpart and predestined mate, whose existence may be certainly known, *à priori* as it were, and *à posteriori* also, accord- ingly as one proves faithful to the grace of God and his highest aspirations, which took that deep hold on Oliphant which he never shook off. Having found his counterpart, as he believed, in the beautiful and noble woman who is commemorated with him in these volumes, he married and lived with her in unbroken con- tinence, thus striving for, and confident of having attained, a union far more close than that of ordinary marriage; one, too, that, in the case of the survivor, sensibly outlasted death. Oliphant was in no sense a spiritualist; perhaps it would be truer to say that his attitude towards mediums, induced hypnotic states, and endeavors to peer into the future was identical with that of Catho- lics. He thought they were works of the devil, sure to be dangerous, and likely to be fatal to the souls of those who prac- tised them. And it was not by seeking for anything of the sort, but much to his surprise, as one must infer from the account given to his wife's mother in a letter, that within a week after her death he found himself again in conscious union with her. "There is no analogy with mediumship or spiritualism," he says, "for I am never more conscious of her than when all my facul- ties are on the alert." He misses " her sweet companionship," and at first the work to which they had given their lives and the common object for which they had labored, " and which formed a tie transcending any which could arise from natural marriage," seemed suddenly checked.

"But now all that is passed. Henceforward I live in her, as she will, if I am faithful to my highest aspirations, live in me; we are indissolubly bound to all eternity—more firmly wedded now than we could ever be below."

Perhaps we have given too much space to beliefs and apprehensions such as these. But in a time when the vast majority of minds outside the Church are going astray in so much more dangerous directions; when their spiritualism leads to the ghastly pessimism of Schopenhauer and Von Hartmann, and their materialism to the conception of a mechanical universe to which nothing is wanting but a supreme Mechanician; and when one sees the result of their teachings on all sides in a world which is denying God, and going bodily over to the devil by a natural sequence, one recognizes with relief any aspiration towards what is good and pure, any faith, however formally erroneous, whose direct object is the Word Incarnate, and any hope which looks, through Him, for a blessed eternal life as the reward of patience and well-doing here. As to the special case of the Oliphants, there are several theories which may be advanced. Some may think that their singular intercommunion of life and sympathy, uninterrupted even by the death of one of them, is a pure delusion; to which view, often suggested, is opposed the unanimous testimony of all who knew them, that in the affairs of ordinary life this pair showed perfect sanity. and exceptionally good judgment. Diabolical agency may be suspected, and at once admitted as a not improbable factor, although it must also be owned that peace, purity, unselfishness, absence of pride, hope in God and faith in Christ, which they seemed to possess, do not usually accompany Satan's persistent interference. It is not incredible that some of the phenomena which the Oliphants believed in and experienced may belong to the arcana of nature itself, to those "things in heaven and earth not dreamt of in our philosophies," but concerning which so much has been learned in these days of man's rapid advance in knowledge. And if it be objected that all their hopes and beliefs co-existed with the gravest formal errors, and notably with an aversion from Catholicity, it may be replied that the Church herself allows us to hold that many belong to her soul who are not of her visible body. "All the baptized are mine," said Pius IX. to the Emperor Wilhelm. At any rate, one may hope that so much unselfish devotion to high ideals, so much purity, such charity in word and deed as these two showed, were rewarded by a gleam of supernatural light and joy.

From Shadow to Sunlight * is a very silly little tale, badly constructed, and for the most part written in a worse style than should be pardoned even to a semi-royal author. No one but the Marquis of Lorne, at least, at any stage of dinner, ever saw an American girl's "flashing eyes and pearly teeth shining between her lovely lips" either with or without "surprise." His hero is always delightful; in his solemn asseveration that he "would die for his sovereign," the present Empress of India and mother-in-law of the author, as well as in his account of the gradual opening of his eyes to the craft and duplicity of the Jesuits after his conversion and ordination to the priesthood in their order. He writes this all down, "just how it was," in the letter containing his proposal to marry the young lady whose eyes occupied the abnormal position above referred to; and when she

"retired to her room to read it . . . her prevalent feeling was expressed when she concluded in the words 'What a horrid shame!' He came to receive his sentence next morning, and was unanimously acquitted by the judge and jury. He certainly would never have feared another earthly tribunal so much as he did that of the Wincott party, and I doubt if even the General of the Jesuits could have infused into him a tithe of the fear that secretly possessed him as he approached the door. To judge from his face, when he left the door, the grand inquisition within had not put him to the torture."

So Mary married him, "and now speaks with a very British accent," says the marquis, and after she became Mary Chisholm "has never since the day we quoted her as using the expression ever again said 'that she felt badly.'" With a British property, a British accent, and a British ex-priest for a husband, how could she? Perhaps she has even been presented at court, and so her poor little American cup now runneth over.

A very good little story,† from the French of Emile Richebourg, is *Le Million du Père Raclot.* It is both innocent and entertaining, like the *Abbé Constantin* of Halévy—a combination too infrequent in French novels chosen for translation.

---

* *From Shadow to Sunlight.* By the Marquis of Lorne, G.C.M.G. (Authorized edition.) New York: D. Appleton & Co.

† *Old Raclot's Million.* Adapted from the French of Emile Richebourg by Mrs. Benjamin Lewis. New York: Cassell Publishing Co.

Not so entertaining but equally innocuous is Mrs. Clara Bell's translation * from the Dutch of Van Lennep's *Story of an Abduction*. It has the further advantage of being strictly historical, if that be considered a great advantage when the incidents narrated are of no special importance that one can discover to humanity at large. There are a good many people who, like the late William George Ward, would care as little for Cæsar's crossing the Rubicon as for John Smith's crossing the street, considered purely in themselves. To such we do not pressingly recommend this tale of the abduction of Catharine d'Orléans, amusing as it is in parts— more especially as any interest they may take in the final disposition of the heroine will be thwarted by the fact that this belongs neither to history nor fiction.

Miss Bacon's book † is full of interesting and suggestive details concerning Japanese women from their cradles to their graves. She has been qualified to give them by a long residence in Japan, where she enjoyed unrestrained intercourse, both as teacher and friend, with the girls and women of whom she writes. Her sympathy, too, is intelligent and generous. We cannot but think she has done a wise and womanly thing in pointing out with such a firm hand the heaven-wide distinction between the Eastern and the Western woman's ideal of personal virtue, and insisting that the memory of it shall be kept in mind when the tales of certain travellers are told. The Japanese girl-child of every rank, she says in brief, from the possible empress down, is trained solely with a view to making her the always amiable and absolutely obedient servant of the men of her family; her father, her husband, her son rule her in turn; and she is taught that no service is too menial, and no sacrifice too great, to be offered by her if they require or can be benefited by it. For her obedience and loyalty are the supreme virtues, to be preserved if necessary at the cost of all others. For the good of father or husband she must brave any danger, endure any dishonor, or perpetrate any crime. She is responsible to no one except on this score. The Japanese maiden, says Miss Bacon, grows to womanhood as pure and modest as our own girls; but, she adds, it is not expected of any woman in America " that she exist solely for the good of some one else, in whatever way he chooses to use her, during all the years of her life." To this observer the sense of duty seemed to be so strongly developed in the Japanese women

* *Story of an Abduction in the Seventeenth Century.* By J. Van Lennep. New York; W. S. Gottsberger & Co.

† *Japanese Girls and Women.* By Alice Mabel Bacon. New York and Boston: Houghton, Mifflin & Co.

that neither fear, shame, nor dread of ridicule will excuse them in their own eyes from performing what is demanded by it. On the other hand, the Japanese husband and father, who is to his women the objective centre of duty, finds his own in the will of his rulers. Neither one nor the other recognizes any personal identity apart from their function as part of the social organism.

Miss Bacon's account of the exquisite manners, the polish and refinement of social intercourse among the Japanese, which threaten to become things of the past under the influence of our ruder Western civilization, is very pleasant. One wonders in reading it, however, if " modern " instead of " Western " would not be the better adjective. There was surely a time within the memory of some of us when even American children were taught manners and reverence for age—and a time, too, when something like the still-existing Japanese distaste for "anything suggestive of trade or barter," which makes them rank merchants lower in the social scale than farmers and artisans, might have been found without going so far to look for it. The difference is not so much geographical as temporal ; the modern man, having become to a greater extent a worshipper of Mammon, has put most of his pride as well as certain of his virtues in his pocket, as a necessary preliminary to filling that receptacle with more tangible possessions. Miss Bacon's volume is, we believe, the pioneer one in its special field, and though it hardly exhausts the subject, it is unlikely that it will soon be superseded.

I.—THE MASS.*

This little book, of one hundred and twenty-two pages, is well printed on excellent paper, but it is to be regretted that the illustrations were not better chosen, especially those of the last chapter, which, far from being artistic, are in several cases quite incorrect as to the position and attitude of priest and server : as, for instance, the celebrant is made to stand on the gospel side of the altar for the introit and collect ; while for the latter the server is made to kneel upon the predella directly in front of the unveiled chalice ; also the illustration marked *Consecration* should read *The Elevation*, and that reading *Ite, missa est* should be *The Blessing*.

However, while *The Holy Mass Explained* cannot be com-

* *The Holy Mass Explained.* By the Rev. F. X. Schouppe, S.J. New York and Cincinnati: Fr. Pustet & Co.

pared to Canon Oakeley's most valuable and exhaustive work on
the same subject, it will probably be read with great profit by a
great number of people to whom the great English churchman's
work would never be known, and we must thank Father O'Hare
most warmly for the labor he has undergone in adding to the
list of Catholic publications, which now, thanks be to God, is fast
becoming a long one and a valuable one to America.

2.—KATERI TEKAKWITHA.[*]

Charlevoix, Parkman, Clark, Kip, Schoolcraft, Shea, and a host
of others have told in glowing periods the heroic deeds of those
members of the Society of Jesus who "endured with a superhuman endurance" all that savage cruelty could inflict on them in
their endeavors to draw the North American Indian to Christ. In
the works of these historians of a race of martyrs mention, often
frequent, is made of the Indian maid Catherine, "the lily of the
Mohawks," "the Genevieve of New France"; but this is the first
complete life of the saintly maiden the church is now petitioned
to raise to the honor of her altars that we have in English.

Miss Walworth, in her very modest preface to this excellent
work, says: "If this book, embodying the result of my researches, should fail to interest the reader, it will not be for any
lack of enthusiasm on my part, or of kind encouragement and
competent assistance from others."

We cannot conceive that any one, even the most blasé of
novel-readers, would find the book pall on him. As a story it
is exquisitely told; as a history it is full of deep research, and is
of a learning that may be styled profound. The pictures of Indian life and Indian customs are exceedingly well transcribed and
are of much interest. The chapter which contains the account
of the baptism of Catherine is a fine piece of word-painting, and
a genuine piece of realism. We commend this chapter in particular to those who fancy that to be realistic is to be photographic.

It is, however, as a veritable history of a saintly heroine, of a
people and time that our English-speaking readers know mostly
from non-Catholic sources, that the book has its greatest value
We owe much to those not of the household who have well told
the story of Catholic heroism in North America, but we owe

[*] *The Life and Times of Kateri Tekakwitha, the Lily of the Mohawks.* By Ellen H.
Walworth. Buffalo: Peter Paul & Brother.

more to Catholics like Miss Walworth and Shea, whose perception of the supernatural is keen because of their gift of faith.

3.—THE PHOTOCHRONOGRAPH.*

An interesting account of the most promising use yet made of photography in the observation of transits. The idea of recording transits photographically, so as to get rid of what is called the "personal equation" of individual observers, as well as to secure greater accuracy, is not absolutely new, but the method employed by Fathers Hagen and Targis is in various respects original and remarkably simple and ingenious.

It is hardly to be expected that the photographic method will ever entirely supersede the usual one, as it seems to be necessarily time-consuming in comparison ; but it will be very serviceable for the brighter and more important stars, and will also furnish one of the best means for determining the amount of the personal equation in just the kind of phenomena in which it is desirable to know it. An application also of the method which would seem to be of special value is that in the telegraphic determination of longitudes. There is little doubt that in this, as in various other ways, the new method, with the further improvements to it which will no doubt be devised, will become a regular adjunct to astronomical observation in all parts of the world.

Georgetown College Observatory : The Photochronograph and its Application to Star Transits. Washington, D. C. : Stormont & Jackson.

THE COLUMBIAN READING UNION.

ALL COMMUNICATIONS RELATING TO READING CIRCLES, LISTS OF BOOKS, ETC., SHOULD BE ADDRESSED TO THE COLUMBIAN READING UNION, NO. 415 WEST FIFTY-NINTH STREET, NEW YORK CITY.

A SHORT time ago the writer of these notes had the pleasure of meeting two of the leading minds connected with the Catholic Reading Circles of Boston. The conversation was directed chiefly to one topic, viz., the results secured and the practical advantages gained by the members. The information given showed that under the guiding influence and encouragement of the Reading Circles many remarkable instances of latent talent had been developed, and that undeniable proofs attested the growth of a taste for studious reading, not only among graduates of academies and high schools, but also among those who earn their own living. Another testimony of the progress made in Boston comes to us in writing :

" The circles in Boston are all prospering and seem to maintain the interest of the members. There is one circle that has not resumed this year, on account of the transfer of the Rev. Director. The young ladies have not had the courage to ask for another, lest he might be withdrawn also, and they do not desire to continue the work by themselves. This is, of course, an unwise action on their part, as the work they did last year was so well planned and so excellently carried out that there is no reason why it should not continue. I wish very much to have a reunion of all the circles of Boston and vicinity this year, as it was too late when proposed last year. I feel that the results would be, to say the least, satisfactory. While it is possible that I may be expecting too much, still I do not think there will be any harm done. The enthusiasm of the people would be aroused with all the material at hand. Accept my best wishes for long-continued success of all the circles throughout the land, and the assurance of my active desire to assist the good work as far as is possible."

We have steadily urged the advantages of local option in arranging programmes for the meetings of Reading Circles. In no other way can the work be adjusted to suit the needs of different localities. The question box has proved to be a useful device for eliciting the practical topics which members wish to have explained. We are very much pleased to get the following account of the St. Agnes Reading Circle, which was established in connection with St. Ignatius Church, Baltimore, Md., early in September, 1890:

"The chief aim of the circle is improvement in using our best judgment to determine what to read and how to read. The plan of our work is to take some book—as *Fabiola*—and study it with care. To do this, four members are appointed each month to take several chapters and analyze them, bring out the pith of the work, and lay it before the members in an epitomized form. These papers, so prepared, are each limited to five minutes. Those who do the work improve themselves in analyzing and learn how to read any other work to the best advantage, as well as help others to do the same. But in order to make it a pleasure to learn our meetings are relieved of dryness and tedium, being diversified with recitations and musical selections. Each meeting is looked forward to as a pleasant recreation, in which study, improvement, and pleasure are combined. Our members are required to belong to a Sodality of the Blessed Virgin, or of the Sacred Heart, in any Catholic church in the city, and to pay one dollar a year, in advance or quarterly, as the member desires.

"There are two divisions: the workers and the listeners. When a lady becomes a member she decides whether she will be merely a listener and participator in the good things prepared by the workers. By this means all are reached, even those who have had but few opportunities; and in course of time some who entered as listeners feel themselves prepared to take a place among the workers.

"The money buys books which are selected to suit the scope of the book under study. These are not simply historical, but consist of stories relating to the period under consideration. Thus we get a pleasurable novel and learn history at the same time. In order to circulate these books, the names of members, arranged in order of nearness of residence, are printed, and each one is furnished with a copy. A member is allowed two weeks to read the book, and then passes it to the next on the list. And to keep these books in order they must be reviewed by the librarian at each meeting.

"At our first meeting, president, secretary, librarian, treasurer, etc., were appointed; also a committee on reading, whose duty it is to prepare a programme and map out the work to be done each month, and a committee on questions. These questions are placed in a box by any member who desires to have some difficulty solved, and may embrace any subject. They are read to the circle, and those which require searching in encyclopædias, etc., are distributed among the members of the committee, and the answers returned at the next meeting. If they meet with the approbation of the circle they are copied into a book kept for that purpose, where they may be reviewed when occasion requires.

The question which is occupying us at present is the Inquisition. One member studies up the Protestant view, and another gives the Catholic view. It will be likely to give us entertainment and food for thought for several meetings. We also have short sketches of American authors and selections from their works.

"After we finish the analysis of *Fabiola*, an historical novel, we propose to have a paper or two on the spread of the church up to that time; one also on the geography of Rome; one on the Coliseum and another on the Catacombs; others on the ideals of true womanhood, maidenhood, etc., as set forth in the person of Pancratius, mother of Fabiola, etc. None of these papers are to occupy over five minutes, if possible.

"I will give a programme of one of our meetings, which will outline the whole. We begin with music, and then the secretary reads the minutes of the last meeting. Then a sketch of our author, Cardinal Wiseman, after which the written selections on *Fabiola*. A recitation or reading follows. We have had Father Ryan's 'Song of the Mystic,' Longfellow's 'Golden Legend,' a selection from *Ben Hur*, etc.; then a vocal solo, after which our questions are answered or discussed, and new business transacted, as receiving new members, exchanging books, etc. The meeting closes with music. We have spent from one hour to one hour and a half pleasantly and profitably, and we retire wishing the next meeting were not a whole month away."

A correspondent in Ottawa, Ontario, is diffident about expressing his opinions on matters pertaining to the Columbian Reading Union. He asks:

"What can I say that has not been already and much better said by men and women whose opinions on such matters are of much weight? The removal of the woeful apathy of the Catholic body in regard to distinctively Catholic literature is certainly a work of crying necessity; and that your plan is a most important move in that direction must be patent to all who have given the question a moment's consideration. But, without in the slightest degree underrating the immense influence for good of your Reading Circles in other spheres, it seems to me that Catholic institutions of learning should be the most hopeful fields for your labor. For if the great object of education be to create an appetite for knowledge, surely the developing of a taste for the wholesome mental food which Catholic writers serve up for Catholic readers should be an important feature of Catholic school work; and what more efficient means for the development of such a taste could be devised than those afforded by the Columbian Reading Union? The object of Catholic schools is the turning out of sterling Catholics. But how can their graduates resist the evil influences which will in after-life surround them if they have not, during the years in which the mind takes on its permanent character, acquired a taste

for good reading? How often and how speedily the work of the
schools is nullified by the reading of books that by unseen degrees
warp the conscience, create false ideals, and malform the character.
As Charles Dudley Warner has truly said : " When one has learned
how to read and not what to read, he is in great peril." If in
every college and convent and advanced school there were in
operation one of your Reading Circles, so many of the young
men and maidens who go forth on commencement days with a
display of oratorical fireworks would not ' be drawn into the current of fashion 'until they can scarcely be distinguished from their
non-Catholic friends and acquaintances.' There would be a greater
demand for Catholic books. The subscription lists of THE
CATHOLIC WORLD and other first-class periodicals would grow
rapidly, and Columbian Reading Circles and Catholic Truth Societies would spring up all over the land. It is too bad that you
have met with, as you tell us in the April CATHOLIC WORLD,
such scant encouragement in these quarters, whence co-operation
should have come without special invitation."

This is the opinion of a man well informed on the needs of
the day, and holding an official position which keeps him in
close contact with the busy world. He represents a class of men
from whom we hope to receive many communications, showing
how Catholic literature may be utilized as an educational force
in school and out of school. The academy should not be a barrier
to any good educational influence. While it is desirable to have
the protection of sacred walls for young people, their future work
as Catholics in society must not be forgotten. As an aid to faith
it is by far better to have a knowledge of Catholic authors and
the noble thoughts they have adorned in beautiful language, than
to spend valuable time on trying to paint grotesque imitations of
flowers and in endless thumping on the piano. We have learned
on reliable authority that in one of our Catholic colleges the
dangerous stories of Charles Lever, which ridicule many Catholic
doctrines, are in constant circulation among the students. In that
library, and perhaps this is not the only case of the kind, the
best recent works of fiction by Catholic writers are not to be
found.

The Directors of the Catholic Educational Exhibit for the
World's Columbian Exposition, to be held in 1893, were called together for a meeting on July 1, at Chicago. A communication was read in behalf of the Columbian Reading Union to the
effect that it would be generally acceptable to the managers of
educational institutions to see at the Columbian Exposition an

exhibit of books suitable for school libraries, giving special prominence to the works of Catholic authors. Exact information
should be obtained concerning each book, as to cost and adaptability to scholars according to age. It should not be merely a
collection of text-books, but should represent the best we have in
Catholic literature, graded to suit the needs of young folks from
ten to twenty years of age. This plan would rigorously exclude
the bulky subscription books which are to be seen—they are not
made to be used—in so many Catholic homes on marble-top
tables, unsightly monuments of bad taste and abominable printing.
It is high time to call a halt to this wasteful expenditure of
money by our Catholic people for ponderous articles in the shape
of books which are rarely opened to the children, lest the caricatures of sacred subjects, called pictures, might be soiled. Publishers doing a legitimate trade in books that are worth buying
will no doubt gladly co-operate with the plan suggested to the
directors of the Catholic Educational Exhibit. We propose this
subject for discussion in the Reading Circles after vacation, and we
hope the members of our Union and others will send us a statement of their opinions.

*

The New Orleans *Morning Star and Catholic Messenger* has
published a letter from a correspondent at Memphis, Tenn. It is
one of the best letters on the subject of Catholic Reading Circles
which has yet appeared. We hope the writer will continue the
good work in Tennessee, and send us an account of the prospects
in that locality :

"One of the most pleasing evidences of the progressive character of Catholic thought in our day, and one that betokens a far-
reaching influence for good both within and without the pale of the
church, is the plan of forming Reading Clubs or circles in the interest
of literary culture in general, and for the specific purpose of bringing Catholic readers into a more intimate acquaintance with the
works of our standard Catholic authors.

"Until quite recently it was a subject of just reproach that
even our best-read brethren of the laity were unacquainted with
the varied productions which Catholic genius has contributed to
the literature of our time. But, thanks to the efforts which have
been made within the past few years, the day is not far distant
when the Catholic young man or woman who cannot claim acquaintance with the novels of a Christian Reid, a Kathleen O'Meara,
the delightful volumes of a Georgiana Fullerton, a Mrs. Sadlier,
or an Eliza Allen Starr, will be looked upon as occupying an

anomalous position among the well-informed of their faith. To the Paulist Fathers, always alive to the highest welfare of our Catholic people, •belongs the credit of having been the first to suggest the formation of Catholic Reading Circles. THE CATHOLIC WORLD, ever on the alert, has entered upon the practical solution of the objections, imaginary and otherwise, raised by well-meaning but captious supporters of the scheme, and by its timely and wise counsel has done noble work in behalf of the New Crusade.

"The 'Columbian Reading Union of New York,' which owes its formation and efficiency to the above-mentioned magazine, is the nucleus of a large number of Reading Circles, which in turn owe their existence to the Union of which they are practically the offshoots—partaking in all the benefits of aggregation to the parent organization. These circles, according to accounts furnished by those who should know best, are giving great satisfaction to the members composing them, and altogether the prospects are most encouraging. The question occurs: What shall we do? What are we doing for this most laudable enterprise? These are questions that should be answered in a spirit of generous resolve for the cause in question. They are questions that apply to the humblest sodality member as well as to the most prominent parishioner; all can aid materially in this new undertaking; ways and means may easily be found in every parish to accomplish something worthy of the growing needs of the hour; an interchange of books among a dozen or more members of a parish; a contribution of books to a Reading Club Library; the reading of standard Catholic authors at meetings of sodalities already in existence; in a word, any initial movement looking to the desired end is not to be despised; provided only each one is disposed to help his less favored associate in the good work. Of course the scope of these clubs will eventually be enlarged; they will doubtless gradually include some, perhaps many, non-Catholics, to whom every facility should be granted to share in the benefits of acquaintance with Catholic authors. It is strange, indeed, that we have been so slow to recognize the merit of so many Catholic writers whose names are an ornament to our literature. Philosophy, poetry, history, fiction, and science have been enriched by the labors of men and women who should have been raised long ago to the rank to which their great talents entitle them. It is easy to understand that those outside the fold will not be slow to slight the worth of Catholic writers when we within are so indifferent to their claims upon our attention.

"Let us hope, however, that the act of justice which has been decreed by Catholic opinion in the United States may meet with heartfelt sympathy everywhere. An auspicious beginning has been made; who will set limits to the beneficent results that must accrue? We may safely predict a rapid multiplication of the standard Catholic authors' works to meet the inevitable increased demand of readers. Good reading will no longer be a luxury to Catholics of humble means; under the new condition of things ‧ such excellent works as *Callista*, *Fabiola*, and the like will not be sealed treasures any longer. Readers and authors will share in the benefits sure to be derived. An invigorating mental tonic will be supplied to those who were wont to excite their jaded powers with the highly spiced products of the secular press, while a new incentive will be ‚afforded to the best efforts of the best Catholic authors, and encouragement extended to rising talent in the literary world. The Catholic press of the land should enlist its best energies in the movement and failure will be impossible. In a free and generous advocacy of the new idea Catholic magazines and newspapers will find themselves benefited in no small measure. A consensus of opinion regarding it, it appears to me, would be most opportune; let correspondents speak out their opinions; let one and all aid by voice and pen. It is a work in which all can take part. It is eminently fitting that all who love the Holy Church should make themselves worthy of the benediction which her illustrious head imparts to all who assist in the spread of Catholic literature. It is, in fact, a duty from which no one can conscientiously exempt himself in this age of rationalism, when the minds of so many are inoculated with the poison which distils from a godless horde of depraved writers, and the hearts are corrupted by the insidious venom that is filtered through the so-called realistic novels of our day. If the law of saving charity is imperative let us prove its force by beginning with those who are united to us by the bonds of a common faith. The ravages already made by the human wolves that linger about the sheepfold may be irreparable. Future attacks will be warded off by the safeguards which prudence and piety will suggest. '*Tolle et lege*.' ARION."

*

One of our tireless members has not forgotten the good work even during the hot weather. She writes:

"I came here to learn of the marked success of a little Reading Circle conducted by Sister ——. She takes a personal interest in the members collectively and individually, assists them in their essays, has a plan for every week's reading at home and at meetings, and makes current events the main topics for consideration. It is the personality of this religious which insures success. I hope we shall yet come to having a lecture bureau and courses delivered to each circle about the country. Is the 'Catholic Truth Society' to do this? I have also felt that the lecture on the Madonna in Art, by Father O'Conner, S.J., would be most acceptable.

"There is a lady now residing at this place who has organized history classes and goes to several adjacent cities during the week.

They have been kept up for five years, and though the members drop out, others are waiting to take their turn. Occasionally she has an entertainment, and the ladies impersonate the characters of a period in conversation, quoting largely from the writers and in costume. She prepares a series of questions, gives her references, writes an essay, and expects her pupils to read, study, and talk at class—not read aloud—at least five minutes on the topic of the day. Here is a suggestion for some of our Catholic women."

St. Joseph's Academy at Washington, Ga., has a flourishing Reading Circle, which sends us this favorable account:

"It is some time since we have forwarded a report of our circle. Our interest, however, has not abated, and we are more and more delighted with the advantages afforded by membership with the Columbian Reading Union. We have read *Fabiola*, *Callista*, and *Martyrs of the Coliseum*, and will next turn our attention to *The Middle Ages*. Our plan is to assign a certain number of pages for private reading, and then questions are asked upon the matter read. We also give miscellaneous queries, and thus enlarge our store of general knowledge. Our meetings are very pleasant and the improvement evident. A number of our former graduates have joined our circle, and we hope to interest all pupils of St. Joseph's in true intellectual advancement."

Before the end of the year 1891 we hope to get at least a few lines from every Catholic Reading Circle in the United States. For many reasons it will be interesting to ascertain the territorial boundaries of the movement, and to what extent the Catholic educational institutions are represented among the Reading Circles. We shall be pleased to have reports also from parochial libraries, and from Catholic Young Men's Societies.

M. C. M.

WITH THE PUBLISHER.

As was announced in our last issue, THE CATHOLIC WORLD will on August 1 · take possession of its new quarters, "The Columbus Press," 120 and 122 West Sixtieth Street. The name given to its new home is most appropriate. And not only because of the approaching centenary, but because the name is freighted with significance; it is another way of telling the purpose of the magazine.

∗
∗ ∗

For, before all else, Columbus was a Christ-bearer; his highest purpose was to bring Christ to those who knew him not, and modern historical research has abundantly emphasized this fact. And this same purpose created THE CATHOLIC WORLD. It has a great mission to a great people. It lives and speaks to-day as another Columbus, and its history for the past quarter of a century is eloquent of its fidelity to its mission and of its success. In many respects its history is a repetition of the story of that elder Columbus; of prejudice vanquished, of enemies made friends; of straitened resources, of the dangers of unknown seas; because, *pace majorum*, when it sailed from its Palos in April, 1865, just after a great civil war, it was the pioneer over the unexplored sea of American Catholic periodical literature. It brought to many, and it still brings, Christ to those who knew him not, or knew him imperfectly, saw him dimly. Its mission fits it for its new dwelling: the name, Columbus, has a character as well as a history that fits THE CATHOLIC WORLD.

∗
∗ ∗

Upon this new conquest of THE CATHOLIC WORLD, the possession of its own home after twenty-five years of all sorts of weather, we congratulate the readers of the magazine: they have been (to pursue the similitude, and yet not make it quite threadbare) the Isabellas of its purpose. The Publisher congratulates them. There are few, perhaps, who know as well as he does how much in the past and the present depended on them. There is no one more ready than he to give them the praise they deserve. And he would like to have each of his readers perfectly convinced of this truth; it ought to penetrate to the marrow of the bone. Each and every reader of THE CATHOLIC WORLD ought to be sensible of the share he or she has in the present success of the magazine. It is yours; it belongs to you, and without you it could not tell its glorious story to-day.

And you are not going to let it end here, are you? If on you so much depends for the purpose of the magazine, and so much depends for its future, the glory of the past and the share you—you who are reading these lines—have had in it by every title of right, you will not cease in your efforts for the future. The realization of every possibility associated with the new condition of things rests largely with you, and the thought gives you fresh courage and renewed zeal. There is much you can do, and have not done yet.

You know, for instance, many of your friends, especially those who are not of the Church and yet are by no means hostile to its teachings; who are not Catholics for the reason that they do not know why they should become members of Christ's fold; who are ignorant of the spirit of the Church, and vaguely imagine it to be what you know it is not: un-American, demanding slavish service and the thousand and one perverted and unjust things that are said of us by the wicked or the ignorant. You, dear reader, are going to put THE CATHOLIC WORLD in the way of such a one. The Publisher could quote many letters that would tell you of the good that has been wrought, under God, through such means; but you don't need it. You have a conscience, and that conscience tells you that you must be a "bearer of Christ" to some one; it tells you, and you know its truth, that this is the mission and end of THE CATHOLIC WORLD.

But enough; this is becoming something of a sermon, with Columbus for a text, and the Publisher will talk of something else.

The value of the contributions of Catholic missionaries to science, especially to philology, has frequently been noted, and is always warmly acknowledged by the scholar. A recent instance of this

is furnished by a *Zulukafir Grammar*, written by Father Ambro-
sious, one of the Trappist missionaries in Zululand and printed at
their missionary station of Mariannhill.   The work has been highly
praised by the German philologists and is commended to all students
of the Bantu class of languages.   A recent letter from Paris tells
us of the publication by the École spéciale des langues orientales
vivantes of the *Account of Persia in* 1660 by the Capuchin Father
Raphael du Mans, a contemporary of Sir John Chardin and Jean de
Thevenot.

It may be of interest to some of our readers to learn of the
early publication of a new volume by William J. Henderson (author
of *The Story of Music*), containing a series of essays on Wagner, the
history of piano-forte playing, Schumann's symphonies, and kindred
topics.   It will be issued from the press of Longmans, Green &
Co., of this city.

That this is an age of easy ways to difficult things and "air-
lines" to distant points is illustrated in a recent publication intended
for dull talkers, called *Conversational Openings and Endings*.   It
somehow gives the impression that there are people to whom conversation becomes little else than a more or less elaborate game
of chess, in which commonplaces have a higher rank than pawns
and the chances of stalemate are abundant.   Can artifice go further?

***

Ginn & Co., Boston, have in preparation *Specimens of the Pre-
Shakesperian Drama*, edited, with an introduction and notes, by
John Matthews Manly, Ph.D., assistant-professor in Brown University.   The work will be in two volumes, the first of which will
contain Miracle Plays, Moralities and Interludes; the second, Roi-
ster Doister, Gorboduc, and plays of Lyly, Greene, and Peele.
In no instance will an extract be given; each play will be printed as a whole.   There will be a general introduction, tracing the
growth of the drama from the Miracle Plays to Shakespeare; and
each play will be provided with a special introduction.   The notes
will be devoted chiefly to the elucidation of the text, and an index to the notes will facilitate reference to the subjects treated in
them.

The first book to be published by Harper & Brothers under
the new copyright law is the life of *The Right Honorable William
E. Gladstone*, by G. W. E. Russell.   This is the fourth volume in
the new series of political biographies entitled *The Queen's Prime
Ministers*, edited by Stuart J. Reid, of which the other three are

devoted to *Lord Beaconsfield, Sir Robert Peel,* and *Viscount Melbourne.*

The Worthington Company has just ready *Columbia : a Story of the Discovery of America,* by John R. Musick. This is the first of a series of twelve volumes by Mr. Musick which is to cover important periods of American history, so that the series will be a complete history of the United States in twelve stories, each of which, however, will be complete in itself. The next volume will be entitled *Estevan : a Story of the Spanish Conquests.* Each volume will be fully illustrated.

The *Memoirs of Moltke,* shortly to be published in Berlin by E. S. Mittler & Sohn, will fill several volumes, and the contents promise to be of much interest. They will contain : (1) A family history written by the field-marshal, a number of documents relating to his youth and travels, his own notes about his life at Kreisau, and his confession of faith, written down shortly before his death ; (2) several essays written by Moltke ; (3) a brief history of the war of 1870-71, written by himself ; (4) his correspondence with friends on private and public affairs ; (5) his speeches ; and (6) remembrances and stories of his life, communicated by his friends. The different volumes will be published consecutively and simultaneously in Germany, England, and America.

Benziger Brothers will publish early in the autumn :

> *The Good Christian.* Vols. vii. and viii. of Hunolt's Sermons. 2 vols. 8vo, cloth, *net,* $5.
>
> *Hand-book of the Christian Religion.* From the German of Rev. Father Welmers, S.J. 12mo, cloth, *net,* $1.50.
>
> *Natural Theology.* By Rev. Bernard Boedder, S.J. A new volume of the "Stonyhurst Philosophy Series." 12mo, cloth, *net,* $1.50.
>
> *Simplicity in Prayer.* 32mo, cloth, *net,* 30 cents.

They have in preparation :

> *Christian Anthropology.* By Rev. John Thein. 8vo, cloth, *net,* $2.50.
>
> *General Principles of the Religious Life.* From the German, by Very Rev. Boniface F. Verheyen, O.S.F. 32mo, cloth.

BOOKS RECEIVED.

A HISTORY OF ST. JOHN'S COLLEGE, Fordham, N. Y. By Thomas Gaffney Taaffe. New York: The Catholic Publication Society Co.; London: Burns & Oates.

THE EPIC OF THE INNER LIFE. By John F. Genung. Boston and New York: Houghton, Mifflin & Co.

THE ISRAELITE BEFORE THE ARK, AND THE CHRISTIAN BEFORE THE ALTAR; OR, A HISTORY OF THE WORSHIP OF GOD. By L. De Goesbriand, Bishop of Burlington, Vt. Burlington: The Free Press Association.

THE LIFE OF FATHER JOHN CURTIS, S.J. By the author of *Tyborne*. Dublin: M. H. Gill & Son; New York: The Catholic Publication Society Co.

CURSUS VITÆ SPIRITUALIS. Auctore R. P. D. Carolo Joseph Moritio, Congregationis S. Bernardi. Ratisbon, New York, and Cincinnati: Fr. Pustet & Co.

DEVOTION TO ST. ANTHONY OF PADUA. By the Rev. Clement Deymann, O.S.F. San Francisco: A. Waldteufel.

PAMPHLETS RECEIVED.

THE CHILD OF MARY; A Melodrama in Three Acts. By the Right Rev. Mgr. J. de Concilio, D.D. Jersey City, N. J.: Published by the Author.

"THE CONTEST BETWEEN THE CIVIL LAW OF ROME AND THE COMMON LAW OF ENGLAND." By Martin F. Morris, LL.D., Professor in the Law School of Georgetown University. Washington: Printed for the University.

AGNOSTICISM. By the Right Rev. J. L. Spalding, D.D., Bishop of Peoria. The Catholic Truth Society of America, St. Paul, Minnesota.

REPORT OF THE INTERNAL COMMERCE OF THE UNITED STATES FOR 1890. By S. G. Brock. Washington: Government Printing-Office.

THE
CATHOLIC WORLD.

VOL. LIII.   SEPTEMBER, 1891.   No. 318.

SOCIALISM AND LABOR.

THE unique position, as well as the exalted personal character of Leo XIII., could not fail to attract world-wide attention to the recent Encyclical Letter, wherein he deals with questions upon which current opinion is everywhere directed.

The fact that the Head of so powerful and so conservative
an organization as the Catholic Church deems it imperative to
turn the thoughts and efforts of his fellow-believers to the pressing need of discovering some way by which the condition of the
masses who toil with their hands may be improved, is not merely a signal example of the importance now given to the problems raised by the New Socialism, but it is also an evidence of
a desire within the church itself to enter in a more active manner into the struggles of the modern world to develop a higher
and more Christian civilization.

The words of the Holy Father, now before all readers, are
distinct and elaborate, and they need no comment. Let us,
while we study them in a reverent spirit, turn our attention to
the godlike work in which he asks us to co-operate. The deep
import of the Encyclical lies in the authoritative pronouncement
that the mission of the church is not only to save souls, but
also to save society; that the earthly and temporal interests of
men not less than their spiritual welfare are of concern to this
divine institution, which is Catholic not only in its teaching and
its organization, but also in its sympathies. To make truth, justice, and love prevail, which is the meaning of the prayer, "Thy
kingdom come, Thy will be done on earth," and which is the
great aim and end of the church, all human forces should conspire: for "it is with this," says the Pope, "as with the Provi-

dence which governs the world: results do not happen unless all the causes co-operate."

The interest which all who think take in the laboring classes, whether it spring from sympathy or fear, is a characteristic feature of the age.

Their condition seems to be the great anomaly in our otherwise progressive and brilliant civilization. Whether when compared with the lot of the slaves and serfs of former times that of the modern laborer is fortunate, is not the question. He is not placed in the midst of the poverty and wretchedness of a rude and barbarous society, but in the midst of boundless wealth and great refinement. He lives, too, in a democratic age, in which all men profess to believe in equality and liberty; in an age in which the brotherhood of the race is proclaimed by all the organs of opinion. He has a voice in public affairs, and since laborers are the majority, he is, in theory at least, the sovereign. They who govern profess to do everything by the authority of the people, in their name and for their welfare; and yet, if we are to accept the opinions of the Socialists, the wage-takers, who in the modern world are the vast multitude, are practically shut out from participation in our intellectual and material inheritance. They contend that the poor are, under the present economic system, the victims of the rich, just as in the ancient societies the weak were the victims of the strong; so that wage-labor, as actually constituted, differs in form rather than in its essential results from the labor of slaves and serfs. And even dispassionate observers think that the tendency of the present system is to intensify rather than to diminish the evils which do exist; and that we are moving towards a state of things in which the few will own everything, and the many be hardly more than their hired servants. In America, they admit that sparse population and vast natural resources, which as yet have hardly been touched, help to conceal this fatal tendency, which is best seen in the manufacturing and commercial centres of Europe, where the capitalistic method of production has reduced wage-earners to a condition of pauperism and degradation which is the scandal of Christendom and a menace to society; and Leo XIII. but expresses the thought and sentiment of all enlightened and generous minds when he declares that "there can be no question whatever but some remedy must be found, and quickly found, for the misery and wretchedness which press so heavily at this moment upon the great majority of the very poor."

The present condition of labor is the result of gradually evolved processes, running through centuries.

The failure of the attempt of Charlemagne to organize the barbarous hordes which had overspread Europe into a stable empire was followed by an era of violence and lawlessness, of wars and invasions, from which society sought refuge in the feudal system. The strong man, as temporal or spiritual lord, was at the top of the feudal hierarchy, and under him the weak formed themselves into classes. The serf labored a certain number of days for himself, and a certain number for his lord. In the towns the craftsmen were organized into guilds which protected the interests of the members. The mendicant poor were not numerous, and their wants were provided for by the bishops and the religious orders.

Then the growth of towns and the development of trade and commerce brought wealth to the burghers, who became a distinct class, while domestic feuds and foreign wars, especially the Crusades, weakened and impoverished the knights and barons. The printing-press and the use of gunpowder in war helped to further undermine the feudal power, while the discovery of America, the turning of the Cape of Good Hope, and the Protestant revolution threw all Europe into a ferment from which new social conditions were evolved. The peasants who had been driven from the land by the decay of the great baronial houses, and the confiscation of the property of the church, flocked into the towns or became vagabonds. The poor became so numerous that permanent provision had to be made for them, and poor laws were consequently devised. It was the contemplation of their misery which caused Sir Thomas More to write the following words, which sound as though they had been taken from some modern Socialist address :

"Therefore, I must say that, as I hope for mercy, I can have no notion of all the other governments that I see or know than that they are a conspiracy of the rich, who on pretence of managing the public, only pursue their private ends, and devise all the ways and arts they can find out ; first that they may without danger preserve all that they have so ill acquired, and then that they may engage the poor to toil and labor for them at as low rates as possible, and oppress them as much as they please. And if they can but prevail to get these contrivances established by the show of public authority, which is considered as the representative of the whole people, then they are accounted laws."

The master-workman who, in the middle ages, employed but two or three apprentices and as many journeymen, gave way to a class of capitalists, enriched by the confiscated wealth of the church, by the treasures imported from America and the Indies, and by the profits of the slave-traffic, who at once prepared to take advantage of the stimulus to industry given by the opening of a vast world market. As late as the middle of the last century, however, manufacturing was still carried on by masters who employed but a small number of hands, and had but little capital invested in the business; and the modern industrial era, with its factory system, properly begins with our marvellous mechanical inventions and the use of steam as a motive power. Machinery made production on a large scale possible, and threw the whole business into the hands of capitalists, while laborers are left with nothing but their ability to work, which they are forced to sell at whatever price it will bring. The capitalist's one aim is to amass wealth, and he buys human labor just as he buys machinery or raw material, at the lowest rate at which it can be obtained. It is either denied that the question of wages has an ethical aspect, or it is maintained that the competition among capitalists themselves, which under the present system of production is' inevitable, compels employers to ignore considerations of equity. Hence it comes to be held that whatever increases profits is right. The hours of labor are prolonged, the sexes are intermingled, children are put to work in factories, sanitary laws are violated; wares are made in excess of demand; and, in consequence of the resulting glut of the markets, wages are still further lowered or work is stopped; and the laborers, whether they continue to work or whether they strike, or are forced into idleness, are threatened with physical and moral ruin. The further development of the system is, in the opinion of many observers, towards the concentration of capital in immense joint-stock companies and syndicates, whose directors, by buying competing concerns and also legislatures and judges, make opposition impossible, and render the condition of laborers still more hopeless.

This brief sketch of the history and nature of industrialism is sufficient to account for the existence of the various socialistic theories and movements of the present day. The word Socialism, which first came into use in the early part of this century, stands rather for a tendency than for a definite body of principles and methods, and this tendency is one of which men of very different and even opposite opinions approve: and a Socialist may be a theist or an atheist, a spiritualist or a materialist, a Christian or an agnostic. The general implication is the need of greater equality in the condition of human beings. The aim, therefore, is to bring about a social arrangement in which all will receive a fair share of the good things of life; and the best way to secure this, socialists commonly think, is to render the will of the individual more completely subordinate to that of the community. The methods by which this may be accomplished are not necessarily violent or revolutionary. In the opinion of many serious writers, socialism is the logical outcome of tendencies which are held to prevail throughout the civilized world. Our views of liberty, equality, and fraternity, they say, must necessarily lead not merely to the reign of the people, to a universal democracy, but must embody themselves in a state which will own both land and capital, and will control both production and distribution; for only in this way can all be made free and equal, and the brotherhood of the race become something better than ironical cant. Already the state has widened its sphere of action. It has passed laws to regulate industry, it has taken charge of education, and there are many indications that the tendency is to assume that whatever concerns the health, happiness, and morals of the people should be subject to state control. The massing of capital in great corporations is the beginning of a movement, it is thought, which will end in the transference of all capital to the one sole corporate state. The different labor unions and co-operative societies are regarded as schools in which the working classes are receiving the education needed to prepare them for the work of universal intelligent co-operation. The Socialists hold, also, that the moral progress of the modern world points in the same direction. There is a wider sympathy, a new sense of justice, a desire to come to the help of the weak and wronged, a consciousness of the responsibility, not of individuals alone but of society, which must lead to a readjustment of the social order in accordance with the sentiments of the more humane temper which is characteristic of our age. And is not all this, in part at least, a result of the teaching and example of Christ himself, who came to preach the Gospel to the poor, to heal the infirm and to bring relief to the overburdened, and who thus gave the impulse which has finally developed into our humanitarian faith, hope, and love? A large number of Socialists, it is true, are atheists and materialists, but the earnest desire to discover some means whereby justice may be done the people, whereby they may be relieved from their poverty and misery, and the resulting vice and crime, is in intimate harmony with the gentle and loving spirit of Him who passed no sorrow by.

From the general principle that it is the duty of the rich and strong to use at least part of their wealth and strength in the service of their fellow-men, and first of all in the service of the poor and helpless, no good or wise man will dissent. Here, then, is a common ground whereon all, whatever their philosophic and religious opinions and beliefs may be, can meet. Disagreement arises only when we come to discuss how this may best be done. If, however, the discussion is to be useful, it is necessary that we first get a true view of the condition of the classes to whose relief we wish to come.

Are the evils from which they suffer really as great and desperate as the Socialist agitators would have us believe? Are laborers worse paid, worse fed, worse clothed, and worse housed than, for instance, in the early part of this century? Do they labor a greater number of hours, and is their work more severe and exhausting now than then?

Is the tendency of the present system to make them unintelligent, brutal, and reckless? Is the present economic system an organization of the ruling classes to keep the laborers in poverty and permanent subjection? Is it a fact, in a word, that we are drifting towards a state of things in which the few shall own everything and the many nothing?

If these questions are to receive an affirmative answer, then the method of production by private competitive capital should be condemned, for it not only, in this case, works injustice to large multitudes, but must, if permitted to continue in operation, finally lead to social ruin. It is easily intelligible that those who believe that private capitalism is essentially vicious, should look to Socialism as a ground for hope, and that they should find in the supposed tendencies of the present economic developments a reason for thinking that the reign of individualism is nearing its end.*

The democracy upon which light is streaming from many sources, which all the forces and struggles of society are helping to organize more thoroughly, and which is rapidly becoming conscious of its superior power, could not be expected to accept as permanent a system which makes of the mass of the people a herd of proletarians, dependent upon uncertain wage-labor. Already, under democratic influence, the state has assumed functions formerly performed by individuals, families, and minor communities, and under the pressure of the growing sense of the responsibility of society for the welfare of all its members, it tends to widen the sphere of its activity and to take greater control of the lives of citizens.

And as it always happens when the stream of tendency sets strongly in a given direction, those who oppose not less than those who favor hasten the coming of the new order. Events, in fact, solve the great problems, and our discussions are but the foam that crests the waves. Thus, it is conceivable that the efforts of competitive capital to save itself by forming colossal companies and syndicates, may be found in the end to facilitate the transference of the whole to the collective management of society.

The era of the small producer, it is plain, has passed away. Indeed, the greatest sufferers among laborers, at present, are the victims of what is known as the Sweating System, which is an unhealthy survival of the method of domestic production. If the choice, then, is between the massing of capital in a few hands and its complete control by the state, there can be little doubt as to what the final decision will be.

But the question whether the Socialist view of the actual condition of labor and of the tendencies of the present economic order, is the true view, still remains to be answered.

There are reasons which should lead us to look upon the assertions of the Socialist agitators with a certain distrust. The temper of reformers is enthusiastic, and hence they almost inevitably exaggerate the evils they seek to correct. The crowd is fond of reckless statement, and its leaders not unfrequently win and hold their pre-eminence by the boldness with which they deal in passionate rhetoric. It is well known, too, that when patients begin to improve they become irritable; and this is true also of suffering bodies of men. The hopeless become resigned. The negro slaves began and ended the day's work to the sound of their own melodies; and when women were treated like slaves the indignities they suffered called forth no clamorous protests. The discontent and agitation which now exist among the working classes are not, then, a proof that their condition is altogether evil or that it is growing worse, while the testimony of the leaders in the labor-movements is, for the reasons I have given, open to suspicion.

No enlightened mind doubts the superiority of our civilization over that of all preceding centuries, and yet when was there ever so much fault-finding as now with the evils and shortcomings of political, social, and domestic life?

We have even a literature which proclaims that life itself is worthless; and there is evidently a number of readers who are interested in arguments which go to show that marriage, free institutions, popular education, civilization, and Christianity have all broken down and failed to bring the good they promised and which the human heart craves.

Our gains seem to have served only to make us more conscious of what we still lack, and in the light of our intellectual, moral, and material progress we easily persuade ourselves that what has been achieved is little more than the promise of better things to be. Then our implements of almost magical power and delicacy, and the ease and rapidity with which by their aid we are able to overcome mere physical obstacles, have made us impatient. We rebel against the teaching which inculcates the wisdom of making haste slowly, and we imagine that by teaching people to read and write, and by proper legislative enactments, we may do away with ignorance, poverty, and crime as easily as we drain swamps or recover exhausted soil. In this our temper is unphilosophic and misleading. Social development depends upon laws which legislation can modify only to a limited extent, and a prerequisite to all effective and desirable social transformations is a corresponding change in the character of both the masses and their rulers and employers. Now, alterations in the character of a people are the result of slow processes, carried on through successive generations, and hence it is a mistake to suppose that a change in the machinery of government will suddenly produce an equivalent change in the thought and conduct of men. The futility of mere paper constitutions has been proven by experiments which leave no room for doubt. Mexico, for example, has had republican institutions since the early part of this century, but the condition of the masses of its people is no better than was that of the slaves in the Southern States.

Putting aside, then, as impracticable all schemes for bringing on an era of universal comfort and contentment by mechanical changes in the constitution of society, let us strive to get a clear view of the results and tendencies of the actually existing system of competitive capitalistic production.

In the first place, it is a fact that, neither in Europe nor in the United States, is there a chasm between the enormously rich and the very poor, but there is a gradation of possession from the beggar to the great capitalist. Most of what is said about the poverty and misery of the working class is applicable only to what has been called the social residuum, which may be compared to the stragglers and camp-followers of an army; and the social gulf is not between rich men and steady, thrifty laborers, but rather between these latter and the crowd of loafers and criminals. That the cause of this disparity of condition is moral rather than economic, whoever observes may see; and this fact gives emphasis to the great truth that all real amelioration in the lot of human beings depends on their religious, moral, and intellectual state. Money does not make a miser rich nor its lack a true man poor. The most competent authorities, basing their opinion upon exhaustive statistical study and careful observation, hold that the condition of laborers during the industrial period has been one of gradual improvement. In England, from 1688 to 1800, there was an increase of less than fifty per cent. in the number of laborers, and an increase of six hundred and ten per cent. in their total earnings; and from 1800 to 1883 workers increased a little over four hundred per cent. and their income about six hundred per cent. Wages have risen both in amount and in purchasing power. The hours of labor have become fewer, and the rate of mortality has decreased. "Taken as a whole," says Professor Levi, who is a recognized authority on questions of statistics, "the working classes of the United Kingdom may be said to be stronger in physique, better educated, with more time at their command, in the enjoyment of greater political rights, in a more healthful relation towards their employers, receiving higher wages and better able to effect some savings, in 1884 than they were in 1857." And in England the conditions are less favorable to the laboring classes than in some other countries, far less favorable than they are in our own. It is densely populated; it imports much of its food; nearly all the land is owned by a few thousand families; its workmen have been crippled and dwarfed by laws made in the interest of employers; and production and distribution are regulated according to the principles of free trade, which we here in America, at least, are taught to believe has a tendency to lower wages.

In the United States, it is plain, there is no gulf between the very rich and the very poor, but a gradation of widely distributed wealth. More than eight million families are landowners, and of the thirteen million families among whom the wealth of the country is divided, eleven million families are said to belong to the wage-earning class. We have, indeed, a few enormously rich men, but it will be found difficult to hold these great fortunes together, and if plutocrats should persist in abusing the power which money gives, the people will know how to protect themselves against the tyrants.

If private property is not a crime, and that it is not even radical Socialists admit, then wealth however great, if it be honestly acquired and justly used, must be respected. Much of the material progress of our country is due to the energy and foresight of men who, if they have grown rich themselves, have made possible the comfortable and independent existence of thousands. Diatribes against wealthy men oftener spring from unworthy passions than from any sense of wrongs inflicted by them. Duties and responsibilities are personal, and the poor are bound not less than the rich to do what they are able to promote the common welfare. The obligation of service is universal, and to encourage jealousy and hatred of the rich among the poor is to do harm to the interests and character of both. If the rich are sometimes selfish and heartless, they are quite as often generous and helpful. Like other men, they are conscious of the irresistible leaning of human nature to the side of justice, and if a sort of all-embracing good-will is characteristic of Americans, we may hope that all efforts to cause class-hatred to prevail here will prove futile. At all events, the condition of laborers under the régime of competitive production, whatever grievances they still may have, are not so desperate as to make us willing to run the risk of putting in jeopardy the two things we have learned to value the most—Liberty and Individuality. Many of our social arrangements are doubtless provisional only. In various ways our age is transitional, and such an age is necessarily one of exceptional hardship for the weak; but in an era of change the last thing the wise will counsel is the rushing into visionary and untried schemes of reform; and such a scheme, where there is question of a whole people, the New Socialism certainly is. In small communities even the Socialist theory has been found impracticable except where celibacy has been made a condition of membership. The social order is an organism infinitely complex, the outcome of many forces, whose action and interaction, beginning in the obscure and mysterious regions where life and mind first manifest themselves, have been going on for unnumbered ages; and it has so intertwined itself with man's very nature that we may say he is what he is in virtue of the society of which he is the product. By it our language, our literature, our laws, and much of our religion have been developed. To make desirable, or possible even, a radical change in this order, such as that implied by Socialism, our nature itself would have to become other. Until this changes man will continue to believe that he has the right to own property, and he will continue to look upon the possession of a home and of other things whereby a comfortable existence for himself and his wife and children is secured, as among the chief boons of life. The owner of the poorest cabin would not barter it for the promises of the Socialist paradise. The passion for independence, for liberty, which, inborn in our portion, at least, of the Aryan race, has been strengthened and intensified by centuries of heroic struggles, makes us averse to social schemes which, if practical at all, can succeed only by controlling and regulating all the affairs of life, by turning the whole nation into an industrial army, where each one is under orders to keep the place and do the duties assigned him. There is nothing we so much dislike as interference—we who think it better to be insulted than to have even advice proffered. In America we know our politicians too well to be able to believe that captains of industry, under the control of a supreme council, to whom power vastly greater than that which politicians and bosses have ever exercised would necessarily be given in a Socialist government, could safely or wisely be entrusted with the management of all our nearest and dearest concerns.

If, indeed, the root-principle of the New Socialism, as set forth by Marx, and before him by Ricardo, that labor is the sole source of value, and that therefore capital is robbery, were true, it would certainly be a powerful argument against the existing economic order, and would drive honest men to look with approval upon projects to substitute in its place some method of production and distribution which would not be in open conflict with the current ideas of morality. Neither religion nor humanity permits us to acquiesce in a system of organized plunder, and if this is what competitive capitalism is, the transformation of society, if needs be by revolution, is an end for which all good men might well labor. If we assume, with the school of Ricardo, that all wealth, all exchange value, is the result exclusively of labor, then to the laborers all wealth rightfully belongs, and capitalists have acquired what they possess by the spoliation of the true owners; and the collectivism of Marx, who proposes to turn all land and capital over to the state, which undertakes to pay every one the full worth of his work, is a logical development. Political economists, however, now generally agree in holding that the theory of Ricardo, which makes labor the only source of value, is untenable; for capital, which is required for production, must be accepted as a factor in determining values, and its owner therefore is entitled to a fair reward for the service his capital renders. It may be said that capital itself is the result of labor, but it must be admitted that it is also the result of abstinence from consumption. While one man consumes the equivalent of his entire work, another consumes but part, and thus gradually accumulates a capital, which he invests in some machine, for instance, and thereby acquires a right to whatever value the machine may add to manufactured products. His machine has become his fellow-laborer, and if large and perfect enough, will do the work of many men. What right can the state have to take from him this labor-saving instrument, which he has invented or paid for with money honestly earned? The fallacy of the Socialist assumption lies in attributing to labor a value of its own, independently of the worth of its product. The labor spent in doing useless things has no value; at least, no social value. He who makes what nobody wants has his labor for his pains. The question is not what amount of labor an object has cost, but what service can it render. A man may devote years to learning to walk the tight-rope, but if I do not care for such attainments and exhibitions, I will not pay to see him perform. Values, then, cannot be estimated in terms of labor, which is nevertheless the task the Socialists have set themselves. How shall we determine the worth of the labor expended in perfecting a plan such as that which led Columbus to discover America? What is the worth of Newton's labor in evolving the theory of gravitation, of Shakspere's in writing "Hamlet," of Wagner's in composing "Parsifal," of Gutenberg's in making his type, or of Watt's in building his steam-engine? Without the genius of inventors and discoverers, without the foresight and enterprise of investors and capitalists, there would be little for laborers to do, and society would drift into general poverty.

Far, then, from being the sole source of value, labor, to have worth, must be provided with the raw materials and forces of nature; must be stimulated and directed by intelligence, and must produce things which human beings want; and capital, which is not so much the result of labor as of abstinence from consumption, which leaves a surplus of the labor product to be invested in profit-bearing enterprises, necessarily shares also in the determination of values. The present economical system, then, is not, as Socialists affirm, organized injustice, though it must be admitted that it often leads to wrongs which cripple the lives of multitudes, and produce an incalculable amount of physical and moral evil. Indeed, the present inequalities in the distribution of wealth affect the moral sense so painfully that we cannot look upon them as irremovable. We may not, however, trample on rights to secure greater distributive justice, or approve of schemes which if they promise a greater abundance of material things to the poor, would lead to a general enfeeblement and lowering of human life. In a Socialist state, in which the universal ideal is that of physical well-being and comfort, the sublimer moods which make saints, heroes, and men of genius possible would no longer be called forth. If all receive the same reward, whatever their labor, spontaneity would come to an end and progress cease, and such an equality would finally come to be a universal equality in indolence, poverty, and low thinking; while from an ethical point of view, it would seem to be unjust that the same reward should be given to every kind of labor.

If different rewards are given for different kinds of work, the practical difficulties in determining the social value of the different kinds of labor appear to be insuperable, especially when we consider that in the Socialist state there are to be no special payments, no money to serve as a universal standard of value. What shall be the basis of comparison for fixing the relative value of the work of a carpenter, a nurse-maid, a schoolmaster, and a minister of religion? If it be said that each shall receive according to the amount and social utility of his or her productive labor, how is this rule to be applied? Every product is the result of the operation of many forces, natural, mechanical, and human, and to decide what part of the value is due to the labor of any special workman is extremely difficult, if not impossible. If we accept the formula, "To each in proportion to the number of hours of his work," which is said to be in the strictest sense the theoretical basis of Socialism, then skilled and unskilled labor will be paid alike; and since the acquirement of skill is the result of long and painful processes, who would take infinite pains when by so doing he would gain nothing? And how shall we apply this time-measure to agricultural labor, to domestic service, to woman's work in the family, where she has at once the offices of wife, mother, nurse, and housekeeper? If skilled labor receives a greater reward than the unskilled the principle of equality is abandoned, while the relative values of the two kinds of labor must be arbitrarily assumed. Not only, then, is the Socialist theory of the source of value unsatisfactory, but the methods by which it is proposed to bring about a more equal distribution of wealth are either impracticable or, if applied, would lead to greater evils than those from which we actually suffer. There would, indeed, have to be, a radical change in man's moral nature before it would be safe to entrust to any body of men such power as the managers of the Social-ist state would inevitably acquire. It is with power as with money—those who love it never have enough; and in fact if the whole economic management of society, together with the education of the young, were turned over to a special governing and directing class, its power would necessarily have to be almost unlimited. The whole people would be marshalled like an army, and unquestioning obedience would be demanded and enforced. The right of the people to elect their officers gives no assurance that their favorites will be worthy or capable. What universal suffrage does to bring the best and the wisest into power is now well known. The policy and the candidates of the people are the policy and the candidates of wire-pullers and bosses. They who should once get hold of the vast and complex machinery by which it is proposed to govern the Social-ist state would most probably remain in power; and when we reflect that all the printing-presses of the country would be under their control, and that there would be no reason for the existence of political parties, it is difficult to see how they could be driven from office. The selfishness which, under the régime of competitive capitalism, makes so many employers of labor heartless and tyrannical, would assert itself also in the new order; for a change of government is like a change of clothes, it leaves the man what he was. It is incredible that the per-versity of human passion may be corrected by mechanical ap-pliances. Its source lies within, where lie also the aids to noble life; and until there is a universal change of heart, a social theory which assumes that every man loves all men as much as he loves himself is utopian. Observant minds, belonging to dif-ferent schools of thought, agree in holding that in the modern world egotism is more intense than it was in the middle ages, at least so far as there is question of the love of money, which now is the form all our selfish passions naturally take; for money means power, it means self-indulgence, it means the satis-faction of vanity, it means honor and place. Mere intellectual training is powerless to correct this vice or to bring about any great moral improvement. It tends to change the form of vice rather than to make us virtuous; or, if we should take a more hopeful view of what secular education is able to do, the time is certainly distant when ·the masses can be called educated, in any real sense of the word.

Though we cannot accept the fundamental principles of Socialism or Collectivism as true, and though we are persuaded that society cannot successfully be established upon them as a basis, there are none the less bonds of sympathy between us and the Socialists. The desire, which in the case of many of them is doubtless earnest and sincere, to come to the relief of the poor, to find some means by which their lot may be made less miserable, springs from a divine impulse. It is Christian and human ; and the anti-religious spirit of modern Socialism comes from an unphilosophic and unhistoric view of the forces which create civilization and give promise of a better future. Atheism and materialism fatally strengthen and intensify man's selfish passions, by merging life's whole significance and worth into the present transitory existence. If there is no order of absolute truth and right, no future for the individual, then pleasure is the chief good, and both instinct and reason impel to indulgence and to the overthrow of society, if society makes the enjoyment of life impossible. Hence the socialism of materialists and atheists logically leads to anarchy. Nothing could be more sad than that the multitude should be driven to look for deliverance from their wrongs and sorrows to leaders who deny God, and man's kinship with the infinitely true and perfect One, who tell them that there is no living heavenly Father, but only an unconscious Earth-Mother, on whose senseless body Life and Death play their horrid farce. The grasping avarice and heartless methods of employers and capitalists, who generally profess to be Christians, are arguments against religion which the preachers of atheism find effective in addressing the victims of our present economic system ; while the decay of faith has greatly diminished the persuasive force of appeals in favor of patient resignation and submission. They who lose faith and hope and love, lose patience too ; and it is futile to preach the sacredness of wealth to the poor when their miserable lives are the sad witnesses to the immorality of the means by which it is acquired.

Who can read the history of rack-renting in Ireland, or the story of the Sweating System in the *Bitter Cry of Outcast London*, without feeling that a social order which makes such things possible ought to be changed or destroyed ?

Who can consider the mental, moral, and physical state of certain classes of emigrants who land upon our shores by the thousand, without asking ourselves whether the countries from which these people come are civilized and Christian? Has the passion of humanity which Christ came to inspire, and which was a living principle in his early followers, died in Christian Europe? There the very poor certainly are excluded from our spiritual and material inheritance, and it would seem that the standing armies which are kept up by the various powers are maintained rather for the purpose of holding the impoverished masses in subjection than for defence against foreign aggression. It is as though the ruling classes in Europe had entered into a conspiracy to ferment national jealousy and hatred, that they may have a pretext for keeping intact their military organizations, which, while they overawe the people, help to reduce them to still greater poverty and wretchedness. There Socialism may have a meaning, and since there are never wanting with us people who think it the proper thing to take whatever infection may prevail in Europe, it was inevitable that certain dilettants and idiosyncratics should seek to persuade us that America too ought to have its Socialism. We began, however, as the most completely individualist people of which history makes record, and our experience has not tended to weaken our faith in the power of freedom, intelligence, and industry to solve the great social problems. Should our plutocrats, instead of making themselves public benefactors, become public malefactors, a modification in the laws of inheritance, together with other legal measures which would readily suggest themselves, would be sufficient to abate the nuisance. For the rest, we are convinced that the great aim should be not to provide for all men, but to train and educate all men to take care of themselves. The tendency of good government is to make government less necessary, and the influence of the religion of Christ not only creates purer morals and sympathies, but it also mitigates the conflict between the church and the world.

As men become more enlightened and human, they perceive that the aims of the best civil government are not really distinct from those of true religion. Man's salvation here and hereafter is the end for which all society exists, and hence it is the duty both of the church and the state to labor for freedom, knowledge, and righteousness; in other words, for humanity. The nineteen centuries which have passed since Christ was born have put new forces into our hands, which, if we but use them with wisdom and in the spirit of Christian love, may teach that the Saviour came not to redeem the individual alone, but to transform society. We have at our disposal the vast treasure of science, which is ever increasing, and which, if we but have understanding and a heart, may be made to bless alike the rich and the poor with greater knowledge of the causes of physical evil, of hygienic and sanitary laws, which shall become more and more able to forestall disease. We shall make education universal, but we shall educate with a view to health of body and soul quite as much, at least, as with a view to sharpen the mental faculties. We shall gradually come to understand that there is no conflict between religion and science, but that both are manifestations of God's wisdom and love, meant to console, strengthen, and save man. The minister of religion will love knowledge and the man of science will be reverent and devout. When co-operation becomes universal not among laborers alone, but when the men of wealth and the men of toil, the men of religion and the men of science, the spiritual guides and the temporal rulers, all unite for the common good of the whole people, a new era will dawn. All will then recognize that intelligence and morality are the basis of human life; and that as right intelligence leads to faith in God, so is that faith the fountain-head of the generous and fervid moods which make righteousness prevail. We shall understand more thoroughly that the causes of vice and crime are the chief causes also of poverty and all other social evils.

And while this truer view will weaken confidence in the mechanical appliances and patent remedies of reformers and empyrics, it will confirm our faith in the efficacy of pure religion, of right education, and of whatever else nourishes and strengthens the faculties within.

Then shall a more perfect society grow round us—a society complex and various, yet free and orderly, rich in art, vocal in literature, strong in sympathy, victorious through the power of holiness and love.

J. L. SPALDING.

Peoria, Ill.

THE DEACON'S TRIAL.

A CLEAR, cold November day was drawing to a close, and giving promise, through a peculiarly brilliant sunset, of warmer weather on the morrow.

The country roads were seamed with deep grooves worn by the heavy wheels of numerous stone-wagons bearing away great gray slabs from a celebrated quarry.

The noise of one of these burdened vehicles almost drowned the voices of two men who had stopped on the highway to exchange salutations.

One of them bestrode a fine colt, that he held in check with a quiet exhibition of good horsemanship; the other was an elderly man seated in a narrow buggy, hung upon high springs. The leathered top was flung half way back, and the large, ruddy face of the driver was thrust beyond the cavernous enclosure, in order to catch the words of his neighbor. "I do not suppose," said the horseman, "that the deacon's trial will come off before the middle of the month; Squire Pierson's been sick."

"No, I an't heard no date fixed; thought maybe there might be somebody down to the office to-night that would be likely to know. I declare for it, it's hard on the deacon to be fetched up afore folks at his age along o' that blamed cow. I never see her, but Wells and Walters both say she's a first-rate milker and they're *sup*pœnaed to testify that she wa'n't no kicker when deacon had her."

"Yes, I feel sorry for him, very sorry; but it was a poor trade for Mrs. Baldwin. I don't quite understand it. The cow—Deb, they call her—was warranted to be all right, and Mrs. Baldwin says she went straight over and told the deacon about it; but he was short with her, and she made up her mind that he knew something of the trick before. Going to get our Indian summer yet, I guess; that will help us out on our husking. Good-night."

Mr. Whitridge sat quite still for a moment after his companion had left him, and then, swinging the reins across the back of his pony-built horse, jogged slowly forward. Half a mile further on he halted before a big, square frame structure, whose front was liberally belettered—the most effective decoration being the announcement, in large type, that Samuel Tibbetts, proprietor, was also " Postmaster of the U. S."

There was a motley group gathered about the red-hot stove within, and as Mr. Whitridge entered some of the men nodded familiarly. But a topic of great interest was on hand. Several voices were discernible in the dispute, and more than one of them rang out in angry tones.

Ordinarily the distribution of the mail absorbed the whole attention of the persons present, and no greater altercation arose than might arise over the authorship of a letter allotted to the box of a rich spinster ; but to-night this curiosity of the bystanders had received a counter-blow. In a moment of comparative sobriety and order in the discussion, a tall, thin man with a sallow face and a piping voice strode across the store, and, while peering into the square glass compartment supposed to contain his correspondence, he said with great earnestness: "Cheatin' a woman is a low-down, low-lived trick; and I don't care who does it, I'm for havin' him hung." This bold sentiment provoked a smile, and it was a second or two before any champion of the abused deacon gathered courage to attack the speaker.

"Nobody denies the meanness of cheatin' man or woman— 'specially a woman—but what *I* say is, that it don't stand to reason a man like the deacon is goin' to risk his reputation— leavin' out his soul—for a few dollars."

"He didn't count on Mrs. Baldwin suing him," said another. "You know just as well as I do that Deacon Wilder's as close as the bark on an apple-tree, and such folks takes a good many chances. For my part, I was always suspicious of the true convertin' of several of our church pillers. Some of 'em are hollow—you can stand by that."

Mr. Whitridge, whose mind inclined toward the innocence of the accused, was not a man of independent thought. He was rather weakening now in his defence, and as the door opened to admit Deacon Wilder he shrank back from the light emitted by the glowing stove, and crept into the gloom of the back store, whose darkness was intensified by the dingy oil lamp on the counter.

Deacon Wilder came irresolutely into the circle. He was a small man, with thick, iron-gray hair and full beard. His head was bowed, not by years but habit, as if a continual consciousness of physical inferiority had humbled him.

One or two of his defenders rose and shook hands with him,

and he saw fit to lengthen his grave face and speak in a funereal voice; but no one alluded directly to his misfortune.

Meantime the postmaster and his wife, whom he had called from the dwelling in the rear of the store to assist in distributing the mail, had finished their task, and now announced it to the assembly by vigorously thrusting aside the "show-winder" that shut them off from the view of the public.

Mr. Whitridge was among the first to receive his weekly paper, and was well on his way to the door, congratulating himself that he had not been recognized by the deacon, when a woman's hand was thrust outside the square opening, and, as she waved it wildly, she cried: "Mr. Whitridge, if you're a-goin' by the North road, wisht you'd take this postal card to Miss Jones. It come yesterday, but none of 'em an't been in; and as it says her mother's comin' to-morrer, I reckon likely she'll want to make some extras beforehand."

He turned slowly around and grudgingly received the card, which he deposited in his pocket, and through the stress of the uncomfortable circumstances connected with it, utterly forgot to deliver!

Some of the men lingered to do a little "trading," and among these, when the deacon had circumspectly departed, the subject of his "counsel" was approached.

"Mrs. Baldwin 'll beat him sure as *you* live, whoever he gets; for she's goin' to have that young chap from the city, Peaseley. They do says he's a buster. He's been to college and to law school, and now he's just carryin' everything before him."

This information rather abashed the other side, who knew that Deacon Wilder had already put his case into the hands of the old town stand-by, John Snell. They contented themselves with that comfortable assumption of the triumph of the "right" which lends a bold front to many an unpopular cause.

The little company next decided that it would be far better for all concerned to delay the trial until Squire Pierson's health would permit him to "sit," rather than let the case fall under strange jurisdiction. The cost was canvassed, some present declaring that the losing party would have to fork over to Peaseley not less than fifteen dollars and car-fare, while Snell was always reasonable in his charges, and possibly his service could be secured for five.

"Who's *sup*pœnaed?" asked the thin man. "I an't heard much about the particulars afore to-night."

"Wells and Walters · is on for the deacon. They'll both swear Deb was all right when he had her."

"She's that slim-tailed, yallerish brown cow he bought at the vandoo over to Lysander, an't she? I bid on her myself, but I soon see the deacon meant to have her, so I drew in my horns."

"Lucky you didn't get her; the suit might 'a' been on your hands."

"No, I don't never law much. It mostly costs more'n it comes to, I cal'late."

The thin man, who had a semi-judicial cast of mind, now came forward again, both arms laden with packages, and added: "There's one question that pesters me. I'd like to have some of you tell me *why*, if Deb was all right and a good milker, the deacon ever come to sell her to Mrs. Baldwin. He an't made of the stuff that don't hold on to the good things of this world when once he gets 'em. Now, there was a reason somewhere for the sellin'. Butter's high; Deb come in in September, and will give her full stint up to Christmas, fallin' off then, perhaps, till fresh feed along in the spring. Them as had owned her told to the vandoo that she don't dry up but a little while afore calving. Them things works in my mind."

A dead silence ensued, and it seemed a clear case against the deacon until one of his defenders, unable to turn the tide of argument, resorted to strategy.

"Haw, haw!" he laughed as he shook his shaggy head, "*you* ought to have been a lawyer; you've got some of their big points. You can hint and look mysterious, and wink away a good man's reputation without even waiting for the trial to come up. Deacon Wilder will clear all this carcumstantial evidence away, now *I* tell ye, when he comes to be put on the stand." He then arose and walked off, leaving his hearers as thoroughly convinced of the rascality of lawyers in general, and the innocence of the accused, as if the verdict of the Supreme Court had been published in all its length and breadth.

Mrs. Baldwin, too, had her sympathizers. She was an exceptionally tidy housekeeper, and in the early afternoon sat down to complete a garment upon her sewing-machine. Scarcely, however, had she filled the bobbin and oiled the driving-wheel, when the click of the gate-latch aroused her curiosity, and she looked up in time to see the minister's wife hurrying toward the house. She smoothed her tightly drawn hair, tied the strings of her white apron a little more precisely, and opened the door.

· "I do declare, Mrs. Brown, this is kind."

The visitor, who was a plump little body, with a pale face beaming with smiles, and curling hair fast growing gray, did not at once reply, but put into the hand of her hostess a large can of Bartlett pears.

"There's just a sample of what our tree did last year, or rather of what the tree and me did together. They an't done up pound for pound, so they won't hurt any one."

Mrs. Baldwin duly admired the gift and complimented the well-known skill of the giver ; then she sighed.

"It does me good to have you come, for I didn't rightly know just how you and dominie would take this lawsuit betwixt me and the deacon, but I *couldn't* do elsewise than sue him in justice to myself, for of all the kickin' creatures Deb's the very worst."

"Now don't tell me a word of it," said the cheery new-comer. "I told Elisha this morning that I couldn't stan' it another day without comin' over, and just speakin' out plain and sayin' that I can't *possibly* understand how such a thing came round between two such good folks as you are—two worthy soldiers of the Cross."

Mrs. Baldwin interrupted her : "I can soon tell my side."

"Not a word, not a breath !" protested Mrs. Brown.

"All I have got to say *is* that I believe in you both, and *no-body* can make me think that either of you started out to do wrong. There's a misunderstandin' *some*where. Now, Elisha, he mourns over the trial comin' on ; for, says he, 'it's a positive disgrace to the church'; but I tell him, Would you have bad feelin's goin' along year after year, breedin' unchristian thoughts in secret, when through a public suit the real truth may be brought forward, and we shall all see that Deacon Wilder is the same good man we always believed him to be, and Mrs. Baldwin has only made a very common mistake in prejudgin' him. That's what I told him when I was pourin' tea, and he quite chirked up. So now, it's all over between us two, and we can visit to our hearts' content.

Mrs. Baldwin was surprised into acquiescence, and they chatted away over mite societies and grab-bags, the prevalence of measles and the missionary box, until the advent of other callers warned the little peace-maker that she might not be able to hold her own in face of the enemy's reinforcement, and therefore it would be wise to beat a hasty retreat.

Mrs. Sylvester and Martha Janes, her step-daughter, had no

such scruples. as the minister's wife. They entered boldly upon the subject close at heart, and as the plaintiff proceeded to state her wrongs, with an ardor increased by recent forced suppression, they repeatedly expressed their conviction that Deacon Wilder was a wolf in sheep's clothing.

"Nobody'll ever make me believe he could have milked Deb twice a day for two months and more, and not found out that she was up to tricks. No more do I think, as I told mother coming over—no, it was whilst we were frying the ham for dinner—that he won't shy out of it all when he's up before the justice."

"I don't see how he's goin' to git round the actual facts," said Mrs. Sylvester in a deep bass voice. "Justice *is* justice in these United States; tan't as if it was in Germany. Elmiry Goodsell was tellin' me, last time I see her, about some of their doin's over there, and it beats all! Harnessin' a woman up with a cow to drag fodder! As for me, I don't *want* to travel in benighted parts. New York State's good enough for the Sylvesters, and the Janeses too I reckon, where a woman's word o' mouth can stand law like any man's."

"You are quite right; but I worry myself awful, sometimes, thinking of the trial. How am I going to get up on top of the witness-box and tell how mean one of the pillars of our church has been, and to a sister in Christ too? It's a nightmare to me."

"Well now I wouldn't allow myself to fret over it. Janes says you have got a high-up lawyer, one that can pull you through if anybody can."

This point of view was entirely new to Mrs. Baldwin. The absolute truth of the statement she expected to make in public was to her sufficient warrant for what she was about to do. There *was* nothing else. Deb kicked; and she had told the deacon about it, and he had refused to make it right notwithstanding the fact that he had warranted the cow to be a first-class animal. The idea of her lawyer "pulling her through" savored of corruption. She absolutely blazed with indignation. "Do you think I'm goin' to lie over a little thing like Deb, or put the deacon to shame just to favor a spleen against him? Why what *are* we coming to? I'd rather be hitched to a cart *with* kickin' Deb than to hurt a hair of anybody's head, let alone bein' pulled through." Her visitors were less sensitive beings, and marvelled much at any reluctance to "beat" the deacon in whatever way it might be accomplished.. To them a verdict was like a written character—endorsed by the powers that be, and therefore able to sustain one through life. They felt uncomfortable in Mrs. Baldwin's presence after her outburst, and with many assurances of good will they departed, leaving her a wiser but far less contented woman.

She had entered upon the lawsuit from a firm conviction that she had been imposed upon—"cheated," as she plainly worded it—but now there crept into her mind a suspicion that there might be those, other than the fierce partisans of the defendant, who thought it possible for her to be mistaken, or—and this was still worse—those who deemed her action instigated by malice.

While she was yet thinking about the matter a paper was served upon her, stating that the trial would come off on the "tenth day of December." "Well, I s'pose there's no stoppin' it now unless I give folks a chance to think I'm a thief more 'an ever. And I reckon the best way is, as Mrs. Brown says, to let the lawyers get at the truth, and *then* the public will know it." She sighed again and returned to the oiling of her sewing-machine, perhaps dimly wishing that the wheels of life could be kept running smoothly with as little trouble.

The tenth day of December brought the first snow-storm of the season. In the early morning Mrs. Whitridge had examined all the signs through whose consultation she had established a certain local reputation as weather prophet, and she announced to her husband at breakfast-time that if he intended going to the deacon's trial he had better fix up things at the barn in winter shape.

"I hadn't thought of this bein' more'n a squall," he replied.

"*I* say, two foot o' snow will be on the ground before the deacon's free."

"That an't tellin' we'll be snowed under to-day nor to-morrow," he laughed. "When once a man gets into the hands of the lawyers there's no knowin' when they'll let up on him. But I reckon you'll see me back before midnight. I'm goin' to get Hiram to do my share of the chores, so as not to bother you."

This arrangement seemed satisfactory, and Mr. Whitridge started off soon after nine o'clock with a clear conscience.

The "justice office" was in a small building detached from the Pierson homestead, but standing very close to the old house, as if afraid to venture from under the shadow of its progenitor. And yet the little structure had a certain independence of its own. Its architectural proportions were not at all in harmony

with the parental edifice, for it had a flat tin roof bordered with
an enormous weight of cornice and a "stoop" that dwarfed the
suggestive little entrance to the large gabled building. This
stoop was, on this auspicious occasion, tenanted at an early hour
by men from the far and near farms, grouped under the head
of "neighbors." They chiefly were dressed in the garments reserved for Sundays and holidays, which gave something of a
festive look to the assembly.

The door stood open and the squire within was making welcome those who had summoned courage to approach "His
Honor."

"Cold day for the deacon," suggested the man who had
volunteered to "fix the fire." "I hope not, sir," answered the
justice, quite forgetting, in his perception of the double meaning
of the phrase, that any suspicion might attach to his reply. Then,
suddenly remembering his relation to the event, he stammered:
"Leastwise for neither him nor Mrs. Baldwin, nor none of us,
since you're fireman." Having thus restored his injured dignity,
he peered among the people outside and exclaimed:

"I declare for it, the dominie and Mrs. Brown's a-comin'!
Fetch two rush-bottomed chairs—the wooden ones sits hard—
and kinder help me to straighten out. I had no idee ladies
would be here; but this *is* a case— Howd'y do, dominie?
Goin' to see Mrs. Baldwin through, Mrs. Brown? Well I guess
it's comin' out right all round. Here's a couple of seats engaged
for you—reserved seats, as I might say."

His embarrassment was great, and he sought to relieve it by
being as jocular as possible. The minister misinterpreted his
humor.

"Ah! it is true, then, the story I heard last night—that the
parties in the case have come to an agreement; that is well."

"No, no, no! Suit's called in ten minutes. Here comes the
plaintiff and her counsel now."

When Mrs. Baldwin entered Mrs. Brown whispered to her
husband and he politely offered the lady his chair, his wife urging it upon her with the suggestion: "You will feel more like
home having a woman next you."

Mrs. Baldwin smiled a very forced smile, and bethought herself to introduce her lawyer to the minister.

"I am glad to know you, Mr. Peaseley," said the latter gravely. "But I regret that it should be under the present circumstances."

The other, who was quite young, well dressed, and with abundant self-possession, made answer pleasantly: "We lawyers do not regard our duties so seriously. Indeed, I feel that we are virtually peace-makers, for oftentimes our clients are simply blind to certain facts that are brought out in the trial, and even if one party *has* the costs to pay they are better friends ever after."

He moved away and arranged his effects upon a small table near the judge's desk.

Within a moment his example was followed by John Snell, an ungainly man, whose slow motions were unequal to the impatience of the throng that now swept in a disorderly way into the little building.

No one paid any attention to the formal opening of the case, so absorbed was the general attention upon the appearance of the respondent. He seemed to have aged in the past month, and his gray head drooped lower than ever upon his breast. He did not even notice the friendly efforts of Mrs. Brown, who conscientiously endeavored to distribute her sympathies without fear or favor.

When, however, Mr. Peaseley had finished his short statement and the name of Mrs. Mehitable Susan Baldwin was called, every eye was fixed upon the plaintiff. She was a sturdy woman, but now it almost seemed as if she would faint, so white and tremulous did she instantly become. The voice of the justice recalled her:

"Step right for'ard, Mrs. Baldwin; don't be afeard; you're among friends and goin' to speak the truth."

Certainly nothing could have inspired her with more daring than this illy conceived sally. She walked firmly forward, dropped her shawl on the bench beside her, and began:

"I don't know as there's any call to say beforehand, squire, that I'll tell the truth. I an't givin' to lyin'."

Her counsel interrupted: "One moment, if you please. Mrs. Baldwin, after you are sworn, you will kindly say nothing but in reply to my questions."

The oath was administered and the ordinary formula requiring personal identification.

"You are an unmarried woman?"

"No, sir; I'm a widow."

"You are at present, then, unmarried, and managing the farm and dairy on Springhill, where you live."

"Yes; me and Mr. Smothers."

"Mr. Smothers rents a portion of your farm. Has he anything to do with the dairy?"

"No, sir; I han't got· but' two cows besides Deb, and I do my own milkin' and churnin'."

"When did you buy the cow, Deb, from Deacon Wilder?"

"On the second day of November. last; and I wish to gracious I had a-done as· I wanted and milked her right afore his eyes."

"Slowly, if you please. Did Deacon Wilder tell you she did not kick?"

"I never said he did."

Visible excitement now amid the spectators.

"What did he tell you?"

"He said she was a first-class animal, gentle an' kind, and he showed me the mornin's milk with cream on it an' the butter she made the week afore; an' I told him it was about milkin' time, an' I'd try her if he'd fetch a pail, an—"

"Slowly, madam. What did the deacon say then?"

"Why, he said that it wa'n't worth while, since I had my good clo's on."

"Then he did not seem willing to have you milk her?" ·

"No, sir, he didn't. I can't say that it wa'n't just goodness on his part for my clo's, but it looked kinder strange to me when I got home and talked it over with Smothers."

It evidently looked strange to the assembly also, for they whispered and nodded without regard to the deacon's proximity.

"When you agreed to take Deb there was nothing more said about her habits?".

"Not a word. I had asked all the questions I wanted to; and I will.say for the deacon that he did not stretch it a bit about her butter-makin'. She's a first-class animal there."

"How did you discover that she kicked?"   ▪

"Land alive! I reckon it didn't take me long to know. Why I was jam up agin the fence, and the milk pourin' all over me out of the pail, upsot."

Everybody save the accused began to laugh. Even good Mrs. Brown shook behind her handkerchief.

The justice had leaned back against his tall chair with his eyes shut, as he had once seen a distinguished judge in the Supreme Court do; but at this point Mr. Peaseley called his attention by saying with severity: "I must remind your honor that there is too much levity here."

His honor looked wildly around, and, reaching for his pen, stammered: "I'd—I'd a-seen that point if there hadn't been so much noise."

Only a few of those present understood why it was a

moment or two before the case was resumed. Then the justice nodded as if to announce that the objection was noted, and Mr. Peaseley went on. " Did you ever attempt to milk Deb again?"

" Of course I did. Smothers can't do it; he's got his own chores ·to 'tend to. 'Tan't pleasant," she added, submissively; " but it's got to be done, and if a widder woman keeps cows she *must* milk 'em."

" Did Deb ever kick again?"

" Of course she did. I wouldn't have complained to the deacon about *onct*, but she kep' it up. So I reckoned it was a way she had."

" But—but "—the young city lawyer was a little bewildered here—" but how could you manage to milk her if she knocked you over every time?" This seemed like improbability, and he was nonplussed. Not so the audience, ·who laughed loudly at his discomfiture. Even the witness was scarcely able to restrain her merriment.

" Why, I *tied* her down. I guess you never see a kickin' cow; but if you'll come home with me, I'll show you how to fix Deb. I strap her hind legs too."

" That will do," said her interrogator sharply.

And now the figure of the deacon was seen edging through the crowd. He held up his hand and spoke with decision: " I don't know but it's agin the law, squire; but if you and these gentlemen can fix it so as it'll stan', I wisht you would. I want to tell my story right here and now, an' leave it to you to lay the penalty."

" Hold on, deacon!" cried John Snell. " Your turn's comin'; first let them get through with their witnesses."

" I don't keer for no witnesses. When you hear my statement you won't. I've hated to talk about my folks; but that what's laid on my mind is all gone now. I guess I can tell it straight."

There was something so pathetic in the whole bearing of the speaker that the young lawyer was touched. He leaned over the table, and a whispered discussion took place between court and counsel. Then Mr. Snell arose and announced, in a wandering way, that it had been agreed between the parties to refer the case directly to the court without argument or further examination of witnesses. The sole evidence to be presented would be a verbal statement from the respondent.

The interest of the spectators was quadrupled. Mrs. Baldwin forgot to sit down, and in fact remained standing throughout the recital.

"I had Deb," said the deacon, slowly stroking his rough beard, "just nine weeks afore the plaintiff bought her. Deb's a *good* cow; a leetle narvous, three-quarters Jersey, gives six quarts to a milkin', and rich at that. I hated to sell her, but—(here there was a slight movement in the throng) now I didn't cal'late to tell this, nor to bring Elizabeth Snyder's name into court at all. I thought maybe I could manage to answer the questions so as to satisfy the justice without that. I didn't know nothin' about Deb's kickin', but night afore last I was up to Snell's office, an' I see plain enough that it had got to come out *why* I sold her; an' I wrestled hard to find what was the right way for a Christian man to act. At last it was borne in on me that I must tell the *truth*, the *hull* truth, an' nothin' *but* the truth." He paused and wiped the perspiration from his brow. "You all know somethin' of the way I'm sitiwated. The hand of the Lord was laid heavy on me three year ago, when he took Sary home to himself; but I thought I'd be able to get along with Elizabeth Snyder's housekeepin'; but a sister-in-law han't like a wife—got your interest to heart; an' I'm bound to say mine has got a temper."

"I should say as much," escaped from Mrs. Baldwin's lips, and various nods and winks were exchanged across the room.

"There han't much money in farmin' onless dairyin', and we—that is, Sary an' me—had laid up somethin' from our cows; but Elizabeth Snyder lately sot her foot down that she *wouldn't* make butter. I tried it after Deb come, but I didn't hev fust-rate luck, so I thought to sell off my extra cows, and get along the best way I could. And when Mrs. Baldwin come over to look at Deb, I *hated* to hev Elizabeth Snyder tell her how poor my butter was, fer she had larfed at me considerable. So I kinder told her off all about Deb as fast as I could, an' hurried her away, while my sister-in-law was over to the Newells. I hadn't no idee Deb kicked. I thought when Mrs. Baldwin come to tell me of it, and I think now, it's only because she an't used to havin' a woman round her. So I smoothed it over, thinkin' likely she never'd have no more trouble; but if I'd been more of a man and not so afraid o' trouble with Elizabeth Snyder, I'd told the right reason in the start. And now I'm punished enough, an' stan' ready to pay whatever you think is right, squire; that's all I've got to say. Mrs. Baldwin's a good woman and a Christian, allowin' her to hev been a leetle hasty in goin' to law."

He went quietly back to his seat, and in the short stillness that ensued the justice rapidly came to a decision. He struck the desk before him with his ruler, and without further ceremony of any kind announced:

"This court has seen fit to hear Deacon Wilder's side of the question presented without counsel, and the same now renders a verdict in favor of the widow, since the cow kicked, whether the deacon knew it or not. I don't think he oughter pay her much; she's got a good milkin' critter, and he'll have to settle with the lawyers and the court. I shouldn't wonder if an X would make it all right with Mrs. Baldwin." He gathered up his papers and somebody opened the outer door.

The storm had increased and there was a prospect of the roads being drifted, so the surprise and sympathy of the assembled farmers were disposed of in few words, as they wended their way to their various vehicles.

Only the dominie and his wife waited to shake hands with the contestants when they had concluded the conversation they were engaged in.

"Deacon," says Mrs. Baldwin, "I'm just ashamed o' myself to think of all this pester I've brought upon you; and I don't want to waste no words, but I'll just put it out sharp that I won't never touch your ten dollars, an' I just believe every word you said. Deb prob'bly never *was* milked by a woman before. I don't know as I blame her for bein' mad about it; 'tan't a woman's business."

"No more it an't," replied the deacon, "an' if you won't take the money I don't see no way of recompensin' you, but to do your milkin' for you."

"Oh! deacon, that's too much trouble; it's full three mile."

"Yes, it's a good ways," he answered reflectively; "but p'raps you might think well of fetching Deb and all your belongin's over to my house. I feel sure," he added with more spirit since Mrs. Baldwin did not resent this—"I feel sure we hev the same interest to heart, and two pews adjoinin', with each one in it, don't speak so well for a lovin' Christian spirit as if we sot together."

S. M. H. G.

THE WITNESS OF SCIENCE TO RELIGION.

VI.—CHRIST STANDING IN THE SUN.—(*Conclusion.*)

I AM now to sum up these fragmentary, yet, as I hope, not random or unfruitful thoughts. And I end as I began. The universe of matter, of force, of life, and of spirit is one; not because all its elements are identical (for that I should strenuously deny), but because they conspire to the same purpose, belong to a great harmonious organism, and have been framed on the pattern of a consistent, however varied, Ideal. In like manner, the mind which contemplates reality is one. Many as are the types of intellectual genius, disparate as I grant the senses to be and the instruments which extend their power and grasp even to "the loftiest star of unascended Heaven," I maintain, with the voice of all science, that the laws of thought are and must be valid throughout the universe. And as science is the necessary and normal product of the human intellect, so is natural Religion. The one cannot be true if the other is false. To the greatest of German philosophers, "the starry Heavens above, and the Moral Law within," were equal certitudes. And rightly. For the mind which beheld in those constellations innumerable, law and order, rhythm and arrangement, self-balancing through countless ages, knew by as certain a method, though more secret, that, as Plato says, "this is the law of the gods in Heaven—the worse to the worse, the better to the better, like to like, in life and in death, and in every state of being or of suffering."[*] The world is a unity; the mind has its axioms which cannot be rejected, save at the cost of universal scepticism; and man's nature and destiny, being subject to the reason which is in all things, are themselves to be interpreted according to reason.

But, then, let us not be deluded by appearances. "They err," again remarks Plato, speaking of natural philosophers in his own day, "who know not that the soul is before the body, and before all other things, and the author and ruler of them all in their vicissitudes. And if the soul is prior to the body, then the things of the soul are prior to the things of the body. In other words, opinion, attention, mind, art, law, are prior to sensible qualities; and the first and greater works of creation are the re-

[*] Here and elsewhere I am quoting Plato's *Laws*, chiefly book x.

sults of art and mind." This ancient doctrine, as profound as it is satisfactory, derives every day fresh confirmation at the hands of inductive science. The "sensible qualities" of things we know to be a kind of perspective, not capricious indeed, yet changing with the angle of sense (if I may so call it) from which we view them. Every creature, great or small, lives and moves in its own sensible world, unshared by another; and, in strict science, no two ever saw the same band of the spectrum, or heard identically the same sounds. The realities which make up to our senses the material universe, lie in themselves beyond our microscopes; and we do not see them, but reason to their existence. If "atoms" be assumed as those realities, then it has been shown that in diameter they must extend less than one-millionth of a millimetre—a dimension which no instrument of ours can grasp. Yet within this inconceivably narrow space, infusoria may perhaps exist with their limbs and organs entire. On the atomic theory, that which we call matter is an infinite number, combined in infinite ways, of infinitesimal realities, far beyond the ken whether of senses or of microscopes. The visible is made of things invisible, that change but never perish. And the solid which we imagine ourselves to see is but an infinite network.

What determines these vicissitudes without end? Energy, science answers; energy, which has neither size nor dimensions, which though everywhere present occupies no space, and which as gravitation is acting every moment in all parts of the universe, yet requires not the tiniest measured interval to make itself felt from shore to shore of the galaxies and the nebulas. And energy, like the atoms over which it rules, is indestructible. Still we ask, Does energy move itself? Can it change its own direction or suspend its activity? What power do we know of that controls energy? The answer comes, we know of such a power, and it is Life or Will. The atoms and forces which make up all we see of a living organism are subject to a principle, as real as these are, yet neither an atom nor an energy but superior to both of them, and distinctly marked by its own characteristics. First, we perceive it in living protoplasm as the something which makes it move, which weaves the tissues and the organs, which transforms dead matter into living, and which rules the cycle of changes called life, returning into itself from seed to fruit, *ab ovo ad ovum.* Next, we are aware of it as self-conscious, as feeling, knowing, and choosing, never as an atom, but in ourselves as a Monad determining its own acts. And thus we learn that the essential principle in man is the spirit, while the body is a fleeting stream.

The body, like all visible matter, is a mere network, a perspective calculated for the senses, an outward form or limit, within which the ceaseless rush of particles is hurried along. And even as atoms are indestructible, and energies never can fail, so is the spirit immortal. Compared with spirit, the body is a phantom, a thing woven literally of air, and sun, and carbonic acid gas, but having in itself neither stay, nor subsistence, nor coherence. To fancy that it is the prime or sole reality is to take the shadow for the substance from which it is cast. These things are known familiarly to the chemist, the physicist, and the physiologist. All three have clear and convincing evidence that the speck of living protoplasm did not make itself, and that something else which is not protoplasm, nor mere dynamic energy, and least of all dead inert matter, does make it live and move and be, while they are looking on at the present miracle.

Take a step farther. The living protoplasm has a past behind it, a future in front of it—a history and a destiny. On the huge rock-tablets of our planet that history may be read, though in broken and disjointed fragments. The earth has been part of a flaming cloud, then a sun, afterwards a chaos of solid and liquid, by and by reduced to a habitation fit for living things to dwell in. But life on its surface must be comparatively recent; and consciousness dates from yesterday—that is to say, from perhaps fifty or a hundred thousand years ago. Evolution, in the sense of "orderly succession," is a fact. There is progress, and there has always been adaptation. The universe which from one point of view is an immense system of energies acting through space, from another is a hierarchy of mental laws, and from a third the home of life and spirit. While in every stage we observe how organisms are fitted to their surroundings, when we turn over the leaves of the geological record, we cannot fail to perceive an upward growth. Viewing, therefore, merely that scene which inductive knowledge unrolls before us, we shall grant that the movement of things is from the unconscious to the living, from matter to personality, from the lowest to the highest. But we must never lose sight of the governing experience, namely, that before the visible comes the invisible, before the solid and tangible comes the infinitesimal; and that energy determines all changes. Hence, if we pursue the history of protoplasm far enough, we shall find ourselves carried across the boundary of sense; and knowing that "mind and art came first," we shall affirm with confidence an Ever-Living by whose act the earthly life was brought into existence. How do we know that mind came first? Because, if it did not, this particle of living matter would be adapted neither to its surroundings, nor to itself, and the vicissitudes it underwent being all at random, it could never result in the organism which we see, and which is destined to be the parent of other organisms in perpetual succession. All protoplasm, whether to-day or a million years back, must have been set up in reason, ordered and guided to the issues of life, and kept from dissolving amid the cross-currents and unceasing storms of influence that rain down upon it from every side. As we cannot eliminate purpose and yet explain the individual organism, so must purpose be incessantly at work in the production and development of the species to which our individual is assigned. The adaptation of certain membranes, liquids, and threads of nerve to the light, and of the light to them, will alone give us the satisfactory account we are seeking, of the origin of the eye. Repeat this argument, not ten thousand times, but ten million times ten thousand, and ask yourself what is its cumulative force, when in the single instance it is so convincing? Then you will begin to realize that life must come from life, and that behind and beneath the myriad existences which fill even this tiny corner of space, there is a Life abiding and eternal.

So much for the past. And what shall we predict of the future? That progress will continue; that we stand on the threshold of eternity; that the ascension of the spirit, having come thus far, cannot pause or be turned back? Doubtless, it is a most warrantable induction. But will the person survive, and under what conditions? Let me ask in turn, Why should he not? Science does not forbid him. Nay more, science points out the manner in which he may survive, and offers him a physical basis of immortality. It is science which declares that man is the son of his deeds; that no past is ever annihilated; and that the newest creature bears about in its very tissues the record and memorial of what it has been. Still more significant is the remarkable witness of facts that, as species move upwards, the individual becomes in a proportionate degree single and distinct. In the ascending stages of culture and civilization, memory tends to become more vivid, accurate, persistent, and introspective. High intelligence is lonely and self-centred. ·Shakespeare, or· Goethe, or Newman, almost fulfils the profound and curious dictum of St. Thomas, that "every angel is a species." Whether we take the moral, the mystic, or the intellectual genius, our truest verdict in each case will be that he is unique—like himself; unlike every one else. He is a world of his own, and his biography tells us how inevitably he' was marked off from the beginning to pursue his way through the wilderness alone; yet in the company of an Ideal which drew · him ever onwards, and which made him the strange - and wonderful creation he at length became. Therefore, personality is the scope of evolution.

If now, excluding Chance or Hazard, and putting mind first, science has decided that "the things of the soul are prior to the things of the body," it follows that in the spiritual nature of man we hold the clue to his destiny. The law of progressive adaptation must in every instance imply a certain want of harmony between the capacities of a creature intended to live under different forms, and the surroundings in which at a given moment it may be found. But in man, the provisional character of his present being, the incompleteness of life, and the partial failure which attends ever upon his most notable success, are facts glaring enough to have originated Pessimism and to cry aloud for explanation. I see no possible reply to these difficulties, no answer which does not speedily drift into the wildest unreason, if we restrict man's existence to the cycle of time through which he is seen travelling. Clothe the human spirit with the idea of purpose, and immortality is the one reasonable conclusion. Deny him an. Hereafter, and you make of his faculties, achievements, and aspirations a horrible tragedy without meaning or dénouement. Why does he exist? His conscience affirms that there is a Law of Righteousness under which he was born, and which corresponds in the spiritual world to the law of gravitation ruling over the physical, even as the law of contradiction rules over logic and the realm of thought. There is an objective Moral Order, revealed to us with unerring certitude, "the Moral Law within," as clear to the mind's apprehension as the sky, and its thousands of starry worlds to the outward vision. At this point it signifies little whether men say they have discovered the law of virtue by calculations of utility, or, as I maintain, by direct insight apart from all reckoning. Grant me the law which affirms justice, and I will prove that it looks forward to judgment. "The good soul, which has intercourse with the Divine Nature, passes into a holier and better place. The evil soul, in like manner, as she grows worse, changes her place for the worse. Thou art not so little that thou canst creep into the earth, or so high that thou canst mount to Heaven; but either here, or in the world below, or in some yet more savage place, thou shalt pay the penalty." Thus

Plato once again records the inductions of conscience, adding, "This is likewise the explanation of the prosperity of the · wicked, in whose actions thou seemedst as in a looking-glass to behold the neglect of the gods, not knowing how they make all things work together and contribute to the great whole."

"Their relation to the great whole." Consider this pregnant sentence and meditate upon it. The whole, I have said, is not only matter, but is sense, life, and spirit. Can we divine its scope? In particular, and as it were by sketching some definite plan which it is carrying on to fulfilment, I, for my part, would not venture; such an enterprise is too high for me. But while I refrain from impotent guessing, I can never doubt that the purpose of the whole is some true and lofty ideal of perfection, is Righteousness established everlastingly, conscious Being crowned with happiness, and a certain magnificent participation of the creature in its Creator's bliss. The Final Cause and the Efficient are one; and manifestly it is goodness, beauty, and joy which have been poured abroad throughout the universe for their own sake; while in no single instance can we discover that Nature delights in the mere infliction of pain. Death itself, I have remarked, is not an end but an instrument. Suffering is the condition of the noblest virtue. And free-will alone can hurt itself. In laying down these truths I do not overlook my engagement to proceed by induction and appeal to experience. I say these things are known to our most intimate and assured experience. The incompleteness of the present life is a fact, and progress a real principle, and justice the law of the nature of things. From all which I conclude that man is an immortal being, destined to live hereafter according to the choice he has deliberately made. He creates by free-will the light or darkness in which he is to abide for ever.

Here, then, at last, we have united into a system the elements which go to make up Natural Religion. For it cannot exist at all without such a distinction between its object and its subject as shall justify the "transcendent admiration," the fear and awe, which we call worship. Neither is it moral, if justice be absent from it; or holy, unless it cleanse the heart and demand inward purity in all who revere its precepts; or true, if it deny any facts, from those of astronomy to the incidents of yesterday's chronicle. Its purpose must be union with the supreme All Holy and All Righteous; and its end life everlasting. The final outcome is personal, self-conscious existence in an ordered world, of which the ground and mainstay shall be that enduring Reality which at the same time is ever an entrancing and attractive Ideal. For in no other way can stability be combined with progress, or eternity with happiness, or the beginnings of things with their successful and triumphant issue in a nobler world. Faith, hope, and charity are, therefore, natural virtues. I mean faith in the unseen, hope in immortality, and love of the beauty of Holiness. For the conscious union of creature and Creator is love; and this is the true meaning of detachment, when the phenomenal and the transitory are surrendered for the sake of the eternal; and when we care not for self apart from its perfection, but only for that which makes self perfect. This, too, is what some have aimed at in their unsubstantial dream of Nirvana; for perhaps they looked to the Divine as that in which they should live somehow, even though absorbed and, as it were, annihilated. But science points rather to a heightened personality and knows nothing of the Nirvana in which substance is swallowed up. Progress means more life, not dissolution of the whole into homogeneous parts. The movement of things is not a curve returning upon itself, like a "serpent of eternity." We must think of it as an ascending spiral, in which the present, while it exceeds, does yet contain as it exalts the past.

· And so I find myself "alone with the Alone." As I began by looking out of my own mind and in its light considering the material universe spread before me, so I end by returning into the deeps of the spirit and beholding there some reflection of the First and Final Cause. At every step I have employed, more truly than I have trusted, my intellect. Have I taken anything else for granted? Does it appear that I have broken with the method prescribed to me by induction? Or that science forbids me to attempt an explanation of man and the world as products of an Eternal Mind, rooted and founded in an Everpresent Life which bears them up and bears them onward? Or is the Ideal of Righteousness shown to be an idle fancy because what is best for the whole involves pain and imperfection in various of the parts? Can it be denied, again, that unless we accept this surely most high and winning philosophy, we are cast upon the rocks of Nescience, and our moral being as well as our intellectual must make shipwreck there? And is the burden so intolerable to a scientific mind, of applying to the whole that sane and clear hypothesis which it is ever using to detect the relation of part with part and order with order? The actual choice, · we have seen, is Mind or no Mind. A middle term between these cannot be imagined, and does not exist. It would be held an overwhelming argument for any view that it stands or falls with the laws of thought. I have shown, it appears to me, that Natural Religion is a chapter, and that the most convincing, of inductive science. To the sceptic who denies all certain knowledge, science and religion may well seem to be audacious affirmations of that which lies beyond our ken. But to the men of inductive research I say, that if they wish me to believe in their science, it is only fair and logical that they should be-lieve in my religion. For both are established by the like men-tal process; and he who denies the one should by parity of argument reject the other. "Either, then, he shall teach us that we were wrong in saying that the soul is the original of all things," and banish from the world mathematical order and scientific harmony, or, "if he is not able to say anything better, then he must yield to us, and live for the remainder of his life in the conviction that there is a God."

Yes, and a just and provident God. Since nothing is plainer than that the universe is one; and all its powers and elements conspire to the same end; and that which is seemingly the least turns out to be the most réal; and every slightest movement of an eyelid reverberates to the ever-widening horizons of time and space. The reign of law cannot be imagined, nor those "exact calculations," according to which the Heavens move and all their host, be at all comprehended, unless we grant that the Mind which is in every particular pervades the whole. And thus, while the multitude are apt to think that "those who handle these matters by the help of astronomy and the accompanying acts of demonstration may become godless, because they see things hap-pening by necessity, and not by an intelligent will bent on the accomplishment of good," we shall maintain that just the oppo-site is the conclusion to be drawn. For mind or spirit is the most ancient of realities, and governs all by its own laws, and stamps the universe as with a seal of perfection. And the high-est law, which can never be repealed, but is steadfast and triumphant whatever betide, is the rule of Righteousness. For the inductions of psychology are there to persuade us that, "even if a man have health and wealth, and a sovereignty which lasts, and is mighty in strength and courage, and has besides the gift of immortality, and none of the so-called evils which counterpoise these goods, but only the injustice and insolence of his own nature," such a one is miserable rather than happy. Shall we not agree with the divine philosopher whom I am quoting when he goes on to say, that to be rich in the goods of fortune but to live without justice and virtue, "is the greatest of evils if life be immortal; but not so great if the bad man lives a very short time"? Recompense to an evil soul is by the nature of the case retribution; and so Juvenal:

> "Evertere domus totas optantibus ipsis
> Di faciles; nocitura toga, nocitura petuntur
> Militia."

But I am passing, you will say, from science to history. There is no real break, I answer. History, too, is a record of facts to be interpreted by the axioms of reason and conscience. While as an individual I am, and must for ever be, alone, living and dying to myself, yet as sharing in the common intellect of the species and having a like origin and destiny, I move with a great multitude. My religion has been taught me from without no less than from within. Does the witness of history agree with that of science? Look up, I say, at the glorious sun of Reason shedding its light on the worlds beyond worlds of intellectual natures; and see who stands therein, radiant with heavenly sheen, yet like unto the Son of Man. The mightiest and most beautiful of all inductions, is that which has been founded on the life and the person of Christ. He is at once the measure of the universe, and the ideal, the incarnate Humanity, the rays and glories of which in other men are scattered and obscure. In Him all religious ideas meet and are crowned. God, Conscience, Immortality; the Resurrection of the flesh; the taking of Humanity unto the Godhead; the triumph of goodness by suffering, and of love by self-sacrifice—surely, "the demonstration of all this would be the best and noblest preamble of all our laws." But unless Jesus of Nazareth lived in vain, and His existence was a mockery, and His death the highest achievement of atheism and scepticism— a scandal which declares that there is no law of justice in things, and that the world is a moral chaos—He has given us the demonstration we were seeking. Science, however, content to have led us along the steep until we have attained this fair prospect, and begin to fasten our gaze upon the revelation of God *in facie Christi Jesu*, now draws modestly behind, and like Virgil when Dante needed his guidance no longer, abandons its disciple to better and holier hands:

> " Io vidi già nel cominciar del giorno
> La parte oriental tutta rosata,
> E l'altro ciel di bel sereno adorno;
> E la faccia del Sol nascere ombrata,
> Si che, per temperanza di vapori,
> L'occhio lo sostenea lunga fiata."*

> * *Purgatorio*, xxx. 22-28.

The Incarnation is the centre of man's history, and the pledge of his future. It transfigures science. But science in disclosing the eternal laws, has shown us how all things are governed by "an intelligent will bent on the accomplishment of good." The sun of Reason is at once the shrine and the tabernacle of that true Christianity in which old ,and new receive their fulfilment, and the Divine Light is tempered to human eyes.

WILLIAM BARRY.

TEKAKWITHA.

OUR readers will hail a new biography now lying on the table before us. It is entitled *The Life and Times of Kateri Tekakwitha, the Lily of the Mohawks*, 1656–1680, by Ellen H. Walworth, author of *An Old World as seen through Young Eyes*. For the production of⸗ this work in print we are indebted to the press of Peter Paul, & Brother, of Buffalo, an enterprising, growing, and pushing firm of publishers.

We are led to review this book from an early and some-what intimate acquaintance with the author and her surround-ings, and not a little from a sympathetic interest in Indian archæology, and still more particularly in this Mohawk Lily and that beautiful valley where her beautiful life first took root. We know the valley well. Many of the localities so vividly emphasized in this book are to be counted among the sweet-est haunts of our boyhood. We thank the fair author for bring-ing them back to us, and for giving us such strong reasons to love them better than ever.

Our first acquaintance with the name and life of Tekakwitha dates back as far as 1853 or 1854. In an interview with John Gilmary Shea, the historian, then a young man and growing into fame, he spoke of this rare Indian maiden in terms so glowing that we have never lost sight of her since. He spoke of her as a saint who ought to be canonized, and whose canonization was even then looked forward to as a probability by many prelates both in Canada and in the United States. To our eyes ever since she presides over the Mohawk Valley like a guardian spirit, whose prayers at the throne of grace are a perpetual benediction to it and to our country. We were impatient to know the exact spot where in it her life originated, and where her home was be-

fore she fled from her wrathful uncle and revengeful tribesmen
to the new Mohawk mission founded by the Jesuits on the
southern shore of the Saint Lawrence. We asked Mr. Shea, as
the man who should know if any one knew. He could not tell
us. It was somewhere, he thought, on the heights that circle
Fonda, in Montgomery County; precisely where, no one could
tell. It was doubtful if any one would ever know. We consulted Dr. O'Callaghan with no better results.

In fine, although memories of Indian wars and trade with Indians, in Tekakwitha's life, hovered over the valley, there was for
these no special foothold to which we could direct our attention
and say:

> " It is the spot, I know it well,
> Of which our old traditions tell.'

Battles were fought along the line of this valley of intense
interest to the American historian and archæologist, to which
names were attached and the results known, but these had no
local habitation. Catholic missionaries had trodden through the
valley with bleeding feet. Some of these had left mutilated fingers along its trails, and sometimes their scalps had been hung
up to dry in the Indian lodges; but just where, no one could
tell. Tekakwitha herself, sweet Indian saint, had taken part in
many tragic scenes. Indian castles had been burnt to the ground
before her eyes. Mohawk warriors had contended with Mohe-
gans, Delawares, Andastes, Eries, and other warlike tribes, and
her hands had supplied lead for the defence of her home and
water to quench burning palisades. But just where all this happened no one knew. In fact, until lately few cared to know.
Now, however, a great interest has gathered about these matters,
and many are eagerly asking for information.

Miss Ellen Walworth steps in opportunely with hands full of
gathered treasures. It has cost her much time and great labor
to gather up these things. The preface to her book shows what
research has been employed, what manuscripts have been de-
ciphered and transcribed, what libraries have been ransacked,
what clues have been sought for in conversations with eminent
historians to furnish her with materials. But this has been only
a small part of her task. A perusal of the very first chapter of
her book reveals an intimate acquaintance with Indian habits,
costumes, industries, tools and weapons, rites and customs, traits
of Indian character. These things are not easily acquired or in
any short time, but they are described by her with an easy
familiarity.

Another thing quite delightful in the book is, that the author knows perfectly well the localities which she describes. She has been there. She has climbed, the hills, forded the brooks, followed the trails. She has gathered trophies from the fields where once old wigwams clustered. She has inspected the ash-heaps blackening the soil where once old lodge-fires blazed. She has visited the corn-fields and counted the corn-pits. She has picked up beads, mussel-shells, bones of the wild deer, teeth of the bear, thrown aside after Indian festivals; and she has stood where the bones of Indian warriors lay before her, just disinterred from their resting places. She has sketched the sites of Iroquois castles and villages with an enthusiastic and busy pencil; and when she describes them she gives a life and color to the scenery which we could get from no stranger.

In fine, the "young eyes" which in 1873 looked eagerly upon the "Old World," and came home to report to us what they saw, are now telling us of old things which they have found in this our New World, and which the most of us have never seen. What was only prehistoric myth in the hands of Schoolcraft, Longfellow, Hoffman, and others is now acquired history. Hiawatha is no longer a beautiful dream of a supposed Indian bard who,

> "In the Vale of Tawasentha,
> In the green and pleasant valley,
> Sang the song of Hiawatha."

He is no longer the great-grandson of the Moon and the son of the great West-wind, Mudjekeewis, who pelted his unnatural father with vast fragments of rock torn from the cliffs of the Rocky Mountains; he is now simply an historical personage, an Onondaga chief, whose epoch is familiar to us and whose dwelling place we know. He lived on the shores of Cross Lake, an expansion of the Seneca River. Minnehaha is no longer a child of the Mississippi valley. She was a genuine New-Yorker, and her merriest and loudest laughter broke forth when the great chief saw her leap the rapids of the Oswego River, smiling back on him as she glided into Lake Ontario.

The daughter of Hiawatha was not slain by a marvellous bird of prodigious size swooping down upon her on the bank of Onondaga Lake, as the legend reads in Clark's "Onondaga," but she was cruelly trampled to death by connivance of another fierce eagle, Atotarho, the great sachem and war-chief of the Onondagas, who drove their grief-stricken father into exile among the Mohawks. Thanks to the researches of Dr. Horatio

Hale, we know much of the lives of these great chiefs, the principal founders of the Long House, or celebrated League of the Six Nations. *Miss Walworth introduces us to much of this myth-land now turned into history, all in truth that is necessary to understand and illustrate the life and times of the Lily of the Mohawks, and those who neglect the intellectual feast which she offers us in this volume will miss a rare treat.

The life of Tekakwitha is concurrent with the heroic missionary work done in the Mohawk Valley by a succession of martyrs and confessors of the Jesuit order. Much of all this is introduced in Miss Walworth's narrative. In this same narrative are also introduced many other matters of great import. New England savages, resisting the entreaties of their missionary, Eliot, come rushing into the valley, threatening its inhabitants and the work of the blackrobes with ruin. In the midst of all this life of missionary labor, of long and persevering privation and suffering, frequently crowned with martyrdom ; the marching of disciplined soldiery and the light footsteps of Indian braves on the warpath ; the smoke of burning villages ; relieved now and then by peaceful times devoted to hunting and fishing, still almost always a life of wandering, glided the form of Tekakwitha. She was a contemplative spirit, shunning society and loving the deep silence of the forest, yet destined to become more famous and more widely known, both in the United States and in Canada, than any of the generals or great sachems who once challenged the attention of this western world. In this book she comes to the front with all the romance which the wild woods can give her, with all that lustre of holiness which heroic Christian virtues shed around her—a true child of the forest, with a spirit as pure and beautiful as any angel of the cloister.

Old Albany knew her footsteps. She came with her tribe to the fishing village at the mouth of the Norman's Kill. Many burials took place at this spot. The Kenwood Convent now stands built above Indian graves. Her uncle, a warlike chief of the Turtles, was also a trader, bringing furs to the Dutch of Beaverwyck, and sometimes sitting with them in council as early as when Pieter Schuyler, the first mayor, was a boy. Passing back again to her forest home, her canoe glided under the stockades of Corlaer, now Schenectady. On her flight northward from that angry uncle she climbed the heights at Amsterdam, now a

" —clattering factory town
Where the choked Choctanunda plunges down.'

This escape of the saintly maiden from the rapids on the Mohawk to the grander rapids on the St. Lawrence, above Montreal, took place in the autumn of the year 1677. It introduces
us to a new epoch in her life. She is no longer a convert
struggling to maintain her faith in a community of heathen
savages, but where all around her are striving for Christian perfection she is a leading spirit, marching far before the rest, and
leading a life which the most zealous of her companions regard
as marvellous. Here the Lily of the Mohawks wins her new
title, "the Genevieve of New France." She stands on ground
destined to take its name from her. It is called the "Côte St.
Catherine."

Thus far we have spoken chiefly of the subject of this biography, and such surroundings as are necessary to characterize
and illustrate it. What these are Miss Walworth has taught us
herself to understand and appreciate. It would be a sad oversight if we should leave unnoticed the thoughtful method and
admirable art with which she has fulfilled her task. She has
never for a moment forgotten that the life of Tekakwitha, when
presented with the severest truth and most scrupulous accuracy,
is always by sheer necessity a romance in real life. This calls
for a certain freedom from such conventional rules as would reduce a beautiful history to an elaborated skeleton. During the
first part of her life, whether heathen or Christian, Kateri is
made to stand before us a true child of the forest, with her Indian leggings and moccasins on, with the leathern skirt and
tunic, her dark eyes gleaming from under the usual blanket of
an Indian squaw. When standing better revealed in the Christian sunlight of the mission village of the Sault, surrounded by
all the practices of Catholic devotion and trained to perfection
by the best of spiritual guides, her thoughtful biographer is still
careful to give us the picture of a living and breathing woman,
and not a saint analyzed into a corpse. We are not obliged to
read through one chapter on her humility, another on her obedience, followed by others on faith, hope, charity, and then, last
and longest of all, a catalogue of miracles, all wonderful to relate, but without a moral. All through, our Indian virgin has
breath in her body and life in her soul. Moreover, we are glad
to notice that the style of the author is also varied with equal
good judgment. It is not modelled after Cæsar's Commentaries,
always historical with perfect angularity, nor always dancing off
to gyrate among the clouds and flowers and birds and breezes.
She does not stop to moralize at given stations. In fine, she is

about as free from mannerism as can be expected from any author. All this enables us conscientiously to recommend this book
as a most readable composition, well studied and truthful, and
yet full of life, blood, and color.

All Catholics in Canada and the United States who have become interested in this fair flower of the American forest sympathize with their bishops in solemn council, and with her red
brethren, who have so earnestly petitioned the Holy Father to
put the church's seal upon the sanctity of their "Little Sister."
When the business of her canonization is seriously taken up at
Rome, that will be the time to catalogue her virtues according
to the formal methods of the Sacred Congregation of Rites. The
American public will be glad to look upon that life as it was
really lived—a beautiful whole, a lily with all its life and color
well blended. So a loving hand has given it to us in the present volume.

We could very willingly indulge in a much longer and more
elaborate review of this timely book, but limits of space have
been assigned to us and we must hasten to a close.

Near the eastern bank of the little Portage Creek, on the
southern side of the St. Lawrence, and overlooking the rocks and
floods of the great Sault St. Louis near Montreal, stands a tall
wooden cross which can be seen from afar and from many directions. It marks the grave of Tekakwitha, a spot where she
loved to pray when living, and where her body was buried.
Very recently a solid granite monument, in form of a sarcopha-
gus, has also been placed there by loving hands to her memory.
An inscription on its upper surface, in the Iroquois language,
bears this testimony to the beauty of her character:

ONKWE ONWE-KE KATSITSIIO TEIOTSITSIANEKARON.

That is: "She is the Fairest Flower of the Red Race." A
more valuable and a more lasting monument than this, however,
is the book itself. The granite could only cover a few feet of
ground where her precious body was laid to rest, but the book
itself preserves to us the memory of her beautiful soul, her grand
and noble fortitude, and the sanctity and sweetness which made
her life so lovely.

We close this remarkable volume and lay it down with a
sigh, and have only these last words to utter, which we do with
all our heart: "*She is the Fairest Flower of the Red Race.*"

Note to the Foregoing Article.

Bishop Kip, of the Protestant Episcopal diocese of California, in his *Early Jesuit Missions* has reproduced in print a letter from Cholenec, missionary in Canada, to his superiors, containing a condensed account of the life of his spiritual pupil, Kateri Tekakwitha. Kip does not fail to praise, in the preface to this book, the zeal and self-sacrifice of the missionaries to whose labors Christianity owes this star of virtue and so many other converts from the American wilderness. It would have been well if he could have ended this generous tribute in a more generous way. Human respect, however, stepped in, as it often does, and he blotted a truthful page in deference to the prejudices of kinsfolk in religion less generous. He says in his preface :

" There is one thought, however, which has constantly occurred to us in the preparation of these letters, and which we cannot but suggest. Look over the world and read the history of the Jesuit missions. After one or two generations they have always come to naught. There is not a recorded instance of their permanency, or their spreading each generation wider and deeper, like our own missions in India. Thus it has been in China, Japan, South America, and our own land. For centuries the Jesuit foreign missionaries have been like those ' beating the air.' And yet greater devotion to the cause than theirs has never been seen since the apostles' days. Why, then, was this result? If ' the blood of the martyrs be the seed of the church,' why is this the only instance in which it has not proved so? Must there not have been something wrong in the whole system, some grievous errors mingled with their teaching, which thus denied them a measure of success proportioned to their efforts ? "

How contrary to actual fact comes in this treacherous after-stab in the side is simply marvellous. Caughnawaga on the St. Lawrence, the very mission of Mohawk converts to which Tekakwitha fled from the older Caughnawaga in the Mohawk valley, contains thirteen hundred Catholic Indians whose faith is an inheritance of two centuries and a quarter, the lasting fruit of the early Jesuit missionaries and martyrs commemorated by Bishop Kip. The same may be said of the mission at Regis, the majority of Indians there being Catholics, with a Catholic church and priest. The like is true of the Sulpitian mission at Oka, Lake of the Two Mountains.

It was long before the fruits of the missions among the Iroquois were made to disappear from the United States. Two centuries of political intrigue and persecution and violation of treaties, during the greater part of which it was death by law in New York even for white men to be Catholics, have failed to obliterate the work of the missions.

During a Redemptorist mission at Wilmington, Del., Father Alexander Czwitkowitz carried the sacraments to a very old and bed-ridden Indian, who had fought on the Brandywine under La Fayette. He was an Onondaga and the son of a chief. About ten years ago an old squaw, said to be 104 years old, died in the Catholic faith on the reservation near Syracuse. She, too, was a relic from the old Jesuit missions—so far as we know, the last one left. The writer of this article. saw her in her own house, and conversed with her through an interpreter.

In no sense of the word have the missions in China, Japan, and South America been failures. In spite of the unparalleled persecutions of anti-Christian and un-Christian governments, the converted tribes of South America never relapsed into paganism. They are Catholic to-day. When, after centuries of exclusion, Europeans were permitted to enter China and Japan, thousands of Catholics were found in the former, and in the latter country to the number of 25,000. So far from the fruits of the Catholic missions having perished, they appear to be imperishable, and the blood of the martyrs has been the seed of the church in these lands.

THE POPULAR SCIENCE MONTHLY ON THE MIRACLES OF ST. FRANCIS XAVIER.*

IN a series of articles, entitled "New Chapters in the Warfare of Science," *The Popular Science Monthly* entertains us with a chapter or two on Miracles and Medicine. The scope of these studies is to present new difficulties against religion and Christianity, from the side of those who put their faith in Evolution. Miracles, which indicate the interposition of a supernatural and divine will in the affairs of this world, happen to find no adequate expression in prevalent scientific formulas. Quite otherwise. Indeed, on barely touching them, Science beholds them dissolving into the thin air of legend, and of a credulity somewhat pious and somewhat pardonable up to this.

Among the other estimable parts of the disquisition which Dr. A. D. White expends on the miracles of ⸜St. Francis Xavier, the very choicest element, as I take it, is that little phrase in which he seems to promise "a more extended discussion of this subject hereafter." There is some reason to believe, and I trust it is so, that this gentle phrase covers a more coarsely sounding idea, to wit, that he has not as yet studied the subject at all. His tentative article, therefore, is naturally inferior to the future extended discussion which he promises; and the few blemishes which mar the present production need not be supposed' to attach either to the integrity of his purpose or the solidity of his prospective erudition.

This part of his general discussion on the Warfare of Science is of a kind which, for the present stage of science manifested in it, would dispense an inquirer from consulting any other part. The same possibly might' be said whatever chapter it was that an inquirer first lighted on; he would prefer to encounter such erudition at a later stage of evolution, when, as the writer gently says, "the future extended discussion of the subject hereafter" will be in order. For, in the chapter before us, his set purpose being to explain away, by a theory of legendary evolution, the recorded miracles of St. Francis Xavier, he seems to omit · everything which, on the face of it, is too difficult to explain away; and on the residue he exercises some

* *The Popular Science Monthly*, May, 1891. "New Chapters in the Warfare of Science." Part I. By Andrew D. White, LL.D., L.H.D., ex-President of Cornell University.

ingenuity. The logical instinct at bottom, however little of it appears on the surface, is very correct. Every miracle in the history of the church has to go. If one remains, it were useless to deny the rest. For one proves as much as a thousand.

Selecting the history of St. Francis Xavier, whereby all the rest shall stand or fall, the writer contends that the miracles· recorded of him are a legendary growth ; that, from the small beginnings of certain trivial facts, the story of his miracles grew with time. To show this he makes selections of his own, which he presents in a way of his own. He quotes books which he has not read ; for otherwise ·he could scarcely quote them for what they do not contain, nor omit to see what they do contain. Not only does he cite some books which do exist for what is not in them, but he quotes an author and book that never existed for what he seems to have read therein. As there is a world of testimony regarding the deeds and life of St. Francis Xavier, he ventures just once, in the course of his article, to take a look askance at the evidence in a juridical process ; but, with a scientific instinct, he discharges against it the argument of his imagination, and then withdraws promptly into the legendary mist. "We can well imagine," he says, with some complacency in the conclusiveness of his logic, "what treasures of grace an obsequious viceroy, only too anxious to please a devout king, could bring together by means of the hearsay of ignorant, compliant natives through all the little towns of Portuguese India ! " This is the way that evolution addresses itself to facts. We, for our part, need not imagine what the issue is likely to be. We have it before us. To discredit anything which stands in his way, it is enough for the writer to throw out in a note some invidious suggestion, and then refer in general to some writer or other whom he does not expect to see consulted, for his reference is not distinct. Once, indeed, he condescends to apply a strictly logical criterion for testing the authenticity of historical accounts. However, he does so only when he has omitted this very criterion at an earlier place, where it would have been of use but against him, and he brings it forward at a later juncture, where it is of no use whatever, but does him no harm, while it lends an air of erudition. Not to weary the reader with more generalities, before descending to particulars, I will mention in the last place that, as to the miracles of St. Francis Xavier, he rests the arguments for their historical authenticity on such assumptions as show that he cannot be assumed to understand either the facts or the law of the case.

Let us distinguish two elements in this characteristic piece of periodical erudition. One is the manner in which a scientific evolutionist goes about demolishing facts. The other is the matter, or the particular edifice, which, on this occasion, he has set himself to pull down. I shall first consider the manner of this evolutionist philosopher.

The life of St. Francis Xavier was a public one of the most singularly brilliant order, sufficiently honored, in this respect, by the marked attention which it has always commanded in the non-Catholic world, and non-Catholic literature. In the course of his ten years of Eastern ministry he dealt personally with millions of people, speaking a variety of tongues, in all the countries of Hindustan, Cochin China, Japan. During those same years, while he was riveting the eyes of all the East upon himself and his movements, Europe too was looking on, and was receiving accounts, through public and private sources, of the many wonders which he was performing in the sight of the nations. Maffei, who addresses Philip II. of Spain in 1588, and dedicates to his majesty the *History of the East*, finished up to date from the time of the first Portuguese discovery by sea, stops, in the course of his general relation, some three times to follow St. Francis Xavier alone, as if the saint summed up in himself a part of the general history. Having given forty-eight pages in all to the progress of Xavier, and coming to the saint's funeral at Goa, the historian apologizes for not saying more. "Others," says Maffei, "recounted his infallible predictions and miracles—many more, indeed, than we have touched upon, hurrying on, as we have done, to fulfil another purpose."*

While Xavier's own gift as a letter-writer made him communicate without stint the varied information which he gathered concerning the field for religion, and the progress of the faith in those new parts, a marked contrast was visible between his letters, as far as they concerned himself or his works, and the other letters which were transmitted at the same time from the religious and official world in the East, as well as from members of the Society of Jesus. Orlandini, who was a contemporary of the saint, but of a younger generation, notes the contrast thus : "He writes about his own affairs sparingly and dryly, while at the same time very much is written about him, profusely and copiously, both by people in the world and by members of the order."† Particularly at the European universities did St. Francis intend to stimulate the activity of apostolic

* Lib. xv. p. 668, Edit. Cadonj, 1614.   † *Historiæ Soc. Jes.*, lib. viii. n. 129.

zeal; hence the fulness of his accounts, but not about himself.
With all his zeal, it cost him little to practise Christian humility.
Nor does it enter into the idea of sanctity, as conceived by the
Catholic Church, that a man should extol and advertise himself.

So prominent, nevertheless, was the miraculous side of Francis Xavier's ministry, that during the first thirty-five years after
his death, the more ordinary personal effects of his life were left
in the background, and the supernatural wonder-worker was the
figure before the world. A desire became pronounced to know
more and more about the intimate workings of his personal
sanctity. A life was called for which should bring them out
into greater prominence. This was the reason why Tursellini
wrote. He says in his preface: "I saw, indeed, that the chief
events in Xavier's life were inserted with magnificence enough
in the histories of others; but I could not help taking it amiss
that, during more than thirty-five years, not one had undertaken
to consign to a volume of its own a life adorned with all kinds
of virtues." Then, modestly undertaking the work himself, at
the instance of others, Tursellini goes on to affirm "that of the
literary records which are extant, and which have come to my
hands, I will select only such facts as have been ascertained on
certain authority, to wit, from people who have either seen
themselves what they report, or have received it from those who
did see."

With this object, therefore, of showing Francis Xavier himself, and not of recording his miraculous exploits, Tursellini
writes the life. Yet he cannot omit a fair account of the miracles. To the well-informed writer in *The Popular Science Monthly*
these miracles, as recorded in Tursellini, appear "few and small."
For once he is right; but in a sense quite different from what
he intends. "Few and small" as they are, I will just count
them up; and, being "few and small," they give us an inkling
of the world of miraculous exploits which Tursellini does not
touch, but only classifies here and there in general summaries.

From book i., chapter x., in which the biographer tells of
Xavier's arrival in Lisbon, to chapter iii., book vi., Tursellini records fifty-one distinct miracles and prophecies, besides summaries of others, all before Xavier's death. Then, in the following
chapter, he recounts nine distinct prodigies, besides summaries of
others, all after death. Among the prodigies distinctly recorded
by Tursellini are most of those subsequently chosen by the
court in Rome for juridical examination, on which to base the

* De Vita Francisci Xaverii, lib. i. præfatio.

process of canonization. He describes the raising of four persons from the dead; the loss of the skiff in the storm and its miraculous recovery, with that most supernatural wonder of "bilocation" when Francis was in two places at the same time, both in the lost skiff, during the three days of its tossing about at the mercy of the storm, and in the ship, among the remaining passengers; the famous intimidation of the Badages, by throwing himself into the thick of the fight; the curing of a leper; "very many sick persons cured, many energumens delivered from evil spirits." At the funeral of the saint, about a year after his death, Tursellini goes on to recount that

"Francis was extolled to the skies, and his extraordinary deeds were recounted, his prophecies, his miracles, by those who either had seen and been witnesses of them, or had received the accounts from competent witnesses; all India, as with one voice, celebrating the sanctity of Xavier. And now new miracles were added to the old. Very many of those who had flocked to the spectacle (of his body miraculously preserved before their eyes at Goa, whereas he had died nearly a year before off the coast of China) affirmed under oath that certain persons came thither, some maimed in limb or decrepit, others suffering from various diseases; and that, by merely touching St. Francis Xavier's body, they had gone away sound and well."

All this is from Tursellini, the great authority with the writer in *The Popular Science Monthly* because the miracles recorded in Tursellini are "few and small," and therefore he is authorized to contradict all later accounts. Perhaps the erudite doctor can still reply that personally he does not believe even Tursellini and the sworn witnesses. This will be quite consistent with the rest of his demonstration, and with the original assumption underlying all, which is that we are on no account to demur to his own testimony, albeit he is not a witness, nor is he sworn to deliver the truth.

The later editions of Tursellini are fuller than the first one, because in the interval a new revelation of matter had become available for the purposes of the historian. He can explain the matter best himself. In a special *Præfatio ad Lectorem*, prefixed to the edition of 1596, he thus speaks of the earlier issue, published only two years before:

"I wrote some years ago the life of St. Francis Xavier with all possible fidelity and diligence. It was published in my absence; and when I came to see it I scarcely recognized it, so spoiled and overlaid was it with faults in the execution. Nor was it less faulty in that respect than deficient in matter.* The reason of this was that formerly, by command of the King of Portugal, the Viceroy of India had, indeed, investigated the recorded deeds of Francis, and had for the most part communicated and sent on the accounts of Xavier's brilliant career within the Portuguese dominion. But not all of these had been included, only such being entered as could be obtained from competent witnesses then within reach; and as to the rest, particularly as to what he had done among the Chinese and Japanese, however memorable and illustrious, all this remained for the most part in silence and obscurity. Now, however, when this part of his history, as narrated by those who at that time were in China or Japan, came at length into my hands, I was not unwilling to translate the records into Latin as soon as possible, and insert them faithfully in their own places. . . . Of the new records so great was the abundance and brilliancy that, not to expand the original four books out of proportion, I had to extend them into six."

And at the beginning of the sixth book the author returns to the same point, dwelling in one entire chapter on the authentic character of the records, the sworn testimonies, the access he has had to them, and other points, regarding testimony, truth and fidelity, which it would be quite in harmony with the interests of science to bring before the notice of popular writers to-day, of *vulgarisateurs* in magazines, if only they thought it worth their while to regard such indifferent matters. But as probably they will not, and our space is limited, we pass on.

We may observe that, up to the date of Tursellini, and much later still, there was an evolution going on, not of facts, but of testimonies and processes—a phenomenon so ordinary, in the drawing up of authentic history, that we see in our own days new lives of Washington, new lives of Charles V., new lives even of Julius Cæsar, issuing from the archives of history. These characters lived a good many generations ago, and we are not aware that judicial bodies are in session upon the deeds and records which concern them. In the case of St. Francis Xavier juridical processes were in order from the day his incorrupt body reached Goa till his canonization was an accomplished fact, seventy years later; during which period the eye-witnesses, their children and grandchildren, were within reach. That these witnesses were thus within reach, during the process of investigation, escaped the writer in the *Popular Monthly*. But the moment that their day was past, they sail within reach of his ken; and, with a flourish of erudition, not without a flavor of logical taste, he brings in the criterion with solemnity.

---

* Adeo multis eam mendis inquinatam atque oblitam vidi. Nec mendosa magis quam manca prodiit in lucem.

He says: "It must be remembered that Bouhours, writing ninety years after Tursellini, could hardly have had access to any really new sources. Xavier had been dead one hundred and thirty years, and of course all the natives upon whom he had wrought his miracles, and their children and grandchildren, were gone." So says this writer, with solemnity, acumen, and truth. And therefore we résumé in his own words, replying: It must be remembered that Tursellini, writing ninety years before Bouhours, and only forty years after the death of Xavier, could really have had access to new sources; and the natives upon whom he had wrought his miracles, and their children and grandchildren, were not gone. This scientific writer does not see deep enough into his own argument to catch the manifest retort staring out of it, nor to feel the rebound of a blank argument exploding. This is what I referred to before, when I said that he omits a strictly logical criterion at an earlier part of his discussion, where it would be of use but against him, and brings it forward at a later stage, where it is of no use whatever, only it does him no harm, while it lends an air of erudition.

It is of no use whatever as against Bouhours, for we shall see that our critic misses the point of the question with this later biographer, who, it is true, like other biographers of a later date, brings forward new facts, new miracles, wrought through the intercession of St. Francis Xavier. They are such as the earlier biographers had not mentioned, nor the process of canonization contained. But it was for the very recondite reason that the miracles in question, the manifold resurrections, had not yet been wrought; they have been going on since; they are going at present, like the standing miracle of the saint's body incorrupt to-day at Goa. And, of course, this scientist is not credulous enough to imagine that Tursellini should have prophesied, or that the Roman courts of canonization should have prophesied, what miracles were yet to come! When he dispenses himself, in truest scientific fashion, from verifying matters of palpable fact before his eyes; as, for instance, that of the body remaining incorrupt to-day at Goa, which fact is recorded in every one of the documents and authors ostentatiously paraded by him—a fact which is a miracle of the first order, alone sufficient to make everything else credible regarding St. Francis Xavier; when science can perform this feat of non-verification, and suppression of a palpable, visible fact, it should not be scandalized that men of the sixteenth and early seventeenth centuries did not prophesy what miracles in the centuries to come St. Francis Xavier was still going to work! Yet, innocently enough, the critic speaks thus: "In the time of Tursellini, four cases [of raising the dead to life] had been developed; in 1622, at the canonization proceedings, three were mentioned; but by the time of Father Bouhours, there were twenty-five." Charming! As if the twenty-five had evolved out of the three! In 1715 the number was not twenty-five but twenty-seven, recognized, says D'Aurignac, by the court of Rome at that date; but of the twenty-seven "fourteen had been wrought within a few years" previous to this date of 1715. D'Aurignac continues, at the same date, 1715, "the Bishop of Malacca had authenticated eight hundred miracles in his diocese alone.* Our legendary evolution imagines that all had developed out of an original small stock, an original suggestion, so to say, of proto-plasmic legend. The thought reveals the growth of a system, and how the wish is father to the products of this science.

Meanwhile, the recognized credit of proceedings in the Roman courts threatened to deal a fatal blow to the somewhat fanciful array of thought and imagination which figures in the pages of the *Science Monthly*. Hence the learned writer must endeavor to parry it. He does so, far on in the article, at the end of a long note full of references, such as might be readily gathered from encyclopædias or dictionaries. There he throws out this profound suggestion: "For some very thoughtful remarks as to the worth-lessness of the testimony to miracles presented during the canon-ization proceedings at Rome, see Maury, *Legendes Pieuses*." That is all! Not another word about the Roman processes, their juri-dical and protracted examinations, the evidence of eye-witnesses. We conclude that the proceedings of the Roman courts must be excellent indeed, if this is all that can be said against them.

He has so little use for evidence of any kind that he never once faces it. He is provoked to do so, if ever a writer was, by the constant reference made to it in the documents which he makes us believe he is using. The bull of canonization is explicit on the subject of the juridical processes and investigations. He cannot have quoted his page from Cardinal Del Monte's speech or *Relatio in Consistorio secreto coram S. D. N. Gregorio Papa XV. facta*, without having his taste for the evidence keenly whetted. Nay, he quotes from Father Coleridge, to the right and the left; but, with a sensitive instinct and a marked agility, he skips over the evidence between. Speaking of Xavier's gift of tongues, he quotes from Coleridge certain passages which refer to the saint's use of interpreters—such passages as an intelligence clerk could

* *Histoire de St. François de Xavier*, par J. M. S. d'Aurignac; 1862, 8mo, part v. p. 261.

have hunted up for him. He leaves out the evidence between the passages. Nay, on the very same page to which he refers in Father Coleridge, as against Xavier's gift of tongues, he does not see this note, only two lines long, and therefore not over-tedious to read: "We hope," says Coleridge, "to give a short abstract of the results of the evidence as to the gift of tongues, in the case of St. Francis, further on (book v. note 2).* The writer in the *Monthly* carefully eschews that note, though he refers to the pages there. Indeed, he eschews what is in the pages themselves, or he could never have written that unintelligible critique on the gift of tongues with which he has filled two of his own valuable pages.

It is to be presumed that a clerk looked up "tongues" in the table of contents of Father Coleridge, gave the number of the page to the doctor, who in due form entered the number, and, on the strength of this and other such original work, catalogued a list of works in a long note, as if he had consulted them. To this he could add with perfect conscientiousness: "In addition to these, I have compared, for a more extended discussion of this subject hereafter, a very great number of editions of these and other biographies of the saint, with speeches, etc." Now, among these that he has thus compared, I notice the Life by Vitteleschi, 1622. He quotes Vitteleschi several times in his text. Who is Vitteleschi, that wrote a life of St. Francis Xavier? There is no such person and no such life. I cannot identify the work quoted, unless it be an edition of the same Tursellini whom he has just named. Naturally, the later edition of Tursellini, in 1621, would have the imprimatur of a later general, Mutius Vitteleschi, possibly under date of 1622. If that is the explanation, and it is the only one I can find, then the learned writer, supposing he ever saw any of the books which he cites, does not see that he is comparing the same work with itself, identical in its words. Yet he has a brilliant demonstration of legendary evolution, based precisely upon the difference between Tursellini in 1596 telling a story about Xavier and Vellio, and "twenty-six years later, Vitteleschi, in his Life of Xavier, telling the story"! He is showing how each biographer "surpassed his predecessor in the multitude of miracles." And he goes on to prove this broad thesis, in his own characteristic way, by a solitary example: "One example will suffice to show the process!" And what is this classic example, to show biographer improving on biographer? Apparently, the

---

* *Life and Letters of St. Francis Xavier*, by Rev. J. H. Coleridge, S.J., vol. i. book ii. ch. ii. p. 173, edition of 1886.

same biographer and the same page, quoted from different edi-tions; for the difference between the two accounts is so slight that we suspect the variable quantity is in the translations, not in the originals. However, this scientific writer is none the wiser for the ineptitude. He is pleased with the amplitude of his demon-stration. And he contributes* this logic as "New Chapters in Science."

We might entertain ourselves in like manner with the doctor's reference to Maffei's *History of India.* Says the critic: "Though he [Maffei] gave a biography of Xavier which shows fervent ad-miration for his subject, he dwelt very lightly on the alleged mira-cles." It is novel to be told that, in a history 718 pages long, forty-eight pages devoted to the prominent figure of St. Francis Xavier is a biography which, by what it does not say, is to dis-credit what full biographies do say. And yet, as to Maffei's tes-timony about the miracles, nothing could be fuller. I have quoted it a few pages above.

Nor would our literary amusement be inferior if we could catechize this scientific writer upon the other names which figure in his pages—Acosta, Nunes, De Quadros—as well as on a little history and geography, as to how De Quadros, a missionary in the depths of Ethiopia, could be appealed to, in 1555, for evi-dence as to what Xavier had been doing in Hindustan up to three years before. When did the telegraph or the steam pack-ets come into use between Hindustan and Ethiopia; or even the penny-post? Why run off to Ethiopia for testimony about Xavier, when all India was alive with the facts? Why? Pre-cisely because all India was alive with the knowledge of the facts, and Europe too, that the modern investigator runs off to Ethiopia for testimony, and says he does not find it!

But there is an assumption underlying all this, yes, and an assertion overtopping all, both of which I shall briefly consider, and so finish these animadversions on the manner of addressing one's self to a scientific question.

The assumption is that, if St. Francis Xavier wrought mira-cles, his own letters should prove them, by the accounts which he himself gives of them. The assertion is, that no contemporary documents have anything about the miracles—except some "fee-ble beginning."

The assumption looks a little weak. To strengthen it, and reassure it, he thinks it necessary to have Xavier's own biogra-phers accept it.

Accordingly he passes it off on them in these terms: "*It*

seems to have been felt as somewhat strange at first that Xavier had never alluded to any of these wonderful miracles." So he fathers the assumption upon the biographers; that they, of course, expected to have the saint preach about his own miracles. Now, the doctor's assumption being thus slipped into the question, the legendary evolution can go on apace; or, to use his own terms, "the process of incubation goes on." For, at once all the accounts of Xavier's humility, and his blushing at the very mention of his having raised the dead, may come in as "subsidiary legends." Says the doctor: "Ere long a subsidiary legend was developed, to the effect that one of the brethren asked him one day if he had raised the dead, whereat he blushed deeply and cried out against the idea, saying, 'And so I am said to have raised the dead!' etc."

A subsidiary legend! Let us dissect the critical mind which uses those two words in this subject matter. First, "subsidiary"; it so happens that his own Tursellini has this account, at the very beginning of the line of biographers; therefore, neither is it a subsidiary element, nor has the doctor read Tursellini.* Secondly, "legend"; it must indeed be a legend, for the idea of a saint's being humble and modest, if not a legend, must, to a mind like this writer's, be a miracle. And of course that cannot be. Therefore it is a legend.

This class of mind, which would invite a clinical study, sinks the saints of the Catholic Church, if they are wonder-workers like St. Francis Xavier, into the crowd of "Jansenists at the cemetery of St. Medard," and "of the various Protestant sects at Old Orchard and elsewhere"; if, like St. Vincent de Paul, they are devoted to a life of mercy in the walks of civilization, it sinks them amid the Florence Nightingales, Howards, Franckes, and the rest. It is not strange. In a mist we cannot distinguish features. And I suppose the primordial mist wherein the incubation of evolution goes on is no exception to the rule. All colors are alike in the dark.

Now for the assertion: which is, that no contemporary document has anything about Xavier's miracles except "a feeble beginning." This extraordinary assertion rests upon an assumption of its own—that we prove matters of fact by documents. Usually, in matters of fact, witnessed with eye and ear, common-sense people refer to the evidence of eye and ear; and court-rooms, acting on this common-sense principle, test the intelligence and credibility of witnesses. It was in this manner,

---

* *Vita*, lib. ii. ch. x. p. 162, edit. 1614.

certainly, that all the investigations had to be rigidly conducted at Goa, from the time of Francis Xavier's funeral, and
again at Rome, up to the date of his canonization. Not so
with this scientific critic of facts. He says: "No account of a
miracle wrought by him appears either in his letters or in any
contemporary document." But first, we may ask, why does he
never make mention of eye-witnesses until he comes to Bouhours, one hundred and thirty years after Xavier's death? Is it
because then he is at a safe distance from them? Secondly,
what does he mean by contemporary documents? Newspapers,
telegraphic dispatches? He is not distinct. If he means these
we need not demur. If he means the self-glorification of sectarian ministers belonging to Bible societies, we need only refer
him to Macaulay for an estimate of their work in Hindustan;
and Macaulay wrote from personal observation there. But if he
insinuates that the letters of Xavier's contemporaries, the sworn
and recorded testimonies of eye-witnesses, the uniform consent
of whole populations, who without having scientific versatility
could possibly have native truth and common sense, and could
see what they saw and say so—if he insinuates that all these
did not testify to an endless number of miracles performed by
St. Francis Xavier, then we need only animadvert upon this
writer's frame of mind, by repeating his assertion and entire
demonstration in all its naked majesty and integrity: "No account of a miracle wrought by him appears either in his own
letters or in any contemporary document." We need only
rehearse the remoter demonstrations thence deduced. For, without adding any element to this proof, except a faulty enumeration of contemporaries, one of them being a missionary off in
Ethiopia, he proceeds to say abruptly, three pages later on:
"As we have seen, the missionaries of Xavier's time wrote
nothing regarding his miracles, and certainly the ignorant natives
of India and Japan did not commit any account of his miracles
to writing." "As we have seen!" To prove nothing and then
quote it! That is Herbert Spencer's most approved style of
demonstration. Finally, since this writer wants contemporary
documents, we need only turn round on him with an argument
ad hominem, and ask him, Why does he not take account of the
contemporary documents regarding the actual miracle going on
of St. Francis Xavier's body remaining incorrupt at Goa, subject
to inspection and verification?*

---

* The latest solemn exposition of Xavier's body was on December 3, 1890, and continued
during fifteen days. For an account of the immense concourse, and an indication of the miracles, see *Civilta Cattolica*, May 2, 1891, pp. 371-6.

As we cannot suppose that a dignified ex-president of Cornell University has followed such a manner of scientific treatment without some adequate occasion or sufficient reason, nor that, in undertaking to give this "simple statement" of "the evolution of miraculous accounts generally," he has deliberately intended to play the part of a partisan libeller of the Catholic Church, creed, and saints, we are of necessity thrown back on the line of his own reflections, and we must endeavor to explain away the discredit which, at first sight, seems to be thrown upon him. This can be done in two ways—in his own words, and in the light of some facts, which we can readily throw upon the subject.

Adapting his own words, we may benignly understand things thus: "It would be utterly unphilosophical to attribute" all this "as a whole to conscious fraud; whatever part" infidelity and *prêtrophobia* "may have taken in sundry discreditable developments, the mass of" evolutionary fancies and "legends grow up mainly in good faith, and as naturally as elms along watercourses or flowers upon the prairie." And again I adapt his words: "It is hardly necessary to attribute to" a scientist of this kind "a conscious attempt to deceive. The simple fact is that, as a rule, he thinks, speaks, and writes in obedience to the natural laws, which govern the luxuriant growth of myth and legend, in the warm atmosphere of love and devotion, which constantly arises" about a fond idea and a pet theory, "in times when there is little care for scientific evidence, and when he who believes most is thought most meritorious." These words of his own, adjusted to himself, suit the writer in *The Popular Science Monthly;* hence we may invite him to taste of his own condiments.

In the second place, a few facts would throw light upon the evolution of this article; and go far towards exonerating the critic, by showing whence he has taken all this matter. To be sure, this matter is given under the head of "New Chapters in the Warfare of Science." But that need not prevent me from indicating where it is all copied from, and how old it is. So we shall pass on to what I had signalized for criticism in the second place. For, after the writer's manner, I had undertaken to criticise his matter.

THOMAS HUGHES, S.J.

(TO BE CONCLUDED.)

THE ENCYCLICAL AND AMERICAN IRON-WORKERS
AND COAL-MINERS.

WHAT is known as the Labor Problem is the puzzle of the age. It has taxed the best minds in two hemispheres and the highest statesmanship to find an adequate solution. After years of close and careful study of the industrial question in its various phases honest men are still widely apart both in theory and the practical results of their investigation. And this applies to those who have been actual participants, whether on the side of labor or capital, in some of the most important labor contests of our day, just as much as it does to the looker-on or speculative thinker. Writers on political economy are no more agreed in their views and the application of their remedies than are the representatives of labor and capital. From the rankest Socialism to ultra-conservatism we discover every grade of opinion and doctrine.

So much disturbance has been created in society by the growth of false teaching on this subject and the frequent outbreak of strikes and lock-outs, that there is scarcely a nation that has not found it necessary to fully examine the question. Only a short time ago the young emperor of Germany succeeded in holding a labor conference in Berlin, which was attended by representatives from fourteen different countries. The business of this conference was to bring about an amelioration in the conditions of factory and mining labor. It settled upon five or six most important points, such as suspension of labor on Sunday, restriction of the work of children to those of a certain age, and the limitation of the work of women. In England a royal commission is at present engaged in investigating the labor question. The report of the commission on the eight-hour day and the condition of the working-men, especially in the mining and great manufacturing centres, will be looked for with much interest. Already steps have been taken to hold a general labor congress in Chicago during the Columbian Exposition of 1893. This congress will be arranged with the co-operation of the most distinguished students of labor problems and leaders in the industrial world. In its scope and aims there is everything in this movement to commend it. Its promoters are confident that the best results will follow from this labor congress; that a way may be found by which equal and exact justice will be finally rendered to employer and employed; the wasted possibilities of unorganized and unskilled, and therefore unproductive, labor shall be exchanged for trained and protective industry, which will nowhere allow poverty to be a necessity; and a means found for ending the suicidal war which at present threatens the world of industry; in short, that a peaceable and satisfactory solution will be reached of the grave questions in controversy and a higher and better industrial system established. These are high and noble aims. The true friends of the working-man and the capitalist, the students and specialists in industrial topics, and the representatives of the various organizations of labor and capital should aid in making the proposed congress a success. It would be to the lasting credit and glory of the United States, and the capacity of our people to solve the most difficult social and economic problems, if this Chicago Labor Congress should succeed in what it proposes.

But the clearest and fullest light comes to us on this vast and important subject, the Industrial Question, from that quarter toward which men's eyes have been anxiously directed. In the Encyclical of Leo XIII., *On the Condition of Labor*, the highest expectations of all who looked with interest for its promulgation are fulfilled. It is, indeed, the most important utterance, most opportunely given, of the Statesman-Pope. And that is much to say with the remembrance of his preceding encyclicals on the Christian Constitution of States and Human Liberty. Presented to the world in the midst of the religious feast of Pentecost, may we not hope that it shall be understood, in all languages, with something like the reverence paid to the inspired discourses of the Apostles? And may it assist in renewing the worn-out and unbalanced machinery of a suffering world!

It has been remarked that a century ago, in 1791, the French Revolution, by a definitive decree, abolished the corporations which formed the base of the ancient industrial order. In 1891 Leo XIII. promulgates a new economical charter at the very moment when industrial society, founded on the Manchester doctrines, tends towards ruin. And for this act of his the Pope receives a special message of congratulation from the present Republican government of France. Leo has well chosen this fateful hour to teach the world the true social gospel. After all, men must be brought to see that the Papacy is the only international power to-day in existence possessed of sufficient authority and strength, sufficiently sure of itself, and rich in light and energy, to attempt the supreme task of reconciling the contending forces of society. Across the "tottering thrones and drooping sceptres," Leo. XIII. notes the rising tide of democracy; he sees that the old order must give way to the new; that the twentieth century will be—what Cardinal Manning prophesies— the People's Century. It is Leo's harmonizing the eternal teachings of the Gospel with the actual necessities of the modern world that bestows on this Encyclical the character of a message of arbitration and makes it "the truce of God." And all this is accomplished with a perfect knowledge of the whole question; filled though it is with intrinsic and technical difficulties, with varying and constantly changing conditions. The composition of the Encyclical presupposes an acquaintance with the whole range of the vast literature of the subject of which it treats. This he has reduced to a clear and accurate statement of the entire case under the most important heads. It is only a master mind who could bear this Atlas-burden, and make such a synthesis.

All Christian tradition is embodied in its teaching. In reading the Encyclical the mind almost unconsciously reflects on the transforming action of the church in the world. It recalls the days of those celebrated monasteries where the religious became shoemakers, masons, carpenters, laborers, mingling manual labor with meditation and the chanting of the praises of God. It takes us back to the Apostles, who taught the rich to make due provision for the wants of the poor, so that "neither was there any one needy among them"; it revives the memories of the guilds of former ages; it suggests a picture of the artisan-monk, who in the austere silence of the Trappist's life realizes the dignity of labor. Nay, more, it carries the mind and heart of the reader back to Him who taught that "the laborer is worthy of his hire," and whose example, as the Carpenter of Nazareth, has merited for the working-man in every land that Christian nobility which constitutes his greatness before man and God.

What specially strikes one in studying this Encyclical is the fatherly tenderness and sympathy that is displayed by the Pope. He deals with the problems nearest the hearts of the common people : the right of private property in land ; the limits of the state's rights in relation to the higher rights of parents; the relations of capital and labor; the sacred rights of the wage-earner; differences between employers and employed ; strikes; the proper regulation of the hours of labor; and, lastly, working-men's guilds, insurance and beneficial societies.

In the first place, he clearly lays down the inviolability of private property, especially in land. For obvious reasons this teaching is of special interest, since it sets aside as false and contrary to sound morals the doctrines of Henry George and the Anti-Poverty Society. He shows how it is for the best interest of the wage-earner to maintain and stand by the true Catholic doctrine. He considers the methods of cure proposed by the Socialists as utterly futile, or as infinitely worse than the present evils of competition.

Having dealt with the fundamental principle of private property, the Pope proceeds to point out the necessity of religion for the solution of the difficulty.

"It is the church," writes Leo XIII., "that proclaims from the Gospel those teachings by which the conflict can be ended, or at least be made far less bitter than it is; the church uses its efforts not only to enlighten the mind, but to direct by its precepts the life and conduct of men; the church improves and ameliorates the condition of the working-man by numerous useful organizations; does its best to enlist the services of all ranks in discussing and endeavoring to meet, in the most practical way, the claims of the working classes; and acts on the decided view that for these purposes recourse should be had, in due measure and degree, to the help of the law and of state authority."

With this object in sight, after denouncing speculators in human labor, he urges the state to safeguard those boards of arbitration, wherever they exist, that help the workman to secure fair wages.

Let us examine closely the words of the Encyclical on this subject of wages; because ever since labor became free all the great disturbances in the industrial world have been chiefly caused by a difference between labor and capital on the rate of wages. It is here that the interests of employer and employed begin to diverge, and it is on the question of wages that strikes and lock-outs mostly originate. In an inquiry into the origin of strikes and lock-outs made at the last census, out of a total of 813 labor contests investigated 582, or over 71 per cent., were caused by differences as to rate of wages. Of these 582 contests 86 per cent. were for advances in wages, and 14 per cent. against reductions.

While these exact proportions will not hold in all years, nor in all sections and industries, it is safe to say that by far the most prolific sources of labor disputes are differences as to wages. It will also be found that many disputes that are not primarily disputes about wages have a direct bearing on rates of wages, and are important only because of such bearing. Apart from rates of wages the causes of these differences are legion. Trouble may arise concerning the basis of computing wages ; the method, time, or frequency of payment ; the store-system ; hours of labor ; the holidays and weekly half-holiday ; apprenticeship ; administration and methods of work, such as shop-rules, labor-saving machinery, piece-work, objectionable workmen ; trades-unions and their rules, and a thousand and one causes that we daily hear of. Notwithstanding their number, however, it will be found that all causes of difference readily group themselves into three general classes :

1st.—Differences as to future contracts.

2d.—Disagreements as to existing contracts.

3d.—Disputes on some matter of sentiment.

In the first division would be classified differences as to future rates of wages, and those arising from attempts to change or abrogate existing agreements, customs, or methods, or to introduce new ones. Disagreements under the second class arise either upon matters of fact or construction, having in view existing agreements, customs, or methods, and not necessarily involving the validity of the contracts themselves, nor any change in their terms. Under the third head are included those quarrels that grow out of the offended *amour propre* either of the individual or the organization.

It is in the first of these classes, " Differences as to future contracts," which, as stated, includes questions as to future rates of wages, that disputes most frequently occur and in which the gravest difficulties arise in harmonizing conflicting interests and hostile views. What is " a fair day's wage for a fair day's work," is a difficult and complex problem to solve. Concerning its solution there are honest differences of opinion even upon the basis or principle on which it shall be decided. With the ebb and flow of the tides of business, of prices and demand, so frequent in these days of the increased effectiveness of labor and rapid transportation ; with the constant changes in methods of production or conditions of work, and the introduction of improved machinery, so common in this age of invention, comes an ever-recurring necessity for a revision of the contracts or agreements governing the relation of employer and employed, and with it the possibility of differences as to what changes the new conditions demand.

Let us take, for instance, the iron and steel business, the

glass trade, or the coke industry of Western Pennsylvania, and we shall see at once how easy it is for difficulties to arise, unless there be found some means of forestalling them. The competition of trade, high or low tariff, the facilities and cheapness of transportation, the methods of production, and other conditions imply the necessity for frequent revision of agreements as to the rates of wages. Here in Pittsburgh, which is the heart and centre of the iron and steel interests of the country, the Amalgamated Association of Iron and Steel Workers holds an annual convention to determine the scale or rate of wages for the ensuing year. When the scale is agreed upon by the workers it is then submitted to the employers, and where differences are found they are eventually adjusted by conferences of both parties. This arrangement has worked successfully for years, there being only one notable instance, nine years ago, when it failed, and the result was a bitter and prolonged fight. The miners, coke and glass workers, have much more trouble in settling the question of wages. With them strikes and lock-outs are much more frequent, and are attended, as in the case of the terrible strike recently in the Pennsylvania coke region, where many lives were sacrificed and valuable property destroyed, with painful and disastrous results. The writer has witnessed the most intense suffering and want among workmen and their families as the consequence of these disturbances. And his limited experience is repeated by almost every clergyman in the mining and coking district of this State. Whilst preparing this paper I have been called upon by three or four poor men from the Connellsville coke region, who told a pitiful tale. " Father," said one man—and the tears came hot and fast as he spoke—" I have left behind me a wife and six children who are without a morsel of bread. Were it not for the aid of our good priest and some kind neighbors they would be starving. I am willing to work," he continued, " but I have been blacklisted by the operators and can find nothing to do." " Why not try something else for a living? Did you not belong to the labor union? Why does it not help you?" In answer to the first question he replied : " Father, you can see I am an old man now and it is useless for me to look for any other kind of work; employers do not want a man like me." " And how about the union? Did you not receive assistance from the ———s ? " To this he answered : " I had always a fear of joining them because I thought the church was opposed to the organization; and, furthermore, from what I could make out from hearsay, I honestly did not like some of their ways of doing business." The case of the others was similar, except that they belonged to the labor union, and, as they alleged, for that reason would not be taken back to work now that the strike was ended.

It is right here, on this important matter of wages, and on that of the usefulness and benefits of labor associations, that Americans especially will find in the Encyclical of Leo XIII. sound and practical principles of guidance. Let us analyze what he has laid down.

In the first place, it is to be observed that there is a wide divergence between the Pope's teaching and the views of most of modern political economists, for these proclaim that supply and demand is the great law that always and everywhere determines the rate of wages. And they insist that this law is inflexible. Hence it is held by the advocates of this cruel law that the working-man should be satisfied with the market price of his labor, whether that be high or low. Profits or the selling price of the manufactured article have no direct bearing on the rate of compensation that the working-man receives. His wages are fixed by the inexorable law of supply and demand in the labor market. In combating this heartless doctrine of the modern school of political economists, Leo XIII. lays down certain principles that ought to be accepted by all just and right-thinking persons. He insists that sound ideas are necessary on this most important matter. Here is what he says: "Wages, we are told, are fixed by free consent; and therefore the employer, when he pays what was agreed upon, has done his part and is not called upon to do anything further." In proving how false and unjust is this view of the relationship existing between the employer and the employed the Pope calls attention to the fact that man's labor has two notes or characteristics. It is, in the first instance, personal, inasmuch as the muscular power or exertion put forth by the laborer is individual or personal to him, and he employs it for his personal benefit. The second characteristic of labor is that it is *necessary*, as without the results of labor man cannot sustain life. "Self-preservation is a law of nature which it is wrong to disobey." After directing attention to these two characteristics of labor, the Encyclical reads:

"Now, if we were to consider labor merely so far as it is personal, doubtless it would be within the workman's right to accept *any rate* of wages whatever; for in the same way as he is free to work or not, so he is free to accept a small remuneration or none at all. *But this is a mere abstract proposition.*

The labor of the working-man is not only his personal attribute, but it is *necessary;* and this makes all the difference. The preservation of life is the bounden duty of each and all, and to fail therein is a crime. It follows, then, that each one has a right to procure what is required to live, and the poor can procure it in no other way than by work and wages."

The Holy Father proceeds to show that wages should not be measured by what is merely required to keep the working-man and his family alive. The Pope has no faith in the bread-and-water theory; or in the scaling-down process to the lowest *minimum* of wages that is often practised by wealthy corporations and grasping employers. No, he does not believe in this; and he says so in unmistakable language. After stating that it is usual for workmen and employers to agree to make a contract as to wages—and under all ordinary circumstances this contract is binding, though the case may arise when the workman is not morally bound to stick to the agreement—the Pope adds: "There is a dictate of nature more imperious and more ancient than any bargain between man and man : that the remuneration must be enough to support the wage-earner in *reasonable and frugal comfort*." And equally important is the statement that immediately follows this. "If," he writes, "through necessity or fear of a worse evil, the workman accepts harder conditions because an employer or contractor will give him no better, he is the victim of force and injustice." This extract from the Encyclical sets before us the true basis—and the lowest at that—upon which the rate of wages is to be computed. And it also furnishes an answer to those who cry out against the working-men who sometimes break agreements into which they had been forced by fear or necessity to enter. The laborer is not a piece of machinery to be purchased at the least possible cost, or thrown aside as worthless when it is of no further use. Nor is he a mere animal needing provision for bodily wants only. No, he is infinitely higher than that monstrous conception which the materialistic philosophy of these times furnishes. He is a man, with God-given faculties, of high and noble dignity, having the most sacred relations and owing the most solemn duties to his Maker, and having spiritual and mental aspirations that require to be satisfied just as much as the wants of the body—nay, more than they do. He should, therefore, have the means of reasonably meeting these wants. And it is only when capitalists and economists get this true idea of the working-man that the wage question, the eight-hour question, Sunday work, and other questions can be satisfactorily settled.

Now let us take a practical example that will fully illustrate these principles. In Pennsylvania there are thousands of men employed in the coal-mining and coke region. The labor of these workers is hard, unhealthy, and, in the case of the miners, attended with more or less danger to life. The labor, especially of the miner, might be classed as skilled. Taking account, therefore, of these circumstances the wages of this class ought to be such as to enable the miner and his family to live in "*reasonable and frugal comfort.*" What are average wages paid in the bituminous coal districts of this State? Perhaps the figures will furnish an explanation of the recent strike in the Connellsville coke-field, which, in its terrible results, arrested the attention of the whole country.

A bulletin just issued by Census Superintendent Porter shows that in 1889 the average number of persons in the mines of Fayette County was 6,567. The total amount of wages paid was $2,644,425. This is an average of about $420 a year to each person, or head of family, or about $1.35 a day. And from this is to be deducted the tolls levied in the "Pluck-me" stores which still flourish in the coal regions. In Westmoreland County the miners averaged 9,109 in number, and were paid in wages $4,064,950, or an average to each person of about $445. In Alleghany County the sum of $3,497,893 was paid to 9,386 miners, or an annual average wage to each miner of about $373.

Any one examining these figures must see at a glance the difficulties the head of a family has to meet in housing, feeding, and clothing himself, wife, and four or five children on a dollar and thirty-five cents a day! The payment of $373 a year, which is the rate received by the average miner in Alleghany County, divided in a family where there are five persons to be supported, means about $75 to each person, or *a dollar and a half a week.* Of course "reasonable and frugal comfort," of which Pope Leo XIII. speaks as due to the laborer, is out of the question on such compensation as this.

It may be said that the census calculation was based on the average wages paid the miner within the year, and not on the average wages received while the miner was actually at work. If the calculation were made on the latter basis the rate would be much higher. The answer is, that the miner has to support himself and his family the year round on what he earns in a year; and this is, therefore, the proper basis on which to figure.

If he works six days and earns $15, and then is idle six days, his average daily pay for the twelve days is $1.25.

Again, it is said that the miners are themselves largely to blame for their condition. They inaugurate a strike on little or no cause; if work is suspended in the mines because of excess of production or dulness in the coal trade, the miners, as a class, will remain in idleness for months rather than work at anything else; and, lastly, they are improvident and generally intemperate in their habits. Consequently, it is held, they themselves are in a large measure responsible for their hard lot.

While it must be admitted that there is some ground for these charges, the experience of the writer for four or five years as resident pastor in a mining district proves them to be in the main unfounded. I witnessed a number of strikes, and I often thought that the miners lent too ready an ear to the agitator or the advocate of violent measures; I also felt that thrift, foresight, and a little more domestic economy would do much to improve their surroundings and make their home-life more enjoyable. I saw that intemperance worked its dreadful havoc here as elsewhere. But making the most ample allowance for these things, what the Holy Father aptly calls "*the cruelty of grasping speculators*" in human labor supplies the true explanation of the miners' situation to-day. And it is useless to look for any improvement as long as the ordinary operator or capitalist sees no higher estimate on human beings than mere instruments for making money.

Under the store-system, to which reference has already been made, any coal operator cannot fail to get rich in a few years if he employs a considerable number of men; and this largely at the expense of the miner. I knew a "gentleman" who, having failed in business in one of our large towns, was made superintendent of a coal-mine by the owners, to whom he was related by marriage. He opened a company's store on his own account, and with the profits from this store and an ordinary salary he was able to retire from the mining village within a few years a rich man. And this is not by any means an isolated instance. The history of the coal region will furnish many similar cases.

To protect themselves against injustice of this sort; to maintain and secure the highest standard of wages that the worker in the various departments of labor is entitled to; to guard their sacred rights and interests, the Encyclical recognizes and encourages the formation of working-men's associations or societies. These societies the Pope would wish to see fashioned after the

Catholic guilds of a former day, but subject to such changes as the requirements of this age, custom, or other circumstances may demand. What those who have the real interests of labor at heart must do is to place at the head of these organizations the right persons. Leaders are needed of the highest and strongest character, of great firmness, tact, and superior executive ability; in a word, those whose aim will be to safeguard the interests and promote the welfare of the society without infringing on the rights of employers or others. Societies, no matter what the avowed objects may be, that are managed by "invisible leaders and on principles far from compatible with Christianity and the public well-being," must be avoided. And the rank and file of labor organizations should see to it that persons of this stamp never control the society. We all know how much suffering and misery have been brought to numberless working-men's homes through the false and, I do not hesitate to say, wicked counsel of selfish and designing leaders. It is the influence of such men that forces labor organizations to adopt, and try to enforce, measures that are unjust and tyrannical. By the enactment of these unjust and objectionable methods strife and ill-feeling are engendered, and the good-will and sympathy of the community in general are lost at times when the cause of labor needs the strong support of public sentiment.

To sum up the teaching of the Pope on this subject of labor associations, he believes in the fullest freedom of industrial workers to organize for mutual self-help and protection; he would have all labor unions based on Christian principles and kept under the restraint of religious motives; and he would have the most devoted, disinterested, and earnest religious men placed at the head of these unions.

As a result of the Encyclical, I read the other day in one of our daily papers the statement that an effort will be made here in Pittsburgh, and it is hoped elsewhere, to establish industrial organizations of which both the wage-earners and employers shall be members, and in which they shall co-operate for the promotion of friendly relations with each other. Leo XIII. has given expression to a strong desire for the formation of such bodies ; because he sees, what has been confirmed by experience, that where conferences are held in the proper spirit between employers and employed the best results follow. Strikes are oftentimes prevented, differences and disputes are amicably settled, confidence is restored, and a better and more kindly feeling established all around.

This method of conference has been successfully followed for years by the Amalgamated Association of Iron and Steel Workers of Pennsylvania in arranging the rate of wages, the hours of work, and all matters of importance to the men or the mill-owners. By this means strikes are averted, and it would be well if this plan for adjusting labor differences were more generally adopted in all kinds of industry all over the United States. As long as the present wage-system exists it is the simplest and most effective mode of settling labor disputes; and should conciliation and conference fail, recourse ought to be had to arbitration. Better, too, to arbitrate in the beginning than at a late stage of a prolonged strike or lockout. Strikes are no sufficient remedy for a labor grievance. They are rather a means, and oftentimes, if not in all instances, a drastic means of directing attention to a grievance. In the great majority of strikes the strikers lose. They are either starved into submission, or provoked by the capitalist into deeds of violence and unlawful conduct; then the state steps in and helps to end the strike. They are a relic of barbarism.

The Encyclical casts a strong white light on all these points that are now raised in the industrial world. It is a message of peace and good-will to all men. It lays down the eternal principles of right and justice for the guidance of rich and poor, worker and capitalist. It does not array class against class. It rather points out the line of duty for each to follow, while it aims to establish and strengthen right relations between labor and capital. It is a reassurance, if there be need of it, that the church is the friend of the working-man the world over; and a declaration that it is part of her divine mission to teach justice and charity to all men.

Such is Leo XIII.'s solution of the labor problem. It is a standing solution. May the closing century witness its fruits and blessings!

MORGAN M. SHEEDY.

Pittsburgh, Pa.

CONVENTION OF THE NATIONAL EDUCATION
ASSOCIATION IN TORONTO.

THE National Education Association of the United States held its annual meeting in Toronto from the 14th to the 17th of July. Two years ago the Minister of Education for Ontario invited the association to hold its next meeting there, but they were unable to do so. Last year another invitation was given to them by Mr. James L. Hughes, Inspector of Public Schools for Toronto. This met with better success.

About the earnestness with which, not alone the leaders but the rank and file of the profession, entered on the work of the convention there can be no doubt; about the practical value of the meeting there may be room for doubt. Seeing that the meeting in Toronto was intended to be, and was as far as its promoters could make it, a glorification of the unreligious or state system of education as the be-all and end-all in the training of youth, it may be well to set forth a few of the more important points connected with the convention, points bearing especially on this view of the end and aim of the meeting.

As has been already stated in the pages of THE CATHOLIC WORLD, the British North America Act guarantees to the religious minority in each of the two older provinces of Canada, Quebec and Ontario, the safety and perpetuation of their denominational schools. Protestant schools for the Protestant minority in Quebec, Catholic schools for the Catholic minority in Ontario. These schools are under the care of, and are supported by, the state as far as it supports the so-called public schools.

But mark the difference between Catholic Quebec and Protestant Ontario in the *development* of the system of denominational schools. In Catholic Quebec there is a *complete* system for the minority—Protestant elementary schools, Protestant high-schools, a Protestant normal school, a Protestant Council of Public Instruction, all supported by the Catholic government of Quebec. In Protestant Ontario the development of the system of Catholic schools for Catholic children stops with the elementary schools. No Catholic high-schools supported by the state, no Catholic normal school, no Catholic Council of Public Instruction. There is a lesson in liberality here: he that runs may read. And while the Catholic minority in Ontario fully appreciate the state's recognition of their elementary schools in which religious is combined with secular education, where the faith of their children is safe, they cannot shut their eyes to the extended privileges of the more fortunate minority in Quebec.

It may not be out of place here to notice how the very just complaint of Ontario Catholics, based on this state of affairs, is met. It is said: " The public schools of Quebec are Catholic, consequently Protestant children cannot conscientiously attend them; the public schools in Ontario are non-sectarian, consequently Catholics are quite safe in attending them." Are the " public " schools of Ontario non-sectarian? I have a long experience of the so-called non-sectarian or public schools, and can say, *no* public school conducted by a Protestant teacher in Ontario is a safe one for a Catholic child. It may be granted that in many such schools glaring or serious dangers to faith and morals do not appear; but there is always some danger. The whole atmosphere of such schools is Protestant; and a Protestant teacher can no more put away his Protestantism from his teaching than he can put away his thinking faculty. As one having over fifty years' experience of public schools, I desire to place this opinion on record. The history of some of the public schools in the States, presented to us of late in the newspapers, is part proof of this. Let me say once and for all to Catholic parents, the whole public-school system is tainted with either Protestantism or irreligion. And if the facts I shall set forth respecting the convention in Toronto do not bear this out, then I will cheerfully acknowledge my error.

Holding these opinions, it was with a good deal of interest I and other friends of Catholic education watched the arrangements made for the convention in Toronto, the programme of work, the special line to be taken in the various papers and addresses.

Let me first introduce the prime mover in bringing the association to Toronto, Mr. James L. Hughes. I do not know whether his fame as the bitterest and most unscrupulous foe to Catholic schools has reached the reading and thinking public of the States; but it can hardly have failed to do so. Some years ago he was comparatively unknown. How he reached his present " bad eminence " it would take too long to tell. Some say that the hope of one day being Minister of Education in a sound Orange Provincial government had much to do with it. Up to the present these hopes, if they ever existed, have not been realized. Let us pray, for the sake of peace and the fair fame of this province, they may ever remain so.

It was, therefore, with little or no wonder we saw the elaborate programme of a meeting to be held in a city, the capital of a province where denominational schools are recognized and supported by the state, silent on the subject of these schools, as if the local committee dreaded lest the visitors should learn something about them. It was to be expected that in such a city as Toronto, possessing as it does the highest (if there are any highest) and the lowest types of Orangemen and bigotry, and with such an active enemy as Mr. Hughes, Catholic schools would be quietly ignored, or damned with faint praise, and the so-called non-sectarian schools lauded to the skies.

For this, however, I believe the local committee is wholly to blame, and not the executive of the National Education Association. A late meeting of the association shows that they are not afraid to hear the principles of Catholic education discussed. These principles will not down, they are eternal; and so we find at the convention some who were called on to "curse" denominational schools very unexpectedly, and to the no small consternation of the local managers of the meetings, turned to "bless" instead.

The beginning of the convention was bad. The dark shadow of intolerance came over it then, and, I am sorry to say, remained over it to the close. The first day's proceedings included the addresses of welcome and the answers thereto. Of these I shall refer to three only. That of the Minister of Education for Ontario, who, if rumor speaks true, had almost been left off the programme by the local committee, was pointed and in good taste. That of the Rev. Mr. Rexford, an Anglican clergyman from Quebec, secretary of the Protestant Council of Public Instruction, and who represented the Chief Superintendent of Education of that province, must have somewhat surprised the "locals." Speaking with authority—and the statement coming from a Protestant came with all the more effect—he tore to shreds the flimsy stories which do duty so frequently about the ignorance of the *habitants* of Quebec. A writer in THE CATHOLIC WORLD some time ago pointed out the utter falsehood of such stories. Mr. Rexford showed that Quebec stands high in educational matters; that she has built up a literature which ranks first in the Dominion to-day; that her universities, high-schools, and elementary schools are doing a work equal to any other institutions on this continent. And using the language of *la belle France*, he presented to the convention the greetings of the province in the tongue of six-sevenths of its people.

Short, direct, and appropriate addresses were given by the leading American visitors. To one of these I wish to refer. It seemed to strike the key-note of the work of the convention. If this statement does injustice to a large body of apparently intelligent and liberal-minded men and women, I am sorry for it; but up to the present no repudiation of the sentiments uttered has come from the executive or any member of the association, either publicly or privately. Many watched in Toronto for this repudiation; it did not come; it has not come. The following is a newspaper summary of the address referred to:

"Professor P. Marcellus Marshall, of Chamita, New Mexico, responded for the south-west. He said: People of Canada, officers, and citizens of Toronto: 800,000 square miles of mountains and of valleys in the 'Southland' of the west heard your invitations so loud and so strong, and now respond to your welcomes so free and so warm. The land of the cactus and the pine; the land of the orange and the palm; the land of earth's most barren wastes and of her richest ever-producing fields; the land in parts of which it burns by day and freezes by night, and in other parts of which it neither burns nor freezes during all the rolling year; the land of Montezuma's children of the sun, which by the Romish Spaniard was later overrun, but in which American civilization is merely just begun, . . . has lifted up her golden ears, and heard and come, at your invitation, to this fair Canada land, to this beautiful, moral, Protestant city of Toronto, chaste Queen of the North, and now, from her life-giving air and cloudless skies and unfathomed possibilities, responds with all her warm, southern, Spanish heart to your grand and gracious welcome. Boasting houses and towns, with dwellers now as they were when Columbus came, she also boasts a middle civilization as well as the newest of the name. The red man still bends his bow upon the game; the Pueblo dances to Montezuma and Malinche, and elects his governors and his captains once a year; the Mexican, son of Spanish 'Conquistador,' in his utter illiteracy yet bows down to sticks and stones, carries his fetiches about his fields in solemn procession to pray for rain, and sheds his own blood to absolve his own sins—an ignoble, superstitious slave of Rome and Romanism; the American has come with rail and wire, with printing-press and Protestant missionary, with light and law and learning, and 'the desert begins to bloom as a rose.' 'San Miguel College,' founded before Harvard University, and the public school-master who cannot write his own name, must now do or die for ever. The seven empires of the south-west respond, 'Viva Canada, Viva Toronto, Viva la Reina Victoria!'"

The Minister of Education, in his explanation of the school system of Ontario, gave simply the fact of the existence of the Catholic schools; and gave statistics to show their standing in the province. This is really all he was called on to do by the circumstances; he did no more.

The address of Dr. Gates, President of Amherst College, was eloquent if his ideas were a little peculiar. He said that the great object of common-school education is to find a man, or to make a man. His list of men partook somewhat of the blasphemous—Christ, Martin Luther, Cromwell, etc. This association of names is peculiar and—painful.

On the evening of the last day of the convention two remarkable addresses were delivered, one by Rev. Professor Clarke, Trinity University, Toronto; the other by Goldwin Smith. Professor Clarke, who on short notice took the place of Professor Meiklejohn, of Aberdeen University, spoke of the progress of elementary education in England. He made some very important admissions—that it was not until 1832 or '34 the state did *anything* for the education of the masses. Who, then, attended to this? The teachers of parochial schools, whose salaries were often paid out of the poor pittance of the clergymen. These parochial schools simply followed out a recognized principle—the child belonged to the parent and to God, and not to the state. There could be no mistaking his admiration of and faith in such a system of education.

Goldwin Smith spoke for a few minutes. He said that, beginning with his own remembrance of things, the two great principles of education, parental control and state control, were the subject of discussion. His own leanings were evidently in the direction of the former.

It is likely that the proceedings of the convention will be officially published. If so, they will repay a careful reading and will afford much food for thought. The friends of Catholic education have, in one sense, no reason to regret the peculiar coloring placed on the proceedings of the convention. Even Protestant public opinion is unmistakably moving round to the Catholic position in this matter. It is one of the signs of the times.

M. A.

MADAME GRADOT.

IN the yards and upon the rear walls of our row of tenement houses the sun had been shining for an hour or more; but now, grown tired, it may be, of loitering there and with the few flowering plants and the climbing vines which the Little Madame had cultivated with such loving care and so successfully, it had reached the furthest corner of my room. It seemed to me that only the day before I had had to dress quickly to be in time for our breakfast, if I waited before rising for the sunlight to come near that corner; but the days were rapidly growing longer, and now I could easily wait for it to chase the shadows a long way up the wall.

Through the open windows I could hear the discordant cry of a parrot kept by some fellow-tenant, possibly for his own amusement but certainly to the annoyance of his neighbors. The clothes-line man had already begun his rounds, and sometimes, as he would discern some broken, frayed line hanging from the high centre pole at the back of every house, he would intermit his curious, unintelligible call to ask, "Fix your line, lady?" in a high, far-reaching voice. Now, too, through the doors, I could hear Mme. Gradot's quick and earnest voice as she tried to waken her husband.

"Jean, Jean!" she called, "you must get up; it is time. Ah! see the bright sun; it is kissing now, it is kissing just the end of your nose. It will make it so red."

But Jean rebelled and muttered sleepily, and I could hear the bed creak as he turned and settled himself for still another nap. But the little woman was inexorable.

"You must, you must," she repeated. "How lazy, how lazy you are! Are you not lazy?"

And Jean, finally yielding, was soon up, and presently I heard him, as he was about to leave his room, ask if I was not to be called for breakfast.

"No, no; go, and do not disturb him. He is not busy as you are, and his employer is so kind," Mme. Gradot replied.

Jean laughed in his cheery way, and soon I heard his steps through the hall and down the stairs. He was now, as he had been for many years, a foreign-corresponding clerk in a large house down-town, where the pay was small and the hours long;

but he was always good-natured, and as fond and proud of the little woman who took such good care of him as he had been when thirty years ago he had come to America with her, newly wedded, in search of fame and fortune.

Now as he went away I heard her murmur to herself, as she came nearer to the door, "Ah, the poor Jean! why do they have to work so early?" And I wondered how long she had been about her daily duties.

"I must be at work, too," I thought; but as I tried to rise a sharp pain in my shoulder reminded me that I had fallen badly the day before and had had to come earlier than usual to the Little Madame, for so Jean and I always thought of our home-coming. When I would meet him down-town, as I did infrequently, he would shake me warmly by the hand and ask, "You come early to the Little Madame to-night?"

Mme. Gradot was always good to me, and she had always been willing to let me take my own time before breakfast. A long time ago, soon after she had given her consent to let me have the little room there was no other use for, Jean had urged her to call me; but as I entered the little room which served her as kitchen, dining-room, and living-room as well on cold days, I had heard her say:

"Let the poor child sleep."

"Such a woman should have a pedestal," I cried as I lifted her bodily upon the dresser. This distressed her greatly, her dignity was so ruffled, and for the only time since I had known her she was angry with Jean; but then, he had laughed zealously. In a minute, however, she forgave us both, and, maybe, we were the better friends.

Now this morning I was glad to be reminded that I was not busy and could easily enough take a holiday; but what a holiday it was to be—to be spent in bed with a strained shoulder! But still I worried a little, for I knew that the little woman would be anxious lest my breakfast might be spoiled. I tried to smile cheerfully as her bright face looked in at the door, but I must have failed, for she came to me quickly.

"You are not sick?" she asked; "you have not fever?"

"No," I answered, and then I told her that my fall had been worse than I thought.

"Oh," she said, as she kissed me, "you are so patient, and so like my son."

Her words hurt a little and made me wince, for I knew there was then no reason why I should not be patient, and Jean had told me too much of their son to make me wish to seem like him.

"The dear little woman must never know," he had said to me, and I had agreed with him. "You see," he went on, "so many drinking-shops are needed to keep us happy in these slums—you call them slums?—and the boy liked them too well. And—but I hope he will come back never."

But his mother always looked for her son, and often she asked Jean whether he thought the day of his return could be far off, much to the discomfiture of the good man. Sometimes I wondered whether, if he should return, we might find that I had stolen his place in his mother's heart; but if he did not, none of us need care for that.

"You will stay in bed to-day?" now she said to me, passing her warm, smooth hand over my forehead.

"Yes," I answered, "I am glad to think that I must."

"'Glad?' Then we shall make it a *fête* day. What shall we have for the dinner, then?"

"O madame!" I replied, "I cannot do justice to one of your marvellous dinners to-day."

"'Marvellous?' she repeated doubtfully; "I do not know, but good? Yes. It will be so good, you can eat, oh! all of it. The soup as clear as that," she went on, holding her thumb and finger close together and before me, and then slowly separating them. "What else? The sweetbreads, perhaps? Oh! I know where to get them, and—and—everything. You shall see."

And she hurried out of the room, but only to return in a minute penitent.

"You will not tell, Jean?" she said, shaking her finger at me.

"Certainly not," I replied, laughing; "but what is it I am not to tell him?"

"The poor child's breakfast, I forgot." And her grief was so real that, hungry though I was, I almost wished she had not now remembered it; but before I could reply to her at all she had hurried out to prepare it.

"You will let me sit here while you eat it, the breakfast?" she asked, when she brought the simple meal to me, and had managed to make me comfortable as I sat up in bed.

"Why did you not call Jean?" she continued presently. "He is so big he could have lifted you so high, so high."

And she was full of tender solicitude until convinced that, although it was wiser for me to remain in bed, I was in no great pain.

The house in which we lived was still a new one, and its tenants were pleasanter and better people than many of those who live in these tenements. The world, they say, grows better as it grows older and better worth the living in, and it may be so; but it is not so with all the small worlds within the world. Dirt will accumulate, and there is much wear and tear in these hastily built houses tenanted by so many. Long ago I noticed that as the houses grew older the tenants changed in character for the worse. We had now been in this house, in a newly developed part of the city, for nearly a year, and I was not surprised to learn that Madame Gradot was looking forward eagerly to the completion of a new and particularly ugly block of houses being built not far from us.

" But," she said, after I had finished my breakfast, and the room had been cleaned as well as it could be—" but it is not nice. I do not like it, these apartments. When my boy gets back—oh! so soon—we shall have in the country a little place. It will cost nothing—only one thousand dollars, not a bit more. What is that for two great men? And you will come too," she added with a little cry. " We could not live without you. No, no! "

For a little time she was silent, and I could fancy that she was already building for herself her little cottage in the sunlight.

"Think," she went on shortly, "what we shall have: in every room the blessed sun, and flowers, oh! so many. And—and—and pigeons. We will not live in the country without pigeons, no."

" Is that all? " I asked; but though I laughed, I took great pleasure in her joy and happiness in the delightful forecast.

" We shall have a whole big yard to dry the clothes; no big pole like that, and pulleys, no. They creak so, ugh! " she went on with a little shrug of disgust. " Oh! you do not see all the day from the window the clothes. They make the dogs bark, I tell you. But you will let me go or we shall not have the dinner."

Then, smiling brightly at me, she left me to get along alone as best I could. Truly it was not difficult, for I had much to think of, but chiefly I thought of the Little Madame herself. I fancied her in the little home in the country she wished for so much, with the pigeons and the sunlight, and I wondered if she would be so much happier there. And then I wondered whether the little house would ever be hers at all, for Jean had told me how most of the money they had struggled so to save for their country home and their old age ˙ had been squandered by their son, or spent in one of the many efforts they had made to save him from the consequences of his folly.

· The day was drawing to a close; Madame Gradot had long ago returned from her trip to market, and had told me with glee of her successful search.

"We who go late," she said, "have not the choice; but the price! Ah! you should see."

She had finished her work and had even arranged the table, and in my room, too, so that I might not have to be moved far; and now we were waiting patiently in the lengthening shadows for Jean's return. But Madame Gradot did not like the shadows; nor, indeed, could she bear any dark spot whatever, and now as again her talk was of the place we should have near by in the country, she spoke only of how bright it would be, and pretty and clean.

"Ah! yes, so clean always. Is it not good I am so small?" then she asked, as she reached over on the floor to pick up some speck her bright eyes had found.

At last Jean returned to us, and then we soon found that the dinner was quite as marvellous as I expected, and as good as the Little Madame had promised that it should be. Then Jean brought to us from a small stock he had had, I do not know how long, a bottle of excellent claret, and as he carefully withdrew the cork and then held it still on the corkscrew toward us, that we might enjoy its fragrance, he said:

"This shall be a *fête* day, veritably."

"If I but had your appetite," I said. "How lucky you are to be so hungry!"

"Yes," he assented; "and you?"

"I shall do better to-morrow," I answered. "Can we have so good a dinner to-morrow, madame?"

"Every night, always. Never fear."

Then when we had finished, and the table and the plates had been taken to the kitchen and duly put away, Jean told us of his day and of the letters he had written to his firm's agents in France, and of how his heart would sometimes follow them there.

"Now, Jean, see," said Madame Gradot. "We need more light. You must not think it is dark here. But we have been talking to-day of the home in the country, Jean. It must come soon. We are growing old, so old"; and she gently stroked Jean's hand.

Madame Gradot liked to have me read to them; but on this evening we talked until Jean grew sleepy and the good woman took him off to bed. I felt that her "Good-night" was indeed a benediction.

Slowly the summer ran its course. For many days the air as it reached us seemed parched by its passage over the heated paving stones. The Little Madame was always cheerful; but she did not bear the heat well. She grew thinner, and I noticed that she was more willing to rest than she had been always. Her eyes grew sometimes dull, and when she did not know that any one was looking at her there was a listlessness in her manner and appearance strangely unlike her. The lines in her face deepened, too. Jean watched her closely, and I saw that he was greatly troubled; but he hid his trouble; even to himself, he would not admit that she could be seriously ill.

"How well you look this morning!" he would say to her; but his smile, meant to be reassuring, was of the sorry kind one can stop so easily and so quickly.

"Yes," she said simply, and she smiled too in response; for she was brave and determined not to show her suffering.

I tried to take her with me to some good doctor; but she rebelled and would not admit that she could need a doctor's care. But Jean and I took counsel together, and we decided that soon we would send her away into the country to stay until cooler weather should come again. There, we thought, she would be sure to regain her health and strength. We talked the matter over many times together, and we found great pleasure in our discussion of the places to which we might send her, and many were the plans we formed for her enjoyment. At length we selected the place we believed might do. It was said to be cool, it was not far, and it was not too expensive for Jean's meagre purse.

With Jean's approval, almost indeed at his request, I made a journey there to be sure that there might be no mischance. The small house was prettily situated on a little level spot among some near-by mountains. The trees were bending in the breeze, and the shadows of the leaves were dancing and playing in the sunlight. In the room they showed me there was no hint of spot or stain. It would surely do, I thought. On my return Jean was enthusiastic, and we went together to tell the Little Madame of the change in store for her.

"The sun?" Jean asked.

"Is everywhere," I answered.

"It is clean, and—and—there are pigeons?"

"Clean? Yes. I do not know about the pigeons, but there are birds in plenty."

"Singing?" he asked.

"Yes," I replied, enjoying his earnestness, "singing all day."

"Then she will be happy, of a truth?"

"We need not fear, I think, Jean," I responded.

The day was a warm one, one of the warmest we had had, and oppressive. Along the streets there were not many stirring, for we were then too early to meet the home-returning working-men; but many women were gathered in front of the houses, lazily fanning sleepy, white-faced children in their arms.

"She will soon be away from this," Jean said; "it is good. No," he went on, "it is not fair. You must wait for me." And he laughingly held me back that I might not reach the Little Madame first, for I was much younger and quicker. We were surprised that she was not upon the landing to meet us; but as we entered the room almost together we saw her form upon the floor. A glance upward told the story. In the dreadful heat her thoughts must have turned to the country home she so wished for, and she had climbed upon the ladder to look upon their little store of savings, safe hidden away at the top of the dresser, perhaps to add to it, and there had fallen as we found her. We placed her gently on the bed, and soon the doctor came, followed quickly by the priest.

When consciousness returned and, true to the faith she had lived up to her life long, her peace had been made with the good God, I told her the story of our plans, and described to her the house in the mountains and the sunlight to which we hoped soon to take her. She smiled, but she shortly beckoned us to her, and she kissed me and then Jean. Jean's kiss was the last thing she knew. She did not linger long.

We knew what she would have wished, and in the quiet country church-yard wherein she sleeps there is no hint of suffering or sorrow. Upon her grave no stone stands to remind us of her virtues, but all summer the grass grows and the flow-ers bloom, and it may be that the birds stopping there to rest sing sweeter than their fellows.

W. M. BANGS.

THE LIFE OF FATHER HECKER.*

CHAPTER XXX.

THE APOSTOLATE OF THE PRESS.

ONE Sunday forenoon, happening to cross Broadway near a
fashionable Protestant church, we saw the curb on both sides
of the street lined with carriages, and the coachmen and foot-
men all reading the morning papers. The rich master and his
family were in the softly-cushioned pews indoors, while their servants studied the news of the world and worshipped at the
shrine of the Press outside: a spectacle suggestive of many
things to the social reformer. But to a religious mind it was an
invitation to the *Apostolate of the Press*. The Philips of our day
can evangelize the rough charioteer by means of the written
word as easily as they can his cultured master.

To Father Hecker the Press was the highest opportunity for
religion. The only term of comparison for it is some element of
nature like sunlight or the atmosphere. In the Press civilized
man lives and breathes. Father Hecker was as alive to the injury done to humanity by bad reading as a skilful physician is
to the malaria which he can smell and fairly taste in an infected
atmosphere; and he ever strove to make the Press a means of
enlightenment and virtue. He began to write for publication
almost immediately after his arrival in America as a Redemptorist missionary; the *Questions of the Soul* and the *Aspirations
of Nature* were composed amidst most absorbing occupations between 1853 and 1858. Throughout life he was ever asking himself and others how the Press could be cleansed, and how its
Apostolate could be inaugurated. To this end he was ready to
devote all his efforts, and expend all his resources and those of
the community of which he was the founder. It is true that no
man of his time was better aware of the power of the spoken
word, and few were more competent to use it, the natural and
Pentecostal vehicle of the Holy Spirit to men's souls. But he
also felt that the providence of God, in making the Press of our
day an artificial medium of human intercourse more universal
than the living voice itself, had pointed it out as a necessary adjunct to the oral preaching of the truth. He was convinced that

religion should make the Press ˙its own. He would not look
upon it as an extraordinary aid, but maintained that the ordinary provision of Christian instruction for the people should ever
be two-fold, by speech and by print: neither the Preacher without the Press nor the Press without the Preacher. He was
heard to say that in reading Montalembert's *Monks of the West*
he had been struck with the author's eloquent apostrophe to the
spade, the instrument of civilization and Christianity for the
wild hordes of the early middle ages. Much rather, he said,
should we worship the Press as the medium of the light of God
to all mankind. He felt that the Apostolate of the Press might
well absorb the external vocation of the most active friends of
religion.

In the Press he found a distinct suggestion from above of a
change of methods for elevating men to truth and virtue. In
the spring of 1870, while on his way home from the Vatican
Council, he wrote to Father Deshon from Assisi:

"I felt as if I would like to have peopled that grand and
empty convent with inspired men and printing-presses. For
evidently the special battle-field of attack and defence of truth
for half a century to come is the printing-press."

He believed in types as he believed in pulpits. He believed
that the printing-office was necessary to the convent. To him
the Apostolate of the Press meant the largest amount of truth
to the greatest number of people. By its means a small band
of powerful men could reach an entire nation and elevate its
religious life.

This being understood, one is not surprised at the extent of
his plans for this Apostolate. He was never able to carry them
out fully. Not till some years after the founding of the community could he make a fair beginning, although the first volume of
the Paulist Sermons appeared in 1861. Delays were inevitable
from the difficulties incident to the opening of the house and
church in Fifty-ninth Street, and these were aggravated by the
war, which for over four years bred such intense excitement as to
interfere with any strong general interest in matters other than
political. But the very month it ended, in April, 1865, Father
Hecker started THE CATHOLIC WORLD. Its purpose was to
speak for religion in high-grade periodical literature. The year
following he founded The Catholic Publication Society, with the
purpose of directing the entire resources of the Press into a

missionary apostolate. In 1870 he began *The Young Catholic.*
In literary merit and in illustrations it equalled any of the juvenile publications of that period, and was the pioneer of all the
Catholic journals in the United States intended for children.
And finally, in 1871, he projected the establishment of a first-
class Catholic daily, securing within a year subscriptions for
more than half the money necessary for the purpose, when the
work was arrested by the final breaking down of his health.

THE CATHOLIC WORLD was considered a hazardous venture.
At the time it was proposed, such modest attempts at Catholic
monthlies as had struggled into life had long ceased to exist.
The public for such a magazine seemed to be small. The priesthood had little leisure for reading, being hardly sufficient in number for their most essential duties; the educated laymen were
not numerous, nor remarkable for activity of mind in matters of
religion; nearly the entire Church of America was foreign by
birth or parentage, and belonged to the toiling masses of the
people: "not many rich, not many noble." And, Father Hecker
was asked, whom are you going to get to write for the magazine? How many Catholic literary men and women do you know
of? Prudence, therefore, stood sponsor to courage. The cautious policy of an eclectic was adopted, and for more than a
year the magazine, with the exception of its book reviews, was
made up of selections and translations from foreign periodicals.
The late John R. G. Hassard, who had already succeeded as a
journalist, was chosen by Father Hecker as his assistant in the
editorial work. Efforts were at once made to secure original articles; but before the magazine was filled by them three or four
years were spent in urgent soliciting, in very elaborate sub-edit-
ing of MSS., and in reliance on the steady assistance of the
pens of the Paulist Fathers. As a compensation, THE CATHO-
LIC WORLD has introduced to the public many of our best
writers, and first and last has brought our ablest minds on both
sides of the water into contact with the most intelligent Catholics in the United States. All through its career it has represented Catholic truth before the American public in such wise as
to command respect, and has brought about the conversion of
many of its non-Catholic readers. Since its beginning it has
been forced to hold its own against the claims of not unwelcome
rivals, and against the almost overwhelming attractions of the
great illustrated secular monthlies, to say nothing of the vicissitudes of the business world; and it has succeeded in doing so.
Father Hecker's purpose in establishing it has been realized, for

it has ever been a first-rate Catholic monthly of general literature, holding an equal place with similar publications in the
world of letters. He was its editor-in-chief till the time of his
death, except during three years of illness and absence in
Europe. He conducted it so as to occupy much of the field
open to the Apostolate of the Press, giving solid doctrine in
form of controversy, and discussing such religious truths as were
of current interest. He kept its readers informed of the changeful moods of non-Catholic thought, and furnished them with
short studies of instructive eras and personages in history.
These graver topics have been floated along by contributions of
a lighter kind, by good fiction and conscientious literary criticism. Meantime, the social problems which had perplexed
Father Hecker himself in his early life, have caught the attention of the slower minds of average men, or rather have been
thrust upon them; and their consideration, ever in his own sympathetic spirit, now forms a prominent feature of THE CATHOLIC
WORLD.

The Young Catholic was an enterprise dear to his heart. His
interest in it was constant and minute, and some of the articles
most popular with its young constituency were from his own
pen. It has always been edited by Mrs. George V. Hecker, assisted by a small circle of zealous and enlightened writers. It
has held its way, but has had to encounter the not unusual fate
of bold pioneers. It created its own rivals by demonstrating the
possibilities of juvenile Catholic journalism, calling into existence
more than a score of claimants for the support which it alone
at first solicited. The lowest estimate of juvenile publications of a
purely secular tone yearly sold in America carries the figure far
into the millions. Some of these, and it is well to know that they
are the most widely sold, are first-rate in a literary point of
view and employ the best artists for the pictures. To say that
they are secular but feebly expresses the totally unmoral influence they for the most part exert. They are the extension of
the unreligious school into the homes of the people. When
Father Hecker and Mrs. George V. Hecker and their associates
began *The Young Catholic*, this vast mirage of the desert of life
had but glimmered upon the distant horizon; they saw it coming and they did their best to point Catholic youth away from
it and lead it to the real oasis of God, with its grateful shade,
its delicious fruits, and its ever-flowing springs of the waters of
life.

As already said, The Catholic Publication Society was begun a year after THE CATHOLIC WORLD was started, its aim being to turn to the good of religion, and especially to the conversion.of non-Catholics, all the uses the press is capable of. It was a missionary work in the broadest sense, seeking to enlist not only the clergy but especially the laity in an organized Apostolate of the Press, to enlighten the faith of Catholics and to spread it among their Protestant fellow-citizens. Its first work was to be the issuing of tracts and pamphlets telling the plain truth about the Catholic religion. Local societies, to be established throughout the country, were to buy these publications at a price less than cost, and distribute them gratis to all classes likely to be benefited. To catch the eye of the American people, to affect their hearts, to supply their religious wants with Catholic truth, were objects kept in view in preparing the tracts. Although some of them were addressed to Catholics, enforcing important religious duties, nearly all of them were controversial. More than seventy different tracts were printed first and last, and many hundreds of thousands, indeed several millions, of them distributed in all parts of the country, public, charitable, and penal institutions being, of course, fair field for this work. They were all very brief, few of them covering more than four small-sized pages. "Three pages of truth have before now overturned a life-time of error," said Father Hecker. The tract *Is it Honest?* though only four pages of large type, or about twelve hundred words, created a sensation everywhere, and was answered by a Protestant minister with over fifty pages of printed matter, or about fifteen times more than the tract itself. One hundred thousand copies of this tract were distributed in New York City alone. It is printed herewith as a specimen, both as to style and matter, of what one may call the aggressive-defensive tactics in Catholic controversy:

IS IT HONEST

To say that the Catholic Church prohibits the use of the Bible—

When anybody who chooses can buy as many as he likes at any Catholic bookstore, and can see on the first page of any one of them the approbation of the Bishops of the Catholic Church, with the Pope at their head, encouraging Catholics to read the Bible, in these words: "The faithful should be excited to the reading of the Holy Scriptures," and that not only for the Catholics of the United States, but also for those of the whole world besides?

IS IT HONEST

To say that Catholics believe that man by his own power can forgive sin—

When the priest is regarded by the Catholic Church only as the agent of our Lord Jesus Christ, acting by the power delegated to him, according to these words, "Whose sins you shall forgive, they are forgiven them; and whose sins you shall retain, they are retained?" (St. John xx. 23.)

Is it Honest

*To repeat over and over again that Catholics pay the priest to pardon their
sins—*

When such a thing is unheard of anywhere in the Catholic Church—

When any transaction of the kind is stigmatized as a grievous sin, and ranked
along with murder, adultery, blasphemy, etc., in every catechism and work on
Catholic theology ?

Is it Honest

*To persist in saying that Catholics believe their sins are forgiven merely by
the confession of them to the priest, without a true sorrow for them, or a
true purpose to quit them—*

When every child finds the contrary distinctly and clearly stated in the catechism, which he is obliged to learn before he can be admitted to the sacraments ?
Any honest man can verify this statement by examining any Catholic catechism.

Is it Honest

*To assert that the Catholic Church grants any indulgence or permission to com-
mit sin—*

When an "indulgence," according to her universally received doctrine, was
never dreamed of by Catholics to imply, in any case whatever, any permission to
commit the least sin ; and when an indulgence has no application whatever to sin
until after sin has been repented of and pardoned ?

Is it Honest

*To accuse Catholics of putting the Blessed Virgin or the Saints in the place of
God or the Lord Jesus Christ—*

When the Council of Trent declares that it is simply useful to ask their intercession in order to obtain favor from God, through his Son, Jesus Christ our Lord,
who alone is our Saviour and Redeemer—

When "asking their prayers and influence with God " is exactly of the same
nature as when Christians ask the pious prayers of one another?

Is it Honest

*To accuse Catholics of paying divine worship to images or pictures, as the
heathen do—*

When every Catholic indignantly repudiates any idea of the kind, and when
the Council of Trent distinctly declares the doctrine of the Catholic Church in regard to them to be, "that there is no divinity or virtue in them which should appear to claim the tribute of one's veneration"; but that "all the honor which is
paid to them shall be referred to the originals whom they are designed to represent ? " (Sess. 25.)

Is it Honest

To make these and many other similar charges against Catholics—

When they detest and abhor such false doctrines more than those do who
make them, and make them, too, without ever having read a Catholic book, or
taken any honest means of ascertaining the doctrines which the Catholic Church
really teaches?

Remember the commandment of God, which says: "Thou shalt not bear
false witness against thy neighbor."

Reader, would you be honest, and do no injustice ? Then examine the doctrines of the Catholic Church; read the works of Catholics. See both sides.
Examine, and be fair, for AMERICANS LOVE FAIR PLAY.

In preparing these little messengers of truth every style of writing was used, narrative, allegory, dialogue, and positive argument. They are as good reading to-day as when first issued, and the volume which they form may be placed in an inquirer's hands with excellent effect. To keep them agoing Father Hecker laid all his friends of any literary ability under contribution, the series being opened by Archbishop Spalding with a tract on *Religious Indifferentism.* Did space permit, an entire list of the subjects dealt with might be given, and the reader could the better see how they embrace the entire controversy between Catholics and Protestants and infidels, many of the tracts being masterpieces of popular argumentation.

As to the business side of these enterprises, Father Hecker confided it to Mr. Lawrence Kehoe, who was publisher of THE CATHOLIC WORLD and of *The Young Catholic* from their beginning until the Paulists became their own publishers, shortly before Mr. Kehoe's death. He was placed in charge of the Publication Society as manager when it was started, and so continued until the formation of the present firm, remaining then the active partner in its management. No more ardent advocate of a good cause could be desired than Lawrence Kehoe. Father Hecker cherished him as a friend, and he was his zealous and efficient agent in his entire Apostolate of the Press.

The purpose of the Publication Society was missionary, and the intention was that its books, tracts, and pamphlets should be either given away or sold at cost price, or below it. Therefore it was necessary to secure funds for the running expenses. The reader has seen that this was to have been done by the contributions of subsidiary societies. To aid in the formation of these and to solicit contributions in money, circulars were sent to all the clergy of the United States. Only a few made any practical response. But the meeting of the Second Plenary Council of Baltimore in 1866, the same year the Society was founded, was opportune. The bishops were induced to take the matter up, and a decree, of which the following is a translation, was enacted. After speaking of the need of supplying Catholic literature at a low price the Council proceeds:

"Since a society with this object in view, known as The Catholic Publication Society, has been founded in New York, and has been so far conducted with commendable diligence and with notable success, we therefore consider it to be entirely worthy of the favor and assistance of prelates and priests, as

well as of the Catholic people in general. That the whole country may the better and more certainly share ·in its advantages,
we advise . and ,exhort the bishops to establish branches of this
society in their dioceses, by means of whose officers the publications of the society may be distributed. But as without great
expenditure of money these societies cannot · be kept up and
must fail of success, the bishops shall therefore appoint a yearly
collection for their support, to be taken up in all the principal
churches, or shall make other provision for the same purpose
according to their best judgment." (Con. Plen. Balt., § 500.)

From the Pastoral Letter of the same Council we extract the
following :

·"In connection with this matter [the Catholic Press] we earnestly recommend to the faithful of our charge The Catholic
Publication Society, lately established in the city of New York
by a zealous and devoted clergyman. Besides the issuing of
short tracts with which this society has begun, and which may
be usefully employed to arrest the attention of many whom
neither inclination nor leisure will allow to read larger works,
this Society contemplates the publication of Catholic books,
according as circumstances may permit and the interests of religion appear to require. From the judgment and good taste
evinced in the composition and selection of such tracts and
books as have already been issued by this Society, we are encouraged to hope that it will be eminently effective in making
known the truths of our holy religion, and dispelling the prejudices which are mainly owing to want of information on the
part of so many of our fellow-citizens. For this it is necessary that a generous co-operation be given both by clergy and
laity to the undertaking, which is second to none in importance among the subsidiary aids which the inventions of modern
times supply to our ministry for the diffusion of Catholic
truth."

How elated Father Hecker was by this action of the Council,
and how over-sanguine, as the event proved, of the future of the
Society, is shown by the following extracts from letters to a
friend :

"My efforts in the recent Council were completely successful,
owing to the many prayers offered to God—yours not the least.
Could you have seen the letters from different quarters, from
good pious nuns, and persons loving and serving and fearing
God in the world, written to me, and their writers all praying
and doing works of mercy and mortification for the purposes I
had in view, you could not wonder at my success. God did it.
What is more, I was fully conscious of the fact, and it is this
that made my great joy.

"The Catholic Publication Society has the unanimous consent, and sympathy, and co-operation of the entire episcopate
and clergy. Every year there is a collection to be taken up in
the principal churches for its support. I have drawn an elephant, but I do not feel like the man who did not know what
to do with him after he had got him."

"It is good in God to place me in a position in which I can
act efficiently. The disposition towards me is, I know, most
pleasant and favorable. I have been placed where I shall be at
liberty to act and direct action. Quietly pray for me as the
Holy Spirit may suggest. On my part I will also seek the same
guidance. How good God is to give it!"

The Council had hardly adjourned when it began to be plain
that in legislating for The Catholic Publication Society the prelates had been over-stimulated by the zeal of Archbishop Spalding and the personal influence of Father Hecker himself, who
was present in his capacity of Superior of the Paulists. He
went among the bishops and pleaded for the Apostolate of the
Press with characteristic vigor, and with his usual success.
Aided by the archbishop, he lifted the Fathers of the Council
for a moment above what in their sober senses they deemed
the exclusive duty of the hour. This was to provide churches
and priests, and schools and school-teachers, for the people. Already far too numerous for their clergy, the Catholic people
were increasing by immigration alone at the rate of more than
a quarter of a million a year. Every effort must be con-
centrated, it was thought, and every penny spent, in the vast
work of housing and feeding the wandering flocks of the
Lord. And certainly the magnitude of the task and the success attained in performing it can excuse the indifference shown
to the Apostolate of the Press, if anything can excuse it. But it
seemed otherwise to Father Hecker, as it does now to us. For
the Catholic people could have been better and earlier cared for
in their ·spiritual concerns if furnished with the abundant supply
of good reading which the carrying out of Father Hecker's plan
would have given them, and that at no great expense. What
substitute for a priest is equal to a good book? What vocation
to the priesthood has not found its origin in the pages of a
good book, or at any rate been fostered by its devout lessons?
And all history as well as experience proves that the best guarantee of the faith of a Catholic, moving amidst kindly-disposed
non-Catholic neighbors, is the aggressive force of missionary zeal.

The Publication Society, if brought into active play, would have done much to create this zeal, and would have supplied its best arms of attack and defence by an abundance of free Catholic reading. It would have helped on every good work by auxiliary forces drawn from intelligent faith and instructed zeal.

A closer view of the case shows that antecedents of a racial and social character among the people had something to do with the apathy we have been considering. To a great degree it still rests upon us, though such organized efforts as the Catholic Truth Society of St. Paul, Minnesota, and the Holy Ghost Society of New Orleans indicate a change for the better.

Had Father Hecker continued in good health there is a chance, though a desperate one, that he might have overcome all obstacles. Many zealous souls would have followed his lead. As a specimen we may name the Vicar-General of San Francisco, Father Prendergast, who, with the help of a few earnest friends, raised several thousand dollars in gold in that diocese alone. But in 1871 Father Hecker's strength began to fail, and in the following year his active life was done. As already shown, it had been the intention to establish branch societies everywhere, whose delegates would regularly meet and control the entire work, giving the Church in America an approved, powerful auxiliary dominantly made up of laymen. In that sense the Society never was so much as organized, the number of branch societies not at any time warranting such a step as a general meeting of their representatives. The money actually collected was all spent in printing and circulating the tracts and other publications given away or sold below cost, Father Hecker and the Paulists managing the entire work. When the collections gave out, Mr. George V. Hecker contributed a large sum for continuing the undertaking. The result was his finding himself in the publishing business, which he was compelled to place as far as possible on a basis to meet the current outlay. The Society, as far as its name went, thus became a Catholic publishing firm, with Mr. Hecker mainly involved financially and Mr. Kehoe in charge of the business. Mr. Hecker sunk a small fortune in the Apostolate of the Press, much of it during the hard times between 1873 and 1876. The history of the whole affair is as curious as it is instructive, and hence we have given a pretty full account of it. It weighed heavy on Father Hecker's heart, though he astonished his friends by the equanimity with which he accepted its failure. His work, if it did not perish in a night like the prophet's gourd, withered quickly into very singular form and narrow proportions. The amazement of Protestant bigots at the appearance of the Catholic tracts, speechless and clamorous by turns; the quaker guns of the Second Plenary Council, and the bright dreams of a vigorous attack upon the enemy all along the line and by all classes of clergy and laity—how Father Hecker did in after years discuss these topics, and how he did inspire all about him with his own enthusiastic hopes of a future and more successful effort! When he went to Europe in 1873, too feeble to hope for recovery, leaving the enterprise behind him in the same condition as his own broken health, how unmurmuring was his submission to the Divine and human wills which had brought all to naught!

Not more than a few words need be said of his undertaking to · buy a New York daily paper. It happened that in 1871 a prominent journal, a member of the Associated Press, could be bought for three hundred thousand dollars. In an instant, as it seems, Father Hecker grasped the opportunity. By personal appeals to the rich men of the city more than half the sum required was subscribed, Archbishop McCloskey heading the list with a large amount. But soon the doctors had to be called in, and the enterprise went no further.

How Father Hecker appeared to men when advocating the Apostolate of the Press, and how he spread the forceful majesty of Catholicity over his personal surroundings, is shown by Mr. James Parton's words in the article in the *Atlantic Monthly* already quoted from: " The special work of this [the Paulist] community is to bring the steam printing-press to bear upon the spread of the Catholic religion in the United States." The resistless missionary power *latent* in the Church is thus spoken of by the same writer:

"What a powerful engine is this! Suppose the six ablest and highest Americans were living thus, freed from all worldly cares, in an agreeable, secluded abode, yet near the centre of things, with twelve zealous, gifted young men to help and cheer them, a thousand organizations in the country to aid in distributing their writings, and in every town a spacious edifice and an eager audience to hang upon their lips. What could they *not* effect in a lifetime of well-directed work?"

What follows, taken from a letter of Father Hecker's while sick in Europe in 1874, shows one of his aims in the Apostolate of the Press. It is suggestive of a result since attained, at least partially, in more than one religious community in America:

"Monsignor Mermillod desired, early in the fall, that I should see Canon Schorderet, of this place [Fribourg in Switzerland], as he was engaged zealously with the press. This was one of my principal reasons for visiting this place. My surprise has been most gratifying in finding that he has organized, or rather be-gun, an association of girls to set types, etc., who live in com-munity and labor for the love of God in the Apostolate of the Press. He publishes several newspapers and journals. The house in which the members live is also the store and the pub-lishing house. Each girl has her own room. They are under the patronage of St. Paul. The canon is filled with the idea of St. Paul as the great patron of the Press, *the first Christian journalist.* What has long been my dream of a movement of this nature has found here an incipient realization. Our views in regard to the mission of the press, and the necessity of run-ning it for the spread and defence of the faith as a form of Christian sacrifice in our day, are identical. You can easily fancy what interest and consolation our meeting and conversation must be to each other. His movement is the completion of The Catholic Publication Society of New York."

As there may be some curiosity about Father Hecker's prin-ciples as a public writer, in point of view of ecclesiastical authority, we give the following from a letter written just before the Vatican Council:

"1. Absolute and unswerving loyalty to the authority of the Church, wherever and however expressed, as God's authority upon earth and for all time.

"2. To seek in the same dispositions the true spirit of the Church, and be unreservedly governed by it as the wisdom of the Most High.

"3. To keep my mind and heart free from all attachments to schools, parties, or persons in the Church, Hecker included, so that nothing within me may hinder the light and direction of the Holy Spirit.

"4. In case any conflict arises concerning what Hecker may have spoken or written, or any work or movement in which he may be engaged, to re-examine. If wrong, make him retract at once. If not, then ask: Is the question of that importance that it requires defence, and the upsetting of attacks? If not of this importance, then not to delay and perhaps jeopardize the pro-gress of other works, and condemn Hecker to simple silence.

"5. In the midst of the imperfections, abuses, scandals, etc., of the human side of the Church, never to allow myself to think. or to express a word which might seem to place a truth of the Catholic faith in doubt, or to savor of the spirit of disobedience.

"6. With all this in view, to be the most earnest and ardent friend of all true progress, and to work with all my might for its promotion through existing organizations and authorities."

CHAPTER XXXI.

THE VATICAN COUNCIL.

In 1867 Father Hecker visited Europe in company with Father Hewit for the purpose of opening business relations between The Catholic Publication Society and English, Irish, and Continental publishers, as well as to attend the Catholic Congress of Malines held in the summer of that year. The latter purpose was the chief inducement for the journey. The Archbishop of New York favored the project of holding a Catholic Congress in America, and encouraged Father Hecker to study the proceedings at Malines with this end in view. Their stay at Malines was full of instruction, as they heard there the renowned orators, Dupanloup and Montalembert, as well as others of note. The Catholic Congress of American laymen held in Baltimore a few years ago, and whose good effects are still felt, would have been assembled twenty years earlier if Father Hecker could have brought it about. These meetings were part of his scheme for that *moral* organization of Catholic forces which he knew to be so necessary for the fruitful working of the *official* unity of the Church.

In the early part of the year 1869 Pius IX. wrote Father Hecker an autograph letter commending the various religious works which he and his community were engaged in, especially the Apostolate of the Press, and giving them all his blessing.

"I have good news to tell you," he wrote to a friend. "The Holy Father has written me the 'tallest' kind of a letter, endorsing every good work in which I am engaged. Hurrah for Catholicity at Fifty-ninth Street! My private opinion is that the Holy Father has gone too far in his endorsement of Hecker. He has made me feel ashamed of myself and humiliated."

When Pius IX. called together the Council of the Vatican

Father Hecker was urged by friends, among them several bishops, to go to Rome for the occasion. The late Bishop Rosecrans, of Columbus, Ohio, not being able to attend himself, appointed Father Hecker his Procurator, or proxy. Before his departure he preached a sermon on the Council in the Paulist Church, which was printed in THE CATHOLIC WORLD for December, 1869. He devoted the greater part of it to quieting the wild forebodings of timid Catholics and combating the prognostics of outright anti-Catholics. He concluded by asking the people to pray that the hopes of a new and brighter era for religion, to date from this great event, might be fulfilled; for it was commonly believed and expressly intended that the entire state of the Church should be considered and legislated upon at the Council. The breaking out of the Franco-Prussian war, as is well known, together with the seizure of Rome by the Piedmontese, frustrated these hopes as to all but the very first part of the work laid out for the Council.

Father Hecker arrived in Rome on the 26th of November, 1869. When the preliminary business of organization had been finished it was announced that the procurators of absent bishops would not be admitted to the Council, as the number of prelates present in person was exceedingly large. But, he writes home:

"The Archbishop of Baltimore has made me his theologian of his own accord. This gives me the privilege of reading all the documents of the Council, of knowing all that takes place in it, its discussions, etc. As his theologian I take part in the meetings and deliberations of the American hierarchy, which is, as it were, a permanent council concerning the interests of the Church in the United States, in which I feel a strong and special interest."

Father Hecker had ever been a firm believer in the doctrine of papal infallibility, as was the case with all American Catholics, prelates, priests, and people. Shortly before leaving for the Council we heard him say: "I have always heard the voice of Rome as that of truth itself." This he also showed very plainly in his farewell sermon. Speaking of the dread of undue papal influence over the bishops in the Council, he exclaimed: "All I have to say is, that if the Roman Court prevail [in the deliberations of the Council], it is the Holy Ghost who prevails through the Roman Court." But the tone of the controversy on the subject of papal infallibility, which soon deafened the world, was too sharp for his nerves, and he abstained from mingling in it. As a matter of fact he determined to get away from Rome early in the spring of 1870. If the reader would know what we deem to have been Father Hecker's frame of mind about the proceedings of the Council we refer him to Bishop J. L. Spalding's excellent life of his uncle, the then Archbishop of Baltimore, whose views of both doctrine and policy were, as far as we can judge, shared by Father Hecker, who was his intimate and beloved friend.

But his stay in the Eternal City, at this time more than ever before the focus of all religious truth, as well as the object of all human expectancy, had not been uneventful. Very much against his will he preached one of the sermons of the course given during the octave of the Epiphany, in the Church of San Andrea della Valle, and later on another, on an important occasion, in place of Archbishop Spalding, who had fallen ill. Much of his time he spent with the American bishops and the distinguished priests who were with them; he renewed the old-time friendships of his stay in Rome twelve years before, seeing a good deal of Archbishop Connolly, of Halifax, N. S.; he made new friends, too, among whom he names especially Mrs. Craven, the author of the *Récit d'une Sœur;* and he formed acquaintance with leading men and women of all nationalities.

" There is not a day passes," he wrote home, " that I do not make the acquaintance of persons of great importance, or acquire the knowledge of matters equally important for me to know; and I gain more in a day than one could in years at other times. For we may say that the intelligence, the science and sanctity of the Church are now gathered into this one city. Yet my heart is in my work at home."

He had two private audiences with Pius IX., which, though of course brief, were very interesting; the Pope remembered him, and expressed his interest in him and his work in America. The following extracts from letters to his brother George, written very soon after reaching Rome, recall an old friend:

"I do not know whether I told you of my interview with Cardinal Barnabo. He received me literally with open arms. After an hour's conversation on several matters he ended by saying: 'The affection and esteem which I had for you when you were here before has been increased by your labors since then, and my door is always open for you, and I shall always be glad to see you.' He entertains a high idea of the importance of THE CATHOLIC WORLD."

"I had a most pleasant interview a few evenings since with Cardinal Barnabo," he writes in April, 1870, shortly before leaving. "Among other things he said : 'You ought to be grateful to God for three reasons : first, He drew you out of heresy ; second, He saved you from shipwreck in Rome ; third, He has given you talents, etc., to do great things for His Church in your country.' He takes great interest in the Paulists."

Not alone in Rome did he meet with friends, but what follows, written home in December, 1869, tells that his name and his vocation had been made familiar to many observant persons in Europe :

"It surprises me to find my name familiar everywhere I have been on my travels. But magazines, newspapers, telegrams, and what-not have turned the world into a whispering gallery. But the less a man is known to men the more he knows of God ; so it seems to me, as a rule. Yet great activity may flow as a consequence of intimate union with Him whom theologians call *Actus Purissimus.* From the fact of his being known, I entertain no better idea of Father Hecker than I ever did ; and could I get him again in the United' States, he will be more devoted than ever to his work."

Father Hecker gave his view of the bearing of the Vatican Council on the future of religion in a letter which will be found below. It concerns what we have already spoken of at some length and what we shall again refer to, namely, the relation between the inner and outer action of the Holy Ghost as factors in the soul's sanctification. We heard Father Hecker several times affirm that he received special illumination from God on this subject while in Rome during the Council, and that something like the very words in which properly to express himself were then given to him. It was written in the summer of 1872, but we quote it here before bidding adieu to Rome and accompanying him in his short pilgrimage among the great shrines of Italy :

"These two months past I have been driven away from home to one place and another by poor health. . . . The definition of the Vatican Council completes and fixes for ever the external authority of the Church against the heresies and errors of the last three centuries. . . . None but the declared enemies of the Church and misdirected Catholics can fail to see in this the directing influence of the Holy Ghost.

" The Vatican Council has placed the Church in battle array, unmasked the concealed batteries of her enemies; the conflict will be on a fair and open field, and it will be decisive. The recent hostility of the governments of Europe, and especially of Italy, against the Church, has shown the wisdom of the Vatican Council in preparing the Church to meet the crisis. The defini-tion leaves no longer any doubt in regard to the authority of the Chief of the Church.

" For my part I sincerely thank the Jesuits for their influence in bringing it about, even though that were as great as some people would have us believe. . . . This had to be done before the Church could resume her normal course of action. What is that ? Why, the divine external authority of the Church completed, fixed beyond all controversy, her attention and that of all her children can now be turned more directly to the divine and interior authority of the Holy Ghost in the soul. The whole Church giving her attention to the interior inspira-tions of the Holy Spirit, will give birth to her renewal, and enable her to reconquer her place and true position in Europe and the whole world. For we must never forget that the im-mediate means of Christian perfection is the interior direction of the Holy Spirit, while the *test* of our being directed by the Holy Spirit and not by our fancies and prejudices, is our filial obedience to the divine external authority of the Church.

" If for three centuries the most influential schools in the Church gave a preponderance in their teaching and· spiritual direction to those virtues which are in direct relation to the ex-ternal authority of the Church, it must be remembered that the heresies of that period all aimed at the destruction of this au-thority. The character of this teaching, therefore, was a neces-sity. There was no other way of preserving the children of the Church from the danger of this infection. If the effect of this teaching made Catholics childlike, less manly and active than others, this was under the circumstances inevitable.

" The definition of the Vatican Council, thanks to the Jesuits, now gives us freedom to turn our attention in another direction, and to cultivating other virtues. If one infidel was equal to two Catholics in courage and action in the past, in the future one Catholic, moved by the Holy Spirit, will be equal to half-a-dozen or a thousand infidels and heretics.

" The stupid Döllingerites do not see or understand that what they pretend to desire—the renewal of the Church—can only be accomplished by the reign of the Holy Spirit throughout the Church, and that this can only be brought about by a filial submission to her divine external authority. Instead of their insane opposition to the definition of the Vatican Council and to the Jesuits, whose influence they have exaggerated beyond all measure, they ought to embrace both with enthusiasm, as opening the door to the renewal of the Church and a brighter and more glorious future. . . . To my view there is no other way or hope for such a future."

He left Rome and his many warm friends there early in the spring of 1870, and, as he thought, for the last time. He was full of courage, he was conscious of not only perfect agreement with every credential of orthodoxy, but of interior impulses of a marvellously inspiring kind. In a very familiar letter to his brother's family he says that just before his departure, while standing in one of the great piazzas, looking at the concourse of representatives of all nations passing back and forth, gathered to take counsel with the Vicar of Christ for the well-being of the human race, he was so exhilarated that he could hardly refrain from calling out, " *Three cheers for Paradise, and one for the United States !* "

" I return with new hope and fresher energy," he writes, " for that better future for the Church and humanity which is in store for both in the United States. This is the conviction of all intelligent and hopeful minds in Europe. They look to the other side of the Atlantic not only with great interest, but to catch the light which will solve the problems of Europe. Our course is surely fraught with the interests, hopes, and happiness of the race. I never felt so much like acquitting myself as a Christian and a man. The convictions which have hitherto directed my course have been deepened, confirmed, and strengthened by recent experience here, and I return to my country a better Catholic and more an American than ever."

That he might say Mass daily and at convenient hours while in Rome, crowded as it was at the time with bishops and priests, he obtained leave to do so in his own rooms. He made little pilgrimages to the great shrines of the Holy City, especially those of the Apostles and the typical martyrs, not forgetting, of course, his favorite modern saints, Philip Neri and Ignatius

Loyola. The following are extracts from letters home telling of his celebration of St. Paul's Conversion and of the martyrdom of St. Agnes. The reader will remember that the "association of women" here mentioned was one of his earliest ideas, and one of the many whose realization Providence has given over, let us hope, to some souls especially favored by Father Hecker's gifts:

"I pray much for each member of the community, and for light to guide it in the way of God. Within a short period much light has been given to me, and the importance of our work and its greatness have impressed me greatly, more than ever before. Yesterday I went to the Basilica of St. Paul, being the feast of his conversion, especially to invoke his aid. I felt that my visit was not in vain. . . . I forgot no one of our dear community. . . . On the 21st I said Mass in the catacombs of St. Agnes; it was the day of her feast. More than twenty persons were present, friends and acquaintances. I gave eleven communions, and made a little discourse at the close of the Holy Sacrifice. The scene was most solemn and affecting.

"What did I pray for? [during my Mass in St. Agnes's Catacomb]. For you all, especially for the future. What future? How shall I name it? The association of women in our country to aid the work of God through the Holy Church for its conversion. My convictions become fixed, and my determination to begin the enterprise consecrated.

"At the close of the Mass I made a short discourse. Think of it, preaching once more in the Catacombs, surrounded with the tombs where the martyrs are laid and where the voice of the martyrs had spoken! You can imagine that the impression was profound and solemn on us all. It was a piece of fool-hardiness on my part to open my lips and speak, when everything around us spoke so impressively and solemnly to our hearts. I will attempt to interpret this speech: In the days of Agnes, Christians were called upon to resist and conquer physical persecution. In our day we are called upon to overcome intellectual and social opposition. They conquered! We shall conquer! Agnes tells us there is no excuse for cowardice. Agnes was young, Agnes was weak, Agnes was a girl, and she conquered! One Agnes can conquer the opposition of the nineteenth century. Such in substance was my discourse. The whole scene caused every one to be bathed in tears."

After leaving Rome he went straight to Assisi, for whose

saint he had ever felt a very powerful attraction. He thus describes his impressions :

"The people that I have seen about here have a milder countenance and a more cheerful look, more refined and human than the Italians around Rome. They are to the other Italians what the Swabians are to the other Germans. It is easy for the Minnesinger of the human, to become the Minnesinger of Divine love.

"I could have kissed the stones of the streets of the town when I remembered that St. Francis had trodden these same streets, and the love and heroism which beat in his heart. . . . I said Holy Mass at the tomb of St. Francis, and in presence of his body this morning—a votive Mass of the Saint. It seems I could linger weeks and weeks around this holy spot. . . . What St. Francis did for his age one might do for one's own. He touched the chords of feeling and of aspiration in the hearts of the men and women of his time and organized them for action. St. Dominic did the same for the intellectual wants of the time. Why not do this for our age? Who shall so touch the springs of men's hearts and reach their minds as to lead them to the desire of united action, and organize them so as to bring forth great results? There is no doubt that the age wants this. Who is there that is inspired from a higher sphere of life, and sees into the future, so as to be able to speak to men and to invite them to do the work of God in our day? Who takes all humanity into his heart, and with the past and present at once in his mind can inspire men to live and act for the divine future?"

He also visited the Holy House at Loretto, and, passing through Venice and Milan to see the great churches of these cities, "the despair of all modern church-builders," as he says, he came finally to Genoa. ·

"I turned my steps," he writes, "to the general hospital; and why? Because the interest of my heart was there, and has been there for upward of twenty years. It is the spot where St. Catherine of Genoa labored for the miserable, loved God, and sanctified her soul. Her body is in a crystal case, uncorrupted, withered in appearance but not unpleasant to the sight. When the curtain was withdrawn and I could see her face and her feet, which were uncovered, I could not help exclaiming with the Psalmist, 'God is wonderful in His saints!' I cannot express what an attraction I have always felt for St. Catherine of Genoa. She knew how to reconcile the greatest fidelity to the interior attrait and ·guidance of the Holy Spirit with perfect filial obedience to the external and divine authority of the Holy Church. She knew how to reconcile the highest degree of divine contemplation with. the greatest extent of works of external charity. She was a heroic lover of God, for she resisted His gifts, lest she might forget the Giver in them, and be hindered the entire possession of Him, and the complete union of her soul with Him. As a virgin she was pure, a model as a wife, and as a widow a saint ! Her writings on the spiritual life are masterpieces, and though a woman, no man has surpassed, if any has equalled, the eloquence of her pen."

He procured an excellent copy of St. Catherine's portrait preserved at the hospital, and brought it home with him. He had done the same for Sts. Philip and Ignatius before leaving Rome. St. Catherine's picture represents a handsome face, earnest, simple, and joyful ; she is dressed plainly as a devout woman living in the world, lovely to look upon and inspiring love of God and man in the beholder.

Father Hecker's stay in Europe during the winter of 1869–70 and the following spring awakened in his soul aspirations towards a wide and enduring religious movement in the Old World, similar to that which he had started in the New. At the time he did not anticipate any personal share in it other than encouragement and direction from America. The reader will learn in the sequel that these aspirations were again felt, and that with renewed force, when he returned to Europe in ill health three years later.

What follows is from a pocket diary, and from a letter home :

" The work that Divine Providence has called us to do in our own country, were its spirit extended throughout Europe, would be the focus of new light and an element of regeneration. Our country has a providential position in our century in relation to Europe, and our efforts to Catholicize and sanctify it give it an importance, in a religious aspect, of a most interesting and significant character."

" I do not wish to cross the Atlantic ever again, and therefore would like to finish with Europe and Italy. As for the notable men of the day, I have seen many of them—enough of them. My present experience in one way and another seems to have prepared me to lay a foundation for action which will be suitable not only for the present but for centuries to come. No one of my, previous convictions have been disturbed, but much strengthened and enlarged and settled. I see nothing, practically, in which I am engaged, that, were it in my power, I would now wish to alter or abandon. I shall return with the resolution to continue them with more confidence, more zeal, more energy."

He arrived in New York in June, 1870.

CHAPTER XXXII.

THE LONG ILLNESS.

We have now arrived at the last period of Father Hecker's life, the long illness which completed his meed of suffering and of merit, and gradually drew him down to the grave. It will not be expected that we shall treat extensively of this subject; nor can one who writes in the beginning of the '90s about the closing scenes of a life which ended late in the '80s go very much into detail without bringing in the living. As to Father Hecker's latter days in this world, it may be said that his joy and courage and buoyancy of spirits, as well as his hopeful outlook upon men and things, were all tried in the furnace of extreme bodily suffering as well as of the most excruciating mental agony.

Four distinct epochs divide Father Hecker's life: one when in early days he was driven from home and business and ultimately into the Church by aspirations towards a higher life; another marks the extraordinary dealings of God with his soul during his novitiate and time of studies; the third was the struggle in Rome which produced the Paulist community; the fourth and last was the illness which we are now to consider. The closing scenes of his life are scattered over more than sixteen years, filled with almost every form of pain of body and darkness of soul.

From severe colds, acute headaches, and weakness of the digestive organs Father Hecker was a frequent sufferer. But towards the end of the year 1871 his headaches became much more painful, his appetite left him, and sleeplessness and excitability of the nervous system were added to his other ailments. Remedies of every kind were tried, but without permanent relief, and, although he lectured and preached and did his other work all winter and most of the following spring, his weakness increased, until by the summer of 1872 he was wholly incapacitated. The winter of 1872–3 was spent in the South without notable improvement, and early in the following summer, acting upon the advice of physicians, he went to Europe. "Look upon me as a dead man," he said with tears as he bade the community farewell; "God is trying me severely in soul and body, and I must have the courage to suffer crucifixion." He also assured us that whatever action should be taken in adopting the Constitutions, then under consideration, had his hearty approval beforehand. He was accompanied to Europe by Father Deshon, from whom he parted with deep emotion at Ragatz, a health resort in Switzerland.

Father Hecker remained more than two years in Europe, trying every change of climate and scene, and every other remedy advised by physicians, and returned to New York in October, 1875, with unimproved health. He had derived most benefit from a journey up the Nile in the winter of 1873–4, and a short visit to the Holy Land in the following spring. While in Europe his mind was busy, and he managed to meet many of his old friends' there, and formed new and important acquaintances. In February, 1875, he published his pamphlet, *An Exposition of the Church in View of the Present Needs of the Age*, which contains his estimate of the evils of our times, especially in Europe, and the adequate remedy for them. On his return to New York he was too weak to bear the routine of the house in Fifty-ninth Street and lived with his brother George till the fall of 1879, when he removed to the convent, remaining with the community till his death nine years afterwards.

As to the physical sufferings of those last sixteen years, they were never such as to impair Father Hecker's mental soundness. He never had softening of the brain, as the state of his nerves before going to Europe seemed to indicate; nor had he heart disease, as was for a time suspected. His mental powers were intact from first to last, though his organs of speech were sometimes too slow for his thoughts. His digestion had been impaired by excessive abstinence in early manhood, dating back to a time before he was a Catholic, and his nervous system, also, had been injured by that means, as well as by the pressure of excessive work in later life. Gradual impoverishment of the blood was the result, and the dropping down of nervous force, till at last the body struck work altogether. Four or five years before his death Father Hecker became subject to frequent attacks of angina pectoris, said to be the most painful of all diseases. During the sixteen years of illness every symptom of bodily illness was aggravated by the least attention to community affairs or business matters, and also by interior trials which will presently be described.

He was not unwilling to trace his breaking down to excessive austerity in former years. Once when asked for advice about corporal mortification he answered: "Don't go too fast. Remember St. Bernard's regret for having gone too far with such things in his youth. For my part, for many years I practised frightful penances, and now I fear that much of my physical helplessness is due to that cause." His state was not one of utter debility, though that quickly resulted if watchfulness were relaxed, or from application to responsible duties. But his strength never was "much to speak of," "only so, so," to use his own expressions, which signified a very small amount of the power of exertion or endurance in the muscles and nerves.

"What about my health?" he wrote from Europe. "There are days when I feel quite myself, and then others when I sink down to the bottom. My condition of mind and body often perplexes me, and there is nothing left me but to abandon all into the hands of Divine Providence. The end of it all is entirely in the dark, and were there not parallel epochs in my past life, and similar things in the lives of some others which I have read, my perplexity would be greater."

And again, from Ragatz, in the summer of 1875:

"My state of health is much the same. I found last week that my pulse was bounding in a few hours from the sixties into the nineties without any apparent cause. Yesterday I determined to consult the leading physician here. He examined me, and, like all others, attributes everything to my nerves, resulting from impoverished blood. I say to myself: 1st, How long will the machine keep working in this style? 2d, There will be a smash-up some day. 3d, Or perhaps I shall be able to get up more steam and run it a while longer. Who knows?"

And in another letter from the same place:

"Even here, freed from all [labors], it often seems to me that a good breeze, if it struck me in the right place, would drive the soul out of my body, so lightly is it connected with it, so slightly do they hold together."

As already said, his trip to Egypt had given him a temporary relief, and this was due, so he supposed, to utter change of scene and to solitude. When it was over he wrote as follows:

"This trip has been in every respect much more to my benefit than my most sanguine expectations led me to hope. It seems to me almost like an inspiration, such have been its beneficial effects to my mind and body. In Nubia there reigned profound silence and repose, and in lower Egypt, although there is more activity and evidence of modern life, still it is quiet and tranquil. I feel somewhat like one who has been in solitude for three or four months."

"My daily régime," he writes to his brother and Mrs. Hecker, from Italy, "has not changed these two years which I have spent in Europe. If I rise before nine I feel it the whole day. In the morning I awake about seven for good, and take a cup of tea with some bread and butter. I then read; sometimes, not often, I write a note in bed, and rise about nine or ten. I take a lunch at twelve and dine at six. My appetite is not much at any time. My sleep, so so. [All through his illness he went to bed at nine or shortly after.] I feel for the most part like a man balancing whether he will keep on swimming or go under the water. Sometimes I take a nap two or three times a day—if I can get it. There are weeks when I do not and cannot put my pen to paper. To write a note is a great effort. . . . Though my strength is so little my mind is not unoccupied, and I keep up some reading."

Just in what way his spiritual difficulties accelerated his bodily decline it is hard to say, for he was generally extremely reticent as to his interior life. A few words dropped unawares and at long intervals, and carefully taken down at the time, give fleeting glimpses into a soul which was a dark chamber of sorrow, though it was sometimes peaceful sorrow. To this we can fortunately add some sentences written in an unusually confidential mood in letters from Europe. Before his illness he was over-joyful, or so it seemed to some to whom this trait of his was a temptation. "Why," it was said, "religion seems to have no penitential side to Father Hecker at all." From the day of his ordination until his illness began he might have made the Psalmist's words his own: "There be many that say, Who shall show us any good? Lord, Thou hast set upon us the light of Thy countenance, Thou hast put gladness in my heart." But

now the light of that radiant joy.had faded away, and the face
of God, though as present as ever before, loomed over him dark,
threatening, and. majestic. He had studied spiritual doctrine too
well not to be ready for this trial, nor had it been sent to him
without warning. Nevertheless the sensible presence of God's
love had been so vivid and constant that he could alternate the
joy of labor with that of prayer with the greatest ease. And
now it was an alternation, not of choice but of dire compulsion,
between bitter, helpless inaction, and a state of prayer which was
a mere dread of an all-too-near Judge. It seemed to him as if
he had boasted, "I said in my abundance I shall not be
moved for ever," and now he must end the inspired sentence,
"Thou hast turned away Thy face from me and I became
troubled." When this obscuration of the Divine Love first
grew upon him the misery of it was intolerable and was borne
with extreme difficulty. The pain was lessened at intervals as
time passed on, and before a year had elapsed, his letters
from Europe, though they did not before complain of desolation, now show its previous existence by hailing the advent of
seasons of interior peace. But from beginning to end of this
entire period of his life we have not found a word of his
speaking of joy. And again, even the peace would go and the
desolation return; the face of God, not any time smiling, had
lost its calm regard and was once more bent frowning upon
him. The following extracts from letters written from Switzerland in the autumn of 1874, and within a month of each other,
tell of these alternations of storm and calm :

"As to my health these last ten days I cannot say much.
My interior trials have been such that it would be impossible
that my health should improve under them. As long as they
last I must expect to suffer. I see nothing before me but darkness, and there is nothing within my soul but desolation and
bitterness. Cut off from all that formerly interested me, banished as it were from home and country, isolated from everything, the doors of heaven shut, I feel overwhelmed with misery
and crushed to atoms. My being away from my former duties
is a negative relief ; it frees me from the .additional burden and
trouble which would necessarily fall upon me if I were within
reach."

"There remains nothing for me but to confide in, to follow,
and abandon myself to that Guide who has directed me from
the beginning. I read Job, Jeremias, and Thomas à Kempis,

and meditate on the sufferings of Our Lord and the character of His death. I recall to mind what I have read on these matters in spiritual writers and the Lives of the Saints. I reflect how from the very nature of the purification of the soul this darkness, bitterness, and desolation must be; but not a drop of consolation is distilled into my soul. The only words which come to my lips are "My soul is sad unto death," and these I repeat and repeat again. At all times, in rising and in going to bed, in company and at my meals, I whisper them to myself, while to others I appear cheerful and join in the talk. At the most I can but die; this is the lot of all, and no one can tell the moment when.

"Withal, I try to have patience, resignation, endurance, and trust in God, waiting on His guidance and leaving all in His hands."

"Since my last I have had some relief from my interior trials, and no sooner does this take place than my body recovers some of its strength. It would not have been possible for me to have borne much longer the desolation which filled my soul. Each new trial, when passed, leaves me more quiet and tranquil. Past periods of my life give me hope that this trial will also come to an end. What will that be? How will it happen? and when? God alone knows. He that has led me so many years still guides me, and resistance to His will is worse than vain. Judging from that same past, my expectations to return to my former labors are not sanguine. It seems to me sometimes that I am cut off from these to be prepared for a deeper and broader basis for future action. But whether this will be so or not, is in the hands of God. Whatever He wills me to do, I must do it. My own will has become null, and all that is left for me to do is to wait on His good pleasure and His own time. To act or not to act, to suffer or not to suffer, to speak or to keep silence, to return to my former labors or never to return, to live on or die, all have become indifferent to me. I am in God's hands, with no will of my own; for He has taken it, and it is for Him to do with me whatever He pleases. If this be a source of pain to others, none but God knows what it has cost me. There is nothing, therefore, left but to wait in trust on God's will and His mercy and good pleasure."

And again the darkened heavens are above him:

"Death invited, alas! will not come. What a relief it would be from a continuous and prolonged death!"

The obscurity of the drawing óf the Holy Ghost, as well as of God's designs, and his incessant fretting against this, partly involuntary and, as he confesses, partly voluntary also, "disturbs my health and reduces my strength."

Next to the evil self-company of an unforgiven sinner there is no loneliness so sad as that of the invalid. He needs company most who is worst company for himself. Yet Father Hecker has not left a single word which would suggest that during more than two years of absence from all his life associates in religion, as well as from his blood kindred, whom he loved with a powerful love, he felt the lack of human companionship. One reason for this was his contemplative nature, and this was the main reason. He was born to be a hermit, and was an active liver only by being born again for 'a special vocation. Another reason was that his mind was so constituted that, when subjected to trial, it rested better when quite out of sight of everybody and everything associated with past responsibilities. He bade adieu to Father Deshon when the latter left him at Ragatz with sorrow, but without reluctance; and when a year afterwards it was suggested that one of the community should come to Europe and keep him company, he refused without hesitation, saying that his companion would be burdened with a sick man's infirmities, or the sick man distressed by his companion's inactivity on his account. But towards the very end of his life there were times when he felt the need of congenial company and was extremely grateful for it. But this did not happen often, and when it did it was because the waves of despondency which submerged him were heavier and darker than usual.

The following extract from a letter shows this state of mind:

"As I get somewhat more accustomed to my separation from all that was so dear to me, the strangeness of my position seems to me more and more inexplicable. All the things which are going on in Fifty-ninth Street were once all to me, and nothing appeared beyond. To be separated from all; to look upon one's past as a dream; to become a stranger to one's self, wandering from city to city, from country to country, ever in a strange land and among strangers; to be attached to nothing; to see no definite future; to be an enigma to one's self; to find no light in any one to guide me, isolated from all except God—who will explain what all this means? where it will end? and how soon? As I become resigned to this state of things my health suffers less. Occasionally my interior trials and struggles are almost insupportable, but less so than if I were surrounded by those who have an affection for me. To worry others without their being able to give me any relief would only increase my suffering, and finally become unbearable. All is for the best! God's will be done!"

What he wrote to a friend suffering from illness he applied to himself; he made spiritual profit, as best he might, from separation from the men and the vocation he loved so well:

"I can sympathize with you more completely in your sickness being myself not well. To be shut off from the world, and cut off from human activity—and this is what it means to be sick—gives the soul the best conditions to love God alone, and this is Paradise upon earth. Blessed sickness! which detaches the soul from all creatures and unites it to its sovereign Good. But one's duties and responsibilities, what of these in the meantime? We must give them all up one day, and why not now? We think ourselves necessary, and others try to make us believe the same; there is but little truth and much self-love in this. 'What else do I require of thee,' says our Lord in Thomas à Kempis, 'than that thou shouldst resign thyself integrally to Me.' This is what our Lord is fighting for in our souls."

Yet in having his life-work torn away from him he was like a man whose leg has been crushed and then amputated, the phantom of the lost limb aching in every muscle, bone, and nerve. This was partly the secret of his pain while in Europe, at the mere thought of his former active life; it haunted him with memories of its lost opportunities, its shortcomings in motive or achievement, or what he fancied to be such, in view of the Divine justice, now always reckoning with him.

He was ever cheerful in word, even when the pallor of his face and the blazing of his eyes betrayed his bodily and spiritual pain. "The end of religion is joy, joy here no less than joy hereafter," he once insisted, and he argued long and energetically for the proposition; but meantime he was racked with inner agony and was too feeble to walk alone. In his letters and diaries he speaks of his illness and of its symptoms as of those of another person of whom he was giving news.

His wanderings in Europe were like gropings after the Divine will in the midst of the spirit's night, often in anguish, often in tranquillity, never in his former bounding joy, always with submission, beforehand, at the moment, and afterwards. Although the Divine will gave a cold welcome, he sought no other refuge.

"There are a thousand things," he writes, "that would worry me if I would only let them, but with God's help I keep them off at arm's length. His grace suffices, or in His presence all the things of this world disappear. God alone has been always the whole desire of my heart, and what else can I wish than that His will may be wholly fulfilled in me. Having rooted everything else out of my heart, and cut me off from all things, what other desire can I have than that He who has begun the work should finish it according to His design. It is not important that I should know what that design is; it is enough that I am in His hands, to do with me whatever He pleases. To be and to live in His presence is all."

And again :

"The mind quiet both as to the past and the future, contented with the present moment : as to the past, leaving it out of sight ; as to the future, unsolicitous. As to the present, satisfied to be outwardly homeless, cut off from all past friendships and relations. The present gives me all the conditions required for preparation for the future. Any time these two years past I would have made an entire renunciation of all relations to my past labors and position, but waited as a dictate of prudence. Now I feel ready to make it with calmness and in view of all its consequences."

"No sooner do I set my mind to pray than God fills it with Himself," Father Hecker was once heard to say. And this power of prayer by no means left him after 1872; only that the God who filled him was no longer revealed as the Supreme Love, but as the Supreme Majesty. "There was once a priest," he said, speaking of himself, "who had been very active for God, until at last God gave him a knowledge of the Divine Majesty. After seeing the Majesty of God that priest felt very strange and was much humbled, and knew how little a thing he was in comparison with God." Comparison with God! It was this that gave him, as it did Job, a terror of the Divine justice beyond words to express, and impressed that air of spiritual dejection upon him which struck his old friends as so strongly in contrast with his former happy and vivacious manners. "You

will never know," he once said, while being helped into bed
after a very sad day, "how much I have suffered till you are
in heaven." Meantime this awful Deity, so prompt to enter
Father Hecker's mind, coming at times like a withering blast
from the desert, was still the only. attraction of his soul, the
only object of his love. He could no more keep his mind off
God now than he could before, and now God killed him, and
then He made him alive. The ideas of the Divine goodness,
patience, mercy, and love which formerly welled up in abundant floods at the thought of God, at the same thought now
were dried up and disappeared. "Oh!" he once exclaimed, "if
I could only be sure that I shall not be damned!" This was
said unawares while listening to the life of a saint. The
reader will, therefore, understand that Father Hecker's inner
trouble was not a state of mere aridity, a difficulty of concentration of mind on spiritual things, or a vagrancy of
thought; it was a perpetual facing of his Divine Accuser and
Judge, a trembling woe at the sight of Infinite Majesty on the
part of one for whom the Divine love was the one necessary
of life for soul and body. Yet he knew that this was really
a higher form of prayer than any he had yet enjoyed, that
it steadily purified his understanding by compelling ceaselessly
repeated acts of faith in God's love, purified his will by constant resignation of every joy except God alone—God received
by any mode in which it might please the Divine Majesty to
reveal Himself. He was, therefore, willing, nay, in a true sense,
glad thus to walk by mere faith and live by painful love. "I
should deem it a misfortune if God should cure me of my
infirmities and restore me to active usefulness, so much have
I learned to appreciate the value of my passive condition of
soul." This he said less than three years before his death.
And about the same time, to a very intimate friend: "God
revealed to me in my novitiate that at some future time I
should suffer the crucifixion. I have always longed for it;
but oh, now that it has come it is hard, oh, it is terrible!"
And this he said weeping.

One aspect of the Divine Majesty which threatened for years
to overpower him was the Last Judgment. "God has given me
to see the terrors of the day of judgment," he once said, "and
it has tried me with dreadful severity; but it is a wonderfully
great privilege." Humility grew upon him day by day. No
one who knew him well in his day of greatest power could
think him a proud man, but his confidence in his vocation,

and in himself as God's representative, had been immense. The following, from a memorandum, shows how he ended:

"I told him how courageous I felt. *Answer :* That is the way I used to feel. I used to say, O Lord! I feel as if I had the whole world on my shoulders; and all I've got to say is, O Lord! I am sorry you've given me such small potatoes to carry on my back. But now—well, when a mosquito comes in I say, Mosquito, have you any good to do me? Yes? Then I thank you, for I am glad to get good from a mosquito."

TRIFLES.

WHAT hand of artist ever wrought,
    What craftsman carved from gold or gem,
Such chalice, passing skill or thought,
    As flashes from the lily's stem?

What Crœsus quaffed with royal lip,
    What lord hath ever lifted up,
Such vintage as the bee doth sip
    From out the violet's cunning cup?

On crown of king, or brow of earl,
    Or throat of girl, have ever been
Such precious jewels, as empearl
    O' morns the meadow grasses green?

Such song to sing to harp or lyre
    In hall, hath any bard been born,
As that wild-warbling, woodland choir
    That thrills before the feet of Morn?

Nay! these are God's alone, and He,
    Inscrutable, confounds us still,
While Art doth worship reverently,
    And own the wisdom of His will.

PATRICK J. COLEMAN.

THE OLD WORLD SEEN FROM THE NEW.

THE failure of the New Unionism of England in its recent conflicts with capital has met with what may be deemed ample compensation. In the first place, the judges of the Court of Queen's Bench have unanimously reversed decisions of lower courts which would have dealt a death-blow to its practical methods. Intimidation is, of course, unlawful; but what is intimidation? Is it intimidation for the officials of trade-unions to tell an employer that unless he dismisses non-union men they will call out all the union men employed by him? Is it intimidation to tell a man that unless he joins a particular union all the members of that union will strike for the sake of exacting his dismissal? The lower courts held that there was legal intimidation in both these cases; the high court has decided that there is no such intimidation, and has thereby rendered such proceedings, whatever may be thought of them from the moral, unimpeachable from the legal point of view.

The second event, which will undoubtedly afford consolation to the new unionists, is one which has taken place not in the Old World but in one of its dependencies. It bears, however, upon their most recently declared policy, that of seeking relief by legislation rather than by striking, and will doubtless be a strong incentive to the adoption of this course. In New South Wales the party in power was lately defeated, and went to the country. The working-men found then the opportunity of carrying out what they had resolved upon as a result of last year's strike. They brought forward their own candidates, cutting themselves loose from both the old-established rival parties; and they have succeeded in carrying a sufficient number to enable the Labor Party to hold the balance of power in the legislature. The ministerialists number forty-eight, the opposition fifty-six, the labor party thirty-one. They are, therefore, in a position to secure for the working classes all that they can in fairness demand, for on them the existence of governments depends. They have resolved for the present to support Sir Henry Parkes, the actual premier, and he will in recompense introduce as government measures bills for constituting courts of arbitration and conciliation in connection with labor disputes, for regulating coal-mining, for amending the mining law, and for regulating factories and workshops with special reference to the employment of women and children.

———◆———

Let us hope that, as sometimes happens, the possession of power will bring with it the sense to use power wisely. For if we may put reliance in the evidence of a member of the legis-lature of one of the other Australian colonies, the most dis-astrous consequences have resulted there from the ill-advised and arbitrary conduct of working-men under the impulsion of a knot of disturbers, fluent of speech but utterly bereft of conscience, who make a profession of agitation. "Northern Australia," he says, "produces the finest cotton I have seen, but the pods are dropped for want of picking. The whites will not tolerate colored labor, although they themselves cannot work in the tropics. Vast sugar-estates have been abandoned. Rich mines of silver, gold, and tin cannot be worked because of the un-reasonable attitude of labor; in fact, a territory teeming with wealth has been turned into what is little better than a desert." But we have no doubt that a keen sense of their own personal interests will avert such consequences in New South Wales.

———◆———

• Another legal decision will tend materially to ameliorate the lot of working-men, especially of those engaged in dan-gerous occupations.. The maxim, *Scienti et volenti non fit in-juria*, has been so interpreted by employers, and by the courts of law, that a workman injured by defective machinery or other negligence on his employer's part, could not recover damages if he continued to work after he had discovered such imperfection or negligence and called attention to it. It was assumed that if a man knew the danger even of this voluntary kind, he was willing and agreed to take the risk upon himself by the fact of his remaining. The House of Lords, however, in the case of "Smith. (pauper) against Charles Baker and Sons," has reversed the decision of the Court of Appeal, and as the House of Lords is the highest legal tribunal, the law is now authoritatively inter-preted and finally settled. A workman, consequently, is not de-barred from his remedy because he is aware of the danger, where the risk arises from the negligence of the employer. If the risk, however, is incident to his work and inseparable from it, he of course has no claim for compensation; the consent to the risk being necessarily involved in the acceptance of the work. Perhaps the workmen will have a more friendly feeling

for the House of Lords when they see it maintaining their
claims against the adverse decisions of lower courts.

The Royal Commission on Labor has been the means of
showing how little the proposers of startling remedies for industrial evils have thought out their own suggestions. Among
these remedies the extension of the direct employment of labor
by the state takes, as is well known, a leading position. Nor is
it by any means an untried expedient. Among other examples,
the dockyards in England employ many thousands of skilled
laborers, and, sad to relate, their outcries of discontent have
been heard throughout the length and breadth of the land. In
the examination of Mr. Ben Tillett, who is perhaps the most
respected of the new unionist leaders, these facts were put
before him as an objection to his proposal for the municipaliza-
tion of the London docks, and he was asked to suggest some
practical method for removing the difficulties. It then appeared
that he had nothing better to propose than that the state
should make those private employers whom it is the object of
the agitation to displace the exemplars and models for the state
in its dealings with its employees. Such is the superficiality of
some of those who think that if only they had their own way
everything would be right.   ·

That the relations between employers—even large employers—
of labor and their employees are not always those of conflict and
of efforts to get the advantage one of the other, is proved by
the reports of the Provident Banks of the South-eastern and
the Metropolitan Railway Companies. These banks were established by the directors for the purpose of giving encouragement
to their workmen to save their earnings. One of them has been
in existence for twenty years. By act of Parliament the deposits
form a first charge on the property of the companies, so that
the security is absolute. The rate of interest is four per cent.
When it is borne in mind that consols pay only two and three-
quarters per cent., and that the railway company could at any
time borrow money for three per cent., this is a very high rate.
Another advantage is that the smallest and the largest sums are
taken on deposit, sums as low as one penny and as high as the
depositor wishes. The pence of the children of the employees
are also received. The management of the banks is left in the
hands of the employees, in order that the directors may not know
who deposit nor the amount of deposits. These can be with,

drawn at a week's notice and for any purpose; in this respect these banks are distinguished from the Friendly Societies, from which deposits can be withdrawn only in case of sickness, old age, or death. The success has been so great that out of 10,000 persons employed by the company 4,000 are depositors, and the experiment, which was begun by the Great Eastern Railway Company, has been followed by nine of the other great companies, who have obtained similar powers from Parliament. The number of depositors amounts to some 20,000, and the amount of deposits to over £1,500,000. Hopes are entertained that the method which has proved so successful for railway operatives may be extended to other branches of labor. Special difficulties stand in the way; there is not the same ample security; but public-spirited men of skill and experience have the matter in hand, and we may look for some fruit from their labors.

So powerful is the interest excited by social questions that at the conference held a few weeks ago of the Catholic Tract Society—a society established for the purpose of disseminating cheap Catholic literature—almost the whole of the papers read dealt with these questions. The subjects discussed were sanitary dwellings for the poor, the protection of young servants, the prevention of cruelty to children, penny banks, the present evils of the drink-traffic, the reform of the poor law, the better organization of laymen and lay-women for the social and religious improvement of Catholic working people, the formation of social clubs for Catholic young men, and the best way of hindering mixed marriages. With the exception of the last, all these questions were primarily social in their character. And this course was not adopted without the sanction of the very highest authority. A letter was read from Cardinal Rampolla, who wrote in the name of the Pope that His Holiness approved the subjects which had been chosen for discussion, and affirming that those who endeavor to make the social question clear, and to ward off the dangers and evils that might otherwise arise, are worthy of all praise, and especially Catholic societies which act for this object,

It is too early yet to estimate the effect of the Pope's Encyclical on employers and employed, but a few facts give ground for hope that its influence will be great on both parties in the conflict. Mr. Stead, who is a warm sympathizer with working-men, has testified in the *Review of Reviews* to the most complete recognition accorded in the Encyclical to their claims, and has given what may be truly called a masterly analysis of the document. On the other hand, the Earl of Wemyss and March, who is as warm a defender of the rights of property and capital as Mr. Stead is of those of labor, said at a meeting of the Liberty and Property Defence League that there were only two directions in which they could gain encouragement. The first of these was the Vatican; and the ground of his confidence in the Vatican was the soundness of the principles laid down by the Pope in the Encyclical. It is said, too, that many employers of labor in the north of England have distributed great numbers of copies of the Encyclical among their workmen, while in Lyons it has been given away by thousands in the streets. Belgian Catholic papers are strongly advising a wide-spread distribution among the classes which have been affected by the anti-religious press of that country as a means of removing the prejudices which have been infused into their minds.

The Free, or rather the Assisted, Education proposals of the government have gone through Parliament with but little modification, and now the question arises whether the present settlement may be looked upon as permanent. On the one hand, the Liberals have pledged themselves to the bringing the schools under popular local control. Even the Marquis of Ripon, although a Catholic, found the bonds of party so strong that he felt compelled to give his adhesion to this policy. Moreover, although the bill is intended by its promoters to safeguard the voluntary and religious schools, many friends of those schools are fearful that certain provisions will operate seriously to their detriment. Opinion, however, on this point is greatly divided. On the other hand, voluntary schools have for their defence one of the most potent of influences. To supplant them will cost the rate-payers an enormous sum of money, and although politicians of the kind to which the enemies of the religious schools belong are willing enough to take other people's money, they have a strong objection to part with their own. Now, the school board rate, which Mr. Forster anticipated would amount at the most to three pence in the pound, is already one shilling in London, and will increase; while in other places it is even more. If the cost of the voluntary schools were added, the rates would be intolerable. This constitutes a practical safeguard of religious education. A second will be found in the zeal and earnestness of their supporters, which we believe will not be found wanting in the future as they have not been in the past. In 1870 it was anticipated that the school boards would carry everything before them; but, on the contrary, the voluntary schools have more than held their own, and would we believe, if the law allowed, drive out the board schools.

For experience brings wisdom, and it is probable that the English statesmen and people will learn and take warning from the experiments made by others who are less opposed to change. In the debate in the House of Lords on the second reading of the Free Education Bill, the Duke of Argyll cited the colony of Victoria as an example of the actual developments: "Twenty years ago public education was established in that colony. It began with what has been called the system of concurrent endowment, under which public money was given to the various denominational schools. But what happened? Very soon the doctrine was laid down that the state had no religion, then the logical inference was drawn that the state should teach no religion, and then came the illogical inference that the state should not tolerate religion. The result is that now not only is the Bible excluded from all schools, but even extracts are excluded which contain the name of God or any reference to religion." The duke then proceeds to pay a tribute of praise to the Catholics of this colony: "I am sorry to say that both the Presbyterians and the Episcopalians submitted to this scheme, although all regret it now. The Roman Catholics had the high honor of standing alone and refusing to pull down in their schools the everlasting standard of conscience. This resistance on the part of the Roman Catholics I believe may be the germ of a strong reaction against secularism—against what I venture to call the pure paganism of the education of the colony." We commend the entire speech of a Scotch Presbyterian in its defence of the dogmatic religious instruction of the young, in its exposure of the intolerance of those who are called Liberals, to the attention of his co-religionists in this State and country, for they are the stoutest defenders here of secular education.

Notwithstanding the refusal of France and Portugal to ratify the Brussels Convention, some hope may yet be entertained that the efforts made to extirpate the slave-trade in Africa may not be altogether fruitless. Cardinal Lavigerie made an earnest appeal to the French government, and an extension of the time for ratification has been signed. The fact that the present French Assembly has rejected the convention by a large majority in the past does not render it at all impossible for the same body to accept it in the future. Meanwhile in England the government proposes to depart from long-recognized principles and to make a grant of money to a private company, in order to enable the British East Africa Company to construct a railway from the sea-coast to Lake Victoria Nyanza. The object of the railway and of the grant is to facilitate the execution of the provisions of the Brussels Convention for the suppression of the slave-trade. Germany also proposes to work actively against this gigantic evil, and to raise the money the German emperor has projected a state lottery. We fear that many who heartily sympathize with the end proposed will find it hard to approve the means.

———————◆———————

A new association, called "The Catholic Association," has been formed in England for the organization of Catholics generally and locally into a compact body for the advancement of Catholic interests. These interests include the election of Catholics as Poor Law guardians, members of school boards and other bodies of a non-political character, for all interference in politics is wisely and almost necessarily placed outside the sphere of its action. It is proposed, also, to create a fund for aiding struggling missions and helping in the establishment of new ones; for assisting in paying off the debts on churches and school buildings; for the support of children in danger of losing the faith, and for assisting the interests of teachers in Catholic schools. It wishes actively to co-operate with existing societies, guilds, leagues, etc., and to promote their objects as far as possible. The chief promoter is a layman—Mr. Edward Lucas—and it has the warm support of many distinguished priests, such as Father Nugent and Father Lockhart. The new association has received the approbation of Cardinal Manning, who is deeply interested in its success. We hope that it will solve one of the problems which most urgently cries for solution—how to interest Catholic laymen in the defence of Catholic objects and the supply of Catholic wants, and that it will afford a much-needed field for a useful exercise of their energies.

———————◆———————

The Royal Irish Academy has had the honor of revealing to the world the results of some recent Egyptian researches which, whether we consider the objects discovered, the manner of the discovery, and the possible results, -form a subject of great interest and importance.   The discoveries consist of important fragments of a lost play of Euripides, the "Antiope"; passages from the "Phædo" of Plato, and a large number of wills and private letters, chiefly of Greek soldiers settled in Egypt.   Of these literary treasures the discoverer is Mr. Flinders Petrie, who has already done so much by his researches in Egypt to confirm the Scriptural narratives.   One of the . most remarkable features of the new "find" is that it places the world in possession of manuscripts of the classics which are of far higher antiquity than any known hitherto found.   Almost all actual texts are based upon manuscripts of late mediæval date; all are post-Alexandrian. The wills found by Mr. Petrie enabled the editors to fix the dates with certainty, and to their wonder, surprise, and delight they found that they belonged to the period of the early Ptolemies; that is to say, to the third century before Christ.   But the character of the handwriting showed that the fragments of the literary texts were even of an earlier date than the official documents, and there is reason to believe that if not actually written in the time of the authors, they are not of a much later period.

Judged by the amount of matter these remains contain there is doubtless reason for disappointment; for, in addition to the wills and private letters, of the "Antiope" there are only three pages, and a little over one hundred intelligible lines; of the "Phædo," between three and four pages, and a few scanty fragments from the poets and other writers.   But their value cannot be measured by mere quantity.   The antiquity of this manuscript fragment of the "Phædo" enables students to see a version of this work before it passed under the editorial care of the Alexandrian scholars; and the comparison of the two leads to the somewhat painful conclusion—which had already been suggested by the head-master of Westminster school—that these Alexandrian editors were in the habit of "improving" the original texts by adding rhetorical and other embellishments. As a consequence there is room for doubting whether we at present possess the real text of any of the Greek classical writers.   One of the smaller fragments leads to a similar conclusion.   It consists of the beginnings and endings of thirty-five hexameter lines.   This Mr. Bury, of Dublin, has conclusively identified as a portion of the eleventh book of the "Iliad." Now, of these thirty-five lines, five, or one-seventh of the whole, are not found in the text of Homer as the grammarians have bequeathed it to us. Is the inference legitimate that they have treated the rest of the text with the same freedom?

———————◆———————

But perhaps the immediate source of the discovery is of equal interest to the object discovered. Mummy cases, as a rule, are made of wood, but Mr. Flinders Petrie found at Gurob, in the Fayoum, a number made of a sort of carton or papier-mache, consisting of layers of papyrus torn into small pieces and stuck together. It had been suggested some sixty years ago, by the Egyptologist Letronne, that discoveries might be made from this source. The same idea occurred independently to Mr. Petrie, and did not remain with him merely a barren idea. Examining the mummy case, he thought he detected writing on some of the scraps, and forthwith set to work to separate and clean the various fragments. He was subsequently assisted by Dr. Mahaffy, Professor Sayce, and others, and what has now been given to the world has been rescued by their efforts from a mass of lime, glue, and other substances which have destroyed the greater part. However, there are many mummy cases made of similar carton, and if scholars equally painstaking can be found, may we not hope that far greater treasures will be brought to light? May we not even hope that, as has been suggested, a first century gospel will enable students of the Scriptures to get nearer to the original text?

———————◆———————

The chief political events during the past month have been an unwonted series of visits of various representatives of the opposed forces in Europe—those who are included in the Triple Alliance and who sympathize with it, on the one hand, and those who are left out, on the other. First, there was the visit of the British fleet to Fiume, where the Emperor-King was received on board the admiral's flag-ship. At Venice similar occurrences took place, except that here the King of Italy made a speech which rendered it perfectly clear to all hostile critics that England was fully committed. to the Alliance. The visit in state of the German Emperor to England, together with the subsequent less conspicuous visit of the Prince of Naples, tended only to make assurance doubly sure. As a set-off for the other side, the young King of Servia went to St. Petersburg, and the French fleet paid a visit to Cronstadt, and was received with all the honor possible. That the most absolute and unbending despotism, which has any claim to be looked upon as civilized, should manifest such demonstrative affection for the country which sup-

poses itself to be the type and chief representative of the principles of liberty and freedom, is but another example of how
little is the power of abstract principles when they come into
conflict with the concrete necessities of life. Of the normal
antagonism between the two countries one incident furnishes an
illustration. The French national anthem (if we may call it so)
is the "Marseillaise"; in Russia this hymn is positively unlawful.
On all such occasions as this public visit of the French fleet, it
is looked upon as indispensable that the respective national
anthems should be performed. What was to be done? A compromise was made. While the music was allowed, other words
were fitted to it, and in this way the wonted courtesy was
shown to the visitors and the Russian public saved from con-
tamination.

———————◆———————

Friends of the French Republic were beginning to congratulate themselves that it was at last giving proofs of stability, and
we do not say that they are not entitled to do so. However,
when on one day its Chamber of Deputies passes a vote equivalent to a vote of censure on the Foreign Minister, and a vote
which would render the unfriendly relations with Germany still
more unfriendly, and on the next day, without there being any
change of circumstances, reverses the preceding day's decision,
there seems reason for warning these friends not to be too confident. The wider and wider acceptance by the clergy of the
republic as the established form of government, forms a solid
ground for belief in its permanent establishment. The movement has taken the form of an active political association, which
eliminates from its programme all dynastic questions and seeks
to band Catholics together in defence of Catholic interests. It
will support any candidate, whether Bonapartist, Orleanist, or
Republican, who will pledge himself to defend those interests.
The Bishop of Grenoble has taken the initiative, and it is said
that a number of other bishops are about to follow his example.
He has created a Diocesan Electoral Committee, representing
some six hundred parochial committees. When the organization
is perfected it is intended that, as the parochial committees are
subordinate to the Diocesan Committee, so the diocesan committee itself will be subordinate to a Central Committee sitting
in Paris. From this it seems clear that the Catholics of France
have determined at last to exert themselves in defence of their
faith.

———————◆———————

It is not often that mention has to be made of Switzerland,

but two constitutional changes which have been made in that little country deserve notice. The right of minorities to be represented in proportion to their strength finds advocates in England, and also, we believe, in this country. The canton of Ticino has, by a system of proportional representation, secured for them their fair share of power. But for Switzerland as a whole a more far-reaching change has been made, which places it far in advance of all other countries in giving to each citizen a direct voice in legislation. For many years the Swiss constitution has enabled the citizens to vote directly upon any measure which had passed the legislature, provided a sufficient number (fifty thousand, we believe) made a requisition for this reference. This, however, had reference only to laws which had gone through the legislative chamber, and gave the people the power merely to negative measures passed by their representatives. The new power enables fifty thousand citizens to submit to the chambers any constitutional change they think proper, and this proposal must be discussed by the chambers. This is the nearest approach yet made to making the people themselves, and not their representatives, the direct law-makers.

The other countries of Europe scarcely call for mention. Portugal is still in the throes of a financial crisis. Spain is in hopes that by the new bank charter she has secured herself against like dangers. The Balkan states—the European centre of disturbance—preserve their unstable equilibrium, marriages past and future forming the only pressing anxiety. In Russia, the crops having failed in the larger part of the empire, there are grave fears of a famine. Hopes have arisen for the persecuted Jews. Mr. Arnold White, who was sent by Baron Hirsch to make inquiries, has prevailed upon the Russian authorities to allow them to depart from the empire without having to pay for the privilege, and permission has been granted for the establishment of emigration committees for the purpose of providing means and information to the emigrants. The money Baron Hirsch and other wealthy Jews are ready to provide, but the precise destination is not yet fixed.

TALK ABOUT NEW BOOKS.

A CLEVER and delicately-touched story,* from the modern woman's point of view, is Mme. Jeanne Mairet's *An Artist*, not altogether well translated by Anna Dyer Page. With little plot, few characters, and no striking incident—save, perhaps, the midnight scene in Diane's studio—the author has given a clear, definite impression of her motive, and produced her effect in an easy, apparently effortless way which almost conceals her art. Her heroine is an interesting type of one of the many new developments of what is often, and not inaptly, called the "woman's age." Religion plays no visible part in this development, it is true; but in the career of a French *jeune fille bien élevée* a preliminary Christian training of some sort may almost be taken for granted. Diane Verryot is, at all events, a pure-minded, high-principled, and courageous young creature, to whom necessity and a true artistic vocation have early imparted the safeguards of industry and self-reliance. Her father, once a painter of reputation, though in a period when painting was by no means the thing it is to-day in Paris, and now a vain and disappointed old man, long incapacitated from work by a paralytic shock, has become a recluse. He lives with Diane, a young woman of twenty-four when her story opens, in a house of his own in Paris, too dilapidated for other tenancy, in the garden of which he had once built a huge studio. This he no longer visits, but lives surrounded by all that remains of its former luxurious fittings in his own room. A man of expensive though refined tastes, immensely vain of his early reputation, yet half-conscious that he could not have maintained it against the newer school, he has gradually wasted all his own fortune, as well as that which Diane had inherited from her mother, in the purchase of rare but not otherwise valuable engravings, and when the story begins is in reality his daughter's pensioner, and though not entirely ignorant of the fact, and chafing under it, yet accepting it as the natural due, not merely of his paternity, but of his superiority as man and artist.

The awakening comes when Diane's talent is on the point of achieving a success certain to cast his own by contrast still

---

* *An Artist.* Translated from the French of Mme. Jeanne Mairet by A. D. Page. **New** York : Cassell Publishing Co.

more into the shade. Up till then he has systematically ignored it, not even looking at her work, and treating it as a mere pastime in which she must be indulged but not encouraged. The suspicion that she may have passed him on his own road is a hideous wound to his vanity and pride. Unwilling to go openly to the studio and watch Diane at her easel, he takes to going there at night, as Diane soon discovers and is very near betraying, seeing in it, as she at first hopes, a late development of fatherly interest. The old man is too much of an artist not to recognize the value of her work and the fact that it proceeds from an original talent which plainly owes nothing to his train-ing or traditions. Worse still, he judges correctly, for the first time in his life, such of his own canvases as still hang on the walls, and finds them "as atrocious as they were painful to him." Madame Mairet's analysis of the mental states of the old painter at this period seems painfully real. Never having loved any one but himself in his life, this love tortures him cruelly in his help-less age. He hates this art which makes his own seem an-tiquated, and he hates the author of it. And on the night when Diane's portrait is finished, in an access of envious spite, he passes his sleeve over her frail pastel, reducing it to a dirty, whitish mass. And, as he tries to give his malice the effect of accident, paralysis once more lays its hand on him, and there he dies.

Enough of a story might have been made of this alone. But the author had not yet fully elaborated her theme. Diane was to suffer still more deeply from that new form of masculine jealousy which is treading hard upon its older, better-known, and once almost sole development. She marries, and from mutual love, another artist, and finds in him another jealous rival when her successes threaten to surpass his. Though her love is great enough to make her try to abnegate her indi-viduality and become "only a wife," as she should have been "only a daughter" in an acceptation of those relations which is passing, the struggle to do so, when complicated by an infidelity, not of the heart but of the senses, on the part of her husband, becomes too much for her and she again resumes her beloved work in secret. Virtual separation follows, which Diane will not terminate when Bernard becomes "repentant," even though his repentance is accompanied by a magnanimous willingness that she shall use her talent as she will. "I do not love you," she replies to his protestations. "I will not become your wife again from a sense of duty. I placed my ideal too high; you lowered it; there is nothing left." In the· end, however, Diane's love rekindles; the tie made by their child is strong; moreover, being a Frenchwoman, she feels too readily the force of M. Limes's remark when, in reply to her charge that Bernard had "·betrayed her shamefully," he says: "What can you do about it now? *You are not going to judge us men as you would judge yourself, I hope.*" Some day, let us hope, when women generally become seriously inspired to conquer the right to their own individuality, this sentiment too will be recognized by them as the chief bar to their success, but also as one which it rests indispensably on them, and them alone, to put away.

Marie Bashkirtseff's *Letters,** vivacious and clever as they are, add little to the knowledge of her personality gained from her Journal. They are less frankly egotistical, as might have been expected; but it is the outside of the same inside that she and her friends were anxious to reveal before. It must be said in their excuse, or justification, that neither is commonplace. How real was her intention to make the public her confidant in the interests of art, is shown by a curious anonymous letter she sent to Edmond de Goncourt the same year she died, and which apparently elicited no response. In it she offers him this Journal as material, stipulating only for profound secrecy on his part, as she "resides in Paris, goes into society, and the people whom she mentions· are all living." M. de Goncourt, one may conjecture, probably experienced some pangs later on for having shown the cold shoulder to so much generosity, pleading merely to expend itself. In the same year she carried on a witty but not at all compromising correspondence with another author whose works she admired, and wrote to Zola, saying that she had read every word he had published, and "cherished the impossible dream of an epistolary friendship" with him. This also appears to have gained no response.· All these letters were anonymous, as were two she sent a year earlier to "M. Alexandre D——," presumably Dumas. In this, after asking him to "be for once the spiritual director of a woman who desires to consult you as she would a priest, regarding a serious matter," she tells him that in his books he seems "to be as great and good as possible," and that if he shows himself scornful now, he will destroy one of her "most cherished illusions," and proposes a meeting at the "ball of the Opera House, the only place where I can see you." With a difference, these letters remind

* *Letters of Marie Bashkirtseff*. Translated by Mary J· Serrano. New York: Cassell Publishing Co.

one of those inflicted on the Duke of Wellington by Miss J. Dumas would seem to have met her with a serious rebuke, which she acknowledges in a second and curious epistle wherein she says: " The guidance of which I stand in need I shall ask from Him who suggested to me the thought of asking it from you. . . . I shall see you, doubtless, on Saturday at the Chamber," she concludes. "The divorce law will be proposed. Apropos of divorces, I announce to you that of my admiration from your person."

An excellent book, well written and most interesting, is Mr. James Jeffrey Roche's *Story of the Filibusters.** It forms one of Fisher Unwin's "Adventure Series," but is published in this country by Macmillan & Co. Besides giving a full account of the various attempts made by Walker, "the gray-eyed man of destiny," to establish his own rule in Nicaragua with a view to aid the slave-holders of our Southern States in maintaining the "peculiar institution," it also presents a brief but graphic sketch of earlier filibusters, from the Norsemen down. The latter and most amusing half of the book is occupied by an abridgment of the biography of Colonel David Crockett, the last survivor of the Alamo, and as to his real self almost a myth, so much has the actual man been obscured by the traditional "Davy Crockett." As a matter of fact, he is better worth knowing and quite as irresistibly droll.

Felicia † seems a curious sort of book to be produced by a young lady of twenty-three, which is said to have been Miss Fanny Murfree's age when it was written. Clever it undeniably is, both in plan and execution, but in neither is it novel. The theme, indeed, reminds one of that charming Russian story, *Asbein*, where an ill-assorted marriage somewhat like that imagined by Miss Murfree was handled in a much more convincing manner. The chief difference is that Boris Lensky and Natalie were a real man and a real woman, while Hugh Kennett and Felicia fall into quite another category. Unlike those juvenile precocities of whom Olive Schreiner and Rudyard Kipling are the most modern and convincing specimens, but among whom Amélie Rives must also be counted, Miss Murfree produces the impression of having been born old in taste and judgment, and of not having been able to correct the mistake by genuine first-hand observation or spontaneity of feeling. Still, she writes so

---

* *The Story of the Filibusters.* By James Jeffrey Roche. New York: Macmillan & Co.
† *Felicia.* A Novel. By Fanny N. D. Murfree. New York and Boston: Houghton, Mifflin & Co.

well that, when she shall have thrown off her allegiance to Mr.
Henry James, and descended from what has at present very
much the air of the teacher's desk, there is no saying that she
may not in time find her way back to the true fountain of youth,
direct contact with nature.

It is impossible that Mr. Fuller's book * should ever be popular, but it is certain that it will long be a favorite among people
of cultivation who enjoy delicate satire and relish a good literary
style. Though it can hardly be said that the satire of *The
Chevalier of Pensieri-Vani* is at all times delicate, yet in the
main it is so. Rancorous it never is, for when Mr. Fuller becomes indignant or disgusted, he at once ceases to be satirical
and says plainly what he means. For example, when speaking
of the "once-lovely convent-isle of Sant' Elena," and the way
in which Italy, "the Modern, the United," and the "brutal
Progresso" have "trampled the olive down, together with a
hundred other gracious and tender things," his indignation is
too great and honest to permit him either to grin or to
smile.

The story of the book is a slight one, but inasmuch as it is
but a line on which to hang many exquisite pictures of Italian
scenery and modern Italian life among the upper classes, whose
pursuits are mainly artistic, this does not matter. The most
amusing chapter is that which gives an account of the discovery
of the "Iron Pot" that was unearthed one day in the garden
•of "San Sabio," and became the subject of much dispute among
German and Italian archæologists, some of whom contended that
it was of Etruscan make in pre-historic times. The Iron Pot
threatened even to dissolve friendly relations between Italy and
Germany, but was finally shown to be no older than Garibaldian
times. This chapter suggests some of the best of Carlyle's satirical work, and is exceedingly clever. *The Chevalier of Pensieri-Vani* is, in fact, a remarkably clever piece of writing
throughout.

It would be little for one who has never found Mr. George
Moore otherwise than offensive as a novelist, to say that as a critic
he is a much pleasanter companion. Everything in his volume†
of *Impressions and Opinions* is entertaining, and for the most part
well put. He has a faculty of imparting his impression and
sharing his knowledge of a book, a picture, a man, between
whom and his reader he is the sole connecting link, which is

---

* *The Chevalier of Pensieri-Vani.* By Henry B. Fuller. Boston: J. G. Cupples.
† *Impressions and Opinions.* By George Moore. New York: Charles Scribner's Sons.

the product, one must suppose, of a keen, sympathetic knowledge of his subject united to a perfectly clear mental conception of it, and of his own means of rendering it. He is not, perhaps, eminently persuasive—one may retain, if he has it already, his preference for the French art of the nineteenth century above the English art of the eighteenth, in face of Mr. Moore's verdict to the contrary, but at all events he will not fail to understand his convictions and his expressed grounds for them. In style he is not oppressively literary, and seldomer than most critics who are encouraged to collect their fugitive essays from the periodical press does he make an isolated remark so individual or so epigrammatic that its form remains inseparable from its substance. It is he, nevertheless, who says that "to succeed in England you must offer a new reading of the Book of Genesis; to succeed in France you must offer medals." And again, in writing of "Art for the Villa," "Of the many enigmas which life offers for our distraction, I know none more insoluble than the prices artists put on their pictures."

A second translation from Señora Pardo Bazan's realistic novels* of contemporary life confirms an impression gained from its predecessor, *A Christian Woman.* A good Christian, if one may judge from her total attitude towards the doctrine, morality, practices, devotions, and professional teachers of Catholicity, she seems to wish to aim a blow from that stand-point in favor of a greater equality in marriage than she has found prevalent. That, at all events, is what we read between the lines of Lucia's *Wedding Trip*, as we read it in the history of Carmen's pitiful venture into matrimony. Divorce is a sin and as impossible as adultery to a Christian woman, Señora Pardo Bazan seems to say, and therefore, fathers and spiritual directors, take greater heed how the Christian girl contracts marriage! Do not give her purity and innocence into the hands of corrupt and vicious husbands, and then hope for all the graces of the sacrament. Only the highest Christian virtue can stand that test, and the most that can be hoped for, ordinarily, is that the living holocaust shall lie quietly on the altar and endure in silence the pangs of a burning against which she should have been guarded as if it were a sin instead of a sacrifice. The very docility with which she accepts your teaching as to her duty as a wife, should enlist you, who are men, to guard her innocence more sacredly. Lucia is charmingly painted. So are the delightful glimpses given by the author of life in northern Spain, and

---

* *A Wedding Trip.* By Emilia Pardo Bazan. New York : Cassell Publishing Co.

such health resorts as Vichy and Biarritz. Her talent has great distinction and her hand is very sure.

One of the brightest and most entertaining novels* we have seen in many months is Maarten Maartens' *An Old Maid's Love.* One does not read a dozen lines of its first chapter without arriving at the persuasion that he has come upon a new flavor and a pleasant one. There are a thousand fine things in it, both as to matter and manner, but the best of all is the portrait of that wrong-headed, right-hearted, delightful, Calvinistic old maid, Suzanna Varelkamp. The story is too long and too complicated to be retold in the most elementary fashion; moreover, the Mephisto, the evil genius of Suzanna's life and that of the darling nephew who is her love, is what the old lady calls "an idolatrous child of Rome," and very far from being a credit to her religion. But the moral lesson of the book is good, notwithstanding, and for freshness and charm, and a certain knowingness concerning human nature in out-of-the-way aspects, it would be hard to match it among recent novels. There are some curious situations in it—as, for example, where Suzanna, after thanking God in all sincerity that it was impossible for her to kill her dangerous guest, is only saved from the consummation of that crime by sheer accident and a good deal of warm water. And again when, in her attempt to save Arnout's honor and his soul by making his actions conform to her private notions of how alone that salvation can be effected in the circumstances he has created, she goes to the Count de Mongelas and buys his consent to divorce his wife at the sacrifice of all her fortune. Good, too, is her return upon herself when at last God has been gracious to her, Arnout has come back repentant, and the woman she has hated has heaped coals of fire upon her head.

"'She is a better woman than I,' she said; 'she, the wicked creature, is a better woman than I. She lived more truly, more straightly than I. I love him, and I have been working hard to mould his lot as I thought best. And whether the means be right or wrong, what has it mattered to me as long as I could have my own way, and do as I thought best? Yes, that is what it has always been: as I thought best. Even murder, if I deemed that it would attain what I thought best. And if I thought my best was better, then the world was mad, and God. was wrong. And what has my wisdom led to from the beginning? I have built up with all my labor the very things I desired to destroy. It was I who sent the lad forth from his home in the very moment when I was yearning to retain him. And

* *An Old Maid's Love.* By Maarten Maartens. New York: Harper & Brothers.

it was I who was welding the chain which must fetter him for
ever at the moment when this woman was loosening it to let
him free. Oh, the unwisdom of our wisdom when it begins to
doubt of conscience, when it tells us and reasons out to us that
evil is not evil because it leads to good! Oh, the wretchedness
of going wrong!'

"She sat for a long time undisturbed in the silence, alone with
her thoughts. Then she got up from the table and went to a
little cupboard in the corner, and took up a Bible which lay
there. She opened it at the fifty-first Psalm, and she read the
Psalm through solemnly without flinching. During all these
troubled weeks she had calmly continued her reading, but she
had shrunk, with a nameless feeling of terror, from that agonized
cry of the repentant King of Israel. It was the Psalm which
Arnout had whistled on the summer evening when he wandered
down the lane, and came upon the carriage upset in the middle
of the road. She shrank from it; from the tune, from the
words, from the awful, overwhelming, 'Deliver me from blood-
guiltiness, O God.' And now, with its meaning sinking deep
into her spirit, with all the reminiscences of that fateful evening
returning upon her, she read it through sorrowfully, calmly, from
end to end."

*Philippa*** is a pretty little tale, laid for the most part in certain well-known Normandy coast resorts, like Trouville and Vil-
lers-sur-Mer, which are sketched in with a good deal of verisimilitude. Belonging to the "Unknown" series, it is, of course, full
of mystery of a not very impenetrable nature, and, her griefs
terminating blissfully by the time she is twenty, Philippa makes
quite as good a thing of life as if she had not been handicapped
at the start by a—but it would be unfair to reveal the mystery
in that way.

Miss Christine Faber has a great deal of cleverness and "go"
about her work, which will be sure to make it popular among
the young people for whom and concerning whom she writes.
Her latest story,† *A Chivalrous Deed*, though badly named, such
a marriage as it characterizes not ranging properly under such a
category, is amusing and full of incident. Would that it were
also possible to describe this interest and fun as elevating or re-
fining in its quality. Unfortunately, the best that can be said
about it is that it is not morally harmful. As a specimen of
book-making it could not easily be worse than it is, being full of
gross errors of spelling, punctuation, and, in fact, of bad proof-
reading of all descriptions. A writer who succeeds so well in
making children interesting to each other, and who skirts so

* *Philippa; or, Under a Cloud.* By Ella. New York: Cassell Publishing Co.
† *A Chivalrous Deed.* By Christine Faber. New York: P. J. Kenedy.

cleverly the dangerous snare of "goodiness" while keeping well within the limits of goodness, would be a real and great accession to the ranks of Catholic literature could she prune her style and terrorize her publisher into giving her work a proper setting.

Better in all those qualities wherein Miss Faber's work is lacking, but less sparkling and vivacious, and more conventional, is a volume * of Mrs. Anna Hanson Dorsey's containing *Two Ways* and *Tomboy*. Mrs. Dorsey is an old favorite with our young people, however, and these stories may be new only to the present writer. Each of them is entertaining and well-written.

The series of articles in the *Fortnightly Review* concerning Russia, by E. B. Lanin, which turns out to be the collective signature of several writers—writers with an astonishing evenness and similarity of style and sentiment be it said—have been collected into a volume † and brought out by Benjamin R. Tucker. It forms a terrible indictment of a great nation. If the half of such papers as those entitled respectively "Russian Prisons: the Simple Truth" and "Sexual Morality in Russia" are to be taken as a literal fact—and that is what their writers claim and seem to establish by documentary evidence— it must be avowed that the horrors of hell itself could not easily surpass those already existing upon earth. The Swedenborgian hell would be a Paradise compared with the terrible *étape* prisons, in which convicts of all sorts, as well as such guiltless members of their families as choose to accompany them into exile, are quartered on their way to Siberia. Certainly, the tale suggests the reflection by which of old King David governed his choice of punishments: that it is better to fall into the hands of God than into those of men. St. Catherine of Genoa hints the same thing when she says that man, when he abandons himself to evil, is worse than the devil, seeing that he has a body and can use it to such vile purpose.

In other points, as for instance that of dishonesty, the indictment against a whole people on the score of such anecdotes as that which opens chapter iv. is like enough too sweeping. That instance, we are very sure, could be paralleled much nearer home without any one of us being willing to accept it as a proof of a general lack of common honesty among Americans. We remember the astonishment with which a woman of our acquaintance, who had established a flourishing business, received

* *Two Ways* and *Tomboy*. By Anna H. Dorsey. Baltimore : John Murphy & Co.
† *Russian Traits and Terrors*. By E. B. Lanin. Boston : Benj. R. Tucker.

the effusive thanks of a large Boston firm with whom she had had extensive transactions. When their account was presented and examined, it became evident that the bill against her was less by a hundred dollars than it should have been, and she called their attention to the fact. One of the Boston men wrote her in terms so complimentary of her integrity, and at the same time so indicative of surprise that she should have been at pains to rectify a mistake in her favor, that she counted the praise so near an insult as to justify her in putting the pertinent question: "What, then, would you have done in my place?" Does one thence conclude that commercial morality is at a hopelessly low ebb in the United States?

The paper on "The Jews in Russia" it would be well to read in connection with Professor Goldwin Smith's article in the August issue of the *North American Review*, "New Light on the Jewish Question," wherein he points out that it is as a financier and usurer that the Jew is hated, and not as a deicide. The press of all European nations, Professor Smith says, is for the most part owned or largely subsidized by Jewish capitalists; hence, when it deals with moot questions between them and the Christians who feel that they are being eaten out of house and home by the Jew's characteristic hunger after the goods of this world, its statements of fact should be taken with a grain of salt. Perhaps a walk down the length of Broadway, and a careful study of the business signs there by one who retains any recollection of the shop-fronts of thirty or forty years ago, would serve to intensify his appreciation of the points of the *North American* article.

———————◆————————

I.—THE BOOK OF JOB.*

Professor Genung, of Amherst College, in this new study of the Book of Job, has fulfilled his task in both a reverent and a critical spirit. The sublime Book of Job is shrouded in a cloud of mystery. The period and author of the book, and the question as to its strictly historical character, have been matters for a controversy which is not yet determined, and perhaps never will be.

Professor Genung's opinion that it is an Epic Poem, by an unknown author contemporary with Isaiah, is ingeniously defended, and seems quite compatible with its inspiration if the

---

* *The Epic of the Inner Life.* Being the Book of Job translated anew and accompanied with Notes and an Introductory Study. By John F. Genung. Boston and New York: Houghton, Mifflin & Co. 1891.

poem is regarded as founded on a true history. Without considering any particular passages of doubtful rendering, we may say that the translation is correct, and it is certainly very good in a literary point of view. The interpretation and notes show much thought, and, although it cannot be expected that they should be regarded as an adequate exposition by Catholic scholars, we think they will be found very serviceable in many ways to those who make this sublime book an object of special study.

2.—BLESSED THOMAS MORE.*

"He hath put down the mighty from their seat, and hath exalted the humble." Surely we may well apply these words to the blessed martyr whose glorious name gives title to this excellent work of Father Bridgett. He was humble in his life and dealings with his fellow-men, and so merited to be exalted to the martyr's crown; having first been divested of the greatest honors which a man of the world could bear in the days when Blessed Thomas More lived, he was born again to everlasting life.

We welcome this life coming from the pen of Father Bridgett, whose valuable, accurate, and scholarly works we have had the pleasure of reading, some of them more than once or twice, and of noticing in these pages. When the life of Blessed John Fisher appeared we longed for that of Thomas More, and now we are hoping that God will spare our author to write the life of Blessed Margaret Pole.

We have read many of the lives of the great chancellor, martyr, and patriot. A new one like this is a delightful month's spiritual reading. The letters quoted and the extracts from some manuscripts unpublished hitherto give us a deeper insight into his character than we have had before.

More was a man of the most profound humility, and it seems as if he practised it in an heroic degree. Consequently he was a man who had the highest respect for the authority of the church as the divine teacher. Had he not combined these two virtues in so close a union, he had never given his life for the faith. He was an illustrious example of a great genius controlled by reason, by piety, and the love of God. The world

---

* *Life and Writings of Sir Thomas More, Lord Chancellor of England, and Martyr under Henry VIII.* By the Rev. T. E. Bridgett, C.SS.R. London: Burns & Oates; New York: The Catholic Publication Society Co.

had no charms for him. When at court his heart was in the domestic circle. His world there was his family, and yet he was willing at the voice of God to leave his earthly love, and serve his country, and finally his God, unto death. He never sought advancement, and when he was preferred to the highest office in the gift of his royal master, he discharged his duties with extraordinary wisdom and great simplicity.

To the student who wishes to study the times of the Reformation in England Father Bridgett's books are invaluable. To the layman of our day the life should be a hand-book. It is the life of a man in the world and not of it. A man twice married, with a family of children, and yet living the life of a confessor, and meriting to crown a work well done with the martyr's palm. A man who served his country faithfully and well, but whose country was too ungrateful to give him the reward he deserved. We hope this book will circulate among Catholic lay people.

3.—A HISTORY OF THE WORSHIP OF GOD.*

Divine Revelation, as the author of this book conclusively shows, teaches the necessity of divine worship. And this worship, which is of obligation, he proves to be of two kinds, viz.: internal, or the homage of the mind and heart toward God, and the external, which, as he deduces from Holy Scripture, has from the beginning been divinely instituted, and has always been sacrificial. Beginning with the sacrifice offered by Abel, he gives a continuous history of the true worship of God until the institution by our Divine Lord of the Most Holy Sacrifice of the altar—the central glory of the Catholic Church.

No one who reads this book can fail to see that the Holy Mass is the only form of Christian worship which links "the pure oblation" of the New Dispensation with the sacrifices of the Old.

We most heartily second the wish of the devout author that this book may be extensively circulated among all Catholics, and particularly among the laity. Although not professedly a controversial work, it will be a great help in bringing non-Catholic believers of the Bible to a knowledge of the truth.

----

* *A History of the Worship of God.* By Right Rev. L. De Goesbriand, D.D., Bishop of Burlington, Vt. Burlington : The Free Press Association.

4.—FATHER CURTIS. *

The author of *Tyborne*, *Forgotten Heroines*, and other charming books, has, it seems to us, done no better work than this little biography of a very saintly man. The life of Father Curtis may be summed up in the following extract taken from one of his letters: " God delights in joy; it is one of the most certain means to secure his favors." And from the following descriptive of his penitents : " His confessional was thronged with his dear poor, who were his favorites—an assembly of poor, miserable, deaf, blind, lame, half-alive people, in many shapes and forms, all most sorrowful, and some quite repulsive." A man of no mean learning, of a joyous, robust nature, he found his greatest happiness in ministering to the abject poor, so as well to merit the title of the "Apostle to the Poor." And this we take to be a greater miracle of grace than those other miracles he is believed to have wrought, or that of the miraculous manifestation at his grave.

He was an Irishman, born in 1794, and died in 1885 at the good old age of ninety-one. Most of his life was spent in Dublin after he became a priest, either as rector in Gardner Street, or as provincial. Apropos of his love for his countrymen, it may not be out of place to quote a witticism contained in a letter of his to a friend on the loss of a parrot : " I offer my sincere condolence on the loss of the beautiful parrot. What a wondrous bird ! It did more than O'Connell or Grattan ever could realize—it blended together in beauteous harmony the orange and the green." Indefatigable in all good works for the raising up of the poor, he had a helping hand for all, lay or religious, engaged in God's service. He held in particular and high esteem the Christian Brothers.

He lived constantly in the presence of God. In one of his instructions to novices he says : " All authority comes from God, and superiors are only his representatives. You should be superior to every superior ; let *God* be your superior. He cannot mistake or forget. Try to please him. I wish to impress on your mind, and on the mind of every religious, that you must not be depending upon your superiors ; you must learn to depend upon God alone, and not on creatures."

* *The Life of Father John Curtis, of the Society of Jesus.* By the author of *Tyborne*, etc. Revised by Father C. Purbrick, S.J. Dublin : M. H. Gill & Son ; New York : The Catholic Publication Society Co.

5.—A BOOK FOR YOUNG MEN. *

The author has written a useful book for young men in a pleasant, confidential vein, and the title he has given it is a particularly taking one to the energetic youth of America. That "Young America " is energetic no one denies. That a vast amount of energy is wasted in the pursuit of false ideals, that aims are energetically pursued without any ideal at all, is sometimes the case even in America. Is it not the creed of certain modern philosophers that belief in the ideal is always to be reprehended? Father Feeny, however, without sharing this error, deals little in ideals.

The book is both negative and affirmative. It tells why some young men do not "get on," and why others do. It shows that it is not impracticable to mingle God in all our actions, and might very easily have shown that all the most truly successful men the world has ever seen, all the true benefactors of the human race, have been men of God.

All in all, it is a book calculated to do good, and may be read with profit not alone by the class for whom it has been written, but by all teachers of youth as well. The strain of hopefulness in which .the book is written is particularly pleasing.

6.—AN EXPLANATION OF THE EPISCOPAL INSIGNIA. †

This explanation of the episcopal insignia, by a Roman canon, need only be mentioned to recommend it sufficiently to all who are interested in Catholic rites, ceremonies, and vestments.

7.—HEALTH WITHOUT MEDICINE. ‡

A tiny booklet containing practical and sensible directions about hygienic habits and exercises.

---

* *How to Get On.* By the Rev. Bernard Feeny. New York, Cincinnati, Chicago: Benziger Bros.

† *De Insignibus Episcoporum Commentaria.* Auctore Petro Josepho Rinaldi-Bussi. New York: Fr. Pustet. 1891.

‡ *Health Without Medicine.* Theodore H. Mead. New York: Dodd, Mead & Co.

THE COLUMBIAN READING UNION.

A FRIENDLY DISCUSSION OF PLANS FOR THE DIFFUSION OF
GOOD BOOKS.

" Were a wholesome book as rare as an honest friend,
    To choose the book be mine : the friend let another take.
    Choose discreetly, and well digest the volume most suited to thy case,
    Touching not religion with levity, nor deep things when thou art wearied."—*Tupper*.

"I am not a reading man. There was a time when I was fond of a good book, but I seldom open one now." The speaker was a middle-aged, good-humored man. His name was Paul Carrollton.

"Nor I, Paul," exclaimed his companion. "My business absorbs the most of my time, and whenever I happen to have a leisure half-hour, I find quite enough in the daily papers to interest me."

"The daily papers," observed the third speaker—a tall, well-built, handsome young man—"are well enough in their way, from a worldly stand-point, but as sensible men, my friends—as I know you are—you must acknowledge that we were endowed with a mind for nobler—"

"Hold on!" interrupted Paul; "stop right there, Francis. No polemical discussion under my roof this evening, if you please."

"You are mistaken, Paul, I assure you," said the young man. "I hadn't the remotest idea of introducing a theological subject. Yet I am convinced that a few words on the question of healthy literature will not be out of place beneath your hospitable roof."

The foregoing conversation took place in the cosey parlor of my friend and host, Paul Carrollton, in an important town in the State of New York. The immediate cause of the talk on reading was the somewhat abrupt appearance in our midst of a canvasser for a New York publishing house, bearing a recently issued, bulky volume under his arm, for which he asked an exorbitant price.

Our young friend Francis was an enthusiast on the subject of good literature.

"I never saw such a book-worm as you are, Francis," observed Paul.

"I confess I have an unquenchable thirst, almost, for good, solid, healthful reading," said Francis. "I prefer historical or scientific subjects, but I also find much profit and amusement in works of fiction, such as Newman's *Callista*, Wiseman's *Fabiola*, and Walter Scott's historical novels."

"For my part," exclaimed our host, "I am as willing as any man living to pay for a good book, if I could only be assured of its worth, but there is a great quantity of trashy literature sold nowadays in beautifully bound covers."

"I agree with you there," said Francis. "For the sake of my children's morals, I wouldn't allow one of them to go within a mile of such books."

"But," said Paul, "how are we to distinguish between the good and the bad? Now you, Francis, belong to the same church as I do; so do our friends here; but with all due respect to you for your book knowledge, I must honestly say that I consider the prayer-book has quite enough good reading for me and for my family. Yes, sir; a man can pull through well enough, without bothering his head so much in search of book-learning. That's my argument, Francis. Don't you think I'm near the mark?"

"Your argument, Paul, will hardly bear inspection. What you say might have been more to the point some years back, when our fathers first came here. In those days, I must admit, the man who could barely write his name stood as good a chance of pushing his way ahead in the battle of life as the college graduate of to-day. However, things have changed amazingly since then; this is a more progressive age."

"Francis, you are right. A man who has lived his life-time here in America must be pretty short-sighted if he fails to notice the wonderful change that has taken place in less than half a century. And now you have mentioned it, I begin to think that a young man needs a well-informed head on his shoulders in this age of competition."

"You must also admit, Paul, that it would be a most difficult task to make a young man bright and clear-headed without the aid of books. The diffusion of clear, sound literature is as essential to sustain the mental faculties of youth as eating is to their material existence." 'I believe that good books are as necessary as wholesome food.

"But," said Paul, "how are we going to discriminate between good and bad; and where are our libraries? Just take this town of ours for example. I am an old citizen and a taxpayer, and should know what I am talking about. Now, this town, as near as I can calculate, contains about ten thousand inhabitants. Well, at a close guess I suppose we may count here at least three thousand Catholics. Again I ask, Where are our libraries? It is true we have a public library, and I am one of the board of directors. It is a great benefit to our society people, but if you hunt the shelves for works relating to our Catholic literature, you'll have your journey for nothing."

"Can you inform me how many of our Catholic authors are admitted to that library?" asked Francis.

"Well, now, that's a puzzler," replied Paul; "but to be frank with you, I must say I haven't the least idea."

"Can it be possible, Paul—an old citizen like you, a taxpayer, and a member of the board of directors. You astonish me."

"It's a fact, nevertheless, Paul. Before you questioned me I had never given the matter a thought."

"I venture to say," replied Francis, "that we have only one Catholic representative among the directors, and that one is yourself, and you have done nothing to make them acquainted with the treasures of Catholic literature."

"Which shows how careless I have been," said Paul.

"My advice is," answered Francis, "that you introduce this question at the next meeting of the board of directors, and any information they may require as to books by Catholic authors, to be placed on their shelves, can be obtained by addressing the Columbian Reading Union at 415 West 59th St., New York City. Just make a memorandum of that in your note-book, and do not forget to use it at the next meeting of the board. I am proud to say we enjoy a better state of affairs in our town. We have made quite an advance there."

"This town," said Paul, "is about a century or so behind the age, I should judge. The wheels of progress seem to have come to a stand-still here; the axle-tree wants a thorough greasing, in my opinion. But to come to the point. What change is this you speak of respecting our Catholic literature in your town?"

"Oh!" said Francis, "I was about to allude to our Reading Circle."

"'Reading Circle!'" echoed Paul.

"Reading Circle; that is the name of our club."

"Turn on the gas, Francis, if you please, for I am as much in the dark as ever."

"The Reading Circle of which I speak is associated with our parochial library. It was established but a short time since, but it has proved to be a wonderful success."

"Who was the founder of your Reading Circle?" inquired Paul.

"We owe much of our success," replied Francis, "to the Columbian Reading Union."

"'The Columbian Reading Union!'" exclaimed Paul. "Is that another society?"

"Certainly," said Francis. "Don't you remember that I called your attention to it when speaking of the board of directors?"

"How stupid I am!" said Paul. "So you did. And I also made a note of it. Well, you say your Reading Circle has been aided by the Columbian Reading Union? Explain how?"

"Yes," said Francis, "you must know that the central organization was established in New York by the Paulist Fathers for the diffusion of wholesome literature. The Reading Circle to which I belong is one of its branches. The movement awakened interest in all directions, and now there is scarcely a town or city of any pretension without its Catholic Reading Circle."

"God speed the good work!" cried Paul excitedly; "that is the fervent wish of my heart."

"It *is* a good work," continued Francis, "and merits the success it has already achieved. Our young people need no longer speak of Catholic literature as if it were something worthless. Every Reading Circle in the country is supplied by the Columbian Reading Union of New York with guide-lists, enumerating the works of our best writers."

"It is an excellent plan, Francis, and I don't wonder at its success. Now just think how many there are of us Catholics in the United States who up to this period have lain fallow, as it were, where our literature was concerned; but as far as human foresight can go, I see in this new movement a means of extricating ourselves at last from the Dismal Swamp of neglect. But what is the reason that we are still without a Reading Circle in this miserable, snail-paced old town of ours?"

"Remember," said Francis, "that Rome was not built in a day, and you know it is never too late to mend. Your Reading Circle has already been thought of."

"Thought of!" exclaimed Paul; "what does that signify?"

"To hasten matters," said Francis, "I saw Father M—— this very afternoon; he intends to organize a Reading Circle next

Sunday. What do you think of that, Paul? I see the news has had a talismanic effect on your features already. A moment or two ago your face was as long as a fiddle. There is a spark of life left in this plodding old town after all, you see; for in about a fortnight from now your Reading Circle will be in full swing, shining forth like a bright star in a dark sky."

"Francis, my dear fellow," cried Paul, starting from his seat, his face beaming with delight, "you have made me as great an enthusiast on the question of good reading as yourself. Think of what a benefit it will be to our growing-up boys and girls, as well as a source of pleasure to ourselves!"

"The Reading Circle," said Francis, "will also be hailed as a boon by the writer and publisher, as well as by the reading public in general. A noted Catholic writer has said: 'The author who writes a Catholic story in this country has no audience, and no publisher; secular publishing houses will not take his books, and religious ones cannot afford to take them. They do not pay the publisher, even when the author has paid half the price of publication."

"Well, now, that's pretty hard," said Paul. "I don't see, for the life of me, why any writer who is obliged to exercise his brains for the welfare of humanity should be left out in the cold for the want of proper support, any more than the man that digs in the mine or guides the plough. For my own part —although, as I have already observed, I am not much of a reading man—I have always had a special admiration for the author whose writings afforded me either pleasure or instruction."

"Such an avowal," said Francis, "does credit to you. This question of reviving and encouraging the growth of our own literature to-day reminds me forcibly of a somewhat similar topic which was agitated more than half a century ago. One of the most gifted writers of that period, in advocating the requirements of art in Ireland, asks the following question: 'Where is your Temple of Art?' He then instances the support given to art by the rulers of other nations; but assuming that it may be contended that in the Emerald Isle the professions of painting and sculpture are not of sufficient importance to justify the serious contemplation of collecting funds for the purpose of erecting an Irish National Gallery and School of Arts, he writes thus: 'Egypt is a wilderness; we only remember that she was. But of our recollections of her old name which is the most lively—the most interesting? which most absorbs our sympathy, commands our respect? Is it our, recollection of her wealth, her commerce? No! it is her mind, and not her wealth; her philosophy, and not her arms; her arts, and not her commerce. Her foster-child, Greece, has left us a greater variety of models for admiration. Her laws, her arms, her poets, orators, heroes, either were more distinguished, or history has better defined or transmitted them to us.'"

"I respect the talents of the painter and the sculptor as much as any man," said Paul, "but in my humble opinion the writer of a good book is as much entitled to admiration as either of them."

"I agree with you," said Francis; "and if it was right for ancient Greece and Rome to honor art, science, and literature in the early ages of the world, is it not right and proper that we of the old faith should be equally proud to encourage the Catholic writer of to-day? Or is civilization tending backward?"

"It looks very much as if we were inclined that way, Francis. The mighty dollar appears to be the magnet of attraction. Now, if we who are hunting after worldly wealth—I include myself, you see—could only realize the fact that a genuine book is of more solid value than a nugget of gold—"

"An American writer," said Francis, "in the early part of this century summed up the value of good books in these words:

"'In the best books great men talk to us, give us their most precious thoughts, and pour their soul into ours. God be thanked for books! They are the voices of the distant and the dead, and make us heirs of the spiritual life of past ages. Books are the true levellers. They give to all who will faithfully use them the society, the spiritual presence, of the best and greatest of our race. No matter how poor I am, no matter though the prosperous of my own time will not enter my obscure dwelling, if the sacred writers will enter and take up their abode under my roof; if Milton will cross my threshold to sing to me of Paradise, and Shakspere to open to me the worlds of imagination and the workings of the human heart, and Franklin to enrich me with his practical wisdom, I shall not pine for want of intellectual companionship, and I may become a cultivated man, though excluded from what is called the best society in the place where I live.'"

"The Reading Circle you speak of is like a rainbow of hope," said Paul; "but give me an idea of the plan you have adopted."

"The plan of our Reading Circle is simply this," replied Francis: "each member is to pay one dollar for initiation, the money to be used in buying books. The fly-leaf of each book contains a printed list of members, arranged according to residence. To every member will be sent one or two books, which may be retained two weeks, and must then be passed to the one whose name follows. on the list; all books to be passed the first and fifteenth of each month, and the dates when received and when passed to be noted by each member. In the forming of a club," continued Francis, "it is necessary to avoid too heavy reading, which would soon discourage all but those above the average literary taste. Books of fiction should be circulated with more solid work."

"How are your meetings conducted?" inquired Paul. "I suppose they afford you sufficient enjoyment?"

"They please me immensely," replied Francis. "I can truthfully say, that the time is spent pleasantly and profitably at the regular meetings of our Reading Circle. The exercises begin with the reading of the minutes of the previous meeting. This is followed by quotations containing good, wholesome thoughts that impress the members in the course of their readings. The readings are selected from a literary stand-point; hence standard periodicals are frequently consulted. For instance, every month at least one selection from THE CATHOLIC WORLD is rendered. The members subscribe to this magazine and circulate it weekly, so that each member in turn is supplied with a copy. An original story was given as a Christmas contribution at one of our meetings. Sometimes, however, we devote the whole evening to one special subject, or one celebrated character, such as Shakspere, Longfellow, or St. Patrick. A modern author, whose works are familiar to most Catholic readers, in describing what our young people must have, says:

"'How much better is it not for them to read good books, and wholesome books, and solid books, under proper guidance, than to devour indiscriminately all kinds of printed matter? In the one case, whatever they read will assist in forming the mind or building up the character; in the other, naught comes of it all but distraction, waste, and loss of time. Why devour trash when all the great writers and thinkers and singers of the world are at their disposal to inspire them with noble thoughts and glorious aspirations?'"

"My dear Francis," said Paul, "I am delighted to have had the pleasure of this evening's conversation. You have expanded my mind with new ideas, for I really believe that, like Rip Van Winkle, it has been under the influence of a twenty years' sleep until you have disturbed its slumber. You have broken the spell at last, and opened my eyes to the blessed light of day."

"I am glad," said Francis, "that I have been fortunate enough to make one convert at least. Your snail-paced, slow-coach old town, Paul, as you term it, is at length on the sure road to success, and will soon have many an ardent supporter of studious reading, now that you are about to set the example. It has been said that our Catholic literature, like the grand old Celtic language, was either dead or forgotten; but, thank Heaven, we are now able to fling back the lie! Already our traducers begin to realize the mettle we are made of. A glorious era is at length dawning before us. Our long-neglected writers, whose luminous pens have spread the light of truth in characters of gold, are becoming better known, and their works are receiving more attention from printers and publishers. It is no longer necessary for a Catholic author to 'become a colorless, lifeless *littérateur*, or else to follow false gods, become un-Catholic, and wallow in the muck of realistic popularity.' Every thinking Catholic will hail the movement as the first one to give the Catholic writer hope of having a little home where he may securely tend the vine and olive and uproot the noxious weed.

"Long may the Columbian Reading Union continue to wield its potent influence, as the advance guard in the crusade for the spread of Catholic literature in the United States! No department of its work is more important than that of trying to secure, through the united efforts of Reading Circles, a suitable recognition of Catholic authors in every public library."

B. O. C.

WITH THE PUBLISHER.

DURING the past month the mail brought us many hearty and outspoken words of congratulation and encouragement, the result of the announcement in our last issue of the changes in the fortunes of THE CATHOLIC WORLD which point so clearly to greater efficiency and give so unmistakable an assurance of greater success. This issue of the magazine is the first that comes from its new, its own home, THE COLUMBUS PRESS. And though there have been delays inseparable from conditions that involve moving, new machinery, and new employees, the work produced is of a quality that will bear comparison with the best of our contemporaries, not only in matter, but also in typography. It must be plain to all our readers that the magazine is beautifully printed from its brand-new dress of type. It is true that this feature of fine typography is but a means to the end and aim of THE CATHOLIC WORLD, but in these days especially the cause of Truth cannot ignore and must enlist every aid of this character.

And so everything already augurs success in this new venture of the magazine. The Publisher, however, wishes to call the attention of his readers to a fact which he regards of special significance at the present time. It is certainly as happy a coincidence as it was unexpected to find that the first sheets that came off the new press of THE CATHOLIC WORLD contained that chapter in the *Life of Father Hecker* which embodied all his ideas on the subject of the Apostolate of the Press.

The Publisher asks his readers to give that chapter a careful study. All that he has ever said of the value of Printer's ink as a vehicle for Divine truth has been derived from the words, spoken and written, of the great man who founded THE CATHOLIC WORLD, and it may be of interest to note that in the plan and scope of the new COLUMBUS PRESS one of his ideals has been realized, one of his prophecies has been fulfilled. The convent and the printing-office have been united.

The results of that union, the good that will thence be effected, rest under God's providence with us—with the reader as well
as with the editors and publisher. Don't say that this is the
same old story, that the Publisher has repeated it again and
again, and that it is high time to change. The Publisher thinks
otherwise, and so will you if you examine your own conscience.
He knows that he cannot say it too often and too strongly,
that the best fruits of the work of the magazine are to be realized by its readers; that upon them rests its continuance, upon
them rests the successful achievement of its purpose. He has
not yet convinced all his readers of this truth; he has not yet
brought it clearly home to you, dear reader of these lines,
that you have a share and an important share in the work of
the Apostolate of the Press. And he won't change his key until
he has convinced you of this, until he has made you feel the
pressure of your duty in this respect.

———————◆———————

Don't allow yourself to think that somebody else can do this
better than you, for this would be self-deception and you would
not permit the thought in any other matter of pure business or
even charity. As a reader of THE CATHOLIC WORLD you have
a share in the good it can accomplish, you are a stock-holder
in the company of all those who in one way or another work to
secure the greatest good to the greatest number. And if your
interest is genuine, you must and will do whatever falls in your
way to boom that stock and secure the highest dividends at
the Great Reckoning. Don't hide the magazine in a napkin;
put it out at interest. Let it become known—for though it has
now been in existence some twenty-seven years, it is surprising
to find how many otherwise well-informed Catholics there are
who are ignorant of its very existence, or who at least know
nothing of the aims and purposes of its publication.

———————◆———————

All this, I repeat, has been said before, but the almost daily
experience of the Publisher makes it clear that it cannot now
be said too often, especially as the managers of the magazine
have now undertaken the burden of debt and increased expense
in order the better to secure the realization of the original plans
of its founder. There are some of our readers who are already
full of the spirit that should belong to those who see in
THE CATHOLIC WORLD something more than the profit that can
come to themselves individually; there are those that find it an

aid to the pulpit in the battle for the cause of Truth. Of such is the gentleman who this year repeats his generosity of the past, remitting the price of a year's subscription to the magazine to be sent "where it will do the most good." It would be out of place to state here the good that was the outcome of that expenditure last year; it would involve disclosures of too personal and local a character; but the magazine went to a South-western town where a priest is never seen, and it has already prepared the way for the Truth by the conquest it has made over Prejudice and by the demand it created in the place for books explanatory of Catholic doctrine. At the present moment the Publisher has on his desk an order for five different books on the Church's teaching, to be sent to a little town in Iowa into which only one copy of THE CATHOLIC WORLD finds its way. But it goes to an earnest and fearless Catholic layman and this order is the first-fruits of his missionary spirit. It is something of this spirit that should possess you, dear reader, and the Publisher begs you to read and ponder that chapter in Father Hecker's life in which he speaks of the Press and its opportunities for the cause of Truth, in this land particularly.

A recent writer in the *Academy*, in speaking of the evils wrought by biased and unscientific historians—evils so great that they often mean the deception of several generations of a trusting public—says that, while the operation of destroying these myths is not laborious, it is very thankless and is often unheeded. How often this has been the experience of the Catholic in argument with well-meaning Protestants needs no proving here; but the writer's summary of the Luther "Bible Myths" is so well put that we venture to quote it at length:

"Take, for example, the whole range of Luther myths, and especially the Luther Bible myth. It used to be asserted, hardly forty years ago, that Luther refound the Latin Bible as a rare book in the Erfurt Library. This card-house toppled down so soon as it was demonstrated that the Vulgate had been printed in hundreds of thousands of copies within the first thirty years of the printing-press. Then a new card-house arose—Luther had first given the Bible in the vernacular to the German people. This toppled down also when it was shown that the German Bible had been printed eighteen times before Luther's version appeared, and that his September Bible was but a slight modification of the old text. The next card-house was

the theory that the pre-Lutheran German Bible was not only
due to Waldensian heretics, but that the very printers and illustrations were tainted with heresy. Here. there was plenty of
scope for show of learning and for knitting hypothesis to hypothesis. The trials of Waldensians in Strassburg and Augsburg
were drawn from the archives and printed alongside accounts of
the early printers of these towns. The heretics were found to
have Bibles in their pockets; what more natural than that they
should have been on their way to take them to the printers?
But not only the printers, the engravers were also 'Reformers
before the Reformation' for these sectarian historians!"

Mr. Andrew Lang in *Scribner's Magazine* for this month has
a somewhat summary way of disposing of the difficulty of advising "a course of reading." "Distrust a course of reading," he
says. "People who really care for books, *read all of them.*
There is no other course." When one remembers that this
piece of advice is addressed to the young, its wisdom can be
questioned in spite of Mr. Lang's acknowledged place as a
guide in matters literary.

Of interest to teachers is the latest addition to Dr. Rolfe's
"English Classics for School Reading," a series of *Tales from
Scottish History*, selected from the works of standard authors.
The tales are carefully graded and annotated, and the series is
in the line of the plea made by Mr. George E. Hardy in the
July issue of the *Educational Review* for the abolition of the
ordinary "reader" from the school-room, and the substitution
of reading matter that has rank as literature, properly graded
and prepared for children. Mr. Hardy speaks from experience
both of the evils of the old system and a careful and prolonged
trial of the new plan in his own school, and we earnestly recommend the reading of his article to all those of our readers who
have an interest in school work.

The Will and the Way Stories is the title of a recent volume
by Mrs. Jessie Benton Fremont, the wife of the famous Path-
finder. It is a collection of her adventures in the early days
when her husband was a power in the Far West. D. Lothrop
Co. publish the volume.

Macmillan & Co. have just issued the first part of a new
Dictionary of Political Economy edited by R. H. Inglis Palgrave,
on the same lines as Sir George Grove's well-known *Dictionary
of Music*.

Major Wissmann, the writer who gave such striking testimony to the efficiency of the Catholic missionaries in Africa as
compared with the labors of the Evangelical bodies, is about to

issue, through Messrs. Chatto .& Windus of London, another book of African travel, which he. calls *My Second Journey through Equatorial Africa.*

It is announced that Mr. Walt. Whitman will write no more. He has completed his peculiar literary work with his last book, entitled *Good-by, my Fancy.*

Macmillan & Co., the publishers of Mr. Joseph Pennell's work on *Pen Drawing and Pen Draughtsmen,* have issued another book by the same author, descriptive of the river Thames, under the title *The Stream of Pleasure.* The work is enriched by ninety illustrations by the author.

Harper & Bros. have published:

> *A King of Tyre.* A Tale of the Times of Ezra and Nehemiah. By James M. Ludlow, author of *The Captain of the Janizaries.*
>
> *As We Were Saying.* A volume of essays by Charles Dudley Warner.
>
> *The Uncle of an Angel and other Stories,* by Thomas A. Janvier.

The Catholic Publication Society Co. has just issued:

> *The Life of Father John Curtis, S.J.* By the author of "; Tyborne."
>
> *The Memoirs of Richard Robert Madden, M.D.* Edited by his son, Thomas More Madden, M.D.

The same firm announces:

> *The Autobiography of Archbishop Ullathorne.* With Selections from his letters. By Augusta Theodosia Drane.
>
> *Ireland and St. Patrick.* A Study of the Saint's Character, and of the results of his Apostolate. By the Rev. W. B. Morris, of the Oratory.
>
> *Life of the Curé of Ars.* From the. French of the Abbé Monnin. Edited by the Cardinal-Archbishop of Westminster. A new and cheap edition.
>
> *Life of St. Francis di Geronimo, S.J.* By A. M. Clarke. (New volume. Quarterly Series.)
>
> *The Spirit of St. Ignatius,* Founder of the Society of Jesus. Translated from the French of the Rev. Father Xavier de Franciosi, of the same Society.
>
> *Succat ;* or, Sixty Years of the Life of St. Patrick. By the Very Rev. Mgr. Robert Gradwell.

BOOKS RECEIVED.

Un Couvent de Religieuses Anglaises à Paris. Par l'Abbé F. M. Th. Cédoz. Paris: Victor Lecoffre; London: Burns & Oates.

The Divine Order of Human Society. By Professor Robert Ellis Thompson, S.T.D. Philadelphia: John D. Wattles.

Lourdes: Histoire Médicale. Par Docteur Boissarie. Paris: Librairie Victor Lecoffre.

The Little Grain of Wheat. Suggestions of Devotion. Compiled by F. A. Spencer, O.P. Boston: T. B. Noonan & Co.

PAMPHLETS RECEIVED.

L'Angelus. Par Claude-Charles Charaux. Paris: Didot et Cie.

La Civilisation et La Pensée. Par C.-C. Charaux. Grenoble: F. Allier Père et Fils.

Address of James F. Tracy. Albany: Argus Company.

The Church and Poverty. By John Brisben Walker.

Kansas State Board of Agriculture. Topeka: Hamilton Printing Co.

Violet Nevin: The Story of a Mixed Marriage. By her Uncle. Liverpool: J. C. Conolly.